CRUDEN'S
HANDY CONCORDANCE

CRUDEN'S
HANDY CONCORDANCE

Edited and Adapted by
CHARLES H. H. WRIGHT, D.D.

to which is added an
INDEX TO THE HOLY BIBLE
OF
PERSONS, PLACES AND SUBJECTS
Mentioned in Scripture

ZONDERVAN
PUBLISHING HOUSE
OF THE ZONDERVAN CORPORATION
GRAND RAPIDS, MICHIGAN 49506

This American Edition is published
by special arrangement with
Pickering & Inglis, Ltd., London and Glasgow

First printing 1963

ISBN 0-310-22931-6

Printed in the United States of America

83 84 85 86 87 88 — 40 39 38 37 36 35 34 33 32 31

This Concordance has been specially prepared with a view to facilitate reference to every subject or text in the Bible. As it is intended to be used in conjunction with the Index of Persons, Places, and Subjects, the words appearing under that Index have not been repeated. It is confidently believed that the arrangement adopted in this Concordance will meet with the approval of every Bible student. The plan adopted is based on Cruden's well-known Concordance. The word is first given in heavy black letter, and the texts in which the word occurs follow in the order of the Books in the Bible.

CRUDEN'S
HANDY CONCORDANCE

CONCORDANCE
TO THE
HOLY BIBLE

ABASE, Job 40. 11. behold proud, and *a.* him.
Is. 31. 4. lion will not *a.* himself.
Ezek. 21. 26. and *a.* him that is high.
Dan. 4. 37. walk in pride, he is able to *a.*
Matt. 23. 12 ; Lk. 14. 11 ; 18. 14. exalt himself shall be *a.*
Phil. 4. 12. I know how to be *a.*
2 Cor. 11. 7. offence in *a.* myself.
Abated, Gen. 8. 3, 11. waters were *a.*
Lev. 27. 18. be *a.* from thy estimation.
Deut. 34. 7. nor was Moses' force *a.*
Jud. 8. 3. then their anger was *a.*
Abhor, Lev. 26. 11. my soul shall not *a.* you.
1 Sam. 27. 12. made his people to *a.* him.
Job 42. 6. I *a.* myself and repent.
Ps. 5. 6. Lord will *a.* bloody man.
119. 163. I hate and *a.* lying.
Prov. 24. 24. nations shall *a.* him.
Jer. 14. 21. do not *a.* us for name's sake.
Amos 6. 8. I *a.* the excellency of Jacob.
Rom. 12. 9. *a.* that which is evil.
Ex. 5. 21. made savour to be *a.*
Job 19. 19. my inward friends *a.* me.
Ps. 89. 38. thou hast cast off and *a.*
Prov. 22. 14. *a.* of the Lord shall fall therein.
Ezek. 16. 25. made thy beauty to be *a.*
Is. 66. 24. an *a.* to all flesh.
Abide, Ex. 16. 29. *a.* every man in his place.
Num. 31. 19. *a.* without camp seven days.
1 Sam. 5. 7. ark shall not *a.* with us.
Job 24. 13. nor *a.* in paths of light.
Ps. 15. 1. who shall *a.* in tabernacle.
91. 1. shall *a.* under the shadow.
Eccl. 1. 4. the earth *a.* for ever.
Joel 2. 11. day terrible, who can *a.* it?
Matt. 10. 11 ; Mk. 6. 10 ; Lk. 9. 4. there *a.*
Lk. 19. 5. I must *a.* at thy house.
24. 29. *a.* with us.
John 3. 36. wrath of God *a.* on him.
14. 16. another Comforter, that he may *a.*
15. 6. if a man *a.* not in me.
1 Cor. 3. 14. if any man's work *a.*
13. 13. now *a.* faith, hope, charity.
2 Tim. 2. 13. yet he *a.* faithful.
1 John 3. 6. whosoever *a.* in him, sinneth not.
3. 15. no murderer hath eternal life *a.* in him.
Ability, Ezra 2. 69. they gave after their *a.*
Dan. 1. 4. had *a.* to stand in the palace.
Matt. 25. 15. to every man according to *a.*
Acts 11. 29. according to *a.* to send.
1 Pet. 4. 11. as of the *a.* God giveth.
Able, Deut. 16. 17. every man give as he is *a.*
Josh. 23. 9. no man been *a.* to stand.

Able—Continued.
1 Sam. 6. 20. who is *a.* to stand before God ?
1 Ki. 3. 9. who is *a.* to judge ?
2 Chr. 2. 6. who is *a.* to build ?
Prov. 27. 4. who is *a.* to stand before envy ?
Dan. 3. 17 ; 6. 20. God is *a.* to deliver.
Matt. 3. 9. God is *a.* of these stones.
9. 28. believe ye that I am *a* ?
20. 22. are ye *a.* to drink of cup ?
22. 46. no man was *a.* to answer.
John 10. 29. none is *a.* to pluck.
Acts 6. 10. not *a.* to resist wisdom.
Rom. 8. 39. *a.* to separate us from love of God.
1 Cor. 10. 13. tempted above that ye are *a.*
2 Cor. 3. 6. *a.* ministers of New Testament.
Eph. 3. 18. *a.* to comprehend with all saints.
Phil. 3. 21. *a.* to subdue all things.
Heb. 2. 18. *a.* to succour them that are tempted.
Heb. 7. 25. *a.* to save to the uttermost.
Jas. 4. 12. *a.* to save and destroy.
Jude 24. *a.* to keep you from falling.
Rev. 5. 3. no man *a.* to open book.
6. 17. who shall be *a.* to stand ?
Abode, 2 Ki. 19. 27 ; Is. 37. 28. I know thy *a.*
John 14. 23. we will come, and make our *a.*
Gen. 49. 24. his bow *a.* in strength.
Ex. 24. 16. glory of the Lord *a.* on Sinai.
John 1. 32. Spirit, and it *a.* on him.
1. 39. they came and *a.* with him.
8. 44. a murderer, and *a.* not in truth.
Acts 14. 3. long time *a.* speaking boldly.
18. 3. Paul *a.* with them, and wrought.
Abolish, Is. 2. 18. idols he shall utterly *a.*
Ezek. 6. 6. your works may be *a.*
2 Cor. 3. 13. end of that which is *a.*
Eph. 2. 15. *a.* in his flesh the enmity.
2 Tim. 1. 10. Christ who hath *a.* death.
Abominable, Lev. 11. 43. not make yourselves *a.* with.
Deut. 14. 3. shalt not eat any *a.* thing.
Job. 15. 16. how much more *a.* is man ?
Ps. 14. 1 ; 53. 1. they have done *a.* works.
Is. 14. 19. cast out like an *a.* branch.
65. 4. froth of *a.* things.
Jer. 44. 4. this *a.* thing that I hate.
Tit. 1. 16. in works they deny him, being *a.*
1 Pet. 4. 3. walked in *a.* idolatries.
Abomination, Gen. 43. 32 ; 46. 34. *a.* to Egyptians.
Lev. 11. 10. be an *a.* to you.
Deut. 7. 25. it is *a.* to the Lord.
25. 16. all that do unrighteously are *a.*
Prov. 3. 32 ; 11. 20. the froward *a.* to the Lord.

7

Abomination—*Continued.*
Prov. 8. 7. wickedness an *a.* to my lips.
15. 8, 9, 26. sacrifice, etc., of wicked *a.*
28. 9. even his prayer shall be a *a.*
Is. 44, 19. the residue thereof an *a.*
Ezek. 33. 29. land desolate because of *a.*
Dan. 11. 31 ; Matt. 24. 15 ; Mk. 13. 14. *a.* of
  desolation.
Lk. 16. 15. esteemed among men, *a.* in sight
  of God.
Rev. 21. 27. not enter that worketh *a.*
Abound, Prov. 28. 20. faithful shall *a.* with
  blessings,
Matt 24. 12. because iniquity shall *a.*
Rom. 5. 20. that the offence might *a.*
15. 13. that ye may *a.* in hope.
1 Cor. 15. 58. always *a.* in work of the Lord.
2 Cor. 1. 5. as sufferings *a.*, so consolation *a.*
Phil. 4. 12. I know how to *a.*
2 Pet. 1. 8. these things be in you, and *a.*
Rom. 5. 15. grace by Jesus Christ hath *a.* to
  many.
Above, John 3. 31. He that cometh from *a.* is
  a. all.
John 8. 23. I am from *a.*
19. 11. power given thee from *a.*
Gal. 4. 26. Jerusalem is *a.*
Eph. 4. 6. one God who is *a.* all.
Col. 3. 2. set your affection on things *a.*
Jas. 1. 17. every perfect gift is from *a.*
Absent, Gen. 31. 49. when we are *a.* one from
  another.
1 Cor. 5. 3. as *a.* in body.
2 Cor. 5. 8. willing to be *a.* from body.
10. 1. being *a.* am bold towards you.
Abstain, Acts 15. 20. *a.* from pollutions of
  idols.
1 Thes. 5. 22. *a.* from all appearance of evil.
1 Pet. 2. 11. *a.* from fleshly lusts.
1 Tim. 4. 3. commanding to *a.* from meats.
Abstinence, Acts 27. 21. after long *a.* Paul
  stood forth.
Abundance, Deut. 33. 19. suck of the *a.* of the
  seas.
1 Sam. 1. 16. out of *a.* of my complaint.
1 Ki. 18. 41. sound of *a.* of rain.
Ps. 72. 7. *a.* of peace.
Eccl. 5. 10. loveth *a.* with increase.
5. 12. *a.* of rich not suffer to sleep.
Is. 60. 5. the *a.* of the sea shall be.
66. 11. with the *a.* of her glory.
Matt. 12. 34 ; Lk. 6. 45. out of *a.* of heart.
  ,,   13. 12 ; 25. 29. he shall have more *a.*
Lk. 12. 15. life consisteth not in *a.*
2 Cor. 8. 2. *a.* of their joy abounded.
12. 7. through *a.* of revelations.
Abundant, Ex. 34. 6. Lord God *a.* in goodness.
Is. 56. 12. as this day and more *a.*
1 Tim. 1. 14. grace was exceeding *a.*
1 Pet. 1. 3. according to his *a.* mercy.
Abundantly, Gen. 1. 20. let waters bring
  forth *a.*
Job 36. 28. clouds drop and distil *a.*
Ps. 36. 8. *a.* satisfied with fatness.
145. 7. *a.* utter the memory.
Is. 55. 7. he will *a.* pardon.
John 10. 10. might have life more *a.*
1 Cor 15. 10. I laboured more *a.* than.
Eph. 3. 20. able to do exceeding *a.*
Tit. 3. 6. shed *a.* through Jesus Christ.
2 Pet. 1. 11 entrance ministered *a.*
Abuse, 1 Sam. 31. 4 lest uncircumcised *a.* me.
1 Cor. 7. 31. use world as not *a.*
9. 18. that I *a.* not my power.

Accept, Deut. 33. 11. *a.* the work of his hands.
2 Sam. 24. 23. the Lord thy God *a.* thee.
Job 13. 8 ; 32. 21. will ye *a.* his person.
Ps. 20. 3. and *a.* thy burnt sacrifice.
Mal. 1. 13. should I *a.* this?
Gen. 4. 7. shalt thou not be *a.* ?
Ex. 28. 38. *a.* before the Lord.
Jer. 42. 2. let our supplication be *a.*
Lk. 4. 24. no prophet is *a.*
Acts 10. 35. he that worketh righteousness
  is *a.*
2 Cor. 5. 9. present or absent, we may be *a.*
Eph. 1. 6. made us *a.* in the beloved.
Ps. 19. 14. let the meditation of my heart
  be *a.*
Is. 61. 2 ; Lk. 4. 19. to proclaim the *a.* year
  of the Lord.
Rom. 12. 1. sacrifice, holy, *a.* to God.
1 Tim. 1. 15. worthy of all *a.*
Heb. 12. 28. serve God *a.* with fear.
Access, Rom. 5. 2. by whom also we have *a.*
Eph. 2. 18. both have *a.* to the Father.
3. 12. boldness and *a.* by faith.
Accomplish, Ps. 64. 6. they *a.* a diligent search.
Is. 55. 11. it shall *a.* that I please.
Lk. 9. 31. decease he should *a.* at Jerusalem.
Prov. 13. 19. desire *a.* is sweet.
Is. 40. 2. her warfare is *a.*
Lk. 12. 50. how am I straitened till it be *a.* .
1 Pet. 5. 9. afflictions are *a.* in brethren.
Accord, Acts 1. 14. with one *a.* in prayer.
2. 46. daily with one *a.* in temple.
4. 24. their voice to God with one *a.*
Phil. 2. 2. being of one *a.* of one mind.
According, Ex. 12. 25. *a.* as he hath promised.
Ps. 33. 22. *a.* as we hope in thee.
62. 12. to every man *a.* to his work.
103. 10. nor rewarded us *a.* to iniquities.
Rom. 8. 28. the called *a.* to his purpose.
12. 6. gifts differing *a.* to grace.
2 Cor. 8. 12. *a.* to that a man hath.
Account, Ps. 144. 3. man, that thou makest *a.*
  of him.
Matt. 12. 36. give *a.* in the day of judgment.
Lk. 16. 2. give *a.* of thy stewardship.
Rom. 14. 12. every one give *a.* to God.
1 Pet. 4. 5. give *a.* to him ready to judge
  quick and dead.
Gal. 3. 6. *a.* to him for righteousness.
Accursed, Deut. 21. 23. hanged is *a.* of God.
Josh. 6. 18. keep yourselves from the *a.* thing.
Rom. 9. 3. wish myself *a.* from Christ.
1 Cor 12. 3. no man by spirit calleth Jesus *a.*
Gal. 1. 8, 9. preach other Gospel, be *a.*
Accusation, Ezra 4. 6. an *a.* against Judah.
Lk. 19. 8. anything by false *a.*
Matt. 27. 37 ; Mk. 15. 26. over his head his *a.*
1 Tim. 5. 19. against elder, receive not *a.*
2 Pet. 2. 11 ; Jude 9. railing *a.*
Accuse, Prov. 30. 10. *a.* not servant to master.
Lk. 3. 14. neither *a.* any falsely.
John 5. 45. think not that I will *a.* you to
  the Father.
1 Pet. 3. 16. that falsely *a.* your good conver-
  sation.
Tit. 1. 6. not *a.* of riot.
Rom. 2. 15. thoughts *a.* or excusing.
Acknowledge, Ps. 32. 5 ; 51. 3. I *a.* my sin.
Prov. 3. 6. in all thy ways *a.* him.
Is. 63. 16. though Israel *a.* us not.
Jer. 14. 20. we *a.* our wickedness.
Hos. 5. 15. till they *a.* their offence.
1 John 2. 23. he that *a.* the son.
Col. 2. 2. to the *a.* of the mystery of God.

Concordance

Acquaint, Job 22. 21. *a.* thyself with him.
Ps. 139. 3. *a.* with my ways.
Is. 53. 3. *a.* with grief.
Acquit, Job 10. 14. not *a.* me from mine iniquity.
Nah. 1. 3. Lord will not at all *a.* wicked.
Actions, 1 Sam. 2. 3. by the Lord *a.* are weighed.
Acts, Jud. 5. 11. rehearse righteous *a.* of the Lord.
Ps. 145. 4, 6. speak of thy mighty *a.*
150. 2. praise him for his mighty *a.*
Is. 28. 21. his *a.* his strange *a.*
Adder, Gen. 49. 17. Dan shall be an *a.*
Ps. 58. 4. like the deaf *a.* that stops.
91. 13. thou shalt tread on the *a.*
140. 3. *a.* poison is under their lips.
Prov. 23. 32. wine stingeth like an *a.*
Addicted, 1 Cor. 16. 15. *a.* themselves to the ministry.
Adjure, Josh. 6. 26. Joshua *a.* them at that time.
1 Sam. 14. 24. Saul had *a.* the people.
1 Ki. 22. 16. how many times shall I *a.* thee.
Matt. 26. 63. I *a.* thee by the living God.
Mk. 5. 7 I *a.* thee by God torment not.
Acts 19. 13. we *a.* you by Jesus.
Administration, 1 Cor. 12. 5. there are differences of a.
2 Cor 9. 12. for the *a.* of this service.
8. 19. *a.* by us to the glory.
Admiration, Jude 16. having men's persons in *a.*
Rev. 17. 6. I wondered with great *a.*
2 Thes. 1. 10. to be *a.* in all them.
Admonish, Eccl. 4. 13. who will no more be *a.*
Eccl. 12. 12. by these, be *a.*
Acts 27. 9. Paul *a.* them.
Rom. 15. 14; Col. 3. 16. *a.* one another.
1 Thes. 5. 12. over you in Lord, and *a.* you.
2 Thes. 3. 15. *a.* him as a brother.
Heb. 8. 5. Moses was *a.* of God.
Admonition, 1 Cor. 10. 11. are written for our *a.*
Eph. 6. 4. bring them up in the *a.*
Tit. 3. 10. after first and second *a.*
Ado, Mk. 5. 39. why make ye this *a.*
Adoption, Rom. 8. 15. received the spirit of *a.*
Rom. 8. 23. waiting for the *a.*
9. 4. to whom pertaineth the *a.*
Gal. 4. 5. might receive the *a.* of sons.
Eph. 1. 5. predestinated us to the *a.*
Adorn, Is. 61. 10; Rev. 21. 2. as a bride *a.* herself.
Lk. 21. 5. temple *a.* with goodly stones.
1 Tim. 2. 9; 1 Pet. 3. 3, 5. women *a.*
Tit. 2. 10. *a.* the doctrine of God.
Advantage, Lk. 9. 25. what is a man *a.*?
Rom. 3. 1. what *a.* hath the Jew?
1 Cor 15. 32. what *a.* if the dead?
2 Cor 2. 11. lest Satan get *a.* of us.
Jude 16. in admiration because of *a.*
Adversary, Ex. 23. 22. I will be *a.* to thy *a.*
Num. 22. 22. angel stood for *a.*
Job 31. 35. that mine *a.* had written a book.
Ps. 74. 10. how long shall *a.* reproach?
Is. 50. 8. who is mine *a.*?
Matt. 5. 25. *a.* quickly lest *a.* deliver.
Lk. 18. 3. saying, avenge me of mine *a.*
1 Cor. 16. 9. there are many *a.*
Phil. 1. 28. nothing terrified by your *a.*
1 Tim. 5. 14. give no occasion to *a.*
1 Pet. 5. 8. your *a.* the devil.
Heb. 10. 27. shall devour the *a.*

Adversity, 1 Sam. 10. 19. save you out of all *a.*
2 Sam. 4. 9. my soul out of all *a.*
Ps. 10. 6. I shall never be in *a.*
94. 13. give rest from days of *a.*
Prov. 17. 17. brother is born for *a.*
Eccl. 7. 14. in the day of *a.* consider.
Is. 30. 20. bread of *a.*
Heb. 13. 3. remember them which suffer *a.*
Advice, Jud. 20. 7. give your *a.* and counsel.
1 Sam. 25. 33. blessed be thy *a.*
2 Sam. 19. 43. our *a.* not be first.
Prov. 20. 18. with good *a.* make war.
2 Cor 8. 10. herein I give my *a.*
Advise, 2 Sam. 24. 13 ; 1 Chr. 21. 12. *a.* and see.
1 Ki. 12. 6. how do ye *a.* that I?
Prov. 13. 10. with well *a.* is wisdom.
Acts 27. 12. the more part *a.* to depart.
Afar off, Gen. 22. 4. Abraham saw the place *a.*
Ps. 139. 2. understandest my thoughts *a.*
Jer. 23. 23. at hand, not a God *a.*
Acts 2. 39. promise to all *a.*
Eph. 2. 17. preached peace to you *a.*
Heb. 11. 13. seen promises *a.*
Affairs, Ps. 112. 5. guide *a.* with discretion.
Eph. 6. 21. know my *a.*
2 Tim. 2. 4. entangled himself with *a.*
Affect, Lam. 3. 51. mine eye *a.* mine heart.
Gal. 4. 17. they zealously *a.* you.
4. 18. good to be zealously *a.*
Acts 14. 2. minds evil *a.* against brethren.
Affection, 1 Chr. 29. 3. set *a.* to house of God.
Rom. 1. 31 ; 2 Tim. 3. 3. without natural *a.*
Rom. 12. 10. be kindly *a.* one to another.
Gal. 5. 24. crucified flesh with *a.*
Col. 3. 2. set your *a.* on things above.
2 Cor 7. 15. his inward *a.*
Afflict, Ex. 1. 11. taskmasters to *a.* them.
Ruth 1. 21. Almighty hath *a.* me.
1 Ki. 11. 39. I will *a.* seed of David.
Ps. 44. 2. how thou didst *a.* the people.
82. 3. do justice to the *a.*
90. 15. the days wherein thou hast *a.*
116. 10. I was greatly *a.*
140. 12. Lord will maintain cause of *a.*
Prov. 22. 22. neither oppress the *a.*
Is. 53. 4. smitten of God and *a.*
63. 9. in all their *a.* he was *a.*
Nah. 1. 12. I will *a.* thee no more.
2 Cor. 1. 6. whether we be *a.* it is.
1 Tim. 5. 10. if she have relieved the *a.*
Heb. 11. 37. destitute *a.* tormented.
Jas. 4. 9. be *a.* and mourn.
5. 13. is any among you *a.*?
Affliction, Ex. 3. 7 ; Acts 7. 34. seen *a.* of my people.
Deut. 16. 3 ; 1 Ki. 22. 27 ; 2 Chr. 18. 26. bread of *a.*
2 Chr. 20. 9. cry to thee in *a.*
Job 5. 6. *a.* cometh not forth of the dust.
30. 16, 27. days of *a.*
36. 8. cords of *a.*
Ps. 34. 19. many are *a.* of righteous.
119. 50. this is my comfort in *a.*
Is. 30. 20. water of *a.*
48. 10. furnace of *a.*
Jer. 16. 19. refuge in day of *a.*
Hos. 5. 15. in *a.* will seek me early.
Mk. 4. 17. *a.* ariseth for the word's sake.
Acts 20. 23. bonds and *a.* abide me;
2 Cor. 2. 4. out of much *a.* I wrote.
4. 17. light *a.* but for a moment.
8. 2. great trial of *a.*
Phil. 1. 16. add *a.* to my bonds.
1 Thes. 1. 6. received word in much *a.*

Affliction—*Continued.*
Heb. 10. 32. great fight of *a.*
11. 25. suffer *a.* with people of God.
Jas. 1. 27. visit fatherless in *a.*
Affright, Is. 21. 4. fearfulness *a.* me.
Mk. 16. 5 ; Lk. 24. 37. they were *a.*
Rev. 11. 13. remnant were *a.*
Afraid, 1 Sam. 18. 29. Saul yet the more *a.*
Job 3. 25. that I was *a.* of is come.
9. 28. I am *a.* of sorrows.
Ps. 27. 1. of whom shall I be *a.?*
56. 3. what time I am *a,*
65. 8. *a.* at thy tokens.
77. 16. waters saw thee and were *a.*
91. 5. not be *a.* for terror by night.
112. 7. *a.* of evil tidings.
Matt. 14. 27 · Mk. 5. 36 ; 6. 50 ; John 6. 20. be not *a.*
Mk. 9. 6 ; Lk. 2. 9. sore *a.*
Gal. 4. 11. I am *a.* of you.
1 Pet. 3. 6. not *a.* with any amazement.
2 Pet. 2. 10. not *a.* to speak evil of dignities.
Afresh, Heb. 6. 6. they crucify son of God *a.*
Afterwards, Ps. 73. 24. *a.* receive me to glory.
Prov. 20. 17. deceit sweet, but *a.*
29. 11. wise keepeth till *a.*
John 13. 36. thou shalt follow me *a.*
1 Cor. 15. 23. *a.* they that are Christ's.
Gal. 3. 23. faith *a.* revealed.
Heb. 12. 11. *a.* yieldeth fruit of righteousness.
Against, Gen. 16. 12. hand *a.* every man.
Matt. 10. 35. man *a.* his father.
12. 30. he not with me, is *a.* me.
Lk. 2. 34. for a sign spoken *a.*
Acts 28. 22. sect everywhere spoken *a.*
Age, Job 5. 26. come to grave in a full *a.*
Ps. 39. 5. my *a.* is as nothing before thee.
Eph. 2. 7. *a.* to come he might shew.
Col. 1. 26. mystery hid from *a.*
Aged, 2 Sam. 19. 32. Barzillai very *a.* man.
Tit. 2. 2. that the *a.* men be sober.
Philem. 9. such an one as Paul the *a.*
Agony, Lk. 22. 44. being in an *a.* he prayed.
Agree, Amos 3. 3. two walk except they be *a.*
Matt. 5. 25. *a.* with adversary quickly.
18. 19. if two shall *a.* on earth.
Acts 23. 20. Jews have *a.* to desire thee.
1 John 5. 8. these three *a.* in one.
2 Cor. 6. 16. what *a.* hath temple?
Aground, Acts 27. 41. they ran the ship *a.*
Aha, Ps. 40. 15. desolate, that say unto me *a.*
70. 3. be turned back that say *a. a.*
Aileth, Gen. 21. 17. what *a.* thee, Hagar?
Jud. 18. 23. Micah, what *a.* thee?
1 Sam. 11. 5. what *a.* the people?
Ps. 114. 5. what *a.* thee, O sea?
Is. 22. 1. what *a.* thee now?
Air, 2 Sam. 21. 10. birds of the *a.* to rest.
Job 41. 16. no *a.* can come between.
Eccl. 10. 20. bird of the *a.* carry voice.
Matt. 8. 20. birds of the *a.* have nests.
1 Cor. 9. 26. not as one that beateth the *a.*
Eph. 2. 2. prince of power of the *a.*
1 Thes. 4. 17. to meet the Lord in the *a.*
Rev. 9. 2. sun and *a.* were darkened.
Alarm, Jer. 4. 19 ; 49. 2. *a.* of war.
Joel 2. 1. sound *a.* in holy mountain.
Zeph. 1. 16. *a.* against the fenced cities.
Alas, 2 Ki. 6. 5, 15. *a.* my master
Ezek. 6. 11. stamp, and say *a.*
Joel 1. 15. *a.* for the day of the Lord.
Amos 5. 16. say in highways *a. a.*
Rev. 18. 10. *a. a.* that great city.

Alien, Deut. 14. 21. sell it to an *a.*
Ps. 69. 8. an *a.* unto my mother's children.
Eph. 2. 12. *a.* from commonwealth.
Heb. 11. 34. armies of the *a.*
Alienated, Eph. 4. 18. *a.* from life of God.
Col. 1. 21. that were sometime *a.*
Alike, Job 21. 26. lie down *a.* in dust.
Ps. 33. 15. fashioneth their hearts *a.*
139. 12. darkness and light both *a.*
Eccl. 9. 2. all things come *a.* to all.
Rom. 14. 5. esteemeth every day *a.*
Alive, Deut. 4. 4. *a.* every one this day.
1 Sam. 2. 6. killeth and maketh *a.*
15. 8. he took Agag *a.*
Ezek. 18. 27. save soul *a.*
Lk. 15. 24, 32. son was dead, and is *a.*
24. 23. angels who said he was *a.*
Acts 1. 3. shewed himself *a.*
Rom. 6. 11, 13. *a.* unto God.
1 Cor. 15. 22. in Christ all be made *a.*
1 Thes. 4. 15. *a.* and remain.
Rev. 1. 18. I am *a.* for evermore.
2. 8. which was dead, and is *a.*
Allow, Lk. 11. 48. that ye *a.* the deeds.
Rom. 7. 15. that which I do, I *a.* not.
1 Thes. 2. 4. as we were *a.* of God.
Allure, Hos. 2. 14. *a.* her into the wilderness.
2 Pet. 2. 18. they *a.* through lusts.
Almighty, Gen. 17. 1. I am the *a.* God.
Ex. 6. 3. by the name of God *a.*
Job 11. 7. find out the *a.* to perfection.
32. 8. inspiration of the *a.*
Ps. 91. 1. under shadow of the *a.*
Rev. 1. 8. was and is to come, the *a.*
4. 8. Lord God *a.,* which was.
Alms, Matt. 6. 1. do not your *a.* before men.
Lk. 11. 41. give *a.* of such things.
Acts 3. 3. seeing Peter and John, asked *a.*
10. 2. Cornelius gave much *a.*
24. 17. to bring *a.* to my nation.
Alone, Gen. 2. 18. not good man should be *a.*
Num. 11. 14 ; Deut. 1. 9. bear all these people *a.*
Deut. 32. 12. Lord *a.* did lead him.
Ps. 136. 4. who *a.* doeth great wonders.
Hos. 4. 17. Ephraim joined to idols, let him *a.*
Matt. 4. 4 ; Lk. 4. 4. not live by bread *a.*
14. 23 ; Lk. 9. 18. Jesus was *a.*
John 8. 16 ; 16. 32. I am not *a.*
Heb. 9. 7. went high-priest *a.* once.
Jas. 2. 17. faith is dead, being *a.*
Altar, Ps. 26. 6. so will I compass thine *a.*
Ps. 43. 4. then will I go to *a.* of God.
Matt. 5. 23. bring thy gift to *a.*
1 Cor. 9. 13 ; 10. 18. partakers with *a.*
Heb. 7. 13. gave attendance at the *a.*
13. 10. we have an *a.*
Alter, Ps. 89. 34. not *a.* thing gone out.
Dan. 6. 8. law of Medes and Persians, which *a.* not.
Lk. 9. 29. fashion of countenance *a.*
Altogether, Ps. 14. 3 ; 53. 3. *a.* become filthy.
Ps. 50. 21. *a.* such an one as thyself.
Cant. 5. 16. he is *a.* lovely.
Acts 26. 29. almost and *a.* such as I.
Always, Job 7. 16. I would not live *a.*
Ps. 103. 9. not *a.* chide.
Matt. 28. 20. I am with you *a.*
Mk. 14. 7 ; John 12. 8. me ye have not *a.*
Lk. 18. 1. men ought *a.* to pray.
2 Cor. 6. 10. yet *a.* rejoicing.
Phil. 4. 4. rejoice in the Lord *a.*
Amazed, Matt. 19. 25. disciples exceedingly *a.*
Mk. 2. 12 ; Lk. 5. 26. *a.* and glorified God.

Amazed—*Continued.*
Mk. 14. 33. he began to be sore *a.*
Lk. 9. 43. *a.* at mighty power of God.
Acts 9. 21. all that heard Saul were *a.*
1 Pet. 3. 6. not afraid with any *a.*
Amend, Jer. 7. 3 ; 26. 13 ; 35. 15. *a.* your ways.
John 4. 52. hour when he began to *a.*
Amiable, Ps. 84. 1. how *a.* are thy tabernacles.
Amiss, 2 Chr. 6. 37. we have done *a.*
Dan. 3. 29. speak anything *a.*
Lk. 23. 41. hath done nothing *a.*
Jas. 4. 3. because ye ask *a.*
Angel, Gen. 48. 16. the *a.* who redeemed me.
Ex. 23. 23. my *a.* shall go before th.ee.
Ps. 34. 7. *a.* of Lord encampeth.
Is. 63. 9. *a.* of his presence saved them.
Hos. 12. 4. he had power over the *a.*
Matt. 13. 39. the reapers are the *a.*
Mk. 12. 25 ; Lk. 20. 36. as *a.* in heaven.
John 5. 4. *a.* went down at a certain season.
Acts 6. 15. saw as face of an *a.*
1 Cor. 6. 3. we shall judge *a.*
2 Thes. 1. 7. with his mighty *a.*
Heb. 2. 16. took not nature of *a.*
13. 2. entertained *a.* unawares.
1 Pet. 1. 12. *a.* desire to look into.
Rev. 5. 11. voice of many *a.* about throne.
Anger, Ex. 4. 14. *a.* of Lord kindled against
Moses.
Deut. 13. 17. fierceness of his *a.*
Ps. 30. 5. his *a.* endureth but a moment.
37. 8. cease from *a.*
90. 7. we are consumed by thine *a.*
Is. 5. 25. his *a.* is not turned away.
Hos. 14. 4. mine *a.* is turned away.
Col. 3. 8. put off *a.*
Angry, Gen. 18. 30. let not Lord be *a.*
Ps. 2. 12. kiss the son, lest he be *a.*
7. 11. God is *a.* with the wicked.
Eccl. 7. 9. be not hasty to be *a.*
Is. 12. 1. though thou wast *a.* with me.
Jon. 4. 9. I do well to be *a.*
Matt. 5. 22. whoso is *a.* with brother.
Eph. 4. 26. be *a.* and sin not.
Rev. 11. 18. the nations were *a.*
Anguish, Ex. 6. 9. hearkened not for *a.*
Job 7. 11. I will speak in *a.* of spirit.
Ps. 119. 143. trouble and *a.* take hold.
John 16. 21. remember not *a.* for joy.
Rom. 2. 9. tribulation and *a.* on every soul.
Anoint, Ex. 28. 41. shalt *a.* them.
1 Sam. 15. 1. the Lord sent me to *a.* thee king.
2 Sam. 14. 2. *a.* not thyself with oil.
Is. 21. 5. arise and *a.* shield.
Mk. 14. 8. *a.* my body to burying.
Lk. 7. 46. my head thou didst not *a.*
John 9. 6. *a.* eyes of blind man.
12. 3. Mary *a.* feet of Jesus.
2 Cor. 1. 21. hath *a.* us is God.
1 John 2. 27. the same *a.* teacheth.
Jas. 5. 14. *a.* with oil in name of the Lord.
Rev. 3. 18. *a.* thine eyes with eyesalve.
Answer, Gen. 41. 16. Pharaoh an *a.* of peace.
Job 19. 16. he gave me no *a.*
Prov. 15. 1. a soft *a.* turneth away wrath.
Cant. 5. 6. I called him, he gave no *a.*
John 1. 22. that we may give *a.*
19. 9. Jesus gave him no *a.*
1 Pet. 3. 15. be ready to give an *a.*
3. 21. *a.* of good conscience.
Job 13. 22. call thou, and I will *a.*
Ps. 65. 5. by terrible things wilt thou *a.*
Eccl. 10. 19. money *a.* all things.
Lk. 21. 14. not to meditate what ye *a.*

Answer—*Continued.*
2 Cor. 5. 12. somewhat to *a.*
Col. 4. 6. how ye ought to *a.*
Apart, Ps. 4. 3. Lord hath set *a.* godly.
Matt. 14. 13. desert place *a.*
Mk. 6. 31. come ye yourselves *a.*
Appear, Gen. 1. 9. let the dry land *a.*
Ex. 23. 15. none *a.* before me empty.
Ps. 42. 2. when shall I come, and *a.*
90. 16. let thy work *a.*
Cant. 2. 12. flowers *a.* on earth.
Is. 1. 12. ye come to *a.* before me.
Matt. 6. 16. *a.* unto men to fast.
23. 28. outwardly *a.* righteous.
Rom. 7. 13. that it might *a.* sin.
2 Cor. 5. 10. all *a.* before judgment seat.
Col. 3. 4. Christ our life shall *a.*
1 Sam. 16. 7. man looketh on outward *a.*
1 Thes. 5. 22. abstain from all *a.* of evil.
Tit. 2. 13. looking for glorious *a.*
Appoint, Job 14. 5. thou hast *a.* his bounds.
30. 23. house *a.* for all living.
Ps. 79. 11 ; 102. 20. preserve those *a.* to die.
Matt. 24. 51 ; Lk. 12. 46. *a.* him his portion.
Acts 6. 3. seven men whom we may *a.*
1 Thes. 5. 9. God hath not *a.* to wrath.
Apprehend, Acts 12. 4. when he *a.* Peter.
2 Cor. 11. 32. garrison desirous to *a.*
Phil. 3. 12. I may *a.* that for which.
Approach, Ps. 65. 4. blessed whom thou
causest to *a.*
Is. 58. 2. take delight in *a.* God.
Lk. 12. 33. where no thief *a.*
1 Tim. 6. 16. light no man can *a.*
Heb. 10. 25. as ye see the day *a.*
Approve, Ps. 49. 13. their posterity *a.* their
sayings.
Acts 2. 22. a man *a.* of God.
Rom. 16. 10. *a.* in Christ.
Phil. 1. 10. *a.* things that are excellent.
2 Tim. 2. 15. show thyself *a.*
Aright, Ps. 50. 23. ordereth his conversation *a.*
Ps. 78. 8. set not their heart *a.*
Prov. 15. 2. useth knowledge *a.*
23. 31. wine, when it moveth itself *a.*
Jer. 8. 6. they spake not *a.*
Arise, Josh. 1. 2. *a.* go over this Jordan.
1 Ki. 18. 44. there *a.* a little cloud.
Ps. 68. 1. let God *a.*
88. 10. shall the dead *a.* and praise thee ?
102. 13. *a.* and have mercy on Zion.
112. 4. to upright *a.* right.
Is. 60. 1. *a.* shine, thy light is come.
Mal. 4. 2. sun of righteousness *a.*
Mk. 5. 41 ; Lk. 8. 54. damsel, *a.*
Lk. 7. 14. young man, *a.*
15. 18. I will *a.* and go to my father.
Eph. 5. 14. *a.* from the dead, and Christ.
2 Pet. 1. 19. till the day-star *a.*
Arm, Ex. 15. 16. by greatness of thine *a.*
Job. 40. 9. hast thou an *a.* like God ?
Ps. 89. 13. thou hast a mighty *a.*
Is. 53. 1 ; John 12. 38. to whom is the *a.* of
the Lord revealed.
Armour, Rom. 13. 12. *a.* of light.
2 Cor. 6. 7. by *a.* of righteousness.
Eph. 6. 11. put on whole *a.* of God.
Array, Job 6. 4. the terrors of God set in *a.*
Matt. 6. 29 ; Lk. 12. 27. not *a.* like one of
these.
1 Tim. 2. 9. not with costly *a.*
Rev. 7. 13. *a.* in white robes.
Arrow, 2 Ki. 13. 17. the *a.* of the Lord's
deliverance.

Arrow—*Continued.*
Ps. 91. 5. *a.* that flieth by day.
38. 2. thine *a.* stick fast.
45. 5. *a.* sharp in heart of enemies.
Ezek. 5. 16. evil *a.* of famine.
Ascend, Ps. 24. 3. who shall *a.* into hill of Lord.
Ps. 139. 8. if I *a.* up into heaven.
68. 18 ; Eph. 4. 8. *a.* on high.
John 1. 51. angels of God *a.*
3. 13. no man hath *a.* to heaven.
Rev. 8. 4. smoke of incense *a.*
Ascribe, Deut. 32. 3. *a.* greatness to God.
Job 36. 3. *a.* righteousness to my Maker.
Ps. 68. 34. *a.* ye strength to God.
Ashamed, Ps. 25. 3. let none that wait on thee be *a.*
Ps. 31. 1. let me never be *a.*
34. 5. their faces were not *a.*
Is. 45. 17. not be *a.*, world without end.
Jer. 6. 15 ; 8. 12. were they *a.* ?
Mk. 8. 38. *a.* of me and my words.
Rom. 1. 16. not *a.* of Gospel.
5. 5. hope maketh not *a.*
2 Tim. 2. 15. workman not needing to be *a.*
Heb. 11. 16. not *a.* to be called their God.
1 Pet. 4. 16. suffer as Christian, not be *a.*
1 John 2. 28. *a.* before him at his coming.
Aside, Mk. 7. 33. *a.* from the multitude.
Heb. 12. 1. let us lay *a.* every weight.
Ask, Ps. 2. 8. *a.* of me, and I shall give.
Jer. 6. 16. *a.* for the old paths.
50. 5. they shall *a.* way to Zion.
Matt. 7. 7 ; Lk. 11. 9. *a.* and it shall be given.
John 14. 13 ; 15. 16. *a.* in my name.
Eph. 3. 20. above all we *a.*
Jas. 1. 5. lack wisdom, let him *a.* of God.
1 Pet. 3. 15. *a.* reason of hope.
1 John 3. 22 ; 5. 14. whatsoever we *a.*
Asleep, Matt. 8. 24 ; Mk. 4. 38. but he was *a.*
Matt. 26. 40 ; Mk. 14. 40. disciples *a.*
1 Cor. 15. 6. some are fallen *a.*
1 Thes. 4. 13. them that are *a.*
2 Pet. 3. 4. since fathers fell *a.*
Ass, Num. 22. 30. am not I thine *a.* ?
Prov. 26. 3. bridle for *a.*
Is. 1. 3. *a.* his master's crib.
Zech. 9. 9 ; Matt. 21. 5. riding on an *a.*
Lk. 13. 15. each loose his *a.* on Sabbath.
14. 5. *a.* fallen into pit.
John 12. 14. had found a young *a.* sat.
2 Pet. 2. 16. the dumb *a.* speaking.
Assay, Job 4. 2. if we *a.* to commune with thee.
Acts 9. 26. Saul *a.* to join disciples.
16. 7. they *a.* to go to Bithynia.
Heb. 11. 29. Egyptians *a.* to do.
Assembly, Ps. 22. 16. *a.* of wicked.
Ps. 89. 7. God feared in *a.* of his saints.
Eccl. 12. 11. nails fastened by masters of *a.*
Heb. 10. 25. forsake not the *a.*
Assurance, Is. 32. 17. effect of righteousness *a.*
Acts 17. 31. whereof he hath given *a.*
Col. 2. 2. full *a.* of understanding.
1 Thes. 1. 5. Gospel came in much *a.*
Heb. 6. 11. full *a.* of hope.
10. 22. draw near in full *a.* of faith.
See 1 John 3. 19.
Astonished, Job. 26. 11. pillars of heaven are *a.*
Is. 52. 14. as many were *a.* at thee.
Jer. 2. 12. be *a.* O ye heavens.
Dan. 8. 27. was *a.* at the vision.
Matt. 7. 28 ; 22. 33 ; Mk. 1. 22 ; 11. 18 ; Lk. 4. 32. *a.* at his doctrine.

Astonished—*Continued.*
Lk. 2. 47. *a.* at his understanding and answers.
5. 9. *a.* at draught of fishes.
24. 22. women made us *a.*
Acts 9. 6. Saul trembling and *a.*
12. 16. saw Peter, they were *a.*
13. 12. deputy believed, being *a.*
Astonishment, Deut. 28. 37. become an *a.* and a proverb.
Ps. 60. 3. drink wine of *a.*
Jer. 8. 21. *a.* hath taken hold.
Ezek. 23. 33. filled with cup of *a.*
Athirst, Matt. 25. 44. when saw we thee *a.*
Rev. 21. 6. I will give to him that is *a.*
22. 17. let him that is *a.* come.
Atonement, Lev. 23. 28 ; 25. 9. day of *a.*
2 Sam. 21. 3. wherewith shall I make *a.*
Rom. 5. 11. by whom we have received *a.*
Attain, Ps. 139. 6. high, I cannot *a.* to it.
Rom. 9. 30. Gentiles *a.* to righteousness.
Phil 3. 11. if I might *a.* to resurrection of dead.
1 Tim 4. 6. doctrine, whereunto thou hast *a.*
Attend, Ps. 17. 1 ; 61. 1 ; 142. 6. *a.* to my cry.
Prov. 4. 1. *a.* to know understanding.
Acts 16. 14. *a.* to things spoken by Paul.
Rom 13. 6. ministers *a.* continually.
Attendance, 1 Tim. 4. 13. give *a.* to reading.
Heb. 7. 13. no man gave *a.* at altar.
Attentive, Neh. 1. 6 ; Ps. 130. 2. let thine ears be *a.*
Lk. 19. 48. people were very *a.*
Audience, 1 Chr. 28. 8. in *a.* of our God.
Lk. 7. 1 ; 20. 45. in *a.* of people.
Acts 13. 16. ye that fear God, give *a.*
22. 22. they gave him *a.* to this word.
Author, 1 Cor. 14. 33. God is not *a.* of confusion.
Heb. 5. 9. he became *a.* of salvation.
12. 2. Jesus, the *a.* and finisher.
Authority, Matt. 7. 29 ; Mk. 1. 22. as one having *a.*
Matt. 8. 9 ; Lk. 7. 8. I am a man under *a.*
21. 23. by what *a.*
Mk. 1. 27 ; Lk. 4. 36. with *a.* he commandeth unclean spirits.
Mk. 13. 34. gave *a.* to his servants.
Lk. 9. 1. power and *a.* over all devils.
19. 17. have *a.* over ten cities.
22. 25. exercise *a.* called benefactors.
John 5. 27. *a.* to execute judgment.
Acts 8. 27. eunuch of great *a.*
1 Cor. 15. 24. put down all *a.*
1 Tim. 2. 2. kings, and all in *a.*
2. 12. suffer not a woman to usurp *a.*
Tit. 2. 15. rebuke with all *a.*
1 Pet. 3. 22. angels and *a.* made subject to.
Rev. 13. 2. dragon gave him great *a.*
Availeth, Gal. 5. 6. in Christ, circumcision *a.* not.
Jas. 5. 16. prayer of righteous *a.* much.
Avenge, Lev. 19. 18. thou shalt not *a.*
Deut. 32. 43. *a.* blood of his servants.
Josh. 10. 13. sun stood still till people *a.*
1 Sam. 24. 12. the Lord Judge, and *a.*
2 Sam. 22. 48 ; Ps. 18. 47. God *a.* me.
Is. 1. 24. I will *a.* me of mine enemies.
Lk. 18. 3. *a.* me of mine adversary.
Rom. 12. 19. *a.* not yourselves.
Rev. 19. 2. God hath *a.* blood of his servants.
Avenger, Deut. 19. 6. lest *a.* pursue the slayer.
Ps. 8. 2. thou mightest still the *a.*
44. 16. enemy and *a.*
1 Thes. 4. 6. the Lord is the *a.*

Avoid, Prov. 4. 15. *a.* it, pass not by it.
Rom. 16. 17. cause divisions, *a.* them.
1 Tim. 6. 20. *a.* profane babblings.
2 Tim. 2. 23. unlearned questions *a.*
Tit. 3. 9. *a.* foolish questions.

Awake, Ps. 17. 15. satisfied, when I *a.* with thy likeness.
Ps. 57. 8; 108. 2. *a.,* psaltery and harp, I will *a.*
Prov. 23. 35. when shall I *a.*
Is. 51. 9; 52. 1. *a., a.,* put on strength.
Dan. 12. 2. sleep in the dust shall *a.*
Joel. 1. 5. *a.,* ye drunkards, weep.
Zech. 13. 7. *a.* O sword.
Mk. 4. 38. asleep, and they *a.* him.
Lk. 9. 32. when *a.,* they saw his glory.
Rom. 13. 11. high time to *a.*
1 Cor. 15. 34. *a.* to righteousness.
Eph. 5. 14. *a.* thou that sleepest.

Awe, Ps. 4. 4. stand in *a.* sin not.
33. 8. inhabitants of world stand in *a.* of.
119. 161. my heart standeth in *a.*

Axe, 1. Ki. 6. 7. hammer nor *a.* was heard.
2 Ki. 6. 5. *a.* head fell into water.
Ps. 74. 5. famous as he had lifted up *a.*
Is. 10. 15. shall the *a.* boast?
Matt. 3. 10; Lk. 3. 9. the *a.* is laid to root.

BABBLER, Eccl. 10. 11; Acts 17. 18.
Babbling, Prov. 23. 29; 1 Tim. 6. 20; 2 Tim. 2. 16.
Babe, Ps. 8. 2; Matt. 21. 16. out of mouth of *b.*
Ps. 17. 14. leave their substance to *b.*
Is. 3. 4. *b.* shall rule over them.
Matt. 11. 25; Lk. 10. 21. revealed to *b.*
Rom. 2. 20. teacher of *b.*
1 Cor. 3. 1. *b.* in Christ.
1 Pet. 2. 2. as newborn *b.*

Back, Ps. 21. 12. shalt make them turn their *b.*
129. 3. ploughers plowed on my *b.*
Prov. 26. 3. rod for the fool's *b.*
Is. 38. 17. cast my sins behind thy *b.*
50. 6. I gave my *b.* to the smiters.
Jer. 2. 27; 32. 33. turned to me *b.* and not face.
Rom. 11. 10. bow down their *b.* always.

Backbiting, Ps. 15. 3. that *b.* not with his tongue.
Prov. 25. 23. *a b.* tongue.
Rom. 1. 30. *b.* haters of God.
2 Cor. 12. 20. lest there be debates, *b.*

Backsliding, Jer. 2. 19. thy *b.* shall reprove thee.
3. 12. return, thou *b.* Israel, saith Lord.
Hos. 4. 16. Israel slideth back as *b.* heifer.
14. 4. I will heal their *b.*

Backward, 2. Ki. 20. 10; Is. 38. 8. shadow return *b.*
Job. 23. 8. *b.* I cannot perceive.
Ps. 40. 14; 70. 2. driven *b.*
Is. 59. 14. judgment is turned *b.*
Jer. 7. 24. they went *b.* and not forward.
John 18. 6. they went *b.* and fell to the ground.

Bad, Gen. 24. 50. cannot speak *b.* or good.
2 Sam. 13. 22. Absalom spake good nor *b.*
Matt. 13. 48. good, but cast the *b.* away.
2 Cor. 5. 10. done, whether good or *b.*

Bag, Deut. 25. 13. in thy *b.* divers weights.
1 Sam. 17. 40. smooth stones in a *b.*
Job. 14. 17. transgression sealed in a *b.*
Prov. 7. 20. taken a *b.* of money.
Is. 46. 6. lavish gold out of *b.*
Mic. 6. 11. *b.* of deceitful weights.
Hag. 1. 6. *b.* with holes.
Lk. 12. 33. *b.* that wax not old.
John 12. 6; 13. 29. Judas a thief, and had the *b.*

Bake, Ex. 16. 23. *b.* that you will *b.* to-day.
Lev. 26. 26. ten women shall *b.*
1 Sam. 28. 24. women at Endor did *b.*
Is. 44. 15. he *b.* bread.

Baker, Gen. 40. 1. *b.* had offended the king.
41. 10. put in ward both chief *b.*
1 Sam. 8. 13. your daughters to be *b.*
Jer. 37. 21. bread out of *b.* street.
Hos. 7. 4. as oven heated by the *b.*

Balance, Lev. 19. 36; Ezek. 45. 10. just *b.*
Job 31. 6. weighed in even *b.*
Ps. 62. 9. laid in *b.* are vanity.
Prov. 11. 1 : 20. 23. a false *b.* is abomination.
16. 11. just weight and *b.* are Lord's.
Is. 40. 12. weighed hills in *b.*
46. 6. weigh silver in the *b.*
Dan. 5. 27. weighed in the *b.* and found wanting.
Hos. 12. 7. *b.* of deceit in his hand.
Rev. 6. 5. a pair of *b.*

Bald, 2 Ki. 2. 23. go up, thou *b.* head.
Jer. 48. 37; Ezek. 29. 18. every head *b.*

Baldness, Lev. 21. 5. not make *b.* on their head.
Deut. 14. 1. any *b.* between your eyes.
Is. 3. 24. instead of well set hair *b.*
22. 12. the Lord did call to *b.*
Mic. 1. 16. enlarge thy *b.* as eagle.

Ball, Is. 22. 18. he will toss thee like a *b.*

Balm, Gen. 37. 25. Ishmaelites bearing *b.*
Jer. 8. 22. is there no *b.* in Gilead?

Bands, Ps. 2. 3; 107. 14. break their *b.* asunder.
Ps. 73. 4. there are no *b.* in their death.
Is. 58. 6. to lose the *b.* of wickedness.
Hos. 11. 4. drew them with *b.* of love.
Zech. 11. 7. two staves, beauty and *b.*
Lk. 8. 29. he brake *b.* and was driven.
Acts 16. 26. every one's *b.* were loosed.
Col. 2. 19. all the body by *b.*
Matt. 27. 27; Mk. 15. 16. gathered to him whole *b.*
Acts 10. 1. *b.* called the Italian *b.*
23. 12. certain of the Jews *b.*

Bank, 2 Sam. 20. 15. cast up a *b.* against the city.
Ezek. 47. 7. at *b.* of river many trees.
Lk. 19. 23. my money into the *b.*

Banner, Ps. 20. 5. in name of God set up *b.*
Cant. 6. 4. terrible as an army with *b.*
2. 4. his *b.* over me was love.
Is. 13. 2. lift ye up a *b.* on mountain.

Banquet, Est. 5. 4. let Haman come to *b.*
Job 41. 6. companions make a *b.* of him.
Cant. 2. 4. brought me to the *b.* house.
Amos 6. 7. *b.* of them that stretched.
1 Pet. 4. 3. we walked in lusts, *b.*

Baptism, Matt. 20. 22; Mk. 10. 38; Lk. 12. 50. baptized with *b.*
Matt. 21. 25; Mk. 11. 30; Lk. 20. 4. *b.* of John.
Mk. 1. 4; Lk. 3. 3; Acts 13. 24. *b.* of repentance.
Rom. 6. 4; Col. 2. 12. buried with him by *b.*
Eph. 4. 5. one Lord, one faith, one *b.*
Heb. 6. 2. doctrine of *b.*
1 Pet. 3. 21. whereunto even *b.*

Baptize, Matt. 3. 11; Mk. 1. 8; Lk. 3. 16. *b.* with Holy Ghost.
Mk. 10. 39. the baptism I am *b.* withal.
16. 16. he that believeth and is *b.*
Lk. 3. 7. multitude came to be *b.*
Lk. 7. 30. Pharisees and lawyers being not *b.*
John 1. 33. he that sent me to *b.*
4 1, 2. Jesus made and *b.* more.

Baptize—*Continued.*
Acts 2. 38. repent and be *b.*
8. 12. were *b.* both men and women.
8. 36. what doth hinder me to be *b.*?
9. 18. Saul arose, and was *b.*
10. 47. that these should not be *b.*?
18. 8. many believed, and were *b.*
22. 16. be *b.* and wash away thy sins.
Rom. 6. 3 ; Gal. 3. 27. *b.* into Jesus Christ.
1 Cor. 1. 13. *b.* in name of Paul.
10. 2. were all *b.* in cloud.
12. 13. all *b.* into one body.
15. 29. *b.* for the dead.

Barbarians, Acts 28. 4. *b.* saw venomous beast.
Rom. 1. 14. debtor both to Greeks and *b.*
1 Cor. 14. 11. to him a *b.*, and he a *b.*
Col. 3. 11. neither Greek nor Jew, *b.*

Barber, Ezek. 5. 1. take thee a *b.* razor.

Bare, Ex. 19. 4. *b.* you on eagle's wings.
Deut. 1. 31. thy God *b.* thee as.
Is. 53. 12. he *b.* the sin of many.
63. 9. he *b.* them all the days of old.
Matt. 8. 17. himself *b.* our sicknesses.
1 Pet. 2. 24. his own self *b.* our sins.
Rev. 22. 2. the tree of life *b.* twelve.
Is. 52. 10. the Lord hath made *b.*
1 Cor. 15. 37. that shall be but *b.* grain.

Barn, Job 39. 12. gather thy seed into *b.*
Matt. 6. 26 ; Lk. 12. 24. nor gather into *b.*
13. 30. gather wheat into *b.*
Lk. 12. 18. pull down my *b.*

Barrel, 1 Ki. 17. 14. the *b.* of meal shall not.
18. 33. fill four *b.* with water.

Barren, 2 Ki. 2. 19. water naught, and ground *b.*
Ps. 107. 34. turneth fruitful land into *b.*
113. 9. the *b.* woman to keep house.
Is. 54. 1. sing, O *b.*, thou that didst not bear.
Lk. 23. 29. blessed are the *b.* and.
2 Pet. 1. 8. be neither *b.* nor unfruitful.

Base, Job 30. 8. children of *b.* men.
Mal. 2. 9. I have made you *b.*
Acts 17. 5. fellows of *b.* sort.
1 Cor. 1. 28. *b.* things of the world.
2 Cor. 10. 1. who in presence am *b.*

Basket, Deut. 28. 5. blessed shall be thy *b.*
Amos 8. 1. of summer fruit.
Matt. 14. 20 ; Mk. 6. 43 ; Lk. 9. 17 ; John 6. 13. twelve *b.*
Matt. 15. 37 ; Mk. 8. 8. seven *b.*
Matt. 16. 9 ; Mk. 8. 19. how many *b.*?

Battle, 1 Sam. 17. 47 ; 2 Chr. 20. 15. *b.* is the Lord's.
2 Sam. 11. 1 ; 1 Chr. 20. 1 ; when kings go forth to *b.*
1 Chr. 5. 20. they cried to God in the *b.*
Job 39. 25. war horse smelleth *b.* afar off.
Ps. 18. 39. girded with strength to *b.*
24. 8. the Lord mighty in *b.*
55. 18. delivered my soul from the *b.*
Eccl. 9. 11. nor *b.* to strong.
Jer. 50. 22. sound of *b.* in land.
1 Cor. 14. 8. who shall prepare to *b.*?
Rev. 16. 14. *b.* of that great day.

Beam, 1 Sam. 17. 7. spear like a weaver's *b.*
Ps. 104. 3. who layeth *b.* in waters.
Matt. 7. 5 ; Lk. 6. 42. cast out *b.*

Bear, Gen. 4. 13. punishment greater than I can *b.*
Ex. 20. 16 ; Lk. 11. 48 ; John 1. 7 ; 8. 18 ; Acts 23. 11 ; 1 John 1. 2 ; 5. 8. *b.* witness.
Lev. 24. 15 ; Heb. 9. 28. *b.* sin.
Num. 11. 14 ; Deut. 1. 9. not able to *b.* people.
Est. 1. 22 ; Jer. 5. 31. *b.* rule.

Bear—*Continued.*
Ps. 75. 3. I *b.* pillars of the earth.
91. 12 ; Matt. 4. 6 ; Lk. 4. 11. they shall *b.* thee up.
Prov. 18. 14. wounded spirit who can *b.*?
Is. 52. 11. clean that *b.* vessels of Lord.
Jer. 31. 19. *b.* reproach of youth.
Lam. 3. 27. *b.* yoke in youth.
Matt. 3. 11. shoes not worthy to *b.*
27. 32 ; Mk. 15. 21 ; Lk. 23. 26. *b.* cross.
John 16. 12. cannot *b.* them now.
Acts 9. 15. chosen vessel to *b.* my name.
Rom. 15. 1. *b.* infirmities of the weak.
1 Cor. 13. 7. charity *b.* all things.
15. 49. shall *b.* image of the heavenly.
Gal. 6. 2. *b.* one another's burdens.
Jas. 3. 12. can fig-tree *b.* olive-berries.

Bear, Is. 11. 7. cow and *b.* shall feed.
Is. 59. 11. we roar all like a *b.*
Hos. 13. 8. as a *b.* bereaved.
Amos. 5. 19. as if a man did flee from a lion and a *b.*

Beard, 2 Sam. 10. 5 ; 1 Chr. 19. 5. till *b.* be grown.
Ps. 133. 2. even Aaron's *b.*
Ezek. 5. 1. cause razor to pass on *b.*

Bearing, Gen. 1. 29. every herb *b.* seed.
Ps. 126. 6. *b.* precious seed.
John 19. 17. *b.* cross.
Rom. 2. 15 ; 9. 1. conscience *b.* witness.
2 Cor. 4. 10. *b.* about in body dying of Jesus.
Heb. 13. 13. *b.* his reproach.

Beast, Gen. 3. 1. serpent more subtil than any *b.*
Ps. 49. 12. like *b.* that perish.
73. 22. as a *b.* before thee.
Prov. 12. 10. regardeth life of *b.*
1 Cor. 15. 32. fought with *b.*
Jas. 3. 7. every kind of *b.* is tamed.
2 Pet. 2. 12. as natural brute *b.*

Beat, Is. 2. 4 ; Mic. 4. 3. *b.* swords into.
Lk. 12. 47. *b.* with many stripes.
1 Cor. 9. 26. not as one that *b.* the air.
2 Cor. 11. 25. thrice was I *b.* with rods.

Beauty, 1 Chr. 1. 29 ; 2 Chr. 20. 21 ; Ps. 29. 2 ; 96. 9. *b.* of holiness.
Ps. 27. 4. behold *b.* of the Lord.
48. 2. *b.* for situation.
50. 2. perfection of *b.*
Is. 33. 17. see the king in his *b.*
53. 2. no *b.* that we should desire him.
52. 7 ; Rom. 10. 15. how *b.* are the feet.

Bed, Job 7. 13. when I say, my *b.* shall comfort.
33. 15. in slumberings upon the *b.*
Ps. 41. 3. make all his *b.* in his sickness.
63. 6. when I remember thee upon my *b.*
Is. 28. 20. *b.* is shorter than a man.
Matt. 9. 6 ; Mk. 2. 9 ; John 5. 11. take up thy *b.*

Befall, Gen. 42. 4 ; 44. 29. mischief *b.* him.
49. 1 ; Deut. 31. 29 ; Dan. 10. 14. *b.* in last days.
Jud. 6. 13. why is all this *b.* us?
Ps. 91. 10. no evil *b.* thee.
Eccl. 3. 19. *b.* men *b.* beasts.
Acts 20. 22. things that shall *b.* me.

Beg, Ps. 109. 10. let his children *b.*
Matt. 27. 58 ; Lk. 23. 52. *b.* body of Jesus
Lk. 16. 3. to *b.* I am ashamed.
John 9. 8. he that sat and *b.*
Gal. 4. 9. the *b.* elements.

Begin, Ezek. 9. 6. *b.* at my sanctuary.
2 Cor. 3. 1. do we *b.* to commend?
1 Pet. 4. 17. judgment *b.* at house of God.

Beginning, Ps. 111. 10 ; Prov. 9. 10. *b.* of wisdom.
Eccl. 7. 8. better end of a thing than *b.*
Matt. 24. 8 ; Mk. 13. 8. *b.* of sorrows.
John 2. 11. *b.* of miracles.
Col. 1. 18. who is the *b.* of the first-born.
Heb. 3. 14. the *b.* of our confidence.
Begotten, Ps. 2. 7 ; Acts 13. 33 : Heb. 1. 5 ; 5. 5. this day have I *b.* thee.
John 1. 14. as of the only *b.* of the Father.
3. 16. God gave only *b.* son.
1 Pet. 1. 3. *b.* us again to a lively hope.
Heb. 1. 6. when he bringeth in first *b.*
Beguile, Gen. 3. 13. serpent *b.* me.
29. 25. wherefore hast thou *b.* me?
Josh. 9. 22. wherefore have ye *b.* us ?
2 Cor. 11. 3. lest as the serpent *b.* Eve.
2 Pet. 2. 14. *b.* unstable souls.
Begun, Gal. 3. 3. having *b.* in the spirit.
Phil. 1. 6. hath *b.* good work.
Behalf, Job 36. 2. speak on God's *b.*
Rom. 16. 19. I am glad on your *b.*
Phil. 1. 29. in *b.* of Christ.
Behave, 1 Chr. 19. 13. let us *b.* valiantly.
Ps. 101. 2. I will *b.* wisely.
Is. 3. 5. child shall *b.* proudly.
1 Cor. 13. 5. charity doth not *b.* unseemly.
1 Thes. 2. 10. how unblameably we *b.*
1 Tim. 3. 15. in the house of God.
Behind, Is. 38. 17. all my sins *b.* thy back.
1 Cor. 1. 7. ye come *b.* in no gift.
Phil. 3. 13. forgetting things *b.*
Col. 1. 24. fill up that which is *b.*
Behold, Job 19. 27. my eyes shall *b.* and not another.
Ps. 27. 4. to *b.* beauty of Lord.
37. 37. *b.* the upright man.
Hab. 1. 13. of purer eyes than to *b.*
Matt. 18. 10. their angels *b.* face.
John 17. 24. they may *b.* my glory.
19. 5. *b.* the man.
2 Cor. 3. 18. as in a glass.
Jas. 1. 23. like man *b.* natural face.
Believe, Num. 14. 11. how long ere they *b.* me?
2 Chr. 20. 20. *b.* in Lord, *b.* his prophets.
Ps. 78. 22. they *b.* not in God.
Prov. 14. 15. simple *b.* every word.
Is. 28. 16. that *b.* not make haste.
53. 1 ; John 12. 38 ; Rom. 10. 16. who nath *b.* our report?
Matt. 8. 13. as thou hast *b.*, so be it.
9. 28. *b.* ye that I am able ?
18. 6 ; Mk. 9. 42. little ones which *b.*
27. 42. come down from cross, and we will *b.*
Mk. 1. 15. repent and *b.* Gospel.
5. 36 ; Lk. 8. 50. be not afraid, only *b.*
9. 23. if thou canst *b.* all things possible.
11. 24. *b.* that ye receive them.
Lk. 1. 1. things most surely *b.*
8. 13. which for a while *b.*
24. 25. slow of heart to *b.*
John 1. 7. all men through him might *b.*
3. 12. *b.* heavenly things.
5. 47. how shall ye *b.* my words.
6. 36. seen me, and *b.* not.
7. 48. have any of the rulers *b.* ?
10. 38. *b.* the works.
11. 15. to intent ye may *b.*
12. 36. *b.* in the light.
14. 1. ye *b.* in God, *b.* also in me.
16. 30. we *b.* thou camest from God.
17. 21. world may *b.*
20. 31. written that ye might *b.*
Acts 8. 37. I *b.* Jesus Christ is Son of God.
13. 39. all that *b.* are justified.

Believe—*continued.*
Acts 16. 34. *b.* with all his nouse.
27. 25. I *b.* God that it shall be as.
Rom 1. 16. power of God to every one that *b.*
3. 22. on all them that *b.*
4. 11. father of all that *b.*
9. 33. *b.* on him shall not be ashamed.
10. 14. how shall they *b.?*
1 Cor. 1. 21. by preaching to save them that *b.*
2 Cor 4. 13. we *b.* therefore speak.
Gal. 3. 22. promise to them that *b.*
1 Thes. 1. 7. ensamples to all that *b.*
2 Thes. 1. 10. admired in all that *b.*
Heb. 10. 39. *b.* to saving of soul.
11. 6. must *b.* that he is.
Jas. 2. 19. devils *b.*, and tremble.
1 Pet. 2. 7. to you which *b.* he is precious.
1 John 4. 1. *b* not every spirit.
5. 1. whoso *b.* Jesus is the Christ.
Belly, Gen. 3. 14. upon thy *b* shalt thou go.
Job 15. 2. *b.* with east wind.
Ps. 22. 10. my God from my mother's *b.*
Jon. 1. 17 ; Matt. 12. 40. in *b.* of fish.
Matt. 15. 17 ; Mk. 7. 19. into *b.* and is cast out
John 7. 38. out of his *b.* flow rivers.
Rom. 16. 18. serve their own *b.*
1 Cor. 6. 13. meats for *b.*, and *b.* for meats.
Phil. 3. 19. whose God is their *b.*
Tit. 1. 12. Cretians slow *b.*
Rev. 10. 9. it shall make thy *b.* bitter.
Belong, Gen. 40. 8. interpretations *b.* to God.
Deut. 29. 29. secret things *b.* to Lord.
Ps. 68. 20. to God *b.* issues from death.
94. 1. God, to whom vengeance *b.*
Dan. 9. 7. righteousness *b.* to thee.
Mk. 9. 41. because ye *b.* to Christ.
Lk. 19. 42. things that *b.* to thy peace.
Heb. 5. 14. strong meat *b.* to them.
Beloved, Deut. 33. 12. *b.* of Lord dwell in safety.
Neh. 13. 26. Solomon *b.* of his God.
Ps. 60. 5 ; 108. 6. thy *b.* may be delivered.
127. 2. so he giveth his *b.* sleep.
Cant. 5. 1. drink abundantly, O *b.*
Dan. 9. 23 ; 10. 11, 19. greatly *b.*
Matt. 3. 17 ; 17. 5. *b.* son.
Rom. 9. 25. *b.* which was not *b.*
11. 28. *b.* for the fathers' sakes.
Eph. 1. 6. accepted in the *b.*
Col. 3. 12. elect of God, holy and *b.*
4. 9 ; Philem. 16. *b.* brother.
Rev. 20. 9. compassed *b.* city.
Bend, Ps. 11. 2. the wicked *b.* their bow.
Is. 60. 14. afflicted thee, come *b.* to thee.
Jer. 46. 9. Lydians, that *b.* the bow.
Ezek. 17. 7. vine did *b.* her roots.
Beneath, Deut. 4. 39. earth *b.* there is none.
Is. 14. 9. hell from *b.* is moved.
John 8. 23. ye are from *b.*
Benefactors, Lk. 22. 25. exercise authority are called *b.*
Benefit, Ps. 68. 19. daily loadeth us with *b.*
103. 2. forget not all his *b.*
116. 12. what render for all his *b.* ?
1 Tim. 6. 2. partakers of the *b.*
Bereave, Eccl. 4. 8. *b.* my soul of good.
Jer. 15. 7 ; 18. 21. *b.* them of children.
Hos. 13. 8. as a *b.* bear.
Beseech, Ex. 33. 18. I *b.* show me thy glory.
Ps. 80. 14. return, we *b.*, O God.
Mal. 1. 9. *b.* God, he be gracious.
Matt. 8. 5 ; Lk. 7. 3. centurion *b.* him.
Rom. 12. 1. *b.* you by the mercies of God.
2 Cor. 5. 20. as though God did *b.* you.
Philem. 9. for love's sake *b.* thee.

Beset, Ps. 139. 5. *b.* me behind and before.
Heb. 12. 1. sin which doth easily *b.* us.
Beside, Mk. 3. 21. said, he is *b.* himself.
Acts 26. 24. Paul, thou art *b.* thyself.
2 Cor. 5. 13. whether we be *b.* ourselves.
Besought, Ex. 32. 11 ; Deut. 3. 23 ; 1 Ki. 13. 6 ;
Jer. 26. 19. *b.* the Lord.
Matt. 8. 31 ; Lk. 8. 31. devils *b.* him.
John 4. 40. *b.* that he would tarry.
2 Cor. 12. 8. I *b.* the Lord thrice.
Best, Ps. 39. 5. man at his *b.* state is vanity.
Lk. 15. 22. *b.* robe.
1 Cor. 12. 31. covet *b.* gifts.
Bestow, Lk. 12. 17. no room to *b.* my fruits.
1 Cor. 15. 10. grace *b.* on me not in vain.
Gal. 4. 11. lest I have *b.* labour in vain.
1 John 3. 1. manner of love Father *b.*
Betray, Matt. 24. 10. shall *b.* one another.
26. 16 ; Mk. 14. 11 ; Lk. 22. 6. opportunity to *b.*
Matt. 27. 4. *b.* innocent blood.
1 Cor. 11. 23. same night he was *b.*
Better, 1 Sam. 15. 22. to obey *b.* than sacrifice.
1 Ki. 19. 4. I am not *b.* than my fathers.
Ps. 63. 3. loving kindness *b.* than life.
Prov. 16. 16. *b.* to get wisdom than gold.
Eccl. 4. 9. two are *b.* than one.
7. 1. *b.* a good name than.
7. 10. former days *b.* than these.
Matt. 6. 26. are ye not much *b.* than they ?
12. 12. man *b.* than a sheep.
Lk. 5. 39. old wine *b.*
Phil. 1. 23. with Christ far *b.*
2. 3. esteem other *b.* than themselves.
Heb. 1. 4. *b.* than the angels.
8. 6. mediator of a *b.* covenant.
12. 24. blood speaketh *b.* than Abel.
2 Pet. 2. 21. *b.* not to have known the way.
Beware, Jud. 13. 4. *b.*, and drink not wine.
Job 36. 18. *b.* lest he take thee away.
Matt. 7. 15. *b.* of false prophets.
16. 6 ; Mk. 8. 15 ; Lk. 12. 1. *b.* of the leaven.
Mk. 12. 38 ; Lk. 20. 46. *b.* of scribes.
Lk. 12. 15. *b.* of covetousness.
Phil. 3. 2. *b.* of dogs, *b.* of evil workers.
Col. 2. 8. *b.* lest any man spoil you.
Bewitched, Acts 8. 9. Simon *b.* the people.
Gal. 3. 1. who hath *b.* you?
Bewray, Prov. 27. 16. ointment of his right
hand *b.* itself.
29. 24. cursing, and *b.* it not.
Is. 16. 3. *b.* not him that wandereth.
Matt. 26. 73. thy speech *b.* thee.
Beyond, Num. 22. 18. *b.* the word of the Lord.
Mk. 6. 51 : 7. 37. amazed *b.* measure.
2 Cor. 8. 3. *b.* their power willing.
Gal. 1. 13. *b.* measure I persecuted.
1 Thes. 4. 6. that no man go *b.*
Bind, Job. 38. 31. canst *b.* influences of Pleiades.
Ps. 118. 27. *b.* the sacrifice with cords.
Prov. 6. 21. *b.* them upon thine heart.
Is. 61. 1. to *b.* up brokenhearted.
Hos. 6. 1. smitten, and will *b.* us up.
Matt. 12. 29 ; Mk. 3. 27. first *b.* the strong man.
16. 19 ; 18. 18. *b.* on earth.
23. 4. *b.* heavy burdens grievous.
Acts 9. 14. authority to *b.* all that.
22. 4. *b.* and delivering men.
Bird, Ps. 11. 1. flee as a *b.* to mountain.
124. 7. our soul is escaped as a *b.*
Prov. 1. 17. net spread in sight of any *b.*
6. 5. as a *b.* from the fowler.
Eccl. 10. 20. *b.* shall tell the matter.
Cant. 2. 12. time of singing of *b.*
Matt. 8. 20 ; Lk. 9. 58. *b.* of air have nests.

Birth, Eccl. 7. 1. better than the day of one's *b.*
Matt. 1. 18. the *b.* of Jesus Christ.
14. 6 ; Mk. 6. 21. Herod's *b.*-day.
John 9. 1. blind from *b.*
Gal. 4. 19. of whom I travail in *b.*
Heb. 12. 16. for one morsel sold *b.*-right.
Bishop, 1 Tim. 3. 1. if a man desire office of *b.*
Tit. 1. 7. *b.* must be blameless.
1 Pet. 2. 25. the *b.* of your souls.
Bit, Ps. 32. 9. must be held in with *b.*
Jas. 3. 3. we put *b.* in horses' mouths.
Bite, Prov. 23. 32. at last it *b.* like serpent.
Mic. 3. 5. prophets that *b.* with teeth.
Gal. 5. 15. if ye *b.* and devour one another
Bitter, Ex. 12. 8 ; Num. 9. 11. with *b.* herbs.
Ex. 15. 23. waters were *b.*
Deut. 32. 24. devoured with *b.* destruction.
Job 13. 26. writest *b.* things.
Is. 5. 20. that put *b.* for sweet.
Jer. 2. 19. an evil thing and *b.*
Matt. 26. 75 ; Lk. 22. 62. Peter wept *b.*
Col. 3. 19. be not *b.* against them.
Bitterness, 1 Sam. 15. 32. surely the *b.* of death
is past.
Job 10. 1 ; 21. 25 ; Is. 38. 15. in *b.* of soul.
Prov. 14. 10. heart knoweth own *b.*
Zech. 12. 10. be in *b.* for him as one that is
in *b.*
Acts 8. 23. in the gall of *b.*
Eph. 4. 31. let all *b.* be put away.
Heb. 12. 15. lest any root of *b.*
Black, Cant. 1. 5. I am *b.* but comely.
Matt. 5. 36. one hair white or *b.*
Heb. 12. 18. ye are not come to *b.*
Jude 13. to whom is reserved *b.*
Blame, 2 Cor. 6. 3. that ministry be not *b.*
Gal. 2. 11. because he was to be *b.*
Eph. 1. 4. holy and without *b.*
Blameless, Lk. 1. 6. in ordinances of Lord *b.*
1 Cor. 1. 8. *b.* in the day of our Lord.
Phil. 2. 15. may be *b.* and harmless.
3. 6. righteousness in the law *b.*
2 Pet. 3. 14. ye may be found *b.*
Blaspheme, 2 Sam. 12. 14. occasion to enemies
to *b.*
Ps. 74. 10. enemy *b.* thy name.
Is. 52. 5. my name continually is *b.*
Matt. 9. 3. Scribes said this man *b.*
Mk. 3. 29. *b.* against Holy Ghost.
Acts 26. 11. I compelled them to *b.*
Rom. 2. 24. name of God is *b.*
1 Tim. 1. 20. may learn not to *b.*
Jas. 2. 7. they *b.* that worthy name.
Blasphemy, Matt. 12. 31. all manner of *b.*
26. 65 ; Mk. 14. 64. he hath spoken *b.*
John 10. 33. stone thee not, but for *b.*
Col. 3. 8. now ye also put off *b.*
Blemish, Dan. 1. 4. children in whom was no *b.*
Eph 5. 27. holy and without *b.*
1 Pet. 1. 19. lamb without *b.* and spot.
Bless, Gen. 12. 3. *b.* them that *b.* thee.
22. 17. in *b.* I will *b.* thee.
32. 26. not let thee go except thou *b.*
Num. 6. 24. Lord *b.* and keep thee.
Deut. 28. 3. *b.* in city, *b.* in field.
1 Chr. 4. 10. Oh that thou wouldest *b.* me.
Ps. 67. 1. be merciful to us, and *b.* us.
132. 15. I will abundantly *b.* her provision.
Prov. 10. 7. memory of just is *b.*
Is. 32. 20. *b.* are ye that sow.
65. 16. *b.* himself in God of truth.
Matt. 5. 44 ; Lk. 6. 28 ; Rom. 12. 14. *b.* them
that curse.
Acts 20. 35. more *b.* to give than receive.

Bless—*Continued.*
2 Cor. 11. 31. *b.* for evermore.
1 Tim. 1. 11. glorious Gospel of *b.* God.
Tit. 2. 13. looking for that *b.* hope.
Jas. 1. 12. *b.* that endureth temptation.
Rev. 14. 13. *b.* are dead which die in Lord.

Blessing, Gen. 27. 35. thy brother taken thy *b.*
Deut. 23. 5; Neh. 13. 2. Lord turned curse into *b.*
Job 29. 13. *b.* of him ready to perish.
Ps. 129. 8. *b.* of the Lord be on you.
Prov. 10. 22. *b.* of Lord maketh rich.
Is. 65. 8. destroy it not, a *b.* is in it.
Mal. 3. 10. pour you out a *b.*
Rom. 15. 29. fulness of *b.* of Gospel.
1 Cor. 10. 16. cup of *b.* which we bless.
Eph. 1. 3. blessed us with all spiritual *b.*
Heb. 6. 7. earth receiveth *b.* from God.
Jas. 3. 10. proceed *b.* and cursing.
Rev. 5. 12. worthy to receive honour and *b.*

Blind, Ex. 23. 8. the gift *b.* the wise.
John 12. 40. he hath *b.* their eyes.
2 Cor. 3. 14. their minds were *b.*
1 John 2. 11. darkness hath *b.*
Job 29. 15. I was eyes to the *b.*
Matt. 11. 5; Lk. 7. 21. the *b.* receive sight.
2 Pet. 1. 9. he that lacketh these things is *b.*

Blindness, Rom. 11. 25. *b.* in part has happened.
Eph. 4. 18. because of *b.* of their heart.

Blood, Gen. 9. 6. whoso sheddeth man's *b.*
Deut. 32. 43. avenge *b.* of his servants.
2 Sam. 1. 16. thy *b.* be on thy head.
Ps. 30. 9. what profit in my *b.*
51. 14. deliver me from *b.* guiltiness.
72. 14. precious shall *b.* be in his sight.
Is. 1. 15. your hands are full of *b.*
9. 5. garments rolled in *b.*
Ezek. 9. 9. land is full of *b.*
Zeph. 1. 17. their *b.* poured out as dust.
Matt. 9. 20; Mk. 5. 25; Lk. 8. 43. woman with issue of *b.*
Matt. 16. 17. flesh and *b.* hath not revealed.
27. 25. his *b.* be on us and on our children.
Mk. 14. 24; Lk. 22. 20; 1 Cor. 11. 25. new testament in my *b.*
John 1. 13. born not of *b.*
6. 54. whoso drinketh my *b.*
19. 34. came thereout *b.*
Acts 15. 20; 21. 25. abstain from *b.*
17. 26. made of one *b.*
20. 28. church purchased with his *b.*
Rom. 3. 25. through faith in his *b.*
5. 9. justified by his *b.*
1 Cor. 11. 27. guilty of body and *b.* of the Lord.
15. 50. flesh and *b.* cannot inherit.
Eph. 1. 7; Col. 1. 14. redemption through his *b.*
Heb. 9. 22. without shedding of *b.*
10. 29; 13. 20. *b.* of the covenant.
1 Pet. 1. 19. with precious *b.* of Christ.
1 John 1. 7. *b.* of Jesus Christ cleanseth us.
5. 8. the spirit, water, and *b.*
Rev. 7. 14; 12. 11. *b.* of the Lamb.

Blossom, Num. 17. 5. the man's rod shall *b.*
Is. 35. 1. desert shall *b.* as the rose.
Hab. 3. 17. fig tree shall not *b.*

Blot, Ex. 32. 32; Ps. 69. 28. *b.* out of book.
Deut. 29. 20. *b.* out his name from under heaven.
Is. 44. 22. *b.* out, as thick cloud.
Acts 3. 19. that your sins be *b.* out.
Col. 2. 14. *b.* out the handwriting.

Boast, 1 Ki. 20. 11. not *b.* as he that putteth it off.
Ps. 44. 8. in God we *b.* all the day.
49. 6. *b.* themselves in their riches.
Prov. 27. 1. *b.* not of to-morrow.
Rom. 11. 18. *b.* not against branches.
Eph. 2. 9. not of works, lest any man should *b.*
Jas. 3. 5. tongue *b.* great things.

Body, Job 19. 26. worms destroy this *b.*
Prov. 5. 11. flesh and *b.* are consumed.
Matt. 5. 29. *b.* cast into hell.
6. 22; Lk. 11. 34. *b.* full of light.
Mk. 5. 29. felt in *b.* that she was healed.
John 2. 21. the temple of his *b.*
Acts 19. 12. from his *b.* were brought.
Rom. 6. 6. *b.* of sin destroyed.
7. 24. *b.* of this death.
8. 23. the redemption of our *b.*
1 Cor. 6. 19. *b.* is the temple of the Holy Ghost.
13. 3. though I give my *b.* to be burned.
2 Cor. 5. 8. absent from the *b.*
12. 2. whether in *b.*, or out of the *b.*
Gal 6. 17. I bear in *b.* marks.
Phil. 3. 21. who shall change our vile *b.*
Col. 1. 18. head of the *b.* the church.
Heb. 10. 5. a *b.* hast thou prepared me.
Jas. 3. 6. tongue defileth the whole *b.*
1 Pet. 2. 24. in his own *b.* on tree.

Bodily, Lk. 3. 22. Holy Ghost descended in a *b.* shape.
2 Cor. 10. 10. his *b.* presence is weak.
Col. 2. 9. fulness of the Godhead *b.*
1 Tim. 4. 8. *b.* exercise profiteth little.

Bold, Prov. 28. 1. righteous are *b.* as a lion.
John 7. 26. he speaketh *b.*
Rom. 15. 15. have written more *b.*
2 Cor. 7. 4. great is my *b.* of speech.
Eph. 3. 12. we have *b.* and access.
Heb. 4. 16. let us come *b.* to throne.
10. 19. *b.* to enter into holiest.
1 John 4. 17. have *b.* in day of judgment.

Bond, Acts 8. 23. in *b.* of iniquity.
Eph. 4. 3. *b.* of peace.
Col. 3. 14. *b.* of perfectness.
Ps. 116. 16. thou hast loosed my *b.*
Acts 20. 23. *b.* abide me.
23. 29; 26. 31. worthy of death or *b.*
Heb. 11. 36. others had trial of *b.* and.

Bondage, Ex. 1. 14. lives bitter with hard *b.*
John 8. 33. never in *b.* to any man.
Rom. 8. 15. not received spirit of *b.*
Gal. 5. 1. not entangled with yoke of *b.*
Heb. 2. 15. lifetime subject to *b.*

Bondwoman, Gen. 21. 10; Gal. 4. 30. cast out *b.*

Bone, Gen. 2. 23. this is *b.* of my bones.
Ex. 12. 46; Num. 9. 12. neither shall ye break a *b.* thereof.
Job 19. 20. my *b.* cleaveth to my skin.
Ps. 51. 8. *b.* thou hast broken may rejoice.
Prov. 14. 30. envy the rottenness of the *b.*
Ezek. 37. 1. valley full of *b.*
Matt. 23. 27. full of dead men's *b.*
Lk. 24. 39. spirit hath not flesh and *b.*
John 19. 36. a *b.* of him shall not be broken.
Eph. 5. 30. we are members of his *b.*

Book, Job. 19. 23. printed in a *b.*
31. 35. adversary had written a *b.*
Ps. 40. 7; Heb. 10. 7. volume of the *b.*
69. 28. let them be blotted out of *b.*
139. 16. in thy *b.* all my members.
Is. 34. 16. seek ye out of the *b.* of the Lord.

Book—*Continued.*
  Mal. 3. 16. *b.* of remembrance.
  Lk. 4. 17. when he opened the *b.*
  John 21. 25. world could not contain *b.*
  Phil. 4. 3 ; Rev. 3. 5 ; 13. 8 ; 17. 8 ; 20. 12 ;
    21. 27.ᵇ *b.* of life.
  Rev. 22. 19. take away from words of *b.*

Booth, Lev. 23. 42. dwell in *b.* seven days.
  Job 27. 18. as a *b.* the keeper maketh.
  Jon. 4. 5 ; Jonah made him a *b.*

Born, Job. 5. 7. man *b.* to trouble.
  Ps. 22. 31. a people that shall be *b.*
  87. 4. this man was *b.* there.
  Prov. 17. 17. a brother is *b.* for adversity.
  Eccl. 3. 2. a time to be *b.*
  Is. 9. 6. unto us a child is *b.*
  66. 8. shall a nation be *b.* at once ?
  Matt. 2. 4. where Christ should be *b.*
  Lk. 2. 11. to you is *b.* this day.
  John 1. 13 ; 1 John 4. 7 ; 5. 1, 4, 18. *b.* of God.
  John 3. 3 ; 1 Pet. 1. 23. *b.* again.
  1 Cor. 15. 8. as one *b.* out of due time.
  1 Pet. 2. 2. as new-*b.* babes.

Borne, Ps. 55. 12. an enemy, then I could have
    b. it.
  Is. 53. 4. *b.* our griefs.
  Matt. 20. 12. *b.* burden and heat of day.
  23. 4 ; Lk. 11. 46. grievous to be *b.*

Borrow, Deut. 15. 6 ; 28. 12. shalt lend, but
    not *b.*
  Ps. 37. 21. wicked *b.* and payeth not.
  Prov. 22. 7. the *b.* is servant to lender
  Matt. 5. 42. from him that would *b.* of thee.

Bosom, Ps. 35. 13. prayer returned into own *b.*
  Prov. 6. 27. take fire in his *b.*
  Is. 40. 11. carry lambs in *b.*
  Lk. 16. 22. carried into Abraham's *b.*
  John 1. 18. in the *b.* of the Father.
  13. 23. leaning on Jesus' *b.*

Bosses, Job 15. 26. thick *b.* of his bucklers.

Bottle, Gen. 21. 14. *b.* of water.
  Jud. 4. 19. a *b.* of milk.
  1 Sam. 1. 24 ; 10. 3 ; 16. 20 ; 2 Sam. 16. 1. a *b.*
    of wine.
  Ps. 56. 8. put tears into *b.*
  119. 83. like *b.* in smoke.
  Hab. 2. 15. puttest thy *b.* to him and.
  Matt. 9. 17 ; Mk. 2. 22 ; Lk. 5. 37. new wine
    into old *b.*

Bough, Gen. 49. 22. Joseph is a fruitful *b.*
  Jud. 9. 49. cut down every man his *b.*
  Job 14. 9. bring forth *b.* like a plant.
  Ps. 80. 10. *b.* like goodly cedars.
  Ezek. 31. 3, 14. top among thick *b.*

Bought, Lk. 14. 18. I have *b.* a piece of ground.
  1 Cor. 6. 20 ; 7. 23. ye are *b.* with a price.
  2 Pet. 2. 1. denying Lord that *b.* them.

Bound, Job 36. 8. if they be *b.* in fetters.
  Ps. 107. 10. being *b.* in affliction.
  Prov. 22. 15. foolishness is *b.* in heart of
    child.
  Is. 61. 1. opening of prison to them *b.*
  Acts 20. 22. I go *b.* in spirit.
  2 Tim. 2. 9. word of God is not *b.*
  Heb. 13. 3. in bonds, as *b.* with them.

Bountiful, Ps. 13. 6. Lord hath dealt *b.*
  119. 17. deal *b.* with thy servant.
  Prov. 22. 9. a *b.* eye shall be blessed.
  Is. 32. 5. nor churl said to be *b.*
  2 Cor. 9. 6. he that soweth *b.* shall reap *b.*

Bowels, 2 Cor. 6. 12. straitened in your own *b.*
  Phil. 1. 8. long after you in *b.* of Christ.
  2. 1. if there be any *b.* and mercies.
  1 John 3. 17. *b.* of compassion.

Brake, Ex. 32. 19 ; Deut. 9. 17. tables and *b.*
    them.
  2 Ki. 23. 14 ; 2 Chr. 34. 4. Josiah *b.* the images.
  Ps. 76. 3. *b.* the arrows of the bow.
  107. 14. *b.* their bands in sunder.
  Matt. 14. 19 ; 15. 36 ; 26. 26 ; Mk. 6. 41 ; 14. 22 ;
    Lk. 9. 16 ; 22. 19 ; 1 Cor. 11. 24. blessed and *b.*

Branch, Job 14. 7. tender *b.* will not cease.
  Ps. 80. 15. *b.* thou madest strong.
  Prov. 11. 28. righteous flourish as *b.*
  Is. 60. 21. the *b.* of my planting.
  Jer. 23. 5. raise a righteous *b.*
  Matt. 13. 32 ; Lk. 13. 19. birds lodge in *b.*
  Matt. 21. 8 ; Mk. 11. 8 ; John 12. 13. cut down *b.*
  John 15. 5. I am the vine, ye are the *b.*
  Rom. 11. 16. if root be holy, so *b.*

Brand, Jud. 15. 5. he had set the *b.* on fire.
  Zech. 3. 2. *b.* plucked out of the fire.

Brass, Num. 21. 9. serpent of *b.*
  Deut. 8. 9. out of whose hills mayest dig *b.*
  28. 23. the heavens shall be *b.*
  Ps. 107. 16. broken the gates of *b.*
  1 Cor. 13. 1. as sounding *b.*

Brawler, Prov. 25. 24. *b.* woman.
  1 Tim. 3. 3. a bishop must be no *b.*
  Tit. 3. 2. to be no *b.*

Breach, Lev. 24. 20. *b.* for *b.*, eye for eye
  Ps. 106. 23. not Moses stood in the *b.*
  Is. 58. 12. the repairer of the *b.*
  Lam. 2. 13. thy *b.* is great like the sea.

Bread, Deut. 8. 3 ; Matt. 4. 4 ; Lk. 4. 4. man
    not live by *b.* alone.
  Ruth 1. 6. visited people in giving them *b.*
  1 Sam. 21. 4. hallowed *b.*
  1 Ki. 17. 6. ravens brought *b.* and flesh.
  Job 22. 7. withholden *b.* from hungry.
  33. 20. life abhorreth *b.* and soul.
  Ps. 132. 15. satisfy poor with *b.*
  Prov. 9. 17. *b.* eaten in secret.
  12. 11 ; 20. 13 ; (28. 19.) satisfied with *b.*
  Eccl. 11. 1. cast *b.* on waters.
  Is. 33. 16. *b.* given, and water sure.
  55. 2. money for that which is not *b.*
  Matt. 4. 3 ; Lk. 4. 3. stones be made *b.*
  Matt. 6. 11 ; Lk. 11. 3. give us our daily *b.*
  Matt. 15. 26 ; Mk. 7. 27. not meet to take
    children's *b.*
  Lk. 24. 35. known in breaking *b.*
  John 6. 35, 48. I am *b.* of life.
  Acts 2. 46. breaking *b.* from house to house.
  1 Cor. 11. 23. night he was betrayed, took *b.*
  2 Thes. 3. 8. did we eat *b.* for nought?

Break, Cant. 2. 17 ; 4. 6. day *b.* and shadows
    flee.
  Is. 42. 3 ; Matt. 12. 20. bruised reed shall he
    not *b.*
  Jer. 4. 3 ; Hos. 10. 12. *b.* up your fallow
    ground.
  Matt. 5. 19. *b.* one of these least command-
    ments.
  Acts 21. 13. to weep and *b.* my heart.
  1 Cor. 10. 16. bread which we *b.*

Breath, Gen. 2. 7 ; 6. 17 ; 7. 15. *b.* of life.
  Job 12. 10. in whose hand is *b.* of all.
  Ps. 146. 4. his *b.* goeth forth, he returneth.
  150. 6. that hath *b.* praise the Lord.
  Is. 2. 22. cease from man, whose *b.*
  Lam. 4. 20. the *b.* of our nostrils.
  Dan. 5. 23. in whose hand thy *b.* is.
  Acts 17. 25. he giveth to all life and *b.*

Breathe, Ps. 27. 12. such as *b.* out cruelty.
  Ezek. 37. 9. O breath, *b.* on these.
  John 20. 22. he *b.* on them, and said.
  Acts 9. 1. Saul *b.* out threatenings.

Brethren, Gen. 13. 8. no strife, for we be *b.*
Ps. 122. 8. for my *b.* and companions' sakes.
133. 1. for *b.* to dwell together in unity.
Matt. 23. 8. all ye are *b.*
Mk. 10. 29 ; Lk. 18. 29. no man left house or *b.*
Rom. 8. 29. first-born among many *b.*
Heb. 2. 11. not ashamed to call them *b.*
1 Pet. 1. 22. unfeigned love of the *b.*
1 John 3. 14. because we love the *b.*
Bribe, 1 Sam. 12. 3. have I received any *b.* ?
Ps. 26. 10. right hand is full of *b.*
Is. 33. 15. hands from holding *b.*
Job 15. 34. tabernacles of *b.*
Brick, Gen. 11. 3. make *b.* had *b.* for stone.
Ex. 5. 7. straw to make *b.*
Is. 9. 10. the *b.* are fallen down.
65. 3. incense on altars of *b.*
Bride, Is. 61. 10. as a *b.* adorneth with jewels.
Jer. 2. 32. can a *b.* forget her attire ?
Rev. 18. 23. voice of *b.* heard no more.
21. 2. as a *b.* adorned for her husband.
22. 17. Spirit and the *b.* say come.
Bridegroom, Ps. 19. 5. as a *b.* coming out of
chamber.
Matt. 9. 15 ; Mk. 2. 19 ; Lk. 5. 34. while the
b. is with them.
Matt. 25. 1. to meet the *b.*
John 3. 29. because of *b.* voice.
Bridle, 2 Ki. 19. 28 ; Is. 37. 29. my *b.* in thy lips.
Ps. 39. 1. keep my mouth with a *b.*
Prov. 26. 3. a *b.* for the ass.
Is. 30. 28. a *b.* in jaws of the people.
Jas. 1. 26. *b.* not his tongue.
3. 2. able to *b.* whole body.
Bright, Job 37. 11. scattereth his *b.* cloud.
Is. 60. 3. to *b.* of thy rising.
62. 1. righteousness go forth as *b.*
Dan. 12. 3. wise shine as *b.* of firmament.
Hab. 3. 4. his *b.* was as the light.
Matt. 17. 5. *b.* cloud overshadowed.
Acts 26. 13. a light above *b.* of sun.
2 Thes. 2. 8. *b.* of his coming.
Heb. 1. 3. the *b.* of his glory.
Rev. 22. 16. the *b.* and morning star.
Broad, Ps. 119. 96. thy commandment is ex-
ceeding *b.*
Is. 33. 21. a place of *b.* rivers.
Matt. 7. 13. *b.* way to destruction.
23. 5. make *b.* their phylacteries.
Broken, Ps. 34. 18 ; 51. 17. *b.* heart.
Matt. 21. 44. shall fall on stone, shall be *b.*
John 10. 35. scripture cannot be *b.*
19. 36. bone shall not be *b.*
Eph. 2. 14. *b.* down middle wall.
Brook, 1 Sam. 17. 40. five stones out of the *b.*
Ps. 42. 1. as hart panteth after *b.*
110. 7. drink of the *b.* in way.
John 18. 1. went over *b.* Cedron.
Broth, Jud. 6. 19. Gideon put the *b.* in a pot.
Is. 65. 4. *b.* of abominable things.
Brother, Prov. 17. 17. a *b.* is born for adversity.
18. 19. a *b.* offended is harder to be won.
18. 24. friend closer than *b.*
Eccl. 4. 8. neither child or *b.*
Matt. 10. 21 ; Mk. 13. 12. *b.* deliver up *b.*
1 Cor. 6. 6. *b.* goeth to law with *b.*
2 Thes. 3. 15. admonish as a *b.*
1 John 2. 10. loveth his *b.* abideth in light.
Brotherly, Rom. 12. 10. affectioned with *b.* love.
1 Thes. 4. 9. as touching *b.* love.
Heb. 13. 1. let *b.* love continue.
2 Pet. 1. 7. to godliness. *b.* kindness.
Bruise, Gen. 3. 15. *b.* thy head, *b.* his heel.
Is. 1. 6. but wounds and *b.*

Bruise—*Continued.*
Is. 53. 10. pleased the Lord to *b.* him.
Lk. 9. 39. the Spirit *b.* him.
Rom. 16. 20. God of peace shall *b.* Satan.
Brutish, Ps. 92. 6. a *b.* man knoweth not.
Prov. 30. 2. I am more *b.* than any.
Jer. 10. 21. pastors are become *b.*
Buckler, 2 Sam. 22. 31 ; Ps. 18. 30. a *b.* to all
that trust.
Ps. 18. 2. Lord is my God, my *b.*
91. 4. his truth shall be thy *b.*
Prov. 2. 7. *b.* to them that walk uprightly.
Buffet, Matt. 26. 67 ; Mk. 14. 65. and *b.* him.
1 Cor. 4. 11. to present hour *b.*
2 Cor. 12. 7. messenger of Satan to *b.* me.
1 Pet. 2. 20. when *b.* for your faults.
Build, Gen. 11. 4. go to, let us *b.* a city.
Ps. 51. 18. *b.* walls of Jerusalem.
127. 1. except the Lord *b.* the house.
Eccl. 3. 3. a time to *b.* up.
Is. 58. 12 ; 61. 4. *b.* old waste places.
Matt. 7. 24 ; Lk. 6. 48. wise man *b.* on rock.
Lk. 14. 30. began to *b.* you up.
Acts 20. 32. able to *b.* you up.
Rom. 15. 20. *b.* on another man's foundation.
1 Cor. 3. 12. if any *b.* on this foundation.
Eph. 2. 22. in whom ye are *b.* together.
Heb. 3. 4. every house is *b.* by some man.
Builder, Ps. 118. 22 ; Matt. 21. 42 ; Mk. 12. 10;
Lk. 20. 17 ; Acts 4. 11 ; 1 Pet. 2. 7. stone
which *b.* refused.
1 Cor. 3. 10. as a wise master-*b.*
Heb. 11. 10. whose *b.* and maker is God.
Building, 1 Cor. 3. 9. ye are God's *b.*
2 Cor. 5. 1. we have a *b.* of God.
Eph. 2. 21. in whom *b.* fitly framed.
Bulrush, Ex. 2. 3. an ark of *b.*
Is. 18. 2. send ambassadors in vessels of *b.*
58. 5. bow his head like a *b.*
Bulwark, Deut. 20. 20. *b.* against the city.
Ps. 48. 13. mark well her *b.*
Is. 26. 1. salvation for walls and *b.*
Bundle, Gen. 42. 35. every man's *b.* of money.
1 Sam. 25. 29. soul bound in *b.* of life.
Cant. 1. 13. a *b.* of myrrh.
Matt. 13. 30. bind the tares in *b.*
Acts 28. 3. Paul gathered a *b.* of sticks.
Burden, Ps. 55. 22. cast thy *b.* on the Lord.
Eccl. 12. 5. grasshopper shall be a *b.*
Matt. 11. 30. my *b.* is light.
20. 12. borne *b.* and heat of day.
23. 4 ; Lk. 11. 46. heavy *b.*
2 Cor. 12. 16. I did not *b.* you.
12. 13. I was not *b.* to you.
Gal. 6. 5. every man bear his own *b.*
Burial, Eccl. 6. 3. that he have no *b.*
Jer. 22. 19. with the *b.* of an ass.
Matt. 26. 12. she did it for my *b.*
Acts 8. 2. carried Stephen to his *b.*
Burn, Gen. 44. 18. let not thine anger *b.*
Is. 27. 4. I would *b.* them together.
Ps. 39. 3. while musing the fire *b.*
89. 46. shall thy wrath *b.* like fire ?
Prov. 26. 23. *b.* lips and wicked heart.
Is. 9. 18. wickedness *b.* as the fire.
33. 14. dwell with everlasting *b.*
Mal. 4. 1. day that shall *b.* as oven.
Matt. 13. 30. bind tares to *b.* them.
Lk. 3. 17. chaff he will *b.*
12. 35. loins girded and lights *b.*
24. 32. did not our heart *b.* ?
John 5. 35. he was a *b.* and shining light.
1 Cor. 13. 3. give body to be *b.*
Heb. 6. 8. whose end is to be *b.*

Burn—*Continued.*
Heb. 12. 18. not come to mount that *b.*
Rev. 19. 20. cast into a lake *b.*
Burnt offering, Ps. 46. 6. *b.* thou hast not required.
51. 16. thou delightest not in *b.*
Is. 61. 8. I hate robbery for *b.*
Jer. 6. 20. your *b.* not acceptable.
Hos. 6. 6. knowledge of God more than *b.*
Mk. 12. 33. to love neighbour is more than *b.*
Heb. 10. 6. in *b.* for sin no pleasure.
Bury, Matt. 8. 21; Lk. 9. 59. suffer me to *b.* my father.
Matt. 27. 7. field to *b.* strangers.
John 19. 40. manner of Jews is to *b.*
Rom. 6. 4; Col. 2. 12. *b.* with him by baptism.
1 Cor. 15. 4. he was *b.* and rose.
Bushel, Matt. 5. 15; Mk. 4. 21; Lk. 11. 33. a candle, and put it under a *b.*
Business, 1 Sam. 21. 8. king's *b.* requireth haste.
Ps. 107. 23. do *b.* in great waters.
Prov. 22. 29. man diligent in *b.*
Eccl. 5. 3. dream through multitude of *b.*
Lk. 2. 49. about my Father's *b.*
Rom. 12. 11. not slothful in *b.*
1 Thes. 4. 11. study to do your own *b.*
Butter, Gen. 18. 8. Abraham took *b.* and milk.
Jud. 5. 25. she brought *b.* in lordly dish.
Ps. 55. 21. words smoother than *b.*
Is. 7. 15, 22. *b.* shall he eat.
Buy, Lev. 22. 11. *b.* any soul with money.
Deut. 2. 6. *b.* meat for money.
Prov. 23. 23. *b.* the truth.
Is. 55. 1. *b.* and eat, *b.* wine and milk.
Matt. 14. 15; Mk. 6. 36. *b.* victuals.
Matt. 25. 9. go to them that sell, and *b.*
John 4. 8. disciples were gone to *b.* meat.
6. 5. whence shall we *b.* bread.
13. 29. *b.* things we have need of.
1 Cor. 7. 30. *b.* as though they possessed not.
Jas. 4. 13. *b.* and sell, and get gain.
Rev. 3. 18. *b.* of me gold tried.
13. 17. no man might *b.* save.
18. 11. no man *b.* her merchandise.
Buyer, Prov. 20. 14. it is naught, saith *b.*
Is. 24. 2. as with the *b.* so the seller.
Ezek. 7. 12. let not *b.* rejoice.
By-and-By, Matt. 13. 21; Mk. 6. 25; Lk. 17. 7; 21. 9.
Byword, Job 17. 6; 30. 9. a *b.* of the people.
Ps. 44. 14. a *b.* among the heathen.

CAGE, Jer. 5. 27. as a *c.* is full of birds.
Rev. 18. 2. Babylon, *c.* of every unclean bird.
Cake, Jud. 7. 13. a *c.* tumbled into host.
2 Sam. 6. 19. to every man a *c.* of bread.
1 Ki. 17. 12. I have not a *c.*
19. 6. a *c.* baken on coals.
Hos. 7. 8. Ephraim is a *c.* not turned.
Calamity, Deut. 32. 35. day of their *c.* is at hand.
2 Sam. 22. 19; Ps. 18. 18. prevented me in day of *c.*
Ps. 57. 1. until these *c.* be overpast.
Prov. 1. 26. I will laugh at your *c.*
17. 5. he that is glad at *c.*
19. 13. foolish son is *c.* of father.
27. 10. brother's house in day of *c.*
Calf, Ex. 32. 4; Deut. 9. 16; Neh. 9. 18; Ps. 106. 19. made a molten *c.*
Is. 11. 6. *c.* and young lion together.
Lk. 15. 23. bring fatted *c.*
Calling, Rom. 11. 29. *c.* of God without repentance.
1 Cor. 7. 20. abide in same *c.*

Calling—*Continued.*
Eph. 1. 18. the hope of his *c.*
Phil. 3. 14. prize of high *c.* of God.
2 Thes. 1. 11. worthy of this *c.*
2 Tim. 1. 9. called us with holy *c.*
Heb. 3. 1. partakers of heavenly *c.*
2 Pet. 1. 10. make *c.* and election sure.
Calm, Ps. 107. 29. maketh storm a *c.*
Jon. 1. 11. sea may be *c.* unto us.
Matt. 8. 26; Mk. 4. 39; Lk. 8. 24. great *c.*
Calves, Hos. 14. 2. render the *c.* of our lips.
Mic. 6. 6. *c.* of a year old.
Heb. 9. 19. blood of *c.* and sprinkled.
Camp, Ex. 14. 19. angel, which went before *c.*
Num. 11. 26. they prophesied in *c.*
Deut. 23. 14. Lord walketh in midst of *c.*
Heb. 13. 13. go forth to him without the *c.*
Is. 29. 3. I will *c.* against thee round about.
Candle, Job. 29. 3. his *c.* shined on my head.
Ps. 18. 28. the Lord will light my *c.*
Prov. 20. 27. spirit of man is *c.* of Lord.
24. 20. *c.* of wicked be put out.
Matt. 5. 15; Mk. 4. 21; Lk. 8. 16. light a *c.*
Rev. 18. 23. *c.* shine no more in thee.
22. 5. need no *c.* nor light of sun.
Canker, 2 Tim. 2. 17. their word will eat as *c.*
Jas. 5. 3. your gold and silver is *c.*
Captain, Josh. 5. 14. *c.* of the Lord's host.
2 Chr. 13. 12. God himself is our *c.*
Heb. 2. 10. *c.* of their salvation perfect.
Rev. 19. 18. eat the flesh of *c.*
Captive, Ex. 12. 29. first-born of *c.*
Is. 52. 2. loose thyself, O *c.* daughter of Zion.
2 Tim. 2. 26. taken *c.* by him at will.
3. 6. lead *c.* silly women laden.
Captivity, Ps. 68. 18; Eph. 4. 8. led *c.* captive.
Rom. 7. 23. into *c.* to law of sin.
2 Cor. 10. 5. bringing into *c.* every thought.
Carcase, Matt. 24. 28. *c.* is there will eagles be.
Heb. 3. 17. whose *c.* fell in wilderness.
Care, Matt. 13. 22; Mk. 4. 19; Lk. 8. 14. *c.* of this world.
1 Cor. 9. 9. doth God take *c.* for oxen?
12. 25. have the same *c.* one for another.
2 Cor. 11. 28. *c.* of all the churches.
1 Pet. 5. 7. casting all your *c.* on him.
Ps. 142. 4. no man *c.* for my soul.
John 12. 6. not that he *c.* for the poor.
Acts 18. 17. Gallio *c.* for none of these things.
Phil. 2. 20. naturally *c.* for your state.
Careful, Jer. 17. 8. not be *c.* in year of drought.
Dan. 3. 16. not *c.* to answer thee.
Lk. 10. 41. *c.* about many things.
Phil. 4. 6. be *c.* for nothing.
Heb. 12. 17. he sought it *c.* with tears.
Carnal, Rom. 7. 14. *c.* sold under sin.
8. 7. *c.* mind is enmity against God.
2 Cor. 10. 4. weapons of warfare not *c.*
Heb. 7. 16. law of a *c.* commandment.
Carriage, Jud. 18. 21. cattle and *c.* before them.
Is. 46. 1. your *c.* were heavy laden.
Acts 21. 15. we took up our *c.*
Carry, Ex. 33. 45. *c.* us not up hence.
Is. 40. 11. *c.* lambs in his bosom.
53. 4. *c.* our sorrows.
63. 9. *c.* them all days of old.
Mk. 6. 55. began to *c.* in beds.
Lk. 10. 4. *c.* neither purse nor scrip.
John 5. 10. not lawful to *c.* thy bed.
21. 18. *c.* thee whither thou wouldst not.
1 Tim. 6. 7. can *c.* nothing out of world.
Eph. 4. 14. *c.* about with every wind.
Heb. 13. 9. *c.* about with divers doctrines.
Jude 12. clouds *c.* about of winds.

Cart, 2 Sam. 6. 3. set ark on a new c.
Is. 5. 18. draw sin as with a c. rope.
Amos 2. 13. c. full of sheaves.
Case, Ps. 144. 15. happy people in such a c.
Matt. 5. 20. in no c. enter heaven.
John 5. 6. long time in that c.
Cast, Ps. 22. 10. I was c. on thee from womb.
Prov. 16. 33. the lot is c. into lap.
Is. 25. 7. covering c. over all people.
Matt. 5. 29; Mk. 9. 45. whole body c. into hell.
Matt. 21. 21. say to mountain, be c. into sea.
Mk. 9. 38; Lk. 9. 49. one c. out devils.
Lk. 21. 1. c. gifts into treasury.
2 Cor. 10. 5. c. down imaginations.
1 Pet. 5. 7. c. all care upon him.
1 John 4. 18. love c. out fear.
Castaway, 1 Cor. 9. 27. lest I be a c.
Catch, Ps. 10. 9. to c. the poor.
Matt. 13. 19. devil c. away that which was sown.
Mk. 12. 13. to c. him in his words.
Lk. 5. 10. c. men.
John 10. 12. wolf c. and scattereth sheep.
Cattle, Gen. 46. 32. their trade to feed c.
Deut. 2. 35; 3. 7; Josh. 8. 2. the c. take for prey.
Ps. 50. 10. c. on a thousand hills.
Caught, Gen. 22. 13. ram c. by horns.
Mk. 12. 3. they c. the servant.
John 21. 3. that night they c. nothing.
Acts 8. 39. the Spirit c. away Philip.
2 Cor. 12. 2. a man c. up to third heaven.
1 Thes. 4. 17. be c. up together with them.
Cause, Ps. 140. 12. Lord will maintain the c.
Eccl. 7. 10. what is c. that former days.
Is. 51. 22. pleadeth c. of his people.
Matt. 19. 5; Mk. 10. 7; Eph. 5. 31. for this c. shall.
1 Cor. 11. 30. for this c. many are sickly.
2 Cor. 4. 16. for which c. we faint not.
1 Tim. 1. 16. for this c. I obtained mercy.
Ps. 67. 1; 80. 3. God c. his face to shine.
Matt. 10. 21; Mk. 13. 12. c. parents to be put to death.
Rom. 16. 17. mark them who c. divisions.
Cease, Deut. 15. 11. poor never c. out of land.
Job 3. 17. wicked c. from troubling.
Ps. 37. 8. c. from anger.
46. 9. he maketh wars to c.
Prov. 19. 27. c. to hear the instruction.
23. 4. c. from thine own wisdom.
Eccl. 12. 3. grinders c., because few.
Is. 1. 16. c. to do evil.
Acts. 20. 31. I c. not to warn.
1 Cor 13. 8. tongues, they shall c.
1 Thes. 5. 17. pray without c.
1 Pet. 4. 1. hath c. from sin.
Cedar, 2 Sam. 7. 2. I dwell in a house of c.
2 Ki. 14. 9. thistle sent to c.
Ps. 92. 12. grow like a c. in Lebanon.
Celestial, 1 Cor. 15. 40. there are c. bodies.
Certain, Ex. 3. 12. c. I will be with thee.
Lk. 23. 47. c. this was a righteous man.
1 Cor. 4. 11. no c. dwelling-place.
1 Tim. 6. 7. it is c. we can carry nothing.
Heb. 10. 27. a c. looking for of judgment.
Chaff, Ps. 35. 5. let them be as c. before wind.
Jer. 23. 28. what is c. to the wheat?
Matt. 3. 12; Lk. 3. 17. burn up c. with fire.
Chain, Gen. 41. 42; Dan. 5. 7. put a gold c. about his neck.
Mk. 5. 3. bind him, no, not with c.

Chain—Continued.
Acts 12. 7. Peter's c. fell off.
2 Tim. 1. 16. not ashamed of my c.
2 Pet. 2. 4. into c. of darkness.
Jude 6. everlasting c.
Chamber, 2 Ki. 4. 10. little c. on wall.
Ps. 19. 5. as bridegroom cometh out of c.
104. 3. beams of c. in the waters.
Is. 26. 20. enter into thy c.
Ezek. 8. 12. c. of imagery.
Matt. 24. 26. in secret c.
Acts 9. 37; 20. 8. in upper c.
Change, Job 14. 14. till my c. come.
Heb. 7. 12. of necessity a c. of law.
Ps. 15. 4. sweareth, and c. not.
102. 26. as a vesture shalt thou c. them.
Mal. 3. 6. I am the Lord, I c. not.
Rom. 1. 23. c. glory of uncorruptible God.
1 Cor. 15. 51. we shall all be c.
2 Cor. 3. 18. c. from glory to glory.
Phil. 3. 21. c. our vile body.
Charge, Job 1. 22. nor c. God foolishly.
Ps. 91. 11; Matt. 4. 6; Lk. 4. 10. give angels c.
Acts 7. 60. lay not sin to their c.
Rom. 8. 33. who shall lay anything to c.?
1 Cor. 9. 18. gospel without c.
1 Tim. 1. 18. this c. I commit to thee.
6. 17. c. them that are rich.
Chargeable, 2 Cor. 11. 9. I was c. to no man.
1 Thes. 2. 9. we would not be c.
Charity, 1 Cor. 8. 1. c. edifieth.
13. 4. c. suffereth long.
Col. 3. 14. above all, put on c.
1 Tim. 1. 5. end of commandment is c.
2 Tim. 2. 22. follow faith, c.
1 Pet. 4. 8. c. shall cover the multitude of sins.
2 Pet. 1. 7. to brotherly kindness c.
Jude 12. spots in your feasts of c.
Chaste, 2 Cor. 11. 2. present you as c. virgin.
1 Pet. 3. 2. your c. conversation.
Chasten, Ps. 6. 1; 38. 1. nor c. me in displeasure.
94. 12. blessed is man whom thou c.
Prov. 19. 18. c. thy son while there is hope.
2 Cor. 6. 9. as c., and not killed.
Heb. 12. 6; Rev. 3. 19. whom Lord loveth he c.
Chastisement, Job 34. 31. I have borne c.
Is. 53. 5. c. of our peace was upon him.
Heb. 12. 8. if ye be without c.
Cheek, Matt. 5. 39; Lk. 6. 29. smiteth on right c.
Cheer, Eccl. 11. 9. thine heart c. thee.
Zech. 9. 17. corn shall make young men c.
John 16. 33; Acts 23. 11. be of good c.
Rom. 12. 8. he that sheweth mercy, with c.
2 Cor. 9. 7. God loveth a c. giver.
Cherish, Eph. 5. 29. c. flesh, as Lord the church.
1 Thes. 2. 7. as a nurse c. children.
Chide, Ex. 17. 2. the people did c.
Ps. 103. 9. he will not always c.
Chief, Matt. 20. 27. whosoever will be c. among you.
Lk. 22. 26. he that is c., as he that serveth.
Eph. 2. 20. Jesus Christ being c. corner stone.
Chiefest, Cant. 5. 10. c. among ten thousand.
Mk. 10. 44. be c. shall be servant.
2 Cor. 11. 5. behind c. apostles.
Child, Gen. 37. 30. c. is not, and I whither.
42. 22. do not sin against the c.
Ps. 131. 2. quieted myself as a weaned c.
Prov. 20. 11. even a c. is known by his doings.
22. 6. train up a c. in way.
Is. 9. 6. unto us a c. is born.
65. 20. c. shall die an hundred years old.
Jer. 1. 6. I cannot speak, for I am a c.

Child—*Continued.*
Mk. 9. 36. Jesus took a *c.* and set him in the midst.
10. 15. receive kingdom of God as little *c.*
Lk. 1. 66. what manner of *c.*
John 4. 49. come down ere *c.* die.
Acts 4. 27. against thy holy *c.* Jesus.
1 Cor. 13. 11. when I was a *c.*
Gal. 4. 1. heir as long as he is a *c.*
2 Tim. 3. 15. from a *c.* hast known the Scriptures.

Children, Ps. 34, 11. come ye *c.*, hearken to me.
45. 16. instead of fathers shall be *c.*
128. 3. thy *c.* like olive plants.
1s. 8. 18 ; Heb. 2. 13. I and *c.* given me.
Is. 63, 8. *c.* that will not lie.
Ezek. 18. 2. *c.* teeth are set on edge.
Matt. 15. 26 ; Mk. 7. 27. not take *c.* bread.
Matt. 19. 14 ; Mk. 10. 14 ; Lk. 18. 16. suffer little *c.*
Lk.16.8. *c.* of this world wiser than *c.* of light.
John 12.36 ; Eph. 5. 8. ; 1 Thes. 5. 5.*c.*of light.
Rom. 8.16; Gal. 3. 26; 1 John 3. 10. *c.* of God.
Eph. 5. 6 ; Col. 3. 6. *c.* of disobedience.
Eph. 6. 1 ; Col. 3. 20. *c.*, obey your parents.

Choke, Matt. 13. 22 ; Mk. 4. 19. deceitfulness of riches *c.* the word.
Mk. 5. 13 ; Lk. 8. 33. *c.* in sea.
Lk. 8. 14. are *c.* with cares.

Choose, Ps. 65. 4. blessed is man thou *c.*
Prov. 1. 29. did not *c.* fear of Lord.
16. 16 ; 22. 1. rather to be *c.*
Jer. 8. 3. death shall be *c.* rather than life.
Matt. 20. 16 ; 22. 14. many called, few *c.*
Lk. 10. 42. Mary hath *c.* good part.
14. 7. how they *c.* chief rooms.
John 15. 16. ye have not *c.* me.
Acts 9. 15. he is a *c.* vessel.
Rom. 16. 13. *c.* in the Lord.
1 Cor. 1. 27, 28. God hath *c.* foolish things.
Eph. 1. 4. according as he hath *c.* us.
Heb. 11. 25. *c.* to suffer affliction.
1 Pet. 2. 4. *c.* of God, and precious.

Christ, Matt. 16. 16. thou art the *C.*
24. 5. many shall come, saying I am *C.*
Mk. 9. 41. because ye belong to *C.*
Lk. 24. 46. it behoved *C.* to suffer.
John 4. 25. Messias, which is called *C.*
6. 69. we are sure that thou art that *C.*
Acts 8. 5. preached *C.* to them.
Rom. 5. 8. while yet sinners. *C.* died for us.
1 Cor. 1. 24. *C.* the power of God.
3. 23. ye are *C.'s*, and *C.* is God's.
Gal. 3. 13. *C.* hath redeemed us from.
Eph. 3. 17. that *C.* may dwell in your hearts.
5. 14. *C.* shall give thee light.
Phil. 1. 21. to me to live is *C.*
3. 8. that I may win *C.*
Heb.13. 8. *C.* the same, yesterday and to-day.
1 Pet. 1. 11. the spirit of *C.* did signify.
1 John 2. 22. denieth that Jesus is the *C.*
Rev. 20. 4. they reigned with *C.* a thousand years.

Christian, Acts 11. 26. first called *C.* at Antioch.
Acts 26. 28. almost persuadest me to be a *C.*
1 Pet. 4. 16. if any suffer as a *C.*

Church, Matt. 16. 18. on this rock I will build my *c.*
18. 17. tell it to the *c.*
Acts. 2. 47. Lord added to *c.* daily.
7. 38. the *c.* in the wilderness.
14. 23. ordained elders in every *c.*
16. 5. *c.* established in faith.
19 37. robbers of *c.*

Church—*Continued.*
Acts. 20. 28. feed the *c.* of God.
Rom. 16. 5 ; 1 Cor. 16. 19 ; Philem. 2. *c.* in house.
Eph. 1. 22. head over all things to *c.*
5. 25. as Christ loved the *c.*
Col. 1. 18. head of the body, the *c.*
Heb. 12. 23. the *c.* of the first-born.

Circuit, 1 Sam. 7. 16. from year to year in *c.*
Job 22. 14. walketh in *c.* of heaven.
Ps. 19. 6. his *c.* unto the ends of.
Eccl. 1. 6. returneth according to his *c.*

Circumcise, Gen. 17. 11. ye shall *c.* foreskin.
Lk. 1. 59. they came to *c.* the child.
John 7. 22. ye on Sabbath *c.* a man.
Acts 15. 1. except ye be *c.* ye.
Gal. 5. 2. if ye be *c.*, Christ shall profit nothing.
Phil. 3. 5. *c.* the eighth day.

Circumcision, Rom. 3. 1. what profit is there of *c.* ?
15. 8. Jesus Christ minister of *c.*
Gal. 5. 6 ; 6. 15. in Christ neither *c.* availeth
Eph. 2. 11. by that called *c.* in flesh.
Phil. 3. 3. the *c.* which worship God.
Col. 2. 11. *c.* without hands.
3. 11. neither *c.* nor uncircumcision.

Circumspect, Ex. 23. 13. in all things, be *c.*
Eph. 5. 15. see that ye walk *c.*

Cistern, 2. Ki. 18. 31 ; Is. 36. 16. drink every one of his *c.*
Eccl. 12. 6. wheel broken at the *c.*
Jer. 2. 13. hewed out *c.*, broken *c.*

City, Gen. 4. 17. Cain builded a *c.*
Num. 35. 6 ; Josh. 15, 59. *c.* of refuge.
2 Sam. 19. 37. I may die in mine own *c.*
Ps. 46. 4. make glad *c.* of God.
107. 4. found no *c.* to dwell in.
127. 1. except Lord keep *c.*
Prov. 8. 3. wisdom crieth in *c.*
16. 32. than he that taketh a *c.*
Eccl. 9. 14. a little *c.*, and few men.
Is. 22. 2. a tumultuous *c.* a joyous *c.*
26. 1. we have a strong *c.*
33. 20. *c.* of our solemnities.
Zech. 8. 3. a *c.* of truth.
Matt. 5. 14. *c.* set on a hill.
21. 10. all the *c.* was moved.
23. 34. persecute them from *c.* to *c.*
Lk. 10. 8. into whatsoever *c.* ye enter.
19. 41. he beheld *c.* and wept.
Acts 8. 8. great joy in that *c.*
Heb. 11. 10. a *c.* that hath foundations.
12. 22. the *c.* of living God.
13. 14. no continuing *c.*
Rev. 3. 12. name of the *c.* of my God.
20. 9. compassed beloved *c.*

Clap, Ps. 47. 1. *c.* your hands, all ye people.
98. 8. let the floods *c.* their hands.
Is. 55. 12. the trees shall *c.* their hands.
Lam. 2. 15. all that pass by *c.* their hands.

Clave, Gen. 22. 3. Abraham *c.* wood for burnt-offering.
Ruth 1. 14. Ruth *c.* to her mother-in-law.
2 Sam. 23. 10. his hand *c.* to the sword.
Neh. 10. 29. they *c.* to their brethren.
Acts 17. 34. certain men *c.* to Paul.

Clay, Job. 4. that dwell in houses of *c.*
10. 9. thou hast made me as *c.*
13. 12. bodies like to bodies of *c.*
33. 6. I am formed out of *c.*
Ps. 40. 2. out of the miry *c.*
Is. 64. 8. we the *c.*, thou our potter.
Jer. 18. 6. as *c.* is in the potter's hand.

Clay—*Continued.*
Dan. 2. 33. part of iron, part of *c.*
John 9. 6. made *c.*, and anointed.
Rom. 9. 21. potter power over *c.*

Clean, 2. Ki. 5, 12, wash and be *c.*
Job. 14. 4. *c.* thing out of an unclean ?
15. 15. heavens not *c.* in his sight.
Ps. 19. 9. fear of the Lord is *c.*
24. 4. he that hath *c.* hands.
51. 10. create in me *c.* heart.
77. 8. is his mercy *c.* gone for ever ?
Prov. 16. 2. ways *c.* in his own eyes.
Is. 1. 16. wash you, make you *c.*
52. 11. be *c.* that bear vessels of the Lord.
Ezek. 36. 25. then will I sprinkle *c.* water on you.
Matt. 8. 2 ; Mk. 1. 40 ; Lk. 5. 12. thou canst make me *c.*
Matt. 23. 25 ; Lk. 11. 39. make *c.* the outside.
Lk. 11. 41. all things *c.* unto you.
John 13. 11. ye are not all *c.*
15. 3. *c.* through the word.
Acts 18. 6. I am *c.*
Rev. 19. 8. arrayed in fine linen *c.* and white.

Cleanse, Ps. 19. 12. *c.* from secret faults.
73. 13. I have *c.* my heart in vain.
119. 9. a young man *c.* his way.
Matt. 8. 3. his leprosy was *c.*
10. 8 ; 11, 5 ; Lk. 7. 22 *c.* lepers.
Matt. 23. 26. *c.* first that which is within.
Lk. 4. 27, none was *c.*, saving Naaman.
17. 17. were not ten *c.* ?
Acts 10. 15 ; 11. 9. what God hath *c.*
2 Cor. 7. 1. let us *c.* ourselves.
Eph. 5. 26. might *c.* it with washing.
Jas. 4. 8. *c.* your hands, ye sinners.
1 John 1. 7. *c.* us from all sin.

Clear, Gen. 44. 16. how shall we *c.* ourselves ?
Ex. 34. 7. by no means *c.* the guilty.
2 Sam. 23. 4. *c.* shining after rain.
Job 11. 17. thine age be *c.* than noonday.
Ps. 51. 4. *c.* when thou judgest.
Cant. 6. 10. *c.* as the sun.
Zech. 14. 6. light shall not be *c.*
Matt. 7. 5 ; Lk. 6. 42. see *c.* to pull out mote.
Mk. 8. 25. saw every man *c.*
Rom. 1. 20. things from creation *c.* seen.
2 Cor. 7. 11. approved yourselves to be *c.*
Rev. 21. 11 ; 22. 1. *c.* as crystal.

Cleave, Josh. 23. 8. *c.* to the Lord your God.
Job 29. 10 ; Ps. 137. 6 ; Ezek. 3. 26. tongue *c.* to roof of mouth.
Ps. 119. 25. my soul *c.* to dust.
Acts 11. 23. with purpose of heart *c.*
Rom. 12. 9. *c.* to that which is good.

Clefts, Cant. 2. 14. dove in *c.* of the rock.
Is. 2. 21. to go into *c.* for fear.
Jer. 49. 16 ; Obad. 3. dwellest in the *c.*

Clerk, Acts 19. 35. town *c.* had appeased.

Climb, Amos 9. 2. though they *c.* up to heaven.
Lk. 19. 4. *c.* up a tree.
John 10. 1. *c.* up some other way.

Cloak, Is. 59, 17. clad with zeal as a *c.*
Matt. 5. 40 ; Lk. 6. 29. let him have thy *c* also.
John 15. 22. no *c.* for their sin.
1 Thes. 2. 5. *c.* of covetousness.
1 Pet. 2. 16 *c.* of maliciousness.

Clods, Job 21, 33, *c.* of valley be sweet.
Is. 28. 24. ploughman break the *c.*
Joel, 1. 17. seed rotten under *c.*

Close, Num. 16. 33. earth *c.* upon them.
Is. 29. 10. Lord *c.* your eyes.
Prov. 18. 24. friend sticketh *c.* than a brother.
Lk. 9. 36. they kept it *c.*

Clothe, Ps. 65. 13. pastures *c.* with flocks.
93. 1. Lord is *c.* with majesty.
132. 9. priests be *c.* with righteousness.
132. 16. *c.* with salvation.
Prov. 31. 21. household *c.* with scarlet.
Is. 50. 3. *c.* heavens with blackness.
61. 10. *c.* with garments of salvation.
Matt. 6. 30 ; Lk. 12. 28. *c.* grass of field.
Matt. 11. 8 ; Lk. 7. 25. a man *c.* in soft raiment ?
Matt. 25. 36. 43. naked, and ye *c.* me.
Mk. 1. 6. *c.* with camel's hair.
5. 15 ; Lk. 8. 35. *c.*, and in right mind.
Mk. 15. 17. *c.* Jesus with purple.
Lk. 16. 19. *c.* in purple and fine linen.
2 Cor. 5. 2. desiring to be *c.* upon.
1 Pet. 5. 5. be *c.* with humility.
Rev. 3. 18. that thou mayest be *c.*
19. 13. *c.* with a vesture dipped in blood.

Clothes, Deut. 29. 5 ; Neh. 9. 21. *c.* not waxen old.
Matt. 24. 18. not return to take *c.*
Mk. 5. 28. if I touch but his *c.*
Lk. 2. 7. in swaddling *c.*
19. 36. spread *c.* in the way.
24. 12 ; John 20. 5. linen *c.* laid.
John 11. 44. bound with grave-*c.*
Acts 7. 58. laid down *c.* at Saul's feet.
22. 23. cried out, and cast off *c.*

Clothing, Ps. 45. 13. *c.* of wrought gold.
Prov. 27. 26. lambs for thy *c.*
Is. 59, 17. garments of vengeance for *c.*
Matt. 7. 15. in sheep's *c.*
Mk. 12. 38. love to go in long *c.*
Acts 10. 30. a man in bright *c.*
Jas. 2. 3. to him that weareth gay *c.*

Cloud, Gen. 9. 13. I set my bow in the *c.*
Ex. 13. 21 ; 14. 24 ; Neh. 9. 19. pillar of *c.*
1 Ki. 18. 44. a little *c.*
Ps. 36. 5. faithfulness reacheth to *c.*
97. 2. *c.* and darkness round about him.
104. 3. maketh *c.* his chariot.
Prov. 3. 20. *c.* drop down dew.
Eccl. 12. 2. nor *c.* return after rain.
Is. 5. 6. the *c.* that they rain not.
44. 22. blotted out as thick *c.*
60, 8. fly as a *c.*
Dan. 7. 13 ; Lk. 21. 27. Son of man with *c.*
Hos. 6. 4 ; 13. 3. goodness as morning *c.*
Matt. 17. 5 ; Mk. 9. 7 ; Lk. 9. 34. *c.* overshadowed.
Matt. 24. 30 ; 26. 64 ; Mk. 13. 26 ; 14. 62. in *c.* with power.
1 Cor. 10. 1. fathers under *c.*
1 Thes. 4. 17. caught up in *c.*
2 Pet. 2. 17. *c.* carried with tempest.
Jude 12. *c.* without water.
Rev. 1. 7. he cometh with *c.*

Cloven, Lev. 11. 3. *c.* footed, that eat.
Acts. 2. 3. *c.* tongues.

Coal, Prov. 6. 28. hot *c.*, and not be burned.
25. 22 ; Rom. 12. 20. heap *c.* of fire.
Is. 6. 6. seraphim having live *c.* in hand.
John 18. 18 ; 21. 9. fire of *c.*

Coat, Matt. 5. 40. take away thy *c.*
10. 10 ; Mk. 6. 9. neither provide two *c.*
Lk. 6. 29, to take *c.* also.
John 19. 23. *c.* without seam.
21. 7. fisher's *c.*
Acts. 9. 39. the *c.* which Dorcas made.

Cock, Matt. 26. 34 ; Mk. 14. 30 ; Lk. 22. 34. *c.* crow, deny me.
Mk. 13. 35. cometh at *c.* crowing.

Coffin, Gen 50, 26. Joseph was put in a *c.*

Cold, Prov 20. 4. by reason of *c.*
    25. 13. *c.* of snow in harvest.
    25. 25. *c.* waters to thirsty soul.
    Matt. 10. 42. cup of *c.* water.
    24. 12. love of many wax *c.*
    2 Cor. 11. 27. in *c.* and nakedness.
    Rev. 3. 15. neither *c.* nor hot.
Collection, 2 Chr. 24. 6. to bring in the *c.*
    1 Cor. 16. 1. concerning *c.* for saints.
College, 2 Ki. 22. 14; 2 Chr. 34. 22. dwelt in *c.*
Comely, Ps. 33. 1 ; 147. 1. praise is *c.*
    Cant. 1. 5. I am black but *c.*
    1 Cor. 7. 35. for that which is *c.*
    Is. 53. 2. no form or *c.*
Comfort, Ps. 119. 50. *c.* in affliction.
    Matt. 9. 22; Mk. 10. 49; Lk. 8. 48 ; 2 Cor.
    13. 11. be of good *c.*
    Acts 9. 31. *c.* of Holy Ghost.
    Rom. 15. 4. patience and *c.* of scriptures.
    2 Cor. 1. 3. God of all *c.*
    7. 13. were comforted in your *c.*
    Phil. 2. 1. if any *c.* of love.
    Ps. 23. 4. rod and staff *c.* me.
    Is. 40. 1. *c.* ye, *c.* ye, my people.
    61. 2. *c.* all that mourn.
    66. 13. as one whom his mother *c.*
    Matt. 5. 4. that mourn, they shall be *c.*
    Lk. 16. 25. he is *c.*, and thou art tormented.
    John 11. 19. to *c.* them.
    Rom. 1. 12. I may be *c.* with you.
    2 Cor. 1. 4. able to *c.* them.
    1 Thes. 4. 18. *c.* one another with these words.
Comfortable, Is. 40. 2. speak ye *c.* to Jerusalem.
    Hos. 2. 14. I will speak *c.* to her.
    Zech. 1. 13. Lord answered with *c.* words.
Comforter, Job 16. 2. miserable *c.* are ye all.
    Ps. 69. 20. looked for *c.*, but found none.
    John 14. 16 ; 15. 26 ; 16. 7. the Holy Ghost the *c.*
Command, Gen. 18. 19. he will *c.* his children.
    Deut. 28. 8. Lord shall *c.* the blessing.
    Ps. 33. 9. he *c.*, and it stood fast.
    42. 8. Lord will *c.* his loving kindness.
    Lk. 8. 25. he *c.* even the winds.
    9. 54. *c.* fire from heaven.
    John 15. 14. if ye do whatsoever I *c.*
    Acts 17. 30. *c.* all men everywhere.
    Heb. 12. 20. could not endure that *c.*
Commander, Is. 55. 4. leader and *c.* to people.
Commandment, Ps. 119. 86. *c.* are faithful.
    119. 96. *c.* exceeding broad.
    119. 127. I love thy *c.*
    119. 143. thy *c.* are my delight.
    Matt. 15. 9; Mk. 7. 7; Col. 2. 22. the *c.* of men.
    John 13. 34; 1 John 2. 7; 2 John 5. a new *c.*
    Rom. 7. 12. *c.* is holy, just, and good.
    1 Cor. 7. 6 ; 2 Cor. 8. 8. not by *c.*
    Eph. 6. 2. first *c.* with promise.
    1 Tim. 1. 5. end of the *c.* is charity.
Commend, Lk. 16. 8. Lord *c.* unjust steward.
    23. 46. into thy hands I *c.* spirit.
    Acts 20. 32. I *c.* you to God.
    Rom. 3. 5. unrighteousness *c.* righteousness
    of God.
    5. 8. God *c.* his love toward us.
    2 Cor. 3. 1 ; 5. 12. *c.* ourselves.
    4. 2. *c.* to every man's conscience.
    10. 18. not he that *c.* himself is approved.
Commit, Ps. 37. 5. *c.* thy way to the Lord.
    John 2. 24. Jesus did not *c.* himself.
    5. 22. hath *c.* judgment to Son.
    Rom. 3. 2. *c.* oracles of God.
    2 Cor. 5. 19. *c.* to us word of reconciliation.
    1 Tim. 6. 20. keep that which is *c.* to thee.
    1 Pet. 2. 23. *c.* himself to him that judgeth.

Common, Eccl. 6. 1. evil, and it is *c.* among men.
    Mk. 12. 37. the *c.* people heard him gladly.
    Acts 2. 44; 4. 32. all things *c.*
    10. 14; 11. 8. never eaten anything *c.*
    1 Cor. 10. 13. temptation *c.* to men.
    Eph. 2. 12. aliens from *c.*-wealth.
    Jude 3. write of *c.* salvation.
Commune, Job 4. 2. if we *c.* with thee.
    Ps. 4. 4; 77. 6. *c.* with own heart.
Communicate, Gal. 6. 6. let him that is taught *c.*
    1 Tim. 6. 18. be willing to *c.*
    Hob. 13. 16. do good and *c.*
Communication, Matt. 5. 37. let your *c.* be yea.
    Lk. 24. 17. what manner of *c.*
    1 Cor. 15. 33. evil *c.* corrupt good manners.
    Eph. 4. 29. let no corrupt *c.* proceed.
Communion, 1 Cor. 10. 16. *c.* of blood, *c.* of body.
    2 Cor. 6. 14. what *c.* hath light with darkness?
    13 14. *c.* of Holy Ghost be with you.
Compact, Ps. 122. 3. Jerusalem is a city *c.*
    Eph. 4. 16. the whole body *c.*
Company, Ps. 55. 14. walked to house of God
    in *c.*
    68. 11. great was the *c.* of those.
    Mk. 6. 39; Lk. 9. 14. sit down by *c.*
    2 Thes. 3. 14. have no *c.* with him.
    Heb. 12. 22. innumerable *c.* of angels.
Compare, Ps. 89. 6. who in heaven *c.* to Lord?
    Prov. 3. 15; 8. 11. not to be *c.* to wisdom.
    Is. 40. 18. what likeness will ye *c.* unto him?
    46. 5. to whom will ye *c.* me?
    Lam. 4. 2. *c.* to fine gold.
    Rom. 8. 18. not worthy to be *c.* with the glory.
    1 Cor 2. 13. *c.* spiritual things with spiritual.
Comparison, Jud. 8. 2. I done it *c.* of you?
    Hag. 2. 3. in your eyes in *c.* of it.
    Mk. 4. 30. with what *c.* shall we.
Compass, 2 Ki. 3. 9; Acts 28. 13. fetched a *c.*
    Prov. 8. 27. *c.* on face of the deep.
    2 Sam. 22. 5. waves of death *c.* me.
    Ps. 18. 4; 116. 3. sorrows of death *c.* me.
    26. 6. *c.* thine altar.
    32. 7. *c.* with songs of deliverance.
    Is. 50. 11. *c.* yourselves with sparks.
    Matt. 23. 15. *c.* sea and land.
    Lk. 21. 20. Jerusalem *c.* with armies.
    Heb. 5. 2. himself *c.* with infirmity.
    12. 1. *c.* about with cloud of witnesses.
Compassion, Is. 49. 15. she should not have *c.*
    Lam. 3. 22. his *c.* fail not.
    Matt. 9. 36; 14. 14; Mk. 1. 41; 6. 34. Jesus
    moved with *c.*
    Matt. 18. 33. *c.* on thy fellow-servant.
    20. 34. had *c.* on them, and touched.
    Mk. 5. 19. the Lord hath had *c.*
    9. 22. have *c.* and help us.
    Lk. 7. 13. Lord saw her, he had *c.*
    10. 33. Samaritan had *c.*
    15. 20. father had *c.* and ran.
    Rom. 9. 15. I will have *c.* on whom I will.
    Heb. 5. 2. have *c.* on ignorant.
    1 John 3. 17. shutteth up bowels of *c.*
    Jude 22. of some have *c.*
Compel, Matt. 5. 41. *c.* thee to go a mile.
    27. 32; Mk. 15. 21. *c.* to bear cross.
    Lk. 14. 23. *c.* to come in.
    Acts 26. 11. I *c.* them to blaspheme.
    Gal. 2. 3. was *c.* to be circumcised.
Complain, Job 7. 11. I will *c.* in bitterness of
    soul.
    Ps. 77. 3. I *c.* and my spirit was overwhelmed.
    144. 14. no *c.* in our streets.
    Lam. 3. 39. wherefore doth a living man *c.*?
    Jude 16. these are murmurers, *c.*

Complaint, 1 Sam. 1. 16. out of abundance of my c.
Job 23. 2. to-day is my c. bitter.
Ps. 142. 2. I poured out my c. before him.
Complete, Col. 2. 10. ye are c. in him.
4. 12. stand c. in all.
Comprehend, Is. 40. 12. c. dust of the earth.
John 1. 5. the darkness c. it not.
Eph. 3. 18. able to c. with all saints.
Conceal, Ps. 40. 10. not c. thy loving kindness
Prov. 12. 23. prudent c. knowledge.
25. 2. glory of God to c. a thing
Jer. 50. 2. publish and c. not.
Conceit, Prov. 18. 11. as high wall in own c.
26. 12. a man wise in his own c.
Rom. 11. 25. lest wise in your own c.
12. 16. be not wise in own c.
Conceive, Job 15. 35; Is. 59. 4. c. mischief.
Ps. 51. 5. in sin did mother c. me.
Is. 7. 14. a virgin shall c.
Acts 5. 4. c. this in thine heart?
Jas. 1. 15. when lust hath c.
Concern, Ps. 138. 8. Lord perfect that c. me.
Acts 28. 31. things which c. Christ.
Concerning, Lk. 24. 27. things c. himself.
Rom. 9. 5. as c. the flesh Christ came.
16. 19. simple c. evil.
Phil. 4. 15. c. giving and receiving.
1 Thes. 5. 18. will of God c. you.
1 Pet. 4. 12. c. fiery trial.
Conclude, Rom. 3. 28. we c. a man is justified.
11. 32. c. them all in unbelief.
Gal. 3. 22. hath c. all under sin.
Condemn, Job 9. 20. my mouth shall c. me.
10. 2. I will say to God, do not c. me.
Is. 50. 9. who is he shall c. me?
Matt. 12. 7. not have c. guiltless.
12. 42; Lk. 11. 31. rise in judgment and c.
Mk. 14. 64. all c. him to be guilty.
Lk. 6. 37. c. not, and ye shall not be c.
John 3. 17. God sent not his Son to c. the world.
Rom. 8. 3. c. sin in the flesh.
8. 34. who is he that c.?
Jas. 5. 6. ye c. and killed the just.
1 John 3. 21. if our heart c. us not.
Condemnation, John 3. 19. this is the c., that light.
Rom. 5. 16. judgment by one to c.
8. 1. there is no c. to them in Christ.
2 Cor. 3. 9. ministration of c.
1 Tim. 3. 6. the c. of the devil.
Jas. 5. 12. lest ye fall into c.
Condescend, Rom. 12. 16. c. to men of low estate.
Coney, Lev. 11. 5. c. unclean unto you.
Ps. 104. 18. rocks a refuge for the c.
Prov. 30. 26. c. a feeble folk.
Confection, Ex. 30. 35. make a c. after art.
1 Sam. 8. 13. your daughters to be c.
Confess, Lev. 26. 40. if they c. their iniquity.
Ps. 32. 5. I said, I will c. my transgression.
Prov. 28. 13. whoso c. and forsaketh.
Matt. 10. 32; Lk. 12. 8. c. me before men.
John 9. 22. if any man did c.
12. 42. did not c. him lest.
Acts 23. 8. Pharisees c. both.
Rom. 14. 11; Phil. 2. 11. every tongue c.
Heb. 11. 13. c. they were strangers.
Jas. 5. 16. c. your faults one to another.
1 John 1. 9. if we c. our sins.
4. 2. every spirit that c. Christ.
Rev. 3. 5. I will c. his name before my Father.

Confidence, Ps. 65. 5. the c. of all the ends of the earth.
118. 8. than put c. in man.
Prov. 14. 26. in fear of Lord is strong c.
Is. 30. 15. in c. shall be your strength.
Eph. 3. 12. access with c. by faith.
Phil. 3. 3. no c. in the flesh.
Heb. 3. 6. hold fast c.
10. 35. cast not away c.
1 John 3. 21. we have c. toward God.
5. 14. this is the c. we have in him.
Confirm, Is. 35. 3. c. the feeble knees.
Mk. 16. 20. c. the word with signs.
Acts 14. 22. c. souls of disciples.
Rom. 15. 8. c. promises made.
Confirmation, Phil. 1. 7. in the c. of the Gospel.
Heb. 6. 16. an oath for c.
Conflict, Phil. 1. 30. same c. ye saw in me.
Col. 2. 1. what c. I have for you.
Conform, Rom. 8. 29. c. to image of his Son.
12. 2. not c. to this world.
Phil. 3. 10. made c. to his death.
Confound, Gen. 11. 7. c. their language.
Ps. 22. 5. fathers trusted, and were not c.
40. 14; 70. 2. ashamed and c.
Acts 2. 6. multitude were c.
1 Pet. 2. 6. believeth shall not be c.
Confused, Is. 9. 5. battle is with c. noise.
Acts 19. 32. the assembly was c.
Confusion, Dan. 9. 7. to us belongeth c. of faces.
Acts 19. 29. city was filled with c.
1 Cor. 14. 33. God not author of c.
Congregation, Lev. 16. 33. atonement for all the c.
Num. 14. 10. all the c. bade stone them.
Neh. 5. 13. all the c. said, Amen.
Ps. 1. 5. nor sinners in c. of the righteous.
22. 22. in midst of c. will I praise.
Prov. 21. 16. in the c. of the dead.
Joel 2. 16. sanctify the c.
Acts 13. 43. when the c. was broken up.
Conquerors, Rom. 8. 37. we are more than c.
Rev. 6. 2. c. and to conquer.
Conscience, Acts 24. 16. c. void of offence.
Rom. 2. 15; 9. 1; 2 Cor. 1. 12. c. bearing witness.
1 Tim. 1. 5, 19; Heb. 13. 18; 1 Pet. 3. 16. a good c.
Heb. 9. 14. purge c. from dead works.
10. 22. hearts sprinkled from evil c.
Consecrate, 1 Chr. 29. 5. to c. his service to the Lord.
Mic. 4. 13. I will c. their gain to Lord.
Heb. 7. 28. Son, who is c. for evermore.
10. 20. living way, which he hath c.
Consent, Ps. 50. 18. a thief, thou c. with him.
Prov. 1. 10. if sinners entice thee, c. not.
Zeph. 3. 9. to serve with one c.
Lk. 14. 18. with one c. began to make excuse.
Consider, Deut. 32. 29. wise to c. latter end.
Ps. 8. 3. when I c. thy heavens.
41. 1. blessed is he that c. the poor.
48. 13. c. her palaces.
50. 22. c. this, ye that forget God.
119. 153. c. mine affliction.
Prov. 6. 6. go to ant, c. her ways.
23. 1. c. diligently what is before thee.
Eccl. 5. 1. they c. not that they do evil.
7. 14. in days of adversity c.
Is. 1. 3. my people think not c.
Jer. 23. 20; 30. 24. in latter days ye shall c.
Ezek. 12. 3. it may be they will c.
Hag. 1. 5, 7. c. your ways.
Matt. 6. 28; Lk. 12. 27. c. the lilies.

Consider—*Continued.*
Matt. 7. 3. *c.* not the beam.
Lk. 12. 24. *c.* the ravens.
John 11. 50. nor *c.* it is expedient.
Gal. 6. 1. *c.* thyself, lest thou also be tempted.
Heb. 3. 1. *c.* the Apostle and High Priest.
7. 4. *c.* how great this man was.
12. 3. *c.* him that endured.
13. 7. *c.* the end of their conversation.
Consist, Lk. 12. 15. life *c.* not in the abundance.
Col. 1. 17. by him all things *c.*
Consolation, Job 15. 11. are the *c.* of God small?
Lk. 6. 24. ye have received your *c.*
Rom. 15. 5. the God of *c.*
Phil. 2. 1. if there be any *c.* in Christ
2 Thes. 2. 16. everlasting *c.*
Heb. 6. 18. strong *c.*
Constrain, Job 32. 18. the spirit in me *c.* me.
Matt. 14. 22 ; Mk. 6. 45. Jesus *c.* disciples.
Lk. 24. 29. *c.* him, saying, abide.
2 Cor. 5. 14. love of Christ *c.* us.
1 Pet. 5. 2. the oversight, not by *c.*
Consult, Ps. 62. 4. only *c.* to cast him down.
Matt. 26. 4. *c.* that they might take Jesus.
Mk. 15. 1. chief priests held a *c.*
John 12. 10. *c.* to put Lazarus to death.
Consume, Ex. 3. 2. bush was not *c.*
Deut. 4. 24 ; 9. 3 ; Heb. 12. 29. a *c.* fire.
Jud. 6. 21. fire out of rock *c.* flesh.
1 Ki. 18. 38 ; 2 Chr. 7. 1. fire fell, and *c.* the sacrifice.
Job 4. 9. by breath of his nostrils *c.*
20. 26. fire not blown shall *c.* him.
Ps. 39. 11. his beauty to *c.* away.
Mal. 3. 6. therefore ye are not *c.*
Lk. 9. 54. fire to *c.* them, as Elias did.
Gal. 5. 15. take heed that ye be not *c.*
Jas. 4. 3. may *c.* it on your lusts.
Contain, 1 Ki. 8. 27 ; 2 Chr. 2. 6 ; 6. 18. heaven of heavens cannot *c.* thee.
John 21. 25. world not *c.* the books.
1 Pet. 2. 6. it is *c.* in scripture.
Contemn, Ps. 10. 13. wicked *c.* God.
15. 4. in whose eyes a vile person is
107. 11. *c.* counsel of Most High.
Ezek. 21. 10. it *c.* rod of my son.
Contempt, Job 12. 21 ; Ps. 107. 40. *c.* on princes.
Ps. 123. 3. exceedingly filled with *c.*
Prov. 18. 3. wicked cometh, then cometh *c.*
Dan. 12. 2. awake to everlasting *c.*
Contemptible, Mal. 2. 9. I made you *c.*
2 Cor. 10. 10. his speech *c.*
Contend, Is. 49. 25. I will *c.* with him that *c.*
50. 8. who will *c.* with me?
Jer. 12. 5. how canst thou *c.* with horses ;
Jude 3. earnestly *c.* for the faith.
Content, Job 6. 28. now therefore be *c.*
Mk. 15. 15. willing to *c.* the people.
Lk. 3. 14. be *c.* with your wages.
Phil. 4. 11. I have learned to be *c.*
1 Tim. 6. 6. godliness with *c.* is great gain.
Heb. 13. 5. be *c.* with such things as ye have.
Contention, Prov. 13. 10. by pride cometh *c.*
18. 18. lot causeth *c.* to cease.
23. 29. who hath *c.*?
Acts 15. 39. the *c.* was sharp.
1 Cor. 1. 11. there are *c.* among you.
Phil. 1. 16. preach Christ of *c.*
Tit. 3. 9. avoid *c.* and strivings.
Continual, Gen. 6. 5. imagination evil *c.*
Ps. 34. 1 ; 71. 6. praise *c.* in my mouth.
40. 11. truth *c.* preserve me.
73. 23. I am *c.* with thee.

Continual—*Continued.*
Prov. 6. 21. bind them *c.* on thine heart.
Is. 14. 6. smote with a *c.* stroke.
52. 5. my name is *c.* blasphemed.
Lk. 18. 5. lest by her *c.* coming.
24. 53. were *c.* in the temple.
Acts 6. 4. give ourselves *c.* to prayer.
Rom. 9. 2. I have *c.* sorrow in my heart.
Heb. 7. 3. abideth a priest *c.*
Continue, Ps. 36. 10. *c.* thy loving kindness.
72. 17. name shall *c.* as long as the sun.
Is. 5. 11. *c.* till wine inflame them.
Lk. 6. 12. he *c.* all night in prayer.
John 8. 31. if ye *c.* in my word.
15. 9. *c.* ye in my love.
Acts 1. 14 ; 2. 46. *c.* with one accord.
14. 22. exhorting them to *c.* in faith.
Rom. 6. 1. shall we *c.* in sin?
12. 12 ; Col. 4. 2. *c.* in prayer.
Gal. 3. 10. that *c.* not in all things.
Col. 1. 23 ; 1 Tim. 2. 15. if ye *c.* in faith.
Heb. 7. 23. not suffered to *c.* by reason.
13. 14. here have we no *c.* city.
Jas. 4. 13. *c.* there a year, and buy.
2 Pet. 3. 4. all things *c.* as they were.
1 John 2. 19. no doubt have *c.* with us.
Contradiction, Heb. 7. 7. without *c.* less is blessed.
12. 3. endured such *c.* of sinners.
Acts 13. 45. with envy, *c.* and blaspheming
Contrary, Matt. 14. 24. wind was *c.*
Acts 18. 13. *c.* to the law.
26. 9. *c.* to name of Jesus.
Gal. 5. 17. *c.* the one to the other.
Col. 2. 14. handwriting *c.* to us.
1 Thes. 2. 15. *c.* to all men.
1 Tim. 1. 10. *c.* to sound doctrine.
1 Pet. 3. 9. railing, but *c.* blessing.
Contrite, Ps. 34. 18. such as be of *c.* spirit.
51. 17. *c.* heart, wilt not despise.
Is. 57. 15. that is of a *c.* spirit, to revive heart of *c.* ones.
66. 2. of *c.* spirit and trembleth.
Controversy, Jer. 25. 31. a *c.* with the nations.
Mic. 6. 2. Lord hath a *c.* with his people.
1 Tim. 3. 16. without *c.* great is the mystery.
Convenient, Prov. 30. 8. feed me with food *c.*
Mk. 6. 21. a *c.* day was come.
Acts 24. 25. when I have a *c.* season.
Rom. 1. 28. things which are not *c.*
Eph. 5. 4. foolish talking, jesting, not *c.*
Conversation, Ps. 37. 14. such as be of *c.* upright *c.*
50. 23. ordereth his *c.* aright.
Eph. 2. 3. had our *c.* in times past.
Phil. 1. 27. *c.* as becometh the Gospel.
3. 20. our *c.* is in heaven.
Heb. 13. 5. *c.* without covetousness.
1 Pet. 1. 15 ; 2 Pet. 3. 11. holy *c.*
1 Pet. 2. 12. your *c.* honest among Gentiles.
Convert, Ps. 19. 7. law of Lord perfect, *c.* soul.
51. 13. sinners be *c.* unto thee.
Is. 6. 10 ; Matt. 13. 15 ; Mk. 4. 12 ; John 12. 40 , Acts 28. 27. lest they *c.*
Matt. 18. 3. except ye be *c.*
Lk. 22. 32. when *c.* strengthen thy brethren.
Acts 3. 19. repent and be *c.*
Jas. 5. 19. do err, and one *c.* him.
Convince, John 8. 46. which of you *c.* me of sin?
1 Cor. 14. 24. he is *c.* of all.
Tit. 1. 9. able to *c.* gainsayers.
Cook, 1 Sam. 8. 13. daughters to be *c.*
9. 23. Samuel said to the *c.*, bring.

Cool, Gen. 3. 8. walking in c. of the day.
  Lk. 16. 24. and c. my tongue.
Copper, Ezra 8. 27. two vessels of fine c.
  2 Tim. 4. 14. Alexander the c. smith.
Copy, Deut. 17. 18. write a c. of law.
  Josh. 8. 32. on stones c. of law of Moses.
  Ezra 4. 11 ; 5. 6. c. of letter sent.
Corban, Mk. 7. 11. it is c. that is, a gift.
Cord, Josh. 2. 15. let spies down by a c.
  Ps. 2. 3. let us cast away their c.
  118. 27. bind the sacrifice with c.
  Prov. 5. 22. holden with the c. of sins.
  Eccl. 4. 12. a threefold c.
  12. 6. silver c. loosed.
  Is. 5. 18. draw iniquity with c.
  54. 2. lengthen thy c.
  Hos. 11. 4. c. of a man.
  John 2. 15. scourge of small c.
Corn, Gen. 42. 2 ; Acts 7. 12. c. in Egypt.
  Deut. 25. 4 ; 1 Cor. 9. 9 ; 1 Tim. 5. 18. ox treadeth c.
  Jud. 15. 5. let foxes go into standing c.
  Job 5. 26. like as a shock of c.
  Ps. 65. 9. thou preparest them c.
  72. 16. handful of c. in the earth.
  Prov. 11. 26. he that withholdeth c.
  Zech. 9. 17. c. shall make men cheerful.
  Matt. 12. 1 ; Mk. 2. 23 ; Lk. 6. 1. pluck ears of c.
  Mk. 4. 28. full c. in the ear.
  John 12. 24. a c. of wheat fall into ground.
Corner, Ps. 118. 22 ; Eph. 2. 20. head stone of c.
  144. 12. daughters as c. stones.
  Is. 28. 16 ; 1 Pet. 2. 6. a precious c. stone.
  Is. 30. 20. teachers removed into c.
  Matt. 6. 5. pray in c. of the streets.
  Rev. 7. 1. four c. of the earth.
Correct, Ps. 39. 11. dost c. man.
  Prov. 3. 12. whom Lord loveth he c.
  Jer. 30. 11 ; 46. 28. I will c. thee in measure.
  Heb. 12. 9. fathers which c. us.
Correction, Prov. 3. 11. neither be weary of his c.
  Jer. 2. 30 ; 5. 3 ; 7. 28 ; Zeph. 3. 2. receive c.
  2 Tim. 3. 16. Scripture profitable for c.
Corrupt, Gen. 6. 11. the earth was c.
  Matt. 6. 19 ; Lk. 12. 33. moth c.
  Matt. 7. 17 ; 12. 33 ; Lk. 6. 43. a c. tree.
  1 Cor. 15. 33. evil communications c.
  Eph. 4. 22. put off old man, which is c.
  1 Tim. 6. 5 ; 2 Tim. 3. 8. men of c. minds.
  Jas. 5. 2. your riches are c.
Corruptible, Rom. 1. 23. image like to c. man.
  1 Cor. 9. 25. a c. crown.
  15. 53. c. must put on incorruption.
  1 Pet. 1. 18. not redeemed with c. things.
Corruption, Ps. 16. 10 ; 49. 9 ; Acts 2. 27 ; 13. 35. not see c.
  Jon. 2. 6. brought up life from c.
  Acts 2. 31. neither his flesh did see c.
  Rom. 8. 21. bondage of c.
  1 Cor. 15. 42. sown in c.
  Gal. 6. 8. of flesh reap c.
  2 Pet. 1. 4. the c. that is in world.
  2. 12. perish in their own c.
Cost, 2 Sam. 24. 24 ; 1 Chr. 21. 24. offer of that which c. nothing.
  Lk. 14. 28. sitteth not down and counteth c.
  John 12. 3. spikenard c.
  Rev. 18. 19. made rich by her c.
Couch, Lk. 5. 19. let him down with c.
  Acts 5. 15. laid sick on c.
Council, Matt. 5. 22. in danger of c.
  Lk. 22. 66. led Jesus into their c.
  Acts 5. 27. set them before c.
  6. 12. brought Stephen to c.

Counsel, Neh. 4. 15. brought c. to nought.
  Job 38. 2 ; 42. 3. darkeneth c. by words.
  Ps. 1. 1. c. of the ungodly.
  33. 11 ; Prov. 19. 21. c. of Lord standeth.
  Ps. 55. 14. took sweet c. together.
  73. 24. guide me with thy c.
  Prov. 1. 25. set at nought all my c.
  Is. 28. 29. wonderful in c.
  40. 14. with whom took he c. ?
  Jer. 32. 19. great in c., mighty in working.
  Mk. 3. 6 ; John 11. 53. took c. against Jesus.
  Acts 2. 23. determinate c. of God.
  5. 38. if this c. be of men.
  20. 27. declare all the c. of God.
  1 Cor. 4. 5. make manifest c. of the heart.
  Eph. 1. 11. after the c. of his own will.
  Heb. 6. 17. the immutability of his c.
  Rev. 3. 18. I c. thee to buy gold tried in fire.
Counsellor, Ps. 119. 24. thy testimonies my c.
  Prov. 11. 14 ; 15. 22 ; 24. 6. in multitude of c.
  Mk. 15. 43 ; Lk. 23. 50. an honourable c.
  Rom. 11. 34. who hath been his c. ?
Count, Gen. 15. 6 ; Ps. 106. 31 ; Rom. 4. 3 ; Gal. 3. 6. c. for righteousness.
  Ps. 44. 22. c. as sheep for the slaughter.
  Is. 32. 15. field be c. for a forest.
  Matt. 14. 5 ; Mk. 11. 32. c. him as a prophet.
  Lk. 21. 36 ; Acts 5. 41 ; 1 Tim. 5. 17. c. worthy.
  Acts 20. 24. neither c. I my life dear.
  Phil. 3. 8. I c. loss for Christ.
  3. 13. c. not myself to have apprehended.
  Heb. 10. 29. c. blood an unholy thing.
  Jas. 1. 2. c. it all joy.
  2 Pet. 3. 9. as some men c. slackness.
Countenance, Num. 6. 26. Lord lift up his c. on thee.
  1 Sam. 16. 7. look not on his c.
  Neh. 2. 2. why is thy c. sad?
  Job 14. 20. thou changest his c.
  Ps. 4. 6 ; 44. 3 ; 89. 15 ; 90. 8. light of thy c.
  Prov. 15. 13. merry heart maketh cheerful c.
  Eccl. 7. 3. by sadness of c., heart made better.
  Is. 3. 9. c. doth witness against them.
  Matt. 6. 16. hypocrites, of a sad c.
  28. 3 ; Lk. 9. 29. c. like lightning.
  Rev. 1. 16. his c. as the sun shineth.
Country, Josh. 7. 2. go up and view the c.
  Prov. 25. good news from a far c.
  Matt. 13. 57 ; Mk. 6. 4 ; Lk. 4. 24 ; John 4. 44. in his own c.
  Matt. 21. 33 ; 25. 14 ; Mk. 12. 1. went to far c.
  Lk. 4. 23. do here in thy c.
  Acts 12. 20. their c. nourished by king's c.
  Heb. 11. 9. sojourned as in strange c.
Courage, Deut. 31. 6 ; Josh. 10. 25 ; Ps. 27. 14 ; 31. 24. be of good c.
  Acts 28. 15. thanked God, and took c.
Course, Acts 20. 24 ; 2 Tim. 4. 7. finished my c.
  2 Thes. 3. 1. word may have free c.
  Jas. 3. 6. the c. of nature.
Court, Ps. 65. 4. that he may dwell in thy c.
  84. 2. soul fainteth for the c. of the Lord.
  92. 13. flourish in the c. of our God.
  100. 4. enter into his c. with praise.
  Is. 1. 12. to tread my c.
  Lk. 7. 25. live delicately in kings' c.
Covenant, Gen. 17. 11. a token of the c. betwixt.
  Ex. 31. 16. Sabbath for a perpetual c.
  Num. 18. 19 ; 2 Chr. 13. 5. c. of salt.
  Ps. 105. 8 ; 106. 45. he remembereth his c. for ever.
  Is. 28. 18. your c. with death disannulled.
  Matt. 26. 15 ; Lk. 22. 5. they c. with him.
  Acts 3. 25. children of the c.

Covenant—*Continued.*
Rom. 9. 4. to whom pertaineth the *c.*
Eph. 2. 12. strangers from *c.* of promise.
Heb. 8. 6. mediator of a better *c.*
13. 20. blood of the everlasting *c.*

Cover, Ex. 15. 5. depths *c.* them.
33. 22. I will *c.* thee.
1 Sam. 28. 14. old man *c.* with a mantle.
Ps. 32. 1 ; Rom, 4. 7. blessed whose sin is *c.*
Ps. 73. 6. violence *c.* as garment.
147. 8. *c.* heaven with clouds.
Prov. 28. 13. he that *c.* sins shall not prosper.
Is. 26. 21. earth no more *c.* her slain.
30. 1. *c.* with a covering.
Matt. 8. 24. ship *c.* with waves.
10. 26 ; Lk. 12. 2. there is nothing *c.*
1 Cor. 11. 7. a man not to *c.* head.
1 Pet. 4. 8. charity *c.* multitude of sins.

Covering, Job 22. 14. thick clouds are a *c.* to him.
26. 6. destruction hath no *c.*
Is. 28. 20. *c.* narrower than he can wrap.

Covert, Ps. 61. 4. trust in *c.* of thy wings.
Is. 4. 6. a tabernacle for a *c.*
32. 2. a man be as a *c.* from tempest.

Covet, Ex. 20. 17 ; Deut. 5. 21 ; Rom. 7. 7. thou shalt not *c.*
Prov. 21. 26. he *c.* greedily all the day.
Hab. 2. 9. *c.* an evil covetousness.
Acts 20. 33. I have *c.* no man's silver.
1 Cor. 12. 31. *c.* earnestly the best gifts.

Covetous, Ezek. 33. 31. their heart goeth after *c.*
Mk. 7. 22. out of heart proceedeth *c.*
Rom. 1. 29. filled with all *c.*
1 Cor. 6. 10 ; Eph. 5. 5. nor *c.* inherit kingdom.
2 Tim. 3. 2. men shall be *c.*
Heb. 13. 5. conversation without *c.*
2 Pet. 2. 3. through *c.* make merchandise.

Cow, Job 21. 10. their *c.* casteth not.
Is. 11. 7. *c.* and the bear shall feed.

Craft, Mk. 14. 1. take him by *c.*
Acts 18. 3. because he was of same *c.*
19. 27. our *c.* is in danger.
Rev. 18. 22. no *c.* be found any more.

Craftiness, Job 5. 13 ; 1 Cor. 3. 19. wise in their *c.*
Lk. 20. 23. he perceived their *c.*
2 Cor. 4. 2. not walking in *c.*
Eph. 4. 14. carried by cunning *c.*
2 Cor. 12. 16. being *c.* I caught you.

Create, Ps. 51. 10. *c.* in me a clean heart.
Is. 40. 26. who hath *c.* these things.
65. 17. I *c.* new heavens and new earth.
Jer. 31. 22. the Lord hath *c.* a new thing.
Mal. 2. 10. hath not one God *c.* us?
1 Cor. 11. 9. neither man *c.* for woman.
Eph. 2. 10. *c.* in Christ Jesus.
4. 24. after God is *c.* in righteousness.
Col. 1. 16. by him were all things *c.*
Rev. 4. 11. hast *c.* all things, for thy pleasure are and were *c.*

Creation, Mk. 10. 6. from *c.* male and female.
13. 19. as was not from the *c.*
Rom. 1. 20. from *c.* are clearly seen.
8. 22. whole *c.* groaneth.
2 Pet. 3. 4. continue as from the *c.*
Rev. 3. 14. beginning of *c.* of God.

Creator, Eccl. 12. 1. remember *c.* in youth.
Is. 40. 28. *c.* of ends of the earth.
Rom. 1. 25. creature more than *c.*
1 Pet. 4. 19. as to a faithful *c.*

Creature, Mk. 16. 15 ; Col. 1. 23. preach Gospel to every *c.*
Rom. 8. 19. expectation of the *c.*

Creature—*Continued.*
2 Cor. 5. 17 ; Gal. 6. 15. a new *c.*
Col. 1. 15. first-born of every *c.*
1 Tim. 4. 4. every *c.* of God is good.
Heb. 4. 13. neither any *c.* not manifest.

Creditor, Deut. 15. 2. *c.* that lendeth shall.
2 Ki. 4. 1. *c.* to take my two sons.
Lk. 7. 41. *c.* had two debtors.

Creep, Lev. 11. 31. unclean all that *c.*
Ps. 104. 20. beasts of the forest *c.* forth.
148. 10. all *c.* things praise the Lord.
Ezek. 8. 10. form of *c.* things portrayed.
Acts 10. 12 ; 11. 6. Peter saw *c.* things.
Jude 4. certain men *c.* in unawares.

Crimson, 2 Chr. 2. 7. cunning to work in *c.*
Is. 1. 18. though your sins be like *c.*
Jer. 4. 30. though thou clothest with *c.*

Crooked, Ps. 125. 5. aside to their *c.* ways.
Eccl. 1. 15 ; 7. 13. *c.* cannot be made straight.
Is. 40. 4 ; 42. 16 ; Lk. 3. 5. *c.* shall be made straight.
Is. 45. 2. make the *c.* places straight.
59. 8 ; Lam. 3. 9. *c.* paths.
Phil. 2. 15. in midst of a *c.* nation.

Cross, Matt. 16. 24 ; Mk. 8. 34 ; 10. 21 ; Lk. 9. 23. take up *c.*
Matt. 27. 32 ; Mk. 15. 21 ; Lk. 23. 26. compelled to bear *c.*
John 19. 25. there stood by *c.*
1 Cor. 1. 17 ; Gal. 6. 12 ; Phil. 3. 18. *c.* of Christ.
1 Cor. 1. 18. preaching of the *c.*
Gal. 5. 11. offence of the *c.*
6. 14. glory save in the *c.*
Eph. 2. 16. reconcile both by the *c.*
Phil. 2. 8. the death of the *c.*
Col. 1. 20. peace through the blood of the *c.*
2. 14. nailing it to his *c.*
Heb. 12. 2. for joy endured the *c.*

Crown, John 19. 9. taken the *c.* from my head.
31. 36. bind it as a *c.* to me.
Ps. 65. 11. thou *c.* the year.
103. 4. *c.* thee with loving kindness.
Prov. 4. 9. *c.* of glory deliver to thee.
12. 4. virtuous woman is a *c.*
16. 31. hoary head a *c.* of glory.
Is. 28. 1. woe to the *c.* of pride.
Matt. 27. 29 ; Mk. 15. 17 ; John 19. 2. a *c.* of thorns.
1 Cor. 9. 25. to obtain a corruptible *c.*
Phil. 4. 1. my joy and *c.*
1 Thes. 2. 19. *c.* of rejoicing.
2 Tim. 4. 8. a *c.* of righteousness.
Jas. 1. 12 ; Rev. 2. 10. *c.* of life.
1 Pet. 5. 4. a *c.* of glory.
Rev. 3. 11. that no man take thy *c.*
19. 12. on his head were many *c.*

Crucify, Matt. 20. 19. to Gentiles to *c.* him.
27. 31 ; Mk. 15. 20. led away to *c.* him.
John 19. 20, 41. where Jesus was *c.*
Acts 2. 23. by wicked hands ye have *c.*
Rom. 6. 6. old man is *c.* with him.
1 Cor. 1. 23. we preach Christ *c.*
2. 2. save Jesus Christ and him *c.*
2 Cor. 13. 4. though he was *c.* through weakness.
Gal. 2. 20. I am *c.* with Christ.
3. 1. Christ set forth *c.*
5. 24. have *c.* the flesh.
Heb. 6. 6. *c.* to themselves afresh.

Cruel, Ps. 25. 19. hate me with *c.* hatred.
27. 12. breathe out *c.*
71. 4. deliver out of hand of *c.*
Prov. 11. 17. *c.* troubleth his own flesh.
12. 10. tender mercies of wicked are *c.*

28

Cruel—*Continued.*
Prov. 27. 4. wrath is *c.*
Cant. 8. 6. jealousy is *c.*
Heb. 11. 36. trial of *c.* mockings.

Crumbs, Matt. 15. 27 ; Mk. 7. 28. dogs eat of *c.*
Lk. 16. 21. to be fed with the *c.*

Cry, Ex. 3. 7. I have heard their *c.*
1 Sam. 5. 12. *c.* of the city went up to heaven.
Job 34. 28. he heareth the *c.* of the afflicted.
Ps. 9. 12. forgetteth not *c.* of humble.
34. 15. his ears open to their *c.*
88. 2. incline thine ear to my *c.*
Prov. 21. 13. stoppeth his ears at *c.* of the poor.
Matt. 25. 6. at midnight there was a *c.*—made.
Ex. 14. 15. wherefore *c.* thou unto me.
Job 29. 12. I delivered the poor that *c.*
Ps. 34. 17. righteous *c.* Lord heareth.
147. 9. food to young ravens which *c.*
Prov. 8. 1. dotn not wisdom *c.* ?
Is. 58. 1. *c.* aloud, spare not.
65. 14. shall *c.* for sorrow of heart.
Matt. 12. 19. he shall not strive nor *c.*
20. 31 ; Mk. 10. 48 ; Lk. 18. 39. *c.* the more.
Lk. 18. 7. elect, who *c.* day and night.
John 7. 37. Jesus *c.,* if any man thirst.
Acts 19. 32 ; 21. 34. some *c.* one thing, and some another.
Rom. 8. 15. whereby we *c.,* Abba, Father.
Jas. 5. 4. hire of labourers *c.*

Crying, Prov. 19. 18. soul spare for his *c.*
Is. 65. 19. voice of *c.*
Matt. 3. 3 ; Mk. 1. 3 ; Lk. 3. 4 ; John 1. 23. one in wilderness.
Heb. 5. 7. prayers, with strong *c.*
Rev. 21. 4. no more death, nor *c.*

Crystal, Job 28. 17. *c.* cannot equal it.
Ezek. 1. 22. as colour of terrible *c.*
Rev. 4. 6. a sea of glass, like *c.*
21. 11. light of city clear as *c.*
22. 1. a pure river, clear as *c.*

Cubit, Deut. 3. 11. after the *c.* of a man.
Matt. 6. 27 ; Lk. 12. 25. one *c.* to stature.

Cumber, Lk. 10. 40. *c.* about much serving.
13. 7. why *c.* it the ground?

Cunning, Gen. 25. 27. Esau was a *c.* hunter.
Ex. 31. 4. to devise *c.* works in gold.
Ps. 137. 5. let my hand forget her *c.*
Is. 40. 20. he seeketh a *c.* workman.
Jer. 9. 17. send for *c.* women.
Dan. 1. 4. children *c.* in knowledge.
Eph. 4. 14. carried about by *c.* craftiness.
2 Pet. 1. 16. not followed *c.* devised fables.

Cup, Ps. 23. 5. my *c.* runneth over.
116. 13. I will take *c.* of salvation.
Matt. 10. 42 ; Mk. 9. 41. *c.* of cold water.
Matt. 20. 22 ; Mk. 10. 39. drink of my *c.*
23. 25 ; make clean outside of *c.*
26. 27. Mk. 14. 23 ; Lk. 22. 17 ; 1 Cor. 11. 25. took the *c.*
Matt. 26. 39 ; Mk. 14. 36 ; Lk. 22. 42. let this *c.* pass.
Lk. 22. 20 ; 1 Cor. 11. 25. this *c.* is New Testament.
John 18 11. *c.* which my Father hath given.
1 Cor. 10. 16. *c.* of blessing we bless.
11. 26. as often as ye drink this *c.*

Cure, Jer. 33. 6. I will *c.* them.
Matt. 17. 18. child *c.* that very hour.
Lk. 7. 21. in that hour he *c.* many.
9. 1. power to *c.* diseases.
13. 32. I do *c.* to-day.

Curse, Deut. 11. 26. I set before you blessing and *c.*
23. 5. turned *c.* into blessing.

Curse—*Continued.*
Mal. 3. 9. ye are cursed with a *c.*
Gal. 3. 10. are under the *c.*
Rev. 22. 3. no more *c.*
Gen. 8. 21. I will not *c.* ground.
Ex. 22. 28. not *c.* ruler of thy people.
Lev. 19. 14. not *c.* the deaf.
Num. 23. 8. how shall I *c.* whom God hath not ?
Jud. 5. 23. *c.* ye Meroz, *c.* ye bitterly.
Job 2. 9. *c.* God, and die.
Ps. 62. 4. they bless, but *c.* inwardly.
Is. 8. 21. *c.* their king, and God.
Mal. 2. 2. I will *c.* your blessings.
Matt. 5. 44 ; Lk. 6. 28 ; Rom. 12. 14. bless them that *c.* you.
Matt. 26. 74 ; Mk. 14. 71. he began to *c.*
Mk. 11. 21. fig tree thou *c.*
John 7. 49. who knoweth not the law are *c.*
Gal. 3. 10. *c.* every one that continueth not.
Jas. 3. 9. therewith *c.* we men.

Custom, Matt. 9. 9 ; Mk. 2. 14 ; Lk. 5. 27. receipt of *c.*
Matt. 17. 25. of whom do kings take *c.* ?
Lk. 1. 9. according to *c.* of priest's office.
4. 16. as Jesus' *c.* was.
John 18. 39. ye have a *c.*
Acts 16. 21. teach *c.* which are not lawful.
Rom. 13. 7. *c.* to whom *c.*
1 Cor. 11. 16. we have no such *c.*

Cymbal, 1 Cor. 13. 1. I am as tinkling *c.*

Cypress, Is. 44. 14. he taketh the *c.*

DAILY, Ps. 13. 2. sorrow in my heart *d.*
42. 10. *d.* to me, where is thy God?
68. 19. *d.* loadeth us.
Prov. 8. 30. I was *d.* his delight.
Dan. 8. 11 ; 11. 31 ; 12. 11. *d.* sacrifice taken away.
Matt. 6. 11 ; Lk. 11. 3. our *d.* bread.
Lk. 9. 23. take up cross *d.*
Acts 2. 47. added to church *d.*
6. 1. the *d.* ministration.
16. 5. churches increased *d.*
17. 11. searched the Scriptures *d.*
1 Cor. 15. 31. I die *d.*
Heb. 3. 13. exhort *d.*
7. 27. needeth not *d.* to offer.
Jas. 2. 15. destitute of *d.* food.

Dainty, Job 33. 20. his soul abhorreth *d.* meat.
Ps. 141. 4. let me not eat of their *d.*
Prov. 23. 3. be not desirous of *d.*

Damage, Prov. 26. 6. drinketh *d.*
Dan. 6. 2. king should have no *d.*
Acts 27. 10. voyage will be with *d.*
2 Cor. 7. 9. *d.* by us in nothing.

Damnation, Matt. 23. 14 ; Mk. 12. 40 ; Lk. 20. 47. ye shall receive greater *d.*
Mk. 3. 29. in danger of eternal *d.*
John 5. 29. to the resurrection of *d.*
Rom. 3. 8. whose *d.* is just.
13. 2. receive to themselves *d.*
1 Cor. 11. 29. eateth and drinketh *d.*
2 Pet. 2. 3. their *d.* slumbereth not.

Damned, Mk. 16. 16. believeth not be *d.*
Rom. 14. 23. doubteth is *d.* if he eat.
2 Thes. 2. 12. be *d.* who believeth not.
2 Pet. 2. 1. bring in *d.* heresies.

Damsel, Gen. 34. 3. he loved the *d.*
34. 4, 12. me this *d.* to wife.
Matt. 14. 11 ; Mk 6. 28. head given to *d.*
Mk. 5. 39. *d.* is not dead.
Acts 12. 13. a *d.* came to hearken.
16. 16. *d.* possessed with a spirit.

Dance, Ex. 32. 19. he saw calf and *d.*
1 Sam. 18. 6. came out singing and *d.*
2 Sam. 6. 14. David *d.* before the Lord.
Ps. 30. 11. my mourning into *d.*
  149. 3; 150. 4. praise him in the *d.*
Eccl. 3. 4. a time to *d.*
Is. 13. 21. satyrs shall *d.* there.
Matt. 11. 17; Lk. 7. 32. piped, and ye have not *d.*
Matt. 14. 6; Mk. 6. 22. daughter of Herodias *d.*
Danger, Matt. 5. 21. in *d.* of judgment.
Mk. 3. 29. *d.* of eternal damnation.
Acts 19. 27. not only craft is in *d.*
  27. 9. when sailing was now *d.*
Dare, Rom. 5. 7. some would even *d.* to die.
  15. 18. *d.* to speak of anything.
1 Cor. 6. 1. *d.* any of you go to law?
2 Cor. 10. 12. *d.* not make ourselves of number.
Dark, Job 12. 25. they grope in the *d.*
  22. 13. can he judge through *d.* cloud?
  38. 2. that *d.* counsel by words.
Ps. 49. 4; Prov. 1. 6. *d.* sayings.
Ps. 69. 23; Rom. 11. 10. let eyes be *d.*
Ps. 88. 12. wonders be known in the *d.*
Eccl. 12. 2. stars be not *d.*
  12. 3. look out of windows be *d.*
Zech. 14. 6. light not clear nor *d.*
Matt. 24. 29; Mk. 13. 24. sun be *d.*
Lk. 23. 45. sun *d.,* and veil rent.
John 20. 1. when it was yet *d.*
Rom. 1. 21. foolish heart was *d.*
Eph. 4. 18. understanding *d.*
2 Pet. 1. 19. shineth in a *d.* place.
Rev. 9. 2. sun and the air were *d.*
Darkness, Gen. 1. 2. *d.* was upon the deep.
Ex. 14. 20. it was a cloud and *d.* to them.
Deut. 5. 22. spake out of thick *d.*
  28. 29. grope as the blind in *d.*
1 Sam. 2. 9. wicked be silent in *d.*
2 Sam. 22. 10; Ps. 18. 9. *d.* under his feet.
1 Ki. 8. 12; 2 Chr. 6. 1. dwell in thick *d.*
Job 3. 5. *d.* and shadow of death.
  30. 26. waited for light, there came *d.*
Ps. 91. 6. pestilence that walketh in *d.*
  97. 2. clouds and *d.* are round about him.
  112. 4. to upright ariseth light in *d.*
  139. 12. *d.* and light alike to thee.
Prov. 20. 20. lamp put out in *d.*
Eccl. 2. 13. as far as light excelleth *d*
Is. 58. 10. thy *d.* as noonday.
  60. 2. *d.* cover the earth, gross *d.*
Joel 2. 2. day of clouds and thick *d.*
Matt. 6. 23; Lk. 11. 34. body full of *d.*
Matt. 8. 12; 22. 13; 25. 30. outer *d.*
  10. 27f; Lk. 12. 3. what I tell in *d.,* speak.
Lk. 1. 79; Rom. 2. 19. light to them that sit in *d.*
Lk. 22. 53; Col. 1. 13. the power of *d.*
Lk. 23. 44. *d.* over all the earth.
John 1. 5. *d.* comprehended it not.
  3. 19. loved *d.* rather than light.
  12. 35. walk while ye have light, lest *d.*
Acts 26. 18. turn from *d.* to light.
Rom. 13. 12; Eph. 5. 11. works of *d.*
1 Cor. 4. 5. hidden things of *d.*
2 Cor. 4. 6. light to shine out of *d.*
  6. 14. what communion hath light with *d.?*
Eph. 6. 12. rulers of the *d.* of this world.
1 Thes. 5. 5. not of the night, nor of *d.*
Heb. 12. 18. ye are not come to *d.*
1 Pet. 2. 9. out of *d.* into marvellous light.
2 Pet. 2. 4. chains of *d.*
1 John 1. 5. in him is no *d.* at all.
  2. 8. the *d.* is past

Dart, Job 41. 26. nor the *d.* cannot hold.
Prov. 7. 23. till *d.* strike.
Eph. 6. 16. to quench fiery *d.*
Heb. 12. 20. thrust through with a *d.*
Dash, Ps. 2. 9; Is. 13. 16; Hos. 13. 16. *d.* in pieces.
Ps. 91. 12; Matt. 4. 6; Lk. 4. 11. *d.* thy foot.
Ps. 137. 9. *d.* little ones against stones.
Daughter, Gen. 24. 23, 47. whose *d.* art thou?
Deut. 28. 53. eat flesh of sons and *d.*
Jud. 11. 35. Jephtah said, alas, my *d.!*
2 Sam. 12. 3. lamb was unto him as a *d.*
Ps. 45. 9. king's *d.* among honourable women.
  144. 12. our *d.* as corner stones.
Prov. 30. 15. horseleech hath two *d.*
  31. 29. many *d.* have done virtuously.
Eccl. 12. 4. the *d.* of music.
Is. 22. 4; Jer. 9. 1; Lam. 2. 11; 3. 48. *d.* of my people.
Jer. 6. 14. healed hurt of *d.*
Mic. 7. 6; Matt. 10. 35; Lk. 12. 53. *d.* riseth against mother.
Matt 15. 28. her *d.* was made whole.
Lk. 8. 42. one only *d.*
  13. 16. this woman, *d.* of Abraham.
John 12. 15. fear not, *d.* of Zion.
Heb. 11. 24. refused to be called **son** of Pharaoh's *d.*
1 Pet. 3. 6. whose *d.* ye are.
Dawn, Ps. 119. 147. I prevented the *d.* of the morning.
Matt. 28. 1. as it began to *d.*
2 Pet. 1. 19. till the day *d.*
Day, Gen. 1. 5. God called the light *d.*
  32. 26. let me go, *d.* breaketh.
Deut. 4. 10. *d.* thou stoodest before Lord.
  4. 32. ask of *d.* that are past.
2 Ki. 7. 9. this *d.* is a *d.* of good tidings.
1 Chr. 23. 1; 2 Chr. 24. 15. full of *d.*
1 Chr. 29. 15; Job 8. 9. our *d.* as a shadow.
Job 19. 25. stand at latter *d.* upon the earth.
  21. 30. reserved to *d.* of destruction.
  32. 7. I said, *d.* should speak.
Ps. 2. 7; Acts 13. 33; Heb. 1. 5. this *d.* have I begotten thee.
Ps. 19. 2. *d.* unto *d.* uttereth speech.
  84. 10. a *d.* in thy courts.
Prov. 4. 18. more and more to perfect *d.*
  27. 1. what a *d.* may bring forth.
Eccl. 7. 1. *d.* of death better than *d.* of birth.
  12. 1. while the evil *d.* come not.
Cant. 2. 17; 4. 6. till the *d.* break.
Is. 10. 3. in the *d.* of visitation.
  27. 3. Lord will keep it night and *d.*
  65. 20. an infant of *d.*
Ezek. 30. 2. woe worth the *d.!*
Zech. 4. 10. *d.* of small things.
Mal. 3. 2. who may abide *d.* of his coming?
Matt. 7. 22. many will say in that *d.*
  24. 36; Mk. 13. 32. that *d.* knoweth no man.
Matt 25. 13. ye know not the *d.* nor the hour.
Lk. 18. 7. elect, which cry *d.* and night.
  21. 34. that *d.* come upon you unawares.
  23. 43. to-*d.* shalt thou be with me.
John 6. 39. raise it again at last *d.*
  8. 56. Abraham rejoiced to see my *d.*
  9. 4. I must work while it is *d.*
Acts 17. 31. he hath appointed a *d.*
Rom. 2. 5. wrath against *d.* of wrath.
  14. 6. regardeth *d.* to the Lord.
1 Cor. 3. 13. the *d.* shall declare it.
2 Cor. 6. 2. the *d.* of salvation.
Eph. 4. 30. sealed to *d.* of redemption.
Phil. 1. 6. perform it until *d.* of Christ.

Day—*Continued.*
1 Thes. 5. 2 ; 2 Pet. 3. 10. *d.* cometh as a thief.
1 Thes. 5. 5. children of the *d.*
Heb. 10. 25. as ye see the *d.* approaching.
13. 8. Jesus Christ same to-*d.* and for ever.
2 Pet. 1. 19. till the *d.* dawn.
3. 8. one *d.* as a thousand years.
Rev. 6. 17. great *d.* of his wrath is come.
Daysman, Job 9. 33. nor any *d.* betwixt us.
Dead, Lev. 19. 28. cuttings for the *d.*
1 Sam. 24. 14 ; 2 Sam. 9. 8 ; 16. 9. *d.* dog.
Ps. 31. 12. forgotten as a *d.* man.
88. 5. free among the *d.*
115. 17. the *d.* praise not the Lord.
Prov. 21. 16. congregation of the *d.*
Eccl. 9. 5. *d.* know not anything.
10. 1. *d.* flies cause ointment.
Is. 26. 19. thy *d.* men shall live.
Jer. 22. 10. weep not for the *d.*
Matt. 8. 22. let the *d.* bury their *d.*
9. 24 ; Mk. 5. 39 ; Lk. 8. 52. maid not *d.*, but.
Matt. 11. 5 ; Lk. 7. 22. deaf hear, *d.* raised.
Matt. 22. 31 ; Mk. 12. 26. touching resurrection of *d.*
Matt. 23. 27. full of *d.* men's bones.
28. 4. keepers became as *d.* men.
Mk. 9. 10. rising from the *d.* should mean.
Lk. 15. 24, 32. was *d.*, and is alive again.
16. 31. though one rose from the *d.*
John 5. 25. *d.* shall hear.
6. 49. did eat manna, and are *d.*
11. 25. though *d.*, yet shall he live.
Acts 10. 42 ; 2 Tim. 4. 1. judge of quick and *d.*
Rom. 6. 2, 11 ; 1 Pet. 2. 24. *d.* to sin.
Rom. 7. 4 ; Gal. 2. 19. *d.* to the law.
Rom. 14. 9. Lord both of *d.* and living.
1 Cor. 15. 15. if the *d.* rise not.
2 Cor. 5. 14. then were all *d.*
Eph. 2. 1 ; Col. 2. 13. *d.* in trespasses and sins.
Eph. 5. 14. arise from the *d.*
Col. 1. 18. first-born from the *d.*
1 Thes. 4. 16. *d.* in Christ shall rise first.
1 Tim. 5. 6. *d.* while she liveth.
Heb. 6. 1 ; 9. 14. from *d.* works.
11. 4. being *d.* yet speaketh.
Jas. 2. 17, 20, 26. faith *d.*
1 Pet. 4. 6. preached to them that are *d.*
Jude 12. twice *d.*
Rev. 1. 5. first-begotten of the *d.*
3. 1. a name that thou livest, and art *d.*
14. 13. blessed are the *d.*
20. 12. the *d.* small and great.
20. 13. sea gave up *d.*
Deadly, Ps. 17. 9. from my *d.* enemies.
Mk. 16. 18. drink any *d.* thing.
Jas. 3. 8. tongue full of *d.* poison.
Deaf, Lev. 19. 14. shalt not curse the *d.*
Ps. 38. 13. I as a *d.* man, heard not.
58. 4. like *d.* adder that stoppeth.
Is. 29. 18. in that day *d.* hear words.
35. 5. ears of the *d.* be unstopped.
Matt. 11. 5 ; Lk. 7. 22. the *d.* hear.
Mk. 7. 32. brought to him one *d.*
9. 25. thou *d.* spirit, come out.
Deal, Lev. 19. 11. nor *d.* falsely.
Job 42. 8. *d.* with you after folly.
Ps. 75. 4. *d.* not foolishly.
119. 17 ; 142. 7. *d.* bountifully with.
Prov. 12. 22. they that *d.* truly are his delight.
Is. 21. 2 ; 24. 16. treacherous dealer *d.* treacherously.
26. 10. in land of uprightness *d.* unjustly.
Jer. 6. 13 ; 8. 10. every one *d.* falsely.
Hos. 5. 7. have *d.* treacherously against Lord.

Deal—*Continued.*
Mk. 10. 48. the more a great *d.*
Lk. 2. 48. why hast thou thus *d.* with us?
John 4. 9. no *d.* with Samaritans.
Acts 7. 19. *d.* subtilly with kindred.
Rom. 12. 3. as God hath *d.* to every man.
Dear, Jer. 31. 20. is Ephraim my *d.* son?
Acts 20. 24. neither count I my life *d.*
Eph. 5. 1. followers of God, as *d.* children.
Col. 1. 13. into kingdom of his *d.* son.
Dearth, Gen. 41. 54. *d.* was in all lands.
2 Ki. 4. 38 ; Acts 7. 11. was a *d.* in the land.
Neh. 5. 3. buy corn because of *d.*
Acts 11. 28. there should be great *d.*
Death, Num. 23. 10. let me die *d.* of righteous.
Jud. 5. 18. jeoparded lives to the *d.*
Ruth 1. 17. if ought but *d.* part thee and me.
1 Sam. 15. 32. the bitterness of *d.* past.
20. 3. but a step between me and *d.*
2 Sam. 1. 23. in *d.* not divided.
22. 5 ; Ps. 18. 4 ; 116. 3. waves of *d.* compassed.
Job 3. 21. long for *d.*, but it cometh not.
7. 15. my soul chooseth *d.*
Ps. 6. 5. in *d.* no remembrance.
13. 3. lest I sleep the sleep of *d.*
23. 4. valley of shadow of *d.*
48. 14. our guide even unto *d.*
68. 20. unto God belong issues from *d.*
73. 4. no bands in their *d.*
89. 48. what man shall not see *d.*?
102. 20. loose those appointed to *d.*
116. 15. precious is *d.* of his saints.
Prov. 7. 27. chambers of *d.*
8. 36. they that hate me love *d.*
Cant. 8. 6. love is strong as *d.*
Is. 9. 2 ; Jer. 2. 6. land of the shadow of *d.*
Is. 25. 8 ; 1 Cor. 15. 56. swallow up *d.* in victory.
Jer. 8. 3. *d.* chosen rather than life.
Ezek. 18. 32 ; 33. 11. no pleasure in *d.*
Hos. 13. 14. O *d.*, I will be thy plagues.
Matt. 15. 4 ; Mk. 7. 10. let him die the *d.*
Matt. 16. 28 ; Mk. 9. 1 ; Lk. 9. 27. not taste of *d.*
Matt. 26. 38 ; Mk. 14. 34. my soul is sorrowful to *d.*
Mk. 5. 23 ; John 4. 47. at point of *d.*
Lk. 2. 26. should not see *d.* before.
23. 22. found no cause of *d.*
John 5. 24 ; 1 John 3. 14. passed from *d.* to life.
John 8. 51, 52. keep my saying shall never see *d.*
11. 4. sickness not unto *d.*
12. 33 ; 18. 32 ; 21. 19. signifying what *d.*
Acts 2. 24. having loosed the pains of *d.*
Rom. 5. 10 ; Col. 1. 22. reconciled by the *d.*
Rom. 6. 5. planted in likeness of his *d.*
6. 23. wages of sin is *d.*
8. 2. law of sin and *d.*
1 Cor. 3. 22. life or *d.*, all are yours.
11. 26. show the Lord's *d.* till he come.
15. 21. by man came *d.*
15. 55. O *d.*, where is thy sting?
2 Cor. 2. 16. savour of *d.* unto *d.*
Phil. 2. 8. *d.*, even *d.* of the cross.
Heb. 2. 9. taste *d.* for every man.
Jas. 1. 15. sin bringeth forth *d.*
Rev. 1. 18. keys of hell and of *d.*
2. 10. be faithful unto *d.*
21. 4. no more *d.*
Debate, Prov. 25. 9. *d.* cause with neighbour.
Is. 58. 4. ye fast for strife and *d.*
Rom. 1. 29. full of envy, *d.*
2 Cor. 12. 20. I fear lest there be *d.*

Debt, 2 Ki. 4. 7. pay thy *d.*, and live.
Neh. 10. 31. leave exaction of every *d.*
Prov. 22. 26. be not sureties for *d.*
Matt 6. 12. forgive us our *d.*
18. 27. forgave him the *d.*
Rom. 4. 4. reward reckoned of *d.*
Debtor, Matt. 23. 16. swear by gold, is a *d.*
Rom. 1. 14. I am *d.* to the Greeks.
8. 12. we are *d.*, not to the flesh.
Gal. 5. 3. *d.* to do the whole law.
Decease, Is. 26. 14. *d.* they shall not rise.
Lk. 9. 31. spake of his *d.*
2 Pet. 1. 15. after my *d.* in remembrance.
36. 3. words of this mouth are *d.*
Deceit, Ps. 10. 7. mouth full of *d.*
38. 12. imagine *d.* all the *d.*
50. 19. tongue frameth *d.*
72. 14. redeem their soul from *d.*
Prov. 12. 5. counsels of wicked are *d.*
20. 17. bread of *d.* is sweet.
31. 30. favour is *d.*   [heart.
Jer. 14. 14; 23. 26. prophesy the *d.* of their
17. 9. the heart is *d.* above all things.
Hos. 11. 12. compasseth me with *d.*
Amos 8. 5. falsifying balances by *d.*
Zeph. 1. 9. fill masters' houses with *d.*
Matt. 13. 22; Mk. 4. 19. the *d.* of riches.
Mk. 7. 22. out of heart proceed *d.*
Rom. 3. 13. they have used *d.*
2 Cor. 4. 2. not handling word of God *d.*
11. 13. false apostles, *d.* workers.
Eph. 4. 22. according to *d.* lusts.
Col. 2. 8. vain *d.*, after tradition.
Deceive, Deut. 11. 16. take heed that your heart
be not *d.*
2 Ki. 19. 10; Is. 37. 10. let not thy God *d.* thee.
Jer. 20. 7. O Lord, thou hast *d.* me, and I
37. 9. *d.* not yourselves.   [was *d.*
Obad. 3. pride of heart *d.* thee.
Matt. 24. 4; Mk. 13. 5. no man *d.* you.
Matt. 24. 24. *d.* the very elect.
John 7. 12. nay, but he *d.* the people.
1 Cor. 6. 9; 15. 33; Gal. 6. 7. be not *d.*
2 Cor. 6. 8. as *d.*, and yet true.
Eph. 4. 14. they lie in wait to *d.*   [*d.* you.
5. 6; 2 Thes. 2. 3; 1 John 3. 7. let no man
2 Tim. 3. 13; worse and worse, *d.*, and being *d.*
1 John 1. 8. no sin, we *d.* ourselves.
Deck, Job 40. 10. *d.* thyself with majesty.
Is. 61. 10. as a bridegroom *d.* himself.
Jer 4. 30. though thou *d.* with gold.
Rev. 18. 16. city that was *d.*
Declare, 1 Chr. 16. 24; Ps. 96. 3. *d.* glory among
heathen.
Job 21. 31. *d.* his way to his face.
38. 4. *d.* if thou hast understanding.
Ps. 2. 7. I will *d.* decree.
9. 11. *d.* among the people his doings.
19. 1. heavens *d.* glory of God.
40. 10. I have *d.* thy faithfulness.
66. 16. I will *d.* what he hath done.
118. 17. live, and *d.* the works of the Lord.
145. 4. shall *d.* thy mighty acts.
Is. 12. 4. *d.* his doings among people.
41. 26; 45. 21. who hath *d.* from beginning?
45. 19. I *d.* things that are right.
53. 8; Acts 8. 33. who shall *d.* his generation?
Is. 66. 19. *d.* my glory among Gentiles.
John 17. 26. have *d.* thy name, and will *d.* it.
Acts. 13. 32. we *d.* glad tidings.
20. 27. *d.* the counsel of God.
Rom 1. 4. *d.* to be Son of God with power.
1 Cor. 3. 13. the day shall *d.* it.
1 John 1. 3. have seen, *d.* we to you.

Decline, Deut. 17. 11. thou shalt not *d.* from
sentence.
2 Chr. 34. 2. *d.* neither to right nor left.
Ps. 102. 11; 109. 23. days like a shadow that *d.*
119. 51. not *d.* from thy law.
Prov. 4. 5. neither *d.* from words of my mouth.
Decrease, Gen. 8. 5. the waters *d.* continually.
Ps. 107. 38. suffereth not their cattle to *d.*
John 3. 30. he must increase, I *d.*
Decree, Job 22. 28. thou shalt *d.* a thing, and
it shall be.
28. 26. made a *d.* for the rain.
Ps. 148. 6. a *d.* which shall not pass.
Prov. 8. 15. princes *d.* justice.
Is. 10. 1. that *d.* unrighteous *d.*
Acts 16. 4. delivered the *d.* to keep.
Dedicate, Deut. 20. 5. a new house, not *d.* it.
1 Ki. 7. 51; 1 Chr. 18. 11. which David had *d.*
1 Chr. 26. 27. of spoil they did *d.*
Ezek. 44. 29. every *d.* thing shall be theirs.
Deed, Ex. 9. 16. in very *d.* for this cause.
2 Sam. 12. 14. by this *d.* hast given occasion
Ezra 9. 13. come upon us for our evil *d.*
Neh. 13. 14. wipe not out my good *d.*
Ps. 28. 4; Is. 59. 18; Jer. 25. 14. according to
their *d.*
Lk. 11. 48. ye allow the *d.* of your fathers.
23. 41. due reward of our *d.*
24. 19. a prophet mighty in *d.*
John 3. 19. because their *d.* were evil.
8. 41. ye do the *d.* of your father.
Rom. 2. 6. render to every man according to
his *d.*
Acts 7. 22. Moses, mighty in word and *d.*
Rom. 3. 20. by *d.* of law no flesh justified.
Col. 3. 9. put off old man with his *d.*
Jas. 1. 25. shall be blessed in his *d.*
2 Pet. 2. 8. vexed with unlawful *d.*
1 John 3. 18. not love in word, but in *d.*
Deep, Gen. 1. 2. darkness on face of *d.*
7. 11; 8. 2. fountains of *d.*
Deut. 33. 13. the *d.* that coucheth beneath.
Job 38. 30. face of *d.* is frozen.
Ps. 36. 6. thy judgments are a great *d.*
42. 7. *d.* calleth to *d.*
107. 24. see his wonders in the *d.*
Is. 63. 13. led them through *d.*
Matt. 13. 5. no *d.* of earth.
Lk. 5. 4. launch out into *d.*
6. 48. digged *d.*, and laid foundation.
8. 31. command to go into the *d.*
John 4. 11. the well is *d.*
1 Cor. 2. 10. searcheth *d.* things of God.
Defence, Num. 14. 9. their *d.* is departed.
Job 22. 25. the Almighty shall be thy *d.*
Ps. 7. 10. my *d.* is of God.
59. 9; 62. 2. God is my *d.*
89. 18; 94. 22. Lord is *d.*
Eccl. 7. 12. wisdom a *d.*, money a *d.*
Is. 33. 16. place of *d.* the munitions of rocks.
Acts 19. 33. would have made his *d.*
Phil. 1. 7. in *d.* of the Gospel.
Defend, Ps. 5. 11. shout for joy, because thou
d. them.
59. 1. *d.* me from them that rise up.
82. 3. *d.* the poor and fatherless.
Zech. 9. 15. Lord of hosts shall *d.* them.
Acts 7. 24. *d.* him, and avenged.
Defile, Ex. 31. 14. that *d.* Sabbath be put to
death.
Num. 35. 33. blood *d.* the land.
Is. 59. 3. your hands are *d.* with blood.
Jer. 2. 7; 16. 18. *d.* my land.
Ezek. 23. 38. they have *d.* my sanctuary.

32

Defile—*Continued.*
Dan. 1. 8. would not *d* himself with meat.
Matt. 15 11; Mk. 7. 15. *d.* a man.
John 18. 28. lest they should be *d.*
1 Cor. 3. 17. if any *d.* temple of God.
Heb. 12. 15. thereby many be *d.*
Jude 8. filthy dreamers *d.* the flesh.
Rev. 3. 4. have not *d.* their garments.

Defraud, Lev. 19. 13. shalt not *d.* neighbour.
1 Sam. 12. 3. whom have I *d.?*
Mk. 10. 19; 1 Cor. 7. 5. *d.* not.
1 Cor. 6. 7. rather suffer yourselves to be *d.*
2 Cor. 7. 2. we have *d.* no man.
1 Thes. 4. 6. no man *d.* his brother.

Degree, Ps. 62. 9. men of low *d.*, of high *d.*
Lk. 1. 52. exalted them of low *d.*
1 Tim. 3. 13. purchase a good *d.*
Jas. 1. 9. brother of low *d.* rejoice.

Delay, Ps.119.60. *d.* not to keep commandments.
Matt. 24. 48; Lk. 12. 45. lord *d.* his coming.
Acts 9. 38. not *d.* to come to them.

Delicate, 1 Sam. 15. 32. Agag came *d.*
Prov. 29. 21. he that *d.* bringeth up his servant.
Is. 47. 1. no more called tender and *d.*
Lam. 4. 5. that did feed *d.* are desolate.
Lk. 7. 25. that live *d.* are in king's courts.

Delight, Deut.10.15.Lord had a *d.* in thy fathers
1 Sam. 15. 22. hath Lord as great *d.* in offerings?
2 Sam. 15. 26. I have no *d.* in thee.
Job 22. 26. have *d.* in Almighty.
Ps. 1. 2. his *d.* is in law of Lord.
16. 3. the excellent, in whom is my *d.*
119. 24. thy testimonies are my *d.*
119. 77, 174. thy law is my *d.*
Prov. 8. 30. I was daily his *d.*
11. 1. just weight is Lord's *d.*
12. 22. that deal truly are his *d.*
18. 2. fool hath no *d.* in understanding.
Cant. 2. 3. under his shadow with great *d.*
Is. 58. 13. call Sabbath a *d.*
Jer. 6. 10. no *d.* in word of Lord.
Job 27. 10. will he *d.* himself in Almighty?
Ps. 37. 4. *d.* thyself also in Lord.
40. 8. I *d.* to do thy will, O Lord.
51. 16. *d.* not in burnt-offering.
94. 19. thy comforts *d.* my soul.
Is. 1. 11. I *d.* not in blood of bullocks.
42. 1. elect, in whom my soul *d.*
55. 2. soul *d.* itself in fatness.
Mic. 7. 18. he *d.* in mercy.
Mal. 3. 1. messenger of covenant ye *d.* in.
Rom. 7. 22. I *d.* in law after inward man.

Deliver, Ex. 3. 8; Acts 7. 34. come down to *d.* them.
Deut. 32. 39; Is. 43. 13. any *d.* out of my hand.
Josh 2. 13. *d.* our lives from death.
1 Sam. 12. 21. which cannot profit nor *d.*
2 Chr. 32. 13. were gods able to *d.* their lands?
Job 5. 19. *d.* thee in six troubles.
36. 18. great ransom cannot *d.*
Ps. 33. 19. to *d.* their soul from death.
56. 13. *d.* my feet from falling.
91. 3. *d.* thee from snare of fowler.
Prov. 24. 11. forbear to *d.* them.
Eccl. 8. 8. small wickedness *d.* those.
Is. 50. 2. have I no power to *d.?*
Jer. 1. 8. I am with thee to *d.* thee.
43. 11. *d.* such as are for death to death.
Dan. 3. 17. God is able to *d.*, and will *d.*
Amos 2. 14. neither mighty *d.* himself.
Matt. 6. 13; Lk. 11. 4. *d.* us from evil.

Deliver—*Continued.*
Matt. 11. 27, Lk. 10. 22. all things *d.* to me of my Father.
Matt. 27. 43. let him *d.* now.
Acts 2. 23 being *d.* by counsel of God.
Rom. 4. 25. was *d.* for our offences.
2 Cor. 4. 11. *d.* to death for Jesus' sake.
1 Thes. 1. 10. *d.* us from the wrath to come.
Jude 3. faith once *d.* to the saints.

Deliverance, Gen. 45. 7. to save by a great *d.*
2 Ki. 5. 1. Lord had given *d.* to Syria.
1 Chr. 11. 14. Lord saved by great *d.*
Ps. 32. 7. compass me with songs of *d.*
Lk. 4. 18. preach *d.* to the captives.
Heb. 11. 35. not accepting *d.*

Delusion, Is. 66. 4. I will choose their *d.*
2 Thes. 2. 11. send them strong *d.*

Demonstration, 1 Cor. 2. 4. in *d.* of the Spirit.

Den, Jud. 6. 2. Israel made them *d.*
Job 37. 8. then the beasts go into *d.*
Is. 11. 8. put hand on cockatrice' *d.*
Jer. 7. 11. is this house a *d.* of robbers?
Matt. 21. 13; Mk. 11. 17; a *d.* of thieves.
Heb. 11. 38. they wandered in *d.*

Deny, Josh. 24. 27. lest ye *d.* your God.
Prov. 30. 9. lest I be full, and *d.* thee.
Matt. 10. 33. shall *d.* me before men.
16. 24. let him *d.* himself and take.
Lk. 20. 27. which *d.* resurrection.
2 Tim. 2. 13. he cannot *d.* himself.
Tit. 1. 16. in works they *d.* him.

Depart, Gen. 49. 10. sceptre shall not *d.* from Judah.   [God.
2 Sam. 22. 22; Ps. 18. 21. have not *d.* from my
Job 21. 14; 22. 17 they say to God, *d.*
28. 28. to *d.* from evil is understanding.
Ps. 34. 14; 37. 27. *d.* from evil and do good.
Prov. 22. 6. when old, he will not *d.* from it.
Matt. 14. 16. they need not *d.*
25. 41. *d.* from me, ye cursed.
Lk. 2. 29. lettest thy servant *d.* in peace.
4. 13. devil *d.* for a season.
5. 8. *d.* from me, I am a sinful man, O Lord.
John 13. 1. when Jesus knew he should *d.*
2 Cor.12.8. besought that it might *d.* from me.
Phil. 1. 23. having a desire to *d.*
1 Tim. 4. 1. some shall *d.* from faith.
2 Tim. 2. 19. nameth Christ, *d.* from iniquity.

Depth, Job 28. 14. *d.* saith, it is not in me.
Ps. 33. 7. he layeth up *d.* in storehouses.
77. 16. the *d.* were troubled.
106. 9. led through *d.* as through wilderness.
130. 1. out of the *d.* have I cried.
Prov. 8. 24. when no *d.* I was brought forth.
25. 3. heaven for height, earth for *d.*
Matt. 18. 6. better drowned in *d.* of sea.
Mk. 4. 5. no *d.* of earth.
Rom. 8. 39. nor height nor *d.* separate.
11. 33. O the *d.* of the riches.

Deputy, 1 Ki. 22. 47. a *d.* was king.
Acts 13. 8. to turn *d.* from the faith.
19. 38. are *d.* let them implead.   [in *d.*

Derision, Job 30. 1. younger than I have me
Ps. 2. 4. the Lord shall have them in *d.*
44. 13; 79. 4. a *d.* to them round us.
59. 8. have heathen in *d.*
Jer. 20. 7, 8. in *d.* daily.
Lam. 3. 14. I was a *d.* to my people.
See Lk. 16. 14; 23. 35.

Descend, Ps. 49. 17. glory not *d.* after him.
Ezek. 26. 20; 31. 16. them that *d.* into pit.
Matt. 7. 25, 27. rains *d.*, and floods came.
Mk. 1. 10; John 1. 32. Spirit *d.*
Mk. 15. 32. let Christ *d.* now from cross.

33

Descend—Continued.
Rom. 10. 7. who shall d. into deep?
Eph. 4. 10. he that d. is same that ascended.
Jas. 3. 15. this wisdom d. not.
Rev. 21. 10. city d. out of heaven.

Descent, Lk. 19. 37. the d. of Mount of Olives.
Heb. 7. 6. he whose d. is not counted.

Describe, Josh. 18. 4. go through land, and d. it.
Rom. 4. 6. as David d. the blessedness.
10. 5. Moses d. righteousness of the law.

Desert, Ps. 78. 40. oft did they grieve him in d.
102. 6. like an owl of the d.
Is. 13. 21; 34. 14; Jer. 50. 39. wild beasts of
d. shall lie there.
Is. 35. 1. the d. shall rejoice.
35. 6; 43. 19. streams in the d.
40. 3. in d. a highway for our God.
Jer. 17. 6. like the heath in the d.
25. 24. people that dwell in d. shall drink.
Matt. 24. 26. say, behold, he is in the d.
Lk. 9. 10. aside privately into a d. place.
John 6. 31. did eat manna in the d.
Heb. 11. 38. they wandered in d.

Desire, Job 14. 15. d. to work of thine hands.
Ps. 10. 3; 21. 2; Rom. 10. 1. heart's d.
Ps. 38. 9. all my d. is before thee.
54. 7; 59. 10; 92. 11; 112. 8. d. on enemies.
92. 11; 112. 10. d. of the wicked.
145. 16. the d. of every living thing.
Prov. 10. 24; 11. 23. the d. of the righteous.
13. 19. d. accomplished is sweet.
21. 25. the d. of slothful killeth him.
Eccl. 12. 5. d. shall fail.
Ezek. 24. 16, 21, 25. the d. of thine eyes.
Mic. 7. 3. great man uttereth mischievous d.
Hab. 2. 5. enlargeth d. as hell.
Hag. 2. 7. the d. of all nations.
Lk. 22. 15. with d. I have d. to eat.
Rom. 10. 1. my heart's d. for Israel.
Eph. 2. 3. fulfilling d. of flesh and min-
Phil. 1. 23. having a d. to depart.

Desired, 1 Ki. 2. 20. I d. one small petition.
Job 13. 3. I d. to reason with God.
Ps. 19. 10. more to be d. than gold.
27. 4. one thing I d. of the Lord.
40. 6. sacrifice and offering thou didst not d.
45. 11. king greatly d. thy beauty.
73. 25. none on earth I d. besides thee.
Prov. 3. 15. all thou canst d. not to be compared.
13. 4. soul of sluggard d. and hath not.
Is. 53. 2. no beauty that we should d. him.
Hos. 6. 6. I d. mercy and not sacrifice.
Matt. 13. 17. have d. to see those things.
20. 20. d. a certain thing of him.
Mk. 9. 35. if any d. to be first.
10. 35. do for us whatsoever we d.
11. 24. what things ye d., when ye pray.
Lk. 10. 24. kings have d. to see.
16. 21. d. to be fed with crumbs.
22. 15. have d. to eat this passover.
Acts 3. 14. d. a murderer to be granted.
1 Cor. 14. 1. d. spiritual gift.
Gal. 4. 9. ye d. again to be in bondage.
Phil. 4. 17. not because I d. a gift.
Heb. 11. 16. they d. a better country.
Jas. 4. 2. ye d. to have, and cannot obtain.
1 Pet. 1. 12. the angels d. to look into.
2. 2. as babes, d. sincere milk of the word.

Desirous, Prov. 23. 3. be not d. of his dainties.
Lk. 23. 8. Herod was d. to see him.
2 Cor. 11. 32. d. to apprehend me.
Gal. 5. 26. not be d. of vain-glory.

Desolate, Ps. 25. 16. have mercy, for I am d.
40. 15. let them be d. for a reward.
69. 25; Acts 1. 20. let their habitation be d.
Ps. 143. 4. my heart within me is d.
Is. 54. 1; Gal. 4. 27. more are children of d.
Jer. 2. 12. be very d., saith the Lord.
32. 43; 33. 12. d. without man or beast.
Dan. 11.31; 12.11. abomination that maketh d.
Mal. 1. 4. return and build the d. places.
Matt. 23. 38; Lk. 13. 35. house left to you d.
Rev. 18. 19. in one hour is she made d.

Desolation, 2 Ki. 22.19. they should become a d.
Ps. 46. 8. what d. he hath made in the earth.
74. 3; Jer. 25. 9; Ezek. 35. 9. perpetual d.
Prov. 1. 27. when your fear cometh as d.
3. 25. the d. of the wicked.
Is. 47. 11. d. come on thee suddenly.
61. 4. raise up former d., the d. of many
generations.
Zeph. 1. 15. a day of wasteness and d.
Matt. 12. 25; Lk. 11. 17. kingdom divided
brought to d.
Lk. 21. 20. know d. thereof is nigh.

Despair, 1 Sam. 27. 1. Saul shall d. of me, to
seek me.
Eccl. 2. 20. to cause my heart to d.
2 Cor. 4. 8. perplexed, not in d.

Despise, Lev. 26. 15. if ye d. my statutes.
1 Sam. 2. 30. that d. me shall be lightly
esteemed.   [chastening.
Job 5. 17; Prov. 3. 11; Heb. 12. 5. d. not
Ps. 51. 17. contrite heart thou wilt not d.
73. 20. thou shalt d. their image.
102. 17. he will not d. their prayer.
Prov. 1. 7. fools d. wisdom.
6. 30. men do not d. a thief.
15. 5. fool d. father's instruction.
23. 22. d. not mother when old.
Is. 33. 15. he that d. gain of oppressions.
53. 3. he is d., and rejected.
Ezek. 20. 13, 16. they d. my judgments.
Amos 2. 4. they d. the law of the Lord.
Zech. 4. 10. who hath d. day of small things?
Mal. 1. 6. wherein have we d. thy name?
Matt. 6. 24; Lk. 16. 13. hold to one, d. the
other.
Lk. 10. 16. d. you, d. me, d. him that sent me.
Rom. 2. 4. d. thou the riches of his goodness.
1 Cor. 11. 22. d. ye the church of God.
1 Thes. 4. 8. d. not man, but God.
5. 20. d. not prophesyings.
Tit. 2. 15. let no man d. thee.
Heb. 12. 2. endured cross, d. the shame.
Jas. 2. 6. ye have d. the poor.

Despisers, Acts 13. 41. behold, ye d. wonder.
2 Tim. 3. 3. fierce, d. of those good.

Despite, Ezek. 25. 6. with thy d. against the
land of Israel.
Heb. 10. 29. done d. to spirit of grace.

Despitefully, Matt. 5. 44; Lk. 6. 28. that d.
use you.
Acts 14. 5. assault to use them d.
Rom. 1. 30. haters of God d.

Destitute, Ps. 102. 17. will regard prayer of d.
Prov. 15. 21. folly is joy to him that is d. of
1 Tim. 6. 5. men d. of the truth.   [wisdom.
Heb. 11. 37. being d., afflicted, tormented.
Jas. 2. 15. if a brother or sister be d.

Destroy, Gen. 18. 23. d. righteous with the
2 Sam. 1. 14. d. Lord's anointed.   [wicked.
Job 19. 10. he hath d. me on every side.
19. 26. though worms d. this body.
Ps. 40. 14; 63. 9. seek my soul to d. it.
101. 8. I will d. all wicked of the land.

Destroy—*Continued.*

Prov. 1. 32. prosperity of fools shall *d.* them.
Eccl. 9. 18. one sinner *d.* much good.
Is. 11. 9; 65. 25. not *d.* in all my holy mountain.
Jer. 17. 18. *d.* them with double destruction.
Hos. 13. 9. thou hast *d.* thyself.
Matt. 5. 17. not come to *d.*, but to fulfil.
10. 28. fear him that is able to *d.*
12. 14; Mk. 3. 6; 11. 18. they might *d.* him.
Matt. 21. 41. miserably *d.* those wicked men.
Mk. 1. 24; Lk. 4. 34. art thou come to *d.* us?
Mk. 12. 9; Lk. 20. 16. *d.* the husbandmen.
Mk. 14. 58. say, I will *d.* this temple.
Lk. 6. 9. is it lawful to save life, or to *d.* it?
9. 56. not come to *d.* men's lives.
17. 27. flood came, and *d.* them all.
John 2. 19. *d.* this temple, and I will raise.
Rom. 14. 15. *d.* not him with thy meat.
Gal. 1. 23. preacheth the faith he once *d.*
2 Thes. 2. 8. *d.* with brightness of his coming.
Jas. 4. 12. able to save and to *d.*
1 John 3. 8. *d.* the works of the devil.

Destruction, Deut. 32. 24. be devoured with bitter *d.*
2 Chr. 22. 4. his counsellors to his *d.*
26. 16. heart lifted up to his *d.*
Est. 8. 6. endure to see *d.* of my kindred.
Job 5. 21. neither be afraid of *d.*
18. 12. *d.* is ready at his side.
26. 6. *d.* hath no covering.
31. 23. *d.* from God was a terror to me.
Ps. 90. 3. thou turnest man to *d.*
91. 6. the *d.* that wasteth at noonday.
103. 4. redeemeth thy life from *d.*
Prov. 1. 27. your *d.* cometh as a whirlwind.
10. 29; 21. 15. *d.* shall be to workers of
16. 18. pride goeth before *d.* [iniquity.
18. 7. a fool's mouth is his *d.*
27. 20. hell and *d.* are never full.
Is. 14. 23. the besom of *d.*
59. 7. wasting and *d.* in their paths.
Jer. 17. 18. destroy them with double *d.*
Lam. 2. 11; 3. 48; 4. 10. *d.* of the daughter of my people.
Hos. 13. 14. O grave, I will be thy *d.*
Matt. 7. 13. broad is way that leadeth to *d.*
Rom. 3. 16. *d.* and misery are in their ways.
9. 22. vessels of wrath fitted to *d.*
Phil. 3. 19. many walk, whose end is *d.*
1 Thes. 5. 3. then sudden *d.* cometh.
2 Thes. 1. 9. punished with everlasting *d.*
2 Pet. 2. 1. bring on themselves swift *d.*
3. 16. wrest Scriptures to their own *d.*

Determine, Ex. 21. 22. pay as the judges *d.*
1 Sam. 20. 7. be sure evil is *d.* by him.
Job 14. 5. seeing his days are *d.*
Dan. 11. 36. that that is *d.* shall be done.
Lk. 22. 22. Son of man goeth, as it was *d.*
Acts 3. 13. Pilate was *d.* to let him go.
17. 26. hath *d.* the times appointed.
1 Cor. 2. 2. I *d.* not to know anything save Christ, and him crucified. See Acts 2. 23.

Detestable, Jer. 16. 18; Ezek. 5. 11; 7. 20; 11. 18; 37. 23. *d.* things.

Device, Est. 9. 25. *d.* return on his own head.
Ps. 21. 11. imagined mischievous *d.*
33. 10. maketh *d.* of the people of none effect.
140. 8. further not his wicked *d.*
Prov. 1. 31. be filled with their own *d.*
19. 21. many *d.* in a man's heart.
Eccl. 9. 10. no work nor *d.* in grave.
Jer. 18. 12. walk after our own *d.*
Acts 17. 29. stone graven by man's *d.*
2 Cor. 2. 11. not ignorant of his *d.*

Devil, Matt. 4. 1. Jesus led to be tempted of *d.*
9. 32; 12. 22. dumb man possessed with *d.*
11. 18; Lk. 7. 33. they say he hath a *d.*
Matt. 13. 39. enemy that sowed is the *d.*
25. 41. fire prepared for the *d.* and his angels.
Mk. 7. 29. *d.* is gone out of thy daughter.
Lk. 4. 33. had a spirit of an unclean *d.*
John 6. 70. and one of you is a *d.*
7. 20; 8. 48. thou hast a *d.*
10. 20. many said, he hath a *d.*
13. 2. *d.* having put into heart of Judas.
Acts 13. 10. thou child of the *d.*
Eph. 4. 27. neither give place to the *d.*
6. 11. able to stand against wiles of the *d.*
1 Tim. 3. 6. fall into condemnation of the *d.*
2 Tim. 2. 26. recover out of the snare of the *d.*
Heb. 2. 14. had power of death, that is the *d.*
Jas. 4. 7. resist *d.* and he will flee.
1 Pet. 5. 8. your adversary the *d.*
1 John 3. 8. to destroy works of *d.*
See Jas. 3. 15.

Devise, Ps. 36. 4. he *d.* mischief on his bed.
Prov. 3. 29. *d.* not evil against thy neighbour.
14. 22. do they not err that *d.* evil?
16. 9. a man's heart *d.* his way.
Is. 32. 8. the liberal *d.* liberal things.
2 Pet. 1. 16. cunningly *d.* fables.

Devoted, Lev. 27. 28; Num. 18. 14. every *d.* thing.
Ps. 119. 38. servant who is *d.* to thy fear.

Devotions, Acts 17. 23. as I beheld your *d.*

Devour, Gen. 49. 27. in morning *d.* prey.
Ex. 24. 17; Is. 29. 6; 33. 14. *d.* fire.
Lev. 10. 2. fire from Lord *d.* them.
2 Sam. 11. 25. sword *d.* one as well as another.
22. 9; Ps. 18. 8. fire out of his mouth *d.*
Ps. 80. 13. beasts of field *d.* it.
Is. 1. 20. ye shall be *d.* with sword.
Jer. 3. 24. shame hath *d.* the labour.
Ezek. 23. 37. pass through fire to *d.* them.
Hos. 8. 14; Amos 1. 14; 2. 2. it shall *d.* palaces.
Joel 2. 3. a fire *d.* before them.
Amos 4. 9. fig trees and olive trees, palmer-worm *d.* them.
Zeph. 1. 18; 3. 8. *d.* by fire of jealousy.
Matt. 13. 4; Mk. 4. 4; Lk. 8. 5. fowls *d.* them.
Matt. 23. 14; Mk. 12. 40; Lk. 20. 47. *d.* widow's houses.
Lk. 15. 30. this thy son hath *d.* thy living.
2 Cor. 11. 20. if a man *d.* you.
Gal. 5. 15. ye bite and *d.* one another.
Heb. 10. 27. which shall *d.* the adversaries.

Devout, Lk. 2. 25. Simeon was just and *d.*
Acts 2. 5; 8. 2. *d.* men.
13. 50. *d.* women.

Dew, Gen. 27. 28. God gave thee of the *d.*
Deut. 32. 2. my speech distil as the *d.*
Jud. 6. 37. if *d.* on fleece only.
2 Sam. 1. 21. let there be no *d.*
17. 12. light on him as *d.* falleth.
1 Ki. 17. 1. there shall not be *d.* nor rain.
Job 38. 28. who hath begotten the drops of *d.*?
Ps. 110. 3. hast the *d.* of thy youth.
Prov. 3. 20. clouds drop down *d.*
Is. 18. 4. like *d.* in heat of harvest.
Dan. 4. 33. body wet with *d.*
Hos. 6. 4; 13. 3. as the early *d.* it passeth away.
Hag. 1. 10. heaven is stayed from *d.*
Zech. 8. 12. heaven give their *d.*

Diadem, Job 29. 14. my judgment as a *d.*
Is. 28. 5. for a *d.* of beauty to.
62. 3. a royal *d.* in hand of God.
Ezek. 21. 26. remove the *d.*

Diamond, Jer. 17. 1. sin is written with the point of a *d.*

35

Die, Gen. 2. 17; 20. 7; 1 Sam. 14. 44; 22. 16;
    1 Ki. 2. 37. 42; Jer. 26. 8; Ezek. 3. 18;
    33. 8, 14. thou shalt surely d.
Gen. 3. 3 ; Lev. 10. 6 ; Num. 18. 32 ; lest ye d.
Gen. 27. 4 ; 45. 28 ; Prov. 30. 7. before I d.
Gen. 46. 30. now let me d.
Ex. 10. 28. seest my face shall d.
    21. 12. smiteth a man that he d.
Lev. 7. 24; 22. 8; Deut. 14. 21; Ezek. 4. 14;
    that d. of itself.
Num. 23. 10. let me d. death of righteous.
Ruth 1. 17 ; where thou d. will I d.
2 Sam. 12. 18. the child d.
2 Ki. 20. 1 ; Is. 38. 1. shalt d., and not live.
Job 2. 9. curse God and d.
    14. 14. if a man d., shall he live again?
Ps. 49. 17. when he d. he shall carry nothing
    away.
    82. 7. ye shall d. like men.
Prov. 5. 23. he shall d. without instruction.
Eccl. 2. 16. how d. the wise man?
    9. 5. living know they shall d.
Is. 66. 24; Mk. 9. 44. worm shall not d.
Jer. 27. 13; Ezek. 18. 31; 33. 11. why will ye d.?
Ezek. 18. 4. soul that sinneth shall d.
Jon. 4. 3. it is better for me to d. than live.
Matt. 15. 4; Mk. 7. 10. let him d. the death.
Matt. 26. 35 ; Mk. 14. 31. though I should d.
    with thee.
Lk. 16. 22. beggar d. the rich man also d.
    20. 36. neither can they d. any more.
John 4. 49. come down ere my child d.
    11, 21; 32. my brother had not d.
    12. 24. except a corn of wheat d.
    19. 7. by our law he ought to d.
Acts 25. 11. I refuse not to d.   [one d.
Rom. 5. 7. scarcely for a righteous man will
    7. 9. sin revived, and I d.
1 Cor. 15. 3. Christ d. for our sins.
2 Cor. 5. 14. if one d. for all.
Phil. 1. 21. to d. is gain.
1 Thes. 4. 14. if we believe that Jesus d.
Heb. 9. 27. appointed unto men once to d.
Rev. 2. 2. things that are ready to d.
    14. 13. blessed are the dead who d. in the
    Lord.
Dying, 2 Cor. 4. 10. the d. of Lord Jesus.
    6. 9. as d., and, behold, we live.
Heb. 11. 21. by faith Jacob, when d.
Differ, 1 Cor. 4. 7. who maketh thee to d.?
    15. 41. one star d. from another.
Difference, Lev. 10. 10. d. between holy and
    unholy.
Ezek. 22. 26. they have put no d. between.
Acts 15. 9. put no d. between us.
Rom. 3. 22; 10. 12. for there is no d.
Jude 22. of some have compassion, making a d.
Dig, Deut. 6. 11; Neh. 9. 25. wells d., which
    thou d. not.
Deut. 8. 9. out of hills mayest d. brass.
Ps. 7. 15; 57. 6. d. a pit, and is fallen.
Matt. 21. 33. d. a winepress.
    25. 18. d. in earth, and hid lord's money.
Lk. 13. 8. let it alone till I d. about it.
16. 3. I cannot d., to beg I am ashamed.
Dignity, Eccl. 10. 6. folly is set in great d.
2 Pet. 2. 10; Jude 8. these speak evil of d.
Diligence, Prov. 4. 23. keep heart with all d.
Lk. 12. 58. art in way, give d.
Rom. 12. 8. he that ruleth with d.
2 Tim. 4. 9. do thy d. to come.
2 Pet. 1. 10. give d. to make calling sure.
Diligent, Josh. 22. 5. take d. heed to do the
    commandments.

Diligent—*Continued*.
    Ps. 64. 6. accomplish a d. search.
Prov. 10. 4. hand of d. maketh rich.
    22. 29. man d. in his business.
Lk. 15. 8. seek d. till she find it.
Acts 18. 25. taught d. the things of the Lord.
Heb. 12. 15. looking d. lest any man fail.
Dim, Deut. 34. 7. eye not d., nor force abated.
Job 17. 7. mine eye is d. by sorrow.
Is. 32. 3. that see, shall not be d.
Lam. 4. 1. how is gold become d.!
See Is. 8. 22; 9. 1.
Diminish, Ex. 5. 8; Deut. 4. 2; 12. 32. not d.
    ought.   [be d.
Prov. 13. 11. wealth gotten by vanity shall
Rom. 11. 12. d. of them be riches of Gentiles.
Dine, Gen. 43. 16. d. with me at noon.
Lk. 11. 37. Pharisee besought him to d.
John 21. 12. Jesus saith, come and d.
Dinner, Prov. 15. 17. better is a d. of herbs.
Matt. 22. 4. I have prepared my d.
Lk. 14. 12. when thou makest a d.
Dip, Gen. 37. 31. d. coat in the blood.
2 Ki. 5. 14. Naaman d. in Jordan.
Matt. 26. 23 ; Mk. 14. 20. d. hand in dish.
John 13. 26. when he had d. the sop.
Rev. 19. 13. a vesture d. in blood.
Direct, Ps. 5. 3. in morning will I d. my prayer
Prov. 3. 6. he shall d. thy paths.
Eccl. 10. 10. wisdom is profitable to d.
Is. 40. 13. who hath d. the Spirit of the Lord?
Jer. 10. 23. not in man to d. his steps.
2 Thes. 3. 5. d. your hearts into love of God.
Disannul, Is. 14. 27. the Lord hath purposed,
    who shall d. it.?
Gal. 3. 17. this covenant law cannot d.
Heb. 7. 18. there is a d. of commandment.
Discern, 2 Sam. 19. 35. can I d. between good
    and evil?   [bad.
1 Ki. 3. 9. that I may d. between good and
    3. 11. understanding to d. judgment.
Eccl. 8. 5. wise d. time and judgment.
Jon. 4. 11. not d. between right and left.
Mal. 3. 18. d. between righteous and wicked
Matt. 16. 3 ; Lk. 12. 56. d. face of sky.
1 Cor. 2. 14. because they are spiritually d.
    11. 29. not d. the Lord's body.   [thoughts.
Heb. 4. 12. the word of God is a d. of the
Discharge, 1 Ki. 5. 9. cause them to be d.
Eccl. 8. 8. there is no d. in that war.
Disciple, Matt. 10. 1 ; Lk. 6. 13. Jesus called
    his twelve d.
Matt. 10. 24 ; Lk. 6. 40. d. not above his
    master.   [of a d.
Matt. 10. 42. give cup of water in the name
    20. 17. Jesus took d. apart.
    22. 16. Pharisees sent their d.
    26. 56. all the d. forsook him and fled.
    28. 7 ; Mk. 16. 7. go, tell his d. he is risen.
Mk. 2. 18; Lk. 5. 33. why do d. of John fast?
Lk. 19. 37. d. began to rejoice and praise God.
John 1. 35. John stood, and two of his d.
    6. 66. many of his d. went back.
    8. 31 ; 13. 35. then are ye my d. indeed.
    19. 26 ; 20. 2. d. whom Jesus loved.
    21. 24. this is the d. which testifieth.
Acts 9. 1. breathing out slaughter against d.
    11. 26. d. called Christians first in Antioch.
    20. 7. d. came together to break bread.
    21. 16. an old d.
Discipline, Job 36. 10. he openeth their ear to d.
Discomfited, Josh. 10. 10. Lord d. them before
    Israel.
Jud. 4. 15. Lord d. Sisera.

Discomfited—*Continued.*
Jud. 8. 12. Gideon *d.* all the host.   [them.
2 Sam. 22. 15 ; Ps. 18. 14. lightnings, and *d.*
Is. 31. 8. his young men shall be *d.*

Discord, Prov. 6. 14. he soweth *d.*
6. 19. he that soweth *d.* among brethren.

Discourage, Num. 32. 7. wherefore *d.* ye the
heart of the children of Israel?
Deut. 1. 21. fear not, neither be *d.*
Is. 42. 4. he shall not fail nor be *d.*
Col. 3. 21. children, lest they be *d.*

Discover, 1 Sam. 14. 8. we will *d.* ourselves to
them.
2 Sam. 22. 16 ; Ps. 18. 15. the foundations of
the world were *d.*
Job 12. 22. he *d.* deep things.
Prov. 25. 9. *d.* not a secret to another.
Ezek. 21. 24 your transgressions are *d.*

Discretion, Ps. 112. 5. guide affairs with *d.*
Prov. 2. 11. *d.* shall preserve thee.
19. 11. the *d.* of a man def-rreth his anger.
Is. 28. 26. his God doth instruct him to *d.*
Jer 10. 12. stretched heavens by *d.*

Disease, Ex. 15. 26 ; Deut. 7. 15. none of these
d. on you.
Deut. 28. 60. bring on thee all the *d.* of Egypt.
Ps. 103. 3. who healeth all thy *d.*
Eccl. 6. 2. vanity, and it is an evil *d.*
Matt. 4. 24 ; Mk. 1. 34. Lk. 4. 40. all taken
with divers *d.*

Disfigure, Matt. 6. 16. hypocrites *d.* their faces.

Disguise, 1 Sam. 28. 8. and Saul *d.* himself.
1 Ki. 14. 2. Jeroboam said, *d.* thyself.
20 38. one of his prophets *d.* himself.
22. 30 ; 2 Chr. 18. 29. I will *d.* myself.

Dish, Jud. 5. 25. butter in a lordly *d.*
2 Ki. 21. 13. as a man wipeth a *d.*
Matt. 26. 23 , Mk. 14. 20. that dippeth with
me in *d.*

Dishonour, Ps. 35. 26 ; 71. 13. [shame with]
Prov. 6. 33. and *d.* shall he get. [clothed with]
Mic. 7. 6. son *d.* father.
John 8. 49. I honour my Father, ye do *d.* me.
Rom. 9. 21 one vessel to honour, another to *d.*
1 Cor. 15. 43. it is sown in *d.*
2 Cor. 6. 8. by honour and *d.* [some to *d.*
2 Tim. 2. 20. are vessels, some to honour,

Dismayed, Deut. 31. 8 ; Josh. 1. 9 ; 8. 1 , 10. 25 ;
1 Chr. 22. 13 ; 28. 20 ; 2 Chr. 20. 15 ; 32. 7.
fear not, nor be *d.*
Is. 41. 10 ; Jer. 1. 17 ; 10. 2 ; 23. 4 ; 30. 10 ; 46.
27 ; Ezek. 2. 6 ; 3. 9. be not *d.*
Jer. 8. 9 ; 10. 2. the wise men are *d.*
17. 18. let them be *d.*, let not me be *d.*
Obad. 9. thy mighty men shall be *d.*

Disobedience, Rom. 5. 19. by one man's *d.*
many were made sinners.
Eph. 2. 2. worketh in children of *d.*
5. 6 ; Col. 3. 6. wrath on children of *d.*
Heb. 2. 2. every *d.* received just recompense
of reward. [just.

Disobedient, Lk. 1. 17. turn *d.* to wisdom of
Acts 26. 19. not *d.* to heavenly vision.
Rom. 1. 30 ; 2 Tim. 3. 2. *d.* to parents.
1 Tim. 1. 9. law is made for lawless and *d.*
Tit. 3. 3. we ourselves were sometimes *d.*
1 Pet. 2 7. to them which be *d.*
3. 20 spirits, which sometime were *d.*

Disorderly, 2 Thes. 3. 6. withdraw from brother
that walketh *d.*
3. 11. some walk among you *d.*

Disperse, Jud. 12. 9 ; 2 Cor. 9. 9. he hath *d.*
Prov. 15. 7. lips of wise *d.* knowledge.
John 7. 35. will he go to the *d.*?

Displease, Num. 11. 1. it *d.* the Lord.
22. 34. if it *d.* thee, I will get me back.
2 Sam. 11. 27. thing David had done *d.* Lord.
1 Ki. 1. 6. father had not *d.* him at any time.
Ps. 60. 1. thou hast been *d.*
Prov. 24. 18. lest the Lord see it, and it *d.* him.
Is. 59. 15. it *d.* him there was no judgment.
Dan. 6. 14. king *d.* with himself.
Jon. 4. 1. it *d.* Jonah exceedingly.
Hab. 3. 8. was Lord *d.* against rivers.
Matt. 21. 15. Scribes saw it, they were *d.*
Mk. 10. 14. Jesus was much *d.*
Lk 12. 20. Herod was highly *d.* with.

Displeasure, Deut. 9. 19. I was afraid of hot *d.*
Jud. 15. 3. though I do them a *d.*
Ps. 2. 5. vex them in his sore *d.*
6. 1 ; 38. 1. neither chasten me in hot *d.*

Disposing, Prov. 16. 33. *d.* thereof is of Lord.
Acts 7. 53. *d.* of angels. [him.

Dispute, Job 23. 7. the righteous might *d.* with
Mk. 9. 34. *d.* who should be greatest.
Acts 17. 17. Paul *d.* in the synagogue.
1 Cor. 1. 20. where is the *d.* of this world?
Phil. 2. 14. do all things without *d.*
1 Tim. 6. 5. perverse *d.*

Disquiet, 1 Sam. 28. 15. why hast thou *d.* me to
bring me up?
Ps. 42. 5, 11 ; 43. 5. O my soul, why art thou
d. within me?

Dissemble, Josh. 7. 11. they have stolen and *d.*
Ps. 26. 4. nor will I go in with *d.*
Prov. 26. 24. he that hateth *d.*
Gal. 2. 13. the other Jews *d.*

Dissension, Acts 15. 2. had no small *d.*
23. 7. arose a *d.* between Pharisees.

Dissolve, Ps. 75. 3. inhabitants thereof are *d.*
Is. 24. 19. the earth is clean *d.*
Dan. 5. 16. thou canst *d.* doubts.
2 Cor. 5. 1. house of this tabernacle be *d.*
2 Pet. 3. 11. all these things shall be *d.*

Distaff, Prov. 31. 19. her hands hold *d.*

Distil, Deut. 32. 2. my speech *d.* as dew.
Job 36. 28. the clouds *d.* on man.

Distract, Ps. 88. 15. I suffer thy terrors, I am *d.*
1 Cor. 7. 35. attend without *d.*

Distress, Gen. 35. 3. answered in day of my *d.*
42. 21. therefore is this *d.* come upon us.
Jud. 11. 7. why are ye come when in *d.*?
2 Sam. 22. 7 ; Ps. 18. 6 ; 118. 5 ; 120. 1. in my
d., I called on the Lord.
1 Ki. 1. 29. redeemed my soul out of all *d.*
Neh. 2. 17. ye see the *d.* we are in.
Ps. 4. 1. enlarged me in *d.*
25. 17 ; 107. 6, 13, 19, 28. out of *d.*
Prov. 1. 27. I will mock when *d.* cometh.
Is. 25. 4. a strength to needy in *d.*
Lk. 21. 25. on earth *d.* of nations.
Rom. 8. 35. shall *d.* separate us?
2 Cor. 12. 10. take pleasure in *d.*

Distribute, Neh. 13. 13. their office was to *d.*
Lk. 18. 22. sell and *d.* to poor. [he *d.*
John 6. 11. when Jesus had given thanks,
Rom. 12. 13. *d.* to necessity of saints.
1 Cor. 7. 17. as God hath *d.* to every man.
2 Cor. 9. 13. your liberal *d.*

Ditch, 2 Ki. 3. 16. make valley full of *d.*
Ps. 7. 15. fallen into *d.* he made.
Matt. 15. 14 ; Lk. 6. 39. both fall into *d.*

Divers, Deut. 22. 9. not sow with *d.* seeds.
22. 11. not wear garment of *d.* sorts.
25. 13. not have in bag *d.* weights.
25. 14. *d.* measures, great and small.
Prov. 20. 10, 23. *d.* weights and measures
abomination.

Divers—*Continued.*
Matt. 4. 24; Mk. 1. 34; Lk. 4. 40. sick with *d.* diseases.
Matt. 24. 7; Mk. 13. 8; Lk. 21. 11. earthquakes in *d.* places.
Mk. 8. 3. *d.* of them came from far.
1 Cor. 12. 10. *d.* kinds of tongues.
2 Tim. 3. 6; Tit. 3. 3. *d.* lusts.
Heb. 1. 1. God, who in *d.* manners, spake.
Jas. 1. 2. joy when ye fall into *d.* temptations.

Diversities, 1 Cor. 12. 6. *d.* of operations, but same God.
12. 28. *d.* of tongues.

Divide, Gen. 1. 18. to *d.* light from darkness.
Ex. 14. 16. stretch hand over the sea, and *d.* it.
Lev. 11. 4; Deut. 14. 7. that *d.* the hoof.
1 Ki. 3. 25. *d.* living child in two.
Ps. 68. 12; Prov. 16. 19; Is. 9. 3; 53. 12. *d.* spoil.
Matt. 12. 25; Mk. 3. 24; Lk. 11. 17. kingdom or house *d.*
Lk. 12. 13. that he *d.* inheritance with me.
15. 12. he *d.* unto them his living.
Acts 14. 4; 23. 7. the multitude was *d.*
1 Cor. 1. 13. is Christ *d.?*
2 Tim. 2. 15. rightly *d.* word of truth.
Heb. 4. 12. piercing to *d.* asunder.

Divination, Num. 22. 7. rewards of *d.* in hand.
Acts 16. 16. damsel with a spirit of *d.*

Divine, Gen. 44. 15. wot ye not that I can *d.?*
Ezek. 13. 9. prophets that *d.* lies.
Mic. 3. 11. prophets *d.* for money.
Heb. 9. 1. ordinances of *d.* service.
2 Pet. 1. 4. partakers of *d.* nature.

Diviner, Deut. 18. 14. nations hearkened to *d.*
Is. 44. 25. that maketh *d.* mad.
Jer. 27. 9. hearken not to your *d.*
29. 8. let not your *d.* deceive you.

Division, Ex. 8. 23. put a *d.* between my people.
Jud. 5. 15. for *d.* of Reuben great thoughts of heart.
Lk. 12. 51. I tell you nay, but rather *d.*
John 7. 43; 9. 16; 10. 19. a *d.* because of him.
Rom. 16. 17. mark them which cause *d.*
1 Cor. 3. 3. among you *d.*

Do, Gen. 18. 25. shall not Judge of all *d.* right?
Deut. 27. 26. words of law, to *d.* them.
Eccl. 9. 10. what thy hand findeth to *d.*, *d.* it with might.
Is. 45. 7. I the Lord *d.* all these things.
Matt. 7. 12. that men should *d.* to you, *d.* ye even so.
Lk. 10. 28. this *d.*, and thou shalt live.
22. 19; 1 Cor. 11. 24. this *d.* in remembrance of me.
John 15. 5. without me ye can *d.* nothing.
Acts 1. 1. all Jesus began to *d.*
9. 6. Lord, what wilt thou have me to *d.?*
Rom. 7. 15. what I would, that *d.* I not.
1 Cor. 10. 31. ye *d.*, all to glory of God.
Gal. 5. 17. ye cannot *d.* the things ye would.
Phil. 4. 13. I can *d.* all things through Christ.
Heb. 4. 13. God with whom we have to *d.*
Jas. 1. 22. be ye *d.* of the word.   [rain.

Doctrine, Deut. 32. 2. my *d.* shall drop as the Is. 28. 9. make to understand *d.*
Jer. 10. 8. the stock is a *d.* of vanities.
Matt. 7. 28; 22. 33; Mk. 1. 22; 11. 18; Lk. 4. 32. astonished at his *d.*   [ments of men.
Matt. 15. 9; Mk. 7. 7. teaching for *d.* command-
Matt. 16. 12. the *d.* of the Pharisees.
Mk. 1. 27; Acts 17. 19. what new *d.* is this?
John 7. 17. do his will, he shall know of the *d.*
Acts 2. 42. continued in apostles' *d.*
Rom. 6. 17. obeyed that form of *d.*

Doctrine—*Continued.*
Rom. 16. 17. contrary to the *d.*
Eph. 4. 14. every wind of *d.*
1 Tim. 1. 10. contrary to sound *d.*
5. 17. labour in word and *d.*
2 Tim. 3. 16. scripture profitable for *d.*
Tit. 2. 1. things which become sound *d.*
2. 10. adorn the *d.* of God our Saviour.
Heb. 6. 1. principles of the *d.* of Christ.
6. 2. the *d.* of baptisms.
13. 9. not carried about with strange *d.*

Dog, Ex. 11. 7. against Israel shall not a *d.* move.
Deut. 23. 18. not bring price of a *d.* into house.
Jud. 7. 5. that lappeth as a *d.* lappeth.
1 Sam. 17. 43; 2 Ki. 8. 13. am I a *d.?*
2 Sam. 9. 8. upon such a dead *d.* as I am.
Ps. 22. 20. darling from power of the *d.*
59. 6. make a noise like a *d.*
Prov. 26. 11; 2 Pet. 2. 22. as a *d.* returneth.
Eccl. 9. 4. living *d.* better than dead lion.
Is. 56. 10. they are all dumb *d.*
Matt. 7. 6. give not that which is holy to *d.*
15. 27; Mk. 7. 28. the *d.* eat of crumbs.
Lk. 16. 21. the *d.* licked his sores.
Phil. 3. 2. beware of *d.*
Rev. 22. 15. without are *d.*

Doing, Ex. 15. 11. fearful in praises, *d.* wonders.
Jud. 2. 19. ceased not from their own *d.*
Ps. 9. 11; Is. 12. 4. declare his *d.*
66. 5. he is terrible in his *d.*
77. 12. I will talk of thy *d.*
118. 23; Matt. 21. 42; Mk. 12. 11; the Lord's *d.*
Acts 10. 38; went about *d.* good.
Rom. 2. 7. patient continuance in well-*d.*
2 Cor. 8. 11. perform the *d.* of it.
Gal. 6. 9; 2 Thes. 3. 13. weary in well-*d.*
Eph. 6. 6. *d.* the will of God.
1 Pet. 2. 15. with well-*d.* put to silence.
3. 17. better suffer for well-*d.*
4. 19. commit souls in well-*d.*   [the *d.*

Dominion, Gen. 27. 40. when thou shalt have 37. 8. shalt thou have *d.* over us?
Num. 24. 19. he that shall have *d.*
Neh. 9. 37. have *d.* over our bodies.
Job 25. 2. *d.* and fear are with him.
Ps. 8. 6. have *d.* over the works of thy hands.
19. 13; 119. 133. let not sins have *d.* over me.
72. 8. have *d.* from sea to sea.
103. 22. bless the Lord in all places of his *d.*
Is. 26. 13. other lords have had *d.* over us.
Dan. 4. 34; 7. 14. *d.* is an everlasting *d.*
Matt. 20. 25. princes of Gentiles exercise *d.*
Rom. 6. 9. death hath no more *d.*
6. 14. sin shall not have *d.*
2 Cor. 1. 24. not have *d.* over your faith.
Eph. 1. 21. far above might and *d.*
Col. 1. 16. whether they be thrones or *d.*
1 Pet. 4. 11; 5. 11, Rev. 1. 6. to whom be praise, glory, and *d.* for ever.

Door, Gen. 4. 7. sin lieth at the *d.*
Ex. 12. 7. strike blood on *d.* post.
Num. 12. 5; 16. 18. stood in *d.* of tabernacle.
Job 38. 17. the *d.* of the shadow of death.
Ps. 24. 7. ye everlasting *d.*
84. 10. rather be a *d.*-keeper.
141. 3. keep the *d.* of my lips.
Prov. 8. 3. wisdom crieth at the *d.*
26. 14. as *d.* turneth on hinges.
Is. 26. 20. enter, and shut thy *d.* about thee.
Hos. 2. 15. for a *d.* of hope.
Matt. 6. 6. when thou hast shut thy *d.*
24. 33; Mk. 13. 29. near, even at the *d.*
Matt. 25. 10. and the *d.* was shut.
27. 60; 28. 2; Mk. 15. 46. *d.* of sepulchre.

Door—*Continued.*
Mk. 2. 2. no room, not so much as about the *d.*
John 10. 1. that entereth not by the *d.*
10. 7, 9. I am the *d.* of the sheep.
18. 16. Peter stood at the *d.* without
Acts 14. 27. opened *d.* of faith.
1 Cor. 16. 9. great *d.* and effectual.
2 Cor. 2. 12. *d.* opened to me of the Lord.
Col. 4. 3. God would open a *d.* of utterance.
Jas. 5. 9. judge standeth before the *d.*
Rev. 3. 8. I set before thee an open *d.*
3. 20. I stand at the *d.*, and knock.
Dote, Jer. 50. 36. and they shall *d.*
1 Tim. 6. 4. *d.* about questions.
Double, Gen. 43. 12. take *d.* money.
Ex. 22. 4. theft be found, restore *d.*
Deut. 15. 18. worth a *d.* hired servant.
2 Ki. 2. 9. a *d.* portion of thy spirit.
1 Chr. 12. 33. not of *d.* heart.   [which is.
Job 11. 6. secrets of wisdom are *d.* to that
Ps. 12. 2. with a *d.* heart do they speak.
Is. 40. 2. received *d.* for all her sins.
Jer. 16. 18. recompense their sin *d.*
17. 18. with *d.* destruction.
1 Tim. 3. 8. deacons not *d.* tongued.
5. 17. elders worthy of *d.* honour.
Jas. 1. 8. a *d.*-minded man is unstable.
4. 8. purify your hearts, ye *d.*-minded.
Doubt, Deut. 28. 56. thy life shall hang in *d.*
Dan. 5. 12. dissolving of *d.*
Matt. 14. 31. wherefore didst thou *d.*
21. 21. if ye have faith, and *d.* not.
Mk. 11. 23. and shall not *d.* in his heart.
John 10. 24. how long dost thou make us to *d.?*
Acts 5.24. they *d.* whereunto this would grow.
Rom. 14. 23. he that *d.* is damned if he eat.
Gal. 4. 20. I stand in *d.* of you.
1 Tim. 2. 8. pray without wrath and *d.*
See Lk. 12. 29; Rom. 14. 1.
Doubtless, Ps. 126. 6. *d.* come again with rejoicing.
Is. 63. 16. *d.* thou art our Father.
Phil. 3. 8. yea *d.* I count all but loss.
Dove, Gen. 8. 9. the *d.* found no rest.
Ps. 55. 6. that I had wings like a *d.*
74. 19. the soul of thy turtle *d.*
Cant. 5. 12. his eyes are as eyes of *d.*
Is. 59. 11. we mourn sore like *d.*
60. 8. flee as *d.* to their windows.
Matt. 3. 16; Mk. 1. 10; Lk. 3. 22; John 1. 32. descending like a *d.*
Matt. 10. 16. be harmless as *d.*
21. 12; Mk. 11. 15; John 2. 14. that sold *d.*
Down, 2 Ki. 19. 30; Is. 37. 31. take root *d.*
Ps. 59. 15. let them wander up and *d.*
109. 23. I am tossed up and *d.*
139. 2. thou knowest my *d.* sitting.
Eccl. 3. 21. spirit of the beast that goeth *d.*
Zech. 10. 12. walk up and *d.* in his name.
Acts 27. 27. were driven up and *d.*
Dowry, Gen. 30. 20. endued me with good *d.*
34. 12. ask me never so much *d.*
Ex. 22. 17. pay according to the *d.*
1 Sam. 18. 25. king desireth not *d.*   [of *d.*
Dragon, Deut. 32. 33. their wine is the poison
Job 30. 29. I am a brother to *d.*
Ps. 74. 13. breakest the heads of the *d.*
91. 13. the *d.* shalt thou trample.
148. 7. praise the Lord, ye *d.*
Is. 34. 13; 35. 7. the habitation of *d.*
43. 20. *d.* and owls shall honour me.
Jer. 9. 11. make Jerusalem a den of *d.*
Rev. 20. 2. laid hold on the *d.*, that old serpent.

Drank, Gen. 9. 21. Noah *d.* of the wine.
1 Sam. 30. 12. nor *d.* water three days and nights.
1 Ki. 17. 6. he *d.* of the brook.   [gold.
Dan. 5. 4. they *d.*, and praised the gods of
Mk. 14. 23. and they all *d.* of it.
John 4. 12. our father Jacob *d.* thereof.
1 Cor. 10. 4. they *d.* of that spiritual rock.
Draught, Matt. 15.17; Mk. 7. 19. cast out into *d.*
Lk. 5. 4. let down nets for a *d.*
5. 9. astonished at *d.* of fishes.
Draw, Job 21.33. every man shall *d.* after him.
Ps. 28. 3. *d.* me not away with the wicked.
73. 28. it is good to *d.* near to God.
Eccl. 12. 1. nor years *d.* nigh when.
Cant. 1. 4. *d.* me, we will run after thee.
Is. 5. 18. *d.* iniquity with cords.
12. 3. *d.* water from wells of salvation.
Jer. 31.3. with loving-kindness have I *d.* thee.
Matt. 15. 8. people *d.* nigh with their mouth.
Lk. 21. 28. your redemption *d.* nigh.
John 4. 11. thou hast nothing to *d.* with.
6. 44. except the Father *d.* him.
12. 32. I will *d.* all men unto me.
Heb. 7. 19. by which we *d.* nigh to God.
10. 22. let us *d.* near with a true heart.
Jas. 4. 8. *d.* nigh to God, he will *d.* nigh.
Dread, Gen. 28. 17. how *d.* is this place!
Ex. 15. 16. *d.* shall fall upon them.
Deut. 1. 29. *d.* not, nor be afraid.
2. 25; 11. 25. begin to put *d.* of thee.
Is. 8. 13. let him be your fear and *d.*
Dan. 9. 4. the great and *d.* God.
Mal. 4. 5. the great and *d.* day of the Lord.
Dream, Gen. 31. 11. angel spake to Jacob in a *d.*
1 Ki. 3. 5. Lord appeared to Jacob in a *d.*
Job 33. 15. in a *d.*, in a vision of the night.
Ps. 73. 20. as a *d.* when one awaketh.
Eccl. 5. 3. a *d.* cometh through the multitude of business.
Joel 2. 28; Acts 2. 17. old men *d.*
Matt. 1. 20. angel of the Lord appeared in a *d.*
Dress, Gen. 2. 15. put man in garden to *d.* it.
Deut. 28. 39. plant vineyards, and *d.* them.
2 Sam. 12. 4. *d.* poor man's lamb.
Lk. 13. 7. said to *d.* of vineyard.
Heb. 6. 7. for them by whom it is *d.*
Drew, Gen. 47. 29. time *d.* nigh that Israel must die.
Ex. 2. 10. because I *d.* him out of the water.
Josh. 8. 26. Joshua *d.* not his hand back.
Ruth 4. 8. *d.* off his shoe.
1 Ki. 22. 34; 2 Chr. 18. 33. man *d.* a bow.
2 Ki. 9. 24. Jehu *d.* bow with full strength.
Jer. 38. 13. *d.* up with cords.
Hos. 11. 4. *d.* them with cords of a man.
Zeph. 3. 2. she *d.* not near to her God.
Matt. 21. 34. when time of fruit *d.* near.
Lk. 15. 25. elder son *d.* nigh to house.
24. 15. Jesus himself *d.* near.
Acts 5. 37. *d.* away much people.
7. 17. time of the promise *d.* near.   [ye go.
Drink, Lev. 10. 9. do not drink strong *d.* when
Num. 6. 3. Nazarite separate from strong *d.*
20. 8. give congregation *d.*
Deut. 14. 26. bestow money for strong *d.*
29. 6. nor drunk strong *d.* forty years.
Prov. 20. 1. strong *d.* is raging.
Is. 5. 11. may follow strong *d.*
28. 7. erred through strong *d.*
Mic. 2. 11. I will prophesy of strong *d.*
Hab. 2. 15. that giveth his neighbour *d.*
Matt. 25. 35. thirsty, and ye gave me *d.*
John 4. 9. a Jew, askest *d.* of me.

Drink—*Continued.*
John 6. 55. my blood is *d.* indeed.
Rom. 12. 20. if thine enemy thirst, give him *d.*
14.17. the kingdom of God is not meat and *d.*
1 Cor. 10. 4. drink same spiritual *d.*
Col. 2. 16. judge you in meat or *d.*

Drink, Ex. 15. 24. wha' shall we *d.*?
17. 1. no water for people to *d.*
Num. 5. 24. *d.* bitter water.
Jud. 4. 19. water to *d.*, for I am thirsty.
2 Ki. 18. 31 ; Is. 36. 16 ; Prov. 5. 15. *d.* every one water of his cistern.
Ps. 36. 8. *d.* of the river of thy pleasures.
60. 3. *d.* the wine of astonishment.
80. 5. givest them tears to *d.*
110. 7. he shall *d.* of the brook in the way.
Prov. 31. 4. it is not for kings to *d.* wine.
Cant. 5. 1. *d.*, yea *d.* abundantly.
Is. 22. 13 ; 1 Cor. 15. 32. let us eat and *d.*
Is. 65. 13. my servants shall *d.*, but ye shall be thirsty.
Jer. 35. 6. we will *d.* no wine.
Zech. 9. 15. they shall *d.*, and make a noise.
Matt. 10. 42. whosoever shall give to *d.*
20. 22 ; Mk. 10. 38. are ye able to *d.*?
Matt. 26. 27. saying, *d.* ye all of it.   [new.
26. 29 ; Mk. 14. 25 ; Lk. 22. 18. when I *d.* it.
Matt. 26. 42. may not pass except I *d.* it.
Mk. 9. 41. shall give you cup of water to *d.*
16. 18. if they *d.* any deadly thing.
John 7. 37. let him come to me and *d.*
Rom. 14. 21. not good to *d.* wine.
1 Cor. 11. 25. as oft as ye *d.* it.

Drive, Gen. 4. 14. thou hast *d.* me out.
Ex. 6. 1. with a strong hand *d.* out.
Deut. 4. 38 ; Josh. 3. 10. to *d.* out nations from before thee.
Job 30. 5. they were *d.* forth from among.
Ps. 44. 2. didst *d.* out the heathen.
68. 2. as smoke, so *d.* them away.
Prov. 22. 15. rod shall *d.* it away.
25. 23. north wind *d.* away rain.
Dan. 4. 25 ; 5. 21. they shall *d.* thee from men.
Hos. 13. 3. as chaff *d.* with whirlwind.
Lk. 8. 29. he was *d.* of the devil.
Jas. 1. 6. like wave *d.* with wind.

Drop, Deut. 32. 2. my doctrine *d.* as the rain.
33. 28 ; Prov. 3. 20. heavens *d.* dew.
Job 36. 28. which the clouds do *d.*
Ps. 65. 11. thy paths *d.* fatness.
68. 8. heavens *d.* at presence of God.
Is. 40. 15. as *d.* of a bucket.
45. 8. *d.* down, ye heavens.
Joel 3. 18 ; Amos 9. 13. the mountains shall *d.* down new wine.
Lk. 22. 44. sweat as it were great *d.* of blood.

Dross, Ps. 119. 119. the wicked like *d.*
Prov. 25. 4. take *d.* from silver.
Is. 1. 22. thy silver is become *d.*
Ezek. 22. 18. house of Israel *d.*

Drought, Gen. 31. 40. in day *d.* consumed me.
Ps. 32. 4. my moisture into the *d.* of summer.
Is. 58. 11. Lord shall satisfy thy soul in *d.*
Jer. 17. 8. not be careful in year of *d.*
Hos. 13. 5. know thee in land of *d.*
Hag. 1. 11. and I called for a *d.*

Drown, Cant. 8. 7. neither can floods *d.* it.
1 Tim. 6. 9. which *d.* men in perdition.

Drunk, 1 Sam. 1. 15. I have *d.* neither wine nor.
2 Sam. 11. 13. David made Uriah *d.*
1 Ki. 20. 16. was drinking himself *d.*
Job 12. 25 ; Ps. 107. 27. stagger like a *d.* man.
Jer. 23. 9. I am like a *d.* man.

Drunk—*Continued.*
Lam. 5. 4. we have *d.* water for money.
Matt. 24. 49 ; Lk. 12. 45. drink with the *d.*
Acts 2. 15. not *d.* as ye suppose.
1 Cor. 11. 21. one is hungry, and another *d.*
Eph. 5. 18. *d.* with wine, wherein is excess.
1 Thes. 5.7. they that be *d.*, are *d.* in the night.

Drunkard, Deut. 21. 20. our son is a glutton and a *d.*
Ps. 69. 12. I was the song of the *d.*
Prov. 23. 21. *d.* shall come to poverty.
Is. 24. 20. the earth shall reel like a *d.*
1 Cor. 6. 10. nor *d.* inherit kingdom of God.

Drunkenness, Deut. 29. 19. to add *d.* to thirst.
Eccl. 10. 17. eat for strength, not for *d.*
Ezek. 23. 33. filled with *d.*
Lk. 21. 34. overcharged with *d.*
Rom. 13. 13. not in rioting and *d.*

Dry, Gen 8. 13. face of ground was *d.*
Josh. 3. 17. priests stood firm on *d.* ground.
Jud. 6. 37. it be *d.* on all the earth.
Ps. 107. 33. water springs into *d.* ground.
Prov. 17. 22. a broken spirit *d.* the bones.
Is. 32. 2. as rivers in a *d.* place.
44. 3. pour floods on *d.* ground.
53. 2. as a root out of a *d.* ground.
Hos. 9. 16. their root is *d.* up.
Matt. 12. 43 ; Lk. 11. 24. through *d.* places.
Mk. 5. 29. fountain of blood *d.* up.
11. 20. saw the fig tree *d.* up.

Due, Lev. 10. 13, 14. it is thy *d.*, and thy son's *d.*
Lev. 26. 4 ; Deut. 11. 14. rain in *d.* season.
Ps. 104. 27; 145. 15 ; Matt. 24. 45 ; Lk. 12. 42. meat in *d.* season.
Prov. 15. 23. word spoken in *d.* season.
Matt. 18. 34. pay all that was *d.*
Lk. 23. 41. the *d.* reward of our deeds. [godly.
Rom. 5. 6. in *d.* time Christ died for the un-
1 Cor. 15. 8. as of one born out of *d.* time.
Gal. 6. 9. in *d.* season we shall reap.
1 Pet. 5. 6. he may exalt you in *d.* time.

Dull, Matt. 13. 15 ; Acts 28. 27. ears are *d.*
Heb. 5. 11. seeing ye are *d.* of hearing.

Dumb, Ex. 4. 11. who maketh the *d.*?
Ps. 38. 13. I was as a *d.* man.
Prov. 31. 8. open thy mouth for the *d.*
Is. 35. 6. the tongue of the *d.* shall sing.
53. 7; Acts 8. 32. as sheep before shearers is *d.*
Hab. 2. 19. woe to him that saith to *d.* stone.
Matt. 9. 32 ; 12. 22 ; Mk. 9. 17. *d.* man.
1 Cor. 12. 2. carried away to *d.* idols.
2 Pet. 2. 16. the *d.* ass speaking.   [*d.* hill.

Dung, 1 Sam. 2. 8; Ps. 113. 7. lifteth beggar from
Lk. 13. 8. till I dig about it, and *d.* it.
14. 35. neither fit for land nor *d.* hill.
Phil. 3. 8. count all things but *d.*

Durable, Prov. 8. 18. *d.* riches are with me.
Is. 23. 18. be for *d.* clothing.
See Matt. 13. 21.

Dust, Gen. 2. 7. Lord God formed man of *d.*
3. 14. *d.* shalt thou eat.
3. 19. *d.* thou art, and unto *d.*
18. 27. who am but *d.* and ashes.
Job 2. 12. sprinkled *d.* upon heads.
34. 15. man shall turn again to *d.*
42. 6. I repent in *d.* and ashes.
Ps. 22. 15. brought me into *d.* of death.
30. 9. shall the *d.* praise thee?
102. 14. servants favour *d.* thereof.
103. 14. remembereth that we are *d.*
119. 25. my soul cleaveth to the *d.*
Eccl. 12. 7. then shall *d.* return to the earth.
Is. 40. 12. comprehended *d.* of the earth.
Dan. 12. 2. many that sleep in *d.* shall awake.

Dust—*Continued.*
Matt. 10. 14; Mk. 6. 11; Lk. 9. 5. shake off *d.* from feet.
Acts 13. 51. they shook off the *d.*
22. 23. they threw *d.* into the air.
Duty, Eccl. 12. 13. the whole *d.* of man.
Lk. 17. 10. done that which was our *d.* to do.
Rom. 15. 27. their *d.* is to minister in carnal things.
Dwell, Deut. 12. 11. cause his name to *d.* there.
2 Ki. 19. 15; Ps. 80. 1; Is. 37. 16. which *d.* between cherubims.
Ps. 23. 6. will *d.* in house of the Lord.
84. 10. than to *d.* in tents of wickedness.
132. 14. here will I *d.*
133. 1. good for brethren to *d.* together.
Is. 33. 14. who shall *d.* with devouring fire.
57. 15. I *d.* in the high and holy place.
John 6. 56. *d.* in me, and I in him.
14. 17. he *d.* with you, and shall be in you.
Acts 7. 48; 17. 24. God *d.* not in temples.
Rom. 7. 17. sin that *d.* in me.
8. 11. by his Spirit that *d.* in you. [head.
Col. 2. 9. in him *d.* all the fulness of the God-
3. 16. word of Christ *d.* in you richly.
1 Tim. 6. 16. *d.* in the light.
2 Tim. 1. 14. Holy Ghost who *d.* in us.
2 Pet. 3. 13. wherein *d.* righteousness.
1 John 3. 17. how *d.* the love of God in him.
4. 12. God *d.* in us.

EAGLE, Ex. 19. 4. I bare you on *e.* wings.
Deut. 32. 11. as an *e.* stirreth her nest.
2 Sam. 1. 23. swifter than *e.*
Ps. 103. 5. youth renewed like *e.*
Is. 40. 31. mount up with wings as *e.*
Matt. 24. 28; Lk. 17. 37. *e.* be gathered.
Ear, Ex. 21. 6; Deut. 15. 17. master shall bore *e.*
2 Ki. 19. 16; Ps. 31. 2. bow down thine *e.*
Neh. 1. 6, 11. let thy *e.* be attentive.
Job 42. 5. heard by hearing of *e.*
Ps. 10. 17. cause thine *e.* to hear.
94. 9. he that planted the *e.*
Prov. 18. 15. *e.* of wise seek knowledge.
Is. 59. 1. *e.* is heavy that it cannot hear.
Matt. 10. 27. what ye hear in the *e.*
1 Cor. 2. 9. eye hath not seen nor *e.* heard.
1 Sam. 8. 12; Is. 30. 24. *e.* the ground.
Early, Ps. 46. 5. God shall help her and that right *e.*
63. 1. my God, *e.* will I seek thee.
90. 14. satisfy us *e.* with thy mercy.
Prov. 8. 17. seek me *e.* shall find me.
Hos. 5. 15. in affliction they will seek me *e.*
6. 4; 13. 3. as the *e.* dew.
Jas. 5. 7. the *e.* and latter rain.
Earnest, Job 7 2. as servant *e.* desireth shadow.
Lk. 22. 44. in agony he prayed more *e.*
Rom. 8. 19. the *e.* expectation of the creature.
1 Cor. 12. 31. covet *e.* the best gifts.
2 Cor. 1. 22; 5. 5. the *e.* of the Spirit.
Eph. 1. 14. the *e.* of our inheritance.
Jude 3. *e.* contend for the faith.
Earth, Gen. 1. 10. God called the dry land *e.*
6. 11. *e.* was corrupt before God.
Ex. 9. 29; Deut. 10. 14; Ps. 24. 1; 1 Cor. 10. 26. *e.* is the Lord's. [Lord.
Num. 14. 21. all the *e.* filled with glory of the
16. 30. if the *e.* open her mouth.
Deut. 32. 1. O *e.,* hear the words of my mouth.
Josh. 23. 14. going way of all the *e.*
1 Sam. 2. 8. pillars of the *e.* are Lord's.
1 Ki. 8. 27; 2 Chr. 6. 18. will God dwell on the *e.*?

Earth—*Continued.*
Job 19. 25. stand at latter day upon the *e*
38. 4. when I laid foundations of the *e.*
Ps. 2. 8. uttermost parts of the *e.*
33. 5. *e.* is full of the goodness of the Lord.
46. 2. not fear, though *e.* be removed.
58. 11. a God that judgeth in the *e.*
65. 9. thou visitest the *e.,* and waterest it.
72. 6. showers that water the *e.* [glory.
72. 19. let the whole *e.* be filled with his
73. 25. none on *e.* I desire beside thee.
99. 1. Lord reigneth, let *e.* be moved.
102. 25; 104. 5; Prov. 8. 29; Is. 48. 13. laid the foundation of the *e.*
Ps. 148. 13. his glory is above the *e.*
Prov. 3. 19. Lord founded the *e.*
8. 23. from everlasting, or ever *e.* was.
Eccl. 1. 4. the *e.* abideth for ever.
12. 7. dust return to *e.*
Is. 11. 9. *e.* full of knowledge of the Lord.
40. 28. Creator of ends of *e.* fainteth not.
45. 22. be saved, all ends of the *e.*
Jer. 22. 29; Mic. 1. 2. O *e., e., e.,* hear word of the Lord.
Ezek. 34. 27. the *e.* shall yield her increase.
Hos. 2. 22. the *e.* shall hear the corn.
Zech. 4. 10. eyes of Lord run through *e.*
Matt. 5. 5. meek shall inherit the *e.*
Mk. 4. 28. *e.* bringeth forth fruit of herself.
Lk. 2. 14. on *e.* peace.
23. 44. darkness over all the *e.* [of the *e.*
John 3. 31. he that is of *e.* is *e.,* and speaketh
12. 32. Son of man lifted up from the *e.*
Acts 8. 33. his life is taken from the *e.*
1 Cor. 15. 47. first man is of the *e., e.* [the *e.*
Col. 3. 2. set your affection not on things or
Heb. 6. 7. *e.* drinketh in the rain.
12. 25. refused him that spake on *e.*
Jas. 3. 15. this wisdom is *e.*
2 Pet. 3. 10. the *e.* shall be burned up.
Rev. 5. 10. we shall reign on the *e.*
21. 1. a new *e.*
Earthquake, 1 Ki. 19. 11. Lord was not in the *e.*
Zech. 14. 5. ye fled before the *e.*
Matt. 24. 7; Mk. 13.8; Lk. 21.11. famines and *e.*
Matt. 27. 54. centurion saw the *e.*
28.2; Acts 16.26; Rev.6.12. there was a great *e.*
Ease, Deut. 28. 65. shalt thou find no *e.*
Job 12. 5. thought of him that is at *e.*
21. 23. dieth, being wholly at *e.*
Ps. 25. 13. his soul shall dwell at *e.*
Is. 32. 9. rise up, ye women at *e.*
Amos 6. 1. woe to them that are at *e.*
Matt. 9. 5; Mk. 2. 9; Lk. 5. 23. whether is *e.* to say.
Matt. 11. 30. my yoke is *e.* and burden light.
19. 24; Mk. 10. 25; Lk. 18. 25. *e.* for camel.
Lk. 12. 19. take thine *e.* and be merry.
1 Cor. 13. 5. charity is not *e.* provoked.
Heb. 12. 1. sin which doth so *e.* beset us.
East, Gen. 3. 24. *e.* of the garden of Eden.
29. 1. land of the people of the *e.*
41. 6, 23, 27. thin ears blasted with *e.* wind.
Ex. 10. 13; 14. 21. Lord brought an *e.* wind.
Job 1. 3. greatest of all the men of the *e.*
38. 24. scattereth *e.* wind on the earth.
Ps. 48. 7. breakest ships with *e.* wind.
75. 6. promotion cometh not from *e.*
103. 12. as far as *e.* from west.
Is. 27. 8. stayeth rough wind in day of *e.* wind.
43. 5; Zech. 8. 7. bring thy seed from the *e.*
Ezek. 8. 16. faces toward the *e.*
Hos. 12. 1. Ephraim followeth *e.* wind.
13. 15. an *e.* wind shall come.

East—Continued.
Jon. 4. 5. sat on e. side of city.
Matt. 2. 1. wise men from the e.
  8. 11; Lk. 13. 29. many come from e.
  24. 27. as lightning out of the e.
Eat, Gen. 2. 16. of every tree thou mayest e.
  3. 17. in sorrow shalt thou e.
1 Ki. 19. 5; Acts 10. 13; 11. 7. angel said,
  arise and e.
2 Ki. 6. 28. give thy son, that we may e. him.
Neh. 5. 2. corn, that we may e., and live.
  8. 10. e. the fat, drink the sweet.
Ps. 22. 26. the meek shall e. and be satisfied.
  69. 9; John 2. 17. zeal of thine house hath
  e. me up.
Ps. 78. 25. man did e. angels' food.
  102. 9. have e. ashes like bread.
Prov. 1. 31; Is. 3. 10. e. fruit of own way.
Cant. 5. 1. e., O friends; drink, yea, drink
  abundantly.   [the land.
Is. 1. 19. if obedient, ye shall e. the good of
  7. 15, 22. butter and honey shall he e.
  11. 7; 65. 25. lion e. straw like ox.
  55. 1. come ye, buy and e.
  65. 13. my servants shall e., but ye shall be
  hungry.
Jer. 31. 29; Ezek. 18. 2. the fathers have e.
  sour grapes.
Hos. 4. 10; Mic. 6. 14; Hag. 1. 6. e. and not
  have enough.
Matt. 6. 25; Lk. 12. 22. what ye shall e.
Matt. 12. 4. e. showbread, which was not
  lawful to e.
  14. 16; Mk. 6. 37; Lk. 9. 13. give ye them to e.
Matt. 15. 20. to e. with unwashen hands.
  15. 27; Mk. 7. 28. dogs e. of crumbs.
Matt. 26. 26; Mk. 14. 22; 1 Cor. 11. 24. take e.,
  this is my body.
Mk. 6. 31. no leisure, so much as to e.
  11. 14. no man e. fruit of thee.
Lk. 10. 8. e. such things as are set before you.
  12. 19. take thine ease, e., drink.
  15. 23. let us e. and be merry.
  24. 43. he took it, and did e. before them.
John 4. 32. meat to e. ye know not of.
  6. 53. except ye e. the flesh.
Acts 2. 46. did e. their meat with gladness.
  9. 9. Saul did neither e. nor drink.
Rom. 14.2. one believeth he may e. all things.
1 Cor. 10. 31. whether ye e. or drink.
  11. 29. he that e. unworthily.
2 Thes. 3. 10. any work not, neither e.
2 Tim. 2. 17. e. as doth a canker.
Jas. 5. 3. e. your flesh as fire.
Rev. 2. 7. e. of the tree of life.
  2. 17. give to e. of hidden manna.
  19. 18. e. flesh of kings.
Edify, Rom. 14. 19. one may e. another
  15. 2. please his neighbour to e.
1 Cor. 8. 1. charity e.
  10. 23. all things lawful, but e. not.
  14. 26. let all things be done to e.
Eph. 4. 12. the e. of the body of Christ.
1 Tim. 1. 4. minister questions rather than e.
Effect, Ps. 33. 10. devices of people of none e.
Is. 32. 17. the e. of righteousness quietness.
Matt. 15. 6; Mk. 7. 13. command of God of
  none e.
Rom. 4. 14; Gal. 3. 17. promise of none e.
1 Cor. 1. 17. lest cross of Christ be of none e.
Gal. 5. 4. Christ is become of no e.
Effectual, 1 Cor. 16. 9. a great door and e.
Eph. 3. 7; 4. 16. the e. working.
Jas. 5. 16. the e. prayer of a righteous man.

Egg, Job 6. 6. any taste in white of e.?
Is. 59. 5. hatch cockatrice' e.
Jer. 17. 11. partridge sitteth on e.
Lk. 11. 12. if he ask an e.
Elder, Gen. 25. 23; Rom. 9. 12. e. serve younger.
Job 15. 10. aged men, much e. than thy father.
Ps. 107. 32. praise in assembly of e.
Matt. 15. 2; Mk. 7. 3. tradition of the e.
Tit. 1. 5. ordain e. in every city.   [report.
Heb. 11. 2. by faith the e. obtained a good
Jas. 5. 14. call for e. of church.
1 Pet. 5. 1. the e. I exhort, who am an e.
Elect, Is. 42. 1. mine e., in whom my soul de-
  lighteth.
  65. 9. mine e. shall inherit it.   [shortened.
Matt. 24. 22; Mk. 13. 20. for e. sake those days
Matt. 24. 31; Mk. 13. 27. gather together his e.
Lk. 18. 7. God avenge his own e.
Rom. 8. 33. lay anything to charge of God's e.
Col. 3. 12. put on as the e. of God.
1 Tim. 5. 21. charge thee before e. angels.
1 Pet. 1. 2. e. according to the foreknowledge.
  2. 6. corner-stone, e., precious.   [ing to e.
Election, Rom. 9. 11. purpose of God accord-
1 Thes. 1. 4. knowing your e. of God.
2 Pet. 1. 10. your calling and e. sure.
Elements, Gal. 4. 9. the weak and beggarly e.
2 Pet. 3. 10. the e. melt with heat.
Eloquent, Ex. 4. 10. I am not e.
Is. 3. 3. Lord doth take away e. orator.
Acts 18. 24. an e. man.   [sent e. away.
Empty, Gen. 31. 42; Mk. 12. 3; Lk. 1. 53; 20. 10.
Ex. 23. 15; 34. 20; Deut. 16. 16. none shall
  appear before me e.
Eccl. 11. 3. clouds e. themselves on the earth.
Is. 24. 1. the Lord maketh earth e.
  29. 8. hungry awaketh, his soul is e.
Hos. 10. 1. Israel is an e. vine.
Matt. 12. 44. when come, he findeth it e.
Emulation, Rom. 11. 14. may provoke to e.
Gal. 5. 20. works of the flesh are e.   [me.
Encamp, Ps. 27. 3. though an host e. against
  34. 7. angel of Lord e. round.
  53. 5. bones of him that e. against thee.
Encourage, Deut. 1. 38; 3. 28; 2 Sam. 11. 25. e.
  him.
Ps. 64. 5. they e. themselves in an evil matter.
Is. 41. 7. carpenter e. goldsmith.
End, Gen. 6. 13. the e. of all flesh is come.
Num. 23. 10. let my last e. be like his.
Deut. 32. 29. consider their latter e.   [long?
Job 6. 11. what is mine e., that I should pro-
  16. 3. shall vain words have an e.?
Ps. 9. 6. destructions come to perpetual e.
  37. 37. the e. of that man is peace.
  39. 4. make me to know my e.
  102. 27. thy years have no e.
  107. 27. are at their wit's e.
Prov. 14. 12. the e. thereof are ways of death.
  19. 20. be wise in thy latter e.
Eccl. 4. 8. no e. of all his labour.
  7. 8. better is the e. of a thing than.
  12. 12. of making books there is no e.
Is. 9. 7. of his government shall be no e.
Jer. 8. 20. harvest past, summer e.
  31. 17. there is hope in thine e.
Lam. 4. 18; Ezek. 7. 2; Amos 8. 2. e. is near.
  e. is come.
Ezek. 21. 25; 35. 5. iniquity shall have an e.
Dan. 8. 19. at the time appointed e. shall be.
Dan. 12. 8. what shall be the e. of these?
Hab. 2. 3. at the e. it shall speak, and not
  tarry.
Matt. 10. 22; 24. 13; Mk. 13. 13. endureth to e.

End—*Continued.*
Matt. 13. 39. harvest is *e.* of the world.
24. 3. what sign of the *e.* of the world?
24. 6; Mk. 13. 7; Lk. 21. 9. the *e.* is not yet.
Matt. 24. 31. gather from one *e.* of heaven.
28. 20. I am with you, even unto the *e.*
Mk. 3. 26. cannot stand, but hath an *e.*
Lk. 1. 33. of his kingdom there shall be no *e.*
22. 37. things concerning me have an *e.*
John 18. 37. to this *e.* was I born.
Rom. 6. 21. the *e.* of those things is death.
6. 22. the *e.* everlasting life.
10. 4. Christ is *e.* of law for righteousness.
1 Tim. 1. 5. the *e.* of commandment is charity.
Heb. 6. 8. whose *e.* is to be burned.
7. 3. neither beginning nor *e.* of life.
9. 26. once in the *e.* hath he appeared.
13. 7. considering *e.* of their conversation.
Jas. 5. 11. ye have seen *e.* of the Lord.
1 Pet. 1. 9. receiving the *e.* of your faith.
4. 17. what shall the *e.* be of them that obey not Gospel?
Rev. 21. 6; 22. 13. the beginning and the *e.*
Endless, 1 Tim. 1. 4. heed to *e.* genealogies.
Heb. 7. 16. after power of an *e.* life.
Endue, Gen. 30. 20. *e.* me with good dowry.
2 Chr. 2. 13. cunning man *e.* with understanding.
Lk. 24. 49. till ye be *e.* with power.
Jas. 3. 13. *e.* with knowledge.
Endure, Gen. 33. 14. as children be able to *e.*
Est. 8. 6. can I *e.* to see the evil? [ever.
Ps. 9. 7; 102. 12; 104. 31. the Lord shall *e.* for
30. 5. weeping may *e.* for a night.
72.5.fear thee as long as the sun and moon *e.*
72. 17. his name shall *e.* for ever.
106. 1; 107. 1; 118. 1; 136. 1; 138. 8; Jer. 33. 11. his mercy *e.* for ever.
111. 3; 112. 3, 9. his righteousness *e.* for ever.
Prov.27.24. doth crown *e.* to every generation?
Ezek. 22. 14. can thy heart *e.*? [the end.
Matt. 24. 13; Mk. 13. 13. he that shall *e.* to
Mk. 4. 17. *e.* but for a time.
1 Cor. 13. 7. charity *e.* all things.
2 Tim. 2. 3. *e.* hardness as a good soldier.
Heb. 10. 34. in heaven a better and *e.* substance.
12. 7. if ye *e.* chastening.
Jas. 1. 12. blessed is man that *e.* temptation.
5. 11. we count them happy who *e.*
1 Pet. 1. 25. the word of the Lord *e.* for ever.
2. 19. for conscience *e.* grief.
Enemy, Ex. 23. 22. I will be *e.* to thine *e.*
Deut. 32. 31. our *e.* themselves being judges.
Jud. 5. 31. so let all thine *e.* perish.
1 Ki. 21. 20. hast thou found me, O mine *e.*?
Ps. 8. 2. mightest still the *e.* and avenger.
72. 9. his *e.* shall lick the dust.
127. 5. speak with *e.* in the gate. [bread.
Prov. 25. 21; Rom. 12. 20. if he hunger give
Is. 59. 19. when *e.* shall come in like a flood.
63. 10. he was turned to be their *e.*
Mic. 7. 6. man's *e.*, men of his own house.
Matt. 5. 43. said, thou shalt hate thine *e.*
Lk. 19. 43. thine *e.* shall cast a trench.
Rom. 5. 10. if when *e.* we were reconciled.
Gal. 4. 16. am I become your *e.*?
2 Thes. 3. 15. count him not as an *e.*
Jas. 4. 4. friend of the world is the *e.* of God.
Engrave, Zech. 3. 9. I will *e.* the graving thereof.
2 Cor. 3. 7. ministration of death *e.*
Enjoin, Job 36. 23. who hath *e.* him his way?
Philem. 8. *e.* what is convenient.
Heb. 9. 20. blood which God hath *e.*

Enjoy, Lev. 26. 34; 2 Chr. 36. 21. land *e.* her Sabbaths.
Eccl. 2. 1. *e.* pleasure, this also is vanity.
2. 24; 3. 13; 5. 18. his soul *e.* good.
1 Tim. 6. 17. giveth all things to *e.*
Heb. 11. 25. than *e.* pleasures of sin.
Enlarge, Gen. 9. 27. God shall *e.* Japheth.
Deut. 12.20. when the Lord shall *e.* thy border.
Ps. 4. 1. thou hast *e.* me in distress.
25. 17. troubles of my heart are *e.*
119. 32. when thou shalt *e.* my heart.
Is. 5. 14. hell hath *e.* herself.
60. 5. heart shall fear and be *e.*
Matt. 23. 5. *e.* borders of garments.
2 Cor. 6. 11. our heart is *e.*
Enlighten, Ps. 18. 28. Lord will *e.* my darkness.
19. 8. command of Lord is pure, *e.* the eyes.
97. 4. his lightnings *e.* world.
Eph. 1. 18. eyes of understanding *e.*
Heb. 6. 4. impossible for those once *e.*
Enmity, Gen. 3. 15. I will put *e.* between.
Rom. 8. 7. carnal mind is *e.* against God.
Eph. 2. 15. abolished in his flesh the *e.*
Jas. 4. 4. friendship of world is *e.* with God.
Enough, Gen. 33. 9. I have *e.*
45. 28. it is *e.*, Joseph is yet alive.
Ex. 36. 5. people bring more than *e.*
2 Sam. 24. 16; 1 Ki. 19. 4; 1 Chr. 21. 15; Mk. 14. 41; Lk. 22. 38. it is *e.*
Prov. 30. 15. four things say not, it is *e.*
Hos. 4. 10; Hag. 1. 6. eat, and have not *e.*
Mal. 3. 10. not room *e.* to receive it.
Matt. 10. 25. it is *e.* for disciple.
25. 9. lest there be not *e.*
Lk. 15. 17. bread *e.* and to spare.
Enquire, Ex. 18. 15. people come to *e.* of God.
2 Sam. 16. 23. as if a man *e.* at oracle of God.
Ps. 27. 4. to *e.* in his temple.
78. 34. returned, and *e.* early after God.
Eccl. 7. 10. thou dost not *e.* wisely.
Is. 21. 12. if ye will *e.*, *e.* ye.
Ezek. 14. 3. should I be *e.* of at all by them.
36. 37. I will yet for this be *e.* of.
Matt. 10. 11. *e.* who in it is worthy.
Lk. 22. 23. to *e.* among themselves.
1 Pet. 1. 10. of which salvation the prophets *e.*
Enrich, 1 Sam. 17. 25. king will *e.* them.
Ps. 65. 9. greatly *e.* it with river of God.
Ezek. 27. 33. didst *e.* kings of earth.
2 Cor. 9. 11. being *e.* in everything.
Ensample, 1 Cor. 10. 11. happened to them for *e.*
Phil. 3. 17. as ye have us for an *e.*
2 Thes. 3. 9. to make ourselves an *e.*
1 Pet. 5. 3. being *e.* to the flock.
Ensign, Ps. 74. 4. set up their *e.* for signs.
Is. 5. 26. he will lift up an *e.*
11. 12. set up an *e.* for the nations.
30. 17. till ye be left as *e.* on hill.
Entangle, Matt. 22. 15. how they might *e.* him.
Gal. 5. 1. be not *e.* with yoke of bondage.
2 Tim. 2. 4. *e.* himself with affairs of life.
Enter, Job 22. 4. will he *e.* into judgment?
Ps. 100. 4. *e.* his gates with thanksgiving.
118. 20. gate into which righteous *e.*
Is. 2. 10. *e.* into the rock.
26. 2. righteous nation may *e.* in.
26. 20. *e.* thou into thy chambers.
Matt. 5. 20. in no case *e.* into kingdom of heaven.
6. 6. when thou prayest, *e.* into thy closet.
7. 13; Lk. 13. 24. *e.* in at straight gate.
Matt. 18.8; Mk. 9.43. better to *e.* into life halt.
Matt. 19. 17. if thou wilt *e.* into life, keep commandments.

Enter—*Continued.*
Matt. 25. 21. *e.* into joy of Lord.
Mk. 14. 38 ; Lk. 22. 46. watch and pray, lest
    ye *e.* into temptation.
Lk. 13. 24. many will seek to *e.*, but not able.
John 3. 5. he cannot *e.* into kingdom of God.
    10. 9. by me if any man *e.* in.   [of God.
Acts 14. 22. through tribulation *e.* kingdom
Rom. 5. 12. sin *e.* into the world.
1 Cor. 2. 9. neither have *e.* into heart of man.
Heb. 4. 6. *e.* not in because of unbelief.
    6. 20. forerunner is for us *e.*
    10. 19. *e.* into holiest by blood of Jesus.
Rev. 21. 27. *e.* into it, anything that defileth.
Entice, Jud. 14. 15. *e.* thy husband, that he
    may declare.
Prov. 1. 10. if sinners *e.* thee.
1 Cor. 2. 4 ; Col. 2. 4. with *e.* words.
Envy, Job 5. 2. *e.* slayeth the silly one.
Ps. 73. 3. I was *e.* at the foolish.
Prov. 14. 30. *e.* is the rottenness of the bones.
    27. 4. who is able to stand before *e.*?
Eccl. 9. 6. their *e.* is perished.
Is. 26. 11. ashamed for their *e.*   [him.
Matt. 27. 18 ; Mk. 15. 10. for *e.* they delivered
Acts 7. 9. patriarchs moved with *e.*
13. 45. Jews filled with *e.*
Rom. 1. 29. full of *e.*
1 Cor. 3. 3. among you *e.* and strife.
13. 4. charity *e.* not.
2 Cor. 12. 20. I fear lest there be *e.*
Gal. 5. 21. works of flesh are *e.*, murders.
Phil. 1. 15. preach Christ even of *e.*
Tit. 3. 3. living in malice and *e.*
Jas. 4. 5. spirit in us lusteth to *e.*
Epistle, 2 Cor. 3. 2. ye are our *e.*
2 Thes. 2. 15. taught by word or *e.*
2 Pet. 3. 16. as in all his *e.* speaking.
Equal, Ps. 17. 2. eyes behold things that are *e.*
55. 13. a man mine *e.*
Prov. 26. 7. legs of lame not *e.*
Is. 40. 25 ; 46. 5. to whom shall I be *e.* ?
Ezek. 18. 25. way of the Lord is not *e.*
33. 17. their way is not *e.*
Matt. 20. 12. hast made them *e.* to us.
Lk. 20. 36. *e.* to the angels.
John 5. 18 ; Phil. 2. 6. *e.* with God.
Col. 4. 1. give servants what is *e.*
Equity, Ps. 98. 9. judge the people with *e.*
Prov. 1. 3. receive instruction of *e.*
2. 9. understand judgment and *e.*
Eccl. 2. 21. a man whose labour is in *e.*
Is. 11. 4. reprove with *e.*
59. 14. truth is fallen, and *e.* cannot enter.
Mal. 2. 6. he walked with me in *e.*
Err, Ps. 95. 10. people that do *e.* in their heart.
119. 21. do *e.* from thy commandments.
Prov. 19. 27. instruction that causeth to *e.*
Is. 3. 12 ; 9. 16. that lead thee cause to *e.*
35. 8. men shall not *e.*   [Scriptures.
Matt. 22. 29 ; Mk. 12. 24. do *e.*, not knowing
1 Tim. 6. 21. have *e.* concerning the faith.
Jas. 1. 16. do not *e.*, my brethren.
5. 19. if any do *e.*, from truth.
Error, Ps. 19. 12. who can understand his *e.* ?
Eccl. 5. 6. neither say it was an *e.*
10. 5. an evil I have seen as an *e.*
Is. 32. 6. to utter *e.* against the Lord.
Matt. 27. 64. last *e.* worse than first.
Jas. 5. 20. converteth sinner from *e.*
2 Pet. 3. 17. led away with *e.* of the wicked.
1 John 4. 6. the spirit of *e.*
Heb. 9. 7. offered for *e.* of people.
Jude 11. ran after *e.* of Balaam.

Escape, Gen. 19. 17. *e.* for thy life, *e.* to moun-
    tain.
1 Ki. 18. 40 ; 2 Ki. 9. 15. let none of them *e.*
Job 11. 20. the wicked shall not *e.*
19. 20. *e.* with the skin of my teeth.
Ps. 55. 8. hasten my *e.* from storm.
71. 2. deliver me, and cause me to *e.*
Prov. 19. 5. he that speaketh lies shall not *e.*
Eccl. 7. 26. whoso pleaseth God shall *e.*
Is. 20. 6. how shall we *e.* ?
Matt. 23. 33. how *e.* damnation of hell?
Lk. 21. 36. accounted worthy to *e.*
Acts 27. 44. they *e.* all safe to land.   [to *e.*
1 Cor. 10. 13. with temptation make a way
Heb. 12. 25. if they *e.* not who refused.
2 Pet. 1. 4. *e.* corruption in the world.
Eschew, Job 1. 1 ; 2. 3. feared God, and *e.* evil.
1 Pet. 3. 11. let him *e.* evil, do good.
Especially, Ps. 31. 11. *e.* among my neighbours.
Gal. 6. 10. *e.* the household of faith.
1 Tim. 5. 17. *e.* they who labour in word.
2 Tim. 4. 13. *e.* the parchments.
Espy, Gen. 42. 27. *e.* the money.
Josh. 14. 7. sent me to *e.* out.
Jer. 48. 19. stand by the way, and *e.*
Ezek. 20. 6. land I had *e.* for them.
Establish, Gen. 17. 19. I will *e.* my covenant.
Ps. 40. 2. *e.* my goings.
89. 2. faithfulness shalt *e.* in heavens.
90. 17. *e.* work of our hands.
Prov. 3. 19. Lord hath *e.* the heavens.
16. 12. throne is *e.* by righteousness.
20. 18. every purpose is *e.* by counsel.
Is. 16. 5. in mercy shall throne be *e.*
Jer. 10. 12 ; 51. 15. he *e.* world by wisdom.
Matt. 18. 16. two witnesses, every word *e.*
Rom. 3. 31. yea, we *e.* the law.   [ness.
10. 3. going about to *e.* their own righteous-
Heb. 8. 6. *e.* upon better promises.
13. 9. the heart be *e.* with grace.
1 Pet. 5. 10. God of all grace *e.* you.
Estate, Ps. 136. 23. remembered us in low *e.*
Eccl. 1. 16. I am come to great *e.*
Lk. 1. 48. low *e.* of his handmaiden.
Rom. 12. 16. condescend to men of low *e.*
Jude 6. angels who kept not first *e.*
Esteem, Deut. 32. 15. lightly *e.* rock of salvation.
1 Sam. 2. 30. despise me shall be lightly *e.*
Job 36. 19. will he *e.* thy riches?
Ps. 119. 128. I *e.* all thy precepts.
Is. 53. 4. did *e.* him smitten.
Lk. 16. 15. highly *e.* among men, is
Rom. 14. 5. one man *e.* one day above another.
14. 14. that *e.* anything unclean.
Phil. 2. 3. let each *e.* other better.
1 Thes. 5. 13. *e.* highly for work's sake.
Heb. 11. 26. *e.* reproach of Christ greater
    riches.
Estranged, Job 19. 13. acquaintance are *e.*
Ps. 58. 3. wicked *e.* from the womb.
78. 30. not *e.* from their lust.
Ezek. 14. 5. they are all *e.* from me.
Eternal, Deut. 33. 27. the *e.* God is thy refuge.
Is. 60. 15. make thee an *e.* excellency.
Matt. 19. 16 ; Mk. 10. 17 ; Lk. 10. 25 ; 18. 18.
    do that I may have *e.* life.
Matt. 25. 46. righteous unto life *e.*
Mk. 3. 29. in danger of *e.* damnation.
10. 30. receive in world to come *e.* life.
John 3. 15. believeth in him have *e.* life.
4. 36. gathereth fruit into life *e.*
5. 39. Scriptures, in them *e.* life.
6. 54. drinketh my blood hath *e.* life.
6. 68. thou hast words of *e.* life.

Eternal—*Continued.*
John 10. 28. I give unto my sheep *e.* life.
   12. 25. hateth life, shall keep it to life *e.*
   17. 2. give *e.* life to as many.
Acts 13. 48. as many as were ordained to *e.* life.
Rom. 2. 7. who seek for glory, *e.* life.
   5. 21. grace reign to *e.* life.
   6. 23. gift of God is *e.* life.
2 Cor. 4. 17. an *e.* weight of glory.
   4. 18. things not seen are *e.*
   5. 1. an house *e.* in the heavens.
Eph. 3. 11. according to *e.* purpose.
1 Tim. 1. 17. to king *e.* be honour.
   6. 12, 19. lay hold on *e.* life.
Tit. 1. 2; 3. 7. in hope of *e.* life.
Heb. 5. 9. author of *e.* salvation.
   6. 2. doctrine of *e.* judgment.
   9. 12. obtained *e.* redemption for us.
1 Pet. 5. 10. called to *e.* glory by Christ.
1 John 1. 2. *e.* life which was with the Father.
   2. 25. this is the promise, even *e.* life.
   5. 11. record that God hath given *e.* life.
   5. 20. this is true God, and *e.* life.
Jude 7. vengeance of *e.* fire.
Eternity, Is. 57. 15. lofty one that inhabiteth *e.*
Evening, Jud. 19. 9. day draweth towards *e.*
1 Sam. 14. 24. cursed that eateth till *e.*
1 Ki. 17. 6. brought bread morning and *e.*
Ps. 90. 6. in the *e.* it is cut down.
   104. 23. goeth to his labour until the *e.*
   141. 2. prayer be as the *e.* sacrifice.
Eccl. 11. 6. in *e.* withhold not thine hand.
Jer. 6. 4. shadows of *e.* stretched out.
Zech. 14. 7. at *e.* time shall be light.
Matt. 14. 23. when *e.* was come. he was there alone.
Lk. 24. 29. abide, for it is toward *e.*
Event, Eccl. 2. 14; 9. 3. one *e.* to them all.
   9. 2. one *e.* to righteous and wicked.
Ever, Gen. 3. 22. lest he eat, and live for *e.*
Deut. 5. 29; 12. 28. be well with them for *e.*
   32. 40. lift up hand and say, I live for *e.*
Job 4. 7. who *e.* perished innocent?
Ps. 9. 7. Lord shall endure for *e.*
   22. 26. your heart shall live for *e.*
   23. 6. dwell in the house of the Lord for *e.*
   33. 11. counsel of the Lord standeth for *e.*
   45. 6; Heb. 1. 8. thy throne, O God, is for *e.* and *e.*
Ps. 51. 3. my sin is *e.* before me.
   61. 4. I will abide in tabernacle for *e.*
   73. 26. God is my strength and portion for *e.*
   93. 5 holiness becometh thine house for *e.*
   102. 12. thou shalt endure for *e.*
   103. 9. not keep his anger for *e.*
   132. 14. this is my rest for *e.*
   146. 6. Lord keepeth truth for *e.*
Prov. 27. 24. riches are not for *e.*
Eccl. 1. 4. the earth abideth for *e.*
Is. 26. 4. trust in Lord for *e.*
   32. 17. quietness and assurance for *e.*
   40. 8. word of God shall stand for *e.*
Lam. 3. 31. Lord will not cast off for *e.*
Matt. 21. 19; Mk. 11. 14. no fruit grow on thee for *e.*
John 6. 51. he that eateth shall live for *e.*
   12. 34. heard that Christ abideth for *e.*
   14. 16. comforter abide for *e.*
1 Thes. 4. 17. so shall we *e.* be with the Lord.
Heb. 7. 25. he *e.* liveth to make intercession.
13. 8. **Christ the same yesterday, to-day, and for** *e.*

Everlasting, Gen. 21. 33; Is. 40. 28. Rom. 16. 26. the *e.* God.
Ex. 40. 15; Num. 25. 13. covenant of an *e.* priesthood.
Deut. 33. 27. underneath are *e.* arms.
Ps. 24. 7. be ye lift up, ye *e.* doors.
   90. 2. from *e.* to *e.* thou art God.
   103. 17. mercy of Lord from *e.* to *e.*
   119. 142. thy righteousness is *e.*
   139. 24. lead me in the way *e.*
Prov. 8. 23. I was set up from *e.*
   10. 25. righteous is an *e.* foundation.
Is. 9. 6. called the *e.* Father.
   26. 4. in Jehovah is *e.* strength.
   35. 10; 51. 11; 61. 7. *e.* joy.
   45. 17. with *e.* salvation.
   54. 8. with *e.* kindness.
   55. 13. for an *e.* sign.
   56. 5; 63. 12. an *e.* name.
   60. 19, 20. Lord shall be an *e.* light.
Jer. 31. 3. loved thee with an *e.* love.
Dan. 4. 34; 7. 14. an *e.* dominion.
Mic. 5. 2. goings forth of old from *e.*
Hab. 3. 6. the *e.* mountains.
Matt. 18. 8; 25. 41. into *e.* fire.
   19. 29. shall inherit *e.* life.
   25. 46. go into *e.* punishment.
Lk. 16. 9. into *e.* habitations.
John 3. 16, 36. believeth on the Son hath *e.* life.
   4. 14. water springing up into *e.* life.
   12. 50. his commandment is life *e.*
Rom. 6. 22. ye have the end *e.* life.
Gal. 6. 8. of the Spirit reap life *e.*
2 Thes. 1. 9. punished with *e.* destruction.
   2. 16. given us *e.* consolation.
Jude 6. angels reserved in *e.* chains.
Rev. 14. 6. having the *e.* Gospel.
Evermore, Ps. 16. 11. pleasures for *e.*
   37. 27. do good, and dwell for *e.*
   86. 12. will glorify thy name for *e.*
   113. 2. blessed be name of Lord for *e.*
   121. 8. Lord preserve thy going out *e.*
   133. 3. the blessing, life for *e.*
John 6. 34. Lord, *e.* give us this bread.
1 Thes. 5. 16. rejoice *e.*
Heb. 7. 28. Son, who is consecrated for *e.*
Rev. 1. 18. I am alive for *e.*
Every, Gen. 6. 5. *e.* imagination of heart evil.
Deut. 4. 4. alive *e.* one of you this day.
Ps. 32. 6. for this shall *e.* one that is godly
   119. 101. refrained from *e.* evil way.
Prov. 2. 9. *e.* good path.
   14. 15. simple believeth *e.* word.
   30. 5. *e.* word of God is pure.
Eccl. 3. 1. a time to *e.* purpose.
Is. 45. 23; Rom. 14. 11. *e.* knee shall bow.
Matt. 4. 4. by *e.* word that proceedeth.
Lk. 19. 26. to *e.* one which hath.
2 Cor. 10. 5. bring into captivity *e.* thought.
Eph. 1. 21; Phil. 2. 9. far above *e.* name.
1 Tim. 4. 4. *e.* creature of God is good.
2 Tim. 2. 21. prepared to *e.* good work.
Heb. 12. 1. lay aside *e.* weight.
Jas. 1. 17. *e.* good and perfect gift.
1 John 4. 1. believe not *e.* spirit.
Evidence, Jer. 32. 10. I subscribed the *e.*
Heb. 11. 1. faith *e.* of things not seen.
Evident, Job 6. 28. it is *e.* to you if I lie.
Gal. 3. 1. Christ hath been *e.* set forth.
   3. 11. no man justified by the law is *e.*
Phil. 1. 28. an *e.* token of perdition.
Heb. 7. 14. it is *e.* our Lord sprang out of Judah.

Evil, Gen. 6. 5; 8. 21. thoughts of heart only *e*.
  37. 20, 33. an *e*. beast hath devoured him.
  47. 9. few and *e*. days of life been.
  Deut. 29. 21. Lord shall separate him to *e*.
  30. 15. set before thee death and *e*.
  31. 29. *e*. befall you in latter days.
  Job 2. 10. receive good and not *e*.
  30. 26. looked for good, then *e*. came.
  Ps. 23. 4. I will fear no *e*.
  34. 21. *e*. shall slay the wicked.
  91. 10. no *e*. shall befall thee.
  97. 10. ye that love the Lord, hate *e*.
  Prov. 12. 21. no *e*. shall happen to the just.
  15. 3. beholding the *e*. and good.
  Is. 1. 4. a seed of *e*.-doers.
  5. 20. call *e*. good, and good *e*.
  7. 15. refuse the *e*. and choose the good.
  57. 1. righteous taken from the *e*. to come.
  Jer. 17. 17. art my hope in the day of *e*.
  44. 11. set my face against you for *e*.
  Ezek. 7. 5. an *e*., an only *e*. is come.
  Jon. 3. 10; 4. 2. God repented of the *e*.
  Hab. 1. 13. purer eyes than to behold *e*.
  Matt. 5. 11. all manner of *e*. against you.
  6. 34. sufficient unto day is *e*. thereof.
  7. 11; Lk. 11. 13. if ye, being *e*.
  Matt. 27. 23; Mk. 15. 14; Lk. 23. 22. what *e*. hath he done?
  Mk. 9. 39. lightly speak *e*. of me.
  Lk. 6. 35. kind to the unthankful and *e*.
  John 3. 20. doeth *e*. hateth light.
  18. 23. if I have spoken *e*.
  Acts 23. 5. not speak *e*. of ruler.
  Rom. 7. 19. the *e*. I would not, that I do.
  12. 17. recompense to no man *e*. for *e*.
  12. 21. overcome *e*. with good.
  1 Cor. 13. 5. charity thinketh no *e*.
  Eph. 5. 16. because the days are *e*.   [for *e*.
  1 Thes. 5. 15; 1 Pet. 3. 9. let no man render *e*.
  1 Thes. 5. 22. abstain from all appearance of *e*.
  1 Tim. 6. 10. love of money root of all *e*.
  Tit. 3. 2. speak *e*. of no man.
  Jas. 3. 8. tongue an unruly *e*.
  3 John 11. follow not *e*. but good.
Exact, Neh. 5. 10. might *e*. of them.
  Ps. 89. 22. enemy not *e*. of them.
  Is. 58. 3. in fast you *e*. all labours.
  60. 17. will make *e*. righteousness.
  Lk. 3. 13. *e*. no more than is appointed.
Exalt, Ex. 15. 2. my father's God, I will *e*. him.
  1 Sam. 2. 10. shall *e*. horn of anointed.
  1 Chr. 29. 11. thou art *e*. as head above all.
  Ps. 34. 3. let us *e*. his name together.
  89. 16. in righteousness shall they be *e*.
  92. 10. my horn shalt thou *e*.
  97. 9. art *e*. far above all gods.
  108. 5. be thou *e*. above the heavens.
  Prov. 4. 8. *e*. her, and she shall promote thee.
  11. 11. by blessing of upright the city is *e*.
  14. 34. righteousness *e*. a nation.
  Is. 2. 2; Mic. 4. 1. mountain of Lord's house be *e*. among the hills.
  Is. 40. 4. every valley shall be *e*.
  52. 13. my servant shall be *e*.
  Ezek. 21. 26. *e*. him that is low.
  Matt. 11. 23; Lk. 10. 15. *e*. to heaven.
  Matt. 23. 12; Lk. 14. 11; 18. 14. *e*. himself shall be abased.
  Acts 5. 31. him hath God *e*.
  2 Cor. 12. 7. be *e*. above measure.
  Phil. 2. 9. God hath highly *e*. him.
  2 Thes. 2. 4. *e*. himself above all called God.
  1 Pet. 5. 6. may *e*. you in due time.

Exalt—*Continued.*
  Examine, Ezra 10. 16. sat down to *e*. matter.
  Ps. 26. 2. *e*. me, O Lord, prove me.
  Acts 4. 9. if we this day be *e*.
  22. 24. be *e*. by scourging.
  1 Cor. 11. 28. let a man *e*. himself.
  2 Cor. 13. 5. *e*. yourselves, prove.
Example, John 13. 15. I have given you an *e*.
  1 Cor. 10. 6. these things were our *e*.
  Phil. 3. 17. ye have us for an *e*.
  1 Tim. 4. 12. an *e*. of believers.
  Heb. 4. 11. fall after same *e*. of unbelief.
  1 Pet. 2. 21. Christ suffered, leaving an *e*.
  Jude 7. set forth for an *e*. suffering.
Exceed, Deut. 25. 3. forty stripes, and not *e*.
  Matt. 5. 20. except righteousness *e*.
  2 Cor. 3. 9. ministration *e*. in glory.
Exceeding, Gen. 15. 1. thy *e*. great reward.
  27. 34. an *e*. bitter cry.
  Num. 14. 7. land is *e*. good.
  Ps. 21. 6. *e*. glad with thy countenance.
  43. 4. God, my *e*. joy.
  119. 96. thy commandment is *e*. broad.
  Prov. 30. 24. four things are *e*. wise.
  Eccl. 7. 24. which is *e*. deep.
  Jon. 1. 16. men feared the Lord *e*.
  3. 3. an *e*. great city.
  4. 6. *e*. glad of the gourd.
  Matt. 2. 10. rejoiced with *e*. great joy.
  4. 8. an *e*. high mountain.
  5. 12. rejoice and be *e*. glad.
  19. 25. they were *e*. amazed.
  26. 38; Mk. 14. 34. my soul is *e*. sorrowful.
  Mk. 6. 26. king was *e*. sorry.
  9. 3. his raiment *e*. white.
  Lk. 23. 8. Herod was *e*. glad.
  Acts 7. 20. Moses was *e*. fair.
  26. 11. being *e*. mad against them.
  Rom. 7. 13. sin might become *e*. sinful.
  2 Cor. 4. 17. *e*. weight of glory.
  7. 4. *e*. joyful in tribulation.
  Gal. 1. 14. *e*. zealous of traditions.
  Eph. 1. 19. *e*. greatness of his power.
  2. 7. the *e*. riches of his grace.
  3. 20. able to do *e*. abundantly.
  1 Thes. 3. 10. praying *e*. that.
  2 Thes. 1. 3. your faith groweth *e*.
  1 Pet. 4. 13. be glad with *e*. joy.
  2 Pet. 1. 4. *e*. great and precious promises.
  Jude 24. present you faultless with *e*. joy.
Excel, Gen. 49. 4. unstable as water, shalt not *e*.
  Ps. 103. 20. angels that *e*. in strength.
  Prov. 31. 29. thou *e*. them all.
  Eccl. 2. 13. wisdom *e*. folly.
  2 Cor. 3. 10. the glory that *e*.
Excellency, Gen. 49. 3. *e*. of dignity.
  Ex. 15. 7. the greatness of thine *e*.
  Job 4. 21. doth not their *e*. go away.
  37. 4. thundereth with voice of his *e*.
  40. 10. deck with majesty and *e*.
  Ps. 62. 4. cast him down from his *e*.
  Is. 60. 15. I will make thee an eternal *e*.
  1 Cor. 2. 1. I came not with *e*. of speech.
  2 Cor. 4. 7. that the *e*. of the power may be of God.
  Phil. 3. 8. count all things but loss for the *e*.
Excellent, Job 37. 23. Almighty is *e*. in power.
  Ps. 8. 1, 9. how *e*. is thy name in earth.
  16. 3. *e*. in whom is all my delight.
  36. 7. how *e*. is thy loving-kindness!
  Prov. 8. 6. I will speak of *e*. things.
  12. 26. righteous more *e*. than neighbour.
  17. 27. of an *e*. spirit.

Excellent—*Continued.*
Is. 12. 5. Lord hath done *e.* things.
28. 29. *e.* in working.
Dan. 5. 12; 6. 3. *e.* spirit in Daniel.
Rom. 2. 18; Phil. 1. 10. things that are *e.*
1 Cor. 12. 31. a more *e.* way.
Heb. 1. 4. obtained a more *e.* name.
2 Pet. 1. 17. a voice from the *e.* glory. [me.

Except, Gen. 32. 26. not let go, *e.* thou bless
Deut. 32. 30. *e.* their Rock had sold them.
Ps. 127. 1. *e.* the Lord build the house.
Is. 1. 9; Rom. 9. 29. *e.* Lord had left remnant.
Amos 3. 3. can two walk, *e.* agreed?
Matt. 5. 20. *e.* your righteousness exceed that
     of the scribes.
18. 3. *e.* ye be converted.
24. 22; Mk. 13. 20. *e.* days be shortened.
Mk. 7. 3. Pharisees *e.* they wash oft.
Lk. 13. 3. *e.* ye repent, ye shall perish.
John 3. 2. do miracles *e.* God be with him?
3. 3. *e.* a man be born again.
4. 48. *e.* ye see signs and wonders.
6. 53. *e.* ye eat flesh of the Son of man.
19. 11. no power, *e.* it were given from above.
20. 25. *e.* I see print of the nails.
Acts 15. 1. *e.* ye be circumcised, ye cannot.
26. 29. as I am, *e.* these bonds.
Rom. 10. 15. how preach, *e.* they be sent?
1 Cor. 15. 36. not quickened, *e.* it die.
2 Thes. 2. 3. *e.* there come a falling away.
2 Tim. 2. 5. not crowned, *e.* he strive lawfully.

Excess, Matt. 23. 25. within are full of *e.*
Eph. 5. 18. wine wherein is *e.*
1 Pet. 4. 4. *e.* that ye run not to the same *e.*

Exchange, Gen. 47. 17. bread in *e.* for
Matt. 16. 26; Mk. 8. 37. give in *e.* for his soul.
Matt. 25. 27. put money to *e.*

Exclude, Rom. 3. 27. where is boasting? it is *e.*
Gal. 4. 17. they would *e.* you, that.

Excuse, Lk. 14. 18. they began to make *e.*
Rom. 1. 20. they are without *e.*
2. 15. thoughts accusing or *e.*
2 Cor. 12. 19. think we *e.* ourselves.

Execute, Num. 8. 11. that they may *e.* service
     of the Lord.
Deut. 33. 21. he *e.* justice of the Lord.
1 Chr. 6. 10; 24. 2; Lk. 1. 8. *e.* priest's office.
Ps. 9. 16. Lord is known by the judgment he *e.*
103. 6. Lord *e.* righteousness and judgment.
149. 7. to *e.* vengeance upon heathen.
John 5. 27. authority to *e.* judgment.
Rom. 13. 4. minister of God to *e.* wrath.
Jude 15. to *e.* judgment on all.

Exercise, Ps. 131. 1. *e.* myself in things too high.
Jer. 9. 24. *e.* loving-kindness. [minion.
Matt. 20. 25; Mk. 10. 42; Lk. 22. 25. *e.* do-
Acts 24. 16. I *e.* myself to have a conscience.
1 Tim. 4. 7. *e.* thyself to godliness.
Heb. 5. 14. senses *e.* to discern good and evil.
12. 11. fruit of righteousness unto them
     which are *e.*
2 Pet. 2. 14. heart *e.* with covetous practices.

Exhort, Acts 2. 40. with many words did he *e.*
27. 22. I *e.* you to be of good cheer.
Rom. 12. 8. he that *e.*, on *e.*
1 Tim. 6. 2. these things teach and *e.*
2 Tim. 4. 2. *e.* with all long-suffering.
Tit. 1. 9. able to *e.* and convince.
2. 15. *e.* and rebuke with authority.
Heb. 3. 13. *e.* one another daily.
13. 22. suffer the word of *e.* [perish.

Expectation, Ps. 9. 18. *e.* of poor shall not
62. 5. wait on God, my *e.* from him.
Prov. 10. 28; 11. 7. *e.* of wicked perish.

Expectation—*Continued.*
Is. 20. 5. ashamed of their *e.*
Rom. 8. 19. *e.* of creature.
Phil. 1. 20. my earnest *e.* and hope. [die.

Expedient, John 11. 50. *e.* for us that one man
16. 7. *e.* for you that I go away.
1 Cor. 6. 12; 10. 23. all things not *e.*
2 Cor. 8. 10. this is *e.* for you.
12. 1. it is not *e.* for me to glory. [me.

Experience, Gen. 30. 27. by *e.* the Lord blessed
Eccl. 1. 16. my heart had *e.* of wisdom.
Rom. 5. 4. patience worketh *e.*, and *e.* hope.

Expound, Jud. 14. 14. they could not *e.* riddle.
Mk. 4. 34. when alone, he *e.* all things.
Lk. 24. 27. he *e.* to them the scriptures.
Acts 28. 23. *e.* the kingdom of God.

Express, Heb. 1. 3. being *e.* image of person.
1 Tim. 4. 1. Spirit speaketh *e.* some.

Extend, Ps. 16. 2. my goodness *e.* not to thee.
109. 12. none to *e.* mercy.
Is. 66. 12. I will *e.* peace like river.

Extinct, Job 17. 1. my days are *e.*
Is. 43. 17. they are *e.*, they are quenched.

Extol, Ps. 30. 1; 145. 1. I will *e.* thee.
68. 4. *e.* him that rideth on heavens.
Is. 52. 13. my servant shall be *e.*
Dan. 4. 37. I *e.* the king of heaven.

Extortion, Ezek. 22. 12. thou hast gained by *e.*
Matt. 23. 25. within they are full of *e.*

Extortioner, Ps. 109. 11. let *e.* catch all he hath.
Is. 16. 4. the *e.* is at an end.
Lk. 18. 11. I am not as other men, *e.*
1 Cor. 5. 11. if any be an *e.*
6. 10. nor *e.* inherit kingdom of God.

Eye, Gen. 3. 7. *e.* of both were opened.
27. 1. his *e.* were dim.
Ex. 21. 24; Lev. 24. 20; Deut. 19. 21; Matt.
     5. 38. *e.* for *e.*
Num. 10. 31. be to us instead of *e.*
Deut. 4. 19. lest thou lift up *e.* to heaven.
16. 19. gift doth blind *e.* of wise.
32. 10. kept him as apple of his *e.*
34. 7. his *e.* was not dim.
1 Ki. 1. 20. *e.* of all Israel upon thee.
8. 29, 52; 2 Chr. 6. 20, 40. *e.* open towards
     this house.
2 Ki. 6. 17. Lord opened *e.* of young man.
2 Chr. 16. 9; Zech. 4. 10. *e.* of Lord run to
     and fro.
Job 10. 18. and no *e.* had seen me.
19. 27. mine *e.* shall behold, and not another.
29. 11. when the *e.* saw me.
29. 15. I was *e.* to the blind.
Ps. 11. 4. his *e.* try children of men.
19. 8. commandment enlightening the *e.*
33. 18. *e.* of Lord on them that fear him.
34. 15; 1 Pet. 3. 12. *e.* of Lord on the righteous.
Ps. 36. 1. no fear of God before his *e.*
94. 9. formed *e.* shall he not see?
119. 18. open mine *e.*
121. 1. lift up mine *e.* to hills.
132. 4. not give sleep to mine *e.*
141. 8. mine *e.* are unto thee, O God.
145. 15. *e.* of all wait upon thee.
Prov. 10. 26. as smoke to the *e.*
20. 12. the seeing *e.* Lord hath made.
22. 9. bountiful *e.* shall be blessed.
23. 29. who hath redness of *e.*?
27. 20. *e.* of man are never satisfied.
Eccl. 1. 8. *e.* not satisfied with seeing.
2. 14. wise man's *e.* are in his head.
11. 7. pleasant for the *e.* to behold the sun.
Is. 1. 15. I will hide mine *e.* from you.
32. 3. *e.* of them that see not be dim.

Eye—Continued.

Is. 33. 17. thine *e.* shall see the king in his beauty.

42. 7. to open the blind *e.* to bring.

52. 8. they shall see *e.* to *e.*

64. 4; 1 Cor. 2. 9. neither hath *e.* seen.

Jer. 5. 21; Ezek. 12. 2. have *e.* and see not.

Jer. 9. 1. mine *e.* a fountain of tears.

13. 17. mine *e.* shall weep sore.

14. 17. mine *e.* run down with tears.

16. 17. mine *e.* are on their ways.

24. 6. I will set mine *e.* upon them for good.

Ezek. 24. 16, 25. the desire of thine *e.*

Hab. 1. 13. of purer *e.* than to behold evil.

Matt. 6. 22; Lk. 11. 34. light of the body is

Matt. 13. 16. blessed are your *e.*   [the *e.*

18. 9. if *e.* offend thee, pluck it out.

Mk. 8. 18. having *e.*, see ye not?

Lk. 4. 20. *e.* were fastened on him.

24. 16. their *e.* were holden.

John 9. 6. anointed *e.* of blind man.

11. 37. could not this man, which opened *e.* ?

Gal. 3. 1. before whose *e.* Christ has been set.

Eph. 1. 18. *e.* of your understanding enlightened.   [him.

Heb. 4. 13. all things are opened unto *e.* of

1 John 2. 16. the lust of the *e.*

FABLES, 1 Tim. 1. 4. nor give heed to *f.*

2 Tim. 4. 4. shall be turned unto *f.*

Tit. 1. 14. not giving heed to *f.*   [devised *f.*

2 Pet. 1. 16. have not followed cunningly

Face, Gen. 3. 19. in sweat of *f.* eat bread.

16. 8. I flee from *f.* of my mistress.

32. 30. I have seen God *f.* to *f.*

Ex. 3. 6. Moses hid his *f.*

33. 11. Lord spake to Moses *f.* to *f.*

34. 29. skin of his *f.* shone.

34. 33; 2 Cor. 3. 13. put a veil on his *f.*

Lev. 19. 32. honour the *f.* of old man.

Num. 6. 25. Lord make his *f.* shine on thee.

Deut. 1. 17. not be afraid of *f.* of man.

1 Sam. 5. 3. Dagon was fallen on his *f.*

1 Ki. 19. 13. wrapped his *f.* in his mantle.

2 Ki. 4. 29. lay staff on *f.* of child.

2 Chr. 6. 42; Ps. 132. 10. turn not away the *f.* of thine anointed.

Ezra 9. 7; Dan. 9. 8. confusion of *f.*

Job 1. 11; 2. 5. curse thee to thy *f.*

13. 24; Ps. 44. 24; 88. 14. wherefore hidest thou thy *f.* ?   [ness.

Ps. 17. 15. I will behold thy *f.* in righteous-

27. 9; 69. 17; 102. 2; 143. 7. hide not thy *f.*

31. 16; 119. 135. make thy *f.* to shine.

34. 5. their *f.* were not ashamed.

84. 9. look upon *f.* of thine anointed.

89. 14. mercy and truth go before *f.*

Prov. 27. 19. in water *f.* answereth to *f.*

Eccl. 8. 1. wisdom maketh *f.* to shine.

Is. 25. 8. wipe tears from off all *f.*

53. 3. hid as it were our *f.* from him.

Jer. 2. 27. turned their back, and not *f.*

16. 17. ways not hid from my *f.*

50. 5. to Zion, with *f.* thitherward.

Dan. 10. 6. his *f.* as appearance of lightning.

Hos. 5. 5. testifieth to his *f.*

Matt. 6. 17. anoint head, and wash *f.*

11. 10; Mk. 1. 2; Lk. 7. 27. messenger before *f.*

Matt. 16. 3; Lk. 12. 56. discern *f.* of sky.

Matt. 17. 2. his *f.* did shine as sun.

18. 10. angels behold *f.* of my Father.

Lk. 2. 31. prepared before *f.* of all people.

22. 64. struck him on *f.*

Acts 2. 25. I foresaw Lord before my *f.*

Face—Continued.

1 Cor. 13. 12. then see *f.* to *f.*

2 Cor. 3. 18. we all with open *f.* beholding.

Gal. 2. 11. I withstood him to the *f.*

Jas. 1. 23. beholding natural *f.* in a glass.

Fade, Is. 1. 30. whose leaf *f.*

40. 7. grass withereth, flower *f.*

64. 6. we all *f.* as a leaf.

Jer. 8. 13. the leaf shall *f.*

Ezek. 47. 12. whose leaf shall not *f.*

Jas. 1. 11. rich man shall *f.* away.

1 Pet. 1. 4; 5. 4. inheritance that *f.* not away.

Fail, Gen. 47. 16. for your cattle, if money *f.*

Deut. 28. 32. eyes shall *f.* with longing.

Josh. 21. 45; 23. 14; 1 Ki. 8. 56. there *f.* not any good thing.

1 Sam. 17. 32. let no man's heart *f.*

1 Ki. 2. 4; 8. 25. shall not *f.* a man on throne.

17. 14. neither shall cruse of oil *f.*

Job 14. 11. as waters *f.* from the sea.

Ps. 12. 1. the faithful *f.* among men.

31. 10; 38. 10. my strength *f.* me.

77. 8. doth his promise *f.* for ever?

119. 123. mine eyes *f.* for thy salvation.

Eccl. 10. 3. wisdom *f.* him.

12. 5. desire shall *f.*

Is. 15. 6. the grass *f.*

19. 5. waters shall *f.*

32. 10. the vintage shall *f.*

38. 14. mine eyes *f.* with looking.

42. 4. not *f.* nor be discouraged.

Jer. 15. 18. as waters that *f.*

Lam. 3. 22. his compassions *f.* not.

Hab. 3. 17. labour of olive shall *f.*

Lk. 12. 33. treasure in heaven that *f.* not.

16. 17. one tittle of law to *f.*

21. 26. hearts *f.* them for fear.

22. 32. that thy faith *f.* not.

1 Cor. 13. 8. charity never *f.*

Heb. 1. 12. thy years shall not *f.*

11. 32. time would *f.* me to tell.

12. 15. lest any man *f.* of grace of God.

Fain, Job 27. 22. *f.* flee out of his hand.

Lk. 15. 16. *f.* fill belly with husks.

Faint, Gen. 25. 29. came from field, and was *f.*

Deut. 25. 18. smote when thou wast *f.*

Jud. 8. 4. *f.*, yet pursuing.

Ps. 27. 13. I had *f.*, unless I had believed.

107. 5. their soul *f.* in them.

Is. 1. 5. whole heart *f.*

40. 28. creator of earth *f.* not.

40. 29. giveth power to the *f.*

40. 30 ; Amos 8. 13. even youths shall *f.*

Is. 40. 31. walk, and not *f.*

Matt. 15. 32 ; Mk. 8. 3. lest they *f.* by the way.

Lk. 18. 1. always to pray, and not *f.*   [*f.* not.

2 Cor. 4. 1, 16. as we have received mercy, we

Gal. 6. 9. in due season shall reap, if we *f.* not.

Heb. 12. 3. wearied and *f.* in your minds.

12. 5. nor *f.* when thou art rebuked.

Fair, Gen. 6. 2. daughters of men were *f.*

Job 37. 22. *f.* weather out of the north.

Ps. 45. 2. *f.* than children of men.

Prov. 11. 22. a *f.* woman without discretion.

Cant. 1. 8 ; 5. 9 ; 6. 1. thou *f.* among women.

6. 10. *f.* as the moon.

Is. 5. 9. many houses great and *f.*

54. 11. lay stones with *f.* colours.

Jer. 12. 6. though they speak *f.* words.

Dan. 1. 15. their countenances appeared *f.*

Matt. 16. 2. it will be *f.* weather.

Acts 7. 20. Moses was exceeding *f.*

Rom. 16. 18. by *f.* speeches deceive.

Gal. 6. 12. to make *f.* shew in flesh.

Faith, Deut. 32. 20. children in whom is no *f.*
Hab. 2. 4; Rom. 1. 17; Gal. 3. 11; Heb. 10. 38.
   just shall live by *f.*
Matt. 6. 30; 8. 26; 14. 31; 16. 8; Lk. 12. 28.
   O ye of little *f.*
Matt. 8. 10; Lk. 7. 9. so great *f.*   [their *f.*
Matt. 9. 2; Mk. 2. 5; Lk. 5. 20. Jesus seeing
Matt. 9. 22; Mk. 5. 34; 10. 52; Lk. 8. 48; 17. 19.
   thy *f.* hath made thee whole.
Matt. 15. 28. great is thy *f.*
   17. 20. *f.* as a grain of mustard seed.
   21. 21. if ye have *f.,* and doubt not.
   23. 23. judgment, mercy, and *f.*
Mk. 4. 40. how is it ye have no *f.?*
   11. 22. have *f.* in God.
Lk. 7. 50. thy *f.* hath saved thee.
   8. 25. where is your *f.?*
   17. 5. Lord increase our *f.*
   18. 8. shall Son of man find *f.* on earth?
   22. 32. that thy *f.* fail not.
Acts 3. 16. the *f.* which is by him.
   6. 5; 11. 24. a man full of *f.*
   14. 9. perceiving he had *f.* to be healed.
   14. 22. exhorting to continue in the *f.*
   14. 27. opened the door of *f.*
   15. 9. purifying their hearts by *f.*
   16. 5. established in the *f.*
   20. 21. *f.* toward our Lord Jesus Christ.
   26. 18. sanctified by *f.*
Rom. 1. 5. grace for obedience to *f.* [*f.* to *f.*
   1. 17. righteousness of God revealed from
   3. 3. make *f.* of God without effect.
   3. 28 ; 5. 1; Gal. 2. 16; 3. 24. justified by *f.*
Rom. 4. 5. *f.* counted for righteousness.
   5. 2. we have access by *f.*
   10. 8. the word of *f.,* which we preach.
   10. 17. *f.* cometh by hearing.
   12. 3. the measure of *f.*
   12. 6. prophesy according to proportion of *f.*
   14. 1. weak in *f.* receive ye.
   14. 23. what is not of *f.* is sin.
1 Cor. 2. 5. your *f.* not stand in wisdom.
   13. 2. though I have all *f.*
   13. 13. now abideth *f.*
   15. 14. your *f.* is also vain.
   16. 13. stand fast in the *f.*
2 Cor. 4. 13. having the same spirit of *f.*
   5. 7. we walk by *f.,* not by sight.
   13. 5. examine whether ye be in the *f.*
Gal. 1. 23. preach the *f.* which once destroyed.
   2. 20. I live by the *f.* of Son of God.
   3. 2. by the hearing of *f.*
   3. 12. the law is not of *f.*
   3. 23. before *f.* came, we were under
   5. 6. *f.* which worketh by love.
   5. 22. fruit of the Spirit is *f.*
   6. 10. the household of *f.*
Eph. 3. 12. access by *f.*
   4. 5. one Lord, one *f.*
   4. 13. in the unity of the *f.*
   6. 16. taking shield of *f.*
Phil. 1. 27. striving for the *f.* of the Gospel.
Col. 2. 5. the stedfastness of your *f.*
1 Thes. 3. 2 ; 2 Thes. 1. 11. your work of *f.*
1 Thes. 5. 8 ; the breastplate of *f.*
2 Thes. 1. 11. fulfil work of *f.* with power.
   3. 2. all men have not *f.*
1 Tim. 1. 5 ; 2 Tim. 1. 5. *f.* unfeigned.
1 Tim. 1. 19. holding *f.* and a good conscience.
   2. 15. if they continue in *f.*
   3. 13. great boldness in the *f.*
   4. 1. some shall depart from the *f.*
   5. 8. he hath denied the *f.*
   6. 10, 21. erred from the *f.*

Faith—Continued.
1 Tim. 6. 12. fight the good fight of *f.*
2 Tim. 2. 18. overthrow *f.* of some.
   3. 8. reprobate concerning the *f.*
   4. 7. I have kept the *f.*
Tit. 1. 1. the *f.* of God's elect.
Heb. 4. 2. word, not being mixed with *f.*
   6. 1. not laying again the foundation of *f.*
   10. 22. draw near in full assurance of *f.*
   10. 23. hold fast the profession of our *f.*
   11. 1. *f.* is substance of things hoped for.
   11.6. without *f.* it is impossible to please God.
   11. 39. a good report through *f.*
   12. 2. author and finisher of our *f.*
   13. 7. whose *f.* follow.
Jas. 1. 3 ; 1 Pet. 1. 7. the trying of your *f.*
Jas. 1. 6. let him ask in *f.*
   2. 1. have not *f.* with respect of persons.
   2. 14. man say he hath *f.,* can *f.* save him?
   2. 17. *f.* without works is dead.
   2. 22. *f.* wrought with his works.
   5. 15. the prayer of *f.* shall save.
1 Pet. 1. 9. the end of your *f.*
   5. 9. resist stedfast in the *f.*
2 Pet. 1. 1. like precious *f.* with us.
   1. 5. add to your *f.* virtue.
1 John 5. 4. overcometh the world, even our *f.*
Jude 3. earnestly contend for the *f.*
   20. your most holy *f.*
Rev. 2. 13. hast not denied my *f.*
   2. 19. I know thy works, and *f.*
   13. 10. patience and *f.* of the saints.
   14. 12. that keep the *f.* of Jesus. [house.
Faithful, Num. 12. 7; Heb. 3. 2, 5. Moses *f.* in
2 Sam. 20.19. one of them that are *f.* in Israel.
Neh. 7. 2. a *f.* man, and feared God.
   9. 8. found his heart *f.* before thee.
Ps. 12. 1. the *f.* fail among men.
   89. 37. a *f.* witness in heaven.
   101. 6. the *f.* of the land.
   119. 86. thy commandments are *f.*
   119. 138. thy testimonies are very *f.*
Prov. 11. 13. a *f.* spirit concealeth.
   13. 17. a *f.* ambassador is health.
   14. 5 ; Jer. 42. 5. a *f.* witness.
Prov. 20. 6. a *f.* man, who can find?
   27. 6. *f.* are the wounds of a friend.
   28. 20. *f.* man shall abound with blessings.
Is. 1. 21, 26. *f.* city.
Matt. 24. 45 ; Lk. 12. 42. who is a *f.* and wise
Matt. 25. 21. well done, good and *f.* servant. [servant?
   25. 23 ; Lk. 19. 17. *f.* in a few things.
Lk. 16. 10. *f.* in least is *f.* also in much.
Acts 16. 15. if ye have judged me *f.*
1 Cor. 1. 9 ; 10. 13. God is *f.*
   4. 2. required in stewards that a man be *f.*
Eph. 6. 21 ; Col. 1. 7 ; 4. 7. a *f.* minister.
1 Thes. 5. 24. *f.* is he that calleth you.
2 Thes. 3. 3. Lord is *f.,* who shall stablish you.
1 Tim. 1. 15 ; 4. 9; 2 Tim. 2. 11 ; Tit. 3. 8. a *f.*
   saying.
2 Tim. 2. 13. he abideth *f.*
Heb. 2. 17. a *f.* high priest.
   3. 2. *f.* to him that appointed him.
   10. 23 ; 11. 11. he is *f.* that promised.
1 Pet. 4. 19. as unto a *f.* creator.
1 John 1. 9. he is *f.* and just to forgive.
Rev. 2. 10. be thou *f.* unto death.
   17. 14. called, and chosen, and *f.*
   21. 5; 22. 6. these words are true and *f.*
Faithfully, 2 Ki. 12. 15 ; 22. 7. they dealt *f.*
2 Chr. 34. 12. men did the work *f.*
Jer. 23. 28. let him speak my word *f.*
3 John 5. thou doest *f.* whatsoever thou doest.

Faithfulness, 1 Sam. 26. 23. Lord render to man his *f.*

Ps. 5. 9. no *f.* in their mouth.

36. 5. thy *f.* reacheth unto the clouds.

40. 10. I have declared thy *f.*

89. 8. or to thy *f.* round about thee.

92. 2. good to shew forth thy *f.* every night.

119. 90. thy *f.* is unto all generations.

143. 1. in thy *f.* answer me.

Is. 11. 5. *f.* shall be the girdle of his reins.

25. 1. thy counsels of old are *f.*

Lam. 3. 23. great is thy *f.*

Faithless, Matt. 17. 17; Mk. 9. 19; Lk. 9. 41. O *f.* generation.

John 20. 27. be not *f.* but believing.

Fall, Prov. 16. 18. haughty spirit before a *f.*

Jer. 49. 21. earth moved at noise of *f.*

Matt. 7. 27. great was the *f.* of it.   [many.

Lk. 2. 34. child set for the *f.* and rising of

Rom. 11. 12. if *f.* of them be riches of world.

Fall, Gen. 45. 24. see ye *f.* not out by the way.

1 Sam. 3. 19. let none of his words *f.* to ground.

14. 45; 2 Sam. 14. 11; 1 Ki. 1. 52; Acts 27. 34. not hair of head *f.* to ground.

2 Sam. 1. 19, 25. how are the mighty *f.*

3. 38. a great man *f.* this day.

24. 14; 1 Chr. 21. 13. let us *f.* into the hand of God.   [Lord.

2 Ki. 10. 10. shall *f.* nothing of word of the

Job 4. 13; 33. 15. deep sleep *f.* on men.

Ps. 5. 10. let them *f.* by their own counsels.

16. 6. lines *f.* in pleasant places.

37. 24. though he *f.* not utterly cast down.

56. 13; 116. 8. deliver my feet from *f.*

72. 11. kings shall *f.* down before him.

91. 7. a thousand shall *f.* at thy side.

145. 14. Lord upholdeth all that *f.*

Prov. 11. 5. wicked shall *f.* by his own wickedness.

11. 14. where no counsel is, the people *f.*

24. 16. wicked shall *f.* into mischief.

24. 17. rejoice not when thine enemy *f.*

26. 27; Eccl. 10. 8. diggeth a pit shall *f.* therein.

Eccl. 4. 10. if they *f.* one will lift up.

11. 3. where the tree *f.* there it shall be.

Is. 14. 12. how art thou *f.* from heaven !

40. 30. the young men shall utterly *f.*

Jer. 8. 4. shall they *f.* and not arise?

46. 6. they shall stumble and *f.*

49. 26; 50. 30. young men *f.* in her streets.

Ezek. 6. 7. slain shall *f.* in the midst.

Dan. 3. 5. *f.* down and worship image.

Hos. 10. 8; Lk. 23. 30; Rev. 6. 16. say to hills, *f.* on us.   [arise.

Mic. 7. 8. O mine enemy, when I *f.* I shall

Matt. 10. 29. not one sparrow *f.* to ground.

12. 11. if it *f.* into a pit on Sabbath.

15. 14; Lk. 6. 39. both *f.* into the ditch.

Matt. 15. 27. crumbs which *f.* from master's table.   [stone.

21. 44; Lk. 20. 18. whoso shall *f.* on this

Matt. 24. 29; Mk. 13. 25. stars shall *f.* from heaven.

Lk. 8. 13. in time of temptation *f.* away.

10. 18. Satan as lightning *f.* from heaven.

John 12. 24. except a corn of wheat *f.* into ground.

Rom. 14. 13. occasion to *f.* in brother's way.

1 Cor. 10. 12. standeth, take heed lest he *f.*

15. 6, 18. some are *f.* asleep.

Gal. 5. 4. ye are *f.* from grace.

1 Tim. 3. 6. *f.* into condemnation of the devil.

Fall—Continued.

1 Tim. 6. 9. rich *f.* into temptation.

Heb. 4. 11. lest any *f.* after same example.

10. 31. fearful thing to *f.* into hands of living God.

Jas. 1. 2. joy when ye *f.* into temptations.

5. 12. lest ye *f.* into condemnation.

2 Pet. 1. 10. do these things, ye shall never *f.*

3. 17. lest ye *f.* from your stedfastness.

Rev. 14. 8; 18. 2. Babylon is *f.*, is *f.*

Falling, Ps. 56. 13; 116. 8. deliver my feet from *f.*

Lk. 22. 44. great drops of blood *f.* down.

Acts 1. 18. Judas *f.* headlong.

1 Cor. 14. 25. so *f.* down, he will worship God.

2 Thes. 2. 3. except there come a *f.* away.

Jude 24. that is able to keep from *f.*

Fallow, Jer. 4. 3; Hos. 10. 12. break *f.* ground.

False, Ex. 20. 16; Deut. 5. 20; Matt. 19. 18. thou shalt not bear *f.* witness.

Ex. 23. 1. thou shalt not raise a *f.* report.

2 Ki. 9. 12. it is *f.*, tell us now.

Job 36. 4. my words shall not be *f.*

Ps. 27. 12. *f.* witnesses are risen up.

119. 104, 128. I hate every *f.* way.

120. 3. thou *f.* tongue.   [a *f.* witness

Prov. 6. 19; 12. 17; 14. 5; 19. 5; 21. 28; 25. 18.

11. 1; 20. 23. a *f.* balance.

Zech. 8. 17. love no *f.* oath.

Matt. 24. 24; Mk. 13. 22. *f.* Christs and *f.* prophets.   [Christ.

Matt. 26. 59; Mk. 14. 56. *f.* witness against

Lk. 19. 8. any thing by *f.* accusation.

Acts 6. 13. set up *f.* witnesses, who said.

1 Cor. 15. 15. we are found *f.* witnesses of God.

2 Cor. 11. 26. in perils among *f.* brethren.

2 Pet. 2. 1. there shall be *f.* teachers.

Falsehood, 2 Sam. 18. 13. should have wrought *f.*

Job 21. 34. in answers remaineth *f.*

Ps. 7. 14. he hath brought forth *f.*

144. 8, 11. right hand of *f.*

Is. 28. 15. under *f.* have we hid ourselves.

57. 4. a seed of *f.*

59. 13. words of *f.*

Hos. 7. 1. they commit *f.*

Mic. 2. 11. walking in the spirit and *f.*

Falsely, Lev. 6. 3; 19. 12; Jer. 5. 2; 7. 9; Zech. 5. 4. swear *f.*

Ps. 44. 17. nor have we dealt *f.*

Jer. 5. 31; 29. 9. prophets prophesy *f.*

Matt. 5. 11. say evil against you *f.*

Lk. 3. 14. nor accuse any *f.*

1 Tim. 6. 20. opposition of science *f.* so called.

1 Pet. 3. 16. *f.* accuse good conversation.

Fame, Num. 14. 15. have heard *f.* of thee.

Josh. 9. 9. we heard the *f.* of God.

1 Ki. 10. 1; 2 Chr. 9. 1. *f.* of Solomon.

Job 28. 22. we have heard *f.* with ears.

Is. 66. 19. isles that have not heard *f.*

Zeph. 3. 19. get them *f.* in every land.

Matt. 4. 24; Mk. 1. 28; Lk. 4. 14, 37; 5. 15. *f.* of Jesus.

Matt. 9. 26; the *f.* thereof went abroad.

14. 1. Herod heard of the *f.* of Jesus.

Familiar, Job 19. 14. my *f.* friends have forgotten me.

Ps. 41. 9. my *f.* friend lifted heel.

Is. 8. 19; 19. 3. *f.* spirits.

Jer. 20. 10. my *f.* watched for halting.

Family, Gen.12.3; 28.14. in thee all *f.* be blessed.

Deut. 29. 18. lest a *f.* turn away from God.

Ps. 68. 6. setteth the solitary in *f.*

Jer. 31. 1. God of all the *f.* of Israel.

Zech. 12. 12. every *f.* apart.

Eph. 3. 15. whole *f.* in heaven and earth.

Famine, Gen. 12. 10. *f.* was grievous in land.
41. 27. seven years' *f.*
2 Sam. 21. 1. a *f.* in days of David.
1 Ki. 8. 37; 2 Chr. 20. 9. if there be *f.*
1 Ki. 18. 2; 2 Ki. 6. 25. sore *f.* in Samaria.
2 Ki. 8. 1. the Lord hath called for a *f.*
Job 5. 20. in *f.* he shall redeem thee.
Ps. 33. 19. to keep them alive in *f.*
37. 19. in days of *f.* they shall be satisfied.
Is. 51. 19. destruction, *f.*, and sword.
Jer. 24. 10; 29. 17. I will send *f.* among them.
Lam. 5. 10. skin black, because of *f.*
Ezek. 5. 16. evil arrows of *f.*
36. 29. I will lay no *f.* upon you.
Amos 8. 11. a *f.*, not of bread.   [places.
Matt. 24. 7; Mk. 13. 8; Lk. 21. 11. *f.* in divers
Lk. 15. 14. a mighty *f.* in that land.
Famish, Gen. 41. 55. all land of Egypt was *f.*
Prov. 10. 3. Lord will not suffer righteous to *f.*
Is. 5. 13. their honourable men are *f.*
Zeph. 2. 11. he will *f.* gods of earth.
Fan, Is. 30. 24. provender winnowed with the *f.*
Jer. 15. 7. I will *f.* them with a *f.*
51. 2. send fanners that shall *f.* her.
Matt. 3. 12; Lk. 3. 17. whose *f.* is in his hand.
Far, Gen. 18. 25. that be *f.* from thee.
Deut. 12. 21; 14. 24. too *f.* from thee.
Jud. 19. 11; Mk. 6. 35; Lk. 24. 29. day *f.* spent.
1 Sam. 2. 30; 22. 15; 2 Sam. 20. 20; 23. 17. be
     it *f.* from me.
Job 5. 4. his children *f.* from safety.
11. 14; 22. 23. put iniquity *f.* away.
19. 13. he hath put my brethren *f.* from me.
34. 10. *f.* be it from God to do wickedness.
Ps. 22. 1. why so *f.* from helping me?   [me.
22. 11; 35. 22; 38. 21; 71. 12. be not *f.* from
97. 9. Lord exalted *f.* above all gods.
103. 12. as *f.* as east from west, so *f.*
Prov. 31. 10. her price is *f.* above rubies.
Eccl. 2. 13. as *f.* as light excelleth darkness.
Is. 43. 6; 60. 9. bring sons from *f.*
57. 19. peace to him that is *f.* off.
Matt. 16. 22. be it *f.* from thee, Lord.
Mk. 12. 34. not *f.* from the kingdom.
13. 34. as a man taking a *f.* journey.
Acts 17. 27. not *f.* from every one of us.
2 Cor. 4. 17. *f.* more exceeding weight of glory.
Eph. 1. 21. *f.* above all principality.
2. 13. who were *f.* off, are made nigh.
4. 10. ascended up *f.* above all heavens.
Phil. 1. 23. with Christ, which is *f.* better.
Heb. 7. 15. it is yet *f.* more evident.
Farthing, Matt. 5. 26. till hast paid the utter-
     most *f.*
10. 29. are not two sparrows sold for a *f.* ?
Mk. 12. 42. two mites, which make a *f.*
Fashion, Job 10. 8; Ps. 119. 73. thine hands
     have *f.* me.
Ps. 33. 15. he *f.* hearts alike.
139. 16. in continuance were *f.*
Is. 45. 9. shall the clay say to him that *f.* it?
Mk. 2. 12. never saw it on this *f.*
Lk. 9. 29. the *f.* of his countenance.
1 Cor. 7. 31. the *f.* of this world passeth away.
Phil. 2. 8. found in *f.* as a man.
3. 21. be *f.* like to his glorious body.
Jas. 1. 11. the grace of *f.* perisheth.
Fast, 2 Sam. 12. 23. child is dead, wherefore
     should I *f.*?
Ps. 33. 9. he commanded, and it stood *f.*
65. 6. strength setteth *f.* the mountains.
Is. 58. 4. ye *f.* for strife.
58. 6. is not this the *f.* that I have chosen?
Zech. 7. 5. did ye at all *f.* unto me?

Fast—Continued.
Matt. 6. 16. when ye *f.* be not as hypocrites.
Mk. 2. 19. can children of bridechamber *f.*?
Lk. 18. 12. I *f.* twice in the week.
Fasten, Eccl. 12. 11. as nails *f.* by masters of
     assemblies.
Is. 22. 25. nail *f.* in the sure place.
Lk. 4. 20. eyes of all were *f.* on him.
Acts 11. 6. when I had *f.* mine eyes.
Fasting, Neh. 9. 1. were assembled with *f.*
Ps. 35. 13. I humbled my soul with *f.*
69. 10. chastened my soul with *f.*
109. 24. my knees weak through *f.*
Matt. 17. 21; Mk. 9. 29. this kind goeth not
     out but by *f.*
Mk. 8. 3. send them away *f.*
1 Cor. 7. 5. give yourselves to *f.* and prayer.
2 Cor. 11. 27. in *f.* often.
Fat, Gen. 45. 18. shall eat the *f.* of the land.
Lev. 3. 16. all the *f.* is the Lord's.
Deut. 32. 15. Jeshurun waxed *f.*, and kicked.
Neh. 8. 10. eat the *f.*, and drink the sweet.
Ps. 17. 10. inclosed in their own *f.*
92. 14. shall be *f.* and flourishing.
Prov. 11. 25. liberal soul be made *f.*
13. 4. soul of diligent be made *f.*
15. 30. good report maketh the bones *f.*
Is. 25. 6. feast of *f.* things.
Father, Gen. 17. 4; Rom. 4. 17. a *f.* of many
     nations.   [children.
Ex. 20. 5; Num. 14. 18. iniquity of *f.* upon
Jud. 17. 10; 18. 19. be to me a *f.* and a priest.
2 Sam. 7. 14. I will be his *f.*, he my son.
1 Ki. 19. 4. not better than my *f.*
2 Ki. 2. 12; 13. 14. cried, my *f.*, my *f.*
6. 21. my *f.*, shall I smite them?
Ezra 7. 27. blessed be the Lord God of our *f.*
Job 29. 16. I was a *f.* to the poor.
31. 18. brought up with me as with a *f.*
38. 28. hath the rain a *f.*?
Ps. 27. 10. when my *f.* and mother forsake me.
68. 5. a *f.* of fatherless is God.
103. 13. as a *f.* pitieth his children.
Prov. 3. 12. correcteth, as *f.* the son.
4. 1. hear the instruction of a *f.*
10. 1; 15. 20. wise son maketh a glad *f.*
Is. 9. 6. name called everlasting *f.*
63. 16; 64. 8. doubtless thou art our *f.*
Jer. 31. 9. I am a *f.* to Israel.
31. 29; Ezek. 18. 2. *f.* have eaten sour grapes.
Mal. 1. 6. if I be a *f.*, where is mine honour?
2. 10. have we not all one *f.*?
Matt. 5. 16, 45. your *F.* in heaven.
6. 9; Lk. 11. 2. our *F.* which art in heaven.
Matt. 10. 37. he that loveth *f.* or mother more
     than me.
23. 9. call no man *f.* on earth.
25. 34. ye blessed of my *F.*
Mk. 13. 32. hour knoweth no man but the *F.*
14. 36; Rom. 8. 15; Gal. 4. 6. Abba, *F.*
Lk. 10. 22. who the *F.* is, but Son.
11. 11. if a son ask bread of a *f.*
15. 21. *f.*, I have sinned.
16. 27. I pray thee *f.* send him.
22. 42. *F.*, if thou be willing, remove cup.
23. 34. *F.*, forgive them.
John 1. 14. as of the only begotten of the *F.*
3. 35; 5. 20. *F.* loveth the Son.
4. 23. shall worship the *F.* in spirit.
5. 22. the *F.* judgeth no man.   [sent me.
5. 37; 8. 16; 12. 49; 14. 24. the *F.* which hath
6. 37. all the *F.* giveth me.
6. 46; 14. 9. hath seen the *F.*
10. 15. as the *F.* knoweth me.

Father—*Continued.*

John 12. 27. *F.*, save me from this hour.
13. 1. should depart unto the *F.*
14. 6. no man cometh unto the *F.* but by me.
15. 1. my *F.* is the husbandman.
16. 32. not alone, for the *F.* is with me.
17. 1. *F.*, the hour is come.
20. 17. I ascend to my *F.* and your *F.*
Rom. 4. 11. the *F.* of all that believe.
1 Cor. 8. 6. is but one God, the *F.*
2 Cor. 1. 3. *F.* of mercies, God of all comfort.
6. 18. I will be a *f.* unto you.
Gal. 1. 24. zealous of the traditions of my *f.*
4. 2. the time appointed of the *f.*
Eph. 4. 6. one God and *F.* of all.
Phil. 2. 11. to the glory of the *F.*
Col. 1. 19. it pleased the *F.* that in him.
Heb. 1. 5. I will be to him a *F.*
7. 3. without *f.*, without mother.
12. 9. the *F.* of spirits.
Jas. 1. 17. the *F.* of lights.
1 John 1. 2. life which was with the *F.*
2. 1. an advocate with the *F.*　　[stowed.
3. 1. what manner of love the *F.* hath be-
5. 7. three bear record, the *F.*, the Word, and Holy Ghost.

Fatherless, Ex. 22. 22. not afflict *f.*
Deut. 10. 8; Ps. 82. 3; Is. 1. 17. execute judgment of *f.*
Ps. 10. 14. the helper of the *f.*
109. 9. let his children be *f.*
Prov. 23. 10. the fields of the *f.*
Is. 1. 23; Jer. 5. 28. judge not *f.*
Jer. 49. 11. leave thy *f.* children.
Hos. 14. 3. in thee the *f.* findeth mercy.
Mal. 3. 5. witness against those that oppress *f.*
Jas. 1. 27. pure religion to visit *f.*　　[earth.

Fatness, Gen. 27. 39. thy dwelling be *f.* of the
Ps. 36. 8. satisfied with *f.* of thine house.
63. 5. satisfied as with marrow and *f.*
65. 11. thy paths drop *f.*
73. 7. their eyes stand out with *f.*
Is. 55. 2. let soul delight itself in *f.*
Rom. 11. 17. partakest of *f.* of olive trees.

Fault, Gen. 41. 9. I remember *f.* this day.
1 Sam. 29. 3. I found no *f.* in him.
Ps. 19. 12. cleanse me from secret *f.*
Dan. 6. 4. find no occasion or *f.* in him.
Matt. 18. 15. tell him his *f.*　　[this man.
Lk. 23. 4; John 18. 38; 19. 4. I find no *f.* in
Rom. 9. 19. why doth he yet find *f.*?
1 Cor. 6. 7. utterly a *f.* among you.
Gal. 6. 1. if a man be overtaken in a *f.*
Heb. 8. 8. finding *f.* with them.
Jas. 5. 16. confess your *f.* one to another.
1 Pet. 2. 20. if, when buffeted for your *f.*
Rev. 14. 5. without *f.* before the throne.

Faultless, Heb. 8. 7. if first covenant had been *f.*
Jude 24. able to present you *f.*　　[the keeper.

Favour, Gen. 39. 21. Joseph *f.* in the sight of
Ex. 3. 21; 11. 3; 12. 36. *f.* in sight of Egyptians.
Ps. 5. 12. with *f.* wilt thou compass him.
30. 5. in his *f.* is life.
45. 12. rich shall entreat thy *f.*
89. 17. in thy *f.* our horn exalted.
102. 13. set time to *f.* her is come.
112. 5. a good man sheweth *f.*
Prov. 13. 15. good understanding giveth *f.*
14. 35; 19. 12. the king's *f.*
31. 30. *f.* is deceitful.
Is. 60. 10. in my *f.* I had mercy.
Dan. 1. 9. brought Daniel into *f.*
Lk. 2. 52. Jesus increased in *f.*
Acts 2. 47. having *f.* with all the people.

Favourable, Jud. 21. 22. be *f.* for our sakes.
Job 33. 26. God will be *f.* unto him.
Ps. 77. 7. will Lord be *f.* no more?
85. 1. hast been *f.* to thy land.

Fear, Gen. 9. 2. the *f.* of you on every beast.
20. 11. the *f.* of God not in this place.
Ex. 15. 16. *f.* shall fall upon them.
Deut. 2. 25; 1 Chr. 14. 17. *f.* of thee on nations.
Ps. 2. 11. serve the Lord with *f.*
5. 7. in thy *f.* will I worship.
19. 9. *f.* of the Lord is clean.
34. 11. I will teach you the *f.* of the Lord.
36. 1; Rom. 3. 18. no *f.* of God before his eyes.
53. 5. in *f.*, where no *f.* was.
90. 11. to thy *f.* so is thy wrath.　　[wisdom.
111. 10; Prov. 9. 10. *f.* of Lord beginning of
Prov. 1. 7. *f.* of Lord beginning of knowledge.
1. 26. mock when *f.* cometh.
3. 25. not afraid of sudden *f.*
14. 26. in *f.* of Lord is strong confidence.
19. 23. *f.* of the Lord tendeth to life.
29. 25. *f.* of man bringeth a snare.
Is. 8. 12. neither *f.* ye their *f.*
14. 3. Lord shall give thee rest from *f.*
24. 17. *f.* and the pit are upon thee.
29. 13. their *f.* toward me is taught by men.
Jer. 30. 5. a voice of *f.*, not of peace.
32. 40. I will put my *f.* in their hearts.
Mal. 1. 6. if master, where is my *f.*?
Matt. 14. 26. disciples cried out for *f.*
28. 4. for *f.* of him keepers did shake.
Luke 21. 26. hearts failing them for *f.*
Rom. 13. 7. *f.* to whom *f.* is due.
1 Cor. 2. 3. with you in weakness and *f.*
2 Cor. 7. 11. what *f.*, what desire!
Eph. 6. 5; Phil. 2. 12. with *f.* and trembling.
Heb. 2. 15. through *f.* of death.
12. 28. with reverence and godly *f.*
1 Pet. 1. 17. pass time of sojourning in *f.*
1 John 4. 18. no *f.* in love, cast out *f.*
Jude 23. others save with *f.*

Fear, Gen. 42. 18. this do, and live, for I *f.* God.
Ex. 14. 13. *f.* not, stand still, and see.
Deut. 4. 10. that they may learn to *f.* me.
28. 58. *f.* this glorious name.
2 Ki. 17. 39. the Lord your God ye shall *f.*
1 Chr. 16. 30; Ps. 96. 9. *f.* before him, all the earth.
Job 1. 9. doth Job *f.* God for nought?
Ps. 23. 4. I will *f.* no evil, for thou.
27. 1. whom shall I *f.*?
31. 19. goodness for them that *f.* thee.
34. 9. *f.* the Lord, ye his saints.
52. 6. righteous also shall see and *f.*
72. 5. *f.* thee as long as sun endureth.
86. 11. unite my heart to *f.* thy name.
103. 11. great is his mercy to them that *f.* him.
115. 11. ye that *f.* the Lord, trust in the Lord.
118. 4. *f.* Lord say, his mercy endureth.
130. 4. forgiveness that thou mayest be *f.*
145. 19. fulfil desire of them that *f.* him.
Prov. 3. 7. *f.* the Lord, depart from evil.
28. 14. happy is the man that *f.* always.
Eccl. 3. 14. that men should *f.* before him.
5. 7. but *f.* thou God.
12. 13. *f.* God, and keep his commandments.
Is. 8. 12. neither *f.* ye their fear.
35. 4. say to them of fearful heart, *f.* not.
41. 10; 43. 5. *f.* not, I am with thee.
Jer. 5. 24. nor say they, let us *f.* the Lord.
10. 7. who would not *f.* thee?
23. 4. and they shall *f.* no more.
Dan. 6. 26. that men *f.* before God of Daniel.

Fear—*Continued.*
Mal. 4. 2. to you that *f.* my name shall sun
    of righteousness arise.
Matt. 10. 28; Lk. 12. 5. *f.* him who is able.
Matt. 21. 26; Mk. 11. 32; Lk. 20. 19. we *f.* the
    people.
Mk. 4. 41. they *f.* exceedingly.
   5. 33. woman *f.* and trembling came.
   6. 20. Herod *f.* John.
Lk. 1. 50. his mercy on them that *f.* him.
   9. 34. *f.* as they entered cloud.
   12. 32. *f.* not, little flock.
   18. 2. a judge who *f.* not God.   [man.
   19. 21. I *f.* thee, because thou art an austere
   23. 40. dost not thou *f.* God?
John 9. 22. because they *f.* the Jews.
   12. 15. *f.* not, daughter of Zion.
Acts 10. 22. one that *f.* God.
   13. 16. that *f.* God, give audience.
   13. 26. whosoever among you *f.* God.
Rom. 8. 15. spirit of bondage again to *f.*
   11. 20. be not high-minded, but *f.*   [as.
2 Cor. 12. 20. I *f.* lest I shall not find you such
1 Tim. 5. 20. rebuke, that others may *f.*
Heb. 4. 1. let us *f.*, lest a promise being
   made.
   5. 7. was heard, in that he *f.*
   13. 6. not *f.* what man can do.
1 John 4. 18. that *f.* is not perfect in love.
Rev. 2. 10. *f.* none of those things.
Fearful, Ex. 15. 11. like thee, *f.* in praises.
Ps. 139. 14. *f.* and wonderfully made.
Is. 35. 4. say to them of *f.* heart.
Matt. 8. 26; Mk. 4. 40. why are ye *f.*
Lk. 21. 11. *f.* sights in divers places.
Heb. 10. 27. *f.* looking for of judgment.
   10. 31. *f.* thing to fall into hands of God.
Fearfulness, Ps. 55. 5. *f.* and trembling are
Is. 21. 4. *f.* affrighted me.   [come.
   33. 14. *f.* surprised the hypocrites.
Feast, Num. 29. 12. ye shall keep a *f.* to Lord.
Job 1. 4. his sons *f.* in their houses.
Ps. 35. 16. hypocritical mockers in *f.*
Prov. 15. 15. merry heart continual *f.*
Eccl. 7. 2; Jer. 16. 8. the house of *f.*
Eccl. 10. 19. a *f.* is made for laughter.
Is. 1. 14. your appointed *f.* my soul hateth.
   25. 6. Lord make to all people a *f.*
Amos 8. 10. turn your *f.* into mourning.
Matt. 23. 6; Mk. 12. 39; Lk. 20. 46. uppermost
   rooms at *f.*
Matt. 26. 5; Mk. 14. 2. not on the *f.* day.
Lk. 2. 42. after the custom of the *f.*
   14. 13. when thou makest a *f.*
   23. 17. release one at the *f.*
John 6. 4. the passover, a *f.* of the Jews.
   7. 8. go ye up to this *f.*
   7. 37. that great day of the *f.*
   13. 29. buy what we need against the *f.*
Acts 18. 21. I must keep this *f.*   [leaven.
1 Cor. 5. 8. let us keep the *f.* not with old
   10. 27. that believe not, bid to *f.*
Jude 12. spots in your *f.* of charity.
Fed, Gen. 48. 15. God who *f.* me all my life.
Deut. 8. 3. he *f.* thee with manna.
Ps. 37. 3. verily thou shalt be *f.*
   81. 16. *f.* them with finest of wheat.
Is. 1. 11. I am full of fat of *f.* beasts.
Jer. 5. 7. when I *f.* them to the full.
Ezek. 34. 8. shepherds *f.* themselves, not
   flock.
Matt. 25. 37. hungered, and *f.* thee.
Lk. 16. 21. desiring to be *f.* with crumbs.
1 Cor. 3. 2. I have *f.* you with milk.

Feeble, Neh. 4. 2. what do these *f.* Jews?
Job 4. 4; Is. 35. 3; Heb. 12. 12. the *f.* knees.
Ps. 105. 37. not one *f.* person.
Prov. 30. 26. the conies a *f.* folk.
Jer. 6. 24. our hands wax *f.*
Ezek. 7. 17; 21. 7. all hands shall be *f.*
1 Thes. 5. 14. comfort the *f.* minded.
Feed, Gen. 37. 12. to *f.* their father's flock.
   46. 32. their trade to *f.* cattle.
1 Ki. 17. 4. commanded ravens to *f.* thee.
   22. 27; 2 Chr. 18. 26. *f.* him with bread and
   water of affliction.
Ps. 28. 9. *f.* them, and lift them up.
   49. 14. death shall *f.* on them.
Prov. 10. 21. lips of righteous *f.* many.
   30. 8. *f.* me with food convenient.
Is. 5. 17. lambs shall *f.* after their manner.
   11. 7. cow and bear shall *f.*
   40. 11. he shall *f.* his flock like a shepherd.
   61. 5. strangers shall *f.* your flocks.
   65. 25. the wolf and lamb shall *f.* together.
Jer. 3. 15. pastors, *f.* you with knowledge.
   6. 3. *f.* every one in his place.
Lam. 4. 5. *f.* delicately are desolate.
Hos. 12. 1. Ephraim *f.* on wind.
Zech. 11. 4. *f.* flock of the slaughter.
Matt. 6. 26. your heavenly Father *f.* them.
Lk. 12. 24. sow not, yet God *f.* them.
John 21. 15. *f.* my lambs.
Rom. 12. 20. if enemy hunger, *f.* him.
1 Pet. 5. 2. *f.* the flock of God.
Rev. 7. 17. lamb shall *f.* and lead them.
Feel, Gen. 27. 21. that I may *f.* thee.
Acts 17. 27. if haply they might *f.* after.
Feeling, Eph. 4. 19. who being past *f.*
Heb. 4. 15. touched with *f.* of our infirmities.
Feet, Gen. 49. 10. lawgiver from between his *f.*
Ex. 3. 5; Acts 7. 33. shoes off thy *f.*
Deut. 2. 28. I will pass through on my *f.*
Josh. 3. 15. *f.* of priests dipped in Jordan.
1 Sam. 2. 9. keep *f.* of his saints.
2 Sam. 22. 34; Ps. 18. 33; Hab. 3. 19. he
   maketh my *f.* like hind's *f.*
2 Sam. 22. 37; Ps. 18. 36. my *f.* did not slip.
2 Ki. 13. 21. dead man stood on his *f.*
Neh. 9. 21. their *f.* swelled not.
Job 29. 15. *f.* was I to the lame.
Ps. 8. 6; 1 Cor. 15. 27; Eph. 1. 22. all things
   under his *f.*
Ps. 22. 16. pierced my hands and *f.*
   25. 15. pluck my *f.* out of the net.
   40. 2. set my *f.* on a rock.
   56. 13; 116. 8. deliver my *f.* from falling.
   73. 2. my *f.* were almost gone.
   115. 7. *f.* have they, but walk not.
   119. 105. thy word is a lamp to my *f.*
   122. 2. our *f.* shall stand within thy gates.
Prov. 1. 16; 6. 18; Is. 59. 7. *f.* run to evil.
Prov. 4. 26. ponder the path of thy *f.*
   19. 2. he that hasteth with his *f.*
Cant. 7. 1; Is. 52. 7. how beautiful are *f.*
Is. 52. 7; Nah. 1. 15. the *f.* of him that
   bringeth good tidings.
   60. 13. place of my *f.* glorious.
Ezek. 24. 17. put shoes upon thy *f.*
Dan. 10. 6; Rev. 1. 15; 2. 18. *f.* like brass.
Nah. 1. 3. clouds are the dust of his *f.*
Matt. 7. 6. trample them under *f.*   [of *f.*
   10. 14; Mk. 6. 11; Lk. 9. 5; Acts 13. 51. dust
Matt. 18. 8. rather than having two *f.*
Lk. 1. 79. guide our *f.* into way of peace.
   7. 38. she kissed his *f.*, and anointed them.
   10. 39. Mary sat at Jesus' *f.*
   24. 39. behold my hands and my *f.*

Feet—Continued.
John 11. 2; 12. 3. wiped *f.* with her hair.
13. 5. washed disci_les' *f.*
Acts 3. 7. his *f.* received strength.
5. 9. *f.* of them that buried thy husband.
14. 8. a man impotent in his *f.*
22. 3. at *f.* of Gamaliel.
Rom. 3. 15. *f.* swift to shed blood.
10. 15. the *f.* of them that preach Gospel.
16. 20. bruise Satan under your *f.* [need.
1 Cor. 12. 21. nor head to the *f.*, I have no
Eph. 6. 15. your *f.* shod with preparation.
Heb. 12. 13. straight paths for your *f.*
Rev. 1. 17. I fell at his *f.* as dead.
22. 8. I fell at his *f.* to worship.
Feign, 1 Sam. 21. 13. David *f.* himself mad.
1 Ki. 14. 5. *f.* herself another woman.
Ps. 17. 1. prayer not out of *f.* lips.
Jer. 3. 10. turned to me *f.*, saith Lord.
Lk. 20. 20. *f.* themselves just men.
2 Pet. 2. 3. with *f.* words make merchandise.
Fell, Gen. 4. 5. his countenance *f.*
44. 14. Joseph's brethren *f.* before him.
Josh. 6. 20; Heb. 11. 30. the wall *f.* down.
1 Ki. 18. 38. fire of Lord *f.*, and consumed.
Ps. 78. 64. their priests *f.* by sword.
Dan. 4. 31. there *f.* a voice from heaven.
Jon. 1. 7. lot *f.* on Jonah. [shipped.
Matt. 2. 11. wise men *f.* down and wor-
7. 25; Lk. 6. 48. house *f.* not.
Matt. 18. 29. servant *f.* down, saying.
Lk. 5. 8. Peter *f.* down at Jesus' knees.
10. 30, 36. *f.* among thieves.
13. 4. on whom tower *f.*
15. 20. his father *f.* on his neck.
John 18. 6. went backward and *f.*
Acts 1. 26. Judas by transgression *f.*
1. 26. lot *f.* on Matthias.
7. 60. said this, he *f.* asleep.
9. 4. Saul *f.* and heard a voice.
2 Pet. 3. 4. since fathers *f.* asleep.
Fellow, Gen. 19. 9. this *f.* came in to sojourn.
Ex. 2. 13. why smitest thou thy *f.*?
1 Sam. 21. 15. this *f.* to play the madman.
2 Sam. 6. 20. as one of the vain *f.*
1 Ki. 22. 27; 2 Chr. 18. 26. put this *f.* in prison.
Ps. 45. 7; Heb. 1. 9. oil of gladness above thy *f.*
Zech. 13. 7. the man that is my *f.*
Matt. 11. 16. like children calling to their *f.*
24. 49. begin to smite his *f.* servants.
26. 61. this *f.* said, I am able to destroy.
26. 71 ; Lk. 22. 59. this *f.* was also with Jesus.
Lk. 23. 2. found this *f.* perverting nation.
John 9. 29. as for this *f.*
Acts 17. 5. lewd *f.* of the baser sort.
22. 22. away with such a *f.*
24. 5. found this man a pestilent *f.*
Eph. 2. 19. *f.* citizens with the saints.
Phil. 4. 3. *f.* labourers.
3 John 8. *f.* helpers to the truth.
Rev. 19. 10; 22. 9. thy *f.* servant.
Fellowship, Acts 2. 42. in doctrine and *f.*
1 Cor. 1. 9. called to the *f.* of his son.
10. 20. not have *f.* with devils.
2 Cor. 6. 14. what *f.* hath righteousness!
8. 4 *f.* of ministering to saints.
Gal. 2. 9. gave the right hand of *f.*
Eph. 3. 9. what is *f.* of the mystery.
5. 11. have no *f.* with works of darkness.
Phil. 1. 5. your *f.* in the Gospel.
2. 1. if there be any *f.* of the spirit.
3. 10. the *f.* of his sufferings.
1 John 1. 3. our *f.* is with the Father.
1. 7. we have *f.* one with another.

Female, Matt. 19. 4; Mk. 10. 6. made them
male and *f.*
Gal. 3. 28. in Christ neither male nor *f.*
Fervent, Acts 18. 25; Rom. 12. 11. *f.* in spirit.
2 Cor. 7. 7. your *f.* mind toward me.
Jas. 5. 16. *f.* prayer of righteous availeth.
1 Pet. 1. 22. with a pure heart *f.*
4. 8. have *f.* charity among yourselves.
2 Pet. 3. 10. melt with *f.* heat.
Few, Gen. 29. 20. they seemed but a *f.* days.
47. 9. *f.* and evil have the days of my life been.
1 Sam. 14. 6. to save by many or *f.*
Neh. 7. 4. city large, but people *f.*
Job 14. 1. man is of *f.* days.
16. 22. when a *f.* years are come.
Eccl. 5. 2. let thy words be *f.*
12. 3. grinders cease because *f.*
Matt. 7. 14. *f.* there be that find it.
9. 37; Lk. 10. 2. the labourers are *f.*
Matt. 20. 16; 22. 14. many called, *f.* chosen.
25. 21. faithful in a *f.* things.
Lk. 13. 23. are there *f.* that be saved?
Heb. 12. 10. for a *f.* days chastened us.
Rev. 2. 14, 20. a *f.* things against thee.
Field, Gen. 23. 20. *f.* and cave made sure.
Deut. 5. 21. neither shalt covet his *f.*
21. 1. if one be found slain in *f.*
Ps. 96. 12. let the *f.* be joyful.
Prov. 24. 30. the *f.* of the slothful.
Is. 5. 8. woe to them that lay *f.* to *f.*
Jer. 26. 18 ; Mic. 3. 12. plowed like a *f.*
Matt. 6. 28. consider lilies of the *f.*
13. 38. the *f.* is the world.
13. 44. treasure hid in a *f.*
27. 8; Acts 1. 19. the *f.* of blood.
John 4. 35. lift up eyes, and look on *f.*
Jas. 5. 4. labourers which reaped your *f.*
Fierce, Gen. 49. 7. their anger, for it was *f.*
Deut. 28. 50. nation of a *f.* countenance.
Dan. 8. 23. a king of *f.* countenance.
Matt. 8. 28. devils, exceeding *f.*
Lk. 23. 5. they were more *f.*
2 Tim. 3. 3. men shall be incontinent, *f.*
Jas. 3. 4. ships driven of *f.* winds.
Fiery, Num. 21. 6. Lord sent *f.* serpents.
Deut. 33. 2. a *f.* law for them.
Ps. 21. 9. make them as a *f.* oven. i
Is. 14. 29. a *f.* flying serpent.
Dan. 3. 6. a *f.* furnace.
Eph. 6. 16. able to quench *f.* darts.
Heb. 10. 27. judgment and *f.* indignation.
1 Pet. 4. 12. concerning the *f.* trial.
Fig, Gen. 3. 7. sewed *f.* leaves for aprons.
1 Ki. 4. 25 ; Mic. 4. 4. dwelt under *f.* tree.
2 Ki. 18. 31 ; Is. 36. 16. eat every one of his
f. tree.
2 Ki. 20. 7 ; Is. 38. 21. take lump of *f.*
Hab. 3. 17. although *f.* tree shall not blossom.
Matt. 7. 16; Lk. 6. 44. do men gather *f.* of
thistles.
Matt. 21. 19; Mk. 11. 13. saw *f.* tree in way.
Lk. 21. 29. behold the *f.* tree.
Jas. 3. 12. can the *f.* tree bear olive berries?
Rev. 6. 13. *f.* tree casteth untimely *f.*
Fight, Ex. 14. 14; Deut. 1. 30; 3. 22; 20. 4. Lord
f. for you.
Deut. 1. 41. we will go up and *f.*
Josh. 23. 10. Lord God that *f.* for you.
1 Sam. 4. 9. quit like men, and *f.*
17. 10. give me a man that we may *f.*
25. 28. *f.* the battles of the Lord.
Ps. 35. 1. *f.* against them that *f.* against me.
144. 1. teacheth my fingers to *f.*
John 18. 36. then would my servants *f.*

Fight—*Continued.*
Acts 5. 39; 23. 9. *f.* against God.
1 Cor. 9. 26. so *f.* I, not as one that.
2 Cor. 7. 5. without were *f.*
1 Tim. 6. 12. *f.* the good *f.* of faith.
2 Tim. 4. 7. I have fought a good *f.*
Heb. 10. 32. endured great *f.* of afflictions.
  11. 34. valiant in *f.*
Jas. 4. 1. wars and *f.* among you.

Figure, Deut. 4. 16. the similitude of any *f.*
Rom. 5. 14. *f.* of him that was to come.
Heb. 9. 9. which was a *f.* for time.
  11. 19. whence he received him in a *f.*
1 Pet. 3. 21. the like *f.* even baptism.

Fill, Gen. 1. 22. *f.* waters in the seas.
Num. 14. 21; Ps. 72. 19; Hab. 2. 14. earth *f.*
  with glory of Lord.
Ps. 81. 10. open mouth, I will *f.* it.
  104. 28. openest hand, are *f.* with good.
Prov. 1. 31. be *f.* with own devices.
  3. 10. barns be *f.* with plenty.
  14. 14. *f.* with his own ways.
  20. 17. mouth be *f.* with gravel.
Matt. 5. 6. hunger, shall be *f.*
Mk. 7. 27. let the children first be *f.* [Ghost.
Lk. 1. 15; Acts 4. 8; 9. 17; 13. 9. *f.* with Holy
Lk. 1. 53. hath *f.* hungry with good.
John 16. 6. sorrow hath *f.* your heart. [ness.
Acts 14. 17. *f.* our hearts with food and glad-
Rom. 15. 14. *f.* with all knowledge.
Eph. 1. 23. fulness of him that *f.* all in all.
  3. 19. be *f.* with fulness of God.
  5. 18. be *f.* with the Spirit.
Phil. 1. 11. *f.* with fruits of righteousness.
Col. 1. 24. *f.* up what is behind.
Rev. 15. 1. in them is *f.* up wrath of God.

Filth, Is. 4. 4. washed away the *f.* of Zion.
1 Cor. 4. 13. as the *f.* of the world. [all *f.*

Filthiness, 2 Cor. 7. 1. cleanse ourselves from
Eph. 5. 4. nor let *f.* be once named.
Jas. 1. 21. lay apart all *f.*
Rev. 17. 4. cup full of abominations and *f.*

Filthy, Job 15. 16. how much more *f.* is man?
Ps. 14. 3; 53. 3. altogether become *f.*
Is. 64. 6. all our righteousness as *f.* rags.
Zech. 3. 3. Joshua clothed with *f.* garments.
Col. 3. 8. put off *f.* communication.
1 Tim. 3. 3; Tit. 1. 7; 1 Pet. 5. 2. *f.* lucre.
2 Pet. 2. 7. Lot vexed with *f.* communication.
Jude 8. *f.* dreamers defile the flesh.
Rev. 22. 11. he that is *f.*, let him be *f.*

Finally, 2 Cor. 13. 11; Eph. 6. 10; Phil. 3. 1;
  4. 8; 2 Thes. 3. 1; 1 Pet. 3. 8. *f.* brethren.

Find, Num. 32. 23. be sure your sin will *f.* you
2 Chr. 2. 14. to *f.* out every device. [out.
Job 9. 10. things past *f.* out.
  23. 3. where I might *f.* him.
Prov. 2. 5. shalt *f.* knowledge of God.
  4. 22. my words life to those that *f.* them.
  8. 17; Jer. 29. 13. seek me early shall *f.* me.
Prov. 8. 35. whoso *f.* me, *f.* life.
  18. 22. whoso *f.* a wife, *f.* a good thing.
Eccl. 9. 10. what thy hand *f.* to do, do it.
  11. 1. shalt *f.* it after many days.
Is. 58. 13. not *f.* thine own pleasure.
Jer. 6. 16; Matt. 11. 29. *f.* rest to your souls.
Matt. 7. 7; Lk. 11. 9. seek, and ye shall *f.*
Matt. 10. 39. loseth life, shall *f.* it.
Mk. 13. 36. lest he *f.* you sleeping.
Lk. 6. 7. they might *f.* accusation.
  13. 7. seeking fruit, and *f.* none.
  15. 8. seek diligently till she *f.* it.
Rom. 7. 21. I *f.* a law that when I would do
  good.

Find—*Continued.*
Rom. 11. 33. his ways past *f.* out.
2 Tim. 1. 18. may *f.* mercy in that day.
Heb. 4. 16. *f.* grace to help.
Rev. 9. 6. seek death, and shall not *f.* it.

Fine, Job 28. 1. place for gold where they *f.* it.
Ps. 19. 10. more to be desired than *f.* gold.
  81. 16; 147. 14. the *f.* of the wheat.
Prov. 8. 19. wisdom better than *f.* gold.
  25. 12. as an ornament of *f.* gold.
Is. 13. 12. man more precious than *f.* gold.
Mk. 15. 46. Joseph bought *f.* linen.
Rev. 19. 8. granted to be arrayed in *f.* linen.

Finger, Ex. 8. 19. this is the *f.* of God. [God.
  31. 18; Deut. 9. 10. tables written with *f.* of
1 Ki. 12. 10; 2 Chr. 10. 10. little *f.* thicker.
Ps. 8. 3. thy heavens, work of thy *f.*
  144. 1. who teacheth my *f.* to fight.
Prov. 7. 3. bind them on thy *f.*
Is. 58. 9. putting forth of the *f.*
Dan. 5. 5. the *f.* of a man's hand.
Matt. 23. 4; Lk. 11. 46. not move with *f.*
Lk. 11. 20. with *f.* of God cast out.
  16. 24. the tip of his *f.*
John 8. 6. with his *f.* wrote on ground.
  20. 25. put my *f.* into print of nails.
  20. 27. reach hither thy *f.*

Finish, Gen. 2. 1. heavens and earth were *f.*
1 Chr. 28. 20. not fail till thou hast *f.*
Dan. 9. 24. *f.* transgression.
Lk. 14. 28. sufficient to *f.*
John 4. 34. to do his will, and *f.* his work.
  5. 36. works given me to *f.*
  17. 4. I have *f.* the work.
  19. 30. he said, it is *f.*
Acts 20. 24. I might *f.* my course.
Rom. 9. 28. he will *f.* the work.
2 Cor. 8. 6. *f.* in you the same grace.
Heb. 4. 3. works *f.* from foundation of world.
  12. 2. Jesus, author and *f.* of faith.
Jas. 1. 15. sin, when it is *f.*

Fire, Gen. 22. 7. behold the *f.* and the wood.
Ex. 3. 2. the bush burned with *f.*
Lev. 10. 2. *f.* from the Lord, and devoured.
  18. 21; Deut. 18. 10; 2 Ki. 17. 17; 23. 10. pass
  through *f.*
Num. 16. 46. take censer, and put *f.* therein.
Deut. 4. 11. mountain burned with *f.*
  5. 5. ye were afraid by reason of the *f.*
Jud. 6. 21. rose up *f.* out of rock.
1 Ki. 18. 24. God that answereth by *f.*
  19. 12. the Lord was not in the *f.*
1 Chr. 21. 26. Lord answered by *f.*
Ps. 39. 3. I was musing, the *f.* burned.
  46. 9. he burneth chariot in the *f.*
  74. 7. they have cast *f.* into thy sanctuary.
Prov. 6. 27. can man take *f.* in bosom?
  26. 20. where no wood is, the *f.* goeth out.
Is. 9. 19. as the fuel of the *f.*
  43. 2. walkest through *f.* not be burned.
  64. 2. when melting *f.* burneth.
  66. 15. the Lord will come with *f.*
  66. 24; Mk. 9. 44. neither their *f.* be quenched.
Jer. 20. 9. word as a *f.* in my bones.
Ezek. 36. 5; 38. 19. in the *f.* of my jealousy.
Dan. 3. 27. upon bodies, *f.* had no power.
Hos. 7. 6. it burneth as a flaming *f.*
Nah. 1. 6. fury poured out like *f.*
Zech. 2. 5. a wall of *f.* round about.
  3. 2. a brand plucked out of the *f.*
Mal. 3. 2. like a refiner's *f.*
Matt. 3. 10; 7. 19; Lk. 3. 9; John 15. 6. every
  tree that bringeth not good fruit cast into *f.*
Matt. 3. 11; Lk. 3. 16. baptise with *f.*

Fire—*Continued.*
Matt. 13. 42. cast them into furnace of *f.*
  17. 15 ; Mk. 9. 22. oft he falleth into *f.*
Matt. 18. 8 ; 25. 41 ; Mk. 9. 43. everlasting *f.*
Lk. 9. 54. wilt thou that we command *f.* ?
  12. 49. come to send *f.* on earth.
  17. 29. same day it rained *f.* and brimstone.
Acts 2. 3. cloven tongues like as of *f.* [try.
1 Cor. 3. 13. revealed by *f.*, and the *f.* shall
  3. 15. saved, yet so as by *f.*
2 Thes. 1. 8. in flaming *f.* taking vengeance.
Heb. 1. 7. his ministers a flame of *f.*
  11. 34. through faith, quenched violence of *f.*
Jas. 3. 5. great matter, little *f.* kindleth.
1 Pet. 1. 7. gold tried with *f.*
2 Pet. 3. 7. reserved unto *f.*
  3. 12. heavens being on *f.*
Jude 7. vengeance of eternal *f.*
  23. pulling them out of the *f.*
Rev. 3. 18. buy gold tried in the *f.*
  15. 2. a sea of glass mingled with *f.*
  20. 9. *f.* came down from God.
  20. 14. death and hell cast into lake of *f.*

First. Deut. 9. 18, 25. I fell before the Lord, as at the *f.* [house.
Ezra 3. 12 ; Hag. 2. 3. the glory of the *f.*
Job 15. 7. art thou the *f.* man born ?
Prov. 3. 9. honour the Lord with *f.* fruits.
  18. 17. *f.* in his own cause.
Is. 43. 27. thy *f.* father hath sinned.
Matt. 5. 24. *f.* be reconciled to thy brother.
  6. 33. seek ye *f.* the kingdom of God.
  7. 5 ; Lk. 6. 42. *f.* cast beam out of own eye.
Matt. 8. 21 ; Lk. 9. 59. *f.* to go and bury my father. [than *f.*
Matt. 12. 45. last state of that man worse
  17. 10 ; Mk. 9. 12. Elias must *f.* come.
Matt. 22. 38 ; Mk. 12.28.the *f.*commandment
Mk. 4. 28. *f.* the blade, then the ear.
  9. 35. If any desire to be *f.*, same shall be last.
  13. 10. Gospel must *f.* be published.
Lk. 11. 38. that he had not *f.* washed.
  14. 28. sitteth not down *f.*
  17. 25. but *f.* must he suffer many things.
John 1. 41. he *f.* findeth his own brother.
  5. 4. whosoever *f.* stepped in.
Acts 11. 26. called Christians *f.* at Antioch.
  26. 23. Christ *f.* that should rise from the dead.
Rom. 2. 9. of the Jew *f.*
  8. 23. the *f.* fruits of the Spirit.
  8. 29. *f.* born among many brethren.
  11. 16. if the *f.* fruit be holy.
1 Cor. 12. 28. *f.* apostles, secondarily prophets.
  15. 20, 23. Christ the *f.* fruits of them that slept.
  15. 45. the *f.* man was made a living soul.
  15. 47. the *f.* man is of the earth.
2 Cor. 8. 5. *f.* gave own selves to the Lord.
  8. 12, if there be *f.* a willing mind.
Eph. 1. 12. who *f.* trusted in Christ.
  6. 2. *f.* commandment with promise.
Col. 1. 15. *f.*-born of every creature.
1 Thes. 4. 16. dead in Christ shall rise *f.*
2 Thes. 2. 3. a falling away *f.*
1 Tim. 1. 16. in me *f.* Christ might shew.
  5. 4. learn *f.* to shew piety at home.
2 Tim. 2. 6. husbandman must be *f.* partaker.
Tit. 3. 10. after *f.* and second admonition.
Heb. 5. 12. which be the *f.* principles.
  7. 27. offer *f.* for his own sins.
  10. 9. he taketh away the *f.*
Jas. 3. 17. wisdom from above is *f.* pure.
1 Pet. 4. 17. if judgment *f.* begin at us.

First—*Continued.*
1 John 4. 19. because he *f.* loved us.
Jude 6. angels who kept not *f.* estate.
Rev. 2. 4. thou has left thy *f.* love.
  20. 5. this is the *f.* resurrection.
  21. 1. *f.* heaven and *f.* earth passed away.

Fish. Gen. 1. 26; Ps. 8. 8. dominion over *f.* of sea.
Deut. 4. 18. likeness of any *f.* in waters.
Eccl. 9. 12. *f.* taken in an evil net.
Hab. 1. 14. makest men as *f.* of the sea.
Matt. 7. 10. if he ask a *f.* ?
  14. 17 ; Mk. 6. 38 ; Lk. 9. 13 ; John 6. 9. five loaves and two *f.*
Matt. 17. 27. take up the *f.* that first cometh.
Lk. 24. 42. gave him piece broiled *f.*
John 21. 9. they saw *f.* laid.
1 Cor. 15. 39. one flesh of beasts, another of *f.*

Fishers. Jer. 16. 16. *f.*, and they shall fish them.
Matt. 4. 19 ; Mk. 1. 17. make you *f.* of men.
John 21. 7. girt *f.* coat to him.

Fit. Lev. 16. 21. away by hand of a *f.* man.
Job. 34. 18. is it *f.* to say to a king ?
Lk. 9. 62. is *f.* for kingdom of God.
  14. 35. not *f.* for land or dunghill.
Acts 22. 22. it is not *f.* that he should live.
Rom. 9. 22. vessels of wrath *f.* to destruction.
Col. 3. 18. submit, as it is *f.* in the Lord.

Fitly. Prov. 25. 11. a word *f.* spoken, apples of gold.
Eph. 2. 21. all the building *f.* framed.
  4. 16. whole body *f.* joined. [sword.

Flame. Gen. 3. 24. at Garden of Eden a *f.*
Ex. 3. 2 ; Acts 7. 30. angel in *f.* of fire.
Jud. 13. 20. angel ascended in *f.*
Job. 41. 21. a *f.* goeth out of his mouth.
Ps. 29. 7. voice of Lord divideth *f.* of fire.
Is. 5. 24. as the *f.* consumeth chaff.
  29. 6. the *f.* of devouring fire.
  43. 2. neither shall *f.* kindle.
  66. 15. rebuke with *f.* of fire.
Ezek. 20. 47. the *f.* shall not be quenched.
Joel 2. 3. behind them a *f.* burneth.
Lk. 16. 24. tormented in this *f.*
Heb. 1. 7. who maketh ministers as *f.* of fire.
Rev. 1. 14 ; 2. 18 ; 19. 12. eyes as *f.* of fire.

Flatter. John 17. 5. that speaketh *f.* to friends.
  32. 21, 22. give *f.* titles.
Ps. 5. 9. they *f.* with their tongue.
  12. 2. with *f.* lips and double heart.
  36. 2. he *f.* himself in his own eyes.
Prov. 20. 19. meddle not with him that *f.*
  26. 28. a *f.* mouth worketh ruin.
  29. 5. man that *f.* spreadeth a net.
1 Thes. 2. 5. neither used we *f.* words.

Flee. Gen. 19. 20. this city is near to *f.* unto.
Lev. 26. 17, 36. shall *f.* when none pursueth.
Num. 10. 35 ; Ps. 68. 1. that hate thee, *f.* before thee.
Neh. 6. 11. should such a man as I *f.* ?
Job 14. 2. he *f.* as a shadow.
  27, 22. would fain *f.* out of his hand.
Ps. 11. 1. how say ye to my soul, *f.*
  139. 7. whether shall I *f.* from presence ?
Prov. 28. 1. the wicked *f.* when no man pursueth
Cant. 2. 17 ; 4. 6. till shadows *f.* away.
Is. 35. 10 ; 51. 11. sighing shall *f.* away.
Amos 5. 19. as if a man did *f.* from a lion.
Matt. 3. 7 ; Lk. 3. 7. to *f.* from wrath to come.
Matt. 10. 23, when persecuted in one city, *f.* to another.
  24. 16; Mk. 13. 14; Lk. 21. 21. *f.* to mountains.
John. 10. 5. stranger not follow, but *f.* from him.

Flee—*Continued.*
John 10. 13. the hireling *f.*
1 Tim. 6. 11. *f.* these things.
2 Tim. 2. 22. *f.* youthful lusts.
Jas. 4. 7. resist the devil, he will *f.*
Rev. 9. 6. death shall *f.* from them.

Flesh, Gen. 2. 24; Matt. 19. 5; Mk. 10. 8; 1 Cor.
   6. 16; Eph. 5. 31. one *f.*
Gen. 6. 12. all *f.* had corrupted his way.
6. 13. end of all *f.* is come.
7. 21. all *f.* died that moved.
Lev. 17. 14. life of all *f.* is the blood.
19. 28. not make cuttings in your *f.*
Num. 16. 22; 27. 16. God of spirits of all *f.*
1 Ki. 17. 6. ravens brought bread and *f.*
2 Chr. 32. 8. with him is an arm of *f.*
Neh. 5. 5. our *f.* is as *f.* of our brethren.
Job 10. 11. clothed me with skin and *f.*
19 26. in my *f.* shall I see God.
Ps. 16. 9; Acts 2. 26. my *f.* shall rest in hope.
Ps. 65. 2. to thee shall all *f.* come.
Prov. 4. 22. my sayings health to *f.*
11. 17. the cruel troubleth his own *f.*
Eccl. 12. 12. much study is weariness of *t.*
Is. 40. 6; 1 Pet. 1. 24. all *f.* is grass.
Ezek. 11. 19; 36. 26. a heart of *f.*
Joel 2. 28; Acts 2. 17. pour Spirit on all *f.*
Matt. 16. 17. *f.* and blood hath not revealed it.
24. 22; Mk. 13. 20. there should no *f.* be
   saved.   [weak,
Matt. 26. 41; Mk. 14. 38. Spirit willing, *f.*
Lk. 24. 39. Spirit hath not *f.* and bones.
John 1. 14. the Word was made *f.*
6. 52. can this man give us his *f.?*
6 63. the *f.* profiteth nothing.
17. 2. power over all *f.*   [ing to *f.*
Acts 2. 30; Rom. 1. 3. seed of David accord-
Rom. 3. 20. shall no *f.* be justified.
8 3 God sending Son in likeness of sinful *f.*
8. 9. not in the *f.*, but in the Spirit.
9 5 of whom as concerning the *f.* Christ
   came.
13. 14. make not provision for the *f.*
1 Cor. 1. 29. that no *f.* should glory.
15. 50. *f.* and blood cannot inherit kingdom.
2 Cor. 4. 11. life of Jesus be manifest in *f.*
12. 7. a thorn in the *f.*
Gal. 1. 16. I conferred not with *f.* and blood.
2. 16. works of law no *f.* be justified.
2. 20. life I now live in the *f.*
5. 17. the *f.* lusteth against the Spirit.
Eph. 2. 3. lusts of *f.*, desires of *f.*
Phil. 3. 3. no confidence in the *f.*   [blood.
Heb. 2. 14. children are partakers of *f.* and
9. 13. to the purifying of the *f.*
1 Pet. 4. 1. Christ hath suffered in the *f.*
1 John 4. 3; 2 Jonn 7. confess not that Christ
   is come in *f.*

Fleshly, 2 Cor. 1. 12. not with *f.* wisdom.
3. 3. in *f.* tables of the heart.
Col. 2. 18. puffed up by his *f.* mind.
1 Pet. 2. 11. abstain from *f.* lusts.

Flock, Is. 40. 11. he shall feed *f.* like a shepherd.
Jer. 13. 20. where is the *f.*, thy beautiful *f.*
Ezek. 24. 5. take the choice of the *f.*
34. 12. as a shepherd seeketh out his *f.*
34. 31. the *f.* of my pasture, are men.
Hab. 3. 17. though the *f.* shall be cut off.
Zech. 11. 7. the poor of the *f.*
Matt. 26. 31. sheep of *f.* shall be scattered.
Lk. 12. 32. fear not, little *f.*
Acts 20. 28. take heed to all the *f.*
1 Pet. 5. 2. feed the *f.* of God.
5. 3. being ensamples to the *f.*

Flood, Gen. 6. 17. even I, bring a *f.* of waters.
Josh. 24. 2. on other side of the *f.*
Job 22. 16. foundation overflown with *f.*
28. 11. he bindeth *f.* from overflowing.
Ps. 29. 10. Lord sitteth upon the *f.*
32. 6. in *f.* of great waters.
66. 6. they went through *f.* on foot.
90. 5. carriest them away as with a *f.*
Cant. 8. 7. neither can *f.* drown love.
Is. 44. 3. I will pour *f.* on dry ground.
59. 19. enemy come in like a *f.*
Matt. 7. 25. the *f.* came, and the winds blew.
24. 38. in days before the *f.*
24. 39; Lk. 17. 27. knew not till *f.* came.
2 Pet. 2. 5. bringing in *f.* on world of ungodly.

Floor, 2 Sam. 24. 21. to buy the threshing-*f.* of
   thee.
1 Ki. 6. 30. overlaid *f.* of house with gold.
Hos. 9. 1. loved a reward on every corn-*f.*
Mic. 4. 12. gather as sheaves into the *f.*
Matt. 3. 12; Lk. 3. 17. purge his *f.*

Flourish, Ps. 72. 7. in his days shall the
   righteous *f.*
90. 6. in the morning it *f.*
92. 12. righteous shall *f.* like the palm tree.
92. 13. they shall *f.* in courts of our God.
103. 15. as flower, so he *f.*
132. 18. upon himself shall crown *f.*
Prov. 11. 28. righteous shall *f.* as branch.
14. 11. tabernacle of upright shall *f.*
Eccl. 12. 5. when the almond tree shall *f.*
Is. 17. 11. in morning thou shalt make seed *f.*
Ezek. 17. 24. have made dry tree to *f.*
Phil. 4. 10. your care of me hath *f.* again.

Flow, Ps. 147. 18. wind to blow, and waters *f.*
Cant. 4. 16. that the spices may *f.* out.
Is. 2. 2. all nations shall *f.* unto it.
48. 21. caused waters to *f.* out of rock.
60. 5. shalt see, and *f.* together.   [Lord.
Jer. 31. 12. shall *f.* to the goodness of the
Mic. 4. 1. people shall *f.* to mountain of Lord.
John 7. 38. shall *f.* living water.

Flower, 1 Sam. 2. 33. shall die in *f.* of age.
Job 14. 2. cometh forth as a *f.*
Cant. 2. 12. the *f.* appear on the earth.
Is. 28. 1, 4. glorious beauty is a fading *f.*
40. 6. as the *f.* of the field.
40. 7; Nah. 1. 4; Jas. 1. 10; 1 Pet. 1. 24. *f.* fadeth.

Fly, Job 5. 7. as sparks *f.* upward.
Ps. 55. 6. then would I *f.* away.
90. 10. soon cut off, and we *f.* away.
Prov. 23. 5. riches *f.* away.
Is. 60. 8. *f.* as a cloud.
Hab. 1. 8. they shall *f.* as the eagle.
Rev. 14. 6. angel *f.* in midst of heaven.
19. 17. fowls that *f.* in midst of heaven.

Fold, Is. 13. 20. shepherds make their *f.*
Hab. 3. 17. flock cut off from the *f.*
John 10. 16. one *f.*, and one shepherd.

Follow, Ex. 23. 2. shalt not *f.* multitude to do
   evil.
Num. 14. 24. hath *f.* me fully.
32. 12; Deut. 1. 36. wholly *f.* Lord.
Ps. 23. 6. goodness and mercy shall *f.* me.
63. 8. my soul *f.* hard after thee.
Is. 5. 11. that they may *f.* strong drink.
Hos. 6. 3. if we *f.* on to know the Lord.
Matt. 4. 19; 8. 22; 9. 9; 16. 24; 19. 21; Mk
2. 14; 8. 34; 10. 21; Lk. 5. 27; 9. 23; John
1. 43; 21. 22. Jesus said, *f.* me.   [thee.
Matt. 8. 19; Lk. 9. 57, 61. Master, I will *f.*
Mk. 10. 28; Lk. 18. 28. we left all, and *f.* thee.
Mk. 16. 17. signs *f.* them that believe.
Lk. 22. 54. Peter *f.* afar off.

Follow—*Continued.*

John 10. 27. sheep hear my voice, and *f.* me.
13. 37. Lord, why cannot I *f.* thee?
Rom. 14. 19. *f.* things that make for peace.
1 Cor. 10. 4. drank of rock that *f.* them.
14. 1. *f.* after charity.
Phil. 3. 12. I *f.* after, if that I may.
1 Thes. 5. 15. *f.* that which is good.
1 Tim. 5. 24. some men they *f.* after.
6. 11 ; 2 Tim. 2. 22. *f.* righteousness.
Heb. 12. 14. *f.* peace with all men.
13. 7. whose faith *f.* considering end.
1 Pet. 1. 11. testified glory that should *f.*
2. 21. example, that ye should *f.* his steps.
2 Pet. 1. 16. not *f.* cunningly devised fables.
2. 2. shall *f.* pernicious ways.
3 John 11. *f.* not that which is evil.
Rev. 14. 4. they that *f.* the Lamb.
14. 13. and their works do *f.* them.

Follower, Eph. 5. 1. be ye *f.* of God, as dear children.
1 Thes. 1. 6. *f.* of us and of the Lord.
Heb. 6. 12. *f.* of them who through faith.
1 Pet. 3. 13. if ye be *f.* of that which is good.

Folly, Josh. 7. 15. wrought *f.* in Israel.
1 Sam. 25. 25. and *f.* is with him.
Job 4. 18. his angels he charged with *f.*
24. 12. God layeth not *f.* to them.
42. 8. lest I deal with you after *f.*
Ps. 49. 13. this their way is their *f.*
85. 8. let them not turn again to *f.*
Prov. 5. 23. in his *f.* he shall go astray.
13. 16. a fool layeth open his *f.*
14. 8. the *f.* of fools is deceit.
16. 22. instruction of fools is *f.*
26. 4. answer not a fool according to his *f.*
Eccl. 1. 17. to know wisdom and *f.*
2. 13. wisdom excelleth *f.*
7. 25. the wickedness of *f.*
10. 6. *f.* is set in great dignity.
Is. 9. 17. every mouth speaketh *f.*
2 Cor. 11. 1. bear with me a little in my *f.*
2 Tim. 3. 9. their *f.* shall be manifest.

Food, Gen. 3. 6. tree good for *f.*
Deut. 10. 18. in giving stranger *f.*
Job 23. 12. esteemed his words more than *f.*
38. 41. who provideth for raven *f.* ?
Ps. 78. 25. man did eat angels' *f.*
104. 14. bring forth *f.* out of the earth.
136. 25. giveth *f.* to all flesh.
Prov. 30. 8. feed me with *f.* convenient.
Ezek. 48. 18. increase thereof be for *f.*
Acts 14. 17. filling our hearts with *f.*
2 Cor. 9. 10. minister bread for your *f.*
1 Tim. 6. 8. having *f.* and raiment.
Jas. 2. 15. destitute of daily *f.*

Fool, 1 Sam. 26. 21. I have played the *f.*
2 Sam. 3. 33. died Abner as a *f.* dieth?
Ps. 14. 1; 53. 1. *f.* said in his heart.
92. 6. neither doth *f.* understand this.
Prov. 1. 7. *f.* despise wisdom.
10. 8, 10. a prating *f.* shall fall.
10. 21. *f.* die for want of wisdom.
11. 29. the *f.* shall be servant to the wise.
12. 15. way of *f.* right in own eyes.
13. 20. companion of *f.* shall be destroyed.
14. 9. *f.* make a mock of sin.
15. 5. a *f.* despiseth his father's instruction.
16. 22. the instruction of *f.* is folly.
17. 28. a *f.*, when he holdeth his peace, is counted wise.
18. 2. a *f.* hath no delight in understanding.
20. 3. every *f.* will be meddling.
29. 11. a *f.* uttereth all his mind.

Fool—*Continued.*

Eccl. 2. 14. *f.* walketh in darkness.
2. 16. no remembrance of wise more than *f.*
5. 3. a *f.* voice known by multitude of words.
7. 4. heart of *f.* in house of mirth.
Is. 35. 8. wayfaring men, though *f.*
Jer. 17. 11. at his end he shall be a *f.*
Matt. 5. 22. whoso shall say, thou *f.*
23. 17; Lk. 11. 40. ye *f.* and blind.
Lk. 12. 20. thou *f.*, this night.
24. 25. O *f.*, and slow of heart.
1 Cor. 3. 18. let him become a *f.*
15. 36. thou *f.*, that thou sowest.
2 Cor. 11. 16. let no man think me a *f.*
12. 11. I am become a *f.* in glorying.
Eph. 5. 15. walk not as *f.*, but as wise.

Foolish, Deut. 32. 6. O *f.* people.
2 Sam. 24. 10 ; 1 Chr. 21. 8. I have done very *f.*
Job 1. 22. nor charged God *f.*
2. 10. as one of the *f.* women.
5. 3. I have seen the *f.* taking root
Ps. 5. 5. *f.* not stand in thy sight.
73. 3. I was envious at the *f.*
Prov. 9. 6. forsake the *f.*, and live.
17. 25; 19. 13. a *f.* son is grief.
Eccl. 7. 17. neither be thou *f.*
Jer. 4. 22. my people are *f.*
Matt. 7. 26. be likened unto a *f.* man.
25. 2. five were wise, and five *f.*
Rom. 1. 21. their *f.* heart was darkened.
2. 20. an instructor of the *f.*
1 Cor. 1. 20. made *f.* wisdom of this world.
Gal. 3. 1. O *f.* Galatians.
Eph. 5. 4. nor *f.* talking.
2 Tim. 2. 23 ; Tit. 3. 9. *f.* questions avoid.
Tit. 3. 3. we were sometimes *f.*

Foolishness, 2 Sam. 15. 31. counsel into *f.*
Ps. 69. 5. O God, thou knowest my *f.*
Prov. 22. 15. *f.* is bound in heart of child.
24. 9. thought of *f.* is sin.
Eccl. 10. 13. the beginning of words is *f.*
1 Cor. 1. 18. to them that perish *f.*
1. 21. the *f.* of preaching.
1. 23. Christ crucified, to Greeks *f.*
1. 25. the *f.* of God is wiser than men.
2. 14. things of Spirit are *f.* to him.
3. 19. wisdom of world *f.* with God.

Foot, Gen. 41. 44. without thee no man lift *f.*
Deut. 8. 4. nor did thy *f.* swell.
29. 5. shoe is not waxen old on *f.*
Ps. 26. 12. my *f.* standeth in an even place.
38. 16. when my *f.* slippeth.
66. 6. went through the flood on *f.*
91. 12; Matt. 4. 6; Lk. 4. 11. dash *f.* against a stone.
Ps. 121. 3. not suffer *f.* to be moved.
Prov. 3. 23. thy *f.* shall not stumble.
4. 27. remove thy *f.* from evil.
25. 17. withdraw *f.* from neighbour's house.
Eccl. 5. 1. keep thy *f.* when thou goest.
Is. 1. 6. from sole of *f.* to head no soundness.
Matt. 5. 13. salt trodden under *f.*
14. 13. people followed on *f.*
18. 8; Mk. 9. 45. if thy *f.* offend thee.
John 11. 44. dead, bound hand and *f.*
1 Cor. 12. 15. if the *f.* say, because I am not.
Heb. 10. 29. trodden under *f.* the Son of God.

Forbear, 2 Chr. 35. 21. *f.* meddling with God.
Neh. 9. 30. many years didst thou *f.* them.
Job 16. 6. though I *f.*, what am I eased?
Ezek. 2. 5 ; 3. 11. whether hear or *f.*
1 Cor. 9. 6. power to *f.* working.
Eph. 4. 2; Col. 3. 13. *f.* one another in love.
1 Thes. 3. 1. we could no longer *f.*

58

Forbid, Num. 11. 28. Joshua said *f.* them.
  Mk. 9. 39; Lk. 9. 50. *f.* him not.
  Mk. 10. 14; Lk. 18. 16. suffer little children
    and *f.* them not.
  Lk. 6. 29. *f.* not to take coat.
  23. 2. *f.* to give tribute.
  Acts 10. 47. can any *f.* water?
  1 Cor. 14. 39. *f.* not to speak with tongues.
  1 Thes. 2. 16. *f.* us to speak to Gentiles.
Force, Deut. 34. 7. nor natural *f.* abated.
  Ezra 4. 23. made them cease by *f.*
  Matt. 11. 12. the violent take it by *f.* [by *f.*
  John 6. 15. perceived they would take him
  Heb. 9. 17. a testament is of *f.* after. [of *f.*
  23. 2. *f.* to give tribute.
Forefathers, Jer. 11. 10. turned to iniquities
  2 Tim. 1. 3. whom I serve from my *f.*
Forehead, Ex. 28. 38. it shall always be on his *f.*
  1 Sam. 17. 49. stone sunk in his *f.*
  Ezek. 3. 9. as adamant I made thy *f.*
  16. 12. put jewel on thy *f.*
  Rev. 7. 3; 9. 4. sealed in their *f.*
  22. 4. his name shall be in their *f.*
Foreigner, Ex. 12. 45. a *f.* not eat thereof.
  Deut. 15. 3. of a *f.* exact it again.
  Eph. 2. 19. ye are no more *f.*
Foreknow, Rom. 8. 29. whom he did *f.*, he also.
  11. 2. not cast away people he *f.*
  1 Pet. 1. 2. elect according to *f.* of God.
Foreordained, 1 Pet. 1. 20. who verily was *f.*
Forerunner, Heb. 6. 20. whither *f.* is for us
  entered.   [evil.
Foresee, Prov. 22. 3; 27. 12. prudent man *f.* the
  Gal. 3. 8. the scripture *f.* that God.
Forest, Ps. 50. 10. every beast of *f.* is mine.
  104. 20. beasts of *f.* do creep forth.
  Is. 29. 17; 32. 15. field esteemed as *f.*
  44. 23. break forth into singing, O *f.*
  Jer. 5. 6. lion out of *f.* shall slay them.
  21. 14. will kindle a fire in the *f.*
  26. 18; Mic. 3. 12. high places of the *f.*
  Jer. 46. 23. they shall cut down her *f.*
  Amos 3. 4. will a lion roar in the *f.*?
Forewarn, Lk. 12. 5. will *f.* whom ye shall fear.
  1 Thes. 4. 6. as we also have *f.* you.
Forgat, Jud. 3. 7. children of Israel *f.* Lord.
  Ps. 78. 11. they *f.* his works.
  106. 21. *f.* God their Saviour.
  Lam. 3. 17. I *f.* prosperity.
Forgave, Sam. 32. 5. *f.* iniquity of my sin.
  78. 38. he *f.* their iniquity.
  Matt. 18. 27. *f.* him the debt.
  Lk. 7. 42. he frankly *f.* them both.   [I it.
  2 Cor. 2. 10. if I *f.* anything, for your sakes *f.*
  Col. 3. 13. as Christ *f.* you, so do ye.   [seen.
Forget, Deut. 4. 9. lest thou *f.* things eyes have
  6. 12; 8. 11. beware lest thou *f.* the Lord.
  2 Ki. 17. 38. covenant ye shall not *f.*
  Job 8. 13. so are the paths of all that *f.* God.
  Ps. 9. 17. all nations that *f.* God.
  10. 12. O Lord, *f.* not the humble.
  13. 1. how long wilt thou *f.* me?
  50. 22. consider, ye that *f.* God.
  74. 19. *f.* not congregation of thy poor.
  78. 7. that they might not *f.* works of God.
  102. 4. I *f.* to eat my bread.
  103. 2. *f.* not all his benefits.
  137. 5. if I *f.* thee, O Jerusalem.
  Prov. 2. 17. *f.* the covenant of her God.
  3. 1. *f.* not my law.
  31. 5. lest they drink, and *f.* law.
  Is. 49. 15. can a woman *f.* child?
  51. 13. *f.* Lord thy Maker.
  Jer. 2. 32. can a maid *f.* her ornaments?
  23. 27. cause my people to *f.* my name.

Forget—*Continued.*
  Lam. 5. 20. why dost *f.* us for ever?
  Phil. 3. 13. *f.* those things which are behind.
  Heb. 6. 10. God not unrighteous to *f.*
  13. 16. to communicate *f.* not.
  Jas. 1. 24. *f.* what manner of man.
Forgive, Ex. 32. 32. if thou wilt *f.* their sin.
  34. 7; Num. 14. 18. *f.* iniquity and trans-
    gression.
  1 Ki. 8. 30; 2 Chr. 6. 21. hearest, *f.*
  2 Chr. 7. 14. then will I hear, and *f.*
  Ps. 25. 18. *f.* all my sins.
  32. 1; Rom. 4. 7. whose transgression is *f.*
  Ps. 86. 5. good and ready to *f.*
  103. 3. who *f.* all thine iniquities.
  Jer. 31. 34. I will *f.* their iniquity.
  Dan. 9. 19. O Lord, hear, O Lord, *f.*
  Matt. 6. 12; Lk. 11. 4. *f.* us, as we *f.*
  Matt. 9. 6; Mk. 2. 10; Lk. 5. 24. power to *f.* sins.
  Matt. 18. 35. if ye from your hearts *f.* not.
  Mk. 2. 7; Lk. 5. 21. who can *f.* sins?
  Mk. 11. 25. *f.* that your Father may *f.*
  Lk. 6. 37. *f.*, and ye shall be *f.*
  7. 49. who is this *f.* sins also?
  17. 3. if brother repent, *f.* him.
  23. 34. Father *f.* them, they know not.
  2 Cor. 2. 7. ye ought rather to *f.*
  2. 10. to whom ye *f.* I *f.* also.
  Eph. 4. 32. as God hath *f.* you.
  Col. 2. 13. quickened, having *f.* all trespasses.
  1 John 1. 9. faithful and just to *f.*
Forgiveness, Ps. 130. 4. *f.* with thee, that thou
  mayest be feared.
  Dan. 9. 9. to the Lord our God belong *f.*
  Mk. 3. 29. hath never *f.*
  Acts 5. 31. exalted to give *f.*   [sins.
  13. 38. through this man is preached *f.* of
  Eph. 1. 7; Col. 1. 14. in whom we have *f.*
Forgotten, Deut. 32. 18. *f.* God that formed
  thee.
  Job 19. 14. my familiar friends have *f.* me.
  Ps. 9. 18. needy not always be *f.*
  10. 11. said in heart, God hath *f.*
  31. 12. I am *f.* as a dead man.
  42. 9. why hast thou *f.* me?
  44. 20. if we have *f.* name of our God.
  77. 9. hath God *f.* to be gracious?
  119. 61. I have not *f.* thy law.
  Eccl. 2. 16. in days to come all *f.*
  9. 5. memory of them is *f.*
  Is. 17. 10. *f.* the God of thy salvation.
  49. 14. Zion said, Lord hath *f.* me.
  65. 16. the former troubles are *f.*
  Jer. 2. 32; 13. 25; 18. 15. my people have *f.*
  3. 21. have *f.* the Lord their God.
  30. 14. all thy lovers have *f.* thee.
  50. 6. have *f.* their resting-place.
  Ezek. 22. 12; 23. 35. thou hast *f.* me.
  Hos. 8. 14. Israel hath *f.* his Maker.
  Matt. 16. 5; Mk. 8. 14. *f.* to take bread.
  Lk. 12. 6. not one *f.* before God.
  Heb. 12. 5. ye have *f.* the exhortation.
  2 Pet. 1. 9. *f.* that he was purged.
Form, Gen. 1. 2. the earth was without *f.*
  1 Sam. 28. 14. what *f.* is he of?
  Job 4. 16. I could not discern the *f.*
  Is. 52. 14. his *f.* more than sons of men.
  53. 2. he hath no *f.* nor comeliness.
  Ezek. 10. 8. the *f.* of a man's hand.
  43. 11. shew them *f.* of the house.
  Dan. 3. 19. *f.* of visage changed.
  3. 25. *f.* of fourth like Son of God.
  Mk. 16. 12. he appeared in another *f.*
  Rom. 2. 20. hast *f.* of knowledge.

Form—*Continued.*
Rom. 6. 17. obeyed that *f.* of doctrine.
Phil. 2. 6. being in *f.* of God.
2 Tim. 1. 13. *f.* of sound words.
   3. 5. having a *f.* of godliness.
Formed, Gen. 2. 7. God *f.* man of the dust.
Deut. 32. 18. forgotten God that *f.* thee.
2 Ki. 19. 25; Is. 37. 26. that I have *f.* it.
Job 26. 13. his hand *f.* crooked serpent.
   33. 6. I also am *f.* of clay.
Ps. 90. 2. or ever thou hadst *f.* the earth.
   94. 9. he that *f.* the eye.
   95. 5. his hands *f.* the dry land.
Prov. 26. 10. great God that *f.* all things.
Is. 43. 1. he that *f.* thee, O Israel.
   43. 7; 44. 21. I have *f.* him.
   43. 10. before me was no god *f.*
   43. 21. this people have I *f.* for myself.
   44. 2. *f.* thee from the womb.
   45. 18. God that *f.* the earth.
   54. 17. no weapon *f.* against thee.
Rom. 9. 20. shall thing *f.* say to him that *f.* it?
Gal. 4. 19. till Christ be *f.* in you.
Former, 1 Sam. 17. 30. answered after *f.* manner.
Job 8. 8. enquire of the *f.* age.
Ps. 79. 8. remember not *f.* iniquities.
   89. 49. where are thy *f.* loving-kindnesses?
Eccl. 1. 11. no remembrance of *f.* things.
   7. 10. *f.* days better than these.
Is. 42. 9. *f.* things are come to pass.
   43. 18. remember not the *f.* things.
   46. 9. remember the *f.* things of old.
   48. 3. declared *f.* things from beginning.
   65. 16. *f.* troubles are forgotten.   [rain.
Jer. 5. 24; Hos. 6. 3; Joel 2. 23. *f.* and latter
Jer. 10. 16; 51. 19. the *f.* of all things.
Hag. 2. 9. greater than glory of *f.* house.
Mal. 3. 4. pleasant as in *f.* years.
Eph. 4. 22. concerning the *f.* conversation.
Rev. 21. 4. the *f.* things are passed away.
Forsake, Deut. 4. 31; 31. 6; 1 Chr. 28. 20. he will not *f.* thee.
Deut. 31. 16. this people will *f.* me.
   32. 15. he *f.* God that made him.
Josh. 1. 5; Heb. 13. 5. I will not fail nor *f.* thee.   [off.
1 Chr. 28. 9. if thou *f.* him, he will cast thee
2 Chr. 15. 2. if he *f.* him, he will *f.* you.
Neh. 10. 39. we will not *f.* house of our God.
   13. 11. why is house of God *f.*?
Job 6. 14. he *f.* fear of the Almighty.
Ps. 22. 1; Matt. 27. 46; Mk. 15. 34. why hast thou *f.* me?
Ps. 37. 8. cease from anger, *f.* wrath.
   37. 25. not seen the righteous *f.*
   94. 14. nor will he *f.* his inheritance.
   119. 8. *f.* me not utterly.
   138. 8. *f.* not works of thine own hands.
Prov. 2. 17. *f.* the guide of her youth.
   4. 6. *f.* her not, she shall preserve thee.
Is. 17. 9. as a *f.* bough.
   32. 14; Jer. 4. 29; Ezek. 36. 4. *f.* city.
Is. 55. 7. let the wicked *f.* his way.
   62. 4. no more be termed *f.*
Jer. 2. 13; 17. 13. *f.* fountain of living waters.
Matt. 19. 27; Lk. 5. 11. we have *f.* all.   [fled.
Matt. 26. 56; Mk. 14. 50. disciples *f.* him, and
Lk. 14. 33. whoso *f.* not all he hath.
2 Cor. 4. 9. persecuted, but not *f.*
Heb. 10. 25. not *f.* assembling of ourselves.
   11. 27. by faith Moses *f.* Egypt.
2 Pet. 2. 15. have *f.* right way.
Forswear, Matt. 5. 33. not *f.* thyself.

Foul, Job 16. 16. my face is *f.* with weeping.
Matt. 16. 3. it will be *f.* weather.
Mk. 9. 25. he rebuked the *f.* spirit.
Rev. 18. 2. Babylon, hold of every *f.* spirit.
Found, Gen. 6. 8. Noah *f.* grace in eyes of the   [Lord.
   8. 9. the dove *f.* no rest.
   27. 20. how hast thou *f.* it so quickly?
   44. 16. God hath *f.* out the iniquity.
Num. 15. 32. *f.* a man gathering sticks.
1 Ki. 21. 20. hast thou *f.* me, mine enemy?
2 Ki. 22. 8. I *f.* book of the law.
2 Chr. 19. 3. good things *f.* in thee.
Job 33. 24. I have *f.* a ransom.
Ps. 32. 6. when thou mayest be *f.*
   69. 20. comforters, but *f.* none.
   84. 3. sparrow hath *f.* an house.
   107. 4. *f.* no city to dwell in.   [I *f.*
Eccl. 7. 28. one man among a thousand have
Cant. 3. 4. I *f.* him whom my soul loveth.
Is. 65. 1; Rom. 10. 20. *f.* of them that sought me not.
Ezek. 22. 30. I sought for a man, but *f.* none.
Dan. 5. 27. weighed, and *f.* wanting.
Matt. 8. 10; Lk. 7. 9. *...* *f.* so great faith.
Matt. 13. 46. *f.* one pearl of great price.
   20. 6. *f.* others standing idle.
   21. 19; Mk. 11. 13; Lk. 13. 6. *f.* nothing thereon.   [them asleep.
Matt. 26. 43; Mk. 14. 40; Lk. 22. 45. he *f.*
Mk. 7. 2. they *f.* fault.
Lk. 2. 46. they *f.* him in the temple.
   7. 10. they *f.* the servant whole.
   15. 6. I have *f.* the sheep.
   15. 9. I have *f.* the piece of money.
   15. 32. was lost, and is *f.*
   23. 14. I have *f.* no fault.
   24. 2. *f.* the stone rolled away.
John 1. 41, 45. we have *f.* the Messias.
Acts 7. 11. our fathers *f.* no sustenance.
   9. 2. if he *f.* any of this way.
   17. 23. I *f.* an altar with inscription.
   24. 5. *f.* this man a pestilent fellow.
Rom. 7. 10. to life, I *f.* to be unto death.
1 Cor. 15. 15. we are *f.* false witnesses.
Phil. 2. 8. being *f.* in fashion as a man.
Heb. 11. 5. Enoch was not *f.*
   12. 17. he *f.* no place of repentance.
Rev. 3. 2. not *f.* thy works perfect.
Foundation, Josh. 6. 26; 1 Ki. 16. 34. lay the *f.* in first-born.
2 Sam. 22. 16; Ps. 18. 7, 15. *f.* were discovered.
Job 4. 19. whose *f.* is in the dust.
   38. 4. when I had laid *f.* of earth?
Ps. 11. 3. if *f.* be destroyed.
   82. 5. all the *f.* out of course.
   102. 25. of old laid *f.* of earth.
   137. 7. rase it even to the *f.*
Prov. 10. 25. righteous an everlasting *f.*
Is. 28. 16. I lay in Zion a *f.*
   48. 13. my hand laid *f.* of the earth.
   58. 12. the *f.* of many generations.
Matt. 13. 35. kept secret from *f.* of the world.
Lk. 6. 48. laid the *f.* on a rock.
John 17. 24. lovedst me before *f.* of world.
Rom. 15. 20. build on another man's *f.*
1 Cor. 3. 10. wise master-builder, laid *f.*   [prophets.
   3. 11. other *f.* can no man lay.
Eph. 2. 20. on the *f.* of the apostles and
1 Tim. 6. 19. laying up a good *f.*
2 Tim. 2. 19. the *f.* of God standeth sure.
Heb. 4. 3. works finished from *f.* of world.
   6. 1. not laying *f.* of repentance.
   11. 10. a city that hath *f.*
Rev. 13. 8. Lamb slain from *f.* of world.

Fountain, Gen. 7. 11; 8. 2. *f.* of deep.
  Deut. 8. 7. a land of *f.*
  Ps. 36. 9. with thee is the *f.* of life.
  114. 8. flint into a *f.* of waters.
  Prov. 5. 18. let thy *f.* be blessed.
  8. 24. no *f.* abounding with water.
  13. 14. law of wise a *f.* of life.
  14. 27. fear of Lord a *f.* of life.
  25. 26. as a troubled *fi*
  Eccl. 12. 6. pitcher broken at the *f.*
  Cant. 4. 12. a *f.* sealed.
  4. 15. a *f.* of gardens.
  Jer. 2. 13; 17. 13. forsaken *f.* of living waters.
  9. 1. mine eyes a *f.* of tears.
  Zech. 13. 1. in that day shall be a *f.* opened.
  Mk. 5. 29. *f.* of her blood dried up.
  Jas. 3. 11. doth a *f.* send forth.
  Rev. 7. 17. lead them to living *f.*
  21. 6. of the *f.* of life freely.
Fragments, Matt. 14. 20; Mk. 6. 43; Lk. 9. 17;
  John 6. 13. took up the *f.*
  Mk. 8. 19. how many baskets of *f.*?
  John 6. 12. gather up *f.* that remain.
Frail, Ps. 39. 4. may know how *f.* I am.
Frame, Jud. 12. 6. could not *f.* to pronounce it.
  Ps. 50. 19. thy tongue *f.* deceit.
  94. 20. *f.* mischief by a law.
  103. 14. he knoweth our *f.*
  Is. 29. 16. shall thing *f.* say of him that *f.* it?
  Eph. 2. 21. in whom the building fitly *f.*
  Heb. 11. 3. worlds *f.* by word of God.
Free, Ex. 21. 2; Deut. 15. 12. in seventh year
  go out *f.*
  Deut. 24. 5. shall be *f.* at home one year.
  2 Chr. 29. 31. as were of *f.* heart offered.
  Ps. 51. 12. uphold me with thy *f.* Spirit.
  88. 5. *f.* among the dead.
  Is. 58. 6. to let the oppressed go *f.*
  Hos. 14. 4. I will love them *f.*
  Matt. 10. 8. *f.* ye have received, *f.* give.
  17. 26. then are the children *f.*
  Mk. 7. 11. say it is Corban, he shall be *f.*
  John 8. 32. truth shall make you *f.*
  8. 36. if Son make you *f.*, ye shall be *f.*
  Acts 22. 28. I was *f.* born.
  Rom. 3. 24. justified *f.* by his grace.
  5. 15. not as offence, so is *f.* gift.
  5. 18. being made *f.* from sin.
  8. 2. *f.* from the law of sin and death.
  8. 32. with him *f.* give us all things.
  1 Cor. 9. 1. am I not *f.*?
  12. 13; Eph. 6. 8. whether bond or *f.*
  Gal. 3. 28; Col. 3. 11. there is neither bond
  nor *f.*
  Gal. 5. 1. liberty wherewith Christ made us *f.*
  2 Thes. 3. 1. word have *f.* course.
  1 Pet. 2. 16. as *f.*, and not using liberty.
  Rev. 21. 6. of the fountain of life *f.*
  22. 17. water of life *f.*
Fret, Ps. 37. 1, 7, 8; Prov. 24. 19. *f.* not thyself.
  Prov. 19. 3. his heart *f.* against the Lord.
  Is. 8. 21. when hungry they shall *f.*
Friend, Ex. 33. 11. as a man to his *f.*
  Deut. 13. 6. if thy *f.* entice thee.   [hatest *f.*
  2 Sam. 19. 6. lovest thine enemies and
  Job 6. 14. pity be showed from his *f.*
  19. 14. my *f.* have forgotten me.
  42. 10. when he prayed for his *f.*
  Ps. 35. 14. as though he had been my *f.*
  41. 9. my familiar *f.* hath lifted heel.
  88. 18. lover and *f.* hast put far from me.
  Prov. 6. 1. if thou be surety for thy *f.*
  14. 20. the rich hath many *f.*
  17. 17. a *f.* loveth at all times.

Friend—Continued.
  Prov. 18. 24. a *f.* that sticketh closer than a
  brother.
  19. 4. wealth maketh many *f.*
  27. 6. faithful are wounds of a *f.*
  27. 17. man sharpeneth countenance of his *f.*
  Cant. 5. 16. beloved, this is my *f.*
  Is. 41. 8. seed of Abraham my *f.*
  Lam. 1. 2. her *f.* have dealt treacherously.
  Mic. 7. 5. trust not in a *f.*
  Matt. 11. 19; Lk. 7. 34. a *f.* of publicans.
  Matt. 20. 13. *f.*, I do thee no wrong.
  22. 12. *f.*, how camest thou hither?
  26. 50. *f.*, wherefore art thou come?
  Mk. 3. 21. when his *f.* heard of it.
  5. 19. Jesus saith, go home to thy *f.*
  Lk. 11. 5. which of you shall have a *f.*?
  14. 10. *f.*, go up higher.
  14. 12. a dinner, call not thy *f.*
  16. 9. *f.* of the mammon.
  John 3. 29. *f.* of the bridegroom rejoiceth.
  11. 11. our *f.* Lazarus sleepeth.
  15. 13. lay down his life for his *f.*
  19. 12. thou art not Cæsar's *f.*
  Jas. 2. 23. Abraham was called the *f.* of God.
  4. 4. a *f.* of the world is the enemy of God.
Froward, Deut. 32. 20. a very *f.* generation.
  2 Sam. 22. 27; Ps. 18. 26. with *f.* wilt shew
  thyself *f.*
  Ps. 101. 4. a *f.* heart shall depart.
  Prov. 2. 12. a man that speaketh *f.* things.
  3. 32. the *f.* is abomination to the Lord.
  4. 24. put away *f.* mouth.
  11. 20; 17. 20. a *f.* heart.
  16. 28. a *f.* man soweth strife.
  21. 8. the way of man is *f.*
  22. 5. thorns are in the way of the *f.*
  1 Pet. 2. 18. servants, be subject to the *f.*
Fruit, Gen. 1. 29. every tree wherein is *f.*
  Num. 13. 26. showed them the *f.* of the land.
  Deut. 26. 2. take the first of all *f.*
  Ps. 72. 16. *f.* thereof shake like Lebanon.
  132. 11. of *f.* of thy body will I set.
  Prov. 8. 19. my *f.* is better than gold.
  11. 30. *f.* of the righteous a tree of life.
  12. 14; 18. 20. satisfied by the *f.* of mouth.
  Cant. 2. 3. his *f.* was sweet to my taste.
  Is. 3. 10; Mic. 7. 13. *f.* of their doings.
  27. 6. fill face of the world with *f.*
  28. 4. the hasty *f.* before summer.
  57. 19. I create the *f.* of the lips.   [doings.
  Jer. 17. 10; 21. 14; 32. 19. according to *f.* of
  Hos. 10. 13. ye have eaten the *f.* of lies.
  Amos 8. 1. a basket of summer *f.*
  Mic. 6. 7. *f.* of body for sin of soul.
  Hab. 3. 17. neither shall *f.* be in the vines.
  Hag. 1. 10. earth is stayed from her *f.*
  Matt. 3. 8; Lk. 3. 8. *f.* meet for repentance.
  Matt. 12. 33. make tree good, and his *f.* good.
  21. 19. let no *f.* grow on thee.
  26. 29; Mk. 14. 25. drink of *f.* of the vine.
  Mk. 4. 28. earth bringeth forth *f.* of herself.
  Lk. 13. 7. I come seeking *f.* on this fig tree.
  John 4. 36. *f.* to life eternal.
  15. 4. branch cannot bear *f.* of itself.
  Rom. 6. 21. what *f.* had ye in those things?
  7. 4. bring forth *f.* unto God.
  Gal. 5. 22; Eph. 5. 9. the *f.* of the Spirit.
  Phil. 4. 17. I desire *f.* that may abound.
  2 Tim. 2. 6. first partaker of the *f.*
  Heb. 12. 11. peaceable *f.* of righteousness.
  13. 15. offer *f.* of our lips.
  Jas. 5. 7. waiteth for the precious *f.*
  Jude 12. trees whose *f.* withereth, without *f.*

61

Frustrate, Ezra 4.'5. hired to _f._ their purpose.
Is. 44. 25. _f._ the tokens of the liars.
Gal. 2. 21. I do not _f._ the grace of God.
Fulfil, Ps. 20. 4. the Lord _f._ all thy counsel.
145. 19. _f._ desire of them that fear him.
Matt. 3. 15. to _f._ all righteousness.
5. 17. not come to destroy, but to _f._
5. 18; 24. 34. till all be _f._
Mk. 13. 4. what sign when all shall be _f. t_
Lk. 21. 22. all written may be _f._
22. 16. till it be _f._ in kingdom of God.
John 3. 29; 17. 13. my joy is _f._
Acts 13. 22. who shall _f._ all my will.
13. 33. God hath _f._ the same unto us.
Rom. 8. 4. righteousness of law be _f._ in us.
13. 10. love is the _f._ of the law.
Gal. 5. 14. all the law is _f._ in one word.
6. 2. so _f._ the law of Christ.
Eph. 2. 3. _f._ the desires of flesh and mind.
Phil. 2. 2. _f._ ye my joy.
Col. 1. 25. to _f._ the Word of God.
2 Thes. 1. 11. _f._ good pleasure of his goodness.
Jas. 2. 8. if ye _f._ the royal law.
Full, Num. 22. 18; 24. 13. give house _f._ of silver.
Deut. 6. 11. houses _f._ of good things.
34. 9. Joshua was _f._ of spirit of wisdom.
Ruth 1. 21. I went out _f._
2 Ki. 6. 17. the mountain was _f._ of horses.
Job 5. 26. come to grave in _f._ age.
14. 1. of few days, and _f._ of trouble.
Ps. 10. 7; Rom. 3. 14. his mouth is _f._ of
Ps. 73. 10. waters of a _f._ cup.   [cursing.
74. 20. _f._ of habitations of cruelty.
119. 64. the earth is _f._ of thy mercy.
Prov. 27. 20. hell and destruction are never _f._
30. 9. lest I be _f._, and deny thee.
Eccl. 1. 7. yet the sea is not _f._
Is. 1. 11. I am _f._ of burnt offerings.   [Lord.
11. 9. earth shall be _f._ of knowledge of the
Jer. 6. 11. I am _f._ of the fury of the Lord.
Hab. 3. 3. earth _f._ of his praise.
Zech. 8. 5. streets _f._ of boys and girls.
Matt. 6. 22; Lk. 11. 36. body _f._ of light.
Lk. 6. 25. woe unto you that are _f._
John 1. 14. _f._ of grace and truth.
15. 11; 16. 24. that your joy might be _f._
Acts 6. 3; 7. 55. _f._ of _h_ ly Ghost.
1 Cor. 4. 8. now ye are _f._
Phil. 4. 12. I am instructed to be _f._
2 Tim. 4. 5. make _f._ proof of thy ministry.
Heb. 5. 14. meat to them of _f._ age.
1 Pet. 1. 8. joy unspeakable and _f._ of glory.
Fully, Num. 14. 24. Caleb hath followed me _f._
Eccl. 8. 11. heart is _f._ set to do evil.
Acts 2. 1. day of Pentecost was _f._ come.
Rom. 14. 5. let every man be _f._ persuaded.
Rev. 14. 18. her grapes are _f._ ripe.
Fulness, 1 Chr. 16. 32; Ps. 96. 11; 98. 7. let sea
roar, and _f._ thereof.
Ps. 16. 11. in thy presence is _f._ of joy.
24. 1; 1 Cor. 10. 26, 28. earth is Lord's, and
_f._ thereof.
John 1. 16. of his _f._ have we received.
Rom. 11. 25. the _f._ of the Gentiles.
Gal. 4. 4. when _f._ of time was come.
Eph. 1. 23. the _f._ of him that filleth all in all.
3. 19. filled with the _f._ of God.
4. 13. the stature of the _f._ of Christ.
Col. 1. 19. in him should all _f._ dwell.
2. 9. the _f._ of the Godhead bodily.
Furious, Prov. 22. 24. with a _f._ man thou shalt
not go.
29. 22. a _f._ man aboundeth in transgression.
Nah. 1. 2. the Lord is _f._ See 2 Ki. 9. 20.

Furnace, Gen. 19. 28. smoke went as smoke of
a _f._
Deut. 4. 20. Lord hath taken you out of _f._
Ps. 12. 6. as silver tried in a _f._
Prov. 17. 3; 27. 21. _f._ for gold.
Is. 48. 10. in _f._ of affliction.
Dan. 3. 6, 11. into midst of fiery _f._
Matt. 13.)42. into a _f._ of fire.
Furnish, Ps. 78. 19. can God _f._ table in wilder-
ness?
Matt. 22. 10. wedding _f._ with guests.
Mk. 14. 15; Lk. 22. 12. shew a room _f._
2 Tim. 3. 17. _f._ unto all good works.
Further, Job 38. 11. hitherto shalt thou come,
but no _f._
Matt. 26. 65; Mk. 14. 63; Lk. 22. 71. what _f._
need of witnesses?
Lk. 24. 28. as though he would have gone _f._
Acts 4. 17. that it spread no _f._
2 Tim. 3. 9. they shall proceed no _f._
Fury, Gen. 27. 44. till thy brother's _f._ turn
Is. 27. 4. _f._ is not in me.
51. 20. they are full of _f._ of the Lord.
Jer. 21. 5. I will fight against you in _f._
25. 15. the wine cup of this _f._
Zech. 8. 2. I was jealous with great _f._

GAIN, Job 22. 3. is it _g._ to make ways perfect?
Prov. 1. 19; 15. 27. greedy of _g._
3. 14. the _g._ thereof better than gold.
28. 8. by usury and unjust _g._
Ezek. 22. 13, 27. dishonest _g._
Dan. 11. 39. he shall divide the land for _g._
Mic. 4. 13. consecrate their _g._ to the Lord.
Matt. 16. 26; Mk. 8. 36; Lk. 9. 25. if he _g._ the
world.
Matt. 25. 22. have _g._ other two talents.
Lk. 19. 15. had _g._ by trading.
Acts 16. 16. brought masters much _g._
19. 24. no small _g._ to craftsmen.
1 Cor. 9. 19. that I might _g._ the more.
2 Cor. 12. 17. did I make a _g._ of you?
Phil. 1. 21. to die is _g._
3. 7. what things were _g._ to me.
1 Tim. 6. 5. supposing that _g._ is godliness.
Jas. 4. 13. buy and sell, and get _g._
Gainsay, Lk. 21. 15. adversaries not able to _g._
Acts 10. 29. came without _g._
Rom. 10. 21. stretched hands to a _g._ people.
Tit. 1. 9. able to convince _g._
Jude 11. perished in the _g._ of Core.
Gall, Deut. 32. 32. their grapes are grapes of _g._
Ps. 69. 21. gave me _g._ for meat.
Lam. 3. 19. wormwood and _g._
Matt. 27. 34. vinegar mingled with _g._
Acts 8. 23. in _g._ of bitterness.
Garden, Gen. 3. 23. sent him forth from _g._
13. 10. as the _g._ of the Lord.
Deut. 11. 10; 1 Ki. 21. 2. as a _g._ of herbs.
Cant. 4. 12. a _g._ enclosed.
5. 1. I am come into my _g._
6. 2. gone down into his _g._
Is. 1. 8. as a lodge in a _g._
1. 30. as a _g._ that hath no water.
58. 11; Jer. 31. 12. like a watered _g._
Is. 61. 11. as the _g._ causeth things sown to
spring forth.
Jer. 29. 5. plant _g._, and eat the fruit.
Ezek. 28. 13. in Eden the _g._ of God.
36. 35. desolate land like _g._ of Eden.
Joel 2. 3. land as _g._ of Eden before them.
John 18. 1. over brook Cedron, where was a _g._
18. 26. did not I see thee in the _g._?
19. 41. a _g._, and in _g._ a new sepulchre.

Garment, Gen. 39. 16. laid up his g.
Josh. 7. 21. a goodly Babylonish g.
2 Ki. 5. 26. is it a time to receive g.?
7. 15. all the way was full of g.
Ps. 22. 18. they part my g. among them.
102. 26; Is. 50. 9; 51. 6; Heb. 1. 11. wax old as a g.
Ps. 104. 2. cover with light, as with a g.
109. 18. clothed with cursing as with his g.
Prov. 20. 16; 27. 13. his g. that is surety.
30. 4. who hath bound the waters in a g.?
Is. 52. 1. put on thy beautiful g.
61. 3. g. of praise for spirit of heaviness.
Joel 2. 13. rend your heart and not your g.
Matt. 9. 16; Mk. 2. 21; Lk. 5. 36. new cloth to old g.
Matt. 9. 20; Mk. 5. 27; Lk. 8. 44. hem of g.
Matt. 21. 8; Mk. 11. 8. spread g. in way.
Matt. 23. 5. enlarge borders of g.
27. 35; Mk. 15. 24. parted g., casting lots.
Mk. 11. 7; Lk. 19. 35. cast g. on colt.
Mk. 13. 16. not turn back again to take g.
Lk. 24. 4. in shining g.
Acts 9. 39. showing the coats and g.
Jas. 5. 2. your g. are moth eaten.
Jude 23. the g. spotted by the flesh.
Rev. 3. 4. not defiled their g.
Gate, Gen. 28. 17. the g. of heaven.
Ps. 118. 20. this g. of the Lord.   [enter.
Is. 26. 2. open the g., that righteous may
60. 11. thy g. shall be open continually.
60. 18. thy walls salvation, and g. praise.
Matt. 7. 13; Lk. 13. 24. strait g.
Matt. 16. 18. g. of hell shall not prevail.
Heb. 13. 12. Jesus suffered without the g.
Rev. 21. 25. g. not shut at all by day.
Gather, Gen. 41. 35. let them g. all the food.
Ex. 16. 17. g. some more, some less.
Deut. 30. 3; Ezek. 36. 24. will g. thee from all nations.
Ps. 26. 9. g. not my soul with sinners.
104. 28. that thou givest them, they g.
Prov. 10. 5. that g. in summer is wise son.
Is. 27. 12. ye shall be g. one by one.
40. 11. he shall g. the lambs.
54. 7. with great mercies will I g. thee.
Matt. 3. 12; Lk. 3. 17. g. wheat into garner.
Matt. 6. 26. nor g. into barns.
7. 16; Lk. 6. 44. do men g. grapes off thorns?
Matt. 12. 30; Lk. 11. 23. he that g. not scattereth.
Matt. 13. 28. wilt thou that we g. them up?
25. 32. before him shall be g. all nations.
John 6. 12. g. up fragments.
15. 6. men g. them, and cast them.
Gave, Num. 21. 44; 2 Chr. 15. 15; 20. 30. Lord
Job 1. 21. the Lord g.   [g. them rest.
Ps. 21. 4. he asked life, and thou g. it.
Eccl. 12. 7. spirit return to God, who g. it.
Matt. 21. 23; Mk. 11. 28; Lk. 20. 2. who g. thee this authority?
Lk. 15. 16. no man g. unto him.   [God.
John 1. 12. he g. power to become sons of
3. 16. God g. his only-begotten Son.
10. 29. my Father, who g. them.
Acts 2. 4. as the Spirit g. them utterance.
26. 10. I g. my voice against them.
1 Cor. 3. 6. God g. the increase.
Gal. 2. 20. loved me, and g. himself for me.
Eph. 4. 8. g. gifts unto men.
1 Tim. 2. 6. who g. himself a ransom.
Generation, Gen. 7. 1. righteous in g.
Deut. 32. 5. a perverse and crooked g.
Ps. 14. 5. God is in the g. of the righteous.

Generation—Continued.
Ps. 22. 30. it shall be accounted for a g.
78. 4. shew to g. to come praises of the Lord.
95. 10; Heb. 3. 10. grieved with his g.
Ps. 145. 4. one g. shall praise thy works.
Prov. 27. 24. doth crown endure to every g.?
30. 12. there is a g. pure in own eyes.
Eccl. 1. 4. one g. passeth away.
Is. 34. 10. from g. to g. it shall lie waste.
53. 8; Acts 8. 33. who shall declare his g.?
Dan. 4. 3, 34. his dominion from g. to g.
Matt. 3. 7; 12. 34; 23. 33; Lk. 3. 7. g. of vipers.
Matt. 11. 16; Lk. 7. 31. whereunto shall I liken this g.?
Matt. 17. 17; Mk. 9. 19; Lk. 9. 41. faithless, perverse g.   [shall not pass.
Matt. 24. 34; Mk. 13. 30; Lk. 21. 32. this g.
Mk. 8. 38. ashamed of me in this sinful g.
Lk. 16. 8. children of world in g. wiser.
1 Pet. 2. 9. ye are a chosen g.   [seek.
Gentiles, Is. 11. 10. root of Jesse, to it shall G.
60. 3. the G. shall come to thy light.
Matt. 6. 32. after all these things G. seek.
10. 5. go not into way of G.
John 7. 35. to the dispersed among G.
Acts 9. 15. to bear my name before G.
18. 6. from henceforth I will go to the G.
Rom. 3. 9. proved Jews and G. under sin.
11. 12. diminishing of them riches of the G.
15. 11. praise the Lord, all ye G.   [riches
Eph. 3. 8. preach among G., unsearchable
2 Tim. 1. 11. I am appointed a teacher of G.
1 Pet. 2. 12. conversation honest among G.
Rev. 11. 2. the court is given to the G.
Gentle, 1 Thes. 2. 7. we were g. among you.
2 Tim. 2. 24. servant of the Lord must be g.
Jas. 3. 17. wisdom from above, pure and g.
1 Pet. 2. 18. subject not only to the g.
Gentleness, 2 Sam. 22. 36; Ps. 18. 35. thy g. made me great.
2 Cor. 10. 1. I beseech you by g. of Christ.
Gal. 5. 22. fruit of the Spirit is g.
Gift, Ex. 23. 8; Deut. 16. 19. take no g., for g. blindeth.
2 Chr. 19. 7. with Lord is no taking of g.
Ps. 45. 12. daughter of Tyre with a g.
68. 18; Eph. 4. 8. g. for men.
Ps. 72. 10. kings of Sheba shall offer g.
Prov. 17. 8. a g. is as a precious stone.
Eccl. 3. 13; 5. 19. it is the g. of God.
7. 7. a g. destroyeth the heart.
Is. 1. 23. every one loveth g.
Matt. 5. 23. bring thy g. to the altar.
7. 11; Lk. 11. 13. know how to give good g.
Matt. 15. 5; Mk. 7. 11. a g., by whatsoever thou mightest be profited.
Lk. 21. 1. casting g. into treasury.
John 4. 10. if thou knewest the g. of God.
Acts 8. 20. thought the g. of God may be purchased.
Rom. 1. 11. some spiritual g.
5. 15. not as offence, so is free g.
6. 23. the g. of God is eternal life.
11. 29. g. of God without repentance.
12. 6. g. differing according to grace.
1 Cor. 12. 4. diversities of g.
14. 1, 12. desire spiritual g.
2 Cor. 9. 15. thanks to God for unspeakable g.
Eph. 2. 8. faith is the g. of God.
Phil. 4. 17. not because I desire a g.
1 Tim. 4. 14. neglect not g. in thee.
2 Tim. 1. 6. stir up g. in thee.
Heb. 6. 4. tasted of heavenly g.
Jas. 1. 17. every good and perfect g.

63

Gird, 2 Sam. 22. 40 ; Ps. 18. 39. hast g. me with strength.

Ps. 45. 3. g. sword on thy thigh.

Joel 1. 13. g. yourselves, and lament.

John 21. 18. when old, another shall g. thee.

Eph. 6. 14. having your loins g.

Girdle, Is. 11. 5. righteousness be g. of loins.

Matt. 3. 4 ; Mk. 1. 6. John had a leathern g.

Rev. 1. 13. girt about with golden g.

Girl, Joel 3. 3. they have sold g. for wine.

Zech. 8. 5. streets full of g.

Give, Gen. 28. 22. I will g. the tenth.

Deut. 16. 17 ; Ezek. 46. 5, 11. every man g. as he is able.

Ps. 2. 8. I shall g. thee the heathen.

29. 11. Lord will g. strength.

37. 4. g. thee the desires of thine heart.

84. 11. Lord will g. grace and glory.

Prov. 23. 26. my son, g. me thine heart.

Is. 55. 10. that it may g. seed to the sower.

Jer. 17. 10 ; 32. 19. g. every man according to his ways.

Hos. 11. 8. how shall I g. thee up?　　[ways.

Matt. 5. 42. g. to him that asketh.

6. 11 ; Lk. 11. 3. g. us daily bread.

Matt. 10. 8. freely ye have received, freely g.

16. 26 ; Mk. 8. 37. what shall a man g. in exchange for soul?　　[poor.

Matt. 19. 21 ; Mk. 10. 21. go sell, and g. to the

Lk. 6. 38. g., and it shall be g.

John 4. 14. the water I shall g. him.

6. 37. all that the Father g. me.

10. 28. I g. to them eternal life.

14. 16. he shall g. you the Comforter.

14. 27. not as the world g., g. I.

Acts 3. 6. such as I have, g. I thee.

6. 4. we will g. ourselves to prayer.

20. 35. more blessed to g. than to receive.

Rom. 8. 32. with him also freely g. us all things.

1 Cor. 2. 12. things freely g. of God.

2 Cor. 9. 7. g. not grudgingly.

1 Tim. 4. 13. g. attendance to reading.

6. 17. who g. us richly.

Jas. 1. 5. that g. to all men liberally

4. 6. g. more grace, g. grace to humble.

1 Pet. 4. 11. of the ability that God g.

Glad, Ex. 4. 14. he will be g. in heart.

Job 3. 22. g. when they can find the grave.

Ps. 16. 9. my heart is g.

21. 6. made him g. with thy countenance.

34. 2 ; 69. 32. humble shall hear, and be g.

46. 4. streams make g. the city of God.

90. 15. make us g.

122. 1. I was g. when they said.

126. 3. great things, whereof we are g.

Prov. 10. 1 ; 15. 20. a wise son maketh a g.

Is. 35. 1. wilderness be g. for them.　　[father.

Lk. 8. 1. g. tidings of the kingdom.

15. 32. make merry, and be g.

John 8. 56. saw my day, and was g.

11. 15. I am g. for your sakes.　　[was g.

Acts 11. 23. when he had seen grace of God,

1 Pet. 4. 13. ye may be g. also.　　[blow.

Gladness, Num. 10. 10. in day of g. ye shall

2 Sam. 6. 12. David brought ark with g.

Neh. 8. 17. there was very great g.

Ps. 4. 7. thou hast put g. in my heart.

45. 7 ; Heb. 1. 9. the oil of g.

Ps. 51. 8. make me to hear joy and g.

97. 11. g. is sown for the upright.

100. 2. serve the Lord with g.

Is. 35. 10 ; 51. 11. they shall obtain joy and g.

Acts 2. 46. did eat with g. of heart.

12. 14. opened not gate for g.

14. 17. filling our hearts with food and g.

Glass, 1 Cor. 13. 12. we see through a g.

2 Cor. 3. 18. beholding as in a g.

Jas. 1. 23. man beholding face in a g.

Rev. 4. 6. sea of g. like unto crystal.

21. 18, 21. city pure gold, like clear g.

Glean, Lev. 19. 10 ; Deut. 24. 21. not g. vineyard.

Jer. 6. 9. they shall g. the remnant.

Mic. 7. 1. as grape g. of the vintage.

Glorify, Ps. 22. 23. all seed of Jacob g. him.

86. 9. all nations shall g. thy name.

Is. 60. 7. I will g. house of my glory.

Dan. 5. 23. God hast thou not g.

Matt. 5. 16. g. your Father in heaven.

15. 31. they g. the God of Israel.

Lk. 4. 15. being g. of all.

John 7. 39. because Jesus was not yet g.

11. 4. that the Son of God might be g.

12. 16. when Jesus was g.

12. 28. Father, g. thy name.

13. 32. God shall also g. him.

14. 13. that Father may be g. in Son.

15. 8. herein is my Father g.

17. 1. g. thy Son, that thy Son may g. thee.

21. 19. by what death he should g. God.

Acts 4. 21. men g. God for what was done.

Rom. 1. 21. they g. him not as God.

8. 17. suffer with him, that we may be g.

1 Cor. 6. 20. g. God in body and spirit.

2 Thes. 1. 10. to be g. in his saints.

3. 1. that word of Lord may be g.

Heb. 5. 5. Christ g. not himself.

1 Pet. 4. 14. on your part he is g.

Rev. 15. 4. fear thee, and g. thy name.

Glorious, Ex. 15. 11. g. in holiness.

Deut. 28. 58 ; 1 Chr. 29. 13. this g. name.

Neh. 9. 5. blessed be thy g. name.

Ps. 45. 13. king's daughter g. within.

66. 2. make his praise g.

72. 19. blessed be his g. name for ever.

87. 3. g. things are spoken of thee.

145. 5. speak of g. honour of majesty.

Is. 28. 1. whose g. beauty is a fading flower.

60. 13. place of my feet g.

63. 1. g. in his apparel.

Jer. 17. 12. a g. high throne.

Lk. 13. 17. rejoiced for g. things done.

Rom. 8. 21. g. liberty of children of God.

2 Cor. 3. 8. ministration of spirit rather g.

4. 4. light of g. gospel.

Eph. 5. 27. present it a g. church.

1 Tim. 1. 11. the g. gospel of the blessed God.

Tit. 2. 13. the g. appearing of the great God.

Glory, Ex. 33. 18. shew me thy g.

Num. 14. 21 ; Ps. 72. 19 ; Is. 6. 3. earth filled with g. of Lord.

1 Sam. 4. 21. the g. is departed from Israel.

Ps. 8. 1. thy g. above the heavens.

24. 7, 10. the king of g.

73. 24. afterward receive me to g.

84. 11. Lord will give grace and g.

85. 9. that g. may dwell in our land.

89. 17. thou art g. of their strength.

145. 11. speak of the g. of thy kingdom.

Prov. 3. 35. the wise shall inherit g.

17. 6. the g. of children are their fathers.

20. 29. the g. of young men is their strength.

Is. 24. 16. songs, even g. to the righteous.

42. 8. my g. will I not give to another.

60. 7. will glorify house of my g.

Jer. 2. 11. my people have changed their g.

Ezek. 31. 18. to whom art thou thus like in g.

Dan. 2. 37 ; 7. 14. God hath given power and g.

Hos. 4. 7. change their g. into shame.

Hag. 2. 7. I will fill thy house with g.

64

Glory—*Continued.*

Matt. 6. 2. that they may have *g.* of men.
6. 29; Lk. 12. 27. Solomon in all his *g.*
Matt. 16. 27; Mk. 8. 38. come in *g.* of Father.
Matt. 24. 30; Mk. 13. 26; Lk. 21. 27. Son coming with power and *g.*
Lk. 2. 14; 19. 38. *g.* to God in the highest.
4. 6. power will I give thee and *g.*
9. 31. appeared in *g.*, and spake.
24. 26. to enter into his *g.*
John 1. 14. we beheld his *g.*
8. 50. I seek not mine own *g.*
17. 5. the *g.* I had with thee.
17. 24. that they may behold my *g*
Acts 7. 2. God of *g.* appeared.
12. 23. he gave not God the *g.*
Rom. 3. 23. come short of *g.* of God.
8. 18. not worthy to be compared with the *g.*
9. 23. he had afore prepared unto *g.*
11. 36; Gal. 1. 5; 2 Tim. 4. 18; Heb. 13. 21; 1 Pet. 5. 11. to whom be *g.* for ever and ever.
1 Cor. 2. 8. not crucified the Lord of *g.*
10. 31. do all to the *g.* of God.
15. 40. *g.* of celestial, *g.* of terrestrial.
15. 43. sown in dishonour, raised in *g.*
2 Cor. 3. 18. are changed from *g.* to *g.*
4. 17. an eternal weight of *g.*
Eph. 1. 6. praise of *g.* of his grace.
3. 21. to him be *g.* in the church.
Phil. 4. 19. according to his riches in *g.*
Col. 1. 27. Christ in you, the hope of *g.*
3. 4. appear with him in *g.*
1 Tim. 3. 16. received up into *g.*
Heb. 1. 3. the brightness of his *g.*
2. 10. in bringing many sons to *g.*
3. 3. this man was counted worthy of more *g.*
Jas. 2. 1. faith of Jesus, Lord of *g.*
1 Pet. 1. 8. joy unspeakable and full of *g.*
1. 24. the *g.* of man as flower of grass.
2. 20. what *g.* is it, if when buffeted?
4. 14. the spirit of *g.* and of God.
5. 10. called us to eternal *g.*
2 Pet. 1. 17. voice from the excellent *g.*
Rev. 4. 11; 5. 12. worthy to receive *g.*
7. 12. blessing and *g.* to our God.
21. 23. the *g.* of God did lighten it.

Gnash, Job 16. 9; Ps. 37. 12. he *g.* on me.
Ps. 35. 16. they *g.* on me with teeth.
Matt. 8. 12; 13. 42; 22. 13; 24. 51; 25. 30; Lk. 13. 28. *g.* of teeth.
Mk. 9. 18; he foameth, and *g.* with teeth.
Acts 7. 54. they *g.* on me with teeth.

Gnat, Matt. 23. 24. strain at a *g.* and swallow a camel.

Go, Gen. 32. 26. let me *g.*, for the day breaketh.
Ex. 23. 23; 32. 34. angel shall *g.* before thee.
33. 14. my presence shall *g.* with thee.
Deut. 31. 6. thy God, he it is that doth *g.*
Ruth 1. 16. whither thou *g.*, I will *g.*
2 Sam. 12. 23. I shall *g.* to him, he shall not return.
1 Ki. 2. 2. I *g.* the way of all the earth.
Ps. 32. 8. teach thee in way thou shalt *g.*
139. 7. whither shall I *g.* from thy Spirit?
Prov. 22. 6. train child in way he should *g.*
30. 29. three things which *g.* well.
Matt. 5. 41. to *g.* a mile, *g.* twain.
8. 9. I say *g.*, and he *g.*
10. 6. *g.* rather to lost sheep of Israel.
28. 19. *g.* ye, and teach all nations.
Lk. 10. 37. *g.* and do likewise.
John 6. 68. Lord, to whom shall we *g.*?
14. 2. I *g.* to prepare a place for you.
19. 12. if thou let this man *g.*

God, Gen. 5. 22; 6. 9. walked with *G.*
16. 13. thou *G.* seest me.
32. 28. power with *G.*
48. 21. *G.* shall be with you.   [lie.
Num. 23. 19. *G.* is not a man, that he should
Deut. 33. 27. the eternal *G.* is thy refuge.
1 Sam. 17. 46. may know there is a *G.* in Israel.
2 Sam. 22. 32; Ps. 18. 31. who is *G.* save the Lord?
1 Ki. 18. 21. if the Lord be *G.*, follow him.
18. 39. the Lord, he is the *G.*
2 Ki. 19. 15. thou art *G.*, even thou.
Job 22. 13; Ps. 73. 11. how doth *G.* know?
Ps. 14. 1; 53. 1. fool said, there is no *G.*
22. 1; Matt. 27. 46. my *G.*, my *G.*, why hast thou forsaken me?
Ps. 86. 10; Is. 37. 16. thou art *G.* alone.
Eccl. 5. 2. *G.* is in heaven.
Is. 44. 8. is there a *G.* beside me?
45. 22. I am *G.*, there is none else.
Jer. 31. 33; 32. 38. I will be their *G.*
Hos. 11. 9. I am *G.*, and not man.
Jon. 1. 6. arise, call upon thy *G.*
Mic. 6. 8. walk humbly with thy *G.*
Matt. 1. 23. *G.* with us.   [mammon.
6. 24; Lk. 16. 13. ye cannot serve *G.* and
Matt. 19. 17; Mk. 10. 18; Lk. 18. 19. there is none good but one, that is *G.*
Matt. 22. 32. *G.* is not *G.* of the dead.
Mk. 12. 32. there is one *G.*, and none other.
John 1. 1. the Word was *G.*
3. 2. do miracles, except *G.* be with him.
4. 24. *G.* is a Spirit.
17. 3. life eternal, to know thee, the true *G.*
Acts 10. 34. *G.* is no respecter of persons.
Rom. 8. 31. if *G.* be for us, who against us?
1 Cor. 8. 6. but one *G.*, the Father.
15. 28. that *G.* may be all in all.   [you.
2 Cor. 13. 11. *G.* of love and peace shall be with
2 Thes. 2. 4. above all that is called *G.*
1 Tim. 3. 16. *G.* was manifest in the flesh.
Heb. 3. 4. he that built all things is *G.*
8. 10. I will be to them a *G.*
11. 16. not ashamed to be called their *G.*
1 John 1. 5. *G.* is light.
4. 8, 16. *G.* is love.
Rev. 21. 4. *G.* shall wipe away all tears.

God (an idol), Ex. 32. 1. make us *g.*, which shall go before us.
Jud. 6. 31. if he be a *g.*, let him plead.
17. 5. Micah had a house of *g.*
Ps. 16. 4. hasten after another *g.*
Is. 44. 15. maketh a *g.*, and worshippeth it.
45. 20. pray to a *g.* that cannot save.
Amos 5. 26; Acts 7. 43. star of your *g.*
Jon. 1. 5. cried every man to his *g.*
Acts 12. 22. the voice of a *g.*, not of a man.
14. 11. the *g.* are come down to us.
1 Cor. 8. 5. there be *g.* many.   [unto gold.

Godhead, Acts 17. 29. not to think *G.* is like
Rom. 1. 20. his eternal power and *G.*
Col. 2. 9. all the fulness of the *G.* bodily.

Godliness, 1 Tim. 3. 16. the mystery of *g.*
4. 8. *g.* is profitable unto all things.
6. 5. supposing that gain is *g.*
2 Tim. 3. 5. a form of *g.*
Tit. 1. 1. the truth which is after *g.*
2 Pet. 1. 3. pertain to life and *g.*
3. 11. in all holy conversation and *g.*

Godly, Ps. 12. 1. the *g.* man ceaseth.
2 Cor. 1. 12. in *g.* sincerity.
7. 10. *g.* sorrow worketh repentance.
2 Tim. 3. 12. all that will live *g.* in Christ.

Godly—*Continued.*

Tit. 2. 12. live *g.* in this world.
Heb. 12. 28. reverence and *g.* fear.
2 Pet. 2. 9. Lord knoweth how to deliver *g.*
3 John 6. bring forward after a *g.* sort.

Going, 2 Sam. 5. 24; 1 Chr. 14. 15. sound of *g.* in trees.

Ps. 17. 5. hold up my *g.*
40. 2. established my *g.*
Prov. 5. 21. pondereth all his *g.*
20. 24. man's *g.* are of the Lord.   [old.
Mic. 5. 2. whose *g.* forth have been from of

Gold, Ex. 20. 23. nor shall make gods of *g.*
Deut. 8. 13. when thy *g.* is multiplied.
1 Ki. 20. 3. silver and *g.* is mine.
Job 28. 1. a vein for silver, a place for *g.*
31. 24. if I made *g.* my hope.
Ps. 19. 10. more to be desired than *g.*
Prov. 16. 16. better to get wisdom than *g.*
25. 11. like apples of *g.*
Is. 60. 17. for brass I will bring *g.*
Lam. 4. 1. how is *g.* become dim?   [mine.
Hag. 2. 8. the silver is mine, and the *g.* is
Zech. 13. 9. I will try them as *g.* is tried.
Matt. 23. 16. swear by *g.* of the temple.
Acts 3. 6. silver and *g.* have I none.
1 Cor. 3. 12. build on this foundation, *g.*
2 Tim. 2. 20. vessels of *g.* and silver.
Heb. 9. 4. ark overlaid with *g.*
Jas. 2. 2. man with a *g.* ring.
5. 3. your *g.* is cankered.   [than of *g.*
1 Pet. 1. 7. trial of your faith more precious
Rev. 3. 18. to buy of me *g.* tried.
21. 18. city was pure *g.*

Gone, Num. 16. 46. wrath *g.* out from the Lord.
Deut. 23. 23. that which is *g.* out of thy lips.
Ps. 42. 4. I had *g.* with the multitude.
73. 2. my feet were almost *g.*
77. 8. is his mercy clean *g.* for ever?
103. 16. wind passeth over, it is *g.*
109. 23. I am *g.* like the shadow.
Cant. 2. 11. the rain is over and *g.*
Is. 53. 6. we all like sheep have *g.* astray.
Mk. 5. 30 ; Lk. 8. 46. virtue had *g.* out of him.
John 12. 19. the world is *g.* after him.
Acts 16. 19. hope of their gains was *g.*
Rom. 3. 12. they are all *g.* out of the way.
Jude 11. *g.* in the way of Cain.

Good, Gen. 32. 12. I will surely do thee *g.*
50. 20. God meant it unto *g.*
Neh. 5. 19 ; 13. 31. think upon me for *g.*
Job 2. 10. shall we receive *g.?*
22. 21. thereby *g.* shall come to thee.
Ps. 4. 6. who will shew us any *g.?*
14. 1; 53. 1; Rom. 3. 12. none doeth *g.*
Ps. 34. 12. loveth days that he may see *g.*
86. 17. shew me a token for *g.*
Prov. 3. 27. withhold not *g.* from them.
11. 17. doeth *g.* to his own soul.
Eccl. 7. 20. that doeth *g.* and sinneth not.
9. 18. one sinner destroyeth much *g.*
Matt. 12. 29 ; Mk. 3. 27. spoil his *g.*
Matt. 26. 24. been *g.* for that man.
Lk. 12. 19. much *g.* laid up.
15. 12. the portion of *g.*
16. 1. accused that he had wasted his *g.*
19. 8. half of my *g.* I give to the poor.
Acts 10. 38. who went about doing *g.*
14. 17. he did *g.*, and gave us rain.
Rom. 8. 28. all things work together for *g.*
13. 4. minister of God for *g.*
1 John 3. 17. this world's *g.*
Rev. 3. 17. rich, and increased with *g.*

Good, Gen. 1. 4, 12, 31. God saw it was *g.*
2. 18. not *g.* that man should be alone.
26. 29. we have done nothing but *g.*
27. 46. what *g.* shall my life do me?
Deut. 2. 4; Josh. 23. 11. take *g.* heed.
1 Sam. 2. 24. it is no *g.* report I hear.
12. 23. I will teach you the *g.* way.
25. 15. men were very *g.* to us.
1 Ki. 8. 56. no word of *g.* promise failed.
2 Ki. 20. 19; Is. 39. 8. *g.* is word of the Lord.
Ezek. 8. 18. *g.* hand of our God upon us.
Neh. 9. 20. thy *g.* spirit to instruct.
Ps. 25. 8. *g.* and upright is the Lord.
34. 8. taste and see that the Lord is *g.*
37. 23. steps of *g.* man ordered by Lord.
45. 1. my heart is inditing a *g.* matter.
112. 5. a *g.* man sheweth favour.
145. 9. the Lord is *g.* to all.
Prov. 12. 25. a *g.* word maketh the heart glad.
15. 23. word in season, how *g.* is it?
22. 1. a *g.* name rather to be chosen than riches.
Eccl. 9. 2. one event to the *g.* and clean.
Is. 55. 2. eat ye that which is *g.*
Jer. 6. 16. the *g.* way, and walk therein.
29. 10. I will perform my *g.* work.
Lam. 3. 27. it is *g.* that a man bear yoke.
Zech. 1. 13. Lord answereth with *g.* words.
Matt. 7. 11 ; Lk. 11. 13. how to give *g.* gifts.
Matt. 9. 22 ; Lk. 8. 48. be of *g.* comfort.
Matt. 19. 17; Lk. 18. 19. none *g.*, save one.
Matt. 25. 21. well done, thou *g.* servant.
Mk. 9. 50 ; Lk. 14. 34. salt is *g.*, but.
Lk. 2. 14. peace on earth, *g.* to men.
6. 38. *g.* measure pressed down.
10. 42. Mary hath chosen that *g.* part.
12. 32. your Father's *g.* pleasure to give.
23. 50. Joseph was a *g.* man, and a just.
John 1. 46. can any *g.* thing come out of Nazareth?
2. 10. kept *g.* wine until now.
10. 11. I am the *g.* shepherd.
10. 33. for a *g.* work we stone thee not.
Rom. 7. 12. the commandment holy, just, and *g.*
12. 2. that *g.* and perfect will of God.
1 Cor. 15. 33. evil communications corrupt *g.* manners.
2 Cor. 9. 8. abound to every *g.* work.
Gal. 6. 6. communicate in all *g.* things.
Col. 1. 10. fruitful in every *g.* work.
1 Thes. 5. 21. hold fast that which is *g.*
1 Tim. 1. 8. the law is *g.*
4. 4. every creature of God is *g.*
Tit. 2. 14. zealous of *g.* works.
Heb. 6. 5. tasted the *g.* word of God.
Jas. 1. 17. every *g.* gift.

Goodly, Gen. 39. 6. Joseph was a *g.* person.
49. 21. he giveth *g.* words.
Ex. 2. 2. he was a *g.* child.
Num. 24. 5. how *g.* are thy tents, O Jacob
Deut. 3. 25. let me see that *g.* mountain.
6. 10. *g.* cities which thou buildest not.
8. 12. when thou hast built *g.* houses.
Josh. 7. 21. a *g.* Babylonish garment.
1 Sam. 9. 2. a choice young man, and a *g.*
16. 12. David was *g.* to look to.
Ps. 16. 6 ; Jer. 3. 19. a *g.* heritage.
Ps. 80. 10. boughs were like *g.* cedars.
Zech. 11. 13. a *g.* price I was prized at.
Matt. 13. 45. seeking *g.* pearls.
Jas. 2. 2. a man in *g.* apparel.

Goodness, Ex. 33. 19. I will make all my *g.* pass before thee.
34. 6. the Lord God abundant in *g.*
2 Chr. 6. 41. let thy saints rejoice in *g.*
Ps. 16. 2. my *g.* extendeth not to thee.
27. 13. believed to see the *g.* of the Lord.
31. 19. how great is thy *g.*
33. 5. earth is full of the *g.* of the Lord.
65. 11. thou crownest the year with thy *g.*
107. 9. he filleth the hungry soul with *g.*
145. 7. the memory of thy *g.*
Prov. 20. 6. proclaim every one his *g.*
Jer. 31. 12. flow together to *g.* of the Lord.
Hos. 6. 4. your *g.* is as a morning cloud.
Rom. 2. 4. the riches of his *g.*
11. 22. the *g.* and severity of God.
2 Thes. 1. 11. fulfil good pleasure of his *g.*
Gospel, Mk. 1. 15. repent, and believe the *g.*
8. 35. lose life for my sake and *g.*
13. 10. the *g.* must be published.
Acts 20. 24. the *g.* of the grace of God.
Rom. 1. 16. I am not ashamed of *g.* of Christ.
15. 29. the blessing of the *g.* of Christ.
2 Cor. 4. 3. if our *g.* be hid.
Gal. 1. 7. pervert *g.* of Christ.   [cision.
2. 7. the *g.* of uncircumcision, *g.* of circum-
Eph. 6. 15. preparation of the *g.* of peace.
Col. 1. 23. be not moved from the hope of the *g.*
1 Tim. 1. 11. *g.* of the blessed God.
2 Tim. 1. 10. immortality to light through *g.*
Rev. 14. 6. having everlasting *g.* to preach.
Government, Is. 9. 7. of increase of his *g.* shall be no end.
22. 21. I commit thy *g.* to his hand.
1 Cor. 12. 28. *g.,* diversities of tongues.
2 Pet. 2. 10. them that despise *g.*
Grace, Ps. 45. 2. *g.* is poured into thy lips.
84. 11. Lord will give *g.*
Prov. 1. 9. an ornament of *g.*
3. 34; Jas. 4. 6. giveth *g.* to the lowly.
Zech. 4. 7. crying *g.,* *g.* unto it.
12. 10. spirit of *g.* and supplications.
John 1. 14. full of *g.* and truth.
1. 17. *g.* and truth came by Jesus Christ.
Acts 4. 33. great *g.* was upon them all.
14. 3. the word of his *g.*
Rom. 1. 7; 1 Cor. 1. 3; 2 Cor. 1. 2; Gal. 3;
Eph. 1. 2; Phil. 1. 2; Col. 1. 2; 1 Thes. 1. 1;
2 Thes. 1. 2. *g.* and peace.
Rom. 3. 24. justified freely by his *g.*
5. 2. access into this *g.*   [abound.
5. 20. where sin abounded, *g.* did much more
6. 14. under *g.*
11. 5. the election of *g.*
2 Cor. 4. 15. *g.* redound to the glory of God.
8. 9. know the *g.* of our Lord.
12. 9. my *g.* is sufficient for thee.
Gal. 5. 4. ye are fallen from *g.*   [of *g.*
Eph. 1. 7. forgiveness, according to riches
2. 5, 8. by *g.* ye are saved through faith.
4. 29. minister to hearers.
6. 24. *g.* be with all that love our Lord.
Col. 4. 6. let your speech be always with *g.*
2 Thes. 2. 16. good hope through *g.*
1 Tim. 1. 2; 2 Tim. 1. 2; Tit. 1. 4; 2 John 3. *g.,* mercy, and peace.
2 Tim. 2. 1. be strong in the *g.* in Christ.
Heb. 4. 16. come boldly to the throne of *g.*
10. 29. done despite to the Spirit of *g.*
12. 28. let us have *g.* to serve God.
13. 9. heart established with *g.*
Jas. 1. 11. the *g.* of the fashion perisheth.
4. 6. he giveth more *g.*

1 Pet. 1. 2; 2 Pet. 1. 2. *g.* and peace be multi-plied.
1 Pet. 3. 7. heirs of *g.*
5. 5. giveth *g.* to the humble.
2 Pet. 3. 18. grow in *g.*
Jude 4. turning *g.* of God into lasciviousness.
Rev. 1. 4. *g.* from him, who is, and was.
Gracious, Gen. 43. 29. God be *g.* to thee.
Ex. 22. 27. I will hear, for I am *g.*
33. 19. I will be *g.* to whom I will be *g.*
Num. 6. 25. Lord be *g.* unto thee.
2 Sam. 12. 22. tell whether God will be *g.?*
Neh. 9. 17, 31. a God *g.,* merciful.
Ps. 77. 9. hath God forgotten to be *g.?*
Is. 30. 18. Lord will wait that he may be *g.*
Hos. 14. 2. receive us *g.*
Amos 5. 15. may be the Lord will be *g.*
Jon. 4. 2. I knew that thou art a *g.* God.
Mal. 1. 9. beseech God, he will be *g.* to us.
Lk. 4. 22. wondered at the *g.* words.
1 Pet. 2. 3. tasted that the Lord is *g.*
Grant, 1 Sam. 1. 17. God *g.* thee thy petition.
1 Chr. 4. 10. God *g.* what he requested.
Job 6. 8. God *g.* the thing I long for.
Prov. 10. 24. desire of righteous shall be *g.*
Matt. 20. 21; Mk. 10. 37. *g.* that my two sons may sit.
2 Tim. 1. 18. Lord *g.* he may find mercy.
Rev. 3. 21. will I *g.* to sit with me in my throne.   [of *g.*
Grape, Gen. 49. 11. washed clothes in blood
Lev. 19. 10. nor gather *g.* of vineyard.
Deut. 32. 14. drink the blood of the *g.*
Cant. 2. 13. vines with tender *g.* give good smell.
Is. 5. 2. looked it should bring forth *g.*
17. 6; 24. 13. gleaning *g.*
Jer. 8. 13. there shall be no *g.* on the vine.
31. 29; Ezek. 18. 2. fathers have eaten sour *g.*
Matt. 7. 16. do men gather *g.* of thorns?
Lk. 6. 44. nor of brambles gather they *g.*
Rev. 14. 18. her *g.* are fully ripe.
Grass, Gen. 1. 11. let the earth bring forth *g.*
Deut. 32. 2. as showers upon the *g.*
2 Ki. 19. 26; Ps. 129. 6; Is. 37. 27. as *g.* on house-tops.
Ps. 72. 6. like rain upon the mown *g.*
90. 5. like *g.* which groweth up.
102. 4. my heart is withered like the *g.*
103. 15. as for man, his days are as *g.*
Prov. 27. 25. the tender *g.* sheweth itself.
Is. 40. 6; 1 Pet. 1. 24. all flesh is *g.*
Mic. 5. 7. as showers upon the *g.*
Matt. 6. 30; Lk. 12. 28. if God so clothe the *g.*
Jas. 1. 10. as *g.* he shall pass away.
Grave, Gen. 37. 35. will go down to *g.* to my son.
42. 38; 44. 31. with sorrow to the *g.*
Ex. 14. 11. no *g.* in Egypt.
Job 5. 26. come to *g.* in full age.
7. 9. goeth to *g.* come up no more.
14. 13. hide me in the *g.*
17. 1. the *g.* are ready for me.
33. 22. his soul draweth near to the *g.*
Ps. 6. 5. in *g.* who shall give thanks?
30. 3. brought my soul from the *g.*
49. 15; Hos. 13. 14. the power of the *g.*
Eccl. 9. 10. no wisdom in the *g.*
Is. 38. 18. the *g.* cannot praise thee.
53. 9. he made his *g.* with the wicked.
Matt. 27. 52. the *g.* were opened.
Lk. 11. 44. as *g.* which appear not.
John 5. 28. all in the *g.* shall hear his voice.
1 Cor. 15. 55. O *g.,* where is thy victory?

Grave, 2 Chr. 2. 7. send a man that can *g*.
Job 19. 24. were *g*. with an iron pen.
Is. 19. 16. I have *g*. thee upon palms of hands.
Jer. 17. 1. is *g*. upon table of heart.
Hab. 2. 18. that the maker hath *g*. it.
Gravity, 1 Tim. 3. 4. in subjection with *g*.
Tit. 2. 7. in doctrine shewing *g*.
Great, Gen. 12. 2; 18. 18; 46. 3. make a *g*. nation.
48. 19. he also shall be *g*.   [a *g*. God.
Deut. 10. 17; 2 Chr. 2. 5. the Lord your God is
Deut. 29. 24. the heat of this *g*. anger. [me *g*.
2 Sam. 22. 36; Ps. 18. 35. gentleness hath made
2 Ki. 5. 13. bid thee do some *g*. thing.
2 Chr. 2. 5. the house is *g*., for *g*. is our God.
Job 32. 9. *g*. men are not always wise.
36. 18. a *g*. ransom.
Ps. 14. 5; 53. 5. there were they in *g*. fear.
31. 19. how *g*. is thy goodness !
92. 5. how *g*. are thy works !
139. 17. how *g*. is the sum of them !
Is. 53. 12. divide him a portion with the *g*.
Jer. 32. 19. *g*. in counsel.
Matt. 5. 12; Lk. 6. 23. *g*. is your reward.
Matt. 20. 26. whosoever will be *g*. among you.
22. 38. the first and *g*. commandment.
Lk. 10. 2. the harvest is *g*.
16. 26. a *g*. gulf is fixed.
Acts 8. 9. giving out that he was some *g*. one.
19. 28, 34. *g*. is Diana of Ephesians.
1 Tim. 3. 16. *g*. is mystery of godliness.
Heb. 2. 3. so *g*. salvation.
12. 1. so *g*. a cloud of witnesses.
Jas. 3. 5. how *g*. a matter a little fire kindleth !
Greater, Gen. 4. 13. punishment *g*. than I can
Ex. 18. 11. Lord is *g*. than all gods. [bear.
Deut. 1. 28. people *g*. and taller than we.
Job 33. 12. that God is *g*. than man.
Hag. 2. 9. glory of latter house *g*. than former.
Matt. 11.11; Lk. 7.28. not risen a *g*. than John.
Matt. 12. 6. one *g*. than the temple.
12. 42; Lk. 11. 31. a *g*. than Solomon is here.
John 1. 50. thou shalt see *g*. things.
4. 12; 8. 53. art thou *g*. than our father?
5. 20 ; 14. 12. *g*. works than these.
10. 29 ; 14. 28. my Father is *g*. than all.
13. 16 ; 15. 20. servant not *g*. than Lord.
15. 13. *g*. love hath no man than this.
19. 11. he that delivered me hath *g*. sin.
Heb. 6. 13. he could swear by no *g*.
9. 11. *g*. and more perfect tabernacle.
11. 26. the reproach of Christ *g*. riches.
1 John 3. 20. God is *g*. than our heart.
4. 4. *g*. is he in you than he in the world.
5. 9. witness of God is *g*.
3 John 4. no *g*. joy than to hear that.
Greatest, Jer. 31. 34; Heb. 8. 11. all know me
    from least to the *g*.
Matt. 13. 32. it is the *g*. among herbs.
18. 1. who is *g*. in kingdom of heaven?
Mk. 9. 34; Lk. 9. 46. who should be *g*.
1 Cor. 13. 13. the *g*. of these is charity.
Greatly, Gen.3.16. I will *g*. multiply thy sorrow.
Ex. 19. 18. whole mount quaked *g*.
1 Sam. 12. 18. the people *g*. feared the Lord.
2 Sam. 24. 10 ; 1 Chr. 21. 8. I have sinned *g*.
1 Chr. 16. 25 ; Ps. 48. 1 ; 96. 4 ; 145. 3. the Lord
    is *g*. to be praised.
Ps. 21. 1. in thy salvation *g*. rejoice.
28. 7. my heart *g*. rejoiceth.
47. 9. God is *g*. exalted.   [of saints.
89. 7. God is *g*. to be feared in the assembly
Dan. 9. 23; 10. 11. thou art *g*. beloved.
Mk. 5. 38. wept and wailed *g*.
12. 27. ye do *g*. err.

Greatness, Ex. 15. 7. *g*. of thine excellency.
Deut. 32. 3. ascribe ye *g*. unto our God.
1 Chr. 29. 11. thine is the *g*., power, and glory.
Ps. 79. 11. according to *g*. of thy power.
145. 3. his *g*. is unsearchable.
Prov. 5. 23. in *g*. of folly go astray.
Is. 40. 26. by *g*. of his might.
63. 1. travelling in *g*. of strength.
Dan. 4. 22. thy *g*. reacheth heaven.
Eph. 1. 19. the exceeding *g*. of his power.
Greedy, Ps. 17. 12. a lion that is *g*. of prey.
Prov. 1. 19 ; 15. 27. *g*. of gain.
Is. 56. 11. they are *g*. dogs.
1 Tim. 3. 3. not *g*. of filthy lucre.
See Eph. 4. 19.
Grief, 1 Sam. 1. 16. out of abundance of *g*.
2 Chr. 6. 29. every one shall know his own *g*.
Job 6. 2. oh that my *g*. were weighed !
Ps. 31. 10. my life is spent with *g*.
Eccl. 1. 18. in much wisdom is much *g*.
Is. 53. 3. a man acquainted with *g*.
Heb. 13. 17. do it with joy, not *g*.   [man.
Grieve, Gen. 6. 6. it *g*. Lord that he had made
45. 5. be not *g*. that ye sold me.
1 Sam. 2. 33. the man to *g*. thy heart.
Ps. 78. 40. how oft did they *g*. him?
95. 10. forty years was I *g*.
139. 21. am not I *g*. with those that?
Lam. 3. 33. doth not willingly *g*. men.
Mk. 3. 5. being *g*. for hardness of their hearts
10. 22. he went away *g*.
John 21. 17. Peter was *g*. because.
Acts 4. 2. being *g*. that they taught the people.
Rom. 14. 15. if brother be *g*. with meat.
Eph. 4. 30. *g*. not the Holy Spirit of God.
Grievous, Gen. 12. 10. famine was *g*. in the
    land.
50. 11. a *g*. mourning to the Egyptians.
Ps. 10. 5. his ways are always *g*.
Prov. 15. 1. *g*. words stir up anger.
Eccl. 2. 17. work wrought under sun *g*.
Is. 21. 2. a *g*. vision is declared.
Jer. 30. 12 ; Nah. 3. 19. thy wound is *g*.
Matt. 23. 4; Lk. 11. 46. burdens *g*. to be borne.
Acts 20. 29. *g*. wolves enter among you.
Phil. 3. 1. to me indeed is not *g*.
Heb. 12. 11. no chastening joyous, but *g*.
1 John 5. 3. his commandments are not *g*.
Grind, Is. 3. 15. *g*. the faces of the poor.
Lam. 5. 13. took young men to *g*.
Matt. 21. 44; Lk. 20. 18. it will *g*. him to
    powder.
See Eccl. 12. 3.
Groan, Ex. 2. 24. God heard their *g*.
Job 24. 12. men *g*. from out of the city.
Joel 1. 18. how do the beasts *g*. !
Rom. 8. 23. we ourselves *g*. within.
2 Cor. 5. 2. we *g*. desiring to be clothed.
Gross, Is. 60. 2. *g*. darkness cover the people.
Matt. 13. 15 ; Acts 28. 27. waxed *g*.
Ground, Gen. 2. 5. not a man to till *g*.
Ex. 3. 5 ; Acts 7. 33. holy *g*.
Job 5. 6. nor trouble spring out of *g*.
Ps. 107. 33. turneth springs into dry *g*.
Is. 35. 7. parched *g*. shall become a pool.
Jer. 4. 3; Hos. 10. 12. break your fallow *g*.
Zech. 8. 12. *g*. shall give her increase.
Matt. 13. 8 ; Lk. 8. 8. fell into good *g*.
Mk. 4. 26. cast seed into *g*.
Lk. 13. 7. why cumbereth it the *g*.?
14. 18. I have bought a piece of *g*.
19. 44. lay thee even with the *g*.
John 8. 6. he wrote on the *g*.
12. 24. a corn of wheat fall into *g*.

Grounded, Is. 30. 32. where *g.* staff shall pass.
Eph. 3. 17. being rooted and *g.* in love.
Col. 1. 23. in the faith, *g.* and settled.
Grow, Gen. 48. 16. let them *g.* into a multitude.
2 Sam. 23. 5. though he make it not to *g.*
Ps. 92. 12. *g.* like cedar on Lebanon.
104. 14; 147. 8. grass to *g.* for cattle.
Is. 53. 2. he shall *g.* up before him.
Hos. 14. 5. he shall *g.* as the lily.
Mal. 4. 2. ye shall *g.* up as calves.   [they *g.*
Matt. 6. 28; Lk. 12. 27 consider the lilies how
Matt. 13. 10. let both *g.* together.
21. 19. no fruit *g.* on thee henceforward.
Mk. 4. 27. seed *g.* up, he knoweth not how.
Acts 5. 24. doubted whereunto this would *g.*
Eph. 2. 21. *g.* unto a holy temple.
2 Thes. 1. 3. your faith *g.* exceedingly.
1 Pet. 2. 2. milk of word that ye may *g.*
2 Pet. 3. 18. *g.* in grace.
Grudge, Lev. 19. 18. not bear *g.* against people.
2 Cor. 9. 7. let him give, not *g.*
Jas. 5. 9. *g.* not one against another.
1 Pet. 4. 9. use hospitality without *g.*
Guide, Ps. 25. 9. meek will he *g.* in judgment.
32. 8. I will *g.* thee with mine eye.
48. 14. our *g.* even unto death.
73. 24. *g.* me with thy counsel.
112. 5. *g.* his affairs with discretion.
Prov. 2. 17. forsaketh *g.* of her youth.
6. 7. having no *g.*, overseer, or ruler.
Is. 58. 11. Lord shall *g.* thee continually.
Jer. 3. 4. thou art the *g.* of my youth.
Matt. 23. 16, 24. ye blind *g.*
Lk. 1. 79. *g.* our feet into the way of peace.
John 16. 13. he will *g.* you into all truth.
Rom. 2. 19. a *g.* of the blind.
Guile, Ex. 21. 14. if a man slay with *g.*
Ps. 32. 2. in whose spirit is no *g.*
34. 13; 1 Pet. 3. 10. keep lips from speaking *g.*
John 1. 47. an Israelite, in whom is no *g.*
2 Cor. 12. 16. I caught you with *g.*
1 Pet. 2. 1. laying aside malice and *g.*
2. 22. nor was *g.* found in his mouth.
Guiltless, Ex. 20. 7; Deut. 5. 11. Lord will not
   hold him *g.*
Josh. 2. 19. we will be *g.*
2 Sam. 3. 28. *g.* of blood.   [the *g.*
Matt. 12. 7. ye would not have condemned
Guilty, Gen. 42. 21. verily *g.* concerning our
   brother.   [the *g.*
Ex. 34. 7; Num. 14. 18. by no means clear
Rom. 3. 19. all the world *g.* before God.
1 Cor. 11. 27. *g.* of the body and blood.
Jas. 2. 10. offend in one point, he is *g.* of all.

HABITATION, Ex. 15. 2. I will prepare him
   an *h.*
15. 13. guided them to thy holy *h.*
2 Chr. 6. 2. have built an house of *h.*
Ps. 26. 8. I have loved *h.* of thy house.
33. 14. from the place of his *h.*
69. 25. let their *h.* be desolate.
71. 3. be thou my strong *h.*
74. 20. full of *h.* of cruelty.   [throne.
89. 14. justice and judgment the *h.* of thy
91. 9. made the Most High thy *h.*
107. 7, 36. might go to a city of *h.*
132. 13. Lord hath desired it for his *h.*
Prov. 3. 33. he blesseth the *h.* of the just.
Is. 32. 18. dwell in a peaceable *h.*
Lk. 16. 9. receive into everlasting *h.*
Acts 17. 26. hath determined bounds of *h.*
Eph. 2. 22. an *h.* of God through the Spirit.
Jude 6. angels which left their own *h.*

Hail, Job 38. 22. hast thou seen the treasures
   of the *h.* ?
Ps. 105. 32. he gave them *h.* for rain.
148. 8. fire and *h.*, snow and vapours.
Is. 28. 17. the *h.* shall sweep away refuge of
   lies.   [with sorrow.
Hair, Gen. 42. 38; 44. 29. bring down gray *h.*
Jud. 20. 16. sling stones at *h.* breadth.
1 Ki. 1. 52. not an *h.* fall to earth.
Job 4. 15. the *h.* of my flesh stood up.
Ps. 40. 12; 69. 4. more than the *h.* of my head.
Matt. 3. 4; Mk. 1. 6. raiment of camel's *h.*
Matt. 5. 36. not make one *h.* white or black.
10. 30; Lk. 12. 7. the *h.* of your head are
   numbered.
John 11. 2; 12. 3. wiped feet with *h.*
1 Cor. 11. 14. if a man have long *h.*
1 Tim. 2. 9. not with broided *h.*
1 Pet. 3. 3. plaiting the *h.*
Hallow, Ex. 20. 11. blessed Sabbath, and *h.* it.
Lev. 22. 32. I am the Lord, who *h.* you.
25. 10. shall *h.* the fiftieth year.
Num. 5. 10. every man's *h.* things.
1 Ki. 9. 3. I have *h.* this house.
Jer. 17. 22. *h.* ye the Sabbath day.
Ezek. 20. 20; 44. 24. and *h.* my Sabbaths.
Matt. 6. 9; Lk. 11. 2. *h.* be thy name.
Halt, 1 Ki. 18. 21. how long *h.* ye between two
   opinions?
Ps. 38. 17. I am ready to *h.*
Jer. 20. 10. my familiars watched for my *h.*
Matt. 18. 8; Mk. 9. 45. better to enter into
   life *h.*
Lk. 14. 21. bring hither *h.* and blind.
John 5. 3. blind, *h.*, waiting for moving of
   the water.   [the tree.
Hand, Gen. 3. 22. put forth his *h.*, and take of
16. 12. his *h.* against every man.
24. 2; 47. 29. put thy *h.* under my thigh.
Ex. 14. 8; Num. 33. 3. Israel went out with
   an high *h.*
Ex. 21. 24; Deut. 19. 21. *h.* for *h.*
Ex. 33. 22. cover with my *h.* while I pass.
Num. 11. 23. is Lord's *h.* waxed short?
22. 29. would there were a sword in mine *h.*
Deut. 8. 17. my *h.* hath gotten this wealth.
33. 3. all his saints are in thy *h.*
Jud. 7. 2. saying, my own *h.* hath saved me.
1 Sam. 5. 6. *h.* of Lord heavy on them.
12. 3. of whose *h.* have I received any bribe?
26. 18. what evil is in mine *h.* ?
28. 21. I have put my life in my *h.*
2 Sam. 24. 14; 1 Chr. 21. 13. let us fall into *h.*
   of the Lord.
1 Ki. 18. 44. cloud like a man's *h.*
Ezra 7. 9; 8. 18; Neh. 2. 8. good *h.* of God.
Neh. 2. 18. strengthened their *h.* for work.
Job 12. 10. in whose *h.* is soul of every living
   thing.
17. 9. hath clean *h.* shall be stronger.
40. 14. that thine own *h.* can save.
Ps. 16. 11. at right *h.* pleasures for evermore.
24. 4. clean *h.* and pure heart.
31. 5. into thy *h.* I commit my spirit.
32. 4. day and night thy *h.* heavy.
80. 17. thy *h.* on man of thy right *h.*
90. 17. establish thou the work of our *h.*
119. 73. thy *h.* made and fashioned me.
137. 5. let my right *h.* forget her cunning.
139. 10. there shall thy *h.* lead me.
Prov. 3. 16. in left *h.* riches and honour.
10. 4. *h.* of diligent maketh rich.
11. 21; 16. 5. though *h.* join in *h.*
12. 24. *h.* of diligent shall bear rule.

69

Hand—*Continued.*

Prov. 19. 24; 26. 15. slothful man hideth his *h.*
22. 26. be not of them that strike *h.*
Eccl. 2. 24. this was from *h.* of God.
9. 10. whatsoever thy *h.* findeth to do.
11. 6. in evening withhold not thine *h.*
Is. 1. 12. who hath required this at your *h.*?
5. 25; 9. 12; 10. 4; 14. 27. his *h.* is stretched out still.
40. 12. measured waters in hollow of *h.*
53. 10. pleasure of Lord shall prosper in his *h.*
56. 2. keepeth his *h.* from doing evil.
Jer. 18. 6. as clay in the potter's *h.*
Ezek. 7. 17; 21. 7. all *h.* shall be feeble.
Dan. 4. 35. none can stay his *h.*
Joel 2. 1. day of Lord is nigh at *h.*
Mic. 7. 3. do evil with both *h.* earnestly.
Matt. 3. 2; 4. 17; 10. 7. kingdom of heaven at *h.*
3. 12; Lk. 3. 17. whose fan is in his *h.*
Matt. 18. 8; Mk. 9. 43. if thy *h.* offend.
Matt. 26. 18. my time is at *h.* [sinners.
Mk. 14. 41. Son of man is betrayed into *h.* of
16. 19. sat on right *h.* of God.
Lk. 9. 44. delivered into *h.* of men.
22. 21. *h.* that betrayeth is with me.
John 10. 29. to pluck out of my Father's *h.*
20. 27. reach hither thy *h.*
1 Cor. 12. 15. because I am not the *h.*
2 Cor. 5. 1. house not made with *h.*
Phil. 4. 5. the Lord is at *h.*
Col. 2. 11. circumcision without *h.*
1 Thes. 4. 11. work with your own *h.*
2 Thes. 2. 2. the day of Christ is at *h.*
1 Tim. 2. 8. lifting up holy *h.*
Heb. 9. 24. not entered places made with *h.*
10. 31. fall into *h.* of living God.
Jas. 4. 8. cleanse your *h.*
1 Pet. 4. 7. end of all things is at *h.* [life.
1 John 1. 1. our *h.* have handled of Word of

Handle, Gen. 4. 21. father of such as *h.* harp.
Jud. 5. 14. that *h.* pen of writer.
Ps. 115. 7. hands, but they *h.* not.
Prov. 16. 20. that *h.* a matter wisely.
Jer. 2. 8. they that *h.* the law.
Ezek. 27. 29. all that *h.* the oar.
Mk. 12. 4. sent him away shamefully *h.*
Lk. 24. 39. *h.* me, and see.
2 Cor. 4. 2. not *h.* word of God deceitfully.
1 John 1. 1. have *h.* Word of life.

Handmaid, Ps. 86. 16. save the son of thy *h.*
116. 6. thy servant, and son of thy *h.*
Lk. 1. 38. behold the *h.* of the Lord.

Hang, Num. 25. 4. *h.* them before the Lord.
Deut. 21. 23; Gal. 3. 13. he that is *h.* is accursed.
Job 26. 7. he *h.* the earth on nothing.
Ps. 137. 2. we *h.* our harps upon the willows.
Matt. 18. 6; Mk. 9. 42; Lk. 17. 2. millstone *h.* about neck. [prophets.
Matt. 22. 40. on these *h.* the law and the
27. 5. Judas went and *h.* himself.
Heb. 12. 12. lift up the hands which *h.* down.
Mk. 11. 13. if *h.* he might find fruit.
Lk. 14. 29. lest *h.* after he hath laid foundation. [God.
Acts 5. 39. *h.* ye be found to fight against
17. 27. if *h.* they might feel after him.

Happen, Prov. 12. 21. no evil *h.* to the just.
Eccl. 2. 14. one event *h.* to them all.
Is. 41. 22. let them shew us what shall *h.*
Jer. 44. 23. therefore this evil is *h.*
Lk. 24. 14. talked of things that had *h.*
Rom. 11. 25. blindness is *h.* to Israel.

Happen—*Continued.*

1 Cor. 10. 11. things *h.* for ensamples.
Phil. 1. 12. things which *h.* to me.
1 Pet. 4. 12. as though some strange thing *h.*
2 Pet. 2. 22. it is *h.* according to proverb.

Happy, Deut. 33. 29. *h.* art thou, O Israel.
Job 5. 17. *h.* is the man whom God correcteth.
Ps. 144. 15. *h.* is that people whose God is the Lord.
Prov. 3. 13. *h.* that findeth wisdom.
14. 21. *h.* is he that hath mercy on the poor.
16. 20. whoso trusteth in Lord, *h.* is he.
28. 14. *h.* is the man that feareth alway.
Jer. 12. 1. why are they *h.* that deal treacherously?
Mal. 3. 15. now we call the proud *h.*
John 13. 17. if ye know these things, *h.* if ye do them.
Rom. 14. 22. *h.* is he that condemneth not.
Jas. 5. 11. we count them *h.* that endure.
1 Pet. 3. 14; 4. 14. *h.* are ye. [Lord?

Hard, Gen. 18. 14. is any thing too *h.* for the
Deut. 1. 17. cause that is too *h.*
26. 6. Egyptians laid on *h.* bondage.
2 Sam. 3. 39. sons of Zeruiah too *h.* [tions.
1 Ki. 10. 1; 2 Chr. 9. 1. to prove with *h.* questions.
2 Ki. 2 10. thou hast asked a *h.* thing.
Job 41. 24. as *h.* as piece of nether millstone.
Prov. 13. 15. way of transgressors is *h.*
Jer. 32. 17, 27 there is nothing too *h.* for thee.
Ezek. 3. 5, 6. to a people of *h.* language.
Matt. 25. 24. I knew thou art an *h.* man.
Mk. 10. 24. how *h.* for them that trust in riches.
John 6. 60. this is an *h.* saying.
Acts 9. 5; 26. 14. *h.* to kick against the pricks.
Heb. 5. 11. many things *h.* to be uttered.
2 Pet. 3. 16. things *h.* to be understood.
Jude 15. convince all of *h.* speeches.

Harden, Ex. 4. 21; 7. 3; 14. 4. I will *h.* Pharaoh's heart.
14. 17. *h.* hearts of Egyptians.
Deut. 15. 7. shalt not *h.* thy heart.
2 Ki. 17. 14; Neh. 9. 16. *h.* their necks.
Job 6. 10. I would *h.* myself in sorrow.
9. 4. who hath *h.* himself against him?
Ps. 95. 8; Heb. 3. 8, 15; 4. 7. *h.* not your hearts.
Prov. 21. 29. a wicked man *h.* his face.
28. 14. he that *h.* his heart. [neck.
29. 1. he that, being often reproved, *h.* his
Is. 63. 17. why hast thou *h.* our heart?
Dan. 5. 20. his mind was *h.* in pride.
Mk. 6. 52; 8. 17. their heart *h.*
John 12. 40. he hath *h.* their heart.
Rom. 9. 18. whom he will *h.*
Heb. 3. 13. lest any of you be *h.* [hearts.

Hardness, Mk. 3. 5. grieved for *h.* of their
16. 14. upbraided them for *h.* of heart.
Rom. 2. 5. *h.* and impenitent heart.
2 Tim. 2. 3. endure *h.*, as good soldier.

Harm, Lev. 5. 16. make amends for *h.* done.
2 Ki. 4. 41. no *h.* in the pot.
1 Chr. 16. 22; Ps. 105. 15. do prophets no *h.*
Prov. 3. 30 if he hath done thee no *h.*
Acts 16. 28. do thyself no *h.*
28. 5. he felt no *h.*
1 Pet. 3. 13. who will *h.* you, if followers of good? [doves.

Harmless, Matt. 10. 16. wise as serpents, *h.* as
Phil. 2. 15. may be *h.*, the sons of God.
Heb. 7. 26. holy, *h.*, and undefiled.

Harp, 1 Sam. 16. 16. cunning player on an *h.*
Job 30. 31. my *h.* is turned to mourning.
Ps. 49. 4. dark saying upon the *h.*

Harp—*Continued.*

Ps. 137. 2. hanged *h.* on the willows.
Is. 5. 12. *h.* and viol are in their feasts.
1 Cor. 14. 7. whether pipe or *h.*
Rev. 14. 2. harping with their *h.*

Harvest, Gen. 8. 22. *h.* shall not cease.
Ex. 23. 16 ; 34. 22. the feast of *h.*
1 Sam. 6. 13. men reaping their *h.*
12. 17. is it not wheat *h.* to-day?
Job 5. 5. whose *h.* the hungry eateth up.
Prov. 6. 8. the ant gathereth food in *h.*
10. 5. he that sleepeth in *h.*
25. 13. cold of snow in time of *h.*
26. 1. as rain in *h.*
Is. 9. 3. according to the joy in *h.*
16. 9. the *h.* is fallen.
17. 11. *h.* shall be a heap in day of grief.
18. 4. dew in heat of *h.*
Jer. 5. 17. they shall eat up thine *h.*
8. 20. the *h.* is past, the summer ended.
Joel 3. 13 ; Rev. 14. 15. put in sickle, for the
     h. is ripe.
Matt. 9. 37. the *h.* is plenteous.
9. 38 ; Lk. 10. 2. the Lord of the *h.*
Matt. 13. 30. both grow together until *h.*
Mk. 4. 29. he putteth in sickle, because *h.* is
     come.
John 4. 35. the fields are white to *h.*

Haste, Ex. 12. 11. shall eat it in *h.*
1 Sam. 21. 8. king's business required *h.*
Ps. 31. 22 ; 116. 11. I said in my *h.*
Prov. 19. 2. he that *h.* with feet sinneth.
28. 22. he that *h.* to be rich.
Is. 52. 12. ye shall not go out with *h.*
60. 22. the Lord will *h.* it.
Zeph. 1. 14. day of the Lord *h.* greatly.
Mk. 6. 25. came in *h.* to the king.

Hasty, Prov. 14. 29. he that is *h.* of spirit
     exalteth folly.
29. 20. seest thou a man *h.* in words?
Eccl. 5. 2. let not thy heart be *h.*
7. 9. be not *h.* in thy spirit.
Is. 28. 4. as *h.* fruit before summer.
Dan. 2. 15. why is the decree so *h.*?

Hate, Gen. 24. 60. possess gate of those that
     h. them.
Lev. 19. 17. shalt not *h.* thy brother.
26. 17. that *h.* you shall reign over you.
2 Chr. 19. 2. love them that *h.* the Lord.
Ps. 34. 21. they that *h.* righteous shall be
     desolate.
83. 2. that *h.* thee have lifted up the head.
97. 10. ye that love the Lord, *h.* evil.
139. 21. do not I *h.* them that *h.* thee?
Prov. 1. 22. how long will ye *h.* knowledge?
8. 13. fear of the Lord is to *h.* evil.
13. 24. he that spareth rod, *h.* son.
15. 10. he that *h.* reproof shall die.
Eccl. 3. 8. a time to *h.*
Is. 1. 14. your feasts my soul *h.*
61. 8. I *h.* robbery for burnt-offering.
Amos 5. 15. *h.* the evil and love the good.
Mic. 3. 2. who *h.* good, and love evil.
Zech. 8. 17. these are things that I *h.*
Mal. 1. 3 ; Rom. 9. 13. I loved Jacob, and *h.*
     Esau.   [*h.* you.
Matt. 5. 44 ; Lk. 6. 27. do good to them that
Matt. 6. 24. either he will *h.* the one.
10. 22 ; Mk. 13. 13 ; Lk. 21. 17. ye shall be *h.*
Matt. 24. 10. betray and *h.* one another.
Lk. 6. 22. blessed are ye when men shall
     h. you.
14. 26. *h.* not his father and mother.
John 3. 20. *h.* not the light.

Hate—*Continued.*

John 7. 7. the world cannot *h.* you.
12. 25. he that *h.* his life.
15. 18 ; 1 John 3. 13. marvel not if world *h.*
                     [you.
Rom. 7. 15. what I *h.*, that do I.
Eph. 5. 29. no man ever yet *h.* his own flesh.
1 John 2. 9 ; 3. 15 ; 4. 20. *h.* his brother.

Haughty, 2 Sam. 22. 28. thine eyes are upon
     the *h.*
Ps. 131. 1. my heart is not *h.*
Prov. 16. 18. a *h.* spirit before a fall.
Is. 3. 16. daughters of Zion are *h.*
10. 33. the *h.* shall be humbled.
Zeph. 3. 11. no more be *h.*

Head, Gen. 3. 15. it shall bruise thy *h.*
Josh. 2. 19. blood be upon his *h.*
Jud. 13. 5. no razor come on his *h.*
2 Ki. 2. 3. take thy master from thy *h.* to-day.
4. 19. said, my *h.*, my *h.*
Est. 9. 25. device return on own *h.*
Ps. 7. 16. mischief return on own *h.*
27. 6. now shall my *h.* be lifted up.
38. 4. iniquities gone over mine *h.*
110. 7. therefore shall he lift up the *h.*
141. 5. oil, which shall not break my *h.*
Prov. 10. 6. blessings on *h.* of the just.
25. 22 , Rom. 12. 20. coals of fire on his *h.*
Eccl. 2. 14. the wise man's eyes are in his *h.*
Is. 1. 5. the whole *h.* is sick.
51. 11. everlasting joy upon their *h.*
58. 5. bow down *h.* as bulrush.
59. 17. helmet of salvation on *h.*
Jer. 9. 1. O that my *h.* were waters.
Dan. 2. 38. thou art this *h.* of gold.
Amos 8. 10. bring baldness on every *h.*
Zech. 1. 21. no man did lift up his *h.*
4. 7. bring *h.* stone with shoutings.
6. 11. set crowns on *h.* of Joshua.
Matt. 5. 36. neither swear by thy *h.*
27. 30 ; Mk. 15. 19. smote him on *h.*
Lk. 7. 46. my *h.* thou didst not anoint.
21. 18. shall not an hair of *h.* perish.
John 13. 9. also my hands and my *h.*
1 Cor. 11. 3. the *h.* of every man is Christ.
Eph. 1. 22 ; 4. 15 ; Col. 1. 18. the *h.* of the
     church.
Eph. 5. 23. husband is *h.* of the wife.
Col. 2. 19. not holding the *h.*
Rev. 19. 12. on his *h.* many crowns.

Heal, Ex. 15. 26. I am the Lord that *h.* thee.
Deut. 32. 39. I wound, I *h.*
2 Ki. 2. 22. waters were *h.*
Ps. 6. 2. O Lord, *h.* me.
41. 4. *h.* my soul, for I have sinned.
103. 3. who *h.* all thy diseases.
107. 20. sent his word, and *h.* them.
Is. 6. 10. lest they convert, and be *h.*
53. 5. with his stripes we are *h.*
Jer. 6. 14 ; 8. 11. they have *h.* the hurt slightly.
17. 14. *h.* me, and I shall be *h.*
Lam. 2. 13. who can *h.* thee?
Hos. 6. 1. he hath torn, and he will *h.* us.
14. 4. I will *h.* their backslidings.
Matt. 8. 7. I will come and *h.* him.
10. 8 ; Lk. 9. 2 ; 10. 9. *h.* the sick.
Matt. 12. 10 ; Lk. 14. 3. is it lawful to *h.* on
     Sabbath?
Matt. 13. 15 ; John 12. 40 ; Acts 28. 27. be
     converted, and I should *h.* them.
Mk. 3. 2 ; Lk. 6. 7. whether he would *h.* on
     Sabbath day.
Lk. 4. 18. to *h.* the broken-hearted.
5. 17. power of the Lord present to *h.*
John 4. 47. come and *h.* his son.

Heal—*Continued.*
John 5. 13. he that was *h.* wist not who it was.
Acts 4. 30. stretching thine hand to *h.*
14. 9. that he had faith to be *h.*
Heb. 12. 13. let it rather be *h.*
Jas. 5. 16. pray that ye may be *h.*
1 Pet. 2. 24. by whose stripes ye were *h.*
Healing, Jer. 14. 19. there is no *h.* for us.
Nah. 3. 19. no *h.* of thy bruise.
Mal. 4. 2. arise with *h.* in his wings.
Matt. 4. 23. *h.* all manner of sickness.
Lk. 9. 11. healed them that had need of *h.*
1 Cor. 12. 9, 28. the gifts of *h.*
Rev. 22. 2. for the *h.* of the nations.
Health, Gen. 43. 28. our father is in good *h.*
2 Sam. 20. 9. art thou in *h.*, my brother?
Ps. 42. 11; 43. 5. the *h.* of my countenance.
67. 2. thy saving *h.* may be known.
Prov. 4. 22. they are *h.* to all their flesh.
13. 17. a faithful ambassador is *h.*
16. 24. *h.* to the bones.
Is. 58. 8. thy *h.* shall spring forth.
Jer. 8. 15. looked for a time of *h.*
8. 22. why is not *h.* of my people recovered?
3 John 2. mayest be in *h.*
Heap, Deut. 13. 16. shall be an *h.* for ever.
32. 23. *h.* mischiefs upon them.
Josh. 7. 26. over him a *h.* of stones.
Job 16. 4. I could *h.* up words.
27. 16. though he *h.* up silver.
Ps. 39. 6. he *h.* up riches.
Prov. 25. 22; Rom. 12. 20. *h.* coals of fire.
Eccl. 2. 26. to gather and to *h.* up.
Is. 17. 11. harvest shall be a *h.*
25. 2. thou hast made of a city an *h.*
Jer. 30. 18. city shall be builded on own *h.*
Ezek. 24. 10. *h.* on wood.
Mic. 1. 6. Samaria as an *h.* of the field.
3. 12. Jerusalem shall become *h.*
Hab. 1. 10. they shall *h.* dust.
2 Tim. 4. 3. to themselves teachers.
Jas. 5. 3. ye have *h.* treasure for last days.
Hear, Deut. 4. 10. I will make them *h.* my
   words.
31. 12. *h.* and fear the Lord.
1 Sam. 2. 23. I *h.* your evil dealings.
15. 14. lowing of oxen which I *h.*
1 Ki. 8. 42. they shall *h.* of thy great name.
18. 26. saying, O Baal, *h.* us.
2 Ki. 7. 6. *h.* a noise of chariots.
18. 28; Is. 36. 13. *h.* words of the great king.
1 Chr. 14. 15. when thou *h.* a sound of going.
Neh. 8. 2. all that could *h.* with understand-
Job 5. 27. *h.* it, and know thou it.   [ing.
34. 2. *h.* my words, ye wise men.
Job 42. 4. *h.*, I beseech thee.
Ps. 4. 1; 39. 12; 54. 2; 84. 8; 102. 1; 143. 1. *h.*
  my prayer.
20. 1. Lord *h.* thee, in day of trouble.
27. 7. *h.*, O Lord, when I cry.
51. 8. make me *h.* joy and gladness.
59. 7. who, say they, doth *h.*?
66. 16. come, *h.*, all ye that fear God.
85. 8. I will *h.* what God the Lord will speak.
102. 20. *h.* groaning of the prisoner.
143. 8. to *h.* thy loving-kindness.
Prov. 8. 33. *h.* instruction and be wise.
22. 17. *h.* the words of the wise.
Eccl. 5. 1. more ready to *h.* than give.
7. 5. better to *h.* rebuke of wise.
12. 13. *h.* conclusion of the whole matter.
Is. 1. 2. *h.*, O heavens, and give ear.
6. 9; Mk. 4. 12. *h.*, but understand not.
Is. 33. 13. *h.*, ye that are afar off.

Hear—*Continued.*
Is. 34. 1. let the earth *h.*
42. 18. *h.*, ye deaf.
55. 3 ; John 5. 25. *h.*, and your soul shall live.
Ezek. 3. 27. he that *h.*, let him *h.*
Dan. 9. 17. *h.* prayer of thy servant.
Matt. 11. 5; Mk. 7. 37; Lk. 7. 22. the deaf *h.*
Matt. 13. 17; Lk. 10. 24. *h.* those things which
  ye *h.*   [him.
Matt. 17. 5; Mk. 9. 7. my beloved Son, *h.*
Mk. 4. 24; Lk. 8. 18. take heed what ye *h.*
Lk. 5. 1. pressed on him to *h.* word.
6. 17. came to *h.* him and be healed.
9. 9. who is this of whom I *h.*?
10. 16. he that *h.*, you, *h.* me.
16. 2. how is it that I *h.* this of thee?
19. 48. people very attentive to *h.*
John 5. 25. dead shall *h.* voice of Son of God.
5. 30. as I *h.*, I judge.
6. 60. an hard saying, who can *h.* it?
8. 47. he that is of God, *h.* God's words.
9. 31. God *h.* not sinners.
12. 47. if any man *h.* my words.
14. 24. the word ye *h.* is not mine.
Acts 2. 8. how *h.* we every man in his own
  tongue?
13. 44. whole city came to *h.* word.
17. 21. to tell or *h.* some new thing.
Rom. 10. 14. how *h.* without a preacher?
1 Cor. 11. 18. I *h.* there be divisions.
2 Thes. 3. 11. we *h.* that some walk disorderly.   [thee.
1 Tim. 4. 16. save thyself, and them that *h.*
Jas. 1. 19. swift to *h.*
1 John 5. 15. we know that he *h.* us.
3 John 4. than to *h.* children walk in truth.
Rev. 3. 20. if any man *h.* my voice.
9. 20. neither see, nor *h.*, nor walk.
Heard, Gen. 3. 8. they *h.* voice of the Lord.
16. 11. Lord *h.* thy affliction.
21. 26. neither yet *h.* I of it.
Ex. 2. 24. God *h.* their groaning.
3. 7. I have *h.* their cry.
Num. 11. 1; 12. 2. the Lord *h.* it.
Deut. 4. 12. only ye *h.* a voice.
1 Ki. 6. 7. nor any tool of iron *h.*   [ago?
2 Ki. 19. 25; Is. 37. 26. hast thou not *h.* long
Ezra 3. 13; Neh. 12. 43. noise was *h.* afar off.
Job 15. 8. hast thou *h.* the secret of God?
19. 7. cry out of wrong, but not *h.*
29. 11. when the ear *h.* me, it blessed me.
Ps. 6. 9. Lord hath *h.* my supplication.
10. 17. hast *h.* the desire of the humble.
34. 4. I sought the Lord, and he *h.*
38. 13. I as a deaf man *h.* not.
61. 5. thou hast *h.* my vows.
97. 8. Zion *h.* and was glad.
116. 1. I love the Lord, because he hath *h.*
Cant. 2. 12. voice of turtle is *h.*
Is. 40. 21. have ye not *h.*?
52. 15. that had not *h.*, shall they consider.
60. 18. violence no more be *h.* in land.
Is. 64. 4. not *h.* what he hath prepared.
65. 19. weeping no more be *h.*
66. 8. who hath *h.* such a thing?
Jer. 7. 13. rising early, but ye *h.* not.
51. 46. rumour shall be *h.* in land.
Ezek. 26. 13. harps shall no more be *h.*
Dan. 12. 8. I *h.*, but understood not.
Jon. 2. 2. I cried to the Lord, and he *h.*
Mal. 3. 16. the Lord hearkened, and *h.* it.
Matt. 6. 7. be *h.* for much speaking.
26. 65; Mk. 14. 64. ye have *h.* the blasphemy.
Lk. 12. 3. shall be *h.* in the light.

Heard—*Continued.*
John 4. 42. we have *h.* him ourselves.
8. 6. as though he *h.* not.
11. 41. I thank thee thou hast *h.* me.
18. 21. ask them which *h.* me.   [pricked.
Acts 2. 37. when they *h.* this, they were
4. 4. many which *h.* believed.
4. 20. cannot but speak things we have *h.*
22. 15. witness of what thou hast seen and *h.*
Rom. 10. 14. of whom they have not *h.*
1 Cor. 2. 9. eye hath not seen, or ear *h.*
2 Cor. 12. 4. *h.* unspeakable words.
Eph. 4. 21. if so be ye have *h.* him.
Heb. 2. 3. confirmed by them that *h.*
4. 2. not mixed with faith in them that *h.*
5. 7. was *h.* in that he feared.
Jas. 5. 11. ye have *h.* of patience of Job.
1 John 1. 1. that which we have *h.* and seen.
Rev. 3. 3. remember how thou hast *h.*
10. 4; 14. 2; 18. 4. *h.* a voice from heaven.
Hearer, Rom. 2. 13. not the *h.* of law are just.
Eph. 4. 29. minister grace unto the *h.*
2 Tim. 2. 14. to subverting of the *h.*
Jas. 1. 22. be ye doers of the word, not *h.*
Hearing, Deut. 31. 11. read this law in their *h.*
2 Ki. 4. 31. was neither voice nor *h.*
Job 42. 5. by the *h.* of the ear.
Prov. 20. 12. the *h.* ear, the Lord hath made.
Eccl. 1. 8. nor ear filled with *h.*
Is. 33. 15. stoppeth ears from *h.* blood.
Amos 8. 11. a famine of *h.* the words of the
   Lord.
Matt. 13. 13. *h.,* they hear not.
Mk. 6. 2. many *h.* were astonished.
Lk. 2. 46. *h.* them, and asking questions.
Acts 9. 7. *h.* a voice, but seeing no man.
Rom. 10. 17. faith cometh by *h.*
1 Cor. 12. 17. where were the *h.?*
Gal. 3. 2. or by the *h.* of faith?
Heb. 5. 11. seeing ye are dull of *h.*
Hearken, Deut. 18. 15. a prophet, to him ye
   shall *h.*   [ments.
28. 13; 1 Ki. 11. 38. if thou *h.* to command-
Josh. 1. 17. so will we *h.* unto thee.   [rams.
1 Sam. 15. 22. to *h.* better than the fat of
Ps. 103. 20. angels *h.* to voice of his word.
Is. 55. 2. *h.* diligently unto me.
Dan. 9. 19. O Lord, *h.* and do.
Mic. 1. 2. *h.,* O earth, and all therein.
Mk. 7. 14. *h.* to me, every one of you.
Acts 7. 2. men, brethren, and fathers, *h.*
Heart, Gen. 45. 26. Jacob's *h.* fainted.
Ex. 23. 9. ye know the *h.* of a stranger.
35. 35. hath he filled with wisdom of *h.*
Deut. 11. 13; Josh. 22. 5; 1 Sam. 12. 20. serve
   him with all your *h.*
Deut. 13. 3; 30. 6; Matt. 22. 37; Mk. 12. 30;
   Lk. 10. 27. love the Lord with all your *h.*
Jud. 5. 16. great searchings of *h.*
1 Sam. 10. 9. God gave him another *h.*
16. 7. the Lord looketh on the *h.*
1 Ki. 3. 9. give an understanding *h.*
8. 17; 2 Chr. 6. 7. it was in the *h.* of David.
1 Ki. 11. 4. not perfect, as was *h.* of David.
14. 8. followed me with all his *h.*
1 Chr. 12. 33. not of double *h.*
16. 10; Ps. 105. 3. let the *h.* of them rejoice
   that seek the Lord.
1 Chr. 29. 17; Jer. 11. 20. thou triest the *h.*
2 Chr. 15. 12. seek God of fathers with all *h.*
31. 21. he did it with all his *h.*
32. 25. his *h.* was lifted up.
Neh. 2. 2. nothing else but sorrow of *h.*
Job 9. 4. wise in *h.,* and mighty.

Heart—*Continued.*
Job 29. 13. I caused the widow's *h.* to sing
38. 36. given understanding to the *h.*
Ps. 19. 8. statutes rejoicing the *h.*
27. 3. my *h.* shall not fear.
34. 18. Lord is nigh them of broken *h.*
44. 21. he knoweth secrets of the *h.*
64. 6. the *h.* is deep.
73. 7. more than *h.* could wish.
78. 37. their *h.* was not right.
97. 11. gladness sown for upright in *h.*
139. 23. search me, and know my *h.*
Prov. 4. 23. keep thy *h.* with all diligence.
14. 10. the *h.* knoweth his own bitterness.
23. 7. as he thinketh in his *h.*
31. 11. *h.* of her husband doth trust.
Eccl. 8. 5. a wise man's *h.* discerneth.
Is. 30. 29. ye shall have gladness of *h.*
35. 4. say to them of fearful *h.*
57. 1; Jer. 12. 11. no man layeth it to *h.*
Is. 57. 15. revive *h.* of contrite.
65. 14. sing for joy of *h.*
Jer. 11. 20. that triest reins and *h.*
17. 9. *h.* is deceitful above all things.
24. 7. I will give them a *h.* to know me.
Lam. 3. 65. give them sorrow of *h.*
Ezek. 11. 19. stony *h.* out of flesh.
18. 31. make a new *h.* and new spirit.
36. 26. will give you a *h.* of flesh.
44. 7; Acts 7. 51. uncircumcised in *h.*
Joel 2. 13. rend your *h.*
Mal. 4. 6. turn *h.* of fathers to children.
Matt. 5. 8. blessed are the pure in *h.*
6. 21; Lk. 12. 34. there will your *h.* be also.
Matt. 11. 29. meek and lowly in *h.*
12. 34. out of abundance of the *h.*
Matt. 15. 19; Mk. 7. 21. out of *h.* proceed evil
   thoughts.
Mk. 2. 8. why reason ye in your *h.?*
10. 5; 16. 14. hardness of *h.*
Lk. 21. 14. settle it in your *h.*
24. 25. slow of *h.* to believe.
John 14. 1, 27. let not your *h.* be troubled.
Acts 2. 46. with singleness of *h.*
7. 54. were cut to the *h.*
11. 23. with purpose of *h.*
Rom. 10. 10. with the *h.* man believeth.
1 Cor. 2. 9. neither entered into *h.* of man.
2 Cor. 3. 3. in fleshy tables of the *h.*
5. 12. glory in appearance, not in *h.*
Eph. 3. 17. that Christ dwell in your *h.* by
Col. 3. 22. in singleness of *h.*   [faith.
Heb. 4. 12. discerner of intents of the *h.*
10. 22. draw near with true *h.*
Jas. 4. 8. purify your *h.*
1 Pet. 3. 4. the hidden man of the *h.*
3. 15. sanctify the Lord in your *h.*
Heat, Gen. 8. 22. cold and *h.,* summer and
18. 1. in *h.* of the day.   [winter.
Deut. 29. 24. the *h.* of this great anger.
Ps. 19. 6. nothing hid from *h.* thereof.
Is. 4. 6; 25. 4. a shadow from the *h.*
18. 4. *h.* upon herbs, dew in *h.* of harvest.
19. 10. neither shall *h.* smite them.
Hos. 7. 4. as an oven *h.* by the baker.
Matt. 20. 12. borne burden and *h.* of the day.
Jas. 1. 11. sun risen with burning *h.*
2 Pet. 3. 10. elements melt with *h.*
Heath, Jer. 17. 6; 48. 6. like *h.* in desert.
Heathen, Ps. 2. 1; Acts 4. 25. why do the *h.*
   rage?
Ps. 2. 8. give thee *h.* for inheritance.
9. 5. thou hast rebuked the *h.*
33. 10. bringeth counsel of *h.* to nought.

Heathen—*Continued.*
Ps. 102. 15. the *h.* shall fear name of the Lord.
Matt. 6. 7. vain repetitions, as the *h.* do.
18. 17. let him be as an *h.* man.
Gal. 3. 8. that God would justify the *h.*
Heaven, Gen. 1. 1. God created *h.* and earth.
28. 17. the gate of *h.*
Ex. 20. 22. talked with you from *h.*
Deut. 10. 14; 1 Ki. 8. 27; Ps. 115. 16. the *h.*
and *h.* of heavens.
Deut. 33. 13. the precious things of *h.*
2 Ki. 7. 2. if the Lord make windows in *h.*
Job 15. 15. the *h.* are not clean in his sight.
22. 14. he walketh in the circuit of *h.*
Ps. 8. 3. when I consider thy *h.*
73. 25. whom have I in *h.?*   [Lord?
89. 6. who in *h.* can be compared to the
103. 11. as *h.* is high above the earth.
Prov. 8. 27. when he prepared the *h.* I was
25. 3. the *h.* for height.   [there.
Eccl. 5. 2. for God is in *h.*
Is. 40. 12. who hath meted out *h.?*
65. 17; Rev. 21. 1. new *h.* and new earth.
Is. 66. 1; Acts 7. 49. *h.* is my throne.
Jer. 7. 18. make cakes to queen of *h.*
23. 24. do not I fill *h.* and earth?
31. 37. if *h.* can be measured.
51. 15. hath stretched out the *h.*
Ezek. 32. 7. I will cover the *h.*
Dan. 4. 35. doeth will in army of *h.*
7. 13. with clouds of *h.*
Hag. 1. 10. the *h.* over you is stayed from dew.
Mal. 3. 10. if I will not open windows of *h.*
Matt. 5. 18. till *h.* and earth pass.
5. 34; Jas. 5. 12. nor swear by *h.*
Matt. 24. 30; 26. 64; Mk. 14. 62. Son of man
coming in clouds of *h.*
Mk. 13. 27. elect from uttermost part of *h.*
Lk. 3. 21. the *h.* was opened.
15. 18. I have sinned against *h.*
John 1. 51. ye shall see *h.* open.
6. 31. bread from *h.*
Acts 3. 21. whom the *h.* must receive.
4. 12. none other name under *h.*
Rom. 1. 18. wrath of God revealed from *h.*
1 Cor. 8. 5. whether in *h.* or in earth.
2 Cor. 5. 1. house eternal in the *h.*
Gal. 1. 8. though an angel from *h.* preach.
Eph. 1. 10. gather in one, things in *h.*
3. 15. whole family in *h.* is named.
6. 9; Col. 4. 1. your master is in *h.*
Phil. 3. 20. our conversation is in *h.*
Col. 1. 16. by him all things created in *h.*
Heb. 10. 34. have in *h.* a better substance.
12. 23. written in *h.*
1 John 5. 7. three that bear record in *h.*
Rev. 4. 1. a door opened in *h.*
8. 1. silence in *h.*
11. 19. temple of God in *h.*
12. 1. a great wonder in *h.*   [them.
Heavenly, Matt. 6. 26. your *h.* Father feedeth
Lk. 2. 13. multitude of the *h.* host.
John 3. 12. if I tell you of *h.* things.
Acts 26. 19. not disobedient to *h.* vision.
1 Cor. 15. 48. as is the *h.*, such are they.
Eph. 1. 3; 2. 6; 3. 10. in *h.* places.
Heb. 3. 1. partakers of the *h.* calling.
6. 4. have tasted of the *h.* gift.
8. 5. shadow of *h.* things.
11. 16. an *h.* country.
Heaviness, Ps. 69. 20. full of *h.*
119. 28. my soul melteth for *h.*
Prov. 12. 25. *h.* in the heart maketh it stoop.
14. 13. the end of that mirth is *h.*

Heaviness—*Continued.*
Is. 61. 3. garment of praise for spirit of *h.*
Rom. 9. 2. have great *h.* and sorrow.
Jas. 4. 9. let your joy be turned to *h.*
1 Pet. 1. 6. if need be, ye are in *h.*
Heavy, Ex. 17. 12. Moses' hands were *h.*
18. 18. this thing is too *h.* for thee.
1 Ki. 14. 6. sent with *h.* tidings.
Neh. 5. 18. the bondage was *h.*
Ps. 32. 4. thy hand was *h.* upon me.
Prov. 25. 20. songs to a *h.* heart. ◂
31. 6. wine to those of *h.* hearts.
Is. 6. 10. and make their ears *h.*
58. 6. to undo the *h.* burdens.
Matt. 11. 28. all ye that are *h.* laden.
23. 4. they bind *h.* burdens.
26. 37. he began to be very *h.*
26. 43; Mk. 14. 40. their eyes were *h.*
Hedge, Job 1. 10. not made an *h.* about him.
Prov. 15. 19. way of slothful as an *h.* of
thorns.
Eccl. 10. 8. whoso breaketh an *h.*
Hos. 2. 6. I will *h.* up thy way.
Mk. 12. 1. he set an *h.* about it.
Lk. 14. 23. the highways and *h.*
Heed, 2 Sam. 20. 10. took no *h.* to the sword.
2 Ki. 10. 31. Jehu took no *h.*
Ps. 119. 9. by taking *h.* to thy word.
Eccl. 12. 9. preacher gave good *h.*
Jer. 18. 18. let us not give *h.* to any words.
Acts 3. 5. he gave *h.* unto them.
1 Tim. 1. 4; Tit. 1. 14. neither give *h.* to fables.
1 Tim. 4. 1. giving *h.* to seducing spirits.
Heb. 2. 1. we ought to give more earnest *h.*
Heel, Gen. 3. 15. thou shalt bruise his *h.*
25. 26. Hos. 12. 3. hold on brother's *h.*
Ps. 41. 9; John 13. 18. hath lifted up *h.*
against me.
Ps. 49. 5. iniquity of my *h.* compass me.
Height, Job 22. 12. is not God in *h.* of heaven?
Ps. 102. 19. Lord looked from *h.* of sanctuary.
Prov. 25. 3. the heaven for *h.*
Is. 7. 11. ask it in the *h.* above.
Rom. 8. 39. nor *h.* nor depth be able.
Eph. 3. 18, 19. the *h.* of the love of Christ.
Heir, 2 Sam. 14. 7. we will destroy the *h.*
Prov. 30. 23. handmaid that is *h.* to her mis-
tress.   [the *h.*
Matt. 21. 38; Mk. 12. 7; Lk. 20. 14. this is
Rom. 8. 17. *h.* of God, joint *h.* with Christ.
Gal. 3. 29. *h.* according to the promise.
4. 7. an *h.* of God through Christ.
Eph. 3. 6. Gentiles be fellow-*h.*
Tit. 3. 7. *h.* according to hope of eternal life.
Heb. 1. 14. who shall be *h.* of salvation.
6. 17. the *h.* of promise.
11. 7. became *h.* of righteousness.
Jas. 2. 5. *h.* of the kingdom.
1 Pet. 3. 7. as *h.* together of the grace.
Hell, Deut. 32. 22. fire shall burn to lowest *h.*
2 Sam. 22. 6; Ps. 18. 5. sorrows of *h.* com-
Job 11. 8. deeper than *h.*   [passed me.
26. 6. *h.* is naked before him.
Ps. 9. 17. wicked be turned into *h.*
16. 10; Acts 2. 27. not leave soul in *h.*
Ps. 55. 15. let them go down quick into *h.*
116. 3. pains of *h.* gat hold on me.
139. 8. if I make my bed in *h.*
Prov. 5. 5. her steps take hold on *h.*
7. 27. house is the way to *h.*
9. 18. her guests are in the depths of *h.*
15. 11. *h.* and destruction before the Lord.
15. 24. that he may depart from *h.* beneath.
23. 14. deliver his soul from *h.*

74

Hell—Continued.

Prov. 27. 20. *h.* and destruction are never full.
Is. 5. 14. *h.* hath enlarged herself.
14. 9. *h.* from beneath is moved.
28. 15. with *h.* are we at agreement.
Ezek. 31. 16. when I cast him down to *h.*
32. 21. shall speak out of the midst of *h.*
Amos 9. 2. though they dig into *h.*
Jon. 2. 2. out of the belly of *h.*
Hab. 2. 5. enlargeth his desire as *h.*
Matt. 5. 22. in danger of *h.* fire.
10. 28; Lk. 12. 5. destroy soul and body in *h.*
Matt. 11. 23; Lk. 10. 15. brought down to *h.*
Matt. 16. 18. gates of *h.* shall not prevail.
18. 9; Mk. 9. 47. two eyes to be cast into *h.*
Matt. 23. 15. twofold more the child of *h.*
Lk. 16. 23. in *h.* he lift up his eyes.
Acts 2. 31. his soul was not left in *h.*
Jas. 3. 6. tongue set on fire of *h.*
2 Pet. 2. 4. cast angels down to *h.*
Rev. 1. 18. keys of *h.* and death.
20. 13. death and *h.* delivered up dead.

Help, Gen. 2. 18. an *h.* meet for him.
Deut. 33. 29. the shield of thy *h.*
Job 6. 13. is not my *h.* in me?
Ps. 20. 2. Lord send *h.* from sanctuary.
22. 19; 38. 22. haste thee to *h.* me.
33. 20. he is our *h.* and our shield.
42. 5. the *h.* of his countenance.
46. 1. God a very present *h.* in trouble.
60. 11; 108. 12. vain is the *h.* of man.
63. 7. thou hast been my *h.*
89. 19. laid *h.* on one that is mighty.
94. 17. unless Lord had been my *h.*
121. 1. the hills, from whence cometh my *h.*
124. 8. our *h.* is in name of the Lord.
146. 3. trust not in man, in whom is no *h.*
Is. 10. 3. to whom will ye flee for *h.?*
30. 5. nor be an *h.* nor profit.
Hos. 13. 9. in me is thine *h.*
Mk. 9. 24. *h.* thou mine unbelief.
Acts 21. 28. men of Israel, *h.*
26. 22. having obtained *h.* of God.
Heb. 4. 16. grace to *h.* in time of need.

Helper, Ps. 10. 14. thou art *h.* of the fatherless.
72. 12. deliver him that hath no *h.*
Heb. 13. 6. Lord is my *h.*, I will not fear.

Hen, Matt. 23. 37; Lk. 13. 34. as *h.* gathereth chickens.

Heritage, Job 20. 29. *h.* appointed by God.
Ps. 16. 6; Jer. 3. 19. a goodly *h.*
Ps. 61. 5. *h.* of those that fear thy name.
111. 6. give them *h.* of the heathen.
127. 3. children are an *h.* of the Lord.
Is. 54. 17. *h.* of servants of the Lord.
Mic. 7. 14. feed flock of thine *h.*
1 Pet. 5. 3. lords over God's *h.*

Hid, Gen. 3. 8. Adam and his wife *h.*
Ex. 2. 2. *h.* Moses three months.
3. 6. Moses *h.* his face.
2 Ki. 4. 27. the Lord hath *h.* it from me.
Job 17. 4. *h.* heart from understanding.
Ps. 22. 24. neither *h.* his face from him.
35. 7. they *h.* for me their net.
119. 11. thy word have I *h.* in mine heart.
Is. 53. 3. and we *h.* our faces from him.
Matt. 10. 26; Mk. 4. 22. there is nothing *h.*
Matt. 11. 25; Lk. 10. 21. *h.* from wise.
Matt. 25. 18. went and *h.* his lord's money.
Lk. 19. 42. now they are *h.* from thine eyes.
2 Cor. 4. 3. if our gospel be *h.*
Col. 1. 26. mystery *h.* from ages.
3. 3. your life is *h.* with Christ.
1 Pet. 3. 4. the *h.* man of the heart.

Hide, Gen. 18. 17. shall I *h.* from Abraham?
Job 14. 13. wouldest *h.* me in the grave.
40. 13. *h.* them in the dust together.
Ps. 17. 8. *h.* me under the shadow of thy wings.
27. 5. *h.* me in pavilion.
31. 20. *h.* them in secret of thy presence.
89. 46. how long wilt thou *h.* thyself?
139. 12. darkness *h.* not from thee.
143. 9. I flee to thee, to *h.* me.
Is. 1. 15. I will *h.* mine eyes from you.
2. 10. and *h.* thee in the dust.
26. 20. *h.* thyself for a little moment.
32. 2. a man shall be as an *h.* place.
45. 15. thou art a God that *h.* thyself.
Ezek. 28. 3. no secret they can *h.* from thee.
Jas. 5. 20. and *h.* a multitude of sins.
Rev. 6. 16. *h.* us from the face of him.

High, Gen. 29. 7. lo, it is yet *h.* day.
Job 11. 8. it is as *h.* as heaven.
22. 12. behold stars, how *h.* they are!
41. 34. he beholdeth all *h.* things.
Ps. 18. 27. bring down *h.* looks.
62. 9. men of *h.* degree are a lie.
68. 18. thou has ascended on *h.*
103. 11. as the heaven is *h.* above the earth.
131. 1. in things too *h.* for me.
138. 6. though the Lord be *h.*
139. 6. it is *h.*, I cannot attain unto it.
Eccl. 12. 5. afraid of that which is *h.*
Is. 6. 1. Lord *h.* and lifted up.
32. 15. Spirit poured on us from on *h.*
35. 8. an *h.*-way shall be there.
57. 15. thus saith the *h.* and lofty One.
Matt. 22. 9; Lk. 14. 23. go into the *h.*-ways.
Lk. 1. 78. dayspring from on *h.*
John 19. 31. Sabbath was an *h.* day.
Rom. 12. 16. mind not *h.* things.
13. 11. it is *h.* time to awake.
2 Cor. 10. 5. casting down every *h.* thing.
Phil. 3. 14. prize of the *h.* calling of God.

Higher, Ps. 61. 2. lead me to Rock that is *h.*
Is. 55. 9. heavens *h.* than the earth.
Lk. 14. 10. friend, go up *h.*
Rom. 13. 1. be subject to *h.* powers.
Heb. 7. 26. high priest made *h.* than the heavens.

Hill, Gen. 49. 26. the everlasting *h.*
Deut. 11. 11. a land of *h.* and valleys.
Ps. 2. 6. set my king on holy *h.*
24. 3. who shall ascend the *h.* of the Lord.
43. 3. bring me to thy holy *h.*
50. 10. cattle on a thousand *h.* are mine.
95. 4. strength of the *h.* is his.
98. 8. let the *h.* be joyful together.
121. 1. I will lift up mine eyes to the *h.*
Prov. 8. 25. before the *h.* was I brought forth.
Is. 2. 2. shall be exalted above *h.*
40. 12. weighed the *h.* in balance.
Hos. 10. 8; Lk. 23. 30. to the *h.*, fall on us.
Matt. 5. 14. city set on an *h.*
Lk. 3. 5. every *h.* be brought low.
Acts 17. 22. Paul stood in Mars' *h.*

Hinder, Gen. 24. 56. *h.* me not.
Neh. 4. 8. *h.* the building.
Job 9. 12; 11. 10. who can *h.* him?
Lk. 11. 52. them entering in ye *h.*
Acts 8. 36. what doth *h.* me to be baptized?
1 Cor. 9. 12. lest we should *h.* the gospel.
Gal. 5. 7. run well, who did *h.* you?
1 Thes. 2. 18. Satan *h.* us.
1 Pet. 3. 7. that your prayers be not *h.*

Hire, 1 Ki. 5. 6. to thee will I give *h.*
Mic. 3. 11. priests teach for *h.*
Matt. 20. 8. give them their *h.*
Lk. 10. 7. labourer worthy of his *h.*
15. 17. how many *h.* servants.
Jas. 5. 4. *h.* of labourers which is kept back.
See John 10. 12.   [me *h.*

Hitherto, Josh. 17. 14. the Lord hath blessed
1 Sam. 7. 12. *h.* hath the Lord helped us.
Job 38. 11. *h.* shalt thou come, but no farther.
John 5. 17. my Father worketh *h.*
16. 24. *h.* have ye asked nothing in my name.
1 Cor. 3. 2. *h.* ye were not able to bear it.

Hold, Gen. 21. 18. *h.* him in thine hand.
Ex. 20. 7; Deut. 5. 11. Lord will not *h.* him guiltless.
Est. 4. 11. king *h.* out golden sceptre.
Job 9. 28. thou wilt not *h.* me innocent.
Ps. 18. 35. thy right hand hath *h.* me up.
119. 117. *h.* me up, and I shall be safe.
Prov. 11. 12. man of understanding *h.* his peace.
17. 28. a fool, when he *h.* his peace.
Is. 41. 13. the Lord will *h.* thy hand.
62. 6. never *h.* their peace day nor night.
Jer. 4. 19. I cannot *h.* my peace.
Matt. 6. 24; Lk. 16. 13. he will *h.* to the one.
Mk. 1. 25; Lk. 4. 35. *h.* thy peace, come out.
Rom. 1. 18. *h.* the truth in unrighteousness.
Phil. 2. 29. *h.* such in reputation.
Col. 2. 19. not *h.* the head.
1 Thes. 5. 21. *h.* fast that which is good.
1 Tim. 1. 19. *h.* faith and good conscience.
2 Tim. 1. 13. *h.* fast form of sound words.
Heb. 3. 14. *h.* beginning of confidence.
4. 14; 10. 23. *h.* fast our profession.
Rev. 2. 25. *h.* fast till I come.
3. 11. *h.* that fast which thou hast.

Hole, Ex. 28. 32. be an *h.* in the top of it.
Is. 11. 8. child shall play on *h.* of the asp.
51. 1. *h.* of pit whence ye are digged.
Ezek. 8. 7. a *h.* in the wall.
Hag. 1. 6. to put it in a bag with *h.*
Matt. 8. 20; Lk. 9. 58. foxes have *h.*

Holiness, Ex. 15. 11. glorious in *h.*
28. 36; 39. 30; Zech. 14. 20. *h.* to the Lord.
1 Chr. 16. 29; 2 Chr. 20. 21; Ps. 29. 2; 96. 9. beauty of *h.*
Ps. 30. 4; 97. 12. at remembrance of his *h.*
47. 8. God sitteth on throne of his *h.*
60. 6; 108. 7. God hath spoken in his *h.*
93. 5. *h.* becometh thine house.
110. 3. people willing, in beauties of *h.*
Is. 35. 8. the way of *h.*
63. 15. habitation of thy *h.*
Jer. 31. 23. O mountain of *h.*
Obad. 17. upon mount Zion there shall be *h.*
Lk. 1. 75. might serve him in *h.*
Acts 3. 12. as though by our *h.*
Rom. 1. 4. according to the Spirit of *h.*
6. 22. fruit unto *h.*
2 Cor. 7. 1. perfecting *h.* in fear of God.
Eph. 4. 24. created in righteousness and *h.*
1 Thes. 3. 13. stablish your hearts in *h.*
1 Tim. 2. 15. continue in faith and *h.*
Tit. 2. 3. in behaviour as becometh *h.*
Heb. 12. 10. partakers of his *h.*
12. 14. *h.*, without which no man.

Holy, Ex. 3. 5; Josh. 5. 15. place whereon thou standest is *h.*
Ex. 16. 23. the *h.* Sabbath.
19. 6; 1 Pet. 2. 9. an *h.* nation.
Ex. 20. 8; 31. 14. Sabbath-day to keep it *h.*
Lev. 10. 10. difference between *h.* and unholy.

Holy—*Continued.*
Lev. 20. 7. be ye *h.*
Num. 16. 5. Lord will shew who is *h.*
1 Sam. 2. 2. there is none *h.* as the Lord.
2 Ki. 4. 9. this is an *h.* man of God.
Ps. 20. 6. hear from his *h.* heaven.
22. 3. thou art *h.* that inhabitest.
28. 2. lift hands towards thy *h.* oracle.
86. 2. preserve my soul, for I am *h.*
98. 1. his *h.* arm hath gotten victory.
145. 17. the Lord is *h.* in all his works.
Is. 6. 3; Rev. 4. 8. *h.*, *h.*, *h.* is the Lord.
Is. 27. 13. shall worship in *h.* mount.
52. 10. Lord made bare his *h.* arm.
Is. 58. 13. call Sabbath, *h.* of the Lord.
64. 11. our *h.* and beautiful house.
Ezek. 22. 26. put no difference between *h.* and profane.
Matt. 3. 11; Mk. 1. 8; Lk. 3. 16; John 1. 33; Acts 1. 5. baptize with *H.* Ghost.
Matt. 7. 6. give not that which is *h.*
12. 31; Mk. 3. 29. blasphemy against the *H.* Ghost.
Mk. 8. 38; Lk. 9. 26. in glory with *h.* angels.
Mk. 13. 11. not ye that speak, but the *H.* Ghost.
Lk. 1. 15. filled with the *H.* Ghost.
3. 22. *H.* Ghost descended in bodily shape.
4. 1. Jesus being full of the *H.* Ghost.
12. 12. *H.* Ghost shall teach you.
John 7. 39. *H.* Ghost was not yet given.
14. 26. Comforter, who is the *H.* Ghost.
17. 11. *h.* Father, keep those.
20. 22; Acts 2. 38. receive ye the *H.* Ghost.
Acts 2. 4; 4. 31. all filled with *H.* Ghost.
4. 27. against thy *h.* child Jesus.
5. 3. to lie to the *H.* Ghost.
6. 3. men full of the *H.* Ghost.
7. 51. ye do always resist the *H.* Ghost.
8. 15. that they might receive *H.* Ghost.
9. 31. in comfort of the *H.* Ghost.
10. 38. God anointed Jesus with *H.* Ghost.
15. 28. it seemed good to the *H.* Ghost.
16. 6. forbidden of *H.* Ghost to preach.
19. 2. have ye received the *H.* Ghost.
20. 28. *H.* Ghost hath made you overseers.
Rom. 1. 2. promised in the *h.* scriptures.
7. 12. the commandment is *h.*, just, and good.
11. 16. if first-fruit be *h.*, if root be *h.*
12. 1. a living sacrifice, *h.*, acceptable to God.
14. 17. kingdom of God is joy in the *H.* Ghost.   [teacheth.
1 Cor. 2. 13. words which the *H.* Ghost
3. 17. the temple of God is *h.*
2 Cor. 13. 14. communion of the *H.* Ghost.
Eph. 1. 4; 5. 27. be *h.* and without blame.
2. 21. groweth to an *h.* temple in the Lord.
Col. 1. 22. present you *h.* and unblameable.
1 Thes. 5. 27. all the *h.* brethren.
1 Tim. 2. 8. lifting up *h.* hands.
2 Tim. 1. 9. called us with an *h.* calling.
Tit. 1. 8. bishop must be *h.*   [calling.
Heb. 3. 1. *h.* brethren, partakers of heavenly
7. 26. High Priest became us, who is *h.*
1 Pet. 1. 12. *H.* Ghost sent down from heaven.
1. 15; 2 Pet. 3. 11 *h.* in all conversation.
1 Pet. 2. 5. an *h.* priesthood.
2 Pet. 1. 18. with him in the *h.* mount.
Rev. 3. 7. things saith he that is *h.*
6. 10. O Lord, *h.* and true.
15. 4. not fear thee, for thou art *h.*
21. 10. the *h.* Jerusalem.
22. 11 he that is *h.*, let him be *h.*

Home, Gen. 43. 16. bring these men *h.*
Ex. 9. 19. shall not be brought *h.*
Deut. 24. 5. free at *h.* one year.
Ruth 1. 21. Lord hath brought me *h.* empty.
2 Sam. 14. 13. not fetch *h.* his banished.
1 Chr. 13. 12. bring ark of God *h.*
Job 39. 12. he will bring *h.* thy seed.
Ps. 68. 12. she that tarried at *h.*
Eccl. 12. 5. man goeth to his long *h.*
Lam. 1. 20. at *h.* there is as death.
Hag. 1. 9. when ye brought it *h.*
Matt. 8. 6. my servant lieth at *h.* sick.
Mk. 5. 19. go *h.* to thy friends.
Lk. 9. 61. bid them farewell at *h.*
John 19. 27. disciple took her to his own *h.*
20. 10. went away to their own *h.*
1 Cor. 11. 34. let him eat at *h.*
14. 35. ask their husbands at *h.*
2 Cor. 5. 6. whilst we are at *h.* in the body.
1 Tim. 5. 4. learn to shew piety at *h.*
Honest, Lk. 8. 15. an *h.* and good heart.
Acts 6. 3. men of *h.* report.
Rom. 12. 17 ; 2 Cor. 8. 21. things *h.*
Rom. 13. 13. let us walk *h.*, as in the day.
Phil. 4. 8. whatsoever things are *h.*
1 Pet. 2. 12. conversation *h.* among Gentiles.
Honour, Num. 22. 17. promote thee to *h.*
24. 11. Lord hath kept thee from *h.*
2 Sam. 6. 22. of them shall I be had in *h.*
1 Ki. 3. 13. given thee riches and *h.*
1 Chr. 29. 12. riches and *h.* come of thee.
2 Chr. 1. 11. not asked riches or *h.*
Est. 1. 20. wives shall give their husbands *h.*
Job 14. 21. his sons come to *h.*
Ps. 7. 5. lay mine *h.* in the dust. [with *h.*
8. 5 ; Heb. 2. 7. thou hast crowned him
Ps. 26. 8. place where thine *h.* dwelleth.
49. 12. man being in *h.* abideth not.
66. 2. sing forth the *h.* of his name.
96. 6. *h.* and majesty are before him.
104. 1. thou are clothed with *h.*
145. 5. speak of the *h.* of thy majesty.
Prov. 3. 16. in left hand riches and *h.*
4. 8. she shall bring thee to *h.*
8. 18. riches and *h.* are with me.
15. 33 ; 18. 12. before *h.* is humility.
20. 3. an *h.* to cease from strife.
25. 2. *h.* of kings to search a matter.
26. 1. *h.* is not seemly for a fool.
Eccl. 6. 2. to whom God hath given *h.*
Mal. 1. 6. where is mine *h.* ?
Matt. 13. 57 ; Mk. 6. 4 ; John 4. 44. prophet
not without *h.*
John 5. 41. I receive not *h.* from men.
Rom. 2. 7. in well-doing seek for *h.*
12. 10. in *h.* preferring one another.
13. 7. *h.* to whom *h.* is due.
2 Cor. 6. 8. by *h.* and dishonour.
Col. 2. 23. not in any *h.* to satisfying of flesh.
1 Tim. 5. 17. elders worthy of double *h.*
6. 1. count masters worthy of *h.*
6. 16. to whom be *h.* and power everlasting.
2 Tim. 2. 20. some to *h.*, some to dishonour.
Heb. 3. 3. more *h.* than the house.
5. 4. no man taketh this *h.* unto himself.
1 Pet. 1. 7. found to praise, *h.*, and glory.
3. 7. giving *h.* to the wife.
Rev. 4. 11 ; 5. 12. worthy to receive glory and *h.*

Honour, Ex. 20. 12 ; Deut. 5. 16 ; Matt. 15. 4 ;
19. 19 ; Mk. 7. 10 ; 10. 19 ; Lk. 18. 20 ; Eph.
6. 2. *h.* thy father and mother.   [man.
Lev. 19. 32. thou shalt *h.* the face of the old
1 Sam. 2. 30. them that *h.* me I will *h.*

Honour—*Continued.*
Est. 6. 6. the king delighteth to *h.*
Ps. 15. 4. he *h.* them that fear the Lord.
91. 15. I will deliver him, and *h.* him.
Prov. 3. 9. *h.* the Lord with thy substance.
12. 9. better than he that *h.* himself.
Is. 29. 13. people with lips do *h.* me.
Dan. 4. 37. I extol and *h.* king of heaven.
Mal. 1. 6. a son *h.* his father.
Matt. 15. 8 ; Mk. 7. 6. *h.* me with their lips.
John 5. 23. *h.* the Son as they *h.* the Father.
8. 54. if I *h.* myself, my *h.* is nothing.
1 Tim. 5. 3. *h.* widows that are widows indeed.
1 Pet. 2. 17. *h.* all men, *h.* the king.
Honourable, Num. 22. 15. sent princes more *h.*
1 Chr. 4. 9. more *h.* than brethren.
Ps. 45. 9. daughters among *h.* women.
111. 3. his work is *h.* and glorious.
Is. 3. 3. Lord doth take away *h.* man.
42. 21. magnify the law, and make it *h.*
Lk. 14. 8. lest more *h.* man be bidden.
Hope, Job 7. 6. my days are spent without *h.*
8. 13. the hypocrite's *h.* shall perish.
19. 10. my *h.* hath he removed.
Ps. 16. 9 ; Acts 2. 26. my flesh shall rest in *h.*
39. 7. my *h.* is in thee.
78. 7. might set their *h.* in God.
119. 116. let me not be ashamed of my *h.*
146. 5. happy he whose *h.* is in the Lord.
Prov. 13. 12. *h.* deferred maketh the heart
sick.
14. 32. righteous hath *h.* in his death.
26. 12 ; 29. 20. more *h.* of a fool.
Eccl. 9. 4. to all the living there is *h.*
Jer. 17. 7. blessed whose *h.* the Lord is.
31. 17. there is *h.* in thine end.
Hos. 2. 15. for a door of *h.*
Zech. 9. 12. ye prisoners of *h.*
Acts 23. 6. *h.* and resurrection of the dead.
28. 20. for the *h.* of Israel I am bound.
Rom. 5. 5. *h.* maketh not ashamed.
8. 24. we are saved by *h.*
12. 12. rejoicing in *h.*
15. 13. that ye may abound in *h.*
1 Cor. 13. 13. faith, *h.*, charity.
15. 19. if in this life only we have *h.*
Gal. 5. 5. though the Spirit wait for *h.*
Eph. 1. 18. the *h.* of his calling.
2. 12. having no *h.*, and without God.
Col. 1. 27. Christ in you, the *h.* of glory.
1 Thes. 4. 13. even as others, who have no *h.*
5. 8. for an helmet, the *h.* of salvation.
2 Thes. 2. 16. good *h.* through grace.
Tit. 2. 13. looking for that blessed *h.*
3. 7. the *h.* of eternal life.
Heb. 3. 6. rejoicing of *h.* firm to end.
6. 18. lay hold on *h.* set before us.
1 Pet. 1. 3. begotten us to a lively *h.*
3. 15. a reason of the *h.* that is in you.
1 John 3. 3. every man that hath this *h.*

Hope, Ps. 22. 29. thou didst make me *h.*
31. 24. all ye that *h.* in the Lord.
42. 5 ; 43. 5. *h.* thou in God.
71. 14. I will *h.* continually.
130. 7 ; 131. 3. let Israel *h.* in the Lord.
Lam. 3. 26. good that a man both *h.* and wait.
Rom. 8. 25. if we *h.* for that we see not.
1 Pet. 1. 13. *h.* to the end.
Horn, 2 Sam. 22. 3 ; Ps. 18. 2. the *h.* of my salvation.   [exalted.
Ps. 89. 17. in thy favour our *h.* shall be
132. 17. make *h.* of David to bud.
Lk. 1. 69. raised up *h.* of salvation.

Horrible, Ps. 11. 6. on wicked reign *h.* tempest.
40. 2. brought me up out of *h.* pit.
Jer. 5. 30. *h.* thing committed in land.
Ezek. 32. 10. kings shall be *h.* afraid.

Horror, Gen. 15. 12. a *h.* of great darkness.
Ps. 55. 5. *h.* hath overwhelmed me.
119. 53. *h.* hath taken hold upon me.

Horse, Ex. 15. 21. *h.* and rider thrown into sea.
Ps. 32. 9. be not as the *h.* or mule.
33. 17. a *h.* is a vain thing for safety.
147. 10. he delighteth not in strength of *h.*
Prov. 21. 31. *h.* is prepared against day of battle.
Is. 63. 13. led through deep, as a *h.*
Jer. 8. 6. as *h.* rusheth into battle.
Hos. 14. 3. we will not ride upon *h.*
Zech. 14. 20. upon bells of the *h.*
Jas. 3. 3. we put bits in *h.* mouths.   [to *h.*

Hospitality, Rom. 12. 13; 1 Tim. 3. 2. given
Tit. 1. 8. a lover of *h.*
1 Pet. 4. 9. use *h.* one to another.

Hot, Deut. 9. 19. anger and *h.* displeasure.
Ps. 6. 1 ; 38. 1. neither chasten in thy *h.* displeasure.
Prov. 6. 28. can one go upon *h.* coals.
1 Tim. 4. 2. conscience seared with *h.* iron.
Rev. 3. 15. art neither cold nor *h.*

Hour, Dan. 4. 19. astonied for one *h.*
Matt. 10. 19; Lk. 12. 12. shall be given you in that same *h.*
20. 12. these have wrought but one *h.*
24. 36; Mk. 13. 32. that *h.* knoweth no man.
Matt. 25. 13. ye know neither day nor *h.*
26. 40; Mk. 14. 37. could ye not watch one *h.?*
Mk. 14. 35. if possible the *h.* might pass.
Lk. 10. 21. in that *h.* Jesus rejoiced.
12. 39. what *h.* the thief would come.
22. 59. about the space of one *h.*
John 2. 4. mine *h.* is not yet come.
5. 25 ; 16. 32. the *h.* is coming, and now is.
12. 27. Father, save me from this *h.*
Acts 3. 1. at the *h.* of prayer.
1 Cor. 4. 11. to this present *h.*
Gal. 2. 5. give place, not for an *h.*
Rev. 3. 10. the *h.* of temptation.

House, Gen. 28. 17. none other but the *h.* of God.   [four's *h.*
Ex. 20. 17 ; Deut. 5. 21. shalt not covet neigh-
2 Sam. 6. 11. Lord blessed *h.* of Obed-edom.
Neh. 13. 11. why is the *h.* of God forsaken?
Job 30. 23. the *h.* appointed for all living.
Ps. 65. 4. satisfied with the goodness of thy *h.*
69. 9 ; John 2. 17. the zeal of thine *h.*
Ps. 84. 3. the sparrow hath found an *h.*
Prov. 2. 18. her *h.* inclineth to death.
9. 1. wisdom hath builded her *h.*
12. 7. the *h.* of the righteous shall stand.
14. 11. the *h.* of wicked be overthrown.
Eccl. 7. 2. *h.* of mourning, *h.* of feasting.
12. 3. the keepers of the *h.* shall tremble.
Is. 5. 8. woe unto them that join *h.* to *h.*
64. 11. our holy and beautiful *h.* is burned.
Mic. 4. 2. let us go up to the *h.* of God.
Hag. 1. 4. and this *h.* lie waste.
Matt. 7. 25 ; Lk. 6. 48. beat upon that *h.*
Matt. 10. 12. when ye come into an *h.*
12. 25; Mk. 3. 25. *h.* divided cannot stand.
Matt. 23. 38. your *h.* is left to you desolate.
Lk. 10. 7. go not from *h.* to *h.*
14. 23. that my *h.* may be filled.
15. 8. light candle, and sweep *h.*
18. 14. went down to his *h.* justified.
John 12. 3. the *h.* was filled with odour of ointment.

House—*Continued.*
John 14. 2. in my Father's *h.* are many mansions.
Acts 2. 2. sound from heaven filled *h.*
2. 46. breaking bread from *h.* to *h.*
2 Cor. 5. 1. *h.* not made with hands.
2 Tim. 2. 20. in a great *h.* vessels of gold.
Heb. 3. 4. every *h.* is built by some man.
Pet. 4. 17. judgment begin at *h.* of God.

Household, Gen. 18. 19. command his *h.* after him.
2 Sam. 6. 20. returned to bless his *h.*
Prov. 31. 27. looketh well to her *h.*   [own *h.*
Matt. 10. 36. a man's foes shall be of his
Gal. 6. 10. the *h.* of faith.
Eph. 2. 19. of the *h.* of God.

Humble, Deut. 8. 2. to *h.* thee and prove thee.
Job 22. 29. he shall save *h.* person.
Ps 9. 12. forgetteth not cry of the *h.*
34. 2. the *h.* shall hear thereof.
69. 32. *h.* shall see this and be glad.
113. 6. *h.* himself to behold things in heaven.
Prov. 16. 19. better be of a *h.* spirit.
Is. 57. 15. of contrite and *h.* spirit.   [self.
Matt. 18. 4 ; 23. 12 ; Lk. 14. 11 ; 18. 14. *h.* him-
2 Cor. 12. 21. my God will *h.* me.
Phil. 2. 8. he *h.* himself and became obedient to death.
Jas. 4. 6 ; 1 Pet. 5. 5. giveth grace to the *h.*
See Mic. 6. 8.   [is *h.*

Humility, Prov. 15. 33 ; 18. 12. before honour
22. 4. by *h.* are riches and honour.
Acts 20. 19. *h.* of mind.
Col. 2. 23. wisdom in will-worship and *h.*

Hunger, Deut. 8. 3. he suffered thee to *h.*
Ps. 34. 10. young lions do lack, and suffer *h.*
Prov. 19. 15. an idle soul shall suffer *h.*
Is. 49. 10. shall not *h.* nor thirst.
Jer. 38. 9. he is like to die for *h.*
Matt. 5. 6 ; Lk. 6. 21. blessed are ye that *h.*
Lk. 6. 25. woe unto full, ye shall *h.*
John 6. 35. he that cometh to me shall never *h.*
Rom. 12. 20. if thine enemy *h.,* feed him.
1 Cor. 4. 11. we both *h.* and thirst.
11. 34. if any man *h.,* let him eat at home.
Rev. 7. 16. they shall *h.* no more.

Hungry, Job 22. 7. withholden bread from *h.*
Ps. 50. 12. if I were *h.,* I would not tell thee.
107. 5. *h.* and thirsty, their soul fainted.
107. 9. he filleth *h.* soul with goodness.
Prov. 27. 7. to the *h.* every bitter thing is sweet.
Is. 29. 8. as when a *h.* man dreameth.
32. 6. to make empty soul of the *h.*
65. 13. my servants eat, but ye shall be *h.*
Mk. 11. 12. from Bethany he was *h.*
Lk. 1. 53. filled *h.* with good things.
1 Cor. 11. 21. one is *h.,* and another drunken.
Phil. 4. 12. instructed both to be full and to be *h.*

Hunt, Gen. 27. 5. Esau went to *h.* venison.
1 Sam. 26. 20. as when one doth *h.* a partridge.
Jer. 16. 16. *h.* them from every mountain.
Mic. 7. 2. they *h.* every man his brother.

Hurt, Gen. 4. 23. slain young man to my *h.*
26. 29. that thou wilt do us no *h.*
31. 29. in power of my hand to do *h.*
Ps 15. 4. that sweareth to his own *h.*
Eccl. 8. 9. ruleth over another to his own *h.*
Is. 11. 9. they shall not *h.* nor destroy.
Jer. 6. 14; 8. 11. have healed *h.* slightly.
8. 21. for the *h.* of my people.
25. 7. ye provoke me to your own *h.*

Hurt—*Continued.*
Dan. 6. 23. no manner of *h.* found upon him.
Mk. 16. 18. deadly thing, it shall not *h.*
Lk. 10. 19. nothing shall by any means *h.* you.
Acts 18. 10. no man set on thee to *h.* thee.
27. 10. this voyage be with *h.*
Rev. 7. 3. *h.* not earth, neither sea.
See 1 Tim. 6. 9.

Husband, Ex. 4. 25. a bloody *h.* art thou.
Prov. 12. 4. virtuous wife crown to her *h.*
31. 11. heart of her *h.* doth trust in her.
Is. 54. 5. thy Maker is thy *h.*
John 4. 16. go, call thy *h.*
Rom. 7. 2. *h.* dead, she is loosed.
1 Cor. 7. 16. whether thou shalt save thy *h.*
14. 35. ask their *h.* at home.   [your *h.*
Eph. 5. 22. wives, submit yourselves to
5. 25; Col. 3. 19. *h.,* love your wives.
1 Tim. 3. 12. the *h.* of one wife.
Tit. 2. 4. teach young women to love their *h.*
1 Pet. 3. 1. be in subjection to own *h.*
Rev. 21. 2. as bride adorned for her *h.*

Husbandman, Gen. 9. 20. Noah began to be an *h.*
John 15. 1. I am true vine, my Father is *h.*
2 Tim. 2. 6. the *h.* that laboureth.
Jas. 5. 7. the *h.* waiteth for fruit of earth.

Hymn, Matt. 26. 30; Mk. 14. 26. sung an *h.*
Eph. 5. 19; Col. 3. 16. speaking in psalms
and *h.*

Hypocrisy, Is. 32. 6. iniquity, to practise *h.*
Matt. 23. 28. within ye are full of *h.*
Mk. 12. 15. he, knowing their *h.*
Lk. 12. 1. leaven of Pharisees, which is *h.*
1 Tim. 4. 2. speaking lies in *h.*
Jas. 3. 17. wisdom is pure, and without *h.*

Hypocrite, Job 8. 13. the *h.* hope shall perish.
20. 5. the joy of the *h.* but for a moment.
Is. 9. 17. every one is an *h.*
33. 14. fearfulness surprised *h.*
Matt. 6. 2, 5, 16. as the *h.* do.
7. 5; Lk. 6. 42. thou *h.,* first cast out beam.
Matt. 15. 7; 16. 3; Mk. 7. 6; Lk. 12. 56. ye *h.*
Matt. 22. 18. why tempt ye me, ye *h.?*
23. 13; Lk. 11. 44. woe unto you, *h.*
Matt. 24. 51. appoint him portion with *h.*

Hyssop, Ex. 12. 22. bunch of *h.* and dip it.
1 Ki. 4. 33. cedar-tree, even unto *h.*
Ps. 51. 7. purge me with *h.,* I shall be clean.
John 19. 29. filled sponge, put it on *h.*
Heb. 9. 19. blood with *h.* sprinkled.

IDLE, Ex. 5. 8. they be *i.*
Prov. 19. 15. an *i.* soul shall suffer hunger.
31. 27. eateth not bread of *i.*
Matt. 12. 36. every *i.* word men speak.
20. 3. standing *i.* in market-place.
Lk. 24. 11. words seemed as *i.* tales.
1 Tim. 5. 13. they learn to be *i.*   [grove.

Idol, 1 Ki. 15. 13; 2 Chr. 15. 16. made an *i.* in a
Ps. 96. 5. all gods of the nations are *i.*
115. 4; 135. 15. their *i.* are silver and gold.
Is. 66. 3. as if he blessed an *i.*
Jer. 50. 38. they are mad upon their *i.*
Hos. 4. 17. Ephraim is joined to *i.*
Acts 7. 41. offered sacrifice to the *i.*
15. 20. abstain from pollutions of *i.*
1 Cor. 8. 4. we know an *i.* is nothing.
2 Cor. 6. 16. what agreement hath temple of
God with *i.?*
1 Thes. 1. 9. ye turned to God from *i.*
1 John 5. 21. keep yourselves from *i.*

Idolatry, Acts 17. 16. city wholly given to *i.*
1 Cor. 10. 14. flee from *i.*
Col. 3. 5. covetousness, which is *i.*

Ignorance, Acts 3. 17. through *i.* ye did it.
17. 30. times of this *i.* God winked at.
Eph. 4. 18. alienated through *i.*
1 Pet. 2. 15. put to silence *i.* of foolish men.

Ignorant, Ps. 73. 22. so foolish was I, and *i.*
Is. 56. 10. all *i.,* they are all dumb.
63. 16. though Abraham be *i.* of us.
Acts 4. 13. perceived they were *i.* men.
Rom. 10. 3. being *i.* of God's righteousness.
11. 25. should be *i.* of this mystery.
1 Cor. 14. 38. if any man be *i.,* let him be *i.*
2 Cor. 2. 11. not *i.* of Satan's devices.
Heb. 5. 2. can have compassion on the *i.*
Pet. 3. 8. be not *i.* of this one thing.

Image, Gen. 1. 26. let us make man in our *i.*
Ps. 73. 20. shalt despise their *i.*   [this *i.?*
Matt. 22. 20; Mk. 12. 16; Lk. 20. 24. whose is
Acts 19. 35. *i.* which fell from Jupiter.
Rom. 1. 23. changed glory of God to *i.*
8. 29. be conformed to *i.* of his Son.
1 Cor. 15. 49. we have borne *i.* of earthy.
2 Cor. 3. 18. changed into the same *i.*
Col. 3. 10. after *i.* of him that created.
Heb. 1. 3. the express *i.* of his person.
10. 1. not the very *i.* of things.

Imagination, Gen. 6. 5; 8. 22. *i.* of heart evil.
Deut. 29. 19. walk in *i.* of heart.
1 Chr. 28. 9. Lord understandeth all the *i.* of
    thoughts.   [hearts.
Lk. 1. 51. scattered the proud in *i.* of their
Rom. 1. 21. became vain in their *i.*
2 Cor. 10. 5. casting down *i.*   [vain things'

Imagine, Ps. 2. 1; Acts 4. 25. why do people *i.*
Ps. 62. 3. how long will ye *i.* mischief?
Nah. 1. 9. what do ye *i.* against the Lord?
Zech. 7. 10; 8. 17. let none *i.* evil.

Immortality, Rom. 2. 7. to them who seek for *i.*
1 Cor. 15. 53. this mortal must put on *i.*
1 Tim. 6. 16. hath *i.* dwelling in light.
2 Tim. 1. 10. who brought *i.* to light.
See 1 Tim. 1. 17.

Impart, Job 39. 17. nor *i.* to her understand-
Lk. 3. 11. let him *i.* to him that hath none. [ing.
Rom. 1. 11. may *i.* some spiritual gift.

Impenitent, Rom. 2. 5. thou, after thy *i.* heart.

Impose, Ezra 7. 24. not be lawful to *i.* toll.
Heb. 9. 10. carnal ordinances *i.* on.

Impossible, Matt. 17. 20. nothing shall be *i.*
    unto you.   [is *i.*
19. 26; Mk. 10. 27; Lk. 18. 27. with men it
Lk. 1. 37; 18. 27. with God nothing *i.*
17. 1. it is *i.* but offences will come.
Heb. 6. 4. *i.* for those enlightened.
11. 6. without faith *i.* to please God.

Impute, Lev. 17. 4. blood shall be *i.* to that
    man.   [iniquity.
Ps. 32. 2; Rom. 4. 8. to whom Lord *i.* not
Rom. 5. 13. sin is not *i.* when there is no law.
2 Cor. 5. 19. not *i.* trespasses to them.

Incline, Josh. 24. 23. *i.* your heart to the Lord.
1 Ki. 8. 58. that he may *i.* our hearts to
    keep law.
Ps. 40. 1; 116. 2. Lord *i.* unto me.
78. 1. *i.* your ears to the words.
119. 36. *i.* my heart to thy testimonies.
Jer. 7. 24; 11. 8; 17. 23; 34. 14. nor *i.* ear.

Incorruptible, Rom. 1. 23. changed glory of *i.*
    God.
1 Cor. 9. 25. to obtain an *i.* crown.
15. 52. the dead shall be raised *i.*
1 Pet. 1. 4. an inheritance *i.*

Increase, Lev. 25. 36. take no usury or *i.*
26. 4. the land shall yield her *i.*
Deut. 14. 22. tithe all *i.* of thy seed.

Increase—*Continued.*
Ps. 67. 6; Ezek. 34. 27. earth shall yield her *i.*
Prov. 18. 20. with the *i.* of his lips.
Eccl. 5. 10. not be satisfied with *i.*
Is. 9. 7. *i.* of his government be no end.
1 Cor. 3. 6. God gave the *i.*

Increase, Job 8. 7. thy latter end greatly *i.*
Ps. 62. 10. if riches *i.*, set not heart on them.
115. 14. Lord shall *i.* you more and more.
Prov. 1. 5; 9. 9. a wise man will *i.* learning.
11. 24. that scattereth, and yet *i.*
Eccl. 1. 18. he that *i.* knowledge, *i.* sorrow.
Is. 40. 29. no might, he *i.* strength.
Dan. 12. 4. knowledge shall be *i.*
Hos. 12. 1. he daily *i.* lies.
Lk. 2. 52. Jesus *i.* in wisdom.
17. 5. Lord, *i.* our faith.
John 3. 30. he must *i.*, I decrease.
Acts 6. 7. word of God *i.*
16. 5. churches *i.* daily.
Col. 2. 19. body *i.* with *i.* of God.
1 Thes. 4. 10. that ye *i.* more and more.
Rev. 3. 17. I am rich, and *i.* with goods.
Indeed, Gen. 37. 8. shalt thou *i.* reign over us?
1 Ki. 8. 27; 2 Chr. 6. 18. will God *i.* dwell on the earth?
1 Chr. 4. 10. thou wouldest bless me *i.*
Is. 6. 9. hear ye *i.*, see ye *i.*
Mk. 11. 32. a prophet *i.*
Lk. 24. 34. the Lord is risen *i.*
John 1. 47. an Israelite *i.*
4. 42. that this is *i.* the Christ.   [drink *i.*
6. 55. my flesh is meat *i.*, and my blood is
8. 36. ye shall be free *i.*
Indignation, Ps. 69. 24. pour out thy *i.* on them.
78. 49. wrath, *i.*, and trouble.
Is. 26. 20. till the *i.* be overpast.
Nah. 1. 6. who can stand before his *i.*?
Matt. 20. 24. moved with *i.*
26. 8. they had *i.*
Acts 5. 17. they were filled with *i.*
2 Cor. 7. 11. yea, what *i.*
Heb. 10. 27. fearful looking for of fiery *i.*
Rev. 14. 10. the cup of his *i.*
Inditing, Ps. 45. 1. my heart is *i.* good matter.
Inexcusable, Rom. 2. 1. thou art *i.*, O man.
Infidel, 2 Cor. 6. 15. that believeth with *i.*?
1 Tim. 5. 8. is worse than an *i.*
Infirmity, Ps. 77. 10. this is mine *i.*
Prov. 18. 14. spirit of man will sustain his *i.*
Matt. 8. 17. himself took our *i.*
Rom. 6. 19. the *i.* of your flesh.
8. 26. the Spirit also helpeth our *i.*
15. 1. strong bear the *i.* of the weak.
2 Cor. 12. 10. take pleasure in *i.*
Heb. 4. 15. touched with the feeling of our *i.*
Influences, Job 38. 31. canst bind *i.* of Pleiades?
Ingrafted, Jas. 1. 21. receive with meekness the *i.* word.   [Israel.
Inhabit, Ps. 22. 3. O thou that *i.* praises of
Is. 57. 15. lofty One that *i.* eternity.
65. 21. build houses and *i.* them.
Amos 9. 14. build waste cities and *i.* them.
Zeph. 1. 13. build houses, not *i.* them.
Inhabitant, Gen. 19. 25. overthrew *i.* of cities.
Num. 13. 32. land eateth up *i.*
Jud. 5. 23. curse bitterly the *i.*
Is. 5. 9. houses great without *i.*
6. 11. cities he wasted without *i.*
24. 17. snare on thee, O *i.* of the earth.
33. 24. the *i.* shall not say, I am sick.
Jer. 44. 22. land without an *i.*
Amos 1. 8. I will cut off *i.* from.

Inherit, Gen. 15. 8. shall I know that I shall *i.* it?
Ex. 32. 13. they shall *i.* it for ever.
Ps. 25. 13. his seed shall *i.* the earth.
37. 11; Matt. 5. 5. the meek shall *i.* the earth.
Prov. 3. 35. the wise shall *i.* glory.
14. 18. the simple *i.* folly.
Is. 65. 9. mine elect shall *i.* it.
Matt. 19. 29. shall *i.* everlasting life.
25. 34. *i.* the kingdom prepared.
Mk. 10. 17; Lk. 10. 25; 18. 18. *i.* eternal life.
1 Cor. 6. 9; 15. 50; Gal. 5. 21; not *i.* the kingdom.
Heb. 6. 12. through faith *i.* the promises.
12. 17. when he would have *i.* the blessing.
Rev. 21. 7. he that overcometh shall *i.* all things.
Inheritance, Gen. 31. 14. is there any *i.* for us?
Ex. 15. 17. plant them in thine *i.*
Ps. 16. 5. Lord is portion of mine *i.*
47. 4. he shall choose our *i.* for us.
79. 1. heathen are come into thine *i.*
Prov. 13. 22. a good man leaveth *i.*
20. 21. an *i.* may be gotten hastily.
Eccl. 7. 11. wisdom is good with an *i.*
Matt. 21. 38. let us seize on his *i.*
Mk. 12. 7; Lk. 20. 14. the *i.* shall be ours.
Lk. 12. 13. he divide the *i.* with me.
Acts 20. 32; 26. 18. an *i.* among the sanctified.
Eph. 1. 14. the earnest of our *i.*
Heb. 1. 4. he hath by *i.* obtained more excellent name.
9. 15. receive promise of eternal *i.*
11. 8. place he should receive for *i.*
Iniquity, Ex. 20. 5; 34. 7; Num. 14. 18; Deut. 5. 9. visiting the *i.* of the fathers.
Ex. 34. 7; Num. 14. 18. forgiving *i.* and transgression.
Deut. 32. 4. a God of truth without *i.*
Job 4. 8. they that plow *i.* reap the same.
5. 16. *i.* stoppeth her mouth.
34. 32. if I have done *i.*, I will do no more.
Ps. 25. 11. pardon mine *i.*, for it is great.
32. 2. blessed to whom Lord imputeth not *i.*
51. 5. I was shapen in *i.*
66. 18. if I regard *i.* in my heart.
69. 27. add *i.* to their *i.*
90. 8. thou hast set our *i.* before thee.
103. 3. who forgiveth all thine *i.*
130. 3. if thou shouldest mark *i.*   [vanity.
Prov. 22. 8. he that soweth *i.* shall reap
Is. 1. 4. a people laden with *i.*
5. 18. woe to them that draw *i.*
6. 7. thine *i.* is taken away.
40. 2. her *i.* is pardoned.
53. 5. he was bruised for *i.*
Dan. 9. 24. make reconciliation for *i.*
Hos. 14. 2. take away *i.*, receive us graciously.
Hab. 1. 13. thou canst not look on *i.*
Matt. 24. 12. because *i.* shall abound.
Acts 1. 18. purchased field with reward of *i.*
8. 23. in bond of *i.*
Rom. 6. 19. servants to *i.* unto *i.*
2 Thes. 2. 7. the mystery of *i.* doth work.
2 Tim. 2. 19. depart from *i.*
Tit. 2. 14. redeem us from *i.*
Jas. 3. 6. tongue is a world of *i.*
Ink, Jer. 36. 18. wrote them with *i.* in a book.
2 Cor. 3. 3. not with *i.*, but the Spirit.
2 John 12; 3 John 13. I would not write with *i.*
Inn, Gen. 42. 27. give ass provender in the *i.*
Ex. 4. 24. in the *i.* the Lord met him.
Lk. 2. 7. no room for them in the *i.*
10. 34. brought him to an *i.*

Innocent, Deut. 27. 25. taketh reward to slay *i.*
Job 4. 7. who ever perished, being *i.* ?
9. 23. laugh at the trial of the *i.*
27. 17. the *i.* shall divide the silver.
Ps. 15. 5. taketh reward against the *i.*
19. 13. *i.* from the great transgression.
Prov. 28. 20. haste to be rich shall not be *i.*
Jer. 19. 4. filled this place with blood of *i.*
Matt. 27. 24. I am *i.* of the blood of.

Innumerable, Ps. 40. 12. *i.* evils compassed about.
104. 25. things creeping *i.*
Heb. 11. 12. sand by the sea-shore *i.*
12. 22. come to *i.* company of angels.

Inquisition, Deut. 19. 18. judges shall make diligent *i.*
Est. 2. 23. *i.* was made of the matter.
Ps. 9. 12. when he maketh *i.* for blood.

Inscription, Acts 17. 23. an altar with this *i.*

Inspiration, Job 32. 8. *i.* of Almighty giveth understanding.
2 Tim. 3. 16. Scripture is given by *i.* of God.

Instant, Is. 29. 5. it shall be at an *i.* suddenly.
Lk. 7. 4. they besought him *i.*
Acts 26. 7. twelve tribes *i.* serving God.
Rom. 12. 12. continuing *i.* in prayer.
2 Tim. 4. 2. be *i.* in season, out of season.

Instruct, Neh. 9. 20. thy good Spirit to *i.* them.
Ps. 16. 7. my reins *i.* me in night season.
32. 8. I will *i.* thee, and teach thee.
Is. 28. 26. God doth *i.* him to discretion.
40. 14. who *i.* him, and taught him?
Matt. 13. 52. every scribe *i.* unto the kingdom.
Rom. 2. 18. being *i.* out of the law.
Phil. 4. 12. in all things I am *i.*

Instruction, Job 33. 16. openeth ears, sealeth *i.*
Ps. 50. 17. seeing thou hatest *i.*
Prov. 1. 3. to receive the *i.* of wisdom.
10. 17. in way of life that keepeth *i.*
15. 32. refuseth *i.* despiseth his soul.
16. 22. the *i.* of fools is folly.
23. 12. apply thy heart to *i.*
2 Tim. 3. 16. Scripture is profitable for *i.*

Instrument, Gen. 49. 5. *i.* of cruelty in habitations.
Ps. 7. 13. prepared the *i.* of death.
33. 2; 92. 3. sing with *i.* of ten strings.
Is. 41. 15. sharp threshing *i.*
Ezek. 33. 32. one that can play on an *i.*
Rom. 6. 13. members *i.* of unrighteousness.

Intangle, Matt. 22. 15. how they might *i.* him.
Gal. 5. 1. be not *i.* with yoke of bondage.
2 Tim. 2. 4. *i.* himself with affairs of life.

Integrity, Gen. 20. 5. in *i.* of my heart done this.
Job 2. 3. he holdeth fast his *i.*
31. 6. that God may know my *i.*
Ps. 7. 8. according to my *i.* in me.
25. 21. let *i.* preserve me.
26. 1. I have walked in *i.*
41. 12. thou upholdest me in my *i.*
Prov. 11. 3. the *i.* of the upright.
19. 1. poor that walketh in *i.*
20. 7. just man walketh in his *i.*

Intent, Acts 10. 29. what *i.* ye have sent for me.
Eph. 3. 10. to the *i.* that now to principalities.
Heb. 4. 12. discerner of *i.* of heart.

Intercession, Is. 53. 12. made *i.* for transgressors.
Rom. 8. 26. the Spirit maketh *i.* for us.
1 Tim. 2. 1. prayers and *i.* be made.
Heb. 7. 25. ever liveth to make *i.*

Intreat, Ruth 1. 16. *i.* me not to leave thee.
1 Sam. 2. 25. if a man sin, who shall *i.* ?
Ps. 45. 12. rich shall *i.* favour.
Is. 19. 22. he shall be *i.* of them.
1 Cor. 4. 13. being defamed, we *i.*
1 Tim. 5. 1. *i.* him as a father.
Jas. 3. 17. wisdom is easy to be *i.*

Inventions, Ps. 106. 29. provoked him to anger with *i.*
Prov. 8. 12. knowledge of witty *i.*
Eccl. 7. 29. have sought out many *i.*

Invisible, Rom. 1. 20. *i.* things are clearly seen
Col. 1. 15. the image of the *i.* God.
1 Tim. 1. 17. King immortal, *i.*
Heb. 11. 27. as seeing him who is *i.*

Inward, Job 38. 36. wisdom in the *i.* parts.
Ps. 51. 6. truth in the *i.* parts.
64. 6. *i* thought of every one is deep.
Jer. 31. 33. I will put my law in their *i.* parts
Lk. 11. 39. *i.* part is full of ravening.
Rom. 7. 22. law of God after the *i.* man.
2 Cor. 4. 16. the *i.* man is renewed.

Issues, Ps. 68. 20. to God belong the *i.* from death.
Prov. 4. 23. out of the heart are *i.* of life.

JEALOUS, Ex. 20. 5; 34. 14; Deut. 4. 24; 5. 9;
6. 15; Josh. 24. 19. a *j.* God.
1 Ki. 19. 10, 14. I have been *j.* for Lord.
Ezek. 39. 25. be *j.* for my holy name.
Joel 2. 18. then will the Lord be *j.*
Nah. 1. 2. God is *j.*, and Lord revengeth.
2 Cor. 11. 2. I am *j.* over you.

Jealousy, Deut. 32. 16; 1 Ki. 14. 22. they provoked him to *j.*
Ps. 79. 5. how long, Lord, shall thy *j.* burn?
Prov. 6. 34. *j.* is the rage of a man.
Cant. 8. 6. *j.* is cruel as the grave.
Is. 42. 13. stir up *j.* like man of war.
Ezek. 36. 5. in fire of *j.* have I spoken.
1 Cor. 10. 22. do we provoke Lord to *j.* ?

Jewels, Is. 61. 10. adorneth herself with *j.*
Hos. 2. 13. decked with ear-rings and *j.*
Mal. 3. 17. when I make up my *j.*

Join, Prov. 11. 21; 16. 5. hand *j.* in hand.
Is. 5. 8. that *j.* house to house.
Jer. 50. 5. let us *j.* ourselves to the Lord.
Hos. 4. 17. Ephraim is *j.* to idols.
Matt. 19. 6; Mk. 10. 9. what God hath *j.*
Acts 5. 13. durst no man *j.* himself?
8. 29. go, *j.* thyself to this chariot.
1 Cor. 1. 10. perfectly *j.* in same mind.
6. 17. *j.* to the Lord.
Eph. 4. 16. the whole body fitly *j.*

Joint, Gen. 32. 25. thigh out of *j.*
Ps. 22. 14. all my bones are out of *j.*
Prov. 25. 19. like foot out of *j.*
Eph. 4. 16. which every *j.* supplieth.
Col. 2. 19. body by *j.* knit together.
Heb. 4. 12. dividing of *j.* and marrow.

Journey, Gen. 24. 21. Lord made *j.* prosperous.
Josh. 9. 11. take victuals for your *j.*
1 Ki. 18. 27. or he is in a *j.*
Neh. 2. 6. how long shall thy *j.* be?
Matt. 10. 10; Mk. 6. 8; Lk. 9. 3. nor scrip for your *j.*
Lk. 11. 6. a friend in his *j.*
15. 13. took his *j.* into a far country.
John 4. 6. Jesus, wearied with his *j.*
1 Cor. 11. 26. in *j.* often.

Joy, 1 Chr. 15. 25. went to bring the ark with *j.*
Ezra 6. 16. dedication of house of God with *j.*
Neh. 8. 10. the *j.* of the Lord is your strength.
Job 20. 5. *j.* of hypocrite but for a moment.

Joy—*Continued.*
Job 29. 13. widow's heart to sing for *j.*
　33. 26. he shall see his face with *j.*
　41. 22. sorrow is turned into *j.*
Ps. 16. 11. in thy presence fulness of *j.*
　30. 5. *j.* cometh in the morning.
　43. 4. to God my exceeding *j.*
　48. 2; Lam. 2. 15. the *j.* of the whole earth.
Ps. 51. 12. restore *j.* of thy salvation.
　126. 5. that sow in tears shall reap in *j.*
Prov. 14. 10. not intermeddle with his *j.*
　21. 15. *j.* to the just to do judgment.
Eccl. 2. 10. I withheld not my heart from *j.*
　9. 7. eat thy bread with *j.*
Is. 9. 3. not increased the *j.*
　12. 3. with *j.* shall ye draw water.
　24. 8. the *j.* of the harp ceaseth.
　29. 19. meek shall increase their *j.*
　35. 10; 51. 11. with everlasting *j.*
　60. 15. a *j.* of many generations.
　65. 14. my servants shall sing for *j.* of heart.
Jer. 15. 16. thy word was the *j.* of my heart.
　31. 13. turn their mourning into *j.*
Matt. 13. 20; Lk. 8. 13. with *j.* receiveth it.
Matt. 13. 44. for *j.* goeth and selleth.
　25. 21, 23. the *j.* of thy Lord.
Lk. 15. 10. there is *j.* in presence of the angels.
　24. 41. they believed not for *j.*
John 3. 29. this my *j.* is fulfilled.
　15. 11; 16. 24. that your *j.* might be full.
Acts 20. 24. finish my course with *j.*
Rom. 14. 17. kingdom of God is *j.*
Heb. 12. 2. for the *j.* that was set before
　him.
Jas. 1. 2. count it all *j.* when.
1 Pet. 4. 13; Jude 24. with exceeding *j.*
3 John 4. no greater *j.* than to hear.
Joyful, Ezra 6. 22. Lord hath made them *j.*
Ps. 35. 9. my soul shall be *j.* in the Lord.
　63. 5. praise thee with *j.* lips.
　66. 1; 95. 1; 98. 6. make a *j.* noise.
Eccl. 7. 14. in day of prosperity be *j.*
Is. 56. 7. *j.* in house of prayer.
　61. 10. my soul shall be *j.* in God.
2 Cor. 7. 4. *j.* in all our tribulation.
See Heb. 10. 34.
Judge, Gen. 18. 25. the *J.* of all the earth. [us?
Ex. 2. 14; Acts 7. 27. who made thee a *j.* over
Ps. 50. 6. God is *j.* himself.
　68. 5. a *j.* of the widows.
　94. 2. thou *j.* of the earth.
Is. 3. 2. take away the *j.*
Mic. 7. 3. the *j.* asketh a reward.
Matt. 5. 25; Lk. 12. 58. adversary deliver
　thee to the *j.*
Lk. 12. 14. who made me a *j.* over you?
　18. 6. the unjust *j.*
Acts 10. 42. the *j.* of quick and dead.
2 Tim. 4. 8. the Lord, the righteous *j.*
Heb. 12. 23. to God, the *j.* of all.
Jas. 4. 11. not a doer of the law, but a *j.*
　5. 9. the *j.* standeth before the door.

Judge, Gen. 16. 5. Lord *j.* between me and thee.
Deut. 32. 36; Ps. 7. 8; 50. 4; Heb. 10. 30.
　Lord shall *j.* people.
Ps. 58. 11. he is a God that *j.* in the earth.
　96. 13; 98. 9; Acts 17. 31. he shall *j.* the
　world with righteousness.
Ps. 110. 6. he shall *j.* among the heathen.
Is. 1. 17. *j.* the fatherless.
　5. 3. *j.* betwixt me and my vineyard.
Matt. 7. 1. *j.* not, that ye be not *j.*
Lk. 7. 43. thou hast rightly *j.*

Judge—*Continued.*
John 7. 24. *j.* righteous judgment.
　16. 11. prince of this world is *j.*
Rom. 14. 13. let us not *j.* one another.
Rev. 20. 13. *j.* every man according to works.
Judgment, Ex. 12. 12. against the gods exe-
　cute *j.*
Deut. 1. 17. the *j.* is God's.
　16. 18. judge people with just *j.*
　32. 4. all his ways are *j.* [justice.
2 Sam. 8. 15; 1 Chr. 18. 14. executed *j.* and
Ps. 1. 5. ungodly shall not stand in *j.*
　9. 7. prepared his throne for *j.*
　25. 9. the meek will he guide in *j.*
　37. 6. bring forth thy *j.* as noonday.
　89. 14; 97. 2. justice and *j.* are habitation of
　throne.
　101. 1. I will sing of mercy and *j.*
Prov. 2. 9. then shalt thou understand *j.*
　29. 26. *j.* cometh from the Lord. [and *j.*
Eccl. 8. 6. to every purpose there is time
　11. 9; 12. 14. God will bring into *j.*
Is. 26. 9. when thy *j.* are in the earth.
　28. 17. I will lay *j.* to the line.
　53. 8. taken from prison and from *j.*
Jer. 5. 1. if there be any that executeth *j.*
Hos. 12. 6. keep mercy and *j.*
Matt. 5. 21. in danger of the *j.*
Lk. 11. 42. pass over *j.* love of God.
John 5. 22. committed all *j.* to the Son.
　7. 24. judge righteous *j.*
　9. 39. for *j.* I am come.
　12. 31. now is the *j.* of this world.
　16. 8. reprove the world of *j.*
Acts 8. 33. his *j.* was taken away.
　24. 25. reasoned of *j.* to come.
Rom. 5. 18. *j.* came on all to condemnation.
　14. 10; 2 Cor. 5. 10. we shall all stand before
Heb. 9. 27. after this the *j.* [*j.* seat.
　10. 27. certain fearful looking for of *j.*
1 Pet. 4. 17. *j.* begin at house of God.
Rev. 16. 7; 19. 2. righteous are thy *j.*
Just, Gen. 6. 9. Noah was a *j.* man.
Deut. 32. 4. a God, *j.* and right is he.
Job 9. 2. how should man be *j.* with God?
Prov. 3. 33. God blesseth the habitation of
　4. 18. path of *j.* as shining light. [the *j.*
　10. 7. the memory of the *j.* is blessed.
　12. 21. no evil happen to the *j.* [not.
Eccl. 7. 20. not a *j.* man on earth sinneth
Is. 26. 7. way of *j.* is uprightness.
　45. 21. a *j.* God and a Saviour.
Hab. 2. 4; Rom. 1. 17; Gal. 3. 11; Heb. 10. 38.
　the *j.* shall live by faith.
Matt. 5. 45. sendeth rain on *j.* and unjust.
Lk. 14. 14. recompensed at resurrection of
　15. 7. ninety and nine *j.* persons. [the *j.*
　23. 50. good man and a *j.*
Acts 24. 15. resurrection of *j.* and unjust.
Rom. 2. 13. not hearers of law are *j.*
　3. 26. that he might be *j.*
Phil. 4. 8. whatsoever things are *j.*
Heb. 2. 2. a *j.* recompense of reward.
　12. 23. spirits of *j.* men made perfect.
1 Pet. 3. 18. *j.* for the unjust.
　1 John 1. 9. he is *j.* to forgive sins.
Justice, Gen. 18. 19. keep way of Lord to do *j.*
2 Sam. 15. 4. I would do *j.*
Ps. 82. 3. do *j.* to afflicted and needy.
Prov. 8. 15. by me princes decree *j.*
Is. 9. 7. to establish his throne with *j.*
　59. 4. none calleth for *j.* [earth.
Jer. 23. 5. execute judgment and *j.* in the
　31. 23; 50. 7. habitation of *j.*

Justification, Rom. 4. 25. Christ raised again for our *j*.

5. 18. free gift came on all men to *j*.

Justify, Job 9. 20. if I *j*. myself, my mouth shall condemn me.

25. 4. how can man be *j*. with God.

Ps. 51. 4. be *j*. when thou speakest.

143. 2. in thy sight shall no man living be *j*.

Is. 5. 23. *j*. the wicked for reward.

53. 11. righteous servant *j*. many.

Matt. 11. 19 ; Lk. 7. 35. wisdom is *j*. of her children.

Matt. 12. 37. by thy words thou shalt be *j*.

Lk. 10. 29. he, willing to *j*. himself.

16. 15. ye *j*. yourselves before men.

18. 14. *j*. rather than the other.

Acts 13. 39. all that believe are *j*.

Rom. 3. 24 ; Tit. 3. 7. *j*. freely by his grace.

Rom. 5. 1. being *j*. by faith.

8. 30. whom he *j*. he also glorified.

Gal. 2. 16 ; 3. 11. man is not *j*. by the law.

1 Tim. 3. 16. *j*. in the Spirit.

Justly, Mic. 6. 8. the Lord require but to do *j*. ?

Lk. 23. 41. indeed *j*., for we receive.

1 Thes. 2. 10. how holily and *j*. we behaved.

KEEP, Gen. 18. 19. they shall *k*. the way of the Lord.

28. 15, 20. I am with thee to *k*. thee.

Num. 6. 24. the Lord bless thee, and *k*. thee.

1 Sam. 2. 9. he will *k*. the feet of his saints.

Job 14. 13. O that thou wouldest *k*. me.

Ps. 17. 8. *k*. me as the apple of the eye.

19. 13. *k*. me from presumptuous sins.

34. 13. *k*. thy tongue from evil.

91. 11. his angels charge to *k*. thee.

103. 9. nor will he *k*. anger for ever.

121. 3. he that *k*. thee will not slumber.

127. 1. except the Lord *k*. the city.

141. 3. *k*. the door of my lips.

Prov. 4. 6. love wisdom, she shall *k*. thee.

4. 23. *k*. thy heart with all diligence.

Eccl. 3. 6. a time to *k*. and cast away.

5. 1. *k*. thy foot when thou goest.

12. 13. fear God and *k*. his commandments.

Is. 26. 3. thou wilt *k*. him in perfect peace.

27. 3. I the Lord do *k*. it.

Jer. 3. 5, 12. will he *k*. his anger?

Mic. 7. 5. *k*. the doors of thy mouth.

Hab. 2. 20. let the earth *k*. silence.

Matt. 19. 17. if thou wilt enter life, *k*. the commandments.

Lk. 11. 28. blessed are they that hear the word and *k*. it.

19. 43. enemies shall *k*. thee in on every side.

John 8. 51. *k*. my saying.

12. 25. he that hateth his life shall *k*. it.

14. 23. if a man love me, he will *k*. my words.

17. 15. *k*. them from the evil.

Acts 5. 3. to *k*. back part of the price.

16. 4. delivered the decrees to *k*.

1 Cor. 5. 8. let us *k*. the feast.

9. 27. I *k*. under my body.

15. 2. *k*. in memory what I preached.

Eph. 4. 3. *k*. the unity of the Spirit.

Phil. 4. 7. the peace of God shall *k*. your hearts.

1 Tim. 5. 22. *k*. thyself pure.

6. 20. *k*. that committed to thy trust.

Jas. 1. 27. to *k*. himself unspotted.

1 John 5. 21. *k*. yourselves from idols.

Jude 24. to him that is able to *k*. you.

Rev. 3. 10. I will *k*. thee from hour of temptation.

Keeper, Gen. 4. 9. am I my brother's *k*. ?

Ps. 121. 5. the Lord is thy *k*.   [tremble.

Eccl. 12. 3. when *k*. of the house shall

Cant. 1. 6. made me *k*. of the vineyards.

Acts 16. 27. *k*. of the prison.

Tit. 2. 5. chaste, *k*. at home.

Key, Is. 22. 22. the *k*. of house of David.

Matt. 16. 19. *k*. of kingdom of heaven.

Lk. 11. 52. taken *k*. of knowledge.

Rev. 1. 18. the *k*. of hell and of death.

Kick, Deut. 32. 15. Jeshurun waxed fat and *k*.

1 Sam. 2. 29. *k*. ye at my sacrifice?

Acts 9. 5 ; 26. 14. to *k*. against the pricks.

Kill, Ex. 20. 13 ; Deut. 5. 17 ; Matt. 5. 21 ; Rom. 13. 9. thou shalt not *k*.

Num. 16. 13. to *k*. us in the wilderness.

Deut. 32. 39. I *k*., and I make alive.

2 Ki. 5. 7. am I God to *k*.?

7. 4. if they *k*. us, we sh..ll but die.

Ps. 44. 22. for thy sake are we *k*.

Eccl. 3. 3. a time to *k*.   [the body.

Matt. 10. 28 ; Lk. 12. 4. fear not them that *k*.

Mk. 3. 4. is it lawful to s..ve life, or to *k*.?

John 5. 18 ; 7. 1. the Jews sought to *k*. him.

7. 19. why go ye about to *k*. me?

8. 22. will he *k*. himself?

10. 10. thief cometh to steal and *k*.

Rom. 8. 36. for thy sake we are *k*. all the day.

2 Cor. 3. 6. the letter *k*., spirit giveth life.

6. 9. as chastened and not *k*.

Jas. 4. 2. ye *k*. and desire to have.

5. 6. ye condemned and *k*. the just.

Rev. 13. 10. he that *k*. with sword must be *k*.

Kind, 2 Chr. 10. 7. if thou be *k*. to this people.

Matt. 13. 47. gathered of every *k*.

17. 21 ; Mk. 9. 29. this *k*. goeth not out.

Lk. 6. 35. God is *k*. to unthankful and evil.

1 Cor. 13. 4. charity suffereth long, and is *k*.

Jas. 1. 18. a *k*. of first-fruits.

Kindle, Num. 11. 33 ; Deut. 11. 17 ; 2 Ki. 22. 13.

Ps. 106. 40. wrath of the Lord was *k*.

Ps. 2. 12. his wrath is *k*. but a little.

Prov. 26. 21. a contentious man to *k*. strife.

Hos. 11. 8. my repentings are *k*. together.

Lk. 12. 49. what will I, if it be already *k*.?

Jas. 3. 5. how great a matter a little fire *k*.

Kindness, Josh. 2. 12. shew *k*. to my father's house.

Ruth 3. 10. shewed more *k*. in latter end.

2 Sam. 2. 6. I will requite you this *k*.

Neh. 9. 17. God gracious, of great *k*.

Ps. 17. 7 ; 92. 2. shew thy loving *k*. !

36. 7. how excellent is thy loving *k*. !

51. 1. have mercy according to thy loving *k*.

63. 3. thy loving *k*. is better than life.

103. 4. who crowneth thee with loving *k*.

117. 2. his merciful is *k*. great.   [be a *k*.

141. 5. let the righteous smite me, it shall

143. 8. cause me to hear thy loving *k*.

Is. 54. 8. with everlasting *k*.

Jer. 2. 2. I remember the *k*. of thy youth.

31. 3. with loving *k*. have I drawn thee.

Joel 2. 13 ; Jon. 4. 2. Lord is of great *k*.

2 Cor. 6. 6. by long-suffering, by *k*.

Col. 3. 12. put on *k*., humbleness.

2 Pet. 1. 7. brotherly *k*., to *k*. charity.

King, Gen. 14. 18 ; Heb. 7. 1. Melchizedek, *k*. of Salem.

Num. 23. 21. the shout of a *k*. is among them.

Jud. 8. 18. resembled children of a *k*.

9. 8. trees went forth to anoint a *k*.

1 Sam. 8. 5. now make us a *k*.   [the *k*.

10. 24 ; 2 Sam. 16. 16 ; 2 Ki. 11. 12. God save

Job 18. 14. the *k*. of terrors.

King—*Continued.*
Ps. 2. 6. I set my *K.* upon holy hill.
5. 2 ; 84. 3. my *K.,* and my God.
10. 16 ; 29. 10. the Lord is *K.* for ever.
20. 9. let the *K.* hear us when we call.
24. 10. Lord of hosts is *K.* of glory.
45. 1. things I have made touching the *K.*
72. 1. give the *k.* thy judgments.
74. 12. God is my *K.* of old.
149. 2. children of Zion joyful in *K.*
Prov. 8. 15. by me *k.* reign.
22. 29. the diligent shall stand before *k.*
24. 21. fear the Lord and the *k.*
Eccl. 2. 12. what can the man do that cometh
   after the *k.* ?
10. 16. woe to thee when thy *k.* is a child.
10. 20. curse not the *k.*
Is. 6. 5. mine eyes have seen the *K.*
32. 1. a *K.* shall reign in righteousness.
33. 17. thine eyes see the *K.* in his beauty.
49. 23. *k.* shall be thy nursing fathers.
Jer. 10. 10. the Lord is an everlasting *K.*
23. 5. a *K.* shall reign and prosper.
Matt. 22. 11. when the *k.* came in to see the
Lk. 14. 31. what *k.* going to war? [guests.
19. 38. blessed be the *K.* that cometh.
23. 2. saying that he is Christ a *K.*
John 6. 15. by force, to make him a *K.*
19. 14. behold your *K.!*
Acts 17. 7. there is another *k.,* one Jesus.
1 Tim. 1. 17. now to the *K.* eternal.
6. 15. the *K.* of *k.,* and Lord of lords.
Rev. 1. 6 ; 5. 10. made us *k.* and priests unto
15. 3. thou *K.* of saints. [God.

Kingdom, Ex. 19. 6 a *k.* of priests.
1 Sam. 18. 8. what can he have more but
   the *k.*? [the *k.,* O Lord.
1 Chr. 29. 11 ; Ps. 22. 28 ; Matt. 6. 13. thine is
Ps. 103. 19. his *k.* ruleth over all.
145. 12. the glorious majesty of his *k.*
Dan. 4. 3. his *k.* is an everlasting *k.*
Matt. 4. 23 ; 9. 35 ; 24. 14. gospel of the *k.*
8. 12. children of the *k.* cast out.
12. 25 ; Mk. 3. 24 ; Lk. 11. 17. *k.* divided
   against itself.
Matt. 13. 38. good seed are children of the *k.*
25. 34. inherit the *k.* prepared for you.
26. 29. drink it new in Father's *k.* [the *k.*
Lk. 12. 32. Father's good pleasure to give you
22. 29. I appoint unto you a *k.*
John 18. 36. my *k.* is not of this world.
Acts 1. 6. restore *k.* again to Israel. [the *k.*
1 Cor. 15. 24. when he shall have delivered up
Col. 1. 13. translated us into *k.* of his Son.
Heb. 12. 28. a *k.* that cannot be moved.
Jas. 2. 5. heirs of the *k.* he hath promised.
2 Pet. 1. 11. entrance into everlasting *k.*
Rev. 12. 10. now is come *k.* of our God.

Kiss, Ps. 2. 12. *k.* Son lest he be angry.
85. 10. righteousness and peace *k.* each other.
Lk. 7. 45. thou gavest me no *k.* [holy *k.*
Rom. 16. 16 ; 1 Cor. 16. 20. salute with an

Knew, Gen. 28. 16. the Lord is in this place,
   and I *k.* it not.
Job 23. 3. *k.* where I might find him.
Jer. 1. 5. before I formed thee, I *k.* thee.
Matt. 7. 23. I never *k.* you, depart.
25. 24. I *k.* thee, thou art an hard man.
John 2. 25. Jesus *k.* what was in man.
4. 10. if thou *k.* the gift of God.
1 Cor. 1. 21. world by wisdom *k.* not God.
2. 8. none of princes of world *k.*
2 Cor. 5. 21. who *k.* no sin.
Rev. 19. 12. name written no man *k.*

Know, Gen. 3. 22. to *k.* good and evil.
1 Sam. 3. 7. Samuel did not yet *k.* the Lord.
Job 5. 27. *k.* thou it for thy good.
8. 9. we are but of yesterday, and *k.* nothing.
19. 25. I *k.* that my Redeemer liveth.
22. 13 ; Ps. 73. 11. how doth God *k.*?
Ps. 39. 4. make me to *k.* mine end.
46. 10. be still and *k.* that I am God.
103. 16. the place shall *k.* it no more.
139. 23. *k.* my heart.
143. 8. to *k.* way wherein I should walk.
Eccl. 1. 17. gave my heart to *k.* wisdom.
9. 5. the living *k.* they shall die.
11. 9. *k.* that God will bring to judgment.
Is. 1. 3. the ox *k.* his owner.
52. 6. my people shall *k.* my name.
Jer. 17. 9. the heart is deceitful, who can
   k. it? [*k.* me.
31. 34 ; Heb. 8. 11. *k.* the Lord, for all shall
Hos. 2. 20. thou shalt *k.* the Lord.
Matt. 6. 3. let not thy left hand *k.* what.
7. 11. if ye *k.* how to give good gifts.
13. 11 ; Mk. 4. 11 ; Lk. 8. 10. it is given to
Lk. 19. 42. if thou hadst *k.* [you to *k.*
22. 57. I *k.* him not.
John 4. 42. we *k.* that this is the Christ.
7. 17. he shall *k.* of the doctrine.
10. 14. I *k.* my sheep, and am *k.* of mine.
13. 7. thou shalt *k.* hereafter.
Acts 1. 7. not for you to *k.* the times. [good.
Rom. 8. 28. we *k.* that all things work for
1 Cor. 2. 14. neither can he *k.* them.
13. 9. we *k.* in part.
Eph. 3. 19. to *k.* the love of Christ.
2 Tim. 1. 12. I *k.* whom I have believed.
3. 15. thou hast *k.* the scriptures.
1 John 3. 2. we *k.* that when he shall appear.
Rev. 2. 2 ; 3. 1, 8. I *k.* thy works.
3. 9. make them *k.* I have loved thee.

Knowledge, Gen. 2. 9. tree of *k.* of good and
Num. 24. 16. *k.* of the Most High. [evil.
2 Chr. 1. 11. thou hast asked *k.*
Job 21. 14. we desire not *k.* of thy ways.
Ps. 19. 2. night to night sheweth *k.*
73. 11. is there *k.* in Most High?
94. 10. he that teacheth man *k.*
139. 6. such *k.* is too wonderful.
143. 3. what is man that thou takest *k.*?
Prov. 1. 7. fear of Lord beginning of *k.*
10. 14. wise men lay up *k.*
14. 18. prudent are crowned with *k.*
17. 27. he that hath *k.* spareth his words.
30. 3. nor have the *k.* of the holy.
Eccl. 1. 18. increaseth *k.* increaseth sorrow.
9. 10. nor *k.* in the grave.
Is. 11. 2. the spirit of *k.*
40. 14. who taught him *k.*?
53. 11. by his *k.* justify many.
Dan. 12. 4. *k.* shall be increased.
Hos. 4. 6. destroyed for lack of *k.*
Hab. 2. 14. earth filled with *k.* of Lord.
Lk. 11. 52. taken away key of *k.*
Acts 4. 13. took *k.* of them.
24. 22. more perfect *k.* of that way.
Rom. 3. 20. by the law is *k.* of sin.
10. 2. zeal of God, but not according to *k.*
1 Cor. 8. 1. *k.* puffeth up.
13. 8. *k.* shall vanish away.
2 Cor. 4. 6. light of *k.* of the glory of God.
Eph. 3. 19. love of Christ, which passeth *k.*
Phil. 3. 8. all things loss for the *k.* of Christ.
Col. 2. 3. treasures of wisdom and *k.*
1 Tim. 2. 4 ; 2 Tim. 3. 7. the *k.* of the truth.
2 Pet. 3. 18. grow in grace and *k.* of Lord.

LABOUR, Ps. 90. 10. strength *l.* and sorrow.
104. 23. man goeth to his *l.* till evening.
128. 2. shalt eat the *l.* of thy hands.
Prov. 10. 16. *l.* tendeth to life.
13. 11. he that gathereth by *l.* shall increase.
14. 23. in all *l.* there is profit.
Eccl. 1. 8. all things are full of *l.*
2. 22. what hath man of all his *l.*?
9. 9. portion in thy *l.* under the sun.
Hab. 3. 17. though *l.* of olive fail.
John 4. 38. reap where ye bestowed no *l.*
1 Cor. 15. 58. your *l.* is not in vain.
1 Thes. 1. 3; Heb. 6. 10. your *l.* of love.
1 Thes. 3. 5. our *l.* be in vain.
Rev. 2. 2. I know thy *l.* and patience.
14. 13. rest from their *l.*

Labour, Ex. 20. 9; Deut. 5. 13. six days shalt
Job 9. 29. why then *l.* in vain?   [thou *l.*
Ps. 127. 1. except Lord build, they *l.* in vain.
144. 14. our oxen may be strong to *l.*
Prov. 23. 4. *l.* not to be rich.
Eccl. 4. 8. for whom do I *l.*?
5. 12. sleep of a *l.* man is sweet.
Matt. 11. 28. come to me, all ye that *l.*
John 6. 27. *l.* not for meat that perisheth.
2 Cor. 5. 9. we *l.* to be accepted of God.
Eph. 4. 28. rather *l.*, working with his hands.
1 Tim. 4. 10. *l.* and suffer reproach.
5. 17. that *l.* in word and doctrine.
Heb. 4. 11. *l.* to enter into that rest.
See 1 Cor. 3. 9; Jas. 5. 4.
Lack, Ps. 34. 10. young lions do *l.*   [ledge.
Hos. 4. 6. people destroyed for *l.* of know-
Matt. 19. 20. what *l.* I yet?
Jas. 1. 5. if any man *l.* wisdom, ask of God.
Laden, Is. 1. 4. a people *l.* with iniquity.
Matt. 11. 28. all that are heavy *l.*
Lamb, Gen. 22. 8. God will provide a *l.*
Is. 11. 6. the wolf shall dwell with the *l.*
53. 7; Jer. 11. 19. as a *l.* to the slaughter.
John 1. 29, 36. behold the *L.* of God.
Acts 8. 32. like a *l.*, dumb before shearer.
1 Pet. 1. 19. as of a *l.* without blemish.
Rev. 13. 8. *l.* slain from foundation of world.
15. 3. song of Moses and of the *L.*
Lame, Job 29. 15. eyes to blind, feet to *l.*
Prov. 26. 7. legs of *l.* are not equal.
Is. 35. 6. *l.* man leap as an hart.
Heb. 12. 13. lest that *l.* be turned out of way.
Lamp, 1 Sam. 3. 3. ere *l.* went out.
Ps. 119. 105. thy word is a *l.* to my feet.
132. 17. ordained a *l.* for mine anointed.
Prov. 13. 9. *l.* of wicked shall be put out.
Matt. 25. 1. ten virgins took *l.*
Language, Gen. 11. 1. whole earth of one *l.*
Ps. 19. 3. no *l.* where voice is not heard.
Acts 2. 6. heard them speak in own *l.*
Lap, Jud. 7. 5. that *l.* water as a dog.
Prov. 16. 33. lot is cast into the *l.*
Last, Num. 23. 10. let my *l.* end be like his.
Prov. 23. 32. at the *l.* it biteth like a serpent.
Lam. 1. 9. she remembereth not her *l.* end.
Matt. 12. 45; Lk. 11. 26. *l.* state of that man
   worse.   [first shall be *l.*
Matt. 19. 30; 20. 16; Mk. 10. 31; Lk. 13. 30.
Matt. 27. 64. *l.* error worse than first.
John 6. 39; 11. 24. the *l.* day.
Heb. 1. 2. spoken in *l.* days by his Son.
Latter, Deut. 11. 14. first and *l.* rain.
Job 19. 25. Redeemer stand at *l.* day.
Prov. 19. 20. be wise in *l.* end.
1 Tim. 4. 1. in *l.* times some depart from
   faith.

Laugh, Job 5. 22. at famine thou shalt *l.*
Ps. 2. 4. that sitteth in heavens shall *l.*
Prov. 1. 26. I will *l.* at your calamity.
Eccl. 3. 4. a time to weep, a time to *l.*
Lk. 6. 25. woe unto you that *l.* now!
Law, Deut. 33. 2. from right hand went
   fiery *l.*
Ps. 1. 2. in his law he meditates.
37. 31. the *l.* of his God is in his heart.
119. 70. I delight in thy *l.*
119. 97. how I love thy *l.*
Prov. 13. 14. the *l.* of the **wise** is a fountain
   of life.
29. 18. that keepeth the *l.*, happy is he.
Is. 42. 4. the isles shall wait for his *l.*
Mal. 2. 6. the *l.* of truth was in his mouth.
Matt. 5. 17. not come to destroy the *l.*
22. 40. on two commandments hang *l.*
23. 23. the weightier matters of the *l.*
Lk. 16. 17. for one tittle of the *l.* to fail.
John 1. 17. the *l.* was given by Moses.
7. 51. doth our *l.* judge any man?
19. 7. by our *l.* he ought to die.
Rom. 2. 13. not hearers of the *l.* are just.
3. 20. by deeds of the *l.* no flesh be justified.
7. 12. the *l.* is holy.
7. 16; 1 Tim. 1. 8. the *l.* is good.
Rom. 8. 3. what the *l.* could not do.
10. 4. Christ is the end of the *l.*
Gal. 3. 24. the *l.* was our schoolmaster.
5. 14. all the *l.* is fulfilled in one word.
6. 2. so fulfil the *l.* of Christ.
1 Tim. 1. 9. the *l.* is not made for a righteous
   man.   [things.
Heb. 10. 1. the *l.* having a shadow of good
Jas. 1. 25. perfect *l.* of liberty.
2. 8. the royal *l.*
1 John 3. 4. transgresseth also the *l.*
Lawful, Matt. 12. 10; Mk. 3. 4; Lk. 6. 9. is it *l.*
   to heal on Sabbath?
John 18. 31. not *l.* to put to death.
1 Cor. 6. 12; 10. 23. all things *l.* to me.
2 Cor. 12. 4. words not *l.* to utter.
Lay, Ps. 7. 5. *l.* mine honour in the dust.
Eccl. 7. 2. the living will *l.* it to heart.
Is. 26. 5. lofty city he *l.* low.   [head.
Matt. 8. 20; Lk. 9. 58. not where to *l.* his
Matt. 28. 6. place where the Lord *l.*
Acts 7. 60. *l.* not sin to their charge.
Col. 1. 5. hope which is *l.* up for you.
1 Tim. 6. 12. *l.* hold on eternal life.
Heb. 6. 18. *l.* hold on hope set before us.
12. 1. *l.* aside every weight.
1 Pet. 2. 6. *l.* in Zion a chief corner-stone.
Lead, Ex. 13. 21. pillar of cloud to *l.* them.
Deut. 32. 12. Lord alone did *l.* him.
Ps. 23. 2. he *l.* me beside still waters.
43. 3. send light and truth, let them *l.* me.
61. 2. *l.* me to Rock higher than I.
139. 24. *l.* me in the way everlasting.
143. 10. *l.* me to land of uprightness.
Is. 11. 6. a little child shall *l.* them.
40. 11. gently *l.* those with young.
42. 16. *l.* them in paths not known.
Matt. 6. 13; Lk. 11. 4. *l.* us not into tempta-
   tion.   [blind.
Matt. 15. 14; Lk. 6. 39. if the blind *l.* the
1 Tim. 2. 2. we may *l.* a quiet life.
Rev. 7. 17. Lamb feed and *l.* them.
Leaf, Gen. 8. 11. in dove's mouth was olive *l.*
Ps. 1. 3. his *l.* also shall not wither.
Is. 64. 6. fade as a *l.*
Matt. 21. 19; Mk. 11. 13. found nothing but *l.*
Rev. 22. 2. *l.* for healing of nations.

Lean, Jud. 16. 26. may *l.* on the pillars.
Prov. 3. 5. *l.* not to own understanding.
Amos 5. 19. *l.* his hand on the wall.
John 21. 20. *l.* on his breast at supper.
Heb. 11. 21. *l.* on top of staff.

Learn, Deut. 31. 13. *l.* to fear the Lord.
Is. 1. 17. *l.* to do well.   [more.
2. 4; Mic. 4. 3. neither shall they *l.* war any
Is. 26. 9. inhabitants *l.* righteousness.
Matt. 9. 13. go *l.* what that meaneth.
11. 29. *l.* of me.   [tians.
Acts 7. 22. Moses was *l.* in wisdom of Egyp-
Eph. 4. 20. ye have not so *l.* Christ.
Phil. 4. 11. have *l.* in every state to be content.
Heb. 5. 8. yet *l.* he obedience.

Learning, Prov. 1. 5. wise man will increase *l.*
Dan. 1. 17. God gave them skill in *l.*
Acts 26. 24. much *l.* doth make thee mad.
Rom. 15. 4. things written for our *l.*
2 Tim. 3. 7. ever *l.* and never able.

Least, Gen. 32. 10. not worthy *l.* of mercies.
Matt. 5. 19. one of these *l.* commandments.
11. 11; Lk. 7. 28. he that is *l.* in kingdom of
heaven.
Matt. 25. 40, 45. done it to the *l.* of these.
Lk. 16. 10. faithful in that which is *l.*
Eph. 3. 8. less than the *l.* of all saints.

Leave, Gen. 2. 24; Matt. 19. 5, Mk. 10. 7; Eph.
5. 31. *l.* father and mother.
Ruth 1. 16. entreat me not to *l.* thee.
Ps. 16. 10; Acts 2. 27. not *l.* my soul in hell.
Ps. 27. 9; 119. 121. *l.* me not.
Matt. 18. 12; Lk. 15. 4. *l.* the ninety and
nine.
Matt. 23. 23. and not to *l.* the other undone.
John 14. 27. peace I *l.* with you.
Heb. 13. 5. I will never *l.* thee.

Lees, Is. 25. 6. feast of wines on the *l.*
Jer. 48. 11. Moab hath settled on his *l.*
Zeph. 1. 12. punish men settled on *l.*

Lend, Deut. 15. 6. thou shalt *l.* to many nations.
Ps. 37. 26; 112. 5. merciful and *l.*   [Lord.
Prov. 19. 17. that hath pity on poor, *l.* to the
Lk. 6. 34. if ye *l.* to them of whom.
See Prov. 22. 7.

Less, Is. 40. 17. *l.* than nothing and vanity.
2 Cor. 12. 15. more I love, the *l.* I am loved.
Heb. 7. 7. the *l.* is blessed of better.

Let, Is. 43. 13. work, and who shall *l.* it?
John 19. 12. if thou *l.* this man go.
2 Thes. 2. 7. who now *l.* will *l.*
Heb. 2. 1. lest we should *l.* them slip.

Letter, Rom. 7. 6. not in the oldness of the *l.*
2 Cor. 3. 6. not of *l.*, but of the Spirit.
Gal. 6. 11. how large a *l.* I have written.
See Lk. 23. 38; John 7. 15.

Liars, Ps. 116. 11. said in haste, all men are *l.*
Tit. 1. 12. the Cretians are always *l.*
Rev. 21. 8. all *l.* have their part in lake.

Liberal, Prov. 11. 25. *l.* soul shall be made fat.
Is. 32. 5. the vile shall not be called *l.*
32. 8. the *l.* deviseth *l.* things.
Jas. 1. 5. God, who giveth to all men *l.*

Liberty, Ps. 119. 45. I will walk at *l.*
Is. 61. 1; Jer. 34. 8; Lk. 4. 18. to proclaim *l.*
Acts 26. 32. man might have been set at *l.*
Rom. 8. 21. the glorious *l.* of children of
God.
1 Cor. 8. 9. take heed lest this *l.* of yours.
2 Cor. 3. 17. where the Spirit is, there is *l.*
Gal. 5. 1. stand fast in the *l.* wherewith.
Jas. 1. 25; 2. 12. the law of *l.*
2 Pet. 2. 19. they promise them *l.*

Life, Gen. 2. 7. the breath of *l.*
2. 9; 3. 24; Rev. 2. 7. the tree of *l.*
Lev. 17. 11. the *l.* is in the blood.   [thee *l.*
Deut. 30. 15; Jer. 21. 8. I have set before
Josh. 2. 18. our *l.* for yours.
1 Sam. 25. 29. bound in the bundle of *l.*
2 Sam. 15. 21. whether in death or *l.*
Ps. 16. 11. shew me the path of *l.*
21. 4. asked *l.* of thee, thou gavest it.
30. 5. in his favour is *l.*
34. 12. what man is he that desireth *l.*?
36. 9. with thee is the fountain of *l.*
91. 16. with long *l.* will I satisfy him.
133. 3. even *l.* for evermore.
Prov. 3. 22. so shall they be *l.* to thy soul.
8. 35. whoso findeth me, findeth *l.*
14. 27. fear of Lord is a fountain of *l.*
15. 24. way of *l.* is above to the wise.
Jer. 8. 3. death be chosen rather than *l.*
Matt. 6. 25; Lk. 12. 22. take no thought for
your *l.*
Matt. 18. 8; Mk. 9. 43. to enter into *l.*
Lk. 12. 23. the *l.* is more than meat.
John 1. 4. in him was *l.*
5. 26. as the Father hath *l.* in himself.
5. 40; 10. 10. will not come that ye might
have *l.*
6. 33. the bread of *l.*
8. 12. shall have the light of *l.*
11. 25. the resurrection and the *l.*
14. 6. the way, the truth, and the *l.*
20. 31. believing, ye might have *l.*
Acts 17. 25. seeing he giveth to all *l.*
Rom. 5. 17. shall reign in *l.* by one.
6. 4. walk in newness of *l.*
8. 6. to be spiritually minded is *l.*
11. 15. *l.* from the dead.
1 Cor. 3. 22. *l.* or death, all are yours.
2 Cor. 2. 16. the savour of *l.* unto *l.*
5. 4. mortality swallowed up of *l.*
Eph. 4. 18. alienated from the *l.* of God.
Col. 3. 3. your *l.* is hid with Christ.
1 Tim. 4. 8; 2 Tim. 1. 1. promise of *l.*
2 Tim. 1. 10. brought *l.* to light by Gospel.
Heb. 7. 16. made after power of an endless *l.*
Jas. 1. 12. a crown of *l.*
4. 14. what is your *l.*?
1 John 1. 2. the *l.* was manifested.
2. 16. the pride of *l.*
5. 12. he that hath the Son, hath *l.*
Rev. 22. 1, 17. river of water of *l.*

Light, Gen. 1. 3. God said, let there be *l.*
Ex. 10. 23. Israel had *l.* in their dwellings.
Neh. 9. 19. pillar of fire to shew *l.*
Job 18. 5. the *l.* of the wicked shall be put out.
Ps. 4. 6. the *l.* of thy countenance.
27. 1. the Lord is my *l.*
36. 9. in thy *l.* shall we see *l.*
37. 6. bring forth righteousness as *l.*
97. 11. *l.* is sown for the righteous.
104. 2. who coverest thyself with *l.*
119. 105. a *l.* to my path.
139. 12. darkness and *l.* alike to thee.
Prov. 4. 18. path of just as shining *l.*
Eccl. 11. 7. the *l.* is sweet.
Is. 5. 20. darkness for *l.*, and *l.* for darkness.
30. 26. the *l.* of the moon as *l.* of sun.
60. 1. arise, shine, for thy *l.* is come.
60. 19. Lord be an everlasting *l.*
Hab. 3. 4. his brightness was as *l.*
Zech. 14. 6. the *l.* shall not be clear.
Matt. 5. 14; John 8. 12. the *l.* of the world.
Matt. 5. 16. let your *l.* so shine before men.
6. 22; Lk. 11. 34. the *l.* of the body is the eye

Light—Continued.

Lk. 8. 16 ; 11. 33. enter in may see the *l.*
16. 8. wiser than children of *l.*
John 1. 4. life was the *l.* of men.
3. 19. *l.* is come into the world.
5. 35. a burning and shining *l.*
12. 35. a little while is the *l.* with you.
Acts 22. 6. there shone a great *l.* round.
26. 23. *l.* to people and to the Gentiles.
1 Cor. 4. 5. bring to *l.* hidden things.
2 Cor. 4. 4. *l.* of the Gospel.
4. 6. commanded *l.* to shine out of darkness.
Eph. 5. 8. now are ye *l.*, walk as children of *l.*
5. 14. Christ shall give thee *l.*
1 Thes. 5. 5. children of the *l.*   [proach.
1 Tim. 6. 16. in *l.* which no man can ap-
2 Pet. 1. 19. a *l.* shining in a dark place.
1 John 1. 5. God is *l.*
Rev. 21. 23. the Lamb is the *l.* thereof.
22. 5. they need not *l.* of the sun.   [the *l.*
Lightning, Job 38. 25. who divided a way for
Ps. 18. 14. *l.* and discomfited them.
77. 18 ; 97. 4. *l.* lightened the world.
144. 6. cast forth *l.*, scatter them.   [the east.
Matt. 24. 27 ; Lk. 17. 24. as *l.* cometh out of
Lk. 10. 18. as *l.* fall from heaven.
Likeness, Gen. 1. 26. make man after our *l.*
Ex. 20. 4. not make *l.* of any thing.
Ps. 17. 15. when I awake, with thy *l.*
Is. 40. 18. what *l.* will ye compare?
Acts 14. 11. gods are come down in *l.* of men.
Rom. 6. 5. *l.* of his death, *l.* of his resurrec-
  tion.
8. 3. in the *l.* of sinful flesh.
Phil. 2. 7. was made in the *l.* of men.
Limit, Ps. 78. 41. *l.* Holy One of Israel.
Heb. 4. 7. he *l.* a certain day.
Line, Ps. 16. 6. *l.* fallen in pleasant places.
19. 4. their *l.* is gone through the earth.
Is. 28. 10. *l.* must be upon *l.*
28. 17. judgment will I lay to the *l.*
2 Cor. 10. 16. boast in another man's *l.*
Lion, Ps. 17. 12. like a *l.* greedy of his prey.
91. 13. thou shalt tread on the *l.*
Prov. 28. 1. the righteous are bold as a *l.*
Eccl. 9. 4. living dog better than dead *l.*
Is. 35. 9. no *l.* shall be there.
2 Tim. 4. 17. delivered out of mouth of *l.*
Heb. 11. 33. by faith stopped mouths of *l.*
1 Pet. 5. 8. devil as a roaring *l.*
Lips, Ps. 12. 4. our *l.* are our own.
17. 1. goeth not out of feigned *l.*
63. 5. mouth praise thee with joyful *l.*
140. 3. poison is under their *l.*
Prov. 15. 7. the *l.* of wise disperse knowledge.
Cant. 7. 9. causing *l.* of those asleep to speak.
Is. 6. 5. a man of unclean *l.*   [me.
29. 13 ; Matt. 15. 8. people with *l.* do honour
Heb. 13. 15. fruit of our *l.* giving thanks.
Little, Gen. 30. 30. it was *l.* thou hadst.
Ps. 8. 5 ; Heb. 2. 7. a *l.* lower than the angels.
Ps. 37. 16. a *l.* that a righteous man hath.
Prov. 15. 16. better is a *l.* with fear of Lord.
30. 24. four things *l.* on earth.
Is. 26. 20. hide thyself for a *l.* moment.
28. 10. here a *l.*, and there a *l.*
40. 15. taketh up isles as a *l.* thing.
Lk. 7. 47. to whom *l.* is forgiven.
19. 17. been faithful in a very *l.*
Acts 28. 2. shewed us no *l.* kindness.
1 Cor. 5. 6 ; Gal. 5. 9. a *l.* leaven.
1 Tim. 4. 8. bodily exercise profiteth *l.*
Jas. 4. 14. life a vapour that appeareth for a
  l. time.

Live, Gen. 3. 22. take of tree of life, and *l.* for
  ever.
42. 18. this do, and *l.*
Ex. 33. 20. no man see me and *l.*
Lev. 18. 5 ; Neh. 9. 29 ; Ezek. 20. 11. he shall
  l. in them.   [alone.
Deut. 8. 3 ; Matt. 4. 4 ; Lk. 4. 4. not *l.* by bread
Job 14. 14. if a man die, shall he *l.* again ?
Ps. 69. 32. heart shall *l.* that seek God.
Is. 26. 19. dead men shall *l.*
55. 3. hear, and your soul shall *l.*
Ezek. 3. 21 ; 18. 9 ; 33. 13. he shall surely *l.*
Hos. 6. 2. we shall *l.* in his sight.   [faith.
Hab. 2. 4 ; Rom. 1. 17. the just shall *l.* by
Lk. 10. 28. this do, and thou shalt *l.*
John 5. 25. hear voice of God, and *l.*
11. 25. though he were dead, yet shall he *l.*
Acts 17. 28. in him we *l.* and move.
Rom. 6. 8. we believe we shall *l.* with him.
8. 12. not to *l.* after the flesh.
14. 8. whether we *l.*, we *l.* unto the Lord.
1 Cor. 9. 14. should *l.* of the Gospel.
2 Cor. 6. 9. as dying, and behold we *l.*
13. 4. *l.* with him, by power of God.
Gal. 2. 20. I *l.* by faith of Son of God.
5. 25. if we *l.* in the Spirit.
Phil. 1. 21. for me to *l.* is Christ.
Jas. 4. 15. if the Lord will, we shall *l.*
Rev. 1. 18. I am he that *l.*, and was dead.
3. 1. a name that thou *l.*
20. 4. *l.* with Christ.
Lively, Ps. 38. 19. my enemies are *l.*
Acts 7. 38. who received *l.* oracles.
1 Pet. 1. 3. begotten us again to *l.* hope.
2. 5. ye as *l.* stones are built.
Living, Gen. 2. 7. man became a *l.* soul.
Job 28. 13 ; Ps. 27. 13 ; 116. 9. the land of the *l.*
Job 30. 23. the house appointed for all *l.*
Ps. 69. 28. blotted out of book of the *l.*
143. 2. in thy sight no man *l.* be justified.
145. 16. satisfiest every *l.* thing.
Eccl. 7. 2. the *l.* will lay it to heart.
9. 5. the *l.* know that they shall die.
Cant. 4. 15 ; John 4. 14. a well of *l.* water.
Is. 38. 19. the *l.* shall praise thee.
53. 8. cut off out of the land of the *l.*
Lam. 3. 39. wherefore doth a *l.* man com-
  plain ?   [the God of the *l.*
Matt. 22. 32; Mk. 12. 27 ; Lk. 20. 38. God is
Mk. 12. 44. cast in all her *l.*
Lk. 8. 43. spent all her *l.*
John 6. 51. I am the *l.* bread.
Rom. 12. 1. your bodies a *l.* sacrifice.
Heb. 10. 20. a new and *l.* way.
1 Pet. 2. 4. coming as to a *l.* stone.
Load, Ps. 68. 19. daily *l.* us with benefits.
Is. 46. 1. carriages were heavy *l.*
Lofty, Ps. 131. 1. heart not haughty, nor eyes *l.*
Is. 2. 11 ; 5. 15. *l.* looks be humbled.
26 5. the *l.* city he layeth low.
57. 15. thus saith the high and *l.* one.
Long, Job 6. 8. that God would grant the thing
  I *l.* for !
Ps. 63. 1. my flesh *l.* for thee in a dry land.
84. 2. my soul *l.* for courts of the Lord.
Look, Gen. 19. 17. *l.* not behind thee.
Job 3. 9. *l.* for light, but have none.
33. 27. he *l.* on men.
Ps. 34. 5. they *l.* to him and were lightened.
40. 12. that I am not able to *l.* up.
84. 9. *l.* upon the face of thine anointed.
123. 2. as eyes of servants *l.* to masters.
Is. 17. 7. at that day shall a man *l.* to his
  Maker.

Look—*Continued.*
Is. 45. 22. *l.* unto me, and be saved.
66. 2. to this man will I *l.*
Jer. 8. 15; 14. 19. we *l.* for peace.
40. 4. I will *l.* well to thee.
Mic. 7. 7. I *l.* to the Lord.
Matt. 11. 3; Lk. 7. 19. do we *l.* for another?
Matt. 24. 50. in a day he *l.* not for.   [dom.
Lk. 9. 62. no man *l.* back is fit for the king-
21. 28. then *l.* up.
John 13. 22. disciples *l.* one on another.
Acts 3. 4, 12. said, *L.* on us.
6. 3. *l.* ye out seven men.
2 Cor. 4. 18. we *l.* not at things seen.
Phil. 2. 4. *l.* not every man on his own things.
3. 20. we *l.* for the Saviour.
Tit. 2. 13. *l.* for that blessed hope.
Heb. 9. 28. to them that *l.* shall he appear.
11. 10. he *l.* for a city.
12. 2. *l.* unto Jesus.
1 Pet. 1. 12. angels desire to *l.* into.
2 Pet. 3. 13. we *l.* for new heavens.
Loose, Josh. 5. 15. *l.* thy shoe from off thy foot.
Job 38. 31. canst thou *l.* the bands of Orion?
Ps. 102. 20. *l.* those appointed to death.
116. 16. thou hast *l.* my bonds.
Eccl. 12. 6. or ever the silver cord be *l.*
Is. 58. 6. to *l.* the bands of wickedness.
Matt. 16. 19; 18. 18. *l.* on earth, be *l.* in heaven.
John 11. 44. *l.* him, and let him go.
Acts 2. 24. having *l.* the pains of death.
Lord, Gen. 18. 14. is anything too hard for *L.*?
28. 21. then shall the *L.* be my God.
Ex. 34. 6. the *L.*, the *L.* God, merciful and
gracious.
Deut. 4. 35; 1 Ki. 18. 39. the *L.* is God.
6. 4. the *L.* our God is one *L.*
Ruth 1. 17; 1 Sam. 20. 13. *L.* do so, and more.
1 Sam. 3. 18; John 21. 7. it is the *L.*
Neh. 9. 6; Is. 37. 20. thou art *L.* alone.
Ps. 33. 12. blessed the nation whose God is
100. 3; 118. 27. the *L.* is God.   [the *L.*
Zech. 14. 9. one *L.*, and his name one.
Matt. 7. 21. not every one that saith, *L., L.*
25. 21. the joy of thy *L.*   [Sabbath.
Mk. 2. 28 *L.* is *L.* of man is *L.* of the
Lk. 6. 46; why call ye me *L., L.*?
John 6. 68. *L.*, to whom shall we go?
13. 13. ye call me master and *L.*
Acts 2. 36. crucified, both *L.* and Christ.
9. 5; 26. 15. who art thou, *L.*?
Rom. 10. 12. same *L.* over all.
14. 9. *L.* of the dead and of the living.
1 Cor. 2. 8. *L.* of glory.
15. 47. *L.* from heaven.
Eph. 4. 5. one *L.*, one faith.
Phil. 2. 11. confess Jesus Christ is *L.*
1 Tim. 6. 15. King of kings, *L.* of *l.*
Lose, Eccl. 3. 6. a time to get, a time to *l.*
Matt. 10. 39; 16. 25; Mk. 8. 35; Lk. 9. 24. he
that findeth his life shall *l.* it.   [soul.
Matt. 16. 26; Mk. 8. 36; Lk. 9. 25. *l.* his own
Lk. 15. 4. if he *l.* one sheep.
John 12. 25. that loveth his life shall *l.* it.
Loss, Acts 27. 21. gained this harm and *l.*
1 Cor. 3. 15. he shall suffer *l.*
Phil. 3. 8. I count all things but *l.* for Christ.
Lost, Ps. 119. 176. gone astray like *l.* sheep.
Matt. 10. 6; 15. 24. *l.* sheep of Israel.
18. 11; Lk. 19. 10. to save that which was *l.*
Lk. 15. 24. son was *l.*   [be *l.*
John 6. 12. gather fragments, that nothing
17. 12. none is *l.*, but son of perdition.
2 Cor. 4. 3. Gospel hid to them that are *l.*

Lot, 1 Chr. 16. 18; Ps. 105. 11. the *l.* of your
inheritance.
Ps. 16. 5. thou maintainest my *l.*
125. 3. not rest on *l.* of the righteous.
Prov. 1. 14. cast in thy *l.* among us.
16. 33. the *l.* is cast into the lap.
18. 18. the *l.* causeth contentions to cease.
Is. 34. 17. he hath cast the *l.* for them.
Dan. 12. 13. shalt stand in thy *l.* at end.
Matt. 27. 35; Mk. 15. 24. parted garments
casting *l.*
Acts 8. 21. thou hast no *l.* in this matter.
Love, 2 Sam. 1. 26. passing the *l.* of women.
13. 15. hatred greater than *l.*
Prov. 10. 12. *l.* covereth all sins.
15. 17. better a dinner of herbs where *l.* is.
Eccl. 9. 6. their *l.* and hatred is perished.
Cant. 2. 4. his banner over me was *l.*
8. 7. many waters cannot quench *l.*
Jer. 31. 3. loved thee with everlasting *l.*
Hos. 11. 4. the bands of *l.*
Matt. 24. 12. *l.* of many shall wax cold.
John 5. 42. ye have not the *l.* of God in you.
15. 13. greater *l.* hath no man than this.
17. 26. *l.* wherewith thou hast loved me.
Rom. 8. 35. separate from *l.* of Christ?
13. 10. *l.* worketh no ill.
2 Cor. 5. 14. the *l.* of Christ constraineth us.
Gal. 5. 6. faith which worketh by *l.*
Eph. 3. 19. to know the *l.* of Christ.
1 Thes. 5. 8. breastplate of faith and *l.*
1 Tim. 6. 10. *l.* of money is the root of all evil
Heb. 6. 10. your work and labour of *l.*
13. 1. let brotherly *l.* continue.
1 John 4. 7. *l.* is of God.
4. 10. herein is *l.*, not that we loved God.
4. 18. there is no fear in *l.*
Rev. 2. 4. thou hast left thy first *l.*

Love, Lev. 19. 18; Matt. 19. 19; 22. 39; Mk. 12. 31.
thou shalt *l.* thy neighbour.
Deut. 6. 5; 10. 12; 11. 1; 19. 9; 30. 6; Matt.
22. 37; Mk. 12. 30; Lk. 10. 27. *l.* the Lord
thy God.
Ps. 5. 11. let them that *l.* thy name be joyful.
18. 1. I will *l.* thee, O Lord, my strength.
34. 12. what man is he that *l.* many days?
69. 36. they that *l.* his name.
97. 10. ye that *l.* the Lord, hate evil.
122. 6. they shall prosper that *l.* thee.
Prov. 8. 17. I *l.* them that *l.* me.
17. 17. a friend *l.* at all times.
Eccl. 3. 8. a time to *l.*
Hos. 14. 4. I will *l.* them freely.
Amos 5. 15. hate the evil, and *l.* the good.
Mic. 6. 8. to *l.* mercy, and walk humbly.
Matt. 5. 44; Lk. 6. 27. I say, *l.* your enemies.
Lk. 7. 42. which will *l.* him most?
John 11. 3. he whom thou *l.* is sick.
15. 12, 17. that ye *l.* one another.
21. 15. *l.* thou me?
Rom. 8. 28. for good to them that *l.* God.
13. 8. owe no man anything but to *l.*   [Lord.
Eph. 6. 24. grace be with them that *l.* our
1 Pet. 1. 8. whom having not seen, ye *l.*
2. 17. *l.* the brotherhood.
1 John 4. 19. we *l.* him, because he first *l.* us.
Rev. 3. 19. as many as I *l.*, I rebuke.
Lovely, 2 Sam. 1. 23. *l.* in their lives.
Cant. 5. 16. he is altogether *l.*
Phil. 4. 8. whatsoever things are *l.*
Lover, Ps. 88. 18. *l.* and friend put far from me.
2 Tim. 3. 4. *l.* of pleasure more than *l.* of God.
Tit. 1. 8. *l.* of hospitality, *l.* of good men.

Low, 1 Sam. 2. 7. the Lord bringeth *l*.
Job 5. 11. set on high those that be *l*.
Ps. 49. 2. high and *l*., rich and poor.
62. 9. men of *l*. degree are vanity.
136. 23. remembered us in *l*. estate.
Is. 26. 5. the lofty city he layeth *l*.
Lk. 1. 52. exalted them of *l*. degree.
Rom. 12. 16. men of *l*. estate.
Jas. 1. 10. rich in that he is made *l*.
Lower, Ps. 8. 5; Heb. 2. 7. *l*. than the angels.
Ps. 63. 9. go into *l*, parts of the earth.
Eph. 4. 9. descended into *l*. parts.   [ness.
Lowliness, Eph. 4. 2. walk with *l*. and meek-
Phil. 2. 3. in *l*. of mind.
Lowly, Ps. 138. 6. yet hath he respect to the *l*.
Prov. 3. 34. he giveth grace to the *l*.
11. 2. with the *l*. is wisdom.
Zech. 9. 9. *l*., and riding on an ass.
Matt. 11. 29. I am meek and *l*.
Lust, Ps. 81. 12. gave them up to their own *l*.
Rom. 7. 7. I had not known *l*., except law.
Gal. 5. 24. crucified flesh with *l*.
1 Tim. 6. 9. foolish and hurtful *l*.
2 Tim. 2. 22. flee youthful *l*.
Tit. 2. 12. denying worldly *l*.
Jas. 1. 14. when he is drawn of his own *l*.
1 Pet. 2. 11. abstain from fleshly *l*.
1 John 2. 16. the *l*. of the flesh.   [thereof.
2. 17. the world passeth away, and the *l*.
Jude 16, 18. walking after their *l*.
See Deut. 12. 15; 14. 26; Matt. 5. 28.
Lying, Ps. 31. 18. let the *l*. lips be put to silence.
119. 29. remove from me the way of *l*.
119. 163. I hate and abhor *l*.
Prov. 6. 17. Lord hateth a *l*. tongue.
12. 19. a *l*. tongue is but for a moment.
Is. 59. 13. in *l*. against the Lord.
Jer. 7. 4. trust not in *l*. words.
Jon. 2. 8. observe *l*. vanities, forsake mercy.
Eph. 4. 25. putting away *l*.

MAD, 1 Sam. 21. 13. feigned himself *m*.
Ps. 102. 8. they that are *m*. against me.
Eccl. 2. 2. I said of laughter, it is *m*.
John 10. 20. he hath a devil, and is *m*.
Acts 26. 24. much learning doth make thee *m*.
1 Cor. 14. 23. will they not say, ye are *m*.?
Made, Ex. 2. 14. who *m*. thee a prince over us?
Ps. 104. 24. thy works in wisdom hast thou *m*.
118. 24. this the day the Lord hath *m*.
139. 14. I am wonderfully *m*.
Prov. 16. 4. Lord *m*. all things for himself.
Eccl. 3. 11. he hath *m*. everything beautiful.
7. 29. God hath *m*. man upright.
Is. 66. 2; Acts 7. 50. things hath mine hand *m*.
John 1. 3. all things were *m*. by him.   [are *m*.
Rom. 1. 20. understood by the things that
1 Cor. 9. 22. *m*. all things to all men.
2 Cor. 5. 21. he hath *m*. him to be sin for us.
Gal. 4. 4. *m*. of a woman, *m*. under the law.
Eph. 3. 7; Col. 1. 23. I was *m*. a minister.
Phil. 2. 7. *m*. in the likeness of men.
Heb. 2. 17. to be *m*. like his brethren.
1 John 2. 19. that they might be *m*. manifest.
Magnify, Josh. 3. 7. this day will I begin to
m. thee.   [*m*. him?
Job 7. 17. what is man, that thou shouldest
Ps. 34. 3. O *m*. the Lord with me.
40. 16; 70. 4. say, Lord be *m*.
138. 2. thou hast *m*. thy word above all.
Is. 42. 21. he will *m*. the law.
Lk. 1. 46 my soul doth *m*. the Lord.
Acts 10. 46. speak with tongues, and *m*. God.
Rom. 11. 13. I *m*. mine office.

Maintain, 1 Ki. 8. 45; 2 Chr. 6. 35, 39. *m*. their
cause.
Ps. 16. 5. thou *m*. my lot.
Tit. 3. 8, 14. careful to *m*. good works.
Majesty, 1 Chr. 29. 11. thine, O Lord, is *m*.
Job 37. 22. with God is terrible *m*.
Ps. 29. 4. voice of the Lord is full of *m*.
96. 6. honour and *m*. are before him.
104. 1. thou art clothed with *m*.
145. 12. glorious *m*. of his kingdom.
Heb. 1. 3; 8. 1. on right hand of *m*.
2 Pet. 1. 16. eye-witnesses of his *m*.
Jude 25. to God be glory and *m*.
Maker, Job 4. 17. shall a man be more pure
than his *m*.?
32. 22. my *m*. would soon take me away.
35. 10. none saith, where is God my *m*.?
36. 3. ascribe righteousness to my *m*.
Ps. 95. 6. kneel before the Lord our *m*.
Prov. 14. 31; 17. 5. reproacheth his *m*.
22. 2. the Lord is *m*. of them all.
Is. 17. 7. shall man look to his *m*.?
45. 9. woe to him that striveth with his *m*.
51. 13. forgettest the Lord thy *m*.
54. 5. thy *m*. is thine husband.
Hos. 8. 14. Israel hath forgotten his *m*.
Hab. 2. 18. image the *m*. hath graven.
Heb. 11. 10. whose builder and *m*. is God.
Malice, 1 Cor. 5. 8. not with leaven of *m*.
14. 20. in *m*. be ye children.
Eph. 4. 31. put away from you all *m*.
1 Pet. 2. 1. laying aside all *m*.   [dust.
Man, Gen. 2. 7. Lord God formed *m*. of the
3. 22. the *m*. is become as one of us.
Num. 23. 19. God is not a *m*.
2 Sam. 12. 7. said, thou art the *m*.
Job 4. 17. shall *m*. be more just than God?
5. 7. *m*. is born to trouble.
11. 12. vain *m*. would be wise.
14. 1. *m*. that is born of a woman.
33. 12. God is greater than *m*.
Ps. 49. 12. *m*. being in honour abideth not.
80. 17. let thy hand be on the *m*.
90. 3. thou turnest *m*. to destruction.
104. 23. *m*. goeth forth to his work.
118. 6. I will not fear: what can *m*. do?
Prov. 12. 2. a good *m*. obtaineth favour.
20. 24. *m*. goings are of the Lord.
Eccl. 6. 12. who knoweth what is good for *m*.?
Is. 2. 22. cease ye from *m*.
32. 2. a *m*. shall be a hiding-place.
53. 3. he is a *m*. of sorrows.
Jer. 10. 23. it is not in *m*. to direct his steps.
Lam. 3. 27. it is good for a *m*. that he bear
yoke.
Hos. 11. 9. I am God, and not *m*.
Matt. 6. 24; Lk. 16. 13. no *m*. can serve two
masters.   [authority.
Matt. 8. 9; Lk. 7. 8. I am a *m*. under
Mk. 2. 27. Sabbath was made for *m*.
John 1. 18; 1 John 4. 12. no *m*. hath seen God.
John 2. 25. he knew what was in *m*.
19. 5. behold the *m*.!
1 Cor. 2. 11. what *m*. knoweth things of a *m*.?
2 Cor. 4. 16. though our outward *m*. perish.
Eph. 3. 16. by his Spirit in the inner *m*.
4. 24. that ye put on the new *m*.
Phil. 2. 8. found in fashion as a *m*.
1 Tim. 2. 5. the *m*. Christ Jesus.
1 Pet. 3. 4. hidden *m*. of the heart.   [be *m*.
Manifest, Mk. 4. 22. nothing hid that shall not
John 2. 11. *m*. forth his glory
14. 22. how is it thou wilt *m*. thyself?
1 Cor. 4. 5. make *m*. the counsels of the heart.

89

Manifest—*Continued.*
1 Cor. 15. 27. it is *m.* he is excepted.
2 Cor. 2. 14. maketh *m.* savour of knowledge.
Gal. 5. 19. the works of the flesh are *m.*
2 Thes. 1. 5. a *m.* token of righteous judgment.
1 Tim. 3. 16. God was *m.* in the flesh.
Heb. 4. 13. no creature that is not *m.*
1 John 1. 2. the life was *m.*
  3. 5. he was *m.* to take away our sins.
  4. 9 in this was *m.* the love of God.
Manifold, Ps. 104. 24. how *m.* are thy works!
Lk. 18. 30. receive *m.* more.
Eph. 3. 10. the *m.* wisdom of God.
1 Pet. 1. 6. through *m.* temptations.
  4. 10. stewards of the *m.* grace of God.
Manner, Lev. 23. 31. ye shall do no *m.* of work.
2 Sam. 7. 19. is this the *m.* of man?
Ps. 107. 18. all *m.* of meat.
Cant. 7. 13. all *m.* of pleasant fruits.
Is. 5. 17. lambs shall feed after their *m.*
Matt. 5. 11. say all *m.* of evil against you.
  8. 27; Mk. 4. 41; Lk. 8. 25. what *m.* of man
    is this?
John 19. 40. *m.* of Jews to bury.   [good *m.*
1 Cor. 15. 33. evil communications corrupt
2 Tim. 3. 10. my *m.* of life.
Heb. 10. 25. as the *m.* of some is.
Jas. 1. 24. forgetteth what *m.* of man.
1 Pet. 1. 15. holy in all *m.* of conversation.
2 Pet. 3. 11. what *m.* of persons ought ye
    to be?
1 John 3. 1. what *m.* of love.   [beard.
Mar, Lev. 19. 27. not *m.* the corners of th'
Is. 52. 14. his visage *m.* more than any *m.*
Mk. 2. 22. wine spilled, the bottles be *m.*
Mark, Gen. 4. 15. the Lord set a *m.* on Cain.
Job 18. 2. *m.* and we will speak.
  22. 15. hast thou *m.* the old way?
Ps. 37. 37. *m.* the perfect man.
  48. 13. *m.* well her bulwarks.
  130. 3. if thou shouldest *m.* iniquities.
Lk. 14. 7. *m.* how they chose rooms.
Gal. 6. 17. the *m.* of the Lord Jesus.   [prize.
Phil. 3. 14. I press toward the *m.* for the
Marrow, Ps. 63. 5. soul satisfied as with *m.*
Prov. 3. 8. health and *m.* to the bones.
Is. 25. 6. feast of fat things full of *m.*
Heb. 4. 12. to the dividing asunder of joints
    and *m.*
Marvel, Eccl. 5. 8. *m.* not at the matter.
Matt. 8. 10; Mk. 6. 6; Lk. 7. 9. Jesus
Mk. 5. 20. all men did *m.*
John 5. 28. *m.* not at this.
Acts 3. 12. why *m.* ye at this?
1 John 3. 13. *m.* not if world hate you.
Marvellous, Job 5. 9. *m.* things without
    number.
Ps. 17. 7. shew *m.* loving-kindness.
  98. 1. he hath done *m.* things.   [eyes.
  118. 23; Matt. 21. 42; Mk. 12. 11. *m.* in our
John 9. 30. herein is a *m.* thing.
1 Pet. 2. 9. called you into his *m.* light.
Master, Mal. 1. 6. if I be a *m.*, where is my
    fear?   [scholar.
  2. 12. the Lord will cut off the *m.* and the
Matt. 6. 24; Lk. 16. 13. no man can serve
    two *m.*   [his *m.*
Matt. 10. 24; Lk. 6. 40. disciple not above
Matt. 23. 8, 10. one is your *m.*, even Christ.
Mk. 5. 35; Lk. 8. 49. why troublest thou
    the *m.*?   [here.
Mk. 9. 5; Lk. 9. 33. *m.*, it is good for us to be
Mk. 10. 17; Lk. 10. 25; 18. 18. good *m.*, what
    shall I do?

Master—*Continued.*
Lk. 13. 25. when the *m.* of the house is risen.
John 3. 10. art thou a *m.* of Israel?
  11. 28. the *m.* is come, and calleth for thee.
  13. 13. ye call me *m.*, and ye say well.
Rom. 14. 4. to his own *m.* he standeth or
    falleth.
1 Cor. 3. 10. as a wise *m.* builder.
Eph. 6. 9; Col. 4. 1. *M.* is in heaven.
Tim. 6. 1. count *m.* worthy of honour.
Jas. 3. 1. be not many *m.*
Matter, Deut. 17. 8. if there arise a *m.* too
    hard.
Job 19. 28. the root of the *m.* is found in me.
  32. 18. I am full of *m.*
Ps. 45. 1. my heart is inditing a good *m.*
Prov. 16. 20. that handleth a *m.* wisely.
  18. 13. answereth a *m.* before heareth it.
Eccl. 10. 20. that which hath wings shall tell
    the *m.*
  12. 13. hear conclusion of the whole *m.*
Matt. 23. 23. omitted the weightier *m.*
Acts 18. 14. if it were a *m.* of wrong.
  24. 22. I will know uttermost of the *m.*
1 Cor. 6. 1. dare any having a *m.* go.
2 Cor. 9. 5. ready as a *m.* of bounty.
Jas. 3. 5. how great a *m.* a little fire kindleth!
Mean, Ex. 12. 26. what *m.* ye by this service?
Deut. 6. 20. what *m.* the testimonies?
Josh. 4. 6, 21. what *m.* these stones?
Prov. 22. 29. not stand before *m.* men.
Is. 2. 9; 5. 15. the *m.* man.
Mk. 9. 10. what the rising from the dead
    should *m.*
Acts 21. 39. a citizen of no *m.* city.
Means, Ex. 34. 7; Num. 14. 18. by no *m.* clear
    the guilty.   [brother.
Ps. 49. 7. none can by any *m.* redeem his
Matt. 5. 26. shalt by no *m.* come out.
Lk. 5. 18. sought *m.* to bring him.
  10. 19. nothing shall by any *m.* hurt you.
John 9. 21. by what *m.* he now seeth.
Acts 4. 9. by what *m.* he is made whole.
1 Cor. 9. 22. that I might by all *m.* save some.
2 Cor. 11. 3. lest by any *m.* as the serpent.
Gal. 2. 2. lest by any *m.* I should run in
    vain.
Phil. 3. 11. by any *m.* attain.
2 Thes. 2. 3. no man deceive you by any *m.*
Measure, Deut. 25. 15. a just *m.* shalt thou
    have.
Job 11. 9. the *m.* is longer than the earth.
  28. 25. he weigheth the waters by *m.*
Ps. 39. 4. to know the *m.* of my days.
  80. 5. tears to drink in great *m.*
Is. 40. 12. comprehended dust of earth in a *m.*
Jer. 30. 11; 46. 28. correct thee in *m.*
Ezek. 4. 11. thou shalt drink water by *m.*
Matt. 7. 2; Mk. 4. 24; Lk. 6. 38. with what
    m. ye mete.
Matt. 13. 33; Lk. 13. 21. three *m.* of meal.
Matt. 23. 32. fill up *m.* of your fathers.
Mk. 6. 51. were amazed beyond *m.*
Lk. 6. 38. good *m.* pressed down.
John 3. 34. God giveth not the Spirit by *m.*
Rom. 12. 3. to every man the *m.* of faith.
2 Cor. 10. 13. not boast of things without
    our *m.*
  12. 7. exalted above *m.*
Gal. 1. 13. beyond *m.* I persecuted.
Eph. 4. 7. the *m.* of the gift of Christ.
  4. 13. to the *m.* of the stature.
Rev. 6. 6. a *m.* of wheat for a penny.
  21. 17. according to the *m.* of a man.

Measure, Num. 35. 5. *m.* from without the city.
Is. 40. 12. who hath *m.* the waters?
65. 7. I will *m.* former work into bosom.
Jer. 31. 37. if heaven can be *m.*   [be *m.*
33. 22; Hos. 1. 10. sand of the sea cannot
2 Cor. 10. 12. *m.* themselves by themselves.
Rev. 11. 1. rise and *m.* the temple of God.
21. 15. a golden reed to *m.* the city.

Meat, Gen. 1. 29. it shall be for *m.*
27. 4. savoury *m.*
1 Ki. 19. 8. he went in strength of that *m.*
Job 33. 20. his soul abhorreth dainty *m.*
38. 41. they wander for lack of *m.*
Ps. 42. 3. my tears have been my *m.*
59. 15. wander up and down for *m.*
69. 21. they gave me gall for my *m.*
104. 27. thou mayest give them their *m.*
145. 15; Matt. 24. 45. *m.* in due season.
Prov. 6. 8. the ant provideth her *m.*
31. 15. giveth *m.* for her household.
Is. 65. 25. dust shall be the serpent's *m.*
Ezek. 4. 10. thy *m.* shall be by weight.
Dan. 1. 8. not defile himself with king's *m.*
Hab. 3. 17. fields yield no *m.*   [than *m.?*
Matt. 6. 25; Lk. 12. 23. is not the life more
Matt. 10. 10. wcr'kman worthy of his *m.*
15. 37; Mk. 8. 8. of. the broken *m.·*
Matt. 25. 35. hungered, ye gave me *m.*
Lk. 8. 55. he commanded to give her *m.*
24. 41; John 21. 5. have ye any *m.?*
John 4. 34. my *m.* is to do the will of him
   that sent me.
6. 27. labour not for the *m.* that perisheth.
Acts 2. 46. eat their *m.* with gladness.
Rom. 14. 15. if thy brother be grieved with
   thy *m.?*
14. 17. kingdom of God is not *m.* and drink.
1 Cor. 3. 2. fed with milk, not with *m.*
6. 13. *m.* for the belly.
8. 8. *m.* commendeth us not to God.
10. 3. eat the same spiritual *m.*
Col. 2. 16. let no man judge you in *m.*
Heb. 5. 14. strong *m.* belongeth to them of
   full age.
12. 16. for one morsel of *m.* sold birthright.

Meddle, 2 Ki. 14. 10; 2 Chr. 25. 19. why *m.* to
   thy hurt?
Prov. 20. 19. *m.* not with him that flattereth.
24. 21. *m.* not with them given to change.
26. 17. that *m.* with strife.

Mediator, Gal. 3. 19. by angels in hand of a *m.*
1 Tim. 2. 5. there is one *m.*, Jesus Christ.
Heb. 8. 6. the *m.* of a better covenant.
9. 15. the *m.* of the New Testament.
12. 24. Jesus the *m.* of the new covenant.

Medicine, Prov. 17. 22. doeth good like a *m.*
Jer. 30. 13. thou hast no healing *m.*
Ezek. 47. 12. the leaf shall be for *m.*

Meditate, Gen. 24. 63. Isaac went out to *m.*
Josh. 1. 8. thou shalt *m.* therein.
Ps. 1. 2. in his law doth he *m.*
63. 6. *m.* in night watches.
77. 12; 143. 5. *m.* of all thy works.
Is. 33. 18. thine heart shall *m.* terror.
Lk. 21. 14. settle not to *m.* before.
1 Tim. 4. 15. *m.* on these things.
See Ps. 19. 14; 104. 34; 119. 97.

Meek, Num. 12. 3. Moses was very *m.*
Ps. 22. 26. the *m.* shall eat and be satisfied.
25. 9. the *m.* will he guide in judgment.
37. 11; Matt. 5. 5. the *m.* shall inherit the
   earth.
Ps. 147. 6. the Lord lifteth up the *m.*
149. 4. beautify the *m.* with salvation.

Meek—*Continued.*
Is. 29. 19. the *m.* shall increase their joy.
61. 1. good tidings to the *m.*
Matt. 11. 29. I am *m.* and lowly.
21. 5. thy king cometh to thee, *m.*
1 Pet. 3. 4. ornament of a *m.* and quiet spirit.

Meekness, Ps. 45. 4. because of truth and *m.*
1 Cor. 4. 21. shall I come in spirit of *m.?*
2 Cor. 10. 1. by the *m.* of Christ.
Gal. 5. 23. fruit of the Spirit is *m.*
6. 1. restore in the spirit of *m.*
Col. 3. 12. put on *m.*, long-suffering.
1 Tim. 6. 11. follow after *m.*
2 Tim. 2. 25. in *m.* instructing.
Tit. 3. 2. shewing all *m.* to all men.   [word.
Jas. 1. 21. received with *m.* the engrafted
1 Pet. 3. 15. reason of hope in you with *m.*

Meet, Gen. 2. 18. an help *m.* for him.
Matt. 3. 8. fruits *m.* for repentance.
15. 26; Mk. 7. 27. not *m.* to take children's
   bread.
Acts 26. 20. works *m.* for repentance.
1 Cor. 15. 9. not *m.* to be called an apostle.
Col. 1. 12. made us *m.* to be partakers.
Heb. 6. 7. herbs *m.* for them by whom it is
   dressed.

Meet, Prov. 22. 2. the rich and poor *m.* together.
Is. 14. 9. hell is moved to *m.* thee.
Amos 4. 12. prepare to *m.* thy God.
Matt. 8. 34. city came to *m.* Jesus.
25. 1. went forth to *m.* the bridegroom.
1 Thes. 4. 17. in the clouds to *m.* the Lord.

Melody, Is. 23. 16. make sweet *m.*
Amos 5. 23. not hear *m.* of thy viols.
Eph. 5. 19. making *m.* to the Lord.

Member, Ps. 139. 16. in thy book all my *m.*
   written.
Matt. 5. 29. one of thy *m.* should perish.
Rom. 7. 23. another law in *m.* warring.
1 Cor. 6. 15. your bodies are *m.* of Christ.
12. 14. the body is not one *m.*
Eph. 4. 25. we are *m.* one of another.
5. 30. *m.* of his body.
Jas. 3. 5. the tongue is a little *m.*
4. 1. lusts that war in your *m.*

Memory, Ps. 109. 15. he may cut off *m.* of them.
145. 7. utter the *m.* of thy goodness.
Prov. 10. 7. the *m.* of the just is blessed.
Eccl. 9. 5. the *m.* of them is forgotten.
Is. 26. 14. made their *m.* to perish.

Men, 1 Sam. 2. 26. in favour with Lord and *m.*
2 Chr. 6. 18. will God dwell with *m.?*
Ps. 9. 20. know themselves to be but *m.*
Eccl. 12. 3. the strong *m.* shall bow them-
Is. 31. 3. the Egyptians are *m.*, and not God.   [selves.
46. 8. shew yourselves *m.*
Matt. 7. 12; Lk. 6. 31. that *m.* should do to
   you, do ye even so to them.
1 Cor. 16. 13. quit you like *m.*
1 Thes. 2. 4. not as pleasing *m.*, but God.
1 Pet. 2. 17. honour all *m.*

Mention, Ex. 23. 13; Josh. 23. 7. make no *m.*
   of other gods.   [ness.
Ps. 71. 16. I will make *m.* of thy righteous-
Is. 12. 4. make *m.* that his name is exalted.
26. 13. we will make *m.* of thy name.
63. 7. I will *m.* the loving-kindnesses of the
   Lord.
Amos 6. 10. may not *m.* name of Lord.
Rom. 1. 9; Eph. 1. 16; 1 Thes. 1. 2. *m.* of you
   in my prayers.
Heb. 11. 22. made *m.* of departing of Israel.

Merchandise, Prov. 3. 14. *m.* of it better than
      m. of silver.   [Lord.
  Is. 23. 18. her *m.* shall be holiness to the
  Matt. 22. 5. one to his farm, another to
    his *m.*
  John 2. 16. my Father's house an house of *m.*
  2 Pet. 2. 3. make *m.* of you.
  Rev. 18. 11. no man buyeth their *m.* any
    more.   [the *m.*
Merchant, Gen. 23. 16. current money with
  37. 28. Midianites, *m.* men.
  Is. 23. 8. whose *m.* are princes.
  47. 15. thy *m.* shall wander.
  Matt. 13. 45. like a *m.*-man seeking goodly
    pearls.
  Rev. 18. 3. the *m.* of the earth are waxed rich.
  18. 23. thy *m.* were great men of the earth.
Merciful, Ex. 34 6. Lord God *m.* and gracious.
  2 Sam. 22. 26 ; Ps. 18. 25. with the *m.* thou
    wilt shew thyself *m.*
  Ps. 37 26. the righteous is ever *m.*
  67. 1. God be *m.* to us.
  Prov. 11. 17. the *m.* man doeth good to his
    own soul.
  Is. 57. 1. *m.* men are taken away.
  Jer. 3. 12. I am *m.*, saith the Lord.
  Jon. 4. 2. I knew thou art a *m.* God.
  Lk. 6. 36. be ye *m.*, as your Father is *m.*
  18. 13. God be *m.* to me a sinner.
  Heb. 2. 17. a *m.* High Priest.
  8. 12. I will be *m.* to their unrighteousness.
Mercy, Gen. 19. 19. thou hast magnified thy *m.*
  32. 10. not worthy of the least of all the *m.*
  Ex. 33. 19. I will shew *m.* on whom I will
    shew *m.*
  34. 7 ; Dan. 9. 4. keeping *m.* for thousands.
  Num. 14. 18 ; Ps. 103. 11 ; 145. 8. Lord is of
    great *m.*
  1 Chr. 16. 34, 41 ; 2 Chr. 5. 13 ; 7. 3, 6 ; Ezra
    3. 11 ; Ps. 106. 1 ; 118. 1 ; 136. 1 ; Jer. 33. 11.
    his *m.* endureth for ever.
  Ps. 23. 6. goodness and *m.* shall follow me.
  25. 10. all the paths of the Lord are *m.*
  33. 18. that hope in his *m.*
  52. 8. I trust in the *m.* of God.
  59. 10. the God of my *m.*
  62. 12. unto thee belongeth *m.*
  66. 20. not turned his *m.* from me.
  77. 8. is his *m.* clean gone for ever?
  85. 10. *m.* and truth met together.
  89. 2. *m.* shall be built up for ever.
  90. 14. satisfy us early with thy *m.*
  101. 1. I will sing of *m.*
  103. 17. *m.* of the Lord is from everlasting.
  130. 7. with the Lord there is *m.*
  Prov. 3. 3. let not *m.* and truth forsake thee.
  14. 21. he that hath *m.* on the poor.
  21. 21. followeth after *m.* findeth life.
  Is. 54. 10. the Lord hath *m.* on thee.
  60. 10. in my favour had *m.* on thee.
  Jer. 6. 23. they are cruel, and have no *m.*
  Lam. 3. 22. it is of the Lord's *m.*
  Hos. 6. 6 ; Matt. 9. 13. I desired *m.*, and not
    sacrifice.
  Hos. 14. 3. in thee the fatherless find *m.*
  Mic. 6. 8. to do justly, and love *m.*
  7. 18. he delighteth in *m.*
  Hab. 3. 2. in wrath remember *m.*
  Matt. 5. 7. the merciful shall obtain *m.*
  9. 27 ; 15. 22 ; 20. 30 ; Mk. 10. 47 ; Lk. 18. 38.
    thou son of David, have *m.* on me.
  Matt. 23. 23. omitted judgment and *m.*
  Rom. 9. 15, 18. I will have *m.* on whom I
    will have *m.*

Mercy—*Continued.*
  Rom. 11. 30. obtained *m.* through unbelief.
  2 Cor. 1. 3. the Father of *m.*
  4. 1. as we have received *m.*
  Eph. 2. 4. God, who is rich in *m.*
  Tit. 3. 5. according to his *m.* he saved us.
  Heb. 4. 16. that we may obtain *m.*
  10. 28. despised the law, died without *m.*
  Jas. 2. 13. judgment without *m.*, that shewed
    no *m.*
  5. 11. Lord is pitiful, and of tender *m.*
  1 Pet. 1. 3. according to his abundant *m.*
  2. 10. had not obtained *m.*, but now have
    obtained *m.*
  Jude 21. looking for the *m.* of Lord Jesus.
Merry, Gen. 43. 34. they drank, and were *m.*
  Jud. 16. 25. their hearts were *m.*
  19. 6 ; 1 Ki. 21. 7. let thine heart be *m.*
  Prov. 15. 13. *m.* heart maketh cheerful coun-
    tenance.
  17. 22. *m.* heart doeth good like a medicine.
  Eccl. 8. 15. nothing better than to eat and
    be *m.*
  10. 19. wine maketh *m.*
  Lk. 12. 19. take thine ease, eat and be *m.*
  15. 32. it was meet we should be *m.*
  Jas. 5. 13. is any *m.*?
  Rev. 11. 10. rejoice and make *m.*
Message, Jud. 3. 20. a *m.* from God to thee.
  Lk. 19. 14. citizens sent a *m.* after him.
  1 John 1. 5 ; 3. 11. the *m.* we have heard.
Messenger, Job 33. 23. if there be a *m.*
  Prov. 25. 13. faithful *m.*
  Is. 42. 19. as my *m.* that I sent.
  Mal. 3. 1. *m.* of the covenant.
  2 Cor. 12. 7. the *m.* of Satan to buffet.
Midst, Gen. 2. 9. tree of life in the *m.*
  Ps. 46. 5. God is in the *m.*
  102. 24. in the *m.* of my days.
  Prov. 23. 34. lieth down in *m.* of the sea.
  Is. 6. 5. I dwell in *m.* of a people of unclean
    lips.   [thee.
  12. 6 ; Hos. 11. 9. the Holy One in the *m.* of
  Dan. 3. 25. walking in *m.* of the fire.
  9. 27. in the *m.* of the week.
  Matt. 10. 16. as sheep in the *m.* of wolves.
  18. 2 ; Mk. 9. 36. a little child in the *m.*
  Matt. 18. 20. there am I in the *m.*   [the *m.*
  Lk. 24. 36 ; John 20. 19. Jesus himself in
  Rev. 2. 7. in the *m.* of the paradise of God.
  4. 6 ; 5. 6 ; 7. 17. in the *m.* of the throne.
  8. 13. flying through *m.* of heaven.
Might, Deut. 3. 24. do according to thy *m.*
  6. 5. love thy God with all thy *m.*
  8. 17. the *m.* of mine hand hath gotten
    wealth.
  Jud. 6. 14. go in thy *m.*
  2 Sam. 6. 14. David danced with all his *m.*
  1 Chr. 29. 12 ; 2 Chr. 20. 6. in thine hand is
    power and *m.*
  Ps. 145. 6. speak of the *m.* of thy acts.
  Eccl. 9. 10. do it with thy *m.*
  Is. 40. 29. to them that have no *m.*
  Jer. 9. 23. let not mighty man glory in his *m.*
  Zech. 4. 6. not by *m.*, nor by power.
  Eph. 3. 16 ; Col. 1. 11. strengthened with *m.*
  Rev. 7. 12. glory and *m.* be unto God.
Mighty, Gen. 10. 9. he was a *m.* hunter.
  18. 18. become a *m.* nation.   [the *m.*
  Jud. 5. 23. to the help of the Lord against
  2 Sam. 1. 19. how are the *m.* fallen !
  Job 9. 4. God is wise in heart, and *m.* in
    strength.
  34. 20. the *m.* shall be taken away.

Mighty—*Continued.*

Ps. 24. 8. Lord strong and *m.*, *m.* in battle.
45. 3. gird thy sword, O Most *M.*
68. 33. his voice, a *m.* voice.
89. 13. thou hast a *m.* arm.
89. 19. laid help upon one that is *m.*
93. 4. Lord mightier than *m.* waves.
112. 2. his seed shall be *m.* on earth.
Prov. 16. 32. that is slow to anger better than *m.*
23. 11. their Redeemer is *m.*   [Israel.
Is. 1. 24; 30. 29; 49. 26; 60. 16. the *M.* One of
63. 1. *m.* to save.
Jer. 32. 19. *m.* in work.
Amos 2. 14. neither shall *m.* deliver himself.
Matt. 11. 20; 13. 54; 14. 2; Mk. 6. 2. *m.* works.
Lk. 1. 52. he hath put down the *m.*
9. 43. the *m.* power of God.
24. 19. a prophet *m.* in deed and word.
Acts 18. 24. *m.* in the Scriptures.
1 Cor. 1. 26. not many *m.*   [God.
2 Cor. 10. 4. weapons of warfare *m.* through
Eph. 1. 19. the working of his *m.* power.
See Acts 19. 20; Col. 1. 29, Rev. 18. 2.

Milk, Gen. 18. 8. butter and *m.*
49. 12. his teeth be white with *m.*
Jud. 5. 25. he asked water, she gave *m.*
Prov. 30. 33. churning of *m.*
Is. 55. 1. buy wine and *m.*
Lam. 4. 7. Nazarites whiter than *m.*
Ezek. 25. 4. eat fruit, and drink *m.*
1 Cor. 3. 2. I have fed you with *m.*
Heb. 5. 12. such as have need of *m.*
1 Pet. 2. 2. the sincere *m.* of the word.

Mind, 1 Chr. 28. 9. serve God with a willing *m.*
Neh. 4. 6. the people had a *m.* to work.
Job 23. 13. he is in one *m.*, who can turn him?
Ps. 31 12. as a dead man out of *m.*
Prov. 29. 11. a fool uttereth all his *m.*
Is. 26. 3. whose *m.* is stayed on thee.
Matt. 22. 37 Mk. 12. 30; Lk. 10. 27. love the Lord with all thy *m.*
Mk. 5. 15; Lk. 8. 35. sitting in his right *m.*
Lk. 12. 29. neither be of doubtful *m.*
Acts 17. 11. with all readiness of *m.*
20. 19. humility of *m.*
Rom. 8. 7. the carnal *m.* is enmity against God.
11. 34. who hath known the *m.* of the Lord?
12. 16. be of the same *m.*
14. 5. fully persuaded in his own *m.*
1 Cor. 2. 16. we have the *m.* of Christ.
2 Cor. 8. 12. if there be first a willing *m.*
13. 11; Phil. 1. 27; 2. 2. be of one *m.*
Eph. 2. 3. desires of the flesh and *m.*
Phil. 2. 3. in lowliness of *m.*
4. 2. be of the same *m.* in the Lord.
2 Tim. 1. 7. spirit of sound *m.*
Tit. 3. 1. put them in *m.* to be subject.
Heb. 8. 10. put my laws into their *m.*
1 Pet. 1. 13. the loins of your *m.*
See Rom. 12. 16; Phil. 3. 16.

Mindful, Ps. 8. 4; Heb. 2. 6. what is man that thou art *m.* of him?
115. 12. Lord hath been *m.* of us.
Is. 17. 10. not been *m.* of the Rock.
Heb. 11. 15. been *m.* of that country.
2 Pet. 3. 2. be *m.* of words spoken.

Mine, Ex. 19. 5; Ps. 50. 12. all the earth is *m.*
Hag. 2. 8. silver is *m.*, and gold is *m.*
Mal. 3. 17. they shall be *m.*, saith the Lord.
Matt. 20. 23; Mk. 10. 40. is not *m.* to give.
John 17. 10. all *m.* are thine, thine are *m.*

Minister, 1 Ki. 10. 5; 2 Chr. 9. 4. the attendance of his *m.*
Ps. 103. 21. ye *m.* that do his pleasure.
104. 4; Heb. 1. 7. his *m.* a flame of fire.
Matt. 20. 26; Mk. 10. 43. let him be your *m.*
Lk. 4. 20. gave the book to the *m.*
Rom. 13. 4. he is the *m.* of God to thee.
2 Cor. 3. 6. able *m.* of New Testament.
11. 23. are they *m.* of Christ?
Gal. 2. 17. is Christ the *m.* of sin?
Eph. 3. 7; Col. 1. 23. whereof I was made a *m.*
Eph. 6. 21; Col. 1. 7. a faithful *m.*
1 Tim. 4. 6. a good *m.* of Christ.
Heb. 8. 2. a *m.* of the sanctuary.

Minister, Deut. 21. 5. God hath chosen them to *m.*
1 Sam. 2. 11. the child did *m.* to the Lord.
1 Chr. 15. 2. chosen to *m.* for ever.
Ps. 9. 8. *m.* judgment to people.
Is. 60. 10. their kings shall *m.* to thee.
Matt. 20. 28; Mk. 10. 45. not to be *m.* unto, but to *m.*
2 Cor. 9. 10. *m.* bread for your food.
Eph. 4. 29. *m.* grace to the hearers.
Heb. 1. 14. to heirs of salvation.

Ministration, Lk. 1. 23. days of *m.* were accomplished.
Acts 6. 1. widows neglected in daily *m.*
2 Cor. 3. 7. if *m.* of death was glorious.
9. 13. by the experiment of this *m.*   [of *m.*

Ministry, Acts 1. 25. that he may take part
6. 4. we will give ourselves to the *m.*   [ing.
Rom. 12. 7. or *m.* let us wait on our minister-
2 Cor. 4. 1. seeing we have this *m.*
5. 18. the *m.* of reconciliation.
Eph. 4. 12. for the work of the *m.*
Col. 4. 17. take heed to the *m.*
2 Tim. 4. 5. make full proof of thy *m.*
Heb. 8. 6. obtained a more excellent *m.*

Minstrel, 2 Ki. 3. 15. bring me a *m.*
Matt. 9. 23. when Jesus saw the *m.*

Miracle, Ex. 7. 9. saying, shew a *m.*
Deut. 29. 3. thine eyes have seen *m.*
Jud. 6. 13. where be all his *m.*?   [name.
Mk. 9. 39. no man which shall do a *m.* in my
Lk. 23. 8. hoped to have seen some *m.*
John 2. 11. this beginning of *m.*
4. 54. this is the second *m.*
10. 41. said, John did no *m.*
11. 47. this man doeth many *m.*
Acts 2. 22. approved of God by *m.* and signs.
4. 16. a notable *m.* has been done.
1 Cor. 12. 29. are all workers of *m.*?
Heb. 2. 4. God bearing witness with *m.*

Mirth, Neh. 8. 12. the people went to make *m.*
Ps. 137. 3. that wasted us, desired *m.*
Eccl. 2. 1. I will prove thee with *m.*
Is. 24. 11. the *m.* of the land is gone.

Miry, Ps. 40. 2. brought me out of *m.* clay.
Dan. 2. 41. iron mixed with *m.* clay.

Mischief, Gen. 42. 4. lest *m.* befall him.
Job 15. 35. they conceive *m.* and vanity.
Ps. 36. 4. the wicked deviseth *m.*
52. 1. why boastest thou thyself in *m.*?
62. 3. how long will ye imagine *m.*?
Prov. 10. 23. as sport to a fool to do *m.*
24. 16; 28. 14. wicked shall fall into *m.*
Ezek. 7. 26. *m.* shall come upon *m.*
Acts 13. 10. O full of all subtilty and *m.*

Misery, Job 11. 16. thou shalt forget thy *m.*
Prov. 31. 7. remember his *m.* no more.
Eccl. 8. 6. the *m.* of man is great.
Jas. 5. 1. howl for your *m.*   [Rev. 3. 17.
See Job 16. 2; Matt. 21. 41; 1 Cor. 15. 19;

Mixed, Prov. 23. 30. that go to seek *m.* wine.
Is. 1. 22. thy wine *m.* with water.
Heb. 4. 2. not being *m.* with faith.
See Ps. 75. 8; John 19. 39; Rev. 14. 10.
Mock, Gen. 19. 14. he seemed as one that *m.*
1 Ki. 18. 27. Elijah *m.* them.
2 Chr. 36. 16. they *m.* the messengers of God.
Prov. 1. 26. I will *m.* when your fear cometh.
17. 5. *m.* poor, reproacheth Maker.
30. 17. the eye that *m.* at his father.
Lk. 14. 29. begin to *m.* him.
Acts 2. 13. others *m.* said.
Gal. 6. 7. God is not *m.* See Prov. 20. 1; Jude 18.
Moisture, Ps. 32. 4. my *m.* turned to drought.
Lk. 8. 6. because it lacked *m.*
Moment, Ex. 33. 5. into midst of thee in a *m.*
Num. 16. 21. consume them in a *m.*
Job 7. 18. try him every *m.*
34. 20. in a *m.* shall they die.
Ps. 30. 5. his anger endureth but a *m.*
Is. 26. 20. hide thyself as it were for a *m.*
27. 3. I will water it every *m.*
54. 8. I hid my face from thee for a *m.*
Lk. 4. 5. kingdoms of world in a *m.*
1 Cor. 15. 52. all be changed in a *m.*
2 Cor. 4. 17. affliction, which is but for a *m.*
Money, Gen. 23. 9. as much *m.* as field is worth.
2 Ki. 5. 26. is it a time to receive *m.*?
Ps. 15. 5. putteth not out *m.* to usury.
Eccl. 7. 12. *m.* is a defence.
10. 19. *m.* answereth all things.
Is. 52. 3. redeemed without *m.*
55. 1. he that hath no *m.*
Matt. 17. 24; 22. 19. tribute *m.*
25. 18. hid his lord's *m.*
28. 12. gave large *m.* to soldiers.
Mk. 12. 41. people cast *m.* into treasury.
Acts 8. 20. thy *m.* perish with thee.
1 Tim. 6. 10. love of *m.* the root of all evil.
Morrow, Prov. 27. 1. boast not thyself of to-*m.*
Is. 22. 13; 1 Cor. 15. 32. to-*m.* we die.
56. 12. to-*m.* shall be as this day.
Matt. 6. 34. take no thought for the *m.*
Jas. 4. 14. ye know not what shall be on
the *m.*   [than God?
Mortal, Job 4. 17. shall *m.* man be more just
Rom. 6. 12; 8. 11. your *m.* body.
1 Cor. 15. 53. this *m.* must put on immortality.
2 Cor. 4. 11. Jesus manifest in *m.* flesh.
See Rom. 8. 13; 2 Cor. 5. 4; Col. 3. 5.
Mote, Matt. 7. 3; Lk. 6. 41. *m.* in brother's eye.
Mother, Gen. 3. 20. she was *m.* of all living.
Jud. 5. 7; 2 Sam. 20. 19. a *m.* in Israel.
Job 17. 14. said to worm, thou art my *m.*
Ps. 113. 9. a joyful *m.* of children.
Is. 66. 13. as one whom his *m.* comforteth.
Mic. 7. 6; Matt. 10. 35; Lk. 12. 53. daughter
riseth against her *m.*
Matt. 12. 48; Mk. 3. 33. who is my *m.*?
John 2. 1; Acts 1. 14. the *m.* of Jesus.
Gal. 4. 26. Jerusalem, the *m.* of us all.
Mount, Ex. 18. 5; 1 Ki. 19. 8. the *m.* of God.
Job 20. 6; Ps. 107. 26. *m.* to heaven.
Is. 40. 31. *m.* with wings, as eagles.
Mourn, Gen. 37. 34. Jacob *m.* for his son.
Ps. 55. 2. I *m.* in my complaint.
Prov. 5. 11. thou *m.* at the last.
Eccl. 3. 4. a time to *m.*
Is. 61. 2. to comfort all that *m.*
Jer. 31. 13. I will turn their *m.* into joy.
Matt. 5. 4. blessed are they that *m.*
Lk. 6. 25. that laugh, for ye shall *m.*
Jas. 4. 9. *m.* and weep.
See 2 Sam. 14. 2; Eccl. 12. 5.

Mouth, Ps. 8. 2; Matt. 21. 16. out of the *m.* of
babes.
37. 30. *m.* of righteous speaketh wisdom.
63. 11. *m.* that speaketh lies.
103. 5. satisfieth thy *m.* with good things.
Prov. 10. 31. *m.* of the just bringeth forth
wisdom.
18. 7. a fool's *m.* is his destruction.
Eccl. 6. 7. labour of man is for his *m.*
10. 12. words of a wise man's *m.* [with *m.*
Is. 29. 13; Matt. 15. 8. this people draw near
Mal. 2. 6. the law of truth was in his *m.*
Matt. 12. 34; Lk. 6. 45. of abundance of heart
the *m.* speaketh.
Lk. 21. 15. I will give you a *m.* and wisdom.
Rom. 10. 10. with the *m.* confession is made.
1 Cor. 9. 9. not muzzle *m.* of ox
Jas. 3. 10. out of same *m.* proceedeth.
Move, Deut. 32. 21. *m.* them to jealousy.
Ps. 10. 6; 16. 8; 30. 6; 62. 2. I shall not be *m.*
Matt. 21. 10; Acts 21 30. the city was *m.*
Matt. 23. 4. they will not *m.* them.
Acts 17. 28. in him we live and *m.*
20. 24. none of these things *m.* me.
See John 5. 3; Heb. 12. 28.   [and *m.*
Multiply, Gen. 1. 22; 9. 7; 35. 11. be fruitful
Ps. 16. 4. their sorrows shall be *m.*
Is. 9. 3. thou hast *m.* the nation.
Dan. 4. 1; 6. 25; 1 Pet. 1. 2; 2 Pet. 1. 2;
Jude 2. peace be *m.*
Acts 12. 24. word of God grew and *m.*
2 Cor. 9. 10. *m.* your seed sown. [thee a *m.*
Multitude, Gen. 28. 3. God Almighty make
Ex. 23. 2. not follow a *m.* to evil.
Deut. 1. 10; 10. 22; 28. 62; Heb. 11. 12. as
the stars for *m.*
Josh. 11. 4; Jud. 7. 12; 1 Sam. 13. 5; 2 Sam.
17 11; 1 Ki. 4. 20. as sand on seashore
for *m.*
Job 32. 7. *m.* of years should teach wisdom.
Ps. 5. 7; 51. 1; 69. 13. *m.* of thy mercy.
33. 16. no king saved by the *m.* of an host.
94. 19. in the *m.* of my thoughts. [not sin.
Prov. 10. 19. in *m.* of words there wanteth
11. 14; 15. 22; 24. 6. in the *m.* of counsellors.
Eccl. 5. 3. through the *m.* of business.
Jas. 5. 20. hide a *m.* of sins.
1 Pet. 4. 8. charity covereth the *m.* of sins.
Murmur, Ex. 16. 7. that ye *m.* against us.
John 6. 43. *m.* not among yourselves.
1 Cor. 10. 10. neither *m.* as some of them *m.*
Phil. 2. 14. do all things without *m.*
See Jude 16.
Muse, Ps. 39. 3. I was *m.*, the fire burned.
143. 5. I *m.* on work of thy hands.
Lk. 3. 15. all men *m.* in their hearts.
Music, 1 Sam. 18. 6. to meet Saul with *m.*
2 Chr. 7. 6. instruments of *m.*
Lk. 15. 25. his elder son heard *m.*
See Rev. 18. 22.   [kingdom.
Mystery, Mk. 4. 11. to know the *m.* of the
Rom. 11. 25. not to be ignorant of *m.*
16. 25. according to revelation of the *m.*
1 Cor. 15. 51. I shew you a *m.*
Eph. 5. 32. this is a great *m.*
Col. 2. 2. acknowledgment of the *m.* of God.
1 Tim. 3. 16. great is the *m.* of godliness.

NAIL, Jud. 5. 26. she put her hand to the *n.*
Ezra 9. 8. give us a *n.* in holy place.
Is. 22. 23. fasten as a *n.* in sure place.
Dan. 4. 33. his *n.* like bird's claws.
John 20. 25. put finger into print of *n.*
Col. 2. 14. *n.* it to his cross.

Naked, Job 1. 21. *n*. came I, and *n*. shall I return.
Matt. 25. 36. was *n*., and ye clothed me.
1 Cor. 4. 11. to this hour we are *n*.
2 Cor. 5. 3. we shall not be found *n*.
Heb. 4. 13. all things are *n*. to eyes of him.
Jas. 2. 15. if a brother be *n*.
Rev. 3. 17. poor, and blind, and *n*.

Name, Gen. 32. 29. why ask after my *n*.?
48. 16. let my *n*. be named on them.
Ex. 3. 15. this is my *n*. for ever.
20. 24. where I record my *n*.
34. 14. Lord whose *n*. is Jealous.
Deut. 9. 14. blot out *n*. from under heaven.
Neh. 9. 10. so didst thou get thee a *n*.
Job 18. 17. he shall have no *n*.
Ps. 20. 1. the *n*. of God of Jacob.
20. 5. in *n*. of God set up our banners.
44. 20. if we forget *n*. of our God.
72. 17. his *n*. shall endure for ever.
111. 9. holy and reverend is his *n*.
Prov. 10. 7. the *n*. of the wicked shall rot.
18. 10. the *n*. of the Lord is a strong tower.
22. 1. a good *n*. rather than riches.
Cant. 1. 3. thy *n*. is as ointment poured forth.
Is. 55. 13. be to the Lord for a *n*.
56. 5; 63. 12. an everlasting *n*.
57. 15. whose *n*. is Holy.
62. 2. called by a new *n*.
Jer. 10. 6. thou art great, and thy *n*. is great.
44. 26. sworn by my great *n*.
Mic. 4. 5. we will walk in *n*. of our God.
Zech. 14. 9. one Lord, and his *n*. one.
Mal. 1. 6. wherein have we despised thy *n*.?
4. 2. to you that fear my *n*.
Matt. 6. 9; Lk. 11. 2. hallowed be thy *n*.
Matt. 10. 41. receiveth prophet in *n*. of a prophet.
18. 20. gathered together in my *n*.
24. 5; Mk. 13. 6; Lk. 21. 8. many shall come in my *n*.
Mk. 6. 14. his *n*. was spread abroad.
9. 39. do a miracle in my *n*.
Lk. 6. 22. cast out your *n*. as evil.
10. 20. *n*. written in heaven.
24. 47. remission of sins in his *n*.
John 5. 43. if another shall come in his own *n*. [my *n*.
14. 13; 15. 16; 16. 23. whatsoever ye ask in
20. 31. ye might have life through his *n*.
Acts 3. 16. his *n*. through faith in his *n*.
4. 12. none other *n*. under heaven.
Eph. 1 21 far above every *n*. that is named.
Phil. 2. 10. at *n*. of Jesus every knee bow.
4. 3. whose *n*. are in the book of life.
Col. 3. 17. do all in the *n*. of the Lord Jesus.
1 Tim. 6. 1. the *n*. of God be not blasphemed.
Heb. 1. 4. obtained a more excellent *n*.
Jas. 2. 7 that worthy *n*.
1 Pet. 4. 14. reproached for *n*. of Christ.
Rev. 2. 17. a *n*. written, which no man knoweth.
3. 1. thou hast a *n*. that thou livest.
14. 1; 22. 4. Father's *n*. in their foreheads.
15. 4. who shall not fear and glorify thy *n*.?

Name, Eccl. 6. 10. that which hath been is *n*. already.
Is. 61. 6. shall be *n*. priests of the Lord.
Rom. 15. 20. not where Christ was *n*.
Eph. 3. 15. whole family in heaven and earth is *n*.
2 Tim. 2. 19. every one that *n*. the name of Christ.

Narrow, Num. 22. 26. angel of Lord stood in *n*. place.
Is. 28. 20. *n*. that he can wrap himself.
49. 19. land of destruction too *n*.
Matt. 7. 14. *n*. is way that leadeth to life.

Nation, Gen. 20. 4. wilt thou slay a righteous *n*.? [greater *n*.
Num. 14. 12; Deut. 9. 14. I will make thee a
Deut. 28. 50. a *n*. of fierce countenance.
2 Sam. 7. 23; 1 Chr. 17. 21. what *n*. like thy people? [Lord.
Ps. 33. 12. blessed is the *n*. whose God is the
105. 13. went from one *n*. to another.
147. 20. he hath not dealt so with any *n*.
Prov. 14. 34. righteousness exalteth a *n*.
Is. 1. 4. sinful *n*. [against *n*.
2. 4; Mic. 4. 3. *n*. shall not lift sword
9. 3. thou hast multiplied the *n*.
26. 2. that the righteous *n*. may enter in.
40. 17. all *n*. before him are as nothing.
55. 5. shalt call a *n*. thou knowest not.
60. 22. small one become a strong *n*.
66. 8. shall a *n*. be born at once?
Jer. 10. 7. king of *n*.
27. 7; Dan. 7. 14. all *n*. serve him.
Zech. 2. 11. many *n*. be joined to the Lord.
Matt. 24. 7; Mk. 13. 8; Lk. 21. 10. *n*. rise
Lk. 7. 5. he loveth our *n*. [against *n*.
John 11. 50. that the whole *n*. perish not.
Acts 2. 5. devout men out of every *n*.
10. 35. in every *n*. he that feareth God.
17. 26. made of one blood all *n*.
Rom. 10. 19. by a foolish *n*. I will anger you.
Phil. 2. 15. in midst of a crooked *n*.
1 Pet. 2. 9. a holy *n*.
Rev. 5. 9. redeemed out of every *n*.
21. 24. the *n*. who are saved. [law.

Nature, Rom. 2. 14. do by *n*. the things in the
11. 24. olive tree which is wild by *n*.
1 Cor. 11. 14. doth not *n*. teach you?
Gal. 4. 8. which by *n*. are no gods.
Eph. 2. 3. by *n*. the children of wrath.
Heb. 2. 16. took not the *n*. of angels.
Jas. 3. 6. the course of *n*.
2 Pet. 1. 4. partakers of the divine *n*.

Natural, Deut. 34. 7. nor his *n*. force abated.
Rom. 1. 31; 2 Tim. 3. 3. without *n*. affection.
1 Cor. 2. 14. the *n*. man receiveth not things of Spirit.
15. 44. it is sown a *n*. body.
Jas. 1. 23. beholding *n*. face in a glass.

Naught, Prov. 20. 14. it is *n*., saith the buyer.
Is. 49. 4. spent strength for *n*.
52. 3. ye have sold yourselves for *n*. [to *n*.
Acts 5. 38. if work be of men, it will come
Rom. 14. 10. why set at *n*. thy brother?
1 Cor. 1. 28. to bring to *n*. things that are.

Naughtiness, 1 Sam. 17. 28. the *n*. of thy heart.
Prov. 11. 6. taken in their own *n*.
Jas. 1. 21. all superfluity of *n*.

Nay, Matt. 5. 37; Jas. 5. 12. let your communication be yea, yea, *n*., *n*.
Rom. 3. 27. *n*., but by law of faith.
9. 20. *n*., but, O man, who art thou?
2 Cor. 1. 18. our word was not yea and *n*.

Near, Gen. 19. 20. this city is *n*. to flee to.
Jud. 20. 34. knew not evil was *n*.
Ps. 22. 11. trouble is *n*.
Prov. 27. 10. better a neighbour that is *n*.
Is. 55. 6. call upon the Lord while he is *n*.
Obad. 15; Zeph. 1. 14. the day of the Lord is *n*.
Matt. 24. 33. it is *n*., even at the doors.
Mk. 13. 28. ye know that summer is *n*.
Rom. 13. 11. our salvation is *n*.

Necessary, Job 23. 12. his words more than *n.* food.

Acts 15. 28 ; 28. 10. *n.* things.

Tit. 3. 14. good works for *n.* uses.

Heb. 9. 23. it was *n.* patterns should be purified.

Necessity, Lk. 23. 17. of *n.* he must release one.

Rom. 12. 13. distributing to *n.* of saints.

1 Cor. 9. 16. *n.* is laid upon me.

2 Cor. 9. 7 ; Philem. 14. give not as of *n.*

Heb. 9. 16. there must of *n.* be death of testator.

Neck, Prov. 3. 3 ; 6. 21. bind them about thy *n.*

Matt. 18. 6 ; Mk. 9. 42 ; Lk. 17. 2. a millstone about his *n.*

Lk. 15. 20 ; Acts 20. 37. fell on his *n.*

Acts 15. 10. yoke on *n.* of the disciples.

Need, Deut. 15. 8. lend sufficient for his *n.*

Prov. 31. 11. he shall have no *n.* of spoil.

Matt. 6. 8 ; Lk. 12. 30. what things ye have *n.* of.

Matt. 9. 12 ; Mk. 2. 17 ; Lk. 5. 31. whole *n.* not a physician.

Matt. 14. 16. they *n.* not depart.

26. 65 ; Mk. 14. 63 ; Lk. 22. 71. what further *n.* of witnesses ?

Lk. 15. 7. just persons who *n.* no repentance.

John 13. 29. buy things we have *n.* of.

Acts 2. 45 ; 4. 35. as every man had *n.*

1 Cor. 12. 21. cannot say, I have no *n.* of thee.

2 Cor. 3. 1. *n.* we epistles of commendation ?

Phil. 4. 12. to abound and to suffer *n.*

4. 19. God shall supply all your *n.*

Heb. 4. 16. grace to help in time of *n.*

5. 12. ye have *n.* that one teach you.

7. 11. what *n.* that another priest rise ?

1 John 3. 17. seeth his brother have *n.*

Rev. 3. 17. rich, and have *n.* of nothing.

21. 23 ; 22. 5. city, had no *n.* of the sun.

Needful, Lk. 10. 42. one thing is *n.*

Jas. 2. 16. things *n.* to the body.

Needy, Deut. 15. 11. open thy hand to the *n.*

Job 24. 4. they turn the *n.* out of the way.

Ps. 9. 18. the *n.* shall not alway be forgotten.

40. 17 ; 70. 5 ; 86. 1 ; 109. 22. I am poor and *n.*

72. 13. he shall spare the poor and *n.*

113. 7. he lifteth the *n.*

Prov. 31. 9. plead the cause of the poor and *n.*

Is. 25. 4. been a strength to the *n.*

Jer. 22. 16. he judgeth cause of the *n.*

Neglect, Matt. 18. 17. if he shall *n.* to hear.

1 Tim. 4. 14. *n.* not the gift in thee.

Heb. 2. 3. how escape, if we *n.* so great salvation ?

Neighbour, Ex. 20. 16. not bear false witness against thy *n.*

Lev. 19. 18 ; Matt. 19. 19 ; 22. 39. thou shalt love thy *n.* as thyself.

Ps. 15. 3. nor doeth evil to his *n.*

Prov. 14. 20. the poor is hated even of his *n.*

27. 10. better is a *n.* near, than a brother far off.

Eccl. 4. 4. a man is envied of his *n.*

Jer. 22. 13. useth his *n.* service without wages.

31. 34 ; Heb. 8. 11. teach no more every one his *n.*

Hab. 2. 15. that giveth his *n.* drink.

Zech. 8. 16 ; Eph. 4. 25. speak every man truth to his *n.*

Mk. 12. 33. to love his *n.* as himself.

Lk. 10. 29. who is my *n.* ?

Rom. 13. 10. love worketh no ill to his *n.*

15. 2. let every one please his *n.*

Nest, Num. 24. 21. thou puttest thy *n.* in a rock.

Deut. 32. 11. as an eagle stirreth up her *n.*

Job 29. 18. I shall die in my *n.*

Ps. 84. 3. the swallow hath found a *n.*

Prov. 27. 8. as a bird that wandereth from her *n.*

Matt. 8. 20 ; Lk. 9. 58. birds of the air have *n.*

Net, Ps. 25. 15 ; 31. 4. shall pluck my feet out of *n.*

66. 11. thou broughtest us into *n.*

Prov. 1. 17. in vain the *n.* is spread.

Eccl. 9. 12. as fishes taken in an evil *n.*

Mic. 7. 2. hunt his brother with a *n.*

Matt. 4. 18 ; Mk. 1. 16. casting *n.* into sea.

Matt. 13. 47. kingdom of heaven is like unto a *n.*

Mk. 1. 18. they forsook their *n.*

Lk. 5. 5. I will let down the *n.*

John 21. 11. drew the *n.* to land.

New, Num. 16. 30. if Lord make a *n.* thing.

Job 32. 19. like *n.* bottles.

Ps. 33. 3 ; 96. 1 ; 98. 1 ; 149. 1 ; Is. 42. 10. sing to the Lord a *n.* song.

Eccl. 1. 9. no *n.* thing under the sun.

Is. 42. 9 ; 48. 6. *n.* things I declare.

62. 2. called by a *n.* name.

65. 17 ; 66. 22. create *n.* heavens, *n.* earth.

Lam. 3. 23. Lord's mercies are *n.* every morning.

Matt. 9. 16 ; Mk. 2. 21 ; Lk. 5. 36. *n.* cloth to old garment.

Matt. 13. 52. things *n.* and old.

Mk. 1. 27 ; Acts 17. 19. what *n.* doctrine is this ? [you.

John 13. 34. *n.* commandment I give unto

Acts 17. 21. to tell or hear some *n.* thing.

2 Cor. 3. 6. able ministers of *N.* Testament.

5. 17 ; Gal. 6. 15. a *n.* creature.

Eph. 4. 24 ; Col. 3. 10. put on the *n.* man.

Heb. 10. 20. a *n.* and living way.

1 Pet. 2. 2. as *n.*-born babes desire milk of the Word.

Rev. 2. 17 ; 3. 12. a *n.* name.

21. 5. I make all things *n.*

See Rom. 6. 4 ; 7. 6.

News, Prov. 25. 25. good *n.* from a far country.

Nigh, Deut. 30. 14 ; Rom. 10. 8. word is *n.* to thee.

Ps. 34. 18. Lord is *n.* to them of broken heart.

85. 9. his salvation *n.* them that fear him.

145. 18. Lord is *n.* to all that call on him.

Joel 2. 1. day of the Lord is *n.* at hand.

Eph. 2. 13. made *n.* by the blood of Christ.

Heb. 6. 8. is *n.* unto cursing.

Night, Gen. 1. 5. the darkness God called *n.*

Ex. 12. 42. a *n.* to be much observed.

Job 7. 4. when shall the *n.* be gone ?

Ps. 19. 2. *n.* unto *n.* sheweth knowledge.

30. 5. weeping may endure for a *n.*

136. 9 ; Jer. 31. 35. moon to rule by *n.*

Ps. 139. 11. the *n.* shall be light about me.

Is. 21. 11. watchman, what of the *n.* ?

Jon. 4. 10. came up in a *n.*, perished in a *n.*

Lk. 6. 12. he continued all *n.* in prayer.

12. 20. this *n.* thy soul shall be required.

John 9. 4. the *n.* cometh when no man can work.

11. 10. if man walk in the *n.* he stumbleth.

Rom. 13. 12. the *n.* is far spent.

1 Cor. 11. 23. the same *n.* he was betrayed.

1 Thes. 5. 2 ; 2 Pet. 3. 10. cometh as a thief in the *n.*

Rev. 21. 25 ; 22. 5. shall be no *n.* there.

Noble, Neh. 3. 5. the n. put not their necks to work.

Job 29. 10. the n. held their peace.

Is. 43. 14. brought down all the n.

Jer. 2. 21. a n vine.

Lk. 19. 12. n. man went to far country.

Acts 17. 11. Bereans were more n.

1 Cor. 1. 26. not many n. are called.

Noise, Ps. 66. 1 ; 81. 1 ; 95. 1 ; 98. 4 ; 100. 1. make a joyful n.

93. 4. Lord mightier than n. of waters.

2 Pet. 3. 10. heavens pass away with great n.

See Mk. 2. 1 ; Acts 2. 6.

Noisome, Ps. 91. 3. deliver thee from n. pestilence.

Rev. 16. 2. a n. and grievous sore.

Nose, 2 Ki. 19. 28 ; Is. 37. 29. put my hook in thy n.

Ps. 115. 6. n. have they, but smell not.

Prov. 30. 33. the wringing of the n.

Is. 3. 21. the n. jewels.

See Gen. 2. 7 ; Is. 2. 22.

Notable, Matt. 27. 16. a n. prisoner.

Acts 2. 20. before n. day of Lord come.

4. 16. a n. miracle hath been done.

Nothing, Ex. 16. 18 ; 2 Cor. 8. 15. gathered much, had n. over.   [costs n.

2 Sam. 24. 24. neither offer of that which

2 Chr. 14. 11. it is n. with thee to help.

Neh. 8. 10. portions to them for whom n. is prepared.

Job 8. 9. we are of yesterday, and know n.

34. 9. it profiteth a man n.

Ps. 39. 5. mine age is as n. before thee.

49. 17. dieth, he shall carry n. away.

119. 165. n. shall offend them.

Prov. 13. 4. the sluggard desireth, and hath n.

13. 7 that maketh himself rich, yet hath n.

Eccl. 5. 15. he shall take n. of his labour.

Is. 40. 17. all nations before him are as n.

Lam. 1. 12. is it n. to you?

Dan. 4. 35. inhabitants of earth as n.

Matt. 17. 20 ; Lk. 1. 37. n. shall be impossible.

Matt. 21. 19 ; Mk. 11. 13. n. but leaves.

Lk. 7. 42. they had n. to pay.

23. 41. this man hath done n. amiss.   [me.

John 14. 30. prince of this world hath n. in

15. 5. without me ye can do n.

1 Cor. 1. 19. bring to n. the understanding of prudent.

4. 5. judge n. before the time.   [things.

2 Cor. 6. 10. having n., yet possessing all

13. 8. can do n. against the truth.

Gal. 5. 2. Christ shall profit you n.

1 Tim. 4. 4. n. to be refused.

6. 7. we brought n. into this world.

Heb. 7. 19. the law made n. perfect.

Jas. 1. 4. perfect and entire, wanting n.

Nourish, Is. 1. 2. n. and brought up children.

Acts 12. 20. was n. by the king's country.

1 Tim. 4. 6. n. in words of faith.

Jas. 5. 5. have n. your hearts.

See Col. 2. 19.

Number, Job 5. 9 ; 9. 10. things without n.

Ps. 139. 18. more in n. than the sand.

147. 4. he telleth the n. of the stars.

Is. 40. 26. bringeth out their host by n.

Hos. 1. 10 ; Rom. 9. 27. n. of Israel shall be as the sand.

John 6. 10. the men sat down in n.

Acts 6. 1. n. of disciples was multiplied.

16. 5. the churches increased in n.

2 Cor. 10. 12. not make ourselves of the n.

Rev. 13. 17. the n. of his name.

Number, Gen. 13. 16. if a man can n. the dust.

15. 5. tell stars, if able to n. them.

2 Sam. 24. 2 ; 1 Chr. 21. 2. n. the people.

Job 38. 37. who can n. the clouds ?

Ps. 40. 5. more than can be n.

90. 12. so teach us to n. our days.

Eccl. 1. 15. that which is wanting cannot be n.

Is. 53. 12 ; Mk. 15. 28. he was n. with the transgressors.

Matt. 10. 30 ; Lk. 12. 7. hairs of head are all n.

Acts 1. 17 ; he was n. with us.

Rev. 7. 9. a multitude which no man could n.

Nurse, Ex. 2. 7. a n. that she may n. the child.

Is. 60. 4. daughters shall be n. at thy side.

1 Thes. 2. 7. as a n. cherisheth her children.

Nurture, Eph. 6. 4. bring them up in the n. of the Lord.

Nuts, Gen. 43. 11. a present, n. and almonds.

Cant. 6. 11. garden of n.

OATH, 1 Sam. 14. 26. people feared the o.

Eccl. 9. 2. as he that feareth an o.

Lk. 1. 73. the o. which he sware.

Heb. 6. 16. an o. for confirmation.

Jas. 5. 12. sware not by earth, nor other o.

Obedience, Rom. 5. 19. by the o. of one.

16. 26. for the o. of faith.

2 Cor. 10. 5. every thought to o. of Christ.

Heb. 5. 8. yet learned he o.

1 Pet. 1. 2. sanctification of Spirit to o.

Obedient, Ex. 24. 7. all will we do, and be o.

Deut. 4. 30. be o. to voice of Lord.

Prov. 25. 12. wise reprover upon an o. ear.

Is. 1. 19. if o. ye shall eat good of the land.

Acts 6. 7. priests were o. to the faith.

2 Cor. 2. 9. o. in all things.

Eph. 6. 5 ; Tit. 2. 9. servants, be o. to your masters.

Phil. 2. 8. Christ became o. unto death.

1 Pet. 1. 14. as o. children.

Obey, Ex. 5. 2. who is Lord, that I o. him ?

Deut. 11. 27. a blessing, if ye o. Lord.

Josh. 24. 24. Lord's voice will we o.

1 Sam. 15. 22. to o. is better than sacrifice.

Jer. 7. 23. o. my voice, and I will be your God.

26. 13 ; Zech. 6. 15. amend your ways, and o. voice of the Lord.

Acts 5. 29. we ought to o. God rather than men.   [ye o.

Rom. 6. 16. his servants ye are to whom

Eph. 6. 1 ; Col. 3. 20. children, o. your parents in the Lord.

2 Thes. 1. 8 ; 1 Pet. 4. 17. that o. not the Gospel.

Tit. 3. 1. to o. magistrates.

Heb. 5. 9. salvation to all that o. him.

13. 17. o. them that have rule over you.

1 Pet. 3. 1. if any o. not the word.

Obscurity, Is. 29. 18. eyes of blind see out of o.

58. 10. then shall thy light rise in o.

See Prov. 20. 20.

Observe, Gen. 37. 11. his father o. the saying.

Ps. 107. 43. whoso is wise, and will o. these things.

119. 34. o. with my whole heart.

Prov. 23. 26. let thine eyes o. my ways.

Jon. 2. 8. that o. lying vanities.

Matt. 28. 20. teaching them to o. all things.

Mk. 10. 20. all these have I o.

Acts 16. 21. customs not lawful to o.

Gal. 4. 10. ye o. days and months.

See Deut. 18. 10 ; Lk. 17. 20.

Obtain, Prov. 8. 35. shall o. favour of the Lord.
Is. 35. 10; 51. 11. they shall o. joy and gladness.
Lk. 20. 35. worthy to o. that world.
1 Cor. 9. 24. so run, that ye may o.
1 Thes. 5. 9; 2 Tim. 2. 10. to o. salvation.
Heb. 4. 16. o. mercy, and find grace to help.
  11. 35. might o. a better resurrection.
Jas. 4. 2. ye desire to have, and cannot o.

Occasion, Gen. 43. 18. he may seek o. against us. [pheme.
2 Sam. 12. 14. great o. to enemies to blas-
Dan. 6. 4; sought to find o.
Rom. 7. 8. sin taking o. by commandment.
  14. 13. an o. to fall in his brother's way.
2 Cor. 5. 12. give you o. to glory.
  11. 12. cut off o. from them which desire o.
1 Tim. 5. 14. give none o. to the adversary.
1 John 2. 10. none o. of stumbling.

Occupation, Gen. 46. 33; Jon. 1. 8. what is your o.?
Acts 18. 3. by o. they were tent-makers.
  19. 25. with the workmen of like o.
See Lk. 19. 13.

Odour, John 12. 3. the o. of the ointment.
Phil. 4. 18. an o. of a sweet smell.
Rev. 5. 8. golden vials full of o.

Offence, 1 Sam. 25. 31. this shall be no o.
Eccl. 10. 4. yielding pacifieth great o.
Is. 8. 14; Rom. 9. 33; 1 Pet. 2. 8. a rock of o.
Matt. 16. 23. thou art an o. to me.   [of o. !
  18. 7; Lk. 17. 1. woe to the world because
Acts 24. 16. a conscience void of o.
Rom. 5. 15. not as o., so is free gift.
1 Cor. 10. 32 . 2 Cor. 6. 3. give none o.
Gal. 5. 11. then is o. of the cross ceased.
Phil. 1. 10. without o. till the day of Christ.

Offend, Job 34. 31. I will not o. any more.
Ps. 119.165. nothing shall o. them.
Prov. 18. 19. a brother o. is harder to be won.
Hab. 1. 11. he shall pass over and o.
Matt. 5. 29; 18. 9; Mk. 9. 47. if thine eye o. thee.
Matt. 13. 41. gather all things that o.
  18. 6; Mk. 9. 42; Lk. 17. 2. whoso o. one of these.
Matt. 26. 31. be o. because of me.
Rom. 14. 21. whereby thy brother is o.
Jas. 2. 10. yet o. in one point.
See Is. 29. 21 ; Acts 25. 11.

Offer, Ex. 22. 29. to o. the first fruits.
Jud. 5. 2. people willingly o. themselves.
Ps. 50. 23. whoso o. praise.
  116. 17. o. sacrifice of thanksgiving.
Matt. 5. 24. then come and o. thy gift.
  8. 4; Mk. 1. 44; Lk. 5. 14. o. gift Moses commanded.
Lk. 6. 29. one cheek, o. also the other.
Phil. 2. 17. o. in the service of your faith.
2 Tim. 4. 6. now ready to be o.
Heb. 9. 14. o. himself without spot to God.
  9. 28. Christ was once o. to bear sins of many.
See Mal. 1. 10 ; Eph. 5. 2 ; Heb. 10. 18.

Office, Gen. 41. 13. me he restored to o.
1 Sam. 2. 36. put me into priest's o.
Neh. 13. 13. their o. was to distribute.
Ps. 109. 8. let another take his o.
Rom. 11. 13. I magnify mine o.
1 Tim. 3. 1. the o. of a bishop.
Heb. 7. 5. the o. of the priesthood.

Offscouring, Lam. 3. 45. made us as the o.
1 Cor. 4. 13. the o. of all things to this day.

Offspring, Acts 17. 29. we are the o. of God.
Rev. 22. 16. I am the o. of David.

Often, Prov. 29. 1. he that being o. reproved.
Mal. 3. 16. spake o. one to another.
Matt. 23. 37; Lk. 13. 34. how o. would I have gathered !
1 Cor. 11. 26. as o. as ye eat this bread.
2 Cor. 11. 26. in journeyings o.
1 Tim. 5. 23. thine o. infirmities.
Heb. 9. 25. nor offer himself o.

Oil, Ex. 25. 6. take o. for the light.
Ps. 45. 7 ; Heb. 1. 9. with o. of gladness.
Ps. 104. 15. o. to make his face to shine.
  141. 5. an o. which shall not break my head.
Is. 61. 3. o. of joy for mourning.   [of o.?
Mic. 6. 7. will Lord be pleased with rivers
Matt. 25. 3. took no o. with them.
Lk. 7. 46. my head with o. thou didst not anoint.
  10. 34. pouring in o. and wine.

Ointment, Ex. 30. 25. make oil of holy o.
Ps. 133. 2. like the precious o.
Prov. 27. 9. o. and perfume rejoice heart.
Eccl. 7. 1. a good name better than o.
Cant. 1. 3. thy name is as o. poured forth.
Is. 1. 6. nor mollified with o.   [precious o.
Matt. 26. 7; Mk. 14. 3; John 12. 3. box of
Lk. 23. 56. prepared spices and o.

Old, Deut. 8. 4; 29. 5; Neh. 9. 21. thy raiment waxed not o.
Ps. 37. 25. I have been young, and now am o.
  71. 18. when I am o., O God, forsake me not.
Prov. 22. 6. when o. he will not depart from it.
  23. 10. remove not old landmark.
Is. 50. 9. they shall wax o. as garment.
  58. 12. build the o. waste places.
  65. 20. child shall die a hundred years o.
Jer. 6. 16. ask for the o. paths.
Matt. 9. 17; Mk. 2. 22 . Lk. 5. 37. new wine into o. bottles.
John 21. 18. when thou shalt be o.
1 Cor. 5. 7. purge out the o. leaven.
2 Cor. 5. 17. o. things are passed away.
Heb. 8. 13. he hath made the first o.
2 Pet. 2. 5. if God spared not the o. world.
1 John 2. 7. the o. commandment is the Word.

Once, Gen. 18. 32 ; Jud. 6. 39. I will speak but this o.
2 Ki. 6. 10. he saved himself not o.
Job 33. 14 ; Ps. 62. 11. God speaks o.
Is. 66. 8. shall a nation be born at o.?
Rom. 6. 10. he died unto sin o.
  7. 9. I was alive without the law o.
Heb. 9. 26. now o. in end of the world.
Jude 3. contend for faith o. delivered.

One, Gen. 27. 38. hast thou but o. blessing.
Job 9. 3 ; 33. 23. o. of a thousand.
Ps. 89. 19. help on o. that is mighty.
Eccl. 4. 9. two are better than o.
Is. 27. 12. ye shall be gathered o. by o.
Matt. 5. 18. o. jot or tittle not pass from law.
  19. 17 ; Mk. 10. 18 ; Lk. 18. 19. none good but o.
Mk. 10. 21 ; Lk. 18. 22. o. thing thou lackest.
Lk. 10. 42. o. thing is needful.
John 9. 25. o. thing I know.
Eph. 4. 5. o. Lord, o. faith, o. baptism.
Phil. 3. 13. this o. thing I do.

Open, Num. 16. 30. if the earth o. her mouth.
Ps. 49. 4. I will o. my dark saying.
  78. 2. I will o. mouth in a parable.
  81. 10. o. thy mouth wide.
  118. 19. o. to me the gates of righteousness.
  119. 18. o. thou mine eyes.
Prov. 31. 8. o. thy mouth for the dumb.
Is. 22. 22. he shall o. and none shut.

Open—*Continued.*
Is. 26. 2. o. gates, that righteous may enter.
42. 7. to o. the blind eyes.
60. 11. thy gates shall be o. continually.
Mal. 3. 10. o. windows of heaven.
Matt. 25. 11 ; Lk. 13. 25. Lord, o. to us.
Lk. 24. 32. while he o. to us the Scriptures.
Acts 26. 18. to o. their eyes.
Col. 4. 3. would o. to us a door of utterance.
Heb. 4. 13. all things are o. to him.
Rev. 5. 2. who is worthy to o. the book ?
Operation, Ps. 28. 5. they regard not o. of his hands.
Is. 5. 12. nor consider o. of his hands.
1 Cor. 12. 6. there are diversities of o.
Col. 2. 12. through faith of the o.
Opinion, 1 Ki. 18. 21. how long halt between two o. ?
Job 32. 6. durst not show you mine o.
Opportunity, Matt. 26. 16 ; Lk. 22. 6. sought o. to betray him.
Gal. 6. 10. as we have o., do good.
Phil. 4. 10. ye lacked o.
Heb. 11. 15. had o. to have returned. [self.
Oppose, Job 30. 21. with strong hand o. thy-
2 Thes. 2. 4. o. and exalteth himself.
2 Tim. 2. 25. instructing those that o. themselves.
See 1 Tim. 6. 20.
Oppress, Ex. 22. 21 ; 23. 9. neither to o. a stranger.
Lev. 25. 14, 17. ye shall not o. one another.
Deut. 23. 16. shall not o. servant.
1 Sam. 12. 3. whom have I o. ?
Ps. 10. 18. man of earth no more o.
Prov. 14. 31 ; 22. 16. he that o. the poor.
22. 22. nor o. the afflicted.
Jer. 7. 6. if ye o. not the stranger.
Hos. 12. 7. he loveth to o.
Zech. 7. 10. o. not widow nor fatherless.
Acts 10. 38. Jesus healed all that were o.
Jas. 2. 6. do not rich men o. you ? [our o.
Oppression, Deut. 26. 7. the Lord looked on
Job 36. 15. openeth their ears in o.
Ps. 42. 9 ; 43. 2. o. of the enemy.
62. 10. trust not in o.
119. 134. deliver me from o. of man.
Eccl. 4. 1. I considered the o. done.
7. 7. o. maketh a wise man mad.
Is. 54. 14. thou shalt be far from o.
See Ps. 72. 4 ; Jer. 21. 12 ; 22. 3.
Oracle, 2 Sam. 16. 23. inquired at the o. of God.
Ps. 28. 2. I lift up hands towards holy o.
Acts 7. 38. who received the lively o.
Heb. 5. 12. first principles of o. of God.
1 Pet. 4. 11. speak as the o. of God.
Ordain, 1 Chr. 17. 9. I will o. a place for my people. [strength.
Ps. 8. 2. out of mouth of babes hast thou o.
132. 17. I have o. a lamp for mine anointed.
Is. 26. 12. thou wilt o. peace for us.
30. 33. Tophet is o. of old.
Jer. 1. 5. I o. thee a prophet.
Mk. 3. 14. Jesus o. twelve to be with him.
John 15. 16. have o. you, that ye should bring forth fruit.
Acts 10. 42. o. of God to be the judge.
13. 48. as were o. to eternal life.
17. 31. by that man whom he hath o.
Rom. 7. 10. commandment o. to life.
13. 1. powers that be are o. of God.
1 Cor. 2. 7. hidden wisdom God o.
Gal. 3. 19. the law was o. by angels.
Eph. 2. 10. good works which God hath before o.

Ordain—*Continued.*
Heb. 5. 1 ; 8. 3. every high priest is o.
Jude 4. of old o. to this condemnation.
Order, 2 Ki. 20. 1 ; Is. 38. 1. set thine house in o.
Job. 10. 22. a land without o.
23. 4. I would o. my cause.
Ps. 50. 21. I will set them in o. [chisedec.
110. 4 ; Heb. 5. 6 ; 6. 20 ; 7. 11. the o. of Mel-
1 Cor. 15. 23. every man shall rise in his o.
Ordinance, Ex. 15. 25. made a statute and an o.
Is. 58. 2 ; Num. 12. 2. the o. of God.
Mal. 3. 7. gone away from mine o.
Eph. 2. 15. commandments contained in o.
Col. 2. 14. handwriting of o.
Heb. 9. 10. in carnal o.
1 Pet. 2. 13. submit to every o. of man.
Ornament, Prov. 1. 9. an o. of grace to thy head.
Is. 61. 10. decketh himself with o.
Jer. 2. 32. can a maid forget her o. ?
1 Pet. 3. 4. the o. of a meek and quiet spirit.
Ought, Matt. 5. 23. if brother have o. against thee.
23. 23 ; Lk. 11. 42. these o. ye to have done.
Acts 4. 32. neither said o. was his own.
5. 29. we o. to obey God.
Rom. 8. 26. what we should pray for as we o.
Jas. 4. 15. ye o. to say, if the Lord will. [be.
2 Pet. 3. 11. what manner of persons o. ye to
Ours, Mk. 12. 7 ; Lk. 20. 14. and the inheritance shall be o.
1 Cor. 1. 2. Jesus, both theirs and o.
2 Cor. 1. 14. ye are o. in day of the Lord.
Outcast, Ps. 147. 2 ; Is. 11. 12. the o. of Israel.
Jer. 30. 17. because they called thee o.
Outgoings, Josh. 17. 18. the o. of it shall be thine.
Ps. 65. 8. thou makest o. of morning to rejoice.
Outside, Matt. 23. 25 ; Lk. 11. 39. make clean o. of the cup. [appearance.
Outward, 1 Sam. 16. 7. man looketh on o.
Matt. 23. 27. appear beautiful o.
Rom. 2. 28. not a Jew, who is one o.
2 Cor. 4. 16. though our o. man perish.
Oven, Ps. 21. 9. make them as a fiery o.
Hos. 7. 4. as an o. heated by baker.
Mal. 4. 1. day that shall burn as an o.
Matt. 6. 30. is cast into o.
Overcome, Gen. 49. 19. troop shall o. him.
Jer. 23. 9. a man whom wine hath o.
Lk. 11. 22. a stronger shall o. him.
John 16. 33. I have o. the world.
Rom. 12. 21. be not o. of evil, but o. evil.
1 John 5. 4. victory that o. the world. [life.
Rev. 2. 7. to him that o. will I give of tree of
Overpast, Ps. 57. 1. refuge until calamities be o.
Is. 26. 20. hide until indignation be o.
Overseer, 2 Chr. 34. 17. delivered money into hand of o.
Prov. 6. 7. the ant having no o.
Acts 20. 28. Holy Ghost made you o. [an o.
Oversight, Gen. 43. 12. peradventure it was
Neh. 13. 4. the o. of the house of God.
1 Pet. 5. 2. taking the o. not by constraint.
Overtake, Deut. 28. 2. blessings shall come and o. thee.
Gal. 6. 1. if a man be o. in a fault.
1 Thes. 5. 4. day should o. you as a thief.
Overthrow, Gen. 19. 21. I will not o. this city.
Ex. 23. 24. thou shalt o. their gods.
Ps. 140. 4. purposed to o. my goings. [be o.
Jon. 3. 4. yet forty days, and Nineveh shall
Acts 5. 39. if it be of God, ye cannot o. it.
2 Tim. 2. 18. o. the faith of some.

Overturn, Job 12. 15. sendeth waters, they o. earth.
  Ezek. 21. 27. I will o., o., o. it.
Overwhelm, Job 6. 27. ye o. the fatherless.
  Ps. 55. 5. horror hath o. me.
  61. 2. when my heart is o.
  77. 3 ; 142. 3 ; 143. 4. my spirit was o.
  124. 4. then the waters had o. us.
Overwise, Eccl. 7. 16. nor make thyself o.
Owe, Matt. 18. 28. pay me that thou o.
  Lk. 16. 5, 7. how much o. thou?
  Rom. 13. 8. o. no man anything.
  Philem. 19. thou o. to me even thine own self.
Own, 1 Chr. 29. 14. of thine o. have we given thee.
  Ps. 12. 4. our lips are our o.
  Matt. 20. 15. do what I will with mine o.
  John 1. 11. he came to his o., and his o. received him not.
  13. 1. having loved his o.
  15. 19. world would love his o.
  1 Cor. 6. 19. ye are not your o.
  10. 24. let no man seek his o.
  13. 5. charity seeketh not her o.
  Phil. 2. 21. all seek their o. things.   [hurt.
Owner, Eccl. 5. 13. riches kept for o. to their
  Is. 1. 3. the ox knoweth his o.
  Lk. 19. 33. o. said, why loose ye the colt?
  Acts 27. 11. the o. of the ship.
Ox, Ex. 20. 17 ; Deut. 5. 21. not covet neighbour's o.
  1 Sam. 12. 3. whose o. have I taken?
  Is. 11. 7. lion shall eat straw like o.
  Lk. 13. 15. each loose his o. on sabbath.
  14. 19. bought five yoke of o.
  John 2. 14. those in temple sold o.
  Acts 14. 13. priest of Jupiter brought o.
  1 Cor. 9. 9. doth God take care for o.?

PACIFY, Prov. 16. 14. a wise man p. wrath.
  21. 14. a gift in secret p. anger.
  Eccl. 10. 4. yielding p. great offences.
Pain, Ps. 25. 18. look on mine affliction and p.
  116. 3. the p. of hell gat hold upon me.
  Acts 2. 24. having loosed the p. of death.
  Rom. 8. 22. the whole creation travaileth in p.
  Rev. 21. 4. neither shall there be any more p.
Painted, 2 Ki. 9. 30. Jezebel p. her face.
  Jer. 4. 30. rentest face with p.
  22. 14. p. with vermilion.
  Ezek. 23. 40. thou p. thy eyes.
Palace, Ezra 4. 14. maintenance from the p.
  Ps. 45. 15. shall enter into king's p.
  48. 3. God is known in her p. for a refuge.
  122. 7. prosperity within thy p.
  144. 12. after similitude of a p.
  Is. 25. 2. hast made p. of strangers no city.
  Lk. 11. 21. a strong man keepeth his p.
  Phil. 1. 13. bonds are manifest in the p.
Palm, Ps. 92. 12. righteous flourish like p. tree.
  Is. 49. 16. graven thee on p. of hands.
  Matt. 26. 67 ; Mk. 14. 65. smote Jesus with p. of their hands.
  Rev. 7. 9. white robes, p. in their hands.
  ant, Ps. 42. 1. as hart p., so p. my soul.
  Amos 2. 7. that p. after the dust.
Paper, Is. 19. 7. the p. reeds shall wither.
  2 John 12. I would not write with p.
Parable, Num. 23. 7. Balaam took up p.
  Ps. 49. 4. I will incline mine ear to a p.
  Mic. 2. 4. take up a p. against you.
Paradise, Lk. 23. 43. to-day be with me in p.
  2 Cor. 12. 4. was caught up into p.
  Rev. 2. 7. in the midst of p. of God.

Pardon, Ex. 23. 21. not p. your transgressions.
  34. 9 ; Num. 14. 19. p. our iniquity.
  2 Ki. 5. 18. the Lord p. thy servant.
  2 Chr. 30. 18. the good Lord p. every one.
  Neh. 9. 17. a God ready to p.
  Ps. 25. 11. for thy name's sake p. iniquity.
  Is. 55. 7. he will abundantly p.   [iniquity?
  Mic. 7. 18. who is a God like thee, that p.
Parents, Matt. 10. 21 ; Mk. 13. 12. children shall rise up against p.
  Lk. 18. 29. no man that hath left p.
  21. 16. ye shall be betrayed by p.
  John 9. 2. who did sin, this man or his p.?
  Rom. 1. 30 ; 2 Tim. 3. 2. disobedient to p.
  2 Cor. 12. 14. children not lay up for p.
  Eph. 6. 1 ; Col. 3. 20. children, obey your p.
  1 Tim. 5. 4. learn to requite their p.
Part, Josh. 22. 25. ye have no p. in the Lord.
  2 Sam. 20. 1. we have no p. in David.
  Ps. 5. 9. their inward p. is very wickedness.
  51. 6. in hidden p. make me know wisdom.
  118. 7. the Lord taketh my p.
  Mk. 9. 40. he that is not against us is on our p.
  Lk. 10. 42. Mary hath chosen that good p.
  John 13. 8. thou hast no p. with me.
  19. 23. four p., to every soldier a p.
  Acts 8. 21. thou hast neither p. nor lot.
  1 Cor. 13. 9. we know in p., and prophesy in p.
  2 Cor. 6. 15. what p. hath he that believeth with an infidel?
  Heb. 2. 14. himself took p. of the same.

Part, Ruth 1. 17. if ought but death p. thee and me.
  Ps. 22. 18. they p. my garments.
  Lk. 24. 51. while he blessed them, he was p. from them.
  Acts 2. 45. p. them to all men.
Partaker, Ps. 50. 18. p. with adulterers.
  Matt. 23. 30. not been p. in blood of prophets
  Rom. 15. 27. p. of their spiritual things.
  1 Cor. 9. 13. are p. with the altar.
  10. 17. p. of that one bread.
  10. 21. p. of the Lord's table.
  Heb. 3. 1. p. of the heavenly calling.
  1 Pet. 4. 13. p. of Christ's sufferings.
  5. 1. a p. of the glory.
  2 Pet. 1. 4. be p. of the divine nature.
  See Rom. 11. 17.
Partial, Mal. 2. 9. have been p. in the law.
  Jas. 2. 4. are ye not p. in yourselves?
  See 1 Tim. 5. 21 ; Jas. 3. 17.   [of gold.
Partition, 1 Ki. 6. 21. he made a p. by chains
  Eph. 2. 14. the middle wall of p.
Pass, Gen. 41. 32. God will bring it to p.   [over.
  Ex. 12. 13. when I see the blood, I will p.
  33. 22. cover thee while I p. by.
  Is. 43. 2. when thou p. through waters.
  Matt. 5. 18. heaven and earth shall p.
  26. 39 ; Mk. 14. 36. let this cup p.
  Lk. 16. 26. neither can they p. to us.   [life.
  John 5. 24 ; 1 John 3. 14. is p. from death to
  1 Cor. 7. 31 ; 1 John 2. 17. fashion of this world p. away.   [ledge.
  Eph. 3. 19. love of Christ which p. know-
  Phil. 4. 7. peace of God which p. understanding.
  2 Pet. 3. 10. the heavens shall p. away.
Passion, Acts 1. 3. shewed himself alive after his p.
  14. 15. we are men of like p.
Past, 1 Sam. 15. 32. bitterness of death is p.
  Eccl. 3. 15. God requireth that which is p.
  Jer. 8. 20. the harvest is p.

Past—Continued.
Rom. 11. 33. ways p. finding out.
2 Cor. 5. 17. old things p. away.
Eph. 4. 19. being p. feeling.
Pastor, Jer. 2. 8. p. transgressed against me.
  23. 1. woe to p. that destroy sheep.
Eph. 4. 11. gave some p., and teachers.
Pasture, Ps. 74. 1 ; 79. 13 ; 100. 3. sheep of p.
Ezek. 34. 31. flock of my p. are men.
John 10. 9. go in and out, and find p.
Path, Num. 22. 24. angel of Lord stood in p.
Job 28. 7. a p. which no fowl knoweth.
Ps. 16. 11. shew me the p. of life.
  27. 11. lead me in a plain p.
  77. 19. thy p. is in the great waters.
  119. 105. thy Word is a light to my p.
  139. 3. thou compassest my p.
Prov. 4. 18. the p. of the just.
Is. 2. 3 ; Mic. 4. 2. we will walk in his p.
  42. 16. in p. they have not known.
Jer. 6. 16. ask for the old p.
Matt. 3. 3 ; Mk. 1. 3 ; Lk. 3. 4. make his p. straight.
Heb. 12. 13. make straight p. for feet.
Patience, Matt. 18. 26, 29. have p. with me.
Lk. 8. 15. bring forth fruit with p.
  21. 19. in p. possess your souls.
Rom. 5. 3. tribulation worketh p.
  15. 5. with p. wait for it.
  15. 5. the God of p.
2 Cor. 6. 4. as ministers of God in much p.
Col. 1. 11. strengthened with all might to all p.
2 Thes. 1. 4. glory in you for your p.
Tit. 2. 2. faith, charity, p.
Heb. 6. 12. through p. inherit the promises.
  10. 36. ye have need of p.
  12. 1. let us run with p.
Jas. 1. 3. trying of your faith worketh p.
  5. 7. the husbandman hath long p.
  5. 11. ye have heard of the p. of Job.
2 Pet. 1. 6. add to temperance p.
Rev. 3. 10. thou hast kept word of p.
  13. 10 ; 14. 12. here is the p. of saints.
Patiently, Ps. 37. 7. rest in the Lord, wait p.
  40. 1. I waited p. for the Lord.
Heb. 6. 15. after he had p. endured.
1 Pet. 2. 20. if, when ye be buffeted, ye take it p.
See Rom. 2. 7 ; 12. 12 ; 1 Thes. 5. 14.
Pattern, Ex. 25. 40. make them after their p.
1 Tim. 1. 16. in me Christ might shew p.
Tit. 2. 7. shewing thyself a p. of good works.
Heb. 8. 5. according to p. shewed thee.
  9. 23. was necessary that p. of things.
Pavilion, 2 Sam. 22. 12 ; Ps. 18. 11. he made darkness his p.
Ps. 27. 5. he shall hide me in his p.
  31. 20. keep them secretly in a p.
Pay, Deut. 23. 21. shalt not slack to p. vow.
Ps. 22. 25 ; 66. 13 ; 116. 14. will p. my vows.
  76. 11. vow, and p. to the Lord.
Eccl. 5. 4. defer not to p. it.
Matt. 18. 26. I will p. thee all.
  18. 28. p. that thou owest.
  23. 23. ye p. tithe of mint, anise.
Rom. 13. 6. for this cause p. tribute.
Peace, Gen. 28. 21. I come to my father's house in p.
  41. 16. an answer of p.
Num. 6. 26. Lord give thee p.
  25. 12. my covenant of p.
Deut. 29. 19. I shall have p. though I walk.
1 Sam. 25. 6 ; Lk. 10. 5. p. be to house.

Peace—Continued.
2 Ki. 9. 19. what hast thou to do with p. ?
Job 22. 21. acquaint thyself with him, and be at p.
Ps. 4. 8. I will lay me down in p.
  7. 4. evil to him that was at p.
  29. 11. Lord will bless his people with p.
  34. 14 ; 1 Pet. 3. 11. seek p., and pursue it.
Ps. 37. 37. end of upright man is p.
  72. 3. the mountains shall bring p.
  85. 8. he will speak p. to his people.
  122. 6. pray for the p. of Jerusalem.
Eccl. 3. 8. a time of war, a time of p.
Is. 9. 6. Prince of P.
  26. 3. thou wilt keep him in perfect p.
  32. 17. work of righteousness shall be p.
  45. 7. I make p., and create evil.
  48. 18. thy p. been as a river.
  48. 22 ; 57. 21. no p. to the wicked.
  52. 7 ; Nah. 1. 15. the feet of him that publisheth p.
Is. 53. 5. chastisement of our p. on him.
  59. 8 ; Rom. 3. 17. the way of p. they know not.   [no p.
Jer. 6. 14 ; 8. 11. saying p., p., when there is
  8. 15 ; 14. 19. we looked for p.
  29. 7. in p. shall ye have p.
Ezek. 7. 25. seek p., there shall be none.
Dan. 4. 1 ; 6. 25 ; 1 Pet. 1. 2 ; 2 Pet. 1. 2 ; Jude 2. p. be multiplied.
Matt. 10. 13. let your p. come upon it.
  10. 34 ; Lk. 12. 51. to send p. on earth.
Mk. 9. 50. have p. one with another.
Lk. 1. 79. to guide our feet in way of p.
  2. 14. on earth p.
  19. 42. things which belong to thy p.
  24. 36 ; John 20. 19. Jesus said, p. be to you.
John 14. 27. p. I leave, my p. I give you.
  16. 33. that in me ye might have p.
Rom. 1. 7 ; 1 Cor. 1. 3 ; 2 Cor. 1. 2 ; Gal. 1. 3 ; Eph. 1. 2 ; Phil. 1. 2. p. from God our Father.
Rom. 5. 1. we have p. with God.
  8. 6. to be spiritually minded is p.
  10. 15 ; Eph. 6. 15. the gospel of p.
Rom. 14. 17. the kingdom of God is p.
  15. 33 ; 16. 20 ; 2 Cor. 13. 11 ; Phil. 4. 9 ; 1 Thes. 5. 23 ; Heb. 13. 20. the God of p.
1 Cor. 7. 15. God hath called us to p.
2 Cor. 13. 11. live in p.
Gal. 5. 22. fruit of Spirit is love, joy, p.
Eph. 2. 14. he is our p.
  4. 3. unity of Spirit in bond of p.
Phil. 4. 7. p. of God which passeth all understanding.
Col. 1. 2 ; 1 Thes. 1. 1 ; 2 Thes. 1. 2 ; 1 Tim. 1. 2 ; 2 Tim. 1. 2 ; Tit. 1. 4 ; Philem. 3 ; 2 John 3. grace and p. from God.   [hearts.
Col. 3. 15. let the p. of God rule in your
1 Thes. 5. 13. be at p. among yourselves.
2 Tim. 2. 22 ; Heb. 12. 14. follow p. with all men.
Heb. 7. 2. king of p.
Jas. 2. 16. depart in p.
  3. 18. fruit of righteousness is sown in p.
2 Pet. 3. 14. be found of him in p.
Peaceable, Is. 32. 18. people dwell in a p. habitation.
1 Tim. 2. 2. lead a quiet and p. life.
Heb. 12. 11. yieldeth the p. fruit of righteousness.
Jas. 3. 17. wisdom from above is pure, p.
See Gen. 37. 4 ; Rom. 12. 18.

Pearl, Matt. 13. 46. one *p.* of great price.
1 Tim. 2. 9. not with *p.*, or costly array.
Rev. 18. 12, 16. no man buyeth the merchandise of *p.*
    21. 21. every gate was of one *p.*

Pen, Jud. 5. 14. they that handle the *p.*
Job 19. 24. graven with an iron *p.* [writer.
Ps. 45. 1. my tongue is the *p.* of a ready
3 John 13. not with ink and *p.* write.

Penury, Prov. 14. 23. talk of lips tendeth to *p.*
Lk. 21. 4. she of her *p.* cast in all.

People, Ex. 6. 7; Deut. 4. 20 ; 2 Sam. 7. 24 ; Jer.
13. 11. I will take you for a *p.* [and live?
Deut. 4. 33. did ever *p.* hear voice of God
33. 29. who is like *p.* saved by the Lord?
2 Sam. 22. 44; Ps. 18. 43. *p.* I knew not shall serve me.
Ps. 62. 8. ye *p.*, pour out your heart.
144. 15. happy is that *p.*
Prov. 14. 34. sin is a reproach to any *p.*
30. 25. the ants are a *p.* not strong.
Is. 1. 4. a *p.* laden with iniquity.
30. 9 ; 65. 2. this is a rebellious *p.*
Jer. 6. 22; 50. 41. a *p.* cometh from the north.
Jon. 1. 8. of what *p.* art thou?
Mic. 4. 1. *p.* shall flow unto it.
Lk. 1. 17. a *p.* prepared for the Lord.
Rom. 10. 19. by them that are no *p.*
Tit. 2. 14. purify to himself a peculiar *p.*
Heb. 4. 9. remaineth a rest to *p.* of God.
Rev. 5. 9. redeemed us out of every *p.*

Perceive, Deut. 29. 4. a heart to *p.*
Josh. 22. 31. we *p.* the Lord is among us.
Job 23. 8. I cannot *p.* him.
Eccl. 3. 22. *p.* there is nothing better.
Is. 6. 9. see ye indeed, but *p.* not.
33. 19. deeper speech than thou canst *p.*
64. 4. nor *p.* what God hath prepared.
Matt. 13. 14 : Mk. 4. 12 ; Acts 28. 26. ye shall see, and shall not *p.*
Mk. 8. 17. *p.* ye not, neither understand?
Lk. 8. 46. I *p.* virtue is gone out of me.
John 4. 19. I *p.* thou art a prophet.
12. 19. *p.* ye how ye prevail nothing?
Acts 10. 34. *p.* God is no respecter of persons.
1 John 3. 16. hereby *p.* we the love of God.

Perdition, John 17. 12. none lost but son of *p.*
Phil. 1. 28. to them a token of *p.*
2 Thes. 2. 3. be revealed, son of *p.*
1 Tim. 6. 9. which drown men in *p.*
Heb. 10. 39. them who draw back to *p.*
2 Pet. 3. 7. *p.* of ungodly men.

Perfect, Gen. 6. 9. Noah was a just man and *p.*
17. 1. walk before me, and be thou *p.*
Deut. 18. 13. thou shalt be *p.* with the Lord.
32. 4. his work is *p.*
2 Sam. 22. 31 ; Ps. 18. 30. his way is *p.*
Job 1. 1, 8 ; 2. 3. that man was *p.*
Ps. 19. 7. the law of the Lord is *p.*
37. 37. mark the *p.* man.
101. 2. behave myself in a *p.* way.
Prov. 4. 18. path of just shineth to *p.* day.
Ezek. 28. 15. thou wast *p.* in thy ways.
Matt. 5. 48. be ye *p.* as your Father is *p.*
19. 21. if thou wilt be *p.*
John 17. 23. may be made *p.* in one.
Acts 24. 22. having more *p.* knowledge.
Rom. 12. 2. that *p.* will of God.
1 Cor. 2. 6. wisdom among them that are *p.*
2 Cor. 12. 9. strength made *p.* in weakness.
Eph. 4. 13. till we come unto a *p.* man.
Phil. 3. 15. as many as be *p.*
Col. 1. 28. present every man *p.* in Christ.
4. 12. may stand *p.* and complete.

Perfect—*Continued.*
1 Thes. 3. 10. *p.* that which is lacking.
2 Tim. 3. 17. man of God may be *p.*
Heb. 2. 10. make *p.* through sufferings.
7. 19. the law made nothing *p.*
11. 40. without us should not be made *p.*
12. 23. spirits of just men made *p.*
13. 21. make you *p.* in every good work.
Jas. 1. 4. let patience have her *p.* work.
.1. 17. every good and *p.* gift.
1. 25. the *p.* law of liberty.
2. 22. by works was faith made *p.*
3. 2. the same is a *p.* man.
1 John 4. 18. *p.* love casteth out fear.

Perfection, Job 11. 7. canst thou find the Almighty to *p.*?
Ps. 50. 2. out of Zion, *p.* of beauty.
Lk. 8. 14. bring no fruit to *p.*
Heb. 6. 1. let us go on to *p.*
See Acts 18. 26 ; Col. 3. 14.

Perform, Gen. 26. 3; Deut. 9. 5; Lk. 1. 72. *p.* oath I sware to Abraham.
Ex. 18. 18. not able to *p.* it thyself.
Job 5. 12. hands cannot *p.* their enterprise.
Ps. 65. 1. unto thee shall the vow be *p.*
119. 106. I have sworn, and I will *p.* it.
Is. 9. 7. zeal of Lord will *p.* this.
Jer. 29. 10 ; 33. 14. I will *p.* my good word.
Matt. 5. 33. *p.* to the Lord thine oaths.
Rom. 4. 21. he was able also to *p.* [not.
7. 18. how to *p.* that which is good I find
Phil. 1. 6. *p.* it until day of Christ.

Peril, Rom. 8. 35. shall *p.* separate us from Christ?
2 Cor. 11. 26. in *p.* of waters.
See 2 Tim. 3. 1.

Perish, Num. 17. 12. we die, we *p.*, we all *p.*
Deut. 26. 5. a Syrian ready to *p.*
Est. 4. 16. if I *p.*, I *p.*
Job 4. 7. who ever *p.*, being innocent?
29. 13. blessing of him that was ready to *p.*
Ps. 2. 12. lest ye *p.* from the way.
49. 12. like the beasts that *p.*
102. 26. they shall *p.*, but thou shalt endure.
Prov. 11. 10 ; 28. 28. when the wicked *p.*
29. 18. no vision, the people *p.*
31. 6. strong drink to him that is ready to *p.*
Is. 27. 13. they shall come that were ready to *p.* [*p.* not.
Jon. 1. 6 ; 3. 9. God will think on us, that we
Matt. 8. 25 ; Lk. 8. 24. save us, we *p.*
Matt. 26. 52. shall *p.* with the sword.
Mk. 4. 38. carest thou not that we *p.*?
Lk. 15. 17. I *p.* with hunger.
21. 18. there shall not an hair of your head *p.*
John 3. 15, 16. believeth on Son of God should not *p.*
6. 27. labour not for the meat which *p.*
Acts 8. 20. thy money *p.* with thee.
2 Cor. 4. 16. though outward man *p.*
2 Pet. 3. 9. not willing that any should *p.*

Permit, Acts 26. 1. thou art *p.* to speak thyself.
1 Cor. 16. 7. tarry a while if Lord *p.*
Heb. 6. 3. this will we do, if God *p.*
See 1 Cor. 7. 6. [statute.

Perpetual, Ex. 29. 9. priest's office be for *p.*
31. 16. keep Sabbath for *n.* covenant.
Ps. 9. 6. destructions are come to a *p.* end.
74. 3 ; Jer. 25. 9 ; Ezek. 35. 9 ; Zeph. 2. 9. *p.* desolation.
Jer. 8. 5. a *p.* backsliding.
15. 18. why is my pain *p.*?
50. 5. join the Lord in a *p.* covenant.
Hab. 3. 6. the *p.* hills.

Perplexity, Mic. 7. 4. now shall be their *p.*
Lk. 21. 25. distress of nations, with *p.*
See Lk. 24. 4 ; 2 Cor. 4. 8.　　　　　[God?
Persecute, Job 19. 22. why do you *p.* me as
Ps. 7. 1. save me from them that *p.* me.
71. 11. *p.* and take him, none to deliver.
Matt. 5. 11. blessed are ye when men shall *p.* you.
5. 44. pray for them that *p.* you.
John 15. 20. they will also *p.* you.
Acts 9. 4 ; 22. 7 ; 26. 14. why *p.* thou me?
22. 4. *p.* this way unto the death.
Rom. 12. 14. bless them which *p.* you.
1 Cor. 4. 12. being *p.*, we suffer it.
15. 9 ; Gal. 1. 13. I *p.* the church of God.
2 Cor. 4. 9. are *p.* but not forsaken.
Phil. 3. 6. *p.* the church.　　　　　[ariseth.
Persecution, Matt. 13. 21 ; Mk. 4. 17. when *p.*
Mk. 10. 30. shall have lands with *p.*
Rom. 8. 35. shall *p.* separate us from Christ?
2 Cor. 12. 10. I take pleasure in *p.*
Gal. 6. 12. lest they should suffer *p.*
2 Tim. 3. 12. all that will live godly shall suffer *p.*
See 1 Tim. 1. 13.
Person, Lev. 19. 15. nor honour *p.* of mighty.
2 Sam. 14. 14. neither doth God respect any *p.*
Job 22. 29. shall save the humble *p.*
Ps. 15. 4 ; Is. 32. 5. vile *p.*
Ps. 26. 4 ; Prov. 12. 11 ; 28. 19. vain *p.*
Ps. 101. 4. I will not know wicked *p.*　　[men.
Matt. 22. 16 ; Mk. 12. 14. regardest not *p.* of
Matt. 27. 24. innocent of blood of this *p.*
2 Cor. 2. 10. forgave it in the *p.* of Christ.
Heb. 1. 3. the express image of his *p.*　　[be?
2 Pet. 3. 11. what manner of *p.* ought ye to
Jude 16. having men's *p.* in admiration.
Persuade, Matt. 28. 14. we will *p.* him, and secure you.　　　　　[from dead.
Lk. 16. 31. will not be *p.* though one rose
Acts 26. 28. almost thou *p.* me to be a Christian.
Rom. 14. 5. let every man be fully *p.*
2 Cor. 5. 11. we *p.* men.
Gal. 1. 10. do I now *p.* men or God?
2 Tim. 1. 12. am *p.* that he is able to keep.
Heb. 6. 9. are *p.* better things of you.
Pertain, Rom. 15. 17. things which *p.* to God.
1 Cor. 6. 3. things that *p.* to this life.
Heb. 5. 1. things *p.* to God.
2 Pet. 1. 3. all things that *p.* to life.
Perverse, Deut. 32. 5. a *p.* generation.
Job 6. 30. cannot my taste discern *p.* things?
Prov. 4. 24. *p.* lips put far from thee.
17. 20. *p.* tongue falleth into mischief.
23. 33. thine heart shall utter *p.* things.
Matt. 17. 17 ; Lk. 9. 41. O *p.* generation.
Phil. 2. 15. in the midst of a *p.* nation.
1 Tim. 6. 5. *p.* disputings.
Pervert, Deut. 16. 19. a gift doth *p.* words of righteous.
24. 17. thou shalt not *p.* judgment.
Job 8. 3. doth God *p.* judgment.
Prov. 10. 9. he that *p.* his ways shall be known.
Jer. 23. 36. ye have *p.* the words of God.
Mic. 3. 9. ye *p.* all equity.　　　　　[ways?
Acts 13. 10. wilt thou not cease to *p.* right
Gal. 1. 7. would *p.* the gospel of Christ.
Pestilence, Ex. 9. 15. smite thee with *p.*
Ps. 91. 3. deliver thee from noisome *p.*
Hab. 3. 5. before him went *p.*
Matt. 24. 7 ; Lk. 21. 11. there shall be *p.*
See Acts 24. 5.

Petition, 1 Sam. 1. 17. God grant thee thy *p.*
1 Ki. 2. 20. I desire one small *p.*
Est. 5. 6 ; 7. 2 ; 9. 12. what is thy *p.*?
Ps. 20. 5. the Lord fulfil all thy *p.*
Dan. 6. 13. maketh *p.* three times a **day.**
1 John 5. 15. we have *p.* we desired.
Philosophy, Col. 2. 8. lest any spoil **you** through *p.*
See Acts 17. 18.
Physician, Job 13. 4. ye are all *p.* of no value.
Jer. 8. 22. is there no *p.* there?
Matt. 9. 12 ; Mk. 2. 17 ; Lk. 5. 31. they that be whole need not a *p.*　　　　[many *p.*
Mk. 5. 26 ; Lk. 8. 43. suffered many things of
Lk. 4. 23. *p.* heal thyself.
Col. 4. 14. the beloved *p.*
Pictures, Num. 33. 52. shall destroy all their *p.*
Prov. 25. 11. like apples of gold in *p.*
Is. 2. 16. day of Lord on pleasant *p.*　　[bread.
Piece, 1 Sam. 2. 36 ; Prov. 6. 26 ; 28. 21. a *p.* of
Ps. 50. 22. lest I tear you in *p.*
Jer. 23. 29. hammer that breaketh rock in *p.*
Zech. 11. 13 ; Matt. 27. 6, 9. thirty *p.* of silver.
Lk. 14. 18. bought a *p.* of ground.
Pierce, Num. 24. 8. *p.* them with arrows.
2 Ki. 18. 21 ; Is. 36. 6. it will go into his hand and *p.* it.
Ps. 22. 16. *p.* my hands and my feet.
Zech. 12. 10 ; John 19. 37. they shall look on me whom they have *p.*　　　　[rows.
1 Tim. 6. 10. *p.* themselves with many sorrow.
Heb. 4. 12. *p.* to the dividing asunder.
Rev. 1. 7. they also which *p.* him.
Pillar, Gen. 19. 26. a *p.* of salt.
28. 18, 22. Jacob set it for a *p.*
Neh. 9. 12. leddest them by cloudy *p.*
Job 9. 6 ; 26. 11. the *p.* thereof tremble.
1 Tim. 3. 15. the *p.* and ground of the truth.
Rev. 3. 12. him that overcometh will I make a *p.*
Pillow, Gen. 28. 11. Jacob put stones for *p.*
1 Sam. 19. 13, 16. a *p.* of goat's hair.
Ezek. 13. 18. woe to women that sew *p.*
Mk. 4. 38. Jesus was asleep on a *p.*
Pipe, 1 Ki. 1. 40. the people *p.* with *p.*
Is. 5. 12. the harp and *p.* are in their feasts.
Matt. 11. 17 ; Lk. 7. 32. we have *p.* unto you.
1 Cor. 14. 7. how shall it be known what is *p.*?
Pit, Gen. 37. 20. cast him into some *p.*
Ex. 21. 33. if a man dig a *p.*
Num. 16. 30, 33. go down into the *p.*　　[the *p.*
Job 33. 24. deliver him from going down to *p.*
Ps. 28. 1 ; 143. 7 ; Prov. 1. 12. like them that go down into the *p.*
40. 2. brought me out of horrible *p.*
88. 4. counted with them that go to *p.*
Prov. 28. 10. fall into his own *p.*
Is. 24. 17. *p.* and the snare are on thee.
38. 17. the *p.* of corruption.
Matt. 12. 11 ; Lk. 14. 5. fall into a *p.* on Sabbath.　　　　　[fountain.
Pitcher, Eccl. 12. 6. or the *p.* be broken at the
Lam. 4. 2. esteemed as earthen *p.*
Mk. 14. 13 ; Lk. 22. 10. a man bearing a *p.*
Pity, Deut. 7. 16 ; 13. 8 ; 19. 13. thine eye shall have no *p.*
Job 19. 21. have *p.* on me, O friends.
Ps. 69. 20. I looked for some to take *p.*
Prov. 19. 17. he that hath *p.* on poor lendeth to Lord.
Is. 13. 18. they shall have no *p.*
63. 9. in his *p.* he redeemed them.
Jer. 15. 5. who shall have *p.* on thee?
21. 7. he shall not spare, nor have *p.*

Pity—*Continued.*

Ezek. 36. 21. I had p. for my holy name.
Joel 2. 18. the Lord will p. his people.
Zech. 11. 5. their shepherds p. them not.
Matt. 18. 33. as I had p. on thee.
See Ps. 103. 13 ; Jas. 5. 11 ; 1 Pet. 3. 8.

Place, Ex. 3. 5 ; Josh. 5. 15. the p. whereon
thou standest is holy.   [this p.
1 Ki. 8. 29. thine eyes may be open toward
2 Ki. 6. 1 ; Is. 49. 20. the p. is too strait.
Ps. 26. 8. the p. where thine honour dwelleth.
32. 7 ; 119. 114. thou art my hiding p.
33. 14. from the p. of his habitation.
103. 16. the p. thereof shall know it no more.
Prov. 15. 3. the eyes of the Lord are in
every p.
Eccl. 3. 20. all go to one p.
Is. 3. 24. of my feet glorious.
66. 1. where is the p. of my rest?
Mic. 1. 3. the Lord cometh out of his p.
Mal. 1. 11. incense be offered in every p.
Matt. 28. 6 ; Mk. 16. 6. see the p. where the
Lord lay.
Mk. 6. 10. in what p. soever.
Lk. 10. 1. two and two into every p.
14. 9. give this man p.
John 8. 37. my word hath no p. in you.
Acts 2. 1. with one accord in one p.
4. 31. the p. was shaken.
8. 32. the p. of Scripture.
Rom. 12. 19. rather give p. to wrath.
Eph. 4. 27. neither give p. to the devil.
Heb. 12. 17. no p. of repentance.

Plague, Ex. 12. 13. the p. shall not be on you.
Deut. 28. 61. every p. not written.
2 Sam. 24. 21 ; 1 Chr. 21. 22. the p. may be
stayed.   [heart.
1 Ki. 8. 38. know every man the p. of his
Ps. 91. 10. neither any p. come nigh dwelling.
Hos. 13. 14. O death, I will be thy p.
Mk. 5. 34. go in peace, and be whole of p.
Rev. 22. 18. God shall add to him the p.
written.

Plain, Gen. 25. 27. Jacob was a p. man.
Ps. 27. 11. lead me in a p. path.
Prov. 8. 9. they are p. to him that under-
standeth.
15. 19. the way of righteous is made p.
Is. 40. 4. rough places made p.
Mk. 7. 35. he spake p.

Plainly, Ex. 21. 5. if the servant p. say.
Deut. 27. 8. write this law very p.
Is. 32. 4. stammerers shall speak p.
John 10. 24. if thou be Christ, tell us p.
16. 29. now speakest thou p.
Heb. 11. 14. declare p.
See 2 Cor. 3. 12.

Plant, Job 14. 9. bring forth boughs like a p.
Ps. 144. 12. sons as p. grown up.
Is. 5. 7. his pleasant p.
53. 2. as a tender p.
Ezek. 34. 29. a p. of renown.
Matt. 15. 13. every p. my Father hath not
planted.

Plant, 2 Sam. 7. 10 ; 1 Chr. 17. 9. I will p. them.
Ps. 1. 3 ; Jer. 17. 8. like a tree p.
Ps. 92. 13. p. in the house of the Lord.
94. 9. he that p. the ear.
Is. 40. 24. they shall not be p.
Jer. 2. 21. I had p. thee a noble vine.
Lk. 17. 6. be thou p. in the sea.
Rom. 6. 5. if we have been p. together.
1 Cor. 3. 6. I have p.

Play, Ex. 32. 6 ; 1 Cor. 10. 7. people rose up to p.
1 Sam. 16. 17. a man that can p. well.
2 Sam. 6. 21. I will p. before the Lord.
10. 12. let us p. the men.
Job 40. 20. where beasts of field p.
41. 5 wilt thou p. with him?
Ps. 33. 3. p. skilfully with a loud noise.
Is. 11 8. sucking child shall p.
Ezek. 33. 32. can p. well on an instrument.
Zech. 8. 5. boys and girls p. in the streets.

Plead, Jud. 6. 31. will ye p. for Baal?
Job 9. 19. who shall set me a time to p.?
13. 19. who will p. with me?
16. 21. O that one might p. for a man !
Is. 1. 17. p. for the widow.
3. 13. the Lord standeth up to p.
43. 26 let us p. together
Jer. 2. 9. I will yet p. with you.
Lam. 3. 58. O Lord, thou hast p.
Hos. 2. 2. p. with your mother, p.
Joel 3. 2. I will p. with them for my people.

Pleasant, Gen. 3. 6. p. to the eyes.
2 Sam. 1. 23. were p. in their lives.
Ps. 16. 6. lines have fallen in p. places.
106. 24. they despised the p. land.
133. 1. how p. for brethren to dwell together
Prov. 2. 10. knowledge is p. to thy soul.
9. 17. bread eaten in secret is p.
15. 26. the words of the pure are p. words.
16. 24. p. words are as honeycomb.
Eccl. 11. 7. it is p. to behold the sun.
Is. 32. 12. lament for p. fields.
64. 11. our p. things are laid waste.
Jer. 31. 20. is Ephraim a p. child?
Ezek. 33. 32. song of one that hath a p. voice
Dan. 10. 3. I ate no p. bread.
See Prov. 3. 17.

Please, 2 Sam. 7. 29 ; 1 Chr. 17. 27. let it p. thee
Ps. 51. 19. then shalt thou be p. with sacrifices.
69. 31. this also shall p. the Lord.
115. 3 ; 135. 6 ; Jon. 1. 14. God hath done
whatsoever he p.
Prov. 16. 7. when a man's ways p. the Lord.
Is. 53. 10. it p. the Lord to bruise him.
55. 11. accomplish that which I p.
Mic. 6. 7. will the Lord be p. with rams?
Mal. 1. 8. will he be p. with thee?
John 8. 29. I do always those things that
p. him.   [p. God.
Rom. 8. 8. they that are in the flesh cannot
15. 3. even Christ p. not himself.
1 Cor. 1. 21. it p. God by the foolishness of
preaching.
Gal. 1. 10. do I seek to p. men?
Heb. 11. 6. without faith it is impossible to
p. God.   [ness.

Pleasure, 1 Chr. 29. 17. thou hast p. in upright-
Est. 1. 8. according to every man's p.
Job 21. 21. what p. hath he in his house?
22. 3. is it any p. to the Almighty?   [ness.
Ps. 5. 4. not a God that hath p. in wicked-
16. 11. at thy right hand p. for evermore.
51. 18. do good in thy good p.
102. 14. thy servants take p. in her stones.
103. 21. ministers that do his p.
111. 2. sought out all that have p. therein.
149. 4. the Lord taketh p. in his people.
Prov. 21. 17. he that loveth p. shall be poor.
Eccl. 12. 1. I have no p. in them.
Is. 53. 10. the p. of the Lord shall prosper.
58. 13. from doing thy p. on my holy day.
Jer. 48. 38 ; Hos. 8. 8. a vessel wherein is
no p.

Pleasure—*Continued.*
Ezek. 18. 23 ; 33. 11. have I any *p.* that wicked should die?
Mal. 1. 10. I have no *p* in you, saith the Lord.
Lk. 8. 14. choked with *p.* of this life.
12. 32. Father's good *p.*
Eph. 1. 5. the good *p.* of his will.   [good *p.*
Phil. 2. 13. both to will and to do of his
1 Tim. 5. 6. she that liveth in *p.*
Heb. 10. 38. my soul shall have no *p.* in him.
12. 10. chastened us after their own *p.*
Jas. 5. 5. ye have lived in *p.* on the earth.
Rev. 4. 11. for thy *p.* they were created.

Plenteous, Deut. 28. 11 ; 30. 9. Lord shall make thee *p.*
Ps. 86. 5 ; 103. 8. *p.* in mercy.
130. 7. with Lord is *p.* redemption.
Matt. 9. 37. the harvest truly is *p.*

Plenty, Gen. 27. 28. *p.* of corn and wine.
Job 22. 25. *p.* of silver.
37. 23. *p.* of justice.
Prov. 3. 10. barns be filled with *p.*
Jer. 44. 17. *p.* of victuals.

Plentiful, Ps. 68. 9. thou didst send a *p.* rain.
Jer. 48. 33. gladness is taken from *p.* field.
Lk. 12. 16. ground brought forth *p.*   [same.

Plow, Job 4. 8. they that *p.* iniquity reap the
Prov. 20. 4. sluggard will not *p.*
Is. 2. 4 ; Mic. 4. 3. beat swords into *p.*-shares.
Is. 28. 24. doth the plowman *p.* all day to sow?
Joel 3. 10. beat your *p.*-shares into swords.
1 Cor. 9. 10. he that ploweth should *p.* in hope.

Pluck, Deut. 23. 25. thou mayest *p.* the ears.
2 Chr. 7. 20. then will I *p.* them up.
Job 24. 9. they *p.* the fatherless from breast.
Ps. 25. 15. he shall *p.* my feet out of the net.
52. 5. *p.* thee out of thy place.
80. 12. they which pass by *p.* her.
Eccl. 3. 2. a time to *p.* up.   [fire.
Amos 4. 11 ; Zech. 3. 3. a firebrand *p.* out of
Matt. 5. 29 ; 18. 9 ; Mk. 9. 47. if eye offend thee, *p.* it out.
Matt. 12. 1 ; Mk. 2. 23. began to *p.* ears of co n.
John 10. 28. nor shall any *p.* them out of my hand.
Jude 12. twice dead, *p.* up by roots.

Point, Gen. 25. 32. at the *p.* to die.
Jer. 17. 1. written with the *p.* of a diamond.
Mk. 5. 23 ; John 4. 47. at the *p.* of death.
Heb. 4. 15. in all *p.* tempted.
Jas. 2. 10. yet offend in one *p.*

Poison, Deut. 32. 24. the *p.* of serpents.
Ps. 140. 3. adder's *p.* is under their lips.
Jas. 3. 8. tongue is full of deadly *p.*

Pollute, Num. 18. 32. neither *p.* holy things.
Ps. 106. 38. land was *p.* with blood.
Ezek. 20. 31 ; 23. 30 ; 36. 18. ye *p.* yourselves with idols.
Mal. 1. 12. say, the table of the Lord is *p.*
Acts 21. 28. hath *p.* this holy place.

Ponder, Prov. 4. 26. *p.* the path of thy feet.
5. 21. the Lord *p.* all his goings.
Lk. 2. 19. Mary *p.* them in her heart.

Poor, Ex. 30. 15. the *p.* shall not give less.
Lev. 19. 15. shalt not respect person of *p.*
Deut. 15. 11. the *p.* shall never cease.
1 Sam. 2. 8 ; Ps. 113. 7. Lord raiseth up the *p.*
Job 5. 16. the *p.* hath hope.
29. 16. I was a father to the *p.*
36. 15 ; Ps. 72. 12. deliver *p.* in affliction.
Ps. 9. 18. expectation of *p.* not perish.
10. 14. the *p.* committeth himself to thee.
34. 6. this *p.* man cried.
41. 1. blessed that considereth the *p.*

Poor—*Continued.*
68. 10. prepared of thy goodness for the *p.*
82. 4. deliver the *p.* and needy.
132. 15. I will satisfy her *p.* with bread.
140. 12. Lord will maintain the right of the *p.*
Prov. 10. 4. he becometh *p.* that dealeth with a slack hand.
13. 7. there is that maketh himself *p.*   [he.
14. 21. that hath mercy on the *p.* happy is
17. 5. whoso mocketh *p.* reproacheth his Maker.
22. 2. the rich and *p.* meet together.
30. 9. lest I be *p.* and steal.
Is. 14. 32. the *p.* of his people shall trust.
41. 17. when *p.* and needy seek water.
66. 2. to him that is *p.* and of a contrite spirit.
Amos 2. 6. they sold the *p.* for a pair of shoes
Zech. 11. 11. the *p.* of the flock waited on me.
Matt. 5. 3. blessed are the *p.* in spirit.
11. 5. the *p.* have the Gospel preached.
26. 11 ; Mk. 14. 7 ; John 12. 8. ye have the *p.* always with you.
2 Cor. 6. 10. as *p.*, yet making many rich.
8. 9. for your sakes he became *p.*
Jas. 2. 5. hath not God chosen the *p.* ?
Rev. 3. 17. thou knowest not thou art *p.*

Portion, Gen. 31. 14. is there yet any *p.* for us?
Deut. 32. 9. the Lord's *p.* is his people.
2 Ki. 2. 9. a double *p.* of thy spirit.
Job 26. 29. this is the *p.* of a wicked man.
31. 2. what *p.* of God is there from above?
Ps. 16. 5. the Lord is the *p.* of mine inheritance.
63. 10. they shall be a *p.* for foxes.
73. 26. God is my *p.* for ever.
119. 57 ; 142. 5. thou art my *p.*, O Lord.
Prov. 31. 15. giveth a *p.* to her maidens.
Eccl. 2. 10. this was my *p.* of all my labour.
3. 22 ; 5. 18 ; 9. 9. for that is his *p.*
9. 6. neither have they any more *p.* for ever.
11. 2. give a *p.* to seven.
Is. 53. 12. divide him a *p.* with the great.
61. 7. they shall rejoice in their *p.*
Jer. 12. 10. made my pleasant *p.* a desolate wilderness.
Lam. 3. 24. the Lord is my *p.*
Dan. 1. 8. with *p.* of king's meat.
Mic. 2. 4. changed the *p.* of my people.
Matt. 24. 51. appoint him his *p.* with the hypocrites.
Lk. 12. 42. their *p.* in due season.
15. 12. the *p.* of goods that falleth to me.

Possess, Gen. 22. 17 ; 24. 60. thy seed shall *p.* the gate.
Job 7. 3. made to *p.* months of vanity.
13. to *p.* iniquities of youth.
Ps. 139. 13. thou hast *p.* my reins.
Prov. 8. 22. the Lord *p.* me in beginning.
Lk. 18. 12. I give tithes of all I *p.*
21. 19. in patience *p.* your souls.
1 Cor. 7. 30. as though they *p.* not.
2 Cor. 6. 10. yet *p.* all things.   [lasting *p.*

Possession, Gen. 17. 8 ; 48. 4. for an ever-
Ps. 2. 8. uttermost parts for thy *p.*
Prov. 28. 10. good things in *p.*
Matt. 19. 22 ; Mk. 10. 22. had great *p.*
Acts 2. 45. sold their *p.*
Eph. 1. 14. redemption of purchased *p.*

Possible, Matt. 19. 26 ; Mk. 10. 27. with God all things are *p.*   [very elect.
Matt. 24. 24 ; Mk. 13. 22. if *p.* deceive the
Matt. 26. 39 ; Mk. 14. 35. if *p.* let this cup pass from me.

Possible—*Continued.*
Mk. 9. 23. all things are *p.* to him that believeth.
14. 36 ; Lk. 18. 27. all things are *p.* to thee.
Acts 2. 24. not *p.* he should be holden.
Rom. 12. 18. if *p.*, live peaceably.
Heb. 10. 4. not *p.* the blood of bulls.

Posterity, Gen. 45. 7. preserve you a *p.* in the earth.
Ps. 49. 13. yet *p.* approve their sayings.
Dan. 11. 4. not be divided to his *p.*

Pot, Ex. 16. 33. take a *p.*, put manna therein.
2 Ki. 4. 2. not any thing save a *p.* of oil.
4. 40. there is death in the *p.*
Job 41. 31. maketh the deep boil like a *p.*
Prov. 17. 3 ; 27. 21. fining *p.* for silver.
Zech. 14. 21. every *p.* shall be holiness.
Mk. 7. 4. the washing of cups and *p.*
Heb. 9. 4. the golden *p.* with manna.

Pour, Ex. 4. 9. *p.* water on the dry land.
Job 30. 16. now my soul is *p.* out.
36. 27. *p.* rain according to vapour.
Ps. 42. 4. I *p.* out my soul.
45. 2. grace is *p.* into thy lips.
62. 8. *p.* out your heart before him.
Prov. 1. 23 ; Is. 44. 3 ; Joel 2. 28 ; Acts 2. 17. I will *p.* out my Spirit.
Cant. 1. 3. name is as ointment *p.* forth.
Is. 32. 15. till the Spirit be *p.* on us.
44. 3. I will *p.* water on him that is thirsty.
53. 12. *p.* out his soul to death.
Lam. 2. 19. *p.* out thine heart like water.
Nah. 1. 6. fury is *p.* out like fire.
Zech. 12. 10. I will *p.* on house of David.
Mal. 3. 10. if I will not *p.* out a blessing.
Matt. 26. 7 ; Mk. 14. 3. *p.* ointment on his head.
John 2. 15. he *p.* out the changers' money.
Rev. 14. 10. wine of wrath of God *p.* out.

Poverty, Prov. 6. 11 ; 24. 34. *p.* come as one that travelleth.
10. 15. destruction of poor is their *p.*
13. 18. *p.* to him that refuseth instruction.
20. 13 ; 23. 21. come to *p.*
28. 19. shall have *p.* enough.
30. 8. give me neither *p.* nor riches.
31. 7. forget his *p.*   [rich.
2 Cor. 8. 9. that ye through his *p.* might be
Rev. 2. 9. I know thy works and *p.*

Powder, Ex. 32. 20. Moses burnt calf to *p.*
Deut. 28. 24. Lord make rain of land *p.*
2 Ki. 23. 15 ; 2 Chr. 34. 7. stamped the altar to *p.*   [to *p.*
Matt. 21. 44 ; Lk. 20. 18. it will grind him

Power, Gen. 32. 28. as a prince hast *p.* with God.
Ex. 15. 6. right hand glorious in *p.*
Lev. 26. 19. I will break your *p.*
Deut. 8. 18. giveth thee *p.* to get wealth.
2 Sam. 22. 33. God is my strength and *p.*
1 Chr. 29. 11 ; Matt. 6. 13. thine is the *p.*
2 Chr. 25. 8. God hath *p.* to help.
Job 21. 7. why are the wicked mighty in *p.* ?
26. 2. helped him that is without *p.*
37. 23. excellent in *p.* and judgment.
Ps. 49. 15. redeem my soul from *p.* of the grave.
62. 11. belongeth unto God.
65. 6. being girded with *p.*
66. 7. he ruleth by his *p.*
90. 11. who knoweth *p.* of thine anger?
110. 3. people be willing in the day of thy *p.*
145. 11. they shall talk of thy *p.*
Prov. 3. 27. it is in *p.* of thy hand.
18. 21. in *p.* of the tongue.

Power—*Continued.*
Eccl. 5. 19 : 6. 2. *p.* to eat thereof.
8. 4. where word of king is, there is *p.*
Is. 40. 29. he giveth *p.* to the faint.
Jer. 10. 12 ; 51. 15. made earth by his *p.*
Ezek. 30. 6. pride of her *p.* shall come down.
Dan. 2. 37. God hath given thee *p.*
Mic. 3. 8. full of *p.* by the Spirit.
Hab. 2. 9. delivered from the *p.* of evil.
Zech. 4. 6. not by might, nor by *p.*
Matt. 9. 6 ; Mk. 2. 10 ; Lk. 5. 24. Son of man hath *p.* to forgive.   [with *p.*
Matt. 24. 30 ; Lk. 21. 27. coming in clouds
Matt. 28. 18. all *p.* is given me.
Mk. 9. 1. kingdom of God come with *p.*
Lk. 1. 35. the *p.* of the Highest.
4. 6. all this *p.* will I give thee.
4. 32. his word was with *p.*
5. 17. the *p.* of the Lord was present.
9. 43. amazed at the mighty *p.* of God.
12. 5. that hath *p.* to cast into hell.
22. 53. the *p.* of darkness.
24. 49. endued with *p.* from on high.
John 1. 12. *p.* to become sons of God.
10. 18. I have *p.* to lay it down.
17. 2. given him *p.* over all flesh.
19. 10. *p.* to crucify, *p.* to release.
Acts 1. 8. receive *p.* after Holy Ghost is come.
3. 12. as though by our own *p.*
5. 4. was it not in thine own *p.* ?
6. 8. full of faith and *p.*
8. 10. this man is the great *p.* of God.
26. 18. from the *p.* of Satan unto God.
Rom. 1. 20. his eternal *p.* and Godhead.
9. 21. hath not potter *p.* over clay?
13. 2. whosoever resisteth the *p.*
1 Cor. 4. 20. not in word, but in *p.*
15. 43. sown in weakness, raised in *p.*
2 Cor. 4. 7. excellency of *p.* be of God.
Eph. 1. 19. exceeding greatness of his *p.*
2. 2. prince of the *p.* of the air.
3. 7. by the effectual working of his *p.*
Phil. 3. 10. the *p.* of his resurrection.
Col. 1. 13. delivered us from *p.* of darkness.
2 Tim. 1. 7. God hath given spirit of *p.*
3. 5. a form of godliness, but denying the *p.*
Heb. 1. 3. all things by the word of his *p.*
2. 14. might destroy him that had *p.* of death.
7. 16. the *p.* of an endless life.
Rev. 4. 11 ; 5. 12. thou art worthy to receive *p*
See Ps. 29. 4 ; 2 Cor. 10. 10 ; Heb. 4. 12.

Praise, Ex. 15. 11. fearful in *p.*
Deut. 10. 21. he is thy *p.* and thy God.
Jud. 5. 3 ; Ps. 7. 17 ; 9. 2 ; 57. 7 ; 61. 8 ; 104. 33. I will sing *p.*
2 Chr. 23. 13. taught to sing *p.*
Neh. 9. 5. exalted above *p.*
Ps. 22. 3. thou that inhabitest the *p.* of Israel.
22. 25. my *p.* shall be of thee.
33. 1 ; 147. 1. *p.* is comely.   [mouth.
34. 1. his *p.* shall continually be in my
35. 28. tongue shall speak of thy *p.*
50. 23. whoso offereth *p.* glorifieth me.
65. 1. *p.* waiteth for thee, O God.
66. 2. make his *p.* glorious.
71. 8. my mouth be filled with thy *p.*
100. 4. enter his courts with *p.*
106. 2. who can shew forth all his *p.* ?
Prov. 27. 21. so is a man to his *p.*
Is. 42. 12. declare his *p.* in the islands.
60. 18. call thy gates *p.*
61. 3. garment of *p.*
62. 7. a *p.* in the earth.

Praise—*Continued.*
Jer. 13. 11. that they might be to me for a *p.*
Hab. 3. 3. the earth was full of his *p.*
Zeph. 3. 19. get them *p.* and fame.
Matt. 21. 16. thou hast perfected *p.*
John 9. 24. give God the *p.*
12. 43. loved *p.* of men.
Rom. 2. 29. whose *p.* is not of men.
13. 3. thou shalt have *p.* of the same.
1 Cor. 4. 5. every man have *p.* of God.
2 Cor. 8. 18. whose *p.* is in the Gospel.
Eph. 1. 12. *p.* of his glory.
Phil. 4. 8. if there be any *p.*
Heb. 2. 12. in church will I sing *p.*
13. 15. offer sacrifice of *p.*
1 Pet. 1. 7. trial of faith might be found to *p.*
2. 14. for *p.* of them that do well.

Praise, 1 Chr. 29. 13. *p.* thy glorious name.
Ps. 22. 23. ye that fear the Lord, *p.* him.
30. 9. shall the dust *p.* thee?
42. 5, 11 ; 43. 5. I shall yet *p.* him.
45. 17. therefore shall the people *p.* thee.
49. 18. men will *p.* thee when thou doest
well.
63. 3. my lips shall *p.* thee.
67. 3. let the people *p.* thee, O God.
69. 34. let heaven and earth *p.* him.
71. 14. I will yet *p.* thee more and more.
72. 15. daily shall he be *p.*
76. 10. wrath of man shall *p.* thee.
88. 10. shall the dead arise, and *p.* thee?
99. 3. let them *p.* thy great name.
107. 32. *p.* him in the assembly.
115. 17. the dead *p.* not the Lord.
119. 164. seven times a day I *p.* thee.
138. 4. kings of the earth shall *p.* thee.
145. 4. one generation shall *p.* thy works.
145. 10. all thy works shall *p.* thee.
148. 3. *p.* him, sun and moon.
Prov. 27. 2. let another *p.* thee.
31. 31. let her own works *p.* her.
Is. 38. 19. the living shall *p.* thee.
Dan. 2. 23. I thank and *p.* thee, O God.
Joel 2. 26. *p.* the name of the Lord.
Rom. 15. 11. *p.* the Lord, all ye Gentiles.
1 Cor. 11. 22. I *p.* you not.
Rev. 19. 5. saying, *p.* our God.
Prating, Prov. 10. 8. a *p.* fool shall fall.
3 John 10. *p.* against us with malicious
words.
Pray, Gen. 20. 7. he shall *p.* for thee.
1 Sam. 7. 5. I will *p.* for you to the Lord.
12. 23. I should sin in ceasing to *p.*
2 Sam. 7. 27. found in his heart to *p.*
2 Chr. 6. 24. *p.* and make supplication.
Ezra 6. 10. *p.* for the life of the king.
Job 21. 15. what profit if we *p.* to him?
Ps. 5. 2. my God, to thee will I *p.*   [I *p.*
55. 17. evening, morning, and at noon will
122. 6. *p.* for the peace of Jerusalem.
Is. 16. 12. come to sanctuary to *p.*
45. 20. to a god that cannot save.
Jer. 37. 3 ; 42. 2, 20. *p.* for us to the Lord.
Zech. 7. 2. they sent men to *p.* before Lord.
Matt. 5. 44. *p.* for them which despitefully
use you.
6. 5. love to *p.* standing in the synagogues.
14. 23 ; Mk. 6. 46 ; Lk. 6. 12 ; 9. 28. apart to *p.*
Matt. 26. 41 ; Mk. 14. 38 ; Lk. 22. 40. watch
and *p.*, that ye enter not into temptation.
Mk. 11. 24. what ye desire when ye *p.*
Lk. 11. 1. Lord, teach us to *p.*
18. 1. men ought always to *p.*

Pray—*Continued.*
John 14. 16 ; 16. 26. I will *p.* the Father.
17. 9. I *p.* for them, I *p.* not for the world.
Acts 9. 11. behold he *p.*
10. 9. on housetop to *p.*
Rom. 8. 26. know not what we should *p.* for.
1 Cor. 14. 15. I will *p.* with the Spirit.
1 Thes. 5. 17. *p.* without ceasing.
1 Tim. 2. 8. that men *p.* everywhere.
Jas. 5. 14. let them *p.* over him.
5. 16. *p.* one for another.
1 John 5. 16. I do not say he shall *p.* for it.
Prayer, 1 Ki. 8. 28. respect *p.* of thy servant.
2 Chr. 7. 15. ears be attent to the *p.*
Neh. 1. 6. thou mayest hear the *p.*
Job 15. 4. thou restrainest *p.*
22. 27. shalt make thy *p.* to him.
Ps. 66. 2. O thou that hearest *p.*
72. 15. *p.* shall be made continually.
102. 17. he will regard *p.* of the destitute.
109. 4. I give myself to *p.*
Prov. 15. 8. *p.* of upright his delight.
Is. 1. 15. when ye make many *p.*
56. 7 ; Matt. 21. 13 ; Mk. 11. 17 ; Lk. 19. 46 ;
house of *p.*
Dan. 9. 17. hear *p.* of thy servant.
Matt. 17. 21 ; Mk. 9. 29. but by *p.* and fasting.
Matt. 21. 22. whatsoever ye ask in *p.*
23. 14 ; Mk. 12. 40 ; Lk. 20. 47. long *p.*
Lk. 1. 13. thy *p.* is heard.
6. 12. continued all night in *p.*
Acts 3. 1. the hour of *p.*
6. 4. we will give ourselves to *p.*
10. 31. thy *p.* is heard.
12. 5. *p.* was made without ceasing.
16. 13. where *p.* was wont to be made.
Eph. 6. 18. praying with all *p.*   [known.
Phil. 4. 6. by *p.* let your requests be made
1 Tim. 4. 5. it is sanctified by *p.*
Jas. 5. 15. the *p.* of faith shall save the sick.
5. 16. the effectual fervent *p.* of a righteous
man.
1 Pet. 4. 7. watch unto *p.*
Rev. 5. 8 ; 8. 3. the *p.* of saints.
Preach, Neh. 6. 7. appointed prophets to *p.*
Is. 61. 1. anointed me to *p.* good tidings.
Jon. 3. 2. *p.* the preaching I bid thee.
Matt. 4. 17. Jesus began to *p.*
11. 1. he departed thence to *p.*   [ance.
Mk. 1. 4. John did *p.* the baptism of repent-
2. 2. he *p.* the word to them.
3. 14 ; Lk. 9. 2. send them forth to *p.*
Mk. 6. 12. they *p.* that men should repent.
16. 20. they went and *p.* everywhere.
Lk. 9. 60. go and *p.* the kingdom of God.
Acts 5. 42. they ceased not to *p.* Christ.
10. 42. he commanded us to *p.*
13. 38. through this man is *p.* forgiveness.
15. 21. in every city them that *p.* him.
17. 3. Jesus whom I *p.* is Christ.
Rom. 2. 21. thou that *p.* a man should not
steal.   [sent?
10. 15. how shall they *p.*, except they be
1 Cor. 1. 23. we *p.* Christ crucified.
9. 16. woe to me if I *p.* not the Gospel.
9. 27. lest when I have *p.* to others.
15. 11. so we *p.*, and so ye believed.
2 Cor. 4. 5. we *p.* not ourselves.
Gal. 2. 2. the Gospel which I *p.*
Phil. 1. 15. some *p.* Christ of envy and strife.
Col. 1. 28. whom we *p.*, warning every man.
2 Tim. 4. 2. *p.* the word, be instant.
Heb. 4. 2. the word *p.* did not profit.
1 Pet. 3. 19. *p.* to spirits in prison.

Preacher, Eccl. 12. 10. the *p.* sought to find
words. [a *p.*?
Rom. 10. 14. how shall they hear without
1 Tim. 2. 7; 2 Tim. 1. 11. am ordained a *p.*
2 Pet. 2. 5. Noah, a *p.* of righteousness.
Precept, Neh. 9. 14. commandedst them *p.*
Ps. 119. 40. I have longed after thy *p.*
Is. 28. 10, 13. *p.* must be upon *p.*
29. 13. taught by *p.* of men.
Dan. 9. 5. departing from thy *p.*
Mk. 10. 5. he wrote you this *p.*
Precious, Gen. 24. 53; Deut. 33. 13. *p.* things.
1 Sam. 3. 1. the word of the Lord was *p.*
26. 21. my soul was *p.* in thine eyes.
2 Ki. 1. 13. let my life be *p.*
Job 28. 16. it annot be valued with *p.* onyx.
Ps. 49. 8. the redemption of their soul is *p.*
72. 14. *p.* shall their blood be in his sight.
116. 15. *p.* in sight of Lord is death of saints.
126. 6. bearing *p.* seed.
133. 2. like *p.* ointment upon the head.
139. 17. how *p.* are thy thoughts, O God!
Prov. 3. 15. wisdom is more *p.* than rubies.
20. 15. lips of knowledge are a *p.* jewel.
Eccl. 7. 1. good name better than *p.* ointment.
Is. 13. 12. a man more *p.* than gold.
28. 16; 1 Pet. 2. 6. a *p.* corner stone.
Is. 43. 4. thou wast *p.* in my sight.
Jer. 15. 19. take the *p.* from the vile.
Lam. 4. 2. the *p.* sons of Zion.
Jas. 5. 7. husbandman waiteth for *p.* fruit of
earth. [gold.
1 Pet. 1. 7. trial of your faith more *p.* than
1. 19. the *p.* blood of Christ.
2. 7. to you which believe he is *p.*
2 Pet. 1. 1. obtained like *p.* faith.
1. 4. exceeding great and *p.* promises.
Pre-eminence, Eccl. 3. 19. a man hath no *p.*
above a beast.
Col. 1. 18. that he might have the *p.*
3 John 9. Diotrephes, who loveth to have
the *p.*
Prefer, Ps. 137. 6. if I *p.* not Jerusalem. [me.
John 1. 15. he that cometh after is *p.* before
Rom. 12. 10. in honour *p.* one another.
Preparation, Prov. 16. 1. *p.* of the heart of
man. [19. 14. the day of *p.*
Matt. 27. 62; Mk. 15. 42; Lk. 23. 54; John
Eph. 6. 15. feet shod with *p.* of the Gospel of
peace.
Prepare, Ex. 15. 2. I will *p.* him a habitation.
1 Sam. 7. 3. *p.* your hearts to the Lord.
Ps. 61. 7. O *p.* mercy and truth. [poor.
68. 10. thou hast *p.* of thy goodness for the
107. 36. that they may *p.* a city.
Prov. 8. 27. when he *p.* the heavens.
30. 25. they *p.* their meat in summer.
Is. 21. 5. *p.* the table, watch in tower.
40. 3; Mal. 3. 1; Matt. 3. 3; Mk. 1. 3; Lk.
1. 76. *p.* the way of the Lord.
Is. 62. 10. *p.* the way of the people.
Amos 4. 12. *p.* to meet thy God.
Matt. 11. 10. shall *p.* way before thee.
20. 23; Mk. 10. 40. given to them for whom
it is *p.*
Matt. 26. 17; Mk. 14. 12; Lk. 22. 9. where wilt
thou that we *p.*?
John 14. 2. I go to *p.* a place for you.
Rom. 9. 23. vessels of mercy afore *p.*
1 Cor. 2. 9. things God hath *p.*
14. 8. who shall *p.* to battle?
Heb. 10. 5. a body hast thou *p.* me.
11. 16. he hath *p.* for them a city.

Presbytery, 1 Tim. 4. 14. laying on hands of
the *p.*
Presence, Gen. 3. 8. hid from *p.* of the Lord.
47. 15. why should we die in thy *p.*?
Ex. 33. 14. my *p.* shall go with thee.
1 Chr. 16. 33. trees sing at *p.* of Lord.
Job 23. 15. I am troubled at his *p.*
Ps. 16. 11. in thy *p.* is fulness of joy.
31. 20. in the secret of thy *p.*
51. 11. cast me not away from thy *p.*
97. 5. hills melted at the *p.* of Lord.
100. 2. come before his *p.* with singing.
139. 7. whither shall I flee from thy *p.*?
Prov. 14. 7. go from *p.* of a foolish man.
Is. 63. 9. the angel of his *p.* saved them.
64. 2. nations may tremble at thy *p.*
Jer. 23. 39; 52. 3. I will cast you out of my *p.*
Jon. 1. 3. to flee from *p.* of the Lord.
Nah. 1. 5. earth is burned at his *p.*
Zeph. 1. 7. hold thy peace at *p.* of the Lord.
Lk. 13. 26. we have eaten and drunk in thy *p.*
Acts 3. 19. times of refreshing from *p.* of the
Lord.
1 Cor. 1. 29. no flesh should glory in his *p.*
2 Cor. 10. 10. his bodily *p.* is weak. [Lord.
2 Thes. 1. 9. destruction from the *p.* of the
Jude 24. present you faultless before his *p.*
Present, 1 Ki. 10. 25; 2 Chr. 9. 24. brought
every man his *p.*
Ps. 46. 1. God is a very *p.* help in trouble.
Lk. 5. 17. power of the Lord was *p.*
John 14. 25. being yet *p.* with you.
Acts 10. 33. all here *p.* before God.
Rom. 7. 21. do good, evil is *p.* with me.
8. 18. the sufferings of this *p.* time.
12. 1. *p.* your bodies a living sacrifice.
2 Cor. 5. 8. to be *p.* with the Lord.
Gal. 1. 4. deliver us from this *p.* world.
Col. 1. 22. to *p.* you holy, unblameable.
2 Tim. 4. 10. having loved this *p.* world.
Tit. 2. 12. live godly in this *p.* world.
Heb. 12. 11. no chastening for *p.* seemeth
joyous.
2 Pet. 1. 12. established in the *p.* truth.
Preserve, Gen. 32. 30. I have seen God, and my
life is *p.*
45. 7. God sent me to *p.* you a posterity.
Deut. 6. 24. that he might *p.* us alive.
Job 29. 2. in the days when God *p.* me.
Ps. 25. 21. let uprightness *p.* me.
36. 6. thou *p.* man and beast.
79. 11. *p.* thou those that are to die.
121. 8. Lord shall *p.* thy going out and
coming in.
Prov. 2. 11. discretion shall *p.* thee.
20. 28. mercy and truth *p.* the king.
22. 12. eyes of Lord *p.* knowledge.
Is. 49. 8. I will *p.* thee. [*p.* it.
Lk. 17. 33. whosoever shall lose his life, shall
Press, Ps. 38. 2. thy hand *p.* me sore.
Amos 2. 13. I am *p.* under you, as a cart is *p.*
Mk. 2. 4; Lk. 8. 19. could not come nigh for
the *p.*
3. 10. they *p.* on him to touch him.
5. 30. Jesus turned about in the *p.*
Lk. 6. 38. good measure *p.* down.
16. 16. every man *p.* into it.
2 Cor. 1. 8. were *p.* above measure.
Phil. 3. 14. I *p.* toward the mark. [*p.* sins.
Presumptuous, Ps. 19. 13. keep servant from
2 Pet. 2. 10. *p.* are they, self-willed.
Pretence, Matt. 23. 14; Mk. 12. 40. for a *p.*
make long prayers.
Phil. 1. 18. whether in *p.* or truth.

Prevail, Gen. 32. 28. power with God, and
  hast p.
  Ex. 17. 11. when Moses held up his hand
  Israel p.
1 Sam. 2. 9. by strength shall no man p.
2 Chr. 14. 11 ; Ps. 9. 19. let not man p.
Ps. 65. 3. iniquities p. against me.
Eccl. 4. 12. if one p. against him.
Matt. 16. 18. gates of hell shall not p.
John 12. 19. perceive ye how ye p. nothing?
Acts 19. 20. so mightily grew word of God
  and p.   [death p. me.
Prevent, 2 Sam. 22. 6 ; Ps. 18. 5. snares of
Ps. 59. 10. God of mercy shall p. me.
  88. 13. in morning shall my prayer p. me.
  119. 147. I p. the dawning of the morning.
Matt. 17. 25. Jesus p. him, saying.
1 Thes. 4. 15. shall not p. them asleep.
Prey, Gen. 49. 27. in morning he shall devour
  the p.
Ps. 17. 12. like a lion greedy of p.
  124. 6. who hath not given us for a p.
Is. 49. 24. shall the p. be taken from the
  mighty?
Ezek. 34. 22. my flock shall no more be a p.
Price, 2 Sam. 24. 24 ; 1 Chr. 21. 22. I will buy it
  at a p.
Is. 55. 1. buy wine and milk without p.
Matt. 13. 46. one pearl of great p.
  27. 6. it is the p. of blood.
Acts 5. 2. kept back part of the p.
1 Cor. 6. 20 ; 7. 23. bought with a p.
1 Pet. 3. 4. meek spirit is of great p.
Pricks, Num. 33. 55. those that remain shall
  be p. in your eyes.   [against the p.
Acts 9. 5 ; 26. 14. it is hard for thee to kick
See Ps. 73. 21 ; Acts 2. 37.   [man.
Pride, Job 33. 17. that he may hide p. from
Ps. 59. 12. then be taken in their p.
  73. 6. by p. cometh contention.
  13. 10. by p. cometh contention.
  14. 3. in mouth of foolish is rod of p.
  16. 18. p. goeth before destruction.
Is. 28. 1. woe to the crown of p.
Jer. 49. 16. the p. of thine heart hath deceived thee.
1 Tim. 3. 6. being lifted up with p.
1 John 2. 16. p. of life is not of the Father.
Priest, Gen. 14. 18 ; Heb. 7. 1. p. of the most
  high God.
1 Sam. 2. 35. I will raise up a faithful p.
2 Chr. 6. 41 ; Ps. 132. 16. let thy p. be clothed
  with salvation.
2 Chr. 15. 3. Israel without a teaching p.
Ps. 110. 4 ; Heb. 5. 6. a p. for ever after order
  of Melchizedec.
Ic. 24. 2. as with the people, so with the p.
  28. 7. p. and prophet have erred.
  61. 6. be named the p. of the Lord.
Jer. 5. 31. p. bear rule.
  23. 11. prophet and p. are profane.
Mic. 3. 11. the p. teach for hire.
Mal. 2. 7. the p. lips should keep knowledge.
Lk. 10. 31. there came down a certain p.
  17. 14. shew yourselves to the p.
Acts 6. 7. p. were obedient to the faith.
  14. 13. the p. of Jupiter.
Heb. 7. 3. abideth a p. continually.
Rev. 1. 6 ; 5. 10. made us p. to God.
Priesthood, Ex. 40. 15 ; Num. 25. 13. an ever-
  lasting p.
Heb. 7. 24. hath an unchangeable p.
1 Pet. 2. 5. an holy p.
  2. 9. ye are a royal p.

Prince, Gen. 32. 28. as a p. hast thou power
  with God.
Ex. 2. 14. who made thee a p. over us?
2 Sam. 3. 38. a p. is fallen in Israel.   [on p.
Job 12. 21 ; Ps. 107. 40. he poureth contempt
Job 21. 28. where is the house of the p.?
  34. 19. that accepteth not the person of p.
Ps. 45. 16. make p. in all the earth.
  118. 9. than to put confidence in p.
  146. 3. put not your trust in p.
Prov. 8. 15. by me p. decree justice.
  28. 16. a p. that wanteth understanding.
  31. 4. it is not for p. to drink strong drink.
Eccl. 10. 7. p. walking as servants.
Is. 9. 6. the P. of peace.
  10. 8. are not my p. altogether kings?
  23. 8. whose merchants are p.
  32. 1. p. shall rule in judgment.
  34. 12. all her p. shall be nothing.
Hos. 3. 4. Israel shall abide many days
  without a p.
Mic. 7. 3. the p. and judge ask reward.
Matt. 9. 34 ; 12. 24 ; Mk. 3. 22. casteth out
  devils by p. of devils.   [world.
John 12. 31 ; 14. 30 ; 16. 11. the p. of this
Acts 3. 15. killed the P. of life.
  5. 31. him hath God exalted to be a P.
1 Cor. 2. 6. nor wisdom of p. of this world.
Eph. 2. 2. the p. of the power of the air.
Principality, Rom. 8. 38. neither p. nor powers
  able to separate.
Eph. 1. 21. far above all p.
  6. 12. we wrestle against p. and powers.
Col. 2. 15. having spoiled p.
Tit. 3. 1. to be subject to p.
See Prov. 4. 7 ; Heb. 5. 12 ; 6. 1.   [my feet.
Print, Job 13. 27. thou settest a p. on heels of
  19. 23. O that my words were p.
John 20. 25. except I see p. of nails.
Prison, Gen. 40. 3. put butler and baker in p.
Ps. 142. 7. bring my soul out of p.
Eccl. 4. 14. out of p. he cometh to reign.
Is. 53. 8. he was taken from p. and judgment.
  61. 1. opening of the p.
Matt. 5. 25 ; Lk. 12. 58. thou be cast into p.
Matt. 25. 36. in p., and ye came unto me.
Lk. 22. 33. to go with thee to p. and to death.
Acts 5. 18. put apostles in common p.
1 Pet. 3. 19. the spirits in p.
Prisoner, Ps. 79. 11. let sighing of the p. come.
  102. 20. to hear groaning of the p.
Zech. 9. 12. turn to stronghold, p. of hope.
Matt. 27. 15. release to the people a p.
Eph. 3. 1 ; 4. 1 ; Philem. 1. 9. the p. of Jesus.
Private, Gal. 2. 2. to them of reputation.
2 Pet. 1. 20. of any p. interpretation.
Privily, Ps. 11. 2. may p. shoot at the upright.
Prov. 1. 11. lurk p. for the innocent.
Acts 16. 37. do they thrust us out p.?
2 Pet. 2. 1. p. bring in heresies.
Prize, 1 Cor 9. 24. one receiveth the p.
Phil. 3. 14. I press for the p.   [Lord.
Proceed, Gen. 24. 50. the thing p. from the
Deut. 8. 3 ; Matt. 4. 4. every word that p. out
  of mouth of God.
Job 40. 5. I p. no further.
Is. 29. 14. I p. to do a marvellous work.
  51. 4. a law shall p. from me.
Jer. 9. 3. they p. from evil to evil.   [defile.
Matt. 15. 18 ; Mk. 7. 21. p. out of the mouth
John 8. 42. I p. forth from God.
Eph. 4. 29. let no corrupt communication p.
Jas. 3. 10. out of the same mouth p. blessing
  and cursing.

Proclaim, Ex. 33. 19. I will p. the name of the Lord.
Is. 61. 1. to p. liberty to captives. [cometh.
62. 11. the Lord hath p., thy salvation
Lk. 12. 3. shall be p. on housetops.

Profane, Lev. 18. 21; 19. 12; 20. 3; 21. 6; 22. 2. neither shalt thou p. name of God.
Jer. 23. 11. prophet and priest are p.
Matt. 12. 5. priests in temple p. Sabbath.
Acts 24. 6. gone about to p. temple.
1 Tim. 1. 9. the law is for unholy and p.
6. 20; 2 Tim. 2. 16. avoid p. babblings.
Heb. 12. 16. lest there be any p. person.

Profess, Matt. 7. 23. will I p. I never knew you.
Rom. 1. 22. p. themselves to be wise.
1 Tim. 6. 12. hast p. a good profession.
Tit. 1. 16. they p. they know God.

Profit, Gen. 25. 32. what p. shall birth-right do to me?
37. 26. what p. if we slay our brother?
Job 21. 15. what p. if we pray to him?
Ps. 30. 9. what p. is in my blood?
Prov. 14. 23. in all labour there is p.
Eccl. 1. 3; 3. 9; 5. 16. what p. hath a man of his labour?
2. 11. there was no p. under the sun.
5. 9. the p. of the earth is for all.
7. 11. by wisdom there is p.
Jer. 16. 19. things wherein is no p.
Mal. 3. 14. what p. that we have kept?
Rom. 3. 1. what p. of circumcision?
1 Cor. 10. 33. not seeking mine own p.
2 Tim. 2. 14. about words to no p.
Heb. 12. 10. he chasteneth us for our p.

Profit, 1 Sam. 12. 21. vain things which cannot p.
Job 34. 9. it p. nothing to delight in God.
Prov. 10. 2. treasures of wickedness p. nothing.
11. 4. riches p. not in the day of wrath.
Is. 30. 5. a people that could not p.
Jer. 2. 11. changed for that which doth not p.
7. 8. lying words that cannot p.
Matt. 16. 26; Mk. 8. 36. what is a man p. if he gain the world?
1 Cor. 12. 7. given to every man to p. withal.
Gal. 5. 2. Christ shall p. you nothing.
1 Tim. 4. 8. bodily exercise p. little.
Heb. 4. 2. the word preached did not p.
Jas. 2. 14. what doth it p.?

Profitable, Job 22. 2. can a man be p. to God?
Eccl. 10. 10. wisdom is p. to direct. [perish.
Matt. 5. 29. p. that one of thy members
1 Tim. 4. 8. godliness is p. to all things.
2 Tim. 3. 16. scripture is p. for doctrine.

Prolong, Deut. 4. 26; 30. 18. ye shall not p. your days. [my life?
Job 6. 11. what is mine end, that I should p.
Prov. 10. 27. the fear of the Lord p. days.
Is. 53. 10. he shall p. his days.

Promise, Num. 14. 34. know my breach of p.
1 Ki. 8. 56. not failed one word of his good p.
Neh. 5. 13. performeth not p. according to p.
Ps. 77. 8. doth his p. fail?
105. 42. he remembered his holy p.
Lk. 24. 49; Acts 1. 4. p. of the Father.
Acts 2. 39. the p. is to you and your children.
7. 17. the time of the p.
26. 6. hope of the p. made of God.
Rom. 4. 14. the p. is made of none effect.
9. 4. to whom pertain the p.
2 Cor. 1. 20. p. of God in him are yea and amen.

Promise—Continued.
Gal. 3. 17. should make the p. of none effect.
Eph. 2. 12. strangers from covenants of p.
1 Tim. 4. 8. having p. of the life that now is.
Heb. 4. 1. fear, lest a p. being left.
6. 12. through faith inherit the p.
9. 15; 10. 36. the p. of eternal inheritance.
2 Pet. 1. 4. great and precious p.
3. 4. where is the p. of his coming?
3. 9. Lord is not slack concerning his p. [us.
1 John 2. 25. this is the p. he hath promised

Promise, Ex. 12. 25. give according as he p.
Num. 14. 40. will go to place the Lord p.
Deut. 1. 11; 15. 6. Lord bless you as he hath p.
19. 8; 27. 3. give thee the land he p.
26. 18. to be his people, as he p.
1 Ki. 8. 56. Lord hath given rest as he p.
2 Ki. 8. 19; 2 Chr. 21. 7. he p. to give him a light.
Matt. 14. 7. Herod p. with an oath.
Mk. 14. 11. they p. to give him money.
Lk. 1. 72. mercy p. to our fathers. [form.
Rom. 4. 21. what he had p. he was able to per-
Tit. 1. 2. p. before the world began.
Heb. 10. 23; 11. 11. faithful that p.

Promote, Num. 22. 17; 24. 11. p. thee to honour.
Prov. 4. 8. wisdom shall p. thee.

Promotion, Ps. 75. 6. p. cometh not from east.
Prov. 3. 35. shame be p. of fools. [many p.

Proof, Acts 1. 3. shewed himself alive by
2 Cor. 2. 9. might know the p. of you.
13. 3. ye seek a p. of Christ.
2 Tim. 4. 5. make full p. of thy ministry.

Proper, 1 Chr. 29. 3. mine own p. good.
Acts 1. 19. in p. tongue, Aceldama.
1 Cor. 7. 7. every man hath p. gift of God.
Heb. 11. 23. Moses was a p. child.

Prophecy, Matt. 13. 14. is fulfilled the p. of Esaias. [fail.
1 Cor. 13. 8. whether there be p., they shall
1 Tim. 4. 14. gift given thee by p.
2 Pet. 1. 19. a more sure word of p.
1. 21. p. came not by the will of man.
Rev. 1. 3. blessed that hear this p.
19. 10. testimony of Jesus is the spirit of p.
22. 19. if any man take from this p.

Prophesy, Num. 11. 25. they p. and did not cease.
1 Ki. 22. 8. he doth not p. good.
Is. 30. 10. p. not to us right things.
Jer. 5. 31. the prophets p. falsely.
14. 14; 23. 25. the prophets p. lies.
Joel 2. 28; Acts 2. 17. your sons shall p.
Amos 2. 12; Mic. 2. 6. saying, p. not.
Amos 3. 8. Lord hath spoken, who can but p.?
Mic. 2. 11. I will p. of wine. [thou Christ.
Matt. 26. 68; Mk. 14. 65; Lk. 22. 64. p. unto us,
Rom. 12. 6. whether p. let us p.
1 Cor. 13. 9. we p. in part.
14. 3. he that p. speaketh unto men.
14. 39. covet to p.

Prophet, Ex. 7. 1. Aaron shall be thy p.
Num. 11. 29. would all the Lord's people were p.!
Deut. 13. 1. if there arise a p. [up a P.
18. 15; Acts 3. 22; 7. 37. the Lord will raise
Deut. 34. 10. there arose not a p. like Moses.
1 Sam. 3. 20. established to be a p.
10. 12; 19. 24. is Saul also among the p.?
1 Ki. 13. 18. I am a p. as thou art.
18. 22. I only remain a p. of the Lord.
22. 7; 2 Ki. 3. 11; 2 Chr. 18. 6. is there not here a p. of the Lord?

Prophet—*Continued.*
2 Ki. 5. 13. if the *p*. had bid thee do some great thing.
1 Chr. 16. 2. , Ps. 105. 15. do my *p*. no harm.
Ps. 74. 9. there is no more any *p*.
Is. 3. 2. the Lord taketh away the *p*.
Jer. 37. 19. where are now your *p*.?   [them.
Ezek. 2. 5; 33. 33. there hath been a *p*. among
Hos. 9. 7. the *p*. is a fool.
Amos 7. 14. I was no *p*., nor *p*. son.
Mic. 3. 11. the *p*. divine for money.
Zech. 1. 5. the *p*., do they live for ever?
Matt. 2. 5. thus it is written by the *p*.
10. 41. he that receiveth a *p*. in the name of a *p*.   [not without honour.
13. 57; Mk. 6. 4; Lk. 4. 24; John 4. 44. a *p*.
Lk. 4. 24. no *p*. is accepted in his own country.
7. 28. there hath not risen a greater *p*. than John.   [Jerusalem.
13. 33. it cannot be that a *p*. perish out of
24. 19. Jesus, who was a *p*. mighty in deed.
John 4. 19. thou art a *p*.
7. 40. of a truth this is the *P*.
Acts 8. 34. of whom speaketh the *p*. this?
13. 15. reading of the law and the *p*.
26. 27. believest thou the *p*.?
1 Cor. 12. 29. are all *p*.?
14. 32. spirits of *p*. are subject to the *p*.
Eph. 2. 20. built on foundation of *p*.
4. 11. he gave some *p*.
Heb. 1. 1. spake to fathers by the *p*.
Jas. 5. 10. take the *p*., who have spoken.
1 Pet. 1. 10. of which salvation the *p*. enquired.
Rev. 22. 9. I am of thy brethren the *p*.
Propitiation, Rom. 3. 25. whom God hath set forth to be a *p*.
1 John 2. 2; 4. 10. the *p*. for our sins.
Proportion, 1 Ki. 7. 36. to the *p*. of every one.
Job 41. 12. not conceal his comely *p*.
Rom. 12. 6. according to *p*. of faith.
Prosper, Gen. 24. 42. if now thou do *p*. my way.
39. 3. the Lord made all Joseph did to *p*.
Num. 14. 41. transgress, but it shall not *p*.
Deut. 28. 29. thou shalt not *p*. in thy ways.
1 Chr. 22. 13. shalt *p*. if thou takest heed.
2 Chr. 20. 20. believe his prophets, so shall ye *p*.
Neh. 2. 20. the God of heaven will *p*. us.
Ps. 1. 3. whatsoever he doeth shall *p*.
73. 12. the ungodly, who *p*. in the world.
122. 6. they shall *p*. that love thee.
Prov. 28. 13. he that covereth sins shall not *p*.
Eccl. 11. 6. knowest not whether shall *p*.
Is. 53. 10. pleasure of Lord shall *p*.
54. 17. no weapon against thee shall *p*.
55. 11. it shall *p*. in the thing I sent.
Jer. 12. 1. wherefore doth way of wicked *p*.?
23. 5. a King shall reign and *p*.
Dan. 11. 27. speak lies, but it shall not *p*.
1 Cor. 16. 2. as God hath *p*. him.
3 John 2. I wish that thou mayest *p*.
Prosperity, Deut. 23. 6. thou shalt not seek their *p*.
1 Sam. 25. 6. say to him that liveth in *p*.
1 Ki. 10. 7. thy wisdom and *p*.
Job 36. 11. spend their days in *p*.
Ps. 30. 6. in my *p*. I said, I shall never be moved.
73. 3. when I saw the *p*. of the wicked.
118. 25. O Lord, send now *p*.
122. 7. peace be within thy walls, and *p*. within thy palaces.

Prosperity—*Continued.*
Prov. 1. 32. the *p*. of fools shall destroy them.
Eccl. 7. 14. in the day of *p*. be joyful.
Jer. 22. 21. I spake to thee in thy *p*.
Lam. 3. 17. I forgat *p*.   [ney *p*.
Prosperous, Gen. 24. 21. Lord made his jour-
39. 2. he was a *p*. man.
Josh. 1. 8. thou shalt make thy way *p*.
Ps. 45. 4. in thy majesty ride *p*.
Rom. 1. 10. might have a *p*. journey.
Protest, Gen. 43. 3. the man did solemnly *p*.
Zech. 3. 6. the angel of the Lord *p*.
1 Cor. 15. 31. I *p*. by rejoicing in Christ.
Proud, Job 26. 12. he smiteth through the *p*.
40. 11. behold every one that is *p*
Ps. 31. 23. rewardeth the *p*. doer.
40. 4. blessed is the man that respecteth not the *p*.
94. 2. render a reward to the *p*.
101. 5. him that hath a *p*. heart.
119. 21. thou hast rebuked the *p*.
123. 4. soul filled with contempt of the *p*.
138. 6. the *p*. he knoweth afar off.
Prov. 6. 17. the Lord hateth a *p*. look.
15. 25. the Lord will destroy the house of the *p*.
21. 4. high look and a *p*. heart is sin.
Eccl. 7. 8. patient better than *p*. in spirit.
Hab. 2. 5. he is a *p*. man.
Mal. 3. 15. we call the *p*. happy.
Lk. 1. 51. he hath scattered the *p*.
1 Tim. 6. 4. he is *p*., knowing nothing.
Jas. 4. 6; 1 Pet. 5. 5. God resisteth the *p*.
See 1 Sam. 2. 3; Ps. 17. 10; Is. 3. 5.
Prove, Ex. 16. 4. I may *p*. them.
20. 20. God is come to *p*. you.
Deut. 8. 2, 16. humble thee, and *p*. thee.
Jud. 6. 39. let me *p*. thee but this once. ₄
1 Sam. 17. 39. I have not *p*. them.   [mon.
1 Ki. 10. 1; 2 Chr. 9. 1. she came to *p*. Solo-
Ps. 17. 3, thou hast *p*. my heart.
26. 2. examine me, O Lord, *p*. me.
95. 9; Heb. 3. 9. when your fathers *p*. me.
Eccl. 2. 1. I will *p*. thee with mirth.
Mal. 3. 10. *p*. me now herewith.
Lk. 14. 19. I go to *p*. them.
John 6. 6. this he said to *p*. him.
Rom. 12. 2. what is that good will of God.
2 Cor. 13. 5. *p*. your own selves.
1 Thes. 5. 21. *p*. all things.   [word.
Proverb, Deut. 28. 37. become a *p*. and a by-
1 Sam. 24. 13. as saith *p*. of the ancients.
Ps. 69. 11. I became a *p*. to them.
Eccl. 12. 9. preacher set in order many *p*.
Hab. 2. 6. take up a *p*. against him.
Lk. 4. 23. ye will surely say this *p*.
John 16. 29. speakest plainly, and speakest no *p*.
2 Pet. 2. 22. it is happened according to the *p*.
Provide, Gen. 22. 8. God will *p*. himself a lamb.
30. 30. when shall I *p*. for mine own house?
Ps. 78. 20. can he *p*. flesh for people?
Matt. 10. 9. *p*. neither gold nor silver.
Lk. 12. 33. *p*. bags that wax not old.
Rom. 12. 17. *p*. things honest.
1 Tim. 5. 8. if any *p*. not for his own house.
Heb. 11. 40. God having *p*. some better thing for us.
Provision, Gen. 42. 25; 45. 21. *p*. for the way.
Ps. 132. 15. I will bless her *p*.
Dan. 1. 5. king appointed a daily *p*.
Rom. 13. 14. make not *p*. for the flesh.

Provoke, Ex. 23. 21. obey his voice, p. him not.
Num. 14. 11. how long will this people p. me?
Deut. 31. 20. p. me, and break my covenant.
Job 12. 6. they that p. God are secure.
Ps. 78. 40. how oft did they p. him!
106. 29. they p. him with their inventions.
Lk. 11. 53. began to urge, and p. him to speak.
Rom. 10. 19; 11. 11. p. to jealousy.
1 Cor. 13. 5. charity is not easily p.
Eph. 6. 4. p. not your children to wrath.
Heb. 3. 16. when they heard, did p.
10. 24. p. to love and good works.
See Ps. 95. 8; Heb. 3. 8, 15.

Prudent, Prov. 12. 16. a p. man covereth shame.
12. 23. a p. man concealeth knowledge.
14. 8. wisdom of the p. is to understand.
15. 5. that regardeth reproof is p.
16. 21. the wise shall be called p.
19. 14. a p. wife is from the Lord.
22. 3; 27. 12. a p. man foreseeth evil. [sight!
Is. 5. 21. woe to them that are p. in own
52. 13. my servant shall deal p.
Jer. 49. 7. is counsel perished from the p.?
Hos. 14. 9. who is p.?
Amos 5. 13. the p. shall keep silence.
Matt. 11. 25; Lk. 10. 21. hid these things from the wise and p. [ing of the p.
1 Cor. 1. 19. bring to nothing the understand-
See Prov. 8. 12; Eph. 1. 8.

Psalms, Lk. 20. 42. David saith in book of p.
24. 44. which were written in p.
Eph. 5. 19. speaking to yourselves in p.
Col. 3. 16. admonishing one another in p.
Jas. 5. 13. is any merry? let him sing p.

Publican, Matt. 5. 46. do not even the p. the same?
11. 19; Lk. 7. 34. a friend of p. [and a p.
Matt. 18. 17. let him be as an heathen man
21. 31. p. go into kingdom of God.
Lk. 18. 10. the one a Pharisee, the other a p.
19. 2. chief among the p. [Lord.

Publish, Deut. 32. 3. I will p. the name of the
2 Sam. 1. 20. p. it not in Askelon.
Ps. 26. 7. may p. with voice of thanksgiving.
68. 11. great was the company that p. it.
Is. 52. 7; Nah. 1. 15. that p. peace.
Jon. 3. 7. he caused it to be p.
Mk. 1. 45; 5. 20. he began to p. it much.
Lk. 8. 39. p. throughout the whole city.
Acts 13. 49. word of the Lord was p.

Pull, Ps. 31. 4. p. me out of net they laid.
Jer. 12. 3. p. them like sheep for slaughter.
Amos 9. 15. shall no more be p. up.
Matt. 7. 4; Lk. 6. 42. p. mote out of thine eye.
Lk. 12. 18. I will p. down my barns.
14. 5. will not p. him out on Sabbath.
2 Cor. 10. 4. mighty to p. down strongholds.
Jude 23. p. them out of the fire.

Pulpit, Neh. 8. 4. stood upon a p. of wood.

Punish, Prov. 17. 26. to p. the just is not good.
Is. 13. 11. I will p. the world for their evil.
26. 21. Lord cometh to p. inhabitants of the earth.
Jer. 21. 14. p. according to your doings.
Acts 4. 21. how they might p. them.
26. 11. I p. them in every synagogue.
2 Thes. 1. 9. p. with everlasting destruction.
2 Pet. 2. 9. unto the day of judgment to be p.

Punishment, Gen. 4. 13. my p. is greater than I can bear.
1 Sam. 28. 10. no p. shall happen to thee.
Job 31. 3. a strange p. to workers of iniquity.
Prov. 19. 19. a man of wrath shall suffer p.

Punishment—*Continued.*
Lam. 3. 39. a man for the p. of his sins.
4. 6. p. is greater than p. of Sodom.
Ezek. 14. 10. bear p. of their iniquity.
Matt. 25. 46. go away into everlasting p.
Heb. 10. 29. of how much sorer p.
1 Pet. 2. 14. for the p. of evil doers. [Heth.

Purchase, Gen. 25. 10. Abraham p. of sons of
Ruth 4. 10. have I p. to be my wife.
Ps. 74. 2. the congregation thou hast p.
Acts 1. 18. this man p. a field. [money.
8. 20. thought gift of God may be p. with
20. 28. he hath p. with his own blood.
Eph. 1. 14. redemption of p. possession.
1 Tim. 3. 13. p. to themselves a good degree.

Pure, 2 Sam. 22. 27; Ps. 18. 26. with the p. thou wilt shew thyself p. [Maker?
Job 4. 17. shall a man be more p. than his
8. 6. if thou wert p. and upright.
11. 4. my doctrine is p.
16. 17. my prayer is p.
25. 5. stars are not p. in his sight.
Ps. 12. 6. the words of the Lord are p.
19. 8. commandment of the Lord is p.
119. 140. thy word is very p.
Prov. 15. 26. words of the p. are pleasant.
20. 9. who can say, I am p. from sin?
30. 5. every word of God is p.
Mic. 6. 11. shall I count them p.?
Zeph. 3. 9. a p. language.
Acts 20. 26. I am p. from blood of all men.
Rom. 14. 20. all things indeed are p.
Phil. 4. 8. whatsoever things are p.
1 Tim. 3. 9; 2 Tim. 1. 3. a p. conscience.
1 Tim. 5. 22. keep thyself p.
Tit. 1. 15. to the p. all things are p.
Heb. 10. 22. bodies washed with p. water.
Jas. 1. 27. p. religion.
3. 17. wisdom from above is first p.
2 Pet. 3. 1. I stir up your p. minds.
1 John 3. 3. purifieth himself even as he is p.
Rev. 22. 1. a p. river of water of life.

Pureness, Job 22. 30. delivered by p. of hands.
Prov. 22. 11. he that loveth p. of heart.
2 Cor. 6. 6. approving ourselves by p.

Purer, Lam. 4. 7. Nazarites p. than snow.
Hab. 1. 13. thou art of p. eyes.

Purge, Ps. 51. 7. p. me with hyssop.
65. 3. transgressions thou shalt p.
Is. 1. 25. purely p. away thy dross.
6. 7. thy sin is p. [not p.
Ezek. 24. 13. I have p. thee, and thou wast
Mal. 3. 3. p. them as gold. [his floor.
Matt. 3. 12; Lk. 3. 17. he will thoroughly p.
John 15. 2. branch that beareth fruit, he p.
1 Cor. 5. 7. p. out the old leaven.
2 Tim. 2. 21. if a man p. himself from these.
Heb. 1. 14. p. your conscience.
10. 2. worshippers once p.
2 Pet 1. 9. hath forgotten he was p.

Purify, Mal. 3. 3. he shall p. sons of Levi.
Tit. 2. 14. p. to himself a peculiar people.
Jas. 4. 8. p. your hearts, ye double-minded.

Purity, 1 Tim. 4. 12. an example in faith, in p.
5. 2. rebuke with all p. [by counsel.

Purpose, Prov. 20. 18. every p. is established
Eccl. 3. 1, 17; 8. 6. a time to every p.
Is. 1. 11. to what p. are your sacrifices?
Acts 11. 23. with p. of heart.
Rom. 8. 28. the called according to his p.
9. 11. that the p. of God might stand.
Eph. 1. 11. according to the p. of him who
3. 11. eternal p. in Christ. [worketh.
1 John 3. 8. for this p. the Son of God.

Purpose, Is. 14. 27. Lord hath *p.,* who shall disannul it?
2 Cor. 1. 17. do I *p.* according to the flesh?
9. 7. every man as he *p.* in his heart.
Purse, Prov. 1. 14. let us have one *p.*
Matt. 10. 9. neither silver nor brass in your *p.*
Mk. 6. 8. take no money in their *p.*
Lk. 10. 4. carry neither *p.* nor scrip.
Pursue, Deut. 19. 6; Josh. 20. 5. lest avenger *p.*
Job 30. 15. terrors *p.* my soul.
Ps. 34. 14. seek peace, and *p.* it.
Prov. 11. 19. he that *p.* evil, *p.* death.
28. 1. wicked flee when no man *p.*
Put, Gen. 3. 15. I will *p.* enmity between.
Ex. 23. 1. *p.* not thine hand with the wicked.
Lev. 26. 8; Deut. 32. 30. *p.* ten thousand to flight.
Num. 23. 5. Lord *p.* word in Balaam's mouth.
Jud. 12. 3; 1 Sam. 28. 21. I *p.* my life in my hands. [offices.
1 Sam. 2. 36. *p.* me into one of the priest's
1 Ki. 9. 3; 11. 36; 14. 21. to *p.* my name there.
1 Chr. 11. 19. *p.* their lives in jeopardy.
Neh. 2. 12. what God *p.* in my heart.
Job 19. 13. hath *p.* my brethren far from me.
Ps. 4. 7. thou hast *p.* gladness in my heart.
8. 6; Eph. 1. 22; Heb. 2. 8. thou hast *p.* all things under his feet. [from me.
Ps. 88. 18. lover and friend hast thou *p.* far
Is. 5. 20. that *p.* darkness for light. [him.
42. 1; Matt. 12. 18. I have *p.* my Spirit upon
Matt. 19. 6; Mk. 10. 9. let not man *p.* asunder.
Mk. 10. 16. he *p.* his hands on them.
John 5. 7. none to *p.* me into the pool.
1 Cor. 15. 25. *p.* all his enemies under his feet.
Eph. 4. 22; Col. 3. 9. *p.* off the old man.
Philem. 18. *p.* that on my account.
Heb. 6. 6. *p.* him to an open shame. [self.
9. 26. to *p.* away sin by the sacrifice of him-
2 Pet. 1. 14. I must *p.* off this tabernacle.
Jude 5. will *p.* you in remembrance.
Rev. 2. 24. *p.* on you none other burden.

QUAKE, Ex. 19. 18. the mount *q.* greatly.
Joel 2. 10. earth shall *q.* before them.
Matt. 27. 51. earth did *q.,* the rocks rent.
Heb. 12. 21. Moses said, I fear and *q.*
Quarrel, 2 Ki. 5. 7. see how he seeketh a *q.*
Mk. 6. 19. Herodias had a *q.* against John.
Col. 3. 13. if any have a *q.* against any.
Queen, 1 Ki. 10. 1; 2 Chr. 9. 1. the *q.* of Sheba.
Ps. 45. 9. the *q.* in gold of Ophir.
Is. 49. 23. their *q.* nursing mothers.
Dan. 5. 10. the *q.* came to banquet house.
Matt. 12. 42; Lk. 11. 31. the *q.* of the south shall rise up in judgment.
Rev. 18. 7. I sit a *q.,* and am no widow.
Quench, Num. 11. 2. the fire was *q.*
2 Sam. 14. 7. they shall *q.* my coal.
21. 17. *q.* not the light of Israel.
Cant. 8. 7. many waters cannot *q.* love.
Is. 34. 10. shall not be *q.* night nor day.
42. 3; Matt. 12. 20. smoking flax shall he not *q.*
Is. 66. 24. neither shall their fire be *q.*
Mk. 9. 44, 46, 48. where the fire is not *q.*
Eph. 6. 16. able to *q.* fiery darts of wicked.
1 Thes. 5. 19. *q.* not the Spirit.
Heb. 11. 34. *q.* the violence of fire. [with *q.*
Question, 1 Ki. 10. 1; 2 Chr. 9. 1. to prove him
Matt. 22. 46. neither durst ask any more *q.*
Mk. 9. 16. what *q.* ye with them?
11. 29. I will ask you one *q.*

Question—*Continued.*
Acts 18. 15. if it be a *q.* of words.
19. 40. in danger to be called in *q.*
1 Cor. 10. 25. asking no *q.* for conscience' sake.
1 Tim. 6. 4. doting about *q.*
2 Tim. 2. 23; Tit. 3. 9. unlearned *q.* avoid.
Quick, Num. 16. 30; Ps. 55. 15. they go down *q.*
Ps. 124. 3. they had swallowed us up *q.*
Is. 11. 3. make him of *q.* understanding.
Acts 10. 42; 2 Tim. 4. 1; 1 Pet. 4. 5. Judge of *q.* and dead. [ful.
Heb. 4. 12. the word of God is *q.* and power-
Quicken, Ps. 71. 20. thou shalt *q.* me again.
80. 18. *q.* us, and we will call on thy name.
119. 25. *q.* me according to thy word.
143. 11. *q.* me, O Lord, for thy name's sake.
Rom. 8. 11. shall *q.* your mortal bodies.
1 Cor. 15. 36. that which thou sowest is not *q.*
Eph. 2. 1. you hath he *q.* who were dead.
2. 5; Col. 2. 13. *q.* us together with Christ.
1 Pet. 3. 18. *q.* by the Spirit. [so *q.*
Quickly, Gen. 27. 20. how hast thou found it
Ex. 32. 8; Deut. 9. 12. have turned *q.* out of the way.
Num. 16. 46. go *q.* to congregation.
Josh. 2. 5. pursue *q.,* overtake them.
Eccl. 4. 12. threefold cord not *q.* broken.
Matt. 5. 25. agree with thine adversary *q.*
John 13. 27. that thou doest, do *q.*
Rev. 2. 5, 16. repent, else I come *q.*
3. 11; 22. 7, 12, 20. behold, I come *q.*
Quiet, Job 21. 23. one dieth being at ease and *q.*
Ps. 107. 30. glad, because they be *q.*
Eccl. 9. 17. words of wise men are heard in *q.*
Is. 7. 4. take heed, and be *q.*
14. 7. the earth is at rest, and is *q.*
32. 18. in *q.* resting-places.
Jer. 49. 23. sorrow on the sea, it cannot be *q.*
Ezek. 16. 42. I will be *q.*
Acts 19. 36. ye ought to be *q.*
1 Thes. 4. 11. study to be *q.*
1 Tim. 2. 2. a *q.* and peaceable life.
1 Pet. 3. 4. ornament of a meek and *q.* spirit.
Quietness, Jud. 8. 28. the country was in *q.*
Prov. 17. 1. better a dry morsel and *q.*
Eccl. 4. 6. better a handful with *q.*
Is. 30. 15. in *q.* and confidence shall be your strength.
32. 17. effect of righteousness, *q.*
Acts 24. 2. by thee we enjoy great *q.*
2 Thes. 3. 12. exhort that with *q.* they work.
Quit, Ex. 21. 19. that smote him be *q.*
Josh. 2. 20. we will be *q.* of this oath.
1 Sam. 4. 9; 1 Cor. 16. 13. *q.* you like men.
Quiver, Ps. 127. 5. the man that hath *q.* full.
Is. 49. 2. polished shaft, in his *q.*
Jer. 5. 16. their *q.* is as an open sepulchre.
Hab. 3. 16. my lips *q.* at the voice.

RACE, Ps. 19. 5. a strong man to run a *r.*
Eccl. 9. 11. the *r.* is not to the swift.
1 Cor. 9. 24. they which run in a *r.*
Heb. 12. 1. run with patience the *r.*
Rage, 2 Ki. 5. 12. Naaman turned away in a *r.*
19. 27; Is. 37. 28. I know thy *r.*
Ps. 2. 1; Acts 4. 25. why do the heathen *r.?*
Prov. 6. 34. jealousy is the *r.* of a man.
14. 16. the fool *r.,* and is confident.
29. 9. whether he *r.* or laugh.
Raging, Ps. 89. 9. thou rulest the *r.* of the sea.
Prov. 20. 1. strong drink is *r.*
Jon. 1. 15. the sea ceased from her *r.*
Lk. 8. 24. he rebuked the *r.* of the water.
Jude 13. *r.* waves of the sea.

Rags, Prov. 23. 21. shall clothe a man with r.
Is. 64. 6. our righteousness as filthy r.
Jer. 38. 11. took rotten r.

Raiment, Gen. 27. 15. goodly r.
28. 20. if the Lord will give me r.
Deut. 8. 4. thy r. waxed not old.
24. 17. nor take a widow's r. to pledge.
2 Ki. 5. 5. ten changes of r.
Job 27. 16. though he prepare r. as clay.
Ps. 45. 14. be brought to the king in r. of needlework.
Is. 63. 3. I will stain all my r.
Zech. 3. 4. I will clothe thee with r.
Matt. 3. 4. a r. of camel's hair.
6. 25; Lk. 12. 23. the body more than r.
Matt. 11. 8; Lk. 7. 25. a man clothed in soft r.
Matt. 17. 2; Mk. 9. 3; Lk. 9. 29. his r. white as light.
Lk. 23. 34; John 19. 24. they parted his r.
1 Tim. 6. 8. having food and r., let us be content.
Jas. 2. 2. a poor man in vile r.
Rev. 3. 18. buy white r.

Rain, Gen. 8. 2. r. from heaven was restrained.
Lev. 26. 4; Deut. 11. 14; 28. 12. r. in due season.
Deut. 11. 11. drinketh of the r. of heaven.
32. 2. my doctrine shall drop as the r.
2 Sam. 23. 4. clear shining after r.
1 Ki. 17. 1. there shall be no dew nor r.
18. 41. a sound of abundance of r.
Ezra 10. 9. a time of much r.
Job 5. 10. who giveth r. upon the earth.
28. 26. he made a decree for the r.
37. 6. to small r. and to great r.
38. 28. hath the r. a father?
Ps. 72. 6. like r. on the mown grass.
Prov. 25. 14. like clouds without r.
25. 23. the north wind driveth away r.
26. 1. as r. in harvest.
Eccl. 11. 3. if the clouds be full of r.
12. 2. nor clouds return after the r.
Cant. 2. 11. the r. is over and gone.
Is. 4. 6. a covert from storm and r.
30. 23. then shall he give the r.
55. 10. as the r. cometh down from heaven.
Hos. 6. 3. he shall come unto us as the r.
Matt. 5. 45. he sendeth r. on just and unjust.
7. 25. the r. descended, and the floods came.
Acts 14. 17. did good, and gave us r.
Heb. 6. 7. earth drinketh in the r.
See Prov. 27. 15.

Rain, Gen. 2. 5. Lord had not caused it to r.
Ex. 16. 4. I will r. bread from heaven.
Ps. 11. 6. upon the wicked he shall r. snares.
78. 24, 27. and r. down manna.
Ezek. 38. 22. I will r. an overflowing r.
Hos. 10. 12. till he come and r. righteousness.
Jas. 5. 17. Elias prayed it might not r.

Raise, Deut. 18. 15; Acts 3. 22. Lord will r. up a prophet.   [dust.
1 Sam. 2. 8; Ps. 113. 7. he r. poor out of the
Ps. 145. 14; 146. 8. he r. those that be bowed down.
Is. 44. 26. I will r. up decayed places.
Hos. 6. 2. in third day he will r. us up.
Matt. 11. 5; Lk. 7. 22. dead are r. up.
John 2. 19. in three days I will r. it up.
6. 40. I will r. him up at the last day.
Acts 26. 8. why incredible that God should r. the dead?
Rom. 4. 25. was r. again for our justification.
6. 4. as Christ was r. from the dead.

Raise—Continued.
1 Cor. 6. 14. God will r. us up by his power.
2 Cor. 1. 9. trust in God who r. the dead.
4. 14. he shall r. us up by Jesus.
Eph. 2. 6. hath r. us up together.   [r. him.
Heb. 11. 19. accounting that God was able to
Jas. 5. 15. the Lord shall r. him up.
1 Pet. 1. 21. believe in God that r. him.

Ransom, Ex. 21. 30. he shall give for the r. of his life.
30. 12. give every man a r. for his soul.
Job 33. 24. I have found a r.
36. 18. a great r. cannot deliver thee.
Ps. 49. 7. nor give to God a r. for him.
Prov. 6. 35. he will not regard any r.
13. 8. the r. of a man's life are his riches.
Is. 35. 10. the r. of the Lord shall return.
43. 3. I gave Egypt for thy r.
Hos. 13. 14. I will r. them from the grave.
Matt. 20. 28; Mk. 10. 45. to give his life a r. for many.
1 Tim. 2. 6. who gave himself a r. for all.

Rash, Eccl. 5. 2. be not r. with thy mouth.
Acts 19. 36. be quiet, do nothing r.

Rather, Matt. 10. 6. go r. to the lost sheep of Israel.
25. 9. go r. to them that sell.
Mk. 5. 26. but r. grew worse.
Rom. 8. 34. yea r. that is risen again.

Reach, Gen. 11. 4. tower may r. to heaven.
John 20. 27. r. hither thy finger.
2 Cor. 10. 13. a measure to r. unto you.
Phil. 3. 13. r. forth to those things before.

Read, Ex. 24. 7. r. in audience of people.
Deut. 17. 19. the king shall r. therein.
Is. 34. 16. seek out book of Lord, and r.
Matt. 12. 3; Mk. 2. 25; Lk. 6. 3. have ye not r.?
Lk. 4. 16. Jesus stood up to r.   [ye r.
2 Cor. 1. 13. none other things than what
3. 2. our epistle, known and r.
1 Tim. 4. 13. give attendance to r.
Rev. 1. 3. blessed is he that r.

Ready, Deut. 26. 5. a Syrian r. to perish.
Neh. 9. 17. a God r. to pardon.
Job 29. 13. blessing of him r. to perish.
Ps. 38. 17. I am r. to halt.
86. 5. Lord good, and r. to forgive.
Prov. 31. 6. strong drink to him r. to perish.
Eccl. 5. 1. be more r. to hear.
Is. 27. 13. shall come that were r. to perish.
32. 4. tongue of stammerers r. to speak plainly.
Matt. 22. 4; Lk. 14. 17. all things are r.
Matt. 24. 44; Lk. 12. 40. be ye also r.
Matt. 25. 10. they that were r. went in.
Mk. 14. 38. the spirit is r., flesh weak.
Lk. 22. 33. I am r. to go with thee.
John 7. 6. your time is alway r.
Acts 21. 13. I am r. not to be bound only.
Rom. 1. 15. I am r. to preach the Gospel at Rome.
2 Cor. 8. 19. declaration of your r. mind.
1 Tim. 6. 18. r. to distribute.
2 Tim. 4. 6. I am now r. to be offered.
Tit. 3. 1. r. to every good work.
Heb. 8. 13. old is r. to vanish away.
1 Pet. 1. 5. r. to be revealed in last time.
3. 15. be r. always to give an answer.
Rev. 3. 2. the things that are r. to die.
See Acts 17. 11; 2 Cor. 8. 11.

Reap, Lev. 19. 9. when ye r. harvest.
25. 11. in jubilee ye shall not sow nor r.
Job 24. 6. they r. every one his corn.
Ps. 126. 5. that sow in tears, r. in joy.

Reap—*Continued.*
Eccl. 11. 4. he that regardeth clouds shall not *r.*
Hos. 8. 7. shall *r.* the whirlwind.
10. 12. sow in righteousness, *r.* in mercy.
Mic. 6. 15. thou shalt sow, but not *r.*
Matt. 6. 26 ; Lk. 12. 24. they sow not, neither *r.*
Matt. 25. 26 ; Lk. 19. 22. I *r.* where I sowed not.
John 4. 38. to *r.* that whereon ye bestowed no labour.   [sparingly.
2 Cor. 9. 6. that soweth sparingly, shall *r.*
Gal. 6. 7. that shall he also *r.*
Jas. 5. 4. cries of labourers who *r.*
Rev. 14. 15. thrust in sickle and *r.*

Reason, Prov. 26. 16. seven men that can render a *r.*
Eccl. 7. 25. to search out the *r.* of things.
Rom. 8. 20. by *r.* of him who hath subjected.
1 Pet. 3. 15. a *r.* of the hope that is in you.

Reason, 1 Sam. 12. 7. that I may *r.* with you.
Job 9. 14. choose words to *r.* with him.
13. 3. I desire to *r.* with God.
Is. 1. 18. let us *r.* together.   [selves?
Matt. 16. 8 ; Mk. 2. 8. why *r.* ye among your-
Lk. 5. 22. what *r.* ye in your hearts?
24. 15. while they *r.* Jesus drew near.
Acts 24. 25. as he *r.* of righteousness.

Rebel, Num. 14. 9. only *r.* not against the Lord.
1 Sam. 12. 15. if ye will not obey Lord, but *r.*
Neh. 2. 19. will ye *r.* against the king?
Ps. 107. 11. they *r.* against words of God.
Is. 1. 2. have nourished children, and they *r.*
63. 10. they *r.*, and vexed his Holy Spirit.
Hos. 13. 16. Samaria *r.* against God.   [Lord.

Rebellious, Deut. 9. 7 ; 31. 27. *r.* against the
Ps. 66. 7. let not the *r.* exalt themselves.
78. 8. a *r.* generation.
Is. 65. 2. have spread my hands to a *r.* people.
Jer. 5. 23. this people hath a *r.* heart.
Ezek. 24. 3. utter parable to the *r.* house.
See 1 Sam. 15. 23 ; Job 34. 37 ; Prov. 17. 11. -

Rebuke, Deut. 28. 20. Lord shall send on thee *r.*
2 Ki. 19. 3 ; Is. 37. 3. this is a day of *r.*
Ps. 18. 15. at thy *r.* blast of nostrils.
80. 16. perish at *r.* of thy countenance.
104. 7. at thy *r.* they fled.
Prov. 13. 1. a scorner heareth not *r.*
27. 5. open *r.* is better than secret love.
Eccl. 7. 5. better to hear *r.* of wise.
Is. 30. 17. thousand flee at *r.* of one.
Phil. 2. 15. without *r.*

Rebuke, Ps. 6. 1 ; 38. 1. *r.* me not in anger.
Prov. 9. 8. a wise man, and he will love thee.
28. 23. he that *r.* shall find favour.
Is. 2. 4 ; Mic. 4. 3. he shall *r.* many nations.
Zech. 3. 2 ; Jude 9. the Lord *r.* thee.
Matt. 8. 26 ; Mk. 4. 39 ; Lk. 8. 24. he *r.* the wind.
Matt. 16. 22 ; Mk. 8. 32. Peter began to *r.* him.
Lk. 17. 3. if brother trespass, *r.* him.
19. 39. *r.* thy disciples.
1 Tim. 5. 1. *r.* not an elder.
2 Tim. 4. 2. *r.* with all long-suffering.
Tit. 1. 13 ; 2. 15. *r.* sharply.
Heb. 12. 5. nor faint when thou art *r.*
Rev. 3. 19. as many as I love, I *r.*   [*r.* evil?
Receive, Job 2. 10. shall we *r.* good, and not
22. 22. *r.* the law from his mouth.
Ps. 6. 9. the Lord will *r.* my prayer.
24. 5. he shall *r.* blessing from the Lord.
49. 15. God shall *r.* me.

Receive—*Continued.*
Ps. 68. 18. hast *r.* gifts for men.
73. 24. afterwards *r.* me into glory.
Prov. 2. 1. if thou wilt *r.* my words.
Hos. 14. 2. *r.* us graciously.
Matt. 11. 14. if ye will *r.* it, this is Elias.
19. 12. he that is able to *r.* it, let him *r.* it.
21. 22. whatsoever ye ask, believing, ye shall *r.*
Mk. 4. 16 ; Lk. 8. 13. hear and *r.* the word with gladness.
Mk. 11. 24. when ye pray, believe ye *r.*
16. 19 ; Acts 1. 9. he was *r.* up into heaven.
Lk. 16. 9. *r.* you into everlasting habitations.
23. 41. we *r.* reward of our deeds.
John 1. 12. as many as *r.* him.
3. 27. a man can *r.* nothing, except.
5. 43. come in his own name, him ye will *r.*
16. 24. ask, and ye shall *r.*
Acts 2. 38. ye shall *r.* gift of Holy Ghost.
10. 43. shall *r.* remission of sins.
20. 35. more blessed to give than *r.*
Rom. 5. 11. by whom we have *r.* atonement.
14. 1. him that is weak in faith *r.* ye.
1 Cor. 3. 6. every man shall *r.* his own reward.   [livered.
11. 23. I *r.* of the Lord that which I de-
2 Cor. 5. 10. every one may *r.* things done in his body.
Col. 3. 25. he shall *r.* for the wrong done.
Jas. 4. 3. ye ask and *r.* not, because.
1 John 3. 22. whatsoever we ask, we *r.*
Rev. 3. 3. remember how thou hast *r.*
Reckon, Lev. 25. 50. he shall *r.* with him that bought him.
Ps. 40. 5. thy thoughts cannot be *r.* up.
Matt. 18. 24. when he had begun to *r.*
25. 19. lord of servants cometh, and *r.* with them.
Rom. 4. 4. the reward is not *r.* of grace.
6. 11. *r.* yourselves dead to sin.
8. 18. I *r.* the sufferings of this present time.
Recompence, Deut. 32. 35. to me belongeth *r.*
Job 15. 31. vanity shall be his *r.*
Prov. 12. 14. *r.* shall be rendered.
Is. 35. 4. God will come with a *r.*
Hos. 9. 7. the days of *r.* are come.
Joel 3. 4. will ye render me a *r.*?
Lk. 14. 12. and a *r.* be made thee.
Rom. 11. 9. let their table be made a *r.*
2 Cor. 6. 13. now for a *r.*, be ye also enlarged.
Heb. 10. 35. great *r.* of reward.
Recompense, Num. 5. 7. he shall *r.* his trespass.
Ruth 2. 12. the Lord *r.* thy work.
2 Sam. 3. 39. 36. why should the king *r.* me?
Job 34. 33. he will *r.* it whether.
Prov. 20. 22. say not, I will *r.* evil.
Is. 65. 6. I will *r.*, even *r.* into their bosom.
Jer. 16. 18. I will *r.* their iniquity.
25. 14 ; Hos. 12. 2. I will *r.* them according to their deeds.
Lk. 14. 14. for they cannot *r.* thee.
Rom. 12. 17. *r.* to no man evil for evil.
Heb. 10. 30. that hath said, I will *r.*
Reconcile, 1 Sam. 29. 4. should he *r.* himself?
Matt. 5. 24. first be *r.* to thy brother.
Rom. 5. 10. if when enemies we were *r.* to God.
2 Cor. 5. 20. be ye *r.* to God.
Eph. 2. 16. that he might *r.* both to God.
Col. 1. 20. to *r.* all things to himself.
See 2 Cor. 5. 18 ; Heb. 2. 17.

Record, Ex. 20. 24. in places where I *r*. my name.
Deut. 30. 19. I call heaven and earth to *r*.
Job 16. 19. my *r*. is on high.
John 1. 32, 34. bare *r*.
   8. 13. thou bearest *r*. of thyself.
   19. 35. he that saw bare *r*., and his *r*. is true.
Rom. 10. 2. I bear them *r*. they have a zeal
2 Cor. 1. 23. I call God for a *r*.   [of God.
Phil. 1. 8. God is my *r*. how greatly I long.
1 John 5. 7. three that bear *r*.
   5. 11. this is the *r*. that God hath given.
3 John 12. we bear *r*., and our *r*. is true.

Recover, 2 Ki. 1. 2. enquire whether I shall *r*.
   5. 3. the prophet would *r*. him.
Ps. 39. 13. that I may *r*. strength.
Is. 38. 16. *r*. me, and make me live.
Jer. 8. 22. why is not my people *r*. ?
Mk. 16. 18. lay hands on sick, and they shall *r*.
Lk. 4. 18. *r*. of sight to the blind.
2 Tim. 2. 26. may *r*. themselves.

Red, Gen. 25. 30. *r*. pottage.
   49. 12. his eyes shall be *r*. with wine.
2 Ki. 3. 22. water *r*. as blood.
Ps. 75. 8. the wine is *r*.
Prov. 23. 31. look not on wine when *r*.
Is. 1. 18. though your sins be *r*. like crimson.
   27. 2. a vineyard of *r*. wine.
   63. 2. wherefore art thou *r*. in apparel?
Matt. 16. 2. fair weather, for the sky is *r*.

Redeem, Ex. 6. 6. I will *r*. you.
   15. 13. people whom thou hast *r*.
2 Sam. 7. 23. what nation like Israel whom God went to *r*.?
Neh. 5. 5. nor is it in our power to *r*. them.
Job 5. 20. in famine he shall *r*. thee.
   6. 23. *r*. me from hand of mighty.
Ps. 25. 22. *r*. Israel out of all his troubles.
   26. 11. *r*. me, and be merciful to me.
   34. 22. the Lord *r*. the soul of his servants.
   49. 15. God will *r*. my soul from the grave.
   72. 14. he shall *r*. their soul from deceit.
   130. 8. he shall *r*. Israel.
Is. 35. 9. the *r*. shall walk there.
   44. 22. return to me, I have *r*. thee.
   50. 2. is my hand shortened, that it cannot *r*.?
   51. 11. the *r*. of the Lord shall return.
   52. 3. ye shall be *r*. without money.
Hos. 13. 14. I will *r*. them from death.
Lk. 1. 68. Lord hath visited and *r*. his people.
   24. 21. he who should have *r*. Israel.
Gal. 3. 13. *r*. us from the curse of the law.
   4. 5. to *r*. them that were under the law.
Tit. 2. 14. he might *r*. us from all iniquity.
1 Pet. 1. 18. not *r*. with corruptible things.
Rev. 5. 9. thou hast *r*. us to God.

Redeemer, Job 19. 25. I know that my R. liveth.
Ps. 19. 14. O Lord, my strength, and my R.
   78. 35. the high God was their R.
Prov. 23. 11. their R. is mighty.
Is. 49. 26; 60. 16. I the Lord am thy R.
   59. 20. the R. shall come to Zion.
   63. 16. thou art our Father, our R.
Jer. 50. 34. their R. is strong.

Redemption, Lev. 25. 51. give price of his *r*.
Ps. 49. 8. the *r*. of their soul is precious.
   111. 9. he sent *r*. to his people.
   130. 7. with Lord is plenteous *r*.
Lk. 2. 38. them that looked for *r*.
   21. 28. your *r*. draweth nigh.
Rom. 8. 23. the *r*. of our body.
Eph. 1. 7; Col. 1. 14. have *r*. through his blood.
Eph. 4. 30. ye are sealed unto the day of *r*.
Heb. 9. 12. obtained eternal *r*. for us.

Reformation, Heb. 9. 10. until the time of *r*.

Refrain, Gen. 45. 1. Joseph could not *r*. him-
Job 7. 11. I will not *r*. my mouth.   [self.
Ps. 40. 9. I have not *r*. my lips.
   119. 101. I *r*. my feet from every evil way.
Prov. 1. 15. *r*. thy foot from their path.
   10. 19. he that *r*. his lips is wise.
Is. 64. 12. wilt thou *r*. thyself, O Lord?
Acts 5. 38. *r*. from these men.
1 Pet. 3. 10. *r*. his tongue from evil.

Refresh, Ex. 31. 17. on the seventh day Lord rested, and was *r*.
1 Ki. 13. 7. come home, and *r*. thyself.
Job 32. 20. I will speak, that I may be *r*.
Acts 3. 19. when times of *r*. shall come.
Rom. 15. 32. I may with you be *r*.

Refuge, Deut. 33. 27. the eternal God is thy *r*.
Josh. 20. 3. *r*. from avenger of blood.
2 Sam. 22. 3. my high tower and *r*.
Ps. 9. 9. Lord will be a *r*. for the oppressed.
   14. 6. the Lord is his *r*.
   59. 16. my *r*. in the day of trouble.
   71. 7; 142. 5. my strong *r*.
   104. 18. high hills a *r*. for wild goats.
Is. 28. 17. hail shall sweep away *r*. of lies.
Heb. 6. 18. who have fled for *r*.

Refuse, Ex. 16. 28. how long *r*. ye to keep my commandments?
Job 34. 33. whether thou *r*. or choose.
Ps. 118. 22. the stone which the builders *r*.
Prov. 1. 24. I have called, and ye *r*.
   8. 33. be wise, and *r*. it not.   [soul.
   15. 32. he that *r*. instruction despiseth his
   21. 25. his hands *r*. to labour.
Is. 7. 15, 16. may know to *r*. the evil.
Jer. 8. 5. they *r*. to return.
   13. 10. this people *r*. to hear my words.
   31. 15. Rachel *r*. to be comforted.
   38. 21. if thou *r*. to go forth.
Hos. 11. 5. because they *r*. to return.
Zech. 7. 11. they *r*. to hearken.
Acts 7. 35. this Moses whom they *r*.
   25. 11. I *r*. not to die.
1 Tim. 4. 4. nothing to be *r*.
   4. 7. *r*. profane fables.   [speaketh.
Heb. 12. 25. see that ye *r*. not him that
See Lam. 3. 45; Amos 8. 6.

Regard, Ex. 5. 9. let them not *r*. vain words
Deut. 10. 17. that *r*. not persons.
   28. 50. not *r*. person of the old.
1 Ki. 18. 29. nor any that *r*.
Job 3. 4. let not God *r*. it from above.
   4. 20. they perish without any *r*. it.
   34. 19. nor *r*. the rich more than the poor.
   35. 13. nor will the Almighty *r*. it.
   36. 21. *r*. not iniquity.   [Lord.
Ps. 28. 5; Is. 5. 12. they *r*. not works of the
Ps. 31. 6. that *r*. lying vanities.
   66. 18. if I *r*. iniquity in my heart.
   102. 17. he will *r*. the prayer of the destitute.
Prov. 1. 24. no man *r*.
   5. 2. thou mayest *r*. discretion.
   6. 35. he will not *r*. any ransom.
   12. 10. righteous *r*. life of his beast.
   13. 18; 15. 5. he that *r*. reproof.
Lam. 4. 16. the Lord will no more *r*. them.
Dan. 11. 37. *r*. God of his fathers, nor *r*. any god.
Mal. 1. 9. will he *r*. your persons?   [of men.
Matt. 22. 16; Mk. 12. 14. thou *r*. not the person
Lk. 18. 4. fear not God, nor *r*. man.   [Lord.
Rom. 14. 6. he that *r*. the day, *r*. it to the
Phil. 2. 30. not *r*. his life.
Heb. 8. 9. I *r*. them not, saith the Lord.

116

Rehearse, Ex. 17. 14. *r.* it in ears of Joshua.
Jud. 5. 11. *r.* righteous acts of the Lord.
Acts 14. 27. they *r.* all that God had done.
Reign, Gen. 37. 8. shalt thou indeed *r.* over us?
Ex. 15. 18; Ps. 146. 10. the Lord shall *r.* for
    ever.   [you.
Lev. 26. 17. they that hate you shall *r.* over
Deut. 15. 6. thou shalt *r.* over many nations.
Jud. 9. 8. the trees said, *r.* thou over us.
1 Sam. 12. 12. a king shall *r.* over us.
2 Sam. 3. 21. thou mayest *r.* over all.
Job 34. 30. that the hypocrite *r.* not.
Ps. 47. 8. God *r.* over the heathen.
93. 1; 96. 10; 97. 1; 99. 1. the Lord *r.*
Prov. 8. 15. by me kings *r.*
30. 22. a servant when he *r.*
Eccl. 4. 14. out of prison he cometh to *r.*
Is. 24. 23. Lord of hosts shall *r.* in Zion.
32. 1. a king shall *r.* in righteousness.
52. 7. saith unto Zion, thy God *r.*
Jer. 22. 15. shalt thou *r.* because?
23. 5. a king shall *r.* and prosper.
Mic. 4. 7. the Lord shall *r.* over them.
Lk. 19. 14. we will not have this man to *r.*
    over us.
Rom. 5. 17. shall *r.* in life by Jesus Christ.
6. 12. let not sin *r.* in your bodies.
1 Cor. 4. 8. I would to God ye did *r.*
15. 25. he must *r.* till.   [him.
2 Tim. 2. 12. if we suffer, we shall also *r.* with
Rev. 5. 10. we shall *r.* on the earth.
11. 15. he shall *r.* for ever and ever.
19. 6. the Lord God omnipotent *r.*
20. 6. shall *r.* with him a thousand years.
22. 5. they shall *r.* for ever and ever.
Reins, Job 16. 13. he cleaveth my *r.* asunder.
19. 27. though my *r.* be consumed.
Ps. 7. 9. God trieth the hearts and *r.*
16. 7. my *r.* instruct me in night.
26. 2. examine me, try my *r.*
73. 21. thus was I pricked in my *r.*
139. 13. thou hast possessed my *r.*
Prov. 23. 16. my *r.* shall rejoice.   [his *r.*
Is. 11. 5. faithfulness shall be the girdle of
Jer. 11. 20. O Lord, that triest the *r.*
12. 2. thou art far from their *r.*
20. 12. seest the *r.*
Lam. 3. 13. arrows to enter into my *r.*
Rev. 2. 23. I am he who searcheth the *r.*
Reject, 1 Sam. 10. 19. ye have this day *r.* God.
15. 26. Lord hath *r.* thee from being king.
Is. 53. 3. he is *r.* of men.
Hos. 4. 6. thou hast *r.* knowledge.
Matt. 21. 42; Mk. 12. 10; Lk. 20. 17. stone
    which builders *r.*
Mk. 7. 9. ye *r.* the commandment of God.
8. 31; Lk. 9. 22. he shall be *r.* of the elders.
Lk. 17. 25. be *r.* of this generation.
John 12. 48. he that *r.* me, and receiveth not
    my words.
Heb. 12. 17. have inherited blessing, he was *r.*
Rejoice, Deut. 12. 7. shall *r.* in all ye put your
    hand to.
26. 11. thou shalt *r.* in every good thing.
28. 63; 30. 9. the Lord will *r.* over you.
1 Sam. 2. 1. because I *r.* in thy salvation.
1 Chr. 16. 10; Ps. 105. 3. let the heart of them
    r. that seek the Lord.
2 Chr. 6. 41. let thy saints *r.* in goodness.
20. 27; Neh. 12. 43. the Lord had made
    them to *r.*   [great.
Job 31. 25. if I *r.* because my wealth was
39. 21. the horse *r.* in his strength.
Ps. 2. 11. *r.* with trembling.

Rejoice—*Continued.*
Ps. 5. 11. let all that trust in thee *r.*
9. 14. I will *r.* in thy salvation.
14. 7. Jacob shall *r.*
19. 5. *r.* as a strong man to run a race.
33. 21. our heart shall *r.* in him.
35. 19. let not mine enemies *r.* over me.
38. 16. hear me, lest they should *r.* over me.
51. 8. the bones which thou hast broken
    may *r.*
63. 7. in shadow of thy wings will I *r.*
68. 3. let the righteous *r.*
85. 6. that thy people may *r.* in thee.
89. 16. in thy name shall they *r.* all the day.
96. 11. let the heavens *r.*
97. 1. let the earth *r.*
104. 31. the Lord shall *r.* in his works.
107. 42. the righteous shall see it, and *r.*
119. 162. I *r.* at thy word.
149. 2. let Israel *r.* in him that made him.
Prov. 2. 14. who *r.* to do evil.
5. 18. *r.* with the wife of thy youth.
23. 15. if thine heart be wise, my heart
    shall *r.*
24. 17. *r.* not when thine enemy falleth.
29. 2. when righteous are in authority
    people *r.*
Eccl. 2. 10. my heart *r.* in all my labour.
3. 12. for a man to *r.* and do good.
3. 22; 5. 19. than that a man should *r.*
11. 9. *r.*, O young man, in thy youth.
Is. 9. 3. as men *r.* when they divide the spoil.
24. 8. noise of them that *r.* endeth.
29. 19. poor among men shall *r.*
35. 1. the desert shall *r.*
62. 5. as the bridegroom *r.* over the bride.
65. 13. my servants shall *r.*, but ye.
66. 14. when ye see this, your heart shall *r.*
Jer. 32. 41. I will *r.* over them to do them
    good.
Ezek. 7. 12. let not the buyer *r.*
Hos. 9. 1. *r.* not, O Israel, for joy.
Amos 6. 13. which *r.* in a thing of nought.
Mic. 7. 8. *r.* not against me, O enemy.
Hab. 3. 18. yet I will *r.* in the Lord.
Zeph. 3. 17. the Lord will *r.* over thee.
Zech. 9. 9. *r.* greatly, O daughter of Zion.
Matt. 18. 13. he *r.* more of that sheep.
Lk. 1. 14. many shall *r.* at his birth.
6. 23. *r.* ye in that day, and leap for joy.
10. 20. in this *r.* not, but rather *r.* because.
15. 6, 9. *r.* with me.
John 4. 36. and he that reapeth may *r.*
5. 35. willing for a season to *r.*
14. 28. if ye loved me, ye would *r.*
16. 20. ye shall weep, but the world shall *r.*
Acts 2. 26. therefore did my heart *r.*
Rom. 5. 2. *r.* in hope of glory of God.
12. 15. *r.* with them that do *r.*
1 Cor. 7. 30. they that *r.* as though they *r.* not.
13. 6. *r.* not in iniquity, but *r.* in the truth.
Phil. 1. 18. 'I do *r.*, yea, and will *r.*
2. 17. I joy and *r.* with you all.
3. 1; 4. 4. *r.* in the Lord.
1 Thes. 5. 16. *r.* evermore.
Jas. 1 9. let the brother of low degree *r.*
1 Pet. 1. 8. *r.* with joy unspeakable..
Rejoicing, 1 Ki. 1. 45. came up from thence *r.*
Job 8. 21. till he fill thy lips with *r.*
Ps. 19. 8. statutes right, *r.* the heart.
107. 22. declare his works with *r.*
118. 15. voice of *r.* is in tabernacles of
    righteous.
126. 6. shall doubtless come again with *r.*

Rejoicing—*Continued.*
Prov. 8. 31. *r.* in habitable part of earth.
Is. 65. 18. I create Jerusalem a *r.*
Jer. 15. 16. thy word was the *r.* of my heart.
Zeph. 2. 15. this is the *r.* city.
Lk. 15. 5. layeth it on his shoulders *r.*
Acts 5. 41. *r.* that they were counted worthy.
8. 39. went on his way *r.*
Rom. 12. 12. *r.* in hope.
2 Cor. 6. 10. as sorrowful, yet always *r.*
1 Thes. 2. 19. what is our crown of *r.?*
Heb. 3. 6. the *r.* of hope firm to the end.

Relieve, Lev. 25. 35. if brother be poor, thou
shalt *r.* him.
Ps. 146. 9. he *r.* the fatherless.
Is. 1. 17. *r.* the oppressed.
Lam. 1. 16. comforter that should *r.* my soul
is far from me.

Religion, Acts 26. 5. straitest sect of our *r.*
Gal. 1. 14. profited in the Jews' *r.*
Jas. 1. 27. pure *r.* and undefiled before God.

Remain, Gen. 8. 22. while earth *r.*
Ex. 12. 10. let nothing *r.* until the morning.
Deut. 21. 23. his body shall not *r.* on tree.
Josh. 13. 1. *r.* yet much land to be possessed.
1 Ki. 18. 22. I, even I only, *r.* a prophet.
1 Chr. 13. 14. ark *r.* in the family of Obed-
edom.
Job 21. 32. yet shall he *r.* in the tomb.
Prov. 2. 21. the perfect shall *r.* in the land.
Eccl. 2. 9. my wisdom *r.* with me.
Matt. 11. 23. it would have *r.* until this day.
John 6. 12. gather up the fragments that *r.*
Acts 5. 4. whiles it *r.,* was it not thine own?
1 Thes. 4. 15. we who *r.* unto the coming of
the Lord.
Heb. 4. 9. there *r.* a rest to the people of God.
10. 26. there *r.* no more sacrifice for sins.
Rev. 3. 2. strengthen things which *r.* [day.

Remember, Gen. 41. 9. I do *r.* my faults this
Ex. 20. 8. *r.* the Sabbath day to keep it holy.
Num. 15. 39. *r.* all the commandments of
Lord.
Deut. 8. 2. *r.* all the way the Lord led thee.
8. 18. thou shalt *r.* the Lord thy God.
32. 7. *r.* the days of old.   [works.
1 Chr. 16. 12; Ps. 105. 5. *r.* his marvellous
Job 10. 9. *r.* thou hast made me as clay.
24. 20. the sinner shall be no more *r.*
Ps. 20. 7. we will *r.* the name of the Lord.
25. 6. *r.* thy mercies.
63. 6. when I *r.* thee upon my bed.
79. 8. *r.* not against us former iniquities.
89. 47. *r.* how short my time is.
105. 8. he hath *r.* his covenant for ever.
136. 23. who *r.* us in our low estate.
Eccl. 12. 1. *r.* now thy Creator.
Cant. 1. 4. we will *r.* thy love.
Is. 43. 18; 46. 9. *r.* ye not the former things.
Jer. 31. 20, I do earnestly *r.* him still.
Lam. 1. 9. she *r.* not her last end.
Ezek. 16. 61; 20. 43; 36. 31. then shalt thou
r. thy ways.
Hab. 3. 2. in wrath *r.* mercy.
Matt. 26. 75. Peter *r.* the word of Jesus.
Lk. 1. 72. to *r.* his holy covenant.
16. 25. *r.* that thou in thy lifetime.
17. 32. *r.* Lot's wife.   [thy kingdom.
23. 42. Lord, *r.* me when thou comest into
John 15. 20. *r.* the word that I said unto you.
Acts 20. 35. *r.* the words of the Lord Jesus.
Gal. 2. 10. that we should *r.* the poor.
Eph. 2. 11. *r.* that being in time past Gentiles.
Col. 4. 18. *r.* my bonds.

Remember—*Continued.*
2 Tim. 2. 8. *r.* that Jesus Christ was raised
from the dead.
Heb. 8. 12. their iniquities I will *r.* no more.
13. 7. *r.* them that have the rule over you.
Rev. 2. 5. *r.* from whence thou art fallen.
3. 3. *r.* how thou hast received.

Remembrance, Num. 5. 15. bringing iniquity
to *r.*
Deut. 32. 26. make the *r.* of them cease.
2 Sam. 18. 18. no son to keep my name in *r.*
1 Ki. 17. 18. art thou come to call my sin
to *r.?*
Job 18. 17. his *r.* shall perish from the earth.
Ps. 6. 5. in death there is no *r.*
30. 4; 97. 12. give thanks at *r.* of his holiness.
112. 6. the righteous shall be in everlast-
ing *r.*
Eccl. 1. 11. there is no *r.* of former things.
2. 16. no *r.* of wise more than the fool.
Is. 43. 26. put me in *r.*
Lam. 3. 20. my soul hath them in *r.*
Ezek. 23. 19. calling to *r.* days of youth.
29. 16. bringeth their iniquity to *r.*
Mal. 3. 16. a book of *r.* was written.
Lk. 22. 19; 1 Cor. 11. 24. this do in *r.* of me.
John 14. 26. bring all things to your *r.*
Acts 10. 31. thine alms are had in *r.*
2 Tim. 1. 3. I have *r.* of thee.
2. 14. of these things put them in *r.*
Heb. 10. 32. call to *r.* the former days.
2 Pet. 3. 1. stir up your pure minds by way
of *r.*   [sins.

Remission, Matt. 26. 28. blood shed for *r.* of
Mk. 1. 4; Lk. 3. 3. baptism of repentance
for *r.*
Lk. 24. 47. that *r.* should be preached.
Acts 10. 43. whosoever believeth shall re-
ceive *r.*
Rom. 3. 25. for *r.* of sins that are past.
Heb. 9. 22. without shedding of blood no *r.*
See John 20. 23.

Remnant, Lev. 5. 13. the *r.* shall be the priest's.
2 Ki. 19. 4; Is. 37. 4. lift up thy prayer for
the *r.*
Ezra 9. 8. to leave us a *r.*
Is. 1. 9. except Lord had left a *r.*
16. 14. the *r.* shall be very small.
Jer. 23. 3. I will gather the *r.* of my flock.
Ezek. 6. 8. yet will I leave a *r.*
Matt. 22. 6. the *r.* took his servants.
Rom. 11. 5. at present time there is a *r.*

Remove, Deut. 19. 14. not *r.* neighbour's landmark.   [me.
Ps. 36. 11. let not the hand of the wicked *r.*
39. 10. *r.* thy stroke away from me.
46. 2. not fear, though the earth be *r.*
103. 12. so far hath he *r.* our transgressions.
125. 1. as Mount Zion, which cannot be *r.*
Prov. 4. 27. *r.* thy foot from evil.
10. 30. the righteous shall never be *r.*
Eccl. 11. 10. *r.* sorrow from thy heart.
Is. 13. 13. earth shall be *r.* out of her place.
24. 20. earth shall be *r.* like a cottage.
29. 13. have *r.* their heart far from me.
30. 20. yet shall not teachers be *r.*
54. 10. the hills shall be *r.*
Jer. 4. 1. return, then shalt thou not *r.*
Lam. 3. 17. thou hast *r.* my soul from peace.
Matt. 17. 20. say, *r.* hence, it shall *r.*
Lk. 22. 42. if willing, *r.* this cup from me.
1 Cor. 13. 2. so that I could *r.* mountains.
Gal. 1. 6. I marvel ye are so soon *r.*
Rev. 2. 5. else I will *r.* thy candlestick.

Rend, Lev. 10. 6. neither *r.* your clothes.
1 Ki. 11. 11. I will *r.* the kingdom.
Eccl. 3. 7. a time to *r.*
Is. 64. 1. that thou wouldest *r.* the heavens.
Hos. 13. 8. I will *r.* the caul of their heart.
Joel 2. 13. *r.* your heart.
Matt. 7. 6. lest they turn and *r* you.
John 19. 24. not *r.* it, but cast lots.
Render, Deut. 32. 41. I will *r.* vengeance.
1 Sam. 26. 23. the Lord *r.* to every man his
faithfulness.   [ness.
Job 33. 26. he will *r.* to man his righteous-
34. 11. the work of a man shall be *r.* to him.
Ps. 116. 12. what shall I *r.* to the Lord?
Prov. 24. 12; Rom. 2. 6. *r.* to every man ac-
cording to his works.
Prov. 26. 16. seven men who can *r.* a reason.
Hos. 14. 2. so will we *r.* the calves of our lips.
Zech. 9. 12. I will *r.* double.
Matt. 21. 41. *r.* to him fruits in their seasons.
22. 21; Mk. 12. 17; Lk. 20. 25. *r.* unto Cæsar.
Rom. 13. 7. *r.* to all their dues.
1 Thes. 3. 9. what thanks can we *r.* to God?
5. 15; 1 Pet. 3. 9. not *r.* evil for evil.
Renew, Ps. 51. 10. *r.* a right spirit within me.
103. 5. thy youth is *r.* like the eagle's.
104. 30. thou *r.* the face of the earth.
Is. 40. 31. they that wait on the Lord shall
r. their strength.
Lam. 5. 21. *r.* our days as of old.
2 Cor. 4. 16. the inward man is *r.* day by day.
Eph. 4. 23. be *r.* in the spirit of your mind.
Col. 3. 10. new man, which is *r.* in knowledge.
Heb. 6. 6. if they fall away, to *r.* them again.
Renounced, 2 Cor. 4. 2. have *r.* hidden things
of dishonesty.
Renown, Gen. 6. 4; Num. 16. 2. men of *r.*
Is. 14. 20. seed of evil-doers shall never be *r.*
Ezek. 34. 29. a plant of *r.*
Dan. 9. 15. gotten thee *r.* as at this day.
Rent, Gen. 37. 33. Joseph is *r.* in pieces.
Josh. 9. 4. bottles old and *r.*
1 Ki. 13. 3. the altar shall be *r.*
Job 26. 8. the cloud is not *r.* under them.
Matt. 9. 16; Mk. 2. 21. the *r.* is made worse.
Matt. 27. 51; Mk. 15. 38; Lk. 23. 45. veil of
temple was *r.* in twain.   [house.
Repair, 2 Chr. 24. 5. gather money to *r.* the
Is. 61. 4. they shall *r.* waste cities.
Repay, Deut. 7. 10. he will *r.* him to his face.
Job 21. 31. who shall *r.* him what he hath
done?
Is. 59. 18. to islands *r.* recompence.
Lk. 10. 35. when I come again, I will *r.* thee.
Rom. 12. 19. vengeance is mine, I will *r.*
Philem. 19. I have written it, I will *r.* it.
Repent, Gen. 6. 6. it *r.* the Lord.
Ex. 13. 17. lest the people *r.*
32. 14; 2 Sam. 24. 16; 1 Chr. 21. 15; Jer. 26. 19.
Lord *r.* of the evil he thought to do.
Num. 23. 19. neither son of man, that he
should *r.*
Deut. 32. 36. the Lord shall *r.* for his servants.
1 Sam. 15. 29. strength of Israel not *r.*
Job 42. 6. I *r.* in dust and ashes.   [vants.
Ps. 90. 13. let it *r.* thee concerning thy ser-
110. 4; Heb. 7. 21. Lord hath sworn, and
will not *r.*
Jer. 18. 8; 26. 13. if nation turn, I will *r.*
Joel 2. 14. if he will return and *r.*
Matt. 12. 41; Lk. 11. 32. they *r.* at preaching
of Jonas.
Matt. 21. 29. afterward he *r.* and went.
27. 3. Judas *r.* himself.

Repent—*Continued.*
Mk. 6. 12. preached that men should *r.*
Lk. 13. 3. except ye *r.*
15. 7. joy over one sinner that *r.*
17. 3. if thy brother *r.,* forgive him.
Acts 2. 38. *r.* and be baptised.
3. 19. *r.* ye therefore and be converted.
8. 22. *r.* of this thy wickedness.
17. 30. commandeth all men to *r.*
26. 20. they should *r.,* and turn to God.
Rev. 2. 16. *r.,* or else I will come quickly.
3. 19. be zealous therefore and *r.*
Repentance, Hos. 13. 14. *r.* shall be hid from
mine eyes.
Matt. 3. 8; Lk. 3. 8; Acts 26. 20. fruits meet
for *r.*   [sinners to *r.*
Matt. 9. 13; Mk. 2. 17; Lk. 5. 32. to call
Rom. 2. 4. goodness of God leadeth thee to *r.*
11. 9. gifts of God are without *r.*
2 Cor. 7. 10. godly sorrow worketh *r.*   [of *r.*
Heb. 6. 1. not laying again the foundation
6. 6. impossible to renew them again to *r.*
12. 17. he found no place of *r.*
2 Pet. 3. 9. that all should come to *r.*
Repetitions, Matt. 6. 7. use not vain *r.* as the
heathen do.   [against God?
Repliest, Rom. 9. 20. who art thou that *r.*
Report, Gen. 37. 2. their evil *r.*
Ex. 23. 1. thou shalt not raise a false *r.*
Num. 13. 32. an evil *r.* of the land.
Deut. 2. 25. nations who shall hear *r.* of thee.
1 Sam. 2. 24. it is no good *r.* I hear.
1 Ki. 10. 6; 2 Chr. 9. 5. it was a true *r.*
Prov. 15. 30. a good *r.*
Is. 53. 1. who hath believed our *r.?*
Acts 6. 3. men of honest *r.*
10. 22. of good *r.* among the Jews.
2 Cor. 6. 8. by evil *r.* and good *r.*
Phil. 4. 8. whatsoever things are of good *r.*
1 Tim. 3. 7. a bishop must have a good *r.*
Heb. 11. 39. these having obtained a good *r.*

Report, Neh. 6. 6. it is *r.* among the heathen.
Jer. 20. 10. *r.,* say they, and we will *r.* it.
Matt. 28. 15. this saying is commonly *r.*
Acts 16. 2. well *r.* of.
1 Cor. 14. 25. he will *r.* that God is in you.
1 Tim. 5. 10. well *r.* for good works.
Reproach, Gen. 34. 14. that were a *r.* to us.
1 Sam. 17. 26. taketh away the *r.*
Neh. 2. 17. that we be no more a *r.*
Ps. 15. 3. that taketh not up a *r.*
22. 6. a *r.* of men.
69. 7. I have borne *r.*
78. 66. he put them to a perpetual *r.*
119. 22. remove from me *r.*
Prov. 6. 33. his *r.* shall not be wiped away.
14. 34. sin is a *r.* to any people.
18. 3. with ignominy cometh *r.*
Is. 51. 7. fear ye not the *r.* of men.
Jer. 23. 40. I will bring an everlasting *r.*
31. 19. I did bear the *r.* of my youth.
Lam. 3. 30. he is filled full with *r.*
2 Cor. 11. 21. I speak as concerning *r.*
12. 10. take pleasure in *r.*
1 Tim. 4. 10. we labour and suffer *r.*   [riches.
Heb. 11. 26. esteeming the *r.* of Christ greater
13. 13. without the camp, bearing his *r.*

Reproach, Num. 15. 30. doeth presumptuously,
r. the Lord.
2 Ki. 19. 22; Is. 37. 23. whom hast thou *r.?*
Job 27. 6. my heart shall not *r.* me.
Ps. 42. 10; 102. 8. mine enemies *r.* me.

119

Reproach—*Continued.*
Ps. 44. 16. the voice of him that *r.*
69. 9 ; Rom. 15. 3. the *r.* of them that *r.* thee.
Ps. 74. 22. how the foolish man *r.* thee.
119. 42 ; Prov. 27. 11. to answer him that *r.*
me.   [Maker.
Prov. 14. 31 ; 17. 5. oppresseth poor, *r.* his
Lk. 6. 22. men shall *r.* you for my sake.
11. 45. thou *r.* us also.
1 Pet. 4. 14. if ye be *r.* for Christ's sake.

Reprobate, Rom. 1. 28. God gave them to a *r.*
mind.
2 Cor. 13. 5. Christ is in you, except ye be *r.*
2 Tim. 3. 8. *r.* concerning the faith.
Tit. 1. 16. to every good work *r.*

Reproof, Job 26. 11. they are astonished at *r.*
Prov. 1. 23. turn you at my *r.*
15. 5. he that regardeth *r.* is prudent.
2 Tim. 3. 16. Scriptures profitable for *r.*

Reprove, Job 6. 25. what doth your arguing *r.?*
13. 10. he will *r.* if ye accept persons.
22. 4. will he *r.* thee for fear?
40. 2. he that *r.* God, let him answer it.
Ps. 50. 8. I will not *r.* thee for burnt offerings.
50. 21. I will *r.* thee and set in order.
141. 5. let him *r.* me, it shall be excellent oil.
Prov. 9. 8. *r.* not a scorner, lest he hate thee.
19. 25. *r.* one that hath understanding.
29. 1. he that being often *r.*   [liar.
30. 6. lest he *r.* thee, and thou be found a
Is. 11. 4. *r.* with equity for meek of the earth.
Jer. 2. 19. thy backslidings shall *r.* thee.
John 3. 20. lest his deeds should be *r.*
16. 8. he will *r.* the world of sin.
2 Tim. 4. 2. *r.,* rebuke, exhort.   [wisdom.

Reputation, Eccl. 10. 1. him that is *r.* for
Acts 5. 34. had in *r.* among the people.
Gal. 2. 2. privately to them of *r.*
Phil. 2. 7. made himself of no *r.*
2. 29. hold such in *r.*
See Dan. 4. 35.

Request, Jud. 8. 24. I would desire a *r.* of you.
Ezra 7. 6. the king granted all his *r.*
Neh. 2. 4. for what dost thou make *r.?*
Job 6. 8. Oh that I might have my *r.* !   [lips.
Ps. 21. 2. hast not withholden the *r.* of his
106. 15. he gave them their *r.*
Phil. 1. 4. in every prayer making *r.*
4. 6. let your *r.* be made known to God.
See 1 Ki. 19. 4.

Require, Gen. 9. 5. blood of your lives will I *r.*
31. 39. of my hand didst thou *r.* it.
Deut. 10. 12 ; Mic. 6. 8. what doth the Lord *r.?*
Josh. 22. 23 ; 1 Sam. 20. 16. let the Lord *r.* it.
1 Sam. 21. 8. the king's business *r.* haste.
2 Sam. 3. 13. one thing I *r.* of thee.
19. 38. whatsoever thou shalt *r.* I will do.
2 Chr. 24. 22. the Lord look upon it, and *r.* it.
Neh. 5. 12. we will restore, and *r.* nothing.
Ps. 10. 13. he hath said, thou wilt not *r.* it.
40. 6. sin offering hast thou not *r.*
Prov. 30. 7. two things have I *r.* of thee.
Eccl. 3. 15. God *r.* that which is past.
Is. 1. 12. who hath *r.* this at your hand?
Ezek. 3. 18 ; 33. 6. his blood will I *r.* at thine
hand.
Lk. 11. 50. be *r.* of this generation.
12. 20. this night thy soul shall be *r.*
12. 48. of him shall much be *r.*
19. 23. I might have *r.* mine own with usury.
23. 24. gave sentence that it should be as *r.*
1 Cor. 1. 22. the Jews *r.* a sign.
4. 2. it is *r.* in stewards that they be faithful.

Requite, Deut. 32. 6. do ye thus *r.* the Lord?
Jud. 1. 7. as I have done, so God hath *r.* me.
2 Sam. 2. 6. I also will *r.* you this kindness.
16. 12. it may be the Lord will *r.* good for
this.
1 Tim. 5. 4. learn to *r.* their parents.

Rereward, Is. 52. 12. God of Israel will be
your *r.*
58. 8. glory of Lord shall be thy *r.*

Resemble, Jud. 8. 18. each *r.* children of a king.
Lk. 13. 18. whereunto shall I *r.* kingdom of
God?   [ing?

Reserve, Gen. 27. 36. hast thou not *r.* a bless-
Job 21. 30. wicked *r.* to day of destruction.
Jer. 3. 5. will he *r.* his anger for ever?
5. 24. he *r.* the appointed weeks of harvest.
Nah. 1. 2. the Lord *r.* wrath for his enemies.
1 Pet. 1. 4. an inheritance *r.* in heaven.
2 Pet. 2. 17. mist of darkness *r.* for ever.
3. 7. heavens and earth are *r.* unto fire.
Jude 13. to whom is *r.* the blackness of
darkness.   [my years.

Residue, Is. 38. 10. I am deprived of the *r.* of
Mal. 2. 15. the *r.* of the Spirit.
Acts 15. 17. that the *r.* might seek the Lord.

Resist, Zech. 3. 1. Satan at right hand to *r.*
Matt. 5. 39. I say, that ye *r.* not evil.   [to *r.*
Lk. 21. 15. your adversaries shall not be able
Acts 7. 51. ye do always *r.* the Holy Ghost.
Rom. 9. 19. who hath *r.* his will?   [of God.
13. 2. whosoever *r.* the power, *r.* ordinance
Jas. 4. 6 ; 1 Pet. 5. 5. God *r.* the proud.
Jas. 4. 7. *r.* the devil, and he will flee.
1 Pet. 5. 9. whom *r.* stedfast in the faith.

Resort, Ps. 71. 3. whereunto I may *r.*
Mk. 10. 1. the people *r.* to him.
John 18. 2. Jesus ofttimes *r.* thither.
Acts 16. 13. spake to women who *r.* thither.

Respect, Gen. 4. 4. the Lord had *r.* to Abel.
Ex. 2. 25. God had *r.* unto them.
Lev. 26. 9. I will have *r.* unto you.
1 Ki. 8. 28 ; 2 Chr. 6. 19. have *r.* to the prayer
of thy servant.
2 Ki. 13. 23. the Lord had *r.* to them.
2 Chr. 19. 7 ; Rom. 2. 11 ; Eph. 6. 9 ; Col. 3. 25.
no *r.* of persons with God.
Ps. 74. 20. have *r.* unto thy covenant.
119. 117. I will have *r.* to thy statutes.
138. 6. yet hath he *r.* unto the lowly.
Prov. 24. 23 ; 28. 21. not good to have *r.* of
persons.   [One.
Is. 17. 7. his eyes shall have *r.* to the Holy
22. 11. nor had *r.* to him that fashioned it.
2 Cor. 3. 10. had no glory in this *r.*
Phil. 4. 11. not that I speak in *r.* of want.
1 Pet. 1. 17. who without *r.* of persons.

Respect, Lev. 19. 15. thou shalt not *r.* person
of poor.   [ment.
Deut. 1. 17. ye shall not *r.* persons in judg-
Job 37. 24. he *r.* not wise of heart.   [proud.
Ps. 40. 4. blessed is the man that *r.* not

Rest, Ex. 31. 15 ; 35. 2 ; Lev. 16. 31 ; 23. 3, 32 ;
25. 4. the Sabbath of *r.*
Ex. 33. 14. I will give thee *r.*
Lev. 25. 5. a year of *r.* to the land.
Deut. 3. 20 ; Josh. 1. 13. Lord have given *r.*
Jud. 3. 30. the land had *r.* fourscore years.
Ruth 1. 9. Lord grant you may find *r.*
1 Chr. 22. 9. a man of *r.,* and I will give
him *r.*
28. 2. to build a house of *r.*
Neh. 9. 28. after they had *r.* they did evil.
Job 3. 17. there the weary be at *r.*

Rest—*Continued.*

Job 11. 18. thou shalt take thy *r.* in safety.
17. 16. our *r.* together is in the dust.
Ps. 55. 6. then would I fly away, and be at *r.*
94. 13. thou mayest give him *r.*
116. 7. return to thy *r.,* O my soul.
132. 8. arise, O Lord, into thy *r.*
132. 14. this is my *r.* for ever.   [night.
Eccl. 2. 23. his heart taketh not *r.* in the
Is. 11. 10. his *r.* shall be glorious.
14. 3. the Lord shall give thee *r.*
14. 7; Zech. 1. 11. the earth is at *r.*
Is. 28. 12. this is the *r.* wherewith.
30. 15. in returning and *r.* shall ye be saved.
66. 1; Acts 7. 49. where is the place of my *r.?*
Jer. 6. 16. ye shall find *r.* for your souls.
Ezek. 38. 11. I will go to them that are at *r.*
Mic. 2. 10. depart, this is not your *r.*
Matt. 11. 28. I will give you *r.*   [none.
12. 43; Lk. 11. 24. seeking *r.,* and finding
Matt. 26. 45; Mk. 14. 41. take your *r.*
John 11. 13. he had spoken of taking *r.* in sleep.
Heb. 4. 9. remaineth a *r.* to people of God.

Rest, Gen. 2. 2. he *r.* on seventh day.
Ex. 34. 21. in harvest thou shalt *r.*
Num. 11. 25. the Spirit *r.* upon them.
Josh. 3. 13. feet of priests shall *r.*
2 Sam. 21. 10. the birds to *r.* on them by day.
Job 3. 18. there the prisoners *r.* together.
Ps. 16. 9; Acts 2. 26. my flesh shall *r.* in hope.
37. 7. *r.* in the Lord.
Prov. 6. 35. nor will he *r.* content.
Is. 11. 2. Spirit of the Lord shall *r.* upon him.
57. 20. like the sea when it cannot *r.*
63. 14. Spirit of the Lord caused him to *r.*
Dan. 12. 13. thou shalt *r.,* and stand in thy lot.
Mk. 6. 31. come, and *r.* awhile.
2 Cor. 12. 9. power of Christ may *r.* on me.
Rev. 4. 8. they *r.* not, day and night.
14. 13. that they may *r.* from their labours.
Restore, Gen. 42. 25. to *r.* every man's money.
Ex. 22. 4. he shall *r.* double.
Lev. 6. 5. he shall *r.* it in the principal.
Deut. 22. 2. things strayed thou shalt *r.* again.
Ps. 23. 3. he *r.* my soul.
51. 12. *r.* to me the joy of thy salvation.
Is. 1. 26. I will *r.* thy judges.
Jer. 30. 17. I will *r.* health to thee.
Matt. 17. 11; Mk. 9. 12. Elias shall *r.* all things.
Lk. 19. 8. I *r.* him fourfold.
Acts 1. 6. wilt thou *r.* the kingdom?
Gal. 6. 1. *r.* such an one in meekness.
Restrain, Gen. 8. 2. rain from heaven was *r.*
11. 6. nothing will be *r.* from them.
Ex. 36. 6. people were *r.* from bringing.
1 Sam. 3. 13. he *r.* them not.
Job 15. 4. thou *r.* prayer before God.
15. 8. dost thou *r.* wisdom?
Ps. 76. 10. wrath shalt thou *r.*
Acts 14. 18. scarce *r.* they the people.
Resurrection, Matt. 22. 23; Mk. 12. 18; Acts 23. 8; 1 Cor. 15. 12. Sadducees who say there is no *r.*   [life.
John 11. 25. Jesus said, I am the *r.* and the
Acts 17. 18. he preached Jesus and the *r.*
Rom. 6. 5. in likeness of his *r.*
Phil. 3. 10. know the power of his *r.*
Heb. 11. 35. might obtain a better *r.*
Rev. 20. 5. this is the first *r.*

Retain, Job 2. 9. dost thou *r.* thine integrity?
Prov. 4. 4. let thine heart *r.* my words.
11. 16. a gracious woman *r.* honour.
Eccl. 8. 8. no man hath power to *r.* the spirit.
John 20. 23. whosesoever sins ye *r.,* they are *r.*
Rom. 1. 28. did not like to *r.* God.
Return, Gen. 3. 19. to dust shalt thou *r.*
1 Sam. 7. 3; Is. 19. 22; 55. 7; Hos. 6. 1. *r.* to the Lord.
1 Ki. 8. 48. *r.* to thee with all their heart.
2 Ki. 20. 10. let the shadow *r.* backward.
Job 1. 21. naked shall I *r.* thither.
7. 10, he shall *r.* no more.   [ness.
15. 22. believeth not he shall *r.* out of dark-
22. 23. if thou *r.* to the Almighty.
33. 25. shall *r.* to the days of his youth.
Ps. 35. 13. my prayer *r.* into mine own bosom.
73. 10. his people *r.* hither.
90. 3. thou sayest, *r.,* ye children of men.
104. 29. they die, and *r.* to the dust.
116. 7. *r.* to thy rest, O my soul.
Prov. 2. 19. none that go to her *r.* again.
26. 11. as a dog *r.* to his vomit.   [came.
Eccl. 5. 15. naked shall he *r.* to go as he
12. 7. dust *r.* to earth, and spirit *r.* to God.
Is. 21. 12. if ye enquire, enquire ye, *r.* come.   [shall *r.*
35. 10; 51. 11. the ransomed of the Lord
55. 11. it shall not *r.* to me void.
Jer. 4. 1. if thou wilt *r.,* saith the Lord, *r.* unto me.
24. 7. they shall *r.* with their whole heart.
Ezek. 18. 23. that the wicked *r.,* and live.
Hos. 5. 15. I will *r.* to my place.
7. 16. they *r.,* but not to the Most High.
Joel 2. 14. who knoweth if he will *r.* and repent?
Mal. 3. 7. *r.* to me, and I will *r.* to you.
3. 18. then shall ye *r.* and discern.   [house.
Matt. 12. 44; Lk. 11. 24. I will *r.* into my
Matt. 24. 18. neither let him in field *r.* back.
Lk. 8. 39. *r.* to thine own house.   [God.
17. 18. not found that *r.* to give glory to
Acts 13. 34. now no more to *r.* to corruption.
Heb. 11. 15. opportunity to have *r.*   [souls.
1 Pet. 2. 25. now *r.* to the Shepherd of your
Reveal, Deut. 29. 29. things *r.* belong to us and our children   [to him.
1 Sam. 3. 7. nor was the word of the Lord *r.*
Job 20. 27. the heaven shall *r.* his iniquity.
Prov. 11. 13; 20. 19. a talebearer *r.* secrets.
Is. 22. 14. it was *r.* in mine ears.
40. 5. the glory of the Lord shall be *r.*
53. 1; John 12. 38. to whom is the arm of the Lord *r.?*
Jer. 33. 6. I will *r.* abundance of peace.
Dan. 2. 28. there is a God that *r.* secrets.
Amos 3. 7. he *r.* his secret to the prophets.
Matt. 10. 26; Lk. 12. 2. nothing covered that shall not be *r.*   [babes.
Matt. 11. 25; Lk. 10. 21. hast *r.* them unto
Matt. 16. 17. flesh and blood hath not *r.* it.
Lk. 2. 35. thoughts of many hearts may be *r.*
17. 30. in day when Son of man is, *r.*
Rom. 1. 18. wrath of God is *r.* from heaven.
8. 18. glory which shall be *r.* in us.
1 Cor. 2. 10. God hath *r.* them by his Spirit.
3. 13. it shall be *r.* by fire.
Gal. 1. 16. to *r.* his Son in me.
3. 23. faith which should be *r.*
2 Thes. 1. 7. when the Lord Jesus shall be *r.*
2. 3. that man of sin be *r.*
1 Pet. 1. 5. ready to be *r.* in last time.
5. 1. partaker of the glory that shall be *r.*

Revelation, Rom. 2. 5. r. of righteous judgmen of God.
16. 25. r. of the mystery.
1 Cor. 14. 26. every one hath a r.
2 Cor. 12. 7. through abundance of the r.
Rev. 1. 1. r. of Jesus Christ which God gave.

Revellings, Gal. 5. 21. works of the flesh are r.
1 Pet. 4. 3. we walked in lusts, r. [him.

Revenge, Jer. 20. 10. we shall take our r. on
Nah. 1. 2. the Lord r., and is furious.
2 Cor. 7. 11. what r. it wrought in you!
10. 6. readiness to r. all disobedience.
See Num. 35. 19; Rom. 13. 4. [the r.

Revenue, Ezra 4. 13. thou shalt endamage
Prov. 8. 19. my r. is better than silver.
16. 8. a little is better than great r.
Is. 23. 3. harvest of river is her r.
Jer. 12. 13. shall be ashamed of your r.

Reverence, Ps. 89. 7. to be had in r. of all.
Matt. 21. 37; Mk. 12. 6; Lk. 20. 13. they will r. my son.
Heb. 12. 9. we gave them r.
12. 28. that we may serve God with r.
See Ps. 111. 9.

Revile, Ex. 22. 28. thou shalt not r. the gods.
Matt. 5. 11. blessed when men shall r. you.
27. 39. they that passed by r. him.
Mk. 15. 32. they that were crucified r. him.
1 Cor. 4. 12. being r. we bless.
1 Pet. 2. 23. when he was r., r. not again.
See Is. 51. 7; 1 Cor. 6. 10.

Revive, Neh. 4. 2. will they r. the stones?
Ps. 85. 6. wilt thou not r. us again?
138. 7. thou wilt r. me.
Is. 57. 15. to r. the spirit of the humble.
Hos. 6. 2. after two days will he r. us.
14. 7. they shall r. as corn.
Hab. 3. 2. r. thy work in midst of years.
Rom. 7. 9. when the commandment came, sin r.
14. 9. Christ both died, rose, and r.

Revolt, Is. 1. 5. ye will r. more and more.
31. 6. children of Israel have deeply r.
59. 13. speaking oppression and r.
Jer. 5. 23. this people are r. and gone.
See Hos. 5. 2.

Reward, Gen. 15. 1. thy exceeding great r
Deut. 10. 17. God who taketh not r.
Ruth 2. 12. a full r. be given thee of the Lord.
2 Sam. 4. 10. thought I would have given him a r.
1 Ki. 13. 7. I will give thee a r.
Job 6. 22. did I say, give a r.?
7. 2. as an hireling looketh for r.
Ps. 15. 5. nor taketh r. against innocent.
19. 11. in keeping them is great r.
58. 11. there is a r. for the righteous.
70. 3. let them be turned back for a r.
91. 8. shalt see the r. of the wicked.
Prov. 11. 18. a sure r.
24. 20. no r. to the evil man.
Eccl. 4. 9. they have a good r. for labour.
9. 5. neither have they any more a r.
Is. 1. 23. every one followeth after r.
5. 23. justify the wicked for r.
40. 10; 62. 11. his r. is with him.
Dan. 5. 17. give thy r. to another.
Hos. 9. 1. thou hast loved a r.
Mic. 7. 3. the judge asketh for a r. [heaven.
Matt. 5. 12; Lk. 6. 23. great is your r. in
Matt. 5. 46. what r. have ye?
6. 2, 5, 16. they have their r.
10. 41. shall receive a prophet's r.
10. 42; Mk. 9. 41. in no wise lose his r.

Reward—*Continued.*
Lk. 6. 35. your r. shall be great.
23. 41. we receive due r. of our deeds.
Acts 1. 18. purchased field with r. of iniquity.
Rom. 4. 4. the r. is not reckoned of grace.
1 Cor. 3. 8. every man shall receive his own r.
9. 18. what is my r.?
Col. 2. 18. let no man beguile you of your r.
3. 24. the r. of the inheritance.
1 Tim. 5. 18. the labourer is worthy of his r.
Heb. 2. 2; 10. 35; 11. 26. recompence of r.
2 l et. 2. 13. the r. of unrighteousness.
2 John 8. that we receive a full r.
Rev. 22. 12. I come quickly, my r. is with me.

Reward, Gen. 44. 4. wherefore have ye r. evil?
Deut. 32. 41. I will r. them that hate me.
1 Sam. 24. 19. the Lord r. thee good.
2 Chr. 15. 7. your work shall be r.
20. 11. behold how they r. us.
Job 21. 19. he r. him, and he shall know it.
Ps. 31. 23. plentifully r. the proud doer.
35. 12; 109. 5. they r. me evil for good.
103. 10. notr. us according to our iniquities.
Prov. 13. 13. feareth commandment be r.
17. 13. whoso r. evil, evil shall not depart.
25. 22. the Lord shall r. thee.
26. 10. both r. the fool, and r. transgressors.
Jer. 31. 16. thy work shall be r.
Matt. 6. 4, 18. Father shall r. thee.
16. 27. he shall r. every man according to his works.
2 Tim. 4. 14. the Lord r. him.
Rev. 18. 6. r. her even as she r. you.
See Heb. 11. 6. [of blue.

Ribband, Num. 15. 38. on fringe of borders a r.

Rich, Gen. 14. 23. lest thou shouldest say, I have made Abraham r.
Ex. 30. 15. the r. shall not give more.
Lev. 25. 47. if a stranger wax r.
1 Sam. 2. 7. the Lord maketh poor and maketh r. [other poor.
2 Sam. 12. 1. two men in city, one r., the
Job 15. 29. he shall not be r.
Ps. 45. 12. the r. shall entreat thy favour.
49. 16. be not afraid when one is made r.
Prov. 10. 4. hand of diligent maketh r.
10. 22. blessing of the Lord maketh r.
14. 20. the r. hath many friends.
18. 23. the r. answereth roughly.
21. 17. he that loveth wine shall not be r.
22. 2. the r. and poor meet together.
23. 4. labour not to be r.
28. 11. the r. man is wise in his own conceit.
Eccl. 10. 20. curse not the r. in thy bedchamber.
Is. 53. 9. with the r. in his death.
Jer. 9. 23. let not the r. man glory.
Hos. 12. 8. Ephraim said, I am r.
Zech. 11. 5. blessed be the Lord, for I am r.
Mk. 12. 41. many that were r. cast in much.
Lk. 1. 53. the r. he hath sent empty away.
6. 24. woe to you r., for.
12. 21. that is not r. toward God.
14. 12. call not thy r. neighbours.
18. 23. sorrowful, for he was very r.
Rom. 10. 12. the same Lord is r. to all.
1 Cor. 4. 8. now ye are full, now ye are r.
2 Cor. 6. 10. poor, yet making many r.
8. 9. r., yet for your sakes he became poor.
Eph. 2. 4. God who is r. in mercy.
1 Tim. 6. 18. be r. in good works. [faith?
Jas. 2. 5. hath not God chosen the poor r. in
Rev. 3. 17. because thou sayest, I am r.

Riches, Gen. 31. 16. the *r*. God hath taken.
1 Sam. 17. 25. enrich with great *r*.
1 Ki. 3. 11 ; 2 Chr. 1. 11. neither hast asked *r*.
1 Chr. 29. 12. *r*. and honour come of thee.
Job 36. 19. will he esteem thy *r*.?
Ps. 39. 6. he heapeth up *r*.
49. 6. boast themselves in their *r*.
52. 7. trusted in abundance of his *r*. [them.
62. 10. if *r*. increase, set not your heart on
73. 12. the ungodly increase in *r*.
104. 24. O Lord, the earth is full of thy *r*.
112. 3. wealth and *r*. shall be in his house.
Prov. 8. 18. *r*. and honour are with me.
11. 4. *r*. profit not in day of wrath.
13. 8. ransom of a man's life are his *r*.
23. 5. *r*. make themselves wings.
27. 24. *r*. are not for ever.
30. 8. give me neither poverty nor *r*.
Eccl. 4. 8. nor his eye satisfied with *r*.
5. 13. *r*. kept for the owners.
Is. 45. 3. I will give thee hidden *r*.
Jer. 17. 11. he that getteth *r*., and not by
right. [ness of *r*.
Matt. 13. 22; Mk. 4. 19; Lk. 8. 14. deceitful-
Mk. 10. 23. how hardly shall they that
have *r*. [ness?
Rom. 2. 4. despisest thou the *r*. of his good-
9. 23. make known the *r*. of his glory.
11. 33. O the *r*. of wisdom of God ! [grace.
Eph. 1. 7. redemption according to the *r*. of
2. 7. the exceeding *r*. of his grace.
3. 8. the unsearchable *r*. of Christ. [Christ.
Phil. 4. 19. according to his *r*. in glory by
Col. 1. 27. what the *r*. of the glory.
1 Tim. 6. 17. nor trust in uncertain *r*.
Heb. 11. 26. reproach of Christ greater *r*.
Jas. 5. 2. your *r*. are corrupted.
Rev. 5. 12. worthy is the Lamb to receive *r*.
18. 17. so great *r*. come to nought.
See Col. 3. 16.

Ride, Deut. 33. 26. who *r*. upon the heaven.
Ps. 45. 4. in thy majesty *r*. prosperously.
66. 12. hast caused men to *r* over our heads.
68. 4, 33. extol him that *r*. on the heavens.
Is. 19. 1. the Lord *r*. on a swift cloud.
Zech. 9. 9. thy king cometh unto thee *r*.

Ridges, Ps. 65. 10. thou waterest the *r*. thereof.

Right, Gen. 18. 25. shall not the Judge of all
do *r*.? [is *r*.
Deut. 6. 18; 12. 25; 21. 9. thou shalt do that
21. 17. the *r*. of the first-born is his.
Ruth 4. 6. redeem thou my *r*.
Neh. 9. 33. thou hast done *r*.
Job 34. 6. should I lie against my *r*.?
36. 6. he giveth *r*. to the poor.
Ps. 9. 4. thou hast maintained my *r*.
17. 1. hear the *r*., O Lord. [poor.
140. 12. the Lord will maintain the *r*. of the
Prov. 16. 13. they love him that speaketh *r*.
Jer. 17. 11. that getteth riches, and not by *r*.
Ezek. 21. 27. till he comes whose *r*. it is.

Right, Gen. 24. 48. Lord who led me in *r*. way.
Deut. 32. 4. God of truth, just and *r*. is he.
1 Sam. 12. 23. I will teach you good and *r*.
way.
2 Sam. 15. 3. thy matters are good and *r*.
Job 6. 25. how forcible are *r*. words !
34. 23. he will not lay on man more than *r*.
35. 2. thinkest thou this to be *r*.?
Ps. 19. 8. the statutes of the Lord are *r*.
45. 6. sceptre of thy kingdom is a *r*. sceptre.
51. 10. renew a *r*. spirit within me.
119. 75. thy judgments are *r*.

Right—Continued.
Prov. 4. 11. I have led thee in *r*. **paths.**
8. 6. opening of my lips shall be *r*. **things.**
12. 5. thoughts of righteous are *r*.
14. 12 ; 16. 25. there is a way that seemeth *r*.
21. 2. every way of a man is *r*. in his own eyes
Is. 30. 10. prophesy not *r*. things.
Hos. 14. 9. the ways of the Lord are *r*.
Amos 3. 10. they know not to do *r*.
Matt. 20. 4. whatsoever is *r*. I will give you.
Mk. 5. 15 ; Lk. 8. 35. in his *r*. mind.
Lk. 12. 57. why judge ye not what is *r*.? [me.
Eph. 6. 1. obey your parents, this is *r*.
2 Pet. 2. 15. forsaken the *r*. way.

Righteous, Gen. 7. 1. thee have I seen *r*. before
18. 23. wilt thou destroy *r*. with wicked?
20. 4. wilt thou slay a *r*. nation?
Num. 23. 10. let me die the death of the *r*.
Deut. 25. 1 ; 2 Chr. 6. 23. they shall justify *r*.
Jud. 5. 11 ; 1 Sam. 12. 7. *r*. acts of the Lord.
1 Sam. 24. 17. thou art more *r*. than I.
1 Ki. 2. 32. two men more *r*. than he.
Job 4. 7. where were the *r*. cut off?
9. 15. though I were *r*., yet would I not
answer.
15. 14. what is man, that he should be *r*.?
Ps. 1. 5. the congregation of the *r*.
1. 6. the Lord knoweth the way of the *r*.
5. 12. thou wilt bless the *r*. with favour.
7. 9. the *r*. God trieth the hearts.
14. 5. God is in generation of the *r*.
34. 17. the *r*. cry, and the Lord heareth them.
37. 16. a little that a *r*. man hath.
37. 25. have not seen the *r*. forsaken.
37. 30. mouth of the *r*. speaketh wisdom.
55. 22. never suffer the *r*. to be moved.
58. 11. there is a reward for the *r*.
64. 10. the *r*. shall be glad in the Lord.
92. 12. the *r*. shall flourish like palm tree.
112. 6. *r*. shall be in everlasting remembrance.
118. 20. gate, into which *r*. shall enter. [of *r*.
125. 3. rod of wicked shall not rest on lot
141. 5. let the *r*. smite me.
146. 8. the Lord loveth the *r*.
Prov. 2. 7. he layeth up wisdom for the *r*.
10. 3. the Lord will not suffer the *r*. to
famish.
10. 16. labour of *r*. tendeth to life.
10. 25. the *r*. is an everlasting foundation.
10. 30. the *r*. shall never be removed.
11. 8. the *r*. is delivered out of trouble.
12. 10. a *r*. man regardeth the life of his
beast.
13. 9. the light of the *r*. rejoiceth.
13. 21. to the *r*. good shall be repaid.
14. 9. among the *r*. there is favour.
14. 32. the *r*. hath hope in his death.
15. 6. in the house of the *r*. is much treasure.
15. 29. he heareth the prayer of the *r*.
18. 10. the *r*. runneth into it, and is safe.
28. 1. the *r*. are bold as a lion. [rejoice.
29. 2. when the *r*. are in authority, people
29. 7. the *r*. considereth cause of the poor.
Eccl. 3. 17. God shall judge *r*. and wicked.
7. 16. be not *r*. overmuch. [God.
9. 1. the *r*. and the wise are in the hand of
9. 2. one event to *r*. and wicked.
Is. 3. 10. say to *r*., it shall be well.
24. 16. songs, even glory to the *r*.
26. 2. that the *r*. nation may enter in.
53. 11. shall my *r*. servant justify many.
57. 1. *r*. perisheth, no man layeth it to heart.
60. 21. thy people shall be all *r*.

Righteous—*Continued.*

Amos 2. 6. they sold the *r.* for silver.

Mal. 3. 18. discern between the *r.* and wicked.

Matt. 9. 13 ; Mk. 2. 17 ; Lk. 5. 32. not come to call the *r.*

Matt. 13. 43. then shall the *r.* shine forth.

23. 28. outwardly appear *r.* to men.

25. 46. the *r.* into life eternal.

Lk. 1. 6. they were both *r.* before God.

18. 9. trusted they were *r.*, and despised others.

23. 47. certainly this was a *r.* man.

John 7. 24. judge *r.* judgment.

17. 25. O *r.* Father.

Rom. 3. 10. there is none *r.*, no, not one.

5. 19. by obedience of one many be made *r.*

2 Tim. 4. 8. the Lord, the *r.* Judge.

Heb. 11. 4. obtained witness that he was *r.*

1 Pet. 3. 12. eyes of the Lord are over the *r.*

4. 18. if the *r.* scarcely be saved.

2 Pet. 2. 8. Lot vexed his *r.* soul.

1 John 3. 7. is *r.*, even as he is *r.*

Rev. 16. 7. true and *r.* are thy judgments.

22. 11. he that is *r.*, let him be *r.* still.

Righteously, Deut. 1. 16 ; Prov. 31. 9. judge *r.*

Ps. 67. 4 ; 96. 10. thou shalt judge the people *r.*

Is. 33. 15. he that walketh *r.* shall dwell on high.

Jer. 11. 20. O Lord, that judgest *r.*

Tit. 2. 12. we should live soberly, *r.*

Righteousness, Gen. 30. 33. so shall my *r.* answer for me.

Deut. 6. 25. it shall be our *r.* if.

33. 19. shall offer sacrifices of *r.*

1 Sam. 26. 23. Lord render to every man his *r.*

Job 29. 14. I put on *r.*, and it clothed me.

35. 2. thou saidst, my *r.* is more than God's.

36. 3. I will ascribe *r.* to my Maker.

Ps. 4. 5. offer the sacrifices of *r.*

9. 8. he shall judge the world in *r.*

17. 15. I will behold thy face in *r.*

23. 3. leadeth me in paths of *r.*

24. 5. *r.* from the God of his salvation.

40. 9. I have preached *r.*

45. 7 ; Heb. 1. 9. thou lovest *r.*

Ps. 85. 10. *r.* and peace have kissed each other.

94. 15. judgment shall return unto *r.*

97. 2. *r.* is the habitation of his throne.

118. 19. open to me the gates of *r.*

132. 9. let thy priests be clothed with *r.*

Prov. 8. 18. riches and *r.* are with me.

10. 2 ; 11. 4. *r.* delivereth from death.

11. 5. *r.* of the perfect shall direct his way.

11. 19. *r.* tendeth to life.

12. 28. in the way of *r.* is life.

14. 34. *r.* exalteth a nation.

16. 8. better is a little with *r.*

16. 12. the throne is established by *r.*

16. 31. crown of glory, if found in way of *r.*

Eccl. 7. 15. a just man that perisheth in his *r.*

Is. 11. 5. *r.* shall be the girdle of his loins.

26. 9. inhabitants of the world will learn *r.*

28. 17. *r.* will I lay to the plummet.

32. 1. a king shall reign in *r.*

32. 17. work of *r.* shall be peace.

41. 10. uphold thee with right hand of my *r.*

59. 16. his *r.* sustained him.

64. 6. our *r.* as filthy rags.

Jer. 23. 6 ; 33. 16. name, the Lord our *r.*

Ezek. 18. 20. the *r.* of the righteous shall be upon him.

Dan. 4. 27. break off thy sins by *r.*

9. 7. O Lord, *r.* belongeth to thee.

9. 24. to bring in everlasting *r.*

Righteousness—*Continued.*

Dan. 12. 3. they that turn many to *r.*

Hos. 10. 12. till he reign *r.* upon you.

Amos 5. 24. let *r.* run down as a stream.

Mal. 4. 2. sun of *r.* arise.

Matt. 3. 15. to fulfil all *r.*

5. 6. that hunger and thirst after *r.*

5. 20. except your *r.* exceed the *r.* of scribes.

21. 32. John came in the way of *r.*

Lk. 1. 75. in *r.* before him.

John 16. 8. reprove the world of *r.*

Acts 10. 35. he that worketh *r.* is accepted.

13. 10. thou enemy of all *r.*

24. 25. as he reasoned of *r.*

Rom. 1. 17 ; 3. 5 ; 10. 3. the *r.* of God.

4. 6. man to whom God imputeth *r.*

4. 11. a seal of the *r.* of faith.

5. 21. grace reign through *r.*

6. 13. members as instruments of *r.*

8. 10. the Spirit is life because of *r.*

9. 30. the *r.* of faith.

10. 4. Christ is the end of the law for *r.*

14. 17. kingdom of God is *r.*, peace.

1 Cor. 1. 30. Christ is made unto us *r.*

15. 34. awake to *r.*

2 Cor. 5. 21. made the *r.* of God in him.

6. 7. the armour of *r.*   [eousness.

6. 14. what fellowship hath *r.* with unright-

Gal. 2. 21. if *r.* come by the law.

Eph. 6. 14. the breastplate of *r.*

Phil. 1. 11. filled with the fruits of *r.*

3. 6. touching the *r.* in the law blameless.

1 Tim. 6. 11 ; 2 Tim. 2. 22. follow *r.*

2 Tim. 4. 8. a crown of *r.*

Tit. 3. 5. not by works of *r.*

Heb. 7. 2. king of *r.*

12. 11. the peaceable fruit of *r.*   [of God.

Jas. 1. 20. wrath of man worketh not the *r.*

3. 18. fruit of *r.* is sown in peace.

1 Pet. 2. 24. dead to sins, should live unto *r.*

2 Pet. 2. 5. a preacher of *r.*

3. 13. new earth wherein dwelleth *r.*

1 John 2. 29. every one that doeth *r.*

Rightly, Gen. 27. 36. is not he *r.* named Jacob?

Lk. 7. 43. said, thou hast *r.* judged.

20. 21. we know thou teachest *r.*

2 Tim. 2. 15. *r.* dividing word of truth.

Riot, Rom. 13. 13. walk not in *r.* drunkenness.

Tit. 1. 6. children not accused of *r.*

1 Pet. 4. 4. that you run not to *r.*

2 Pet. 2. 13. count it pleasure to *r.*

See Prov. 28. 7 ; Lk. 15. 13.

Ripe, Gen. 40. 10. brought forth *r.* grapes.

Ex. 22. 29. offer the first of thy *r.* fruits.

Num. 18. 13. whatsoever is first *r.* shall be thine.

Joel 3. 13. put in sickle, for harvest is *r.*

Rev. 14. 15. harvest of earth is *r.*

Rise, Num. 24. 17. a sceptre shall *r.* out of Israel.

32. 14. ye are *r.* up in your father's stead.

Job 9. 7. commandeth the sun, and it *r.* not.

14. 12. man lieth down, and *r.* not.

31. 14. what shall I do when God *r.* up?

Ps. 27. 3. though war should *r.* against me.

127. 2. it is vain to *r.* up early.   [bird.

Eccl. 12. 4. he shall *r.* at the voice of the

Is. 24. 20. earth shall fall, and not *r.*

33. 10. now will I *r.*, saith the Lord.

60. 1. the glory of the Lord is *r.* upon thee.

Jer. 7. 13 ; 25. 3 ; 35. 14. I spake unto you, *r.* early.

11. *r.* early and protesting.

Lam. 3. 63. sitting down and *r.* up.

124

Rise—Continued.

Matt. 5. 45. he maketh sun to *r.* on evil and good.
20. 19; Mk. 9. 31; 10. 34; Lk. 18. 33; 24. 7. the third day he shall *r.* again.
Matt. 26. 46. *r.*, let us be going.
Mk. 10. 49. *r.*, he calleth thee.
Lk. 11. 7. I cannot *r.* and give thee.
24. 34. the Lord is *r.* indeed.
John 11. 23. thy brother shall *r.* again.
Acts 10. 13. *r.* Peter, kill and eat.
26. 23. the first that should *r.* from the dead.
Rom. 8. 34. Christ that died, yea, rather, that is *r.* again.
15. 12. he that shall *r.* to reign.
1 Cor. 15. 15. if the dead *r.* not.
Col. 3. 1. if ye then be *r.* with Christ.
1 Thes. 4. 16. the dead in Christ shall *r.* first.
River, Gen. 41. 1. he stood by the *r.*
Ex. 7. 19; 8. 5. stretch out hand on *r.*
Josh. 13. 9; 2 Sam. 24. 5. the city in the midst of the *r.*
Jud. 5. 21. *r.* Kishon, that ancient *r.*
2. Sam. 17. 13. draw it into the *r.*
2 Ki. 5. 12. are not *r.* of Damascus better?
Job 28. 10. he cutteth out *r.* among rocks.
29. 6. *r.* of oil.
40. 23. he drinketh up a *r.*
Ps. 1. 3. a tree planted by the *r.*
36. 8. the *r.* of they pleasure.   [make glad.
46. 4. there is a *r.*, the streams whereof
65. 9. enrichest it with *r.* of God.
72. 8. have dominion from the *r.*
119. 136. *r.* of waters run down mine eyes.
137. 1. by *r.* of Babylon we wept.
Eccl. 1. 7. all the *r.* run into the sea.
Is. 32. 2. as of water in a dry ground.
43. 19. I will make *r.* in the desert.
48. 18. then had thy peace been as a *r.*
66. 12. I will extend peace like a *r.*
Lam. 2. 18. let tears run down like a *r.*
Mic. 6. 7. be pleased with *r.* of oil ?
Zech. 9. 10. his dominion from the *r.*
John 7. 38. *r.* of living water.
Acts 16. 13. on Sabbath we went by a *r.* side.
Rev. 22. 1. a pure *r.* of water of life.
Roar, 1 Chr. 16. 32; Ps. 96. 11; 98. 7. let the sea *r.*
Ps. 46. 3. not fear, though waters *r.*
104. 21. young lions *r.* after their prey.
Prov. 19. 12. king's wrath is as the *r.* of a lion.
Is. 59. 11. we *r.* all like bears.
Jer. 6. 23. their voice *r.* like the sea.
25. 30. the Lord shall *r.* from on high.
31. 35. divideth sea, when waves *r.*
Hos. 11. 10. he shall *r.* like a lion.   [of Zion.
Joel 3. 16; Amos 1. 2. the Lord shall *r.* out
Amos 3. 4. will a lion *r.* if he hath no prey ?
Lk. 21. 25. the sea and waves *r.*
1 Pet. 5. 8. the devil as a *r.* lion.
Rob, Prov. 22. 22. *r.* not the poor.
Is. 10. 2. that they may *r.* the fatherless.
42. 22. this is a people *r.* and spoiled.
Mal. 3. 8. will a man *r.* God ?
2 Cor. 11. 8. I *r.* other churches.
See Job 12. 6; Jer. 7. 11; John 10. 1; 2 Cor. 11. 26; Phil. 2. 6.
Robe, Job 29. 14. my judgment was as a *r.*
Is. 61. 10. covered me with *r.* of righteousness.
Matt. 27. 28. put on Jesus a scarlet *r.*
Lk. 15. 22. bring forth the best *r.*
20. 46. scribes walk in long *r.*
Rev. 6. 11. white *r.* were given them.

Rock, Ex. 17. 6. I will stand before thee on the *r.*
33. 22. I will put thee in a clift of the *r.*
Num. 20. 8. speak to the *r.* before their eyes.
24. 21. thou puttest thy nest in a *r.*
Deut. 8. 15. who brought thee water out of the *r.*
32. 4. he is the *R.*
32. 15. lightly esteemed the *R.* of his sal-   [vation.
32. 31. their *r.* is not as our *R.*   [God.
1 Sam. 2. 2. neither is there any *r.* like our
2 Sam. 22. 2; Ps. 18. 2; 92. 15. the Lord is my *r.*   [God ?
2 Sam. 22. 32; Ps. 18. 31. who is a *r.* save our
1 Ki. 19. 11. strong wr nd brake in pieces the *r.*
Job 14. 18. the *r.* is removed out of its place.
19. 24. graven in the *r.* for ever.
Ps. 27. 5; 40. 2. he shall set me upon a *r.*
31. 3; 71. 3. thou art my *r.* and my fortress.
61. 2. lead me to the *r.* that is higher than I.
89. 26; 95. 1. *r.* of salvation.
Prov. 30. 26. make their houses in the *r.*
Cant. 2. 14. that art in the clefts of the *r.*
Is. 17. 10. not mindful of the *r.* of thy strength.
32. 2. as the shadow of a great *r.*   [pieces.
Jer. 23. 29. hammer that breaketh the *r.* in
Matt. 7. 25; Lk. 6. 48. it was founded upon a *r.*
Matt. 16. 18. upon this *r.* I w ll build my church.
Lk. 8. 6. some fell upon a *r.*   [offence.
Rom. 9. 33; 1 Pet. 2. 8. I lay in Zion a *r.* of
1 Cor. 10. 4. drank of that spiritual *r.*
Rev. 6. 16. said to the *r.* fall on us.
Rod, Ex. 4. 4. it became a *r.* in his hand.
Job 21. 9. neither is the *r.* of God upon them.
Ps. 2. 9. break them w th a *r.* of iron.
23. 4. thy *r.* and staff comfort me.
110. 2. the Lord shall send the *r.* of strength.
Prov. 10. 13; 26. 3. a *r.* for back of fools.
13. 24. he that spareth his *r.*
29. 15. the *r.* and reproof give wisdom.
Is. 11. 1. shall come forth a *r.*
Ezek. 20. 37. cause you to pass under the *r.*
Mic. 6. 9. hear the *r.*, and who hath appointed it.
2 Cor. 11. 25. thrice was I beaten with *r.*
Rev. 12. 5. rule nations with a *r.* of iron.
Roof, Gen. 19. 8. under the shadow of my *r.*
Deut. 22. 8. make a battlement for thy *r.*
Job 29. 10; Ps. 137. 6; Ezek. 3. 26. tongue cleaveth to *r* of mouth.
Matt. 8. 8; Lk. 7. 6. I am not worthy thou shouldest come under my *r.*
Mk. 2. 4. they uncovered the *r.*
Room, Gen. 24. 23. is there *r.* for us?
26. 22. the Lord hath made *r.* for us.
Ps. 31. 8. thou hast set my feet in a large *r.*
80. 9. thou preparedst *r.* before it.
Prov. 18. 16. a man's gift maketh *r.* for him.
Mal. 3. 10. there shall not be *r.* enough.
Matt. 23. 6; Mk. 12. 39; Lk. 20. 46. love the uppermost *r.*
Mk. 2. 2. there was no *r.* to receive them.
14. 15; Lk. 22. 12. a large upper *r.*
Lk. 2. 7. no *r.* for them in the inn.
12. 17. no *r.* to bestow my fruits.
14. 7. how they chose out the chief *r.*
14. 22. yet there is *r.*
1 Cor. 14. 16. that occupieth the *r.* of the unlearned.

Root, Deut. 29. 18. a r. that beareth gall.
2 Ki. 19. 30. shall again take r. downward.
Job 5. 3. I have seen the foolish taking r.
    19. 28. the r. of the matter.   [fruit.
Prov. 12. 12. the r. of righteous yieldeth
Is. 5. 24. their r. shall be rottenness.
    11. 1. a Branch shall grow out of his r.
    11. 10; Rom. 15. 12. a r. of Jesse.
Is. 53. 2. as a r. out of a dry ground.
Ezek. 31. 7. his r. was by great waters.
Hos. 14. 5. cast forth his r. as Lebanon.
Mal. 4. 1. shall leave them neither r. nor
    branch.
Matt. 3. 10; Lk. 3. 9. axe is laid to r. of trees.
Matt. 13. 6; Mk. 4. 6; Lk. 8. 13. because they
    had no r.
Rom. 11. 16. if the r. be holy.   [evil.
1 Tim. 6. 10. love of money is the r. of all
Heb. 12. 15. lest any r. of bitterness.
Jude 12. trees plucked up by the r.
Rev. 22. 16. the r. and offspring of David.

Root, 1. Ki. 14. 15. he shall r. up Israel.
Job 18. 14. confidence shall be r. out.
Ps. 52. 5. r. thee out of the land of the living.
Matt. 15. 13. shall be r. up.
Eph. 3. 17. being r. and grounded in love.
Col. 2. 7. r. and built up in him.

Rose, Cant. 2. 1. I am the r. of Sharon.
Is. 35. 1. desert shall blossom as the r.

Rose, Gen. 4. 8. Cain r. up against Abel.
    32. 31. the sun r. upon him.
Josh. 3. 16. waters r. up on an heap.
Ps. 124. 2. when men r. up against us.
Lk. 16. 31. not be persuaded, though one r.
    from the dead.
Rom. 14. 9. Christ both died and r.
1 Cor. 10. 7. people r. up to play.
    15. 4. he was buried, and r. again.
2 Cor. 5. 15. him who died and r. again.

Rot, Prov. 10. 7. name of wicked shall r.
Is. 40. 20. chooseth a tree that will not r.
See Prov. 14. 30 ; Is. 5. 24.

Rough, Is. 27. 8. he stayeth his r. wind.
    40. 4. r. places be made plain.
Lk. 3. 5. r. ways be made smooth.
See Gen. 42. 7 ; Prov. 18. 23.

Royal, Gen. 49. 20. yield r. dainties.   [city?
1 Sam. 27. 5. why should I dwell in the r.
Est. 1. 7. r. wine.
    5. 1 ; 6. 8 ; 8. 15 ; Acts 12. 21. r. apparel.
Jas. 2. 8. if ye fulfil the r. law.
1 Pet. 2. 9. ye are a r. priesthood.
Rubies, Job 28. 18; Prov. 8. 11. price of wisdom
    is above r.
Ruddy, 1 Sam. 16. 12 ; 17. 42. David was r.
Cant. 5. 10. my beloved is white and r.
Lam. 4. 7. more r. than rubies.
Rudiments, Col. 2. 8, 20. the r. of the world.
Ruin, 2 Chr. 28. 23. they were the r. of him.
Ps. 89. 40. hast brought his strongholds
    to r.
Prov. 26. 28. a flattering mouth worketh r.
Is. 25. 2. made of a defenced city a r.
Ezek. 18. 30. iniquity shall not be your r.
Lk. 6. 49. the r. of that house was great.
Acts 15. 16. build again the r. thereof.
Rule, Est. 9. 1. Jews had r. over them.
Prov. 17. 2. a wise servant shall have r.
    19. 10. a servant to have r. over princes.
    25. 28. no r. over his own spirit.
Is. 63. 19. thou never barest r. over them.
1 Cor. 15. 24. put down all r.

Rule—*Continued*.
2 Cor. 10. 13. measure of the r.
Gal. 6. 16. as many as walk according to
    this r.
Phil. 3. 16. let us walk by the same r.
Heb. 13. 7, 17. that have the r. over you.

Rule, Gen. 1. 16. to r. the day.
    3. 16. thy husband shall r. over thee.
Jud. 8. 23. I will not r. over you.
2 Sam. 23. 3. he that r. over men must be just.
Ps. 66. 7. he r. by his power for ever.
    89. 9. thou r. the raging of the sea.
    103. 19. his kingdom r. over all.
    110. 2. r. in midst of enemies.
Prov. 16. 32. that r. his spirit.
Eccl. 8. 9. one man r. over another.
Is. 3. 4. babes shall r. over them.
    32. 1. princes shall r. in judgment.
    40. 10. his arm shall r. for him.
Ezek. 29. 15. no more r. over the nations.
Joel 2. 17. heathen should r. over them.
Mk. 10. 42. who are accounted to r.
Rom. 12. 8. he that r., with diligence.
Col. 3. 15. let the peace of God r. in your
    hearts.
1 Tim. 3. 5. how to r. his house.
    5. 17. elders that r. well.   [people.
Ruler, Ex. 22. 28. thou shalt not curse r. of
Num. 13. 2. every one a r. among them.
Prov. 23. 1. when thou sittest to eat with a r.
    28. 15. a wicked r. over the poor.
Is. 3. 6. be thou our r.
Mic. 5. 2. out of thee shall come r.
Matt. 9. 18. there came a certain r.
    25. 21. I will make thee r.
John 3. 1. a r. of the Jews.
    7. 48. have any of the r. believed on him?
Rom. 13. 3. r. are not a terror to good
    works.
Eph. 6. 12. r. of the darkness of world.
Rumour, Jer. 49. 14. heard a r. from the Lord.
Ezek. 7. 26. r. shall be upon r.
Matt. 24. 6 ; Mk. 13. 7. wars and r. of wars.
Lk. 7. 17. this r. went forth.
Run, 2 Sam. 22. 30 ; Ps. 18. 29. I have r. through
    a troop.   [r. to and fro.
2 Chr. 16. 9; Zech. 4. 10. the eyes of the Lord
Ps. 19. 5. as a strong man to r. a race.
    23. 5. my cup r. over.   [ments.
    119. 32. I will r. the way of thy command-
    147. 15. his word r. very swiftly.
Prov. 1. 16 ; Is. 59. 7. their feet r. to evil.
Cant. 1. 4. we will r. after thee.
Is. 40. 31. they shall r., and not be weary.
    55. 5. nations shall r. to thee.
Jer. 12. 5. if thou hast r. with the footmen.
    51. 31. one post shall r. to meet another.
Hab. 2. 2. that he may r. that readeth.
Zech. 2. 4. r., speak to this young man.
Rom. 9. 16. nor of him that r.
1 Cor. 9. 24. they which r. in a race, r. all.
Gal. 2. 2. lest I should r., or had r. in vain.
    5. 7. ye did r. well.
Heb. 12. 1. let us r. with patience.
1 Pet. 4. 4. that ye r. not to the same excess.
Rush, Is. 17. 13. nations shall r. like r. of many
    waters.
Jer. 8. 6. as horse r. into battle.
Acts 2. 2. sound as of a r. mighty wind.
Rust, Matt. 6. 19, 20. where moth and r. doth
    corrupt.
Jas. 5. 3. the r. of them shall be a witness
    against you.

SABBATH, Ex. 31. 14, 16. ye shall keep the *S.*
Lev. 16. 31; 23. 3, 32. *S.* of rest.
2 Ki. 4. 23. it is neither new moon nor *S.*
Neh. 9. 14. madest known thy holy *S.*
Is. 58. 13. call *S.* a delight.
Ezek. 46. 1. on *S.* it shall be opened.
Amos 8. 5. when will the *S.* be gone?
Mk. 2. 27. the *S.* was made for man. [the *S.*
2. 28; Lk. 6. 5. the Son of man is Lord of
Lk. 13. 15. doth not each on *S.* loose?
John 5. 18. he not only had broken the *S.*
Sacrifice, Gen. 31. 54. Jacob offered a
Ex. 5. 17; 8. 8. do *s.* to the Lord. [giving.
Lev. 7. 12; Ps. 116. 17. offer a *s.* of thanks-
1 Sam. 2. 29. wherefore kick ye at my *s.*?
15. 22. to obey is better than *s.*
Ps. 4. 5. offer *s.* of righteousness.
40. 6; 51. 16. *s.* thou didst not desire.
51. 17. the *s.* of God are a broken spirit.
118. 27. bind the *s.* to horns of the altar.
141. 2. lifting up hands as evening *s.*
Prov. 15. 8. *s.* of wicked an abomination.
17. 1. a house full of *s.* with strife.
21. 3. to do justice is more acceptable than *s.*
Eccl. 5. 1. the *s.* of fools. [your *s.*?
Is. 1. 11. to what purpose the multitude of
Jer. 6. 20. nor are your *s.* sweet to me.
33. 11. that bring *s.* of praise.
Ezek. 39. 17. gather to my *s.* great *s.*
Dan. 8. 11; 9. 27; 11. 31. daily *s.* taken away.
Hos. 6. 6; Matt. 9. 13; 12. 7. I desired mercy,
and not *s.*
Amos 5. 25. have ye offered unto me *s.*?
Zeph. 1. 7. the Lord hath prepared a *s.*
Mk. 9. 49. every *s.* shall be salted.
12. 33. to love the Lord is more than *s.*
Acts 7. 42. have ye offered *s.* forty years?
14. 13. would have done *s.*
Rom. 12. 1. present your bodies a living *s.*
1 Cor. 8. 4; 10. 19, 28. offered in *s.* to idols.
Eph. 5. 2. a *s.* to God for a sweet-smelling
savour.
Phil. 2. 17. offered on *s.* of your faith.
4. 18. a *s.* acceptable, well pleasing to God.
Heb. 9. 26. put away sin by the *s.* of himself.
10. 26. there remaineth no more *s.* for sin.
13. 15. let us offer the *s.* of praise.
1 Pet. 2. 5. to offer up spiritual *s.*

Sacrifice, Ex. 20. 24. thou shalt *s.* burnt-
offerings. [him.
Ezra 4. 2. we seek your God, and do *s.* to
Neh. 4. 2. will they *s.*?
Ps. 54. 6. I will freely *s.* to thee.
107. 22. *s.* sacrifices of thanksgiving.
Eccl. 5. 2. to him that *s.* and that *s.* not.
Hos. 8. 13. they *s.*, but the Lord accepteth not.
Hab. 1. 16. they *s.* unto their net.
1 Cor. 5. 7. Christ our passover is *s.* for us.
10. 20. things Gentiles *s.*, they *s.* to devils.
Rev. 2. 14, 20. things *s.* to idols.
Sad, 1 Sam. 1. 18. countenance no more *s.*
1 Ki. 21. 5. why is thy spirit so *s.*?
Matt. 6. 16. be not of a *s.* countenance.
Mk. 10. 22. he was *s.* at that saying.
Lk. 24. 17. as ye walk and are *s.*
Safe, 2 Sam. 18. 29. is the young man *s.*?
Job 21. 9. their houses are *s.* from fear.
Ps. 119. 117. hold me up, and I shall be *s.*
Prov. 18. 10. righteous runneth into it, and is *s.*
29. 25. whoso trusteth in the Lord shall be *s.*
Lk. 15. 27. received him *s.*
Acts 27. 44. they escaped all *s.* to land.
Phil. 3. 1. to write, for you it is *s.*

Safety, Job 3. 26. I was not in *s.*
5. 4. his children are far from *s.*
11. 18. thou shalt take thy rest in *s.*
Ps. 12. 5. I will set him in *s.*
33. 17. an horse is a vain thing for *s.*
Prov. 11. 14; 24. 6. in the multitude of counsellors is *s.*
21. 31. *s.* is of the Lord.
Is. 14. 30. needy shall lie down in *s.*
Acts 5. 23. prison shut with all *s.*
1 Thes. 5. 3. shall say, peace and *s.*
Saints, Deut. 33. 3. all his *s.* are in thy hand.
1 Sam. 2. 9. keep the feet of his *s.*
Job 15. 15. he putteth no trust in his *s.*
Ps. 16. 3. to the *s.* that are in the earth.
31. 23. love the Lord, all ye his *s.*
37. 28. the Lord forsaketh not his *s.*
50. 5. gather my *s.* together.
89. 7. God is to be feared in assembly of *s.*
97. 10. he preserveth souls of his *s.*
116. 15. precious is the death of his *s.*
132. 9. let thy *s.* shout for joy.
Prov. 2. 8. preserveth way of his *s.*
Dan. 7. 18. the *s.* shall take the kingdom.
Matt. 27. 52. many bodies of the *s.* arose.
Acts 9. 13. evil he hath done to thy *s.*
26. 10. many of the *s.* did I shut up.
Rom. 1. 7; 1 Cor. 1. 2. called to be *s.*
Rom. 8. 27. maketh intercession for the *s.*
12. 13. distributing to the necessity of *s.*
1 Cor. 6. 2. the *s.* shall judge the world.
16. 15. the ministry of *s.*
Eph. 1. 18. his inheritance in the *s.*
2. 19. fellow-citizens with the *s.*
4. 12. perfecting of the *s.*
Col. 1. 12. the *s.* in light.
1 Thes. 3. 13. coming of our Lord with his *s.*
2 Thes. 1. 10. to be glorified in his *s.*
Jude 3. faith once delivered to the *s.*
Rev. 5. 8; 8. 3. the prayers of *s.*
Sake, Gen. 3. 17. cursed is the ground for
thy *s.* [man's *s.*
8. 21. not curse the ground any more for
18. 26. spare the place for their *s.*
Num. 11. 29. enviest thou for my *s.*?
2 Sam. 9. 1. kindness for Jonathan's *s.*
18. 5. deal gently for my *s.*
Neh. 9. 31. for thy great mercies' *s.*
Ps. 6. 4; 31. 16. save me for thy mercies' *s.*
23. 3. he leadeth me for his name's *s.*
44. 22; Rom. 8. 36. for thy *s.* are we killed.
Ps. 143. 11. quicken me for thy name's *s.*
Matt. 10. 39; 16. 25; Mk. 8. 35; Lk. 9. 24. he
that loseth his life for my *s.* [my name's *s.*
Matt. 24. 9; Mk. 13. 13; Lk. 21. 17. hated for
Lk. 6. 22. cast out for Son of man's *s.*
John 11. 15. I am glad for your *s.*
13. 38. wilt thou lay down thy life for my *s.*?
14. 11. believe me for works' *s.*
Acts 26. 7. for hope's *s.* I am accused.
1 Cor. 4. 10. we are fools for Christ's *s.*
2 Cor. 4. 5. your servants for Jesus' *s.*
Col. 1. 24. for his body's *s.*, which is the
church.
1 Thes. 5. 13. esteem them for their work's *s.*
2 Tim. 2. 10. for elect's *s.*
2 John 2. for the truth's *s.*
Salute, Matt. 5. 47. if ye *s.* your brethren only.
10. 12. when ye come into a house, *s.* it.
Mk. 15. 18. began to *s.* him.
Lk. 10. 4. *s.* no man by the way.
2 Cor. 13. 13; Phil. 4. 22. the saints *s.* you.
Phil. 4. 21. *s.* every saint in Christ Jesus.
See Mk. 12. 38; Lk. 1. 29; 1 Cor. 16. 21.

Salvation, Gen. 49. 18. I have waited for thy *s.*
Ex. 14. 13 ; 2 Chr. 20. 17. see the *s.* of the Lord.
Ex. 15. 2. the Lord is become my *s.*
Deut. 32. 15. lightly esteemed the Rock of his *s.* [Israel.
1 Sam. 11. 13 ; 19. 5. Lord wrought *s.* in
2 Sam. 22. 51. he is tower of *s.* for his king.
1 Chr. 16. 23. shew forth from day to day his *s.*
2 Chr. 6. 41. let thy priests be clothed with *s.*
Ps. 3. 8. *s.* belongeth to the Lord.
13. 5. my heart shall rejoice in thy *s.*
25. 5. the God of my *s.*
27. 1 ; 62. 6 ; Is. 12. 2. the Lord is my *s.*
Ps. 37. 39. the *s.* of righteous is of the Lord.
50. 23. to whom will I shew the *s.* of God?
51. 12 ; 70. 4. restore the joy of thy *s.*
68. 20. he that is our God, is the God of *s.*
71. 15. my mouth shall shew forth thy *s.*
74. 12. working *s.* in the midst of the earth.
78. 22. they trusted not in his *s.*
85. 9. his *s.* is nigh them that fear him.
91. 16. will shew him my *s.*
95. 1. Rock of our *s.*
96. 2. shew forth his *s.* from day to day.
98. 3. all ends of earth hath seen *s.* of God.
116. 13. the cup of *s.*
118. 14 ; Is. 12. 2. the Lord is become my *s.*
Ps. 119. 155. *s.* is far from the wicked.
144. 10. that giveth *s.* unto kings.
149. 4. he will beautify the meek with *s.*
Is. 12. 3. the wells of *s.*
26. 1. *s.* will God appoint for walls.
33. 2. be thou our *s.* in time of trouble.
45. 17. saved with an everlasting *s.*
49. 8. in a day of *s.* have I helped thee.
52. 7. feet of him that publisheth *s.*
52. 10. ends of earth shall see the *s.* of God.
59. 16. his arm brought *s.*
59. 17. an helmet of *s.* on his head.
60. 18. call thy walls *S.*
61. 10. the garments of *s.*
Jer. 3. 23. in vain is *s.* hoped for.
Lam. 3. 26. wait for the *s.* of the Lord.
Jon. 2. 9. *s.* is of the Lord.
Hab. 3. 8. ride on thy chariots of *s.*
3. 18. I will joy in the God of my *s.*
Zech. 9. 9. thy King, just, and having *s.*
Lk. 1. 69. raised an horn of *s.* for us.
2. 30. mine eyes have seen thy *s.*
3. 6. all flesh shall see the *s.* of God.
19. 9. this day is *s.* come to this house.
John 4. 22. *s.* is of the Jews.
Acts 4. 12. neither is there *s.* in any other.
16. 17. shew the way of *s.*
Rom. 1. 16. the power of God unto *s.*
10. 10. confession is made to *s.*
13. 11. now is our *s.* nearer.
2 Cor. 6. 2. now is the day of *s.*
7. 10. sorrow worketh repentance to *s.*
Eph. 1. 13. the gospel of your *s.*
6. 17 ; 1 Thes. 5. 8. the helmet of *s.*
Phil. 2. 12. work out your *s.* with fear.
2 Tim. 3. 15. scriptures able to make wise to *s.*
Tit. 2. 11. grace of God that bringeth *s.*
Heb. 1. 14. them who shall be heirs of *s.*
2. 3. if we neglect so great *s.*
2. 10. the captain of their *s.*
5. 9. the author of eternal *s.*
9. 28. appear without sin unto *s.*
1 Pet. 1. 9. end of faith, the *s.* of your souls.
2 Pet. 3. 15. long-suffering of the Lord is *s.*
Jude 3. the common *s.*
Rev. 7. 10. saying, *s.* to our God.
12. 10. now is come *s.* and strength.

Same, Ps. 102. 27 ; Heb. 1. 12. thou art the *s.*
Acts 1. 11. this *s.* Jesus shall come.
Rom. 10. 12. the *s.* Lord over all. [ever.
Heb. 13. 8. the *s.* yesterday, to-day, and for
Sanctify, Ex. 31. 13. the Lord that doth *s.* you.
Lev. 11. 44 ; 20. 7 ; Num. 11. 18 ; Josh. 3. 5 ;
7. 13 ; 1 Sam. 16. 5. *s.* yourselves.
Is. 8. 13. *s.* the Lord of hosts himself.
29. 23. they shall *s.* the Holy One.
66. 17. that *s.* themselves in gardens.
Jer. 1. 5. I *s.* and ordained thee a prophet.
Ezek. 36. 23. I will *s.* my great name.
Joel 1. 14 ; 2. 15. *s.* ye a fast.
John 10. 36. him whom the Father hath *s.*
17. 17. *s.* them through thy truth.
Acts 20. 32 ; 26. 18. an inheritance among *s.*
Rom. 15. 16. being *s.* by the Holy Ghost.
1 Cor. 6. 11. but ye are *s.*
7. 14. unbelieving husband is *s.* by the wife.
Eph. 5. 26. might *s.* and cleanse the church.
1 Thes. 5. 23. the very God of peace *s.* you.
1 Tim. 4. 5. it is *s.* by the word of God.
2 Tim. 2. 21. a vessel *s.* for the Master's use.
Heb. 2. 11. he that *s.,* and they who are *s.*
10. 14. he perfected for ever them that are *s.*
13. 12. that he might *s.* the people.
1 Pet. 3. 15. *s.* the Lord God in your hearts.
See 1 Cor. 1. 30 ; 2 Thes. 2. 13 ; 1 Pet. 1. 2.
Sanctuary, Ex. 15. 17. plant them in the *s.*
25. 8. let them make me a *s.*
Ps. 20. 2. Lord send thee help from the *s.*
63. 2. as I have seen thee in the *s.*
73. 17. till I went into the *s.* of God.
Is. 60. 13. beautify the place of my *s.*
Heb. 9. 1. first covenant had a worldly *s.*
Sand, Gen. 22. 17 ; 32. 12. multiply as the *s.*
Ps. 139. 18. more in number than the *s.*
Prov. 27. 3. stone is heavy, *s.* weighty.
Matt. 7. 26. man built his house on the *s.*
Rev. 20. 8. number of whom is as the *s.*
Sat, Ps. 26. 4. I have not *s.* with vain persons.
Matt. 4. 16. the people who *s.* in darkness
Mk. 16. 19. he *s.* on the right hand of God.
Lk. 7. 15. he that was dead *s.* up.
10. 39. Mary *s.* at Jesus' feet.
19. 30. a colt whereon never man *s.*
John 4. 6. Jesus *s.* on the well.
Acts 3. 10. *s.* for alms at gate of temple.
Satan, 1 Chr. 21. 1. *S.* provoked David.
Job 1. 12. *S.* went from presence of the Lord.
Ps. 109. 6. let *S.* stand at his right hand.
Matt. 12. 26 ; Mk. 3. 23 ; Lk. 11. 18. if *S.* cast out *S.* [hind me, *S.*
Matt. 16. 23 ; Mk. 8. 33 ; Lk. 4. 8. get thee be-
Lk. 10. 18. I beheld *S.* as lightning fall.
Acts 5. 3. why hath *S.* filled thine heart?
26. 18. turn them from the power of *S.*
Rom. 16. 20. God shall bruise *S.* under feet.
2 Cor. 2. 11. lest *S.* get advantage of us.
12. 7. the messenger of *S.* to buffet me.
2 Thes. 2. 9. after the working of *S.*
1 Tim. 1. 20. whom I have delivered unto *S.*
5. 15. some have turned aside after *S.*
Rev. 2. 13. seat where *S.* dwelleth. [ness.
Satiate, Jer. 31. 14. *s.* soul of priests with fat-
46. 10. sword shall be *s.* with blood.
Satisfy, Job 38. 27. to *s.* the desolate ground.
Ps. 17. 15. I shall be *s.* with thy likeness.
22. 26. the meek shall eat and be *s.*
37. 19. in days of famine be *s.*
63. 5. my soul shall be *s.*
90. 14. O *s.* us early with thy mercy.
91. 16. with long life will I *s.* him.

Satisfy—*Continued.*

Ps. 103. 5. who *s.* thy mouth with good things.
105. 40. he *s.* them with bread from heaven.
107. 9. he *s.* the longing soul.
132. 15. I will *s.* her poor with bread.
145. 16. thou *s.* every livin *g* thing.
Prov. 6. 30. if he steal to *s.* his soul.
12. 11. he that tilleth his land shall be *s.*
14. 14. a good man shall be *s.* from himself.
20. 13. open thine eyes, and thou shalt be *s.*
30. 15. three things are never *s.*
Eccl. 1. 8. the eye is not *s.* with seeing.
5. 10. shall not be *s.* with silver.
Is. 9. 20 ; Mic. 6. 14. shall eat, and not be *s.*
53. 11. see of travail of his soul, and be *s.*
58. 11. the Lord shall *s.* thy soul.
Jer. 31. 14. people be *s.* with my goodness.
Hab. 2. 5. he is as death, and cannot be *s.*
Mk. 8. 4. whence is these with bread?

Save, Gen. 45. 7. to *s.* your lives.
Deut. 20. 4. the Lord goeth to *s.* you.
28. 29. no man shall *s.* thee.
Jud. 6. 15. wherewith shall I *s.* Israel?
1 Sam. 14. 6. no restraint to *s.* by many or few.
Job 2. 6. in thine hand, but *s.* his life.
22. 29. he shall *s.* the humble.
Ps. 7. 10. God who *s.* the upright.
34. 18. he *s.* such as be of contrite spirit.
44. 3. neither did their arm *s.* them.
60. 5. *s.* with thy right hand.
69. 35. God will *s.* Zion.
72. 4. he shall *s.* the children of the needy.
86. 2. *s.* thy servant.
109. 31. to *s.* him from those that condemn.
118. 25. *s.* now I beseech thee.
138. 7. thy right hand shall *s.* me.
145. 19. hear their cry, and *s.* them.
Prov. 20. 22. wait on the Lord, and he shall *s.* thee.
Is. 35. 4. your God will come and *s.* you.
45. 20. pray unto a god that cannot *s.*
45. 22. look unto me, and be ye *s.*
59. 1. Lord's hand is not shortened that it cannot *s.*
63. 1. mighty to *s.*
Jer. 2. 28. let them arise, if they can *s.* thee.
8. 20. the summer is ended, and we are not *s.* [to *s.* thee.
15. 20 ; 30. 11 ; 42. 11 ; 46. 27. I am with thee
17. 14. *s.* me, and I shall be *s.*
Hos. 1. 7. I will *s.* them by the Lord.
13. 10. is there any other that may *s.* thee?
Hab. 1. 2. cry to thee, and thou wilt not *s.*
Zeph. 3. 17. he will *s.*
Matt. 1. 21. *s.* his people from their sins.
16. 25 ; Mk. 8. 35 , Lk. 9. 24. whosoever will *s.* his life.
Matt. 18. 11 ; Lk. 19. 10. to seek and to *s.* that which was lost.
Matt. 19. 25 ; Mk. 10. 26 ; Lk. 18. 26. who then can be *s.*?
Matt. 27. 42 ; Mk. 15. 31. he *s.* others, himself he cannot *s.*
Mk. 3. 4 ; Lk. 6. 9. is it lawful to *s.*?
Lk. 9. 56. not to destroy, but to *s.*
23. 35. let him *s.* himself. [be *s.*
John 5. 34. these things I say that ye might
12. 47. I came not to judge, but to *s.*
Acts 2. 40. *s.* yourselves from this generation.
4. 12. none other name whereby we must be *s.*
16. 30. what must I do to be *s.*?

Save—*Continued.*

Rom. 8. 24. we are *s.* by hope.
11. 14 ; 1 Cor. 9. 22. if I might *s.* some.
1 Cor. 1. 21. by foolishness of preaching to *s.* some.
3. 15. *s.* as by fire.
1 Tim. 1. 15. Christ came to *s.* sinners.
4. 16. thou shalt *s.* thyself and them.
Heb. 5. 7. able to *s.* him from death.
7. 25. able to *s.* to the uttermost.
11. 7. an ark to *s.* his house.
Jas. 1. 21. word which is able to *s.* your souls.
2. 14. can faith *s.* him?
4. 12. able to *s.* and destroy.
5. 15. the prayer of faith shall *s.* the sick.
5. 20. shall *s.* a soul from death.
1 Pet. 4. 18. if the righteous scarcely be *s.*
Jude 23. others *s.* with fear.

Saviour, 2 Sam. 22. 3. my refuge, my *s.*
2 Ki. 13. 5. the Lord gave Israel a *s.*
Ps. 106. 21. they forgat God their *s.*
Is. 19. 20. he shall send them a *s.* [no *s.*
43. 11. I am the Lord, beside me there is
45. 15. hidest thyself, O God, the *S.*
45. 21. a just God and a *S.*
60. 16. shalt know I am thy *S.*
63. 8. so he was their *S.*
Lk. 1. 2. 11. born in city of David a *s.*
John 4. 42. this is Christ, the *S.* of the world.
Acts 13. 23. God raised to Israel a *S.*
Eph. 5. 23. Christ is the *s.* of the body.
Phil. 3. 20. whence we look for the *S.*
1 Tim. 4. 10. God who is the *S.* of all men.
Tit. 2. 10. adorn doctrine of God our *S.*
2 Pet. 2. 20. knowledge of the Lord and *S.*
Jude 25. the only wise God our *S.*

Savour, Gen. 8. 21. the Lord smelled a sweet *s.*
Ex. 5. 21. made our *s.* to be abhorred.
Cant. 1. 3. *s.* of thy good ointments.
Matt. 5. 13 ; Lk. 14. 34. if the salt have lost his *s.*? [smelling *s*
Eph. 5. 2. a sacrifice to God for a sweet-
See Matt. 16. 23 ; Mk. 8. 33.

Saw, Gen. 26. 28. we *s.* the Lord was with thee.
Ex. 24. 10. they *s.* the God of Israel.
2 Chr. 15. 9. *s.* the Lord was with him.
25. 21. they *s.* one another in the face.
Job 29. 11. when the eye *s.* me.
Ps. 77. 16. the waters *s.* thee.
114. 3. sea *s.* it, and fled. [God.
Eccl. 2. 24. this I *s.*, it was from hand of
Cant. 3. 3. *s.* ye him whom my soul loveth?
Matt. 17. 8. they *s.* no man.
Mk. 8. 23. asked if he *s.* ought.
Lk. 24. 24. but him they *s.* not.
John 1. 48. under the fig tree I *s.* thee.
8. 56. Abraham *s.* my day.
19. 35. he that *s.* it, bare record.

Say, Gen. 44. 16. what shall we *s.* to my lord?
Ex. 3. 13. what shall I *s.* to them?
Num. 22. 19. know what the Lord will *s.*
Ezra 9. 10. O God, what shall we *s.*?
Job 9. 12 ; Eccl. 8. 4. who will *s.* to him, what doest thou? [yourselves.
Matt. 3. 9 ; Lk. 3. 8. think not to *s.* within
Matt. 7. 22. many will *s.* in that day.
16. 15 ; Mk. 8. 29 ; Lk. 9. 20. whom *s.* ye that I am?
Matt. 23. 3. they *s.*, and do not.
Lk. 7. 40. I have somewhat to *s.* to thee.
John 8. 54. of whom ye *s.* that he is your God.
Heb. 11. 32. what shall I more *s.*?
Jas. 4. 15. ye ought to *s.*, if the Lord will.

Saying, Deut. 1. 23. the *s.* pleased me well.
1 Ki. 2. 38. the *s.* is good.
Ps. 49. 4. my dark *s.* on the harp.
78. 2. utter dark *s.* of old.
Jon. 4. 2. was not this my *s.?*
Matt. 19. 11. all men cannot receive this *s.*
28. 15. this *s.* is commonly reported.
Lk. 9. 44. let these *s.* sink into your ears.
John 4. 37. herein is that *s.* true.
6. 60. an hard *s.*
1 Cor. 15. 54. be brought to pass the *s.*
1 Tim. 1. 15. this is a faithful *s.*   [one die.
Scarcely, Rom. 5. 7. a for a righteous man will
1 Pet. 4. 18. if righteous *s.* be saved.
See Gen. 27. 30; Deut. 8. 9; Acts 14. 18.
Scatter, Gen. 11. 9. thence did the Lord *s.* them.
Lev. 26. 33. I will *s.* you among the heathen.
Num. 10. 35; Ps. 68. 1. let thine enemies be *s.*
Job 37. 11. he *s.* his bright cloud.
38. 24. which *s.* the east wind.
Ps. 68. 30. *s.* the people that delight in war.
92. 9. workers of iniquity shall be *s.*
106. 27. lifted up hand to *s.* them.
147. 16. he *s.* the hoar frost.   [creaseth.
Prov. 11. 24. there is that *s.,* and yet in-
Jer. 23. 1. woe to pastors that *s.* the sheep.
Zech. 13. 7; Matt. 26. 31; Mk. 14. 27. sheep
shall be *s.*
Matt. 9. 36. *s.* as sheep having no shepherd.
12. 30; Lk. 11. 23. he that gathereth not, *s.*
John 10. 12. wolf *s.* the sheep.
Sceptre, Gen. 49. 10. the *s.* shall not depart
from Judah.   [right *s.*
Ps. 45. 6; Heb. 1. 8. *s.* of thy kingdom is a
Scholar, 1 Chr. 25. 8. the teacher as the *s.*
Mal. 2. 12. Lord will cut off master and *s*
Science, Dan. 1. 4. understanding *s*
1 Tim. 6. 20. avoiding oppositions of *s.*
Scorner, Prov. 9. 8. reprove not a *s.* lest he
hate thee.
13. 1. a *s.* heareth not rebuke.
15. 12. a *s.* loveth not one that reproveth.
19. 25. smite a *s.*   [made wise.
21. 11. when *s.* is punished, the simple is
24. 9. the *s.* is abomination to men.
Is. 29. 20. the *s.* is consumed.
Hos. 7. 5. he stretched his hand with *s.*
See Ps. 1. 1; 44. 13; 79. 4; Prov. 19. 28; Is. 28. 14.
Scourge, Job 5. 21. the *s.* of the tongue.
9. 23. if the *s.* slay suddenly.
Is. 10. 26. the Lord shall stir up a *s.*
28. 15. the overflowing *s.*   [him.
Matt. 20. 19; Mk. 10. 34; Lk. 18. 33. shall *s.*
John 2. 15. a *s.* of small cords.
Acts 22. 25. is it lawful to *s.* a Roman?
Heb. 12. 6. the Lord *s.* every son he receiveth.
Scribe, 1 Chr. 27. 32. a wise man and a *s.*
Is. 33. 18. where is the *s.?*
Jer. 8. 8. the pen of the *s.* is in vain.
Matt. 5. 20. exceed the righteousness of the *s.*
13. 52. every *s.* instructed unto the kingdom.
Mk. 12. 38; Lk. 20. 46. beware of the *s.*
1 Cor. 1. 20. where is the *s.?*
Scrip, 1 Sam. 17. 40. David put stones in *s.*
Matt. 10. 10; Mk. 6. 8; Lk. 9. 3; 10. 4. nor *s.*
for your journey.
Lk. 22. 36. let him take his purse and *s.*
Scripture, Dan. 10. 21. what is noted in *s.*
Mk. 12. 10. have ye not read this *s.?*
Acts 8. 32. the place of *s.* which he read.
2 Tim. 3. 16. all *s.* is by inspiration of God.
Jas. 4. 5. do ye think the *s.* saith in vain?
1 Pet. 2. 6. it is contained in *s.*
2 Pet. 1. 20. no *s.* is of private interpretation.

Search, Num. 13. 2. that they may *s.* the land.
1 Chr. 28. 9. the Lord *s.* all hearts.
Job 11. 7. canst thou by *s.* find out God?
13. 9. is it good that he should *s.* you out?
36. 26. neither can the number of his years
be *s.* out.
Ps. 44. 21. shall not God *s.* this out?
139. 23. *s.* me, O God, know my heart.
Prov. 25. 2. honour of kings to *s.* out a matter.
Eccl. 1. 13; 7. 25. I gave my heart to *s*
wisdom.
Is. 40. 28. there is no *s.* of his understanding.
Jer. 17. 10. I the Lord *s.* the heart.
29. 13. when ye *s.* for me with all your heart.
Lam. 3. 40. let us *s.* our ways, and turn.
Ezek. 34. 11. I will *s.* my sheep.
Zeph. 1. 12. I will *s.* Jerusalem with candles.
John 5. 39; Acts 17. 11. *s.* the scriptures.
Rom. 8. 27. he that *s.* hearts knoweth mind
of the Spirit.
1 Cor. 2. 10. the Spirit *s.* all things.
1 Pet. 1. 10. prophets *s.* diligently.
Rev. 2. 23. he which *s.* the reins.
See Ps. 64. 6; 77. 6; Jer. 2. 34.
Seared, 1 Tim. 4. 2. conscience *s.* with hot iron.
Season, Gen. 1. 14. lights be for signs, and *s.*
Deut. 28. 12. give rain in his *s.*
Josh. 24. 7. dwelt in wilderness a long *s.*
2 Chr. 15. 3. for a long *s.* without the true
God.
Job 5. 26. as a shock of corn in his *s.*
Ps. 1. 3. bringeth forth fruit in his *s.*
22. 2. I cry in the night *s.*
Prov. 15. 23. a word spoken in due *s.*
Eccl. 3. 1. to every thing there is a *s.*
Is. 50. 4. know how to speak a word in *s.*
Jer. 5. 24. former and latter rain in his *s.*
33. 20. not be day and night in their *s.*
Dan. 2. 21. changeth the times and *s.*
7. 12. lives prolonged for a *s.*
Matt. 21. 41. render fruits in their *s.*
Lk. 13. 1. were present at that *s.*
23. 8. desirous to see Jesus of a long *s.*
John 5. 4. angel went down at a certain *s.*
5. 35. willing for a *s.* to rejoice.
Acts 1. 7. not for you to know times or *s.*
13. 11. not seeing the sun for a *s.*
24. 25. a convenient *s.*
2 Tim. 4. 2. be instant in *s.* and out of *s.*
Heb. 11. 25. pleasures of sin for a *s.*
1 Pet. 1. 6. though for a *s.* if need be.
See Lk. 9. 50; Lk. 14. 34; Col. 4. 6.
Seat, Job 23. 3. that I might come even to
his *s.!*   [sold doves.
Matt. 21. 12; Mk. 11. 15. the *s.* of them that
Matt. 23. 6; Mk. 12. 39. chief *s.* in the synagogues.
Rev. 2. 13. dwellest where Satan's *s.* is.
Secret, Gen. 49. 6. come not into their *s.*
Job 15. 8. hast thou heard the *s.* of God?
29. 4. the *s.* of God was upon my tabernacle.
Ps. 25. 14. the *s.* of the Lord is with them
that fear him.
27. 5. in *s.* of his tabernacle hide me.
64. 4. may shoot in *s.* at the perfect.
139. 15. when I was made in *s.*
Prov. 3. 32. his *s.* is with the righteous.
9. 17. bread eaten in *s.*
21. 14. a gift in *s.* pacifieth anger.
25. 9. discover not a *s.* to another.
Is. 45. 19; 48. 16. I have not spoken in *s.*
Amos 3. 7. he revealeth his *s.* to his servants.
Matt. 6. 4. thy Father who seeth in *s.*
John 18. 20. in *s.* have I said nothing.

Secret, Deut. 29. 29. *s.* things belong to God.
Jud. 3. 19. I have a *s.* errand.
13. 18. why askest my name, seeing it is *s.* ?
Ps. 19. 12. cleanse thou me from *s.* faults.
90. 8. *s.* sins in light of thy countenance.
91. 1. *s.* place of the Most High.
Prov. 27. 5. open rebuke better than *s.* love.
Matt. 24. 26. he is in *s.* chambers.
Lk. 11. 33. no man putteth candle in *s.* place.

Secretly, Gen. 31. 27. wherefore didst thou flee *s.* ?
1 Sam. 23. 9. Saul *s.* practised mischief.
2 Sam. 12. 12. thou didst it *s.*
Job 4. 12. a thing was *s.* brought to me.
31. 27. my heart hath been *s.* enticed.
Ps. 10. 9. he lieth in wait *s.* as a lion.
31. 20. keep them *s.* in a pavilion.
John 11. 28. she called her sister *s.*
19. 38. a disciple, but *s.* for fear of the Jews.

Sect, Acts 5. 17. the *s.* of the Sadducees.
15. 5. the *s.* of the Pharisees.
24. 5. the *s.* of the Nazarenes.
26. 5. the straitest *s.* of our religion.

Secure, Job 12. 6. they that provoke God are *s.*
Prov. 3. 29. seeing he dwelleth *s.*
Matt. 28. 14. persuade him, and *s.* you.

See, Gen. 11. 5. Lord came down to *s.* the city.
44. 23. you shall *s.* my face no more.
Ex. 12. 13. when I *s.* the blood.
33. 20. there shall no man *s.* me, and live.
Num. 24. 17. I shall *s.* him, but not now.
Deut. 3. 25. let me *s.* the good land.
2 Ki. 6. 17. open his eyes that he may *s.*
Job 7. 7. mine eye shall no more *s.* good.
19. 26. in my flesh shall I *s.* God.
Ps. 14. 2; 53. 2. God looked to *s.* if any.
34. 8. O taste and *s.* the Lord is good.
40. 3. many shall *s.* it, and trust in the Lord.
66. 5. come and *s.* the works of God.
94. 9. he that formed the eye, shall he not *s.* ?
Is. 6. 10. lest they *s.* with their eyes.
30. 20. thine eyes shall *s.* thy teachers.
32. 3. the eyes of them that *s.* not be dim.
33. 17. thine eyes shall *s.* the king in his beauty.
52. 8. they shall *s.* eye to eye.
53. 2. when we shall *s.* him.
Matt. 5. 8. pure in heart shall *s.* God.
11. 4. shew John the things ye *s.* and hear.
12. 38. we would *s.* a sign.
13. 14; Mk. 4. 12; Acts 28. 26. *s.* ye shall *s.*
Matt. 27. 4. *s.* thou to that.
28. 6. come *s.* the place where the Lord lay.
Mk. 8. 18. having eyes, *s.* ye not ?
Lk. 17. 22. desire to *s.* and ye shall not *s.*
John 1. 39; 11. 34; Rev. 6. 1. come and *s.*
John 3. 36. he shall not *s.* life.
9. 25. I was blind, now I *s.*
9. 39. that they who *s.* not, might *s.*
1 Cor. 13. 12. we *s.* through a glass. [him.
Heb. 2. 8. we *s.* not yet all things put under
1 Pet. 1. 8. though now ye *s.* him not.
1 John 3. 2. we shall *s.* him as he is.
Rev. 1. 7. every eye shall *s.* him.

Seed, Gen. 3. 15. enmity between thy *s.* and [her *s.*
Ex. 16. 31. manna, like coriander *s.*
Lev. 19. 19. thou shalt not sow mingled *s.*
26. 16. ye shall sow your *s.* in vain.
27. 16. estimation shall be according to *s.*
Num. 20. 5. it is no place of *s.*
Deut. 11. 10. Egypt where thou sowedst *s.*
14. 22. tithe all the increase of your *s.*
28. 28. thou shalt carry much *s.* into field.
Ps. 126. 6. bearing precious *s.*

Seed—Continued.
Eccl. 11. 6. in the morning sow thy *s.*
Is. 17. 11. make thy *s.* to flourish.
55. 10. that it may give *s.* to the sower.
Jer. 35. 7. sow *s.* nor plant vineyard.
Joel 1. 17. the *s.* is rotten under the clods.
Amos 9. 13. overtake him that soweth *s.*
Hag. 2. 19. is the *s.* yet in the barn ?
Zech. 8. 12. the *s.* shall be prosperous.
Mal. 2. 3. I will corrupt your *s.*
2. 15. might seek a godly *s.*
Matt. 13. 19. *s.* by the way side.
13. 37. that soweth good *s.* is Son of man.
Mk. 4. 26. a man should cast *s.* into ground.
Lk. 8. 11. the *s.* is the word of God.
1 Cor. 15. 38. to every *s.* his own body.
2 Cor. 9. 10. ministreth *s.* to sower.
1 Pet. 1. 23. born again, not of corruptible *s.*
1 John 3. 9. his *s.* remaineth in him.

Seek, Gen. 43. 18. that he may *s.* occasion.
Deut. 4. 29. if thou *s.* him with all thy heart.
23. 6; Ezra 9. 12. thou shalt not *s.* their peace.
1 Ki. 19. 10, 14. they *s.* my life to take it.
1 Chr. 28. 9; 2 Chr. 15. 2. if thou *s.* him he will be found.
2 Chr. 19. 3; 30. 19. prepared heart to *s.* God.
34. 3. Josiah began to *s.* after God.
Ezra 4. 2. we *s.* your God, as ye do.
Neh. 2. 10. to *s.* the welfare of Israel.
Job 5. 8. I would *s.* unto God.
7. 21. shalt *s.* me in the morning.
8. 5. wouldest *s.* unto God betimes.
20. 10. children shall *s.* to please the poor.
Ps. 9. 10. hast not forsaken them that *s.* thee.
10. 15. *s.* out his wickedness till thou find none.
14. 2; 53. 2. if there were any that did *s.*
24. 6. generation of them that *s.* him.
27. 4. one thing have I desired, that will I *s.* after. [I *s.*
27. 8. *s.* ye my face; thy face, Lord, will
34. 14; 1 Pet. 3. 11. *s.* peace and pursue it.
Ps. 63. 1. early will I *s.* thee.
69. 32. your heart shall live that *s.* God.
70. 4. let those that *s.* thee rejoice.
83. 16. that they may *s.* thy name.
104. 21. young lions *s.* meat from God.
119. 2. *s.* him with the whole heart.
122. 9. I will *s.* thy good.
Prov. 1. 28. they shall *s.* me, but not find me.
8. 17. those that *s.* me early shall find me.
23. 35. I will *s.* it yet again. [loveth.
Cant. 3. 2. I will *s.* whom my soul
Is. 1. 17. learn to do well, *s.* judgment.
8. 19. should not a people *s.* unto their God ?
34. 16. *s.* ye out of the book of the Lord.
45. 19. I said not, *s.* ye my face in vain.
Jer. 29. 13. ye shall *s.* me and find.
Lam. 3. 25. Lord is good to the soul that *s.* him.
Ezek. 7. 25. they shall *s.* peace.
34. 16. I will *s.* that which was lost
Dan. 9. 3. I set my face to *s.* by prayer.
Amos 5. 4. *s.* ye me, and ye shall live.
8. 12. to *s.* the word of the Lord.
Zeph. 2. 3. *s.* ye the Lord, all ye meek.
Mal. 2. 7. they should *s.* the law.
Matt. 6. 32. after these things do the Gentiles *s.* [God.
6. 33; Lk. 12. 31. *s.* ye first the kingdom of
Matt. 7. 7; Lk. 11. 9. *s.* and ye shall find.
Matt. 28. 5; Mk. 16. 6. I know that ye *s.* Jesus.

Seek—*Continued.*
Mk. 1. 37. all men *s.* for thee.
Lk. 12. 30. these things the nations *s.*
13. 24. many will *s.* to enter in.
15. 8. doth she not *s.* diligently?
17. 33. whosoever shall *s.* to save his life.
19. 10. the Son of man is come to *s.* and to save.
John 1. 38. Jesus saith, what *s.* ye?
7. 34. ye shall *s.* me, and shall not find me.
Acts 10. 19. three men *s.* thee.
Rom. 2. 7. to them who *s.* for glory.
3. 11. there is none that *s.* after God.
1 Cor. 10. 24. let no man *s.* his own.
13. 5. charity *s.* not her own.
Phil. 2. 21. all *s.* their own things.
Col. 3. 1. *s.* those things which are above.
Heb. 11. 14. declare plainly they *s.* a country.
13. 14. but we *s.* one to come.
Rev. 9. 6. in those days shall men *s.* death.
Seem, Gen. 27. 12. I shall *s.* as a deceiver.
Num. 16. 9. *s.* it but a small thing?
Prov. 14. 12. there is a way that *s.* right.
Lk. 8. 18. taken that which he *s.* to have.
1 Cor. 3. 18. if any *s.* to be wise.
Heb. 4. 1. lest any *s.* to come short.
12. 11. no chastening *s.* to be joyous.
Jas. 1. 26. if any man *s.* to be religious.
Seen, Gen. 32. 30. I have *s.* God face to face.
Ex. 19. 4. ye have *s.* what I did to Egyptians.
20. 22. ye have *s.* that I talked with you.
Jud. 13. 22. die, because we have *s.* God.
2 Ki. 20. 15. what have they *s.* ?
Job 13. 1. mine eye hath *s.* all this.
Ps. 68. 24. they have *s.* thy goings, O God.
Eccl. 6. 5. he hath not *s.* the sun.
Is. 6. 5. mine eyes have *s.* the Lord.
64. 4; 1 Cor. 2. 9. neither hath eye *s.*
Is. 66. 8. who hath *s.* such things?
Jer. 12. 3. thou hast *s.* me, tried heart.
Matt. 6. 1; 23. 5. to be *s.* of men.
9. 33. never so *s.* in Israel.
Mk. 9. 9. tell no man what they had *s.*
Lk. 5. 26. we have *s.* strange things.
24. 23. they had *s.* a vision of angels.
John 1. 18. no man hath *s.* God.
3. 11. we testify that we have *s.*
8. 57. hast thou *s.* Abraham?
14. 9. he that hath *s.* me, hath *s.* the Father.
20. 29. because thou hast *s.*, thou hast believed.
Acts 4. 20. speak things we have *s.*
1 Cor. 9. 1. have I not *s.* Jesus Christ?
1 Tim. 6. 16. whom no man hath *s.*
Heb. 11. 1. evidence of things not *s.*
1 Pet. 1. 8. whom having not *s.*, ye love.
1 John 4. 20. can he love God whom he hath not *s.* ?
Sell, Gen. 25. 31. *s.* me thy birthright.
37. 27. let us *s.* him to Ishmeelites.
1 Ki. 21. 25. Ahab did *s.* himself to work wickedness.
Neh. 5. 8. will ye even *s.* your brethren?
10. 31. victuals on Sabbath day to *s.*
Prov. 23. 23. buy the truth, and *s.* it not.
Joel 3. 8. I will *s.* your sons and daughters.
Amos 8. 6. *s.* the refuse of the wheat.
Matt. 19. 21; Mk. 10. 21; Lk. 18. 22, go and *s.* that thou hast.
Lk. 22. 36. let him *s.* his garment.
Jas. 4. 13. we will buy and *s.*
See Is. 24. 2; Acts 16. 14.

Send, Gen. 24. 7. God shall *s.* his angel.
24. 12. *s.* me good speed this day.
45. 5. God did *s.* me to preserve life.
Ex. 4. 13. *s.* by hand of him whom thou wilt *s.*
Lev. 16. 21. *s.* him away by a fit man.
Jud. 13. 8. man of God thou didst *s.*
Ps. 43. 3. *s.* out thy light and truth.
118. 25. O Lord, *s.* now prosperity.
Is. 6. 8. whom shall I *s.* ?
19. 20. he shall *s.* them a Saviour.
Matt. 9. 38; Lk. 10. 2. *s.* labourers.
Matt. 15. 23. *s.* her away.
Mk. 3. 14. that he might *s.* them to preach.
John 14. 26. whom the Father will *s.* in my name.
17. 8. believed that thou didst *s.* me.
Sent, Gen. 45. 7. God *s.* me before you.
Ex. 3. 14. I AM hath *s.* me to you.
Matt. 15. 24. I am not *s.* but to lost sheep of Israel.   [his son.
21. 37; Mk. 12. 6. last of all he *s.* unto them
John 4. 34. the will of him that *s.* me.
9. 4. work the works of him that *s.* me.
11. 42. may believe thou hast *s.* me.
17. 3. eternal life to know him whom thou hast *s.*   [they be *s.* ?
Rom. 10. 15. how shall they preach except
1 Pet. 1. 12. the Holy Ghost *s.* from heaven.
1 John 4. 9. God *s.* his only-begotten Son.
Sentence, Ps. 17. 2. let my *s.* come forth.
Prov. 16. 10. a divine *s.* in the lips of the king.   [speedily.
Eccl. 8. 11. because *s.* is not executed
Dan. 8. 23. a king understanding dark *s.*
Lk. 23. 24. Pilate gave *s.*
2 Cor. 1. 9. we had the *s.* of death.
Separate, Deut. 19. 2. thou shalt *s.* three cities.
Prov. 16. 28; 17. 9. *s.* friends.
19. 4. the poor is *s.* from his neighbour.
Matt. 25. 32. he shall *s.* them.   [Christ?
Rom. 8. 35. who shall *s.* us from love of
2 Cor. 6. 17. be ye *s.*
Heb. 7. 26. *s.* from sinners.
Serpent, Gen. 3. 1. the *s.* was more subtil.
49. 17. Dan shall be a *s.* by the way.
Num. 21. 9. Moses made a *s.* of brass.
Job 26. 13. his hand formed the crooked *s.*
Ps. 58. 4. like the poison of a *s.*
140. 3. sharpened their tongues like a *s.*
Prov. 23. 32. at last it biteth like a *s.*
Eccl. 10. 8; Amos 5. 19. a *s.* shall bite him.
Is. 14. 29. a fiery flying *s.*
27. 1. the Lord shall punish the *s.*
65. 25. dust shall be the *s.* meat.
Mic. 7. 17. shall lick dust like a *s.*
Matt. 7. 10; Lk. 11. 11. will he give him a *s.* ?
Matt. 10. 16. be ye wise as *s.*
Mk. 16. 18. they shall take up *s.*
John 3. 14. as Moses lifted up the *s.*
1 Cor. 10. 9. were destroyed of *s.*
Rev. 12. 9; 20. 2. that old *s.*, called the Devil.
Servant, Gen. 9. 25. a *s.* of *s.* shall he be.
Ex. 21. 5. if the *s.* plainly say.
Job 7. 2. as a *s.* desireth the shadow.
Ps. 116. 16; 119. 125; 143. 12. I am thy *s.*
Prov. 22. 7. the borrower is *s.* to the lender.
Is. 24. 2. as with *s.*, so with master.
Jer. 2. 14. is Israel a *s.* ?
Matt. 10. 25. enough for *s.* to be as his lord.
25. 21. good and faithful *s.*
Mk. 12. 2. sent to husbandmen a *s.*
Lk. 12. 47. that *s.* which knew his lord's will.
17. 9. doth he thank that *s.* ?

Servant—Continued.

Lk. 20. 10. at the season he sent a s.
John 8. 35. the s. abideth not in house for ever.   [lord.
13. 16 ; 15. 20. the s. is not greater than his
Rom. 1. 1. a s. of Jesus Christ.
1 Cor. 7. 21. art thou called, being a s. ?
Phil. 2. 7. he took the form of a s.
Philem. 16. not as a s., but above a s.
Heb. 3. 5. Moses was faithful as a s.

Serve, Gen. 15. 14. nation they s. will I judge.
25. 23 ; Rom. 9. 12. the elder shall s. the younger.   [nor s. them.
Ex. 20. 5 ; Deut. 5. 9. not bow down to them,
Deut. 6. 13 ; 10. 12 ; 11. 13 ; 13. 4 ; Josh. 22. 5 ;
24. 14 ; 1 Sam. 7. 3 ; 12. 14. thou shalt fear the Lord, and s. him.
Josh. 24. 15. choose you whom ye will s.
2 Sam. 22. 44. people I knew not shall s. me.
1 Chr. 28. 9. s. him with a perfect heart.
Job 21. 15. what is the Almighty, that we should s. him?
Ps. 22. 30. a seed shall s. him.
72. 11. all nations shall s. him.
97. 7. confounded that s. graven images.
Is. 43. 24. made me to s. with thy sins.
56. 6. join themselves to the Lord, to s. him.
Dan. 6. 16. thy God whom thou s. will deliver.
Zeph. 3. 9. to s. him with one consent.
Mal. 3. 14. said, it is vain to s. God.   [ters.
Matt. 6. 24 ; Lk. 16. 13. no man can s. two mas-
Lk. 10. 40. left me to s. alone.
15. 29. these many years do I s. thee.
22. 26. is chief, as he that doth s.   [me.
John 12. 26. if any man s. me, let him follow
Acts 6. 2. leave word of God, and s. tables.
Rom. 7. 6. should s. in newness of spirit.
Gal. 5. 13. by love s. one another.
Col. 3. 24. ye s. the Lord Christ.   [God.
1 Thes. 1. 9. turned from idols to s. the living
Heb. 12. 28. we may s. God acceptably.
Rev. 7. 15. they s. him day and night.

Service, Ex. 12. 26. what mean you by this s. ?
1 Chr. 29. 5. who is willing to consecrate his s. to the Lord?
John 16. 2. will think he doeth God s.
Rom. 12. 1. which is your reasonable s.
Eph. 6. 7. doing s. as to the Lord.
Heb. 9. 1. ordinances of divine s.
Rev. 2. 19. I know thy works and s.

Set, Gen. 9. 13. I do s. my bow in the cloud.
Deut. 7. 7. Lord did not s. his love on you.
11. 26. I s. before you blessing and curse.
30. 15. I s. before thee life and death.
Job 33. 5. s. thy words in order before me.
Ps. 4. 3. Lord s. apart him that is godly.
16. 8. I s. the Lord always before me.
20. 5. we will s. up our banners.
40. 2. s. my feet upon a rock.
91. 14. he hath s. his love upon me.
118. 5. and s. me in a large place.
Eccl. 7. 14. God hath s. one against the other.
Jer. 21. 8. I s. before you way of life.
Matt. 5. 14. a city s. on a hill.
Lk. 11. 6. I have nothing to s. before thee.
23. 11. Herod s. him at nought.
John 3. 33. s. to his seal that God is true.
Acts 18. 10. no man shall s. on thee.
Heb. 6. 18. lay hold on hope s. before us.
Rev. 3. 8. s. before thee an open door.

Settle, Ps. 65. 10. thou s. the furrows thereof.
Lk. 21. 14. s. it in your hearts.
Col. 1. 23. in faith, grounded and s.
1 Pet. 5. 10. God strengthen, s. you.

Sew, Gen. 3. 7. they s. fig leaves together.
Eccl. 3. 7. a time to rend, a time to s.
Ezek. 13. 18. woe to women that s. pillows.
Mk. 2. 21. no man s. new cloth on old garment.

Shade, Ps. 121. 5. the Lord is thy s.

Shadow, Gen. 19. 8. the s. of my roof.
2 Ki. 20. 9. shall the s. go forward?
Job 7. 2. as a servant desireth the s.
14. 2. he fleeth as a s., and continueth not.
Ps. 17. 8. hide me under s. of wings.
91. 1. abide under s. of the Almighty.
102. 11. my days are like a s.   [clineth.
109. 23. I am gone like the s. when it de-
144. 4 ; Eccl. 8. 13. his days are as a s.
Eccl. 6. 12. life he spendeth as a s.   [light.
Cant. 2. 3. I sat under his s. with great de-
2. 17 ; 4. 6. till the s. flee away.
Is. 4. 6. for a s. in the day time.
25. 4. a s. from the heat.
32. 2. as the s. of a great rock.
49. 2 ; 51. 16. in the s. of his hand.
Jer. 6. 4. the s. of evening are stretched out.
Lam. 4. 20. under his s. we shall live.
Hos. 4. 13. the s. thereof is good.
14. 7. they that dwell under his s. shall return.   [of it.
Mk. 4. 32. fowls of air may lodge under s.
Acts 5. 15. the s. of Peter might overshadow.
Col. 2. 17. a s. of things to come.
Heb. 10. 1. the law having a s. of good things.
Jas. 1. 17. with whom is no s. of turning.

Shake, Jud. 16. 20. I will s. myself.
Job 9. 6. s. the earth out of her place.
Ps. 46. 3. though the mountains s.
72. 16. the fruit thereof shall s. like Lebanon.
Is. 2. 19. when he ariseth to s. the earth.
13. 13 ; Hag. 2. 6, 21. I will s. the heavens.
Is. 24. 18. foundations of earth do s.
52. 2. s. thyself from the dust.
Hag. 2. 7. I will s. all nations.
Matt. 10. 14 ; Mk. 6. 11 ; Lk. 9. 5. s. dust off your feet.
Matt. 28. 4. for fear the keepers did s.
Lk. 6. 38. good measure s. together.
2 Thes. 2. be not soon s. in mind.
Heb. 12. 26. I s. not the earth only.

Shame, Ps. 4. 2. how long turn my glory to s. ?
40. 14 ; 82. 17. let them be put to s.
132. 18. enemies will I clothe with s.
Prov. 10. 5 ; 17. 2. a son that causeth s.
Is. 61. 7. for your s. ye shall have double.
Dan. 12. 2. awake, some to s.   [room.
Lk. 14. 9. begin with s. to take the lowest
Acts 5. 41. counted worthy to suffer s.
Phil. 3. 19. whose glory is in their s.
Heb. 6. 6. put him to an open s.
12. 2. endured the cross, despising the s.

Shape, Lk. 3. 22. descended in bodily s.
John 5. 37. nor seen his s.

Sharp, Josh. 5. 2. make thee s. knives.
1 Sam. 13. 20. to s. every man his share.
Ps. 45. 5. arrows s. in the heart.
52. 2. tongue like a s. razor.
57. 4. their tongue a s. sword.
Prov. 25. 18. man that beareth false witness is a s. arrow.
27. 17. iron s. iron, so a man s. his friend.
Acts 15. 39. the contention was so s.
Heb. 4. 12. word of God s. than any sword.

Shed, Gen. 9. 6. by man shall his blood be s.
Matt. 26. 28. is s. for many for remission of sins.
Rom. 5. 5. love of God is s. in our hearts.

133

Shed—*Continued.*
Tit. 3. 6. which he *s.* on us through Jesus Christ.
Heb. 9. 22. without *s.* of blood is no remis- [sion.

Sheep, Gen. 4. 2. Abel was a keeper of *s.*
Num. 27. 17; 1 Ki. 22. 17; 2 Chr. 18. 16; Matt. 9. 36; Mk. 6. 34. as *s.* which have no shep- [of *s.?* herd.
1 Sam. 15. 14. what meaneth this bleating
2 Ki. 5. 26. is it a time to receive *s.?*
Ps. 49. 14. like *s.* they are laid in the grave.
95. 7; 100. 3. we are the *s.* of his hand.
Is. 53. 6. all we like *s.* have gone astray.
Jer. 12. 3. like's. for the slaughter.
Matt. 7. 15. false prophets in *s.* clothing.
10. 6. go to lost *s.* of Israel.
12. 12. how much is a man better than a *s.?*
John 10. 2. he that entereth by the door is shepherd of the
21. 16. feed my *s.*
Heb. 13. 20. Lord Jesus, shepherd of *s.*

Shepherd, Gen. 46. 34. *s.* is abomination to Egyptians.
Ps. 23. 1. the Lord is my *s.*
80. 1. give ear, O *S.* of Israel.
Is. 40. 11. he shall feed his flock like a *s.*
Jer. 50. 6. their *s.* caused them to go astray.
Zech. 11. 17. woe to the idol *s.*
13. 7. awake, O sword, against my *s.*
John 10. 16. shall be one fold, one *s.*
1 Pet. 5. 4. when the chief *s.* shall appear.

Shew, Ps. 39. 6. every man walketh in a vain *s.*
Lk. 20. 47. for a *s.* make long prayers.
Gal. 6. 12. to make a fair *s.* in flesh.
Col. 2. 15. made a *s.* of them openly.

Shew, Ps. 4. 6. who will *s.* us any good?
16. 11. thou wilt *s.* me the path of life.
Is. 60. 6. *s.* forth the praises of the Lord.
John 5. 20. Father *s.* the Son all things.
1 Cor. 11. 26. ye do *s.* the Lord's death.
1 John 1. 2. *s.* unto you eternal life.

Shield, Gen. 15. 1. I am thy *s.* and reward.
Deut. 33. 29. the Lord, the *s.* of thy help.
Ps. 5. 12. compass him as with a *s.*
33. 20; 59. 11; 84. 9. the Lord is our *s.*
84. 11. a sun and *s.*
91. 4. his truth shall be thy *s.*
115. 9. he is their help and *s.*
Prov. 30. 5. a *s.* to them that trust him.
Is. 21. 5. anoint the *s.*
Eph. 6. 16. taking the *s.* of faith.

Shine, Num. 6. 25. Lord make his face *s.* upon thee.
Job 22. 28. light shall *s.* upon thy ways.
29. 3. when his candle *s.* upon my head.
Ps. 31. 16; 119. 135. make thy face to *s.* on thy servant.
104. 15. oil to make his face to *s.*
139. 12. the night *s.* as the day.
Prov. 4. 18. as light that *s.* more and more.
Is. 9. 2. upon them hath the light *s.*
60. 1. arise, *s.* for thy light is come.
Dan. 12. 3. wise shall *s.* as brightness of firmament.
Matt. 5. 16. let your light so *s.* before men.
13. 43. the righteous *s.* as the sun.
17. 2. his face did *s.* as the sun.
2 Cor. 4. 6. God who commanded the light to *s.*
2 Pet. 1. 19. a light that *s.* in a dark place.
1 John 2. 8. the true light now *s.*

Short, Num. 11. 23. is the Lord's hand waxed *s.?*
Job 20. 5. triumphing of wicked is *s.*
Ps. 89. 47. remember how *s.* my time is.
Rom. 3. 23. come *s.* of the glory of God.
9. 28. a *s.* work will Lord make on the earth.
1 Cor. 7. 29. the time is *s.*
See Is. 28. 20; 59. 1; Matt. 24. 22; Mk. 12. 20.

Shout, Num. 23. 21. *s.* of king among them.
Ps. 47. 5. God is gone up with a *s.*
1 Thes. 4. 16. Lord shall descend with a *s.*

Shower, Ps. 65. 10. makest earth soft with *s.*
72. 6. like *s.* that water the earth.
Ezek. 34. 26. cause *s.* to come in season.
Lk. 12. 54. ye say, there cometh a *s.*

Shut, Gen. 7. 16. the Lord *s.* him in.
Ps. 77. 9. hath he *s.* up tender mercies?
Is. 22. 22. he shall open and none shall *s.*
60. 11. thy gates shall not be *s.* day nor night.
Matt. 23. 13. ye *s.* up the kingdom of heaven.
Lk. 4. 25. heaven was *s.* up three years.
Rev. 3. 7. openeth and no man *s.*

Sick, Prov. 13. 12. hope deferred maketh heart *s.*
23. 35. stricken me, and I was not *s.*
Is. 1. 5. whole head is *s.*
33. 24. inhabitant not say, I am *s.*
Matt. 25. 36. was *s.* and ye visited me.
Jas. 5. 15. prayer of faith shall save the *s.*
See 1 Cor. 11. 30. [in *s.*

Sickness, Ps. 41. 3. thou wilt make his bed
Hos. 5. 13. when Ephraim saw his *s.*
Matt. 8. 17. himself bare our *s.*
9. 35. Jesus went about healing *s.*
John 11. 4. this *s.* is not unto death.

Sift, Is. 30. 28. *s.* nations with the sieve.
Amos 9. 9. will *s.* Israel as corn is *s.*
Lk. 22. 31. Satan desired to *s.* you.

Sight, Ex. 3. 3. turn and see this great *s.*
Eccl. 6. 9. better is *s.* of eyes.
Matt. 11. 5; Lk. 7. 21. blind receive their *s.*
Lk. 4. 18. recovering of *s.* to the blind.
18. 42; Acts 22. 13. receive thy *s.*
Lk. 24. 31. he vanished out of their *s.*
2 Cor. 5. 7. we walk by faith, not by *s.*
1 Pet. 3. 4. in *s.* of God of great price.

Sign, Deut. 6. 8; 11. 18. bind for *s.* on hand.
Is. 7. 11. ask thee a *s.* of the Lord.
55. 13. for an everlasting *s.*
Matt. 12. 38; 16. 1; Mk. 8. 11; Lk. 11. 16. we would see a *s.*
Matt. 16. 3. can ye not discern *s.* of times?
Lk. 2. 34. for a *s.* which shall be spoken against.
John 4. 48. except ye see *s.*
Acts 2. 19. I will shew *s.* in the earth.
2. 22. a man approved of God by *s.*
1 Cor. 1. 22. Jews require a *s.*

Silent, 1 Sam. 2. 9. be *s.* in darkness.
Ps. 28. 1. be not *s.* to me.
Zech. 2. 13. be *s.* O all flesh, before the Lord.
See Ps. 94. 17; 1 Tim. 2. 12; 1 Pet. 2. 15.

Silly, Job 5. 2. envy slayeth the *s.* one.
Hos. 7. 11. Ephraim is like a *s.* dove.
2 Tim. 3. 6. lead captive *s.* women.

Similitude, Num. 12. 8. the *s.* of the Lord.
Deut. 4. 12. saw no *s.*
Ps. 144. 12. after the *s.* of a palace.
Rom. 5. 14. after the *s.* of Adam's transgression.
Heb. 7. 15. after *s.* of Melchizedec.
Jas. 3. 9. men made after the *s.* of God.

134

Simple, Ps. 19. 7. making wise the *s.*
116. 6. the Lord preserveth the *s.*
119. 130. it giveth understanding to the *s.*
Prov. 1. 22. how long ye *s.* ones, will ye?
22. 3; 27. 12. the *s.* pass on, and are punished.
Rom. 16. 19. *s.* concerning evil.

Sin, Gen. 4. 7. *s.* lieth at the door.
Ex. 34. 7. forgiving iniquity and *s.*
Deut. 24. 16; 2 Ki. 14. 6; 2 Chr. 25. 4. put to death for his own *s.*
Job 10. 6. thou searchest after my *s.*
Ps. 32. 1. blessed is he whose *s.* is covered.
51. 3. my *s.* is ever before me.
103. 10. not dealt with us after our *s.*
Prov. 10. 19. in multitude of words there wanteth not *s.*
14. 34. *s.* is a reproach to any people.
Is. 30. 1. may add *s.* to *s.*
53. 12. he bare the *s.* of many.
Mic. 6. 7. fruit of body for *s.* of my soul.
Zech. 13. 1. a fountain opened for *s.*
Matt. 12. 31. all manner of *s.* shall be forgiven.
John 1. 29. taketh away the *s.* of the world.
16. 8. Comforter will reprove the world of *s.*
Acts 7. 60. lay not this *s.* to their charge.
Rom. 4. 7. blessed whose *s.* are covered.
5. 20. where *s.* abounded.
6. 1. shall we continue in *s.?*
7. 9. commandment came, *s.* revived.
8. 10. body dead, because of *s.*
14. 23. whatsoever is not of faith is *s.*
2 Cor. 5. 21. made him to be *s.* for us.
Gal. 3. 22. concluded all under *s.*
2 Thes. 2. 3. that man of *s.*
Heb. 9. 26. he appeared to put away *s.*
1 Pet. 2. 24. his own self bare our *s.*
1 John 1. 8. if we say we have no *s.*

Sin, Ex. 9. 27; Num. 22. 34; Josh. 7. 20; 1 Sam. 15. 24; 26. 21; 2 Sam. 12. 13; Job 7. 20; Ps. 41. 4; Matt. 27. 4; Lk. 15. 18. I have *s.*
1 Ki. 8. 46. no man that *s.* not.
Job 10. 14. if I *s.*, thou markest me.
Ps. 4. 4. stand in awe, and *s.* not.
39. 1. that I *s.* not with my tongue.
Prov. 8. 36. he that *s.* against me.
Is. 43. 27. thy first father hath *s.*
Ezek. 18. 4. the soul that *s.*, it shall die.
Hos. 13. 2. now they *s.* more and more.
Matt. 18. 21. how oft shall my brother *s.?*
John 5. 14; 8. 11. *s.* no more.
Rom. 6. 15. shall we *s.* because not under law?
1 Cor. 15. 34. awake to righteousness, and *s.* [not.
Eph. 4. 26. be ye angry, and *s.* not.
Heb. 10. 26. if we *s.* wilfully after.
1 John 3. 9. he cannot *s.*, because born of God.

Sincere, Phil. 1. 10. may be *s.* till day of Christ.
1 Pet. 2. 2. as babes desire *s.* milk of the word.
See Josh. 24. 14; 1 Cor. 5. 8; 2 Cor. 2. 17.

Sing, Ex. 15. 21; 1 Chr. 16. 23; Ps. 30. 4; 95. 1; 98. 1; 149. 1; Is. 12. 5. *s.* to the Lord.
Ps. 66. 2. *s.* forth honour of his name.
100. 2. come before his presence with *s.*
Cant. 2. 12. time of the *s.* of birds.
Eph. 5. 19; Col. 3. 16. *s.* in your hearts.
Rev. 15. 3. they *s.* song of Moses.

Single, Matt. 6. 22; Lk. 11. 34. if eye be *s.*, whole body shall be full of light.
See Acts 2. 46; Eph. 6. 5; Col. 3. 22.

Sinner, Gen. 13. 13. men of Sodom were *s.*
Ps. 1. 1. standeth not in way of *s.*
26. 9. gather not my soul with *s.*
51. 13. *s.* shall be converted to thee.
Prov. 1. 10. if *s.* entice thee.
13. 21. evil pursueth *s.*
Eccl. 9. 18. one *s.* destroyeth much good.
Matt. 9. 13; Mk. 2. 17. came not to call righteous, but *s.*
Matt. 11. 19; Lk. 7. 34. a friend of *s.*
Lk. 7. 37. woman who was a *s.*
15. 7. joy in heaven over one *s.*
18. 13. God be merciful to me a *s.*
John 9. 16. how can a man that is a *s.* do such miracles?
Rom. 5. 8. while we were yet *s.*
Jas. 5. 20. converteth *s.*, save a soul.

Sister, Job 17. 14. said to worm, thou art my *s.*
Matt. 12. 50; Mk. 3. 35. same is my brother and *s.*
John 19. 25. stood by cross his mother's *s.*

Sit, Jud. 5. 10. ye that *s.* in judgment.
2 Ki. 7. 3. why *s.* we here till we die?
Ps. 26. 5. will not *s.* with wicked.
69. 12. they that *s.* in the gate.
110. 1. *s.* thou at my right hand.
Is. 30. 7. their strength is to *s.* still.
Jer. 8. 14. why do we *s.* still?
Mic. 4. 4. *s.* every man under his vine.
Matt. 20. 23; Mk. 10. 37. to *s.* on my right hand.
Jas. 2. 3. *s.* thou here in a good place.
Rev. 3. 21. to *s.* with me in my throne.

Situation, 2 Ki. 2. 19. the *s.* of city is pleasant.
Ps. 48. 2. beautiful for *s.*, joy of earth.

Skill, 1 Ki. 5. 6; 2 Chr. 2. 8. *s.* to hew timber.
2 Chr. 2. 7. men hat can *s.* to grave.
34. 12. all that could *s.* of music.
Dan. 1. 17. God gave them *s.* in wisdom.

Skin, Ex. 34. 29. wist not that *s.* of his face shone.
Job 2. 4. *s.* for *s.* [flesh.
10. 11. thou hast clothed me with *s.* and
19. 20. escaped with *s.* of my teeth.
19. 26. after my *s.* worms destroy body.
Ps. 102. 5. my bones cleave to *s.*
Jer. 13. 23. can the Ethiopian change his *s.?*
Heb. 11. 37. wandered in sheep *s.*

Skip, Ps. 29. 6. maketh them also to *s.*
114. 4. mountains *s.* like rams.
Cant. 2. 8. he cometh *s.* upon the hills.
Jer. 48. 27. thou *s.* for joy. [that.

Slack, Deut. 7. 10. he will not be *s.* to him
Prov. 10. 4. poor that dealeth with *s.* hand.
2 Pet. 3. 9. Lord is not *s.* concerning his promise.

Slain, Gen. 4. 23. I have *s.* a man.
Prov. 7. 26. strong men have been *s.* by her.
22. 13. the slothful man saith, I shall be *s.*
Is. 26. 21. the earth shall no more cover her *s.*
66. 16. the *s.* of the Lord shall be many.
Ezek. 37. 9. breathe upon these *s.*
Acts 2. 23. by wicked hands have *s.*
Eph. 2. 16. by cross, having *s.* the enmity.
Rev. 5. 6. a lamb as it had been *s.*
6. 9. souls of them that were *s.*

Slaughter, Ps. 44. 22; Rom. 8. 36. as sheep for the *s.* [the *s.*
Is. 53. 7; Jer. 11. 19. brought as a lamb to
Jer. 7. 32; 19. 6. valley of *s.*
Acts 9. 1. Saul yet breathing out *s.*
Jas. 5. 5. nourished your hearts as in a day of *s.*

Slay, Gen. 18. 25. far from thee to *s.* righteous.
Job 13. 15. though he *s.* me, yet will I trust him.
Lk. 19. 27. bring hither, and *s.* them.

Sleep, Gen. 2. 21. God caused a deep *s.* to fall on Adam.
1 Sam. 26. 12. a deep *s.* from God. [men.
Job 4. 13 ; 33. 15. when deep *s.* falleth upon
Ps. 13. 3. lest I sleep the *s.* of death.
127. 2. he giveth his beloved *s.*
132. 4. I will not give *s.* to mine eyes.
Prov. 3. 24. thy *s.* shall be sweet.
6. 10 ; 24. 33. yet a little *s.*
Eccl. 5. 12. the *s.* of labouring man is sweet.
Lk. 9. 32. heavy with *s.*
John 11. 13 of taking rest in *s.*
Rom. 13. 11. time to awake out of *s.*

Sleep, Ex. 22. 27. wherein shall he *s.* ?
1 Sam. 3. 3. laid down to *s.*
Job 7. 21. now shall I *s.* in the dust.
Ps. 4. 8. I will lay me down and *s.*
121. 4. shall neither slumber nor *s.*
Prov. 4. 16. they *s.* not, except they have done mischief.
6. 10 ; 24. 33. folding of hands to *s.*
10. 5. he that *s.* in harvest is.
Cant. 5. 2. I *s.,* but my heart waketh.
Dan. 12. 2. many that *s.* in the dust.
Matt. 9. 24 ; Mk. 5. 39 ; Lk. 8. 52. maid is not dead, but *s.*
Matt. 26. 45 ; Mk. 14. 41. *s.* on now.
Lk. 22. 46. why *s.* ye? rise and pray.
John 11. 12. if he *s.,* he shall do well.
1 Cor. 11. 30. for this cause many *s.*
15. 51. we shall not all *s.*
Eph. 5. 14. awake, thou that *s.*
1 Thes. 4. 14. them which *s.* in Jesus.
5. 6. let us not *s.,* as do others.

Slide, Deut. 32. 35. foot shall *s.* in due time.
Ps. 26. 1. I trusted in the Lord, I shall not *s.*
37. 31. none of his steps shall *s.*
Hos. 4. 16. Israel *s.* back.

Slightly, Jer. 6. 14 ; 8. 11. healed my people *s.*

Slip, 2 Sam. 22. 37 ; Ps. 18. 36. my feet did not *s.*
Job 12. 5. he that is ready to *s.*
Ps. 17. 5. that my footsteps *s.* not.
73. 2. my steps had well nigh *s.*
Heb. 2. 1. lest we should let them *s.*

Slothful, Jud. 18. 9. be not *s.* to possess land.
Prov. 18. 9. the *s.* is brother to great waster.
21. 25. the desire of *s.* killeth him.
Matt. 25. 26. thou wicked and *s.* servant.
Rom. 12. 11. not *s.* in business.
Heb. 6. 12. that ye be not *s.*

Slow, Ex. 4. 10. I am *s.* of speech.
Neh. 9. 17. a God *s.* to anger.
Prov. 14. 29. that is *s.* to wrath, is of great understanding.
Lk. 24. 25. *s.* of heart.
Jas. 1. 19. *s.* to speak, *s.* to wrath. [not *s.*

Slumber, Ps. 121. 3. he that keepeth thee will
Prov. 6. 4. give not *s.* to thine eyelids.
Is. 5. 27. none shall *s.* nor sleep.
Nah. 3. 18. thy shepherds *s.*
Matt. 25. 5. while bridegroom tarried, they *s.*
Rom. 11. 8. God hath given them the spirit of *s.*

Small, Ex. 16. 14. *s.* thing, *s.* as hoar frost.
Num. 16. 13. is it a *s.* thing that thou hast brought us? [sight.
2 Sam. 7. 19. ; 1 Chr. 17. 17. a *s.* thing in thy
1 Ki. 19. 12. after fire, still *s.* voice.
Is. 7. 13. is it a *s.* thing to weary men?

Small—Continued.
Is. 54. 7. for a *s.* moment.
60. 22. a *s.* one shall become a strong nation
Zech. 4. 10. the day of *s.* things.
Acts 15. 2. no *s.* dissension.

Smell, Gen. 27. 27. as *s.* of a field which the Lord hath blessed.
Job 39. 25. he *s.* the battle afar off.
Ps. 45. 8. thy garments *s.* of myrrh.
115. 6. noses have they, but they *s.* not.
1 Cor. 12. 17. where were the *s.* ?
Phil. 4. 18. an odour of a sweet *s.*

Smite, Ex. 21. 12. he that *s.* a man.
2 Ki. 6. 21. shall I *s.* them?
Ps. 121. 6. the sun shall not *s.* thee by day.
Prov. 19. 25. *s.* a scorner.
Is. 49. 10. neither shall heat *s.* thee. [him
Lam. 3. 30. giveth his cheek to him that *s.*
Nah. 2. 10. the knees *s.* together.
Zech. 13. 7 ; Matt. 26. 31 ; Mk. 14. 27. awake, O sword, *s.* shepherd.
Mal. 4. 6. lest I *s.* the earth with a curse.
Matt. 5. 39. shall *s.* thee on right cheek.
24. 49. begin to *s.* his fellow servants.
John 18. 23. why *s.* thou me?

Smitten, Deut. 28. 25. Lord cause thee to be *s.* before enemies.
Job 16. 10. they have *s.* me on cheek.
Ps. 102. 4. my heart is *s.*
Is. 53. 4. *s.* of God.
Hos. 6. 1. he hath *s.,* and he will bind.

Smoke, Gen. 19. 28. as the *s.* of a furnace.
Deut. 29. 20. the anger of the Lord shall *s.*
Ps. 37. 20. wicked consume into *s.*
68. 2. as *s.* is driven away.
102. 3. my days are consumed like *s.*
104. 32. he toucheth hills, and they *s.*
119. 83. like a bottle in the *s.*
Prov. 10. 26. as *s.* to the eyes.
Is. 6. 4. the house was filled with *s.*
51. 6. the heavens shall vanish like *s.*
Hos. 13. 3. as the *s.* out of the chimney.
Rev. 19. 3. her *s.* rose up for ever.
See Is. 42. 3 ; Matt. 12. 20.

Smooth, Gen. 27. 11. I am a *s.* man.
1 Sam. 17. 40. five *s.* stones.
Ps. 55. 21. words were *s.* than butter.
Is. 30. 10. speak unto us *s.* things.
Lk. 3. 5. rough ways shall be made *s.*

Smote, Gen. 19. 11. *s.* men with blindness.
Num. 20. 11. Moses *s.* the rock.
Cant. 5. 7. the watchmen *s.* me.
Is. 60. 10. in my wrath I *s.* thee.
Hag. 2. 17. I *s.* you with blasting. [thee
Matt. 26. 68 ; Lk. 22. 64. who is he that *s.*
Lk. 18. 13. publican *s.* upon his breast.
Acts 12. 23. angel of the Lord *s.* him.

Snare, Ex. 10. 7. how long shall this man be a *s.* unto us?
Josh. 23. 13. they shall be *s.* unto you.
1 Sam. 28. 9. wherefore layest thou a *s.* for my life? [vented me.
2 Sam. 22. 6 ; Ps. 18. 5. the *s.* of death pre-
Ps. 11. 6. on the wicked he shall rain *s.*
69. 22. let their table become a *s.*
91. 3. deliver thee from *s.* of fowler.
124. 7. the *s.* is broken.
142. 3. they privily laid *s.* for me.
Prov. 7. 23. as a bird hasteth to the *s.*
13. 14 ; 14. 27. the *s.* of death.
29. 25. fear of man bringeth a *s.*
Eccl. 9. 12. as birds caught in the *s.*
Is. 24. 17 ; Jer. 48. 43. the *s.* are upon thee
Lam. 3. 47. fear and a *s.* is come upon us.

Snare—*Continued.*
Hos. 9. 8. the prophet is *s.* of fowler.
Amos. 3. 5. can a bird fall in a *s.*?
Lk. 21. 35. as a *s.* shall it come.
1 Tim. 3. 7. lest he fall into *s.* of devil.
6. 9. they that will be rich fall into a *s.*
2 Tim. 2. 26. recover out of *s.* of the devil.
Snow, Ex. 4. 6 ; Num. 12. 10 ; 2 Ki. 5. 27. leprous as a *s.*
2 Sam. 23. 20. slew lion in time of *s.*
Job 6. 16. wherein the *s.* is hid.
9. 30. if I wash myself with *s.* water.
37. 6. saith to *s.*, be thou on the earth.
38. 22. the treasures of the *s.*
Ps. 51. 7. I shall be whiter than *s.*
147. 16. he giveth *s.* like wool.
Prov. 25. 13. as cold of *s.* in harvest.
26. 1. as *s.* in summer.
31. 21. she is not afraid of the *s.*
Is. 1. 18. your sins shall be white as *s.*
55. 10. as the *s.* from heaven returneth not.
Lam. 4. 7. Nazarites purer than *s.*
Dan. 7. 9. whose garment was white as *s.*
Matt. 28. 3 ; Mk. 9. 3. raiment white as *s.*
Rev. 1. 14. his hairs white as *s.*
Snuffed, Jer. 14. 6. wild asses *s.* up the wind.
Mal. 1. 13. ye have *s.* at it, saith the Lord.
Soap, Jer. 2. 22. though thou take thee much *s.*
Mal. 3. 2. like fuller's *s.*
Sober, 2 Cor. 5. 13. *s.* for your cause.
1 Thes. 5. 6. let us watch and be *s.*
1 Tim. 3. 2 ; Tit. 1. 8. a bishop must be *s.*
Tit. 2. 2. that aged men be *s.*
1 Pet. 4. 7. be *s.*, and watch unto prayer.
5. 8. be *s.* be vigilant.
See Acts 26. 25 ; Rom. 12. 3 ; Tit. 2. 12.
Soft, Job 23. 16. God maketh my heart *s.*
41. 3. will he speak *s.* words?
Ps. 55. 10. thou makest it *s.* with showers.
Prov. 15. 1. a *s.* answer turneth away wrath.
25. 15. a *s.* tongue breaketh the bone.
Matt. 11. 8. a man clothed in *s.* raiment.
See Ps. 55. 21 ; Is. 38. 15 ; Acts 27. 13.
Sojourn, Gen. 19. 9. this fellow came in to *s.*
47. 4. to *s.* in the land are we come.
2 Ki. 8. 1. *s.* wheresoever thou canst *s.*
Ps. 120. 5. woe is me, that I *s.*
Is. 52. 4. my people went to Egypt to *s.*
Acts 7. 6. should *s.* in a strange land.
Heb. 11. 9. by faith he *s.* in land of promise.
1 Pet. 1. 17. pass the time of your *s.* in fear.
See Lev. 25. 23 ; 1 Chr. 29. 15 ; Ps. 39. 12.
Sold, Gen. 25. 33. *s.* his birthright.
45. 4. whom ye *s.* into Egypt.
Lev. 27. 28. no devoted thing shall be *s.*
Deut. 32. 30. except their Rock had *s.* them.
1 Ki. 21. 20. thou hast *s.* thyself to work evil.
Is. 52. 3. ye have *s.* yourselves for nought.
Joel 3. 3. they have *s.* a girl for wine.
Amos 2. 6. they *s.* the righteous for silver.
Matt. 10. 29. are not two sparrows *s.* for a farthing?
13. 46. went and *s.* all that he had.
18. 25. his lord commanded him to be *s.*
21. 12 ; Mk. 11. 15. cast out them that *s.*
Matt. 26. 9 ; Mk. 14. 5 ; John 12. 5. ointment might have been *s.*
Lk. 17. 28. they bought, they *s.*
Rom. 7. 14. *s.* under sin.
1 Cor. 10. 25. whatsoever is *s.* in the shambles.

Soldier, Ezra 8. 22. ashamed to require *s.*
Matt. 8. 9 ; Lk. 7. 8. having *s.* under me.
Lk. 3. 14. the *s.* demanded, what shall we do?
John 19. 23. to every *s.* a part.
Acts 10. 7. a devout *s.*
2 Tim. 2. 3. endure hardness as a good *s.* of Christ. [Christ.
Sole, Gen. 8. 9. dove found no rest for *s.* of foot.
2 Sam. 14. 25 ; Is. 1. 6. from *s.* of foot to crown. [crown.
Solemn, Num. 10. 10. in your *s.* days.
Ps. 92. 3. sing praise with a *s.* sound.
See Gen. 43. 3 ; 1 Sam. 8. 9 ; Is. 30. 29.
Solitary, Ps. 68. 6. God setteth the *s.* in families.
107. 4. wandered in a *s.* way.
Is. 35. 1. wilderness and *s.* place shall be glad.
Mk. 1. 35. Jesus departed to a *s.* place.
Son, Ps. 2. 12. kiss the *S.*, lest he be angry.
86. 16. save *s.* of thine handmaid.
Prov. 10. 1 ; 15. 20. a wise *s.* maketh a glad father.
Is. 9. 6. unto us a *s.* is given.
14. 12. *s.* of the morning.
Dan. 3. 25 ; Lk. 3. 38 ; John 1. 34 ; Acts 9. 20. the *S.* of God.
Mal. 3. 17. as a man spareth his *s.*
Matt. 11. 27. no man knoweth the *S.*
13. 55 ; Mk. 6. 3 ; Lk. 4. 22. the carpenter's *s.*
Matt. 17. 5. this is my beloved *S.*
22. 42. Christ, whose *s.* is he?
Mk. 14. 61. Christ, *S.* of the Blessed.
Lk. 7. 12. only *s.* of his mother.
12. 53. father divided against the *s.*
John 1. 18 ; 3. 18. only begotten *S.*
5. 23. men should honour the *S.*
8. 36. if the *S.* shall make you free.
17. 12 ; 2 Thes. 2. 3. the *s.* of perdition.
Acts 4. 36. the *s.* of consolation.
23. 6. the *s.* of a Pharisee.
Rom. 8. 3. God sending his own *S.*
8. 32. spared not his own *S.*
Gal. 4. 7. if a *s.*, then an heir.
Heb. 1. 2. God hath spoken to us by his *S.*
5. 8. though he were a *S.*, yet learned he obedience.
12. 6. scourgeth every *s.* whom he receiveth.
1 John 5. 12. he that hath the *S.* hath life.
Song, Ex. 15. 2 ; Ps. 118. 14 ; Is. 12. 2. the Lord is my strength and *s.*
Job 30. 9. I am their *s.*
Ps. 33. 3 ; Is. 42. 10. sing a new *s.*
Ps. 40. 3. he hath put a new *s.* in my mouth.
42. 8. his *s.* shall be with me.
69. 12. I was the *s.* of the drunkards.
137. 4. how shall we sing the Lord's *s.*?
Cant. 1. 1. *s.* of *s.*
Is. 24. 16. we heard *s.*
35. 10. come to Zion with *s.*
Ezek. 33. 32. as a very lovely *s.*
Eph. 5. 19 ; Col. 3. 16. speaking in psalms and spiritual *s.*
Soon, Ex. 2. 18. how is it ye are come so *s.*?
Job 32. 22. my Maker would *s.* take me away.
Ps. 58. 3. go astray as *s.* as born.
90. 10. it is *s.* cut off.
Tit. 1. 7. not *s.* angry.
Sore, Job 5. 18. maketh *s.* and bindeth up
Ps. 118. 13. thou hast thrust *s.* at me.
Matt. 21. 15. they were *s.* displeased.
Acts 20. 37. wept *s.*
See Is. 1. 6 ; Heb. 10. 29.

Sorrow, Gen. 42. 38. with *s.* to the grave.
Job. 6. 10. I would harden myself in *s.*
  41. 22. *s.* is turned into joy.
Ps. 90. 10. their strength is labour and *s.*
  116. 3. I found trouble and *s.*   [no *s.*
Prov. 10. 22. maketh rich, and he addeth
  23. 29. who hath *s.*?   [increaseth *s.*
Eccl. 1. 18. he that increaseth knowledge,
  7. 3. *s.* is better than laughter.
  11. 10. remove *s.* from thy heart.
Is. 17. 11. day of desperate *s.*
  35. 10; 51. 11. *s.* and sighing shall flee away.
  53. 3. a man of *s.*
Jer. 49. 23. there is *s.* on the sea.
Lam. 1. 12. any *s.* like unto my *s.*
Matt. 24. 8; Mk. 13. 8. beginning of *s.*
Lk. 22. 45. sleeping for *s.*
John 16. 6. *s.* hath filled your heart.
2 Cor. 2. 7. overmuch *s.*
  7. 10. godly *s.* worketh repentance.
1 Thes. 4. 13. ye *s.* not as others.
Rev. 21. 4. be no more death, neither *s.*

Sorrowful, 1 Sam. 1. 15. a woman of a *s.* spirit.
Ps. 69. 29. I am poor and *s.*
Prov. 14. 13. even in laughter, the heart is *s.*
Matt. 19. 22; Lk. 18. 23. went away *s.*
Matt. 26. 37. he began to be *s.*
  26. 38; Mk. 14. 34. my soul is exceeding *s.*
John 16. 20. ye shall be *s.*
2 Cor. 6. 10. as *s.*, yet always rejoicing.
See Ps. 38.18; Is. 51.19; Matt. 14. 9; 17. 23.

Sort, Gen. 6. 19. two of every *s.*
Dan. 3. 29. no god can deliver after this *s.*
Acts 17. 5. fellows of baser *s.*
2 Cor. 7. 11; 3 John 6. after a godly *s.*

Sought, Gen. 43. 30. he *s.* where to weep.
Ex. 4. 24. the Lord *s.* to kill him.
1 Chr. 15. 13. we *s.* him not after due order.
2 Chr. 15. 4. when they *s.* him. he was found.
  15. 15. they *s.* him with their whole desire.
Ps. 34. 4; 77. 2. I *s.* the Lord, and he heard me.
  111. 2. *s.* out of all that have pleasure.
  119. 94. I have *s.* thy precepts.
Eccl. 7. 29. they *s.* out many inventions.
  12. 10. preacher *s.* to find out acceptable words.
Is. 62. 12. shalt be called *S.* out.
  65. 1. I am *s.* of them that asked not.
Jer. 10. 21. pastors have not *s.* the Lord.
Lam. 1. 19. they *s.* meat to relieve their souls.
Ezek. 34. 4. neither have ye *s.* that which was lost.
Zeph. 1. 6. those that have not *s.* the Lord.
Matt. 21. 46; Mk. 12. 12; Lk. 20. 19. they *s.* to lay hands on him.
Lk. 2. 49. how is it that ye *s.* me?
  13. 6. he *s.* fruit thereon.
  19. 3. he *s.* to see Jesus.
Rom. 9. 32. they *s.* it not by faith.   [tears.
Heb. 12. 17. though he *s.* it carefully with

Soul, Gen. 2. 7. man became a living *s.*
Deut. 11. 13. serve him with all your *s.*
  13. 3; Josh. 22. 5. love the Lord with all your *s.*   [*s.* of David.
1 Sam. 18. 1. the *s.* of Jonathan was knit with
1 Ki. 8. 48. return with all their *s.*
1 Chr. 22. 19. set your *s.* to seek the Lord.
Job 3. 20. life to the bitter in *s.*   [thing.
  12. 10. in whose hand is the *s.* of every living
  16. 4. if your *s.* were in my *s.* stead.
Ps. 33. 19. to deliver their *s.* from death.
  34. 22. Lord redeemeth *s.* of his servants.
  49. 8. redemption of their *s.* is precious.

Soul—*Continued.*
Ps. 63. 1. my *s.* thirsteth for God.
  103. 1; 104. 1. bless the Lord, O my *s.*
  116. 7. return unto thy rest, O my *s.*
  142. 4. no man cared for my *s.*
Prov. 11. 25. liberal *s.* shall be made fat.
  19. 2. *s.* without knowledge is not good.
Is. 55. 3. hear, and your *s.* shall live.
  58. 10. if thou satisfy the afflicted *s.*
Jer. 31. 12. their *s.* shall be as a garden.
  38. 16. Lord that made this *s.*
Ezek. 18. 4. all *s.* are mine.
Hab. 2. 10. sinned against thy *s.*
Matt. 10. 28. to destroy both *s.* and body.
  16. 26; Mk. 8. 36. lose his own *s.*
Lk. 21. 19. in patience possess your *s.*
Acts 4. 32. of one *s.*
Rom. 13. 1. let every *s.* be subject.
1 Thes. 5. 23. your *s.* and body be preserved.
Heb. 6. 19. an anchor of the *s.*
  10. 39. believe to saving of *s.*
Jas. 5. 24; 1 Chr. 16. 14. 15. *s.* of going in tops
1 Pet. 2. 11. lusts which war against the *s.*
  4. 19. commit the keeping of *s.* to him.
3 John 2. even as thy *s.* prospereth.
Rev. 16. 3. every living *s.* died in sea.

Sound, Lev. 26. 36. the *s.* of a shaken leaf.
2 Sam. 5. 24; 1 Chr. 14. 15. *s.* of going in tops of trees.
1 Ki. 18. 41. a *s.* of abundance of rain.
Job 15. 21. dreadful *s.* in his ears.
Ps. 89. 15. people that know joyful *s.*
Eccl. 12. 4. the *s.* of the grinding is low.
Matt. 24. 31. send angels with a great *s.*
John 3. 8. hearest the *s.*, but canst not tell.
Acts 2. 2. there came a *s.* from heaven.
Rom. 10. 18. their *s.* went into all the earth.
1 Cor. 14. 8. if trumpet give uncertain *s.*
Rev. 1. 15. as the *s.* of many waters.

Sound, Prov. 2. 7; 8. 14. *s.* wisdom.
  14. 30. a *s.* heart is life of the flesh.
Lk. 15. 27. received him safe and *s.*
1 Tim. 1. 10; 2 Tim. 4. 3; Tit. 1. 9; 2. 1. *s.* doctrine.
2 Tim. 1. 7. spirit of a *s.* mind.
  1. 13. the form of *s.* words.

Sound, Joel 2. 1. *s.* an alarm in holy mountain.
Matt. 6. 2. do not *s.* a trumpet before thee.
1 Cor. 15. 52. the trumpet shall *s.*
1 Thes. 1. 8. from you *s.* out word of the Lord.

Sow, Job. 4. 8. they that *s.* wickedness reap the same.
Ps. 126. 5. that *s.* in tears, reap in joy.
Eccl. 11. 4. he that observeth the wind shall not *s.*
  11. 6. in the morning *s.* thy seed.
Is. 32. 20. that *s.* beside all waters.
Jer. 4. 3. *s.* not among thorns.   [mercy.
Hos. 10. 12. *s.* in righteousness, reap in
Mic. 6. 15. thou shalt *s.*, but not reap.
Hag. 1. 6. ye have *s.* much, and bring in little.
Matt. 6. 26. they *s.* not.   [to *s.*
  13. 3; Mk. 4. 3; Lk. 8. 5. sower went forth
Lk. 19. 21. reapest that thou didst not *s.*
John 4. 36. he that *s.* and he that reapeth.
1 Cor. 15. 36. that which thou *s.* is not quickened.
2 Cor. 9. 6. he that *s.* sparingly.   [reap.
Gal. 6. 7. whatsoever a man *s.*, that shall he
See Is. 55. 10; Jer. 50. 16; 2 Cor. 9. 10.

Spake, Ps. 33. 9. he s., and it was done.
78. 19. they s. against God.
Jer. 7. 13. I s. to you, rising early.
Mal. 3. 16. feared the Lord, s. one to another.
John 7. 46. never man s. like this man.
9. 29. God s. to Moses.
Acts 7. 6. God s. on this wise.
1 Cor. 13. 11. I s. as a child.
Heb. 1. 1. God who s. in time past.
12. 25. refused him that s. on earth.
2 Pet. 1. 21. men of God s. as moved.

Spare, Gen. 18. 26. I will s. the place for their sakes.
Neh. 13. 22. s. me according to thy mercy.
Ps. 39. 13. s. me, that I may recover strength.
72. 13. he shall s. poor and needy.
Prov. 13. 24. he that s. the rod.
19. 18. let not thy soul s. for his crying.
Is. 58. 1. not, lift up thy voice.
Jon. 4. 11. should not I s. Nineveh?
Mal. 3. 17. I will s. them as a man s. his son.
Lk. 15. 17. have bread enough and to s.
Rom. 8. 32. he that s. not his Son.
11. 21. lest he also s. not thee.
2 Pet. 2. 4. if God s. not angels.

Spark, Job 5 7. as s. fly upward.
18. 5. the s. of his fire shall not shine.
Is. 1. 31. maker of it shall be as a s.

Sparrow, Ps. 84. 3. the s. hath found an house.
Matt. 10. 31 ; Lk. 12. 7. ye are of more value than man s.

Speak, Gen. 18. 27. taken on me to s. to God.
24. 50. we cannot s. bad or good.
Ex. 4. 14. I know he can s. well.
33. 11. as a man s. to his friend.
34. 34. went in to s. to the Lord.
1 Sam. 3. 9. s. Lord, thy servant heareth.
Job 33. 14. God s. once, yea, twice.
36. 2. yet to s. on God's behalf.
Ps. 85. 8. I will hear what the Lord will s.
145. 21. my mouth shall s. praise of Lord.
Prov. 23. 9. s. not in the ears of a fool.
Eccl. 3. 7. a time to s.
Is. 50. 4. to s. a word in season.
63. 1. I that s. in righteousness.
Hab. 2. 3. at the end it shall s.
Zech. 8. 16; Eph. 4. 25. s. every man the truth.
Matt. 10. 19 ; Mk. 13. 11. how ye shall s.
Matt. 12. 36. every idle word that men shall s.
Lk. 6. 26. when all men s. well of you.
John 3. 11. we s. that we do know.
Acts 4. 20. we cannot but s.
26. 1. permitted to s. for thyself.
1 Cor. 1. 10. that ye all s. the same thing.
2 Cor. 2. 17. in sight of God s. we in Christ.
4. 13. we believe, and therefore s.
1 Thes. 2. 4. s. not as pleasing men.
Tit. 3. 2. to s. evil of no man.
Heb. 12. 25. see that ye refuse not him that s.
Jas. 1. 19. slow to s.

Spear, 1 Sam. 17. 45. thou comest with a s.
Ps. 46. 9. he cutteth the s. in sunder.
Is. 2. 4; Mic. 4. 3. beat s. into pruning hooks.
John 19. 34. with a s. pierced his side.

Spectacle, 1 Cor. 4. 9. we are made a s. to the world.

Speech, Gen. 11. 1. whole earth was of one s.
Ex. 4. 10. I am slow of s.
Deut. 32. 2. my s. shall distil as dew.
1 Ki. 3. 10. Solomon's s. pleased the Lord.
Ps. 19. 2. day unto day uttereth s.
Prov. 17. 7. excellent s. becometh not a fool.
Cant. 4. 3. thy s. is comely.
Is. 29. 4. thy s. shall be low out of the dust.

Speech—Continued.
Is. 33. 19. of deeper s. than thou canst perceive.
Matt. 26. 73. thy s. bewrayeth thee.
1 Cor. 2. 1. not with excellency of s.
2 Cor. 10. 10. his s. is contemptible.
Col. 4. 6. let your s. be alway with grace.
Tit. 2. 8. sound s. that cannot be condemned.
See Matt. 22. 12 ; Lk. 1. 22 ; Acts 9. 7.

Speed, Gen. 24. 12. send me good s.
Is. 5. 26. they shall come with s.
2 John 10. neither bid him God-s.

Speedily, Ps. 31. 2. deliver me s.
69. 17 ; 143. 7. hear me s.
79. 8. let thy mercies s. prevent us.
102. 2. when I call, answer me s.
Eccl. 8. 11. because sentence is not executed s.
Is. 58. 8. thy health shall spring forth s.
Lk. 18. 8. he will avenge them s.

Spend, Job 21. 13. they s. their days in wealth.
36. 11. they shall s. their days in prosperity.
Ps. 90. 9. we s. our years as a tale that is told.　　　　　[bread?
Is. 55. 2. why s. money for that which is not
2 Cor. 12. 15. very gladly s. and be spent for you.

Spent, Gen. 21. 15. the water was s.
47. 18. our money is s.
Lev. 26. 20. your strength be s. in vain.
Job 7. 6. my days are s. without hope.
Ps. 31. 10. my life is s. with grief.
Is. 49. 4. I have s. my strength for nought.
Mk. 5. 26 ; Lk. 8. 43. had s. all that she had.
Acts 17. 21. s. their time to tell some new thing.
Rom. 13. 12. the night is far s.

Spirit, Gen. 6. 3. my s. shall not always strive.
Ex. 35. 21. every one whom his s. made willing.
Num. 11. 17. take of the s. that is on thee.
14. 24. he had another s. with him.
27. 18. a man in whom is the s.　　　[them.
Josh. 5. 1. nor was there any more s. in
2 Ki. 2. 9. a double portion of thy s.
Neh. 9. 20. thou gavest thy good s. to instruct.
Job 15. 13. thou turnest thy s. against God.
26. 4. whose s. came from thee?
32. 8. there is a s. in man.　　　　[my s.
Ps. 31. 5 ; Lk. 23. 46. into thy hand I commit
Ps. 32. 2. in whose s. there is no guile.
51. 10. renew a right s. within me.
78. 8. whose s. was not stedfast.
139. 7. whither shall I go from thy S.?
143. 10. thy s. is good.
Prov. 14. 29. he that is hasty of s.
16. 18. a haughty s. goeth before a fall.
16. 32. he that ruleth his s. is better than.
20. 27. s. of man is candle of Lord.
Eccl. 3. 21. who knoweth s. of man?
8. 8. no man hath power over s. to retain s.
11. 5. knowest not what is the way of the s.
12. 7. the s. shall return to God.
Is. 32. 15. till the s. be poured on us.
42. 1. I have put my S. on him.　　　[me.
61. 1 ; Lk. 4. 18. the S. of the Lord is upon
Mic. 2. 11. walking in the s. and falsehood.
Matt. 26. 41 ; Mk. 14. 38. the s. is willing.
Mk. 1. 10; John 1. 32. the S. descending on him.
Mk. 8. 12. he sighed deeply in his s.
Lk. 1. 80. child waxed strong in s.
8. 55. her s. came again.　　　　　[are.
9. 55. ye know not what manner of s. ye
24. 39. a s. hath not flesh and bones.

Spirit—*Continued.*
John 3. 34. God giveth not the *S.* by measure.
4. 24. God is a *S.*
6. 63. it is the *S.* that quickeneth.
Acts 2. 4. began to speak as the *S.* gave utterance.
6. 10. not able to resist the wisdom and *S.*
17. 16. his *s.* was stirred in him.
23. 8. Sadducees say there is neither angel nor *s.* [the *S.*
Rom. 8. 1. walk not after the flesh, but after
8. 26. the *S.* maketh intercession.
1 Cor. 2. 10. the *S.* searcheth all things.
6. 17. he that is joined to the Lord is one *s.*
15. 45. last Adam was made a quickening *s.*
2 Cor. 3. 6. the letter killeth, but the *S.* giveth life. [liberty.
3. 17. where the *S.* of the Lord is, there is
Gal. 3. 3. having begun in the *S.*
5. 16. walk in the *S.*
5. 22; Eph. 5. 9. the fruit of the *S.*
Gal. 6. 8. he that soweth to the *S.* shall of the *S.* reap.
Eph. 2. 18. we have access by one *S.*
2. 22. habitation of God through the *S.*
4. 4. there is one body, and one *S.*
5. 18. be filled with the *S.*
6. 17. take the sword of the *S.*
Phil. 2. 1. if there be any fellowship of the *S.*
1 Thes. 5. 19. quench not the *S.*
1 Tim. 3. 16. justified in the *S.*
Heb. 1. 14. ministering *s.*
4. 12. dividing asunder of soul and *s.*
9. 14. who through the eternal *S.* offered himself.
Jas. 2. 26. the body without the *s.* is dead.
4. 5. the *s.* lusteth to envy.
1 Pet. 3. 4. ornament of a meek and quiet *s.*
4. 6. live according to God in the *s.*
1 John 4. 1. believe not every *s.*
5. 6. it is the *S.* that beareth witness.
Rev. 1. 10. I was in the *S.* on the Lord's day.
22. 17. the *S.* and the bride say, come.

Spiritual, Hos. 9. 7. the *s.* man is mad.
Rom. 1. 11. impart some *s.* gift.
7. 14. the law is *s.*
15. 27. partakers of their *s.* things.
1 Cor. 2. 13. comparing *s.* things with *s.*
2. 15. he that is *s.* judgeth all things.
3. 1. I could not speak unto you as unto *s.*
9. 11. have sown unto you *s.* things.
10. 3. did all eat the same *s.* meat.
12. 1; 14. 1. *s.* gifts.
15. 44. it is raised a *s.* body.
Gal. 6. 1. ye which are *s.*, restore such an one.
Eph. 1. 3. blessed us with *s.* blessings.
5. 19; Col. 3. 16. in psalms and hymns, and *s.* songs.
Eph. 6. 12. *s.* wickedness in high places.
1 Pet. 2. 5. a *s.* house to offer *s.* sacrifices.
See Rom. 8. 6; 1 Cor. 2. 14; Rev. 11. 8.

Spite, Ps. 10. 14. thou beholdest mischief and *s.*
Spitefully, Matt. 22. 6. they entreated them *s.*
Lk. 18. 32. shall be *s.* entreated.
Spoil, Gen. 49. 27. at night he shall divide the *s.*
Jud. 5. 30. necks of them that take *s.*
1 Sam. 14. 32. the people flew upon the *s.*
2 Chr. 15. 11. they offered to the Lord of the *s.* [prey.
Est. 3. 13; 8. 11. take the *s.* of them for a
Ps. 68. 12. that tarried at home, divided the *s.*
119. 162. rejoice as one that findeth great *s.*

Spoil—*Continued.*
Prov. 16. 19. than to divide the *s.* with the proud.
31. 11. he shall have no need of *s.*
Is. 42. 24. who gave Jacob for a *s.*?
53. 12. he shall divide the *s.* with the strong.
Nah. 2. 9. take *s.* of silver, *s.* of gold.

Spoil, Ex. 3. 22. ye shall *s.* the Egyptians.
Ps. 89. 41. all that pass by the way *s.* him.
Cant. 2. 15. the little foxes that *s.* the vines.
Is. 33. 1. woe to thee that *s.*, and thou wast not *s.*! [do?
Jer. 4. 30. when thou art *s.*, what wilt thou
Matt. 12. 29; Mk. 3. 27. *s.* his goods.
Col. 2. 8. beware lest any man *s.* you.
2. 15. having *s.* principalities. [hath *s.*
Spoken, Gen. 18. 19. Lord bring what he
Num. 23. 19. hath he *s.*, and shall he not make it good?
1 Ki. 18. 24. the people said, it is well *s.*
Ps. 62. 11. God hath *s.* once.
87. 3. glorious things are *s.* of thee.
Prov. 25. 11. a word fitly *s.*
Eccl. 7. 21. take no heed to all words *s.*
Is. 46. 11. I have *s.* it, I will bring it to pass.
Jer. 26. 16. *s.* to us in name of the Lord.
Mal. 3. 13. what have we *s.* against thee?
Mk. 14. 9. shall be *s.* for a memorial.
John 15. 22. if I had not come and *s.*
Acts 19. 36. these things cannot be *s.* against.
Rom. 15. 21. to whom he was not *s.* of.
2 Pet. 2. 2. way of truth be evil *s.* of.
Spot, Num. 28. 3; 29. 17. lambs without *s.*
Deut. 32. 5. their *s.* is not the *s.* of his children.
Cant. 4. 7. there is no *s.* in thee.
Jer. 13. 23. can the leopard change his *s.*?
Eph. 5. 27. a glorious church, not having *s.*
1 Tim. 6. 14. keep commandment without *s.*
Heb. 9. 14. offered himself without *s.*
1 Pet. 1. 19. as a lamb without *s.*
2 Pet. 3. 14. that ye may be found without *s.*
Jude 12. these are *s.* in your feasts.

Sprang, Mk. 4. 8; Lk. 8. 8. fruit that *s.* up.
Acts 16. 29. called for a light, and *s.* in.
Heb. 7. 14. it is evident our Lord *s.* out of Judah.
Spread, 1 Ki. 8. 54. with hands *s.* to heaven.
2 Ki. 19. 14; Is. 37. 14. *s.* letter before the Lord.
Job 9. 8. God who alone *s.* out the heavens.
26. 9. he *s.* his cloud upon it.
36. 30. he *s.* his light upon it.
37. 18. hast thou with him *s.* out the sky?
Ps. 105. 39. he *s.* a cloud for a covering.
Is. 1. 15. when ye *s.* forth your hands.
33. 23. they could not *s.* the sail.
65. 2. *s.* out my hands to a rebellious people.
Jer. 8. 2. they shall *s.* them before the sun.
Ezek. 26. 14. a place to *s.* nets upon.
Hos. 14. 6. his branches shall *s.*
Matt. 21. 8; Mk. 11. 8; Lk. 19. 36. *s.* their garments.
Acts 4. 17. that it *s.* no further.
1 Thes. 1. 8. your faith is *s.* abroad.
Spring, Num. 21. 17. *s.* up, O well.
Job 5. 6. neither doth trouble *s.* out of the ground.
Ps. 85. 11. truth shall *s.* out of the earth.
87. 7. all my *s.* are in thee.
104. 10. he sendeth the *s.* into valleys.
107. 35. he turneth dry ground into water *s.*
Prov. 25. 26. troubled fountain and corrupt *s.*

Spring—*Continued.*

Is. 58. 8. thine health shall *s.* forth.
Joel 2. 22. the pastures do *s.*
Mk. 4. 27. seed should *s.* he knoweth not how.
John 4. 14. a well of water *s.* up.

Sprinkle, Is. 52. 15. so shall he *s.* many nations.
Ezek. 36. 25. *s.* clean water upon you.
Heb. 10. 22. hearts *s.* from an evil conscience.

Spy, Num. 13. 16. Moses sent to *s.* land.
Josh. 2. 1. sent two men to *s.* secretly.
Gal. 2. 4. who came in to *s.* out our liberty.

Stability, Is. 33. 6. the *s.* of thy times.

Staff, Gen. 32. 10. with my *s.* I passed over.
Ex. 12. 11. eat it with *s.* in hand.
Jud. 6. 21. the angel put forth end of his *s.*
2 Ki. 4. 29. lay my *s.* on face of the child.
18. 21; Is. 36. 6. thou trustest on a *s.*
Ps. 23. 4. thy rod and *s.* comfort me.
Is. 3. 1. Lord doth take away the stay and *s.*
9. 4. thou hast broken the *s.* of his shoulder.
10. 15. as if the *s.* should lift up itself.
14. 5. Lord hath broken the *s.* of the wicked.
28. 27. fitches are beaten out with a *s.*
30. 32. where the grounded *s.* shall pass.
Jer. 48. 17. how is the strong *s.* broken !
Zech. 11. 10. took my *s.,* even Beauty.
Mk. 6. 8. take nothing, save a *s.* only.
Heb. 11. 21. leaning on the top of his *s.*

Stagger, Job 12. 25; Ps. 107. 27. *s.* like a drunken man.
Is. 29. 9. they *s.,* but not with strong drink.
Rom. 4. 20. he *s.* not at promise of God.

Stairs, 1 Ki. 6. 8. went up with winding *s.*
Cant. 2. 14. in secret places of the *s.*
Acts 21. 40. Paul stood on the *s.*

Stall, Amos 6. 4. out of the midst of the *s.*
Hab. 3. 17. there be no herd in the *s.*
Mal. 4. 2. grow up as calves of the *s.*
Lk. 13. 15. loose his ox from the *s.*

Stammering, Is. 28. 11. with *s.* lips and another tongue.
32. 4. tongue of *s.* speak plainly.
33. 19. not see a people of *s.* tongue.

Stamp, Ex. 32. 20. *s.* the calf, and ground it.
2 Sam. 22. 43. did *s.* them as the mire.
2 Ki. 23. 15. *s.* high place small to powder.
Jer. 47. 3. at noise of the *s.* of hoofs.
Ezek. 6. 11. *s.* with thy foot.

Stand, Ex. 14. 13; 2 Chr. 20. 17. *s.* still and see the salvation of the Lord. 　　　　[the Lord.
Deut. 29. 10. ye *s.* this day all of you before
1 Ki. 17. 1; 18. 15; 2 Ki. 3. 14; 5. 16. the Lord before whom I *s.* 　　　　[we *s.?*
2 Ki. 10. 4. two kings *s.* not, how then shall
Est. 8. 11. to *s.* for their life. 　　　　[earth.
Job 19. 25. he shall *s.* at latter day on the
Ps. 1. 5. the ungodly shall not *s.* in judgment.
4. 4. *s.* in awe and sin not.
24. 3. who shall *s.* in his holy place?
33. 11. the counsel of the Lord *s.* for ever.
76. 7. who may *s.* in thy sight?
122. 2. our feet shall *s.* within thy gates.
130. 3. if thou shouldest mark iniquities, who shall *s.*?
Prov. 19. 21. counsel of Lord shall *s.*
22. 29. a man diligent shall *s.* before kings.
27. 4. who is able to *s.* before envy?
Eccl. 8. 3. *s.* not in an evil thing.
Is. 40. 8. word of our God shall *s.* for ever.
65. 5. *s.* by, I am holier than thou.
Jer. 6. 16. *s.* ye in the ways, ask for the old paths.
Dan. 12. 13. *s.* in thy lot at end of days.

Stand—*Continued.*

Nah. 2. 8. *s., s.,* shall they cry.
Mal. 3. 2. who shall *s.* when he appeareth?
Matt. 12. 25; Mk. 3. 25; Lk. 11. 17. house divided shall not *s.*
Matt. 20. 6. why *s.* ye all the day idle?
Acts 1. 11. why *s.* ye gazing up into heaven?
Rom. 5. 2. this grace wherein we *s.*
14. 4. God is able to make him *s.*
1 Cor. 16. 13. *s.* fast in the faith.
Gal. 5. 1. *s.* fast in the liberty.
Eph. 6. 13. having done all, to *s.*
Phil. 1. 27. *s.* fast in one spirit.
4. 1; 1 Thes. 3. 8. *s.* fast in the Lord.
2 Tim. 2. 19. the foundation of God *s.* sure.
Jas. 5. 9. the Judge *s.* before the door.
1 Pet. 5. 12. true grace wherein we *s.*
Rev. 3. 20. I *s.* at the door and knock.
6. 17. who shall be able to *s.*? 　　　　[God.
20. 12. the dead, small and great, *s.* before

Star, Num. 24. 17. shall come a *S.* out of Jacob.
Job 38. 7. the morning *s.* sang together.
Dan. 12. 3. they shall shine as a *s.* for ever.
Matt. 2. 2. we have seen his *s.* in the east.
Acts 7. 43. we took up the *s.* of your God.
1 Cor. 15. 41. one *s.* differeth from another *s.*
Jude 13. wandering *s.*
Rev. 9. 1. a *s.* fall from heaven to earth.

State, Ps. 39. 5. man at his best *s.* is vanity.
Matt. 12. 45; Lk. 11. 26. last *s.* worse than the first.

Stature, Num. 13. 32. men of great *s.*
1 Sam. 16. 7. look not on height of his *s.*
Cant. 7. 7. thy *s.* is like to a palm tree.
Is. 10. 33. high ones of *s.* shall be hewn down.
Matt. 6. 27; Lk. 12. 25. not add to *s.*
Lk. 2. 52. Jesus increased in *s.*
19. 3. little of *s.*
Eph. 4. 13. measure of *s.* of the fulness of Christ. 　　　　[nance.

Statute, Ex. 15. 25. he made a *s.* and ordi-
18. 16. make them know the *s.* of God.
Lev. 3. 17; 16. 34; 24. 9. a perpetual *s.*
Ps. 19. 8. the *s.* of the Lord are right.
Ezek. 5. 6. hath changed my *s.*
33. 15. walk in the *s.* of life.

Stay, Gen. 19. 17. neither *s.* in the plain.
Ex. 9. 28. ye shall *s.* no longer.
Num. 16. 48; 25. 8; 2 Sam. 24. 25; Ps. 106. 30. the plague was *s.*
2 Sam. 22. 19; Ps. 18. 18. the Lord was my *s.*
Job 37. 4. he will not *s.* them.
38. 11. here shall thy proud waves be *s.*
38. 37. who can *s.* the bottles of heaven?
Prov. 28. 17. let no man *s.* him.
Cant. 2. 5. *s.* me with flagons.
Is. 26. 3. keep him whose mind is *s.* on thee.
27. 8. he *s.* his rough wind.
29. 9. *s.* yourselves, and wonder.
50. 10. trust in Lord, and *s.* upon his God.
Dan. 4. 35. none can *s.* his hand.
Hag. 1. 10. heaven is *s.,* earth is *s.*
Lk. 4. 42. people came and *s.* him.

Stead, Gen. 30. 2. am I in God's *s.*
Num. 32. 14. risen in your fathers' *s.*
Job 16. 4. if your soul were in my soul's *s.*
34. 24. shall set others in their *s.*
Prov. 11. 8. the wicked cometh in his *s.*
2 Cor. 5. 20. we pray you in Christ's *s.*

Steal, Gen. 31. 27. wherefore didst thou *s.* away?
44. 8. how should we *s.* silver or gold?
Prov. 6. 30. if he *s.* to satisfy his soul.
30. 9. lest I be poor, and *s.*

Steal—*Continued.*
Jer. 23. 30. prophets that *s.* my words.
Matt. 6. 19. thieves break through and *s.*
John 10. 10. thief cometh not, but to *s.*
Eph. 4. 28. him that stole, *s.* no more.

Stedfast, Job 11. 15. thou shalt be *s.*
Ps. 78. 8. spirit was not *s.* with God.
Dan. 6. 26. living God, and *s.* for ever.
Heb. 2. 2 words spoken by angels was *s.*
3. 14. hold our confidence *s.* to end.
6. 19. hope a *r* an anchor, sure and *s.*
1 Pet. 5. 9. whom resist *s.* in the faith.
See Lk. 9. 51 , Acts 7. 55 ; 2 Cor. 3. 13.

Steps, Ex. 20. 26. neither go up by *s.*
1 Sam. 20. 3.—but a *s.* between me and death.
2 Sam. 22. 37 ; Ps. 18. 36. thou hast enlarged
    my *s.*
Job 14. 16. thou numberest my *s.*
31. 4. doth not he count my *s.* ?
31. 7. if my *s.* hath turned out of the way.
Ps. 37. 23, the *s.* of a good man are ordered
    by the Lord.
44. 18. nor have our *s.* declined.
73. 2. my *s.* had well nigh slipped.
119. 133. order my *s.* in thy word.
Prov. 4. 12. thy *s.* shall not be straitened.
16. 9. the Lord directeth his *s.*
Jer. 10. 23. not in man to direct his *s.*
Rom. 4. 12. walk in *s.* of that faith.
2 Cor. 12. 18. walked we not in the same *s.* ?
1 Pet. 2. 21. that ye should follow his *s.*

Steward, Gen. 15. 2. the *s.* of my house.
1 Ki. 16. 9. drunk in house of his *s.*
Lk. 12. 42. that faithful and wise *s.*
16. 8. the lord commended the unjust *s.*
1 Cor. 4. 1. *s.* of the mysteries of God.
1 Pet. 4. 10. as good *s.* of grace of God.

Stick, Num. 15. 32. gathered *s.* on Sabbath.
1 Ki. 17. 12. I am gathering two *s.*
2 Ki. 6. 6. cut down a *s.* and cast it.
Job 33. 21. his bones *s.* out.
Ps. 38. 2. thine arrows *s.* fast in me.
Prov. 18. 24. a friend that *s.* closer than a
    brother.
Ezek. 37. 16. take one *s.*, and write on it.
Acts 28. 3. bundle of *s.*

Stiff, Ex. 32. 9 ; 34. 9 ; Deut. 9. 13 ; 10. 16. a
    s.-necked people.
Ps. 75. 5. speak not with a *s.* neck.
Ezek. 2. 4. impudent children and *s.* hearted.
Acts 7. 51. ye *s.*-necked, ye always resist the
    Holy Ghost.

Still, Ex. 15. 16. as *s.* as a stone.
2 Sam. 14. 32. good to have been there *s.*
2 Ki. 7. 4. if we sit *s.* here, we die.
Job 2. 9. dost thou *s.* retain thine integrity ?
Ps. 8. 2. thou mightest *s.* the enemy.
23. 2. beside the *s.* waters.
46. 10. be *s.*, and know that I am God.
83. 1. be not *s.*, O God.
107. 29. so that the waves thereof are *s.*
Is. 30. 7. their strength is to sit *s.*
42. 14. I have been *s.*, and refrained.
Jer. 8. 14. why do we sit *s.* ?
Mk. 4. 39. said to sea, peace, be *s.* [unjust *s.*
Rev. 22. 11. he that is unjust, let him be
Sting, Prov. 23. 32. it *s.* like an adder.
1 Cor. 15. 55. O death, where is thy *s.* ?
Rev. 9. 10. were *s.* in their tails.
Stir, Num. 24. 9. who shall *s.* him up ?
Deut. 32. 11. as an eagle *s.* up her nest.
1 Sam. 26. 19. if the Lord have *s.* thee up.
1 Chr. 5. 26 ; 2 Chr. 36. 22. God *s.* up the
    spirit.

Stir—*Continued.*
Job 17. 8. the innocent shall *s.* up himself.
41. 10. none dare *s.* him up.
Ps. 35. 23. *s.* up thyself.
80. 2. *s.* up thy strength, and come.
Prov. 15. 18 ; 29. 22. a wrathful man *s.* up
    strife.
Is. 10. 26. the Lord shall *s.* up a scourge.
22. 2. full of *s.*, a tumultuous city.
Lk. 23. 5. he *s.* up the people.
Acts 17. 16. his spirit was *s.* in him.
19. 23. no small *s.* about that way.
2 Tim. 1. 6. *s.* up gift of God in thee.

Stock, Job 14. 8. though the *s.* thereof die.
Is. 40. 24. their *s.* shall not take root.
44. 19. shall I fall down to the *s.* of a tree?
Hos. 4. 12. my people ask counsel at their *s.*
Acts 13. 26. children of the *s.* of Abraham.
Heb. 10. 33. ye were made a gazing *s.*

Stolen, Josh. 7. 11. they have *s.*, and dis-
    sembled.
Prov. 9. 17. *s.* waters are sweet.   [enough?
Obad. 5. would they not have *s.* till they had

Stone, Gen. 11. 3. they had brick for *s.*
28. 18 ; 31. 45 ; 35. 14. set up a *s.* for a pillar.
Josh. 24. 27. this *s.* shall be a witness.
Job 14. 19. the waters wear the *s.*
41. 24. his heart is as firm as a *s.*
Ps. 91. 12 ; Matt. 4. 6 ; Lk. 4. 11. lest thou
    dash thy foot against a *s.*
Ps. 118. 22 ; Matt. 21. 42 ; Mk. 12. 10. the *s.*
    which the builders refused.
Prov. 27. 3. a *s.* is heavy, a fool's wrath
    heavier.   [corner *s.*
Is. 28. 16 ; 1 Pet. 2. 6. a tried *s.*, a precious
Is. 54. 11. I will lay thy *s.* with fair colours.
60. 17. for *s.* I will bring iron.
Dan. 2. 34. a *s.* was cut out without hands.
Hab. 2. 19. that saith to the dumb *s.*, arise.
Hag. 2. 15. before *s.* was laid upon *s.*
Zech. 7. 12. they made their hearts as *s.*
Matt. 7. 9 ; Lk. 11. 11. will he give him a *s.* ?
Matt. 21. 44 ; Lk. 20. 18. whosoever shall fall
    on this *s.*
Matt. 24. 2 ; Mk. 13. 2 ; Lk. 19. 44 ; 21. 6. not
    be left one *s.* upon another.
Mk. 16. 4 ; Lk. 24. 2. found the *s.* rolled
    away.   [bread.
Lk. 4. 3. command this *s.* that it be made
John 1. 42. Cephas, by interpretation a *s.*
11. 39. take ye away the *s.*
Acts 17. 29. that the Godhead is like to *s.*
2 Cor. 3. 3. not in tables of *s.*
1 Pet. 2. 5. ye as lively *s.*, are built up.
See Ezek. 11. 19 ; 36. 26 ; Matt. 13. 5 ; Mk. 4. 5.

Stood, Gen. 18. 22. Abraham *s.* yet before the
    Lord.
Deut. 5. 5. I *s.* between Lord and you.
Josh. 3. 16. waters *s.* up on an heap.
Ps. 33. 9. he commanded, and it *s.* fast.
Lk. 7. 14. they that bare him *s.* still.
24. 36 ; John 20. 19. Jesus himself *s.* in their
    midst.
Acts 23. 11. the Lord *s.* by him.
2 Tim. 4. 16. no man *s.* with me.   [heart *s.*
Stoop, Prov. 12. 25. heaviness maketh the
Is. 46. 2. they *s.*, they bow down.
John 8. 6. Jesus *s.* down, and wrote on
    ground.
Stop, Gen. 8. 2. windows of heaven were *s.*
1 Ki. 18. 44. that the rain *s.* thee not.
Ps. 107. 42. iniquity shall *s.* her mouth.
Prov. 21. 13. whoso *s.* his ears at cry of the
    poor.

142

Stop—*Continued.*
Acts 7. 57. thus *s.* their ears, and ran upon him.
Rom. 3. 19. that every mouth may be *s.*
Tit. 1. 11. whose mouths must be *s.*
Heb. 11. 33. through faith *s.* mouths of lions.
Store, Deut. 28. 5. blessed be thy basket and *s.*
1 Chr. 29. 16. all this *s.* cometh of thine hand.
Ps. 144. 13. our garners affording all manner of *s.*
Nah. 2. 9. none end of the *s.*
Lk. 12. 24. neither have *s.* house nor barn.
1 Cor. 16. 2. let every one lay by him in *s.*
1 Tim. 6. 19. laying in *s.* a good foundation.
2 Pet. 3. 7. by the same word are kept in *s.*
Storm, Job 21. 18. as chaff that the *s.* carrieth away.
Ps. 107. 29. he maketh the *s.* a calm.
Is. 4. 6. a covert from *s.*
25. 4. a refuge from the *s.*
28. 2. as a destroying *s.*
Nah. 1. 3. the Lord hath his way in the *s.*
Mk. 4. 37. there arose a great *s.*
See Ps. 107. 25 ; 148. 8.
Stout, Is. 10. 12. punish fruit of *s.* heart.
Dan. 7. 20. whose look was more *s.*   [me.
Mal. 3. 13. your words have been *s.* against
Straight, Ps. 5. 8. make thy way *s.*
Eccl. 1. 15 ; 7. 13. crooked cannot be made *s.*
Is. 40. 3. make *s.* in desert a highway.
40. 4 ; 42. 16 ; 45. 2 ; Lk. 3. 5. crooked shall be made *s.*
Jer. 31. 9. cause them to walk in a *s.* way.
Matt. 3. 3 , Mk. 1. 3 ; Lk. 3. 4 ; John 1. 23. make his paths *s.*
Acts 9. 11. street which is called *S.*
Heb. 12. 13. make *s.* paths for your feet.
Strain, Matt. 23. 24. at a gnat.
Strait, 2 Sam. 24. 14. I am in a great *s.*
2 Ki. 6. 1. place where we dwell is too *s.*
Job 20. 22. he shall be in *s.*
Is. 49. 20. the place is too *s.* for me.
Matt. 7. 13 ; Lk. 13. 24. enter in at the *s.* gate.
Phil. 1. 23. I am in a *s.* betwixt two.
See Mic. 2. 7 ; Lk. 12. 50 ; 2 Cor. 6. 12.
Strange, Gen. 42. 7. Joseph made himself *s.*
Lev. 10. 1 ; Num. 3. 4 ; 26. 61. offered *s.* fire.
Job 31. 3. a *s.* punishment to workers of iniquity.
Prov. 21. 8. the way of man is froward and *s.*
Is. 28. 21. his *s.* work, his *s.* act.
Zeph. 1. 8. clothed with *s.* apparel.
Lk. 5. 26. we have seen *s.* things to-day.
Acts 17. 20. thou bringest *s.* things to our ears.
Heb. 13. 9. carried about with *s.* doctrines.
1 Pet. 4. 4 they think it *s.* ye run not.
Stranger, Gen. 23. 4 ; Ps. 39. 12 ; 119. 19. I am a *s.*
Ex. 22. 21. thou shalt not oppress a *s.*
1 Chr. 29. 15. we are *s.*, as were all our fathers.
Job 31. 32. the *s.* did not lodge in the street.
Ps. 109. 11. let the *s.* spoil his labour.
146. 9. the Lord preserveth the *s.*
Prov. 2. 16. to deliver thee from the *s.*
11. 15. he th⸱t is surety for a *s.*
14. 10. a *s.* doth not intermeddle.
27. 2. let a *s.* praise thee.
Is. 56. 3. neither let son of the *s.* speak.
Jer. 14. 8. why be as a *s.* in the land ?
Matt. 25. 35. I was a *s.*, and ye took me in.
Eph. 2. 12. *s.* from the covenants.
2. 19. ye are no more *s.*
Heb. 11. 13. confessed they were *s.*
13. 2. be not forgetful to entertain *s.*
1 Pet. 2. 11. I beseech you as *s.* and pilgrims.

Stream, Job 6. 15. as the *s.* of brooks they pass away.
Ps. 124. 4. the *s.* had gone over.
Is. 35. 6. *s.* in the desert.
Amos 5. 24. righteousness as a mighty *s.*
Street, 2 Sam. 22. 43 ; Mic. 7. 10. as mire of the *s.*
Prov. 1. 20. wisdom uttereth her voice in the *s.*
Eccl. 12. 5. the mourners go about the *s.*
Lk. 14. 21. go into *s.* and lanes of city.
Rev. 21. 21. the *s.* of city was pure gold.
Strength, Ex. 15. 2 ; 2 Sam. 22. 33 ; Ps. 18. 2 ; 28. 7 ; 118. 14 ; Is. 12. 2. the Lord is my *s.*
1 Sam. 2. 9. by *s.* shall no man prevail.
15. 29. the *S.* of Israel will not lie.
Job 9. 19. if I speak of *s.*, lo, he is strong.
12. 13. with him is wisdom and *s.*
12. 21. he weakeneth *s.* of the mighty.
Ps. 8. 2. out of mouth of babes hast thou ordained *s.*
18. 32. girdeth me with *s.*
27. 1. the Lord is the *s.* of my life.
29. 11. the Lord will give *s.* to his people.
33. 16. mighty not delivered by much *s.*
46. 1 ; 81. 1. God is our refuge and *s.*
68. 35. God giveth *s.*
73. 26. God is the *s.* of my heart.
84. 5. blessed whose *s.* is in thee.
84. 7. they go from *s.* to *s.*
93. 1. the Lord is clothed with *s.*
96. 6. *s.* and beauty are in his sanctuary.
138. 3. strengenedst me with *s.*
Prov. 10. 29. the way of the Lord is *s.* to upright.
Eccl. 9. 16. wisdom is better than *s.*
Is. 25. 4. a *s.* to the poor, a *s.* to the needy
26. 4. in Jehovah is everlasting *s.*
40. 29. he increaseth *s.*
51. 9. awake, put on *s.*
Lk. 1. 51. he hath shewed *s.* with his arm.
Rom. 5. 6. when we were without *s.*
1 Cor. 15. 56. the *s.* of sin is the law.
Rev. 3. 8. thou hast a little *s.*
5. 12. worthy is the Lamb to receive *s.*
12. 10. now is come salvation and *s.*
Strengthen, Ps. 20. 2. Lord *s.* thee out of Zion.   [ing.
41. 3. Lord will *s.* him on bed of languish-
104. 15. bread which *s.* man's heart.
Is. 35. 3. *s.* ye the weak hands.
Lk. 22. 32. when converted, *s.* thy brethren.
Eph. 3. 16 ; Col. 1. 11. *s.* with might.
Phil. 4. 13. do all things through Christ who *s.* me.
Rev. 3. 2. *s.* the things which remain.
Stretch, Ps. 68. 31. soon *s.* out her hands to God.
Is. 28. 20. shorter than a man can *s.* himself.
Jer. 10. 12 ; 51. 15. he hath *s.* out the heavens.
Matt. 12. 13. *s.* forth thine hand.
2 Cor. 10. 14. we *s.* not beyond measure.
Strike, Job 17. 3 ; Prov. 22. 26. *s.* hands.
Ps. 110. 5. he shall *s.* through kings.
Prov. 7. 23. till a dart *s.* through.
Mk. 14. 65. did *s.* Jesus with their hands.
Strive, Gen. 6. 3. Spirit shall not always *s.*
Ps. 35. 1. plead with them that *s.* with me.
Prov. 3. 30. *s.* not without cause.
Matt. 12. 19. he shall not *s.* nor cry.
Lk. 13. 24. *s.* to enter in at straight gate.
2 Tim. 2. 24. the servant of the Lord must not *s.*

Strong, 1 Sam. 4. 9; 2 Chr. 15. 7; Is. 35. 4.
be *s*.
Job 9. 19. if I speak of strength, he is *s*.
Ps. 19. 5. as a *s*. man to run a race.
24. 8. the Lord *s*. and mighty.
31. 2. be thou my *s*. rock.
71. 7. thou art my *s*. refuge.
89. 8. who is a *s*. Lord like thee?
Prov. 18. 10. name of the Lord is a *s*. tower.
Eccl. 9. 11. the battle is not to the *s*.
Cant. 8. 6. love is *s*. as death.
Is. 26. 1. we have a *s*. city.
40. 26. for that he is *s*. in power.
53. 12. he shall divide the spoil with the *s*.
Jer. 50. 34. their Redeemer is *s*.
Joel 3. 10. let the weak say, I am *s*.
Lk. 11. 21. a *s*. man armed keepeth his
palace.
Rom. 4. 20. *s*. in faith.   [of weak.
15. 1. we that are *s*. ought to bear infirmities
1 Cor. 4. 10. we are weak, ye are *s*.
Heb. 5. 12. need of milk, not of *s*. meat.
11. 34. out of weakness were made *s*.
See Job 17. 9; Jer. 20. 7; 1 Cor. 1. 25; 10. 22.
Stubble, Ex. 15. 7. wrath consumed them as *s*.
Job 21. 18; Ps. 83. 13. as *s*. before the wind.
Is. 33. 11. conceive chaff, bring forth *s*.
41. 2. as driven *s*.
Jer. 13. 24. I will scatter them as *s*.
1 Cor. 3. 12. on this foundation, hay, *s*.
Study, Eccl. 12. 12. much *s*. is a weariness.
1 Thes. 4. 11. that ye *s*. to be quiet.
2 Tim. 2. 15. *s*. to shew thyself approved.
Stumble, Prov. 3. 23. foot shall not *s*.
4. 19. know not at what they *s*.
Is. 5. 27. none shall be weary, nor *s*.
28. 7. they *s*. in judgment.
59. 10. we *s*. at noonday.
Jer. 46. 6; Dan. 11. 19. *s*. and fall.
Mal. 2. 8. ye have caused many to *s*.
Rom. 9. 32. they *s*. at that stumbling-stone.
14. 21. whereby thy brother *s*.
1 Pet. 2. 8. that *s*. at the word.
Subdue, Ps. 47. 3. he shall *s*. the people.
Mic. 7. 19. he will *s*. our iniquities.
1 Cor. 15. 28. when all shall be *s*. unto him.
Phil. 3. 21. able to *s*. all things.
Heb. 11. 33. through faith *s*. kingdoms.
Subject, Lk. 2. 51. Jesus was *s*. to parents.
10. 17. devils are *s*. unto us.
Rom. 8. 7. it is not *s*. to law of God.
8. 20. creature was made *s*. to vanity.
13. 1. let every soul be *s*. to higher powers.
1 Cor. 14. 32. spirits of prophets are *s*. to
prophets.
15. 28. then shall the Son also be *s*. to him.
Eph. 5. 24. as the church is *s*. to Christ.
Heb. 2. 15. all their lifetime *s*. to bondage.
Jas. 5. 17. Elias was *s*. to like passions.
1 Pet. 2. 18. servants, be *s*. to masters.
3. 22. angels and powers made *s*. to him.
5. 5. all of you be *s*. one to another.
Submit, Gen. 16. 9. *s*. thyself under her hands.
2 Sam. 22. 45; Ps. 18. 44. strangers shall *s*.
themselves to me.
Ps. 66. 3. enemies shall *s*. to thee.
68. 30. till every one *s*. himself.
Eph. 5. 22; Col. 3. 18. wives, *s*. yourselves to
husbands.
Jas. 4. 7. *s*. yourselves to God.
1 Pet. 2. 13. *s*. to every ordinance.
Subscribe, Is. 44. 5. another shall *s*. unto
Lord.
Jer. 32. 44. men shall *s*. evidences.

Substance, Gen. 15. 14. they shall come with
great *s*.
Deut. 33. 11. bless, Lord, his *s*.
Job 15. 29. nor shall his *s*. continue.
30. 22. thou dissolvest my *s*.
Ps. 17. 14. they leave their *s*. to babes.
139. 15. my *s*. was not hid from thee.
Prov. 3. 9. honour the Lord with thy *s*.
28. 8. he that by usury increaseth his *s*.
Hos. 12. 8. I have found me out *s*.
Mic. 4. 13. I will consecrate their *s*.
Lk. 8. 3. ministered to him of their *s*.
15. 13. wasted his *s*.
Heb. 10. 34. in heaven a better *s*.
11. 1. faith is *s*. of things hoped for.
Subtil, Gen. 3. 1. serpent was more *s*. than any
beast.
2 Sam. 13. 3. a *s*. man.
Prov. 7. 10. *s*. of heart.
See Gen. 27. 35; Matt. 26. 4; Acts 13. 10.
Subvert, Lam. 3. 36. to *s*. a man in his cause,
Acts 15. 24. *s*. souls.
2 Tim. 2. 14. to the *s*. of hearers.
Tit. 1. 11. who *s*. whole houses.
Suck, Deut. 32. 13. *s*. honey out of rock.
33. 19. *s*. of abundance of the seas.
Job 20. 16. he shall *s*. the poison of asps.
Is. 60. 16. *s*. the milk of the Gentiles.
Matt. 24. 19; Mk. 13. 17; Lk. 21. 23. woe to
them that give *s*. in those days!
Sudden, Job 22. 10. *s*. fear troubleth thee.
Prov. 3. 25. be not afraid of *s*. fear.
1 Thes. 5. 3. then *s*. destruction cometh.
See Prov. 29. 1; Mal. 3. 1: Mk. 13. 36 ; 1 Tim.
5. 22.   [moved.
Suffer, Ps. 55. 22. never *s*. righteous to be
89. 33. nor *s*. my faithfulness to fail.
121. 3. not *s*. thy foot to be moved.
Prov. 10. 3. Lord not *s*. righteous to famish.
19. 15. an idle soul shall *s*. hunger.
Matt. 3. 15. Jesus said, *s*. it to be so now.
8. 21; Lk. 9. 59. *s*. me first to bury my
father.
Matt. 16. 21; 17. 12; Mk. 8. 31; Lk. 9. 22.
must *s*. many things.   [children.
Matt. 19. 14; Mk. 10. 14; Lk. 18. 16. *s*. little
Lk. 24. 46; Acts 3. 18. it behoved Christ to *s*.
Rom. 8. 17. if we *s*. with him.
1 Cor. 3. 15. he shall *s*. loss.
10. 13. will not *s*. you to be tempted.
2 Tim. 2. 12. if we *s*. we shall also reign.
Heb. 11. 25. choosing rather to *s*. affliction.
13. 22. *s*. the word of exhortation.
1 Pet. 2. 21. Christ *s*. for us, leaving us an
example.
Sufficient, Is. 40. 16. not *s*. to burn.
Matt. 6. 34. *s*. to the day is the evil thereof.
2 Cor. 2. 16. who is *s*. for these things?
See 2 Cor. 3. 5; 9. 8.
Sum, Ps. 139. 17. how great is the *s*. of them !
Acts 22. 28. with a great *s*. obtained I this
freedom.
Heb. 8. 1. of the things, this is the *s*.
Summer, Gen. 8. 22 ; Ps. 74. 17. *s*. and winter.
Ps. 32. 4. drought of *s*.
Prov. 6. 8: 30; 25. provideth meat in *s*.
10. 5. he that gathereth in *s*. is a wise son.
26. 1. as snow in *s*.
Is. 28. 4. as hasty fruit before the *s*.
Jer. 8. 20. the *s*. is ended.
Zech. 14. 8. in *s*. and winter shall it be.
Matt. 24. 32; Mk. 13. 28. ye know that *s*. is
nigh.
Sumptuously, Lk. 16. 19. fared *s*. every day.

144

Sun, Josh. 10. 12. *s.*, stand thou still.
Job 9. 7. commandeth *s.* it riseth not.
Ps. 19. 4. he set a tabernacle for the *s.*
84. 11. Lord is a *s.* and shield.
121. 6. the *s.* shall not smite thee by day.
Eccl. 1. 9. no new thing under the *s.*
12. 2. while the *s.* or stars be not darkened.
Cant. 6. 10. clear as the *s.*
Is. 60. 20. thy *s.* shall no more go down.
Mal. 4. 2. the *S.* of righteousness arise.
Matt. 5. 45. he maketh his *s.* to rise on evil
and good.   [the *s.*
13. 43. then shall the righteous shine as
1 Cor. 15. 41. there is one glory of the *s.*
Eph. 4. 26. let not the *s.* go down on your
wrath.
Rev. 21. 23 ; 22. 5. city had no need of the *s.*
Sup, Lk. 17. 8. make ready wherewith I may *s.*
1 Cor. 11. 25. took the cup when he had *s.*
Rev. 3. 20. I will *s.* with him, he with me.
See Lk. 14. 16 ; John 12. 2 ; Rev. 19. 17.
Supplication, 1 Ki. 9. 3. I have heard thy *s.*
Job 9. 15. I would make *s.* to my judge.
Ps. 6. 9. the Lord hath heard my *s.*
Dan. 9. 20. I was presenting *s.* before God.
Zech. 12. 10. spirit of grace and *s.*
Eph. 6. 18. with all prayer and *s.*
Phil. 4. 6. in every thing by *s.*
1 Tim. 2. 1. that *s.* be made for all men.
Supply, Phil. 1. 19. through prayer and *s.* of
Spirit.
4. 19. shall *s.* all your need by Christ.
Support, Acts 20. 35 ; 1 Thes. 5. 14. ye ought to
s. the weak.
Supreme, 1 Pet. 2. 13. whether to the king as *s.*
Sure, Num. 32. 23. be *s.* your sin will find you
out.
2 Sam. 23. 5. covenant ordered and *s.*
Job 24. 22. no man is *s.* of life.
Ps. 111. 7. his commandments are *s.*
Prov. 6. 3. make *s.* thy friend.
Is. 33. 16. bread given, waters *s.*
55. 3 ; Acts 13. 34. the *s.* mercies of David.
2 Tim. 2. 19. the foundation of God stand-
eth *s.*
2 Pet. 1. 10. your calling and election *s.*
1. 19. a more *s.* word of prophecy.
Surety, Ps. 119. 122. be *s.* for thy servant.
Prov. 6. 1. if thou be *s.* for thy friend.
22. 26. be not of them that are *s.*   [ment.
Heb. 7. 22. Jesus made a *s.* of a better testa-
Surfeiting, Lk. 21. 34. lest your hearts be over-
charged with *s.*
Sustain, Ps. 3. 5. I awaked, the Lord *s.* me.
55. 22. burden on Lord, he shall *s.* thee.
Prov. 18. 14. the spirit of man will *s.* his
infirmity.
Is. 59. 16. his righteousness *s.* him.   [tory.
Swallow, Is. 25. 8. he will *s.* up death in vic-
Matt. 23. 24. strain at a gnat, and *s.* a camel.
1 Cor. 15. 54. death is *s.* up in victory.
2 Cor. 5. 4. that mortality might be *s.* up of
life.
See Ps. 84. 3 ; Jer. 8. 7.
Swear, Lev. 19. 12. ye shall not *s.* by my name
Ps. 15. 4. that *s.* to his hurt.   [falsely.
Eccl. 9. 2. he that *s.*, as he that feareth an
Is. 45. 23. to me every tongue shall *s.*   [oath.
65. 16. shall *s.* by the God of truth.
Jer. 4. 2. thou shalt *s.*, the Lord liveth.
23. 10. because of *s.* the land mourneth.
Hos. 4. 2. by *s.* and lying, they break out.
Zech. 5. 3. every one that *s.* shall be cut off.
Matt. 5. 34 ; Jas. 5. 12. *s.* not at all.

Sweat, Gen. 3. 19. in *s.* of face eat bread.
Lk. 22. 44. his *s.* was as drops of blood.
Sweet, Neh. 8. 10. eat the fat, and drink the *s.*
Job 20. 12. though wickedness be *s.*
Ps. 55. 14. we took *s.* counsel together.
104. 34. my meditation of him shall be *s.*
119. 103. how *s.* are thy words to my taste !
Prov. 3. 24. thy sleep shall be *s.*
9. 17. stolen waters are *s.*
13. 19. desire accomplished is *s.*
16. 24. pleasant words are *s.*
20. 17. bread of deceit is *s.* to a man.
27. 7. to the hungry every bitter thing is *s.*
Eccl. 5. 12. sleep of labouring man is *s.*
11. 7. truly the light is *s.*
Cant. 2. 3. his fruit was *s.* to my taste.
Is. 5. 20. that put bitter for *s.*, and *s.* for
bitter.
Jas. 3. 11. at same place *s.* water and bitter.
Rev. 10. 9. in thy mouth *s.* as honey.
See Jud. 14. 18 ; Job 24. 20 ; Prov. 27. 9.
Swelling, Jer. 12. 5. how wilt thou do in *s.* of
Jordan ?
2 Pet. 2. 18. speak *s.* words of vanity.
Swift, Prov. 6. 18. feet *s.* in running to mis-
chief.
Eccl. 9. 11. the race is not to the *s.*
Is. 19. 1. the Lord rideth on *s.* cloud.
Rom. 3. 15. feet are *s.* to shed blood.
See Job 7. 6 ; 9. 25 ; Ps. 147. 15.
Swim, 2 Ki. 6. 6. the iron did *s.*
Is. 25. 11. spread forth hands to *s.*
Ezek. 47. 5. waters to *s.* in.
Swoon, Lam. 2. 11. children *s.* in the streets.
Sword, Gen. 3. 24. cherubim, and a flaming *s.*
Deut. 33. 29. the *s.* of thy excellency.
Jud. 7. 20. *s.* of Lord and Gideon.
Ps. 45. 3. gird thy *s.* on thy thigh.
57. 4. their tongue is a sharp *s.*
Cant. 3. 8. every man hath his *s.* upon his
thigh.   [nation.
Is. 2. 4. nation shall not lift up *s.* against
Jer. 12. 12. the *s.* of the Lord shall devour.
15. 2 ; 43. 11. such as are for the *s.*, to
the *s.*
Zech. 11. 17. the *s.* shall be upon his arm.
13. 7. awake, O *s.*, against my shepherd.
Matt. 10. 34. not to send peace, but a *s.*
Lk. 2. 35. a *s.* shall pierce thy own soul.
Rom. 13. 4. he beareth not the *s.* in vain.
Eph. 6. 17. the *s.* of the Spirit.
Heb. 4. 12. sharper than any two-edged *s.*
Rev. 1. 16 ; 19. 15. out of his mouth went a
sharp *s.*
13. 10. he that killeth with the *s.*, must be
killed with the *s.*
Synagogue, Matt. 13. 54 ; Mk. 6. 2. taught in
their *s.*   [a *s.*
Lk. 7. 5. he loveth our nation, and built us
John 12. 42. lest they should be put out of
the *s.*
16. 2. they shall put you out of the *s.*
Rev. 2. 9 ; 3. 9. the *s.* of Satan.

TABERNACLE, Job 5. 24. thy *t.* shall be in
peace.
Ps. 15. 1. who shall abide in thy *t.* ?
27. 5. in secret of his *t.* shall he hide me.
84. 1. how amiable are thy *t.* !
118. 15. salvation is in *t.* of righteous.
Is. 33. 20. a *t.* that shall not be taken down.
Ezek. 37. 27. my *t.* shall be with them.
2 Cor. 5. 1. if house of this *t.* be dissolved.
5. 4. we that are in this *t.* do groan.

Table, Ps. 23. 5. thou preparest a *t.* before me.
69. 22. let their *t.* become a snare.
128. 3. like olive plants about thy *t,*
Prov. 3. 3; 7. 3. write on *t.* of heart.
9. 2. wisdom hath furnished her *t.*
Is. 21. 5. prepare the *t.*
Jer. 17. 1. graven on *t.* of heart.
Matt. 15. 27; Mk. 7. 28. crumbs from their master's *t.* [devils.
1 Cor. 10. 21. partakers of Lord's *t.,* and *t.* of
2 Cor. 3. 3. fleshy *t.* of the heart.
Take, Ex. 6. 7. I will *t.* you for a people.
20. 7; Deut. 5. 11. not *t.* name of Lord in vain.
Ex. 34. 9. *t.* us for thine inheritance.
Job 23. 10. he knoweth the way that I *t.*
Ps. 27. 10. then the Lord will *t.* me up.
51. 11. *t.* not thy Holy Spirit from me.
116. 13. I will *t.* the cup of salvation.
Hos. 14. 2. *t.* with you words.
Matt. 18. 16. *t.* with thee one or two more.
20. 14. *t.* that thine is, and go thy way.
26. 26; Mk. 14. 22; 1 Cor. 11. 24. *t.,* eat.
Lk. 12. 19. soul, *t.* thine ease.
John 16. 15. he shall *t.* of mine.
1 Cor. 6. 7. why not rather *t.* wrong?
1 Pet. 2. 20. if ye *t.* it patiently.
Rev. 3. 11. that no man *t.* thy crown.
22. 19. if any man *t.* away from this prophecy.
Tale, Ps. 90. 9. we spend our years as a *t.*
Ezek. 22. 9. that carry *t.* to shed blood.
Lk. 24. 11. their words seemed as *t.*
Talent, 2 Ki. 5. 22. a *t.* of silver.
23. 33. a *t.* of gold.
Matt. 18. 24. one owed him ten thousand *t.*
25. 25. I went and hid thy *t.*
Talk, Deut. 5. 24. God doth *t.* with man.
6. 7. *t.* of them when thou sittest.
Job 11. 2. a man full of *t.*
13. 7. will ye *t.* deceitfully for him?
Ps. 71. 24. *t.* of thy righteousness.
77. 12. I will *t.* of thy doings.
145. 11. *t.* of thy power.
Prov. 6. 22. it shall *t.* with thee. [ments.
Jer. 12. 1. let me *t.* with thee of thy judg-
Matt. 22. 15. might entangle him in his *t.*
Lk. 24. 32. while he *t.* with us by the way.
John 9. 37. it is he that *t.* with thee.
14. 30. I will not *t.* much with you.
Eph. 5. 4. nor foolish *t.*
Tame, Mk. 5. 4. nor could any man *t.* him.
Jas. 3. 8. the tongue can no man *t.*
Tarry, Gen. 19. 2. *t.* all night.
Jud. 5. 28. why *t.* the wheels of his chariots?
2 Ki. 7. 9. if we *t.* till morning light.
Ps. 68. 12. she that *t.* at home. [sight.
101. 7. he that telleth lies shall not *t.* in my
Prov. 23. 30. they that *t.* long at the wine.
Is. 46. 13. my salvation shall not *t.*
Hab. 2. 3. though it *t.,* wait for it.
Matt. 25. 5. while the bridegroom *t.*
26. 38; Mk. 14. 34. *t.* ye here and watch.
Lk. 24. 29. he went in to *t.* with them.
John 21. 22. if I will that he *t.* [tized.
Acts 22. 16. why *t.* thou? arise, and be bap-
1 Cor. 11. 33. *t.* one for another.
Heb. 10. 37. will come, and will not *t.*
See Ps. 40. 17; 70. 5.
Taste, Ex. 16. 31. *t.* of manna like wafers.
Num. 11. 8. the *t.* of it as *t.* of fresh oil.
Job 6. 6. is there any *t.* in white of an egg?
12. 11. doth not mouth *t.* meat?
Ps. 34. 8. O *t.* and see that the Lord is good.

Taste—*Continued.*
Ps. 119. 103. how sweet are thy words to my *t.* !
Cant. 2. 3. fruit was sweet to my *t.*
Jer. 48. 11. his *t.* remained in him.
Matt. 16. 28; Mk. 9. 1; Lk. 9. 27. some, which shall not *t.* death.
Lk. 14. 24. none bidden shall *t.* of my supper.
John 8. 52. keep my saying, shall never *t.* of death.
Col. 2. 21. touch not, *t.* not.
Heb. 2. 9. should *t.* death for every man.
6. 4. have *t.* of the heavenly gift.
1 Pet. 2. 3. have *t.* that the Lord is gracious.
Tattlers, 1 Tim. 5. 13. not only idle, but *t.*
Taught, 2 Chr. 6. 27. thou hast *t.* them the good way.
Eccl. 12. 9. he *t.* the people knowledge.
Is. 29. 13. their fear is *t.* by precept of men.
54. 13. thy children shall be *t.* of the Lord.
Jer. 32. 33. though I *t.* them, rising up early.
Matt. 7. 29; Mk. 1. 22. he *t.* as one having authority.
Lk. 13. 26. thou hast *t.* in our streets.
John 6. 45. they shall be all *t.* of God.
Gal. 6. 6. let him that is *t.* in the word.
Eph. 4. 21. if ye have been *t.* by him.
1 John 2. 27. as anointing hath *t.* you.
Teach, Ex. 4. 15. I will *t.* you.
Deut. 4. 10. that they may *t.* their children.
33. 10. they shall *t.* Jacob thy judgments.
1 Sam. 12. 23. I will *t.* you the good way.
2 Chr. 17. 7. to *t.* in cities of Judah.
Job 6. 24. *t.* me, and I will hold my tongue.
21. 22. shall any *t.* God knowledge?
37. 19. *t.* us what we shall say to him.
Ps. 25. 4. *t.* me thy paths.
25. 8. he will *t.* sinners in the way.
34. 11. I will *t.* you the fear of the Lord.
51. 13. then will I *t.* transgressors thy ways.
90. 12. so *t.* us to number our days.
94. 10. he that *t.* man knowledge.
Is. 2. 3 , Mic. 4. 2. he will *t.* us of his ways.
Is. 28. 9. whom shall he *t.* knowledge?
Jer. 31. 34; Heb. 8. 11. *t.* no more every man his neighbour.
Mic. 3. 11. priests *t.* for hire.
Matt. 28. 19. *t.* all nations.
Lk. 11. 1. *t.* us to pray.
John 9. 34. dost thou *t.* us?
14. 26. Holy Ghost shall *t.* you all things.
Acts 5. 42. they ceased not to *t.* and preach.
1 Cor. 11. 14. doth not even nature *t.* you ?
Col. 1. 28. *t.* every man in all wisdom.
3. 16. *t.* and admonishing one another.
1 Tim. 2. 12. I suffer not a woman to *t.*
3. 2 ; 2 Tim. 2. 24. apt to *t.*
1 Tim. 4. 11. these things command and *t.*
2 Tim. 2. 2. faithful men, able to *t.* others.
Tit. 2. 12. *t.* us, that denying ungodliness.
Heb. 5. 12. ye have need that one *t.* you.
Teacher, 1 Chr. 25. 8. as well the *t.* as the scholar. [my *t.*
Ps. 119. 99. more understanding than all
Is. 30. 20. thine eyes shall see thy *t.*
Hab. 2. 18. a *t.* of lies.
John 3. 2. a *t.* come from God.
Rom. 2. 20. a *t.* of babes.
1 Cor. 12. 29. are all *t.* ?
Eph. 4. 11. pastors and *t.*
1 Tim. 1. 7. desiring to be *t.* of the law.
2 Pet. 2. 1. shall be false *t.*

Tear, Job 16. 9. he *t.* me in his wrath.
Ps. 7. 2. lest he *t.* my soul.
　50. 22. lest I *t.* you in pieces.
Hos. 5. 14. I will *t.* and go away.
Mk. 9. 18; Lk. 9. 39. he *t.* him.
Tears, Job 16. 20. mine eye poureth out *t.*
Ps. 6. 6. I water my couch with *t.*
　42. 3. my *t.* have been my meat.
　56. 8. put my *t.* into thy bottle.
　80. 5. the bread of *t.*
　126. 5. they that sow in *t.*
Is. 16. 9. I will water thee with my *t.*
　25. 8. the Lord will wipe away *t.*　[of *t.* !
Jer. 9. 1. Oh that mine eyes were a fountain
　31. 16. refrain thine eyes from *t.*
Lam. 2. 11. mine eyes do fail with *t.*
Ezek. 24. 16. neither shall thy *t.* run down.
Mal. 2. 13. covering altar of Lord with *t.*
Lk. 7. 38. to wash his feet with *t.*
Acts 20. 31. ceased not to warn with *t.*
Heb. 5. 7. offered supplications with *t.*
　12. 17. he sought it carefully with *t.*
Rev. 7. 17; 21. 4. God shall wipe away *t.*
Teeth, Gen. 49. 12. his *t.* shall be white with
　milk.
Job 19. 20. escaped with the skin of my *t.*
Prov. 10. 26. as vinegar to the *t.*
Cant. 4. 2; 6. 6. thy *t.* are like a flock.
Is. 41. 15. an instrument having *t.*　[edge.
Jer. 31. 29; Ezek. 18. 2. children's *t.* are set on
Amos 4. 6. cleanness of *t.*
Matt. 27. 44. cast the same in his *t.*
Tell, Gen. 15. 5. *t.* the stars if thou be able.
　32. 29. *t.* me thy name.
2 Sam. 1. 20. *t.* it not in Gath.
Ps. 48. 13. may *t.* it to the generation follow-
　ing.　　　　　　　　　　[after?
Eccl. 6. 12; 10. 14. who can *t.* what shall be
　10. 20. that which hath wings shall *t.* matter.
Jon. 3. 9. who can *t.* if God will turn?
Matt. 18. 15. *t.* him his fault.
Mk. 11. 33; Lk. 20. 7. we cannot *t.*
John 3. 8. thou canst not *t.* whence.
　4. 25. he will *t.* us all things.　　　[thing.
Acts 17. 21. either to *t.* or hear some new
2 Cor. 12. 2. in or out of the body I cannot *t.*
Temperance, Acts 24. 25. as he reasoned of *t.*
Gal. 5. 23. *t.*, against such there is no law *v.*
2 Pet. 1. 6. add to knowledge *t.*, and to *t.*
Tempest, Job 9. 17. he breaketh me with a *t.*
Ps. 11. 6. on wicked he shall reign a *t.*
　55. 8. I hasten from storm and *t.*
Is. 28. 2. as a *t.* of hail.
　32. 2. a covert from the *t.*
Heb. 12. 18. not come to darkness and *t.*
2 Pet. 2. 17. clouds carried with a *t.*
Temple, 2 Sam. 22. 7; Ps. 18. 6. he did hear
　my voice out of his *t.*
Ps. 27. 4. to enquire in his *t.*　　　[glory.
　29. 9. in his *t.* doth every one speak of his
Is. 6. 1. his train filled the *t.*　　　[his *t.*
Mal. 3. 1. the Lord shall suddenly come to
Matt. 12. 6. one greater than the *t.*
John 2. 19. destroy this *t.*
Acts 7. 48 ; 17. 24. *t.* made with hands.
1 Cor. 3. 16 ; 2 Cor. 6. 16. ye are the *t.* of God.
1 Cor. 6. 19. your body is *t.* of Holy Ghost.
Rev. 7. 15. serve day and night in his *t.*
　21. 22. no *t.* therein.
Temporal, 2 Cor. 4. 18. things seen are *t.*
Tempt, Gen. 22. 1. God did *t.* Abraham.
Ex. 17. 2. wherefore do ye *t.* the Lord?
Deut. 6. 16 ; Matt. 4. 7 ; Lk. 4. 12. shall not *t.*
　the Lord.

Tempt—*Continued.*
Is. 7. 12. I will not ask, neither *t.* the Lord.
Mal. 3. 15. they that *t.* God are delivered.
Matt. 22. 18 ;　Mk. 12. 15 ;　Lk. 20. 23. why *t.*
　ye me?
Acts 5. 9. agreed together to *t.* the Spirit.
　15. 10. why *t.* ye God?
1 Cor. 10. 13. will not suffer you to be *t.*
Gal. 6. 1. lest thou also be *t.*
1 Thes. 3. 5. the tempter have *t.* you.
Heb. 2. 18. hath suffered, being *t.*
　4. 15. in all points *t.* like as we are.
Jas. 1. 13. God cannot be *t.*, neither *t.* he any
　man.
Temptation, Ps. 95. 8 ; Heb. 3. 8. as in day of
　t. in wilderness.
Matt. 6. 13 ; Lk. 11. 4. lead us not into *t.*
Matt. 26. 41 ;　Mk. 14. 38 ;　Lk. 22. 46. lest ye
　enter into *t.*
Lk. 8. 13. in time of *t.* fall away.
1 Cor. 10. 13. there hath no *t.* taken you.
1 Tim. 6. 9. they that will be rich fall into *t.*
Jas. 1. 12. blessed that endureth *t.*
2 Pet. 2. 9. how to deliver out of *t.*
Rev. 3. 10. keep thee from hour of *t.*
Tend, Prov. 10. 16. labour of righteous *t.* to life.
　14. 23. talk of lips *t.* to penury.
　19. 23. fear of Lord *t.* to life.
　21. 5. thoughts of diligent *t.* to plenteous-
　ness.　　　　　　　　　　[was *t.*
Tender, 2 Ki. 22. 19 ; 2 Chr. 34. 27. thine heart
Job 38. 27. cause the *t.* herb to spring.
Is. 47. 1. no more be called *t.*
　53. 2. grow up as a *t.* plant.
Lk. 1. 78. through the *t.* mercy of our God.
Eph. 4. 32. be kind, *t.*-hearted.
Jas. 5. 11. Lord is pitiful, and of *t.* mercy.
Tents, Num. 24. 5. how goodly are thy *t.* !
1 Ki. 12. 16. to your *t.*, O Israel.
Ps. 84. 10. than to dwell in *t.* of wickedness.
Terrible, Ex. 34. 10. a *t.* thing I will do.
Deut. 1. 19 ; 8. 15. that *t.* wilderness.
　7. 21 ; 10. 17 ; Neh. 1. 5 ; 4. 14 ; 9. 32. a mighty
　God and *t.*
Deut. 10. 21 ; 2 Sam. 7. 23. done *t.* things.
Job 37. 22. with God is *t.* majesty.
Ps. 45. 4. thy right hand shall teach thee *t.*
　things.
　47. 2. the Lord Most High is *t.*
　65. 5. by *t.* things in righteousness.
　66. 5. God is *t.* in his doing towards men.
　76. 12. he is *t.* to kings of the earth.
　99. 3. thy great and *t.* name.
　145. 6. the might of thy *t.* acts.
Cant. 6. 4. *t.* as an army with banners.
Is. 25. 4. blast of the *t.* ones.
　64. 3. when thou didst *t.* things.
Joel 2. 11. the day of the Lord is very *t.*
Heb. 12. 21. so *t.* was the sight.
Terrify, Job 7. 14. thou *t.* me through visions.
　9. 34. let not his fear *t.* me.
Lk. 21. 9. when ye hear of wars, be not *t.*
　24. 37. they were *t.* and affrighted.
Phil. 1. 28. in nothing *t.* by adversaries.
Terror, Gen. 35. 5. the *t.* of God.
Deut. 32. 25. the sword without, and *t.*
　within.
Job 18. 11. *t.* shall make him afraid.
　24. 17. in the *t.* of the shadow of death.
　31. 23. destruction was a *t.* to me.
Ps. 55. 4. the *t.* of death are fallen upon me.
　91. 5. not afraid for *t.* by night.
Is. 33. 18. thine heart shall meditate *t.*
　54. 14. thou shalt be far from *t.*

147

Terror—*Continued.*
Jer. 17. 17. be not a *t.* unto me.
  20. 4; Ezek. 26. 21. I will make thee a *t.*
Ezek. 27. 36; 28. 19. thou shalt be a *t.*
Rom. 13. 3. rulers are not a *t.* to good works.
2 Cor. 5. 11. knowing the *t.* of the Lord.
1 Pet. 3. 14. be not afraid of their *t.*

Testament, Matt. 26. 28; Mk. 14. 24. this is my
  blood of new *t.*
Lk. 22. 20; 1 Cor. 11. 25. cup is new *t.*
2 Cor. 3. 6. ministers of new *t.*
Heb. 7. 22. surety of a better *t.*
  9. 16. where a *t.* is, there must be death of
  testator.

Testify, Num. 35. 30. one witness shall not *t.*
Neh. 9. 30. *t.* against them by thy Spirit.
Job 15. 6. thine own lips *t.* against thee.
Is. 59. 12. our sins *t.* against us.
Hos. 5. 5; 7. 10. pride of Israel doth *t.*
Mic. 6. 3. *t.* against me.
John 2. 25. any should *t.* of man.
  3. 11. we *t.* that we have seen.
  5. 39. Scriptures *t.* of me.
  15. 26. he shall *t.* of me.
  21. 24. disciple, who *t.* of these things.
Acts 20. 24. to *t.* gospel of grace of God.
Eph. 4. 17. this I say, and *t.* in the Lord.
1 Tim. 2. 6. gave himself to be *t.* in due time.
Heb. 2. 6. one in a certain place *t.*
1 Pet. 1. 11. *t.* beforehand the sufferings.
1 John 4. 14. we have seen and do *t.*

Testimony, 2 Ki. 11. 12; 2 Chr. 23. 11. gave
  him the *t.*
Ps. 78. 5. he established a *t.* in Jacob.
  93. 5. thy *t.* are very sure.
  119. 24. thy *t.* are my delight.
  119. 59. I turned my feet to thy *t.*
  119. 129. thy *t.* are wonderful.
Is. 8. 16. bind up the *t.*
  8. 20. to the law and to the *t.*
Matt. 10. 18; Mk. 13. 9. for a *t.* against them.
John 3. 32. no man receiveth his *t.*
  21. 24. we know that his *t.* is true.
Acts 14. 3. gave *t.* to the word of his grace.
1 Cor. 2. 1. declaring the *t.* of God.
2 Cor. 1. 12. the *t.* of our conscience.
Heb. 11. 5. Enoch had this *t.*
Rev. 1. 2; 19. 10. the *t.* of Jesus.

Thank, 1 Chr. 29. 13. our God, we *t.* thee.
Matt. 11. 25; Lk. 10. 21; John 11. 41. I *t.*
  thee, O Father.
Rom. 6. 17. God be *t.* ye were.
1 Cor. 1. 4. I *t.* God on your behalf.
2 Thes. 1. 3. we are bound to *t.* God.

Thanks, Dan. 6. 10. he prayed, and gave *t.*
Matt. 26. 27; Lk. 22. 17. he took the cup, and
  gave *t.*
Rom. 14. 6. he giveth God *t.*
1 Cor. 15. 57. *t.* be to God who giveth us the
  victory.   [gift.
2 Cor. 9. 15. *t.* be to God for his unspeakable
Eph. 5. 20. giving *t.* always for all things.
1 Thes. 3. 9. what *t.* can we render?   [the *t.*

Thanksgiving, Neh. 11. 17. principal to begin
Ps. 26. 7. publish with voice of *t.*
  50. 14. offer unto God *t.*
  95. 2. come before his presence with *t.*
  100. 4. enter into his gates with *t.*
Is. 51. 3. *t.* and melody shall be found therein.
Amos 4. 5. offer a sacrifice of *t.*   [known.
Phil. 4. 6. with *t.* let your requests be made
Col. 4. 2. watch in the same with *t.*
1 Tim. 4. 3. to be received with *t.*
Rev. 7. 12. *t.* and honour be to our God.

Thief, Ps. 50. 18. when thou sawest a *t.*
Jer. 2. 26. as the *t.* is ashamed.
Hos. 7. 1. the *t.* cometh in, and robbers.
Joel 2. 9. enter at windows like a *t.*
Matt. 24. 43; Lk. 12. 39. what hour the *t.*
  would come.
Matt. 26. 55; Mk. 14. 48; Lk. 22. 52. are ye
  come as against a *t.?*
Lk. 12. 33. where no *t.* approacheth.
John 10. 1. the same is a *t.* and a robber.
1 Thes. 5. 2; 2 Pet. 3. 10. day of Lord cometh
  as a *t.*
1 Pet. 4. 15. let none suffer as a *t.*   [6. 10.
See Matt. 6. 19; Lk. 10. 30; John 10. 8; 1 Cor.

Thigh, Gen. 24. 2; 47. 29. put hand under *t.*
  32. 25. touched hollow of Jacob's *t.*
Jud. 15. 8. smote them hip and *t.*
Cant. 3. 8. every man hath sword on his *t.*
Rev. 19. 16. he hath on his *t.* a name.

Thine, 2 Chr. 29. 11. *t.*, O Lord, is the greatness.
Ps. 74. 16. the day is *t.*, the night also is *t.*
Is. 63. 19. we are *t.*
Matt. 20. 14. take that is *t.*
Lk. 4. 7. all shall be *t.*
  22. 42. not my will, but *t.* be done.
John 17. 10. all mine are *t.*, and *t.* are mine.

Thing, Gen. 24. 50. the *t.* proceedeth from the
  Lord.
Num. 16. 30. if Lord make a new *t.*
2 Sam. 13. 33. take the *t.* to heart.
2 Ki. 2. 10. thou hast asked a hard *t.*   [for!
Job 6. 8. that God would grant the *t.* I long
  14. 4. who can bring clean *t.* out of unclean?
Eccl. 1. 9. the *t.* that hath been.
  7. 8. better is end of a *t.* than beginning.
Is. 29. 16. shall the *t.* framed say?
  40. 15. isles as a very little *t.*
  43. 19; Jer. 31. 22. a new *t.*
Amos 6. 13. rejoice in a *t.* of nought.
Mk. 1. 27. what *t.* is this?
John 5. 14. lest a worse *t.* come unto thee.
Phil. 3. 16. let us mind the same *t.*
1 Pet. 4. 12. as though some strange *t.*
  happened.   [well.

Think, Gen. 40. 14. *t.* on me when it shall be
Neh. 5. 19. *t.* on me, my God, for good.
Ps. 40. 17. yet the Lord *t.* upon me.
Prov. 23. 7. as he *t.* in his heart.
Jon. 1. 6. if God will *t.* upon us.
Matt. 3. 9. *t.* not to say within yourselves.
  5. 17. *t.* not I am come to destroy.
  6. 7. they *t.* they shall be heard.
  9. 4. why *t.* ye evil in your hearts?
  17. 25; 22. 17. what *t.* thou?
  22. 42. what *t.* ye of Christ?
John 16. 2. will *t.* that he doeth God service.
Rom. 12. 3. not to *t.* more highly than he
  ought to *t.*
1 Cor. 10. 12. let him that *t.* he standeth.
2 Cor. 3. 5. to *t.* anything as of ourselves.
Gal. 6. 3. if a man *t.* himself to be something.
Eph. 3. 20. able to do above all we ask or *t.*
Phil. 4. 8. *t.* on these things.
Jas. 1. 7. let not that man *t.* he shall receive.
  4. 5. do ye *t.* that the scripture saith in
  vain?

Thirst, Ex. 17. 3. to kill us with *t.*
Deut. 29. 19. to add drunkenness to *t.*
Jud. 15. 18. now I shall die for *t.*
Ps. 69. 21. in my *t.* they gave me vinegar.
  104. 11. wild asses quench their *t.*
Is. 41. 17. when their tongue faileth for *t.*
Amos 8. 11. not a *t.* for water, but of hearing.
2 Cor. 11. 27. in hunger and *t.*

Thirst, Ps. 42. 2 ; 63. 1 ; 143. 6. my soul *t.* for God.
Is. 49. 10 ; Rev. 7. 16. shall not hunger nor *t.*
Is. 55. 1. every one that *t.*
Matt. 5. 6. hunger and *t.* after righteousness.
John 4. 14 ; 6. 35. shall never *t.*
7. 37. if any man *t.*, let him come unto me.
19. 28. Jesus saith, I *t.*
Rom. 12. 20. if enemy *t.*, give him drink.
Thirsty, Jud. 4. 19. give me water, I am *t.*
Ps. 63. 1 ; 143. 6. a *t.* land.
107. 5. hungry and *t.*, their soul fainted.
Prov. 25. 25. as cold waters to a *t.* soul.
Is. 21. 14. water to him that was *t.*
29. 8. as when a *t.* man dreameth.
35. 7. *t.* land become springs of water.
44. 3. pour water on him that is *t.*
65. 13. servants drink, but ye shall be *t.*
Matt. 25. 35. I was *t.*, ye gave me drink.
Thistle, Gen. 3. 18. thorns and *t.* shall it bring forth.   [Lebanon.
2 Ki. 14. 9 ; 2 Chr. 25. 18. the *t.* that was in
Job 31. 40. let *t.* grow instead of wheat.
Hos. 10. 8. *t.* come up on their altars
Matt. 7. 16. do men gather figs of *t.*?
Thorn, Num. 33. 55 ; Jud. 2. 3. *t.* in your sides.
Ps. 118. 12. quenched as the fire of *t.*
Prov. 15. 19. way of slothful as hedge of *t.*
22. 5. *t.* are in way of the froward.
24. 31. it was grown over with *t.*
26. 9. as *t.* goeth into the hand.
Eccl. 7. 6. as crackling of *t.* under a pot.
Cant. 2. 2. as the lily among *t.*
Is. 33. 12. as *t.* cut up shall they be burned.
34. 13. *t.* shall come up in her palaces.
55. 13. instead of the *t.* shall come up the fir tree.
Jer. 4. 3. sow not among *t.*
12. 13. sown wheat, shall reap *t.*
Hos. 2. 6. I will hedge up way with *t.*
9. 6. *t.* shall be in their tabernacles.
10. 8. the *t.* shall come up on their altars.
Mic. 7. 4. the most upright is sharper than *t.* hedge.   [of *t.*?
Matt. 7. 16 ; Lk. 6. 44. do men gather grapes
Matt. 13. 7 ; Mk. 4. 7. some fell among *t.*
Matt. 27. 29 ; Mk. 15. 17 ; John 19. 2. platted a crown of *t.*
2 Cor. 12. 7. a *t.* in the flesh.
Thought, Gen. 50. 20. ye *t.* evil against me.
2 Ki. 5. 11. I *t.*, he will surely come out.
Ps. 48. 9. we have *t.* of thy loving-kindness.
50. 21. thou *t.* I was such an one as thyself.
73. 16. when I *t.* to know this.
119. 59. I *t.* on my ways.
Jer. 18. 8. I will repent of the evil I *t.* to do.
Zech. 8. 15. I *t.* to do well.
Mal. 3. 16. for them that *t.* on his name.
Mk. 14. 72. when he *t.* thereon, he wept.
Lk. 12. 17. he *t.* within himself, what shall I do?   [appear.
19. 11. they *t.* the kingdom of God should
John 11. 13. they *t.* he had spoken of rest.
Acts 15. 38. *t.* not good to take him.
26. 8. why should it be *t.* a thing incredible?
1 Cor. 13. 11. I *t.* as a child.   [God.
Phil. 2. 6. *t.* it not robbery to be equal with
Thoughts, Gen. 6. 5. imagination of *t.* of his heart only evil.
1 Chr. 28. 9. the Lord understandeth the *t.*
Job 4. 13. in *t.* from the visions of the night.
42. 2. no *t.* can be withholden from thee.
Ps. 10. 4. God is not in all his *t.*
40. 5. thy *t.* cannot be reckoned.

Thoughts—*Continued.*
Ps. 92. 5. thy *t.* are very deep.
94. 11. the Lord knoweth the *t.* of man.
139. 17. how precious are thy *t.* to me !
139. 23. try me, and know my *t.*
Prov. 12. 5. the *t.* of the righteous are right.
15. 26. the *t.* of the wicked are abomination.
16. 3. thy *t.* shall be established.
Is. 55. 7. let the unrighteous forsake his *t.*
55. 8. my *t.* are not your *t.*
Mic. 4. 12. they know not the *t.* of the Lord.
Matt. 9. 4 ; 12. 25 ; Lk. 5. 22 ; 6. 8 ; 9. 47 ; 11. 17. Jesus knowing their *t.*   [ceed evil *t.*
Matt. 15. 19 ; Mk. 7. 21. out of the heart pro-
Lk. 24. 38. why do *t.* arise in your hearts?
1 Cor. 3. 20. the Lord knoweth the *t.* of the wise.
2 Cor. 10. 5. bringing into captivity every *t.*
Heb. 4. 12. the word of God is a discerner of the *t.*
Jas. 2. 4. are become judges of evil *t.*
Threaten, Acts 4. 17. let us straitly *t.* them.
1 Pet. 2. 23. when he suffered, he *t.* not.
See Acts 9. 1 ; Eph. 6. 9.
Thresh, Is. 41. 15. thou shalt *t.* the mountains.
Jer. 51. 33. it is time to *t.* her.
Mic. 4. 13. arise and *t.*
Hab. 3. 12. thou didst *t.* the heathen.
1 Cor. 9. 10. he that *t.* in hope.
See Lev. 26. 5 ; 1 Chr. 21. 20 ; Is. 21. 10 ; 28. 28.
Throat, Ps. 5. 9 ; Rom. 3. 13. their *t.* is an open sepulchre.
Ps. 115. 7. neither speak they through their *t.*
Prov. 23. 2. put a knife to thy *t.*
Matt. 18. 28. took him by the *t.*
Throne, Gen. 41. 40. in the *t.* will I be greater.
Ps. 11. 4. the Lord's *t.* is in heaven.
47. 8. God sitteth on *t.* of his holiness.
89. 14. justice and judgment are habitation of thy *t.*   [with thee?
94. 20. shall *t.* of iniquity have fellowship
Prov. 20. 28. his *t.* is upholden by mercy.
25. 5. his *t.* shall be established in right-eousness.
Is. 66. 1 ; Acts 7. 49. heaven is my *t.*
Jer. 17. 12. a glorious high *t.*   [tion.
Lam. 5. 19. thy *t.* from generation to genera-
Dan. 7. 9. his *t.* was like the fiery flame.
Matt. 19. 28 ; 25. 31. the Son of man shall sit in the *t.*
Heb. 4. 16. the *t.* of grace.
Rev. 3. 21. to him will I grant to sit on my *t.*
20. 11. a great white *t.*
Throng, Mk. 3. 9. lest they should *t.* him.
5. 24 ; Lk. 8. 42. much people *t.* him.
Lk. 8. 45. the multitude *t.* thee.
Thrust, Ex. 11. 1. he shall surely *t.* you out
Job 32. 13. God *t.* him down, not man.
Ps. 118. 13. thou hast *t.* at me.
Lk. 10. 15. shalt be *t.* down to hell.
13. 28. and you yourselves *t.* out.
John 20. 25. and *t.* my hand into his side.
Heb. 12. 20. stoned or *t.* through.
Rev. 14. 15. *t.* in thy sickle.   [king.
Tidings, 2 Sam. 18. 31. said, *t.*, my lord the
Ps. 112. 7. not be afraid of evil *t.*
Dan. 11. 44. *t.* out of the east.
Lk. 8. 1. showing glad *t.* of kingdom of God.
Rom. 10. 15. glad *t.* of good things.
Time, Ps. 32. 6. in a *t.* when thou mayest be found.
37. 19. not be ashamed in the evil *t.*
41. 1. deliver him in *t.* of trouble.
56. 3. what *t.* I am afraid.

Time—*Continued.*
Ps. 69. 13 ; Is. 49. 8. in an acceptable *t.*
Ps. 89. 47. remember how short my *t.* is.
Eccl. 3. 1. there is a *t.* to every purpose.
9. 11. *t.* and chance happeneth to all.
Is. 60. 22. I will hasten it in his *t.*
Ezek. 16. 8. thy *t.* was the *t.* of love.
Dan. 7. 25. *a. t.* and *t.* and the dividing of *t.*
Hos. 10. 12. it is *t.* to seek the Lord.
Hag. 1. 4. is it *t.* to dwell in houses?
Mal. 3. 11. neither shall vine cast fruit before the *t.*
Mk. 4. 17. endure but for a *t.*
6. 35. now the *t.* is far passed. [tion.
Lk. 10. 44. knewest not the *t.* of thy visita-
John 7. 6. my *t.* is not yet come.
Acts 17. 21. spent their *t.* in nothing else.
Rom. 13. 11. it is high *t.* to awake.
1 Cor. 7. 29. the *t.* is short.
Eph. 5. 16 ; Col. 4. 5. redeeming the *t.*
2 Tim. 4. 6. the *t.* of my departure is at hand.
Heb. 4. 16. grace to help in *t.* of need.
Jas. 4. 14. that appeareth a little *t.*
1 Pet. 1. 17. pass the *t.* of sojourning in fear.
Rev. 10. 6. there should be *t.* no longer.
Title, 2 Ki. 23. 17. what *t.* is that that I see?
John 19. 19. Pilate wrote a *t.*
Tittle, Matt. 5. 18 ; Lk. 16. 17. one *t.* shall not pass from the law.
Together, Prov. 22. 2. rich and poor meet *t.*
Matt. 18. 20. where two or three are gathered *t.*
Rom. 8. 28. all things work *t.* for good.
Token, Ps. 65. 8. they are afraid at thy *t.*
86. 17. show me a *t.* for good.
Phil. 1. 28. an evident *t.* of perdition.
2 Thes. 1. 5. a *t.* of righteous judgment of God.
Tongue, Job 5. 21. hid from scourge of *t.*
20. 12. hide wickedness under his *t.*
29. 10. *t.* cleaved to roof of mouth.
Ps. 5. 9. they flatter with their *t.*
34. 13 ; 1 Pet. 3. 10. keep *t.* from evil.
Prov. 10. 20. *t.* of the just as choice silver.
12. 18 ; 31. 26. *t.* of the wise is health.
12. 19. a lying *t.* is but for a moment.
15. 4. a wholesome *t.* is a tree of life.
18. 21. death and life are in the power of the *t.*
21. 23. whoso keepeth his *t.* keepeth his soul.
25. 15. a soft *t.* breaketh the bone.
Is. 30. 27. his *t.* as a devouring fire.
50. 4. given me the *t.* of the learned.
Jer. 9. 5. taught their *t.* to speak lies.
18. 18. let us smite him with the *t.*
Jas. 1. 26. and bridleth not his *t.*
3. 5. the *t.* is a little member.
3. 8. the *t.* can no man tame.
1 John 3. 18. nor let us love in *t.*
Torment, Matt. 8. 29. art thou come to *t.* us?
Lk. 16. 23. being in *t.*
1 John 4. 18. fear hath *t.*
Rev. 14. 11. the smoke of their *t.*
Torn, Gen. 44. 28. surely he is *t.* in pieces.
Hos. 6. 1. he hath *t.*, and he will heal.
Mk. 1. 26. unclean spirit had *t.* him.
Toss, Ps. 109. 23. I am *t.* up and down.
Is. 22. 18. he will *t.* thee like a ball.
54. 11. *t.* with tempest.
Eph. 4. 14. children *t.* to and fro.
Jas. 1. 6. he that wavereth is like a wave *t.*
Touch, Gen. 3. 3. nor shall ye *t.* it, lest ye die.
1 Chr. 16. 22 ; Ps. 105. 15. *t.* not mine anointed.
Job 5. 19. there shall no evil *t.* thee.
Is. 6. 7. lo, this hath *t.* thy lips.

Touch—*Continued.*
Is. 52. 11 ; 2 Cor. 6. 17. *t.* no unclean thing.
Jer. 1. 9. the Lord *t.* my mouth.
Zech. 2. 8. he that *t.* you, *t.* the apple of his eye. [garment.
Matt. 9. 21 ; Mk. 5. 28. if I may but *t.* his
Mk. 10. 13 ; Lk. 18. 15. children, that he should *t.* them.
Lk. 11. 46. ye yourselves *t.* not the burdens.
John 20. 17. *t.* me not.
Col. 2. 21. *t.* not, taste not.
1 John 5. 18. wicked one *t.* him not.
Tower, Gen. 11. 4. let us build city and *t.*
2 Sam. 22. 3 ; Ps. 18. 2 ; 144. 2. God is my high *t.*
Ps. 61. 3. a strong *t.* from the enemy.
Prov. 18. 10. name of Lord is a strong *t.*
Is. 5. 2 ; Matt. 21. 33 ; Mk. 12. 1. built a *t.*
Tradition, Matt. 15. 2 ; Mk. 7. 5. *t.* of the elders.
Gal. 1. 14. zealous of *t.* of my fathers.
Col. 2. 8. spoil you after *t.* of men. [go.
Train, Prov. 22. 6. *t.* a child in way he should
Is. 6. 1. his *t.* filled the temple.
Traitor, Lk. 6. 16. Judas Iscariot, who was the *t.*
2 Tim. 3. 4. in last days shall men be *t.*
Trample, Ps. 91. 13. dragon *t.* under feet.
Is. 63. 3. I will *t.* them in my fury.
Matt. 7. 6. lest they *t.* them under foot.
Tranquillity, Dan. 4. 27. a lengthening of thy *t.*
Transfigured, Matt. 17. 2 ; Mk. 9. 2. he was *t.* before them.
Transformed, Rom. 12. 2. be ye *t.* by renewing of your mind.
2 Cor. 11. 14. Satan is *t.* into an angel of light.
Transgress, Num. 14. 41 ; 2 Chr. 24. 20. wherefore do ye *t.* commandments of Lord?
1 Sam. 2. 24. ye make the Lord's people to *t.*
Neh. 1. 8. if ye *t.*, I will scatter you.
Ps. 17. 3. my mouth shall not *t.*
25. 3. ashamed who *t.* without cause.
Prov. 28. 21. for a piece of bread that man will *t.*
Amos 4. 4. come to Bethel and *t.*
Hab. 2. 5. he *t.* by wine. [law.
1 John 3. 4. whosoever committeth sin, *t.* the
Transgression, Ex. 34. 7 ; Num. 14. 18. forgiving *t.*
1 Sam. 24. 11. there is no *t.* in my hand.
1 Chr. 10. 13. Saul died for his *t.*
Ezra 10. 6. he mourned because of their *t.*
Job 7. 21. why dost thou not pardon my *t.*?
13. 23. make me to know my *t.*
Ps. 19. 13. innocent from the great *t.*
32. 1. blessed is he whose *t.* is forgiven.
65. 3. as for our *t.*, thou shalt purge them away.
89. 32. I will visit their *t.*
107. 17. fools because of their *t.* are afflicted.
Prov. 17. 9. he that covereth *t.*
Is. 44. 22. blotted out thy *t.*
53. 8. for the *t.* of my people was he stricken.
58. 1. show my people their *t.*
Ezek. 33. 12. not deliver in day of his *t.*
Mic. 1. 5. what is the *t.* of Jacob?
7. 18. that passeth by *t.* of remnant.
Rom. 4. 15. where no law is, is no *t.*
5. 14. after similitude of Adam's *t.*
Transgressor, Ps. 51. 13. then will I teach *t.* thy way.
Prov. 13. 15. the way of *t.* is hard.
21. 18. the *t.* shall be ransom for the upright.
Is. 48. 8. thou wast called a *t.* from the womb.
53. 12 ; Mk. 15. 28 ; Lk. 22. 37. he was numbered with the *t.*
Jas. 2. 11. thou art become a *t.* of the law.

150

Translated, Col. 1. 13. *t.* us into kingdom of
his Son.   [see death.
  Heb. 11. 5. Enoch was *t.* that he should not
Travail, Job 15. 20. wicked man *t.* with pain.
  Ps. 7. 14. he *t.* with iniquity.
  Is. 53. 11. the *t.* of his soul.
  Rom. 8. 22. whole creation *t.* in pain.
  Gal. 4. 19. my children, of whom I *t.*
  1 Thes. 5. 3. destruction cometh as *t.*
Travel, Prov. 6. 11; 24. 34. poverty come as
one that *t.*
  Is. 63. 1. who is this *t.* in his strength?
  Matt. 25. 14. kingdom of heaven is as a man *t.*
  See 2 Sam. 12. 4; Job 31. 32.
Treacherously, Is. 21. 2; 24. 16. treacherous
dealer dealeth *t.*
  33. 1. dealest *t.*
  Jer. 12. 1. why are they happy that deal *t.*?
  Lam. 1. 2. her friends have dealt *t.*
  Hos. 5. 7. they dealt *t.* against the Lord.
  Mal. 2. 10. why do we deal *t.*?
Tread, Deut. 11. 24. whereon your feet *t.*
  25. 4; 1 Cor. 9. 9; 1 Tim. 5. 18. not muzzle
ox when he *t.* corn.
  Job 40. 12. *t.* down wicked in their place.
  Ps. 7. 5. let him *t.* down my life.
  44. 5. through thy name will we *t.* them
under.
  60. 12; 108. 13. shall *t.* down our enemies.
  91. 13. thou shalt *t.* upon lion and adder.
  Is. 1. 12. to *t.* my courts.
  16. 6. to *t.* them down like mire.
  16. 10. treaders shall *t.* out no wine.
  63. 3. I will *t.* them in mine anger.
  Jer. 25. 30. as they that *t.* grapes.
  48. 33. none shall *t.* with shouting.
  Hos. 10. 11. loveth to *t.* out corn.
  Lk. 10. 19. power to *t.* on scorpions.
  Rev. 11. 2. city shall they *t.* under foot.
  19. 15. he *t.* wine-press of wrath.
Treasure, Gen. 43. 23. God hath given you *t.*
  Ex. 19. 5; Ps. 135. 4. a peculiar *t.* to me.
  Deut. 28. 12. Lord shall open his good *t.*
  Job 3. 21. dig more than for hid *t.*
  38. 22. *t.* of the snow, *t.* of hail.
  Prov. 2. 4. searchest as for hid *t.*
  10. 2. *t.* of wickedness profit nothing.
  15. 16. than great *t.* and trouble therewith.
  21. 20. there is a *t.* to be desired.
  Is. 33. 6. the fear of the Lord is his *t.*
  Matt. 6. 21; Lk. 12. 34. where your *t.* is.
  Matt. 12. 35; Lk. 6. 45. out of good *t.* of his
heart.
  Matt. 13. 44. *t.* hid in a field.
  13. 52. bringeth out of his *t.* things new
and old.
  19. 21; Mk. 10. 21; Lk. 18. 22. *t.* in heaven.
  Lk. 12. 21. that layeth up *t.* for himself.
  2 Cor. 4. 7. we have this *t.* in earthen vessels.
  Col. 2. 3. in whom are hid *t.* of wisdom.
  Heb. 11. 26. greater riches than the *t.* in
Egypt.
  Jas. 5. 3. ye have heaped *t.* together.
  See Is. 23. 18; Rom. 2. 5.
Treasury, Matt. 27. 6. not lawful to put into *t.*
  Mk. 12. 41; Lk. 21. 1. Jesus beheld them
casting money into *t.*
Tree, Gen. 1. 29. given you every *t.*
  Deut. 20. 19. the *t.* of field is man's life.
  Job 14. 7. there is hope of a *t.* if cut down.
  24. 20. wickedness shall be broken as a *t.*
  Ps. 1. 3; Jer. 17. 8. like a *t.* planted by rivers.
  Ps. 104. 16. the *t.* of the Lord are full of sap.
  Prov. 3. 18; 11. 30; 13. 12; 15. 4 a *t.* of life.

Tree—*Continued.*
  Eccl. 11. 3. where the *t.* falleth.
  Is. 56. 3. I am a dry *t.*
  61. 3. called *t.* of righteousness.   [any *t.*?
  Ezek. 15. 2. what is the vine *t.* more than
  Matt. 7. 17; Lk. 6. 43. good *t.* bringeth forth
good fruit.   [the *t.*
  1 Pet. 2. 24. bare our sins in his own body on
  Rev. 2. 7. I will give to eat of *t.* of life.
Tremble, Job 9. 6. the pillars of earth *t.*
  26. 11. the pillars of heaven *t.*
  Ps. 60. 2. thou hast made the earth to *t.*
  99. 1. the Lord reigneth, let the people *t.*
  114. 7. *t.* thou earth, at presence of the Lord.
  Eccl. 12. 3. the keepers of the house shall *t.*
  Is. 14. 16. is this the man that made earth *t.*?
  32. 11. *t.* ye women that are at ease.
  64. 2. that the nations may *t.* at thy presence.
  66. 5. ye that *t.* at his word.
  Jer. 5. 22. will ye not *t.* at my presence?
  Joel 2. 10. the heavens shall *t.*
  Amos 8. 8. shall not the land *t.* for this?
  Acts 24. 25. as he reasoned, Felix *t.*
  Phil. 2. 12. work out your salvation with *t.*
  Jas. 2. 19. the devils believe and *t.*
Trespass, Gen. 50. 17. forgive the *t.* of thy
servants.
  Ezra 9. 6. our *t.* is grown unto heavens.
  Ps. 68. 21. as goeth on still in his *t.*
  Matt. 6. 14. if ye forgive men their *t.*
  18. 35. if ye forgive not every one his
brother their *t.*
  Lk. 17. 3. if thy brother *t.* against thee.
  2 Cor. 5. 19. not imputing their *t.*
  Eph. 2. 1. dead in *t.* and sins.
  Col. 2. 13. having forgiven you all *t.*
Trial, Job 9. 23. the *t.* of the innocent.
  2 Cor. 8. 2. a great *t.* of affliction.
  1 Pet. 1. 7. the *t.* of your faith.
Tribes, Ps. 105. 37. not one feeble among their *t.*
  122. 4. whither the *t.* go up.
  Is. 63. 17. for the *t.* of thine inheritance.
  Hab. 3. 9. according to oaths of the *t.*
  Matt. 24. 30. then shall all *t.* of the earth
mourn.
Tribulation, Deut. 4. 30. when thou art in *t.*
  Jud. 10. 14. let them deliver you in *t.*
  1 Sam. 26. 24. deliver me out of all *t.*
  Matt. 13. 21. when *t.* ariseth.
  24. 21. then shall be great *t.*
  John 16. 33. in the world ye shall have *t.*
  Acts 14. 22. we must through much *t.* enter.
  Rom. 5. 3. *t.* worketh patience.
  8. 35. shall *t.* separate us from Christ?
  12. 12. patient in *t.*
  2 Cor. 7. 4. exceeding joyful in *t.*
  Rev. 7. 14. they which came out of great *t.*
Tribute, Gen. 49. 15. a servant to *t.*
  Num. 31. 28. levy a *t.* to the Lord.
  Deut. 16. 10 a *t.* of free-will offering.
  Ezra 4. 20. *t.* and custom was paid to them.
  7. 24. not lawful to impose *t.*
  Prov. 12. 24. the slothful shall be under *t.*
  Matt. 22. 17; Mk. 12. 14; Lk. 20. 22. is it law-
ful to give *t.* unto Cæsar?
  Rom. 13. 7. render *t.* to whom *t.* is due.
Triumph, Ex. 15. 1. he hath *t.* gloriously.
  Ps. 25. 2. let not mine enemies *t.* over me.
  92. 4. I will *t.* in works of thy hands.
  94. 3. how long shall the wicked *t.*?
  106. 47. give thanks, and *t.* in thy praise.
  2 Cor. 2. 14. causeth us to *t.* in Christ.
  Col. 2. 15. a show of them openly, *t.* over
them.

Trodden, Jud. 5. 21. hast *t.* down strength.
Job 22. 15. old way wicked men have *t.*
Ps. 119. 118. thou hast *t.* down all that err.
Is. 63. 3. I have *t.* the wine-press alone.
Mic. 7. 10. now shall she be *t.* as mire.
Matt. 5. 13. salt to be *t.* under foot.
Lk. 8. 5. fell by wayside, and was *t.*
     21. 24. Jerusalem shall be *t.* of Gentiles.
Heb. 10. 29. hath *t.* under foot the Son of
     God.

Trouble, 2 Chr. 15. 4; Neh. 9. 27. when they in
     t. sought the Lord.   [ground.
Job 5. 6. neither doth *t.* spring out of the
     14. 1. man is of few days, and full of *t.*
Ps. 9. 9. Lord will be a refuge in times of *t.*
     22. 11. for *t.* is near.
     27. 5. in time of *t.* he shall hide me.
     46. 1. a very present help in *t.*
     60. 11. give us help from *t.*
     73. 5. they are not in *t.* as other men.
     91. 15. I will be with him in *t.*   [me.
     119. 143. *t.* and anguish have taken hold on
     143. 11. bring my soul out of it.   [of *t.*
Prov. 11. 8; 12. 13. righteous delivered out
Is. 17. 14. at evening-tide *t.*
     26. 16. Lord, in *t.* they visited thee.
     33. 2. our salvation in time of *t.*
Jer. 8. 15. we looked for health, and behold *t.*!
1 Cor. 7. 28. such shall have *t.* in the flesh.
2 Cor. 1. 4. able to comfort them in *t.*

Trouble, Josh. 7. 25. Lord shall *t.* thee this day.
1 Ki. 18. 17. art thou he that *t.* Israel?
Ps. 3. 1. how are they increased that *t.* me!
     46. 3. though waters roar and be *t.*
Prov. 25. 26. is as a *t.* fountain.
Is. 57. 20. wicked are like the *t.* sea.
Dan. 5. 10. let not thy thoughts *t.* thee.
Matt. 24. 6; Mk. 13. 7 be not *t.*
Matt. 26. 10; Mk. 14. 6. why *t.* ye the woman?
Lk. 7. 6. Lord, *t.* not thyself.
     11. 7. *t.* me not, door is shut.
John 11. 33; 12. 27; 13. 21. Jesus was *t.*
     14. 1, 27. let not your heart be *t.*
2 Cor. 4. 8; 7. 5. we are *t.* on every side.
Gal. 6. 17. let no man *t.* me.
Heb. 12. 15. lest any bitterness *t.* you.
See Job 3. 17; John 5. 4.   [breakers.
Truce, 2 Tim. 3. 3. in last days men shall be *t.*
True, Gen. 42. 11. we are *t.* men.
1 Ki. 22. 16. tell me nothing but that which
     is *t.*   [God.
2 Chr. 15. 3. Israel hath been without the *t.*
Neh. 9. 13. thou gavest them *t.* laws.
Ps. 19. 9. judgments of the Lord are *t.*
     119. 160. thy word is *t.* from the beginning.
Jer. 10. 10. the Lord is the *t.* God.
     42. 5. the Lord be a *t.* witness.   [art *t.*
Matt. 22. 16; Mk. 12. 14. we know that thou
Lk. 16. 11. the *t.* riches.
John 1. 9. that was the *t.* light.
     4. 37. herein is that saying *t.*   [ness is not *t.*
     5. 31. if I bear witness of myself, my wit-
     6. 32. the *t.* bread.
     10. 41. all things that John spake were *t.*
     15. 1. the *t.* vine.   [God.
     17. 3; 1 John 5. 20. to know thee the only *t.*
John 19. 35; 21. 24. his record is *t.*
2 Cor. 1. 18. as God is *t.*
     6. 8. as deceivers, and yet *t.*
Phil. 4. 8. whatsoever things are *t.*
Heb. 10. 22. draw near with a *t.* heart.
Rev. 15. 3. just and *t.* are thy ways.
     19. 11. he that sat was Faithful and *T.*

Truly, Num. 14. 21. as *t.* as I live, saith Lord.
Ps. 116. 16. O Lord, *t.* I am thy servant.
Prov. 12. 22. they that deal *t.* are his delight.
Matt. 27. 54. *t.* this was the Son of God.
Lk. 20. 21. teachest way of God *t.*
John 4. 18. in that saidst thou *t.*
Trump, 1 Cor. 15. 52. at last *t.* dead shall be
     raised.
1 Thes. 4. 16. Lord shall descend with *t.*
Trumpet, Num. 10. 2. make thee a *t.*
Matt. 6. 2. do not sound a *t.* before thee.
Rev. 1. 10; 4. 1. I heard voice as of a *t.*
Trust, 2 Sam. 22. 3; Ps. 18. 2; 91. 2. in him will
     I *t.*   [him.
Job 13. 15. though he slay me, yet will I *t.* in
     15. 15. he putteth no *t.* in his saints.
Ps. 25. 2; 55. 23; 56. 3; 143. 8. I *t.* in thee.
     37. 3; 40. 3; 62. 8; 115. 9; Prov. 3. 5; Is. 26. 4.
     t. in the Lord.
Ps. 40. 4. that maketh the Lord his *t.*
     118. 8. it is better to *t.* in the Lord.
     141. 8. in thee is my *t.*
Is. 12. 2. I will *t.*, and not be afraid.
     50. 10. let him *t.* in the name of the Lord.
Jer. 9. 4. *t.* not in any brother.
     49. 11. let thy widows *t.* in me.
Mic. 7. 5. *t.* ye not in a friend.
Nah. 1. 7. the Lord knoweth them that *t.* in
     him.   [Gentiles in
Matt. 12. 21; Rom. 15. 12. in his name shall
Mk. 10. 24. them that *t.* in riches.
Lk. 18. 9. certain which *t.* in themselves.
2 Cor. 1. 9. should not *t.* in ourselves.
1 Tim. 4. 10. we *t.* in the living God.
Truth, Ex. 34. 6. abundant in goodness and *t.*
Deut. 32. 4. a God of *t.*
Ps. 15. 2. speaketh *t.* in his heart.
     25. 10. the paths of the Lord are mercy
     and *t.*
     51. 6. thou desirest *t.* in the inward parts.
     91. 4. his *t.* shall be thy shield.
     117. 2. *t.* of the Lord endureth for ever.
     119. 142. thy law is *t.*
Prov. 12. 19. the lip of *t.* shall be established.
     23. 23. buy the *t.*
Is. 26. 2. nation which keepeth *t.*
     59. 14. *t.* is fallen in the street.
Jer. 9. 3. they are not valiant for the *t.*
Dan. 4. 37. all whose works are *t.*
Zech. 8. 16. speak every man *t.* to his neigh-
     bour.
Mal. 2. 6. law of *t.* was in his mouth.
Mk. 12. 32. Master, thou hast said the *t.*
John 1. 14. full of grace and *t.*   [free.
     8. 32. know the *t.*, and the *t.* shall make you
     14. 6. I am the way, the *t.*, and the life.
     16. 13. Spirit of *t.* will guide you into all *t.*
     18. 38. what is *t.*?   [ness.
Rom. 1. 18. who hold the *t.* in unrighteous-
     2. 2. judgment of God is according to *t.*
1 Cor. 5. 8. unleavened bread of *t.*
2 Cor. 13. 8. we can do nothing against the *t.*
Gal. 3. 1; 5. 7. that ye should not obey the *t.*
Eph. 4. 15. speaking the *t.* in love.
1 Tim. 3. 15. pillar and ground of the *t.*
2 Tim. 2. 15. rightly dividing the word of *t.*
     3. 7. to come to the knowledge of the *t.*
Jas. 3. 14. lie not against the *t.*
     5. 19. if any err from the *t.*
1 John 5. 6. the Spirit is *t.*
Try, 2 Chr. 32. 31. God left him to *t.* him.
Job 7. 18. shouldest *t.* him every moment.
Ps. 26. 2. *t.* my reins and my heart.
     139. 23. *t.* me, and know my thoughts.

Try—*Continued.*
Jer. 9. 7; Zech. 13. 9. I will melt them and *t.* them.
1 Cor. 3. 13. fire shall *t.* every man's work.
1 John 4. 1. *t.* the spirits.
Rev. 3. 18. gold *t.* in the fire.

Turn, Job 23. 13. who can *t.* him?
Ps. 7. 12. if he *t.* not, he will whet his sword.
Prov. 1. 23. *t.* you at my reproof.
Jer. 31. 18. *t.* thou me, and I shall be *t.*
Lam. 5. 21. *t.* us unto thee, O Lord.
Ezek. 14. 6; 18. 32; 33. 9; Hos. 12. 6; Joel 2. 12. repent, and *t.*
Dan. 12. 3. that *t.* many to righteousness.
Zech. 9. 12. *t.* you to the strong hold.
Mal. 4. 6. he shall *t.* heart of fathers.
Matt. 5. 39. *t.* the other also.
Acts 26. 20. they should repent and *t.* to God.
Jas. 1. 17. with whom is no shadow of *t.*

Twain, Is. 6. 2. with *t.* he covered his face.
Matt. 5. 41. to go a mile, go with him *t.*
19. 6; Mk. 10. 8. they are no more *t.*
Matt. 27. 51; Mk. 15. 38. veil of temple was rent in *t.*   [man.
Eph. 2. 15. to make in himself of *t.* one new

Twice, 2 Ki. 6. 10. saved himself, not once nor *t.*
Job 33. 14. God speaketh once, yea *t.*
Ps. 62. 11. *t.* have I heard this.
Mk. 14. 30. before the cock crow *t.*
Lk. 18. 12. I fast *t.* in the week.
Jude 12. *t.* dead, plucked up by the roots.

Twinkling, 1 Cor. 15. 52. in the *t.* of an eye.

UNADVISEDLY, Ps. 106. 33. he spake *u.* with his lips.

Unawares, Ps. 35. 8. destruction come on him *u.*
Lk. 21. 34. that day come on you *u.*
Heb. 13. 2. entertained angels *u.*
Jude 4. are certain men crept in *u.*

Unbelief, Matt. 13. 58. because of their *u.*
Mk. 9. 24. help thou mine *u.*
Rom. 3. 3. shall *u.* make faith without effect?
11. 20. because of *u.* they were broken.
11. 32. God hath concluded them all in *u.*
Heb. 3. 12. an evil heart of *u.*
4. 11. fall after same example of *u.*
See Lk. 12. 46.; 2 Cor. 6. 14.

Unblameable, Col. 1. 22. to present you holy, *u.*
1 Thes. 3. 13. may stablish your hearts *u.*

Uncertain, 1 Cor. 14. 8. if trumpet give an *u.* sound.
1 Tim. 6. 17. nor trust in *u.* riches.

Unchangeable, Heb. 7. 24. hath an *u.* priesthood.   [*u.* and clean.

Unclean, Lev. 10. 10; 11. 47. difference between
Is. 6. 5. I am a man of *u.* lips.
Acts 10. 28. not call any man *u.*
Rom. 14. 14. nothing is *u.* of itself.
2 Cor. 6. 17. touch not the *u.* thing.

Unclothed, 2 Cor. 5. 4. not that we would be *u.*

Uncorruptness, Tit. 2. 7. in doctrine shewing *u.*   [Holy One.

Unction, 1 John 2. 20. ye have an *u.* from the

Undefiled, Ps. 119. 1. blessed are *u.* in way.
Heb. 7. 26. priest, holy, harmless, *u.*
Jas. 1. 27. pure religion and *u.*
1 Pet. 1. 4. an inheritance incorruptible, *u.*

Under, Rom. 3. 9; Gal. 3. 22. all *u.* sin.
1 Cor. 9. 27. I keep *u.* my body.
Gal. 3. 10. as many as are of the works of the law are *u.* the curse.

Understand, Gen. 11. 7. not *u.* one another's speech.
Neh. 8. 7, 13. caused people to *u.* law.
Job 6. 24. cause me to *u.* wherein.
Ps. 19. 12. who can *u.* his errors?
107. 43. shall *u.* loving-kindness of Lord.
119. 100. I *u.* more than the ancients.
139. 2. thou *u.* my thought afar off.
Prov. 2. 5. *u.* fear of the Lord.
8. 5. *u.* wisdom.
20. 24. how can man *u.* his way?
28. 5. they that seek Lord, *u.* all things.
Is. 6. 9. hear ye indeed, but *u.* not.
28. 9. whom make to *u.* doctrine?
32. 4. heart of rash *u.* knowledge.
Jer. 9. 12; Hos. 14. 9. who is wise, that may *u.* this?   [shall *u.*
Dan. 12. 10. the wicked shall not *u.*, the wise
Matt. 15. 10; Mk. 7. 14. hear and *u.*
Matt. 24. 15. whoso readeth, let him *u.*
Lk. 24. 45. might *u.* the Scriptures.
Acts 8. 30. *u.* thou what thou readest?
Rom. 3. 11. there is none that *u.*
15. 21. they that have not heard shall *u.*
1 Cor. 13. 2. though I *u.* all mysteries.
Heb. 11. 3. we *u.* worlds were framed.
See Ps. 73. 17; Matt. 13. 51; 1 Cor. 13. 11; 2 Pet. 3. 16.   [and *u.*

Understanding, Ex. 31. 3; Deut. 4. 6. wisdom
1 Ki. 3. 11. hast asked *u.*
4. 29. God gave Solomon wisdom and *u.*
7. 14. filled with wisdom and *u.*
1 Chr. 12. 32. men that had *u.* of the times.
2 Chr. 26. 5. had *u.* in visions.
Job 12. 13. he had counsel and *u.*
17. 4. thou hast hid their heart from *u.*
28. 12. where is the place of *u.*?
28. 28. to depart from evil is *u.*
32. 8. the Almighty giveth them *u.*
38. 36. who hath given *u.* to the heart?
39. 17. neither imparted to her *u.*
Ps. 47. 7. sing ye praises with *u.*
49. 3. meditation of my heart shall be of *u.*
119. 34. give me *u.*
119. 99. I have more *u.* than my teachers.
147. 5. his *u.* is infinite.
Prov. 2. 2. apply thine heart to *u.*
2. 11. *u.* shall keep thee.
3. 5. lean not to thine own *u.*
3. 13. happy is the man that getteth *u.*
3. 19. by *u.* hath he established the heavens.
4. 5, 7. get wisdom, get *u.*
8. 1. doth not *u.* put forth her voice?
9. 6. go in the way of *u.*
9. 10. the knowledge of the holy is *u.*
14. 29. he that is slow to wrath is of great *u.*
16. 22. *u.* is a wellspring of life.
19. 8. he that keepeth *u.* shall find good.
21. 30. there is no *u.* against the Lord.
23. 23. buy instruction and *u.*
24. 3. by *u.* an house is established.
28. 16. prince that wanteth *u.*
30. 2. have not the *u.* of a man.
Eccl. 9. 11. nor riches to men of *u.*
Is. 11. 2. the spirit of *u.* shall rest on him.
11. 3. make him of quick *u.*
27. 11. a people of no *u.*
29. 14. the *u.* of prudent men shall be hid.
40. 28. there is no searching of his *u.*
Jer. 51. 15. he stretched out heaven by *u.*
Dan. 4. 34. mine *u.* returned to me.
Matt. 15. 16; Mk. 7. 18. are ye without *u.*?
Mk. 12. 33. to love him with all the *u.*
Lk. 2. 47. astonished at his *u.*

Understanding—*Continued.*
Lk. 24. 45. then opened he their *u.*
Rom. 1. 31. without *u.*
1 Cor. 1. 19. bring to nothing *u.* of prudent.
14. 15. pray with the *u.* also.
14. 20. in *u.* be men.
Eph. 1. 18. eyes of *u.* being enlightened.
4. 18. having the *u.* darkened.
Phil. 4. 7. peace of God which passeth all *u.*
Col. 1. 9. filled with all spiritual *u.*
2. 2. riches of God which passeth all *u.*
1 John 5. 20. God hath given us an *u.*

Undertake, Is. 38. 14. *u.* for me.

Undone, Is. 6. 5. woe is me, for I am *u.*
Matt. 23. 23; Lk. 11. 42. not leave other *u.*

Unequal, Ezek. 18. 25, 29. are not your ways *u.?*
2 Cor. 6. 14. be not *u.* yoked.

Unfeigned, 2 Cor. 6. 6. by love *u.*
1 Tim. 1. 5; 2 Tim. 1. 5. faith *u.*
1 Pet. 1. 22. *u.* love of brethren.

Unfruitful, Matt. 13. 22; Mk. 4. 19. becometh *u.*
1 Cor. 14. 14. my understanding is *u.*
Eph. 5. 11. no fellowship with *u.* works of darkness.
2 Pet. 1. 8. neither barren nor *u.*

Ungodly, 2 Sam. 22. 5; Ps. 18. 4. *u.* men made me afraid.
2 Chr. 19. 2. shouldest thou help the *u.?*
Job 16. 11. God hath delivered me to the *u.*
34. 18. is it fit to say, ye are *u.?*
Ps. 1. 1. the counsel of the *u.*
1. 6. the way of the *u.* shall perish.
43. 1. plead my cause against an *u.* nation.
73. 12. these are *u.* who prosper.
Prov. 16. 27. an *u.* man diggeth up evil.
19. 28. an *u.* witness scorneth judgment.
Rom. 5. 6. Christ died for the *u.*
1 Pet. 4. 18. where shall the *u.* appear?
2 Pet. 2. 6. those that after should live *u.*
3. 7. perdition of *u.* men.
Jude 4. *u.* men turning grace of God.
See Rom. 1. 18; 2 Tim. 2. 16; Tit. 2. 12.

Unholy, Lev. 10. 10. difference between holy and *u.*
1 Tim. 1. 9. law is made for the *u.*
2 Tim. 3. 2. men shall be *u.*
Heb. 10. 29. counted blood of covenant an *u.* [thing.

Unity, Ps. 133. 1. for brethren to dwell in *u.*
Eph. 4. 3. endeavouring to keep *u.* of Spirit.
4. 13. till we come in *u.* of the faith.
See Gen. 49. 6; Ps. 86. 11.

Unjust, Ps. 43. 1. deliver me from *u.* man.
Prov. 11. 7. hope of *u.* man perisheth.
28. 8. he that by *u.* gain.
29. 27. an *u.* man is an abomination.
Zeph. 3. 5. the *u.* knoweth no shame.
Matt. 5. 45. he sendeth rain on just and *u.*
Lk. 16. 10. he that is *u.* in least is *u.* in much.
18. 6. hear what the *u.* judge saith.
18. 11. not as other men, *u.*
Acts 24. 15. resurrection of just and *u.*
1 Cor. 6. 1. go to law before the *u.*
1 Pet. 3. 18. Christ suffered, the just for the *u.*
2 Pet. 2. 9. reserve *u.* to day of judgment.
Rev. 22. 11. he that is *u.*, let him be *u.* still.

Unknown, Acts 17. 23. to the *u.* God.
1 Cor. 14. 2. speaketh in *u.* tongue.
2 Cor. 6. 9. as *u.*, and yet well known.

Unlawful, Acts 10. 28. an *u.* thing for a Jew.
2 Pet. 2. 8. vexed his soul with their *u.* deeds.

Unlearned, Acts 4. 13. perceived they were *u.*
1 Cor. 14. 16. occupieth room of *u.*
2 Tim. 2. 23. foolish and *u.* questions avoid.
2 Pet. 3. 16. they that are *u.* wrest.

Unmerciful, Rom. 1. 31. without natural affection, *u.*

Unmindful, Deut. 32. 18. of Rock thou art *u.*

Unmoveable, Acts 27. 41. forepart of ship remained *u.*
1 Cor. 15. 58. be stedfast, *u.*

Unprofitable, Job 15. 3. reason with *u.* talk.
Matt. 25. 30. cast *u.* servant into darkness.
Lk. 17. 10. say, we are *u.* servants.
Rom. 3. 12. are together become *u.*
Philem. 11. in time past *u.*
Heb. 13. 17. not with grief, that is *u.*

Unpunished, Prov. 11. 21; 16. 5; 17. 5; 19. 5; Jer. 25. 29. shall not be *u.*
Jer. 30. 11; 46. 28. not leave thee altogether *u.* [send.
49. 12. thou shalt not go *u.*

Unquenchable, Matt. 3. 12; Lk. 3. 17. burn chaff with *u.* fire.

Unreasonable, Acts 25. 27. it seemeth *u.* to
2 Thes. 3. 2. be delivered from *u.* men.

Unrebukeable, 1 Tim. 6. 14. keep this commandment, *u.* [holy.

Unreprovable, Col. 1. 22. to present you

Unrighteous, Ex. 23. 1. an *u.* witness.
Ps. 71. 4. deliver me out of hand of *u.*
Is. 10. 1. decree *u.* decrees.
55. 7. let *u.* man forsake his thoughts.
Lk. 16. 11. not faithful in *u.* mammon.
Rom. 3. 5. is God *u.* who taketh vengeance?
1 Cor. 6. 9. *u.* shall not inherit the kingdom.
Heb. 6. 10. God is not *u.* to forget.

Unrighteousness, Lev. 19. 15. do no *u.* in judgment.
Ps. 92. 15. there is no *u.* in him.
Lk. 16. 9. mammon of *u.*
John 7. 18. true, and no *u.* in him.
Rom. 1. 18. hold the truth in *u.*
2. 8. them that obey *u.*
3. 5. if our *u.* commend righteousness.
6. 13. instruments of *u.*
9. 14. is there *u.* with God?
2 Cor. 6. 14. what fellowship with *u.?*
2 Thes. 2. 12. had pleasure in *u.*
2 Pet. 2. 13. receive the reward of *u.*
1 John 1. 9. to cleanse us from all *u.*
5. 17. all *u.* is sin.

Unruly, 1 Thes. 5. 14. warn them that are *u.*
Tit. 1. 6. not accused of riot, or *u.*
Jas. 3. 8. the tongue is an *u.* evil.

Unsavoury, Job 6. 6. can that which is *u.* be eaten without salt?

Unsearchable, Job 5. 9. God doeth great things and *u.*
Ps. 145. 3. his greatness is *u.*
Rom. 11. 33. how *u.* are his judgments!
Eph. 3. 8. preach *u.* riches of Christ.

Unseemly, Rom 1. 27. working that which is *u.*
1 Cor. 13. 5. doth not behave *u.*

Unskilful, Heb. 5. 13. is *u.* in the word.

Unspeakable, 2 Cor. 9. 15. thanks to God for his *u.* gift.
12. 4. caught up and heard *u.* words.
1 Pet. 1. 8. rejoice with joy *u.*

Unspotted, Jas. 1. 27. *u.* from the world.

Unstable, Gen. 49. 4. *u.* as water.
Jas. 1. 8. a double-minded man is *u.*
2 Pet. 2. 14. beguiling *u.* souls.
3. 16. that are unlearned and *u.* wrest.

Unthankful, Lk. 6. 35. he is kind to the *u.*
2 Tim. 3. 2. blasphemers, *u.*, unholy.

Untoward, Acts 2. 40. save yourselves from *u.* generation.

Unwashen. Matt. 15. 20; Mk. 7. 2, 5. eat with *u.* hands.

Unwise, Deut. 32. 6. do ye thus requite the Lord, *u.* people?

Hos. 13. 13. an *u.* son.

Rom. 1. 14. debtor to wise and *u.*

Eph. 5. 17. be not *u.* but understanding.

Unworthy, Acts 13. 46. ye judge yourselves *u.*

1 Cor. 6. 2. are ye *u.* to judge?

11. 27. drink cup of Lord *u.*   [cities.

Upbraid, Matt. 11. 20. then began he to *u.*

Mk. 16. 14. he *u.* them with unbelief.

Jas. 1. 5. that giveth liberally, and *u.* not.

Uphold, Ps. 51. 12. *u.* me with thy free Spirit.

54. 4. Lord is with them that *u.* my soul.

119. 116. *u.* me according to thy word.

145. 14. the Lord *u.* all that fall.

Prov. 29. 23. honour shall *u.* humble.

Is. 41. 10. I will *u.* thee with right hand.

63. 5. my servant, whom I *u.*

63. 5. wondered there was none to *u.*

Heb. 1. 3. *u.* all things by word of his power.

Upright, 2 Sam. 22. 26; Ps. 18. 25. with *u.* show thyself *u.*

Job 12. 4. the *u.* man is laughed to scorn.

17. 8. *u.* men shall be astonied.

Ps. 25. 8; 92. 15. good and *u.* is the Lord.

37. 37. mark the perfect man, and behold the *u.*

49. 14. the *u.* shall have dominion.

111. 1. the assembly of the *u.*

112. 4. to the *u.* ariseth light.

125. 4. that are *u.* in their hearts.

140. 13. the *u.* shall dwell in thy presence.

Prov. 2. 21. the *u.* shall dwell in the land.

10. 29. way of Lord is strength to the *u.*

11. 3. the integrity of the *u.*

11. 20. *u.* in their way are his delight.

14. 11. tabernacle of *u.* shall flourish.

15. 8. the prayer of the *u.* is his delight.

28. 10. the *u.* shall have good things.

Eccl. 7. 29. God hath made man *u.*

Hab. 2. 4. his soul is not *u.* in him.

Uprightly, Ps. 15. 2. that walketh *u.* shall abide.

58. 1; 75. 2. judge *u.*   [walk *u.*

84. 11. withhold no good from them that

Prov. 2. 7. a buckler to them that walk *u.*

10. 9; 15. 21; 28. 18; Mic. 2. 7. that walketh *u.*

Is. 33. 15; Amos 5. 10. that speaketh *u.*

Uprightness, 1 Ki. 3. 6. walked in *u.* of heart.

1 Chr. 29. 17. thou hast pleasure in *u.*

Job 4. 6. the *u.* of thy ways.

33. 23. to show unto man his *u.*

Ps. 25. 21. let *u.* preserve me.

111. 8. stand fast, and are done in *u.*

143. 10. lead me into the land of *u.*

Prov. 2. 13. who leave paths of *u.*

28. 6. better is poor that walketh in *u.*

Is. 26. 7. the way of the just is *u.*

Uproar, 1 Ki. 1. 41. city being in an *u.*

Matt. 26. 5; Mk. 14. 2. lest there be an *u.*

Acts 19. 40. in question for this day's *u.*

Upward, 2 Ki. 19. 30; Is. 37. 31. bear fruit *u.*

Job 5. 7. to trouble, as sparks fly *u.*

Eccl. 3. 21. spirit of man goeth *u.*

Is. 38. 14. mine eyes fail looking *u.*

Urge, 2 Ki. 2. 17. *u.* him till he was ashamed.

Lk. 11. 53. began to *u.* him.

See Dan. 3. 22.

Use, Matt. 6. 7. *u.* not vain repetitions.   [it.

1 Cor. 7. 31. that *u.* this world, as not abusing

Gal. 5. 13. *u.* not liberty for occasion.

Eph. 4. 29. good to *u.* of edifying.

Use—*Continued.*

1 Tim. 1. 8. if a man *u.* it lawfully.

2 Tim. 2. 21. meet for master's *u.*

Tit. 3. 14. works for necessary *u.*

1 Pet. 2. 16. not *u.* liberty for cloak.

Usurp, 1 Tim. 2. 12. I suffer not a woman to *u.* authority.

Usury, Deut. 23. 20. thou mayest lend upon *u.*

Ps. 15. 5. putteth not his money to *u.*

Prov. 28. 8. by *u.* increaseth substance.

Is. 24. 2. taker of *u.* so with giver of *u.*

Matt. 25. 27; Lk. 19. 23. received mine own with *u.*

Utter, Job 33. 3. my lips shall *u.* knowledge.

Ps. 19. 2. day unto day *u.* speech.

78. 2. I will *u.* dark sayings.

106. 2. who can *u.* the mighty acts of Lord?

145. 7. shall *u.* memory of goodness.

Prov. 1. 20. wisdom *u.* her voice.

14. 5. false witness will *u.* lies.

23. 33. thine heart shall *u.* perverse things.

29. 11. a fool *u.* all his mind.

Eccl. 5. 2. let not thine heart be hasty to *u.* before God.

Joel 2. 11. Lord shall *u.* his voice.

Rom. 8. 26. groanings that cannot be *u.*

2 Cor. 12. 4. not lawful for a man to *u.*

Heb. 5. 11. things hard to be *u.*   [them *u.*

Utterance, Acts 2. 4. speak as the Spirit gave

1 Cor. 1. 5. ye are enriched in all *u.*

Col. 4. 3. God would open a door of *u.*

Utterly, Ex. 17. 14. *u.* put out remembrance.

Ps. 119. 8. forsake me not *u.*

Is. 6. 11. the land be *u.* desolate.

40. 30. young men shall *u.* fall.

Uttermost, Ps. 2. 8. give *u.* parts for possession.

Matt. 5. 26. till thou hast paid the *u.* farthing.

12. 42. came from *u.* parts to hear.

1 Thes. 2. 16. wrath is come to the *u.*

Heb. 7. 25. save them to the *u.* that come.

VAIL, Matt. 27. 51; Mk. 15. 38; Lk. 23. 45. *v.* of temple was rent.

2 Cor. 3. 14. which *v.* is done away in Christ.

Heb. 6. 19. entereth within the *v.*

Vain, Ex. 5. 9. not regard *v.* words.

20. 7; Deut. 5. 11. not take name of Lord in *v.*

Deut. 32. 47. it is not a *v.* thing for you.

1 Sam. 12. 21. turn not after *v.* things.

2 Ki. 18. 20; Is. 36. 5. they are but *v.* words.

Job 11. 12. *v.* man would be wise.

16. 3. shall *v.* words have an end?

Ps. 2. 1; Acts 4. 25. the people imagine a *v.* thing.

Ps. 26. 4. not sat with *v.* persons.

33. 17. horse is a *v.* thing for safety.

39. 6. every man walketh in a *v.* show.

60. 11; 108. 12. *v.* is the help of man.

89. 47. wherefore hast thou made men in *v.?*

127. 2. it is *v.* for you to rise early.

Prov. 12. 11; 28. 19. followeth *v.* persons.

31. 30. beauty is *v.*

Eccl. 6. 12. all the days of his *v.* life.

Is. 1. 13. bring no more *v.* oblations.

45. 19. I said not, seek ye me in *v.*

49. 4. laboured in *v.*, spent strength in *v.*

Jer. 3. 23. in *v.* is salvation hoped for.

4. 14. how long shall *v.* thoughts?

46. 11. in *v.* shalt thou use medicines.

Mal. 3. 14. ye have said, it is *v.* to serve God.

Matt. 6. 7. *v.* repetitions.

15. 9; Mk. 7. 7. in *v.* do they worship me.

Rom. 1. 21. became *v.* in their imaginations.

13. 4. he beareth not the sword in *v.*

Vain—*Continued.*
1 Cor. 15. 58. your labour is not in *v.*
2 Cor. 6. 1. receive not the grace of God in *v.*
Gal. 2. 2. lest I should run in *v.*
Col. 2. 8. philosophy and *v.* deceit.
1 Tim. 6. 20; 2 Tim. 2. 16. *v.* babbling.
Jas. 1. 26. this man's religion is *v.*
1 Pet. 1. 18. redeemed from *v.* conversation.

Valiant, 1 Sam. 18. 17. be *v.* for me.
  26. 15; 1 Ki. 1. 42. a *v.* man.
Is. 10. 13. put down inhabitants like a *v.* man.
  33. 7. their *v.* ones shall cry without.
Jer. 9. 3. they are not *v.* for the truth.
Heb. 11. 34. waxed *v.* in fight.
See 1 Chr. 19. 13; Ps. 60. 12; 118. 15.

Value, Job 13. 4. physicians of no *v.*
Matt. 10. 31; Lk. 12. 7. ye are of more *v.* than.
Matt. 27. 9. whom they of Israel did *v.*

Vanish, Is. 51. 6. heavens shall *v.* away.
Lk. 24. 31. he *v.* out of their sight.
1 Cor. 13. 8. knowledge, it shall *v.*
Heb. 8. 13. waxeth old, ready to *v.*
Jas. 4. 14. life is a vapour that *v.*

Vanity, 2 Ki. 17. 15. they followed *v.*
Job 7. 3. to possess months of *v.*
  35. 13. God will not hear *v.*
Ps. 4. 2. how long will ye love *v.*?
  12. 2. they speak *v.* every one.
  35. 5. man at his best state is *v.*
  62. 9. are *v.*, and lighter than *v.*
  119. 37. turn eyes from beholding *v.*
  144. 4. man is like to *v.*
Prov. 13. 11. wealth gotten by *v.*
  22. 8. that soweth iniquity shall reap *v.*
  30. 8. remove from me *v.*   [is *v.*
Eccl. 1. 2; 3. 19; 11. 8; 12. 8. *v.* of vanities, all
  11. 10. childhood and youth are *v.*
Is. 5. 18. draw iniquity with cords of *v.*
  30. 28. sift with sieve of *v.*
  40. 17. nations are counted *v.*
Hab. 2. 13. people weary themselves for *v.*
Rom. 8. 20. the creature was made subject
  to *v.*
Eph. 4. 17. walk in *v.* of mind.
2 Pet. 2. 18. swelling words of *v.*
See Jer. 10. 8; Jon. 2. 8; Acts 14. 15.

Variableness, Jas. 1. 17. with whom is no *v.*

Variance, Matt. 10. 35. set a man at *v.* against.
Gal. 5. 20. works of flesh are hatred, *v.*

Vaunt, Jud. 7. 2. lest Israel *v.* against me.
1 Cor. 13. 4. charity *v.* not itself.

Vehement, Cant. 8. 6. love that hath a *v.* flame.
Jon. 4. 8. a *v.* wind.
Mk. 14. 31. Peter spake more *v.*
Lk. 6. 48. stream beat *v.* on house.
2 Cor. 7. 11. what *v.* desire !

Vengeance, Deut. 32. 35; Ps. 94. 1; Heb. 10. 30.
  to me belongeth *v.*
Ps. 58. 10. rejoice when he seeth *v.*   [of *v.*
Prov. 6. 34; Is. 34. 8; 61. 2; Jer. 51. 6. the day
Is. 35. 4. your God will come with *v.*
  59. 17. garments of *v.* for clothing.
Lk. 21. 22. these be days of *v.*
Acts 28. 4. whom *v.* suffereth not to live.
Rom. 12. 19. *v.* is mine, saith Lord.
2 Thes. 1. 8. in flaming fire, taking *v.*
Jude 7. the *v.* of eternal fire.

Verity, Ps. 111. 7. works of his hands are *v.*
1 Tim. 2. 7. a teacher in faith and *v.*

Vessel, Ps. 2. 9. in pieces like a potter's *v.*
  31. 12. I am like a broken *v.*
Jer. 22. 28; Hos. 8. 8. a *v.* wherein is no
  pleasure.
Matt. 25. 4. the wise took oil in their *v.*

Vessel—*Continued.*
Acts 9. 15. he is a chosen *v.* unto me.
Rom. 9. 22, 23. *v.* of wrath, *v.* of mercy.
1 Thes. 4. 4. to possess his *v.* in sanctification.
2 Tim. 2. 21. he shall be a *v.* to honour.
1 Pet. 3. 7. honour to wife, as to weaker *v.*

Vestry, 2 Ki. 10. 22. said to him over *v.*

Vesture, Ps. 22. 18; Matt. 27. 35; John 19. 24.
  they cast lots upon my *v.*
Ps. 102. 26. as a *v.* shalt thou change them.
Heb. 1. 12. as a *v.* shalt thou fold them.
Rev. 19. 13. clothed with *v.* dipped in blood.

Vex, Ex. 22. 21; Lev. 19. 33. thou shalt not *v.* a
  stranger.
2 Sam. 12. 18. how will he *v.* himself ?
Job 19. 2. how long will ye *v.* my soul ?
Ps. 2. 5. shall *v.* them in his displeasure.
Is. 11. 13. Judah shall not *v.* Ephraim.
  63. 10. they rebelled and *v.* Spirit.
2 Pet. 2. 8. *v.* his righteous soul.
See Eccl. 1. 14; 2. 22; Is. 28. 19; 65. 14.

Victory, 1 Chr. 29. 11. thine, O Lord, is the *v.*
Ps. 98. 1. arm hath gotten him *v.*
Is. 25. 8; 1 Cor. 15. 54. he will swallow up
  death in *v.*
Matt. 12. 20. send forth judgment unto *v.*
1 John 5. 4. this is the *v.*, even our faith.

Vigilant, 1 Tim. 3. 2. a bishop must be *v.*
1 Pet. 5. 8. be *v.* because your adversary.

Vile, Deut. 25. 3. thy brother seem *v.*
1 Sam. 3. 13. sons made themselves *v.*
Job. 18. 3. wherefore are we reputed *v.* ?
  40. 4. I am *v.* what shall I answer thee ?
Ps. 15. 4; Is. 32. 5; Dan. 11. 21. a *v.* person.
Jer. 15. 19. take the precious from the *v.*
Rom. 1. 26. God gave them up to *v.* affections.
Phil. 3. 21. who shall change our *v.* body.
Jas. 2. 2. a poor man in *v.* raiment.

Vine, Deut. 32. 32. their *v.* is of the *v.* of Sodom.
Jud. 9. 12. trees said to the *v.*, reign.
  13. 14. not eat anything that cometh of the *v.*
1 Ki. 4. 25. dwelt every man under his *v.*
2 Ki. 18. 31; Is. 36. 16. eat every man of his
  own *v.*
Ps. 80. 8. a *v.* out of Egypt.
  128. 3. thy wife as a fruitful *v.*
Is. 24. 7. the *v.* languisheth.
Jer. 2. 21. I planted thee a noble *v.*
Hos. 10. 1. Israel is an empty *v.*
  14. 7. they shall grow as the *v.*
Mic. 4. 4. sit every man under his *v.*
Matt. 26. 29; Mk. 14. 25; Lk. 22. 18. fruit of
  the *v.*
John 15. 1. I am the true *v.*

Violence, Gen. 6. 11. earth was filled with *v.*
Ps. 11. 5. him that loveth *v.*
  72. 14. redeem their soul from *v.*
  73. 6. *v.* covereth them as a garment.
Prov. 4. 17. they drink the wine of *v.*
Is. 53. 9. because he had done no *v.*
  60. 18. *v.* shall no more be heard.   [w th *v.*
Ezek. 8. 17; 28. 16. they have filled the land
Hab. 1. 2. cry to thee of *v.*
Mal. 2. 16. covereth *v.* with garment.
Matt. 11. 12. kingdom of heaven suffereth *v.*
Lk. 3. 14. do *v.* to no man.
Heb. 11. 34. quenched *v.* of fire.

Virgin, Is. 7. 14; Matt. 1. 23. a *v.* shall conceive.
Matt. 25. 1. kingdom of heaven is like to ten *v.*
2 Cor. 11. 2. present you as chaste *v.* to Christ.

Virtue, Mk. 5. 30; Lk. 6. 19; 8. 46. *v.* had gone
  out of him.
Phil 4. 8. if there be any *v.*
2 Pet. 1. 5. add to faith *v.* to *v.*, knowledge.

Vis   Concordance   Wai

Visage, Is. 52. 14. his *v.* was marred more.
Dan. 3. 19. form of *v.* was changed.
Vision, 1 Sam. 3. 1. there was no open *v.*
Job 20. 8. as a *v.* of the night.
Ps. 89. 19. spakest in *v.* to Holy One.
Prov. 29. 18. where there is no *v.*, the people perish.
Is. 28. 7. they err in *v.*
Hos. 12. 10. I have multiplied *v.*
Joel 2. 28; Acts 2. 17. young men shall see *v.*
Hab. 2. 3. the *v.* is for an appointed time.
Matt. 17. 9. tell the *v.* to no man.
Lk. 1. 22. perceived he had seen a *v.*
24. 33. they had seen a *v.* of angels.
Acts 26. 19. not disobedient to heavenly *v.*
Visit, Gen. 50. 24; Ex. 13. 19. God will *v.* you.
Ex. 20. 5; 34. 7; Num. 14. 18; Deut. 5. 9. *v.* iniquity of the fathers.   [them.
Ex. 32. 34. when I *v.*, I will *v.* their sin upon
Job 7. 18. that thou shouldest *v.* him.
Ps. 8. 4; Heb. 2. 6. the son of man that thou *v.* him.
Ps. 80. 14. look down and *v.* this vine.
106. 4. *v.* me with thy salvation.
Jer. 5. 9; 9. 9. shall I not *v.* for these things?
Matt. 25. 36. I was sick, and ye *v.* me.
Lk. 1. 68. God hath *v.* and redeemed his people.
Acts 7. 23. to *v.* his brethren.
15. 14. God did *v.* Gentiles.
Jas. 1. 27. to *v.* fatherless and widows.
Visitation, Num. 16. 29. visited after *v.* of all men.
Job 10. 12. thy *v.* preserved my spirit.
Is. 10. 3. what will ye do in the day of *v.*?
Jer. 8. 12; 10. 15; 46. 21; Lk. 19. 44. time of *v.*
1 Pet. 2. 12. glorify God in day of *v.*
Vocation, Eph. 4. 1. walk worthy of the *v.*
Voice, Gen. 4. 10. the *v.* of thy brother's blood.
27. 22. the *v.* is Jacob's *v.*
Ex. 23. 21. beware of him, obey his *v.*
24. 3. all the people answered with one *v.*
Deut. 4. 33. did ever people hear *v.* of God and live?
1 Ki. 19. 12. after the fire, a still small *v.*
2 Ki. 4. 31. there was neither *v.* nor hearing.
Job. 30. 31. the *v.* of them that weep.
37. 4. a *v.* roareth.
40. 9. canst thou thunder with a *v.* like him?
Ps. 18. 13. the Highest gave his *v.*
31. 22; 86. 6. the *v.* of my supplications.
42. 4. with the *v.* of joy.
93. 3. the floods have lifted up their *v.*
95. 7; Heb. 3. 7, 15. to-day if ye will hear his *v.*
Ps. 103. 20. hearkening to *v.* of his word.
Prov. 8. 4. my *v.* is to sons of man.
Eccl. 12. 4. rise up at the *v.* of the bird.
Cant. 2. 12. the *v.* of the turtle is heard.
Is. 30. 19. gracious at *v.* of thy cry.
40. 3; Matt. 3. 3; Mk. 1. 3; Lk. 3. 4. the *v.* of him that crieth.
Is. 48. 20. a *v.* of singing.
52. 8. with the *v.* together shall they sing.
65. 19. the *v.* of weeping shall be no more heard.
Jer. 30. 19. the *v.* of them that make merry.
Ezek. 23. 42. a *v.* of a multitude at ease.
33. 32. one that hath a pleasant *v.*
43. 2; Rev. 1. 15. *v.* like a noise of many waters.
Jon. 2. 9. with *v.* of thanksgiving.
Matt. 3. 17; Mk. 1. 11; Lk. 3. 22. a *v.* from heaven.

Voice—*Continued.*
Matt. 12.19. neither shall any man hear his *v.*
John 1. 23. the *v.* of one crying in the wilderness.   [God.
5. 25. the dead shall hear the *v.* of Son of
10. 4. the sheep know his *v.*
12. 30. this *v.* came not because of me.
18. 37. every one that is of the truth heareth my *v.*
Acts 9. 7. hearing a *v.*, but seeing no man.
24. 21. except it be for this one *v.*
26. 10. I gave my *v.* against them.
1 Cor. 14. 19. by my *v.* I might teach others.
Gal. 4. 20. I desire to change my *v.*
1 Thes. 4. 16. descend with *v.* of archangel.
Rev. 3. 20. if any man hear my *v.*
Void, Gen. 1. 2; Jer. 4. 23. earth without form and *v.*
Deut. 32. 28. a nation *v.* of counsel.
Ps. 89. 39. made *v.* the covenant.
119. 126. they have made *v.* thy law.
Prov. 11. 12. he that is *v.* of wisdom.
Is. 55. 11. word not return to me *v.*
Acts 24. 16. a conscience *v.* of offence.
Rom. 3. 31. do we make *v.* the law?
4. 14. faith is made *v.*   [written.
Volume, Ps. 40. 7; Heb. 10. 7. in *v.* of book it is
Vomit, Job 20. 15. swallowed riches, and shall *v.* them.   [his *v.*
Prov. 26. 11; 2 Pet. 2. 22. dog returneth to
Vow, Gen. 28. 20; 31. 13. Jacob vowed a *v.*
Jud. 11. 30. Jephthah vowed a *v.*
Job 22. 27. thou shalt pay thy *v.*
Ps. 22. 25; 66. 13; 116. 14. I will pay my *v.* to the Lord.
50. 14. pay thy *v.* unto the Most High.
61. 8. that I may daily perform my *v.*
65. 1. to thee shall the *v.* be performed.
Prov. 31. 2. the son of my *v.*
Eccl. 5. 4. when thou vowest a *v.*
Is. 19. 21. they shall vow a *v.* unto the Lord.
Jon. 1. 16. feared the Lord, and made a *v.*
Acts 21. 23. which have a *v.* on them.

Vow, Deut. 23. 22. if thou forbear to *v.*
Ps. 76. 11. *v.* and pay to the Lord.
132. 2. *v.* to the mighty God.
Jon. 2. 9. I will pay that I have *v.*

WAGES, Gen. 29. 15. what shall thy *w.* be?
Ex. 2. 9. nurse this child, and I will give *w.*
Jer. 22. 13. useth service without *w.*
Hag. 1. 6. earneth *w.* to put into bag with holes.
Mal. 3. 5. oppress hireling in *w.*
Lk. 3. 14. be content with your *w.*
John 4. 36. he that reapeth receiveth *w.*
Rom. 6. 23. the *w.* of sin is death.
2 Pet. 2. 15. the *w.* of unrighteousness.
Wail, Mic. 1. 8. I will *w.* and howl.
Matt. 13. 42. *w.*, and gnashing of teeth.
Mk. 5. 38. them that *w.* greatly.
Rev. 1. 7. kindreds of earth shall *w.*
18. 15. merchants shall stand afar off *w.*
Wait, 2 Ki. 6. 33. should I *w.* for the Lord any longer?
Job 14. 14. I will *w.* till my change come.
17. 13. if I *w.*, the grave is my house.
29. 23. they *w.* for me as for rain.
Ps. 25. 3; 69. 6. let none that *w.* be ashamed.
27. 14; 37. 34; Prov. 20. 22. *w.* on the Lord.
Ps. 33. 20. our soul *w.* for the Lord.
40. 1. I *w.* patiently for the Lord.
62. 1; 130. 6. my soul *w.* upon God.

157

Wait—*Continued.*
Ps. 65. 1. praise *w.* for thee, O God, in Zion.
104. 27 ; 145. 15. these *w.* upon thee.
123. 2. our eyes *w.* on the Lord.
Prov. 27. 18. he that *w.* on his master.
Is. 25. 9. our God, we *w.* for him.
30. 18. the Lord *w.* to be gracious.
40. 31. they that *w.* on the Lord shall renew.
42. 4. the isles shall *w.* for his law.
59. 9. we *w.* for light.   [quietly *w.*
Lam. 3. 26. good that a man hope and
Hos. 12. 6. *w.* on thy God continually.
Mic. 7. 7. I will *w.* for God of my salvation.
Hab. 2. 3. though the vision tarry, *w.* for it.
Mk. 15. 43. who *w.* for the kingdom of God.
Lk. 2. 25. *w.* for the consolation of Israel.
12. 36. like men that *w.* for their lord.
Acts 1. 4. *w.* for the promise of the Father.
Rom. 8. 25. then do we with patience *w.* for it.
12. 7. let us *w.* on our ministering.
Gal. 5. 5. we *w.* for the hope of righteousness.
1 Thes. 1. 10. to *w.* for his Son from heaven.
Wake, Ps. 139. 18. when I *w.* I am still with
     thee.
Cant. 5. 2. I sleep, but my heart *w.*
Jer. 51. 39. sleep a perpetual sleep, and not *w.*
Joel 3. 9. *w.* up the mighty men.
Zech. 4. 1. angel came, and *w.* me.
1 Thes. 5. 10. whether we *w.* or sleep.
Walk, Gen. 17. 1. *w.* before me, and be perfect.
24. 40. the Lord before whom I *w.*
Ex. 16. 4. whether they will *w.* in my law.
Lev. 26. 12. I will *w.* among you.   [heart.
Deut. 29. 19. though I *w.* in imagination of
Job 22. 14. he *w.* in the circuit of heaven.
Ps. 23. 4. though I *w.* through valley of shadow
     of death.
26. 11. I will *w.* in mine integrity.
48. 12. *w.* about Zion.
55. 14. we *w.* to house of God in company.
56. 13. that I may *w.* before God in light of
     living.
84. 11. from them that *w.* uprightly.
89. 15. shall *w.* in light of thy countenance.
91. 6. the pestilence that *w.* in darkness.
115. 7. feet have they, but *w.* not.
116. 9. I will *w.* before the Lord.
119. 45. I will *w.* at liberty.
138. 7. though I *w.* in midst of trouble.
143. 8. cause me to know way I should go.
Prov. 2. 20. mayest *w.* in way of good men.
10. 9 ; 28. 18. he that *w.* uprightly, *w.* surely.
13. 20. he that *w.* with wise men shall be wise.
19. 1 ; 28. 6. the poor that *w.* in integrity.
Is. 2. 5. let us *w.* in the light of the Lord.
9. 2. the people that *w.* in darkness.
30. 21. this is the way, *w.* in it.
35. 9. the redeemed shall *w.* there.
40. 31. shall *w.* and not faint.
Jer. 6. 16. the good way, and *w.* therein.
10. 23. it is not in man that *w.* to direct his
     steps.
Dan. 4. 37. those that *w.* in pride.
Hos. 14. 9. the just shall *w.* in them.
Amos 3. 3. can two *w.* together, except agreed?
Mic. 6. 8. *w.* humbly with thy God.
Zech. 10. 12. they shall *w.* up and down.
Matt. 11. 5 ; Lk. 7. 22. the lame *w.*
Mk. 16. 12. Jesus appeared to two of them,
     as they *w.*
Lk. 13. 33. I must *w.* to-day and to-morrow.
John 8. 12. shall not *w.* in darkness.
11. 9. if any man *w.* in the day.
Rom. 6. 4. *w.* in newness of life.

Walk—*Continued.*
Rom. 8. 1. who *w.* not after the flesh, but after
     the Spirit.
2 Cor. 5. 7. we *w.* by faith.   [rule.
Gal. 6. 16. as many as *w.* according to this
Eph. 2. 10. ordained that we should *w.* in
     them.
4. 1. *w.* worthy of the vocation.
5. 15. see that ye *w.* circumspectly.
Phil. 3. 18. many *w.* of whom I told you.
Col. 1. 10 ; 1 Thes. 2. 12. that ye might *w.*
     worthy of the Lord.
1 Thes. 4. 1. how ye ought to *w.*
2 Thes. 3. 6. brother that *w.* disorderly.
1 Pet. 5. 8. *w.* about, seeking whom he may
     devour.
1 John 1. 7. if we *w.* in the light.
2. 6. ought so to *w.*, as he *w.*
Walking, Deut. 2. 7. the Lord knoweth thy *w.*
Job 1. 7 ; 2. 2. from *w.* up and down.
31. 26. the moon in brightness.
Dan. 3. 25. four men *w.* in the fire.
Mic. 2. 11. if a man *w.* in the spirit.
Matt. 14. 25. Jesus went *w.* on the sea.
Mk. 8. 24. I see men as trees *w.*   [Lord.
Lk. 1. 6. *w.* in all commandments of the
Acts 9. 31. *w.* in the fear of the Lord.
2 Cor. 4. 2. not *w.* in craftiness.   [the *w.*
Wall, Gen. 49. 22. whose branches run over
Ex. 14. 22. the waters were a *w.* to them.
Num. 22. 24. a *w.* being on this side, a *w.* on
     that.
1 Sam. 25. 16. a *w.* by night and day.   [a *w.*
2 Sam. 22. 30 ; Ps. 18. 29. I have leaped over
1 Ki. 4. 33. hyssop that springeth out of *w.*
2 Ki. 20. 2 ; Is. 38. 2. turned his face to the *w.*
Neh. 4. 6. so built we the *w.*
Ps. 62. 3. as a bowing *w.* shall ye be.
122. 7. peace be within thy *w.*
Prov. 18. 11. as high *w.* in his own conceit.
24. 31. stone *w.* was broken down.
25. 28. like a city without *w.*
Is. 25. 4. as a storm against the *w.*
26. 1. salvation will God appoint for *w.*
59. 10. we grope for the *w.*
60. 18. thou shalt call thy *w.* salvation.
Jer. 15. 20. will make thee a fenced *w.*
Ezek. 8. 7. a hole in the *w.*
Dan. 5. 5. fingers wrote on the *w.*
Joel 2. 7. they shall climb the *w.*   [bit him.
Amos 5. 19. leaned hand on *w.*, and serpent
Hab. 2. 11. the stone shall cry out of the *w.*
Acts 23. 3. thou whited *w.*
Eph. 2. 14. the middle *w.* of partition.
Rev. 21. 14. the *w.* of city had twelve foun-
     dations.
Wallow, Jer. 6. 26 ; Ezek. 27. 30. *w.* in ashes.
Mk. 9. 20. he fell on ground, and *w.* foaming.
2 Pet. 2. 22. sow that was washed, to *w.* in
     the mire.
Wander, Gen. 20. 13. God caused me to *w.*
Num. 14. 33 ; Ps. 107. 40. *w.* in wilderness.
Deut. 27. 18. cursed be he that maketh blind
     to *w.*
Job 12. 24. he causeth them to *w.*
15. 23. he *w.* abroad for bread.
38. 41. ravens *w.* for lack of meat.
Ps. 55. 7. then would I *w.* far off.
59. 15. let them *w.* up and down.
Prov. 27. 8. as a bird that *w.* from nest.
Is. 47. 15. shall *w.* every one to his quarter.
Jer. 14. 10. they loved to *w.*
Amos 8. 12. they shall *w.* from sea to sea.
Heb. 11. 37. they *w.* about in sheep-skins.

Want, Deut. 28. 48. serve thy enemies in w.
Jud. 18. 10. a place where there is no w.
19. 20. let all thy w. lie on me.
Job 31. 19. if I have seen any perish for w.
Ps. 34. 9. there is no w. to them that fear him.
Prov. 6. 11 ; 24. 34. w. as an armed man.
Amos 4. 6. I have given w. of bread.
Mk. 12. 44. she of her w. cast in all.
Lk. 15. 14. he began to be in w.
Phil. 4. 11. not that I speak of w.

Want, Ps. 23. 1. I shall not w.   [thing.
34. 10. that seek Lord, shall not w. any good
Prov. 9. 4. him that w. understanding.
13. 25. the wicked shall w.
Is. 34. 16. none shall w. her mate.
Ezek. 4. 17. that they may w. bread and water.
John 2. 3. when they w. wine.   [no man.
2 Cor. 11. 9. when I w., I was chargeable to
Jas. 1. 4. perfect and entire, w. nothing.
Wanton, 1 Tim. 5. 11. to wax w. against Christ.
Jas. 5. 5. ye have lived and been w.
See Rom. 13. 13 ; 2 Pet. 2. 18.
War, Ex. 32. 17. a noise of w. in the camp.
Num. 21. 14. in book of w. of the Lord.
Josh. 11. 23 ; 14. 15. land rested from w.
2 Ki. 18. 20. strength for w.
1 Chr. 5. 22. the w. was of God.
Job 10. 17. changes and w. are against me.
38. 23. reserved against the day of w.
Ps. 27. 3. though w. should rise against me.
46. 9. he maketh w. to cease.
68. 30. scatter the people that delight in w.
120. 7. I am for peace, they are for w.
Prov. 20. 18. with good advice make w.
Eccl. 3. 8. a time of w.
8. 8. there is no discharge in that w.
Is. 2. 4 ; Mic. 4. 3. nor learn w. any more.
Mic. 2. 8. as men averse from w.
Matt. 24. 6 ; Mk. 13. 7 ; Lk. 21. 9. w. and rumours of w.
Lk. 14. 31. what king going to make w.?
Jas. 4. 1. from whence come w.?
Rev. 12. 7. there was w. in heaven.
13. 7. to make w. with saints.

War, 2 Sam. 22. 35 ; Ps. 18. 34 ; 144. 1. Lord teacheth my hands to w.   [nothing.
Is. 41. 12. they that w. against thee be as
2 Cor. 10. 3. we do not w. after the flesh.
1 Tim. 1. 18. mightest w. a good warfare.
2 Tim. 2. 4. no man that w. entangleth himself.
Jas. 4. 2. ye fight and w., yet ye have not.
1 Pet. 2. 11. lusts which w. against the soul.
Wardrobe, 2 Ki. 22. 14 ; 2 Chr. 34. 22. keeper of the w.
Warfare, Is. 40. 2. her w. is accomplished.
1 Cor. 9. 7. who goeth a w. at his own charges?
2 Cor. 10. 4. weapons of our w. are not carnal.
Warm, Eccl. 4. 11. how can one be w. alone?
Is. 47. 14. there shall not be a coal to w. at.
Hag. 1. 6. ye clothe you, but there is none w.
Mk. 14. 54 ; John 18. 18. Peter w. himself.
Jas. 2. 16. be ye w. and filled.
Warn, Ps. 19. 11. by them is thy servant w.
Ezek. 3. 18 ; 33. 8. to w. the wicked.
Matt. 3. 7 ; Lk. 3. 7. who hath w. you?
Acts 20. 31. I ceased not to w. every one.
Col. 1. 28. w. every man.
1 Thes. 5. 14. w. them that are unruly.
Heb. 11. 7. Noah being w. of God.

Wash, 2 Ki. 5. 10. go, w. in Jordan.
Job 9. 30. if I w. myself with snow water.
14. 19. thou w. away things which grow.
29. 6. when I w. my steps with butter.
Ps. 26. 6. I will w. my hands in innocency.
51. 2. w. me throughly from mine iniquity.
51. 7. w. me, and I shall be whiter than snow.
Is. 1. 16. w. you, make you clean.
Jer. 2. 22. though thou w. thee with nitre.
4. 14. w. thy heart from wickedness.
Ezek. 16. 4. nor wast w. in water.
Matt. 6. 17. when thou fastest, w. thy face.
Mk. 7. 4. except they w., they eat not.
Lk. 7. 38. began to w. his feet with tears.
John 9. 7. go, w. in the pool of Siloam.
13. 5. Jesus began to w. disciples' feet.
Acts 22. 16. w. away thy sins.
1 Cor. 6. 11. but ye are w.   [water.
Heb. 10. 22. having our bodies w. with pure
Rev. 1. 5. that w. us from our sins.
7. 14. have w. their robes.
Waste, Deut. 32. 10 ; Job 30. 3. w. wilderness
1 Ki. 17. 14. barrel of meal shall not w.
Ps. 80. 13. boar out of the wood doth w. it.
91. 6. the destruction that w. at noonday.
Is. 24. 1. the Lord maketh the earth w.
Lk. 15. 13. w. his substance.
16. 1. accused that he had w. his goods.
Gal. 1. 13. persecuted the church, and w. it.
See Prov. 18. 9 ; Is. 54. 16 ; 59. 7 ; 61. 4.
Watch, Ps. 90. 4. as a w. in the night.
141. 3. set a w. before my mouth.
Jer. 51. 12. make the w. strong.
Hab. 2. 1. I will stand upon my w.   [a w.
Matt. 27. 26. sealing the stone, and setting

Watch, Gen. 31. 49. the Lord w. between me and thee.
Job 14. 16. dost thou not w. over my sin?
Ps. 102. 7. I w., and am as a sparrow.
130. 6. more than they that w. for morning.
Is. 21. 5. w. in the watch-tower.
29. 20. all that w. for iniquity are cut off.
Jer. 44. 27. I will w. over them for evil.
Matt. 24. 42 ; 25. 13 ; Mk. 13. 35 ; Lk. 21. 36 ; Acts 20. 31. w. therefore.
Matt. 26. 41 ; Mk. 13. 33 ; 14. 38. w. and pray.
1 Cor. 16. 13. w. ye, stand in faith.
1 Thes. 5. 6 ; 1 Pet. 4. 7. let us w., and be sober.
Heb. 13. 17. they w. for your souls.
Rev. 16. 15. blessed is he that w.   [3. 2.
See Lk. 12. 37 ; 2 Cor. 11. 27 ; Eph. 6. 18 ; Rev.
Water, Gen. 49. 4. unstable as w.
Deut. 11. 11. the land drinketh w. of rain of heaven.   [as w.
Josh. 7. 5. their hearts melted, and became
1 Sam. 26. 11. take the cruse of w.
2 Sam. 14. 14. as w. spilt on the ground.
1 Ki. 22. 27 ; 2 Chr. 18. 26. bread and w. of affliction.
Job 8. 11. can the flag grow without w.?
15. 16. who drinketh iniquity like w.
22. 7. thou hast not given w. to the weary.
38. 30. the w. are hid as with a stone.
Ps. 22. 14. I am poured out like w.
23. 2. beside the still w.
46. 3. though the w. roar and be troubled.
63. 1. a dry and thirsty land, where no w. is.
65. 9. river of God that is full of w.
77. 13. the w. saw thee.
79. 3. blood have they shed like w.
124. 4. then the w. had overwhelmed us.
Prov. 5. 15. drink w. out of thine own cistern.

159

Water—*Continued.*
Prov. 20. 5. counsel is like deep *w.*
25. 25. as cold *w.* to a thirsty soul.
27. 19. as in *w.* face answereth to face.
30. 4. who hath bound the *w.* in a garment?
Eccl. 11. 1. cast thy bread upon the *w.*
Cant. 4. 15; John 4. 14. a well of *w.*
Is. 1. 22. thy wine is mixed with *w.*
3. 1. Lord doth take away the stay of *w.*
11. 9 ; Hab. 2. 14. as the *w.* cover the sea.
32. 20. blessed are ye that sow beside all *w.*
33. 16. his *w.* shall be sure.
35. 6. in wilderness shall *w.* break out.
41. 17. when the poor seek *w.*
43. 2. when thou passest through the *w.*
44. 3. pour *w.* on him that is thirsty.
55. 1. come ye to the *w.*
Jer. 2. 13 ; 17. 13. fountain of living *w.*
9. 1. O that my head were *w.* !
Ezek. 7. 17 ; 21. 7. knees be weak as *w.*
36. 25. then will I sprinkle clean *w.* upon
you.   [thirst for *w.*
Amos 8. 11. not a famine of bread, nor a
Matt. 3. 11 ; Mk. 1. 8 ; Lk. 3. 16 ; John 1. 26.
I baptise you with *w.*   [cold *w.*
Matt. 10. 42. whoso giveth a cup of
Matt. 27. 24. Pilate took *w.*, and washed.
Lk. 8. 23. ship was filled with *w.*
16. 24. dip the tip of his finger in *w.*
John 3. 5. except a man be born of *w.*
4. 15. give me this *w.*
5. 3. waiting for moving of the *w.*
19. 34. came thereout blood and *w.*
Acts 10. 47. can any man forbid *w.* ?
Eph. 5. 26. cleanse it with washing of *w.*
1 Pet. 3. 20. eight souls were saved by *w.*
2 Pet. 2. 17. wells without *w.*
1 John 5. 6. this is he that came by *w.*
Jude 12. clouds they are without *w.*
Rev. 22. 17. let him take the *w.* of life freely.

Water, Gen. 2. 10. river to *w.* the garden.
13. 10. the plain was well *w.*
Deut. 11. 10. *w.* it with thy foot, as a garden.
Ps. 6. 6. *w.* my couch with tears.
72. 6. as showers that *w.* the earth.
104. 13. he *w.* the hills from his chambers.
Prov. 11. 25. he that *w.*, shall be *w.*
Is. 27. 3. I will *w.* it every moment.
55. 10. returneth not, but *w.* the earth.
58. 11 ; Jer. 31. 12. thou shalt be like a *w.*
garden.
1 Cor. 3. 6. I have planted, Apollos *w.*
Wavering, Heb. 10. 23. hold faith without *w.*
Jas. 1. 6. ask in faith, nothing *w.*
Waves, Ps. 42. 7. all thy *w.* are gone over me.
65. 7 ; 89. 9 ; 107. 29. stilleth the *w.*
93. 4. Lord is mightier than mighty *w.*
Is. 48. 18. thy righteousness as *w.* of the sea.
Matt. 8. 24. ship was covered with *w.*
14. 24 ; Mk. 4. 37. tossed with *w.*
Jude 13. raging *w.* of the sea.
Wax, Ps. 22. 14. my heart is like *w.*
68. 2. as *w.* melteth, wicked perish.
97. 5. hills melted like *w.* at presence of
Lord.
Mic. 1. 4. cleft as *w.* before the fire.

Wax, Ex. 22. 24 ; 32. 10. my wrath shall *w.* hot.
Num. 11. 23. is the Lord's hand *w.* short?
Deut. 8. 4 ; 29. 5 ; Neh. 9. 21. raiment *w.* not
old.
Deut. 32. 15. *w.* fat, and kicked.
1 Sam. 3. 2. eyes began to *w.* dim.

Wax—*Continued.*
Ps. 102. 26 ; Is. 50. 9 ; 51. 6 ; Heb. 1. 11. shall
w. old as a garment.   [gross.
Matt. 13. 15 ; Acts 28. 27. people's heart *w.*
Matt. 24. 12. love of many shall *w.* cold.
Lk. 12. 33. bags which *w.* not old.
Way, Gen. 24. 42. if thou prosper my *w.*
Ex. 13. 21. pillar of cloud to lead the *w.*
Josh. 23. 14 ; 1 Ki. 2. 2. the *w.* of all the earth.
1 Sam. 12. 23. I will teach you the good and
right *w.*   [perfect.
2 Sam. 22. 31 ; Ps. 18. 30. as for God, his *w.* is
2 Chr. 6. 27. when thou hast taught them the
good *w.*
Ezra 8. 21. seek of him a right *w.*
Job 3. 23. to a man whose *w.* is hid.
12. 24 ; Ps. 107. 40. to wander where there is
no *w.*   [return.
Job 16. 22. I go the *w.* whence I shall not
22. 15. hast thou marked the old *w.* ?
23. 10. he knoweth the *w.* that I take.
38. 19. where is the *w.* where light dwelleth?
Ps. 1. 6. the Lord knoweth the *w.* of the
righteous.
2. 12. lest ye perish from the *w.*
25. 9. the meek will he teach his *w.*
37. 5. commit thy *w.* unto the Lord.
39. 1. I will take heed to my *w.*
49. 13. this their *w.* is their folly.
67. 2. that thy *w.* may be known.
78. 50. he made a *w.* to his anger.
101. 2. behave wisely in a perfect *w.*
119. 32. I will run the *w.* of thy commandments.
139. 24. lead me in the *w.* everlasting.
Prov. 2. 8. Lord preserveth the *w.* of his
saints.
3. 6. in all thy *w.* acknowledge him.
3. 17. her *w.* are *w.* of pleasantness.
6. 6. consider her *w.*, and be wise.
6. 23 ; 15. 24 ; Jer. 21. 8. the *w.* of life.
Prov. 10. 29. the *w.* of the Lord is strength.
22. 6. train up a child in the *w.* he should go.
Eccl. 11. 5. the *w.* of the spirit.
Is. 30. 21. this is the *w.*, walk ye in it.
35. 8. a *w.*, called the *w.* of holiness.
40. 3 ; Lk. 3. 4. prepare the *w.* of the Lord.
Is. 40. 27. my *w.* is hid from the Lord.
55. 8. neither are your *w.* my *w.*   [not
59. 8 ; Rom. 3. 17. the *w.* of peace they know
Jer. 6. 16. where is the good *w.* ?
10. 23. the *w.* of man is not in himself.
32. 39. I will give them one heart and one *w.*
50. 5. they shall ask the *w.* to Zion.
Ezek. 18. 29. are not my *w.* equal?
Amos 2. 7. turn aside *w.* of the meek.
Nah. 1. 3. the Lord hath his *w.* in the whirlwind.
Hag. 1. 5. consider your *w.*
Mal. 3. 1. he shall prepare the *w.* before me.
Matt. 7. 13. broad is the *w.* that leadeth to
destruction.   [of God in truth.
22. 16 ; Mk. 12. 14 ; Lk. 20. 21. teaching the *w.*
Lk. 15. 20. when he was a great *w.* off.
John 10. 1. but climbeth up some other *w.*
14. 4. the *w.* ye know.
14. 6. I am the *w.*, the truth, and the life.
Acts 16. 17. show unto us the *w.* of salvation.
18. 26. expounded the *w.* of God more
perfectly.
24. 14. after the *w.* which they call heresy.
Rom. 3. 12. they are all gone out of the *w.*
11. 33. his *w.* are past finding out.
1 Cor. 10. 13. make a *w.* to escape.

Way—*Continued.*

1 Cor. 12. 31. a more excellent *w.*
Col. 2. 14. took handwriting out of the *w.*
Heb. 5. 2. compassion on them out of the *w.*
     9. 8. the *w.* into the holiest.
     10. 20. by a new and living *w.*
2 Pet. 2. 2. the *w.* of truth be evil spoken of.
     2. 15. have forsaken the right *w.*
Jude 11. they have gone in the *w.* of Cain.
Rev. 15. 3. just and true are thy *w.*

Weak, 2 Chr. 15. 7. let not your hands be *w.*
Job 4. 3. thou hast strengthened the *w.* hands.
Ps. 6. 2. I am *w.*
Is. 35. 3. strengthen ye the *w.* hands.
Ezek. 7. 17 ; 21. 7. knees *w.* as water.
Joel 3. 10. let the *w.* say, I am strong.
Matt. 26. 41 ; Mk. 14. 38. the flesh is *w.*
Acts 20. 35. ye ought to support the *w.*
Rom. 4. 19. being not *w.* in faith.
     8. 3. the law was *w.* through the flesh.
     14. 1. that is *w.* in the faith.
1 Cor. 1. 27. *w.* things to confound the mighty.
     11. 30. for this cause many are *w.*
2 Cor. 10. 10. his bodily presence is *w.*
     12. 10. when I am *w.* then am I strong.
Gal. 4. 9. how turn ye to the *w.* elements?
1 Thes. 5. 14. support the *w.*   [3. 7.
See 2 Sam. 3. 1 ; Job 12. 21 ; Ps. 102. 23 ; 1 Pet.

Weakness, 1 Cor. 1. 25. the *w.* of God is stronger than men.
     15. 43. it is sown in *w.*, raised in power.
2 Cor. 12. 9. strength is made perfect in *w.*
     13. 4. though he was crucified through *w.*
Heb. 11. 34. out of *w.* were made strong.

Wealth, Deut. 8. 18. Lord giveth power to get *w.*
2 Chr. 1. 11. thou hast not asked *w.*
Job 21. 13. they spend their days in *w.*
     31. 25. if I rejoiced because my *w.* was great.
Ps. 49. 6. they that trust in *w.*
     49. 10. leave *w.* to others.
     112. 3. *w.* and riches shall be in his house.
Prov. 10. 15 ; 18. 11. the rich man's *w.* is his strong city.
     13. 11. *w.* gotten by vanity.
     19. 4. *w.* maketh many friends.
Acts 19. 25. by this craft we have our *w.*
1 Cor. 10. 24. seek every man another's *w.*

Weaned, Ps. 131. 2. as child *w.* of mother.
Is. 11. 8. the *w.* child put his hand.
     28. 9. them that are *w.* from milk.

Weapon, Job 20. 24. he shall flee from from *w.*
Is. 13. 5 ; Jer. 50. 25. the *w.* of his indignation.
Is. 54. 17. no *w.* formed against thee shall prosper.
Ezek. 9. 1. with destroying *w.* in his hand.
2 Cor. 10. 4. the *w.* of our warfare.

Wear, Deut. 22. 5. woman shall not *w.* what pertaineth to man.
Job 14. 19. the waters *w.* the stones.
Dan. 7. 25. *w.* out saints of Most High.
Zech. 13. 4. nor shall they *w.* a rough garment.
Matt. 11. 8. that *w.* soft clothing.
Lk. 9. 12. day began to *w.* away.

Weary, Gen. 27. 46. I am *w.* of my life.
Job 3. 17. there the *w.* be at rest.
     10. 1. my soul is *w.* of life.
     22. 7. not given water to the *w.* to drink.
Ps. 6. 6. I am *w.* with groaning.
Prov. 3. 11. be not *w.* of Lord's correction.
     25. 17. lest he be *w.* of thee.
Is. 5. 27. none shall be *w.* among them.
     7. 13. will ye *w.* God also?
     28. 12. cause the *w.* to rest.

Weary—*Continued.*

Is. 32. 2. as shadow of great rock in a *w.* land.
     40. 28. God fainteth not, neither is *w.*
     40. 31. they shall run, and not be *w.*
     50. 4. a word in season to him that is *w.*
Jer. 9. 5. they *w.* themselves to commit iniquity.
     15. 6. I am *w.* with repenting.
     20. 9. I was *w.* with forbearing.
     31. 25. I have satiated the *w.* soul.
Lk. 18. 15. lest by continual coming she *w.* me.
Gal. 6. 9 ; 2 Thes. 3. 13. let us not be *w.* in well-doing.   [11. 27.
See Job 7. 3 ; Eccl. 12. 12 ; Mal. 1. 13 ; 2 Cor.

Wearied, Is. 43. 24. thou hast *w.* me with thine iniquities.
     47. 13. art *w.* in multitude of counsels.
     57. 10. art *w.* in greatness of way.
Jer. 12. 5. run with footmen, and they *w.* thee.
Ezek. 24. 12. she hath *w.* herself with lies.
Mic. 6. 3. wherein have I *w.* thee?
Mal. 2. 17. wherein have we *w.* the Lord?
John 4. 6. Jesus being *w.* sat on the *w.*
Heb. 12. 3. lest ye be *w.* and faint.

Weather, Job 37. 22. fair *w.* cometh out of the north.   [cold *w.*
Prov. 25. 20. that taketh away a garment in
Matt. 16. 2. fair *w.*, for the sky is red.

Web, Job 8. 14. trust shall be a spider's *w.*
Is. 59. 5. they weave the spider's *w.*

Wedding, Matt. 22. 3. them that were bidden to the *w.*
     22. 11. man had not on a *w.* garment.
Lk. 12. 36. when he will return from the *w.*
     14. 8. when thou art bidden to a *w.*

Wedge, Josh. 7. 21. a *w.* of gold.
Is. 13. 12. a man more precious than golden *w.* of Ophir.

Week, Jer. 5. 24. the appointed *w.* of harvest.
Dan. 9. 27. in the midst of the *w.*
Matt. 28. 1 ; Mk. 16. 2. 9 ; Lk. 24. 1 ; John 20. 1, 19. the first day of the *w.*
Lk. 18. 12. I fast twice in the *w.*

Weep, Gen. 43. 30. he sought where to *w.*
1 Sam. 11. 5. what aileth the people that they *w.*?
     30. 4. no more power to *w.*
2 Sam. 12. 21. thou didst *w.* for the child
Neh. 8. 9. mourn not, nor *w.*
Job 27. 15. his widows shall not *w.*
     30. 25. did not I *w.* for him?
Eccl. 3. 4. a time to *w.*
Is. 22. 4. I will *w.* bitterly.
     30. 19. thou shalt *w.* no more.
Jer. 9. 1. that I might *w.* day and night!
     22. 10. *w.* not for the dead.
Joel 1. 5. awake, ye drunkards, and *w.*
Mic. 1. 10. declare it not, *w.* not.
Mk. 5. 39. why make ye this ado, and *w.*?
Lk. 6. 21. blessed are ye that *w.* now.
     7. 13 ; 8. 52 ; Rev. 5. 5. *w.* not.   [there.
John 11. 31. she goeth to the grave to *w.*
     16. 20. ye shall *w.*, world shall rejoice.
Acts 21. 13. what mean ye to *w.*?
Rom. 12. 15. *w.* with them that *w.*
Jas. 4. 9. be afflicted, mourn, and *w.*

Weeping, 2 Sam. 15. 30. *w.* as they went.
Ezra 3. 13. could not discern noise of joy from *w.*
Job 16. 16. my face is foul with *w.*
Ps. 6. 8. the Lord hath heard the voice of my *w.*
     30. 5. *w.* may endure for a night.

Weeping—*Continued.*
Is. 65. 19. voice of *w.* be no more heard.
Jer. 31. 16. refrain thy voice from *w.*
48. 5. continual *w.* shall go up.
Joel 2. 12. turn with fasting and *w.*
Matt. 8. 12 ; 22. 13 ; 24. 51 ; 25. 30 ; Lk. 13. 28. there shall be *w.*
Lk. 7. 38. stood at his feet behind him *w.*
John 20. 11. Mary stood at sepulchre *w.*
Acts 9. 39. widows stood by *w.*
Phil. 3. 18. now tell you even *w.*
Weigh, Job 6. 2. Oh that my grief were *w.*
31. 6. let me be *w.* in an even balance.
Prov. 16. 2. the Lord *w.* the spirits.
Is. 26. 7. thou dost *w.* the path of the just.
40. 12. who hath *w.* the mountains?
Dan. 5. 27. thou art *w.* in the balances.
Zech. 11. 12. they *w.* thirty pieces of silver.
Weight, Deut. 25. 15. thou shalt have just *w.*
Job 28. 25. to make the *w.* for the winds.
Prov. 11. 1. a just *w.* is his delight.
16. 11. a just *w.* and balance are the Lord's.
Ezek. 4. 16. they shall eat bread by *w.*
2 Cor. 4. 17. a more exceeding *w.* of glory.
Heb. 12. 1. let us lay aside every *w.*
Weighty, Prov. 27. 3. stone is heavy, sand *w.*
Matt. 23. 23. omitted *w.* matters of the law.
2 Cor. 10. 10. his letters, say they, are *w.*
Well, Num. 21. 17. spring up, O *w.*
2 Sam. 23. 15 ; 1 Chr. 11. 17. water of *w.* of Bethlehem. [it a *w.*
Ps. 84. 6. passing through valley of Baca make
Prov. 5. 15. waters of thine own *w.*
10. 11. mouth of righteous man is a *w.* of life.
Cant. 4. 15 ; John 4. 14. *w.* of living water.
Is. 12. 3. the *w.* of salvation.
2 Pet. 2. 17. *w.* without water.

Well, Gen. 4. 7. if thou doest *w.*
29. 6. is he *w.* ?
Ex. 4. 14. I know he can speak *w.*
Deut. 4. 40 ; 5. 16 ; 6. 3 ; 12. 25 ; 19. 13 ; 22. 7 ; Ruth 3. 1 ; Eph. 6. 3. that it may go *w.* with thee.
Ps. 49. 18. when thou doest *w.* to thyself.
Eccl. 8. 12. it shall be *w.* with them that fear God. [with him.
Is. 3. 10. say to the righteous, it shall be *w.*
Jon. 4. 4. doest thou *w.* to be angry?
Matt. 25. 21 ; Lk. 19. 17. *w.* done, good servant.
Lk. 6. 26. when all men speak *w.* of you.
20. 39 ; John 4. 17. thou hast *w.* said.
1 Tim. 5. 17. elders that rule *w.*
Went, Deut. 1. 31. in all the way ye *w.*
Ps. 42. 4. I *w.* with them to the house of God.
Matt. 21. 30. I go, sir, and *w.* not.
Lk. 18. 10. two men *w.* up into temple to pray.
1 John 2. 19. they *w.* out from us.
Wept, Ezra 10. 1 ; Neh. 8. 9. the people *w.* very sore.
Neh. 1. 4. I *w.* before God.
Ps. 137. 1. by rivers of Babylon we *w.*
Lk. 7. 32. we mourned, ye have not *w.*
19. 41. he beheld the city, and *w.* over it.
John 11. 35. Jesus *w.* [*w.* not.
1 Cor. 7. 30. they that weep, as though they
Wheat, Jud. 15. 1 ; Ruth 2. 23 ; 1 Sam. 12. 17. *w.* harvest. [of *w.*
Ezra 7. 22 ; Lk. 16. 7. an hundred measures
Job 31. 40. let thistles grow instead of *w.*
Ps. 81. 16 ; 147. 14. the finest of the *w.*
Jer. 12. 13. they have sown *w.*, but reap thorns.
23. 28. what is the chaff to the *w.* ?
Joel 2. 24. floors shall be full of *w.*

Wheat—*Continued.*
Amos 8. 6. sell refuse of *w.*
Matt. 3. 12 ; Lk. 3. 17. gather his *w.*
Matt. 13. 25. enemy sowed tares among the *w.*
Lk. 22. 31. that he may sift you as *w.*
John 12. 24. except corn of *w.* fall into ground.
1 Cor. 15. 37. it may chance of *w.*
Rev. 6. 6. measure of *w.* for a penny.
Wheel, Ex. 14. 25. took off their chariot *w.*
Jud. 5. 28. why tarry the *w.* of his chariots?
Ps. 83. 13. make them like a *w.*
Prov. 20. 26. king bringeth the *w.* over them.
Eccl. 12. 6. or the *w.* broken at the cistern.
Is. 28. 28. nor break it with the *w.* of his cart.
Jer. 47. 3. at the rumbling of his *w.*
Nah. 3. 2. noise of rattling of the *w.*
Whence, Gen. 42. 7 ; Josh. 9. 8. *w.* come ye?
Job 10. 21 ; 17. 22. I go *w.* I shall not return.
John 7. 28. ye know *w.* I am.
Rev. 7. 13. *w.* came they?
Where, Gen. 3. 9. *w.* art thou?
Ex. 2. 20 ; 2 Sam. 9. 4 ; Job 14. 10. *w.* is he?
Job 9. 24. *w.*, and who is he?
Ps. 42. 3. *w.* is thy God?
Zech. 1. 5. your fathers, *w.* are they?
Lk. 17. 37. *w.* Lord?
Wherewith, Jud. 6. 15. *w.* shall I save Israel?
Mic. 6. 6. *w.* shall I come before the Lord?
Whet, Deut. 32. 41. if I *w.* my glittering sword.
Ps. 7. 12. he will *w.* his sword.
64. 3. who *w.* their tongue like a sword.
Eccl. 10. 10. and he *w.* not the edge. [soul.
While, Ps. 49. 18. *w.* he lived, he blessed his
63. 4. bless thee *w.* I live.
Is. 55. 6. seek Lord *w.* he may be found.
Lk. 8. 13. for a *w.* believe.
18. 4. he would not for a *w.*
Whip, 1 Ki. 12. 11. chastised you with *w.*
Prov. 26. 3. a *w.* for the horse.
Nah. 3. 2. noise of a *w.*
Whisper, 2 Sam. 12. 19. David saw servants *w.*
Ps. 41. 7. all that hate me *w.*
Is. 29. 4. thy speech *w.* out of dust.
See Prov. 16. 28 ; Rom. 1. 29.
Whit, 1 Sam. 3. 18. told every *w.*
John 7. 23. man every *w.* whole.
13. 10. is clean every *w.*
2 Cor. 11. 5. not a *w.* behind apostles.
White, Gen. 49. 12. his teeth be *w.* with milk.
Job 6. 6. is there any taste in the *w.* of an egg?
Eccl. 9. 8. let thy garments be always *w.*
Cant. 5. 10. my beloved is *w.* and ruddy.
Is. 1. 18. sins shall be *w.* as snow. [*w.*
Dan. 12. 10. many shall be purified and made
Matt. 5. 36. canst not make one hair *w.* or black.
John 4. 35. fields are *w.* to harvest.
Rev. 2. 17. a *w.* stone.
3. 4. shall walk with me in *w.*
See Matt. 23. 27 ; Acts 23. 3.
Whole, 2 Sam. 1. 9. my life is yet *w.* in me.
Matt. 9. 12 ; Mk. 2. 17. the *w.* need not a physician. [thee *w.*
Mk. 5. 34 ; Lk. 8. 48 ; 17. 19. faith hath made
John 5. 6. wilt thou be made *w.* ?
Acts 9. 34. Jesus Christ maketh thee *w.*
1 Cor. 12. 17. if the *w.* body were an eye.
See Prov. 15. 4 ; 1 Tim. 6. 3.
Wholly, Num. 32. 11. not *w.* followed me.
Deut. 1. 36 ; Josh. 14. 8. Caleb *w.* followed the Lord.
Jer. 46. 28. not leave thee *w.* unpunished.
Acts 17. 16. city *w.* given to idolatry.
1 Thes. 5. 23. God sanctify you *w.*
1 Tim. 4. 15. give thyself *w.* to them.

Why. Jer. 27. 13 ; Ezek. 18. 31 ; 33. 11. *w.* will ye
die?
Mk. 5. 39. *w.* make ye this ado?
Lk. 2. 48. *w.* hast thou dealt with us?
Acts 14. 15. *w.* do ye these things?
Rom. 9. 20. *w.* hast thou made me thus?
Wicked. Gen. 18. 23. destroy righteous with *w.*
Ex. 23. 7. I will not justify the *w.*
Deut. 15. 9. a thought in thy *w.* heart.
1 Sam. 2. 9. the *w.* shall be silent in darkness.
Job 3. 17. there the *w.* cease from troubling.
8. 22. dwelling-place of the *w.* shall come to
nought.
21. 7. wherefore do the *w.* live?
34. 18. is it fit to say to a king, thou art *w.*?
Ps. 7. 11. God is angry with the *w.*
9. 17. the *w.* shall be turned into hell.
10. 4. the *w.* will not seek God.
11. 6. upon the *w.* he shall rain snares.
34. 21. evil shall slay the *w.*
37. 35. I have seen the *w.* in great power.
58. 3. the *w.* are estranged from the womb.
94. 3. how long shall the *w.* triumph?
119. 155. salvation is far from the *w.*
139. 24. see if there be any *w.* way in me.
145. 20. all the *w.* will he destroy.   [ness.
Prov. 11. 5. *w.* shall fall by his own wicked-
11. 21. the *w.* shall not be unpunished.
15. 29. the Lord is far from the *w.*
28. 1. the *w.* flee when no man pursueth.
Eccl. 7. 17. be not overmuch *w.*
Is. 53. 9. he made his grave with the *w.*
55. 7. let the *w.* forsake his way.
57. 20. the *w.* are like the troubled sea.
Jer. 17. 9. the heart is desperately *w.*
Ezek. 3. 18 ; 33. 8. to warn the *w.*
18. 23. have I any pleasure that the *w.*
should die?
Dan. 12. 10. the *w.* shall do wickedly.
Nah. 1. 3. The Lord will not acquit the *w.*
Matt. 13. 49. sever the *w.* from the just.
Acts 2. 23. by *w.* hands have slain him.
Eph. 6. 16. the fiery darts of the *w.*
Col. 1. 21. enemies by *w.* works.
2 Thes. 2. 8. then shall that *W.* be revealed.
Wickedly. Job 13. 7. will you speak *w.* for God?
34. 12. surely God will not do *w.*
Ps. 73. 8 ; 139. 20. they speak *w.*
74. 3. the enemy hath done *w.*
Mal. 4. 1. all that do *w.*
Wickedness. Gen. 6. 5. God saw *w.* was great.
39. 9. this great *w.*
1 Sam. 24. 13. *w.* proceedeth from the wicked.
Job 4. 8. they that sow *w.*, reap the same.
20. 12. though *w.* be sweet.
22. 5. is not thy *w.* great?
Ps. 55. 15. *w.* is in their dwellings.
84. 10. than to dwell in tents of *w.*
Prov. 4. 17. they eat the bread of *w.*
8. 7. *w.* is abomination to my lips.
10. 2. treasures of *w.* profit nothing.
13. 6. *w.* overthroweth the sinner.
Eccl. 7. 25. the *w.* of folly.
8. 8. neither shall *w.* deliver.
Is. 9. 18. *w.* burneth as the fire.
58. 6. to loose the bands of *w.*
Jer. 2. 19. thine own *w.* shall correct thee.
8. 6. no man repented of his *w.*
14. 20. we acknowledge our *w.*
Ezek. 3. 19. if he turn not from his *w.*
33. 12. in the day he turneth from his *w.*
Hos. 9. 15. for the *w.* of their doings.
10. 13. ye have ploughed *w.*
Mic. 6. 10. treasures of *w.* in house of wicked.

Wickedness—*Continued.*
Mk. 7. 22. out of the heart proceed *w.*
Lk. 11. 39. inward part is full of *w.*
Acts 8. 22. repent of this thy *w.*
Rom. 1. 29. being filled with all *w.*
1 Cor. 5. 8. the leaven of *w.*
Eph. 6. 12. spiritual *w.* in high places.
1 John 5. 19. whole world lieth in *w.*
Wide. Job 29. 23 ; Ps. 35. 21 ; 81. 10. opened
mouth *w.*
Prov. 13. 3. that openeth *w.* his lips.
Matt. 7. 13. *w.* is gate that leadeth to de-
struction.
Wife, Prov. 5. 18 ; Eccl. 9. 9. the *w.* of thy
youth.   [good thing.
Prov. 18. 22. whoso findeth a *w.* findeth a
19. 14. a prudent *w.* is from the Lord.
Hos. 12. 12. Israel served for a *w.*
Lk. 17. 32. remember Lot's *w.*
1 Cor. 7. 14. the unbelieving *w.* is sancti-
fied.
Eph. 5. 23. the husband is the head of the *w.*
1 Pet. 3. 7. giving honour to the *w.*
Rev. 21. 9. the bride, the Lamb's *w.*
Wilderness, Ps. 95. 8. day of temptation in
the *w.*
Is. 35. 1. the *w.* shall be glad.
40. 3 ; Matt. 3. 3 ; Mk. 1. 3 ; Lk. 3. 4 ; John
1. 23. voice of him that crieth in the *w.*
Wiles, Num. 25. 18. they vex you with *w.*
Eph. 6. 11. able to stand against *w.* of
devil.
Will, Deut. 33. 16. the good *w.* of him that
dwelt in the bush.
Ps. 40. 8. I delight to do thy *w.*, O God.
Matt. 6. 10 ; Lk. 11. 2. thy *w.* be done in
earth, as in heaven.
Matt. 7. 21 ; 12. 50. doeth the *w.* of my Father.
18. 14. it is not the *w.* of your Father.
26. 42. thy *w.* be done.
Lk. 2. 14. good-*w.* toward men.
John 1. 13. born not of the *w.* of the flesh.
4. 34. to do the *w.* of him that sent me.
6. 39. this is the Father's *w.*
Acts 21. 14. the *w.* of the Lord be done.
Rom. 7. 18. to *w.* is present with me.
Eph. 5. 17. what the *w.* of the Lord is.
6. 7. with good *w.* doing service.
Phil. 2. 13. both to *w.* and to do.
Jas. 1. 18. of his own *w.* begat he us.
Rev. 22. 17. whosoever *w.*, let him take.
See Rom. 9. 16 ; Heb. 10. 26.
Willing, Ex. 35. 5. whosoever is of a *w.* heart.
1 Chr. 28. 9. serve God with a *w.* mind.
Ps. 110. 3. people shall be *w.* in day of thy
power.
Matt. 26. 41. the Spirit is *w.*
Lk. 22. 42. if thou be *w.*, remove this cup.
John 5. 35. ye were *w.* for a season to rejoice.
Rom. 9. 22. if God *w.* to show wrath.
2 Cor. 5. 8. *w.* rather to be absent.
8. 12. if there be first a *w.* mind.
1 Tim. 6. 18. *w.* to communicate.
2 Pet. 3. 9. not *w.* that any should perish.
Willingly, Jud. 5. 2, 9. people *w.* offered them-
selves.
Lam. 3. 33. the Lord doth not afflict *w.*
Rom. 8. 20. creature was made subject to
vanity, not *w.*   [but *w.*
Philem. 14 ; 1 Pet. 5. 2. not as of necessity,
2 Pet. 3. 5. they *w.* are ignorant.
Win, 2 Chr. 32. 1. he thought to *w.* them.
Prov. 11. 30. he that *w.* souls is wise.
Phil. 3. 8. that I may *w.* Christ.

Wind, Job 6. 26. speeches which are as *w.*
7. 7. remember that my life is *w.*
Ps. 147. 18. he causeth his *w.* to blow.
Prov. 11. 29. he shall inherit *w.*
25. 23. north *w.* driveth away rain.
30. 4. who hath gathered the *w.* in his fists?
Eccl. 11. 4. he that observeth the *w.*
Is. 7. 2. as trees are moved with *w.*
26. 18. as it were brought forth *w.*
27. 8. he stayeth his rough *w.*
32. 2. a hiding-place from the *w.*
Jer. 10. 13; 51. 16. bringeth *w.* out of his treasures.
Ezek. 37. 9. prophesy to the *w.*
Hos. 8. 7. they have sown *w.*
12. 1. feedeth on *w.*
Amos 4. 13. he that createth the *w.*
Matt. 11. 7; Lk. 7. 24. a reed shaken with the *w.*
John 3. 8. the *w.* bloweth where it listeth.
Eph. 4. 14. carried about with every *w.* of doctrine.
Jas. 1. 6. like wave driven with the *w.*

Windows, Gen. 7. 11. *w.* of heaven were opened.
2 Ki. 7. 2, 19. if Lord make *w.* in heaven.
Eccl. 12. 3. they that look out of *w.* be darkened.
Is. 60. 8. fly as doves to their *w.*
Jer. 9. 21. death is come into our *w.*
Mal. 3. 10. if I will not open *w.* of heaven.

Wine, Ps. 104. 15. *w.* that maketh glad the heart.
Prov. 20. 1. *w.* is a mocker.
23. 31. look not on *w.* when it is red.
Is. 5. 11. till *w.* inflame them.
25. 6. *w.* on the lees well refined.
28. 7. they have erred through *w.*
55. 1. buy *w.* and milk.
Hos. 3. 1. love flagons of *w.*
Hab. 2. 5. he transgresseth by *w.*
Eph. 5. 18. be not drunk with *w.*
1 Tim. 3. 3; Tit. 1. 7; 2. 3. not given to *w.*
1 Tim. 5. 23. use *w.* for stomach's sake.
1 Pet. 4. 3. walked in excess of *w.*

Wings, Ex. 19. 4. bare you on eagles' *w.*
Ps. 17. 8; 36. 7; 57. 1; 61. 4; 91. 4. the shadow of thy *w.*
18. 10; 104. 3. fly on *w.* of the wind.
55. 6. Oh that I had *w.* like a dove!
139. 9. if I take *w.* of the morning.
Prov. 23. 5. riches make themselves *w.*
Is. 40. 31. mount with *w.* as eagles.
Mal. 4. 2. with healing in his *w.*
Matt. 23. 37; Lk. 13. 34. as a hen gathereth chickens under *w.*

Wink, Job 15. 12. what do thine eyes *w.* at?
Ps. 35. 19. neither let them *w.*
Prov. 6. 13. a wicked man *w.* with his eyes.
10. 10. he that *w.* causeth sorrow.
Acts 17. 30. ignorance God *w.* at.

Winter, Gen. 8. 22. *w.* shall not cease.
Ps. 74. 17. hast made summer and *w.*
Cant. 2. 11. lo, the *w.* is past.
Matt. 24. 20; Mk. 13. 8. pray that your flight be not in *w.*
1 Cor. 16. 6. I will *w.* with you.

Wipe, 2 Ki. 21. 13. *w.* Jerusalem as a dish.
Neh. 13. 14. *w.* not out good deeds.
Is. 25. 8; Rev. 7. 17; 21. 4. Lord will *w.* away tears from all faces.

Wisdom, Deut. 4. 6. this is your *w.*
Job 4. 21. they die without *w.*
28. 12. where shall *w.* be found?
Ps. 90. 12. apply our hearts to *w.*

Wisdom—*Continued.*
Prov. 4. 5. get *w.,* get understanding.
4. 7. *w.* is the principal thing.
16. 16. better to get *w.* than gold.
19 8. he that getteth *w.* loveth his own soul.
23. 4. cease from thine own *w.*
Eccl. 1. 18. in much *w.* is much grief.
9. 10. there is no *w.* in the grave.
Is. 10. 13. by my *w.* I have done it.
29. 14. the *w.* of their wise men shall perish.
33. 6. *w.* shall be the stability of thy times.
Jer. 10. 12; 51. 15. established the world by *w.*
Matt. 11. 19. *w.* is justified of her children.
13. 54. whence hath this man *w.*?
Lk. 2. 52. Jesus increased in *w.* and stature.
1 Cor. 1. 17. not with *w.* of words.
1. 21. the world by *w.* knew not God.
1. 24. Christ the *w.* of God.   [with God.
3. 19. the *w.* of this world is foolishness
2 Cor. 1. 12. not with fleshly *w.*
Eph. 3. 10. the manifold *w.* of God.
Col. 1. 9. that ye might be filled with all *w.*
4. 5. walk in *w.* toward them without.
Jas. 1. 5. if any lack *w.*
3. 17. the *w.* from above is pure.
Rev. 5. 12. worthy is the Lamb to receive *w.*
13. 18. here is *w.*

Wise, Gen. 3. 6. a tree to make one *w.*
Ex. 23. 8; Deut. 16. 19. the gift blindeth the *w.*
Deut. 32. 29. O that they were *w.*!   [ness.
Job 5. 13. taketh the *w.* in their own crafti-
11. 12. vain man would be *w.*
32. 9. great men are not always *w.*
37. 24. he respecteth not any *w.* of heart.
Ps. 2. 10. be *w.* now, O kings.
19. 7. making *w.* the simple.
94. 8. ye fools, when will ye be *w.*?
107. 43. whoso is *w.,* and will observe.
Prov. 1. 5. a *w.* man will attain *w.* counsels.
3. 7. be not *w.* in thine own eyes.
3. 35. the *w.* shall inherit glory.
9. 12. thou shalt be *w.* for thyself.
11. 30. he that winneth souls is *w.*   [be *w.*
13. 20. he that walketh with *w.* men shall
20. 1. whosoever is deceived thereby is not *w.*
26. 12. a man *w.* in his own conceit.
Eccl. 6. 8. what hath the *w.* more than the fool?
7. 4. heart of *w.* is in house of mourning.
9. 1. the *w.* are in the hand of God.
12. 11. the words of the *w.* are as goads.
Is. 5. 21. woe to them that are *w.* in their own eyes!
Jer. 4. 22. they are *w.* to do evil.
Dan. 12. 3. they that be *w.* shall shine.
Matt. 10. 16. be ye *w.* as serpents.
11. 25. thou hast hid these things from the *w.*
Rom. 1. 22. professing themselves to be *w.*
12. 16. be not *w.* in your own conceits.
16. 19. *w.* to that which is good.
1 Cor. 1. 20. where is the *w.*?
3. 20. Lord knoweth thoughts of the *w.*
4. 10. ye are *w.* in Christ.
Eph. 5. 15. walk not as fools, but as *w.*
2 Tim. 3. 15. to make *w.* unto salvation.

Wisely, Ps. 58. 5. charmers, charming never so *w.*
101. 2. I will behave myself *w.*
Prov. 16. 20. that handleth a matter *w.*
Eccl. 7. 10. thou dost not enquire *w.*
Lk. 16. 8. because he had done *w.*

164

Wiser, 1 Ki. 4. 31. Solomon was *w.* than all men.

Prov. 9. 9. he will be yet *w.*

Lk. 16. 8. in their generation *w.* than children of light.

1 Cor. 1. 25. foolishness of God is *w.* than men.

Wish, Ps. 73. 7. more than heart could *w.*

Rom. 9. 3. could *w.* myself accursed.

2 Cor. 13. 9. *wd w.* even your perfection.

3 John 2. I *w.* thou mayest prosper.

Withdraw, Job 9. 13. if God will not *w.* his anger.

33. 17. that he may *w.* man from his purpose.

Is. 60. 20. neither shall thy moon *w.* itself.

2 Thes. 3. 6. *w.* from brother that walketh disorderly.

Wither, Ps. 1. 3. his leaf shall not *w.*

37. 2. they shall *w.* as the green herb.

90. 6. it is cut down, and *w.*

Is. 40. 7 ; 1 Pet. 1. 24. the grass *w.*

Matt. 13. 6 ; Mk. 4. 6. having no root, *w.*

Matt. 21. 19 ; Mk. 11. 21. the fig tree *w.* away.

John 15. 6. is cast forth as a branch, and *w.*

Jude 12. trees whose fruit *w.*

Withhold, Ps. 40. 11. *w.* not thy mercies.

84. 11. no good thing will he *w.*

Prov. 3. 27. *w.* not good from them to whom it is due.

23. 13. *w.* not correction from the child.

Eccl. 11. 6. *w.* not thy hand.

Within, Ps. 40. 8. thy law is *w.* my heart.

45. 13. king's daughter is all glorious *w.*

Matt. 23. 26. cleanse first that which is *w.*

Mk. 7. 21. from *w.* proceed evil thoughts.

Lk. 11. 7. he from *w.* shall answer.

2 Cor. 7. 5. *w.* were fears.

Without, Gen. 24. 31. wherefore standest thou *w.*?

2 Chr. 15. 3. *w.* the true God.

Prov. 1. 20. wisdom crieth *w.*

2 Cor. 7. 5. *w.* were fightings.

Eph. 2. 12. *w.* God in the world.   [are *w.*

Col. 4. 5 ; 1 Thes. 4. 12 ; 1 Tim. 3. 7. them that

Heb. 13. 12. Jesus suffered *w.* the gate.

Rev. 22. 15. *w.* are dogs.

Withstand, 2 Chr. 20. 6. none is able to *w.* thee.

Eccl. 4. 12. two shall *w.* him.

Acts 11. 17. what was I that I could *w.* God?

Eph. 6. 13. able to *w.* in the evil day.

Witness, Gen. 31. 44. covenant be a *w.* between us.

31. 50. God is *w.* betwixt me and thee.

Josh. 24. 27. this stone shall be a *w.*

Job 16. 19. my *w.* is in heaven.

Ps. 89. 37. a faithful *w.* in heaven.

Prov. 14. 5. a faithful *w.* will not lie.

14. 25. a true *w.* delivereth souls.

24. 28. be not *w.* against thy neighbour.

Is. 55. 4. I have given him for a *w.* to the people.   [us.

Jer. 42. 5. the Lord be a faithful *w.* between

Mal. 3. 5. a swift *w.* against the sorcerers.

Matt. 24. 14. for a *w.* to all nations.

Mk. 14. 55. sought *w.* against Jesus.

John 1. 7. the same came for a *w.*

3. 11. ye receive not our *w.*

5. 37. the Father hath borne *w.* of me.

Acts 14. 17. he left not himself without *w.*

Rom. 2. 15 ; 9. 1. conscience bearing *w.*

Heb. 12. 1. compassed with cloud of *w.*

1 John 5. 9. if we receive *w.* of men.

5. 10. hath the *w.* in himself.

Rev. 1. 5. Jesus Christ the faithful *w.*

Witness, Deut. 4. 26. I call heaven and earth to *w.*

1 Sam. 12. 3. *w.* against me.   [them.

Is. 3. 9. their countenance doth *w.* against

Matt. 26. 62 ; Mk. 14. 60. what is it which these *w.* against thee?

Acts 20. 23. Holy Ghost *w.* in every city.

26. 22. *w.* both to small and great.

Rom. 3. 21. being *w.* by the law and prophets.

1 Tim. 6. 13. before Pilate *w.* a good confession.

Heb. 7. 8. of whom it is *w.* that he liveth.

Wits, Ps. 107. 27. they stagger at their *w.* end.

See Prov. 8. 12.   [lamb.

Wolf, Is. 11. 6. the *w.* shall dwell with the

65. 25. the *w.* and lamb shall feed together.

Matt. 7. 15. inwardly they are *w.*

10. 16. as sheep in the midst of *w.*

John 10. 12. hireling seeth the *w.* coming.

Acts 20. 29. *w.* shall enter among them.

Woman. Gen. 3. 15. enmity between thee and the *w.*

Ps. 48. 6 ; Is. 13. 8 ; 21. 3 ; 26. 17 ; Jer. 4. 31 ;

6. 24 ; 13. 21 ; 30. 6 ; 31. 8 ; 48. 41 ; 49. 22 ;

50. 43. pain as of a *w.* in travail.

Prov. 9. 13. a foolish *w.* is clamorous.

12. 4 ; 31. 10. a virtuous *w.*

14. 1. every wise *w.* buildeth her house.

21. 9. with a brawling *w.* in a wide house.

Eccl. 7. 28. a *w.* among all those have I not found.

Is. 49. 15. can a *w.* forget her sucking child?

54. 6. as a *w.* forsaken.

Jer. 31. 22. a *w.* shall compass a man.

Matt. 5. 28. whoso looketh on a *w.*

15. 28. O *w.*, great is thy faith.

26. 10. why trouble ye the *w.?*

26. 13. this, that this *w.* hath done, be told.

John 2. 4. *w.*, what have I to do with thee?

8. 3. a *w.* taken in adultery.

19. 26. *w.*, behold thy son!

Rom. 1. 27. the natural use of the *w.*

1 Cor. 7. 1. good not to touch a *w.*

11. 7. the *w.* is the glory of the man.

Gal. 4. 4. God sent his Son, made of a *w.*

1 Tim. 2. 12. I suffer not a *w.* to teach.

2. 14. the *w.* being deceived, was in the transgression.

Womb, Gen. 49. 25. blessings of the *w.*

1 Sam. 1. 5. the Lord had shut up her *w.*

Ps. 22. 9. he that took me out of the *w.*

22. 10. I was cast upon thee from the *w.*

110. 3. from *w.* of the morning.

127. 3. the fruit of the *w.* is his reward.

139. 13. thou hast covered me in my mother's *w.*

Eccl. 11. 5. how bones grow in the *w.*

Is. 44. 2 ; 49. 5. Lord formed thee from the *w.*

48. 8. a transgressor from the *w.*

66. 9. to bring forth, and shut the *w.*

Hos. 9. 14. give them a miscarrying *w.*

Lk. 1. 42. blessed is the fruit of thy *w.*

11. 27. blessed is the *w.* that bare thee.

23. 29. blessed are the *w.* that never bare.

Women, Jud. 5. 24. blessed above *w.*

2 Sam. 1. 26. passing the love of *w.*

Ps. 45. 9. among thy honourable *w.*

Prov. 31. 3. give not thy strength to *w.*

Is. 3. 12. *w.* rule over them.

32. 9. ye *w.* that are at ease.

Matt. 11. 11 ; Lk. 7. 28. among them born of *w.*

Matt. 24. 41 ; Lk. 17. 35. two *w.* grinding at the mill.

Lk. 1. 28. blessed art thou among *w.*

1 Cor. 14. 34. let your *w.* keep silence.

Women—*Continued.*
1 Tim. 2. 9. that *w.* adorn themselves in modest apparel.
2 Tim. 3. 6. lead captive silly *w.*
Heb. 11. 35. *w.* received their dead.
1 Pet. 3. 5. holy *w.* adorned themselves.
Wonder, Deut. 13. 1; 28. 46. a sign and *w.*
Ps. 71. 7. I am as a *w.* unto many.
77. 14. thou art the God that doest *w.*
88. 10. wilt thou show *w.* to the dead?
96. 3. declare his *w.* among all people.
136. 4. who alone doeth great *w.*
Is. 20. 3. walked barefoot for a sign and a *w.*
29. 14. I will do a marvellous work and a *w.*
Dan. 12. 6. how long to the end of these *w.?*
Joel 2. 30; Acts 2.19. I will show *w.* in heaven.
Acts 3. 10. they were filled with *w.*

Wonder, Is. 29. 9. stay yourselves, and *w.*
59. 16. he *w.* there was no intercessor.
Hab. 1. 5. regard, and *w.* marvellously.
Lk. 4. 22. they *w.* at the gracious words.
Rev. 17. 8. that dwell on the earth shall *w.*
Wonderful, 2 Sam. 1. 26. thy love was *w.*
Job 42. 3. things too *w.* for me.
Ps. 119. 129. thy testimonies are *w.*
139. 6. such knowledge is too *w.* for me.
Is. 9. 6. his name shall be called *W.*
25. 1. thou hast done *w.* things.
28. 29. Lord, who is *w.* in counsel.   [did.
Matt. 21. 15. when they saw the *w.* things he
   See Ps. 139. 14 ; Dan. 8. 24.
Wondrous, 1 Chr. 16. 9 ; Ps. 26. 7; 105. 2;
   119. 27 ; 145. 5. talk of his *w.* works.   [him?
Job 37. 16. dost thou know the *w.* works of
Ps. 72. 18; 86. 10. God doeth *w.* things.
119. 18. *w.* things out of thy law.
Wont, Matt. 27. 15. the governor was *w.* to release.
Mk. 10. 1. as was his *w.*, he taught.
Lk. 22.39. he went, as he was *w.*, to the mount.
Acts 16. 13. where prayer was *w.* to be made.
Wood, Gen. 22. 7. behold the fire and the *w.*
Deut. 29. 11 ; Josh. 9. 21 ; Jer. 46. 22. hewer of *w.*
Ps. 80. 13. boar of *w.* doth waste it.
141. 7. as one cleaveth *w.*
Prov. 26. 20. where no *w.* is, the fire goeth out.
Is. 60. 17. for *w.* I will bring brass.
1 Cor. 3. 12. on this foundation *w.*, hay.
Wool, Ps. 147. 16. he giveth snow like *w.*
Prov. 31. 13. she seeketh *w.* and flax.
Is. 1. 18. your sins shall be as *w.*
Ezek. 27. 18. merchant in *w.*
Dan. 7. 9 ; Rev. 1. 14. hair like *w.*   [you.
Word, Deut. 4. 2. not add to *w.* I command
8. 3 ; Matt. 4. 4. every *w.* of God.
Deut. 30. 14 ; Rom. 10. 8. the *w.* is nigh.
Job 12. 11. doth not the ear try *w.?*
38. 2. darkeneth counsel by *w.*   [able.
Ps. 19. 14. let the *w.* of my mouth be accept-
68. 11. the Lord gave the *w.*
139. 4. there is not a *w.*, but thou knowest it.
Prov. 15. 23. a *w.* spoken in due season.
25. 11. a *w.* fitly spoken.
Is. 29. 21. make a man an offender for a *w.*
30. 21. thine ears shall hear a *w.* behind thee.
45. 23. the *w.* is gone out of my mouth.
50. 4. how to speak a *w.* in season.
Jer. 5. 13. the *w.* is not in them.
18. 18. nor shall the *w.* perish.
44. 16. the *w.* thou hast spoken.
Dan. 7. 25. speak great *w.* against the Most High.

Word—*Continued.*
Hos. 14. 2. take with you *w.*
Matt. 8. 8. speak the *w.* only.
12. 36. every idle *w.* that men shall speak.
24. 35. my *w.* shall not pass away.
Mk. 4. 14. the sower soweth the *w.*
Lk. 4. 36. what a *w.* is this!
24. 19. a prophet mighty in deed and *w.*
John 1. 1. in the beginning was the *W.*
1. 14. the *W.* was made flesh.
6. 68. thou hast the *w.* of eternal life.
14. 24. the *w.* ye hear is not mine.
15. 3. ye are clean through the *w.* I have spoken.   [me.
17. 8. I have given them the *w.* thou gavest
Acts 13. 15. any *w.* of exhortation.
13. 26. to you is *w.* of salvation sent.
17. 11. received the *w.* with readiness.
20. 32. the *w.* of his grace.
26. 25. the *w.* of truth and soberness.
1 Cor. 4. 20. kingdom of God is not in *w.*, but in power.
2 Cor. 1. 18. our *w.* was not yea and nay.
5. 19. the *w.* of reconciliation.
Gal. 5. 14. all the law is fulfilled in one *w.*
6. 6. him that is taught in the *w.*
Phil. 2. 16. holding forth the *w.* of life.
Col. 3. 17. whatsoever ye do in *w.* or deed.
1 Thes. 1. 5. the Gospel came not in *w.* only.
4. 18. comfort one another with these *w.*
1 Tim. 5. 17. labour in the *w.* and doctrine.
2 Tim. 4. 2. preach the *w.*
Tit. 1. 9. holding fast the faithful *w.*
Heb. 2. 2. if the *w.* spoken by angels was stedfast.
4. 2. the *w.* preached did not profit.
4. 12. the *w.* of God is quick and powerful.
5. 13. is unskilful in the *w.* of righteousness.
6. 5. have tasted the good *w.* of God.
13. 22. suffer the *w.* of exhortation.
Jas. 1. 21. receive the engrafted *w.*
1. 22. be ye doers of the *w.*
3. 2. if any offend not in *w.*
1 Pet. 2. 2. the sincere milk of the *w.*
3. 1. if any obey not the *w.*
2 Pet. 1. 19. a more sure *w.* of prophecy.
3. 5. by the *w.* of God the heavens were of old.
1 John 1. 1. hands have handled of the *W.* of life.
3. 18. not love in *w.* but in deed.
Rev. 3. 10. kept the *w.* of my patience.
Work, Gen. 2. 3. God rested from his *w.*
Ex. 20. 9 ; 23. 12 ; Deut. 5. 13. six days do all thy *w.*
Deut. 4. 28 ; 27. 15 ; 2 Ki. 19. 18; 2 Chr. 32. 19 ;
   Ps. 115. 4 ; 135. 15. the *w.* of men's hands.
Deut. 33. 11. accept the *w.* of his hands.
1 Chr. 29. 1 ; Neh. 4. 19. the *w.* is great.
2 Chr. 34. 12. the men did the *w.* faithfully.
Ezra 6. 7. let the *w.* of the house of God alone.
Neh. 6. 16. they perceived this *w.* was of God.
Job 1. 10. thou hast blessed the *w.* of his hands.
10. 3. despise the *w.* of thine hands.
14. 15. have desire to *w.* of thy hands.
34. 11. the *w.* of a man shall he render unto him.
Ps. 8. 3. the *w.* of thy fingers.
19. 1. the firmament showeth his handy *w.*
33. 4. all his *w.* are done in truth.
90. 17. establish thou the *w.* of our hands.
101. 3. I hate the *w.* of them that turn aside.
111. 2. the *w.* of the Lord are great.

Work—*Continued.*

Ps. 143. 5. muse on *w.* of thy hands.
Prov. 20. 11. whether his *w.* be pure.
24. 12 ;   Matt. 16. 27 ; 2 Tim. 4. 14. render to every man according to his *w.*
Eccl. 3. 17. there is a time for every *w.*
5. 6. why should God destroy *w.* of thine hands?
8. 9. I applied my heart to every *w.*
9. 10. there is no *w.* in the grave.
12. 14. God shall bring every *w.* into judgment.
Is. 5. 19. let him hasten his *w.*   [whole *w.*
10. 12. when the Lord hath performed his
28. 21. do his *w.*, his strange *w.*
49. 4. my *w.* is with God.
64. 8. we are the *w.* of thy hand.
Jer. 32.19. great in counsel, and mighty in *w.*
Hab. 1. 5. I will work a *w.* in your days.
3. 2. revive thy *w.* in the years.   [men.
Matt. 23. 5. all their *w.* they do to be seen of
Mk. 6. 5. he could there do no mighty *w.*
John 6. 29. this is the *w.* of God, that ye believe.
7. 21. I have done one *w.*, and ye all marvel.
9. 3. that the *w.* of God should be made manifest.
10. 32. for which of those *w.* do ye stone me?
14. 12. the *w.* I do shall he do, and greater *w.*
17. 4. I have finished the *w.* thou gavest me.
Acts 5. 38. if this *w.* be of men.
14. 26. the *w.* which they fulfilled.
15. 38. went not with them to the *w.*
Rom. 2. 15. show *w.* of law written.
3. 27. by what law? of *w.*?   [earth.
9. 28. a short *w.* will Lord make on the
11. 6. otherwise *w.* is no more *w.*
13. 12; Eph. 5. 11. the *w.* of darkness.
1 Cor. 3. 13. every man's *w.* shall be made manifest.
9. 1. are not ye my *w.* in the Lord?
Gal. 2. 16. by *w.* of the law shall no flesh be justified.
6. 4. let patience have his own *w.*
Eph. 2. 9. not of *w.*, lest any man boast.
4. 12. the *w.* of the ministry.
Col. 1.21. enemies in your mind by wicked *w.*
1 Thes. 5. 13. esteem them in love for their *w.* sake.
2 Thes. 1. 11. God fulfil *w.* of faith.
2. 17. stablish you in every good word and *w.*
2 Tim. 1. 9. saved us, not according to our *w.*
4. 5. do the *w.* of an evangelist.
Tit. 1. 16. in *w.* they deny him.
Heb. 6. 1 ; 9. 14. from dead *w.*
Jas. 1. 4. let patience have her perfect *w.*
2. 14. if he have not *w.*, can faith save him?
2. 17. faith, if it hath not *w.*, is dead.
2. 22. by *w.* was faith made perfect.
2 Pet. 3. 10. earth and *w.* therein shall be burned up.
1 John 3. 8. might destroy the *w.* of the devil.
Rev. 2. 26. he that keepeth my *w.* to the end.
3. 2. I have not found thy *w.* perfect.
9. 20. repented not of *w.* of hands.
14. 13. their *w.* do follow them.
22. 12. to give every man as his *w.* shall be.

Work, Ex. 34. 21. six days thou shalt *w.*
1 Sam. 14. 6. may be the Lord will *w.* for us.
1 Ki. 21. 20. sold thyself to *w.* evil.
Neh. 4. 6. the people had a mind to *w.*
Job 23. 9. on the left hand, where he doth *w.*
33. 29. all these things *w.* God with man.

Work—*Continued.*

Ps. 58. 2. in heart ye *w.* wickedness.
101. 7. he that *w.* deceit.
119. 126. it is time for Lord to *w.*
Prov. 26. 28. a flattering mouth *w.* ruin.
31. 13. she *w.* with her hands.
Is. 43. 13. I will *w.*, and who shall let it?
44. 12. the smith *w.* in the coals.
Dan. 6. 27. he *w.* signs and wonders.
Mic. 2. 1. woe to them that *w.* evil !
Hag. 2. 4. *w.*, for I am with you.   [up.
Mal. 3. 15. they that *w.* wickedness are set
Matt. 21. 28. go *w.* in my vineyard.
John 5. 17. my Father *w.* hitherto, and I *w.*
6. 28. that we might *w.* the works of God.
6. 30. what dost thou *w.*?
9. 4. the night cometh, when no man can *w.*
Acts 10. 35. he that *w.* righteousness.
Rom. 5. 3. tribulation *w.* patience.
8. 28. all things *w.* together for good.   [all.
1 Cor. 12. 6. it is the same God that *w.* all in
2 Cor. 4. 12. death *w.* in us.   [of glory.
4. 17. *w.* for us a far more exceeding weight
Gal. 5. 6. faith which *w.* by love.
Eph. 1. 11. who *w.* all things after counsel of his will.   [obedience.
2. 2. the spirit that *w.* in children of dis-
3. 20. according to power that *w.* in us.
4. 28. *w.* thing that is good.
Phil. 2. 12. *w.* out your own salvation.
1 Thes. 4. 11. *w.* with your own hands.
2 Thes. 2. 7. the mystery of iniquity doth *w.*
3. 10. if any would not *w.*, neither should he eat.
Heb. 13. 21. *w.* that which is pleasing.
Jas. 1. 20. wrath of man *w.* not righteousness of God.   [image.
Workman. Is. 40. 19. the *w.* melteth a graven
Matt. 10. 10. the *w.* is worthy of his meat.
2 Tim. 2. 15. a *w.* that needeth not to be ashamed.
See Eph. 2. 10.

World, 1 Sam. 2. 8. he set the *w.* upon them.
1 Chr. 16. 30. the *w.* shall be stable.
Job 18. 18. chased out of the *w.*
34. 13. who hath disposed the whole *w.*?
37. 12. upon the face of the *w.*
Ps. 17. 14. from men of the *w.*
24. 1 ; 98. 7 ; Nah. 1. 5. the *w.* and they that dwell therein.
50. 12. the *w.* is mine.
73. 12. the ungodly, who prosper in the *w.*
93. 1 ; 96. 10. the *w.* is established.
Eccl. 3. 11. he hath set the *w.* in their heart.
Is. 14. 21. nor fill the face of the *w.* with cities.
24. 4. the *w.* languisheth.
34. 1. let the *w.* hear.
45. 17. not confounded, *w.* without end.
Matt. 4. 8;   Lk. 4. 5. all the kingdoms of the *w.*
Matt. 5. 14. the light of the *w.*
13. 22 ; Mk. 4. 19. the cares of this *w.*
Matt. 13. 38. the field is the *w.*
13. 40. in the end of this *w.*   [*w.*
16. 26 ; Mk. 8. 36 ; Lk. 9. 25. gain the whole
Matt. 18. 7. woe to the *w.* because of offences !
24. 14 ;   Mk. 14. 9. shall be preached in all the *w.*   [eternal life.
Mk. 10. 30 ; Lk. 18. 30. in the *w.* to come
Lk. 1. 70 ; Acts 3. 21. since the *w.* began.
Lk. 20. 35. worthy to obtain that *w.*
John 1. 10. he was in the *w.*
1. 29. taketh away the sin of the *w.*
3. 16. God so loved the *w.*

World—*Continued.*

John 4. 42; 1 John 4. 14. the Saviour of the *w.*

John 6. 33. bread of God giveth life to the *w.*

8. 12; 9. 5. Jesus said, I am the light of the *w.*

12. 47. I came not to judge the *w.*, but to save the *w.*

14. 27. not as the *w.* giveth, give I unto you.

14. 30. the prince of this *w.* cometh.

15. 18; 1 John 3. 13. if the *w.* hate you.

John 16. 28. I leave the *w.*, and go to the Father.

17. 9. I pray not for the *w.*   [sent me.

17. 21, 23. that the *w.* may believe thou hast

21. 25. the *w.* could not contain the books.

Acts 17. 6. turned the *w.* upside down.

Rom. 3. 19. that all the *w.* may become guilty.

12. 2. be not conformed to this *w.*

1 Cor. 1. 21. the *w.* by wisdom knew not God.

7. 31. they that use this *w.*, as not abusing it.

2 Cor. 4. 4. the god of this *w.* hath blinded.

Gal. 1. 4. deliver us from this present evil *w.*

6. 14. the *w.* is crucified unto me.

Eph. 2. 12. without God in the *w.*

1 Tim. 6. 7. we brought nothing into this *w.*

Heb. 11. 38. of whom the *w.* was not worthy.

Jas. 3. 6. the tongue is a *w.* of iniquity.

4. 4. the friendship of the *w.*

1 John 2. 15. love not the *w.*

3. 1. the *w.* knoweth us not.

5. 19. the whole *w.* lieth in wickedness.

Worm, Ex. 16. 24. neither was there any *w.* therein.

Job 7. 5. my flesh is clothed with *w.* and dust.

17. 14. said to the *w.*, thou art my mother.

19. 26. though *w.* destroy this body.

24. 20. the *w.* shall feed sweetly on him.

25. 6. man, that is a *w.*

Ps. 22. 6. I am a *w.*, and no man.

Is. 14. 11. the *w.* is spread under thee.

41. 14. fear not, thou *w.* Jacob.

66. 24; Mk. 9. 44, 46, 48. their *w.* shall not die.

Acts 12. 23. eaten of *w.*

Wormwood, Deut. 29. 18. a root that beareth *w.*

Jer. 9. 15; 23. 15. feed them with *w.*

Amos 5. 7. who turn judgment to *w.*

Rev. 8. 11. name of star is called *W.*

Worse, 2 Ki. 14. 12; 1 Chr. 19. 16; 2 Chr. 6. 24. put to the *w.*   [than first.

Matt. 12. 45; 27. 64; Lk. 11. 26. last state *w.*

John 5. 14. lest a *w.* thing come unto thee.

1 Cor. 11. 17. not for the better, but for the *w.*

2 Tim. 3. 13. shall wax *w.* and *w.*

2 Pet. 2. 20. the latter end is *w.* with them.

Worship, 1 Chr. 16. 29; Ps. 29. 2; 96. 9. *w.* the Lord in beauty of holiness.

Ps. 81. 9. neither *w.* any strange god.

95. 6. let us *w.* and bow down.

97. 7. *w.* him, all ye gods.

99. 5. *w.* at his footstool.

Is. 27. 13. shall *w.* the Lord in holy mount.

Zeph. 1. 5. that *w.* the host of heaven.

Matt. 4. 9; Lk. 4. 7. if thou wilt *w.* me.

Matt. 15. 9. in vain they do *w.* me.

John 4. 20. the place where men ought to *w.*

4. 22. ye *w.* ye know not what.   [truth.

4. 24. that *w.* him must *w.* in spirit and truth.

Acts 17. 23. whom ye ignorantly *w.*

24. 14. so *w.* I the God of my fathers.

Rom. 1. 25. *w.* the creature more than the Creator.

1 Cor. 14. 25. falling down, he will *w.* God.

Heb. 1. 6. let angels of God *w.* him.

Rev. 4. 10. *w.* him that liveth for ever.

Worth, Job 24. 25. make speech nothing *w.*

Prov. 10. 20. heart of wicked little *w.*

Ezek. 30. 2. woe *w.* the day!   [mercies.

Worthy, Gen. 32. 10. I am not *w.* of thy

1 Ki. 1. 52. show himself a *w.* man.

Matt. 3. 11. whose shoes I am not *w.* to bear.

8. 8; Lk. 7. 6. I am not *w.* thou shouldest come under my roof.

Matt. 10. 10. the workman is *w.* of his meat.

10. 37. that loveth father more than me is not *w.* of me.

22. 8. they which were bidden were not *w.*

Mk. 1. 7; Lk. 3. 16; John 1. 27. I am not *w.* to unloose.

Lk. 3. 8. fruits *w.* of repentance.

7. 7. neither thought I myself *w.*   [hire.

10. 7; 1 Tim. 5. 18. the labourer is *w.* of his

Lk. 15. 19. no more *w.* to be called thy son.

20. 35. accounted *w.* to obtain that world.

Acts 24. 2. very *w.* deeds are done by thee.

Rom. 8. 18. not *w.* to be compared with the glory.

Eph. 4. 1; Col. 1. 10; 1 Thes. 2. 12. walk *w.*

1 Tim. 1. 15; 4. 9. *w.* of all acceptation.

Heb. 10. 29. of how much sorer punishment shall he be thought *w.?*

11. 38. of whom the world was not *w.*

Jas. 2. 7. that *w.* name.

Rev. 3. 4. they are *w.*

4. 11; 5. 12. thou art *w.* to receive glory.

Would, Ps. 81. 11. Israel *w.* none of me.

Prov. 1. 25. ye *w.* none of my reproof.

1. 30. they *w.* none of my counsel.   [men.

Matt. 7. 12; Lk. 6. 31. whatsoever ye *w.* that

Rom. 7. 15. what I *w.*, that do I not.

7. 19. the good that I *w.* I do not.

Gal. 5. 17. cannot do the things that ye *w.*

Rev. 3. 15. I *w.* thou wert cold or hot.

Wound, Ex. 21. 25. give *w.* for *w.*

Job 34. 6. my *w.* is incurable.

Ps. 147. 3. he bindeth up their *w.*

Prov. 20. 30. blueness of a *w.* cleanseth.

27. 6. faithful are the *w.* of a friend.

Is. 1. 6. no soundness, but *w.* and bruises.

Jer. 15. 18. why is my *w.* incurable?

30. 12; Nah. 3. 19. thy *w.* is grievous.

Zech. 13. 6. what are these *w.* in thy hands?

Lk. 10. 34. bound up his *w.*

Rev. 13. 3. his *w.* was healed.

Wound, Deut. 32. 39. I *w.*, and I heal.

Job 5. 18. he *w.*, and his hands make whole.

Ps. 68. 21. God shall *w.* his enemies.

109. 22. my heart is *w.* within me.

Prov. 18. 14. a *w.* spirit who can bear?

Is. 53. 5. he was *w.* for our transgressions.

Hab. 3. 13. thou *w.* head of the wicked.

Wrap, Is. 28. 20. covering narrower than he can *w.* himself in it.

Mic. 7. 3. so they *w.* it up.   [body.

Matt. 27. 59; Mk. 15. 46; Lk. 23. 53. *w.* the

Wrath, Gen. 49. 7. cursed be their *w.*

Num. 16. 46. there is *w.* gone out from the Lord.   [the enemy.

Deut. 32. 27. were it not I feared the *w.* of

Job 5. 2. *w.* killeth the foolish man.

21. 20. drink of *w.* of the Almighty.

36. 18. because there is *w.*, beware.

Ps. 76. 10. the *w.* of man shall praise thee.

90. 7. by thy *w.* are we troubled.

95. 11. to whom I sware in my *w.*

Prov. 15. 1. soft answer turneth away *w.*

16. 14. *w.* of a king is as messengers of death.

27. 4. *w.* is cruel, and anger outrageous.

Wrath—*Continued.*
Eccl. 5. 17. much *w.* with his sickness.
Is. 54. 8. in a little *w.* I hid my face.
Hab. 3. 2. in *w.* remember mercy.
Matt. 3. 7 ; Lk. 3. 7. from the *w.* to come.
Rom. 2. 5. treasurest up *w.* against day of *w.*
12. 19. rather give place to *w.*
Eph. 4. 26. let not sun go down on your *w.*
6. 4. fathers, provoke not your children to *w.*
Col. 3. 8. put off these, *w.*, malice.
1 Thes. 1. 10. delivered us from *w.* to come.
5. 9. God hath not appointed us to *w.*
1 Tim. 2. 8. lifting up holy hands without *w.*
Jas. 1. 19. slow to speak, slow to *w.*
Rev. 6. 16. hide us from *w.* of the Lamb.
Wrest, Ex. 23. 2. to *w.* judgment.
Deut. 16. 19. thou shalt not *w.* judgment.
Ps. 56. 5. every day they *w.* my words.
2 Pet. 3. 16. they that are unstable *w.*
Wrestle, Gen. 32. 24. there *w.* a man with him.
Eph. 6. 12. we *w.* not against flesh.
Wretched, Rom. 7. 24. O *w.* man that I am !
Rev. 3. 17. knowest not thou art *w.*
Wring, Jud. 6. 38. Gideon *w.* dew out of fleece.
Ps. 75. 8. wicked shall *w.* them out.
Prov. 30. 33. *w.* of nose bringeth blood.
Wrinkle, Job 16. 8. thou hast filled me with *w.*
Eph. 5. 27. not having spot or *w.*
Write, Deut.6.9; 11.20. *w.* them on posts of house.
Prov. 3. 3 ; 7. 3. *w.* on table of thy heart.
Is. 10. 19. that a child may *w.* them.
Jer. 22. 30. *w.* this man childless.
31. 33 ; Heb. 8. 10. I will *w.* law in their hearts.
Hab. 2. 2. *w.* the vision on tables.
John 19. 21. *w.* not, the King of the Jews.
Rev. 3. 12. I will *w.* on him my new name.
Written, Ex. 31. 18. *w.* with the finger of God.
Job 19. 23. oh that my words were *w.* !
Ps. 69. 28. let them not be *w.* with righteous.
102. 18. *w.* for the generation to come.
Prov. 22. 20. have not I *w.* excellent things ?
Eccl. 12. 10. that which was *w.* was upright.
Ezek. 2. 10. roll *w.* within and without.
Dan. 5. 24. the writing was *w.*
Matt. 27. 37. set up his accusation *w.*
John 19. 22. what I have *w.*, I have *w.*
1 Cor. 10. 11. *w.* for our admonition.
2 Cor. 3. 2. ye are our epistle *w.* in our hearts.
1 Pet. 1. 16. it is *w.*, be ye holy.
Wrong, Ex. 2. 13. to him that did the *w.*
Deut. 19. 16. to testify what is *w.*
1 Chr. 12. 17. there is no *w.* in mine hands.
16. 21 ; Ps. 105. 14. he suffered no man to do them *w.*
Job 19. 7. I cry out of *w.*, but am not heard.
Jer. 22. 3. do no *w.*, do no violence.
Matt. 20. 13. friend, I do thee no *w.*
Acts 18. 14. a matter of *w.*
1 Cor. 6. 7. why do ye not take *w.*?
Col. 3. 25. doeth *w.* shall receive for the *w.*
Wronged, 2 Cor. 7. 2. we have *w.* no man.
Philem. 18. if he hath *w.* thee.
Wrongfully, Job 21. 27. devices ye *w.* imagine.
Ps. 69. 4. being mine enemies *w.*
1 Pet. 2. 19. suffering *w.*
Wrote, Ex. 24. 4 ; Deut. 31. 9. Moses *w.* all the words of the Lord.
Dan. 5. 5. man's hand *w.* on the wall.
John 8. 6. with his finger *w.* on the ground.
2 John 5. though I *w.* a new commandment.
Wroth, Gen. 4. 6. Lord said, why art thou *w.*?
Deut. 1. 34 ; 3. 26 ; 9. 19 ; 2 Sam. 22. 8 ; 2 Chr. 28. 9 ; Ps. 18. 7 ; 78. 21. Lord heard your words, and was *w.*

Wroth—*Continued.*
2 Ki. 5. 11. Naaman was *w.*
13. 19. man of God was *w.* with him.
Ps. 89. 38. hast been *w.* with thine anointed.
Is. 47. 6. I was *w.* with my people.
54. 9. I have sworn I would not be *w.*
57. 16. neither will I be always *w.*
64. 9. be not *w.* very sore, O Lord.
Lam. 5. 22. thou art very *w.* against us.
Matt. 18. 34. his lord was *w.*
22. 7. the king was *w.*
Wrought, Num. 23. 23. what hath God *w.* !
1 Sam. 6. 6. God had *w.* wonderfully.
11. 13 ; 19. 5. Lord *w.* salvation in Israel.
Neh. 4. 17. every one *w.* in the work.
6. 16. this work was *w.* of God.
Job 12. 9. the hand of the Lord hath *w.* this.
36. 23. who can say, thou hast *w.* iniquity?
Ps. 31. 19. hast *w.* for them that trust in thee.
68. 28. strengthen that which thou hast *w.* for us.   [earth.
139. 15. curiously *w.* in lowest parts of the
Eccl. 2. 17. work *w.* under the sun.
Is. 26. 12. thou hast *w.* all our works in us.
41. 4. who hath *w.* and done it?
Ezek. 20. 9. I *w.* for my name's sake.   [me.
Dan. 4. 2. the wonders God hath *w.* toward
Jon. 1. 11. the sea *w.*, and was tempestuous.
Matt. 20. 12. these last have *w.* but one hour.
26. 10 ; Mk. 14. 6. hath *w.* a good work on me.
John 3. 21. manifest, that they are *w.* in God.
Acts 15. 12. what wonders God had *w.*
18. 3. he abode with them, and *w.*
Rom. 15. 18. things which Christ hath not *w.* by me.   [thing is God.
2 Cor. 5. 5. he that hath *w.* us for the selfsame
Gal. 2. 8. he that *w.* effectually.
Eph. 1. 20. which he *w.* in Christ.
Heb. 11. 33. through faith *w.* righteousness.
Jas. 2. 22. how faith *w.* with his works.
1 Pet. 4. 3. to have *w.* the will of the Gentiles.
2 John 8. lose not those things we have *w.*
Wrung, Lev. 1. 15 ; 5. 9. blood shall be *w.* out.
Ps. 73. 10. waters of cup *w.* to them.
Is. 51. 17. hast *w.* out dregs of cup.

YEA, Matt. 5. 37 ; Jas. 5. 12. let your communication be *y.*, *y.*   [nay.
2 Cor. 1. 17. there should be *y. y.*, and nay
1. 20. promises of God in him are *y.*
Year, Gen. 1. 14. for seasons, days, and *y.*
47. 9. few and evil have the *y.* of my life been.
Ex. 13. 10. keep this ordinance from *y.* to *y.*
Lev. 16. 34. make atonement once a *y.*
25. 5. a *y.* of rest.   [by *y.*
Deut. 14. 22. thou shalt tithe the increase *y.*
32. 7. consider the *y.* of many generations.
1 Sam. 7. 16. went from *y.* to *y.* in circuit.
Job 10. 5. are thy *y.* as man's days?
16. 22. when a few *y.* are come.
32. 7. multitude of *y.* should teach wisdom.
36. 26. neither can the number of his *y.* be searched out.
Ps. 31. 10. my *y.* are spent with sighing.
61. 6. prolong his *y.* as many generations.
65. 11. thou crownest *y.* with thy goodness.
77. 10. *y.* of the right hand of the Most High.
78. 33. their *y.* did he consume in trouble.
90. 4 ; 2 Pet. 3. 8. a thousand *y.* in thy sight.
Ps. 90. 9. we spend our *y.* as a tale that is told.   [and ten.
90. 10. the days of our *y.* are threescore *y.*
102. 24. *y.* are throughout all generations.
102. 27. thy *y.* shall have no end.

Year—*Continued.*
Prov. 4. 10. the *y.* of thy life shall be many.
10. 27. *y.* of the wicked shall be shortened.
Eccl. 12. 1. nor the *y.* draw nigh.
Is. 21. 16. according to the *y.* of an hireling.
29. 1. add ye *y.* to *y.*
61.2 ; Lk. 4. 19. the acceptable *y.* of the Lord.
Is. 63. 4. the *y.* of my redeemed is come.
Jer. 11. 23 ; 23. 12 ; 48. 44. *y.* of their visitation.
17. 8. not be careful in *y.* of drought.
28. 16. this *y.* thou shalt die.
Ezek. 22. 4. thou art come unto thy *y.*
46. 17. it shall be his to the *y.* of liberty.
Joel 2. 2. the *y.* of many generations.
Hab. 3. 2. revive thy work in midst of the *y.*
Lk. 13. 8. let it alone this *y.* also.
Gal. 4. 10. ye observe months and *y.*
Heb. 1. 12. thy *y.* shall not fail.
Jas. 4. 13. continue there a *y.*, and buy.
Yesterday, Job 8. 9. we are of *y.*, and know
nothing.
Heb. 12. 8. Christ the same *y.*, and for ever.
Yield, Gen. 4. 12. ground not *y.* her strength.
Lev. 19. 25. that it may *y.* the increase.
26. 4 ; Ps. 67. 6 ; 85. 12. the land shall *y.* her
increase.
2 Chr. 30. 8. *y.* yourselves to the Lord.
Ps. 107. 37. vineyards, which may *y.* fruits.
Eccl. 10. 4. *y.* pacifieth great offences.
Hos. 8. 7. the bud shall *y.* no meal.
Joel 2. 22. fig tree and vine *y.* their strength.
Hab. 3. 17. though fields shall *y.* no meat.
Matt. 27. 50. Jesus *y.* up the ghost.
Acts 23. 21. do not thou *y.* to them.
Rom. 6. 13. *y.* yourselves to God.
6. 19. *y.* your members to righteousness.
Heb. 12. 11. it *y.* the peaceable fruit of
righteousness.   [fresh.
Jas. 3. 12. no fountain can *y.* salt water and
Yoke, Gen. 27. 40 ; Jer. 30. 8. break his *y.*
Num. 19. 2 ; Deut. 21. 3 ; 1 Sam. 6. 7. on which
never came *y.*
Deut. 28. 48. he shall put a *y.* on thy neck.
1 Ki. 12. 4. thy father made our *y.* grievous.
Is. 9. 4 ; 10. 27 ; 14. 25. thou hast broken the
y. of his burden.
58. 6. that ye break every *y.*
Jer. 2. 20. of old time I have broken thy *y.*
31. 18. as a bullock unaccustomed to the *y.*
Lam. 3. 27. it is good to bear the *y.* in youth.
Hos. 11. 4. as they that take off the *y.*
Matt. 11. 29. take my *y.* upon you.
11. 30. for my *y.* is easy.
Lk. 14. 19. I have bought five *y.* of oxen.
Acts 15.10. to put a *y.* on neck of the disciples.
Gal. 5.1. be not entangled with *y.* of bondage.
Phil. 4. 3. I entreat thee, true *y.*-fellow.
1 Tim. 6. 1. as many as are under the *y.*
Yonder, Gen. 22. 5. I and the lad will go *y.*
Num. 23. 15. while I meet the Lord *y.*
Matt. 17. 20. say, remove to *y.* place.
You, 1 Chr. 22. 18. is not the Lord with *y.*?
2 Chr. 15. 2. the Lord is with *y.*, while ye be
with him.
Jer. 42. 11 ; Hag. 1. 13 ; 2. 4. I am with *y.*
Amos 3. 2. *y.* only have I known.
Matt. 28. 20. I am with *y.* alway.
Lk. 10. 16. he that heareth *y.* heareth me.
13. 28. and *y.* yourselves thrust out.
1 Cor. 6. 11. such were some of *y.*
2 Cor. 12. 14. I seek not yours, but *y.*
Eph. 2. 1 ; Col. 2. 13. *y.* hath he quickened.
Col. 1. 27. Christ in *y.*
1 John 4. 4. greater is he that is in *y.*

Young, Deut. 28. 50. not show favour to the *y.*
32. 11. as an eagle fluttereth over her *y.*
Job 38. 41. when his *y.* ones cry to God.
Ps. 37. 25. I have been *y.*, and now am old.
84. 3. a nest where she may lay her *y.*
147. 9. he giveth food to the *y.* ravens.
Is. 11. 7. their *y.* ones shall lie down together.
40. 11. gently lead those that are with *y.*
John 21. 18. when *y.* thou girdest thyself.
Tit. 2. 4. teach *y.* women to be sober.
Younger, Gen. 25. 23. the elder shall serve the *y.*
Job 30.1.they that are *y.*, have me in derision.
Lk. 22. 26. he that is greatest, let him be as *y.*
1 Tim. 5. 1. intreat the *y.* men as brethren.
1 Pet. 5. 5. ye *y.*, submit yourselves to the
elder.
Yours, 2 Chr. 20. 15. the battle is not *y.*, but
God's.
Lk. 6. 20. for *y.* is the kingdom of God.
1 Cor. 3. 21. all things are *y.*   [his *y.*
Youth, Gen. 8. 21. imagination is evil from
1 Sam. 17. 33. a man of war from his *y.*
2 Sam.19.7.all evil that befell thee from thy *y.*
1 Ki. 18. 12. I fear the Lord from my *y.*
Job 13. 26. to possess the iniquities of my *y.*
29. 4. as I was in days of my *y.*
30. 12. on my right hand rise the *y.*
33. 25. he shall return to the days of his *y.*
36. 14. hypocrites die in *y.*
Ps. 25. 7. remember not the sins of my *y.*
71. 5. thou art my trust from my *y.*
71. 17. thou hast taught me from my *y.*
89. 45. days of his *y.* hast thou shortened.
103. 5. thy *y.* is renewed like the eagle's.
110. 3. thou hast the dew of thy *y.*
129. 1. they have afflicted me from my *y.*
144. 12. as plants grown up in *y.*
Prov. 2. 17. forsaketh the guide of her *y.*
5. 18. rejoice with the wife of thy *y.*
Eccl. 11. 9. rejoice, young man, in thy *y.*
11. 10. childhood and *y.* are vanity.
12. 1. remember thy Creator in days of *y.*
Is. 40. 30. even the *y.* shall faint.
Jer. 2. 2. the kindness of thy *y.*
3. 4. thou art the guide of my *y.*
48. 11. been at ease from his *y.*
Hos. 2. 15. sing, as in the days of her *y.*
Matt. 19. 20 ; Mk. 10. 20 ; Lk. 18. 21. these
have I kept from my *y.*
1 Tim. 4. 12. let no man despise thy *y.*
See 2 Tim. 2. 22.

ZEAL, 2 Ki. 10. 16. see my *z.* for the Lord.
19. 31 ; Is. 37. 32. *z.* of the Lord shall do this.
Ps. 69. 9 ; John 2. 17. the *z.* of thine house.
Ps. 119. 139. my *z.* hath consumed me.
Is. 9. 7. the *z.* of the Lord will perform this.
59. 17. clad with *z.* as a cloak.
63. 15. where is thy *z.*?
Ezek. 5. 13. I the Lord have spoken it in my *z.*
Rom. 10. 2. they have a *z.* of God.
2 Cor. 7. 11. yea what *z.*!
9. 2. your *z.* hath provoked very many.
Phil. 3. 6. concerning *z.*, persecuting church.
Col. 4. 13. he hath a great *z.* for you.
Zealous, Num. 25. 11. he was *z.* for my sake.
Acts 21. 20. they are all *z.* of the law.
22. 3 ; Gal. 1. 14. *z.* towards God.
1 Cor. 14. 12. as ye are *z.* of spiritual gifts.
Tit. 2. 14. people, *z.* of good works.
Rev. 3. 19. be *z.* therefore, and repent.
Zealously, Gal. 4. 17. they *z.* affect you, but
not well.
4. 18. good to be *z.* affected in a good thing.

AN INDEX

OF

PERSONS, PLACES AND SUBJECTS

IN THE

HOLY BIBLE

Aaron, brother of Moses, the first High Priest.
appointed to assist Moses, Ex. 4. 14, 16, 27.
with Moses before Pharaoh, Ex. 5. 1.
his rod becomes a serpent, Ex. 7. 10.
changes the waters into blood, Ex. 7. 20;
causes the plagues of frogs, lice, flies, Ex. 8. 5, 17, 24; of boils, Ex. 9. 10.
along with Hur holds up Moses' hands, Ex. 17. 12.
set apart for the priest's office, Ex. 28.
his sin in making the golden calf, Ex. 32.
spared at Moses' intercession, Deut. 9. 20.
consecration, Ex. 29; Lev. 8.
his duties, to offer sacrifice, Ex. 30. 7; Lev. 9.
his sons (Nadab and Abihu) offer strange fire and die, Lev. 10. 1; Num. 3. 4.
not to drink wine, when going into the tabernacle, Lev. 10. 8.
his sons (Eleazar and Ithamar) censured by Moses, Lev. 10. 16.
his sedition against Moses, Num. 12.
spoken against by Korah, Num. 16. 3.
makes atonement, and the plague is stayed, Num. 16. 46-48.
his rod buds, Num. 17. 8.
excluded from the promised land, Num. 20. 12.
dies on Mount Hor, Num. 20. 28.
his descendants, 1 Chr. 6. 49.
chosen by God, Ps. 105. 26; Heb. 5. 4.
his priesthood inferior to Christ's, Heb. 5; 7. See Ps. 77. 20; 99. 6; 106. 16; Acts 7. 40; Heb. 9. 4.
Abaddon (Apollyon), angel of the bottomless pit, Rev. 9. 11.
Abana and Pharpar, rivers of Damascus, 2. Ki. 5. 12.
Abarim, mountains of, including Nebo, Pisgah, Hor, Num. 27. 12; Deut. 32. 49.
Abba, Father, Mk. 14. 36; Rom. 8. 15; Gal. 4. 6.
Abdon (a judge), Jud. 12. 13.
Abed-nego, one of the three Hebrew captives, Dan. 1. 7.
saved in the fiery furnace, Dan. 3.
Abel, the second son of Adam, his occupation, his offering, his murder, Gen. 4.
righteous, Matt. 23. 35; 1 John 3. 12.
blood of, Lk. 11. 51; Heb. 12. 24.
his faith, Heb. 11. 4.
Abel—Mizraim, mourning of the Egyptians, Gen. 50. 11.
—Shittim, Num. 33. 49.
—Meholah, 1 Ki. 4. 12; 19. 16.

Abiathar, the priest, escapes Saul's vengeance, 1 Sam. 22. 20.
faithful to David, 1 Sam. 23. 6; 30. 7; 2 Sam. 15. 24.
follows Adonijah, 1 Ki. 1. 7.
deposed by Solomon, 1 Ki. 2. 26.
Abib, the Hebrew passover month, Ex. 13. 4; 23. 15; 34. 18.
Abiezer, ancestor of Gideon, Josh. 17. 2; Jud. 6.
Abigail, wife of Nabal, her character, 1 Sam. 25. 3.
becomes David's wfe, 1 Sam. 25. 39.
Abihu, son of Aaron, offers strange fire, and dies, Lev. 10. 2.
Abijah (or Abijam) king of Judah, his evil reign, 1 Ki. 15. 1.
his wars with Jeroboam, 2 Chr. 13.
—(son of Jeroboam), his death foretold, 1 Ki. 14.
Abimelech (king of Gerar), reproved by God about Abraham's wife, Gen. 20. 3; restores her, Gen. 20. 14.
—(another) Isaac rebuked by, and makes a covenant with, Gen. 26.
—son of Gideon, Jud. 8. 31; slays his brethren, and is made king, Jud. 9. 5, 6.
his cruelty, Jud. 9. 48; his death, Jud. 9. 54.
Abinadab receives the ark from the Philistines, 1 Sam. 7. 1; 2 Sam. 6. 3.
Abiram rebels against Moses, Num. 16.
his punishment, Num. 16. 31; 26. 10.
Abishag, the Shunammite, ministers to David, 1 Ki. 1. 3; Adonijah slain on her account, 1 Ki. 2. 25.
Abishai, brother of Joab, 1 Chr. 2. 16.
prevented from slaying Saul, 1 Sam. 26. 9.
and Shimei, 2 Sam. 16. 9; 19. 21;
his valiant deeds, 2 Sam. 21. 17; 23. 18; 1 Chr. 11. 20; 18. 12.
Abner, cousin of Saul, commander of his army, 1 Sam. 14. 50.
taunted by David, 1 Sam. 26. 5, 14.
makes Ish-bosheth king, 2 Sam. 2. 8.
goes over to David, 2 Sam. 3. 8.
treacherously slain by Joab, 2 Sam. 3. 27.
lamented by David, 2 Sam. 3. 31.
Abomination of offerings, Lev. 7. 18; Deut. 17. 1; 23. 18; Prov. 15. 8; Is. 1. 13; 41. 24.
defilement, Deut. 24. 4; Prov. 16. 12; Is. 66 17; Ezek. 16; Rev. 21. 27.
idolatry, Deut. 7. 25, 26; 27. 15; 1 Ki. 11. 5; 2 Ki. 23. 13; Ezek. 18. 12; Mal. 2. 11.
pride and falsity, Prov. 3. 32; 6. 16; 11. 20; 16. 5; 11. 1; 17. 15; 20. 10, 23.

Abomination of the heathen censured, Lev. 18. 26; Deut. 18. 9; 1 Ki. 14. 24; Rom. 1. 18; Col. 5. 3.

of Jerusalem described, Is. 1; 3; Jer. 2; Ezek. 5. 11; 7; 8; 11; 16; 23; Hos. 1.

prayer of the wicked, Prov. 28. 9.

of desolation foretold, Dan. 11. 31; 12. 11; Matt. 24. 15; Mk. 13. 14.

Abraham (Abram) born, Gen. 11. 27.

called by God, and sent to Canaan, Gen. 12. 1-5.

goes down to Egypt, Gen. 12. 10.

makes his wife pass for his sister, Gen. 12. 13; 20. 2.

dispute with and separation from Lot, Gen. 13. 7-11.

receives the promise, Gen. 13. 14; 15. 5.

rescues Lot from captivity, Gen. 14. 14.

blessed by Melchizedek, king of Salem, Gen. 14. 19; Heb. 7. 1.

his faith counted for righteousness, Gen. 15. 6.

God's covenant with him, Gen. 15. 18; 17; Ps. 105. 9.

he and his household circumcised, Gen. 17.

entertains angels, Gen. 18.

pleads for Sodom, Gen. 18. 23.

dismisses Hagar and Ishmael, Gen. 21. 14.

his faith in offering Isaac, Gen. 22.

purchases Machpelah for a burying-place, Gen. 23.

sends for a wife for his son, Gen. 24.

invests Isaac with all his goods, Gen. 25. 5.

death, Gen. 25. 8.

his posterity, Gen. 25. 1.

testimonies to his faith and works, Is. 41. 8; 51. 2; John 8. 31; Acts 7. 2; Rom. 4; Gal. 3. 6; Heb. 11. 8; Jas. 2. 21-24.

Absalom, son of David, 2 Sam. 3. 3.

slays Amnon, 2 Sam. 13. 28.

conspires against David, 2 Sam. 15.

David flees from, 2 Sam. 15. 17.

caught by hair in an oak, 2 Sam. 18. 9.

slain by Joab, 2 Sam. 18. 14.

lamented by David, 2 Sam. 18. 33; 19. 1.

Access to God by faith, Rom. 5. 2; Eph. 2. 18; 3. 12; Heb. 7. 19; 10. 19.

See Isa. 55. 6; Hos. 14. 2; Joel 2. 12; John 14. 6; Jas. 4. 8.

its blessedness, Ps. 65. 4; 73. 28; Is. 2. 3; Jer. 31. 6.

See *Prayer*.

Accursed, what so called, Deut. 21. 23; Josh. 6. 17; 7. 1; 1 Chr. 2. 7; Isa. 65. 20; Gal. 1. 18.

Aceldama, field of blood, Matt. 27. 8; Acts 1. 18.

Achaia, Paul in, Acts 18.

contribution for poor made by those of, Rom. 15. 26; 2 Cor. 9. 2.

See 1 Cor. 16. 15; 2 Cor. 11. 10.

Achan, his trespass and punishment, Josh. 7. 22. 20; 1 Chr. 2. 7.

Achish, king of Gath, succours David, 1 Sam. 21; 10; 27. 2; 28. 1; 29. 6.

See 1 Kings, 2. 39.

Achor, valley of, Achan slain there, Josh. 7. 26. See Hos. 2. 15.

Achsah, Caleb's daughter, Josh. 15. 16; Jud. 1. 13-15.

Adam, created, Gen. 1, and blessed, Gen. 1. 28.

placed in Eden, Gen. 2. 8.

creatures named by, Gen. 2. 20.

ADAM—*Continued*.

his disobedience and punishment, Gen. 3.

hides from God, Gen. 3. 8.

his death, Gen. 5. 5.

his transgression referred to, Job 31. 33; Rom. 5. 14.

first Adam, 1 Cor. 15. 45; 1 Tim. 2. 13.

in, all die, 1 Cor. 15. 22.

the last, 1 Cor. 15. 45.

Addan, a city of the captivity, Ezra 2. 59; Neh. 7. 61.

Admah, city of the plain, destroyed, Gen. 19; Deut. 29. 23; Hos. 11. 8.

Admonish, Jer. 42. 19; Eccl. 4. 13; 12. 12; Acts 27. 9; Rom. 15. 14; Col. 3. 16; 1 Thes. 5. 12; 2 Thes. 3. 15.

Admonition, 1 Cor. 10. 11; Eph. 6. 4; Tit. 3. 10.

Adoni-Bezek, Jud. 1. 5.

Adonijah, fourth son of David, usurps the kingdom, 1 Ki. 1. 5.

is pardoned by Solomon, 1 Ki. 1. 53.

requesting Abishag in marriage, is slain, 1 Ki. 2. 17-25.

Adoni-Zedek, king of Jerusalem, resists Joshua, Josh. 10. 1.

his death, Josh. 10. 26.

Adoption of the children of God described, John 1. 12; 20. 17; Rom. 8. 14; 2 Cor. 6.18; Gal. 4; Eph. 1. 5; Heb. 2. 10; 12. 5; Jas. 1. 18; 1 John 3.

of the Gentiles, Is. 66. 19; Hos. 2. 23; Acts 15. 3; Rom. 8. 15; 9. 24; Gal. 4. 5; Eph. 1. 5; 2; 3; Col. 1. 27.

Adullam, cave of, David's sojourn there, 1 Sam. 22. 1; 1 Chr. 11. 15.

Adultery forbidden, Ex. 20. 14; Deut. 5. 18; Matt. 5. 27; 19. 18; Rom. 13. 9; Gal. 5. 19; Heb. 13. 4.

penalty of, Lev. 20. 10; 1 Cor. 6. 9.

instances of, 2 Sam. 11. 2; Mk. 6. 18; John 8. 3.

in what it consists, Matt. 5. 28; 15. 19; 19. 9; Mk. 7. 21; 10. 11.

spiritual, Jer. 3; 13. 27; Ezek. 16; 23; Hos. 1; 2; Rev. 2. 22.

Adversary, Ex. 23. 22; Matt. 5. 25; 1 Tim. 5. 14.

the devil, resist, 1 Pet. 5. 8, 9.

Adversity, Ps. 31. 7; Heb. 13. 3.

Advocate (Christ) of the Church, 1 John 2. 1.

Aeneas, healing of, Acts 9. 33.

Aenon, John baptizes there, John 3. 23.

Affection to God's house, 1 Chr. 29. 3; Ps. 26. 8; 84.

to God, Ps. 42. 1; 73. 25; 91. 14; 119.

set on things above, Col. 3. 2.

worldly affections to be mortified, Rom. 8. 13; 13. 14; 1 Cor. 9. 27; Gal. 5. 16, 24; 2 Pet. 2. 10.

Afflicted, our duty towards the, Job 6. 14; Ps. 82. 3; Prov. 22. 22; 1 Tim. 5. 10; Jas. 1. 27; 5. 13.

Affliction, the consequence of sin, 2 Sam. 12. 14; Job 4. 8; Ps. 90. 7; Prov. 1. 31; Ezek. 6. 13; Rom. 5. 12.

man born to, Job 5. 6, 7; 14. 1.

foretold, Gen. 15. 13; Is. 10. 12; Jer. 29. 17; 42. 16; Ezek. 20. 37.

sent from God, Num. 14. 33; 2 Ki. 6. 33; Job 10. 15; Ps. 66. 11; Is. 9. 1.

sent in mercy, Gen. 50. 20; Ex. 1. 12; Deut. 8. 16; Ps. 30. 5; 106. 43-44; 119. 75; Is. 54. 7; Ezek. 20. 37; Nah. 1. 12; Matt. 24. 9; John 16. 20, 33; Acts 20. 23; Rom. 8. 18; 2 Cor. 4. 17; Heb. 12. 6; Jas. 5. 10; 1 Pet. 1. 6; 4. 13; Rev. 3. 19; 7. 14.

AFFLICTION—*Continued.*
promises of support under, Ps. 27. 5; 46. 5;
Is. 25. 4; 43. 2; 49. 13; 63. 9; Jer. 16. 19; 59.
17; Nah. 1. 7; Matt. 11. 28; John 14; 2
Cor. 1. 4; Heb. 2. 18; 12; Rev. 3. 10.
comfort under, Is. 61. 2; Jer. 31. 13; Matt. 5.
4; Lk. 7. 13; 2 Cor. 7. 6.
object of, 1 Cor. 11. 32; 1 Pet. 5. 10.
behaviour under, 1 Sam. 1. 11; 3. 18; 2 Sam.
12. 16; 2 Kings 20. 1; Neh. 9. 3; Job 1. 21;
2.10; 5. 17; 13. 15; 34. 31; Ps. 18. 6; 27. 4;
39. 9; 50. 15; 55. 16, 22; 56. 3; 66. 13; 71. 14;
Prov. 3. 11, 12; Jer. 50. 4; Lam. 3. 39; Hos.
6. 1; Mic. 7. 9; Lk. 15. 17; 21. 19; Rom. 12.
12; 2 Cor. 1. 9; 1 Thes. 4.13; 2 Thes. 1. 4;
Heb. 12. 1; James 1. 4; 5. 11; 1 Pet. 2. 20.
supplication under, Judges 4. 3; 1 Sam. 1.
10; 2 Sam. 24. 10; 2 Ki. 19. 16; 2 Ch. 14. 11;
20. 6; Ezra 9. 6; Neh. 9. 32; Job. 10. 2; 13.
23; 33. 26; Ps. 66. 13; Jer. 17. 13; 31. 18;
Lam. 5. 1; Dan. 9; Hab. 3. 2; Matt. 26. 39;
2 Cor. 12. 8; James 5. 13.
deliverance from, Ps. 34. 4, 19; 40. 2; Prov.
12. 13; Is. 63. 9; Jonah 2. 1, 2; 2 Tim. 3. 11;
4. 17, 18.
benefits of, Job 23. 10; 36. 8; Ps. 66. 10; 119.
67, 71; Eccl. 7. 2; Is. 26. 9; 48. 10; Lam. 3.
19, 27, 39; Ezek. 14. 11; Hos. 5. 15; Mic. 6.
9; Zech. 13. 9; John 15. 2; Acts 14. 22;
Rom. 5. 3; Phil. 1. 12; Heb. 12. 10; 1. 3, 12;
1 Pet. 1. 7.
Agabus foretells a famine, Acts 11. 28.
and Paul's suffering at Jerusalem, Acts 21. 10.
Agag, king of Amalek, spared by Saul, but
slain by Samuel, 1 Sam. 15.
spoken of by Balaam, Num. 24. 7.
Agate, Ex. 28. 19; Is. 54. 12.
Agony of Christ in the garden, Matt. 26. 36;
Lk. 22. 44, etc.
Agrippa, Paul's defence before, Acts 25. 22; 26.
his respective decisions, Acts 26. 28, 32.
Agur, his confession and instructions, Prov. 30.
Ahab, king of Israel, 1 Ki. 16. 29.
marries Jezebel, his idolatry, 1 Ki. 16. 31.
meets Elijah, 1 Ki. 18. 17.
defeats the Syrians, 1 Ki. 20. 13.
condemned for sparing Ben-hadad, 1 Ki.
20. 42.
takes Naboth's vineyard, 1 Ki. 21.
his repentance, 1 Ki. 21. 27.
seduced by false prophets, 1 Ki. 22. 6.
mortally wounded at Ramoth-gilead, 1 Ki.
22. 34; 2 Chr. 18.
a false prophet, Jer. 29. 21.
Ahasuerus, king of Persia, Est. 1. 1.
divorces Vashti, Est. 1. 21.
makes Esther queen, Est. 2. 17.
advances Haman, Est. 3.
his decree to destroy the Jews, Est. 3. 12
rewards Mordecai for his loyalty, Est. 6.
hangs Haman, Est. 7. 9.
advances Mordecai, Est. 9. 4; 10.
Ahaz, king of Judah, his wicked reign,
2 Ki. 16.
profanes the temple, 2 Ki. 16. 17.
afflicted by Pekah, king of Israel, 2 Chr. 28.
comforted by Isaiah, Is. 8.
refuses to ask a sign, Is. 7. 12.
Ahaziah, king of Judah, his wicked reign,
2 Ki. 8. 25.
slain by Jehu, 2 Ki. 9. 27; 2 Chr. 22. 9.
—king of Israel 1 Ki. 22. 40, 49.
his sickness and idolatry, 2 Ki. 1.
his death denounced by Elijah, 2 Ki. 1.

Ahijah prophesies against Solomon, 1 Ki. 11. 31.
prophesies against Jeroboam, and foretells
his son's death, 1 Ki. 14. 7.
Ahikam, 2 Ki. 22. 12.
protects Jeremiah, Jer. 26. 24.
Ahimaaz, son of Zadok, serves David, 2 Sam.
15. 27; 17. 17; 18. 19.
Ahimelech, high priest, slain by Saul's order,
for assisting David, 1 Sam. 22. 18.
Ahithophel, his treachery, 2 Sam. 15. 31;
16. 20.
disgrace and suicide, 2 Sam. 17. 1-23.
See Ps. 41. 9; 55. 12; 109.
Aholah and Aholibah, their abominations
figurative of Samaria and Jerusalem.
Ezek. 23.
Aholiab inspired to construct the tabernacle,
Ex. 35. 34; 36.
Ai, men of, defeat Israel, Josh. 7.
but are subdued, Josh. 8.
Alarm, how to be sounded, Num. 10. 5.
Alexander (and Rufus), Mk. 15. 21.
—a member of the council, Acts 4. 6.
—an Ephesian Jew, Acts 19. 33.
—the coppersmith, 1 Tim. 1. 20; 2 Tim. 4. 14
Allegory (of Hagar), Gal. 4. 24.
Alleluia. See *Hallelujah.*
Allon-Bachuth, oak of weeping, Gen. 35. 8;
1 Ki. 13. 14.
Almighty (God) Gen. 17. 1; Ex. 6. 3; Num. 24.
4; Ruth 1. 20; Job 5. 17; Is. 13. 6; Ezek.
1. 24; Rev. 1. 8.
See God.
Almonds, produced by the rod of Aaron,
Num. 17. 8.
See Jer. 1. 11.
Almsgiving, Matt. 6. 1; Lk. 11. 41; 12. 33.
examples of, Acts 3. 2; 10. 2; 24. 17.
Aloes mentioned, Ps. 45. 8; Cant. 4. 14; John
19. 39.
Alpha, Rev. 1. 8, 11; 21. 6; 22. 13.
Altar erected by Noah, Gen. 8. 20. Abram.
Gen. 12. 7, 8; 13. 4, 18; 22. 9. Isaac, Gen.
26. 25. Jacob, Gen. 33. 20; 35. 7. Moses, Ex.
17. 15. Balaam, Num. 23. 1. Reubenites,
Josh. 22. 10. Saul, 1 Sam. 14. 35. Elijah,
1 Ki. 18. 30-32. Solomon, 2 Chr. 4. 1; of
Damascus, 2 Ki. 16. 10.
Jacob commanded to make, Gen. 35. 1.
how built, of earth, Ex. 20. 24.
„   „   of stone, Ex. 20. 25.
„   „   of wood, Ex. 27. 1.
of incense, Ex. 30. 1; 37. 25.
in the temple, 2 Chr. 4. 1.
golden, Rev. 8. 3; 9. 13.
gift brought to, Matt. 5. 23.
we have an, Heb. 13. 10.
Amalek, Gen. 36. 12.
fights with Israel in Rephidim, and is discomfited, Ex. 17. 8-13.
perpetual war declared against, Ex. 17. 16;
Deut. 25. 17.
smitten by Gideon, Jud. 7. 12.
„   by Saul, 1 Sam. 14. 48; 15. 7, 8.
„   by David, 1 Sam. 27. 9; 30. 17.
Amalekite, self-accused of killing Saul, is
slain, 2 Sam. 1.
Amasa, captain of the host of Absalom, 2
Sam. 17. 25.
treacherously slain by Joab, 2 Sam. 20. 9, 10;
1 Ki. 2. 5.
See 1 Chr. 12. 18.
Amaziah, king of Judah, **2 Ki. 14. 1; 2 Chr.**
25. 1.

173

Amaziah—*Continued.*
defeats Edom, 2 Ki. 14. 7; 2 Chr. 25. 11.
defeated by Joash, king of Israel, 2 Ki. 14. 12; 2; 2 Chr. 25. 21.
slain at Lachish, 2 Ki. 14. 19.
—priest of Bethel, Amos, 7. 10.

Ambassadors sent to Hezekiah, 2 Chr. 32. 31; Is. 39.
apostles so called, 2 Cor. 5. 20.

Amber, Ezek. 1. 4, 27; 8. 2.

Ambition reproved, Gen. 11. 4; Matt. 18. 1; 20. 25; 23. 8; Lk. 22. 24.
punishment of, Prov. 17. 19; Is. 14. 12; Ezek. 31. 10.
of Aaron and Miriam, Num. 12.
Korah, Dathan, and Abiram, Num. 16. 3.
Absalom, 2 Sam. 15-18.
Adonijah, 1 Ki. 1. 5.
Babylon, Jer. 51. 53.
James and John, Matt. 20. 21.
man of sin, 2 Thes. 2. 4.
Diotrephes, 3 John 9.

Ambush, Josh. 8. 4; Jud. 20. 29; 2 Chr. 13. 13; 20. 22.

Amen, true, form of assent, Num. 5. 22; Deut. 27. 15., etc.; 1 Cor. 14. 16; 2 Cor. 1. 20.
Christ so called, Rev. 3. 14.

Amethyst, Ex. 28. 19; Rev. 21. 20.

Ammon, children of, Gen. 19. 38.
their possessions to remain inviolate, Deut. 2. 19.
not to enter the congregation, Deut. 23. 3.
subdued by Jephtah, Jud. 11.
slain by Saul, 1 Sam. 11. 11.
insult David's servants, 2 Sam. 10.
chastised by David, 2 Sam. 12. 26.
prophecies concerning, Jer. 25. 21; 49. 1; Ezek. 21. 28; 25. Amos 1. 13; Zeph. 2. 8.

Amnon, son of David, 2 Sam. 3. 2.
his wickedness and death, 2 Sam. 13.

Amon, king of Judah, his wicked reign, 2 Ki. 21. 21; 2 Chr. 33. 22.
killed by his servants, 2 Ki. 21. 23.

Amorites, dispossessed for their iniquities, Gen. 15. 16; Deut. 20. 17; Josh. 3. 10.

Amos declares God's judgment upon the nations, Amos 1; and upon Israel, Amos 3; 4.
his call, Amos 7. 14, 15.
foretells Israel's restoration, Amos 9. 11.

Anakim (giants), Num. 13. 33; Deut. 9. 2.
cut off by Joshua, Josh. 11. 21.

Ananias (and Sapphira), their sin and death. Acts 5.
—(disciple) sent to Paul at Damascus, Acts 9. 10; 22. 12.
—(high priest), [Paul brought before, Acts 22. 30.
smitten by order of, and rebuked by Paul, Acts 23. 2. 3.

Anathema Maranatha, I Cor. 16. 22.

Anathoth, men of, condemned for persecuting Jeremiah, Jer. 11. 21.
See 1 Ki. 2. 26.

Anchor of the soul, Heb. 6. 19.

Ancient of Days, Dan. 7. 22.

Andrew, the apostle, Matt. 4. 18; Mk. 13. 3; John 1. 40; 6. 8; 12. 22; Acts 1. 13.

Andronicus, disciple at Rome, Rom. 16. 7.

Angels, their nature, office and characteristics, 2 Sam. 14. 20; 1 Ki. 19. 5; Neh. 9. 6; Job. 25. 3; 38. 7; Ps. 68. 17; 91. 11; 103. 20; 104. 4; 148. 2; Is. 6. 2; Dan. 6. 22; Matt. 13. 39; 16. 27; 18. 10; 24. 31; 25. 31; Mk.

Angels—*Continued.*
8. 38; Lk. 15. 7; 16. 22; Acts 7. 53; 12; 7. 27. 23; Eph. 1. 21; Phil. 2. 9; Col. 1. 16; 2. 10; 1 Thes. 4. 16; 2 Thes. 1. 7; 1 Tim. 3. 16; 5. 21; Heb. 1. 6; 2. 2; 12. 22; 1 Pet. 1. 12; 3. 22; 2 Pet. 2. 11; Jude 9; Rev. 5. 2; 7; 11; 12. 7; 14. 6; 16; 17.
announce the nativity, Lk. 2. 13.
minister to Christ, Matt. 4. 11; 26. 53; Lk. 22. 43; John 1. 51.
saints shall judge, 1 Cor. 6. 3.
not to be worshipped, Col. 2. 18; Rev. 19. 10; 22. 9.
rebellious, 2 Pet. 2. 4; Jude 6.

Angel of the Lord appears to Hagar, Gen. 16. 7; 21. 17. Abraham, Gen. 18 etc., Lot, Gen. 19. Balaam, Num. 22. 23. Israelites, Jud. 2. Gideon, Jud. 6. 11. Manoah's wife, Jud. 13. 3. David, 2 Sam. 24. 16; 1 Chr. 21. 16. Elijah, 1 Ki. 19. 7. Daniel, Dan. 8. 16; 9. 21; 10. 11; 12. Joseph, Matt. 1. 20. Two women, Matt. 28. 2-5; Mk. 16. Zacharias, Lk. 1. 11. Mary, Lk. 1. 26. The shepherds, Lk. 2. 8-12. The apostles, Acts 5. 19. Peter, Acts 12. 7. Philip, Acts 8. 26. Cornelius, Acts 10. 3. Paul, Acts 27. 23.
See Ps. 34. 7; 35. 5; Zech. 1. 11.

Angels of the churches, Rev. 1. 20; 2; 3, etc.

Anger (human) nature and effects of, Gen. 27. 45; 44. 18; 49. 7; Ex. 32. 19; Ps. 37. 8; 69. 24; Prov. 15. 18; 16. 32; 19. 11; 21. 19; 29. 22; Eccles. 7. 9; Matt. 5. 22; Tit. 1. 7.
See *Wrath.*
cure for, Prov. 15. 1; 21. 14.
to be put away, Eph. 4. 26, 31; Col. 3. 8.
instances of, Gen. 4. 5; 31. 36; Ex. 11. 8; Lev. 10. 16; Num. 22. 27; 1 Sam. 20. 30; 2 Ki. 5. 11; Jon. 4. 1; Matt. 2. 16.
(divine), Gen. 3. 14; 4; Deut. 29. 20; 32. 19; Josh. 23. 16; 2 Ki. 22. 13; Ezra 8. 22; Job 9. 13; Ps. 7. 11; 21. 9; 78. 21, 58; 89. 30; 90. 7; 99. 8; 106. 40; Prov. 1. 30; Is. 1; 3. 8; 9. 13; 13. 9; 47. 6; Jer. 3. 5; 7. 19; 44. 3; Nah. 1. 2; Mk. 3. 5; 10. 14; John 3. 36; Rom. 1. 18; 2. 5; 3. 5; 1 Cor. 10. 22; Eph. 5. 6; Col. 3. 6; 1 Thes. 2. 16; Heb. 3. 18; 10. 26; Rev. 21. 8; 22.
kindled, Ex. 4. 14; Num. 11. 1; 12. 9; Josh. 7. 1; 2 Sam. 6. 7; 24. 1; 2 Ki. 13. 3; Jer. 17. 4; Hos. 8. 5; Zech. 10. 3.
is slow, Ps. 103. 8; Is. 48. 9; Jon. 4. 2; Neh. 1. 3.
deferred, Ps. 103. 9; Is. 48. 9; Jer. 2. 35; 3. 12; Hos. 14. 4; Jon. 3. 9, 10.
instances of, Gen. 19; Ex. 14. 24; Job 9. 13; 14. 13; Ps. 76. 6; 78. 49; 90. 7; Is. 9. 19; Jer. 7. 20; 10. 10; Lam. 1; Ezek. 7; 9; Nah. 1.
reserved for the day of judgment, Rom. 2. 5; 2 Thes. 1. 8; 2 Pet. 3; Rev. 6. 17; 11. 18; 19. 15.
to be dreaded, deprecated, and endured, Ex. 32. 11; 2 Sam. 24. 17; Ps. 2. 12; 6; 27. 9; 30. 5; 38; 39. 10; 74; 76. 7; 79. 5; 80. 4; 85. 4; 90. 11; Is. 64. 9; Jer. 4. 8; Lam. 3. 39; Dan. 9. 16; Mic. 7. 9; Hab. 3. 2; Zeph. 2. 2; 3. 8; Matt. 10. 28; Lk. 18. 13.
propitiation of, by Christ, Rom. 3. 25; 5. 9; 2 Cor. 5. 18; Eph 2. 14; Col. 1. 20; 1 Thes. 1. 10; 1 John 2. 2.
turned away by repentance, 1 Ki. 21. 29; Job 33. 27, 28; Ps. 106. 43; 107. 13, 19; Jer. 3. 12; 18. 7, 8; 31. 18; Joel 2. 14; Lk. 15. 18.

Anise, or dill, a species of parsley, Matt. 22. 23.

Anna, a prophetess, Lk. 2. 36.

Annas, high priest, Lk. 3. 2.
Christ brought to, John 18. 13, 24.
Peter and John before, Acts 4. 6.

Anointed, the (Christ), Is. 61. 1; Lk. 4. 18;
Acts 4. 27; 10. 38.

—the Lord's, 1 Sam. 24. 10; 26. 9.

—mine, 1 Sam. 2. 35; 1 Chr. 16. 22; Ps. 132. 17.

Anointing of Aaron and his sons as priests,
Lev. 6. 20; 8. 10; 10. 7.
Saul as king. 1 Sam. 10. 1. David, 1 Sam.
16. 13.
Solomon, 1 Ki. 1. 39. Elisha, 1 Ki. 19. 16.
Jehu, 2 Ki. 9. Joash, 2 Ki. 11. 12.
Christ by Mary, Matt. 26. 6; Mk. 14. 3; John
12. 3.
Christ by a woman that was a sinner, Lk.
7. 37.
of the sick, James 5. 14.
of the Holy Spirit, 2 Cor. 1. 21; 1 John
2. 20.

Anointing Oil, directions for making, Ex. 30.
22; 37. 29.

Antichrist, 1 John 2. 18, 22; 2 John 7.
See 2 Thes. 2. 9; 1 Tim. 4. 1.

Antioch (in Syria) disciples first called
Christians at, Acts 11. 26.
Barnabas and Saul called to apostleship at,
Acts 13. 1.
Paul withstands Peter at, Gal 2. 11.

—(in Pisidia) visited by St Paul, Acts 13. 14.
Paul and Barnabas persecuted there, Acts
13. 50.

Antipas, a Christian martyr, Rev. 2. 13.

Apelles, saluted by Paul, Rom. 16. 10.

Aphek, defeat of Saul at, 1 Sam. 29. 1.
See Josh. 13. 4; 19. 30; 1 Sam. 4. 1; 1 Ki.
20. 26.

Apollos, an eloquent disciple, Acts 18. 24;
19. 1; 1 Cor. 1. 12; 3. 4.

Apollyon (the destroyer) Rev. 9. 11.

Apostates described, Deut. 13. 13; Matt. 24. 10;
Lk. 8. 13; John 6. 66; Heb. 3. 12; 6. 4;
2 Pet. 3. 17; 1 John 2. 19.
their punishment, Zeph. 1. 4; 2 Thes. 2. 8;
1 Tim. 4. 1; Heb. 10. 26; 2 Pet. 2. 17.

Apostles, calling of the, Matt. 4. 18, 21; 9. 9;
Mk. 1. 16; Lk. 5. 10; John 1. 38.
their appointment and powers, Matt. 10;
16. 19; 18. 18; 28. 19; Mark 3. 13; 16. 15;
Lk. 6. 13; 9. 12. 11; 24. 47; John 20. 23;
Acts 9. 15, 27; 20. 24; 1 Cor. 5. 3; 2 Thes.
3. 6; 2 Tim. 1. 11.
witnesses of Christ, Lk. 1. 2; 24. 33, 48;
Acts 1. 2, 22; 10. 41; 1 Cor. 9. 1; 15. 5;
2 Pet. 1. 16; 1 John 1. 1.
their sufferings, Matt. 10. 16; Lk. 21. 16;
John 15. 20; 16. 2, 33; Acts 4, etc.; 1 Cor.
4. 9; 2 Cor. 1. 4; 4. 8; 11. 23, etc.; Rev.
1. 9, etc.
their names written in heaven, Lk. 10. 20;
Rev. 21. 14.
false, condemned, 2 Cor. 11. 13.

Apparel, exhortations concerning, Deut. 22.
5; 1 Tim. 2. 9; 1 Pet. 3. 3.
of the Jewish women described, Is. 3. 16.

Appeal of Paul to Cæsar, Acts 25. 11.

Appii Forum, Acts 28. 15.

Apple of the eye, Deut. 32. 10; Ps. 17. 8; Prov.
7. 2; Lam. 2. 18; Zech. 2. 8.

Aquila and Priscilla accompany Paul, Acts
18. 2.
instruct Apollos, Acts 18. 26.
their constancy commended, Rom. 16. 3;
1 Cor. 16. 19.

Arabia, Ps. 72. 10, 15.
kings of, pay tribute, 1 Ki. 10. 15; 2 Chr.
9. 14; 17. 11; 26. 7.

Arabians, Is. 13. 20; 21. 13; Jer. 25. 24; Acts
2. 11.

Ararat, mountain on which the ark rested,
Gen. 8. 4.
See Jer. 51. 27.

Araunah (Ornan), Jebusite, sells to David a
site for the temple, 2 Sam. 24. 16; 1 Chr.
21. 15, 18; 22. 1.

Archangel. See *Michael*.

Archelaus, king of Judea, feared by Joseph,
Matt. 2. 22.

Archers, Gen. 21. 20; 49. 23; 1 Sam. 31. 3; Job
16. 13, etc.
Ahab and Josiah killed by, 1 Ki. 22. 34:
2 Chr. 35. 22.

Arcturus, Job. 9. 9; 38. 32.

Archippus exhorted by Paul, Col. 4. 17.
Philem. 2.

Areopagus, Mars' hill, Paul preaches on, Acts
17. 19.

Aretas, king of Damascus, 2 Cor. 11. 32.

Aristarchus, fellow-prisoner of Paul, Acts 19.
29; 20. 4; 27. 2; Col. 4. 10; Philem. 24.

Aristobulus, his household greeted by Paul,
Rom. 16. 10.

Ark (of Noah) described, Gen. 6. 14.
Noah's faith in making, Heb. 11. 7; 1 Pet.
3. 20.

—of bulrushes, Ex. 2. 3.
of God, its construction, Ex. 25. 10; 37. 1.
passes over Jordan, Josh. 3. 15; 4. 11.
compasses Jericho, Josh. 6. 11.
captured by the Philistines, 1 Sam. 4. 5.
their plagues in consequence, 1 Sam. 5.
restored, 1 Sam. 6.
carried to Jerusalem, 2 Sam. 6; 15. 24; 1 Chr.
13; 15; 16.
brought into the temple, 1 Ki. 8. 3; 2 Chr. 5.
See Heb. 9. 4.

Ark in heaven. Rev. 11. 19.

Arm of God, Ex. 15. 16; Deut. 33. 27; Job 40. 9;
Ps. 77. 15; 89. 13; 98. 1; Is. 33. 2; 51. 5; 52. 10;
53. 1; Jer. 27. 5; Lk. 1. 51; Acts 13. 17.

Arms, the everlasting, Deut. 33. 27.

Armageddon, Rev. 16. 16.

Armour, Goliath's described, 1 Sam. 17. 5.
of God, Rom. 13. 12; 2 Cor. 6. 7; Eph. 6. 13;
1 Thes. 5. 8.

Aroer, built by children of Gad, Num. 32. 34.

—boundary of Reuben, Josh. 13. 16.

Artaxerxes (king of Persia), his decree to prevent the building of the walls of Jerusalem, Ezra. 4. 17.

—Longimanus, permits Ezra to restore the
temple, Ezra 7; and Nehemiah to rebuild
Jerusalem, Neh. 2.

Artificer, Tubal-Cain the first, Gen. 4. 22.

Asa, his good reign, 1 Ki. 15. 8.
his prayer against the Ethiopians, 2 Chr.
14. 11.
his zeal, 2 Chr. 15.
wars with Baasha, 1 Ki. 15. 16; 2 Chr. 16.
seeks aid from the Syrians, 2 Chr. 16. 2.
rebuked by Hanani the seer. 2 Chr. 16. 7.
his long reign and death, 2 Chr. 16. 12.

Asahel, his rashness, slain by Abner, 2 Sam.
2. 18-23; 3. 27; 23. 24; 1 Chr. 11. 26.

Asaph, a Levite, musical composer, his part in
the temple service, 1 Chr. 6. 39; 2 Chr. 5.
12; 29. 30; 35. 15; Neh. 12. 46. Psalms 50
and 73 to 83 are ascribed to him.

Ascension of Christ (from Olivet), Lk. 24. 50 ;
  Acts 1. 9 ; Rom. 8. 34 ; Eph. 4. 8 ; 1 Pet. 3. 2.
  prophecies corncerning, Ps. 24. 7-10 ; 68. 18 ;
  John 6. 62 ; 14. 2, 28 ; 16. 5 ; 20. 17.
Asenath, wife of Joseph, Gen. 41. 45 ; 46. 20.
Ashdod, city of Philistines, the ark carried
  there.
  men of, smitten, 1 Sam. 5.
  subdued by Uzziah, 2 Chr. 26. 6.
  prophecies concerning, Jer. 25. 20 ; Amos 1.
  8 ; Zeph. 2. 4 ; Zech. 9. 6.
Asher, son of Jacob, Gen. 30. 13.
  blessed by Jacob, Gen. 49. 20.
  ,,   ,,   Moses, Deut. 33. 24.
  his descendants, Num. 1. 40 ; 26. 44 ; 1 Chr. 7.
  30 ; Luke 2. 36.
  their inheritance, Josh. 19. 24 ; Jud. 5. 17.
  See Ezek. 48. 34 ; Rev. 7. 6.
Ashes, man likened to, Gen. 18. 27 ; Job 30. 19.
  used in mourning, 2 Sam. 13. 19 ; Est. 4. 1 ;
  Job 2. 8 ; 42. 6 ; Is. 58. 5 ; Jon. 3. 6, etc. ;
  Matt. 11. 21.
Ashkelon (Askelon) taken, Jud. 1. 18 ; 14. 19 ;
  1 Sam. 6. 17 ; 2 Sam. 1. 20.
  prophecies concerning, Jer. 25. 20 ; 47. 5 ;
  Amos 1. 8 ; Zeph. 2. 4 ; Zech. 9. 5.
Ashtaroth, goddess of Zidon, worshipped
  by Israel, Jud. 2. 13 ; 1 Sam. 12. 10 ; Solo-
  mon, 1 Ki. 11. 5, 33.
Asp, venomous serpent, Deut. 32. 33 ; Job 20.
  14 ; Is. 11. 8 ; Rom. 3. 13.
Ass, Balaam rebuked by, Num. 22. 28 ; 2 Pet.
  2. 16.
  laws concerning, Ex. 13. 13 ; 23. 4 ; Deut. 22. 10.
  Christ rides on one (Zech. 9. 9) ; Matt. 21 ;
  John 12. 14, etc.
  —(wild) described, Job 39. 5 ; Hos. 8. 9.
Assembling for public worship, Lev. 23 ; Deut.
  16. 8 ; Heb. 10. 25 ;
  David's love for, Ps. 27. 4 ; 42 ; 43 ; 65 ; 84 ;
  87 ; 118. 26 ; 122 ; 134 ; 135.
  See Is. 4. 5 ; Mal. 3. 16 ; Matt. 18. 20.
  instances of, 1 Ki. 8 ; 2 Chr. 5 ; 29 ; 30 ;
  Neh. 8 ; Lk. 4. 16 ; John 20. 19 ; Acts 1.
  13 ; 2. 1 ; 3. 1 ; 13. 2 ; 16. 13 ; 20. 7.
Assurance of faith and hope, Is. 32. 17 ; Col. 2.
  2 ; 1 Thes. 1. 5 ; 2 Tim. 1. 12 ; Heb. 6. 11 ;
  10. 22.
  confirmed by love, 1 John 3. 14, 19 ; 4. 18.
Assyria, Israel carried captive to, 2 Ki. 15.
  29 ; 17.
  army of, miraculously destroyed, 2 Ki. 19.
  35 ; Is. 37. 36.
  prophecies concerning, Is. 8 ; 10. 5 ; 14. 24 ;
  30. 31 ; 31. 8 ; Mic. 5. 6 ; Zeph. 2. 13.
  its glory, Ezek. 31. 3.
Astrologers (Chaldean), their inability, Is. 47.
  13-15 ; Dan. 2 ; 4. 7 ; 5. 7.
Asyncritus, disciple, Rom. 16. 14.
Athaliah, mother of Ahaziah, 2 Ki. 8. 26.
  slays the seed royal, 2 Ki. 11. 1 ; 2 Chr. 22. 10.
  slain by order of Jehoiada, 2 Ki. 11. 16 ;
  2 Chr. 23. 12.
Athens, Paul preaches at, Acts 17. 15 ; 1 Thes.
  3. 1.
  men of, described, Acts 17. 21.
Atonement under the law, Ex. 29. 29 ; 30 ;
  Lev. 1, etc.
  annual day of, Lev. 16 ; 23. 26.
  made by Aaron for the plague, Num. 16. 46.
  made by Christ, Rom. 3. 24 ; 5. 6 ; 2 Cor. 5.
  18 ; Gal. 1. 4 ; 3. 13 ; Tit. 2. 14 ; Heb. 9. 28 ;
  1 Pet. 1. 19 ; 2. 24 ; 3. 18 ; 1 John 2. 2 ; Rev.
  1. 5 ; 13. 8, etc.

Atonement – *Continued.*
  prophecies concerning, Is. 53 ; Dan. 9. 24 ;
  Zech. 13. 1, 7 ; John 11. 50.
  commemorated in the Lord's supper, Matt.
  26. 26 ; 1 Cor. 11. 23.
Attalia, sea-port, Acts 14. 25.
Avenger of blood, deliverance from, Num. 35.
  12 ; Deut. 19. 6 ; Josh. 20.
Azariah (Uzziah), king of Judah, his good
  reign, 2 Ki. 14. 21 ; 2 Chr. 26.
  invades the priest's office, 2 Chr. 26. 16.
  struck with leprosy, 2 Ki. 15. 5 ; 2 Chr 26. 20.
  —prophet, exhorts Asa, 2 Chr. 15.
Azotus (Ashdod), Acts 8. 40.
Baal worshipped, Num. 22. 41 ; Jud. 2. 13 ; 8.
  33 ; 1 Ki. 16. 32 ; 18. 26 ; 2 Ki. 17. 16 ; 19.
  18 ; 21. 3 ; Jer. 2. 8 ; 7. 9 ; 12. 16 ; 19. 5 ; 23.
  13 ; Hos. 2. 8 ; 13. 1, etc.
  his altars and priests destroyed by Gideon,
  Jud. 6. 25 ; by Elijah, 1 Ki. 18. 40 ; by
  Jehu, 2 Ki. 10. 18 ; by Jehoiada, 2 Ki. 11.
  18 ; by Josiah, 2 Ki. 23. 4 ; 2 Chr. 34. 4.
Baalim, 2 Chr. 28. 2 ; Jer. 2. 23.
Baal-Peor, the trespass of Israel concerning,
  Num. 25 ; Deut. 4. 3 ; Ps. 106. 28 ; Hos. 9. 10.
Baal-Perazim, David's victory over Philistines
  at, 2 Sam. 5. 20.
Baal-Zebub, false God of Ekron, Ahaziah
  rebuked for sending to inquire of, 2 Ki. 1. 2.
Baanah and Rechab, for murdering Ish-
  bosheth, slain by David, 2 Sam. 4.
Baasha, king of Israel, destroys the house of
  Jeroboam, 1 Ki. 15. 16, 27.
  Jehu's prophecy against, 1 Ki. 16. 1.
Babel, Nimrod king of, Gen. 10. 10.
  confusion of tongues at the building of,
  Gen. 11.
Babes (as new-born), 1 Pet. 2. 2.
  the humble and teachable so called by Jesus,
  Matt. 11. 25 ; Lk. 10. 21.
Babylon, Gen. 10. 10 ; 2 Ki. 17. 30.
  ambassadors from, come to Hezekiah, 2
  Ki. 20. 12 ; 2 Chr. 32. 31 ; Is. 39.
  Jews carried captive there, 2 Ki. 25 ; 2 Chr.
  36 ; Jer. 39 ; 52.
  their return from, Ezra 1 ; Neh. 2.
  its greatness, Dan. 4. 30.
  taken by the Medes, Dan. 5. 30.
  its fall, Is. 13. 14 ; 21. 2 ; 47 ; 48 ; Jer. 25. 12 ;
  50 ; 51.
  church in, 1 Pet. 5. 13.
  —the Great, Rev. 14. 8 ; 16. 19 ; 17 ; 18.
Baca, valley of misery, Ps. 84. 6.
Backbiting forbidden, Ps. 15. 3 ; Prov. 25. 23 .
  Rom. 1. 30 ; 2 Cor. 12. 20.
Backsliding (turning from God), 1 Ki. 11. 9 ;
  2 Cor. 11. 3 ; Gal. 3. 1 ; 5. 4 ; Rev. 2. 4.
  of Israel, Ex. 32 ; Jer. 2. 19 ; 3. 6, 11 ; 12 ; 22 ;
  Hos. 4. 16 ; 11. 7.
  of Saul, 1 Sam. 15. 11.
  of Solomon, 1 Ki. 11. 3, 4.
  of Peter, Matt. 26. 70-74 ; Ga.. 2. 14.
  God's displeasure at, Ps. 78. 57-59.
  punishment of, Deut. 11. 28 ; Prov. 14. 14 ;
  Jer. 2. 19.
  pardon for, promised, 2 Chr. 7. 14 ; Jer. 3. 12 ;
  31. 20 ; 36. 3 ; Hos. 14. 4.
  return from, Ps. 80. 3 ; 85. 4 ; Lam. 5. 21 ; Jer.
  3. 22 ; Hos. 5. 15.
Badgers' skins used in the tabernacle, Ex. 25.
  5 ; 26. 14.
Balaam requested by Balak to curse Israel, is
  forbidden, Num. 22. 13.
  his anger, Num. 22. 27.

Balaam—*Continued*.
blesses Israel, Num. 23. 19; 24. 1.
his prophecies, Num. 23. 7, 18; 24. 17.
his wicked counsel, Num. 31. 16; Deut. 23. 4.
  See Josh. 24. 9; Jud. 11. 25; Mic. 6. 5; 2 Pet. 2. 15; Jude 11; Rev. 2. 14.
slain, Num. 31. 8; Josh. 13. 22.
Balak, king of Moab. See *Balaam*.
Balances and measures to be just, Lev. 19. 35; Prov. 16. 11.
false, condemned, Prov. 11. 1; Hos. 12. 7; Amos 8. 5; Mic. 6. 11.
Balm of Gilead, Gen. 37. 25.
used figuratively, Jer. 8. 22; 46. 11, etc.
Banner figuratively mentioned, Ps. 60. 4; Cant. 2. 4; 6. 4.
Banquet, royal, Est. 5; 7; Dan. 5.
Baptism of John, Matt. 3. 6; Mk. 1. 4; Lk. 3; John 1. 19; Acts 19. 4.
Pharisees' answer concerning, Matt. 21. 25; Mk. 11. 29; Lk. 20. 4.
appointed by Christ, Matt. 28. 19; Mk. 16. 15; John 3. 22; 4. 1.
its signification, Acts 2. 38; 19. 3; 22. 16; Rom. 6. 3; 1 Cor. 10. 2; 12. 13; 15. 29; Gal. 3. 27; Col. 2. 12; Tit. 3. 5; 1 Pet. 3. 21.
instances of, Acts 8. 12, 38; 9. 18; 10. 48; 16. 15, 33; 1 Cor. 1. 14, 16.
one baptism, Eph. 4. 5.
Barabbas, a robber, released instead of Jesus, Matt. 27. 16; Mk. 15. 6; Lk. 23. 18; John 18. 40.
Barak delivers Israel from Sisera, Jud. 4. 5; Heb. 11. 32.
Barbarians (foreigners), Rom. 1. 14; 1 Cor. 14. 11.
Paul kindly treated by, Acts 28.
Bar-Jesus (Elymas) smitten with blindness, Acts 13. 6.
Barley mentioned, Ex. 9. 31; Ruth 1. 22, etc.; John 6. 9; Rev. 6. 6.
Barnabas, Levite of Cyprus, sells his possessions, Acts 4. 36.
preaches at Antioch, Acts 11. 22.
accompanies Paul, Acts 11. 30; 12. 25; 13; 14; 15; 1 Cor. 9. 6.
their contention, Acts 15. 36.
his error, Gal. 2. 13.
Barrenness of Sarah, Gen. 11. 30; 16. 1; 18. 9; 21.
  ,,   of Rebekah, Gen. 25. 21.
  ,,   cf Rachel, Gen. 29. 31; 30. 1.
  ,,   of Manoah's wife, Jud. 13.
  ,,   of Hannah, 1 Sam. 1.
  ,,   of the Shunammite, 2 Ki. 4. 14.
  ,,   of Elizabeth, Lk. 1.
  See Ps. 113. 9; Is. 54. 1; Gal. 4. 27.
Bartholomew, the apostle, Matt. 10. 3; Mk. 3. 18; Lk. 6. 14; Acts 1. 13.
Bartimæus' blindness cured near Jericho, Mk. 10. 46.
Baruch takes Jeremiah's evidence, Jer. 32. 13; 36.
carried into Egypt, Jer 43. 6.
comforted, Jer. 45.
Barzillai's kindness to David, 2 Sam. 17. 27.
David's gratitude, 2 Sam. 19. 31; 1 Ki. 2. 7.
Bashan conquered, Num. 21. 33; Deut. 3. 1; Ps. 68. 15; 22; 135. 10; 136. 20.
Bastards, not to enter the congregation, Deut. 23. 2.
  See Heb. 12. 8.
Bath, a measure, 1 Ki. 7. 26: 2 Chr. 2. 10; Ezra 7. 22; Is. 5. 10, etc.

Bath-Sheba, her sin with David, 2 Sam. 11; 12.
her request for Solomon, 1 Ki. 1. 15.
  ,,   ,,   for Adonijah, 1 Ki. 2. 19.
Battle, laws concerning, Deut. 20.
of great day of God, Rev. 16. 14.
of Israelites, etc., described, Gen. 14; Ex. 17; Num. 31; Josh. 8; 10; Jud. 4; 7; 8; 11; 20; 1 Sam. 4; 11; 14; 17; 31; 2 Sam. 2; 10; 18; 21. 15; 1 Ki. 20; 22; 2 Ki. 3; 1 Chr. 18-20; 2 Chr. 13; 14. 9; 20; 25.
Battlements to be made to houses, Deut. 22. 8.
Bdellium, Gen. 2. 12.
like manna in colour. Num. 11. 7.
Beard, laws concerning, Lev. 19. 27; 21. 5.
  See 2 Sam. 10. 4; Jer. 41. 5; Ezek. 5. 1.
Beasts, creation of, Gen. 1. 24.
dominion over, given to man, Gen. 1. 26, 28; Ps. 8. 7.
named by Adam, Gen. 2. 20.
preserved, Gen. 7. 2; Ps. 36. 6; 104; 147. 9.
what clean and unclean, Lev. 11; Deut. 14. 4; Acts 10. 12.
laws concerning, Ex. 13. 12; 20. 10; 22; 23. 4; Lev. 27. 9; Deut. 5. 14; Prov. 12. 10.
Daniel's vision of, Dan. 7.
John's vision of, Rev. 4. 7; 13, etc.
Beauty, vanity of, Ps. 39. 11; 49. 14; Prov. 6. 25; 31. 30; Is. 3. 24.
instances of its danger, Gen. 12. 11; 26. 7; 34; 2 Sam. 11; 13, etc.
Beauty and Bands, the two staves so called, Zech. 11. 7.
Beauty of Holiness, 1 Chr. 16. 29; 2 Chr. 20. 21; Ps. 110. 3.
Bedstead of Og, king of Bashan, Deut. 3. 11.
Beelzebub, prince of devils, Matt. 10. 25; 12. 24; Mk. 3. 22; Lk. 11. 15.
Christ's miracles ascribed to, Matt. 9. 34; 12. 24, etc.
Beer-Sheba, Abraham dwells there, Gen. 21. 31; 22. 19; 28. 10.
Hagar relieved there, Gen. 21. 14.
Jacob comforted there, Gen. 46. 1.
Elijah flees to, 1 Ki. 19. 3.
Beginning, the name of Christ, Rev. 1. 8; 3. 14.
of time, Gen. 1. 1; John 1. 1.
of miracles, John 2. 11.
Behemoth described, Job 40. 15.
Bel, an idol, Is. 46. 1; Jer. 50. 2.
Belial, men of, wicked men so called, Deut. 13. 13; Jud. 19. 22.
children of, 1 Sam. 10. 27.
Bells upon the priest's ephod, Ex. 28. 33; 39. 25.
  See Zech. 14. 20.
Belshazzar's profane feast, warning, and death, Dan. 5.
Belteshazzar, Daniel so named, Dan. 1. 7; 4. 8, etc.
Benaiah, valiant acts of, 2 Sam. 23. 20; 1 Chr. 11. 22; 27. 5.
proclaims Solomon king, 1 Ki. 1. 32.
slays Adonijah, Joab, and Shimei, 1 Ki. 2. 25-46.
Ben-Hadad, king of Syria, his league with Asa, 1 Ki. 15. 18.
—war with Ahab, 1 Ki. 20.
baffled by Elisha, 2 Ki. 6. 8.
besieges Samaria, 2 Ki. 6. 24; 7.
slain by Hazael, 2 Ki. 8. 7.
—son of Hazael, wars with Israel, 2 Ki. 13. 3, 25.
  See Jer. 49. 27; Amos 1. 4.
Benjamin (Benoni), youngest son of Jacob. his birth, Gen. 35. 16.

Benjamin—*Continued.*
sent into Egypt, Gen. 43. 15.
Joseph's stratagem to detain, Gen. 44.
Jacob's prophecy concerning. Gen. 49. 27.
his descendants, Gen. 46. 21; 1 Chr. 7. 6.
twice numbered, Num. 1. 36; 26. 38.
blessed by Moses, Deut. 33. 12.
their inheritance, Josh. 18. 11.
their wickedness chastised, Jud. 20; 21.
the first king chosen from, 1 Sam. 9; 10.
support the house of Saul, 2 Sam. 2.
afterwards adhere to that of David, 1 Ki. 12. 21; 1 Chr. 11.
the tribe of Paul, Phil. 3. 5.
See Ezek. 48. 32; Rev. 7. 8.

Berachah (blessing) valley of, why so named. 2 Chr. 20. 26.

Berea, city of Macedonia, Paul preaches at, Acts 17. 10.
people of, commended, Acts 17. 11.

Bethabara, place where John baptized, John 1. 28.

Bethany visited by Christ, Matt. 21. 17; 26. 6. Mk. 11. 1; Lk. 19. 29; John 12. 1.
raising of Lazarus at, John 11. 18.
ascension of Christ at, Lk. 24. 50.

Beth-El, city of Palestine, Jacob's vision there, Gen. 28. 19; 31. 13.
he builds an altar there, Gen. 35. 1.
occupied by the house of Joseph, Jud. 1. 22.
idolatry of Jeroboam at, 1 Ki. 12. 28; 13. 1.
prophets dwell there, 2 Ki. 2. 2, 3; 17. 28.
reformation by Josiah at, 2 Ki. 23. 15.
See Amos 3. 14; 4. 4; 5. 5; 7. 10.

Bethesda, pool of, at Jerusalem, miracles wrought at, John 5. 2.

Beth-Horon, Josh. 10. 10.

Beth-Lehem, Naomi and Ruth return to, Ruth 1-4.
David anointed at, 1 Sam. 16. 13; 20. 6.
well of, mentioned, 2 Sam. 23. 15; 1 Chr. 11. 17.
Christ's birth at, Matt. 2. 1; Lk. 2. 4; John 7. 42.
    ,,   ,, predicted, Mic. 5. 2; Ps. 132. 5, 6.
children of, slain, Matt. 2. 16.

Bethsaida of Galilee, native place of Philip, Peter, and Andrew, Mk. 6. 45; John 1. 44; 12. 21.
blind man cured at, Mk. 8. 22.
condemned for unbelief, Matt. 11. 21.
Christ feeds the five thousand at, Lk. 9. 10-17.

Beth-Shemesh, men of, punished for profanity, 1 Sam. 6. 19.
great battle at, 2 Ki. 14. 11.

Betrothal, laws concerning, Ex. 21. 8; Lev. 19. 20; Deut. 20. 7.

Bezaleel constructs the tabernacle, Ex. 31. 2; 35. 30; 36-38.

Bigthan and Teresh, their conspiracy discovered by Mordecai, Est. 2. 21.

Bildad's answers to Job, Job 8; 18; 25.

Bilhah, Jacob's children by, Gen. 30. 5.

Birds, created and preserved, Gen. 1. 20; 7. 3; Ps. 104. 17; 148. 10; Matt. 8. 20.
used in sacrifices, Gen. 15. 9; Lev. 14. 4; Lk. 2. 24.
what may not be eaten, Lev. 11. 13; Deut. 14. 12.
nests of, Deut. 22. 6.
mentioned figuratively, Prov. 1. 17; 6. 5, etc.; Jer. 12. 9; Amos 3. 5; Rev. 18. 2.

Birthdays celebrated—
of Pharaoh, Gen. 40. 20.
of Herod, Matt. 14. 6; Mk. 6. 21.

Birthright, law concerning, Deut. 21. 15.
despised by Esau, Gen. 25. 31; Heb. 12. 16.
lost by Reuben, 1 Chr. 5. 1.

Births foretold—
of Ishmael, Gen. 16. 11.
of Isaac, Gen. 18. 10.
of Samson, Jud. 13. 3.
of Samuel, 1 Sam. 1. 11, 17.
of Josiah, 1 Ki. 13. 2.
of John the Baptist, Lk. 1. 13.
of Messias, Gen. 3. 15; Is. 7. 14; Mic. 5 Lk. 1. 31.

Bishop, qualifications of, 1 Tim. 3.
See Phil. 1. 1.
of souls (Christ), 1 Pet. 2. 25.

Bitter herbs eaten with the passover, Ex. 12. 3
water healed. Ex. 15. 23.

Blasphemy, Ex. 20. 7; Ps. 74. 18; Is. 52. 5 Ezek. 20. 27; Matt. 15. 19; Lk. 22. 65; Col 3. 8; Rev. 2. 9; 13. 5, 6; 16. 9.
its punishment, death, Lev. 24. 16; 1 Ki. 21, 10.
Christ accused of, Matt. 9. 3; 26. 65; Mk. 2. 7; Lk. 5. 21; John 10. 33.
Naboth, 1 Ki. 21. 13, and Stephen, Acts 6. 13; 7. 54, unjustly stoned for,
occasion to blaspheme given by David, 2. Sam. 12. 14.
See also 1 Tim. 5. 14; 6. 1.
against the Holy Ghost, Matt. 12. 31; Mk. 3. 28; Lk. 12. 10; 1 John 5. 16.

Blemish, offerings must be free from, Ex. 12. 5, etc.; Lev. 1. 3, etc.; Deut. 17. 1, etc.
priests to be without, Lev. 21. 16.
the Church to be without, Eph. 5. 27.
—Lamb without, Christ compared to, 1 Pet. 1. 19.

Blessed, Gen. 12. 3; Ps. 1. 1; 65. 4; 84. 4, 5; 112. 1; Is. 30. 18; Matt. 5. 3-11; 25. 34; Lk. 6. 21; 12. 37; 14. 15; Rom. 4. 6-9.
those chosen and called by God, Ps. 65. 4; Is. 51. 2; Eph. 1. 3, 4; Rev. 19. 9.
who trust and delight in God, Ps. 2. 12; 34. 8; 40. 4; 84. 12; 112. 1; Jer. 17. 7.
who hear and obey, Ps. 119. 2; Matt. 13. 16; Lk. 11. 28; Jas. 1. 25; Rev. 1. 3; 22. 7, 14.
who endures chastisement, Ps. 94. 12.
  ,, temptation, Jas. 1. 12.
who fears the Lord, Ps. 128.
who believe and suffer for Christ, Matt. 16. 16, 17; 11. 6; Lk. 6. 22; Gal. 3. 9.
who die in the Lord, Rev. 14. 13.
sins forgiven, Ps. 32. 1, 2; Rom. 4. 7.
others pronounced blessed, Deut. 15. 10; Ps. 5. 12; 41. 1; 106. 3; 112. 2; 119. 1; Prov. 10. 6; 20. 7; 22. 9; 24. 25; Lk. 14. 13, 14; Rev. 16. 15.
persons blessed: Jacob by Isaac, Gen. 27. 27. Jacob by God, Gen. 48. 3. Joseph and his sons by Jacob, Gen. 48. 9, 14. The twelve tribes by Moses, Deut. 33.

Blessing, form of, Num. 6. 22.
and curse, Deut. 11. 26.
and glory, Rev. 5. 12, 13; 7. 12.

Blind, laws concerning the, Lev. 19. 14; Deut. 27. 18.

Blindness inflicted on the men of Sodom. Gen. 19. 11.
inflicted on the Syrian army, 2 Ki. 6. 18.
    ,, on Saul of Tarsus, Acts 9. 8.
    ,, on Elymas, Acts 13. 11.

B.indness—*Continued.*

healed by Christ, Matt. 9. 27; 12. 22; 20. 30;
Mk. 8. 22; 10. 46; Lk. 7. 21; John 9.
See Ps. 146. 8; Is. 29. 18; 35. 5; 42. 7.

spiritual, Ps. 82. 5; Is. 56. 10; 59. 9; Matt.
6. 23; 15. 14; 23. 16; John 1. 5; 3. 19; 9. 39;
1 Cor. 2. 14; 2 Pet. 1. 9; 1 John 2. 9; Rev.
3. 17.

judicially inflicted, Ps. 69. 23; Is. 6. 9; 44.
18; Matt. 13. 13; John 12. 40; Acts 28. 26;
Rom. 11. 7; 2 Cor. 3. 14; 4. 4.

prayer for deliverance from, Ps. 13. 3; 119. 18.

removed by Christ, Is. 9. 2; 42. 7; Lk. 4. 18;
John 8. 12; 9. 39; 2 Cor. 3. 14; 4. 6; Eph.
5. 8; Col. 1. 13; 1 Thes. 5. 4; 1 Pet. 2. 9.

Blood, eating of, forbidden to man after the
flood, Gen. 9. 4.

eating of, forbidden to the Israelites under
the law, Lev. 3. 17; 7. 26; 17. 10; 19. 26;
Deut. 12. 16; 1 Sam. 14. 32, 33; Ezek. 33. 25.

eating of, forbidden to the Gentile Christians, Acts 15. 20, 29.

water changed into, Ex. 4. 9, 30; 7. 17; Rev.
8. 8; 11. 6.

shedding of human, forbidden, Gen. 9. 5, 6;
Deut. 21. 1-9; Ps. 106. 38; Prov. 6. 16, 17;
Is. 59. 3; Jer. 22. 17; Ezek. 22. 4; Matt.
27. 6.

of legal sacrifices, Ex. 23. 18; 29. 12; 30. 10;
34. 25; Lev. 4. 7; 17. 11; Heb. 9. 13, 19-22;
10. 4.

of the covenant, Ex. 24. 8; Zech. 9. 11; Heb.
10. 29; 13. 20.

—of Christ, 1 Cor. 10. 16; Eph. 2. 13; Heb. 9.
14; 1 Pet. 1. 19; 1 John 1. 7.

in the Lord's Supper, Matt. 26. 28; Mk. 14.
24; Lk. 22. 20; 1 Cor. 11. 25.

redemption by, Eph. 1. 7; Col. 1. 20; Heb.
9. 12, 22; 10. 19; 12. 24; 13. 12; 1 Pet. 1. 2;
Rev. 1. 5; 5. 9; 12. 11.

typified, under the law, Ex. 12. 13; 29. 16; 30.
10; Lev. 1. 5; 4; 16. 15; Heb. 9. 7, etc.

Boanerges (sons of thunder), James and John
surnamed, Mk. 3. 17.

Boasting reproved, 1 Ki. 20. 10; Ps. 49. 6; 52. 1;
94. 4; Prov. 20. 14; 25. 14; 27. 1; Is. 10. 15;
Rom. 1. 30; 11. 18; 2 Cor. 10; Jas. 3. 5; 4. 16.

of Paul, 2 Cor. 7. 14; 8. 24; 9. 3, 4; 11. 10.

excluded under the Gospel, Rom. 3. 27;
Eph. 2. 9.

Boaz, his kindness towards Ruth, Ruth 2; 3; 4.

ancestor of David and Christ, Ruth 4. 17, 22;
Matt. 1. 5; Lk. 3. 23, 32.

—and Jachin (strength and stability), pillars
of the temple, 2 Chr. 3. 17.

Bochim, Israel rebuked by an angel at, Jud. 2. 1.

Israel repents at, Jud. 2. 4, 5.

Body (human) not to be disfigured, Lev. 19.
28; 21. 5; Deut. 14. 1.

to be kept pure, Rom. 12. 1; 1 Cor. 6. 13;
1 Thes. 4. 4.

of Christians, the temple of the Holy Ghost,
1 Cor. 3. 16; 6. 19; 2 Cor. 6. 16.

dead, laws concerning, Lev. 21. 11; Num. 5.
2; 9. 6; 19. 11; Deut. 21. 23; Hag. 2. 13.

to be raised again. Matt. 22. 30; 1 Cor. 15.
12; Phil. 3. 21.

See *Resurrection.*

of Christ (Heb. 10. 5); Lk. 2. 35; John 19. 34.

buried by Joseph, Matt. 27. 58;
Mk. 15. 42; Lk. 23. 50; John 19. 38.

the Church so called, Rom. 12. 4; 1 Cor. 10.
17; 12. 12; Eph. 1. 22; 4. 13; 5. 23; Col. 1.
18; 2. 19; 3. 15.

Boils and blains, the plague of, Ex. 9. 10;
Rev. 16. 2.

See 2 Ki. 20. 7; Job 2. 7.

Boldness through faith, Prov. 28. 1; Is. 50. 7;
Acts 5. 29; Eph. 3. 12; Heb. 10. 19; 1 John
4. 17.

exhortations to, Josh. 1. 7; 2 Chr. 19. 11;
Jer. 1. 8; Ezek. 3. 9; Heb. 4. 16.

of Peter and John, Acts 4. 13; 5. 29. Stephen,
Acts 7. 51. Paul, Acts 9. 27; 19. 8; 2 Cor.
7. 4; Gal. 2. 11. Apollos, Acts 18. 26.

Bond (or vow), law of, Num. 30.

of peace. Eph. 4. 3.

Bondage of Israel in Egypt, Ex. 1-12; Ps.
105. 25; Acts 7. 6.

of Israel in Babylon, 2 Ki. 25; Ezra 1; 9. 7;
Neh. 1; Est. 3; Dan. 1.

spiritual, John 8. 34; Acts 8. 23; Rom. 6. 16;
7. 23; 8. 2; Gal. 2. 4; 4. 3; 1 Tim. 3. 7;
2 Tim. 2. 26; Heb. 2. 14; 2 Pet. 2. 19.

deliverance by Christ, Is. 61. 1; Lk. 4. 18;
John 8. 36; Rom. 8. 2; Gal. 3. 13.

Bondmaid, laws concerning, Lev. 19. 20; 25. 44.

Bondmen, laws concerning, Lev. 25. 39; Deut.
15. 12.

Bondwoman cast out, Gen. 21. 10; Gal. 4. 23.

Bones (Gen. 2. 23).

Joseph's, Gen. 50. 25; Ex. 13. 19; Heb. 11. 22.

scattered as a judgment. 2 Ki. 23. 14; Ps. 53.
5; 141. 7; Jer. 8. 1; Ezek. 6. 5.

vision of the dry bones, Ezek. 37.

of the paschal lamb not broken, Ex. 12. 46.

also Christ's, John 19. 36.

Bonnets of the priests, directions for making
Ex. 28. 40; 29. 9; 39. 28; Ezek. 44. 18.

See *Mitre.*

Book of Life, Ex. 32. 32; Ps. 69. 28; Dan. 12. 1;
Phil. 4. 3; Rev. 3. 5; 13. 8; 17. 8; 21. 27;
22. 19.

opened, Rev. 20. 12.

—of the Law, Deut. 28. 61; 29. 27, etc.; Gal.
3. 10.

found and read, 2 Ki. 22. 8; 23. 2; Neh. 8. 8.

—of Jasher, Josh. 10. 13; 2 Sam. 1. 18.

Books, Eccl. 12. 12; Dan. 9. 2; John 21. 25;
2 Tim. 4. 13.

of various persons, 1 Chr. 29. 29; Chr. 9. 29;
12. 15; 20. 34.

of Solomon, 1 Ki. 4. 32; 11. 41.

of judgment, Dan. 7. 10; Rev. 20. 12.

burned at Ephesus, Acts 19. 19.

Booths used at the feast of tabernacles, Lev.
23. 42; Neh. 8. 14.

Borders of the land determined. Num. 34;
Josh. 1. 4; Ezek. 47. 13.

Boring of the ear, Ex. 21. 6.

See Ps. 40. 6.

Born of God, John 1. 13; 3. 3; 1 Pet. 1. 23;
1 John 3. 9; 5. 1.

Borrowing, law concerning, Ex. 22. 14; Deut.
15. 1, etc.

its consequences, 2 Ki. 6. 5; Prov. 22. 7.

of Israel from the Egyptians, Ex. 3. 22;
12. 35.

Bottle of water, Gen. 21. 14.

See Ps. 119. 83.

Bottles of wine, Josh. 9. 4, 13; 1 Sam. 25. 18;
Hos. 7. 5.

old and new, Job 32. 19; Matt. 9. 17; Mk. 2.
22; Lk. 5. 37, 38.

Bottomless pit, Rev. 9. 1; 11. 7; 17. 8.

Satan bound there, Rev. 20. 1, 2.

Bought with a price, 1 Cor. 6. 20.

179

Bow in the cloud, sign of God's mercy, Gen. 9. 13; Ezek. 1. 28.
(weapon), Gen. 48. 22; Josh. 24. 12; 1 Sam. 18. 4; 2 Sam. 1. 18, 22; 2 Ki. 9. 24; Ps. 44. 6; 78. 57; Jer. 49. 35; Hos. 7. 16; Rev. 6. 2.

Bowels of mercies, Gen. 43. 30; Ps. 25. 6; Is. 63. 15; Lk. 1. 78; Phil. 1. 8; 2. 1; Col. 3. 12, etc.

Bowls, etc., offered by the princes, Num. 7. See Zech. 4. 2.

Bozrah, prophecies concerning, Is. 34. 6; 63. 1; Jer. 48. 24; 49. 13; Amos 1. 12; Mic. 2. 12.

Bramble chosen to reign over the trees, Jud. 9. 14.

Branch (of the Lord), prophecies concerning, Is. 4. 2; Jer. 23. 5; Zech. 3. 8; 6. 12; John 15. 5; Rom. 11. 16.

Brand, as a, plucked from the fire, Amos 4. 11; Zech. 3. 2; Jude 23.

Brass used in construction of the tabernacle and temple, Ex. 25. 3; 26. 11; 1 Ki. 7. 14.
altar of, Ex. 39. 39; 2 Ki. 16. 14.
mentioned figuratively, Lev. 26. 19; Job 6. 12; 1 Cor. 13. 1; Rev. 1. 15.

Bread, man appointed to labour for, Gen. 3. 19.
given from heaven (manna), Ex. 16. 4.
miraculously supplied, 2 Ki. 4. 42; John 6, etc.
a type of Christ, John 6. 31; 1 Cor. 10. 16.
offered before the Lord, Ex. 25. 30; Lev. 8. 26; 24. 5.
hallowed, David obtains from Ahimelech, 1 Sam. 21. 4.
used in the Lord's Supper, Lk. 22. 19; 24. 30; Acts 2. 42; 20. 7; 1 Cor. 10. 16; 11. 23.
unleavened, Gen. 19. 3; Ex. 12. 8; 1 Sam. 28. 24; 2 Ki. 23. 9.
figuratively used, 1 Cor. 5. 8.

Breastplate of the high priest described, Ex. 28. 15; 39. 8.
of righteousness, Eph. 6. 14.
of faith and love, 1 Thes. 5. 8.

Breath (life) dependent upon God, Gen. 2. 7; 6. 17; Job 12. 10; 33. 4; Ps. 104. 29; Ezek. 37. 5; Dan. 5. 23; Acts 17. 25.
—of God, its power, 2 Sam. 22. 16; Job 4. 9; Ps. 33. 6; Is. 11. 4; 30. 28.

Brethren, duty of, towards each other, Gen. 13. 8; Deut. 15. 7; 24. 14; Ps. 133; Matt. 5. 22; 18. 15, 21; 25. 40; John 13. 34; 15. 12, etc.; Rom. 12. 10; 1 Cor. 6; 8. 13; Gal. 6. 1; 1 Thes. 4. 9; 2 Thes. 3. 15; Heb. 13. 1; 1 Pet. 1. 22; 3. 8; 2 Pet. 1. 7; 1 John 2. 9; 3. 17.

Bribery forbidden, Ex. 23. 2, 6; Deut. 16. 19; Job. 15. 34.
denounced, Prov. 17. 23; 29. 4; Eccl. 7. 7; Is. 5. 23; 33. 15; Ezek. 13. 19; Amos 2. 6.
of Delilah, Jud. 16. 5; of Samuel's sons, 1 Sam. 8. 3; of Judas, Matt. 26. 14; of the soldiers, Matt. 28. 12.

Bricks made by Israelites, Ex. 1. 14; 5.

Bride of Christ, the Church, John 3. 29; Rev. 21. 2; 22. 17.

Bridegroom, Christ the heavenly, Matt. 9. 15; John 3. 29.
See Ps. 19. 5; Is. 61. 10; 62. 5.

Brimstone and fire, Sodom destroyed by, Gen. 19. 24.
figurative of torment, Is. 30. 33; Rev. 9. 17; 14. 10; 19. 20; 21. 8.

Broidered work, Ezek. 16. 10.

Brother's widow, law concerning, Deut. 25. 5; Matt. 22. 24.

Bruised (Christ) for us, Is. 53. 5.
reed, Is. 42. 3; Matt. 12. 20; Egypt so called, 2 Ki. 18. 21; Ezek. 29. 6, 7.

Buckler, the Divine, 2 Sam. 22. 31; Ps. 18. 2; 91. 4; Prov. 2. 7.

Budding of Aaron's rod, Num. 17.

Building, the Church compared to, 1 Cor. 3. 9; Eph. 2. 21; Col. 2. 7.

Bundle of life, 1 Sam. 25. 29.

Burden, meaning prophecy, 2 Ki. 9. 25; Is. 13. 15; 17; 19; 21; 22; 23; Nah. 1. 1.
cast on the Lord, Ps. 55. 22.
of affliction, Is. 58. 6; 2 Cor. 5. 4.
of iniquities, Ps. 38. 4.
of Christ, light, Matt. 11. 30; Acts 15. 28; Rev. 2. 24.
bear one another's, Gal. 6. 2.

Burial, deprivation of, a calamity, Deut. 28. 26; Ps. 79. 2; Eccl. 6. 3; Is. 14. 19; Jer. 7. 33; 16. 4; 25. 33; 34. 20.
of Sarah, Gen. 23. 19. Abraham, Gen. 25. 9. Isaac, Gen. 35. 29. Jacob, Gen. 50. Abner, 2 Sam. 3. 31, 32. Christ, Matt. 27. 57; Lk. 23. 50. Stephen, Acts 8. 2.

Burning bush, the Lord appears to Moses in, Ex. 3. 2; Mk. 12. 26; Lk. 20. 37; Acts 7. 35.

Burnt-offerings, law concerning, Lev. 1. 1; 6. 8.
illustrations of, Gen. 8. 20; 22. 13; Ex. 18. 12; 1 Sam. 7. 9; Ezra 3. 4; Job 1. 5.
See Ps. 40. 6; 51. 19; Is. 40. 16; Heb. 10.
the continual, Ex. 29. 38; Num. 28. 3; 1 Chr. 16. 40; 2 Chr. 13. 11.

Bury, let the dead, Lk. 9. 60.
manner of Jews to, John 19. 40.

Busy-bodies censured, Prov. 20. 3; 26. 17; 1 Thes. 4. 11; 2 Thes. 3. 11; 1 Tim. 5. 13; 1 Pet. 4. 15.

Buyer characterised, Prov. 20. 14.

Cæsar Augustus, Lk. 2. 1. Tiberius, Lk. 3. 1. Claudius, time of dearth, Acts 11. 28. Nero, Paul appeals to, Acts 25. 11.

Cæsarea, Peter sent there, Acts 10.
Paul visits, Acts 21. 8.
Paul sent to Felix there, Acts 23. 23.
—Philippi, visited by Christ, Matt. 16. 13; Mk. 8. 27.

Caiaphas, high priest, prophesies concerning Christ, John 11. 49.
his counsel, Matt. 26. 3.
he condemns Him, Matt. 26. 65; Mk. 14. 63; Lk. 22. 71.

Cain kills Abel, Gen. 4. 8.
his punishment, Gen. 4. 11.
See Heb. 11. 4; 1 John 3. 12; Jude 11.

Caleb, faith of, Num. 13. 30; 14. 6.
permitted to enter Canaan, Num. 26. 65; 32. 12; Deut. 1. 36.
his request, Josh. 14. 6.
his possessions, Josh. 15. 13.
gives his daughter to Othniel to wife, Jud. 1. 13.

Calf, golden, Aaron's transgression in making, Ex. 32; Acts 7. 40, 41.
of Samaria, Hos. 8. 5, 6.
calves made by Jeroboam, 1 Ki. 12, 28.

Call of God to repentance and salvation, Ps. 49; 50, etc.; Prov. 1. 20; 2. 8; Is. 1; 45. 20; 55; Jer. 35. 15; Hos. 6; 14; Joel 2; Jon. 3; Matt. 3; 11. 28; John 7. 37; 12. 44; Rom. 8. 28; 9; 10; 11; 2 Cor. 5. 20; Rev. 2. 5; 3. 3, 19; 22. 17.
danger of rejecting, Ps. 50. 17; Prov. 1. 24; 29. 1; Is. 6. 9; 66. 4; Jer. 6. 19; 26. 4; 35. 17;

Call—*Continued.*
Matt. 22. 3; John 12. 48; Acts 13. 46: 18. 6; 28. 24; Rom. 11. 8; 2 Thes. 2. 10; Heb. 2. 1; 12. 25; Rev. 2. 5.

call of Noah, Gen. 6. 13. Abraham, Gen. 12. Jacob, Gen. 28. 12. Moses, Ex. 3. Gideon, Jud. 6. 11. Samuel, 1 Sam 3. Elijah, 1 Ki. 17. Elisha, 1 Ki. 19. 16, 19. Isaiah, Is. 6. Jeremiah, Jer. 1. Ezekiel, Ezek. 1. Hosea, Hos. 1.

call of Amos, Amos 1; 7. 14.

See Mic. 1. 1; Zeph. 1. 1; Hag. 1. 1; Zech. 1. 1.

call of Jonah, Jon. 1.

,,   of Peter, etc., Matt. 4. 18; Mk. 1. 16; Lk. 5; John 1. 39.

call of Paul, Acts 9; Rom. 1. 1; Gal. 1. 1, 11; 1 Tim. 1.

Calling or vocation of the Gospel, Rom. 11. 29; 1 Cor. 1. 26; Eph. 1. 18; 4. 1; Phil. 3. 14; 2 Thes. 1. 11; 2 Tim. 1. 9; Heb. 3. 1; 1 Pet. 2. 9; 2 Pet. 1. 10; Rev. 19. 9.

Calvary, Lk. 23. 33.

Camels mentioned, Gen. 12. 16; 24. 19; Ex. 9. 3; 1 Chr. 5. 21; Job 1. 3.

See Matt. 19. 24.

their flesh unclean, Lev. 11. 4; Deut. 14. 7.

camel's hair, raiment of, Matt. 3. 4.

Camp of Israelites, Ex. 14. 19; Num. 1. 52; 2; 24. 5.

to be kept holy, Lev. 6. 11; 13. 4, 6; Num. 5. 2; Deut. 23. 10; Heb. 13. 11.

Cana, Christ's first miracle at, John 2.

nobleman visits Christ at, John 4. 47.

Canaan, land of, Ex. 23. 31; Josh. 1. 4; Zeph. 2. 5.

promised to Abraham, Gen. 12. 7; 13. 14; 17. 8.

inhabitants of, Ex. 15. 15.

their wickedness at Sodom and Gomorrah, Gen. 13. 13; 19.

Israelites not to walk in their ways, Lev. 18. 3, 24, 30; 20. 23.

See Gen. 28. 1, 6, 8; Jud. 3. 1; 4. 2, 23, 24; 5. 19; Ps. 135. 11; Is. 19. 18.

patriarchs dwell in, Gen. 12. 6; 28; 36; 37.

the spies visit, and their report, Num. 13.

the murmurers forbidden to enter, Num. 14. 22.

also Moses and Aaron, Num. 20. 12; Deut. 3. 23; 32. 48.

Moses sees from Pisgah, Num. 27. 12; Deut. 3. 27; 34. 1.

allotted to children of Israel, Num. 26. 52; Josh. 14.

—a son of Ham, cursed on account of his father's mockery of Noah, Gen. 9. 25.

Candace, queen of Ethiopia, Acts 8. 27.

Candle, figurative, Job 18. 6; 21. 17; Ps. 18. 28; Prov. 20. 27.

parable, Matt. 5. 15; Lk. 8. 16.

Candlestick in the tabernacle, Ex. 25. 31; 37. 17; Lev. 24. 4; Num. 8. 2-4.

in visions, Zech. 4. 2; Rev. 1. 12.

Capernaum, Christ preaches at, Matt. 4. 17; Mk. 1. 21.

miracles at, Matt. 8. 5; 17. 24; John 4. 46; 6. 17.

parables at, Matt. 13. 18, 24; Mk. 4.

condemned for unbelief, Matt. 11. 23; Lk. 10. 15.

Cappadocia, Acts 2. 9; 1 Pet. 1. 1.

Captivity of the Israelites foretold, Lev. 26. 33; Deut. 28. 36.

of the ten tribes, Amos 3; 4; 7. 11.

Captivity—*Continued.*
fulfilled, 2 Ki. 17; 1 Chr. 5. 26.

of Judah foretold, Is. 39. 6; Jer. 13. 19; 20. 4; 25. 11; 32. 28.

fulfilled, 2 Ki. 25; 2 Chr. 36; Ps. 137; Est. 2; Jer. 39; 52; Dan. 1.

their return from, Ezra 1; Neh. 2; Ps. 126.

Care, worldly, forbidden, Matt. 6. 25; Lk. 8. 14; 12. 22; John 6. 27; 1 Cor. 7. 32; Phil. 4. 6; 1 Tim. 6. 8; 2 Tim. 2. 4; Heb. 13. 5.

Martha reproved for, Lk. 10. 41.

(loving) of the Samaritan, Lk. 10. 34.

of Christ for his mother, John 19. 26.

of Paul for the Corinthians, 2 Cor. 7. 12; 11. 28.

of Titus   ,,   2 Cor. 8. 16.

for Paul by Philippians, Phil. 4. 10.

to be cast on God, 1 Pet. 5. 7.

of thoughts, Ps. 39. 1.

Carmel, Nabal's conduct to David at, 1 Sam. 25.

mount, Elijah and the prophets of Baal, 1 Ki. 18.

Shunammite woman meets Elisha at, 2 Ki. 4. 25.

her child restored to life, 2 Ki. 4. 34.

Carnal mind condemned, Rom. 8. 7; 1 Cor. 3. 1; Col. 2. 18.

Carpenters, vision of four, Zech. 1. 20.

sent to David by Hiram, 2 Sam. 5. 11.

Carpenter's Son, Christ reproached as, Matt. 13. 55; Mk. 6. 3.

Cassia, spice, Ex. 30. 24; Ps. 45. 8.

Castor and Pollux, ship so called, Acts 28. 11.

Cattle of Jacob increased, Gen. 30. 43.

of Israelites preserved, Ex. 9. 4.

regulations concerning, Ex. 20. 10; 21. 28; 22. 1; 23. 4; Deut. 5. 14; 22. 1; 25. 4; (1 Cor. 9. 9; 1 Tim. 5. 18).

referred to by Christ, Matt. 12. 11; Lk. 13. 15: 14. 5.

an example of obedience, Is. 1. 3.

Caves of refuge, 1 Sam. 13. 6; Heb. 11. 38.

prophets concealed in, by Obadiah, 1 Ki. 18. 4.

Elijah lodges in, 1 Ki. 19. 9.

Cedar, temple built of, 1 Ki. 5. 6; 6. 15.

Behemoth compared to, Job 40. 17.

Cedars of Lebanon, Jud. 9. 15; Ps. 92. 12; 104. 16; 148. 9; Cant. 5. 15; Is. 2. 13; Ezek. 17. 3.

Cenchrea, seaport of Corinth, church there, Rom. 16. 1.

Paul shaves his head at, Acts 18. 18.

Censers of brass, Lev. 10. 1; 16. 12.

,,   of gold, 1 Ki. 7. 50; Heb. 9. 4; Rev. 8. 3.

,,   of Korah, reserved for holy use, Num. 16. 36.

Centurion, servant of, healed, Matt. 8. 5; Lk. 7. 2.

—at crucifixion acknowledges Christ, Matt. 27. 54; Mk. 15. 39; Lk. 23. 47.

—Cornelius, Acts 10. 1.

—in charge of Paul, Acts 27. 43.

Cephas (Peter) a stone, John 1. 42; 1 Cor. 1. 12; 3. 22; 9. 5; 15. 5; Gal. 2. 9.

See Peter.

Chalcedony, foundation of the heavenly city, Rev. 21. 19.

Chaldeans afflict Job, Job 1. 17.

besiege Jerusalem, 2 Ki. 24. 2; 25. 4; Jer. 37-39.

wise men of, preserved by Daniel, Dan. 2. 24.

prophecies concerning, Is. 23. 13; 43. 14; 47. 1; 48; Hab. 1. 5.

Chapel, the king's, Amos 7. 13.

Charge of God to Moses and Aaron, Ex. 6. 13.
,, of Moses to Joshua, Deut. 31. 7.
,, of David to Solomon, 1 Ki. 2. 1; 1 Chr. 22. 6.
,, of Jehoshaphat to the judges, 2 Chr. 19. 6.
,, of Paul to the elders of Ephesus, Acts 20. 17.
,, of Paul to Timothy, 1 Tim. 5. 21; 2 Tim. 4.
,, of Peter to the elders, 1 Pet. 5.

Chariot of fire, Elijah ascends to heaven in, 2 Ki. 2. 11.

Chariots of war, Ex. 14. 7; 1 Sam. 13. 5; 2 Sam. 10. 18; Ps. 20. 7; Nah. 3. 2.
sent by the king of Syria to take Elisha, 2 Ki. 6. 14.
of fire sent to defend Elisha, 2 Ki. 6. 17.
of God, Ps. 68. 17.

Charity, love to our neighbour, Matt. 22. 39; Mk. 12. 33; Rom. 13. 8-10; 1 Cor. 13; 1 Thes. 1. 3; 3. 6; 4. 9; 1 Tim. 1. 5; 4. 12; 2 Tim. 3. 10; Heb. 6. 10; Jas. 2. 8; 1 Pet. 1. 22; 1 John 2. 10; 3. 14; 4. 11; Rev. 2. 19.
almsgiving, Prov. 19. 17; Matt. 19. 21; Lk. 11. 41; 12. 33; 18. 22; Acts 10. 2, 4; 2 Cor. 9; 3 John 6.
exhortations to, Lev. 19. 18; Deut. 10. 19; Matt. 5. 44; Gal. 5. 14; 6. 10; Eph. 4. 2; 1 John 3. 23; 4. 7, 21; 2 John 5.
commended, 1 Cor. 8. 1; 13; Gal. 5. 6, 22; Eph. 3. 17; 4. 16; 5. 2; Col. 3. 14.
how to be manifested, Lev. 19. 17; 25. 35; Is. 58. 7; Matt. 18. 15; 25. 35; John 13. 35; Rom. 12. 15; 1 Cor. 12. 26; Gal. 5. 13; Eph. 4. 32; 1 Thes. 5. 14; Heb. 6. 10; 1 Pet. 4. 8; 1 John 3. 10, 17.
exemplified by Christ, John 13. 34; 15. 12; Eph. 5. 2, 25; Rev. 1. 5.

Chebar, the river, Ezekiel's visions at, Ezek. 1; 3. 15; 10. 15.

Chedorlaomer, king of Elam, takes Lot prisoner, but subdued by Abram, Gen. 14.

Chemosh, god of Moab, Num. 21. 29; Jud. 11. 24; Jer. 48. 7, 13, 46.
worshipped by Solomon, 1 Ki. 11. 7.

Cherethites (and Pelethites), David's guard, 2 Sam. 15. 18.

Cherubim in garden of Eden, Gen. 3. 24.
for the mercy seat and the temple, Ex. 25. 18; 37. 7; 1 Ki. 6. 23; 2 Chr. 3. 10; Ps. 80. 1; Ezek. 41. 18.
Ezekiel's visions of, Ezek. 1; 10.

Chief Priests, consulted by Herod, Matt. 2. 4.
their persecution of Christ, Matt. 16. 21; Mk. 14. 1; 15. 31; John 7. 32.

Children, the gift of God, Gen. 33. 5; Ps. 127; 128.
a blessing, Prov. 10. 1; 15. 20; 17. 6; 23. 24; 27. 11; 29. 3.
duty of, Ex. 20. 12; Lev. 19. 3, 32; Deut. 5. 16; 30. 2; Prov. 1. 8; 6. 20; 13. 1; 15. 5; 19. 27; 23. 22; 24. 21; 28. 7, 24; Eccles. 12. 1; Eph. 6. 1; Col. 3. 20; 1 Tim. 5. 4; Heb. 12. 9; 1 Pet. 5. 5.
of Bethlehem slain by Herod, Matt. 2. 16 (Jer. 31. 15).
blessed by Christ, Matt. 19. 13; Mk. 10. 13; Lk. 18. 15.
of light, Lk. 16. 8; John 12. 36; Eph. 5. 8; 1 Thes. 5. 5.
of God, Eph. 5. 1; Heb. 12. 5; 1 Pet. 1. 14; 1 John 3. 10.
Examples of *obedient* children

Children *Continued*,
Christ, Lk. 2. 51. Isaac, Gen. 22. 6. Joseph, Gen. 45. 9. Jephthah's daughter, Jud. 11. 36. Samuel, 1 Sam. 2. 26.
Wicked children characterised, 1 Sam. 2. 12, 25; Prov. 15. 5; 17. 21; 19. 13, 26; 28. 7, 24; 30. 11; Is. 3. 5; Ezek. 22. 7.
their punishment, Ex. 21. 15; Deut. 21. 18; 27. 16; 2 Ki. 2. 23; Prov. 30. 17; Mk. 7. 10.
(child) of the devil, Acts 13. 10; 1 John 3. 10.

Chittim, prophecies concerning, Num. 24. 24; Is. 23. 1, 12; Jer. 2. 10; Ezek. 27. 6; Dan. 11. 30.

Christ, Lord Jesus, Matt. 1. 21; Lk. 2. 11; John 1. 41; 4. 42; Acts 11. 17; 13. 23; 15. 11; 16. 31; 20. 21; Rom. 5. 1, 11; 6. 23; 7. 25; 13. 14; 15. 6, 30; 16. 13; 1 Cor. 1. 2, 3, 7, 10; 5. 4; Eph. 5. 23; Phil. 3. 20; 1 Tim. 1. 1, 12; 3. 13; 4. 6; 5. 21; 2 Tim. 1. 10; Tit. 1. 4; 2. 13; 3. 6; Philem. 3. 5, 25; Heb. 13. 8, 21; Jas. 1. 1; 1 Pet. 1. 3; 2 Pet. 1. 1, 11; 2. 20; 3. 18; Jude 1. 4, 17, 21; Rev. 22. 21.
Son of God, Matt. 2. 15; 3. 17; 4. 3, 6; Lk. 1. 32, 35; 3. 22; 4. 3, 9; 4. 34. 41; John 1. 34; 3. 16, 18; 5. 22, 23; 6. 69; 13. 8; 16. 27, 30; 17. 1; 19. 7; Rom. 1. 9; 5. 10; 8. 3, 32; 1 Cor. 1. 9; Gal. 1. 16; 4. 4; Col. 1. 13; 1 Thes. 1. 10; Heb. 1. 2, 5, 8; 3. 6; 4. 14; 5. 5; 6. 6; 1 John 1. 7; 3. 23; 4. 9, 10; 5. 9.
Son of Man, Matt. 8. 20; 10. 23; 11. 19; 12. 8, 32, 40; 13. 37, 41; 16. 13; 17. 9, 22; 24. 27, 30, 44; 25. 31; 26. 2, 24, 45; Mk. 8. 38; 9. 12, 31; 44; 25. 31; 26. 2, 24, 45; Mk. 8. 38; 9. 12, 31; Lk. 5. 24; 6. 22; 9. 22, 56; 11. 30; 12. 8; 17. 22; 18. 8; 19. 10; 21. 36; 22. 48; John 1. 51; 3. 13; 5. 27; 6. 27, 53, 62; 8. 28; 12. 23, 34; 13. 31; Acts 7. 56; Rev. 1. 13.
Prophet, Deut. 18. 15; Nah. 1. 15; Lk. 4. 18, 24; Acts 3. 22.
Priest, Heb. 2. 17; 3. 1; 5. 6; 6. 20; 7; 8.
See Ps. 110. 4.
King, Matt. 2. 2; 21. 5; 25. 34; John 1. 49; 18. 36; Heb. 1. 8; Rev. 1. 5; 11. 15; 17. 14; 19. 16.

LIFE AND WORK ON EARTH:
his miraculous conception and birth predicted, Is. 7. 14; 11. 1; Mic. 5. 2.
accomplished at Bethlehem, Matt. 1. 18; Lk. 1. 31; 2. 6.
announced to shepherds by angels, Lk. 2. 9-14.
wise men of the East do homage to, Matt. 2. 1.
circumcision of, and presentation in the temple, Lk. 2. 21.
carried into Egypt, Matt. 2. 13.
first public appearance (doctors in temple), Lk. 2. 46.
baptised by John, Matt. 3. 13; Mk. 1. 9; Lk. 3. 21; John 1. 32; 3. 24.
his temptation, Matt. 4; Mk. 1. 12; Lk. 4. 1. 14; Lk. 4. 16.
begins to preach and heal, Matt. 4. 12; Mk. 1. 14; Lk. 4. 16.
his selection of disciples, Matt. 4. 18; Mk. 1. 16; Lk. 4. 31; 5. 10; John 1. 38.
his sermon on the mount, Matt. 5; 6; 7.
cleanses the temple, John 2. 14; Ps. 69. 9.
his conversation with Nicodemus, John 3. and with a woman of Samaria, John 4.
refuses to be made king, John 6. 15.
taunted by his kinsmen, John 7. 4.
sufferings and death predicted, Matt. 16. 21; 17. 22; 20. 17; Mk. 8. 31; 9. 31; 10. 32; Lk. 9. 22, 44; 18. 31.
transfiguration on the mount, Matt. 17; Mk. 9; Lk. 9. 28.

Christ—*Continued.*
the people's testimony, Matt. 16. 13; Mk. 8. 27; Lk. 9. 18; John 7. 12.
message to John the Baptist, Lk. 7. 22.
anointed at Simon the Pharisee's house, Lk. 7. 36.
pays tribute at Capernaum, Matt. 17. 24.
inculcates humility on apostles, Matt. 18; Mk. 9. 33; Lk. 9. 46; 22. 24.
goes into Judea, Matt. 19. 1; John 7. 10.
teaches respecting divorce, Matt. 19. 3; Lk. 16. 18.
reproves Herod and Jerusalem, Lk. 13. 32, 34.
pardons woman taken in adultery, John 8. 3.
compares Martha and Mary, Lk. 10. 38-42.
blesses little children, Matt. 19. 13; Mk. 10. 13; Lk. 18. 15.
Zaccheus the publican called by, Lk. 19. 2.
anointed by Mary at Bethany, Matt. 26. 6; Mk. 14. 3; John 12. 3.
rides into Jerusalem, Matt. 21; Mk. 11; Lk. 19. 29; John 12. 12.
drives money changers out of temple, Matt. 21. 12; Mk. 11. 15; Lk. 19. 45.
curses the barren fig tree, Matt. 21. 19; Mk. 11. 12.
Greeks desire to see him, John 12. 20.
  his reply, John 12. 23.
  glorified by the Father, John 12. 28.
his reply to the chief priests, Lk. 20. 3.
  „   to the Pharisees, Matt. 22. 15.
  „   to the Sadducees, Mk. 12. 18.
chief priests conspire to kill, Matt. 26. 3; Mk. 14. 1.
covenant with Judas to betray, Matt. 26. 14; Mk. 14. 10; Lk. 22. 3; John 13. 18.
gives directions for the passover, Matt. 26. 17; Mk. 14. 12; Lk. 22. 7.
foretells Peter's denial, Matt. 26. 34; Mk. 14. 29; Lk. 22. 31.
washes disciples' feet, John 13. 5.
comforts and exhorts his disciples, John 14; 15.
promises the Holy Spirit, John 16.
prays for disciples, John 17.
institutes the Lord's Supper, Matt. 26. 26; Mk. 14. 22; Lk. 22. 19; (1 Cor. 11. 23).
his agony, Matt. 26. 36; Mk. 14. 32; Lk. 22. 39.
betrayed by Judas, Matt. 26. 47; Mk. 14. 43; Lk. 22. 47; John 18. 3.
forbids use of sword, Matt. 26. 52; John 18. 11.
deserted by disciples, Matt. 26. 31, 56; John 18. 15.
taken before Annas and Caiaphas, Matt. 26. 57; Mk. 14. 54; John 18. 13.
and Pilate and Herod, Matt. 27. 2; Mk. 15. 1; Lk. 23; John 18. 28.
acquitted by Pilate, Matt. 27. 23; Mk. 15. 14; Lk. 23. 13; John 18. 38; 19.
yet delivered to be crucified, Matt. 27. 26; Mk. 15. 15; Lk. 23. 24; John 19. 16.
his crucifixion, Matt. 27. 33; Mk. 15. 21; Lk. 23. 33; John 19. 17.
his legs not broken, John 19. 33.
his side pierced, John 19. 34.
his garments divided amongst soldiers, Matt. 27. 35; Mk. 15. 24; Lk. 23. 34; John 19. 24.
yields up the ghost, Matt. 27. 50; Mk. 15. 37; John 19. 30.
acknowledged by centurion to be the Son of God, Matt. 27. 54; Mk. 15. 39. To be righteous, Lk. 23. 47.

Christ—*Continued.*
buried by Joseph and Nicodemus, Matt. 27. 57; Mk. 15. 42; Lk. 23. 50; John 19. 38.
the sepulchre sealed and watched, Matt. 27. 66.
his resurrection, Matt. 28; Mk. 16; Lk. 24; John 20. 21.
appears first to Mary Magdalene, Matt. 28. 1; Mk. 16. 1; Lk. 24. 1; John 20. 1.
to his disciples at various times, Matt. 28. 16; Mk. 16. 12; Lk. 24. 13, 26; John 20; 21; 1 Cor. 15.
shews Thomas his hands and feet, John 20. 27.
charges Peter to feed his lambs, John 21. 15.
ascends into heaven, Mk. 16. 19; Lk. 24. 51; Acts 1. 9, 10.
appears after his ascension to Stephen, Acts 7. 55. To Paul, Acts 9. 4; 18. 9; 22. 6. To John, Rev. 1. 13.
HIS TEACHING :
preaches repentance at Galilee, Matt. 4. 17.
preaches at Nazareth, Lk. 4. 16.
the gospel of the kingdom, Matt. 4. 23; Mk. 1. 14.
testimony concerning John the Baptist, Matt. 11. 7; Lk. 7. 24; 20. 4.
upbraids Chorazin, Bethsaida, Capernaum, Matt. 11. 20; Lk. 10. 13.
concerning his mission, John 5. 17; 7. 16; 8. 12; 10; 12. 30.
on the bread of life, John 6. 26.
traditions of the elders, Matt. 15. 1; Mk. 7. 1.
to Pharisees asking a sign, Matt. 12. 38; 16. 1; Mk. 8. 11; Lk. 11. 16; 12. 54; John 2. 18.
on humility, John 13. 14.
concerning the Scribes and Pharisees, Matt. 23; Mk. 12. 38; Lk. 11. 37; 20. 45.
prophesies the destruction of Jerusalem, and the last times, Matt. 24; Mk. 13; Lk. 13. 34; 17. 20; 19. 41; 21. 5.
his invitation to the weary and heavy laden, Matt. 11. 28.
concerning the Galileans killed by Pilate, Lk. 13. 1.
on suffering for the Gospel's sake, Lk. 14. 26; (Matt. 10. 37.).
on marriage, Matt. 19; Mk. 10.
on riches, Matt. 19. 16; Mk. 10. 17; Lk. 12. 13; 18. 18.
paying tribute, Matt. 22. 15; Mk. 12. 13; Lk. 20. 20.
the resurrection, Matt. 22. 23; Mk. 12. 18.
the two great commandments, Matt. 22. 35; Mk. 12. 28.
the son of David, Matt. 22. 41; Mk. 12. 35; Lk. 20. 41.
the widow's mite, Matt. 41; Lk. 21. 1.
on watchfulness, Matt. 24. 42; Mk. 13. 33; Lk. 21. 34; 12. 35.
the last judgment, Matt. 25. 31.
SERMON ON THE MOUNT, Matt. 5; 6; 7.
See Lk. 6. 20-46.
Lord's prayer, Matt. 6. 9-13; Lk. 11. 2-4.
hearers and doers, Matt. 7. 24; Lk. 6. 46.
epistles to the seven churches in Asia, Rev. 1; 2; 3.
HIS DISCOURSES :
on faith, the centurion's, Matt. 8. 8.
to those who would follow him, Matt. 8. 19; Lk. 9. 23, 57.
on fasting, Matt. 9. 14; Mk. 2. 18; Lk. 5. 33.
on blasphemy, Matt. 12. 31; Mk. 3. 28; Lk. 11. 15.

Christ—*Continued.*
who are his brethren, Matt. 12. 46; Mk. 3. 31; Lk. 8. 19.

His Parables :
the w se and foolish builders, Matt. 7. 24-27.
children of the bridechamber, Matt. 9. 15; Lk. 5. 34, 35.
new cloth and old garment, Matt. 9. 16; Lk. 5. 36.
new wine and old bottles, Matt. 9. 17.
the unclean spirit, Matt. 12. 43.
the sower, Matt. 13. 3, 18; Mk. 4. 3; Lk. 8. 5, 11.
the tares, Matt. 13. 24, 36.
mustard seed, Matt. 13. 31, 32; Lk. 13. 19.
leaven, Matt. 13. 33.
treasure hid in a field, Matt. 13. 44.
pearl of great price, Matt. 13. 45-46.
net cast into the sea, Matt. 13. 47-50.
meats not defiling, Matt. 15. 10-15.
the unmerciful servant, Matt. 18. 23-35.
the labourers, Matt. 20. 1-16.
the two sons, Matt. 21. 28-32.
the w cked husbandmen, Matt. 21. 33-45; Mk. 12. 1; Lk. 20. 9.
the marriage feast, Matt. 22. 2; Lk. 14. 16.
fig tree leafing, Matt. 24. 32-34.
man of the house watching, etc., Matt. 24. 43-51
ten virgins, Matt. 25. 1.
talents, Matt. 25. 14-30; Lk. 19. 12.
kingdom and house divided against themselves, Mk. 3. 24, 25.
strong man armed, Mk. 3. 27; Lk. 11. 21.
seed growing secretly, Mk. 4. 26-29.
lighted candle, Mk. 4. 21; Lk. 11. 33-36.
man going on a long journey, Mk. 13. 34-37.
the creditor and two debtors, Lk. 7. 41-47.
the good Samaritan, Lk. 10. 30-37.
the importunate friend, Lk. 11. 5-9.
the rich fool, Lk. 12. 16-21.
cloud and wind, Lk. 12. 54-57.
the barren fig tree, Lk. 13. 6-9.
chief seats at a feast, Lk. 14. 7-11.
builder of a tower, Lk. 14. 28-30, 33.
king going to war, Lk. 14. 31-33.
savour of salt, Lk. 14. 34, 35.
lost sheep, Lk. 15. 3-7.
lost piece of silver, Lk. 15. 8-10.
prodigal son, Lk. 15. 11-32.
the unjust steward, Lk. 16. 1-8.
rich man and Lazarus, Lk. 16. 19-31.
unprofitable servant, Lk. 17. 7.
the importunate widow, Lk. 18. 1-8.
Pharisee and publican, Lk. 18. 9-14.
the good shepherd, John 10. 1.
vine and branches, John 15. 1.

His Miracles :
water turned into wine, John 2. 6-10.
nobleman's son healed, John 4. 46-53.
centurion's servant healed, Matt. 8. 5-13.
draughts of fishes, Lk. 5. 4-6; John 21. 6.
devils cast out, Matt. 8. 28-32; 9. 32, 33; 15. 22-28; 17. 14-18; Mk. 1. 23-27.
Peter's wife's mother healed, Matt. 8. 14, 15.
lepers cleansed, Matt. 8. 3; Lk. 17. 14.
paralytic healed, Mk. 2. 3-12.
withered hand restored, Matt. 12. 10-13.
impotent man healed, John 5. 5-9.
the dead raised to life, Matt. 9. 18, 19, 23-25; Lk. 7. 12-15; John 11. 11-44.
issue of blood stopped, Matt. 9. 20-22.
the blind restored to sight, Matt. 9. 27-30; Mk. 8. 22-25; John 9. 1-7.

Christ—*Continued.*
the deaf and dumb cured, Mk. 7. 32-35.
the multitude fed, Matt. 14. 15-21; 15. 32-33.
his walking on the sea, Matt. 14. 25-27.
with the tribute-money, Matt. 17. 27.
tempest still, Matt. 8. 23-26; Mk. 4. 37; Lk. 8. 23.
woman healed of infirmity, Lk. 13. 11-13.
dropsy cured, Lk. 14. 2-4.
blighting of the fig tree, Matt. 21. 19.
miracles performed in the presence of the messengers of John, Lk. 7. 21, 22.
many and divers diseases healed, Matt. 4. 23, 24; 14. 14; 15. 30; Mk. 1. 34; Lk. 6. 17-19.
Malchus healed, Lk. 22. 50, 51; (John 18. 10.)
his transfiguration, Matt. 17. 1-8; Mk. 9. 2; Lk. 9. 29.
his resurrection, Lk. 24. 6; John 10. 18.
his appearance to his disciples when the doors were shut, John 20. 19.
his ascension, Acts 1. 9.

His Character :
holy, Lk. 1. 35; Acts 4. 27; Rev. 3. 7.
righteous, Is. 53. 11; Heb. 1. 9.
good, Matt. 19. 16.
faithful, Is. 11. 5; 1 Thes. 5. 24.
true, John 1. 14; 7. 18; 1 John 5. 20.
just, Zech. 9. 9; John 5. 30; Acts 22. 14.
guileless, Is. 53. 9; 1 Pet. 2. 22.
sinless, John 8. 46; 2 Cor. 5. 21.
spotless, 1 Pet. 1. 19.
harmless, Heb. 7. 26.
obedient to God the Father, Ps. 40. 8; John 4. 34; 15. 10.
subject to his parents, Lk. 2. 51.
zealous, Lk. 2. 49; John 2. 17; 8. 29.
meek, Is. 53. 7; Matt. 11. 29.
lowly in heart, Matt. 11. 29.
merciful, Heb. 2. 17.
long-suffering, 1 Tim. 1. 16.
compassionate, Is. 40. 11; Matt. 15. 32; Lk. 7. 13; 19. 41.
benevolent, Matt. 4. 23, 24; 9. 35; Acts 10. 38.
loving, John 13. 1; 15. 13.
self-denying, Matt. 8. 20; 2 Cor. 8. 9.
humble, Lk. 22. 27; Phil. 2. 8.
forgiving, Lk. 23. 34.

His Compassion :
for the weary and heavy-laden, Matt. 11. 28-30.
towards the afflicted, Lk. 7. 13; John 11. 33.
" " diseased, Matt. 14. 14; Mk. 1. 41.
for perishing sinners, Matt. 9. 36; Lk. 19. 41; John 3. 16.
towards the tempted, Heb. 2. 18.
necessary to his priestly office, Heb. 5. 2-10.
an encouragement to prayer, Heb. 4. 15, 16.

His Divine Nature :
the eternal God and Creator, John 1. 1-5; Col. 1. 16, 17; 2. 9; Heb. 1. 2, 3.
equality with God, John 5. 17-23; 10. 30, 38; 16. 15; Phil. 2. 6; 1 Thes. 3. 11; 2 Thes. 2. 16.
Son of God, Matt. 3. 17; 26. 63, 64; John 1. 14, 18; 3. 16, 18; 14. 7-10; 1 John 4. 9.
one with the Father, John 12. 45; 17. 10.
sending the spirit equally with the Father, John 14. 16; 15. 26.
image of God and first-born, Col. 1. 15; Heb. 1. 3.
the Lord of glory, 1 Cor. 2. 8; Jas. 2. 1.
the Lord of all, Acts 10. 36.
Lord of the Sabbath, Matt. 12. 8.
the Lord from heaven, 1 Cor. 15. 47.

Christ—*Continued.*

King of kings and Lord of lords, Rev. 19. 16.
the Judge of men, Matt. 16. 27; 25. 31; 2 Cor. 5. 10.
the true Light, Lk. 1. 78, 79; John 1. 4, 9.
the Way, John. 14. 6; Heb. 10. 19, 20.
the Truth, 1 John 5. 20; Rev. 3. 7.
the Life, John 11. 25; Col. 3. 4; 1 John 5. 11.
manifest in the flesh, John 1. 14; 1 Tim. 3. 16.
head of the Church, Eph. 1. 22.
manifested in his words, Lk. 4. 22; John 7. 46.
     ,,   his works, Matt. 13. 54; John 2. 11; 5. 21; 6. 40.
acknowledged by his disciples, Matt. 16. 16; John 1. 49; 20. 28.
object of Divine worship, Acts 7. 59; Heb. 1. 6; Rev. 5. 12.
his omnipresence, omnipotence, and omniscience, Matt. 18. 20: 28. 20; John 3. 13; 16. 30; 21. 17; Phil. 3. 21; Col. 1. 17; Heb. 1. 8-10.
the Mediator, Gal. 3. 19; Heb. 8. 6; 12. 24.
HIS HUMAN NATURE:
born of a woman, Matt. 1. 18; Lk. 1. 31; Gal. 4. 4.
partaking of our flesh and blood, John 1. 14; Heb. 2. 14.
having a human soul, Matt. 26. 38; Lk. 23. 46; Acts 2. 31.
increasing in wisdom and stature, Lk. 2. 52.
feeling hunger, Matt. 4. 2, 21. 18.
     ,,   thirst, John 4. 7; 19. 28.
     ,,   weariness, John 4. 6.
sleeping, Matt. 8. 24; Mk. 4. 38.
weeping, Lk. 19. 41; John 11. 35.
Man of Sorrows, Is. 53. 3, 4; Lk. 22. 44; John 11. 33; 12. 27.
enduring indignities, Matt. 26. 67; Lk. 22. 64; 23. 11.
scourged, Matt. 27. 26; John 19. 1.
nailed to the cross, Lk. 23. 33; John 19. 18.
buried, Matt. 27. 59, 60; Mk. 15. 46.
like us in all things, Acts 3. 22; Phil. 2. 7, 8; Heb. 2. 17; but without sin, John 8. 46; 18. 38; Heb. 4. 15; 7. 26, 28; 1 Pet. 2. 22; 1 John 3. 5.
asserted by men, Mk. 6. 3; John 7. 27; 19. 5; Acts 2. 22.
denied by Antichrist, 1 John 4. 3; 2 John 7.
evidenced by the senses, John 20. 27; 1 John 1. 1, 2.
attested by himself, Matt. 8. 20; 16. 13.
called Son of David, Matt. 22. 42; Mk. 10. 47; Acts 2. 30; 13. 23; Rom. 1. 3.
the seed of Abraham, Gal. 3. 16; Heb. 2. 16.
one Mediator, the man Christ Jesus, 1 Tim. 2. 5; Heb. 2. 17.
HIS DIFFERENT TITLES:
Adam, the second, 1 Cor. 15. 45.
Advocate, 1 John 2. 1.
Alpha and Omega, Rev. 1. 8; 22. 13.
Amen, Rev. 3. 14.
Apostle of our Profession, Heb. 3. 1.
Author and Finisher of our faith, Heb. 12. 2.
Beginning of the Creation of God, Rev. 3. 14.
Blessed and only Potentate, 1 Tim. 6. 15.
Captain of Salvation, Heb. 2. 10.
Chief Corner Stone, Eph. 2. 20; 1 Pet. 2. 6.
Chief Shepherd, 1 Pet. 5. 4.
Dayspring, Lk. 1. 78.
Desire of all Nations, Hag. 2. 7.
Emmanuel, Is. 7. 14; 8. 8; Matt. 1. 23.

Christ—*Continued.*

Everlasting Father, Is 9. 6.
Faithful Witness, Rev. 1. 5; 3. 14.
First and Last, Rev. 1. 17; 2. 8.
Good Shepherd, John 10. 14.
Governor, Matt. 2. 6.
Great High Priest, Heb. 3. 1; 4. 14.
Head of the Church, Eph. 5. 23; Col. 1. 18.
Heir of all Things, Heb. 1. 2.
Holy One, Mk. 1. 24; Acts 2. 27.
Horn of Salvation, Lk. 1. 69.
I Am, John 8. 58. See Ex. 3. 14.
Just One, Acts 7. 52.
Lamb (of God), John 1. 29, 36; Rev. 5. 6, 12, 13. 8; 21. 22: 22. 3.
Lion of Tribe of Judah, Rev. 5. 5.
Lord God Almighty, Rev. 15. 3; 22. 6.
Lord our Righteousness, Jer. 23. 6.
Messenger of the Covenant, Mal. 3. 1.
Messiah, Dan. 9. 25; John 1. 41.
Morning Star, Rev. 22. 16.
Prince of Life, Acts 3. 15.
Prince of Peace, Is. 9. 6.
Prince of the Kings of the Earth, Rev. 1. 5.
Resurrection and Life, John 11. 25.
Root of David, Rev. 22. 16.
Saviour, 2 Pet. 2. 20; 3. 18.
Shepherd and Bishop of Souls, 1 Pet. 2. 25.
Son of the Blessed, Mk. 14. 61.
Son of the Highest, Lk. 1. 32.
Sun of Righteousness, Mal. 4. 2.
Wonderful, Counsellor, Mighty God, Is. 9. 6.
Word of God, Rev. 19. 13.
Word of Life, 1 John 1. 1.
THE HEAD OF THE CHURCH:
declared by Himself to be head of the corner, Matt. 21. 42.
     ,,   ,, St Paul, Eph. 4. 12, 15; 5. 23.
as such, has pre-eminence in all things, 1 Cor. 11. 3; Eph. 1. 22; Col. 1. 18.
saints complete in, Col. 2. 10.
TYPES OF:
Aaron, Ex. 28. 1: Lev. 16. 15; Heb. 4. 15: 12. 24.
Abel, Gen. 4. 8, 10; Heb. 12. 24.
Adam, Rom. 5. 14; 1 Cor. 15. 45.
David, 2 Sam. 8. 15; Ps. 89. 19; Ezek. 37. 24.
Eliakim, Is. 22. 20. See Rev. 3. 7.
Isaac, Gen. 22. 2; Heb. 11. 17.
Jacob, Gen. 32. 28; John 11. 42; Heb. 7. 25.
Jonah, Jon. 1. 17; Matt. 12. 40.
Joshua, Josh. 1. 5; 11. 23; Acts 20. 32; Heb. 4. 8.
Melchizedek, Gen. 14. 18, 20; Heb. 7. 1.
Moses, Num. 12. 7; Deut. 18. 15; Acts 3. 22; 7. 37; Heb. 3. 2.
Noah, Gen. 5. 29; 2 Cor. 1. 5.
Solomon, 2 Sam. 7. 12; Lk. 1. 32.
Zerubbabel, Zech. 4. 7, 9; Heb. 12. 2, 3.
the ark, Gen. 7. 16; Ex. 25. 16; Ps. 40. 8; Is. 42. 6; 1 Pet. 3. 20, 21.
Jacob's ladder, Gen. 28. 12; John 1. 51.
passover, Ex. 12; 1 Cor. 5. 7.
lamb, Ex. 12. 3; Is. 53. 7; John 1. 29; Acts 8. 32; 1 Pet. 1. 19; Rev. 5. 6; 6. 1; 7. 9; 12. 11; 13. 8; 14. 1; 15. 3; 17. 14; 19. 7; 21. 9; 22. 1.
manna, Ex. 16. 11; John 6. 32; Rev. 2. 17.
rock, Ex. 17. 6; 1 Cor. 10. 4.
first-fruits, Ex. 22. 29; 1 Cor. 15. 20.
brazen altar, Ex. 27. 1, 2; Heb. 13. 10.
laver, Ex. 30. 18; Zech. 13. 1; Eph. 5. 26.
burnt offering, Lev. 1. 2; Heb. 10. 10.

Christ—*Continued.*
peace-offering, Lev. 3; Eph. 2. 14.
sin offering, Lev. 4. 2; Heb. 13. 11.
atonement, sacrifices upon the day of, Lev. 16. 15; Heb. 9. 12.
scapegoat, Lev. 16. 20; Is. 53. 6; Heb. 9. 28.
brazen serpent, Num. 21. 9; John 3. 14.
cities of refuge, Num. 35. 6; Heb. 6. 18.
tabernacle, Heb. 9. 8, 11.
temple, 1 Ki. 6. 1, 38; John 2. 21.
veil, Ex. 40. 21; Heb. 10. 20.
branch, Is. 4. 2; Jer. 23. 5; Zech. 3. 8.
Christs, false, warnings against, Matt. 24. 4, 5, 24; Mk. 13. 22.
Christian, none to be ashamed to suffer as a, 1 Pet. 4. 16.
Christians, disciples first called, at Antioch, Acts 11. 26.
Chrysolite and Chrysoprasus, Rev. 21. 20.
Church of God, Acts 20. 28; 1 Cor. 1. 2; 10. 32; 11. 22; 15. 9; Gal. 1. 13; 1 Tim. 3. 5.
foundation of, Matt. 16. 18; Col. 1. 18.
increase of, Acts 2. 47; Acts 14. 23.
authority of, Matt. 18. 17; 1 Cor. 5. 4.
teaching of, Acts 11. 26; 1 Cor. 12. 28; 14. 4, 5.
persecuted, Acts 8. 3; 12. 1; Gal. 1. 13; Phil. 3. 6.
saluted, Acts 18. 22; Rom. 16. 5; 1 Cor. 16. 19.
loved of Christ, Eph. 5. 25, 29.
Churches, the seven, in Asia, Rev. 1. 4, 11, 20; 2. 7, 11, 17, 29; 3. 6, 13, 22.
Churlish, Nabal so designated, 1 Sam. 25. 3.
Cilicia, disciples there, Acts 15. 23, 41.
the country of Paul, Acts 21. 39; 22. 3; Gal. 1. 21.
Circumcision, the covenant of, Gen. 17. 10.
performed, Gen. 34. 24; Ex. 4. 25; 12. 48, etc.
renewed by Joshua, Josh. 5. 2.
of John, Lk. 1. 59; of Jesus, Lk. 2. 21; of Timothy, Acts 16. 3.
superseded by the Gospel, Acts 15; Gal. 5. 2.
of heart, Deut. 10. 16; 30. 6.
spiritual, Phil. 3. 3; Col. 2. 11.
how far profitable, Rom. 2. 25; 4. 9; 1 Cor. 7. 19; Gal. 5. 6; 6. 15.
Circumspection, exhortations to, Ex. 23. 13; Eph. 5. 15.
Cities, what to be spared, Deut. 20. 10.
what to be destroyed, Deut. 20. 16.
of refuge, Num. 35. 6; Deut. 19; Josh. 20.
Claudia, 2 Tim. 4. 21.
Claudius Lysias, chief captain, rescues Paul, Acts 21. 31; 22. 24; 23. 10.
sends him to Felix, Acts 23. 26.
Clement, fellow-labourer of Paul, Phil. 4. 3.
Cleopas, a disciple, Lk. 24. 18.
Clothing, the first, Gen. 3. 21.
rending, a mark of grief, Gen. 37. 29, 34; Num. 14. 6; Jud. 11. 35; Acts 14. 14.
laws concerning washing, Ex. 19. 10; Lev. 11. 25; Num. 19. 7.
Cloud, pillar of, children of Israel guided by, Ex. 13. 21; 14. 19; Neh. 9. 19; Ps. 78. 14; 105. 39; 1 Cor. 10. 1.
appearance of the Lord in, Ex. 24. 15; 34. 5; Lev. 16. 2; Num. 11. 25; 12. 5; 1 Ki. 8. 10; Ezek. 10. 4; Matt. 17. 5; Lk. 21. 27; Rev. 14. 14.
Collection for the saints, Acts 11. 29; Rom. 15. 26; 1 Cor. 16. 1.
Colosse, brethren at, encouraged and warned, Col. 1; 2.
exhorted to holiness, Col. 3; 4.

Comforter, the Spirit of Truth, John 14. 26; 15. 26; 16. 7.
Command of God to Adam, Gen. 2. 16.
     ,,   ,,   to Moses, Ex. 3. 14.
     ,,   ,,   to Joshua, Josh. 1. 9.
     ,,   of Moses to the sons of Levi, Deut. 31. 10.
     ,,   of Christ to the twelve, Matt. 10. 5; Mk. 16. 15.
     ,,   ,,   to Peter, John 21. 15.
Commandments (ten) delivered, Ex. 20; 31. 18; Deut. 5. 6.
on tables of stone broken, Ex. 32. 19.
renewed, Ex. 34. 1; Deut. 10. 1.
fulfilled by Christ, Matt. 5. 17; 19. 17; 22. 35; Mk. 10. 17; Lk. 10. 25; 18. 18.
Communion of the body and blood of Christ, 1 Cor. 10. 16.
Lord's Supper instituted, Matt. 26. 26; Mk. 14. 22; Lk. 22. 19; 1 Cor. 11. 23.
self-examination and preparation for, Acts 2. 42; 20. 7; 1 Cor. 10. 21; 11. 28.
unworthily partaken of, 1 Cor. 11. 27.
Communion of saints. See *Fellowship.*
Company, evil, to be avoided, Ps. 1. 1; 26. 4; Prov. 1. 10; 2. 12; 4. 14; 12. 11; 13. 20; 14. 7; 22. 24; 24. 19; 29. 3, 24; Rom. 1. 32; 1 Cor. 5. 9; 15. 33; Eph. 5. 7.
Compassion to be shown to the afflicted, etc., Job. 6. 14. Ps. 35. 13; Prov. 14. 21; 19. 17; 28. 8; Zech. 7. 9; Rom. 12. 15; 2 Cor. 11. 29; Gal. 6. 2; Col. 3. 12; Heb. 13. 3; Jas. 1. 27; 1 Pet. 3. 8.
Christ's, Matt. 15. 32; 20. 34; Lk. 7. 13, 21; Heb. 2. 18; 4. 15; 5. 2.
Conceit (pride) reproved, Prov. 3. 7; 12. 15; 18. 11; 26. 5; 28. 11; Is. 5. 21; Rom. 11. 25; 12. 16.
Concupiscence to be mortified, Col. 3. 5; 1 Thes. 4. 5.
Condemnation for sin, universal, Ps. 14. 3; 53. 3; Rom. 3. 12; 19; 5. 12; 6. 23.
for unbelief, etc., Matt. 11. 20; 23. 14; John 3. 18.
by the law, 2 Cor. 3. 6, 9.
of false teachers, 2 Pet. 2. 1; Jude 4.
deliverance from, by Christ, John 3. 18; 5. 24; Rom. 8. 1.
final, Matt. 25. 46; Rev. 20. 15.
Confession of Christ unto salvation, Matt. 10. 32; Mk. 8. 35; John 12. 42; Rom. 10. 9; 2 Tim. 2. 12; 1 John 2. 23; 4. 2.
of sin, Lev. 5. 5; Josh. 7. 19; Hos. 5. 15; 1 John 1. 9.
examples of, Num. 12. 11; 21. 7; Josh. 7. 20; 1 Sam. 7. 15. 24; Ezra 9. 6; Neh. 1. 6; 9; Ps. 51; Dan. 9. 4; Lk. 23. 41.
at the offering of first fruits, Deut. 26. 1.
" one to another," Jas. 5. 16.
Confidence, through faith, Prov. 3. 26; 14. 26; Eph. 3. 12; Heb. 3. 6; 10. 35; 1 John 2. 28; 3. 21; 5. 14.
none in the flesh, Phil. 3. 3.
Congregation (of Israel), all to keep the pass-over, Ex. 12, etc.
sin offering for, Lev. 4. 13, 16, 17.
to stone offenders, Lev. 24. 14; Num. 14. 10; 15. 35.
who not to enter, Deut. 23. 1.
Conies described, Ps. 104. 18; Prov. 30. 26.
pronounced unclean, Lev. 11. 5 Deut. 14. 7.
Conscience, convicts of sin, Gen. 3. 10; 4. 13; 42. 21; 1 Sam. 24. 5; Prov. 20. 27; Matt. 27. 3; Lk. 9. 7; John 8. 9; Rom. 2. 15.

Conscience—*Continued.*
purified by faith, 1 Tim. 1. 19; 3. 9; 2 Tim. 1. 3.
    „   „ blood of Christ, Heb. 9. 14; 10. 2, 22.
a good, Heb. 13. 18; 1 Pet. 3. 16.
effects of a good, Acts 24. 16; Rom. 13. 5; 14. 22; 2 Cor. 1. 12; 1 Pet. 2. 19.
of others to be respected, Rom. 14. 21; 1 Cor. 8; 10. 28.
seared, 1 Tim. 4. 2; defiled, Tit. 1. 15.
ignorant, Acts 26. 9; Rom. 10. 2.
Consecration of priests, Ex. 29; Lev. 8.
    „ of the Levites, Num. 8. 5.
    „ of Christ, Heb. 7; 8; 10. 20.
Consideration, exhortations to, Deut. 4. 39; 32. 29; Job 23. 15; 37. 14; Ps. 8. 3; 50. 22; Prov. 6. 6; Eccl. 4. 1; 5. 1; 7. 13; Hag. 1. 5; Matt. 6. 28; 2 Tim. 2. 7; Heb. 3. 1; 7. 4; 10. 24; 12. 3.
Consolation under affliction, Deut. 33. 27; Job 19. 25; Ps. 10. 14; 23; 34. 6; 41. 3; 42. 5; 51. 17; 55. 22; 69. 29; 71. 9, 18; 73. 26; 94. 19; 119. 50; 126; Eccl. 7. 3; Is. 1. 18; 12. 1; Lam. 3. 22; Ezek. 14. 22; Hos. 2. 14; Mic. 7. 18; Zech. 1. 17; Matt. 11. 28; Lk. 4. 18; 15; John 14; 15; 16; Rom. 15. 4; 16. 20; 1 Cor. 10. 13; 14. 3; 2 Cor. 1. 3; 5. 1; 7. 6; 12. 9; Col. 1. 11; 1 Thes. 4. 14; 5. 11; 2 Thes. 2. 16; Heb. 4. 9; 6. 18; 12; Jas. 1. 12; 4. 7; 2 Pet. 2. 9; Rev. 2. 10; 7. 14; 14.
Conspiracy against Christ, Matt. 26. 3; Mk. 3. 6; 14. 1; Lk. 22. 2; John 11. 55; 13. 18.
against Paul, Acts 23. 12.
Constancy of Ruth, Ruth 1. 14.
of Priscilla and Aquila, Rom. 16. 3, 4.
Contentment, with godliness, great gain, Ps. 37. 16; Prov. 30. 8; 1 Tim. 6. 6.
exhortations to, Ps. 37. 1; Lk. 3. 14; 1 Cor. 7. 20; 1 Tim. 6. 8; Heb. 13. 5.
of Paul, 1 Cor. 4. 11; Phil. 4. 11.
Contribution for saints, Acts 20. 35; Rom. 15. 26; 2 Cor. 8.
Contrite heart not despised by God, Ps. 34. 18; 51. 17; Is. 57. 15; 66. 2.
Controversies, how to be decided, Deut. 17. 8; 19. 16; 21. 5.
Conversation (conduct), upright, Ps. 37. 14; 50. 23; Phil. 3. 20; 1 Tim. 4. 12; Heb. 13. 5; Jas. 3. 13; 1 Pet. 2. 12; 2 Pet. 3. 11.
as becometh the Gospel, 2 Cor. 1. 12; (Gal. 1. 13); Eph. 4. 1; Phil. 1. 27; 1 Pet. 1. 15.
(speech) of the Lord with Moses, Ex. 33. 9.
    of Jesus with Nicodemus, John 3.
    of   „   woman of Samaria, John 4. 7-27.
on the walk to Emmaus, Lk. 24. 13.
of Peter with Cornelius, Acts 10. 27.
of Festus and Agrippa, Acts 26. 31.
Conversion of sinners proceeds from God, 1 Ki. 18. 37; Ps. 19. 7; 78. 34; Prov. 1. 23; Jer. 31. 18; John 6. 44; Acts 3. 26; 11. 21.
See Ps. 51. 13; Is. 1. 16; 6. 10; Ezek. 18. 23; 36. 25; Joel 2. 13; 2 Cor. 5. 17; 1 Thes. 1. 9.
call to, Is. 1. 16; Matt. 3. 2; 4. 17; 10. 7; Acts 2. 38; 17. 30; Jas. 4. 8.
prayer for, Ps. 80. 7; 85. 4; Lam. 5. 21.
instruments of, blessed, Dan. 12. 3; 1 Tim. 4. 16; Jas. 5. 19.
of the Jews, Acts 2. 41; 4. 32; 6. 7.
of Paul, Acts 9; 22; 26.
of the Gentiles foretold, Is. 2. 2; 11. 10; 60. 5. 66. 12.

Conversion—*Continued.*
of the Gentiles fulfilled, Acts 8. 26; 10; 15. 3; Rom. 10; 11; 1 Cor. 1; Eph. 2; 3; 1 Thes. 1.
Coos, Paul sails to, Acts 21. 1.
Copy of the law to be written by the king, Deut. 17. 18.
Corban, a gift, Mk. 7. 11.
Corinth, Paul and Apollos at, Acts 18; 19. 1.
Corinthians, their divisions, etc., censured, 1 Cor. 1; 5; 11. 18; 2 Cor. 13.
their gifts and graces, 2 Cor. 3.
instructed concerning spiritual gifts, 1 Cor. 14; and the resurrection, 1 Cor. 15.
exhorted to charity, etc., 1 Cor. 13; 14. 1; 2 Cor. 8; 9.
their false teachers exposed, 2 Cor. 11. 3, 4, 13.
Paul commends himself to, 2 Cor. 11; 12.
Cornelius, devout centurion, his prayer answered, Acts 10. 3.
sends for Peter, Acts 10. 9.
baptised, Acts 10. 48.
Council of the Jews, Matt. 26. 3, 59; Mk. 15. 1.
the apostles arraigned before, Acts 4; 5. 29.
Paul's discourse before, Acts 23.
Counsel, advantage of good, Prov. 12. 15; 13. 10; 20. 18; 27. 9.
of God, asked by Israel, Jud. 20. 18.
    „   by Saul, 1 Sam. 14. 37.
    „   by David, 1 Sam. 23. 2, 10; 30. 8; 1 Chr. 14. 10.
See Ps. 16. 7; 33. 11; 73. 24; Prov. 8. 14; Eccl. 8. 2; Rev. 3. 18.
danger of rejecting, 2 Chr. 25. 16; Prov. 1. 25, 26; Jer. 23. 18-22; Lk. 7. 30.
of the wicked condemned, Job 5. 13: 10. 3; 21. 16; Ps. 1. 1; 5. 10; 33. 10; 64. 2; 81. 12; 106. 43; Is. 7. 5; Hos. 11. 6; Mic. 6. 16.
Counsellors, safety in multitude of, Prov. 11. 14; 15. 22; 24. 6.
Courage, exhortations to, Num. 13. 20; Deut. 31. 6; Josh. 1. 6; 10. 25; 2 Sam. 10. 12; 2 Chr. 19. 11; Ezra 10. 4; Ps. 27. 14; 31. 24; Is. 41. 6; 1 Cor. 16. 13; Eph. 6. 10.
through faith: Abraham, Heb. 11. 8, 17. Moses, Heb. 11. 25. Israelites, Heb. 11. 29. Barak, Jud. 4. 16. Gideon, Jud. 7. 1. Jephthah, Jud. 11. 29. Samson, Jud. 16. 28. Jonathan, 1 Sam. 14. 6. Daniel, Dan. 6. 10, 23. See *Boldness, Confidence.*
Courses of the Levites, established by David, 1 Chr. 23; 24.
of the singers, 1 Chr. 25.
of the porters, 1 Chr. 26.
of the captains, 1 Chr. 27.
Court of the tabernacle described, Ex. 27. 9; 38. 9.
Courtesy, exhortation to, Col. 4. 6; Jas. 3. 17; 1 Pet. 3. 8.
examples of, Acts 27. 3; 28. 7.
Covenant of God:—
with Noah, Gen. 6. 18; 9. 8.
with Abraham, Gen. 15. 7, 18; 17. 2; (Lk. 1. 72; Acts 3. 25; Gal. 3. 16, 17).
with Isaac, Gen. 17. 19; 26. 3.
with Jacob, Gen. 28. 13 (Ex. 2. 24; 6. 4; 1 Chr. 16. 16).
with the Israelites, Ex. 6. 4; 19. 5; 24; 34. 27; Lev. 26. 9; Deut. 5. 2; 9. 9; 26. 16; 29; Jud. 2. 1; Jer. 11; 31. 33; Acts 3. 25.
with Phinehas, Num. 25. 13.
with David, 2 Sam. 23. 5; Ps. 89. 3.
See Ps. 25. 14.
God mindful of, Deut. 7. 9; 1 Ki. 8. 23; Ps. 105. 8; 111. 5, etc.

Covenant—*Continued.*
danger of despising, Deut. 28. 15; Jer. 11. 2; Heb. 10. 29.

Covenant, signs of :—salt, Lev. 2. 13; Num. 18. 19; 2 Chr. 13. 5. The Sabbath, Ex. 31. 12.
book of the, Ex. 24. 7; 2 Ki. 23. 2; Heb. 9. 19.
—between Abraham and Abimelech, Gen. 21. 27.
    ,,   Joshua and Israelites, Josh. 24. 25.
    ,,   David and Jonathan, 1 Sam. 18. 3; 20. 16; 23. 18.

Covenant, new, Jer. 31. 31; Rom. 11. 27; Heb. 8. 8.
ratified by Christ (Mal. 3. 1), Lk. 1. 68-80; Gal. 3. 17; Heb. 8. 6; 9. 15; 12. 24.
a covenant of peace, Is. 54. 10; Ezek. 34. 25; 37. 26.
unchangeable, Ps. 89. 34; Is. 54. 10; 59. 21.
everlasting, Gen. 9. 16; 17. 13; Lev. 24. 8; Is. 55. 3; 61. 8; Ezek. 16. 60; 37. 26; Heb. 13. 20.

Covetousness described, Ps. 10. 3; Prov. 21. 26; Eccl. 4. 8; 5. 10; Ezek. 33. 31; Hab. 2; Mk. 7. 22; Eph. 5. 5; 1 Tim. 6. 10; 2 Pet. 2. 14.
forbidden, Ex. 20. 17; Lk. 12. 15; Rom. 13. 9.
its evil consequences, Prov. 1. 18; 15. 27; 28. 20; Ezek. 22. 13; 1 Tim. 6. 9.
its punishment, Job 20. 15; Is. 5. 8; 57. 17; Jer. 6. 12; 22. 17; Mic. 2. 1; Hab. 2. 9; 1 Cor. 5. 10; 6. 10; Eph. 5. 5; Col. 3. 5.
of Laban, Gen. 31. 41.
of Balaam, Num. 22. 21 (2 Pet. 2. 15; Jude 11).
of Achan, Josh. 7. 21.
of Saul, 1 Sam. 15. 9.
of Ahab, 1 Ki. 21.
of Gehazi, 2 Ki. 5. 20.
of Judas, Matt. 26. 14.
of Ananias and Sapphira, Acts 5.
of Felix, Acts 24. 26.

Cozbi slain by Phinehas, Num. 25. 15.
Creation of the world, Gen. 1; 2.
See Rom. 1. 20; 8. 22; Rev. 4. 11.
the new, Rev. 22.
Creature, a new, 2 Cor. 5. 17; Gal. 6. 15; Eph. 2. 10; 4. 24. See Rom. 8. 19.
Creatures, the four living, vision of, Ezek. 1. 5.
Creditor, parable of the, Lk. 7. 41.
of two creditors, Matt. 18. 23.
Crescens goes to Galatia, 2 Tim. 4. 10.
Crete visited by Paul, Acts 27. 7.
Cretians, their character, Tit. 1. 12.
Cripple healed at Lystra, Acts 14. 8.
Crispus baptised by Paul, Acts 18. 8; 1 Cor. 1. 14.
Cross, Christ dies upon the, Matt. 27. 32; Phil. 2. 8; Heb. 12. 2.
the preaching of, 1 Cor. 1. 18.
to be taken up, self-denial, Matt. 10. 38; 16. 24.
offence of the, Gal. 5. 11.
persecution for, Gal 6. 12.
Crown (and mitre) of the high priest, Ex. 29. 6; 39. 30; Lev. 8. 9.
of righteousness, 2 Tim. 4. 8.
of life, Jas. 1. 12; Rev. 2. 10.
of glory, 1 Pet. 5. 4.
incorruptible, 1 Cor. 9. 25.
See Rev. 4. 4; 9. 7; 12. 3; 13. 1; 19. 12.
Cruelty condemned, Ex. 23. 5; Ps. 27. 12; Prov. 11. 17; 12. 10; Ezek. 18. 18.
of Simeon and Levi, Gen. 34. 25; 49. 5.
of Pharaoh, Ex. 1. 8.
of Adoni-bezek, Jud. 1. 7.
of Herod, Matt. 2. 16.
See Jud. 9. 5; 2 Ki. 3. 27; 10; 15. 16.

Curse upon the earth in consequence of the fall, Gen. 3. 17.
upon Cain, Gen. 4. 11.
on Canaan, Gen. 9. 25.
upon the breakers of the law, Lev. 26. 14; Deut. 11. 26; 27. 13; 28. 15; 29. 19; Josh. 8. 34; Prov. 3. 33.
uttered by Job on his birth, Job 3. 1.
also by Jeremiah, Jer. 20. 14.
Christ redeems from, Rom. 3; Gal. 3. 13; Rev. 22. 3.

Cursed, who so called, Deut. 27. 15; Ps. 37. 22; Prov. 11. 26; 27. 14; Jer. 11. 3; 17. 5; Lam. 3. 65; Zech. 5. 3; Mal. 1. 14; Matt. 25. 41; Gal. 3. 10; 2 Pet. 2. 14.

Cursing forbidden, Ex. 21. 17; Lev. 24. 15; Ps. 109. 17; Prov. 30. 11; Jas. 3. 10.
to return blessing for, Matt. 5. 44; Rom. 12. 14.

Curtains of the tabernacle described, Ex. 26; 36.
Cushi announces Absalom's death, 2 Sam. 18. 21.
Cutting the flesh forbidden, Lev. 19. 28; Deut. 14. 1.
practised by prophets of Baal, 1 Ki. 18. 28.
Cymbals used in worship, 2 Sam. 6. 5; 1 Chr. 15. 16; 16. 5; Ps. 150. 5.
tinkling, 1 Cor. 13. 1.
Cyprus, disciples there, Acts 11. 19.
Paul and Barnabas preach there, Acts 13. 4.
Barnabas and Mark go there, Acts 15. 39.
Cyrene, disciples of, Acts 11. 20; 13. 1.
Simon of, Mk. 15. 21.
Cyrenius, governor of Syria, Lk. 2. 2.
Cyrus, king of Persia, prophecies concerning, Is. 44. 28; 45. 1.
See Dan. 6. 28; 10. 1.
his proclamation for rebuilding the temple, 2 Chr. 36. 22; Ezra 1.

DAGON, national idol-god of the Philistines, sacrificed to, Jud. 16. 23.
smitten down in temple at Ashdod, 1 Sam. 5. 3, 4.
Saul's head fastened in house of, 1 Chr. 10. 10.
Damaris cleaves to Paul, Acts. 17. 34.
Damascus mentioned, Gen. 15. 2.
subjugated by David, 2 Sam. 8. 6; 1 Chr. 18. 6.
Rezon reigns there, 1 Ki. 11. 24.
Elisha's prophecy there, 2 Ki. 8. 7.
taken by Tiglath-pileser, king of Assyria, 2 Ki. 16. 9.
re-captured by Jeroboam, 2 Ki. 14. 28.
king Ahaz copies an altar there, 2 Ki. 16. 10.
Paul's journey to, Acts 9; 22. 6.
prophecies concerning, Is. 7. 8; 8. 4; 17. 1; Jer. 49. 23; Ezek. 27. 18; Amos 1. 3.
Damnation, denounced upon unbelievers, etc., Matt. 23. 14; Mk. 16. 16; John 5. 29; Rom. 3. 8; 13. 2; 2 Thes. 2. 12; 1 Tim. 5. 12; 2 Pet. 2. 3.

Dan, son of Jacob, Gen. 30. 6.
— tribe of, numbered, Num. 1. 38; 26. 42.
their inheritance, Josh. 19. 40.
blessed by Jacob, Gen. 49. 16.
blessed by Moses, Deut. 33. 22.
take Laish, Jud. 18. 29.
set up idolatry, Jud. 18. 30; 1 Ki. 12. 29.
Dancing as a mark of rejoicing, Ex. 15. 20; 32. 19; Jud. 11. 34; 1 Sam. 21. 11; 2 Sam. 6. 14; Eccl. 3. 4.
of Herodias's daughter pleases Herod, Matt. 14. 6; Mk. 6. 22.

Daniel (Belteshazzar) one of the captives in Babylon, Dan. 1. 3.
  refuses to take the king's meat or drink, Dan. 1. 8.
  has understanding in dreams, Dan. 1. 17.
  interprets the royal dreams, Dan. 2; 4; and the handwriting on the wall, Dan. 5. 17.
  promoted by Darius, Dan. 6. 2.
  conspired against by the princes, Dan. 6. 4.
  disregards the idolatrous decree, Dan. 6. 10.
  cast into the lions' den, Dan. 6. 16.
  his preservation in, Dan. 6. 22.
  his vision of the four beasts, Dan. 7.
    "   of the ram and he-goat, Dan. 8.
  his prayer, Dan. 9. 3.
  promise given of return from captivity, Dan. 9. 20; 10. 10; 12. 13.
  his name mentioned, Ezek. 14. 14, 20; 28. 3.
Darius (the Median) takes Babylon, Dan. 5. 31.
  his decree to fear the God of Daniel, Dan. 6. 25,
—(another) his decree concerning the rebuilding of the temple, Ezra 6.
Darkness divided from light, Gen. 1. 18.
  created by God, Is. 45. 7.
  instances of supernatural, Gen. 15. 12; Ex. 10. 21; 14. 20; Josh. 24. 7; Rev. 8. 12; 9. 2; 16. 10.
  at the crucifixion, Matt. 27. 45; Mk. 15. 33; Lk. 23. 44.
  figurative of punishment, Matt. 8. 12; 22. 13; 2 Pet. 2. 4, 17; Jude 6.
  of the mind, Job 37. 19; Prov. 2. 13; Eccl. 2. 14; Is. 9. 2; 42. 7; John 1. 5; 3. 19; 8. 12; 12. 35; Rom. 13. 12; 1 Cor. 4. 5; 2 Cor. 4. 6; 6. 14; 1 Thes. 5. 4; 1 Pet. 2. 9; 1 John 1. 5; 2. 9.
  powers of, Lk. 22. 53; Eph. 6. 12; Col. 1. 13.
Dathan. See *Abiram.*
Daughters, their inheritance determined, Num. 27. 6; 36.
David, king, son of Jesse, 1 Sam. 16. 11; 1 Chr. 2; Matt. 1.
  anointed by Samuel, 1 Sam. 16. 11.
  plays the harp before Saul, 1 Sam. 16. 19.
  his zeal and faith, 1 Sam. 17. 26, 34.
  kills Goliath of Gath, 1 Sam. 17. 49.
  at first honoured by Saul, 1 Sam. 18.
  Saul afterwards jealous of, 1 Sam. 18. 8, 12.
  tries to kill him, 1 Sam. 18. 10.
  persecuted by Saul, 1 Sam. 19; 20.
  loved by Jonathan, 1 Sam. 18. 1; 19. 2; 20; 23. 16.
  and by Michal, 1 Sam. 18. 28; 19. 11.
  overcomes the Philistines, 1 Sam. 18. 27; 19. 8.
  flees to Naioth, 1 Sam. 19. 18.
  eats of the shewbread, 1 Sam. 21; Ps. 52; Matt. 12. 4.
  flees to Gath, and feigns madness, 1 Sam. 21. 10, 13; Ps. 34; 56.
  dwells in the cave of Adullam, 1 Sam. 22; Ps. 63; 142.
  escapes Saul's pursuit, 1 Sam. 23; Ps. 57; 59.
  twice spares Saul's life, 1 Sam. 24; 26. 5.
  his wrath against Nabal appeased by Abigail, 1 Sam. 25. 23.
  dwells at Ziklag, 1 Sam. 27.
  dismissed from the army by Achish, 1 Sam. 29. 9.
  chastises the Amalekites, 1 Sam. 30. 16.
  kills messenger who brings news of Saul's death, 2 Sam. 1. 15.
  laments the death of Saul and Jonathan, 2 Sam. 1. 17.
  becomes king of Judah, 2 Sam. 2. 4.

David—*Continued.*
  forms a league with Abner, 2 Sam. 3. 13.
  laments his death, 2 Sam. 3. 31.
  avenges the murder of Ishbosheth, 2 Sam. 4. 9.
  becomes king of all Israel, 2 Sam. 5. 3; 1 Chr. 11.
  his victories, 2 Sam. 5; 6; 8; 10; 12. 29; 21. 15; 1 Chr. 18-20; Ps. 60.
  brings the ark to Zion, 2 Sam. 6; 1 Chr. 13; 15.
  his psalms of thanksgiving, 2 Sam. 22; 1 Chr. 16. 7; Ps. 18; 103; 105.
  reproves Michal for despising his religious joy, 2 Sam. 6. 21.
  desires to build God a house, 2 Sam. 7. 2.
  and is forbidden by Nathan, 2 Sam. 7. 4; 1 Chr. 17. 4.
  God's promises to him, 2 Sam. 7. 11; 1 Chr. 17. 10.
  his prayer and thanksgiving, 2 Sam. 7. 18; 1 Chr. 17. 16.
  his kindness to Mephibosheth, 2 Sam. 9.
  his sin concerning Bath-Sheba and Uriah, 2 Sam. 11; 12.
  his repentance at Nathan's parable, 2 Sam 12; Ps. 51.
  troubles in his family, 2 Sam. 13; 14.
  Absalom's conspiracy against him, 2 Sam. 15; Ps. 3.
  Ahithophel's treachery against, 2 Sam. 15. 31; 16; 17.
  cursed by Shimei, 2 Sam. 16. 5; Ps. 7.
  Barzillai's kindness to, 2 Sam. 17. 27.
  his grief at Absalom's death, 2 Sam. 18. 33, 19. 1.
  returns to Jerusalem, 2 Sam. 19. 15.
  pardons Shimei, 2 Sam. 19. 16.
  Sheba's conspiracy against, 2 Sam. 20.
  renders justice to the Gibeonites, 2 Sam. 21.
  his mighty men, 2 Sam. 23. 8; 1 Chr. 11. 10.
  his offence in numbering the people, 2 Sam. 24; 1 Chr. 21.
  regulates the service of the tabernacle, 1 Chr. 26-26.
  exhorts the people to fear God, 1 Chr. 28.
  appoints Solomon his successor, 1 Ki. 1; Ps. 72.
  his charge to Solomon, 1 Ki. 2; 1 Chr. 28. 9; to build a house for the sanctuary, 1 Chr. 22. 6; 28. 10.
  his last words, 2 Sam. 23.
  his death, 1 Ki. 2; 1 Chr. 29. 26.
  the progenitor of Christ, Matt. 1. 1; 9. 27; 21. 9; comp. Ps. 110 with Matt. 22. 41; Lk. 1. 32; John 7. 42; Acts 2. 25; 13. 22; 15. 15; Rom. 1. 3; 2 Tim. 2. 8; Rev. 5. 5; 22. 16.
  prophecies connected with, Ps. 89; 132; Is. 9. 7; 22. 22; 55. 3; Jer. 30. 9; Hos. 3. 5; Amos 9. 11.
Day, the last, foretold, Job 19. 25; Joel 2. 11; Zeph. 1. 14; John 6. 39; 11. 24; 12. 48; Rom. 2. 5; 1 Cor. 3. 13; Rev. 6. 17; 16. 14; 20.
Days, last, mentioned, Is. 2. 2; Mic. 4. 1; Acts 2. 17; 2 Tim. 3. 1; Heb. 1. 2; Jas. 5. 3; 2 Pet. 3. 3.
Dayspring, from on high, Lk. 1. 78.
Day Star, arising in the heart, 2 Pet. 1. 19.
Deacons appointed, Acts 6; Phil. 1. 1.
  their qualifications, Acts 6. 3; 1 Tim. 3. 8.
Dead, the, Job 3. 18; 14. 12; Ps. 6. 5; 88. 10; 115. 17; 146. 4; Eccl. 9. 5; 12. 7; Is. 38. 18.
  resurrection of, Job 19. 26; Ps. 49. 15; Is. 26. 19; Dan. 12. 2, 13; John 5. 25; 1 Cor. 15. 12; 1 Thes. 4. 13.

Devil—*Continued.*
cast out of heaven, Lk. 10. 18.
cast down to hell, 2 Pet. 2. 4; Jude 6.
as serpent causes the fall of man, Gen. 3. 1.
cursed by God, Gen. 3. 14.
appears before God, Job 1. 6; 2. 1.
called Beelzebub, Matt. 12. 24.
    „   Satan, Lk. 10. 18.
    „   Belial, 2 Cor. 6. 15.
    „   Abaddon and Apollyon, Rev. 9. 11.
tempter of Christ, Matt. 4. 3-10; Mk. 1. 13; Lk. 4. 2.
    „   of Eve, Gen. 3.
    „   of David, 1 Chr. 21. 1.
    „   of Job, Job 2. 7.
resisting Joshua, rebuked, Zech. 3.
desired to have Simon, Lk. 22. 31.
enters into Judas Iscariot, Lk. 22. 3; John 13. 3.
    „ into Ananias, Acts 5. 3.
as Prince and God of this world, he hinders the Gospel, Matt. 13. 19; 2 Cor. 4. 4; 1 Thes. 2. 18.
works lying wonders, 2 Thes. 2. 9; Rev. 16. 14.
appears as an angel of light, 2 Cor. 11. 14.
is the father of lies, John 8. 44; 1 Ki. 22. 22.
vanquished by Christ, Matt. 4. 11; who destroys his works, 1 John 3. 8; by His death, Col. 2. 15; Heb. 2. 14.
to be resisted by believers, Rom. 16. 20; 2 Cor. 2. 11; 11. 3; Eph. 4. 27; 6. 16; 2 Tim. 2. 26; Jas. 4. 7; 1 Pet. 5. 9; 1 John 2. 13; Rev. 12. 11.
characterised as proud, 1 Tim. 3. 6.
    „   as powerful, Eph. 2. 2; 6. 12.
    „   as wicked, 1 John 2. 13.
    „   as subtle, Gen. 3. 1; 2 Cor. 11. 3.
    „   as deceitful, 2 Cor. 11. 14; Eph. 6. 11.
    „   as fierce and cruel. Lk. 8. 29; 9. 39, 42; 1 Pet. 5. 8.
shows himself malignant, Job 1. 9; 2. 4.
everlasting fire prepared for, Matt. 25. 41.
to be condemned at the judgment, Jude 6; Rev. 20. 10.
compared to a fowler, Ps. 91. 3.
    „   to a sower of tares, Matt. 13. 25, 28.
    „   to a wolf, John 10. 12.
    „   to a roaring lion, 1 Pet. 5. 8.
called that old serpent, Rev. 12. 9; 20. 2.
the wicked called children of, Matt. 13. 38; Acts 13. 10; 1 John 3. 10.
    „   „ do lusts of, John 8. 44.
    „   „ ensnared by, 1 Tim. 3. 7; 2 Tim. 2. 26.
Devils, sacrifices offered to, Lev. 17. 7; Deut. 32. 17; 2 Chr. 11. 15; Ps. 106. 37; 1 Cor. 10. 20; Rev. 9. 20.
cast out by Christ, Matt. 4. 24; 8. 31; Mk. 5. 2; Lk. 9. 42.
    „   by His apostles, Lk. 9. 1; Acts 16. 16; 19. 12.
confess Jesus to be Christ, Matt. 8. 29; Mk. 1. 24; 3. 11; 5. 7; Lk. 4. 34; Acts 19. 15.
believe and tremble, Jas. 2. 19.
Devout, persons so called : Simeon, Lk. 2. 25; Cornelius, Acts 10. 2; Ananias, Acts 22. 12.
Dew, a blessing, Gen. 27. 28; Deut. 33. 13.
a sign, Jud. 6. 37.
figurative, Deut. 32. 2; Ps. 110. 3; 133. 3; Prov. 19. 12; Is. 26. 19, etc.
Dial of Ahaz, 2 Ki. 20. 11; Is. 38. 8.

Diamond in high priest's breastplate, Ex. 28. 18; 39. 11.
Diana of Ephesians, tumult concerning, Acts 19. 24.
Didymus (Thomas), John 20. 24.
Diligence, exhortations to, in the service of God, etc., Ex. 15. 26; Deut. 4. 9; 6. 7; 13. 14; 24. 8; Josh. 1. 7; Ezra 7. 23; Ps. 37. 10; 112. 1; Prov. 2; 3; 4; 7; 8; Is. 55. 2; Jer. 12. 16; Zech. 6. 15; Lk. 12. 58; Rom. 12. 8; 2 Cor. 8. 7; 1 Tim. 5. 10; Heb. 6. 11; 11. 6; 12. 15; 1 Pet. 1. 5, 10; 2 Pet. 3. 14.
in worldly business, Prov. 10. 4; 12. 24; 13. 4; 21. 5; 22. 29; 27. 23; Rom. 12. 11; 2 Thes. 3. 11.
Dinah, Jacob's daughter, Gen. 30. 21.
outraged by Shechem, Gen. 34. 2.
avenged by Simeon and Levi, Gen. 34. 25.
Dionysius the Areopagite believes, Acts 17. 34.
Diotrephes loves pre-eminence, 3 John 9.
Disciples of Christ :—
seventy sent out, Lk. 10.
three thousand added to the Church. Acts 2. 41.
five thousand believers, Acts 4. 4.
first called Christians at Antioch, Acts 11. 26.
—of John enquire of Christ, Matt. 9. 14; 11. 2.
follow Christ, John 1. 37.
dispute about purifying, John 3. 25.
baptised by Paul, and receive the Holy Ghost, Acts 19. 1.
Discord censured, Prov. 6. 14, 19; 16. 29; 17. 9; 18. 8; 26. 20; Rom. 1. 29; 2 Cor. 12. 20.
Discretion commended, Ps. 34. 12; Prov. 1. 4; 2. 11; 3. 21; 5. 2; 19. 11.
Diseases inflicted by God, Ex. 9; 15. 26; Num. 12. 10; Deut. 28. 60; 2 Ki. 1. 4; 5. 27; 2 Chr. 21. 18; 26. 21; Job 2. 6, 7.
cured by Christ, Matt. 4. 23; 9. 20; John 5. 8.
power given to his disciples to cure, Lk. 9. 1; Acts 28. 8; exercised, Acts 3. 1; 9. 34; Acts 28. 8.
Disguises resorted to, 1 Sam. 28. 8; 1 Ki. 14. 2; 20. 38; 22. 30; 2 Chr. 18. 29; 35. 22.
disfiguring of face for the dead forbidden, Lev. 19. 28; Deut. 14. 1.
Disobedience and its results, Lev. 26. 14; Deut. 8. 11; 27; 28. 15; Josh. 5. 6; 1 Sam. 2. 30; 12. 15; Ps. 78. 10; Is. 3. 8; 42. 24; Jer. 9. 13; 18. 10; 22. 21; 35. 14; Eph. 5. 6; Tit. 1. 16; 3. 3; Heb. 2. 2.
of Adam and Eve, Gen. 3.
of Pharaoh, Ex. 5. 2. Achan, Josh. 7.
of Saul, 1 Sam. 13. 9; 15. Man of God, 1 Ki. 13. 21. Jonah, Jon. 1; 2.
Dispensation of the Gospel, 1 Cor. 9. 17; Eph. 1. 10; 3. 2; Col. 1. 25.
Dispersed of Israel, Est. 3. 8; Is. 11. 12; John. 7. 35.
prophecies concerning, Jer. 25. 34; Ezek. 36. 19; Zeph. 3. 10.
Disputing with God, forbidden, Rom. 9. 20; 1 Cor. 1. 20.
with men, Mk. 9. 33; Rom. 14. 1; Phil. 2. 14; 1 Tim. 1. 4; 4. 7; 6. 20; 2 Tim. 2. 14; Tit. 3. 9.
Dissension concerning circumcision, Acts 15. 1.
Dividing the hoof, unclean beasts, Lev. 11. 4; Deut. 14. 7.
Divination forbidden, Lev. 19. 26; Deut. 18. 10; 1 Sam. 28. 7; 2 Ki. 17. 17; Jer. 27. 9; 29. 8; Ezek. 21. 21.
Divisions, kingdom and house, Matt. 12. 25.
in the Church forbidden, Rom. 16. 17; 1 Cor. 1. 10; 3. 3; 11. 18; 12. 20.
Christ's prayer against, John 17. 21.

Divorce, when permitted, Deut. 24. 1; Matt. 5. 32.
condemned by Christ, Mk. 10. 4.
Doctors, Christ questions, Lk. 2. 46.
of the law, Lk. 5. 17; Gamaliel, Acts 5. 34.
Doctrine of Christ, Matt. 7. 28, 29; Mk. 4. 2;
John 7. 16; Acts 2. 42; 1 Tim. 3. 16; 6. 3;
2 Tim. 3. 16; Tit. 1. 1; Heb. 6. 1; 2 John 9.
adorned by obedience, Rom. 6. 17; 1 Tim. 6.
1; Tit. 2. 7, 10.
no other to be taught, 1 Tim. 1. 3; 4. 6, 13.
those opposed to, to be avoided, Rom. 16. 17;
2 John 10.
Doctrines, false, Jer. 10. 8; Matt. 15. 9; 16. 12;
Eph. 4. 14; 2 Thes. 2. 11; 1 Tim. 4. 1; 2 Tim.
4. 3; Heb. 13. 9; Rev. 2. 14.
to be avoided, Jer. 23. 16; 29. 8; Col. 2. 8;
1 Tim. 1. 4; 6. 20.
Doeg the Edomite slays the priests, 1 Sam. 22. 9.
Dogs, law concerning, Deut. 23. 18.
a term of reproach, 2 Sam. 9. 8; Rev. 22. 15.
figurative of enemies, Ps. 22. 16.
    ,,   of impenitence, Prov. 26. 11; 2 Pet. 2. 22.
false teachers so called, Is. 56. 10.
beware of, Phil. 3. 2.
Dominion of God, Ps. 103. 22; 145. 13; Dan. 4.
3, 34; 7. 27; Col. 1. 16; 1 Pet. 4. 11; Jude 25.
Door of the sheep, Christ the, John 10. 9.
Dorcas (Tabitha) raised from death by Peter,
Acts 9. 40.
Doubtfulness rebuked, Matt. 14. 31; 21. 21;
Lk. 12. 29; Acts 10. 20; 1 Tim. 2. 8.
Dough, offering of, Num. 15. 20; Neh. 10. 37;
Ezek. 44. 30.
Dove, sent out from the ark, Gen. 8. 8.
sacrificial, Gen. 15. 9; Lev. 12. 6; 14. 22.
figuratively mentioned, Ps. 68. 13; 74. 19;
Cant. 1. 15; 2. 14.
Holy Spirit in form of, Matt. 3. 16; Mk. 1.
10; Lk. 3. 22; John 1. 32.
Dragons, Job 30. 29; Ps. 74. 13; Is. 13. 22; 27. 1;
Rev. 12. 3; 13. 2; 16. 13. See Ezek. 29. 3.
poison of, Deut. 32. 33.
Draught of fishes, miraculous, Lk. 5. 4-6;
John 21. 6, 11.
Dreams, vanity of, Job 20. 8; Ps. 73. 20; Eccl.
5. 3; Is. 29. 8; Jer. 23. 28; 27. 9; Zech. 10. 2;
Jude 8.
sent by God, Job 33. 15; Joel 2. 28.
of Abimelech, Gen. 20. 3. Jacob, Gen. 28. 12;
31. 10. Laban, Gen. 31. 24. Joseph, Gen.
37. 5. Pharaoh's servants, Gen. 40. 5.
Pharaoh, Gen. 41. Midianite, Jud. 7. 13.
Solomon, 1 Ki. 3. 5. Nebuchadnezzar, Dan.
2; 4. Joseph, Matt. 1. 20; 2. 13. Wise
men, Matt. 2. 12. Pilate's wife, Matt.
27. 19.
Drink, strong, forbidden, Lev. 10. 9; Num. 6.
3; Jud. 13. 14; Lk. 1. 15.
use of, Prov. 31. 6; 1 Tim. 5. 23.
abuse of, Is. 5. 11, 22.
strong, raging, Prov. 20. 1.
Drink Offerings, law concerning, Ex. 29. 40;
Lev. 23. 13; Num. 6. 17; 15. 5 (Gen. 35. 14).
to idols, Is. 57. 6; Jer. 7. 18; 44. 17; Ezek. 20. 28.
Dromedaries, 1 Ki. 4. 28; Est. 8. 10; Is. 60. 6;
Jer. 2. 23.
Dropsy, cured by Christ, Lk. 14. 2.
Dross, wicked compared to, Ps. 119. 119; Is. 1.
25; Ezek. 22. 18.
Drought, Deut. 28. 24; 1 Ki. 17; Hag. 1. 11.

Drunkenness censured, Is. 5. 11; 28. 1; Joel 1. 5;
Lk. 21. 34; Rom. 13. 13; 1 Cor. 5. 11; Gal.
5. 21; Eph. 5. 18; 1 Thes. 5. 7; 1 Pet. 4. 3.
its punishment, Deut. 21. 20; Amos 6. 7;
Nah. 1. 10; Matt. 24. 49; Lk. 12. 45; 1 Cor.
6. 10; Gal. 5. 21.
of Noah, Gen. 9. 21. Lot, Gen. 19. 33. Nabal,
1 Sam. 25. 36. Elah, 1 Ki. 16. 9. Ben-
hadad, 1 Ki. 20. 16. Belshazzar, Dan. 5. 4.
The Corinthians, 1 Cor. 11. 21.
Dumb healed by Christ, Matt. 9. 32; 12. 22.
not to be oppressed, Prov. 31. 8.
Dumbness of Zacharias, Lk. 1. 20.
Dungeon, Joseph cast into, Gen. 39; 40. 15; also
Jeremiah, Jer. 37. 16; 38. 6.
Dust of the earth, man formed of, Gen. 2. 7;
3. 19; 18. 27; Job 10. 9; 34. 15; Ps. 103. 14;
104. 29; Eccl. 12. 7.
mark of grief, Josh. 7. 6; Job 2. 12; Lam. 2. 10.
Duty of man, the whole, Eccl. 12. 13; Lk. 17. 10.
Dwarfs not to minister, Lev. 21. 20.

EAGLE, unclean, Lev. 11. 13.
described, Job 9. 26; 39. 27; Ezek. 17. 3;
Obad. 4.
one of the four living creatures in the vision
of heaven, Ezek. 1. 10; Rev. 4. 7.
Ear, the, 2 Sam. 7. 22; Ps. 45. 10; 78. 1; 94. 9;
Prov. 15. 31; 20. 12; 22. 17; Is. 50. 4; 55. 3;
Matt. 10. 27.
Ears, he that hath, to hear, Matt. 11. 15; 13.
16; Mk. 4. 9, 23; 7. 16.
have, but hear not, Ps. 115. 6; Is. 42. 20; Ezek.
12. 2; Matt. 13. 14; Mk. 8. 18; Rom. 11. 8.
the Lord's, open to prayer, 2 Sam. 22. 7; Ps.
18. 6; 34. 15; Jas. 5. 4; 1 Pet. 3. 12.
opened by God, Job 33. 16; 36. 15; Ps. 40. 6;
Mk. 7. 35.
Early Rising, Gen. 19. 27; 26. 31; 28. 18; Josh.
3. 1; Jud. 6. 38; 1 Sam. 9. 26; 15. 12; 17. 20;
Mk. 1. 35; 16. 2; John 8. 2; 20. 1; Acts 5. 21.
Earnest of the Spirit, 2 Cor. 1. 22; 5. 5; Eph.
1. 14.
Earth created, Gen. 1. 1; made fruitful, Gen.
1. 11; cursed, Gen. 3. 17; covered by the
flood, Gen. 7. 10; to be consumed by fire,
Mic. 1. 4; Zeph. 3. 8; 2 Pet. 3. 7; Rev. 20. 9.
a new (and heaven), 2 Pet. 3. 13; Rev. 21. 1.
Earthquakes, 1 Ki. 19. 11; Is. 29. 6; Amos 1. 1;
Matt. 27. 54; Acts 16. 26; Rev. 6. 12; 8. 5;
11. 13; 16. 18.
Ease, Is. 32. 9; Amos 6. 1; Lk. 12. 19.
East, men of the, Job 1. 3.
glory of God proceeding from, etc., Ezek.
43. 2; 47. 8.
wise men from, worship Christ, Matt. 2. 1.
Easter, Peter imprisoned till after, Acts 12. 4.
Ebal, mount, curses delivered from, Deut. 27.
13; Josh. 8. 33.
Ebed-Melech, Ethiopian eunuch, intercedes
for and delivers Jeremiah, etc., Jer. 38. 7;
39. 16.
Eben-Ezer, Israelites smitten by Philistines
at, 1 Sam. 4. 1.
"hitherto hath the Lord helped us" (stone
raised by Samuel in memory of defeat of
the Philistines), 1 Sam. 7. 12.
Eden, described, Gen. 2. 8; Adam driven from,
Gen. 3. 24.
figuratively mentioned, Is. 51. 3; Ezek. 28.
13; 31. 9; 36. 35; Joel 2. 3.
Edification, Rom. 14. 19; 15. 2; 1 Cor. 8. 1; 10.
33; 14. 5; 2 Cor. 12. 19; 13. 10; Eph. 4. 12,
29; 1 Thes. 5. 11.

Edom (Idumea), the land of Esau, Gen. 32. 3;
Is. 60. 1.

prophecies concerning, Jer. 25. 21; 49. 7;
Ezek. 25. 13; 35; Amos 1. 11; Obad. 1.

Edomites, the descendants of Esau, Gen. 36.

deny the Israelites passage through Edom,
Num. 20. 18.

their possessions, Deut. 2. 5; Josh. 24. 4.

not to be abhorred, Deut. 23. 7.

subdued by David, 2 Sam. 8. 14.

revolt, 2 Ki. 8. 20; 2 Chr. 21. 8.

subdued by Amaziah, 2 Ki. 14. 7; 2 Chr. 25. 11.

Eglon, king of Moab, oppresses Israel, Jud.
3. 14.

slain by Ehud, Jud. 3. 21.

Egypt, Abram goes down into, Gen. 12. 10.

Joseph sold into, Gen. 37. 36; his advancement, imprisonment, and restoration
there, Gen. 39; 40; 41.

Jacob's sons go to buy corn in, Gen. 42.

Jacob and all his family go there, Gen. 46. 6.

Israelites' bondage there, Ex. 1. 12; 5, etc.

their departure from, Ex. 13. 17; Ps. 78. 12.

army of, pursue and perish in the Red Sea,
Ex. 14.

kings of, harass Judah, 1 Ki. 14. 25; 2 Ki.
23. 29; 2 Chr. 12. 2; 35. 20; 36. 3; Jer. 37. 5.

the "remnant of Judah" taken there, Jer.
43. 7.

Jesus taken to, Matt. 2. 13.

prophecies concerning, Gen. 15. 13; Is. 11. 11;
19; 20; 27. 12; 30. 1; Jer. 9. 26; 25. 19; 43.
8; 44. 28; 46; Ezek. 29-32; Dan. 11. 8; Hos.
9. 3; 11; Joel 3. 19; Zech. 10. 10; 14. 18.

Ehud, judge, delivers Israel, Jud. 3. 15.

Ekron taken, Jud. 1. 18.

men of, smitten with emerods, 1 Sam. 5. 12;
6. 17.

prophecies concerning, Amos. 1. 8; Zeph. 2.
4; Zech. 9. 5.

Elah, king of Israel, 1 Ki. 16. 8, 10.

—valley of, battle in, 1 Sam. 17. 2.

David slays Goliath there, 1 Sam. 17. 49.

Elam, son of Shem, Gen. 10. 22.

—Chedorlaomer, king of, Gen. 14.

Elamites, Acts 2. 9.

Eldad and Medad prophesy, Num. 11. 26.

Elders, seventy, Ex. 24. 1; Num. 11. 16.

officers so called, Gen. 50. 7; Lev. 4. 15;
Deut. 21. 19; 1 Sam. 16. 4; Ezra 5. 5; Ps.
107. 32; Ezek. 8. 1.

of the Church, Acts 14. 23; 15. 4, 23; 16. 4;
20. 17; Tit. 1. 5; Jas. 5. 14; 1 Pet. 5. 1.

Paul's charge to, Acts 20. 17.

Peter's charge to, 1 Pet. 5.

twenty-four, in heaven, Rev. 4. 4; 7. 11; 14. 3.

Eleazar, son of Aaron, and chief priest, Ex. 6.
23; 28; 29; Lev. 8; Num. 3. 2; 4. 16; 16.
36; 20. 26; 27. 22; 31. 13; 34. 17; Josh. 17. 4;
24. 33.

Eleazar, son of Abinadab, keeps the ark,
1 Sam. 7. 1.

—one of David's captains, 2 Sam. 23. 9; 1 Chr.
11. 12.

Elect, Christ so called, 1 Pet. 2. 6; Is. 42. 1.

God's chosen, Is. 45. 1; 65. 9.

under the Gospel, Matt. 24. 22; Mk. 13. 20;
Lk. 18. 7; Rom. 8. 33; 11. 5; Col. 3. 12;
2 Tim. 2. 10; Tit. 1. 1; 1 Pet. 1. 2; 2 John
1. 13.

Election, of God, 1 Thes. 1. 4.

its privileges and duties, Mk. 13. 20; Lk. 18.
7; Rom. 8. 29; 1 Cor. 1. 27; 2 Pet. 1. 10.

Elect Lady, Epistle to, 2 John.

El-Elohe-Israel (God, the God of Israel), Gen.
33. 20.

Elhanan, one of David's warriors, 2 Sam. 21. 19;
23. 24; 1 Chr. 11. 26; 20. 5.

Eli, high priest and judge, blesses Hannah,
1 Sam. 1. 17.

Samuel brought to, 1 Sam. 1. 25.

wickedness of his sons, 1 Sam. 2. 22.

rebuked by man of God, 1 Sam. 2. 27.

destruction of his house foretold, 1 Sam.
3. 11.

his sons slain, 1 Sam. 4. 10, 11.

his death, 1 Sam. 4. 18.

Eli, **Eli**, **lama sabachthani?** Matt. 27. 46; Mk.
15. 34.

Eliakim, chief minister of Hezekiah, confer-
ence with Rab-shakeh, 2 Ki. 18. 18; Is.
36. 11.

sent to Isaiah. 2 Ki. 19. 2; Is. 37. 2.

prefigures kingdom of Christ, Is. 22. 20-25.

—son of Josiah, made king by Pharaoh, and
named Jehoiakim, 2 Ki. 23. 34; 2 Chr. 36. 4.

Elias, Matt. 27. 47, 49; Mk. 15. 35, 36. See
Elijah.

Eliashib, high priest, builds the wall, Neh. 3. 1.

allied unto Tobiah, Neh. 13. 4.

Eliezer, Abraham's steward, Gen. 15. 2.

—son of Moses, Ex. 18. 4; 1 Chr. 23. 15.

—prophet, reproves Jehoshaphat, 2 Chr. 20. 37.

Elihu reproves Job's friends, Job 32; and Job's
impatience, Job 33. 8; and self-righteous-
ness, Job 34. 5.

declares God's justice, Job 33. 12; 34. 10; 35.
13; 36; and power, Job 33-37; and mercy.
Job 33. 23; 34. 28.

Elijah the Tishbite, predicts a great drought,
1 Ki. 17. 1; Lk. 4. 25; Jas. 5. 17.

miraculously fed, 1 Ki. 17. 6; 19. 5.

raises the widow's son, 1 Ki. 17. 21.

slays the priests of Baal, 1 Ki. 18. 40.

flees into the wilderness of Beer-sheba, 1 Ki.
19; Rom. 11. 2.

anoints Elisha, 1 Ki. 19. 19.

denounces Ahab in Naboth's vineyard, 1 Ki.
21. 17.

his prediction fulfilled, 2 Ki. 9. 36; 10. 10.

rebukes Ahaziah, 2 Ki. 1. 3, 16.

calls down fire from heaven, 2 Ki. 1. 10; Lk.
9. 54.

divides Jordan, 2 Ki. 2. 8.

carried up into heaven in a chariot of fire,
2 Ki. 2. 11.

his mantle taken by Elisha, 2 Ki. 2. 13.

appears at Christ's transfiguration, Matt. 17.
3; Mk. 9. 4; Lk. 9. 30.

precursor of John the Baptist, Mal. 4. 5;
Matt. 11. 14; 16. 14; Lk. 1. 17; 9. 8, 19;
John 1. 21.

Eliphaz reproves Job, Job 4; 5; 15; 22.

God's anger against him appeased, Job 42.
7, 8.

Elisabeth, mother of John the Baptist, Lk. 1. 5.

her salutation to Mary, Lk. 1. 42.

Elisha (Eliseus) appointed to succeed Elijah,
1 Ki. 19. 16.

receives his mantle, 2 Ki. 2. 13.

heals the waters with salt, 2 Ki. 2. 22.

bears destroy the children who mock him,
2 Ki. 2. 24.

his miracles:—water, 2 Ki. 3. 16; oil, 2 Ki.
4. 4; Shunammite's son, 2 Ki. 4. 32; death
in the pot, 2 Ki. 4. 40; feeds a hundred
men with twenty loaves, 2 Ki. 4. 44; Naaman's leprosy, 2 Ki. 5. 14; Lk. 4. 27; the

Elisha—*Continued.*
iron swims, 2 Ki. 6. 5; Syrians struck blind, 2 Ki. 6. 18.
prophesies plenty in Samaria when besieged, 2 Ki. 7. 1.
sends to anoint Jehu, 2 Ki. 9. 1.
his death, 2 Ki. 13. 20.
miracle wrought by his bones, 2 Ki. 13. 21.
Elkanah, Samuel's father, 1 Sam. 1.
Elon judges Israel, Jud. 12. 11.
Elymas (Bar-jesus), Acts 13. 6.
Embalming of Jacob, Gen. 50. 2; of Joseph, Gen. 50. 26; of Christ, John 19. 39.
Emeralds, Ex. 28. 18; 39. 11; Rev. 4. 3; 21. 19.
Emerods, threatened, Deut. 28. 27.
Philistines smitten with, 1 Sam. 5. 6.
Emims, giants, Gen. 14. 5; Deut. 2. 10.
Emmanuel (Immanuel), God with us, Is. 7. 14; 8. 8; Matt. 1. 23.
Emmaus, Christ's journey to, and discourse, Lk. 24. 15.
Emulations censured, Gal. 5. 20.
Enchantments forbidden, Lev. 19. 26; Deut. 18. 9; Is. 47. 9.
Endor, witch of, 1 Sam. 28. 7.
Enemies, treatment of, Ex. 23. 4; 1 Sam. 24. 10; 26. 9; Job 31. 29; Prov. 24. 17; 25. 21; Matt. 5. 44; Lk. 6. 35.
God delivers from, 1 Sam. 12. 11; Ezra 8. 31; Ps. 18. 48; 59; 61. 3.
of God, their punishment, Ex. 15. 6; Deut. 32. 41; Jud. 5. 31; Est. 7; 8; Ps. 68. 1; 92. 9; Is. 1. 24; 37. 36; 2 Thes. 1. 8; Rev. 21. 8.
En-Gedi, city of Judah, Josh. 15. 62.
David dwells there, 1 Sam. 23. 29; 24. 1.
See Cant. 1. 14; Ezek. 47. 10.
Engines of war, 2 Chr. 26. 15; Ezek. 26. 9.
Engraving on stones, Ex. 28. 11; Zech. 3. 9.
Enmity between God and man, Rom. 8. 7; Jas. 4. 4.
how abolished, Eph. 2. 15; Col. 1. 20.
Enoch, his godliness and translation, Gen. 5. 24.
his faith, Heb. 11. 5; his prophecy, Jude 14.
En-Rogel, fountain, Josh. 15. 7; 18. 16; 1 Ki. 1. 9.
Enticers to idolatry to be stoned, Deut. 13. 10.
Envy described, Prov. 14. 30; 27. 4; Eccl. 4. 4; Matt. 27. 18; Acts 7. 9; Rom. 1. 29; 1 Cor. 3. 3; 2 Cor. 12. 20; Gal. 5. 21; 1 Tim. 6. 4; Tit. 3. 3; Jas. 4. 5.
forbidden, Ps. 37. 1; Prov. 3. 31; 24. 1, 19; Rom. 13. 13; 1 Pet. 2. 1.
its evil consequences, Job 5. 2; Ps. 106. 16; Prov. 14. 30; Is. 26. 11; Jas. 3. 16.
Joseph sold for, Acts 7. 9; Gen. 37. 28.
Epaphras commended, Col. 1. 7; 4. 12.
Epaphroditus, Paul's joy at his recovery, Phil. 2. 25; his kindness, Phil. 4. 18.
Ephah, a measure, Ex. 16. 36; Lev. 19. 36; Ezek. 45. 10; Zech. 5. 6.
Ephesians, Paul's epistle to, Eph. 1; election, 1. 4; adoption of grace. 1. 6; dead in sin—quickened, 2. 1, 5; adoption of the Gentiles, 2. 13; 3; unity and kindness enjoined, 4-6.
Ephesus visited by Paul, Acts 18. 19; 19. 1; miracles there, Acts 19. 11; tumult there, Acts 19. 24.
Paul's address to the elders of, Acts 20. 17.
„   fight with beasts there, 1 Cor. 15. 32.
Paul tarries there, 1 Cor. 16. 8.
Ephod of the priest, Ex. 28. 4; 39. 2.
of Gideon, Jud. 8. 27.
of Micah, Jud. 17. 5.

Ephphatha ("be opened"), Mk. 7. 34.
Ephraim, younger son of Joseph, Gen. 41. 52.
Jacob blesses Ephraim and Manasseh, Gen. 48. 14.
his descendants numbered, Num. 1. 10, 32; 2. 18; 26. 35; 1 Chr. 7. 20.
their possessions, Josh. 16. 5; 17. 14; Jud. 1. 29.
chastise the Midianites, Jud. 7. 24.
their quarrel with Gideon, Jud. 8. 1; and Jephthah, Jud. 12.
revolt from the house of David, 1 Ki. 12. 25.
chastise Ahaz and Judah, 2 Chr. 28. 6, 7.
release their prisoners, 2 Chr. 28. 12.
carried into captivity, 2 Ki. 17. 5; Ps. 78. 9, 67; Jer. 7. 15.
repenting, called God's son, Jer. 31. 20.
prophecies concerning, Is. 7. 9; 9. 9; 11. 13; 28. 1; Hos. 5-14; Zech 9. 10; 10. 7.
Ephratah (Beth-lehem), Gen. 35. 16; Ps. 132. 6; Mic. 5. 2.
Ephron, the Hittite, sells Machpelah to Abraham, Gen. 23. 10.
Epicureans, philosophers, encounter Paul at Athens, Acts 17. 18.
Erastus ministers to Paul, Acts 19. 22; Rom. 16. 23; 2 Tim. 4. 20.
Esar-Haddon, king of Assyria, 2 Ki. 19. 37; Ezra 4. 2; Is. 37. 38.
Esau, son of Isaac, Gen. 25. 25; (Mal. 1. 2; Rom. 9. 10).
sells his birthright, Gen. 25. 29 (Heb. 12. 16).
deprived of the blessing, Gen. 27. 26.
his anger against Jacob, Gen. 27. 41; and reconciliation, Gen. 33.
his descendants, Gen. 36; 1 Chr. 1. 35.
Eschol, grapes of, Num. 13. 23.
Esther (Hadassah) made queen in place of Vashti, Est. 2. 17.
intercedes for her people, Est. 7. 3, 4, etc.
Ethiopians, invading Judah, subdued by Asa, 2. Chr. 14. 9.
See Num. 12. 1; 2 Ki. 19. 9; Est. 1. 1; Job 28. 19.
prophecies concerning, Ps. 68. 31; 87. 4; Is. 18; 20; 43. 3; 45. 14; Jer. 46. 9; Ezek. 30. 4; 38. 5; Nah. 3. 9; Zeph. 3. 10.
eunuch baptised, Acts 8. 27.
Eunice commended (Acts 16. 1), 2 Tim. 1. 5.
Eunuchs, promise to those who please God, Is. 56. 3.
Christ's declaration concerning, Matt. 19. 12.
Ashpenaz, master of the king's eunuchs, Dan. 1. 3.
Ethiopian, baptised by Philip, Acts 8. 27.
Euphrates, river, Gen. 2. 14; 15. 18; Deut. 11. 24; Josh. 1. 4; 2 Sam. 8. 3; Jer. 13. 4; 46. 2; 51. 63; typical, Rev. 9. 14; 16. 12.
Euroclydon, a wind, Acts 27. 14.
Eutychus, his fall and recovery, Acts 20. 7.
Evangelist, Philip the, receives Paul's company, Acts 21. 8.
work of, Eph. 4. 11; 2 Tim. 4. 5.
Eve created, Gen. 1. 27; 2. 18.
her fall and fate, Gen. 3. See *Adam.*
Evil-Merodach, king of Babylon, restores Jehoiachin, 2 Ki. 25. 27; Jer. 52. 31.
Exaction (usury, etc.), forbidden, Lev. 25. 35; Deut. 15. 2; Prov. 28. 8; Ezek. 22. 12; 45. 9; Lk. 3. 13; 1 Cor. 5. 10.
disclaimed, Neh. 5. 1; 10. 31.
Example of Christ, Matt. 11. 29; John 13. 15; Rom. 15. 5; Phil. 2. 5; 1 Pet. 2. 21.
of the prophets, Heb. 6. 12; Jas. 5. 10.

Example—*Continued*.
of the apostles, 1 Cor. 4. 16; 11. 1; Phil. 3. 17; 4. 9; 1 Thes. 1. 6.
for warning, 1 Cor. 10. 6; Heb. 4. 11; 1 Pet. 5. 3; Jude 7.

Excess forbidden, Eph. 5. 18; 1 Pet. 4. 3.

Exhortation, 1 Thes. 4. 18; 5. 11; Heb. 3. 13; 10. 25.

Experience worketh hope, Rom. 5. 4.

Eye-service forbidden, Eph. 6. 6; Col. 3. 22.

Eyes of the Lord, Deut. 11. 12; 2 Chr. 16. 9; Prov. 5. 3; upon the righteous Ezra 5. 5; Ps. 32. 8; 33. 8; 34. 15; 1 Pet. 3. 12.
See John 10. 21.

Ezekiel sent to house of Israel, Ezek. 2; 3; 33. 7.
his visions of God's glory, Ezek. 1; 8; 10; 11. 22; of the Jews' abominations, Ezek. 8. 5; their punishment, Ezek. 9; 11; the resurrection of dry bones, Ezek. 37; measuring of the temple, Ezek. 40.
intercedes for his people, Ezek. 9. 8; 11. 13.
his dumbness, Ezek. 3. 26; 24. 26; 33. 22.
his parables, Ezek. 15; 16; 17; 19; 23; 24.
exhorts Israel against idols, Ezek. 14. 1; 20. 1; 33. 30.
rehearses Israel's rebellions, Ezek. 20; and the sins of the rulers and people of Jerusalem, Ezek. 22; 23; 24.
predicts Israel's and the nations' doom, Ezek. 21; 35.
prophesies concerning various nations, Ezek. 25-39.

Ezion-Gaber, on the Red Sea, Num. 33. 35; 1 Ki. 9. 26.

Ezra, scribe goes up from Babylon to Jerusalem, Ezra 7. 1; 8. 1.
the commission from Artaxerxes, Ezra 7. 11.
fast ordered by, Ezra 8. 21.
his prayer, Ezra 9. 5.
reproves the people, Ezra 10. 9.
reforms various corruptions, Ezra 10; Neh. 13.

FABLES, unedifying, 1 Tim. 1. 4; 4. 7; 2 Tim. 4. 4; Tit. 1. 14.

Face of God set against them that do evil, Ps. 34. 16; Is. 59. 2; Ezek. 39. 23.
to be sought, 2 Chr. 7. 14; Ps. 31. 16; 80. 2; Dan. 9. 17.
seen by Jacob, Gen. 32. 30.

Faith described, Heb. 11.
justification by, Rom. 3. 28; 5. 1, 16; Gal. 2. 16.
purification by, Acts 15. 9.
sanctification by, Acts 26. 18.
object of, Father, Son, and Holy Ghost, Mk. 11. 22; John 6. 29; 14. 1; 20. 31; Acts 20. 21; 2 Cor. 13. 14.
the gift of God, Rom. 12. 3; 1 Cor. 2. 5; 12. 9; Eph. 2. 8.
in Christ, Acts 8. 12; 2 Tim. 3. 15.
unity of, Eph. 4, 5, 13; Jude 3.
leads to salvation, etc., Mk. 16. 16; John 1. 12; 3. 16, 36; 6. 40, 47; Acts 16. 31; Gal. 3. 11; Eph. 2. 8; Heb. 11. 6; 1 Pet. 1. 9; 1 John 5. 10.
works by love, 1 Cor. 13; Gal. 5. 6; Col. 1. 4; 1 Thes. 1. 3; 1 Tim. 1. 5; Philem. 5; Heb. 10. 23; 1 Pet. 1. 22; 1 John 3. 14, 23.
without works is dead, Jas. 2. 17, 20.
produces peace, joy, hope, etc., Rom. 5. 1; 15. 13; 2 Cor. 4. 13; 1 Pet. 1. 8.
excludes boasting, etc., Rom. 3. 27; 4. 2; 1 Cor. 1. 29; Eph. 2. 9.

Faith—*Continued*.
blessings received through, Mk. 16. 16; John 6. 40; 12. 36; 20. 31; Acts 10. 43; 16. 31; 26. 18; Rom. 1. 17 (Hab. 2. 4); Rom. 3. 21; 4. 16; 5. 1; 2 Cor. 5. 7; Gal. 2. 16; 3. 14, 26; Eph. 1. 13; 3. 12, 17; 1 Tim. 1. 4; Heb. 4. 3; 6. 12; 10. 38; 1 Pet. 1. 5; Jude 20.
miracles performed through, Matt. 9. 22; Lk. 8. 50; Acts 3. 16.
power of, Matt. 17. 20; Mk. 9. 23; 11. 23; Lk. 17. 6.
trial of, 2 Thes. 1. 4; Heb. 11. 17; Jas. 1. 3, 13; 1 Pet. 1. 7.
overcometh the world, 1 John 5. 4.
shield of the Christian, Eph. 6. 16; 1 Thes. 5. 8.
exhortations to continue in, 1 Cor. 16. 13; 2 Cor. 13. 5; Eph. 6. 16; Phil. 1. 27; Col. 1. 23; 2. 7; 1 Thes. 5. 8; 1 Tim. 1. 19; 4. 12; 6. 11; 2 Tim. 2. 22; Tit. 1. 13; Heb. 10. 22; Jude 3.

EXAMPLES OF :
Caleb, Num. 13. 30.
Shadrach, Meshach, and Abednego, Dan. 3. 17.
Daniel, Dan. 6. 10.
Ninevites, Jon. 3. 5.
Peter, Matt. 16. 16.
Nathanael, John 1. 49.
Martha, John, 11. 27.
Stephen, Acts 6. 5.
Ethiopian eunuch, Acts 8. 37.
Barnabas, Acts 11. 24.

Faithfulness commended in the service of God, 2 Ki. 12. 15; 2 Chr. 31. 12; Matt. 24. 45; 2 Cor. 2. 17; 4. 2; 3 John 5.
towards men, Deut. 1. 16; Ps. 141. 5; Prov. 11. 13; 13. 17; 14. 5; 20. 6; 25. 13; 27. 6; 28. 20; Lk. 16. 10; 1 Cor. 4. 2; 1 Tim. 3. 11; 6. 2; Tit. 2. 10.
of Abraham, Gen. 22; Gal. 3. 9.
of Joseph, Gen. 39. 4, 22.
of Moses, Num. 12. 7; Heb. 3. 5.
of David, 1 Sam. 22. 14.
of Daniel, Dan. 6. 4.
of Paul, Acts 20. 20.
of Timothy, 1 Cor. 4. 17.
of God, Ps. 36. 5; 40. 10; 88. 11; 89. 1; 92. 2; 119. 75; Is. 25. 1; Lam. 3. 23.

Fall of man, Gen. 3.
its consequences, sin and death, Gen. 3. 19; Rom. 5. 12; 1 Cor. 15. 21.

False witnesses condemned. See *Deceit, Witnesses*.

Familiar spirits not to be sought after, Lev. 19. 31; Is. 8. 19.
possessors of, to die, Lev. 20. 27.
inquired of by Saul, 1 Sam. 28. 7; 1 Chr. 10. 13.

Famine occurs in Canaan, Gen. 12. 10. Egypt, Gen. 41. Israel, Ruth 1. 1; 2 Sam. 21. 1; 1 Ki. 18. 2; 2 Ki. 6. 25; 7; Lk. 4. 25.
threatened, Jer. 14. 15; 15. 2; Ezek. 5. 12; 6. 11; Matt. 24. 7; Acts 11. 28.
described, Jer. 14; Lam. 4; Joel 1.
(of God's word), Amos 8. 11.

Fast proclaimed, Lev. 23. 27, 29; 2 Chr. 20. 3; Ezra 8. 21; Neh. 9; Est. 4. 16; Joel 2. 15; Jon. 3. 5.
the true and the false, Is. 58; Zech. 7; Matt. 6. 16.

Fasting turned into gladness, Zech. 8. 19.
Christ defends his disciples for not, Matt. 9. 14; Mk. 2. 18; Lk. 5. 33.

Flesh—*Continued.*
God manifest in the, John 1. 14; 1 Tim. 3. 16; 1 Pet. 3. 18; 4. 1; to be acknowledged, 1 John 4. 2; 2 John 7.

Flies, Egyptians plagued by, Ex. 8. 21, 31; Ps. 78. 45; 105. 31.

Flint, water brought from, Num. 20. 11; Deut. 8. 15; Ps. 114. 8; 1 Cor. 10. 4.

Flood threatened, Gen. 6. 17; sent, Gen. 7. 11; Matt. 24. 38; 2 Pet. 2. 5.
assuaged, Gen. 8.

Flour, employed in sacrifices, Ex. 29. 2; Lev. 2. 2.

Food for all creatures, Gen. 1. 29; 9. 3; Ps. 104. 14; 145. 16; 147. 8.

Foolishness, the Gospel so designated, 1 Cor. 1. 18; 2. 14.
worldly wisdom is, with God, 1 Cor. 1. 20; 2. 7; 3. 19.

Fools, their character and conduct, Ps. 14. 1; 49. 13; 53. 1; 92. 6; Prov. 10. 8, 23; 12. 15, 16; 13. 16; 14. 16; 15. 5; 17. 7, 10, 12, 16, 21, 28; 18. 2, 6, 7; 19. 1; 20. 3; 26. 4; 27. 3, 22; Eccl. 4. 5; 5. 1, 3; 7. 4, 9; 10. 2, 14; Is. 44. 25; Matt. 26; 23. 17; 25. 2; Lk. 12. 20; Rom. 1. 22.

Footstool of God: the temple so called, 1 Chr. 28. 2; Ps. 99. 5; 132. 7.
the earth called, Is. 66. 1; Matt. 5. 35; Acts 7. 49.
God's enemies made, Ps. 110. 1; Matt. 22. 44; Heb. 10. 13.

Forbearance, exhortations to, Matt. 18. 33; Eph. 4. 2; 6. 9; Col. 3. 13; 2 Tim. 2. 24.
of God, Ps. 50. 21; Is. 30. 18; Rom. 2. 4; 3. 25; 1 Pet. 3. 20; 2 Pet. 3. 9.

Foreknowledge of God, Acts 2. 23; Rom. 8. 29; 11. 2; Gal. 3. 8; 1 Pet. 1. 2.

Forgetfulness of God, condemned, Deut. 4. 9; 6. 12; Ps. 78. 7; 103. 2; Prov. 3. 1; 4. 5; 31. 5; Heb. 13. 16.
punishment of, Job 8. 13; Ps. 9. 17; 50. 22; Is. 17. 10; Jer. 2. 32; Hos. 8. 14.

Forgiveness, mutual, commanded, Gen. 50. 17; Matt. 5. 23; 6. 14; 18. 21, 35; Mk. 11. 25; Lk. 11. 4; 17. 4; 2 Cor. 2. 7; Eph. 4. 32; Col. 3. 13; Jas. 2. 13.
of enemies, Matt. 5. 44; Lk. 6. 27; Rom. 12. 14, 19.
—of sin, prayed for, Ex. 32. 32; 1 Ki. 8. 30; 2 Chr. 6. 21; Ps. 25. 18; 32; 51; 79. 9; 130; Dan. 9. 19; Amos 7. 2; Matt. 6. 12.
promised, Lev. 4. 20; 2 Chr. 7. 14; Is. 33. 24; 55. 7; Jer. 3. 12; 31. 20, 34; 33. 8; Ezek. 36. 25; Hos. 14. 4; Mic. 7. 18; Lk. 24. 47; Acts 5. 31; 26. 18; Eph. 1. 7; Col. 1. 14; Jas. 5. 15; 1 John 1. 9.

Fornication denounced, Ex. 22. 16; Lev. 19. 20; Num. 25; Deut. 22. 21; 23. 17; Prov. 2. 16; 5. 3; 6. 25; 7; 9. 13; 22. 14; 23. 27; 29. 3; 31. 3; Eccl. 7. 26; Hos. 4. 11; Matt. 15. 19; Mk. 7. 21; Acts 15. 20; Rom. 1. 29; 1 Cor. 5. 9; 6. 9; 2 Cor. 12. 21; Gal. 5. 19; Eph. 5. 5; Col. 3. 5; 1 Thes. 4. 3; 1 Tim. 1. 10; Heb. 13. 4; 1 Pet. 4. 3; Jude 7; Rev. 2. 14; 21. 8; 22. 15.
spiritual, idolatry, etc., Ezek. 16. 29; Hos. 1; 2; 3; Rev. 14. 8; 17. 2; 18. 3; 19. 2.

Forsaking God, danger of, Deut. 28. 20; Jud. 10. 13; 2 Chr. 15. 2; 24. 20; Ezra 8. 22; 9. 10; Is. 1. 28; Jer. 1. 16; 5. 19; 17. 13; Ezek. 9. 9.

Fortress, the Lord compared to a, 2 Sam. 22. 2; Ps. 18. 2; Jer. 16. 19.

Fortunatus ministers to Paul, 1 Cor. 16. 17.

Forty Days, period of the flood, Gen. 7. 17.
giving of the law, Ex. 24. 18.
spying land of Canaan, Num. 13. 25.
Goliath's defiance, 1 Sam. 17. 16.
Elijah's journey to Horeb, 1 Ki. 19. 8.
Jonah's warning to Nineveh, Jon. 3. 4.
fasting of Christ, Matt. 4. 2; Mk. 1. 13; Lk. 4. 2.
Christ's appearances during, Acts 1. 3.

Forty Stripes, Deut. 25. 3; save one, 2 Cor. 11. 24.

Forty Years, manna sent, etc., Ex. 16. 35; Num. 14. 33; Ps. 95. 10.
of peace, Jud. 3. 11; 5. 31; 8. 28.

Foundation, Jesus Christ the one, Is. 28. 16; (Matt. 16. 18); 1 Cor. 3. 11; Eph. 2. 20; Heb. 11. 10; 1 Pet. 2. 6.

Fountain of living waters, Ps. 36. 9; Jer. 2. 13; Joel 3. 18; Zech. 13. 1; 14. 8.
See Is. 12. 3; 44. 3; 55. 1; John 4. 10; Rev. 7. 17; 21. 6.

Four living creatures, vision of, Ezek. 1. 5; 10. 10; Rev. 4. 6; 5. 14; 6. 6.
kingdoms, Nebuchadnezzar's vision of, Dan. 2. 36; Daniel's vision of, Dan. 7. 3, 16.

Fourfold compensation, Ex. 22. 1; 2 Sam. 12. 6; Lk. 19. 8.

Fowls, winged, Gen. 1. 20; 7. 8; Ps. 104. 12; 148. 10.

Foxes, Samson's stratagem with, Jud. 15. 4.
mentioned, Cant. 2. 15; Lam. 5. 18; Matt. 8. 20; Lk. 13. 32.

Frankincense, various uses for, Ex. 30. 34; Lev. 2. 1; Cant. 3. 6; Matt. 2. 11.

Fraud condemned, Lev. 19. 13; Mal. 3. 5; Mk. 10. 19; 1 Cor. 6. 8; 1 Thes. 4. 6. See *Deceit.*

Freewill offerings, Lev. 22. 18; Num. 15. 3; Deut. 16. 10; Ezra 3. 5.

Freewoman and bondwoman, allegory of, Gal. 4. 22.

Friend of God, title of Abraham, 2 Chr. 20. 7; Is. 41. 8; Jas. 2. 23.

Friends, advantages of, Prov. 18. 24; 27. 6, 9, 17; John 15. 13.
danger arising from evil, Deut. 13. 6; Prov. 22. 24; 29. 19; Mic. 7. 5; Zech. 13. 6.
the disciples so called, Lk. 12. 4; John 15. 14; 3 John 14.

Friendship of Jonathan and David, 1 Sam. 18. 1; 19; 20; 2 Sam. 1. 26.
with the world, forbidden, Rom. 12. 2; 2 Cor. 6. 17; Jas. 4. 4; 1 John 2. 15.

Fringes, how worn, Num. 15. 37; Deut. 22. 12; Matt. 23. 5.

Frogs, Egypt plagued with, Ex. 8. 6; Ps. 78. 45; 105. 30.
unclean spirits like, Rev. 16. 13.

Frontlets, Ex. 13. 16; Deut. 6. 8.

Frowardness, results of, Deut. 32. 20; 2 Sam. 22. 27; Job 5. 13; Prov. 2. 12; 3. 32; 4. 24; 10. 31; 11. 20; 16. 28; 17. 20; 21. 8; 22. 5.

Fruits, first three years not to be touched, Lev. 19. 23.
blessed to the obedient, Deut. 7. 13; 28. 4.
of faith meet for repentance, etc., Matt. 3. 8; 7. 16; John 4. 36; 15. 16; Rom. 7. 4; 2 Cor. 9. 10; Gal. 5. 22; Col. 1. 6; Heb. 12. 11; Jas. 3. 17.

Fruit Trees to be preserved in time of war, Deut. 20. 19.

Fugitive servant, law of, Deut. 23. 15.

Furnace, burning fiery, Dan. 3. 6, 11, 15, 17, etc.
figurative. Deut. 4. 20; Is. 48. 10; Ezek. 22. 18.

GAAL conspires against Abimelech, etc. Jud. 9. 26.

Gabbatha (pavement), John 19. 13.

Gabriel, archangel, appears to Daniel, Dan. 8. 16; 9. 21.

to Zacharias, Lk. 1. 19.

to Mary, Lk. 1. 26.

Gad, son of Jacob, Gen. 30. 11.

his descendants, Gen. 46. 16.

blessed by Jacob, Gen. 49. 19.

—tribe of, blessed by Moses, Deut. 33. 20.

numbered, Num. 1. 24; 26. 15.

their possessions, Num. 32; 34. 14.

commended by Joshua, Josh. 22. 1.

accused of idolatry. Josh. 22. 11.

their defence, Josh. 22. 21.

—seer, his message to David, 2 Sam. 24. 11; 1 Chr. 21. 9; 2 Chr. 29. 25.

Gadarenes or **Gergesenes**, miracle wrought in the country of, Matt. 8. 28; Mk. 5. 1; Lk. 8. 26.

Gaius commended, 3 John.

Galatians, Paul visits, Acts 16. 6.

reproved, Gal. 1. 6; 3; and exhorted, Gal. 5; 6.

their love to Paul, Gal. 4. 13.

Galileans, killed by Pilate, Lk. 13. 1.

disciples so called, Acts 1 11; 2. 7.

Galilee, prophecy concerning. Is. 9. 1, Matt. 4. 15.

Christ's work there, Matt. 2. 22; 15. 29; 26. 27. 55; 28. 7; Mk. 1. 9; Lk. 4. 14; 23. 5; 24. 6; Acts 10. 37; 13. 31.

Gallio, deputy of Achaia, dismisses Paul, Acts 18. 12.

Gallows, Haman hanged on, Est. 7. 10.

Gamaliel advises the council, Acts 5. 34.

Paul brought up under, Acts 22. 3.

Games, public, 1 Cor. 9. 24; Phil. 3. 12; 1 Tim. 6. 12; 2 Tim. 2. 5; 4. 7; Heb. 12. 1.

Garden of Eden, Gen. 2. 8.

of Gethsemane, John 18. 1.

Garments of the priests, Ex. 28; 39.

manner of purifying, Lk. 13. 47 (Eccl. 9. 8; Zech. 3. 3; Jude 23).

not to be made of diverse materials, Lev. 19. 19; Deut. 22. 11.

of the sexes not to be exchanged, Deut. 22. 5.

of Christ, lots cast for (Ps. 22. 18); Matt. 27. 35; John 19. 23.

Gates of heaven, Gen. 28. 17; Ps. 24. 7; Is. 26. 2.

of death and hell, Ps. 9. 13; Matt. 16. 18.

of the grave, Is. 38. 10.

the strait and wide, Matt. 7. 13; Lk. 13. 24.

Gath, Goliath of, 1 Sam. 17. 4.

men of, smitten with emerods, 1 Sam. 5. 8.

David flees to, 1 Sam. 27. 4.

taken by David, 1 Chr. 18. 1.

," by Hazael, 2 Ki. 12. 17.

Uzziah breaks down the wall of, 2 Chr. 26. 6.

Gaza, Samson carries away the gates of, Jud. 16.

destruction of, foretold, Jer. 47; Amos 1. 6; Zeph. 2. 4; Zech. 9. 5.

Gedaliah, governor of the remnant of Judah, 2 Ki. 25. 22; (Jer. 40. 5).

treacherously slain by Ishmael, 2 Ki. 25. 25; (Jer. 41).

Gedor conquered by Simeonites, 1 Chr. 4. 41.

Gehazi, servant of Elisha, 2 Ki. 4. 12.

his covetousness and its punishment, 2 Ki. 5. 20.

Genealogies:—Generations of Adam, Gen. 5; 1 Chr. 1; Lk. 3; of Noah, Gen 10; 1 Chr.

Genealogies—*Continued.*

1. 4; of Shem, Gen. 11. 10; of Terah, Gen. 11. 27; of Abraham, Gen. 25; 1 Chr. 1. 28; of Jacob, Gen. 29. 31; 30; 46. 8; Ex. 1. 2; Num. 26; 1 Chr. 2; of Esau, Gen. 36; 1 Chr. 1. 35; of the tribes, 1 Chr. 2; 4; 5; 6; 7; of David, 1 Chr. 3; of Saul, 1 Chr. 8; 9. 35; of Christ, Matt. 1; Lk. 3. 23; endless, 1 Tim. 1. 4. See **Fables.**

Gennesaret, a lake of Palestine, miracles wrought there, Matt. 17. 27; Lk. 5. 1; John 21. 6.

Gentiles, origin of, Gen. 10. 5.

their state by nature, Rom. 1. 21; 1 Cor. 12. 2; Eph. 2; 4. 17; 1 Thes. 4. 5.

their conversion predicted, Is. 11. 10; 42. 1; 49. 6; (Matt. 12. 18; Lk. 2. 32; Acts 13. 47); 62. 2; Jer. 16. 19; Hos. 2. 23; Mal. 1. 11; Matt. 8. 11.

prediction fulfilled, John 10. 16; Acts 8. 37; 10; 14; 15; Eph. 2. 1; 1 Thes. 1. 1.

calling of, Rom. 9. 24.

See Is. 66. 19.

Christ made known to, Col. 1. 27.

Gentleness of Christ, 2 Cor. 10. 1; Matt. 11. 29; (Is. 40. 11).

the fruit of the Spirit, Gal. 5. 22.

exhortations to (1 Thes. 2. 7), 2 Tim. 2. 24; Tit. 3. 2; Jas. 3. 17.

Gerar, herdmen of, strive with Isaac's, Gen. 26. 20.

Gerizim, mount of blessing, Deut. 11. 29; 27. 12; Josh. 8. 33.

Gershom (**Gershon**), son of Levi, Gen. 46. 11; Num. 3. 17

—son of Moses, Ex. 2. 22; 1 ; 3.

Gershonites, their duties in the service of the tabernacle, Num. 4; 7; 10. 17.

Geshur, Absalom dwells there, 2 Sam. 13. 37; 14. 23; (Josh. 13. 13).

Gethsemane, garden of, our Lord's agony there, Matt. 26. 36; Mk. 14. 32; Lk. 22. 39; John 18. 1.

Giants before the flood, Gen. 6. 4.

in Canaan terrify the spies, Num. 13. 33, Deut. 1. 28; (2. 10, 11, 19, 20; 9. 2).

several slain by David and his servants 1 Sam. 17; 2 Sam. 21. 16; 1 Chr. 20. 4.

Gibeah, a city of Benjamin, Jud. 19. 14.

its wickedness, Jud. 19. 22.

punishment of its inhabitants, Jud. 20.

the city of Saul, 1 Sam. 10. 26; 11. 4; 14. 2. 15. 34; 2 Sam. 21. 6.

Gibeon, craft of its inhabitants, Josh. 9.

delivered by Joshua, Josh. 10.

Saul persecutes them, 2 Sam. 21. 1; and David makes atonement, 2 Sam. 21. 3-9.

Solomon's dream at, 1 Ki. 3. 5.

tabernacle of the Lord kept at, 1 Chr. 16. 39; 21. 29; (Is. 28. 21).

Gideon, angel of the Lord appears to, Jud. 6. 11.

destroys the altar and grove of Baal, Jud. 6. 25, 27.

God gives him two signs, Jud. 6. 36-40.

his army reduced, etc., Jud. 7. 2-7.

his stratagem, Jud. 7. 16.

subdues the Midianites, Jud. 7. 19; 8.

makes an ephod of the spoil, Jud. 8. 24

his death, Jud. 8. 32.

See Heb. 11. 32.

Gift of God, John 4. 10; unspeakable, 2 Cor. 9. 15.

the Holy Ghost, Acts 2. 38; 8. 20; 10. 45.

Gifts, spiritual, Ps. 29. 11; 68. 18, 35; 84. 11;
Prov. 2. 6; Ezek. 11. 19; Acts 11. 17; Rom.
12. 6; 1 Cor. 1. 7; 12; 13. 2; 14; Eph. 2. 8;
Jas. 1. 5, 17; 4. 6; 1 Pet. 4. 10.
  temporal, Gen. 1. 26; 9. 1; 27. 28; Lev 26. 4;
Ps. 34. 10; 65. 9; 104; 136. 25, 145. 15; 147;
Is. 30. 23; Acts 14. 17.
  (Corban), Matt. 7. 11; Mk. 7. 11.
Gilboa, Mount, Saul slain there, 1 Sam. 31;
2 Sam. 1. 21.
Gilead, land of, granted to the Reubenites,
etc., Num. 32.
  invaded by the Ammonites, Jud. 10. 17.
  Jephthah made captain of, Jud. 11.
Gilgal, Joshua encamps there, Josh. 4. 19; 9. 6.
  Saul made king there, 1 Sam. 10. 8; 11. 14.
  „ sacrifices at, 1 Sam. 13. 8; 15. 12.
Girdle of the high priest, Ex. 28. 4.
  typical, Jer. 13. 1.
Girgashites, descendants of Canaan, Gen. 10.
15; 15. 21.
  intercourse with, forbidden, Deut. 7. 1.
  driven out, Josh. 3. 10; 24. 11.
Glass, as seen through, darkly, 1 Cor. 13. 12.
See 2 Cor. 3. 18.
  the sea of, Rev. 4. 6; 15. 2.
Gleaning, to be left for the poor and stranger,
Lev. 19. 9; 23. 22; Deut. 24. 19.
  liberality of Boaz concerning, Ruth. 2. 15.
Glorifying God, exhortations to, 1 Chr. 16. 28;
Ps. 22. 23; 50. 15; Rom. 15. 6; 1 Cor. 6. 20;
10. 31; 1 Pet. 2. 12; Rev. 15. 4.
Glory. See under *God.*
Gluttony condemned, Deut. 21. 20; Prov. 23.
1, 20; 25. 16; 1 Pet. 4. 3.
Goats, wild, described, Job 39. 1.
GOD:
  The Lord God Almighty, Gen. 17. 1; Ex. 6. 3;
Num. 24. 4; Ruth 1. 20; Job 5. 17; Ps. 68.
14; 91. 1; 13. 13. 6; Ezek. 1. 24; Joel 1. 15;
2 Cor. 6. 18; Rev. 1. 8.
  The Creator, Gen. 1. 2; Deut. 4. 19; Neh. 9.
6; Job 33. 4; 38; Ps. 8; 19. 1; 33. 6; 89. 11;
94. 9; 104; 136. 146. 6; 148; Prov. 3. 19; 8.
22; Eccl. 12. 1; Is. 37. 16; 40. 28, 43. 7; 44.
8; Jer. 10. 12; 32. 17; Zech. 12. 1; John 1.
3; Acts 17. 24; Rom. 1. 25; 11. 36; Col. 1. 16;
Heb. 1. 10; 3. 4; 11. 3; 1 Pet. 4. 19; Rev. 4. 11.
  HIS DEALINGS WITH
    our first parents, Gen. 3.
    Noah and the sinful world, Gen. 6-9.
    Abraham, Gen. 12-24.
    Lot, Gen. 19.
    Isaac, Jacob, and Esau, Gen. 22; 25; 26; 28.
    Joseph, Gen. 39.
    Moses and Aaron, Ex. 3; 7.
    Pharaoh and Egypt, Ex. 7; 8.
    causes the plagues of blood, Ex. 7. 19;
frogs, lice, and flies, Ex. 8; murrain,
boils, and hail, Ex. 9; locusts and darkness, Ex. 10; death of the firstborn in
Egypt, Ex. 12. 29.
    institutes the passover, Ex. 11; 12; 13.
    preserves the Israelites in their passage
through the Red Sea, Ex. 14.
    the children of Israel during their forty
years' wandering in the wilderness:
sends manna, Ex. 16. 15.
    gives the ten commandments, Ex. 20.
    reveals his glory to Moses, Aaron, and the
elders, Ex. 24.
    makes a covenant with Israel, Ex. 34.
    commands the tabernacle to be made, Ex.
35; to be reared and anointed, Ex. 40.

God (HIS DEALINGS WITH)—*Continued.*
  the children of Israel during their forty
years' wandering in the wilderness:
  delivers the law concerning sacrificial
offerings, Lev. 1; Num. 28.
  sanctifies Aaron, Lev. 8; 9.
  institutes blessings and curses, Lev. 26;
Deut. 27.
  punishes the revolt of Korah, Dathan, and
Abiram, Num. 16.
  causes Aaron's rod to blossom, Num. 17.
  excludes Moses and Aaron from the
promised land for unbelief, Num. 20. 12
  sends fiery serpents, and heals with brazen
serpent, Num. 21.
  Balaam and Balak, Num. 22-24.
  Joshua, at Jericho and Ai, Josh. 1; 3; 4; 6-
7; 8.
  kings of Canaan, Josh. 10-12.
  Gideon, Jud. 6.
  Jephthah, Jud. 11.
  Samson, Jud. 13.
  Naomi and Ruth, Ruth 1-4.
  Hannah, Eli, and Samuel, 1 Sam. 1-3.
  Saul, 1 Sam. 9-31; 1 Chr. 10.
  David, 1 Sam. 16-31; 2 Sam. 1-24; 1 Ki. 1-2
11; 1 Chr. 11-23; 28; 29.
  Solomon, 1 Ki. 1-11; 2 Chr. 1. 9.
  Rehoboam, Jeroboam, 1 Ki. 12-15; 2 Chr.10-12
  Ahab, 1 Ki. 16-22; 2 Chr. 18.
  Elijah, 1 Ki. 17-22; 2 Ki. 2.
  Elisha, 2 Ki. 2-9.
  Hezekiah, 2 Ki. 18-20; 2 Chr. 29-32; Is. 36-39
  Josiah, 2 Ki. 22; 23; 2 Chr. 34; 35.
  the captive Jews in Persia, Est. 1-10.
  the liberated Jews, Ezra 1-10; Neh. 1-13.
  Job and his friends, Job 1; 2; 38-42.
  Isaiah, 2 Ki. 19; 20; 2 Chr. 26; 32.
  Jeremiah, 2 Chr 35; 36; Jer. 26. 34-43.
  Daniel at Babylon, Dan. 1-10.
  Nebuchadnezzar, Dan. 4.
  Shadrach, Meshach, and Abed-nego, Dan. 3
  Jonah, Jon. 1-4.
  HIS REVELATIONS TO
    Isaiah, warning Judah and Israel, Is. 1-12.
    „ warning surrounding nations, Is.
13-23.
    „ of impending judgment, Is. 24; 39.
    „ comforting his people, Is. 40-44, etc.
    Jeremiah, respecting Judah's overthrow on
account of sin, Jer. 1-25; 27-33; 44.
    Ezekiel, concerning
    Judah's captivity, Ezek. 3-7.
    the defiled temple, Ezek. 8-11.
    warnings to Judah, Ezek. 12-19.
    impending judgments, Ezek. 20-23.
    Jerusalem's overthrow, Ezek. 24.
    judgments on other nations, Ezek. 25-32
    exhortations and promises, Ezek. 32-39.
    the New Jerusalem, Ezek. 40-48.
  HIS GOODNESS:
    Ex. 34. 6; Ps. 25. 8; 33. 5; 52. 1; 65. 4; 104.
24; 145. 9; Jer. 31. 12, 14; Nah. 1. 7; Zech.
9. 17; Matt. 5. 45; 19. 17; Rom. 2. 4.
    how manifested, Ps. 31. 19; 68. 10; 86. 5; 119.
68; Lam. 3. 25; Acts 14. 17.
  HIS GIFTS:
    Num. 14. 8; Rom. 8. 32; Jas. 1. 17; 2 Pet. 1. 3.
    dispensed according to his will, Eccl. 2. 26;
Dan. 2. 21; Rom. 12. 6; 1 Cor. 7. 7.
  His Spiritual Gifts:
    Ps. 21. 2; 29. 11; 68. 35; Ezek. 11. 19; Rom.
11. 29.
    are through Christ, Ps. 68. 18, with Eph. 4. 7, 8

God (*His Spiritual Gifts*)—*Continued.*

Christ the chief of, Is. 42. 6; 55. 4; John 3. 16; 4. 10: 6. 32, 33.

to be prayed for, Matt. 7. 7, 11; John 16. 23, 24.

the Holy Ghost, Lk. 11. 13; Acts 8. 20.

rest, Matt. 11. 28; 2 Thes. 1. 7.

grace, Ps. 84. 11; Jas. 4. 6.

wisdom, Prov. 2. 6; Jas. 1. 5.

glory, Ps. 84. 11; John 17. 22.

repentance, Acts 11. 18.

righteousness, Rom. 5. 16, 17.

eternal life, John 6. 27; Rom. 6. 23.

faith, Eph. 2. 8; Phil. 1. 29.

to be used for mutual profit, 1 Pet. 4. 10.

His Temporal Gifts:

rain and fruitful seasons, Gen. 27. 28; Lev. 26. 4, 5; Is. 30. 23; Acts 14. 17.

should make us remember God, Deut. 8. 18.

all good things, Ps. 34. 10; 1 Tim. 6. 17.

all creatures partake of, Ps. 136. 25; 145. 15, 16.

to be used and enjoyed, Eccl. 3. 13; 5. 19, 20; 1 Tim. 4. 4, 5.

food and raiment, etc., Matt. 6. 25-33.

to be prayed for, Zech. 10. 1; Matt. 6. 11.

His Joy Over His People:

1 Chr. 29. 17; Ps. 147. 11; 149. 4; Prov. 11. 20; 15. 8; Zeph. 3. 17; Lk. 15. 7, 10; Heb. 11. 5, 6.

leads him to do them good, etc., Num. 14. 8; Deut. 28. 63; 30. 9; 2 Sam. 22. 20; Is. 65. 19; Jer. 32. 41; 1 Pet. 1. 4.

His Glory:

exhibited in his power, Ex. 15. 1, 6; Rom. 6. 4; holiness, Ex. 15. 11; name, Deut. 28. 58; Neh. 9. 5; majesty, Job 37. 22; Ps. 93. 1; 104. 1; 145. 5, 12; Is. 2. 10; works, Ps. 19. 1; 111. 3.

described as exalted, Ps. 8. 1; 113. 4. Eternal, Ps. 104. 31. Great, Ps. 138. 5. Rich, Eph. 3. 16.

exhibited to Moses, Ex. 34. 5-7, with Ex. 33. 18-23. His Church, Deut. 5. 24; Ps. 102. 16; Is. 60. 1, 2; Rev. 21. 11, 23. Stephen, Acts 7. 55.

exhibited in Christ, John 1. 14; 2 Cor. 4. 6; Heb. 1. 3.

See Num. 14. 21; 1 Chr. 16. 24; Ps. 57. 5; 63. 2; 79. 9; 90. 16: 145. 5, 11; Is. 6. 3; 42. 8; 59. 19; Hab. 2. 14.

His Law:

Given to Adam, Gen. 2. 16, 17, with Rom. 5. 12-14.

  ,,   to Noah, Gen. 9. 6.

  ,,   to the Israelites, Ex. 20. 2; Ps. 78. 5.

  ,,   through Moses, Ex. 31. 18; John 7. 19.

  ,,   through the ministration of angels, Acts 7. 53; Gal. 3. 19; Heb. 2. 2.

described as perfect, Ps. 19. 7; Rom. 12. 2; pure, Ps. 19. 8; exceeding broad, Ps. 119. 96; truth, Ps. 119. 142: holy, just, and good, Rom. 7. 12; spiritual, Rom. 7. 14; not grievous, 1 John 5. 3.

requires perfect obedience, Deut. 27. 26; Gal. 3. 10; Jas. 2. 10.

requires obedience of the heart, Ps. 51. 6; Matt. 22. 37.

man cannot render perfect obedience to, 1 Ki. 8. 46; Eccl. 7. 20; Rom. 3. 10.

man cannot be justified by, Acts 13. 39; Rom. 3. 20, 28; Gal. 2. 16; 3. 11.

all men have transgressed, Rom. 3. 9, 19.

gives the knowledge of sin, Rom. 3. 20; 7. 7.

love is the fulfilling of, Rom. 13. 8, 10; Gal. 5. 14; Jas. 2. 8.

God (*His Law*)—*Continued.*

designed to lead to Christ, Gal. 3. 24.

blessedness of keeping, Ps. 119. 1; Matt. 5. 19; 1 John 3. 22, 24; Rev. 22. 14.

Christ came to fulfil, Matt. 5. 17; (Is. 42. 21).

explained by Christ, Matt. 7. 12; 22. 37-40.

the wicked forsake, etc., 2 Chr. 12. 1; Jer. 9. 13; Ps. 78. 10; Is. 5. 24; 30. 9; Hos. 4. 6.

saints should observe, etc., Ex. 13. 9; Ps. 119. 55, 77, 97, 113; Jer. 31. 33; Mal. 4. 4; Heb. 8. 10.

punishment for disobeying, Neh. 9. 26, 27; Is. 65. 11-13; Jer. 9. 13-16.

His Attributes:

Eternal, Gen. 21. 33; Ex. 3. 14; Deut. 32. 40; 33. 27; Job 10. 5; 36. 26; Ps. 9. 7; 90. 2; 92. 8; 93. 2; 102. 12; 104. 31; 135. 13; 145. 13; Eccl. 3. 14; Is. 9. 6; 40. 28; 41. 4; 43. 13; 48. 12; 57. 15; 63. 16; Jer. 10. 10; Lam. 5. 19; Dan. 4. 3, 34; 6. 26; Mic. 5. 2; Hab. 1. 12; Rom. 1. 20; 16. 26; Eph. 3. 9; 1 Tim. 1. 17; 6. 16; 2 Pet. 3. 8; Rev. 1. 8; 4. 9; 22. 13.

Immutable, Num. 23. 19; 1 Sam. 15. 29; Ps. 33. 11; 119. 89; Mal. 3. 6; Acts 4. 28; Eph. 1. 4; Heb. 1. 12; 6. 17; 13. 8; Jas. 1. 17.

Invisible, Ex. 33. 20; Job 23. 8; John 1. 18; 4. 24; 5. 37; Rom. 1. 20; Col. 1. 15; 1 Tim. 1. 17; 6. 16; Heb. 11. 27; 1 John 4. 12.

Incomprehensible, Job 5. 9; 9. 10; 11. 7; 26. 14; 36. 26; 37. 5; Ps. 36. 6; 40. 5; 106. 2; 139. 6; Eccl. 3. 11; 8. 17; 11. 5; 18. 40. 12; 45. 15; Mic. 4. 12; 1 Tim. 6. 16.

Unsearchable, Job 11. 7; 26. 14; 37. 15; Ps. 145. 13; Eccl. 8. 17; Rom. 11. 33.

Omniscient, Job 26. 6; 34. 21; Ps. 139; Prov. 15. 3; Is. 44. 7; Ezek. 11. 5; Matt. 12. 25; John 2. 24; Rom. 1. 20.

Omnipresent, Jeb 23 9; 26; 28; Acts 17. 27.

Holiness, Gen. 35. 2; Ex. 3. 5; 28. 36; 34. 5; 39. 30; Lev. 11. 44; 21. 8; Josh. 5. 15; 1 Sam. 2. 2; 1 Chr. 16. 10; Ps. 22. 3; 30. 4; 60. 6. See *Psalms.* Is. 6. 3; 43. 15; 49. 7; 57. 15; Jer. 23. 9; Lk. 1. 49; Acts 3. 14; Rom. 7. 12; 1 John 2. 20; Rev. 4. 8; 19. 1.

Justice, Gen. 2. 16; 3. 8; 4. 9; 6. 7; 9. 15; 18. 17; Ex. 32. 33; Lev. 4. 7. 20; 18. 4; 26. 21; Num. 11; 14; 16; 17; 20; 25; 26. 64; 27. 12; 35; Deut. 1. 31; 4. 24; 5; 6; 9. 4; 10. 17; 25. 17; 28. 15; 31. 16; 32. 35, 41; Josh. 7. 1; Jud. 1. 7; 2. 14; 9. 56; 1 Sam. 2. 30; 3. 11; 6. 19; 15. 17; 2 Sam. 6. 7; 12. 1; 22; 24. 11; 1 Ki. 8. 20; 2 Chr. 6. 17; 19. 7; Neh. 9. 33; Ezra 8. 22; Job 4. 17; 8: 10. 3; 11. 11; 12. 6; 13. 15; 14. 15; 34. 10; 35. 13; 37. 23; 40. 8. See *Psalms.* Prov. 11. 21; 15. 8; 28. 9; 30. 5; Eccl. 5. 8; 8. 12; 9. 2; Is. 45. 21; Jer. 5. 3; 9. 24; 23. 20; 32. 19; 50. 7; 51. 9; Lam. 1. 18; Ezek. 7. 27; 16. 35; 18. 10; 33. 17; Dan. 4. 37; 9. 14; Hos. 4; 5; Nah. 1. 3; Hab. 1. 13; Zeph. 3. 5; Mal. 2. 17; 4. 1; Matt. 10. 15; 20. 13; 23. 14; Lk. 12. 47; 13. 27; John 7. 18; Acts 10. 34; 17. 31; Rom. 2. 2; Gal. 6. 7; Eph. 6. 8; Col. 3. 25; Jas. 1. 13; 1 John 1. 9; Rev. 15. 3; 16. 7.

Knowledge, Wisdom, and Power, Gen. 1. 3; 6-9; 41. 16; Ex. 4. 1, 11; 7-10; 12. 29; 14; 15; 33. 18; 34. 5; 35. 30; 36; Num. 11. 23; 12; 22. 9; 23. 4; 24. 1; Deut. 3. 4. 32; 5. 24; 6. 22; 7. 10; 26; 28. 58; 29. 29; 32. 4; Josh. 3; 6; 7. 10. 23. 9; 24; Jud. 2; 1 Sam. 2. 4; 5; 12. 18; 14. 6; 16. 7; 17. 37, 46; 18. 10; 23; 2 Sam. 7. 22; 1 Ki. 8. 27; 22. 22; 1 Chr. 16. 24; 17. 4; 22. 18; 28. 9; 29. 11; 2 Chr. 6. 18; 14. 11; 20. 6; Neh. 9. 5; Job 4. 9; 5. 9; 9:

God (His Attributes)—*Continued.*

10. 4; 11; 12; 19. 6; 21. 17; 22. 23; 26. 6;
33; 34. 22; 35-41. See *Psalms.* Prov. 3. 19;
5. 21; 8. 22; 15. 3; 16. 9; 19. 21; 21. 30;
Eccl. 3. 11; 7. 13; Is. 2. 10; 6. 3; 12. 5; 14.
24; 28. 29; 29. 16; 30. 18; 33. 13; 40. 29; 41.
21; 42. 8; 43. 13; 44. 6, 23; 45. 20; 46. 5; 47.
4; 48. 3; 52. 10; 55. 11; 59. 1; 60. 1; 66. 1;
Jer. 3. 14; 5. 22; 10. 6; 14. 22; 29. 23; 32. 17;
Lam. 3. 37; Ezek. 8. 12; 11. 5; 22. 14; Dan.
2. 20; 3. 17, 29; 4. 34; 6. 26; Joel 2. 11;
Amos 5. 12; 8. 7; Hab. 2. 14; Mal. 3. 16;
Matt. 5. 48; 6. 13; 9. 38; 10. 29; 12. 25; 19.
26; 22. 29; Mk. 5. 30; 12. 15; Lk. 1. 48; 12.
5; 18. 27; John 1. 14; 2. 24; 5. 26; 6. 61;
11. 25; 16. 19; 18. 4; 19. 28; 20. 17; Acts 1.
24; 2. 17; 7. 55; 15. 18; Rom. 1. 20; 4. 17;
8. 29; 11. 34; 15. 19; 16. 27; 1 Cor. 2. 9; 2 Cor.
4. 6; 12. 9; 13. 4; Gal. 2. 8; Eph. 1. 19; 3. 7;
6. 10; Phil. 1. 6; 3. 21; Col. 3. 4; 1 Tim. 1.
12, 17; Heb. 1. 3; 2. 11; 4. 12; Jas. 4. 6;
1 Pet. 1. 2, 20; 1 John 1. 5; 3. 20; Jude 1,
24; Rev. 1. 8; 4. 11; 5. 13; 11. 17; 19. 6;
21. 3.

Faithfulness and Truth, Num. 23. 19; Deut.
7. 8; Josh. 21. 45; 2 Sam. 7. 28; 1 Ki. 8. 56;
Ps. 19. 9; 89. 34; 105. 8; 111. 7; 117; 119. 89,
160; 146. 6; Is. 25. 1; 31. 2; 46. 11; 65. 16;
Jer. 4. 28; Lam. 2. 17; Ezek. 12. 25; Matt.
24. 35; John 7. 28; Rom. 3. 4; 1 Cor. 1. 9;
15. 58; 2 Cor. 1. 18; 1 Thes. 5. 24; 2 Thes. 3.
3; 2 Tim. 2. 13; Tit. 1. 2; Heb. 6. 18; 10.
23; 11. 11; 13. 5; 2 Pet. 3. 9; Rev. 1. 5; 3.
7; 15. 3; 16. 7.

Goodness, Mercy, and Love, Gen. 1. 28; 3. 15;
4. 4; 8; 9; 15. 4; 16. 7; 17; 18. 16; 19. 12;
21. 12; 22. 15; 24. 12; 26. 24; 28. 10; 29. 31;
32. 9, 24; 39. 2; 46; Ex. 1. 20; 2. 23; 3. 7;
6; 16; 17; 20. 6; 22. 27; 23. 20; 29. 45; 32.
14; 33. 12; 34. 6; Lev. 4. 35; 26. 3, 40; Num.
14. 18; 21. 7; Deut. 4. 29; 7. 7; 8; 10. 15;
18. 15; 20. 4; 23. 5; 28. 1; 30; 32. 7, 43; 33;
Josh. 20; Jud. 2. 16; 6. 36; 10. 15; 13; 15.
18; 1 Sam. 2. 9; 7; 25. 32; 2 Sam. 7. 5; 12.
13; 1 Ki. 8. 56; 2 Chr. 16. 9; 30. 9; Ezra 8.
18; Neh. 2. 18; 9. 17; Job 5. 17; 7. 17; 11.
6; 33. 14; 36. 11; 37. 23; Ps. 34. 8; 36. 5;
69. 16; Prov. 8. 30; 11. 20; 18. 10; 28. 13;
Eccl. 2. 26; 8. 11; Is. 25. 4; 27. 3; 30. 18;
38. 17; 40. 29; 43. 1; 48. 9, 17; 49. 15; 54. 7;
55. 3; 63. 7; Jer. 3. 12; 9. 24; 16. 14; 17. 7;
31. 3, 12; 32. 39; 33. 11; 44. 28; Lam. 3. 22;
31; Ezek. 20. 17; 33. 11; Dan. 9. 9; Hos. 2.
19; 11. 4; 13. 14; 14. 3; Joel 2. 13; Mic. 7.
18; Nah. 1. 7; Hab. 3. 18; Zeph. 3. 17;
Mal. 3. 6, 16; 4; Matt. 5. 45; 19. 17; 23. 37;
Lk. 1. 50, 78; 5. 21; 6. 35; 13. 6; John 1. 4,
9; 3. 16; 4. 10; 14; 15. 9; 16. 7; 17; Acts
14. 17; Rom. 2. 4; 3. 25; 5. 8; 8. 32; 9. 22;
11; 2 Cor. 1. 3; 12. 9; 13. 11; Gal. 1. 4; Eph.
2. 3, 17; 4. 6; 1 Tim. 2. 4; 6. 17; 2 Tim. 1.
8, Tit. 3. 4; Heb. 12. 6; Jas. 1. 5, 17; 5. 11;
1 Pet. 1. 3; 3. 20; 2 Pet. 3. 9, 15; 1 John 1;
Jude 21; Rev. 2. 3. See *Psalms.*

Jealousy, Ex. 20. 5; 34. 14; Deut. 4. 24; 5. 9;
6. 15; 29. 20; 32. 16; Josh. 24. 19; Ps. 78.
58; 79. 5; Ezek. 16; 23; Hos. 1. 2; Joel 2.
18; Zeph. 1. 18; Zech. 1. 14; 1 Cor. 10. 22;
Rev. 2. 4.

His Characters:

The Supreme Governor, Gen. 6-9; 11. 8; 12;
14. 20; 18. 14; 22; 25. 23; 26; Ex. 9. 16;
Deut. 7. 7; 1 Sam. 2. 6; 9. 15; 13. 14; 15.
17; 16; 2 Sam. 7. 8; 22. 1; Ps. 10. 16; 22. 28;

God (His Characters)—*Continued.*

24; 33; 74. 12; 75; Is. 6. 5; 40. 13, 43-45;
64. 8; Jer. 8. 19; 10. 10; 18; 19; Dan. 4; 5;
Zech. 14. 9; Lk. 10. 21; Rom. 9; Eph. 1;
1 Tim. 1. 17; 6. 15; Jas. 4. 12.

Judge of All, Gen. 18. 25; Deut. 32. 36; Jud.
11. 27; Ps. 7. 11; 9. 7; 50; -58. 11; 68. 5; 75.
7; 94. 2; Eccl. 3. 17; 11. 9; 12. 14; Is. 2. 4;
3. 13; Jer. 11. 20; Acts 10. 42; Rom. 2. 16;
2 Tim. 4. 8; Heb. 12. 23; Jude 6; Rev. 11.
18; 18. 8; 19. 11.

Searcher of Hearts, 1 Chr. 28. 9; Ps. 7. 9; 44.
21; 139. 23; Prov. 17. 3; 24. 12; Jer. 17. 10;
Acts 1. 24; Rom. 8. 27; Rev. 2. 23.

Refuge and Sanctuary, Deut. 33. 27; 2 Sam.
22. 3; Ps. 9. 9; 46. 1; 57. 1; 59. 16; 62; 71. 7;
91; 94. 22; 142. 5; Is. 8. 14; Ezek. 11. 16;
Heb. 6. 18.

The Saviour, Ps. 106. 21; Is. 43. 3, 11; 45. 15,
49. 26; 60. 16; 63. 8; Jer. 14. 8; Hos. 13. 4;
Lk. 1. 47.

His Names:

Jehovah, Ex. 6. 3; Ps. 83. 18; Is. 12. 2; 26. 4;
usually rendered Lord.

I Am, Ex. 3. 14.

Living God, Deut. 5. 26; Josh. 3. 10.

God of Heaven, Ezek. 5. 11; Neh. 1. 4; 2. 4.

God of Hosts, Ps. 80. 7, 14, 19.

Holy One, Job 6. 10; Ps. 16. 10; Is. 10. 17;
Hos. 11. 9; Hab. 1. 12.

Holy One of Israel, 2 Ki. 19. 22; Ps. 71. 22;
Is. 1. 4; Jer. 51. 5; Ezek. 39. 7.

Lord of Hosts, 1 Sam. 1. 11; Is. 1. 24.

Lord of Lords, Deut. 10. 17; 1 Tim. 6. 15;
Rev. 17. 14.

Mighty God, Ps. 50. 1; Is. 9. 6; 10. 21; Jer.
32. 18.

Most High, Num. 24. 16; Deut. 32. 8; 2 Sam.
22. 14; Ps. 7. 17.

Most High God, Gen. 14. 18; Ps. 57. 2; Dan.
3. 26.

Father of Lights, Jas. 1. 17.

Lord of Sabaoth, Rom. 9. 29; Jas. 5. 4.

King of Kings, 1 Tim. 6. 15; Rev. 17. 14.

The Father, Matt. 11. 25; 28. 19; Mk. 14. 36;
Lk. 10. 21; 22. 42; John 1. 14; Acts 1. 4;
2. 33; Rom. 6. 4; 8. 15; 1 Cor. 8. 6; 15. 24;
2 Cor. 1. 3; 6. 18; Gal. 1. 1, 3, 4; Eph. 1.
17; Col. 1. 19; 2. 2; 1 Thes. 1. 1; Jas. 1. 27;
3. 9; 2 Pet. 1. 17; 1 John 1. 2; Jude 1.

The Son, Matt. 11. 27; Lk. 1. 32; John 1. 18;
Acts 8. 37; 9. 20; Rom. 1. 4; 2 Cor. 1. 19;
Gal. 2. 21; Eph. 4. 13; Heb. 4. 14; 1 John
2. 22; Rev. 2. 18. See *Christ.*

As a Spirit:

"The Holy Ghost," John 4. 24; 2 Cor. 3. 17;
Eternal, Heb. 9. 14.

Omnipresent, Ps. 139. 7.

Omniscient, 1 Cor. 2. 10.

Omnipotent, Lk. 1. 35; Rom. 15. 19.

Author of the new birth, John 3, 5, 6;
1 John 5. 4.

the source of wisdom, Is. 11. 2; John 14. 26;
16. 13; 1 Cor. 12. 8.

the source of miraculous power, Matt. 12.
28; Lk. 11. 20; Acts 19. 11; Rom. 15. 19.

inspiring Scripture, 2 Tim. 3. 16; 2 Pet. 1. 21.

appointing ministers, Acts 13. 2, 4; 20. 28.

directing where to preach the Gospel, Acts
16. 6, 7.

dwelling in saints, John 14. 17; 1 Cor. 6. 19.

sanctifying the Church, Rom. 15. 16; (Ezek.
37. 28).

the witness, Heb. 10. 15; 1 John 5. 8.

God (As a Spirit)—*Continued.*
  convincing of sin, *of righteousness, and of judgment,* John 16. 8-11.

Personality of:
  he strives with sinners, Gen. 6. 3.
  he creates and gives life, Job 33. 4.
  he commissions his servants, etc., Is. 48. 16; Acts 8. 29; 10. 19, 20; 1 Cor. 2. 13.
  he teaches, etc., John 14. 26; 15. 26; 16. 8; 16. 13, 14; 1 Cor. 12. 13.
  helps our infirmities, Rom. 8. 26.
  searches all things, Rom. 11. 33, 34; 1 Cor. 2. 10, 11.
  works according to his own will, 1 Cor. 12. 11.
  he speaks in, and by, the prophets, Acts 1. 16; 1 Pet. 1. 11, 12; 2 Pet. 1. 21.
  See Acts 7. 51; 9. 31: Rom. 15. 16.

The Holy Ghost:
The Comforter:
  given by Christ, Lk. 4. 18; John 14. 26; 15. 26; 16. 7.
  edifies the Church, Acts 9. 31.
  imparts the love of God, Rom. 5. 5.
  communicates joy, Rom. 14. 17; Gal. 5. 22; 1 Thes. 1. 6.
  imparts hope, Rom. 15. 13; Gal. 5. 5.

The Teacher:
  as the spirit of wisdom, Is. 11. 2; 40. 13, 14.
  given to saints, Neh. 9. 20; 1 Cor. 2. 12, 13; Eph. 1. 16, 17.
  See Ezek. 36. 27; Mk. 13. 11; Lk. 2. 26; 12. 12; John 16. 13, 14; Acts 15. 28; 1 Cor. 12. 8.

Emblems of:
  Water, John 3. 5; 7. 38, 39; Eph. 5. 26; Heb. 10. 22; Rev. 22. 17; (Is. 55. 1).
  Fire, Ex. 13. 21; Ps. 78. 14; Is. 4. 4; Mal. 3. 2, 3; Matt. 3. 11; Heb. 12. 29
  Wind, 1 Ki. 19. 11; John 3. 8; Acts 2. 2.
  Oil, Is. 61. 1, 3; Heb. 1. 9; 1 John 2. 20, 27.
  Rain and Dew, Ps. 68. 9; 72. 6; Hos. 6. 3; 10. 12; 14. 5.
  A Dove, Matt. 3. 16.
  A Voice, Is. 6. 8; 30. 21; John 16. 13; Heb. 3. 7.
  Seal, 2 Cor. 1. 22; Eph. 1. 13, 14; 4. 30; Rev. 7. 2.
  Cloven Tongues, Acts 2. 3, 6-11.
  The Gift of the Holy Ghost, Ps. 68. 18; Is. 32. 15; 59. 21; Ezek. 39. 29; Hag. 2. 5; Lk. 11. 13; John 3. 34; 20. 22; Acts 2. 38; 5. 32; 10. 44, 45; 15. 8; 2 Cor. 5. 5; Gal. 3. 14; 1 John 3. 24; 4. 13.

Godliness enjoined, 1 Tim. 2. 2; 4. 7; 5; 6; 2 Pet. 1. 3; 3. 11.
Godly conversation. See *Conversation.*
Gods, judges described as, Ex. 22. 28; Ps. 82. 1; 138. 1; John 10. 34; 1 Cor. 8. 5.
  false, worship of, forbidden, Ex. 20. 3; 34. 17; Deut. 5. 7; 8. 19; 18. 20.
God save the king, 2 Sam. 16. 16.
Gog and Magog, Ezek. 38; 39; Rev. 20. 8.
Gold, Gen. 2. 11; Job 22. 24; Ps. 19. 10; 21. 3; Zech. 4. 2.
  mentioned figuratively, Rev. 3. 18; 21. 18.
Golden candlestick, Ex. 25. 31.
Golgotha, place of a skull, Matt. 27. 33; Mk. 15. 22; Lk. 23. 33; John 19. 17.
Goliath of Gath, 1 Sam. 17; 21. 9; 22. 10.
Gomorrah (and Sodom), Gen. 19. 24, 28; Is. 1. 9; Matt. 10. 15.
Good Shepherd, John 10. 11.
Goshen, land of (Egypt), Israelites placed there, Gen. 45. 10; 46. 34; 47. 4.
  no plagues there, Ex. 8. 22; 9. 26.
—(Canaan), Josh. 10. 41; 11. 16.

Gospel of Christ, characterised, Matt. 4. 23; 24. 14; Mk. 1. 14; Lk. 2. 10; 20. 21; Acts 13. 26; 14. 3; 20. 21; Rom. 1. 2, 9, 16; 2. 16; 10. 8; 16. 25; 1 Cor. 1. 18; 2. 13; 15. 1; 2 Cor. 4. 4; 5. 19; 6. 7; Eph. 1. 13; 3. 2; 6. 15; Phil. 1. 16; Col. 1. 5; 3. 16; 1 Thes. 1. 5; 2. 8; 3. 2; 1 Tim. 1. 11; 6. 3; Heb. 4. 2; 1 Pet. 1. 12, 25; 4. 17.
  preached to Abraham, Gal. 3. 8.
    to the poor and others, Matt. 11. 5; Mk. 1. 15; 13. 10; 16. 15; Lk. 4. 18; 24. 47; Acts 13. 46; 14; 1 Cor. 1. 17; 9. 16; Gal. 2. 2; Rev. 14. 6.
  its effects, Mk. 1. 15; 8. 35; Lk. 2. 10, 14; 19. 8; Acts 4. 32; Rom. 1. 16; 12; 13; 15. 29; 16. 26; 2 Cor. 8; 9; Gal. 1. 16; 2. 14; Eph. 4-6; Phil. 1. 5, 17, 27; Col. 1. 23; 3; 4; 1 Thes. 1; 2; Tit. 2; 3; Jas. 1; 1 & 2 Pet; 1 John 3; Jude 3.
  from whom hid, 1 Cor. 1. 23; 2. 8; 2 Cor. 4. 3.
  rejected by the Jews, Acts 13. 26; 28. 25: Rom. 9; 10; 11; 1 Thes. 2. 16.
Gourd prepared for Jonah, Jon. 4. 6.
Grace of God and Jesus Christ, Ps. 84. 11; Zech. 4. 7; Lk. 2. 40; John 1. 16; Acts 20. 24; Rom. 11. 5; 1 Cor. 15. 10; 2 Cor. 8. 9; 2 Tim. 1. 9; 1 Pet. 5. 5.
  salvation through, Acts 15. 11; Rom. 3. 24; 4. 4; Eph. 2. 5; 2 Thes. 2. 16; Tit. 3. 7; 1 Pet. 1. 10.
  effects of, 2 Cor. 1. 12; Tit. 2. 11; 1 Pet. 4. 10. See *Gospel.*
  prayer for, Rom. 16. 20; 1 Tim. 1. 2; Heb. 4. 16.
  danger of abusing, Rom. 6; Jude 4; and departing from, Gal. 5. 4.
  exhortations concerning, 2 Tim. 1. 9; Heb. 12. 15, 28; 2 Pet. 3. 18
Grapes, laws concerning, Lev. 19. 10; Num. 6. 3; Deut. 23. 24; 24. 21.
  See Jer. 31. 29; Ezek. 18. 2.
Grass brought forth, Gen. 1. 11.
  man compared to, Ps. 37. 2; 90. 5; 103. 15. Is. 40. 6; Jas. 1. 10, 1 Pet. 1. 24.
Grasshoppers, Amos 7. 1.
Grave, law of, Num. 19. 16.
  triumphed over, Hos. 13. 14; John 5. 28; 1 Cor. 15. 55; Rev. 20. 13.
Gravity in bishops and deacons, 1 Tim. 3. 4, 8, 11; Tit. 2. 2, 7.
Greece, prophecies of, Dan. 8. 21; 10. 20; 11. 2; Zech. 9. 13.
  Paul preaches in, Acts 16; 20.
Greeks would see Jesus, John 12. 20.
  believe in him, Acts 11. 21; 17. 4.
Groves for worship, Gen. 21. 33.
  idolatrous, forbidden, Deut. 16. 21; Jud. 6. 25; 1 Ki. 14. 15; 15. 13; 16. 33; 2 Ki. 17. 16; 21. 3; 23. 4.
Grudging forbidden, 2 Cor. 9. 7; Jas. 5. 9; 1 Pet. 4. 9.
Guide, God is, of his people, Ps. 25. 9; 31. 3; 32. 8; 48. 14; 73. 24; Is. 58. 11; Lk. 1. 79; 1 Thes. 3. 11.
Guile forbidden, Ps. 34. 13; 1 Pet. 2. 1; 3. 10. Rev. 14. 5.

HABAKKUK, prophet, his burden, complaint to God, his answer, and prayer, Hab. 1; 2; 3.
Hadad, an Edomite, 1 Ki. 11. 14.
Hadadezer (Hadarezer), king of Zobah, David's wars with, 2 Sam. 8; 10. 15; 1 Chr. 18.
Hadassah, Est. 2. 7.

Hagar, mother of Ishmael, Gen. 16.
fleeing from Sarah is comforted by an angel, Gen. 16. 10, 11.
dismissed with her son, Gen. 21. 14; allegory of, Gal. 4. 24.

Haggai, prophet, Ezra 5 6. 14.
See Hag. 1; 2.

Hail, plague of, Ex. 9. 23; Josh. 10. 11, Ps. 18. 12; 78. 47; 18. 28. 2; Ezek. 13. 11; Hag. 2. 17; Rev. 8. 7; 11. 19; 16. 21.

Hall (of judgment), John 18. 28, 33; 19. 9; Acts 23. 35.

Hallelujah (Alleluia), Ps. 106; 111; 113; 146; 148; 149; 150; Rev. 19. 1, 3, 4, 6.

Hallowed bread. See *Shewbread.*

Ham, son of Noah, cursed, Gen. 9. 22.
his descendants, Gen. 10. 6; 1 Chr. 1. 8, Ps. 105. 23; smitten by the Simeonites, 1 Chr. 4. 40.

Haman's advancement, Est. 3.
hatred to Mordecai, Est. 3. 8.
fall, Est. 7.

Hamath (Syria), Num. 34. 8; Josh. 13. 5, 2 Ki. 14. 28; 17. 24.
conquered, 2 Ki. 18. 34; Is. 37. 13; Jer. 49. 23.

Hamor, father of Shechem, Gen. 34; Acts 7. 16.

Hanani, a prophet, 2 Chr. 16. 7.
—brother of Nehemiah, Neh. 1. 2 : 7. 2; 12. 36.

Hananiah, false prophet, Jer. 28.
his death, Jer. 28. 16.

Hand of God, for blessing, 2 Chr. 30. 12; Ezra 7. 9 : 8. 18; Neh. 2. 18.
for chastisement, Deut. 2. 15; Ruth 1. 13; Job 2. 10; 19. 21; 1 Pet. 5. 6.

Hands, laying on of, Num. 8. 10; 27. 18; Acts 6. 6; 13. 3; 1 Tim. 4. 14; 2 Tim. 1. 6.
washing, as mark of innocence, Deut. 21. 6; Ps. 26. 6; Matt. 27. 24.
lifting up, in prayer, Ex. 17. 11; Ps. 28. 2 · 63. 4; 141. 2; 143. 6; 1 Tim. 2. 8.

Hanging, a punishment, Gen. 40. 22; Num. 25. 4; Est. 7. 10.
the hanged accursed, Deut. 21. 22; Gal. 3. 13.

Hannah's vow and prayer, 1 Sam. 1. 11 answered, 1 Sam. 1. 19.
song, 1 Sam. 2.

Hanun, king of the Ammonites, dishonours David's messengers, 2 Sam. 10. 4; chastised, 2 Sam. 12. 30.

Happy, who so called, Deut. 33. 29; Job 5. 17; Ps. 127. 5; 144. 15; 146. 5; Prov. 3. 13; 14. 21; 28. 14; 29. 18; John 13. 17; Rom. 14. 22 : Jas. 5. 11; 1 Pet. 3. 14 : 4. 14.

Haran, son of Terah, Gen. 11. 26.
—(city of Nahor), Abram comes to, Gen. 11. 31 ; departs from, Gen. 12. 4.
Jacob flees to Laban at, Gen. 27. 43 : 28. 10. 29.

Harbonah, chamberlain of Artaxerxes, Est. 1. 10.
proposes the hanging of Haman, Est. 7. 9.

Hardened heart deprecated, Deut 15. 7 ; 1 Sam. 6. 6; Ps. 95. 8; Heb. 3. 8.
results of, Ex. 7. 13 ; 8. 15 ; Prov. 28. 14 , Dan. 5. 20; John 12. 40.

Harlots, Gen. 34. 31; Lev. 19. 29 ; 21. 7, Deut. 23. 17; Is. 57. 3; Jer. 3. 3 : Matt. 21. 32; 1 Cor. 6. 15.
Rahab of Jericho, Josh. 2. 1.
priests forbidden to marry, Lev. 21. 14.
Solomon's judgment between two, 1 Ki. 3. 16.
figurative of idolatry, Is. 1. 21 . Jer. 2. 20, Ezek. 16 : 23 ; Hos. 2 ; Rev. 17. 18.

Harmless, Christ was, Heb. 7. 26: disciples to be, Matt. 10. 16; Rom. 16. 19 ; Phil. 2. 15.

Harp (and organ), Gen. 4. 21.
played on by David, 1 Sam. 16. 16, 23 : 2 Sam. 6. 5.
used in public worship, 1 Chr. 25. 3; Ps. 33. 2; 81. 2; 150. 3.
in heaven, Rev. 14. 2.

Hart, a clean animal, Deut. 12. 15 : 1 Ki. 4. 23 Is. 35. 6 ; Ps. 42. 1.

Harvest, promise concerning, Gen. 8. 22.
feast of, Ex. 23. 16; 34. 21; Lev. 19. 9. 3 ; 16. 9.
of the world, Jer. 8. 20; Matt. 13. 30, 39; Rev. 14. 15.

Haste to be rich, dangerous, Prov. 28. 22.

Hastiness in speech, etc., censured, Prov. 14. 29; 29. 20; Eccl. 5. 2 ; Dan. 2. 15.

Hatred forbidden, Ex. 23. 5; Lev. 19. 17; Deut. 19. 11 ; Prov. 10. 12, 18; 15. 17; Matt. 5. 43; Gal. 5. 20; Tit. 3. 3 ; 1 John 2. 9; 3. 15; 4. 20.

Haughtiness censured, 2 Sam. 22. 28; Prov. 6. 17 ; 16. 18; 21. 4, 24; Is. 2. 11; 3. 16; 13. 11; 16. 6 ; Jer. 48. 29.

Hawk, unclean, Lev. 11. 16.
described, Job 39. 26.

Hazael, king of Syria, 1 Ki. 19. 15.
Elisha's prediction, 2 Ki. 8. 7.
slays Ben-hadad, 2 Ki. 8. 15.
oppresses Israel, 2 Ki. 9. 14 ; 10. 32; 12. 17; 13. 22.

Hazor, city of Canaan, burnt, Josh. 11. 10; 15. 25.

Head, of the Church, Christ, Eph. 1. 22; 4. 15; 5. 23 ; Col. 1. 18 ; 2. 10.
not holding the Col. 2. 19.

Health of body, Gen. 43. 28 ; 3 John 2.
spiritual, Ps. 42. 11 ; Prov. 3. 8; 12. 18; Is. 58. 8 ; Jer. 8. 15 ; 30. 17 ; 33. 6.

Heart of man, Gen. 6. 5 ; 8. 21 ; Eccl. 8. 11 ; 9. 3 ; Jer. 17. 9 : Matt. 12. 34; 15. 19 ; Lk. 6. 45 ; Rom. 2. 5.
searched and tried by God, 1 Chr. 28. 9 ; 29. 17 ; Ps. 44. 21 ; 139. 23 ; Prov. 21. 2; 24. 12 ; Jer. 12. 3 ; 17. 10 ; 20. 12 ; Rev. 2. 23.
enlightened, etc., by him. 2 Cor. 4. 6 ; Ps. 27. 14 ; Prov. 16. 1 ; 1 Thes. 3. 13 ; 2 Pet. 1. 19.
a new, promised, Jer. 24. 7 ; 31. 32; 32. 39; Ezek. 11. 19 ; 36. 26.

Heathen described, Eph. 2. 12 ; 4. 18 ; 5. 12 ; 1 Cor. 1. 21.
Gospel preached to, Matt. 24. 14; 28. 19 ; Rom. 10. 14; 16. 26 ; Gal. 1. 16.
conversion of, Acts 10. 35; Rom. 15. 16.

Heaven, the firmament, created, Gen. 1. 1, 8, Ps. 8 : 19 ; Is. 40. 22; Rev. 10. 6.
God's dwelling-place, 1 Ki. 8. 30; Ps. 2. 4; 115. 3 ; 123. 1 ; Is. 6. 1 ; 66. 1 ; Ezek. 1. 16; Matt. 6. 9; Acts 7. 49 ; Heb. 8. 1 ; Rev. 4.
its happiness, Ps. 16. 11 ; Is. 49. 10 : Dan. 12. 3 ; Matt. 5. 12 ; 13. 43 ; Lk. 12. 37 ; John 12. 26 ; 14. 1 ; 17. 24 ; 1 Cor. 2. 9 ; 13. 12 ; 1 Pet. 1. 4 ; Rev. 7. 16 : 14. 13 ; 21. 4; 22. 3.
who enter, Matt. 5. 3 ; 25. 34; Rom. 8. 17; Heb. 12. 23 ; 1 Pet. 1. 4 ; Rev. 7. 9, 14.
who excluded from, Matt. 7. 21 ; 25. 41 ; Lk. 13. 27 ; 1 Cor. 6. 9 ; Gal. 5. 21 ; Rev. 21. 8 ; 22. 15.
the new, Rev. 21. 1.

Heavenly Father, Matt. 6. 14, 15, 18 ; Lk. 11. 13.

Heave-Offering, Ex. 29. 27 ; Num. 15. 19 ; Lk. 8. 30.

Heber, Gen. 10. 21 ; Lk. 3. 35.
—the Kenite, Jud. 4. 11.

Hebrews, Abraham and his descendants so called, Gen. 14. 13; 40. 15; 43. 32 ; Ex. 2. 6; 2 Cor. 11. 22; Phil. 3. 5

Hormah, destruction of, Num. 21. 3 ; Jud. 1. 17.

Hornets, as God's instruments of punishment, Ex. 23. 28 ; Deut. 7. 20 ; Josh. 24. 12.

Horns, figuratively mentioned, 1 Sam. 2. 1 ; 2 Sam. 22. 3 ; Ps. 75. 4.
seen in vision, Dan. 7. 7 ; 8. 3 ; Hab. 3. 4 ; Rev. 5. 6 ; 12. 3 ; 13. 1 ; 17. 3.
—of the altar, 1 Ki. 1. 50 ; 2. 28.

Horse described, Job 39. 19 ; Prov. 21. 31 ; Jer. 8. 6.

Horses, kings forbidden to multiply, Deut. 17. 16 ; Ps. 33. 17 ; 147. 10.
vision of, Zech. 1. 8 ; 6 ; Rev. 6.

Hosanna, children sing to Christ, Matt. 21. 9, 15 ; Mk. 11. 9 ; John 12. 13 ; (Ps. 118. 25, 26).

Hosea, prophet, declares God's judgment against idolatrous Israel, Hos. 1 ; 2 ; 4 ; and his mercy, Hos. 2. 14 ; 11 ; 13 ; 14.

Hoshea, last king of Israel, his wicked reign, defeat and captivity, 2 Ki. 15. 30 ; 17.

Hospitality, exhortations to, Rom. 12. 13 ; Tit. 1. 8. Heb. 13. 2 ; 1 Pet. 4. 9.
of Abraham, Gen. 18. Lot, Gen. 19. Laban, Gen. 24. 31. Jethro, Ex. 2. 20. Manoah, Jud. 13. 15. Samuel, 1 Sam. 9. 22. David, 2 Sam. 6. 19. Barzillai, etc., 2 Sam. 17. 27 ; 19. 32. The Shunammite, 2 Ki. 4. 8. Nehemiah, Neh. 5. 18. Matthew, Lk. 5. 29. Zacchaeus, Lk. 19. 6. Lydia, Acts 16. 15. Publius, etc, Acts 28. 2. Gaius, 3 John 5.

Host, the heavenly, 2. 13.
See 1 Chr. 12. 22 ; Ps. 103. 21 ; 148. 2.
of the Lord, Gen. 32. 2 ; Josh. 5. 14 ; 1 Chr. 9. 19.

Hour, the third, of day, Matt. 20. 3 ; Mk. 15. 25 ; Acts 2. 15 ; 23. 23.
the sixth, Matt. 27. 45 ; Mk. 15. 33 ; Lk. 23. 44 ; John 4. 6 ; 19. 14 ; Acts 10. 9.
the ninth, Acts 3. 1 ; 10. 3, 30.
at hand, Matt. 26. 45 ; John 4. 21 ; 5. 25 ; 12. 23 ; 13. 1 ; 16. 21 ; 17. 1.
knoweth no man, Matt. 24. 36, 42 ; 25. 13 ; Mk. 13. 32 ; Rev. 3. 3.
of temptation, Rev. 3. 10 ; judgment, Rev. 14. 7 ; 18. 10.
figurative, Rev. 8. 1 ; 9. 15.
See Matt. 8. 13 ; 9. 22 ; 15. 28 ; Lk. 12. 12 ; John 4. 53 ; Acts 22. 13 ; 1 Cor. 4. 11 ; 8. 7.

House of God, Gen. 28. 17 ; Jud. 20. 18 ; 2 Chr. 5. 14 ; Ezra 5. 8, 15 ; Neh. 6. 10 ; Ps. 84. 10 ; Is. 6. 4 ; 60. 7 ; 64. 11 ; Ezek. 43. 5 ; Mic. 4. 2 ; Zech. 7. 2 ; Matt. 12. 4 ; 1 Tim. 3. 15 ; Heb. 10. 21 ; 1 Pet. 4. 17 ; (heaven), Acts 7. 49 ; (for worship). See *Temple*.

Humility, Prov. 15. 33 ; 22. 4.
enjoined, Mic. 6. 8 ; Matt. 18 ; 20. 25 ; Mk. 9. 33 ; 10. 43 ; Lk. 9. 46 ; 14. 7 ; 22. 24 ; Eph. 4. 2 ; Col. 3. 12 ; Phil. 2. 3 ; Jas. 4. 10 ; 1 Pet. 5. 5.
benefits of, Ps. 34. 2 ; 69. 32 ; Prov. 3. 34 ; Is. 57. 15 ; Matt. 18. 4 ; Lk. 14. 11 ; Jas. 4. 6.

Hunger, Ex. 16. 3 ; Ps. 34. 10 ; Jer. 38. 9 ; Lam. 4. 9 ; Lk. 15. 17 ; 2 Cor. 11. 27 ; Rev. 6. 8.
(and thirst), figurative, Ps. 107. 5 ; Is. 49. 10 ; 55 ; Matt. 5. 6 ; John 6. 35 ; Rev. 7. 16.
See Ps. 146. 7 ; Prov. 25. 21 ; Is. 58. 7 ; Lk. 1. 53 ; Acts 10. 10 ; 1 Cor. 11. 21.

Hur, son of Caleb, Ex. 17. 10 ; 24. 14 ; 1 Chr. 2. 19.

Husbands, Gen. 2. 24 ; Matt. 19. 4 ; 1 Cor. 7. 3 ; Eph. 5. 25 ; Col. 3. 19 ; 1 Pet. 3. 7.
God the husband of his Church, Is. 54. 5 ; Hos. 2. 7.

Husbandman, John 15. 1 ; 2 Tim. 2. 6 ; Jas. 5. 7.
parable of the husbandmen, Matt. 21. 33 ; Mk. 12. 1 ; Lk. 20. 9.

Hushai's loyalty to David, 2 Sam. 15. 32, etc.

Hymenaeus, 1 Tim. 1. 20 ; 2 Tim. 2. 17.

Hymns, Matt. 26. 30 ; Mk. 14. 26 ; Eph. 5. 19 ; Col. 3. 16.

Hypocrisy, Is. 29. 15 ; Matt. 23. 28 ; Mk. 12. 15 ; 1 Tim. 4. 2 ; Rev. 3. 1.
punishment of, Job 8. 13 ; 15. 34 ; 20. 5 ; 36. 13 ; Matt. 24. 51.
denounced, Matt. 6. 2 ; 7. 5 ; 1 Pet. 2. 1.

Hyssop, Ex. 12. 22 ; Lev. 14. 4 ; Num. 19. 6 - Ps. 51. 7 ; Heb. 9. 19.

I AM, the divine name, Ex. 3. 14.
See John 8. 58 ; Rev. 1. 18.

I-chabod, why so called, 1 Sam. 4. 21 ; 14. 3.

Iconium, Gospel preached at, Acts 13. 51 ; 14. 1 ; 16. 2.
Paul persecuted at, 2 Tim. 3. 11.

Idleness reproved, Prov. 6. 6 ; 18. 9 ; 24. 30 ; Rom. 12. 11 ; 1 Thes. 4. 11 ; 2 Thes. 3. 10 ; Heb. 6. 12.
evil of, Prov. 10. 4 ; 12. 24 ; 13. 4 ; 19. 15 ; 20. 4, 13 ; 21. 25 ; Eccl. 10. 18 ; 1 Tim. 5. 13.

Idolatry forbidden, Ex. 20. 2 ; 22. 20 ; 23. 13 ; Lev. 26. 1 ; Deut. 4. 15 ; 5. 7 ; 11. 16 ; 17. 2 ; 18. 9 ; 27. 15 ; Ps. 97. 7 ; Jer. 2. 11 ; 1 Cor. 10. 7, 14 ; 1 John 5. 21.
folly of, 1 Ki. 18. 26 ; Ps. 115. 4 ; 135. 15 ; Is. 40. 19 ; 41 ; 44. 9 ; 46. 1 ; Jer. 2. 26 ; 10.
monuments of, to be destroyed, Ex. 23. 24 ; 34. 13 ; Deut. 7. 5 ; 13. 1.
Israelites guilty of, Ex. 32 : Num. 25 ; Jud. 2. 11 ; 3. 7 ; 8. 33 ; 18. 30 ; 2 Ki. 17. 12. Micah, Jud. 17. Solomon, 1 Ki. 11. 5. Jeroboam, 1 Ki. 12. 28. Ahab, etc., 1 Ki. 16. 31 ; 18. 19. Manasseh, 2 Ki. 21. 4. Ahaz, 2 Chr. 28. 2. Nebuchadnezzar, etc., Dan 3 ; 5. Inhabitants of Lystra, Acts 14. 11. Athenians, Acts 17. 16. Ephesians, Acts 19. 28.
zeal of Asa against, 1 Ki. 15. 12
 „ Jehoshaphat, 2 Chr. 17. 6
 „ Hezekiah, 2 Chr. 30. 13.
 „ Josiah, 2 Chr. 34.
punishment of, Deut. 7. 16 ; 17. 2 ; Jer. 8. 1 ; 16. 1 ; 44. 21 ; Hos. 8. 5 ; 1 Cor. 6. 9 ; Eph. 5. 5 ; Rev. 14. 9 ; 21. 8 ; 22. 15.

Idols, meats offered to, Rom. 14 ; 1 Cor. 8.

Idumaea, land of Edom, Is. 34. 5 ; Ezek. 35. 15 ; 36. 5 ; Mk. 3. 8.

Ignorance, sin offerings for, Lev. 4 ; Num. 15. 22.
effects of, Rom. 10. 3 ; 2 Pet. 3. 5.
Paul's deprecation of, 1 Cor. 10. 1 ; 12 ; 2 Cor. 1. 8 ; 1 Thes. 4. 13 ; 2 Pet. 3. 8.

Illyricum, Gospel preached there, Rom. 15. 19.

Images prohibited, Ex. 20. 4 ; Lev. 26. 1 ; Deut. 16. 22.

Imagination of man, evil, Gen. 6. 5 ; 8. 21 ; Deut. 31. 21 ; Jer. 23. 17 ; Lk. 1. 51.

Immanuel, God with us, Is. 7. 14 ; Matt. 1. 23.

Immortality, of God, 1 Tim. 1. 17 ; 6. 16.
of man, Rom. 2. 7 ; 1 Cor. 15. 53.

Immutability of God's counsel, Heb. 6. 17.

Imputed righteousness, Rom. 4. 6, 22 ; 5.

Incense, Ex. 30. 22 ; 37. 29.
offered, Lev. 10. 1 ; 16. 13 ; Num. 16. 46.
figurative, Rev. 8. 3.

Incest forbidden, Lev. 18 ; 20. 17 ; Deut. 22. 30 ; 27. 20 ; Ezek. 22. 11 ; Amos 2. 7.
cases of, Gen. 19. 33 ; 35. 22 ; 38. 18 ; 2 Sam. 13 ; 16. 21 ; Mk. 6. 17 ; 1 Cor. 5. 1.

India, Est. 1. 1.

Industry commanded, Gen. 2. 15; 3. 23; Prov. 6. 6; 10. 4; 12. 24; 13. 4; 21. 5; 22. 29; 27. 23; Eph. 4. 28; 1 Thes. 4. 11; 2 Thes. 3. 12; Tit. 3. 14.

rewarded, Prov. 13. 11; 31. 13.

Infirmities, human, borne by Christ (Is. 53. 4); Matt. 8. 17; Heb. 4. 15.

Ingathering, feast of, Ex. 23. 16; 34. 22.

Ingratitude to God, Rom. 1. 21.

exemplified: Israel, Deut. 32. 18; Saul, 1 Sam. 15; 24. 17; David, 2 Sam. 12. 7, 9; Nebuchadnezzar, Dan. 5; the lepers, Lk. 17.

punishment of, Prov. 17. 13; Jer. 18. 20.

Inheritance, law of, Num. 27; 36; Deut. 21. 15.

in Christ, Eph. 1. 11; Col. 1. 12; 3. 24; 1 Pet. 1. 4.

Injustice forbidden, Ex. 22. 21; 23. 6; Lev. 19. 15; Deut. 16. 19; 24. 17; Job 31. 13; Ps. 82. 2; Prov. 22. 16; 29. 7; Jer. 22. 3; Lk. 16. 10.

results of, Prov. 1. 7; 28. 8; Mic. 6. 10; Amos 5. 11; 8. 5; 1 Thes. 4. 6; 2 Pet. 2. 9.

Inspiration of Scripture, 2 Tim. 3. 16; Lk. 1. 70; 2 Pet. 1. 21; Heb. 1. 1.

Instruction promised, etc., Job 33. 16; Ps. 32. 8; Prov. 10. 17; 12. 1; 13. 1; Matt. 13. 52; 2 Tim. 3. 16.

hated by wicked, Ps. 50. 17; Prov. 1. 22; 5. 12.

recommended, Prov. 1. 2, 8; 4. 13; 9. 9; 19. 20.

danger of rejecting, Prov. 13. 18; 15. 32.

Integrity, 1 Sam. 12. 3; 2 Ki. 12. 15; 22. 7; Job 2. 3; Ps. 7. 8; 26. 1; 41. 12; Prov. 11. 3; 19. 1; 20. 7.

Intercession of Christ, Lk. 23. 34; Rom. 8. 34; Heb. 7. 25; 1 John 2. 1.

of the Holy Spirit, Rom. 8. 26.

to be made for all men, 1 Tim. 2. 1; Eph. 6. 18; for kings, 1 Tim. 2. 2.

asked for by Paul, Rom. 15. 30; 2 Cor. 1. 11; Col. 4. 3; 1 Thes. 5. 25; 2 Thes. 3. 1; Heb. 13. 18.

Interpretation (of dreams) is of God, Gen. 40. 8; Prov. 1. 6; Dan. 2. 27.

Invisible God, the, Col. 1. 15; 1 Tim. 1. 17; Heb. 11. 27.

Iron, Deut. 3. 11; 2 Sam. 23. 7; Job 28. 2; Prov. 27. 17; Is. 45. 2; Ezek. 27. 12; Dan. 2. 33, 40.

pen of, Job 19. 24.

rod of, figurative, Ps. 2. 9; Rev. 2. 27.

Isaac, his birth promised, Gen. 15. 4; 17. 16; 18. 10; born, Gen. 21. 2.

offered by Abraham, Gen. 22. 7.

marries Rebecca, Gen. 24. 67.

blesses his sons, Gen. 27. 27, 39; 28. 1.

his death, Gen. 35. 29.

Isaiah (Esaias), prophet, Is. 1. 1; 2. 1.

sent to Ahaz, Is. 7; and Hezekiah, Is. 37. 6; 38. 4; 39. 3.

prophesies concerning various nations, Is. 7; 8; 10; 13-23; 45-47.

referred to, Matt. 3. 3; 4. 17; 8. 17; 12. 17; 13. 14; 15. 7; Mk. 1. 2; Lk. 3. 4; 4. 17; John 1. 23; 12. 38; Acts 8. 32; 28. 25; Rom. 9. 27; 10. 16; 15. 12.

Ish-bosheth, son of Saul, 2 Sam. 2. 8; 3. 7; 4. 5.

Ishmael, son of Abraham, Gen. 16. 15; 17. 20; 21. 17; 25. 17.

his descendants, Gen. 25. 12; 1 Chr. 1. 29.

—son of Nethaniah slays Gedaliah, Jer. 40. 14; 41.

Israel, Jacob so called, Gen. 32. 28; 35. 10; Hos. 12. 3.

Israelites, their bondage in Egypt, Ex. 1-12.

the first passover instituted, Ex. 12.

their departure from Egypt, Ex. 12. 31.

Israelites—*Continued.*

pass through the Red Sea, Ex. 14.

miraculously fed, Ex. 15. 23; 16; 17. 1; Num. 11; 20.

God's covenant with, Ex. 19; 20; Deut. 29. 10.

their idolatry, Ex. 32.

See 2 Ki. 17; Ezra 9; Neh. 9; Ezek. 20; 22; 23; Acts 7. 39; 1 Cor. 10. 1.

their rebellious conduct, Deut. 1; 2; 9.

enter and divide Canaan under Joshua, Josh. 1; 12; 13.

governed by judges, Jud. 2; and by kings, 1 Sam. 10; 2 Sam.; 1 & 2 Ki.; 1 & 2 Chr.

their captivity in Assyria, 2 Ki. 17; in Babylon, 2 Ki. 25; 2 Chr. 36; Jer. 39; 52.

their return, Ezra; Neh.; Hag.; Zech.

See Ps. 78; 105; 106; 1 Cor. 10. 6.

Issachar, son of Jacob, Gen. 30. 18; 35. 23.

descendants of, Gen. 46. 13; Jud. 5. 15; 1 Chr. 7. 1.

See Num. 1. 18; 26. 23; Gen. 49. 14; Deut. 33. 18; Josh. 19. 17; Ezek. 48. 33; Rev. 7. 7.

Ithamar, son of Aaron, Ex. 6. 23; Lev. 10. 6; his charge, Num. 4.

Ithiel, Prov. 30. 1.

Ittai's fidelity to David, 2 Sam. 15. 19; 18. 2.

Iturea, Lk. 3. 1.

Ivory, 1 Ki. 10. 22; Is. 21. 13; Ezek. 27. 15; Rev. 18. 12.

Solomon's throne of, 1 Ki. 10. 18; 2 Chr. 9. 17.

palaces, Ps. 45. 8; Amos 3. 15.

JABAL (and Jubal), Gen. 4. 20, 21.

Jabbok, river, Gen. 32. 22.

Jabesh-Gilead, inhabitants of, slain, Jud. 21.

threatened by Ammonites, 1 Sam. 11. 1; delivered by Saul, 1 Sam. 11. 11.

Jabez, prayer of, 1 Chr. 4. 9.

Jabin, king of Hazor, conquered by Joshua, Josh. 11.

—(another), subdued by Barak, Jud. 4.

Jachin, one of the pillars of the temple, 1 Ki. 7. 21; 2 Chr. 3. 17.

Jacinth, Rev. 9. 17; 21. 20.

Jacob, his birth, Gen. 25. 26; birthright, Gen. 25. 33; obtains the blessing, Gen. 27. 27; sent to Padan-aram, Gen. 27. 43; 28. 1; his vision and vow, Gen. 28. 10; marriages, Gen. 29; his sons, Gen. 29. 31; 30; dealings with Laban, Gen. 31; his vision of God's host, Gen. 32. 1; his prayer, Gen. 32. 9; wrestles with an angel, Gen. 32. 24; Hos. 12. 4; reconciled with Esau, Gen. 33; builds an altar, Gen. 35. 1; his grief for Joseph and Benjamin, Gen. 37; 42. 38; 43; goes down to Egypt, Gen. 46; brought before Pharaoh, Gen. 47. 7; blesses his sons, Gen. 48; 49; his death and burial, Gen. 49. 33; 50.

See Ps. 105. 23; Mal. 1. 2; John 4. 5, 6; Rom. 9. 10; Heb. 11. 21.

Jael kills Sisera, Jud. 4. 17; 5. 24.

Jahaziel comforts Jehoshaphat, 2 Chr. 20. 14.

Jair, Gileadite, judge, Jud. 10. 3.

Jairus' daughter, raising of, Matt. 9. 18; Mk. 5. 22; Lk. 8. 41.

James (apostle), son of Zebedee, called, Matt. 4. 21; Mk. 1. 19; Lk. 5. 10.

ordained one of the twelve, Matt. 10. 2; Mk. 3. 14; Lk. 6. 13.

present at Christ's transfiguration, Matt. 17. 1; Mk. 9. 2; Lk. 9. 28.

present at the passion, Matt. 26. 36; Mk. 14. 33.

James—*Continued.*
slain by Herod, Acts 12. 2.
—(apostle), son of Alphæus, Matt. 10. 3; Mk. 3. 18; 6. 3; Lk. 6. 15; Acts 1. 13; 12. 17.
his decision concerning circumcision, etc., Acts 15. 13-29.
See Acts 21. 18; 1 Cor. 15. 7; Gal. 1. 19: 2. 9.
his teaching, epistle, Jas. 1; 2; 3; 4; 5.
Jannes and Jambres, magicians of Egypt, 2 Tim. 3. 8; (Ex. 7. 11).
Japheth, son of Noah, blessed, Gen. 9. 27.
his descendants, Gen. 10. 1; 1 Chr. 1. 4.
Jared, Gen. 5. 15; Lk. 3. 37.
Jasher, book of, Josh. 10. 13; 2 Sam. 1. 18.
Jashobeam, one of David's warriors, 1 Chr. 11. 11.
Jason persecuted at Thessalonica, Acts 17. 5; Rom. 16. 21.
Jasper mentioned, Ex. 28. 20; Ezek. 28. 13; Rev. 4. 3; 21. 11, 18, 19.
Javan, son of Japheth, Gen. 10. 2.
—country of, Is. 66. 19; Ezek. 27. 13, 19.
Javelin, Num. 25. 7; 1 Sam. 18. 10; 19. 10.
Jaw-bone of an ass, Samson uses, Jud. 15. 15.
Jealous (God), Ex. 20. 5; Deut. 29. 20; Ps. 78. 58; Zeph. 1. 18; Zech. 1. 14; 1 Cor. 10. 22.
Jealousy, Prov. 6. 34; Cant. 8. 6.
offering of, Num. 5. 11.
Jebusites, Gen. 15. 21; Num. 13. 29; Josh. 15. 63; Jud. 1. 21; 19. 11; 2 Sam. 5. 6.
Jedidiah, a name of Solomon, 2 Sam. 12. 25.
Jehoahaz, king of Israel, 2 Ki. 10. 35; 13. 4.
—(Shalium), king of Judah, 2 Ki. 23. 31; 2 Chr. 36. 1.
Jehoiachin, king of Judah, 2 Ki. 24. 6; 2 Chr. 36. 8.
Jehoiada, high priest, slays Athaliah, and restores Jehoash, 2 Ki. 11. 4; 2 Chr. 23.
repairs the temple, Jud. 12. 7; 2 Chr. 24. 6.
abolishes idolatry, 2 Chr. 23. 16.
Jehoiakim, made king of Judah, his evil reign, and captivity, 2 Ki. 23. 34; 24. 1; 2 Chr. 36. 4; Dan. 1. 2.
See Jer. 22. 18.
Jehoram, king of Judah, 1 Ki. 22. 50; 2 Ki. 8. 16.
his cruelty and death, 2 Chr. 21. 4, 18.
—(Joram), king of Israel, son of Ahab, 2 Ki. 1. 17; 3. 1; his evil reign, 2 Ki. 3. 2; slain by Jehu, 2 Ki. 9. 24.
Jehoshaphat, king of Judah, 1 Ki. 15. 24; 2 Chr. 17; his death, 1 Ki. 22. 50; 2 Chr. 21. 1.
—valley of, Joel 3. 2.
Jehosheba, 2 Ki. 11; 2 Chr. 22. 11.
Jehovah, Ex. 6. 3; Ps. 83. 18; Is. 12. 2; 26. 4.
—Jireh (the Lord will provide), Gen. 22. 14.
—Nissi (the Lord my banner), Ex. 17. 15.
—Shalom (the Lord send peace), Jud. 6. 24.
Jehu prophesies against Baasha, 1 Ki. 16. 1.
rebukes Jehoshaphat, 2 Chr. 19. 2; 20. 34.
—son of Nimshi, to be anointed king of Israel, 1 Ki. 19. 16; 2 Ki. 9. 1.
his reign, 2 Ki. 9. 10.
Jephthah, judge, his covenant with the Gileadites, Jud. 11. 4.
his message to the Ammonites, Jud. 11. 14.
his rash vow, Jud. 11. 30, 34.
chastises the Ephraimites, Jud. 12.
Jeremiah (prophet), his call and visions, Jer. 1.
his mission, Jer. 1. 17; 7.
his complaint, Jer. 20. 14.
his message to Zedekiah, Jer. 21. 3; 34. 1.
foretells the seventy years' captivity, Jer. 25. 8.

Jeremiah—*Continued.*
apprehended, but delivered by Ahikam, Jer. 26.
denounces Hananiah, Jer. 28. 5.
his letter to the captives in Babylon, Jer. 29.
praying, is comforted, Jer. 32. 16; 33.
writes a roll of a book, Jer. 36. 4; Baruch reads it, Jer. 36. 8.
imprisoned by Zedekiah, Jer. 32; 37; 38.
released by Ebed-melech, Jer. 38. 7.
carried into Egypt, Jer. 43. 4.
various predictions, Jer. 46-51; 51. 59.
See Matt. 2. 17; 16. 14; 27. 9.
Jericho, spies sent there, Josh. 2. 1.
capture of, Josh. 6. 20; (Heb. 11. 30).
rebuilt by Hiel, 1 Ki. 16. 34.
See Josh. 6. 26.
Jeroboam I., promoted by Solomon, 1 Ki. 11. 28.
Ahijah's prophecy to, 1 Ki. 11. 29.
made king, 1 Ki. 12. 20; (2 Chr. 10).
his idolatry, 1 Ki. 12. 26.
his hand withers, 1 Ki. 13. 4.
judgment denounced upon his house, 1 Ki. 14. 7.
his death, 1 Ki. 14. 20.
evil example, 1 Ki. 15. 34
Jeroboam II., 2 Ki. 13. 13; 14. 23-29.
Jerusalem, king of, slain by Joshua, Josh. 10
borders of, Josh 15. 8.
David reigns there, 2 Sam. 5. 6.
the ark brought there, 2 Sam. 6.
preserved from the pestilence, 2 Sam. 24. 16.
temple built at, 1 Ki. 5-8; 2 Chr. 1-7.
sufferings from war, 1 Ki. 14. 25; 2 Ki. 14. 14; 25; 2 Chr. 12; 25; 36; Jer. 39; 52.
capture and destruction by Nebuchadnezzar, Jer. 52. 12-15.
captives return, and Cyrus begins to rebuild the temple, Ezra 1; 2; 3; continued by Artaxerxes, Neh. 2.
wall rebuilt and dedicated, Neh. 12. 38.
presentation of Christ at, Lk. 2. 22.
his public entry into, Matt. 21. 1; Mk. 11. 7, Lk. 19. 35; John 12. 14; laments over it, Matt. 23. 37; Lk. 13. 34; 19. 41; foretells its destruction, Matt. 24; Mk. 13; Lk. 13. 34; 17. 23; 19. 41 , 21.
disciples filled with the Holy Ghost at, Acts 2. 4.
which is above, Gal. 4. 26.
the new, Rev. 21. 2.
Jeshua (Joshua), Neh. 8. 17. See *Joshua.*
Jeshurun, Israel so called, Deut. 32. 15; 33. 5, 26; Is. 44. 2.
Jesse, David's father, Ruth 4. 22.
and his sons sanctified by Samuel, 1 Sam. 16. 5.
his son David anointed to be king, 1 Sam. 16. 13.
his posterity, 1 Chr. 2. 13.
See Is. 11. 1.
Jesting, foolish, censured, Eph. 5. 4.
Jesus Christ. See *Christ.*
Jethro, Moses' father-in-law, Ex. 18. 12.
Jews, Israelites first so called, 2 Ki. 16. 6.
Christ's mission to, Matt. 15. 24; 21. 37; Acts 3. 26.
Christ rejected by, Matt. 11. 20; 13. 15; John 5. 16, 38; Acts 3. 13; 13. 46; 1 Thes. 2. 15.
Gospel first preached to, Matt. 10. 6; Lk. 24. 47; Acts 1. 8.
St Paul's teaching rejected by, Acts 13. 46; 28. 24, 26.

Joshua—*Continued.*
renews the covenant, Josh. 24. 14.
his death, Josh. 24. 29; Jud. 2. 8.
his curse, Josh. 6. 26; fulfilled, 1 Ki. 16. 34.
Josiah, prophecy concerning, 1 Ki. 13. 2; fulfilled, 2 Ki. 23. 15.
his good reign, 2 Ki. 22.
repairs the temple, 2 Ki. 22. 3.
hears the words of the book of the law, 2 Ki. 22. 8.
Huldah's message from God to him, 2 Ki. 22. 15.
ordains the reading of the book, 2 Ki. 23.
his solemn passover, 2 Chr. 35.
slain by Pharaoh-nechoh, 2 Ki. 23. 29.
Jotham, son of Gideon, his parable, Jud. 9. 7.
—king of Judah, 2 Ki. 15. 32; 2 Chr. 27.
Joy, 1 Chr. 12. 40; Ezra 6. 16; Neh. 8. 10; Ps. 16. 11; 89. 16; 149. 2; Is. 35. 2; 60. 15; 61. 10; Hab. 3. 18; Lk. 10. 20; John 15. 11; Rom. 14. 17; Phil. 3. 3; 1 Thes. 1. 6.
of the wicked, folly, Job 20. 5; Prov. 15. 21; Eccl. 2. 10; 7. 6; 11. 9; Is. 16. 10; Jas. 4. 9.
follows grief, Ps. 30. 5; 126. 5; Prov. 14. 10; Is. 35. 10; 61. 3. 66. 10; Jer. 31. 13; John 16. 20; 2 Cor. 6. 10; Jas. 1. 2.
in heaven over repentant sinners, Lk. 15. 7, 10.
of Paul over the churches, 2 Cor. 1. 24; 2. 3; 7. 13; Phil. 1. 4; 2. 2; 4. 1; 1 Thes. 2. 19; 3. 9; 2 Tim. 1. 4; Philem. 7.
of John over his spiritual children, 3 John 4.
expressed by psalmody, Eph. 5. 19; Col. 3. 16; Jas. 5. 13.
Jubal, inventor of harp and organ, Gen. 4. 21.
Judah, son of Jacob, Gen. 29. 35.
pledges himself for Benjamin, Gen. 43. 3.
his interview with Joseph, Gen. 44. 18; 46. 28.
blessed by Jacob, Gen. 49. 8.
his descendants, Gen. 38; 46. 12; Num. 1. 26; 26. 19; 1 Chr. 2-4.
—tribe of, blessed by Moses, Deut. 33. 7.
their inheritance, Josh. 15.
they make David king, 2 Sam. 2. 4; and adhere to his house, 1 Ki. 12; 2 Chr. 10; 11. See *Jews.*
Judas (Jude, Lebbæus, Thaddæus), apostle, brother of James, Matt. 10. 3; Mk. 3. 18; Lk. 6. 16; Acts 1. 13.
his question to our Lord, John 14. 22.
exhorts to perseverance in the faith, Jude 3, 20.
—the Lord's brother, Matt. 13. 55; Mk. 6. 3.
—(Barsabas), Acts 15. 22.
—Iscariot, Matt. 10. 4; Mk. 3. 19; Lk. 6. 16; John 6. 70.
betrays Jesus, Matt. 26. 14, 47; Mk. 14. 10, 43; Lk. 22. 3, 47; John 13. 26; 18. 2.
hangs himself, Matt. 27. 5; (Acts 1. 18).
Judge of all the earth, God, Gen. 18. 25.
Judges, appointment of, Deut. 16. 18; Ezra 7. 25.
their functions, Ex. 18. 21; Lev. 19. 15; Deut. 1. 16; 17. 8; 2 Chr. 19. 6; Ps. 82; Prov. 18. 5; 24. 23.
unjust, 1 Sam. 8. 3; Is. 1. 23; Lk. 18. 2; hateful to God, Prov. 17. 15; 24. 24; Is. 10. 1.
Judgment, cautions concerning, Matt. 7. 1; Lk. 6. 37; 12. 57; John 7. 24; Rom. 2. 1; Jas. 4. 11.
Judgment, the last, foretold, 1 Chr. 16. 33; Ps. 9. 7; 96. 13; 98. 9; Eccl. 3. 17; 11. 9; 12. 14; Acts 17. 31; Rom. 2. 16; 2 Cor. 5. 10; Heb. 9. 27; 2 Pet. 3. 7.

Judgment—*Continued.*
described, Ps. 50; Dan. 7. 9; Matt. 25. 31; 2 Thes. 1. 8; Rev. 6. 12; 20. 11.
hope of Christians respecting, Rom. 8. 33; 1 Cor. 4. 5; 2 Tim. 4. 8; 1 John 2. 28; 4. 17.
Jupiter, Barnabas addressed as, Acts 14. 12; (19. 35.)
Justice, of God, Deut. 32. 4; Job 4. 17; 8. 3; 34. 12; Is. 45. 21; Zeph. 3. 5; 1 John 1. 9; Rev. 15. 3.
to do, enjoined, Lev. 19. 36; Deut. 16. 18; Ps. 82. 3; Prov. 3. 33; 11. 1; Jer. 22. 3; Ezek. 18. 5; 45. 9; Mic. 6. 8; Matt. 7. 12; Phil. 4. 8; Rom. 13. 7; 2 Cor. 8. 21; Col. 4. 1.
Justification by faith, Hab. 2. 4; Acts 13. 39; Rom. 1. 17; 3; 4; 5; Gal. 2. 11.
by works, Jas. 2. 14-26.

KADESH-BARNEA, Israelites murmur there, Num. 13; 14; Deut. 1. 19; Josh. 14. 6.
Kedar, son of Ishmael, Gen. 25. 13; 1 Chr. 1. 29; Ps. 120. 5; Cant. 1. 5; Jer. 2. 10; Ezek. 27. 21.
tribe of, prophecies concerning, Is. 21. 16; 42. 11; 60. 7; Jer. 49. 28.
Kedron (Kidron, Cedron), brook near Jerusalem, crossed by David in affliction, 2 Sam. 15. 23; and by Christ, John 18. 1.
idols destroyed there, 1 Ki. 15. 13; 2 Ki. 23. 6; 2 Chr. 29. 16; Jer. 31. 40.
Keilah, Josh. 15. 44.
David there, 1 Sam. 23. 1, 12.
Kenites, their fate foretold, Num. 24. 22.
Kerchiefs idolatrously used, Ezek. 13. 18.
Keren-Happuch, one of Job's daughters, Job 42. 14.
Kerioth, a city of Judah, Jer. 48. 24, 41; Amos 2. 2.
Keturah, Abraham's descendants by, Gen. 25; 1 Chr. 1. 32.
Key, of David, Is. 22. 22; Rev. 3. 7; keys of heaven, Matt. 16. 19; keys of hell, Rev. 1. 18; 9. 1.
Kid, law concerning, Ex. 23. 19; Deut. 14. 21; Lev. 4. 23; 16. 5; 23. 19.
Kidneys, for sacrifices, burnt, Ex. 29. 13; Lev. 3. 4.
—of wheat, fat of, Deut. 32. 14.
Kindness, exhortations to, Ruth 2; 3; Prov. 19. 22; 31. 26; Rom. 12. 10; 1 Cor. 13. 4; 2 Cor. 6. 6; Eph. 4. 32; Col. 3. 12; 2 Pet. 1. 7.
Kine, Pharaoh's dream of, Gen. 41. 2.
two take back the ark, 1 Sam. 6. 7.
Kings, chosen by God, Deut. 17. 14; 1 Sam. 9. 17; 16. 1; 1 Ki. 11. 35; 19. 15; 1 Chr. 28. 4; Dan. 2. 21.
honour due to, Prov. 24. 21; 25. 6; Eccl. 8. 2; 10. 20; Matt. 22. 21; Rom. 13; 1 Pet. 2. 13, 17.
to be prayed for, 1 Tim. 2. 1.
parable of the king and his servants, Matt. 18. 23; of the king and his guests, Matt. 22. 2.
See Ps. 2. 10; Prov. 25. 2; 31. 4; Is. 49. 23.
King of kings, Ps. 2. 6; 10. 16; 24. 7; 110; Zech. 9. 9; 14. 9; 1 Tim. 1. 17; 6. 15; Rev. 15. 3; 17. 14.
Kingdom of God, 1 Chr. 29. 11; Ps. 22. 28; 45. 6; 145. 11; Is. 24. 23; Dan. 2. 44.
of Christ, Is. 2; 4; 9; 11; 32; 35; 52; 61; 66; Matt. 16. 28; 26. 29; John 18. 36; 2 Pet. 1. 11.
of Heaven, Matt. 3. 2; 8. 11; 11. 11; 13. 11.
who shall enter, Matt. 5. 3; 7. 21; 18. 3; Lk. 9. 62; John 3. 3; Acts 14. 22; Rom. 14. 17; 1 Cor. 6. 9; 15. 50; 2 Thes. 1. 5.
parables concerning, Matt. 13. 24, etc.

Kinsman, right of, Ruth 3. 14; 4.

Kir, 2 Ki. 16. 9; Is. 15. 1; 22. 6; Amos 1. 5; 9. 7.

Kirjath-Jearim, Josh. 9. 17; 18. 14; 1 Chr. 13. 6.
the ark brought to, 1 Sam. 7. 1.
fetched from, 1 Chr. 13. 5; 2 Chr. 1. 4.

Kish, Saul's father, 1 Sam. 9. 1.

Kishon, river, Jud. 4. 7; 5. 21; 1 Ki. 18. 40.

Kiss, holy, salute with, Rom. 16. 16; 1 Cor. 16. 20; 2 Cor. 13. 12; 1 Thes. 5. 26; 1 Pet. 5. 14.
given as mark of affection, Gen 27. 27; 29. 11; 45. 15; 48. 10; 1 Sam. 10. 1; 20. 41; Lk. 7. 38; 15. 20; Acts 20. 37.
given treacherously, 2 Sam. 20. 9; Matt. 26. 48; Lk. 22. 48.
idolatrous, 1 Ki. 19. 18; Job 31. 27; Hos. 13. 2.

Kite, unclean, Lev. 11. 14; Deut. 14. 13.

Kneeling in prayer, 2 Chr. 6. 13; Ezra 9. 5; Ps. 95. 6; Dan. 6. 10; Acts 7. 60; 9. 40; 21. 5; Eph. 3. 14.

Knowledge given by God, Ex. 8. 10; 18. 16; 31. 3; 2 Chr. 1. 12; Ps. 119. 66; Prov. 1. 4; 2. 6; Eccl. 2. 26; Is. 28. 9; Jer. 24. 7; 31. 33; Dan. 2. 21; Matt. 11. 25; 13. 11; 1 Cor. 1. 5; 2. 12; 12. 8.
advantages of, Ps. 89. 15; Prov. 1. 4, 7; 3. 13; 4; 9. 10; 10. 14; Eccl. 7. 12; Mal. 2. 7; Eph. 3. 18; 4. 13; Jas. 3. 13; 2 Pet. 2. 20.
want of, Prov. 1. 22; 19. 2; Jer. 4. 22; Hos. 4. 6; Rom. 1. 28; 1 Cor. 15. 34.
to be prayed for, John 17. 3; Col. 1. 9; 2 Pet. 3. 18; and sought, 1 Cor. 14. 1; Heb. 6. 1; 2 Pet. 1. 5.
abuse of, 1 Cor. 8. 1.
responsibility of, Num. 15. 30; Deut. 17. 12; Lk. 12. 47; John 15. 22; Rom. 1. 21; 2. 21; Jas. 4. 17.
vanity of human, Eccl. 1. 18; Is. 44. 25; 1 Cor. 1. 19; 3. 19; 2 Cor. 1. 12.
of good and evil, tree of, Gen. 2. 9.

Kohath, son of Levi, Gen. 46. 11.
his descendants, Ex. 6. 18; 1 Chr. 6. 2.
their duties, Num. 4. 15; 10. 21; 2 Chr. 29. 12; 34. 12.

Korah (Core), Dathan, etc., their sedition and punishment, Num. 16; 26. 9; 27. 3; Jude 11.

LABAN, hospitality of, Gen. 24. 29.
gives Jacob his two daughters, Gen. 29.
envies and oppresses him, Gen. 30. 27; 31. 1.
his covenant with him, Gen. 31. 43.

Labour, appointed for man, Gen. 3. 19; Ps. 104. 23; 1 Cor. 4. 12.
when blessed by God, Prov. 10. 16; 13. 11; Eccl. 2. 24; 4. 9; 5. 12, 19.

Labourer worthy of hire, Lk. 10. 7; 1 Tim. 5. 18.
parable of the labourers, Matt. 20.

Lachish conquered, Josh. 10. 31; 12. 11.
Amaziah slain at, 2 Ki. 14. 19.

Ladder, Jacob's, Gen. 28. 12.

Laish taken by stratagem, Jud. 18. 14.

Lake of fire, Rev. 19. 20; 20. 10; 21. 8.

Lamb for sacrifices, Gen. 22. 7; Ex. 12. 3; Lev. 3. 7; Is. 1. 11.

Lame, the, excluded from the priest's office, Lev. 21. 18.
animals, not to be offered for sacrifices, Deut. 15. 21; Mal. 1. 8, 13.
healed by Christ, Matt. 11. 5; 21. 14; Lk. 7. 22; and the apostles, Acts 3; 8. 7.

Lamech, descendant of Cain, Gen. 4. 18.
—father of Noah, Gen. 5. 25, 29.

Lamentation for Jacob, Gen. 50. 10.
David's, for Saul and Jonathan, 2 Sam. 1. 17; for Abner, 2 Sam. 3. 31.

Lamentation—*Continued.*
for Josiah, 2 Chr. 35. 25.
for Tyrus, Ezek. 26. 17; 27. 30; 28. 12.
for Pharaoh, Ezek. 32.
for Christ, Lk. 23. 27.
for Stephen, Acts 8. 2.
for Babylon, Rev. 18. 10.

Lamentations of Jeremiah, Lam. 1, etc.

Lamps in the tabernacle, Ex. 25. 37; 27. 20; 30. 7; Lev. 24. 2; Num. 8.
seen in visions, Gen. 15. 17; Zech. 4. 2; Rev. 4. 5.
parable concerning, Matt. 25. 1.

Landmarks not to be removed, Deut. 19. 14; 27. 17; Prov. 22. 28; 23. 10; Job 24. 2.

Languages confounded, Gen. 11.
gift of, by Holy Ghost, Acts 2. 7, 8; 10. 46; 19. 6; 1 Cor. 12. 10.

Laodiceans, Rev. 1. 11; 3. 14.
Paul's epistle to, Col. 4. 16.

Lasciviousness, source of, Mk. 7. 21; Gal. 5. 19.
censured, 2 Cor. 12. 21; Eph. 4. 19; 1 Pet. 4. 3; Jude 4.

Laughter, Gen. 18. 13; Eccl. 2. 2; 3. 4; 7. 3; Ps. 126. 2; Prov. 14. 13.

Laver of brass, Ex. 30. 18; 38. 8; 40. 7; sanctified, Lev. 8. 11.
ten lavers in the temple, 1 Ki. 7. 38.

Law of God, given to Adam, Gen. 2. 16; to Noah, Gen. 9. 3.
promulgated through Moses, Ex. 19; 20; Deut. 1. 5; 5; 6.
requires perfect obedience, Deut. 27. 26; Gal. 3. 10; Jas. 2. 10.
described, Ps. 19. 7; 119; Rom. 7. 12.
all guilty under, Rom. 3. 20.
—(of Moses), ordained, Ex. 21; Lev. 1; Num. 3; Deut. 12.
preserved on stone, Deut. 27. 1; Josh. 8. 32.
read every seventh year, Deut. 31. 9.
preserved in the ark, Deut. 31. 24.
read by Joshua, Josh. 8. 34; by Ezra, Neh. 8.
book of, discovered by Hilkiah, 2 Ki. 22. 8; and read by Josiah, 2 Ki. 23. 2.
fulfilled by Christ, Matt. 5. 17; Rom. 5. 18.
abolished in Christ, Acts 15. 24; 28. 23; Gal. 2-6; Eph. 2. 15; Col. 2. 14; Heb. 7.
Christians redeemed from curse of, John 1. 17; Acts 13. 39; Rom. 10. 4; Gal. 3. 13.

Lawgiver, God, Is. 33. 22; Jas. 4. 12.

Lawsuits censured, 1 Cor. 6. 1.

Lawyers, Christ reproves, Lk. 10. 25; 11. 46; 14. 3.

Lazarus and the rich man, Lk. 16. 19.
—brother of Mary and Martha, raised from the dead, John 11; 12. 1.

Leah, Gen. 29. 31; 30. 17; 31. 4; 33. 2; 49. 31. See Ruth 4. 11.

Learning, advantage of, Prov. 1. 5; 9. 9; 16. 21, 23; Rom. 15. 4.

Leaven not to be used at the passover, Ex. 12. 15; 13. 7; or in meat offerings, Lev. 2. 11; 6. 17; 10. 12.
figuratively mentioned, Matt. 13. 33; 16. 6; Lk. 13. 21; 1 Cor. 5. 6.

Lebanon, forest and mountain, Deut. 3. 25; Jud. 3. 3; 1 Ki. 5. 14.
its cedars, 2 Ki. 14. 9; 2 Chr. 2. 8; Ps. 92. 12; Cant. 3. 9; Is. 40. 16; Hos. 14. 5.

Lebbæus, Matt. 10. 3. See Jude.

Left-handed slingers, Jud. 20. 16.

Legion (of devils), Mk. 5. 9; Lk. 8. 30.
legions of angels, Matt. 26. 53.

Lemuel, king, his lesson, Prov. 31.

Lending, laws concerning, Ex. 22. 25; Lev. 25. 37; Deut. 15. 2; 23. 19; 24. 10.

See Ps. 37. 26; Lk. 6. 34.

Leopard, vision of, Dan. 7. 6; Rev. 13. 2.

figuratively mentioned, Is. 11. 6; Hos. 13. 7.

Lepers expelled from the camp, Lev. 13. 46; Num. 5. 2; 12. 14.

four, of Samaria, 2 Ki. 7. 3.

Leprosy, in a house, Lev. 14. 33.

of Miriam, Num. 12. 10.

of Naaman and Gehazi, 2 Ki. 5.

of Uzziah, 2 Chr. 26. 19.

symptoms of, Lev. 13.

rites observed in healing,. Lev. 14; 22. 4; Deut. 24. 8.

cured by Christ, Matt. 8. 3; Mk. 1. 41; Lk. 5. 12; 17. 12.

Letter and the spirit, Rom. 2. 27; 7. 6; 2 Cor. 3. 6.

Letters:—of David to Joab, 2 Sam. 11. 14; of Jezebel, 1 Ki. 21. 9; of king of Syria, 2 Ki. 5. 5; of Jehu, 2 Ki. 10. 1, of Elijah to Jehoram, 2 Chr. 21. 12; of Hezekiah, 2 Chr. 30. 1; to Artaxerxes, Ezra 4. 7; of Tatnai, Ezra 5. 6; of Sennacherib, Is. 37. 10, 14; of Jeremiah, Jer. 29. 1; of the apostles, Acts 15. 23; of Claudius Lysias to Felix, Acts 23. 25.

Levi, son of Jacob, Gen. 29. 34.

avenges Dinah, Gen. 34. 25; 49. 5. See *Matthew.*

Levites, descendants of Levi, mentioned, Ex. 32. 26.

their service, Ex. 38. 21.

appointed over the tabernacle, Num. 1. 47.

their divisions, Gershonites, Kohathites, Merarites, Num. 3.

their charge, Num. 3. 23; 4; 8. 23; 18.

their inheritance, Num. 35; Deut. 18; Josh. 21.

duty towards, Deut. 12. 19.

their genealogies, 1 Chr. 6; 9.

charged with the temple service, 1 Chr. 23-27.

their sin censured, Mal. 1; 2; Ezek. 22. 26.

Liars, instances:—the devil, Gen. 3. 4. Cain, Gen. 4. 9. Sarah, Gen. 18. 15. Jacob, Gen. 27. 19. Joseph's brethren, Gen. 37. 31, 32. Saul, 1 Sam. 15. 13. Michal, 1 Sam. 19. 14. David, 1 Sam. 21. 2. Prophet of Bethel, 1 Ki. 13. 18. Gehazi, 2 Ki. 5. 22. Ninevites, Nah. 3. 1. Peter, Matt. 26. 72. Ananias, Acts 5. 5. Cretians, Tit. 1. 12.

their doom, Rev. 21. 8, 27; 22. 15.

Liberality commended, Deut. 15. 14; Prov. 11. 25; Is. 32. 8; 2 Cor. 9. 13.

of the Israelites, Ex. 35. 21; Num. 7.

of the early Christians, Acts 2. 45; 4. 34.

of the Macedonians, 2 Cor. 8; 9; Phil. 4. 15.

Libertines, synagogue of, Acts 6. 9.

Liberty of the Gospel, Rom. 8. 21; 2 Cor. 3. 17; Gal. 5. 1; Jas. 1. 25; 2. 12; (Is. 61. 1; Lk. 4. 18).

not to be misused, 1 Cor. 8. 9; Gal. 5. 13; 1 Pet. 2. 16; 2 Pet. 2. 19.

Libnah subdued, Josh. 10. 29; 21. 13; revolts, 2 Ki. 8. 22.

besieged by Assyrians, 2 Ki. 19. 8; Is. 37. 8.

Libya, Jer. 46. 9; Ezek. 30. 5; Dan. 11. 43; Acts 2. 10.

Lice, plague of, Ex. 8. 16; Ps. 105. 31.

Life, the gift of God, Gen. 2. 7; Job 12. 10; Ps. 36. 6; 66. 9; Dan. 5. 23; Acts 17. 28.

long, to whom promised, Ex. 20. 12; Deut. 5. 33; 6. 2; Prov. 3. 2; 9. 11; 10. 27; Eph. 6. 3.

Life—*Continued.*

its shortness and vanity, Job 7. 1; 9. 25; 14. 1; Ps. 39. 5; 73. 19; 89. 47; 90. 5, 9; Eccl. 1. 12; Is. 38. 12; Jas. 4. 14; 1 Pet. 1. 24.

of Hezekiah prolonged, 2 Ki. 20; 2 Chr. 32. 24; Is. 38.

how to be passed, Lk. 1. 75; Rom. 12. 18; 14. 8; Phil. 1. 21; 1 Pet. 1. 17.

Spiritual, Rom. 6. 4; 8; Gal. 2. 20; Eph. 2. 1; Col. 3. 3.

Eternal, the gift of God through Jesus Christ (Ps. 133. 3); John 6. 27, 54; 10. 28; 17. 3; Rom. 2. 7; 6. 23; 1 John 1. 2; 2. 25; Jude 21; Rev. 2. 7; 21. 6.

to whom promised, John 3. 16; 5. 24; 1 Tim. 1. 16.

Light, Gen. 1. 3; Jer. 31. 35.

type of God's favour, Ex. 10. 23; Ps. 4. 6; 27. 1; 97. 11; Is. 9. 2; 60. 19.

God's word is, Ps. 19. 8; 119. 105, 130; Prov. 6. 23.

instances of miraculous, Matt. 17. 2; Acts 9. 3.

Christ the light of the world, Lk. 2. 32; John 1. 4; 3. 19; 8. 12; 12. 35; Rev. 21. 23.

disciples called children of, Eph. 5. 8; 1 Thes. 5. 5; 1 Pet 2. 9.

God is, 1 Tim. 6. 16; 1 John 1. 5.

Lightning, 2 Sam. 22. 15; Job 28. 26; 38. 25; Ps. 18. 14; 144. 6.

surrounding God's throne, Ezek. 1. 13; Rev. 4. 5.

Lily of the valley, Cant. 2. 1; Hos. 14. 5; Matt. 6. 28; Lk. 12. 27.

Linen for sacred vestments, Ex. 28. 42; Lev. 6. 10; 1 Sam. 2. 18; 22. 18.

See Rev. 15. 6.

Lions, Samson kills one, Jud. 14. 5.

David kills one, 1 Sam. 17. 34.

Daniel in the den of, Dan. 6. 18.

prophets slain by, 1 Ki. 13. 24; 20. 36.

parable of young, Ezek. 19.

mentioned figuratively, Gen. 49. 9; (Rev. 5. 5); Num. 24. 9; 2 Sam. 17. 10; Job 4. 10.

Satan likened to a lion, 1 Pet. 5. 8; (Ps. 10. 9).

visions of, Ezek. 1. 10; 10. 14; Dan. 7. 4; Rev. 4. 7.

Living water given by Christ, John 4. 10; 7. 38; Rev. 7. 17.

Lizards, unclean, Lev. 11. 30.

Loaves, miraculous multiplication of, Matt. 14. 17; 15. 32; Mk. 6. 35; Lk. 9. 12; John 6. 5.

Locusts, Ex. 10. 4; Deut. 28. 38; Ps. 105. 34; Rev. 9. 3.

used as food, Lev. 11. 22; Matt. 3. 4.

described, Prov. 30. 27; Nah. 3. 17; Rev. 9. 7.

Log, a liquid measure, Lev. 14. 10.

Lois commended, 2 Tim. 1. 5.

Lord. See *Jehovah.*

Lord's Day, Rev. 1. 10.

Lord's Prayer, Matt. 6. 9.

Lord's Supper. See *Communion.*

Lot (Abram's nephew), his choice, Gen 13. 10.

rescued from captivity by Abram, Gen. 14.

entertains angels, Gen. 19. 1.

saved from the destruction of Sodom, Gen. 19. 16; 2 Pet. 2. 7.

his wife turned into a pillar of salt, Gen. 19. 26; Lk. 17. 28, 32.

Lot, the, decided by God, Lev. 16. 8; Prov. 16. 33.

Canaan divided by, Num. 26. 55; Josh. 15.

Saul chosen king by, 1 Sam. 10. 17.

Christ's garments divided by, Matt. 27. 35; Mk. 15. 24; (Ps. 22. 18).

Matthias chosen by, Acts 1. 26.

Love to God commanded, Deut 6. 5; 10. 12; 11. 1; Josh. 22. 5; Ps. 31. 23; Dan. 9. 4; Matt. 22. 37; 1 John 4; 5.
blessings of, Neh. 1. 5; Ps. 145. 20; 1 Cor. 2. 9; 8. 3.
of husbands, etc., Gen. 29. 20; 2 Sam. 1. 26; Eph. 5. 25; Tit. 2. 4.
to Christ, Matt. 10. 37; Rev. 2. 4.
of the world, censured, 1 John 2. 15.
Lucius of Cyrene, a teacher, Acts 13. 1; Rom. 16. 21.
Lucre, greed of, forbidden, 1 Tim. 3. 3; Tit. 1. 7; 1 Pet. 5. 2.
Luke, the beloved physician, companion of Paul, Col. 4. 14; 2 Tim. 4. 11; Philem. 24; (Acts 16. 12; 20. 5).
Lukewarmness censured, Rev. 3. 16.
Luz (Bethel), Gen. 28. 19.
Lycaonia, Acts 14. 6.
Lycia, Acts 27. 5.
Lydda, miracle at, Acts 9. 32.
Lydia, of Thyatira, Acts 16. 14, 40.
Lying, hateful to God, Prov. 6. 16, 19; 12. 22.
forbidden, Lev. 19. 11; Col. 3. 9.
devil father of, John 8. 44; Acts 5. 3.
Lysanias, Lk. 3. 1.
Lystra, miracle at, Acts 14. 8.
Paul and Barnabas taken for gods, Acts 14. 11.
Paul stoned at, Acts 14. 19.

MAACHAH, queen, her idolatry, 1 Ki. 15. 13; 2 Chr. 15. 16.
Macedonia, Paul's mission there, Acts 16. 9; 17.
liberality of, 2 Cor. 8; 9; 11. 9; Phil. 4. 15.
its churches, 1 & 2 Thes.
Machpelah, field of, Gen. 23.
patriarchs buried there, Gen. 23. 19; 25. 9; 35. 29; 49. 30; 50. 12.
Madness feigned by David, 1 Sam. 21. 13.
threatened, Deut. 28. 28.
Magicians of Egypt, Ex. 7. 11; 8. 19.
of Chaldea, preserved, Dan 2; 4. 7.
Magistrates, Ezra 7. 25; to be obeyed, Ex. 22. 8; Rom. 13; Tit. 3. 1; 1 Pet. 2. 14.
Mahanaim, Jacob's vision at, Gen. 32.
See 2 Sam. 2. 8; 17. 24.
Maher-Shalal-Hash-Baz, Is. 8. 1.
Mahlon and Chilion die in Moab, Ruth 1.
Maidservants, Ex. 20. 10; 21. 7; Deut. 15. 17.
Maimed healed by Christ, Matt. 15. 30.
animal, unfit for sacrifice, Lev. 22. 22.
Majesty of God, 1 Chr. 29. 11; Job 37. 22; Ps. 93; 96; Is. 24. 14; Nah. 1; Hab. 3. See *God*.
of Christ, 2 Pet. 1. 16. See *Christ*.
Makkedah, cave of, Josh. 10. 16.
Malachi complains of Israel's ingratitude, Mal. 1; 2.
foretells the coming of Messiah and his messenger, Mal. 3; 4.
Malchus wounded by Peter, John 18. 10; Matt. 26. 51; Mk. 14. 47.
healed by Jesus, Lk. 22. 51.
Male children, saved from Pharaoh, Ex. 1. 15.
Males to appear before the Lord three times a year, Ex. 23. 17; Deut. 16. 16.
Malefactors, execution of, Deut. 21. 22.
crucified with Christ, Lk. 23. 32.
Malice condemned, Prov. 17. 5; 24. 17; 1 Cor. 5. 8; 14. 20; Eph. 4. 31; Col. 3. 8; Tit. 3. 3; Jas. 5. 9; 1 Pet. 2. 1.
Mammon, worship of, Matt. 6. 24; Lk. 16. 9.
Mamre, Abram dwells there, Gen. 13. 18; 14; 18; 23. 17; 35. 27.

Man created, Gen. 1. 26; 2. 7.
his original dignity, Gen. 1. 27; 2. 25; Eccl 7. 29.
his fall, Gen. 3.
his iniquity, Gen. 6. 5, 12; 1 Ki. 8. 46; Jo. 14. 16; 15. 14; Ps. 14; 51; Eccl. 9. 3; Is. 43. 27; 53. 6; Jer. 3. 25; 17. 9; John 3. 19; Rom 3. 9; 5. 12; 7. 18; Gal. 3. 10; 5. 17; Jas. 1. 13 1 John 1. 8.
his weakness, etc., 2 Chr. 20. 12; Matt. 6. 27; Rom. 9. 16; 1 Cor. 3. 7; 2 Cor. 3. 5.
liable to suffering, Job 5. 7; 14. 1; Ps. 39. 4; Eccl. 3. 2; Acts 14. 22; Rom. 8. 22; Rev. 7. 14.
his ignorance, Job 8. 9; 11. 12; 28. 12; Prov. 16. 25; 27. 1; Eccl. 8. 17; Is. 59. 10; 1 Cor. 1. 20; 8. 2; (Is. 47. 10); Jas. 4. 14.
mortality of, Job 14; Ps. 39; 49; 62. 9; 78. 39; 89. 48; 103. 14; 144. 4; 146. 3; Eccl. 1. 4· 12. 7; Rom. 5. 12; Heb. 9. 27.
vanity of his life, Ps. 49; Eccl. 1. 2.
his whole duty, Eccl. 12. 13; Mic. 6. 8; 1 John 3. 23.
his redemption, Rom. 5; 1 Cor. 15. 49; Gal. 3; 4; Eph. 3; 5. 25; Phil. 3. 21; Col. 1; Heb. 1; 2; Rev. 5.
Manasseh, firstborn son of Joseph, Gen. 41. 51.
his blessing, Gen. 48.
his descendants numbered, etc., Num. 1. 34; 26. 29; Josh. 22. 1; 1 Chr. 5. 23; 7. 14; their inheritance, Num. 32. 33; 34. 14; Josh. 13. 29; 17.
incline to David's cause, 1 Chr. 9. 3; 12. 19; 2 Chr. 15. 9; 30. 11.
—king of Judah, his evil reign, 2 Ki. 21; 2 Chr. 33.
Mandrakes, Gen. 30. 14; Cant. 7. 13.
Maneh, a measure, Ezek. 45. 12.
Manger, Christ laid in, Lk. 2. 7.
Manifestation of Christ, Matt. 17; John 1. 14; 2. 11; 1 John 3. 5.
of God's righteousness, Rom. 3. 21; and love 1 John 4. 9.
of the sons of God, Rom. 8. 19.
of the spirit, 1 Cor. 12. 7.
Manna promised, Ex. 16. 4.
sent, Ex. 16. 14; Deut. 8. 3; Neh. 9. 20; Ps. 78. 24; John 6. 31.
an omer of, laid up in the ark, Ex. 16. 32; Heb. 9. 4.
Israelites murmur at, Num. 11. 6.
ceases on entering Canaan, Josh. 5. 12.
the hidden, Rev. 2. 17.
Manoah, father of Samson, Jud. 13; 16. 31.
Manslaughter, Gen. 9. 6; Ex. 21. 12; Num. 35. 6, 22; Deut. 19. 4; Josh. 20. 1; 1 Tim. 1. 9.
Mansteaxling, Ex. 21. 16; Deut. 24. 7.
Mara, Ruth 1. 20.
Marah, bitter waters healed there, Ex. 15. 23.
Maranatha, 1 Cor. 16. 22.
Marble, 1 Chr. 29. 2; Cant. 5. 15.
Mark, evangelist, Acts 12. 12.
goes with Paul and Barnabas, Acts 12. 25. 13. 5.
contention about, Acts 15. 37.
approved by Paul, 2 Tim. 4. 11.
Marriage instituted, Gen. 2. 18.
honourable, Ps. 128 Prov. 31. 10; Heb. 13. 4.
Christ's discourses about, Matt. 19; Mk. 10.
its obligations, Matt. 19. 4; Rom. 7. 2; 1 Cor. 6. 16; 7. 10; Eph. 5. 31.
parables concerning, Matt. 22; 25.
confined to this world, Matt. 22. 30; Mk. 12. 23.

Marriage—*Continued.*
Paul's opinion on, 1 Cor. 7 ; 1 Tim. 5. 14.
of the Lamb, typical, Rev. 19. 7.
unlawful marriages, Lev. 18 ; Deut. 7. 3 ;
  Josh. 23. 12 ; Ezra 9 ; Neh. 13. 23.
Martha instructed by Christ, John 11. 5, 21.
reproved by him, Lk. 10. 38.
Martyr, Stephen the first, Acts 7 ; 22. 20.
See Rev. 2. 13 ; 17. 6.
Mary, the Virgin, mother of Jesus, Gabriel
  sent to, Lk. 1. 26.
believes, and magnifies the Lord, Lk. 1. 38,
  46 ; John 2. 5.
Christ born of, Matt. 1. 18 ; Lk. 2.
present at the marriage at Cana, John 2. 1.
desires to speak with Christ, Matt. 12. 46 ;
  Mk. 3. 31 ; Lk. 8. 19.
commended to John by Christ at his crucifixion, Matt. 27. 56 ; John 19. 25.
—Magdalene, Lk. 8. 2.
at the cross, Matt. 27. 56 ; Mk. 15. 40 ; John
  19. 25.
Christ appears first to, Matt. 28. 1 ; Mk. 16.
  1 ; Lk. 24. 10 ; John 20. 1.
—sister of Lazarus, commended, Lk. 10. 42.
Christ's affection for, John 11. 5, 33.
anoints Christ's feet, John 12. 3 ; (head),
  Matt. 26. 6 ; Mk. 14. 3.
Massah, Israel's rebellion at, Ex. 17. 7 ; Deut.
  9. 22 ; 33. 8.
Masters, duty of, Ex. 20. 10 ; Lev. 19. 13 ; 25.
  40 ; Deut. 24. 14 ; Job 31. 13 ; Jer. 22. 13 ;
  Eph. 6. 9 ; Col. 4. 1 ; Jas. 5. 4.
Mattan, priest of Baal, slain, 2 Ki. 11. 18 ;
  2 Chr. 23. 17.
Matthew (Levi), apostle, called, Matt. 9. 9 ;
  Mk. 2. 14 ; Lk. 5. 27.
sent out, Matt. 10. 3 ; Mk. 3. 18 ; Lk. 6. 15 ;—
  Acts 1. 13.
Matthias, chosen apostle, Acts 1. 26.
Mazzaroth, Job 38. 32.
Measures of quantity :—Log, Lev. 14. 10, 15,
  21. Cab, 2 Ki. 6. 25. Omer, Ex. 16. 36 ; Lev.
  5. 11 ; 14. 10. Hin, Ex. 29. 40. Bath or
  ephah, Is. 5. 10 ; Ezek. 45. 11. Homer, Is.
  5. 10 ; Ezek. 45. 14. Firkin, John 2. 6.
of length :—handbreadth, Ex. 25. 25 ; Ps. 39.
  5. Span, Ex. 28. 16 ; 1 Sam. 17. 4. Cubit,
  Gen. 6. 15, 16 ; Deut. 3. 11. Fathom, Acts
  27. 28. Furlong, Lk. 24. 13 ; John 11. 18.
  Mile, Matt. 5. 41.
Measuring of the holy city, and new Jerusalem, Ezek. 40 ; Zech. 2. 1 ; Rev. 11. 1 ; 21. 15.
Meat-Offering, Lev. 2 ; 3 ; 6. 14 ; Num. 15 ; Neh.
  10. 33.
Meats, clean and unclean, Lev. 11 ; Deut. 14 ;
  Acts 15. 29 ; Rom. 14 ; 1 Cor. 8. 4 ; Col. 2.
  16 ; 1 Tim. 4. 3.
Medad prophesies, Num. 11. 26.
Meddling censured, 2 Ki. 14. 10 ; Prov. 20. 3 ;
  24. 21 ; 26. 17.
Medes capture Babylon (Is. 21. 2); Dan. 5. 28, 31.
  11 ; Est. 1.
prophecy concerning, Dan. 8. 20.
Mediator, one, Gal. 3. 19, 20 ; 1 Tim. 2. 5 ; Heb.
  8. 6 ; 9. 15 ; 12. 24.
Medicine, typical, Prov. 17. 22 ; Jer. 8. 22 ; 30.
  13 ; 46. 11 ; Ezek. 47. 12.
Meditation encouraged, Ps. 1. 2 ; 19. 14 ; 77. 12 ;
  107. 43 ; 119. 97.
exhortations to, Josh. 1. 8 ; Ps. 4. 4 ; Prov. 4.
  26 ; 1 Tim. 4. 15.
See Gen. 24. 63.

Meekness, Christ an example of, Matt. 11. 29 ;
  Lk. 23. 34 ; 2 Cor. 10. 1 ; (Is. 53. 2 ; John 18. 19).
exhortations to, Zeph. 2. 3 ; Gal. 5. 23 ; 6. 1 ;
  Eph. 4. 2 ; Phil. 2. 2 ; Col. 3. 12 ; 1 Tim. 6.
  11 ; 2 Tim. 2. 25 ; Tit. 3. 2 ; Jas. 1. 21 ; 3. 13 ;
  1 Pet. 3. 4, 15.
blessed of God, Ps. 22. 26 ; 25. 9 ; 37. 11 ;
  (Matt. 5. 5) ; 69. 32 ; 76. 9 ; 147. 6 ; 149. 4 ; Is.
  11. 4 ; 29. 19 ; 61. 1.
of Moses, Num. 12. 3. David, 2 Sam. 16. 9.
  Jeremiah, Jer. 26. 14.
Megiddo, Josh. 17. 11 ; Jud. 1. 27 ; 5. 19.
Ahaziah, 2 Ki. 9. 27, and Josiah slain there,
  2 Ki. 23. 29 ; Zech. 12. 11.
Melchizedek, king of Salem, blesses Abram,
  Gen. 14. 18.
his priesthood above Aaron's, Ps. 110. 4 ;
  Heb. 5. 6, 10 ; 6. 20 ; 7. 1.
Melita, Paul shipwrecked near, Acts 28. 1.
shakes off the viper at, Acts 28. 5.
Melzar favours Daniel, Dan. 1. 11.
Members of the body, types of the Church,
  Rom. 12. 4 ; 1 Cor. 12. 12 ; Eph. 4. 25.
Memorials ordained, Ex. 17. 14 ; 28. 12 ; 30. 16 ;
  Num. 16. 40.
offerings of, Lev. 2. 2 ; Num. 5. 15.
Memory of the just, blessed, Prov. 10. 7.
of the wicked, cut off, Ps. 109. 15 ; Is. 26. 14.
Memphis, in Egypt, Hos. 9. 6.
Menahem, king of Israel, his evil reign, 2 Ki.
  15. 14, 18.
Mene, Mene, Tekel, Upharsin, Dan. 5. 25-28.
Mephibosheth, son of Jonathan, his lameness,
  2 Sam. 4. 4.
David's kindness to, 2 Sam. 9. 1.
slandered by Ziba, 2 Sam. 16. 1 ; 19. 24.
spared by David 2 Sam. 21. 7.
Merab, Saul's daughter, 1 Sam. 14. 49 ; 18. 17.
her five sons hanged by the Gibeonites,
  2 Sam. 21. 8.
Merarites, descendants of Levi, Ex. 6. 19 ;
  1 Chr. 6. 1 ; 23. 21 ; 24. 26.
their duties and dwellings, Num. 4. 29 ; 7. 8 ;
  10. 17 ; Josh. 21. 7 ; 1 Chr. 6. 63.
Merchants, Gen. 37. 25 ; 1 Ki. 10. 15 ; Neh. 13.
  20 ; Is. 23. 8 ; Ezek. 27.
parable of one seeking pearls, Matt. 13. 45.
Merciful, blessed, Prov. 11. 17 ; Matt. 5. 7.
Mercurius, Paul so called, Acts 14. 12.
Mercy, supplication for, Deut. 21. 8 ; 1 Ki. 8.
  30 ; Neh. 9. 32 ; Ps. 51 ; Dan. 9. 16 ; Hab. 3.
  2 ; Matt. 6. 12.
of God, Ps. 78. 38 ; 103. 9 ; Is. 30. 18 ; 54. 7 ;
  Lam. 3. 32.
exhortations to shew, Prov. 3. 3 ; Zech. 7. 9 ;
  Lk. 6. 36 ; Rom. 12. 19 ; (Prov. 25. 21) ; Phil.
  2. 1 ; Col. 3. 12 ; Jas. 2. 13.
Mercy-Seat described, Ex. 25. 17 ; 26. 34 ; 37. 6 ;
  Lev. 16. 13 ; 1 Chr. 28. 11 ; Heb. 9. 5.
Meribah, Israel's rebellion there, Ex. 17. 7 ;
  Num. 20. 13 ; 27. 14 ; Deut. 32. 51 ; 33. 8 ; Ps.
  81. 7.
Merodach-(or Berodach) Baladan, his embassy
  to Hezekiah, 2 Ki. 20. 12 ; 2 Chr. 32. 31 ; Is.
  39 ;—Jer. 50. 2.
Merom, waters of, Josh. 11. 5.
Meroz cursed, Jud. 5. 23.
Meshach. See *Shadrach.*
Meshech, son of Japheth, Gen. 10. 2.
traders of, Ezek. 27. 13 ; 32. 26 ; 38. 2 ; 39. 1.
Mesopotamia (Ur), Abram leaves, Gen. 11. 31 ;
  12. 1 ; 24. 4, 10.
See Acts 2. 9 ; 7. 2.
king of, slain by Othniel, Jud. 3. 8.

Messenger of the covenant, Mal. 3. 1 ; Is. 42. 19.

Messiah, the prince, foretold, Dan. 9. 25.
 (Messias), John 1. 41 ; 4. 25.
 See Is. 9. 6.

Methuselah's great age, Gen. 5. 27.

Micah makes and worships idols, Jud. 17 ; 18.
—prophet (Jer. 26. 18) ; denounces Israel's sin,
 Mic. 1-3 ; 6 ; 7.
 predicts Messiah's coming, Mic. 4 ; 5 ; 7.

Micaiah forewarns Ahab, 1 Ki. 22 ; 2 Chr. 18.

Mice, golden, 1 Sam. 6. 11.

Michael, Dan. 10. 13, 21 ; 12. 1.
 Archangel, Jude 9 ; Rev. 12. 7.

Michal, Saul's daughter, 1 Sam. 14. 49.
 becomes David's wife, 1 Sam. 18. 20.
 given to another, 1 Sam. 25. 44.
 restored to David, 2 Sam. 3. 13.
 rebuked for mocking his religious dancing,
 2 Sam. 6. 16, 20 ; 1 Chr. 15. 29.

Midian, sons of, Gen. 25. 4.
—land of, Ex. 2. 15.
 See 1 Ki. 11. 18 ; Is. 60. 6 ; Hab. 3. 7.

Midianites, their cities destroyed by Moses,
 Num. 31. 1.
 subdued by Gideon, Jud. 6-8.
 See Ps. 83. 9 ; Is. 9. 4 ; 10. 26.

Midnight, Egyptians smitten at, Ex. 12. 29.
 prayer made at, Ps. 119. 62 ; Acts 16. 25 ; 20. 7.
 See Matt. 25. 6 ; Mk. 13. 35.

Midwives of Egypt, Ex. 1. 16, 20.

Mighty men, 2 Sam. 23. 8 ; 1 Chr. 11. 10.

Milcah, Gen. 11. 29 ; 22. 20.

Milcom, false god, 1 Ki. 11. 5, 33 ; 2 Ki. 23. 13.

Miletus, Paul takes leave of elders at, Acts
 20. 15.
 Trophimus left at, 2 Tim. 4. 20.

Milk (and honey), Josh. 5. 6 ; Is. 55. 1.
 mentioned, Cant. 4. 11 ; Is. 7. 22 ; 1 Cor. 3. 2 ;
 Heb. 5. 12 ; 1 Pet. 2. 2.

Mill, women at, Matt. 24. 41.

Millo, house of, Jud. 9. 6.

Millstones, Ex. 11. 5 ; Matt. 24. 41 ; Rev 18. 21.

Mind, devoted to God, Matt. 22. 37 ; Mk. 12. 30 ;
 Rom. 7. 25.
 willingness of, 1 Chr. 28. 9; Neh. 4. 6; 2 Cor. 8. 12.
 united, 1 Cor. 1. 10 ; 2 Cor. 13. 11 ; Phil. 2. 2 ;
 1 Pet. 3. 8.
 See Heb. 8. 10.

Ministering Spirits, Heb. 1. 14.
 See Rom. 15. 25, 27.

Ministers, God's, Ps. 103. 21 ; 104. 4 ; Heb. 1. 7
 (priests), Ex. 28 ; Heb. 10. 11.
 to be honoured, etc., 1 Thes. 5. 12, 13 ; 1 Tim.
 5. 17 ; Heb. 13. 17.
 Christ's, 1 Cor. 3. 5 ; 4. 1 ; 2 Cor. 3. 6 ; 6 ; Eph.
 3. 7 ; 6. 21.
 their qualifications, 1 Tim. 3 ; Tit. 1 ; 1 Pet. 5.

Ministry of the Gospel, Acts 6. 4 ; 20. 24 ; Rom.
 12. 7 ; 1 Cor. 16. 15 ; 2 Cor. 4. 1 ; 5. 18 ; Eph.
 6. 21 ; Col. 1. 7 ; 4. 17 ; 1 Tim. 1. 12.

Miracles performed by Moses and Aaron at
 God's command, Ex. 4. 3 ; 7. 10 ; 7-12 ; 14.
 21 ; 15. 25 ; 17. 6 ; Num. 16. 28 ; 20. 11 ; 21. 8 ;
 by Joshua, Josh. 3 ; 4 ; 6 ; 10. 12 ; by Samson, Jud. 14-16 ; by Samuel, 1 Sam. 12. 18 ;
 by a prophet, 1 Ki. 13. 4 ; by Elijah, 1 Ki.
 17 ; 18 ; 2 Ki. 1 ; by Elisha, 2 Ki. 2-6 ; 13.
 21 ; by Isaiah, 2 Ki. 20. 9 ; by the disciples,
 Lk. 10. 17 ; by Peter, Acts 3 ; 5 ; 9. 32 ; by
 Stephen, Acts 6. 8 ; by Philip, Acts 8. 6 ;
 by Paul, Acts 13 ; 14 ; 16 ; 19 ; 20 ; 28 ; by
 sorcerers and evil spirits, Ex. 7. 11 ; 8. 7 ;
 Matt. 24. 24 ; 2 Thes. 2. 9 ; Rev. 13. 14 ; 16.
 14 ; 19. 20. See Christ.

Miriam, sister of Moses and Aaron, Ex. 15. 20 ;
 Num. 26. 59.
 her song, Ex. 15. 20.
 her sedition against Moses, Num. 12. 1, 2.
 is smitten with leprosy, Num. 12. 10, 15.
 her death, Num. 20. 1.

Mirth, vanity of, Eccl. 2 ; 7. 4.
 See Jer. 7. 34 ; 16. 9 ; Hos. 2. 11.

Mischief, punishment of, Ps. 7. 14 ; 9. 15 ; 140.
 2 ; Prov. 26. 27 ; Is. 33. 1 ; Acts 13. 10.

Mites, the widow's, Mk. 12. 42 ; Lk. 21. 2.

Mitre of the high priest, Ex. 28. 4, 29. 6 ; 39. 28.

Mizpah (Mizpeh), Jacob and Laban meet at,
 Gen. 31. 49.
 Israelites assemble there, Jud. 10. 17 ; 11. 11 ;
 20. 1 ; 1 Sam. 7. 5 ; 10. 17.
—(Moab), 1 Sam. 22. 3.

Mnason, an old disciple, Acts 21. 16.

Moab, Gen. 19. 37 ; his descendants, and terri-
 tory, Deut. 2. 9, 18 ; 34. 5.

Moabites excluded from the congregation,
 Deut. 23. 3.
 subdued by Ehud, Jud. 3. 12 ; by David, 2
 Sam. 8. 2 ; by Jehoshaphat and Jehoram,
 2 Ki. 1. 1 ; 3.
 their destruction, 2 Chr. 20. 23.
 prophecies concerning, Ex. 15. 15 ; Num. 21.
 29 ; 24. 17 ; Ps. 60. 8 ; 83. 6 ; Is. 11. 14 ; 15 ;
 16 ; 25. 10 ; Jer. 9. 26 ; 25. 21 ; 48 ; Ezek. 25.
 8 ; Amos 2. 1 ; Zeph. 2. 8.

Mocking censured, Prov. 17. 5 · 30. 17 ; Jer. 15.
 17 ; Jude 18.
 punished, Gen. 21. 9 ; 2 Ki. 2. 23.
 See 2 Chr. 30. 10 ; 36. 16.
 (of Christ), Matt. 27. 29 ; Lk. 23. 11.

Moderation, 1 Cor. 7. 29 ; Phil. 4. 5.

Modest apparel, 1 Tim. 2. 9 ; 1 Pet. 3. 3.

Moloch (Molech), Lev 18. 21 ; 20. 2.
 worship of, 1 Ki. 11. 7 ; 2 Ki 23. 10 ; Jer. 32.
 35 ; Amos 5. 26 ; Acts 7 43.

Money, Gen. 17. 27 ; 23. 9 ; 42. 25 ; Jer. 32 . 9.
 Mk. 12. 41 , 14. 11.
 love of, censured, 1 Tim. 6. 10.

Months of the Hebrews, Ex. 12. 2 ; 13. 4 . Deut.
 16. 1 ; 1 Ki. 6. 1 ; 8. 2.
 of the Chaldeans, Neh. 1. 1 ; 2. 1.

Moon (the lesser light), Gen. 1. 16.
 referred to, Deut. 33. 14 ; Josh. 10. 12 ; Ps. 8.
 3 , 89. 37 ; 104. 19 ; 121. 6.
 idolatrously worshipped. Deut. 17. 3 ; Job 31.
 26 , Jer. 44. 17.
 feasts of the new, 1 Sam. 20. 5 ; 1 Chr. 23. 31 ;
 Ps. 81. 3 ; Is. 1. 13 ; Hos. 2. 11.

Mordecai discovers conspiracy against Ahasuerus, Est. 2. 21.
 excites Haman's enmity, Est 3. 5.
 his appeal to Esther, Est. 4.
 honoured by the king, Est. 6.
 his advancement, Est. 8. 9 ; 10 . (Ezra 2. 2;
 Neh. 7. 7).

Moriah, mount, Gen. 22.
 David's sacrifice there, 2 Sam. 24. 18 ; 1 Cor.
 21. 18 ; 22. 1.
 site of the temple, 2 Chr. 3. 1.

Mortality of man, Job 19. 26 ; Rom. 8. 11 ; 1 Cor.
 15. 53 ; 2 Cor. 4. 11 ; 5. 4.

Mortgages mentioned, Neh. 5. 3.

Moses, his birth and preservation, Ex. 2 ; (Acts
 7. 20 ; Heb. 11. 23).
 escapes to Midian, Ex. 2. 15.
 called by the Lord, Ex. 3 ; signs shown to
 Ex. 4.
 returns to Egypt, Ex. 4. 20.
 intercedes with Pharaoh for Israel, Ex. 5-12.

Moses—*Continued.*
leads Israel forth from Egypt, Ex. 14.
meets God in mount Sinai, Ex. 19. 3; (24. 18).
delivers the law to the people, Ex. 19. 25; 20-23; 34. 10; 35. 1; Lev. 1; Num. 5; 6; 15; 27-30; 36; Deut. 13-26.
instructed to build the tabernacle, Ex. 25-31; 35; 40; Num. 4; 8; 9; 10; 18; 19.
his anger at Israel's idolatry, Ex. 32. 19.
his intercession, Ex. 32. 11; (33. 12).
again meets God in the mount, Ex. 34. 2.
skin of his face shines, Ex. 34. 29; (2 Cor. 3. 7, 13).
consecrates Aaron, Lev. 8; 9.
numbers the people, Num. 1; 26.
sends out the spies to Canaan, Num. 13.
intercedes for the people, Num. 14. 13.
Korah's rebellion against, Num. 16.
for his unbelief not permitted to enter Canaan, Num. 20. 12; 27. 12; Deut. 1. 35; 3. 23.
leads Israel in the wilderness, Num. 20; 21.
makes the brazen serpent, Num. 21. 9; (John 3. 14).
recounts Israel's history, etc., Deut. 1; 3-12; 27-31.
his charge to Joshua, Deut. 3. 28; 31. 7, 23.
his death, Deut. 34. 5; his body, Jude 9.
seen at Christ's transfiguration, Matt. 17. 3; Mk. 9. 4; Lk. 9. 30.
his meekness, Num. 12. 3; dignity, Deut. 34. 10; faithfulness, Num. 12. 7; Heb. 3. 2.
Moth mentioned, Job 27. 18; Ps. 39. 11; Is. 50. 9; Hos. 5. 12; Matt. 6. 19.
Mother of all living, Eve, Gen. 3. 20.
Mothers, love of, Is. 49. 15; 66. 13.
examples of, Gen. 21. 10; Ex. 2; 1 Sam. 1. 22; 1 Ki. 3. 26; 2 Tim. 1. 5; 2 John.
duty towards, Ex. 20. 12; Prov. 1. 8; 19. 26; 23. 22; Eph. 6. 1.
Mourners, comfort for, Job 29. 25; Rom. 12. 15; 2 Cor. 1. 4; 1 Thes. 4. 18.
Mourning, when blessed, Eccl. 7. 2; Matt. 5. 4, Lk. 6. 21.
for the dead, Gen. 50. 3; Num. 20. 29; Deut. 14. 1; 2 Sam. 1. 17; 3. 31; 12. 16; 18. 33; 19. 1; Eccl. 12. 5; Jer. 6. 26; 9. 17; 22. 18.
of the priests, Lev. 21. 1; Ezek. 44. 25.
Mouth of God, Deut. 8. 3; Matt. 4. 4.
of babes, Ps. 8. 2; Matt. 21. 16.
of fools, Prov. 14. 3; 15. 2; 18. 7; 26. 7.
of the righteous, etc., Ps. 37. 30; Prov. 10. 31; Eccl. 10. 12.
of the wicked, Ps. 32. 9; 63. 11; 107. 42; 109. 2, 144. 8; Prov. 4. 24; 5. 3; 6. 12; 19. 28; Rom. 3. 14; Rev 13. 5.
Mulberry Trees, 2 Sam. 5. 23.
Murder forbidden, Gen. 9. 6; Ex. 20. 13; Lev. 24. 17; Deut. 5. 17; 21. 9; Matt. 5. 21; 1 John 3. 15.
examples:—Gen. 4; Jud. 9; 2 Sam. 3. 27; 4; 12. 9; 20. 8, 1 Ki. 16. 9; 21; 2 Ki. 15. 10; 21. 23; 2 Chr. 24. 21.
its penalty, Gen. 4. 12; 9. 6; Num. 35. 30; Jer. 19. 4; Ezek. 16. 38; Gal. 5. 21; Rev. 22. 15.
source of, Matt. 15. 19; Gal. 5. 21.
Murmuring rebuked, Lam. 3. 39; 1 Cor. 10. 10; Phil. 2. 14; Jude 16.
of Israel, Ex. 15. 23; 16; 17; Num. 11; 16; 20; 21.
Murrain, plague of, Ex. 9. 3; Ps. 78. 50.
Music, invention of, Gen. 4. 21.
soothes Saul, 1 Sam. 16. 14.

Music—*Continued.*
used in worship, 2 Sam. 6. 5; 1 Chr. 15. 28; 16. 42; 2 Chr. 7. 6; 29. 25; Ps. 33; 81; 92; 108; 150; Dan. 3. 5.
at festivities, Is. 5. 12; 14. 11; Amos 6. 5; Lk. 15. 25; 1 Cor. 14. 7.
in heaven, Rev. 5. 8; 14. 2.
Mustard Seed, parable of, Matt. 13. 31; Mk. 4. 30; Lk. 13. 18.
Muzzling the ox, law concerning, Deut. 25. 4; 1 Cor. 9. 9; 1 Tim. 5. 18.
Myrrh, Ex. 30. 23; Est. 2. 12; Ps. 45. 8; Cant. 1. 13; Matt. 2. 11; Mk. 15. 23; John 19. 39.
Myrtles, Is. 41. 19; 55. 13.
vision of, Zech. 1. 8.
Mystery of the kingdom of God made known by Christ, Mk. 4. 11; Eph. 1. 9; 3. 3; 1 Tim. 3. 16; by the disciples to the world, 1 Cor. 4. 1; 13. 2; Eph. 6. 19; Col. 2. 2.
of iniquity, 2 Thes. 2. 7; Rev. 17. 5.
See 1 Cor. 15. 51.

NAAMAN, the Syrian, his leprosy healed, 2 Ki. 5.
See Lk. 4. 27.
Nabal, his conduct towards David, 1 Sam. 25. 10.
Abigail's intercession for, 1 Sam. 25. 18.
his death, 1 Sam 25. 38.
Naboth slain by Jezebel, 1 Ki. 21.
his murder avenged, 2 Ki. 9. 21.
Nadab, son of Aaron, his trespass and death, Lev. 10.
—king of Israel, slain by Baasha, 1 Ki. 14. 20; 15. 25.
Nahash, the Ammonite, subdued by Saul, 1 Sam. 11.
Nahor, Abram's brother, Gen. 11. 26; 22. 20; 24. 10.
Nahum, vision of, Nah. 1-3.
Nails, figuratively mentioned, Ezra 9. 8; Eccl. 12. 11; Is. 22. 23.
Nain, miracle at, Lk. 7. 11.
Name of God, Ex. 34. 5, 14.
See Ex. 6. 3; 15. 3; Ps. 83. 18.
to be reverenced, Ex. 20. 7; Deut. 5. 11; 28. 58; Ps. 34. 3; 72. 17; 111. 9; Mic. 4. 5; 1 Tim. 6. 1.
—of Christ, prayer in, John 14. 13; 16. 23; Rom. 1. 8; Eph. 5. 20; Col. 3. 17; Heb. 13. 15.
miracles performed in, Acts 3. 6; 4. 10; 19. 13.
to be honoured, 2 Tim. 2. 19.
Name given to children at circumcision, Lk. 1. 59; 2. 21.
—value of a good, Prov. 22. 1; Eccl. 7. 1.
Names changed by God, Gen. 17. 5, 15; 32. 27; 2 Sam. 12. 25; by man, Dan. 1. 7; by Christ, Mk. 3. 16, 17.
Naomi's (and Ruth's) history, Ruth 1-4.
Naphtali, son of Jacob, Gen. 30. 8; 35. 25; 46. 24; 49. 21; Deut. 33. 23.
—tribe of, numbered, etc., Num. 1. 42; 10. 27; 13. 14; 26. 48; Jud. 1. 33.
subdue the Canaanites, Jud. 4. 10; 5. 18; 6. 35; 7. 23.
carried captive, 2 Ki. 15. 29.
See Is. 9. 1; Matt. 4. 13.
Narcissus, household of, Rom. 16. 11.
Nathan, the prophet, 2 Sam. 7.
his parable condemning David, 2 Sam. 12. 1.
anoints Solomon king, etc., 1 Ki. 1. 34; 1 Chr. 29. 29; 2 Chr. 9. 29.
—son of David, 2 Sam. 5. 14; Zech. 12. 12; Lk. 3. 31.
Nathanael commended, John 1. 45; 21. 2.

Navy of Solomon, 1 Ki. 9. 26 ; 2 Chr. 8. 17.
of Jehoshaphat, 1 Ki. 22. 48.

Nazareth, Jesus of, Matt. 2. 23 ; 21. 11 ; Lk. 1. 26 ; 2. 39, 51 ; 4. 16 ; John 1. 45 ; 18. 5 ; Acts 2. 22 ; 3. 6.

Nazarites, law of the, Num. 6.

Nebuchadnezzar, king of Babylon, Jer. 20 ; 21 ; 25 ; 27 ; 28 ; 32 ; 34 ; Ezek. 26. 7 ; 29. 19.
captures Jerusalem, 2 Ki. 24 ; 25 , 2 Chr. 36 ; Jer. 37-39 ; 52 ; Dan. 1. 1.
his dreams, Dan. 2 ; 4.
sets up the golden image, Dan. 3.
his degradation, Dan. 4. 33.
his restoration and confession, Dan. 4. 34.

Nebuzar-Adan, captain of the Chaldeans, 2 Ki. 25. 8.
his kindness to Jeremiah, Jer. 39. 11 ; 40. 1.

Necessities, Paul's, 2 Cor. 6. 4 ; 12. 10.

Nehemiah, his grief and prayer for Jerusalem, Neh. 1 ; his visit to, Neh. 2. 9 ; his conduct at, Neh. 4-6 ; 8-10 ; 13.

Nehushtan (the brazen serpent) destroyed by Hezekiah, 2 Ki. 18. 4.

Neighbour, duty towards one's, Ex. 20. 16 ; 22. 26 ; Lev. 19. 18 ; Deut. 15. 2 ; 27. 17 ; Prov. 3. 28 ; 24. 28 ; 25. 8, 17 ; Mk. 12. 31 ; Rom. 13. 9 ; Gal. 5. 14 ; Jas. 2. 8.

Net, parable of, Matt. 13. 47.

Nethinims, the, 1 Chr. 9. 2 ; Ezra 2. 43 ; 7. 7, 24 ; 8. 17.

New Birth, John 3. 3, 6 ; 1 Pet. 1. 23.

Nicanor, one of the seven deacons, Acts 6. 5.

Nicodemus visits Jesus by night, John 3. 1.
defends him before the Pharisees, John 7. 50.
assists at Christ's burial, John 19. 39.

Nicolaitanes, their doctrines condemned, Rev. 2. 6, 15.

Night appointed, Gen. 1. 5 ; (Ps. 19. 2).
figurative, John 9. 4 ; Rom. 13. 12 ; 1 Thes. 5. 5.
none in heaven, Rev. 21. 25 ; (Is. 60. 20).

Nimrod, mighty hunter, Gen. 10. 9.

Nineveh, Jonah's mission to, Jon. 1. 1 ; 3. 2.
repenting, is spared by God, Jon. 3. 5-10 ; (Matt. 12. 41 ; Lk. 11. 32).
the burden of, Nah. 1. 1 ; 2 ; 3.

Nisan, month, Neh. 2. 1 ; Est. 3. 7.

Nisroch, god of Assyria, 2 Ki. 19. 37 ; Is. 37. 38.

No, prophecy concerning, Jer. 46. 25 ; Ezek. 30. 14 ; Nah. 3. 8.

Noah, son of Lamech, Gen. 5. 29.
finds grace with God, Gen. 6. 8.
builds the ark, Gen. 6. 14.
enters it, Gen. 7 ; goes forth from, Gen. 8. 18.
God blesses and makes a covenant with, Gen. 9. 1, 8.
is drunken, etc., Gen. 9. 20.
his death, Gen. 9. 29.

Nob, city of David comes to, 1-Sam. 21. 1.
smitten by Saul, 1 Sam. 22. 19.

Noph, city, warned, Is. 19. 13 ; Jer. 2. 16 ; 46. 14 ; Ezek. 30. 13.

North and South, conflicts of, Dan. 11.

Numbering of the people, by Moses, Num. 1 ; 26 ; by David, 2 Sam. 24 ; 1 Chr. 21.
of the Levites, Num. 3. 14 ; 4. 34.

Nurses, Gen. 35. 8 ; 2 Sam. 4. 4 ; 1 Thes. 2. 7.

Nursing fathers and nursing mothers (kings and queens), Is. 49. 23.

OATH, God ratifies his purpose by, Ps. 132. 11 ; Lk. 1. 73 ; Acts 2. 30 ; Heb. 6. 17.

Oaths, laws about, Lev. 5. 4 ; 6. 3 ; 19. 12 ; Num. 30. 2 ; Ps. 15. 4, Matt. 5. 33 ; Jas. 5. 12.

Oaths—*Continued.*
demanded, Ex. 22. 11 ; Num. 5. 21 ; 1 Ki. 8. 31 ; Ezra 10. 5.
examples of, Gen. 14. 22 ; 21. 31 ; 24. 2 : Josh. 14. 9 ; 1 Sam. 20. 42 ; 28. 10 ; Ps. 132. 2.
rash :—of Esau, Gen. 25. 33 ; of Israel, to the Gibeonites, Josh. 9 19 ; of Jephthah, Jud. 11. 30 ; of Saul at Beth-aven, 1 Sam. 14. 24 ; of Herod to Herodias' daughter, Matt. 14. 7, of the forty Jews, Acts 23. 12, 21.

Obadiah, sent by Ahab to find water, 1 Ki. 18. 3 ; meets Elijah, 1 Ki. 18. 7.
how he hid a hundred prophets 1 Ki. 18. 4, 13.
—prophet, his prediction, Obad. 17.

Obed, son of Boaz, Ruth 4. 17.

Obed-Edom, blessed while keeping the ark, 2 Sam. 6. 10 ; 1 Chr. 13. 14 ; 15. 18, 24 ; 16. 5.
his sons, 1 Chr. 26. 4, 5.

Obedience to God enjoined, Ex. 19. 5 ; 23. 21 ; Lev. 26. 3 ; Deut. 4-8, 11, 29 ; Is. 1. 11 ; Jer. 7. 23 ; 26. 13 ; 38. 20, Acts 5. 29 ; Jas. 1. 25.
its blessings, Ex. 23. 22 ; Deut. 28 ; 30 ; Prov. 25. 12 ; Is. 1. 19 ; Heb. 11. 8 ; 1 Pet. 1. 22 ; Rev. 22. 14.
preferred before sacrifice, 1 Sam. 15. 22 ; Ps. 50. 8 ; Mic. 6. 6.
of Christ, Rom. 5. 19 ; Phil. 2. 8 ; Heb. 5. 8.
of the faith, Rom. 1. 5 ; 16. 26 ; 2 Cor. 7. 15 ; 1 Pet. 1. 2.
due to parents, Eph. 6. 1 ; Col. 3. 20.
to masters, Eph. 6. 5 ; Col. 3. 22 ; Tit. 2. 9.
of wives to husbands, Tit. 2. 5.
to rulers, Tit. 3. 1 ; Heb. 13. 17.

Oblations, Lev. 2 ; 3.
of the spoil, Num. 31. 28.

Oded, prophet, 2 Chr. 28. 9.

Offences to be avoided, Matt. 18. 7 ; 1 Cor. 10. 32 ; 2 Cor. 6. 3 ; Phil. 1. 10.
how to remedy, Eccl. 10. 4 ; Matt. 5. 29 ; 18. 8 ; Mk. 9. 43 ; Rom. 16. 17.
Christ delivered for our, Rom. 4. 25.

Offerings, laws for, Lev. 1 ; 22. 21 ; Deut. 15. 21 ; Mal. 1. 13.
types of Christ, Heb. 9. 14, 28 ; 10. 10.

Og, king of Bashan, Num. 21. 33 ; Deut. 3. 1 ; Ps. 135. 11 ; 136. 20.

Oil for the lamps, Ex. 27. 20 ; Lev. 24. 1.
for anointing, Ex. 30. 31 ; 37. 29.
used in meat offerings, Lev. 2. 1.
miraculously increased, 1 Ki. 17. 12 ; 2 Ki. 4. 1.
figurative, Ps. 23. 5 ; 141. 5 ; Is. 61. 3 ; Zech. 4. 12 ; Matt. 25. 1.

Ointment, Christ anointed with, Matt. 26. 7 ; Mk. 14. 3 ; Lk. 7. 37 ; John 11. 2 ; 12. 3.

Old age, Job 30. 2 ; Ps. 90. 10 ; Eccl. 12 ; Tit. 2. 2.
reverence due to, Lev. 19. 32 ; Prov. 23. 22 ; 1 Tim. 5. 1.

Old man, to put off, Rom. 6. 6 ; Eph. 4. 22 ; Col. 3. 9.

Olive trees, vision of, Zech. 4. 3 ; Rev. 11. 4.
See Jud. 9. 9 ; Ps. 52. 8 ; Rom. 11. 17.

Olivet (Olives), mount, 2 Sam. 15. 30 ; Matt. 21. 1 ; 24. 3 ; Mk. 11. 1 ; 13. 3 ; Lk. 21. 37 ; John 8. 1 ; Acts 1. 12.

Omega, Rev. 1. 8, 11 ; 21. 6 ; 22. 13.

Omri, king of Israel, 1 Ki. 16. 16, 23 ; Mic. 6. 16.

Onesimus, Col. 4. 9 ; Philem. 10.

Onesiphorus, 2 Tim. 1. 16.

Onyx, Ex. 28. 20 ; 39. 13.

Ophir, Gen. 10. 29.
gold of, 1 Ki. 9. 28 ; 10. 11 ; 22. 48 ; 1 Chr. 29. 4 ; 2 Chr. 8. 18 ; Job 22. 24 ; Ps. 45. 9 ; Is. 13. 12.

Oppression forbidden and threatened, Ex. 22. 21; Lev. 25. 14; Deut. 23. 16; 24. 14; Ps. 12. 5; 62. 10; Prov. 14. 31; 22. 16; Eccl. 4. 1; 5. 8; Is. 1. 17; 10; 58. 6; Jer. 22. 17; Ezek. 22. 7; Amos 4. 1; 8. 4; Mic. 2. 2; Mal. 3. 5; Jas. 4.

Oracle of the temple, 1 Ki. 6. 16; 8. 6; 2 Chr. 4. 20; Ps. 28. 2.

of God, 2 Sam. 16. 23.

Oracles (the Holy Scriptures), Acts 7. 38; Rom. 3. 2; Heb. 5. 12; 1 Pet. 4. 11.

Order necessary in the churches, 1 Cor. 14. 40; Tit. 1. 5.

Ordination, mode and use of, Acts 6. 6; 14. 23; 1 Tim. 2. 7; 3; 4. 14; 5. 22; 2 Tim. 2. 2; Tit. 1. 5.

Ornaments, of apparel, etc., Gen. 24. 22; Prov. 1. 9; 4. 9; 25. 12; Is. 3. 18; Jer. 2. 32; 1 Pet. 3. 3.

Ostentation condemned, Prov. 25. 14; 27. 2; Matt. 6. 1.

Ostrich, Job 39. 13; Lam. 4. 3.

Othniel, Josh. 15. 17; Jud. 1. 13; 3. 9.

Outcasts of Israel, promised restoration, Is. 11. 12; 16. 3; 27. 13; Jer. 30. 17; Rom. 11.

Overcoming, glory and reward of, 1 John 2. 13; Rev. 2. 7, 11, 17, 26; 3. 5, 12, 21; 21. 7.

Overseers in building the temple, 1 Chr. 9. 29; 2 Chr. 2. 18.

Ox, treatment of, Ex. 21. 28; 22. 1; 23. 4; Lev. 17. 3; Deut. 5. 14; 22. 1; Lk. 13. 15.

not to be muzzled when treading out the corn, Deut. 25. 4; 1 Cor. 9. 9; 1 Tim. 5. 18.

PADAN-ARAM, Jacob sent there, Gen. 28. 1.

Painting the face, 2 Ki. 9. 30; Jer. 4. 30; Ezek. 23. 40.

Palace, the temple so called, 1 Chr. 29. 1; Ps. 48. 3; 78. 69; 122. 7.

Palestina, predictions about, Ex. 15. 14; Is. 14. 29.

Palm tree and branches, Ex. 15. 27; Lev. 23. 40; Deut. 34. 3; Jud. 1. 16; 3. 13; 2 Chr. 28. 15; John 12. 13; Rev. 7. 9.

Palsy cured by Christ, Matt. 4. 24; 8. 6; 9. 2; Mk. 2. 3; Lk 5. 18; by his disciples, Acts 8. 7; 9. 33.

Pamphylia, Paul preaches there, Acts 13. 13; 14. 24.

Paper reeds of Egypt, Is. 19. 7.

Paphos, Paul at, Acts 13. 6.

Elymas the sorcerer at, Acts 13. 11.

Parables, notable ones in Old Testament, Jud. 9. 8, 15; 2 Sam. 12. 1; 14. 5; 1 Ki. 20. 39; 2 Ki. 14. 9; 2 Chr. 25. 18.

as discourses, Num. 23. 7; 24. 5, 16; Ps. 78. 2; Job 27; Prov. 26. 9.

of the prophets, Is. 5. 1; Jer. 13. 1; 18; 24; 27; Ezek. 16; 17; 19; 23; 24; 31; 33; 37.

of Christ, Matt. 13. 3, 34; Mk. 3. 23; 4. 13; Lk. 8. 10. See *Christ*.

Paradise, Rev. 2. 7; Lk. 23. 43; 2 Cor. 12. 4.

Paran, mount, Gen. 21. 21; Num. 10. 12; 12. 16; 13. 26; Deut. 33. 2; Hab. 3. 3.

Parchments, 2 Tim. 4. 13.

Pardon of sin, 2 Chr. 30. 18; Neh. 9. 17; Job 7. 21; Ps. 25. 11; Is. 55. 7; Jer. 33. 8; 50. 20.

Parents, duty of, Prov. 13. 24; 19. 18; 22. 6, 15; 23. 13; 29. 15; Lk. 11. 13; Eph. 6. 4; Col. 3. 21; 1 Tim. 5. 8; Tit. 2. 4.

duty to. See *Obedience*.

Parthians, Acts 2. 9.

Partiality condemned, Lev. 19. 15; Deut 1. 17; 16. 19; Prov. 18. 5; 24. 23; Mal. 2. 9; 1 Tim. 5. 21; Jas. 2. 4; 3. 17; Jude 16.

Pashur's cruelty to Jeremiah, Jer. 20.

Passover instituted, Ex. 12. 3, 11; 13. 3.

laws relating to, Lev. 23. 4; Num. 9; 28. 16; Deut. 16.

observed under Moses, Ex. 12. 28; Num. 9. 5: under Joshua, Josh. 5. 10; by Hezekiah, 2 Chr. 30. 13; by Josiah, 2 Ki. 23. 21; 2 Chr. 35; by Ezra, Ezra 6. 19.

kept by Christ, Matt. 26. 19; Mk. 14. 12; Lk. 22. 7; John 13.

a type of Christ's death, 1 Cor. 5. 7.

Pastors of the Jews, censured, Jer. 2. 8; 10. 21; 23.

Pasture, spiritual, Ps. 23. 2; 74. 1; 79. 13; 95. 7; 100; Ezek. 34. 14; John 10. 9.

Pathros, in Egypt, Is. 11..11; Jer. 44. 1, 15; Ezek. 29. 14; 30. 14.

Patience commended, Ps. 37. 7; Eccl. 7. 8; Is. 30. 15; 40. 31; Lk. 21. 19; Rom. 12. 12; 1 Thes. 5. 14; 2 Thes. 3. 5; 1 Tim. 3. 3; 6. 11; Heb. 12. 1; Jas. 1. 3; 5. 7; 1 Pet. 2. 20; 2 Pet. 1. 6.

blessings resulting from, Rom. 5. 3; 15. 4; Heb. 6. 12; Rev. 2. 2; 3. 10.

Patmos, John banished there, Rev. 1. 9.

Patriarchs, history of, Gen. 5.

Pattern of the tabernacle, etc., Ex. 25. 9, 40; (Ezek. 43. 10); Heb. 8. 5; 9. 23.

Paul, as a persecutor, Acts 7. 58; 8. 1; 9. 1; 22. 4; 26. 9; 1 Cor. 15. 9; Gal. 1. 13; Phil. 3. 6; 1 Tim. 1. 13.

his miraculous conversion, Acts 9. 3; 22. 6; 26. 12.

as a preacher, Acts 9. 19, 29; 13. 1, 4, 14; 17. 18; (2 Cor. 11. 32; Gal. 1. 17).

stoned at Lystra, Acts 14. 8, 19.

contends with Barnabas, Acts 15. 36.

persecuted at Philippi, Acts 16.

the Holy Ghost given by his hands, Acts 19. 6.

restores Eutychus, Acts 20. 10.

his charge to the elders of Ephesus, Acts 20. 17.

returns to Jerusalem, and persecution there, Acts 21.

his defence before the people, Acts 22; before the council, Acts 23; before Felix, Acts 24; Festus, Acts 25; and Agrippa, Acts 26.

appeals to Cæsar at Rome, Acts 25.

his voyage and shipwreck, Acts 27.

miracles wrought by, at Melita, Acts 28. 3, 8.

arrives at Rome, Acts 28. 1a.

reasons with the Jews, Acts 28. 17.

his love to the churches, Rom. 1. 8; 15; 1 Cor. 1. 4; 4. 14; 2 Cor. 1. 2; 6; 7; Phil. 1; Col. 1: 1 & 2 Thes.

his sufferings, 1 Cor. 4. 9; 2 Cor. 11. 23; 12. 7; Phil. 1. 12; 2 Tim. 2. 11.

divine revelations to, 2 Cor. 12. 1.

defends his apostleship, 1 Cor. 9; 2 Cor. 11; 12; 2 Tim. 3. 10.

commends Timothy, etc., 1 Cor. 16. 10; Phil. 2. 19; 1 Thes. 3. 2.

commends Titus, 2 Cor. 7. 13; 8. 23.

pleads for Onesimus, Philem.

his epistles mentioned by Peter, 2 Pet. 3. 15.

Pavilion, 2 Sam. 22. 12; Ps. 27. 5; 31. 20.

Peace to be prayed for, Jer. 29. 7; Ezra 6. 10; 1 Tim. 2. 2.

bestowed by God, Lev. 26. 6; 1 Ki. 2. 33; 4. 24; 2 Ki. 20. 19; Prov. 16. 7; Is. 45. 7; Jer. 14. 13.

exhortations to maintain, Ps. 34. 14; Matt. 5. 9; Rom. 12. 18; 14. 19; 1 Cor. 7. 15; Eph. 4. 3; 1 Thes. 5. 13; 2 Tim. 2. 22; Jas. 3. 18; 1 Pet. 3. 11.

Peace—*Continued.*
spiritual, gift of God (John 14. 27); Acts 10. 36;
Rom. 1. 7; 5. 1; 8. 6; 14. 17; Phil. 4. 7; Col.
3. 15; 1 Thes. 5. 23; 2 Thes. 3.16; Rev. 1. 4.
preached to the Gentiles, Zech. 9. 10; Eph.
2. 14, 17; 3.
the fruit of the Spirit, Gal. 5. 22.
on earth, Lk. 2. 14; in heaven, Lk. 19. 38.
denied to the wicked, 2 Ki. 9. 31; Is. 48. 22;
59. 8; (Rom. 3. 17); Jer. 12. 12; Ezek. 7. 25.
to whom promised, Ps. 29. 11; 85. 8; 122. 6;
125. 5; 128. 6; 147. 14; John 14. 27; Gal. 6.
16; Eph. 6. 23.
king of, Melchisedec, Heb. 7. 2.
prince of, Christ, Is. 9. 6.
Peace-Offerings, laws concerning, Ex. 20. 24;
24. 5; Lev. 3; 6; 7. 11; 19. 5.
Peacock, 2 Chr. 9. 21; Job 39. 13.
Pearl, parable of, Matt. 7. 6; 13. 45.
See 1 Tim. 2. 9; Rev. 17. 4.
Peculiar people of God, Deut. 14. 2; Ps. 135. 4.
See Tit. 2. 14; 1 Pet. 2. 9.
Pekah, king of Israel, 2 Ki. 15. 25.
his victory over Judah, 2 Chr. 28. 6.
prophecy against, Is. 7. 1.
Pekahiah king of Israel, 2 Ki. 15. 22.
Pelatiah, Ezek. 11. 1, 13.
Pelican, Lev. 11. 18; Deut. 14. 17; Ps. 102. 6.
Peniel (Penuel) scene of Jacob's wrestling with
an angel, Gen. 32. 24.
Gideon's vengeance upon, Jud. 8. 17.
Penny (a Roman coin, equal to sevenpence-
halfpenny), Matt. 20. 2; Mk. 12. 15; Rev. 6. 6.
Pens, Jud. 5. 14; Ps. 45. 1; Is. 8. 1; Jer. 8. 8;
17. 1; 3 John 13.
Pentecost (feast of weeks), how observed, Lev.
23. 9; Deut. 16. 9.
Holy Spirit given then, Acts 2.
People of God, their blessings and privileges,
Deut. 7. 6; 32. 9; 33; 1 Sam. 12. 22; 2 Sam.
7. 23; Ps. 3. 8; 29. 11; 33. 12; 77. 15; 85;
89. 15; 94. 14; 95. 7; 100; 110; 111. 6; 121;
125; 144. 15; 148. 14; 149. 4; Is. 11. 11; 14.
32; 30. 19; 33. 24; 49. 13; 51. 22; 65. 18;
Dan. 7. 27; Joel 2. 18; 3. 16; Zeph. 3. 9, 20;
Matt. 1. 21; Lk. 1. 17; Acts 15. 14; Rom.
11; 2 Cor. 6. 16; Tit. 2. 14; Heb. 4. 9; 8. 10;
1 Pet. 2. 9; Rev. 5. 9; 21. 3.
Peor (Baal), Num. 23. 28; 25. 3, 18; Josh. 22. 17.
Perdition, what leads to, Phil. 1. 28; 1 Tim. 6.
9; Heb. 10. 39; 2 Pet. 3. 7; Rev. 17. 8.
the son of, John 17. 12; 2 Thes. 2. 3.
Perfection of God, Deut. 32. 4; 2 Sam. 22. 31;
Job 36. 4; Matt. 5. 48.
of Christ, Heb. 2. 10; 5. 9; 7. 28.
of God's law, Ps. 19. 7; 119; Jas. 1. 25.
of saints, 1 Cor. 2. 6; Eph. 4. 12; Col. 1. 28;
3. 14; 2 Tim. 3. 17.
See Matt. 5. 48; 2 Cor. 12. 9; Heb. 6. 1; 11. 40.
Perfume, sacred, Ex. 30. 34.
Perga, visited by Paul, Acts 13. 13; 14. 25.
Pergamos, epistle to church of, Rev. 1. 11; 2. 12.
Perizzites, Gen. 13. 7; 15. 20; Jud. 1. 4; 2 Chr. 8. 7.
Perjury forbidden, Ex. 20. 16; Lev. 6. 3; 19.
12; Deut. 5. 20; Ezek. 17. 16; Zech. 5. 4; 8.
17; 1 Tim. 1. 10.
Persecution foretold, Matt. 13. 21; 23. 34; Mk.
10. 30; Lk. 11. 49; John 15. 20; 2 Cor. 4. 9;
2 Tim. 3. 12.
conduct under, Matt. 5. 44; 10. 22; Acts 5.
41; Rom. 12. 14; Phil. 1. 28; Heb. 10. 34;
1 Pet. 4. 13-19.
results of, Matt. 5. 10; Lk. 6. 22; 9. 24; Jas.
1. 2; 1 Pet. 4. 14; Rev. 6. 9; 7. 13.

Perseverance enjoined, Matt. 24. 13; Mk. 13.
13; Lk. 9. 62; Acts 13. 43; 1 Cor. 15. 58; 16.
13; Eph. 6. 18; Col. 1. 23; 2 Thes. 3. 13;
1 Tim. 6. 14; Heb. 3. 6, 13; 10. 23, 38; 2 Pet.
3. 17; Rev. 2. 10, 25.
Persia, kingdom of, 2 Chr. 36. 20; Est. 1. 3;
Ezek. 27. 10; 38. 5; Dan. 6.
prophecies concerning, Is. 21. 2; Dan. 5. 28;
8. 20; 10. 13; 11. 2.
Persis, commended, Rom. 16. 12.
Persons, God no respecter of, Deut. 10. 17;
2 Chr. 19. 7; Job 34. 19; Acts 10. 34; Rom.
2. 11; Gal. 2. 6; Eph. 6. 9; Col. 3. 25; 1 Pet.
1. 17.
Pestilence, threatened for disobedience, Lev.
26. 25; Num. 14. 12; Deut. 28. 21; Jer. 14.
12; 27. 13; Ezek. 5. 12; 6. 11; 7. 15; Matt.
24. 7; Lk. 21. 11.
inflicted, Num. 14. 37; 16. 46; 25. 9; 2 Sam.
24. 15; Ps. 78. 50.
removed, Num. 16. 47; 2 Sam. 24. 16.
Peter, apostle, called, Matt. 4. 18; Mk. 1. 16;
Lk. 5; John 1. 35.
sent forth, Matt. 10. 2; Mk. 3. 16; Lk. 6. 14.
confesses Jesus to be the Christ, Matt. 16.
16; Mk. 8. 29; Lk. 9. 20.
present at the transfiguration, Matt. 17;
Mk. 9. Lk. 9. 28; 2 Pet. 1. 16.
his self-confidence reproved, Lk. 22. 31; John
13. 36.
thrice denies Christ, Matt. 26. 69; Mk. 14.
66; Lk. 22. 57; John 18. 17.
his repentance, Matt. 26. 75; Mk. 14. 72; Lk.
22. 62.
his address to the disciples, Acts 1. 15.
preaches to the Jews, Acts 2. 14; 3. 12.
brought before the council, Acts 4.
rebukes Ananias and Sapphira, Acts 5.
denounces Simon the sorcerer, Acts 8. 18.
restores Æneas and Tabitha, Acts 9. 32, 40.
sent for by Cornelius, Acts 10.
imprisoned and liberated by an angel, Acts
12.
his decision about circumcision, Acts 15. 7.
rebuked by Paul, Gal. 2. 14.
bears witness to Paul's teaching, 2 Pet. 3. 15.
his martyrdom foretold, John 21. 18; 2 Pet.
1. 14.
comforts the church, and exhorts to holy
living, etc., 1 & 2 Pet.
Pharaoh, king of Egypt, Gen. 12. 14.
reproves Abram, Gen. 12. 18.
—his dreams interpreted by Joseph, Gen. 40.
his kindness to Jacob and his family, Gen. 47.
—oppresses the Israelites, Ex. 1. 8.
miracles performed before, and plagues sent,
Ex. 7; 8; 9; 10.
grants Moses' request, Ex. 12. 31.
repenting, pursues Israel, and perishes in
the Red Sea, Ex. 14; (Neh 9. 10; Ps. 135. 9;
136. 15; Rom. 9. 17).
—Solomon's affinity with, 1 Ki. 3. 1.
receives Hadad, Solomon's adversary, 1 Ki.
11. 19.
Pharaoh - Hophra, his fate predicted, Jer. 44.
30.
See Ezek. 29. 3; 30; 31; 32.
Pharaoh-Necho slays Josiah, 2 Ki. 23. 29; 2
Chr. 35. 20.
dethrones Jehoahaz, 2 Ki. 23. 33; 2 Chr. 36. 3.
Pharaoh's daughter preserves Moses, Ex. 2. 5,
10; Acts 7. 21.
Pharez, Gen. 38. 29; Ruth 4. 18.
Pharisee and publican, Lk. 18. 9.

Pharisees censured by Christ, Matt. 5. 20; 16. 6; 21. 43; 23. 2, 13; Lk. 11. 39, 42.
Christ's controversies with, Matt. 9. 34; 19. 3; Mk. 2. 18; Lk. 5. 30; 11. 39; 16. 14.
celebrated ones, Nicodemus, John 3. 1; Simon, Lk. 7; Gamaliel, Acts 5. 34; Saul of Tarsus, Acts 23. 6; 26. 5; Phil. 3. 5.
Christ entertained by, Lk. 11. 37; 14. 1; 7. 36.
people cautioned against, Mk. 8. 15; Lk. 12. 1.
seek a sign from Christ, Matt. 12. 38; 16. 1.
take counsel against Christ, Matt. 12. 14; Mk. 3. 6.
send officers to take him, John 7. 32.
Nicodemus remonstrates with, John 7. 50.
contend about circumcision, Acts 15. 5.
their belief in the resurrection, Acts 23. 8.

Phebe commended, Rom. 16. 1.

Phenice, Paul and Barnabas pass through, Acts 11. 19; 15. 3; (27. 12).

Phenicia, Acts 21. 2.

Philadelphia, church of, commended, Rev. 1. 11; 3. 7.

Philemon, Paul's letter to, concerning Onesimus, Philem.

Philip, apostle, called, John 1. 43.
ordained, Matt. 10. 3; Mk. 3. 18; Lk. 6. 14; John 12. 22; Acts 1. 13.
reproved by Christ, John 14. 8.
— deacon, elected, Acts 6. 5.
preaches in Samaria, Acts 8. 5.
baptizes the eunuch, Acts 8. 27.
his daughters prophesy, Acts 21. 8.
—(brother of Herod), Matt. 14. 3; Mk. 6. 17; Lk. 3. 1, 19.

Philippi, Paul persecuted at, Acts 16. 12.
church at, commended and exhorted, Phil. 1; 2; 3; 4.

Philistia, Gen. 21. 34; Ex. 13. 17; Josh. 13. 2; 2 Ki. 8. 2.

Philistines, Gen. 10. 14; 1 Chr. 1. 12.
fill up Isaac's wells, Gen. 26. 14.
contend with Joshua, Josh. 13; Shamgar, Jud. 3. 31; Samson, Jud. 14; 15; 16; Samuel, 1 Sam. 4; 7; Jonathan, 1 Sam. 14; Saul, 1 Sam. 17; David, 1 Sam. 18.
their wars with Israel, 2 Sam. 4. 1; 28; 29; 31; 2 Chr. 21. 16.
mentioned, Ps. 60. 8; 83. 7; 87. 4; 108. 9; Is. 2. 6; 9. 12; 11. 14; Jer. 25. 20.
their destruction foretold, Jer. 47; Ezek. 25. 15; Amos 1. 8; Obad. 19; Zeph. 2. 5; Zech. 9. 6.

Philologus, Julia, and all saints with them, Rom. 16. 15.

Philosophers mentioned, Acts 17. 18.

Philosophy, vanity of, Col. 2. 8.

Phinehas, son of Eleazar, Ex. 6. 25.
slays Zimri and Cozbi, Num. 25. 7. 11; Ps. 106. 30.
sent against the Midianites, Reubenites, and Benjamites, Num. 31. 6; Josh. 22. 13; Jud. 20. 28.
—son of Eli, his sin and death, 1 Sam. 1. 3; 2. 22; 4. 11.

Phrygia, Acts 16. 6; 18. 23.

Phygellus and Hermogenes censured, 2 Tim. 1. 15.

Phylacteries, Matt. 23. 5.
See Ex. 13. 9, 16; Num. 15. 38.

Physician mentioned, Matt. 9. 12; Mk. 2. 17; Lk. 4. 23; 5. 31.
See Jer. 8. 22.

Piece of silver, 1 Sam. 2. 36; parable of, Lk. 15. 8.

Piety at home, 1 Tim. 5. 4.

Pigeons as offerings, Lev. 1. 14; 12. 6; Num. 6. 10; Lk. 2. 24.

Pi-Hahiroth, Ex. 14. 2.

Pilate, Pontius, governor of Judea, Lk. 3. 1.
destroys the Galileans, Lk. 13. 1.
declares Christ's innocence, but delivers him to be crucified, Matt. 27; Mk. 15; Lk. 23; John 18; 19.
grants the request of Joseph of Arimathæa, Matt. 27. 57; Mk. 15. 42; Lk. 23. 50; John 19. 38.
See Acts 3. 13; 4. 27; 13. 28; 1 Tim. 6. 13.

Pilgrimage, typical, Gen. 47. 9; Ex. 6. 4; Ps. 119. 54; Heb. 11. 13; 1 Pet. 2. 11.

Pillar of salt, Lot's wife turned into, Gen. 19. 26.
See Lk. 17. 32.

Pillars erected by Jacob, Gen. 28. 18; 35. 20; and Absalom, 2 Sam. 18. 18.
in porch of the temple, 1 Ki. 7. 21; 2 Chr. 3. 17; Rev. 3. 12.
of cloud and fire, Ex. 13. 21; 33. 9; Neh. 9. 12; Ps. 99. 7.

Pine tree, Is. 41. 19; 60. 13.

Pisgah, mount, Num. 23. 14; Deut. 3. 27; 34. 1.

Pisidia, Acts 13. 14; 14. 24.

Pison, a river in Eden, Gen. 2. 11.

Pit, the grave, death, Job 17. 16; 33. 18; Ps. 28. 1; 30. 9; 88. 4; 143. 7; Is. 14. 15; 38. 17; Ezek. 26. 20; 32. 18.
as a prison, Is. 24. 22; Zech. 9. 11.

Pitch, used for the ark, etc., Gen. 6. 14; Ex. 2. 3; Is. 34. 9.

Pitcher, Gen. 24. 15, 20; Mk. 14. 13; Lk. 22. 10.
Gideon's use of, Jud. 7.

Pity, Deut. 7. 16; 13. 8; 2 Sam. 12. 6; Job. 19. 21; Ps. 69. 20; Prov. 19. 17; Joel 2. 18; Matt. 18. 33.

Places, idolatrous, 1 Ki. 11. 7; 12. 31; 13; Ps. 78. 58; Ezek. 16. 24.
destruction of, Lev. 26. 30; 2 Ki. 18. 4; 23; 2 Chr. 14. 3; 17. 6; 34. 3; Ezek. 6. 3.

Plagues of Egypt. See *Egypt.*
of Israel. See *Pestilence.*

Plant, figuratively mentioned, Ps. 128. 3; 144. 12; Cant. 4. 13; Is. 5. 7; 53. 2; Jer. 2. 21; Ezek. 34. 29; Matt. 15. 13.

Pleading of God with Israel, Is. 1. 3. 13; 43. 26; Jer. 2. 6; 13; Ezek. 17. 20; 20. 36; 22; Hos. 2., etc.; Joel 3. 2; Mic. 2.
of Job with God, Job 9. 19; 16. 21.

Pleasures, vanity of worldly, Eccl. 2.
effects of, Lk. 8. 14; Jas. 5; 2 Pet. 2. 13.
exhortations against, 2 Tim. 3. 4; Tit. 3. 3; Heb. 11. 25; 1 Pet. 4.

Pledges, limitations of, Ex. 22. 26; Deut. 24. 6.
See Job 22. 6; 24. 3; Ezek. 18. 7; Amos 2. 8.

Pleiades, Job 9. 9; 38. 31; Amos 5. 8.

Plenty, the gift of God, Gen. 27. 28; Deut. 16. 10; 28. 11; Ps. 65. 8; 68. 9; 104. 10; 144. 13; Joel 2. 26; Acts 14. 17.

Ploughing, Deut. 22. 10.
figuratively mentioned, Job 4. 8; Hos. 10. 13; 1 Cor. 9. 10.

Ploughshares beaten into swords, Joel 3. 10.
swords to be beaten into ploughshares, Is. 2. 4; Mic. 4. 3.

Plumb-line and plummet, 2 Ki. 21. 13; Is. 28. 17; Amos 7. 8; Zech. 4. 10.

Poets, heathen, quoted, Acts 17. 28; Tit. 1. 12.

Poison of serpents, Ps. 58. 4; 140. 3; Rom. 3. 13; Jas. 3. 8.

Pollutions under the law, Lev. 5; 11; 13; 15; 21; 22; Num. 5; 9. 6; Ezek. 22.

Priest, high, Ex. 28 ; 39 ; Lev. 8 ; 16.

Priesthood of Christ, Aaron, and Melchizedek, Rom. 8. 34 ; Heb. 2. 17 ; 3 ; 5 ; 7 ; 1 John 2. 1.

Priests, Levitical, Ex. 28. 1 ; Lev. 8.
their duties, etc., Lev. 1 ; 9 ; 21 ; 22 ; Num. 3 ; Deut. 31. 9 ; Josh. 3 ; 4 ; 1 Ki. 8. 3.
slain by command of Saul, 1 Sam. 22. 17.
divided by lot by David, 1 Chr. 24.
denounced for unfaithfulness, Jer. 1. 18 ; 5. 31 ; Hos. 5 ; 6 ; Mic. 3. 11 ; Zeph. 3. 4 ; Mal. 2.

—of Baal, slain, 1 Ki. 18. 40 ; 2 Ki. 10. 19 ; 11. 18.

—Christians called, 1 Pet. 2. 5 ; Rev. 1. 6 ; 5. 10 ; 20. 6.

Prince of peace, Is. 9. 6 ; of life, Acts 3. 15.
—of this world, John 12. 31 ; 14. 30 ; 16. 11 ; of the power of the air, Eph. 2. 2.
—of devils, Christ's miracles ascribed to, Matt. 9. 34 ; 12. 24 ; Mk. 3. 22 ; Lk. 11. 15.

Princes of the tribes, Num. 1. 5.
their offerings, Num. 7.

Principalities and powers, Eph. 6. 12 ; Col. 2. 15.
Christ the head of all, Eph. 1. 21 ; Col. 1. 16 ; 2. 10.

Priscilla (and Aquila), Acts 18 ; Rom. 16. 3 ; 1 Cor. 16. 19.

Prodigal son, parable of, Lk. 15. 11.

Profanity forbidden, Lev. 18. 21 ; 19 12 ; Neh. 13. 18 ; Ezek. 22. 8 ; Mal. 1. 12.

Profession of Christ, to hold fast, 1 Tim. 6. 12 ; Heb. 3. 1 ; 4. 14 ; 10. 23.

Promises of God, Ps. 89. 3 ; Rom. 1. 2 ; Eph. 3. 6 ; 2 Tim. 1. 1 ; Heb. 6. 17 ; 8. 6.
inviolable and precious, Num. 23. 19 ; Deut. 7. 9 ; Josh. 23. 14 ; 1 Ki. 8. 56 ; Ps. 77. 8 ; 105. 42 ; 2 Cor. 1. 20 ; Gal. 3. 21 ; Heb. 6. 17 ; 2 Pet. 1. 4.
of pardon and reconciliation, Ex, 34. 7 ; Ps. 65. 3 ; 130. 4 ; Is. 1. 18 ; 27. 5 ; 43. 25 ; 44. 22 ; 46. 13 ; 53 ; 55 ; Jer. 31. 34 ; 33. 8 ; Ezek. 33. 16 ; 36. 25 ; Rom. 4 ; 5 ; 2 Cor. 6. 18 ; 7. 1 ; Eph. 2. 13.
of strength and help, etc., Ps. 23 ; 37. 17 ; 42. 8 ; 73. 26 ; 84. 11 ; 94. 14 ; 103. 13 ; Is. 25. 8 ; 30. 18 ; 40. 29 ; 41. 10 ; 43. 4 ; 46. 3 ; 49. 14 ; 63. 9 ; Jer. 31. 3 ; Hos. 13. 10 ; 14. 4 ; Zeph. 3. 17 ; Zech. 2. 8 ; 10 ; Rom. 16. 20 ; 1 Cor. 10. 13 ; 15. 57 ; 2 Cor. 6. 18 ; 12. 9 ; Eph. 1. 3 ; 1 Pet. 3. 1 ; 5. 7.
to Adam, Gen. 3. 15 ; to Noah, Gen. 8. 21 ; 9. 9 ; to Abraham, Gen. 12. 7 ; 13. 14 ; 15 ; 17 ; 18. 10 ; 22. 15 ; to Hagar, Gen. 16. 11 ; 21. 17 ; to Isaac, Gen. 26. 2 ; to Jacob, Gen. 28. 13 ; 31. 3 ; 32. 12 ; 35. 11 ; 46. 3 ; to David, 2 Sam. 7. 11 ; 1 Chr. 17. 10 ; to Solomon, 1 Ki. 9 ; 2 Chr. 1. 7 ; 7. 12.
of Christ to his disciples, Matt. 6. 4, 33 ; 7. 7 ; 10 ; 11. 28 ; 12. 50 ; 16. 18, 24 ; 17. 20 ; 19. 28 ; 28. 20 ; Lk. 9-12 ; 12. 32 ; 22. 29 ; John 14-16 ; 20. 21.
to the poor, fatherless, etc., Deut. 10. 18 ; Ps. 9. 8 ; 10. 14 ; 12. 5 ; 68. 5 ; 69. 33 ; 72. 12 ; 102. 17 ; 107. 41 ; 109. 31 ; 113. 7 ; 146. 9 ; Prov. 15. 25 ; 23. 10 ; Jer. 49. 11 ; Hos. 14. 3.
of temporal blessings, Ex. 23. 25 ; Lev. 26. 6 ; Ps. 34. 9 ; 37. 3 ; 91 ; 102. 28 ; 112 ; 121. 3 ; 128 ; Prov. 3. 10 ; Is. 32. 18 ; 33. 16 ; Matt. 6. 25 ; Phil. 4. 19 ; 1 Tim. 4. 8.
exhortation concerning, Heb. 4. 1.
fulfilled in Christ, 2 Sam. 7. 12 ; (Acts 13. 23) ; Lk. 1. 69-73.

Promotion, Ps. 75. 6.

Prophecies respecting Christ, and their fulfilment :—Prophecy, Gen. 3. 15 ; fulfilled, Gal.

Prophecies—*Continued*.
4. 4. Gen. 22. 18—Gal. 3. 16. Ps. 2. 7—Lk. 1. 32, 35. Ps. 132. 11 ; Jer. 23. 5—Acts 13. 23 ; Rom. 1. 3. Is. 7. 14—Matt. 1. 18 ; Lk. 2. 7. Mic. 5. 2—Matt. 2. 1. Hos. 11. 1—Matt. 2. 15. Is. 40. 3 ; Mal. 3. 1—Matt. 3. 1 ; Lk. 1. 17. Ps. 45. 7 ; Is. 11. 2 ; 61. 1—Matt. 3. 16 ; John 3. 34 ; Acts 10. 38. Zech. 9. 9—Matt. 21. 1-5. Is. 53. 2—Mk. 6. 3 ; Lk. 9. 58. Is. 40. 11 ; 42. 3—Matt. 12. 15, 20 ; Heb. 4. 15. Ps. 69. 9—John 2. 17. Ps. 78. 2—Matt. 13. 34, 35. Ps. 118. 22—Matt. 21. 42 ; John 7. 48. Zech. 13. 7—Matt. 26. 31. Zech. 11. 12—Matt. 26. 15. Zech. 11. 13—Matt. 27. 7. Ps. 22. 14, 15—Lk. 22. 42, 44. Is. 53. 4-6 ; Dan. 9. 26—Matt. 20. 28. Is. 53. 7—Matt. 26. 63 ; 27. 12-14. Mic. 5. 1—Matt. 27. 30. Is. 50. 6—John 19. 1. Is. 52. 14 ; 53. 3—John 19. 5. Ps. 22. 1—Matt. 27. 46. Ps. 22. 7, 8—Matt. 27. 39-44. Ps. 22. 16—John 19. 18 ; 20. 25. Ps. 22. 18—Matt. 27. 35. Ps. 69. 21—Matt. 27. 34. Is. 53. 12—Matt. 27. 50 ; Mk. 15. 28. Ex. 12. 46 ; Ps. 34. 20—John 19. 33, 36. Ps. 16. 10—Acts 2. 31. Ps. 68. 18—Lk. 24. 51 ; Acts 1. 9. Ps. 110. 1—Heb. 1. 3. Zech. 6. 13—Rom. 8. 34. Is. 28. 16—1 Pet. 2. 6, 7. Ps. 11. 10 ; 42. 1—Matt. 1. 17, 21 ; John 10. 16 ; Acts 10. 45. Ps. 72. 8 ; Dan. 7. 14—Phil. 2. 9, 11. Is. 9. 7 ; Dan. 7. 14—Lk. 1. 32, 33.

Prophecy, God author of, Is 44. 7 ; 45. 21 ; Lk. 1. 70 ; 2 Pet. 1. 19, 21 ; Rev. 1. 1.
gift of Christ, Eph. 4. 11 ; Rev. 11. 3.
of Holy Ghost, 1 Cor. 12. 10.
Christ the great subject of, Lk. 24. 44 ; Acts 3. 22-24 ; 10. 43 ; 1 Pet. 1. 10, 11.
how to be received, 2 Chr. 20. 20 ; Lk. 24. 25 ; 1 Thes. 5. 20 ; 2 Pet. 1. 19.
false, how tested, Deut. 13. 1 ; 18. 20 ; Jer. 14. 15 ; 23. 16 ; Ezek. 13. 3.

Prophets, sent by God, Is. 58. 1 ; Jer. 1. 4 ; 23. 28 ; 25. 4 ; Ezek. 2. 3.
Christ so called, Matt. 21. 11 ; Lk. 7. 16 ; 22. 64 ; Deut. 18. 15.
others so called :—Aaron, Ex. 7. 1 ; Abraham, Gen. 20. 7 ; Ahijah, 1 Ki. 11. 29 ; Amos, Amos 7. 14 ; Balaam, Num. 24. 2 ; Daniel, Dan. 10 ; 11 ; Matt. 24. 15 ; David, Matt. 13. 35 ; Acts 2. 30 ; Eldad, Num. 11. 26 ; Elijah, 1 Ki. 18. 36 ; Elisha, 2 Ki. 6. 12 ; Ezekiel, Ezek. 1. 3 ; Gad, 1 Sam. 22. 5 ; Habakkuk, Hab. 1. 1 ; Haggai, Ezra 5. 1 ; 6. 14 ; Hag. 1. 1 ; Hananiah, Jer. 28. 17 ; Hosea, Hos. 1. 1 ; Rom. 9. 25 ; Iddo, 2 Chr. 13. 22 ; Isaiah, 2 Ki. 20. 11 ; Is. 1. 1 ; Matt. 3. 3 ; Jehu, 1 Ki. 16. 7 ; Jeremiah, 2 Chr. 36. 12 ; Jer. 1. 5 ; Joel, Joel 1. 1 ; Acts 2. 16 ; John the Baptist, Lk. 7. 28 ; Joshua, 1 Ki. 16. 34 ; Jonah, 2 Ki. 14. 25 ; Jon 1. 1 ; Matt. 12. 39 ; Malachi, Mal. 1. 1 ; Medad, Num. 11. 26 ; Micah, Jer. 26. 18 ; Mic. 1. 1 ; Moses, Deut. 34. 10 ; Nahum, Nah. 1. 1 ; Nathan, 1 Ki. 1. 32 ; Obadiah, Obad. 1 ; Oded, 2 Chr. 15. 8 ; Paul, Acts 13. 9 ; 27. 10 ; Samuel, 1 Sam. 3. 20 ; Zacharias, Lk. 1. 67 ; Zechariah, Zech. 1. 1 ; Zephaniah, Zeph. 1. 1.
—false, Zedekiah, 1 Ki. 22. 11 ; Jer. 29. 21 ; Bar-jesus, Acts 13. 6.
denounced, Deut. 13 ; 18. 20 ; Is. 9. 15 ; Jer. 6. 13 ; 14. 13 ; 23. 34 ; 28. 15 ; 29. 31 ; Ezek. 13. 3 ; 14. 9 ; Matt. 7. 15 ; 24. 11 ; 1 John 4. 1 ; 2 Pet. 2. 1.

Prophetesses, Anna, Lk. 2. 36 ; Deborah, Jud. 4. 4 ; Huldah, 2 Ki. 22. 14 ; Miriam, Ex. 15. 20 ; Noadiah, Neh. 6. 14.

Propitiation for sin, Rom. 3. 25; 1 John 2. 2;
4. 10.

Proselytes, Jewish, Acts 2. 10; 6. 5; 13. 43.

Prosperity of the righteous, Ps. 36. 8; 37. 11;
18; 75. 10; 84. 11; 92. 12; Prov. 3. 2; Eccl.
8. 12.

of the wicked, Job 12. 6; 20. 5; 21. 7; Ps. 17.
10; 37; 73. 3; 92. 7; Eccl. 8. 14; 9. 1; Jer. 12.
dangers of, Deut. 6. 10; Prov. 1. 32; 30. 8;
Lk. 6. 24; 12. 16; 16. 19; Jas. 5. 1.

Proverbs of Solomon, Prov. 1-25; collected
under Hezekiah, 25-29.

various, 1 Sam. 10. 12; 24. 13; Lk. 4. 23; 2
Pet. 2. 22.

Providence of God, Gen. 8. 22; 1 Sam. 6. 7; Ps.
36. 6; 104; 136; 145; 147; Prov. 16; 19; 20;
Matt. 6. 26; 10. 29; Lk. 21. 18; Acts 17. 26.

Prudence, Prov. 12. 16; 23; 13. 16; 15. 5; 16.
21; 18. 15; 19. 14; 22. 3, Hos. 14. 9; Amos
5. 13.

Psalmody, service of song, Jewish, Ex. 15. 1;
1 Chr. 6. 31; 13. 8; 2 Chr. 5. 13; 20. 22; 29.
30; Neh. 12. 27.

Christian, Matt. 26. 30; Mk. 14. 26; Jas. 5. 13.

spiritual songs, Eph. 5. 19; Col. 3. 16.

THE PSALMS

May be divided into Five Parts, as follows:—

I. DAVIDIC (i.—xli).

II. DAVIDIC (xlii.—lxxii).

III. ASAPHIC (lxxiii.—lxxxix).

IV. OF THE CAPTIVITY (xc.—cvi).

V. OF RESTORATION (cvii.—cl).

Or may be classified according to their subjects, thus:—

(I.) PSALMS OF SUPPLICATION.

1. On account of sin, Ps. 6; 25; 32; 38; 51;
102; 130.

2. affliction, Ps. 7; 10; 13; 17; 22; 31; 35;
41-43; 54-57; 59; 64; 69-71; 77; 86; 88;
94; 109; 120; 140-143.

3. persecution, Ps. 44; 60; 74; 79; 80; 83;
89; 94; 102; 123; 137.

4. relative to public worship, Ps. 26; 27; 42;
43; 63; 65; 84; 92; 95-100; 118; 122; 132;
144; 145-150.

5. expressing trust in God, Ps. 3-5; 11; 12;
16; 20; 23; 27; 28; 31; 42; 43; 52; 54;
56; 57; 59; 61-64; 71; 77; 86; 108; 115;
118; 121; 125; 131; 138; 141.

6. the Psalmist's integrity, Ps. 7; 17; 26; 35;
101; 119.

(II.) GRATITUDE.

1. For mercies shown to the Psalmist, Ps. 9;
18; 30; 32; 34; 40; 61-63; 75; 103; 108;
116; 118; 138; 144.

2. to the Church, Ps. 33; 46; 47; 65; 66; 68;
75; 76; 81; 85; 87; 95; 98; 105; 106;
107; 124; 126; 129; 134; 135; 136; 149.

(III.) ADORATION.

1. Of God's goodness and mercy, Ps. 3; 4; 9;
16; 18; 30-34; 36; 40; 46; 65-68; 84; 85; 91;
99; 100; 103. 107; 111; 113; 116; 117; 121;
126; 145; 146.

2. of God's power, majesty, and glory, Ps. 2;
3; 8; 18; 19; 24; 29; 33; 45-48; 50; 65-68;
76; 77; 89; 91-100; 104-108; 110; 111; 113
118; 135; 136; 139; 145-150.

(IV.) DIDACTIC.

1. Shewing the blessings of God's people and
the misery of His enemies, Ps. 1; 3; 4; 5;
7; 9-15; 17; 24; 25; 32; 34; 36; 37; 41; 50;
52; 53; 58; 62; 73; 75; 82; 84; 91; 92; 94;
101; 112; 119; 121; 125; 127-129; 133; 149.

2. the excellence of God's law, Ps. 19; 119.

Psalms—*Continued.*

3. the vanity of human life, etc., Ps. 14; 39;
49; 53; 73; 90..

(V.) PROPHETICAL, TYPICAL, AND HISTORICAL.

Ps. 2; 16; 22; 24; 31; 35; 40; 41; 45; 50;
55; 68; 69; 72; 78; 87; 88; 102; 105; 106;
109; 110; 118; 132; 135; 136.

Psaltery, 2 Sam. 6. 5; 2 Chr. 9. 11; Dan. 3. 5,
10, 15.

Ptolemais, Paul at, Acts 21. 7.

Publicans, Matt. 5. 46; 9. 11; 11. 19; 18. 17; Lk.
3. 12.

some believe in Jesus, Matt. 21. 32; Lk. 5.
27; 7. 29; 15. 1; 19. 2.

parable of Pharisee and publican, Lk. 18. 10.

Publius, of Melita, entertains Paul, Acts 28. 7.

Pul, king of Assyria, 2 Ki. 15. 19; 1 Chr. 5. 26.

Punishments:

burning, Gen. 38. 24; Lev. 20. 14; 21. 9.

hanging, Gen. 40. 22; Deut. 21. 23; Ezra 6.
11; Est. 2. 23; 7. 10.

scourging, Lev. 19. 20; Deut. 25. 1; Matt. 27.
26; Acts 22. 25.

stoning, Lev. 20. 2; 24. 14; 1 Ki. 21. 10; John
8. 59; Acts 7. 58; 14. 19.

beheading, 2 Ki. 6. 31; 10. 7; Matt. 14. 10.

See Heb. 11. 36.

crucifying, Matt. 20. 19; 27. 31, etc.

Purchases, Gen. 23; Ruth 4; Jer. 32. 6.

Purification, laws concerning, Lev. 13-16; Num.
31. 19; 19; (Mal. 3. 3; Acts 21. 24; Heb. 9. 13).

of women, Lev. 12; Est. 2. 12; Lk. 2. 22.

of the heart by faith, Acts 15. 9; 1 Pet. 1. 22;
1 John 3. 3.

See Dan. 12. 10.

Purim, the feast of, Est. 9. 20.

Purity, moral, enjoined, Gal. 5. 16; Eph. 5. 3;
Phil. 2. 15; 4. 8; Col. 3. 5; 1 Tim. 5. 22; Tit.
1. 15; 1 Pet. 2. 11; 2 Pet. 3. 1; 1 John 3. 3.

Purity of God's word and law, Ps. 12. 6; 19. 8;
119. 140; Prov. 30. 5.

Puteoli (Pozzuoli), seaport of Italy, Acts 28. 13.

QUAILS, Israel fed with, Ex. 16. 12.

sent in wrath, Num. 11. 31; Ps. 78. 27; 105. 40.

Quarrelling. See *Strife.*

Quaternions (of soldiers), Acts 12. 4.

Queen of heaven, idolatrous worship of, Jer.
44. 17, 25.

Quick and the dead, Acts 10. 42; 2 Tim. 4. 1;
1 Pet. 4. 5.

Quickening, spiritual, Ps. 71. 20; 80. 18; John
5. 21; 6. 63; Rom. 4. 17; 8. 11; 1 Cor. 15. 45;
2 Cor. 3. 6; Eph. 2. 1; 1 Tim. 6. 13; 1 Pet.
3. 18.

Quicksands, Acts 27. 17.

Quiet, the faithful shall dwell in, Prov. 1. 33;
Is. 30. 15; 32. 17, 18.

to be, enjoined, 1 Thes. 4. 11; 2 Thes. 3. 12;
1 Tim. 2. 2; 1 Pet. 3. 4.

RABBAH (Rabbath), besieged and taken by
Joab, 2 Sam. 11; 12. 26.

prophecies concerning, Jer. 49. 2; Ezek. 21.
20; 25. 5; Amos 1. 14.

Rabbi (master), John 1. 38; 3. 2; Matt. 23. 7, 8.

Rabboni, Christ so named by Mary, John 20. 16.

Rabshakeh reviles Hezekiah, 2 Ki. 18. 19; 19.
1; Is. 36. 4.

Raca (vain fellow), 2 Sam. 6. 20; Matt. 5. 22.

Race, typical, Ps. 19. 5; Eccl. 9. 11; 1 Cor. 9.
24; Heb. 12. 1.

Rachel (Rahel) and Jacob, Gen. 29. 10, 28; 31.
1, 19, 34; 35. 16.

Rage censured, 2 Ki. 19. 27; Ps. 2. 1; Prov. 14. 16.

Rahab, the harlot, Josh. 2; 6. 22.
See Matt. 1. 5; Heb. 11. 31; Jas. 2. 25.
—(Egypt), Ps. 87. 4; 89. 10; Is. 51. 9.

Railing, 1 Sam. 25. 14; 2 Sam. 16. 7; Mk. 15. 29; 1 Cor. 5. 11; 1 Tim. 6. 4; 1 Pet. 3. 9; 2 Pet. 2. 11; Jude 9.

Rain (the deluge), Gen. 7; Ex. 9. 34; 1 Sam. 12. 17; Ps. 105. 32.
withheld, 1 Ki. 17; Jer. 14; Zech. 14. 17; Jas. 5. 17.
emblematic, Lev. 26. 4; Deut. 32. 2; 2 Sam. 23. 4; Ps. 68. 9; Hos. 10. 12.
the gift of God, Matt. 5. 45; Acts 14. 17.

Rainbow, sign of God's covenant with Noah, Gen. 9. 12; Ezek. 1. 28.
in heaven, Rev. 4. 3; 10. 1.

Ram, used in sacrifices, Gen. 15. 9; 22. 13; Ex. 29. 15; Lev. 9; Num. 5. 8.
typical, Dan. 8. 20.
battering, Ezek. 4. 2; 21. 22.

Rams' horns used as trumpets, Josh. 6. 4.

Ramah, Josh. 18. 25; Jud. 4. 5; 1 Sam. 1. 19; 7. 17; 8. 4; 19. 18; 25. 1.

Ramoth-Gilead, Deut. 4. 43; 1 Ki. 22; 2 Ki. 8. 28; 9. 1; 2 Chr. 18; 22. 5.

Ransom, Christ a, Matt. 20. 28; 1 Tim. 2. 6; Job 33. 24.

Ransomed of the Lord, Is. 35. 10; Jer. 31. 11; Hos. 13. 14.

Rashness, Eccl. 5. 2; Prov. 14. 29; Acts 19. 36.

Ravens, Gen. 8. 7; Lev. 11. 15; Deut. 14. 14; 1 Ki. 17. 4; Job 38. 41; Ps. 147. 9; Lk. 12. 24.

Reading of the law, Ex. 24. 7; Josh. 8. 34; 2 Ki. 23; Neh. 8; 9.
—of the prophets, Lk. 4. 16.
—of the epistles, Col. 4. 16; 1 Thes. 5. 27.
See Acts 13. 15.

Reaping, Lev. 19. 9; 23. 10, 22; 25. 5.
figurative, Job 4. 8; Ps. 126. 5; Prov. 22. 8; Matt. 13. 30; John 4. 36; 1 Cor. 9. 11; 2 Cor. 9. 6; Gal. 6. 7; Rev. 14. 15.

Rebekah, history of, Gen. 22; 24. 15, 67; 27. 6, 43; 49. 31; Rom. 9. 10.

Rechabites, Jer. 35. 18.

Reconciliation with God, Is. 53. 5; Dan. 9. 24; Rom. 5; 2 Cor. 5. 19; Eph. 2. 16; Col. 1. 20; Heb. 2. 17.

Record of God, 1 John 5. 7, 10.

Redeemer, the Lord, Job 19. 25; Ps. 19. 14; 78. 35; Prov. 23. 11; Is. 41. 14; 47. 4; 59. 20; 63. 16; Jer. 50. 34; Hos. 13. 14.

Redemption by Christ, Rom. 5; Gal. 1. 4; 3; 4; Eph. 1; 2; Col. 1; Heb. 9; 10; Tit. 2. 14; 1 Pet. 1. 18; Rev. 5. 9.

Redemption of land, etc., Lev. 25; Neh. 5. 8.
of the firstborn, Ex. 13. 11; Num. 3. 12.

Red Dragon, Rev. 12. 3.

Red Horse, vision of, Zech. 1. 8; 6. 2; Rev. 6. 4.

Red Sea, Ex. 14; 15; 1 Ki. 9. 26.

Reed, bruised, 2 Ki. 18. 21; Is. 42; Matt. 12. 20.
a measure, Ezek. 40. 3; Rev. 11. 1; 21. 15.

Refiner, the, Is. 48. 10; Zech. 13. 9; Mal. 3. 2.

Refuge, the divine, Deut. 33. 27; 2 Sam. 22. 3; Ps. 9. 9; 46. 1; 48. 3; Heb. 6. 18.
cities of, Num. 35; Deut. 4. 41; 19; Josh. 20.

Regeneration, Matt. 19. 28; John 1. 13; 3. 3; Tit. 3. 5.

Rehoboam, king of Judah, 1 Ki. 11. 43; 12; 14; 2 Chr. 9. 31; 10; 11; 12.

Rehoboth, Gen. 26. 22.

Rejoicing of the faithful, Lev. 23. 40; Deut. 12. 10; 16. 11; 1 Chr. 16. 10; 2 Chr. 6. 41; Ps. 5. 11; 33; 48. 11; 68. 4; 89. 16; 97. 12; 103; Is. 41. 16; Joel 2. 23; Hab. 3. 18; Zech. 10. 7; Rom. 12. 15; Phil. 3. 1; 4. 4; 1 Thes. 5. 16; Jas. 1. 9; Rev. 12. 12; 18. 20.

Release, year of, Ex. 21. 2; Deut. 15. 1; 31. 10; Jer. 34. 14.

Religion, pure and undefiled, Jas. 1. 27.

Remission of sins, Matt. 26. 28; Mk. 1. 4; Lk. 4. 47; Acts 2. 38; 10. 43; Heb. 9. 22; 10. 18.

Remphan, Acts 7. 43.

Rending the clothes, Gen. 37. 34; 2 Sam. 13. 19; 2 Chr. 34. 27; Ezra 9. 5; Job 1. 20; 2. 12; Joel 2. 13; by the high priest, Matt. 26. 65; Mk. 14. 63.

Repentance, preached by John the Baptist, Matt. 3; Mk. 1. 4; Lk. 3. 3; by Christ, etc., Matt. 4. 17; Mk. 1. 15; 6. 12; Lk. 15; 24. 47; Acts 2. 38; 3. 19; 17. 30.
exhortations to, Job 11. 13; Is. 1; Jer. 3; 4; 5; 26; 31. 18; Ezek. 14. 6; 18; Hos. 6; 12; 14; Joel 1. 8; 2; Zeph. 2; Zech. 1; Mal. 1-4; Rev. 2. 5, 16, 21; 3. 3, 19.

Repetitions, vain, forbidden, Matt. 6. 7.

Rephidim, Amalek subdued there, Ex. 17.

Reproaches, Ps. 69. 9; Rom. 15. 3.
See Lk. 6. 22; 2 Cor. 12. 10; Heb. 10. 33; 1 Pet. 4. 14.

Reprobate, Jer. 6. 30; Rom. 1. 28; 2 Tim. 3. 8; Tit. 1. 16.
See 2 Cor. 13. 5.

Reproof, Prov. 6. 23; 13. 18; 15. 5, 31; 17. 10; 19. 25; 25. 12; 27. 5; 29. 15; Eccl. 7. 5; Eph. 5. 13; 2 Tim. 3. 16.
necessary, Lev. 19. 17; Is. 58. 1; Ezek. 2. 3; 33; 2 Thes. 3. 15; 1 Tim. 5. 20; 2 Tim. 4. 2; Tit. 1. 13; 2. 15.
benefits of, Ps. 141. 5; Prov. 9. 8; 15. 5; 24. 25.
not to be despised, Prov. 1. 25; 5. 12; 10. 17; 12. 1; 15. 10; 29. 1.

Rereward, Is. 52. 12; 58. 8.

Rest, future, promised, Heb. 3. 11; 4.
See Is. 11. 10; 14. 3; 30. 15; Jer. 6. 16; Matt. 11. 28.

Restitution, Ex. 22. 1; Lev. 5. 16; 6. 4; 24. 21; Num. 5. 5; Lk. 19. 8.
See Acts. 3. 21.

Resurrection of the body foretold, Job 19. 26; Ps. 17. 15; Is. 26. 19; Dan. 12. 2.
typified, Ezek. 37.
proclaimed by Christ, Matt. 22. 31; Lk. 14. 14; John 5. 28; 11. 23.
preached by the apostles, Acts 4. 2; 17. 18; 24. 15; 26. 8; Rom. 6. 5; 8. 11; 1 Cor. 15; 2 Cor. 4. 17; Phil. 3. 20; Col. 3. 3; 1 Thes. 4. 15; 5. 23; Heb. 6. 2; 2 Pet. 1. 11; 1 John 3. 2.

Return from captivity, Ezra 1; Neh. 2; Jer. 16. 14; 23; 24; 30; 31; 32; 50. 4, 17, 33; Amos 9. 14; Hag. 1; Zech. 1.

Reuben, son of Jacob, Gen. 29. 32; 30. 14; 35; 37; 42; 49; 1 Chr. 5. 1.

Reubenites, their number and possessions, Num. 1; 2; 26; 32; Deut. 3. 12; Josh. 13. 15; 1 Chr. 5. 18.
dealings of Moses and Joshua with, Num. 32; Deut. 33; Josh. 1. 12; 22.
carried into captivity, 1 Chr. 5. 26; (Rev. 7. 5).

Revelation of Jesus Christ to John, Rev. 1; the messages to the churches, Rev. 2; 3; the glory of heaven, Rev. 4; 5; opening of the seven seals, Rev. 6; 8; the sealing of

Revelation—*Continued.*
God's servants, Rev. 7; the seven trumpets, Rev. 8; 9; 11. 15; the seven thunders, Rev. 10. 4; the two witnesses and the beast, Rev. 11; the woman clothed with the sun, the red dragon, Michael fighting against, overcomes, Rev. 12; 13; of the glory and fall of Babylon, Rev. 14; 17; 18; 19; the seven vials, Rev. 15; 16; the marriage of the Lamb, Rev. 19; the last judgment, Rev. 20; the New Jerusalem, etc., Rev. 21; 22.

Revelations from God:—of mercy, etc., Deut. 29. 29; Job 33. 16; Is. 40. 5; 53. 1; Jer. 33. 6; Dan. 2. 22; Amos 3. 7; Matt. 11. 25; 16. 17; 1 Cor. 2. 10; 2 Cor. 12; Gal. 1. 12; Eph. 3. 9; Phil. 3. 15; 1 Pet. 1. 5; 4. 13.
of wrath, Rom. 1. 18; 2. 5; 2 Thes. 1. 7.

Revenge forbidden, Lev. 19. 18; Prov. 20. 22; 24. 29; Matt. 5. 39; Rom. 12. 19; 1 Thes. 5. 15; 1 Pet. 3. 9.

Reverence due to God, Ex. 3. 5; Ps. 89. 7; 111. 9; Heb. 12. 28; to God's sanctuary, Lev. 19. 30.
from wives to husbands, Eph. 5. 33.

Reviling condemned, Ex. 22. 28; Matt. 5. 22; 1 Cor. 6. 10.
examples of enduring, Is. 51. 7; Matt. 5. 11; 27. 39; 1 Cor. 4. 12; 1 Pet. 2. 23.

Reward to the righteous, Gen. 15. 1; Ps. 19. 11; 58. 11; Prov. 11. 18; 25. 22; Matt. 5. 12; 6. 1; 10. 41; Lk. 6. 35; 1 Cor. 3. 8; Col. 2. 18; 3. 24; Heb. 10. 35; 11. 6; Rev. 22. 12.
threatened to the wicked, Deut. 32. 41; 2 Sam. 3. 39; Ps. 54. 5; 91. 8; 109; Obad. 15; 2 Pet. 2. 13; Rev. 19. 17; 20. 15; 22. 15.

Rezin, king of Syria, 2 Ki. 15. 37; 16. 5, 9; Is. 7. 1.

Rezon of Damascus, 1 Ki. 11. 23.

Rhodes, island of, Acts 21. 1.

Riblah, in Syria, 2 Ki. 23. 33; 25. 6; Jer. 39. 5; 52. 9.

Riches, given by God, 1 Sam. 2. 7; Prov. 10. 22; Eccl. 5. 19.
earthly, Deut. 8. 17; 1 Chr. 29. 12; Ps. 49. 6; Prov. 11. 4; 15. 16; 23. 5; 27. 24; Eccl. 4. 8; 5. 10; 6; Jer. 9. 23; 48. 36; Ezek. 7. 19; Zeph. 1. 18; Matt. 6. 19; 13. 22; 1 Tim. 6. 17; Jas. 1. 11; 5. 2; 1 Pet. 1. 18.
dangers of, Deut. 8. 13; 32. 15; Neh. 9. 25; Prov. 15. 17; 18. 23; 28. 11; 30. 8; Eccl. 5. 12; Hos. 12. 8; Matt. 13. 22; 19. 23; Mk. 10. 22; Lk. 12. 15; 1 Tim. 6. 10; Jas. 2. 6; 5. 1.
proper use of, 1 Chr. 29. 3; Job 31. 16, 24; Ps. 62. 10; Jer. 9. 23; Matt. 6. 19; 19. 21; Lk. 16. 9; 1 Tim. 6. 17; Jas. 1. 9; 1 John 3. 17.
evil use of, Job 20. 15; 31. 24; Ps. 39. 6; 49. 6; 73. 12; Prov. 11. 28; 13. 7, 11; 15. 6; Eccl. 2. 26; 5. 10; Jas. 5. 3.
the true, Lk. 16. 11; Eph. 3. 8; Col. 2. 3; Rev. 3. 18.
end of the wicked rich, Job 20. 16; 21. 13; 27. 16; Ps. 52. 7; Prov. 11. 4; 22. 16; Eccl. 5. 14; Jer. 17. 11; Mic. 2. 3; Hab. 2. 6; Lk. 6. 24; 12. 16; 16. 19; Jas. 5. 1.

Riddle of Samson, Jud. 14. 12.

Righteous, blessings and privileges of the, Job 36. 7; Ps. 1; 5. 12; 14. 5; 15; 32. 34. 15; 37; 52. 6; 55. 22; 58. 10; 64. 10; 89; 92. 12; 97. 11; 112; 125. 3; 146. 8; Prov. 2. 7; 3. 32; 12. 26; 10-13; 28. 1; Is. 3. 10; 26. 2; 60. 21; Ezek. 18; Matt. 13. 43; Acts 10. 35; Rom. 2. 10; 1 Pet. 3. 12; 1 John 3. 7; Rev. 22. 11.

Righteousness, by faith, Gen. 15. 6; Ps. 106. 31; Rom. 4. 3; Gal. 3. 6; Jas. 2. 23.
—of Christ, imputed to the Church, Is. 54. 17; Jer. 23. 6; 33. 16; Hos. 2. 19; Mal. 4. 2; Rom. 1. 17; 3. 22; 10. 3; 1 Cor. 1. 30; 2 Cor. 5. 21; Phil. 3. 9; Tit. 2. 14; 2 Pet. 1. 1.
of the law and faith, Rom. 10.
—of man, Deut. 9. 4; Is. 64. 6; Dan. 9. 18; Phil. 3. 9.

Rimmon, idol, 2 Ki. 5. 18.

Rings, Gen. 41. 42; Ex. 25. 12; 26. 29; Est. 3. 10; Ezek. 1. 18; Lk. 15. 22.

Rioting and revelling, Prov. 23. 20; 28. 7; Lk. 15. 13; Rom. 13. 13; 1 Pet. 4. 4; 2 Pet. 2. 13.

River of life, Rev. 22.
See Ps. 36. 8; 46. 4; 65. 9; Ezek. 47.

Robbery forbidden, Lev. 19. 13; Ps. 62. 10; Prov. 21. 7; 22. 22; 28. 24; Is. 10. 2; 61. 8; Ezek. 22. 29; Amos 3. 10; 1 Cor. 6. 8; 1 Thes. 4. 6.

Robe, scarlet, gorgeous, purple, Matt. 27. 28; Lk. 23. 11; John 19. 2.

Robes, white, Rev. 6. 11; 7. 9.

Rock, water miraculously brought from, Ex. 17. 6; Num. 20. 10; 1 Cor. 10. 4.
figuratively used, Deut. 32. 4, 15; 2 Sam. 22. 2; 23. 3; Ps. 18. 2; 28. 1; 31. 2; 61. 2; Is. 17. 10; 32. 2.
See Matt. 7. 24.

Rod of Moses, Ex. 4; of Aaron, Num. 17; Heb. 9. 4.

Roll of prophecy, Is. 8. 1; Jer. 36. 2; Ezek. 2. 9; 3. 1; Zech. 5. 1.

Romans, St Paul's teaching to.
See epistle to Romans, also *Faith, Works, Righteousness.*

Rome, strangers of, at Pentecost, Acts 2. 10; Jews ordered to depart from, Acts 18. 2; Paul preaches there, Acts 28.

Rose of Sharon, Cant. 2. 1.

Rufus (chosen in the Lord), Rom. 16. 13.

Rulers chosen by Moses, Ex. 18. 25.
of the Jews, John 3. 1; 12. 42.
of the synagogue:—Jairus, Lk. 8. 41; Crispus, Acts 18. 8; Sosthenes, Acts 18. 17.

Ruth, story of, Ruth 1-4.
Christ descended from, Matt. 1. 5.

SABAOTH (Hosts), the Lord of, Rom. 9. 29; Jas. 5. 4.

Sabbath, instituted, Gen. 2. 2; (Heb. 4. 4).
to be kept holy, Ex. 16. 23; 20. 8; 23. 12; 31. 13; 34. 21; 35. 2; Lev. 25. 3; Num. 15. 32; Deut. 5. 12; Neh. 10. 31; 13. 15; Is. 56; 58. 13; Jer. 17. 21; Ezek. 20. 12.
its offerings, Num. 28. 9.
of the seventh year, Ex. 23. 10; Lev. 25. 1.
Christ the Lord of, Mk. 2. 27; Lk. 6. 5.
the Jews' hypocrisy concerning, reproved, Matt. 12; Mk. 2. 23; 3; Lk. 13. 14; John 7. 23.
first day of the week kept as, Acts 20. 7; 1 Cor. 16. 2; Rev. 1. 10.
See Mat 28. 1; Mk. 16. 2, 9; John 20. 1, 19, 26.

Sabeans, Job 1. 15; Is. 45. 14.

Sackcloth, 2 Sam. 3. 31; 1 Ki. 20. 32; Neh. 9. 1; Est. 4. 1; Ps. 30. 11; 35. 13; Jonah 3. 5.

Sacrifices, Lev. 22. 19; Deut. 17. 1.
types of Christ, Heb. 9; 10.

Sacrilege, Rom. 2. 22.

Sadducees, their controversies with Christ, Matt. 16. 1; 22. 23; Mk. 12. 18; Lk. 20. 27; with the apostles, Acts 4. 1; with Paul, Acts 23. 8; their doctrines, Matt. 22. 23; Mk. 12. 18; Acts 23. 8.

Saints, their blessings and privileges, Deut. 33. 2 ; 1 Sam. 2. 9 ; Ps. 145. 10 ; 148. 14 ; 149 ; Prov. 2. 8 ; Dan. 7. 18 ; Zech. 14. 5 ; Rom. 8. 27 ; Eph. 2. 19 ; Col. 1. 12 ; Jude 3 ; Rev. 5. 8.
their duty, 2 Chr. 6. 41 ; Ps. 30. 4 ; 31. 23 ; 34. 9 ; 132. 9 ; Rom. 16. 2, 15 ; 1 Cor. 6 ; 2 Cor. 8 ; 9 ; Eph. 4 ; 6. 18 ; Philem. ; Heb. 6. 10 ; 13. 24.

Salem, Gen. 14. 18 ; Heb. 7. 1.

Salome, Mk. 15. 40 ; 16. 1.

Salt, Lev. 2. 13 ; Mk. 9. 49.
Lot's wife becomes a pillar of, Gen. 19. 26.
of the earth, Matt. 5. 13 ; Lk. 14. 34 ; (Col. 4. 6).

—sea (Siddim), Gen. 14. 3 ; Num. 34. 3, 12 ; Deut. 3. 17 ; Josh. 3. 16 ; 12. 3 ; 15. 1, 2.

Salvation, Ex. 14. 3 ; 15 ; 1 Sam. 11. 13 ; Ps. 3. 8 ; 37. 39, 62. 1 ; 68. 19 ; Is. 33. 2 ; 46. 13 ; 59. 1 ; 63. 5 ; Lam. 3. 26 ; Mic. 7. 7 ; Hab. 3. 18 ; Lk. 1. 69 ; Rev. 7. 10 ; 12. 10 ; 19. 1.
to be wrought out with fear and trembling, Phil. 2. 12.

Samaria (city of), 1 Ki. 16. 24 ; 20. 1 ; 2 Ki. 6. 24.

—(region of), visited by Christ, Lk. 17. 11 ; John 4.
Gospel preached there, Acts 8.

Samaritan, parable of, Lk. 10. 33.
miracle performed on, Lk. 17. 16.

Samson, his deeds, etc., Jud. 13-16.
delivered up to Philistines, Jud. 16. 21.
his death, Jud. 16. 30.

Samuel born and presented to the Lord, 1 Sam. 1. 19, 26.
ministers to the Lord, 1 Sam. 3.
the Lord speaks to, 1 Sam. 3. 11.
judges Israel, 1 Sam. 7 ; 8. 1 ; Acts 13. 20.
anoints Saul king, 1 Sam. 10. 1.
rebukes Saul for disobedience, 1 Sam. 13. 13 ; 15. 16.
anoints David, etc., 1 Sam. 16 ; 19. 18.
his death, 1 Sam. 25. 1 ; 28. 3.
his spirit consulted by Saul, 1 Sam. 28. 12.
as a prophet, Ps. 99. 6 ; Acts 3. 24 ; Heb. 11. 32.

Sanballat, Neh. 2. 10 ; 4 ; 6. 2 ; 13. 28.

Sanctification by Christ, John 17. 19 ; 1 Cor. 1. 2, 30 ; 6. 11 ; Eph. 5. 26 ; Heb. 2. 11 ; 10. 10 ; Jude 1.
by the Spirit, Rom. 15. 16 ; 2 Thes. 2. 13 ; 1 Pet. 1. 2.

Sanctified, the seventh day, Gen. 2. 3.
the firstborn to be, Ex. 13. 2.
the people, Ex. 19. 10 ; Num. 11. 18 ; Josh. 3. 5.
the tabernacle, etc., Ex. 29 ; 30 ; Lev. 8. 10.
the priests, Lev. 8. 30 ; 9 ; 2 Chr. 5. 11.

Sanctuary, God, of His people, Is. 8. 14 ; Ezek. 11. 16.
See Ps. 20. 2 ; 63. 2 ; 68. 24 ; 73. 17 ; 77. 13 ; 78. 54 ; 96. 6 ; 134 ; 150 ; Heb. 8 ; 9.

Sand of the sea, Gen. 22. 17 ; Hos. 1. 10 ; Heb. 11. 12 ; Rev. 20. 8.

Sandals, Mk. 6. 9 ; Acts 12. 8.

Sapphire, Ex. 24. 10 ; 28. 18 ; Ezek. 1. 26 ; 10. 1 ; 28. 13 ; Rev. 21. 19.

Sarah (Sarai), Gen. 12. 14 ; 20. 2. See *Abraham.*
her death and burial, Gen. 23.
See Heb. 11. 11 ; 1 Pet. 3. 6.

Sardine stone, Rev. 4. 3.

Sardis, church of, Rev. 1. 11 ; 3. 1.

Sardius, Ex. 28. 17 ; Ezek. 28. 13 ; Rev. 21. 20.

Sardonyx, Rev. 21. 20.

Satan, Job 1. 7 ; 2. 1 ; Zech. 3. 1 ; Matt. 4. 10. See *Devil.*

Saul, king of Israel, his parentage, anointing by Samuel, prophesying, and acknowledgment as king, 1 Sam. 9 ; 10.

Saul—*continued.*
his disobedience and rejection by God, 1 Sam. 15.
troubled by an evil spirit, 1 Sam. 16. 14.
favours David, 1 Sam. 18. 5 ; seeks to kill him, 1 Sam. 18. 10 ; pursues him, 1 Sam. 20 ; 23 ; 24 ; 26.
slays the priests at Nob, 1 Sam. 22. 9.
enquires of the witch of En-dor, 1 Sam. 28. 7.
his ruin foretold, 1 Sam. 28. 15.
his death, 1 Sam. 31 ; 1 Chr. 10.
his descendants, 1 Chr. 8. 33.

—of Tarsus. See *Paul.*

Saviour, God, Is. 43. 3, 11 ; Jer. 14. 8 ; Hos. 13. 4 ; Lk. 1. 47.
Christ, Lk. 2. 11 ; John 4. 42 ; Acts 5. 31 ; 13. 23 ; Eph. 5. 23 ; 2 Pet. 1. 1 ; 3. 2 ; 1 John 4. 14 ; Jude 25.

Savour, a sweet (of the sacrifices), Gen. 8. 21 ; Ex. 29. 18.
type of Christ, 2 Cor. 2. 14, 15 ; Eph. 5. 2.

Scab, Lev. 13. 1 ; Deut. 28. 27 ; Is. 3. 17.

Scapegoat, Lev. 16. 20, 21 ; (Is. 53. 6).

Sceptre, Gen. 49. 10 ; Num. 24. 17 ; Est. 5. 2 ; Ps. 45. 6 ; Heb. 1. 8.

Schism condemned, 1 Cor. 1 ; 3 ; 11. 18 ; 12. 25 ; 2 Cor. 13. 11.

Schoolmaster, figurative, Gal. 3. 24.

Scoffers, their sin, Ps. 1 ; 2 ; 123. 4 ; Prov. 1. 22, 3. 34 ; 13. 1 ; 14. 6 ; 15. 12 ; 19. 25, 29 ; 21. 24 ; 24. 9 ; Is. 28. 14 ; 29. 20 ; 2 Pet. 3. 3.

Scorpions, Deut. 8. 15 ; Lk. 10. 19 ; Rev. 9. 3.

Scourging, Lev. 19. 20 ; Deut. 25. 3 ; 2 Cor. 11. 24.
of Christ, Matt. 27. 26 ; Lk. 23. 16.

Scribes, 2 Sam. 8. 17 ; 20. 25 ; 1 Ki. 4. 3 ; 2 Ki. 19. 2 ; 22. 8 ; 1 Chr. 27. 32 ; Ezra 7. 6 ; Jer. 36. 26.
and Pharisees, censured by Christ, Matt. 15. 2 ; 23. ; Mk. 2. 16 ; 3. 22 ; Lk. 11. 53 ; 20. 1.
conspire against Christ, Mk. 11. 18 ; Lk. 20. 19 ; 22. 2 ; 23. 10.
persecute Stephen, Acts 6. 12.

Scriptures, the Holy, given by inspiration of God through the Holy Ghost, Acts 1. 16 ; Heb. 3. 7 ; 2 Tim. 3. 16 ; 2 Pet. 1. 21.
to be kept unaltered, Deut. 4. 2 ; Prov. 30. 6 ; Rev. 22. 18.
profitable for doctrine, instruction, etc., Ps. 19. 7 ; 119. 9 ; John 17. 17 ; Acts 20. 32 ; Rom. 15. 4 ; 16. 26 ; 2 Tim. 3. 16.
referred to and expounded by Christ, Matt. 4. 4 ; Mk. 12. 10 ; Lk. 24. 27 ; John 7. 42.
testify of Christ, John 5. 39 ; Acts 10. 43 ; 18. 28 ; 1 Cor. 15. 5.
make wise unto salvation, John 20. 31 ; Rom. 1. 2 ; 2 Tim. 3. 15 ; Jas. 1. 21 ; 2 Pet. 1. 19.
formerly given by God through the prophets, Lk. 16. 31 ; Rom. 3. 2 ; 9. 4 ; Heb. 1. 1 ; in the last days through Jesus Christ, Heb. 1. 2.
fulfilled by Christ, Matt. 5. 17 ; Lk. 24. 27 ; John 19. 24 : Acts 13. 29.
appealed to by the apostles, Acts 2 ; 3 ; 8. 32 ; 17. 2 ; 18. 24 ; 28. 23.
danger of rejecting, John 12. 48 ; Heb. 2. 3 ; 10. 28 ; 12. 25.

Scroll, the heavens compared to, Is. 34. 4 ; Rev. 6. 14.

Scythians, Col. 3. 11.

Sea, God's power over, Ex. 14. 6 ; 15 ; Neh. 9. 11 ; Job 38. 11 ; Ps. 65. 7 ; 66. 6 ; 89. 9 ; 93. 4 ; 107. 23 ; 114 ; Prov. 8. 29 ; Is. 51. 10 ; Nah. 1. 4.

Sheshach, Jer. 25. 26 ; 51. 41.

Sheshbazzar, Ezra 1. 8 ; 5. 14.

Shethar-Boznai and Tatnai oppose rebuilding of temple, Ezra 5. 6.

Shewbread, Ex. 25. 30 ; Lev. 24. 5 ; Heb. 9. 2. given to David, 1 Sam. 21. 6 ; (Matt. 12. 4 ; Mk. 2. 26 ; Lk. 6. 4).

Shibboleth, Jud. 12. 6.

Shield, God, of His people, Gen. 15. 1 ; Deut. 33. 29 ; Ps. 33. 20 ; 84. 11 ; 115. 9 ; Prov. 30. 5. of faith, Eph. 6. 16.

Shields, Solomon's, 1 Ki. 10. 17 ; Goliath's, 1 Sam. 17. 6.

Shiloh, prophecy concerning, Gen. 49. 10.
—site of tabernacle, Josh. 18. 1 ; Jud. 21.19 ; 1 Sam. 1. 3 ; 2. 14 ; 3. 21 ; Ps. 78. 60 ; Jer. 7. 12 ; 26. 6.

Shimei curses David, 2 Sam. 16. 5. slain by Solomon, 1 Ki. 2. 36.

Shining of God's face, Numb. 6. 25 ; Ps. 31. 16 ; 50. 2 ; 67. 1, 80. 1, Dan. 9. 17. skin of Moses' face, Ex. 34. 29 ; 2 Cor. 3. of Christ's countenance, Matt. 17. 2 ; Lk. 9. 29 ; Acts 9. 3 ; Rev. 1. 16. of Christians, as lights of the world, Matt. 5. 16 ; (John 5. 35), Phil. 2. 15 ; and in the kingdom of heaven, Dan. 12. 3 ; Matt. 13. 43. of the Gospel, 2 Cor. 4. 4 ; Is. 9. 2.

Ships, mentioned, Gen. 49. 13 ; Num. 24. 24. a navy formed by Solomon, 1 Ki. 9. 26 ; by Jehoshaphat, 1 Ki. 22. 48. of Tarshish, Ps. 48. 7 ; Is. 2. 16 ; 23. 1 ; 60. 9 ; Ezek. 27. 25.

Shishak, king of Egypt, invades Jerusalem and spoils the temple, 1 Ki. 14. 25 ; 2 Chr. 12.

Shittim-wood for the tabernacle, Ex. 25. 5 ; 27. 1.

Shoes taken off, Ex. 3. 5 ; Deut. 25. 9 ; Josh. 5. 15 ; Ruth 4. 7 ; 2 Sam. 15. 30.

Shoulder in sacrifices, Ex. 29. 22, 27 ; Lev. 7. 34, 10. 14 ; Num. 6. 19.

Shouting, in war, Josh. 6. 5 ; 1 Sam. 4. 5 ; 2 Chr. 13. 15. in worship, 2 Sam. 6. 15 ; Ezra 3. 11 ; Ps. 47. 1 ; Zeph. 3. 14.

Shunem, Josh. 19. 18 , 1 Sam. 28. 4 ; 2 Ki. 4. 8.

Shushan, city, Ahasuerus at, Neh. 1. 1 : Est. 2. 8, 3. 15.

Sickle, Deut. 16. 9 ; 23. 25. typical, Joel 3. 13 ; Mk. 4. 29 ; Rev. 14. 14.

Sickness, Lev. 26. 16 ; Deut. 28. 27 ; 2 Sam. 12. 15 ; 2 Chr. 21. 15. behaviour under, Ps. 35. 13 ; Is. 38. 12 ; Matt. 25. 36 ; Jas. 5. 14. of persons healed miraculously : Hezekiah, 2 Ki. 20. 1 , 2 Chr. 32. 24 ; Lazarus, John 11. 1 ; Peter's wife's mother, Matt. 8. 14 ; Mk. 1. 30 , Lk. 4. 38 ; Dorcas, Acts 9. 37. cured by Christ, Matt. 8. 16 ; 10. 8 ; Mk. 16. 18 ; Lk. 7. 10. See *Affliction.*

Sidon, son of Canaan, Gen. 10. 15.
—(Zidon), city of, Josh. 19. 28 ; 1 Ki. 5 ; Acts 27. 3.

Signs, sun and moon, Gen. 1. 14 ; rainbow, Gen. 9. 13 ; circumcision, Gen. 17. 10 ; Sabbath, Ex. 31. 13 ; Jonas, Matt. 12. 39, false, Deut. 13. 1 ; Matt. 24. 24 , 2 Thes. 2. 9. of the times, Matt. 16. 3. Pharisees ask for, Matt. 12. 38 ; Mk. 8. 11. See 1 Ki. 13. 3 ; Is. 7. 11 ; 8. 18 ; 20. 3 ; Acts 2. 43.

Sihon, king of the Amorites, Num. 21. 21 ; **Deut. 1. 4 ; 2. 26** ; Ps. 135. 11 ; 136. 19.

Silas, companion of Paul, Acts 15. 22 ; 16. 22 ; 17. 4. See 2 Cor. 1. 19 ; 1 Thes. 1. 1 ; 1 Pet. 5. 12.

Silence, Job 2. 13 ; Ps. 39. 2 ; Prov. 10. 19 ; 11. 12 ; 17. 28. women to keep, 1 Tim. 2. 11. in heaven, Rev. 8. 1.

Silk mentioned, Prov. 31. 22 ; Ezek. 16. 10.

Siloam, pool of, miracle there, John 9. 7.

Silver used in the tabernacle, Ex. 26. 19 ; Num. 7. 13. as money, Gen. 23. 15 ; 44. 2 ; Deut. 22. 19 ; 2 Ki. 5. 22.

Simeon, son of Jacob, Gen. 29. 33 ; 34. 7, 25 ; 42. 24. prophecy concerning, Gen. 49. 5. his descendants, Gen. 46. 10 ; Ex. 6. 15 ; Num. 1. 22 ; 26. 12 ; 1 Chr. 4. 24 ; 12. 25.
—blesses Christ, Lk. 2. 25.

Simon, brother of Christ, Matt. 13. 55 ; Mk. 6. 3.
—(Zelotes), apostle, Matt. 10. 4 ; Mk. 3. 18 ; Lk. 6. 15.
—(Pharisee), reproved, Lk. 7. 36.
—(leper), Matt. 26. 6 ; Mk. 14. 3.
—(of Cyrene), bears the cross of Jesus, Matt. 27. 32 ; Mk. 15. 21 ; Lk. 23. 26.
(a tanner), Peter's vision in his house, Acts 9. 43 ; 10. 6.
—(a sorcerer), baptized, Acts 8. 9 ; rebuked by Peter, Acts 8. 18.
—Peter. See *Peter.*

Simple, the (foolish), Prov. 1. 22 ; 8. 5. See Prov. 1. 32 , 7. 7 ; 14. 15.

Simplicity, in Christ, 2 Cor. 1. 12 ; 11. 3 ; Rom. 16. 19.

Sin, origin of, Gen. 3. 6 ; Matt. 15. 19 ; John 8. 44 ; Rom. 5. 12 ; 1 John 3. 8. characterised, Deut. 9. 7 ; Josh. 1. 18 ; Prov. 14. 34 ; 15. 9 ; 24. 9 ; Is. 1. 18 ; Rom. 14. 23 ; Eph. 5. 11 ; Heb. 3. 13 ; 6. 1 ; 9. 14 ; Jas. 1. 15 ; 4. 17 ; 1 John 3. 4 ; 5. 17. all born in, and under, Gen. 5. 3 ; Job 15. 14 ; 25. 4 ; Ps. 51. 5 ; Rom. 3. 9 ; Gal. 3. 22. Christ alone without, 2 Cor. 5. 21 ; Heb. 4. 15 ; 7. 26 ; 1 John 3. 5. Christ's blood redeems from, John 1. 29 ; Eph. 1. 7 ; 1 John 1. 7 ; 3. 5. a fountain opened for, Zech. 13. 1. repented of, and confessed, Job 33. 27 ; Ps. 38. 18 ; 97. 10 ; Prov. 28. 13 ; Jer. 3. 21 ; 1 John 1. 9. striven against and mortified, Ps. 4. 4 ; 19. 13 ; 39. 1 ; 51. 2 ; 139. 23 ; Matt. 6. 13 ; Rom. 8. 13 ; Col. 3. 5 , Heb. 12. 4. excludes from heaven, 1 Cor. 6. 9 ; Gal. 5. 19 ; Eph. 5. 5 ; Rev. 21. 27. wages of, death, Rom. 6. 23. sting of, „ 1 Cor. 15. 56. against the Holy Ghost, Matt. 12. 31 ; Mk. 3. 28 ; Lk. 12. 10. See Heb. 6. 4 ; 10. 26 ; 1 John 5. 16.

Sin (Zin), wilderness of, Ex. 16 ; Num. 13. 21 ; 20 ; 27. 14.

Sinai, mount, Deut. 33. 2 ; Jud. 5. 5 ; Ps. 68. 8, 17 ; Gal. 4. 24.

Sincerity, exhortations to, Josh. 24. 14 ; 1 Cor. 5. 8 ; Eph. 6. 24 ; Tit. 2. 7.

Singing. See *Psalmody.*

Sirion, mount, Deut. 3. 9 ; Ps. 29. 6.

Sisera, Jud. 4. 2, 21 ; 5. 24 ; 1 Sam. 12. 9 ; Ps. 83. 9.

Slander, Ex. 23. 1 ; Ps. 15. 3 ; 31. 13 ; 34. 13 ; (1 Pet. 3. 10) ; 50. 20 , 64. 3 ; 101. 5 ; Prov. 10. 18 ; Jer. 6. 28 ; 9. 4 ; Eph. 4. 31 ; 1 Tim. 3. 11 ; Tit. 3. 2.

Slander—*Continued.*
effects of, Prov. 16. 28; 17. 9; 18. 8; 26. 20, 22;
   Jer. 38. 4; Ezek. 22. 9; Matt. 26. 59; Acts
   6. 11; 17. 7; 24. 5.
behaviour under, Matt. 5. 11; 1 Cor. 4. 12.
   See Rom. 3. 8.

Slaying unpremeditatedly, Num. 35. 11; Deut.
   4. 42; 19. 3; Josh. 20. 3.

Sleep, Gen. 2. 21; 15. 12; 1 Sam. 26. 12; Job 4.
   13; Prov. 6. 4-11; 19. 15; 20. 13.
of death, Ps. 13. 3; Dan. 12. 2; Mk. 13. 36; 1
   Cor. 11. 30; 15. 20; 1 Thes. 4. 14.

Sling, Jud. 20. 16.
Goliath slain by, 1 Sam. 17. 49.
   See 2 Ki. 3. 25; 2 Chr. 26. 14.
figurative, 1 Sam. 25. 29; Prov. 26. 8.

Slothfulness, Prov. 12. 24, 27; 15. 19; 18. 9; 19.
   15, 24; 21. 25; 22. 13; 24. 30; 26. 13-16; Eccl.
   10. 18; Matt. 25. 26; Rom. 11. 8.
condemned, Prov. 6. 4; Rom. 12. 11; 13. 11;
   1 Thes. 5. 6; Heb. 6. 12.

Sluggard, the, Prov. 6. 6, 10. 26; 13. 4; 20. 4;
   26. 16.

Smyrna, church of, Rev. 2. 8.

Snail, unclean, Lev. 11. 30.

Snuffers, gold, Ex. 25. 38; 37. 23.

Sobriety, Rom. 12. 3; 1 Thes. 5. 6; 1 Tim. 2. 9;
   3. 2; Tit. 1. 8; 2. 12; 1 Pet. 1. 13; 4. 7; 5. 8.

Sodom, its wickedness and destruction, Gen.
   13. 13; 18. 20; 19. 4; Deut. 23. 17; 1 Ki. 14. 24.
Lot's deliverance from, Gen. 19.
a warning, Deut. 29. 23; 32. 32; Is. 1. 9; 13.
   19; Lam. 4. 6; Matt. 10. 15; Lk. 17. 29;
   Jude 7; Rev. 11. 8.

Soldiers, admonition to, Lk. 3. 14.
at the crucifixion. John 19. 2, 23, 32.
as guards, Matt. 27. 66, 28. 4, 12; Acts 12. 4;
   23. 10; 27. 42.
of Israel, 2 Sam. 12. 24; 1 Ki. 1,
   2. 24; 1 Chr. 28. 9; 29.

Solomon, king of, 1 Ki. 3. 5; 4. 29; 2 Chr. 1. 7.
asks of God wisdom, 1 Ki. 3. 5; 4. 29; 2 Chr. 1. 7.
his wise judgment, 1 Ki. 3. 16.
his league with Hiram, 1 Ki. 5; 2 Chr. 2.
builds the temple, (2 Sam. 7. 12; 1 Chr. 17.
   11); 1 Ki. 6; 7; 2 Chr. 3-5.
his prayer at the dedication, 1 Ki. 8; 2 Chr. 6.
God's covenant with, 1 Ki. 9; 2 Chr. 7. 12.
visited by the queen of Sheba, 1 Ki. 10; 2
   Chr. 9; (Matt. 6. 29); 12. 42.
David's prayer for, Ps. 72.
his idolatry, rebuke, and death, 1 Ki. 11. 1,
   9, 41; 2 Chr. 9. 29; Neh. 13. 26.
his Proverbs and Canticles, Prov. 1. 1; Eccl.
   1. 1; Cant. 1. 1.

Son of God. See *Christ.*
—of man, Ezek. 2. 1; Matt. 8. 20; Acts 7. 56.

Sons of God, John 1. 6; 38. 7; John 1. 12; Rom.
   8. 14; 2 Cor. 6. 18; Heb. 2. 10; 12. 5; Jas. 1.
   18; 1 John 3. 1.
obligations of, Eph. 5. 1; Phil. 2. 15; 1 Pet.
   1. 13; 2. 9.

Songs:—of Moses, Ex. 15; Num. 21. 17; Deut.
   32; Rev. 15. 3.
of Deborah, Jud. 5; of Hannah, 1 Sam. 2. ;
   of David, 2 Sam. 22 (see *Psalms*); of Mary,
   Lk. 1. 46; of Zacharias, Lk. 1. 68; of the
   angels, Lk. 2. 13; of Simeon, Lk. 2. 29; of
   the redeemed, Rev. 5. 9; 19.

Sorcery, Is. 47. 9; 57. 3; Acts 8. 9; 13. 6; Rev.
   21. 8; 22. 15.

Sorrow, godly, 2 Cor. 7. 10; earthly, Gen. 42.
   38; Job 17. 7; Ps. 13. 2; 90. 10; Prov. 10. 22;
   Is. 35. 10; Lk. 22. 45; Rom. 9. 2; 1 Thes.
   4. 13; consequence of sin, Gen. 3. 16; Ps. 51.

Soul, man endowed with, Gen. 2. 7.
atonement for, Lev. 17. 11.
redemption of, Ps. 34. 22; 49. 8, 15.
its inestimable value, Matt. 16. 26; Mk. 8. 37.

Sour grapes, proverb concerning, Jer. 31. 29;
   Ezek. 18. 2.

South, the king of, Dan. 11.
—queen of, Matt. 12. 42.

Sower, parable of, Matt. 13. 3; Mk. 4. 3; Lk. 8. 5.

Span, a measure, Ex. 28. 16.

Spear, Josh. 8. 18; 1 Sam. 17. 7; John 19. 34.

Spices for religious rites, Ex. 25. 6; 30. 23, 34;
   37. 29; Ps. 45. 8.
for embalming, 2 Chr. 16. 14; Mk. 16. 1; Lk.
   23. 56; John 19. 40.

Spies sent into Canaan by Moses, Num. 13. 3,
   14. 35; Deut. 1. 22; Heb. 3. 17.
sent to Jericho by Joshua, Josh. 2. 1; 6. 17, 23.

Spikenard, Cant. 1. 12.
Christ anointed with, Mk. 14. 3; Lk. 7. 37;
   John 12. 3.

Spirit of God (the Holy Spirit, or Holy Ghost).
   See article *God*.

Spirit, of man, Eccl. 3. 21; 12. 7; Zech. 12. 1;
   1 Cor. 2. 11.
broken, Ps. 51. 17; Prov. 15. 13; 17. 22.
of Christ, Rom. 8. 9; 1 Pet. 1. 11.
of Antichrist, 1 John 4. 3.
born of, John 3. 5; Gal. 4. 29.
fruit of, Gal. 5. 22; Eph. 5. 9.
of truth, John 14. 17; 15. 26; 16. 13.
of bondage, Rom. 8. 15.
of jealousy, Num. 5. 14.
of divination, Acts 16. 16.
of slumber, Rom. 11. 8.
of fear, 2 Tim. 1. 7.

Spirits to be tried, 1 John 4. 1.

Spiritual body, etc., Rom. 1. 11; 1 Cor. 12; 14;
   15. 44; Phil. 3. 21; 1 John 3. 2.
   See 1 Cor. 2. 13; 1 Pet. 2. 5.

Spitting, Num. 12. 14; Deut. 25. 9; Job 30. 10.
endured by Christ (Is. 50. 6); Matt. 26. 67;
   27. 30; Mk. 10. 34; 14. 65; 15. 19.

Spoil, its division, Num. 31. 27.

Sprinkling of blood, the passover, Ex. 12. 22;
   Heb. 11. 28.
the covenant of, Ex. 24. 8; Heb. 9. 13.
cleansing the leper by, Lev. 14. 7.
of oil, Lev. 14. 16.
of the blood of Christ, Heb. 10. 22; 12. 24; 1
   Pet. 1. 2.

Standards of the twelve tribes, Num. 2.

Star, Balaam's prophecy concerning, Num. 24.
   17.
at Christ's birth, Matt. 2. 2.
morning star, Christ, Rev. 22. 16.
great star falls from heaven, Rev. 8. 10; 9. 1.

Stars created, Gen. 1. 16; Job 38. 7.
mentioned, Gen. 15. 5; 37. 9; Jud. 5. 20; 1
   Cor. 15. 41; Heb. 11. 12; Jude 13; Rev. 8.
   12; 12. 1.
not to be worshipped, Deut. 4. 19.

Statutes of the Lord, 1 Chr. 29. 19; Ps. 19. 8;
   119. 12, 16.

Staves for the tabernacle, Ex. 25. 13; 37. 15;
   40. 20; Num. 4. 6.

Steadfastness of the disciples, Acts 2. 42; Col.
   2. 5.
exhortations to, Deut. 10. 20; Job 11. 15; 1
   Cor. 15. 58; 1 Thes. 5. 21; Heb. 3. 14; 4. 14;
   10. 23; 1 Pet. 5. 9; 2 Pet. 3. 17.

Stealing, Ex. 20. 15; 21. 16; Lev. 19. 11; Deut.
   5. 19; 24. 7; Ps. 50. 18; Zech. 5. 4; Matt.
   19. 18; Rom. 13. 9; Eph. 4. 28; 1 Pet. 4. 15.

Stealing—*Continued.*
restitution to be made, Ex. 22. 1; Lev. 6. 4;
  Prov. 6. 30, 31.
Stephen, deacon and first martyr, Acts 6. 5;
  7. 58.
Steward, parable of, Lk. 16. 1.
of God, a bishop is, Tit. 1. 7.
  See 1 Cor. 4. 1; 1 Pet. 4. 10.
Stocks, Job 13. 27; 33. 11; Prov. 7. 22.
Jeremiah put in, Jer. 20. 2.
also Paul and Silas, Acts 16. 24.
Stoics deride Paul, Acts 17. 18.
Stone, corner, Christ is (Ps. 118. 22; Is. 28. 16);
  Matt. 21. 42; Mk. 12. 10; 1 Pet. 2. 6.
Stones, precious, in the high priest's breast-
  plate, Ex. 28. 17.
in the temple, 1 Chr. 29. 2; 2 Chr. 3. 6.
in the New Jerusalem, Rev. 21. 19.
Stoning, Lev. 20. 2; 24. 14; Deut. 13. 10; 17. 5;
  22. 21.
of Achan, Josh. 7. 25.
of Naboth, 1 Ki. 21.
of Stephen, Acts 7. 58.
of Paul, Acts 14. 19; 2 Cor. 11. 25.
Stork, the, Ps. 104. 17; Jer. 8. 7; Zech. 5. 9.
Strange women, 1 Ki. 11. 1; Prov. 2. 16; 5. 3,
  20; 6. 24; 23. 27.
Strangers (among the Israelites), not to be
  oppressed, Ex. 22. 21; 23. 9; Lev. 19. 33;
  Deut. 1. 16; 10. 18; 23. 7; 24. 14; Mal. 3. 5.
regulations as to the passover, the priest's
  office, marriage, and the laws concerning
  them, Ex. 12. 43; 34. 16; Lev. 17. 10; 22. 10;
  24. 16; Num. 1. 51; 18. 7; 19. 10; 35. 15;
  Deut. 7. 3; 17. 15; 25. 5; 31. 12; Josh. 8. 33;
  Ezra 10. 2; Neh. 13. 27; Ezek. 44. 9. See
  Hospitality.
and pilgrims, 1 Pet. 2. 11.
Strength of Israel, the Lord, Ex. 15. 2; 1 Sam.
  15. 29; Ps. 27. 1; 28. 8; 29. 11; 46. 1; 81. 1;
  Is. 26. 4; Joel 3. 16; Zech. 12. 5.
—of sin, the law, 1 Cor. 15. 56; Rom. 7.
—made perfect in weakness, 2 Cor. 12. 9; Heb.
  11. 34; Ps. 8. 2.
Strife, Prov. 3. 30; 17. 14; 25. 8; 26. 17; Rom.
  13. 13; 1 Cor. 3. 3; Gal. 5. 20; Phil. 2. 3, 14;
  2 Tim. 2. 23; Tit. 3. 9; Jas. 3. 14.
its origin, Prov. 10. 12; 13. 10; 15. 18; 16. 28;
  22. 10; 23. 29; 26. 20; 28. 25; 30. 33; 1 Tim.
  6. 4; 2 Tim. 2. 23; Jas. 4. 1.
its results, Lev. 24. 10; Gal. 5. 15; Jas. 3. 16.
reproved, 1 Cor. 1. 11; 3. 3; 6; 11. 17.
Stripes, Deut. 25. 3; 2 Cor. 11. 24.
Stubbornness, punishment of, Deut. 21. 18;
  Prov. 1. 24; 29. 1.
forbidden, 2 Chr. 30. 8; Ps. 32. 9; 75. 4.
of the Jews, 2 Ki. 17. 14; Jer. 5. 3; 7. 28; 32. 33.
Study, excessive, Eccl. 12. 12.
Stumblingblock not to be placed before the
  blind, Lev. 19. 14; Deut. 27. 18.
figurative of offence, Is. 8. 14; Rom. 9. 32;
  14. 21; 1 Cor. 1. 23; 8. 9; 1 Pet. 2. 8.
Submission to God, Jas. 4. 7.
to rulers, Eph. 5. 21; Heb. 13. 17; 1 Pet. 2.
  13; 5. 5.
Succoth (Canaan), Gen. 33. 17; Josh. 13. 27;
  1 Ki. 7. 46; Ps. 60. 6.
punished by Gideon, Jud. 8. 5, 16.
—(in Egypt), Ex. 12. 37; 13. 20.
Sufferings. See *Christ.*
of His followers, Acts 5. 40; 12; 13. 50; 14.
  19; 16. 23; 20. 24; 21; 22; 1 Cor. 4. 11; 2
  Cor. 1. 4; 4. 8; 6. 4; 11. 23; Phil. 1; 1 Tim.
  4. 10; 2 Tim. 3. 10; 1 Pet. 2. 19; 3. 14; 4. 12.

Sun created, Gen 1. 14; Ps. 19. 4; 74. 16; 1 Cor.
  15. 41.
not to be worshipped, Deut. 4. 19; Job 31.
  26; Ezek. 8. 16.
stayed by Joshua, Josh. 10. 12.
brought backward for Hezekiah, 2 Ki. 20. 9.
darkened at crucifixion, Lk. 23. 44.
Sun of righteousness, Mal. 4. 2.
Supper, parable of, Lk. 14. 16.
marriage, of the Lamb, Rev. 19. 9.
Lord's Supper. See *Communion.*
Suretyship, evils of, Prov. 6. 1; 11. 15; 17. 18;
  20. 16; 22. 26; 27. 13.
Swallow, the, Ps. 84. 3; Prov. 26. 2; Is. 38. 14;
  Jer. 8. 7.
Swan, an unclean bird, Lev. 11. 18; Deut. 14. 16.
Swearing, forbidden, Matt. 5. 34; Jas. 5. 12.
Swine, unclean, Lev. 11. 7; Deut. 14. 8; Is. 65. 4.
devils sent into herd of, Matt. 8. 32; Mk. 5.
  13; Lk. 8. 33.
typical of unbelievers and apostates, Matt.
  7. 6; 2 Pet. 2. 22.
Sword of the Lord, Gen. 3. 24; Deut. 32. 41;
  Jud. 7. 18; 1 Chr. 21. 12; Ps. 45. 3; Is. 34.
  5; 66. 16; Jer. 12. 12; 47. 6; Ezek. 21. 4; 30.
  24; 32. 10; Zeph. 2. 12.
Sycamore tree, 1 Ki. 10. 27; Amos 7. 14; Lk.
  19. 4.
Synagogues, Christ teaches in, Matt. 12. 9; Lk.
  4. 16; John 6. 59; 18. 20.
Paul teaches in, Acts 13. 5; 14. 1; 18. 4.
Syrians, Gen. 25. 20; Deut. 26. 5.
subdued by David, 2 Sam. 8; 10.
tributary to Solomon, 1 Ki. 10. 29.
contend with Israel, 1 Ki. 11. 25; 20; 22. 34;
  2 Ki. 6. 24; 7; 8. 13; 13. 7; 16. 6; 2 Chr.
  18. 33.
employed to punish Joash, 2 Chr. 24. 23.
See 2 Chr. 28. 23; Is. 7. 2; Ezek. 27. 16; Hos.
  12. 12; Amos 1. 5.
the Gospel preached to, Matt. 4. 24; Acts 15.
  23; 18. 18; Gal. 1. 21.
Syrophenician woman, Mk. 7. 25, 30.

TABERNACLE of GOD, its construction, Ex.
  25-27; 36-38; 40.
covered by the cloud, Ex. 40. 34; Num. 9. 15.
consecrated by Moses, Lev. 8. 10.
directions concerning its custody and re-
  moval, Num. 1. 50, 53; 3. 4; 9. 18; 1 Chr. 6. 48.
set up at Shiloh, Josh. 18. 1; at Gibeon, 1 Chr.
  21. 29; 2 Chr. 1. 3.
David's love for, Ps. 27. 4; 42; 43; 84; 132.
typical, Heb. 8. 2; 9. 2.
—of witness, Num. 17. 7; 18. 2; 2 Chr. 24. 6;
  Acts 7. 44.
of testimony, Ex. 38. 21.
in heaven, Rev. 15. 5.
Tabernacle, the human body compared to, 2
  Cor. 5. 1; 2 Pet. 1. 13.
Tabernacles, feast of, Lev. 23. 34; Num. 29. 12;
  Deut. 16. 13; 2 Chr. 8. 13; Ezra 3. 4; Zech.
  14. 16; John 7. 2.
Table of the Lord, in the tabernacle, Ex. 25.
  23; 31. 8; 37. 10; 40. 4; Ezek. 41. 22.
profanation of, condemned, Mal. 1. 7, 12.
shewbread placed thereon, Ex. 25. 30; Lev.
  24. 6; Num. 4. 7.
—the Lord's. See *Communion.*
Tables of stone, containing the law, Ex. 24. 12;
  31. 18.
broken by Moses, Ex. 32. 19; Deut. 9. 15.
renewed, Ex. 34; Deut. 10.
See 2 Cor. 3. 3.

Thyatira (Acts 16. 14), angel of, Rev. 1. 11 ; 2. 18.
Tibni's conspiracy, 1 Ki. 16. 21.
Tiglath-Pileser (Tilgath-Pilneser, 1 Chr. 5. 6, 26), 2 Ki. 15. 29 ; 16. 7 ; 2 Chr. 28. 20.
Time, redemption of, Ps. 39. 4 ; 90. 12 ; Eccl. 12. 1 ; Is. 55. 6 ; Matt. 5. 25 ; Lk. 19. 42 ; John 9. 4 ; 12. 35 ; Rom. 13. 11 ; 2 Cor. 6. 2 ; Gal. 6. 9 ; Eph. 5. 16 ; Col. 4. 5.
for all things, Eccl. 3.
the end of, Rev. 10. 6.
Times, the last, signs of, Matt. 16. 3 ; Acts 3. 21 ; 1 Thes. 5. 1 ; 2 Thes. 2 ; 1 Tim. 4. 1 ; 2 Tim. 3. 1.
Timnath-Serah, Joshua buried there, Josh. 24. 30.
Timotheus (Timothy) accompanies Paul, Acts 16. 3 ; 17. 14, 15 ; Rom. 16. 21 ; 2 Cor. 1. 1, 19.
commended, 1 Cor. 16. 10 ; Phil. 2. 19.
See 1 & 2 Tim.
Tirhakah, Sennacherib's war with, 2 Ki. 19. 9.
Tirshatha (governor), Ezra 2. 63 ; Neh. 7. 70.
Tirzah, 1 Ki. 14. 17 ; 15. 21 ; 16. 8, 15 ; 2 Ki. 15. 16 ; Cant. 6. 4.
Tithes paid by Abraham to Melchizedec, Gen. 14. 20 ; Heb. 7. 6.
due to God, Gen. 28. 22 ; Lev. 27. 30 ; Prov. 3. 9 ; Mal. 3. 8.
granted to the Levites, Num. 18. 21 ; 2 Chr. 31. 5 ; Neh. 10. 37 ; Heb. 7. 5.
for the feasts, and poor, Deut. 14. 23, 28.
Titus, Gal. 2. 3.
Paul's love for, 2 Cor. 2. 13 ; 7. 6, 13.
See Titus 1 ; 2 ; 3.
Tobiah, the Ammonite, vexes the Jews, Neh. 4. 3 ; 6. 1, 12 ; 13. 4.
Tongue, unruly, Jas. 3.
to be bridled, Ps. 39. 1 ; Prov. 4. 24 ; 10. 10, 19 ; 14. 23 ; 15. 4 ; 17. 20 ; 18. 6 ; Eccl. 3. 7 ; 10. 12 ; Matt. 5. 22 ; 12. 36 ; Eph. 4. 29 ; 5. 4 ; Col. 3. 8 ; 4. 6 ; Tit. 1. 10 ; 2. 8 ; 3. 2 ; Jas. 1. 26 ; 1 Pet. 3. 10 ; Jude 16.
Tongues, confusion of, Gen. 11.
gift of, Acts 2. 3 ; 10. 46 ; 19. 6 ; 1 Cor. 12. 10 ; 13. 1 ; 14. 2.
Topaz, precious stone, Ex. 28. 17 ; Rev. 21. 20.
Tophet, 2 Ki. 23. 10.
See Is. 30. 33 ; Jer. 7. 31 ; 19. 11.
Torn beasts not to be eaten, Ex. 22. 31 ; Lev. 22. 8 ; Ezek. 4. 14 ; 44. 31.
Tortoise, an unclean animal, Lev. 11. 29.
Touching Christ's garment in faith, Mk. 5. 28 ; 6. 56 ; Lk. 6. 19.
Tower of Babel, Gen. 11.
of Penuel, Jud. 8. 17.
of Shechem, Jud. 9. 46.
of Siloam, Lk. 13. 4.
Traders in Tyre, Ezek. 27.
Traditions of men, Matt. 15. 3 ; Mk. 7. 7 ; Gal. 1. 14 ; Col. 2. 8 ; Tit. 1. 14 ; 1 Pet. 1. 18.
Traitor, Judas, Lk. 6. 16.
Trance of Balaam, Num. 24. 4.
of Peter, Acts 10. 10 ; 11. 5.
of Paul, Acts 22. 17.
Transfiguration of Christ, Matt. 17 ; Mk. 9. 2 ; Lk. 9. 29 ; John 1. 14 ; 2 Pet. 1. 16.
Transformation of Satan and his ministers, 2 Cor 11. 13, 15.
Translation of Enoch, Gen. 5. 24 ; Heb. 11. 5.
of Elijah, 2 Ki. 2.
Treachery, instances of, Gen. 34. 13 ; Jud. 9 ; 1 Sam. 21. 7 ; 22. 9 ; 2 Sam. 3. 27 ; 11. 14 ; 16 ; 20. 9 ; 1 Ki. 21. 5 ; 2 Ki. 10. 18 ; Est. 3 ; Matt. 26. 47 ; Mk. 14. 43 ; Lk. 22. 47 ; John 18. 3.

Treason, instances, 2 Sam. 15-18 ; 20 ; 1 Ki. 1 ; 16. 10 ; 2 Ki. 11 ; 15. 10 ; 2 Chr. 22. 10 ; Est. 2. 21.
Treasury, gifts cast into, Mk. 12. 41 ; Lk. 21. 1.
Tree of life, Gen. 2. 9 ; 3. 22 ; Prov. 3. 18 ; 11. 30 ; Ezek. 47. 7, 12 ; Rev. 2. 7 ; 22. 2, 14.
of knowledge of good and evil, Gen. 2. 17 ; 3.
Trees, laws concerning, Lev. 19. 23 ; 27. 30 ; Deut. 20. 19.
Jotham's parable of the, Jud. 9. 8.
Nebuchadnezzar's vision, Dan. 4. 10.
figuratively mentioned, Num. 24. 6 ; 1 Chr. 16. 33 ; Ps. 1 ; (Jer. 17. 8) ; 92. 12 ; Eccl. 11. 3 ; Cant. 2. 3 ; Is. 41. 19 ; Ezek. 17. 24 ; 31. 5 ; Matt. 3. 10 ; 7. 17 ; 12. 33 ; Lk. 3. 9 ; 6. 43 ; 21. 29 ; Jude 12.
Trespass offerings, laws concerning, Lev. 5 ; 6 ; Num. 5.
Trial, of the heart, God's prerogative, Ps. 26. 2 ; 66. 10 ; Prov. 17. 3 ; Jer. 11. 20 ; 1 Thes. 2. 4.
of faith, Job 23. 10 ; Zech. 13. 9 ; Heb. 11. 17 ; Jas. 1. 3 ; 1 Pet. 4. 12 ; Rev. 3. 10. See *Temptation.*
Tribes of Israel blessed, Gen. 49 ; Num. 23. 20 ; 24 ; Deut. 33.
their order and numbering, Num. 1 ; 2 ; 10. 14 ; 26 ; 2 Sam. 24 ; 1 Chr. 21.
number of those sealed, Rev. 7. 4.
Tribulation connected with the Gospel, Matt. 13. 21 ; 24. 21, John 16. 33 ; Acts 14. 22 ; 1 Thes. 3. 4 ; Rev. 7. 14.
Tribute, Matt. 22. 21 ; Lk. 20. 25 ; Rom. 13. 6 ; 1 Pet. 2. 13.
paid by Christ, Matt. 17. 24.
Troas visited by Paul, Acts 16. 8 ; 20. 5 ; 2 Cor. 2. 12 ; 2 Tim. 4. 13.
Trophimus, companion of Paul, Acts 20. 4 ; 21. 29 ; 2 Tim. 4. 20.
Trumpet, giving uncertain sound, 1 Cor. 14. 8.
the last, 1 Cor. 15. 52 ; 1 Thes. 4. 16.
Trumpets, their use, Num. 10 ; Josh. 6. 4 ; Ps. 81. 3 ; Ezek. 7. 14 ; 33. 3 ; Joel 2. 1.
employed in worship, 1 Chr. 13. 8 ; 15. 24 ; 2 Chr. 5. 12 ; 29. 27 ; Ps. 98. 6.
feast of, Lev. 23. 24 ; Num. 29.
the seven, Rev. 8 ; 9 ; 11.
Trust in God, Ps. 4. 5 ; 34 ; 37. 3 ; 40. 3, 4 ; 62. 8 ; 64. 10 ; 84. 12 ; 115. 9 ; 118. 8 ; Prov. 3. 5 ; 16. 20 ; Is. 26. 4 ; 50. 10 ; 51. 5 ; Jer. 17. 7.
exemplified, 1 Sam. 17. 45 ; 30. 6 ; 2 Ki. 18. 5 ; 2 Chr. 20. 12 ; Dan. 3. 28 ; 2 Tim. 1. 12 ; 4. 18.
blessings resulting from, Ps. 5. 11 ; 26. 1 ; 32. 10 ; 33. 21 ; 34. 8, 22 ; 37. 5, 40 ; 56. 11 ; 112. 7 ; 125 ; Prov. 16. 20 ; 28. 25 ; 29. 25 ; Is. 12. 2 ; 26. 3 ; 57. 13 ; Heb. 13. 6.
Trust in man, riches, etc., vain, Job 31. 24 ; Ps. 20. 7 ; 33. 16 ; 44. 6 ; 49. 6 ; 52. 7 ; 62. 10 · 118. 8 ; 146. 3 ; Prov. 11. 28 ; 28. 26 ; Is. 30. 31 ; Jer. 7. 4 ; 9. 4 ; 17. 5 ; 46. 25 ; 49. 4 ; Ezek. 33. 13 ; Mk. 10. 24 ; 2 Cor. 1. 9 ; 1 Tim. 6. 17.
Truth, of God, Ex. 34. 6 ; Num 23. 19 · Deut. 32. 4 ; Ps. 19. 9 ; 25. 10 ; 33. 4 ; 57. 10 ; 85. 10 ; 86. 15 ; 89. 14 ; 91. 4 ; 96. 13 ; 100. 5 ; 146. 6 ; Is. 25. 1 ; 65. 16 ; Dan. 4. 37 · Mic. 7. 20 ; John 17. 17 ; 2 Cor. 1. 20 ; Rev. 15. 3 ; 16. 7.
word of, Ps. 119. 43 ; 2 Cor. 6. 7 ; Eph. 1. 13 ; Col. 1. 5 ; 2 Tim. 2. 15 ; Jas. 1. 18.
the, the Gospel, John 1. 17 ; 4. 24 ; 5. 33 : 17. 17 ; 18. 37 ; Rom. 2. 8 ; 1 Cor 13. 6 ; 2 Cor. 4. 2 ; Gal. 3. 1 ; Eph. 6. 14 ; 2 Thes. 2. 10 ; 1 Tim. 2. 7 ; 3. 15 ; 4. 3 ; 6. 5 ; 2 Tim. 3. 8 ; 4. 4 ; Tit. 1. 1 ; 1 Pet. 1. 22. **See** *Scriptures, Gospel.*

Vulture, an unclean bird, Deut. 14. 13. See Job 28. 7; Is. 34. 15.

WAFERS used as offerings, Ex. 29. 2. 23; Lev. 2. 4; 8. 26; Num. 6. 15.

Wages to be duly paid, Lev. 19. 13; Deut. 24. 15; Jas. 5. 4.

Waiting upon God, Ps. 27. 14; 37. 34; Prov. 20. 22; Is. 40. 31; 49. 23; Jer. 14. 22; Lam. 3. 25; Hab. 2. 3; Zeph. 3. 8; Lk. 12. 36; Rom. 8. 25; 1 Cor. 1. 7; Gal. 5. 5; 1 Thes. 1. 10; 2 Thes. 3. 5.

Walking with God, Deut. 5. 33; 28. 9; Josh. 22. 5; 1 Ki. 8. 36; Ps. 1; 112; Prov. 2. 7; Is. 2. 3; 30. 21; Jer. 6. 16; 7. 23; Ezek. 37. 24; of Enoch, Gen. 5. 24; of Noah, Gen. 6. 9.

in faith, love, etc., Rom. 6. 4; 8. 1; 13. 13; 2 Cor. 5. 7; Gal. 5. 16; Eph. 5. 2; Phil. 3. 16; Col. 1. 10; 2. 6; 1 John 1. 6; Rev. 3. 4; 21. 24.

Wantonness censured, Is. 3. 16; Rom. 13. 13; 2 Pet. 2. 18.

War, laws of, Deut. 20; 23. 9; 24. 5.

Warning, 2 Chr. 19. 10; Ezek. 3. 17; 33. 3; 1 Thes. 5. 14.

Paul's example, Acts 20. 31; 1 Cor. 4. 14; Col. 1. 28.

Washing, enjoined by the law, Ex. 29. 4; Lev. 6. 27; 13. 54; 14. 8; Deut. 21. 6; 2 Chr. 4. 6. of the feet, Gen. 18. 4; 24. 32; 43. 24; 1 Sam. 25. 41; Lk. 7. 38; 1 Tim. 5. 10. of the hands, Deut. 21. 6; Ps. 26. 6; Matt. 27. 24.

Christ washes disciples' feet, John 13. traditional, censured, Mk. 7. 3; Lk. 11. 38. figuratively mentioned, Job 9. 30; Is. 1. 16; 4. 4; Eph. 5. 26; Tit. 3. 5; Heb. 10. 22. through the blood of Christ, 1 Cor. 6. 11; Rev. 1. 5; 7. 14.

Waste forbidden by Christ, John 6. 12.

Watches, of time, Ex. 14. 24; 1 Sam. 11. 11; Matt. 14. 25; Mk. 6. 48.

Watchfulness enjoined, Matt. 24. 42; 25. 13; 26. 41; Mk. 13. 35; Lk. 12. 35; 21. 36; 1 Cor. 10. 12; Eph. 6. 18; Col. 4. 2; 1 Thes. 5. 6; 2 Tim. 4. 5; 1 Pet. 4. 7; 5. 8; Rev. 3. 2; 16. 15.

Watchmen, their duty, 2 Sam. 18. 25; 2 Ki. 9. 17; Ps. 127. 1; Cant. 3. 3; 5. 7; Is. 21. 5, 11; 52. 8; Jer. 6. 17; 31. 6; Ezek. 3. 17; 33; Hab. 2. 1.

evil, described, Is. 56. 10.

Watch towers, 2 Chr. 20. 24; Is. 21. 5.

Water, miraculously supplied, Gen. 21. 19; Ex. 15. 23; 17. 6; Num. 20. 7; 2 Ki. 3. 20. used in the trial of jealousy, Num. 5. 17. of affliction, 1 Ki. 22. 27. used in baptism, Matt. 3. 11; Acts 8. 36; 10. 47.

Christ walks on, Matt. 14. 25; Mk. 6. 48; John 6. 19.

changed into wine, John 2. 3.

figuratively mentioned, Ps. 65. 9; Is. 41. 17; 44. 3; 55. 1; Jer. 2. 13; Ezek. 47; Zech. 13. 1; John 3. 5; 4. 10; 7. 38; Rev. 7. 17; 21. 6; 22.

Waters of creation, Gen. 1. 2, 6, 9. the flood, Gen 6. 17; 7. 6. fountain of living, Jer. 2. 13; 17. 13. living fountains of, Rev. 7. 17.

Wave offering, Ex. 29. 24; Lev. 7. 30; 8. 27; 23. 11, 20; Num. 5. 25; 6. 20.

Wavering, exhortations against, Heb. 10. 23; Jas. 1. 6.

Way, the, Christ so called, John 14. 6; Heb. 10. 20.

Weak in the faith, Rom. 14; 15; 1 Cor. 8; 1 Thes. 5. 14; Heb. 12. 12.

Paul's example, 1 Cor. 9. 22.

Weaned child, Ps. 131. 2; Is. 11. 8; 28. 9.

Weapons of the Christian, not carnal, 2 Cor. 10. 4.

Weasel, an unclean animal, Lev. 11. 29.

Weaver mentioned, Ex. 35. 35; Job 7. 6; Is. 38. 12.

Web, spider's, Job 8. 14; Is. 59. 5.

Wedding, parable of, Matt. 22. See Lk. 12. 36; 14. 8.

Weeks, feast of, Deut. 16. 9. seventy, prophecy concerning, Dan. 9. 24.

Weeping, Ps. 6. 8; 30. 5; Joel 2. 12; Matt. 8. 12; 22. 13; Lk. 6. 21; 7. 38; Rom. 12. 15; 1 Cor. 7. 30; Phil. 3. 18.

for the dead, etc., Gen. 23. 2; 2 Sam. 1. 24; Eccl. 3. 4; Jer. 9. 17; 22. 10; Ezek. 24. 16; Amos 5. 16; Mk. 5. 39; John 11. 35; 20. 13; 1 Thes. 4. 13.

none in heaven, Rev. 21. 4.

Weights, just, commanded, Lev. 19. 35; Deut. 25. 13; Prov. 11. 1; 16. 11; 20. 10, 23; Ezek. 45. 10; Micah 6. 10.

Well of Beth-lehem, 1 Chr. 11. 17.

Wells of Abraham, Gen. 26. 15; Isaac, Gen. 26. 25; Uzziah, 2 Chr. 26. 10; Jacob, John 4. 6.

Whale mentioned, Gen. 1. 21; Job 7. 12; Ezek. 32. 2.

Jonah swallowed by one, Jon. 1. 17; Matt. 12. 40.

Wheat, Ex. 29. 2; 1 Ki. 5. 11; Ezek. 27. 17. parable concerning, Matt. 13. 25.

Wheels, vision of, Ezek. 1. 15; 3. 13; 10. 9.

Whelps (lions'), parable of, Ezek. 19; Nah. 2. 12.

Whirlwinds, 1 Ki. 19. 11; 2 Ki. 2. 1; Job 37. 9; 38. 1; Is. 66. 15; Jer. 23. 19; Ezek. 1. 4; Nah. 1. 3; Zech. 9. 14.

Whispering, Prov. 16. 28; 26. 20; Rom. 1. 29; 2 Cor. 12. 20. See *Slander, Tale-bearers.*

White horse, Rev. 6. 2; 19. 11; cloud, Rev. 14; throne, Rev. 20. 11.

White raiment, of Christ at the transfiguration, Matt. 17. 2; Mk. 9. 3; Lk. 9. 29. of angels, Matt. 28. 3; Mk. 16. 5. of the redeemed, Rev. 3. 5; 4. 4; 7. 9; 19. 8, 14.

Whole, the, need not a physician, Matt. 9. 12; Mk. 2. 17; Lk. 5. 31.

made, Matt. 12. 13; Mk. 3. 5; Lk. 6. 10. See *Miracles.*

Whore of the great, Rev. 17; 18.

Whoredom condemned, Lev. 19. 29; Deut. 22. 21; 23. 17.

spiritual, Ezek. 16; 23; Jer. 3; Hos. 1; 2. See *Idolatry.*

Whoremongers condemned, Eph. 5. 5; 1 Tim. 1. 10; Heb. 13. 4; Rev. 21. 8; 22. 15.

Wicked, their character and punishment, Deut. 32. 5; Job 4. 8; 5; 15; 18; 20; 21; 24; 27. 13; 30; 36. 12; Eccl. 8. 10; Is. 1; 22; 28; 29; 37. 21; 44. 9; 45. 9; 47; 57-59; 66; Jer. 2; Ezek. 5; 16; 18; 23; Hos. to Mal.; Matt. 5-7; 13. 37; 15; 16; 21. 33; 23; John 5. 29; Rom. 1. 21; 3. 10; 1 Cor. 5. 11; Gal. 5. 19; Eph. 4. 17; 5. 5; Phil. 3. 18; Col. 3. 6; 2 Thes. 2; 1 Tim. 1. 9; 4; 6. 9; 2 Tim. 3. 13; Tit. 1. 10; Heb. 6. 4; Jas. 4; 5; 1 Pet. 4; 2 Pet. 2; 3; 1 John 2. 18; 4; Jude; Rev. 9. 20; 14. 8; 18; 20. 13; 22. 15.

their prosperity not to be envied, Ps. 37. 1; 73; Prov. 3. 31; 23. 17; 24. 1, 19; Jer. 12.

Wolves, unjust judges and false teachers so called, Zeph. 3. 3; Matt. 7. 15; 10. 16; Lk. 10. 3; Acts 20. 29.

Woman, creation of, Gen. 2. 22.
fall of, Gen. 3.
Christ the seed of (Gen. 3. 15); Gal. 4. 4.

Women, duty of the aged, Tit. 2. 3; of the young, 1 Tim. 2. 9; 5. 14; Tit. 2. 4; 1 Pet. 3. See *Wives.*

Wonderful, prophetic name of Christ, Is. 9. 6. See Jud. 13. 18.

Wonders, God's, Ex. 3. 20; Is. 29. 14; Ps. 77. 11; Dan. 6. 27; Acts 7. 36.

Word of God, a name of Christ, John 1. 1, 14; 1 John 1. 1; 5. 7; Rev. 19. 13.

—the Scriptures, Lk. 5. 1; Acts 4. 31; 8. 14; 13. 7; 16. 6.

Words, men to be judged for, Eccl. 5. 2; Ezek. 35. 13; Mal. 2. 17; 3. 13; Matt. 12. 37.

Works of God, Job 9; 37-41; Ps. 8; 19 89; 104; 111; 145; 147; 148; Eccl. 8.17; Jer. 10.12.
—of the law, insufficiency of, Rom. 3. 20; 4. 2; Gal. 3.
—good, the evidence of faith, Acts 26. 20; Jas. 2. 14.
exhortations to, Matt. 5. 16; (Acts 9. 36); 2 Cor. 8; 9; Eph. 2. 10; Phil. 2. 12; 1 Thes. 4. 11; 2 Thes. 2. 17; Heb. 10. 24; 1 Pet. 2. 12.

World created, Gen. 1; 2.
See John 1. 10; Col. 1. 16; Heb. 1. 2.
its corruption by the fall, Rom. 5. 12; 8. 22.
exhortations against conformity to, Rom. 12. 2; Gal. 6. 14; Jas. 1. 27; 4. 4; 1 John 2. 15.

Worm, man compared to, Job 17. 14; 25. 6; Mic. 7. 17.

Wormwood, figurative, Deut. 29. 18; Prov. 5. 4; Lam. 3. 15.
a star so called, Rev. 8. 11.

Worship to be rendered to God alone, Ex. 20. 1; Deut. 5. 7; 6. 13; Matt. 4. 10; Lk. 4. 8; Acts 10. 26; 14. 15; Col. 2. 18; Rev. 19. 10; 22. 8.
how to be performed, Lev. 10. 3; Eccl. 5; Joel 2. 16; John 4. 24; 1 Cor. 11; 14.
exhortations to, 2 Ki. 17. 36; 1 Chr. 16. 29; Ps. 29; 95. 6; 99. 5; 100.

Wrath, Job 5. 2; Ps. 37. 8; Prov. 12. 16; 14. 29; 29. 8; Rom. 12. 19; 13. 5; Gal. 5. 20; Eph. 4. 26; 1 Tim. 2. 8; Jas. 1. 19.
of God, Ps. 106. 23, 32; Rom. 9. 22; Rev. 6. 17; 11. 18; 16. 1; 19. 15.

Wrestling of Jacob with an angel, Gen. 32. 24.

Writing of God, Ex. 31. 18; 32. 16; Dan. 5. 5.

YEAR, beginning of, changed, Ex. 12. 1; Lev. 23. 5.

Yoke of Christ easy, Matt. 11. 30; 1 John 5. 3.

Yokes, typical, Jer. 27.

Young, exhortations to, Lev. 19. 32; Prov. 1. 8; Eccl. 12. 1.
Christ's example, Lk. 2. 46, 51; 1 Pet. 5. 5.

ZACCHÆUS, Lk. 19. 2.

Zachariah, king of Israel, 2 Ki. 14. 29.
smitten by Shallum, 2 Ki. 15. 10.

Zacharias, father of John the Baptist, commended as blameless before God, Lk. 1. 6; is promised a son, Lk. 1. 13; stricken with dumbness for his unbelief, Lk. 1. 18, 20; his recovery and song, Lk. 1. 64, 68.

Zadok, priest, 2 Sam. 8. 17; 15. 24; 20. 25.
anoints Solomon king, 1 Ki. 1. 39.

Zamzummims, giant race, Deut. 2. 20, 21.

Zarephath (Sarepta), Elijah sent there, 1 Ki. 17. 9; raises a widow's child, 1 Ki. 17. 17. See Lk. 4. 26.

Zeal of Phinehas, Num. 25. 7, 11; Ps. 106. 30.
of Jehu, 2 Ki. 10. 16.
of the Jews for the law, Acts 21. 20; Rom. 10. 2.
of Paul for the Jewish religion, Acts 22. 3; Gal. 1. 14; Phil. 3. 6.
Christ an example of, Ps. 69. 9; John 2. 17.
in good works, etc., Gal. 4. 18; Tit. 2. 14; Rev. 3. 19.

Zebah and **Zalmunna,** Jud. 8. 5, 21; Ps. 83. 11.

Zebedee, Matt. 4. 21; Mk. 1. 20.

Zeboim, Gen. 14. 2; 19. 25; Deut. 29. 23; Hos. 11. 8.

Zebul, Jud. 9. 28, 30.

Zebulun, son of Jacob, Gen. 30. 20; 35. 23.
blessed by Jacob, Gen. 49. 13.
his descendants, Num. 1. 30; 26. 26; Deut. 33. 18; Josh. 19. 10; Jud. 4. 6; 5. 14, 18; 6. 35; 2 Chr. 30. 11, 18; Ps. 68. 27; Ezek. 48. 26; Rev. 7. 8.
Christ preaches in the land of (Is. 9. 1); Matt. 4. 13.

Zechariah, son of Jehoiada, stoned in the court of the Lord's house, 2 Chr. 24. 20, 21.
referred to, Matt. 23. 35; Lk. 11. 51.
—the prophet, his exhortations to repentance, his visions and predictions, Zech. 1-14.

Zedekiah, a false prophet, 1 Ki. 22. 11; 2 Chr. 18. 10, 23.
—another, Jer. 29. 22.
—(Mattaniah), king of Judah, his evil reign, 2 Ki. 24. 17; 2 Chr. 36. 10.
his dealings with Jeremiah, Jer. 37. 6, 16; 38.
carried captive to Babylon, 2 Ki. 25; 2 Chr. 36. 17; Jer. 39; 52.

Zephaniah, priest, Jer. 29. 25; 37. 3.
prophet, Zeph. 1; 2; 3.

Zerubbabel (Zorobabel), prince of Judah, Ezra 2. 2.
restores the worship of God, Ezra 3. 1; Neh. 12. 47; Hag. 1. 1, 14; 2. 1; Zech. 4. 6.
See Matt. 1. 12, 13.

Zidon, Gen. 49. 13; Josh. 11. 8; Jud. 10. 6; 18. 7; 1 Ki. 11. 1; Ezra 3. 7; Lk. 4. 26; Acts 12. 20.
prophecies concerning, Is. 23; Jer. 25. 22; 27. 3; 47. 4; Ezek. 27. 8; 28. 21; 32. 30; Joel 3. 4; Zech. 9. 2.

Ziklag, 1 Sam. 27. 6; 30. 1; 2 Sam. 1. 1; 1 Chr. 12. 1.

Zin, wilderness of, Num. 13. 21; Josh. 15. 1.

Zion (mount), 2 Sam. 5. 7; 1 Ki. 8. 1; Rom. 11. 26; Heb. 12. 22; Rev. 14. 1.

Zipporah, wife of Moses, Ex. 2. 21; 4. 20.

Zoan, in Egypt, Num. 13. 22; Ps. 78. 12.

Zoar, Gen. 14. 2; 19. 22; (Is. 15. 5); Deut. 34. 3; Jer. 48. 34.

Zobah, kings of, subdued, 1 Sam. 14. 47; 2 Sam. 8. 3; 1 Ki. 11. 23.

Zophar, Job 2. 11; 11; 20; 42. 7.

Zorah, city of Samson, Josh. 19. 41; Jud. 13. 2, 25; 16. 31.

Zuzims, giants, Gen. 14. 5.